TWELFTH EDITION

LITERATURE
THE HUMAN EXPERIENCE

RICHARD ABCARIAN
California State University, Northridge, Emeritus

MARVIN KLOTZ
Late of California State University, Northridge

SAMUEL COHEN
University of Missouri

Bedford / St. Martin's
A Macmillan Education Imprint

Boston • New York

For Bedford/St. Martin's

Vice President, Editorial, Macmillan Higher Education Humanities: Edwin Hill
Editorial Director, English and Music: Karen S. Henry
Senior Executive Editor: Stephen A. Scipione
Developmental Editor: Alicia Young
Publishing Services Manager: Andrea Cava
Production Supervisor: Robert Cherry
Executive Marketing Manager: Joy Fisher Williams
Project Management: DeMasi Design and Publishing Services
Director of Rights and Permissions: Hilary Newman
Senior Art Director: Anna Palchik
Text Design: Joan O'Connor; DeMasi Design and Publishing Services
Cover Design: William Boardman
Cover Art: Collage Woman #2, © Elizabeth Rosen, 2015/Morgan Gaynin, Inc.
Composition: Cenveo Publisher Services
Printing and Binding: Edwards Brothers Malloy

Manufactured in the United States of America.

0   9   8   7   6   5
f   e   d   c   b   a

For information, write: Bedford/St. Martin's, 75 Arlington Street, Boston, MA 02116 (617-399-4000)

ISBN 978-1-4576-9993-1

Acknowledgments

For Marv

PREFACE FOR INSTRUCTORS

> We all suffer alone in the real world; true empathy's impossible. But if a piece of fiction can allow us imaginatively to identify with a character's pain, we might then also more easily conceive of others identifying with our own. This is nourishing, redemptive; we become less alone inside. It might just be that simple.
> —David Foster Wallace

While committed readers would agree that they read literature because they find it delightful, instructive, or both, many of your students may read literature because it has been assigned to them in a required class. We've prepared every edition of *Literature: The Human Experience* for such students. For them, we choose literature that's entertaining and thought-provoking enough to capture the interest of indifferent or uncommitted readers. We organize that literature to address cradle-to-grave thematic concerns that are compelling and inescapable. Finally, we show students how to connect with what they encounter in the literature through their reading, discussion, and writing. As David Foster Wallace's epigraph suggests, reading literature can forge empathetic links that are consoling, sustaining, and even redemptive. We believe that students' experience of literature in a course should leave them feeling connected, not only to the writing they read and the writers who wrote it, but also to one another—indeed, to the multitudes of others, past and present, whose lives comprise the human experience.

Everything that's new in the twelfth edition furthers these goals. New works by young writers extend our effort to bring students to literature by including writing that speaks, in voices more like theirs, of experiences to which they can connect. New examples of classic literature on timeless themes continue to represent the best that's been thought and said and as well the perennial need for humans to represent their experiences through imaginative work and storytelling. New pairs and clusters of literary works juxtapose classic and recent writing, encouraging critical comparative thinking. New argument-focused questions ask students to engage more actively with selections, pushing them to think critically and write persuasively about literature. Creative new writing topics strengthen the book's emphasis on getting students to see literature—and life—as writers.

FEATURES

A THEMATIC ORGANIZATION THAT CONNECTS LITERATURE TO LIFE.
We believe that students are most immediately engaged by works in which

they can see themselves. The ability of students to connect their experiences to those they read about does not mean they should be assigned nothing but literature about students or Americans or Westerners or young people from anywhere; it does mean that the human experience, in its dazzling variety, can be represented in art and that students can respond to it no matter the different circumstances of reader and writer. In gathering these works, we tried to meet students where they live and take them to places they have never seen. The best way to do this is to concentrate on different themes drawn from human experience and to ask students to read divergent perspectives on these themes. Thus, the anthology is organized into five thematic sections: "Innocence and Experience," "Conformity and Rebellion," "Culture and Identity," "Love and Hate," and "Life and Death." Each section opens with a short introductory essay and questions that invite students to reflect on their own experiences with the chapter's theme.

To enhance teaching flexibility, the thematic structure features two subordinate arrangements of the literature. Embedded in each thematic section, the stories, poems, plays, and essays are grouped by genre; within each genre, selections are arranged chronologically by author's birth date. (The date following the title indicates the selection's first appearance in a book. We have not attempted to date traditional ballads.) The dates, together with an appendix containing biographical notes on the authors, provide students with a brief historical context for each work. So whether you teach literature thematically, generically, or historically—or some combination of the three—the organization of *Literature: The Human Experience* accommodates your approach.

The thematic sections are also punctuated with twenty-four short units that pair or cluster literary works—often classic with contemporary. While promoting comparative critical thinking with their accompanying questions and writing assignments, these compact clusters provide engaging reading for students. For example, "America through Immigrants' Eyes" brings together poets from Phillis Wheatley to Richard Blanco, and in "Love Stinks," poems by Catullus and Aphra Behn are grouped with more modern poets in a cluster about the pain that often accompanies love. The new nonfiction pair "Missing Mothers" couples Jonathan Lethem's powerful reflection on adolescence and loss, "13, 1977, 21," with Ruth Margalit's affecting essay "The Unmothered."

TWO CHAPTERS OFFER SUPPORT FOR READING AND WRITING ABOUT LITERATURE. Two introductory chapters, "Responding to Literature" and "Writing about Literature," give students the tools to think about and appreciate what they read and to put those thoughts into words. In these chapters, we discuss the formal elements of each genre and provide descriptions and samples of various forms of written response and documentation. Throughout the thematic sections, study questions challenge students to analyze works, to make connections between them, and to write about them in a variety of ways. At the end of the book, the "Glossary of Critical Approaches" and the "Glossary of Literary Terms" provide additional resources for students learning about how to approach literature.

NEW TO THIS EDITION

WIDE-RANGING CONTEMPORARY LITERATURE ANCHORED BY A STURDY SELECTION OF CLASSICS.

- *Fiction:* Edwidge Danticat's "The Book of the Dead" and Junot Díaz's "Drown" are new to the Twelfth Edition, as are the classics "Half a Day" by Naguib Mahfouz and Lu Xun's "Diary of a Madman."

- *Poetry:* Selections from Jonathan Swift, Czeslaw Milosz, Léopold Sédar Senghor, and others are new to the anthology, as are modern voices such as Dilruba Ahmed, Tishani Doshi, Chris Abani, and Richard Blanco.

- *Drama:* Edward Albee's *The Sandbox* makes its first appearance in this anthology in the "Life and Death" section.

- *Nonfiction:* The new essays represent some of the most stimulating work in this ever-growing genre, from critically acclaimed essays by John Jeremiah Sullivan and Jonathan Lethem to graphic selections from Allie Brosh and Sabrina Jones—as well as short examples of creative nonfiction from the much-admired online journal *Brevity.*

MORE SUPPORT FOR MAKING ARGUMENTS ABOUT LITERATURE. A new section in the introduction shows students the basic building blocks of argument, and new "Making Arguments" questions throughout the thematic chapters ask students to argue critically about—and with—the literature they're reading.

FOUR NEW CASE STUDIES EXPLORE ARGUMENTS WITHIN THE GENRES. Case studies on debates about Flannery O'Connor (fiction), persuading the people we love (poetry), shifting historical perceptions of a classic American play (drama), and the conditions of modern-day revolutions (nonfiction) show students how literature can make arguments about our world and our lives.

ACKNOWLEDGMENTS

We would like to thank the professors who generously took time to share their ideas about the previous edition of this anthology. They are Amy Amoroso, University of Maine at Augusta; Lauren Angel-Cann, Collin College–Preston Ridge Campus; Leisa Belleau, University of Southern Indiana; Lynn Clarkson, North Shore Community College; Paul Francoeur, University of Massachusetts Lowell; Claire-Marie Hart, North Shore Community College; Nancy Lee-Jones, Endicott College; MaryKate McMaster, Anna Maria College; Marge Morian-Boyle, Dean College; David Mulry, College of Coastal Georgia; Debbie Olson, University of Texas at Arlington; Kirsten Patey-Hurd, Quinsigamond Community College; Thomas Schaefer, Middlesex Community College; Judy Sneller, South Dakota School of Mines and Technology; Frederick White,

Slippery Rock University; and our reviewers who wish to remain anonymous from New Jersey City University and the University of Massachusetts Lowell.

We wish to thank Karissa Lagos, whose precocious writing skills provided us with a superb research paper. We also wish to thank Anita Zubère, who helped untangle some knotty lines of poetry; Roy Merrens for explaining some of the arcane features of the urban London landscape; and Bainbridge Scott, whose knowledge of music made our task easier. Our thanks also go to Mary Lawless for her thoughtful contributions to the introductory chapters on reading and writing and to Michelle McSweeney for her smart and detailed updates to the biographical notes. Experienced and wise people at Bedford/St. Martin's have guided this book along the way. We thank Edwin Hill, Vice President, Editorial, Macmillan Higher Education Humanities. As well, we are grateful to Kalina Ingham, Virginia Creeden, and Angela Boehler for procuring permissions and to Linda DeMasi and Andrea Cava for shepherding the book through production. We thank Billy Boardman for his persistence in creating this edition's vibrant new cover and Vivian Garcia for providing expert advice. We thank Karen Henry, Editorial Director, English and Music, for her encouraging and nurturing leadership. As ever, we owe many thanks to senior executive editor Steve Scipione, as well as heaps of gratitude to editor Alicia Young, for her vision, hard work, and endless patience and good humor. This book would simply not be what it is without their contributions—it would not exist at all. Some of this labor (there's certainly enough to go around) must surely be credited to editorial assistants Jennifer Prince and Stephanie Thomas, for whose efforts we are very grateful.

Finally, we would like to recognize the passing of Marvin Klotz, who with Dick Abcarian created this book dedicated to teaching and learning literature as a human creation and a record of human experience, and who saw it through four decades of use in classrooms around the country. On behalf of all of the students and teachers his work touched, we want to acknowledge Marv.

Richard Abcarian
Samuel Cohen

RESOURCES FOR *LITERATURE: THE HUMAN EXPERIENCE*

Literature: The Human Experience doesn't stop with a book. Online, you'll find both free and affordable premium resources to help students get even more out of the book and your course. You'll also find convenient instructor resources, and even a nationwide community of teachers. To learn more about or order any of the products below, contact your Bedford/St. Martin's sales representative, e-mail sales support (sales_support@bfwpub.com), or visit the Web site at **macmillanhighered.com/experience_literature/catalog**.

GET CLOSE READING HELP FOR YOUR STUDENTS WITH *LAUNCHPAD SOLO FOR LITERATURE*. *LaunchPad Solo for Literature* helps beginning literature students learn and practice close reading and critical thinking skills in an interactive environment. Easy-to-use and easy-to-assign modules based on widely taught literary selections guide students through three common assignment types: responding to a reading, drawing connections between texts, and instructor-led collaborative close reading. In addition, students and instructors have access to nearly 500 reading comprehension quizzes on commonly taught literary selections along with several engaging videos by well-known authors on literary elements such as character, dialogue, and voice. Get all our great resources and activities in one fully customizable space online. Visit **macmillanhighered.com/launchpadsolo/literature**. To order *LaunchPad Solo for Literature* with this print text, use ISBN 978-1-319-05103-7.

GET FREE ONLINE HELP FOR YOUR STUDENTS. *Re:Writing for Literature* provides close reading help, reference materials, and support for working with sources.

- *VirtuaLit Interactive Tutorials* for close reading (fiction, poetry, and drama)
- *AuthorLinks* and biographies for 800 authors
- Quizzes on poetic elements and hundreds of literary works
- Glossary of literary terms
- MLA-style student papers
- A sampler of author videos and additional literature
- Help for finding and citing sources, including access to Diana Hacker's *Research and Documentation Online*

LITERATURE: THE HUMAN EXPERIENCE NOW COMES WITH VIDEO. At no additional cost to students, this book can be packaged with *VideoCentral: Literature*, our growing library of more than fifty video interviews with today's writers. Biographical notes and questions make each video an easy-to-assign module.

See **macmillanhighered.com/videolit/catalog**. To order *VideoCentral: Literature* with this print text, use ISBN 978-1-319-05104-4.

ACCESS YOUR INSTRUCTOR RESOURCES

You have a lot to do in your course. Bedford/St. Martin's wants to make it easy for you to find the support you need—and to get it quickly. Go to **macmillanhighered.com/experience_literature/catalog**.

DOWNLOAD YOUR INSTRUCTOR'S MANUAL. *Editor's Notes for Teaching Literature: The Human Experience* offers teaching ideas for each selection in the anthology as well as additional thematic connections and writing topics. To download the PDF, go to **macmillanhighered.com/experience_literature /catalog**.

GET TEACHING IDEAS YOU CAN USE TODAY. Are you looking for professional resources for teaching literature and writing? How about some help with planning classroom activities?

- **TeachingCentral.** We've gathered all of our print and online professional resources in one place. You'll find landmark reference works, sourcebooks on pedagogical issues, award-winning collections, and practical advice for the classroom—all free for instructors and available at **bedfordstmartins .com/teachingcentral**.

- *LitBits: Ideas for Teaching Literature and Creative Writing.* Our *LitBits* blog—hosted by a growing team of instructors, poets, novelists, and scholars—offers a fresh, regularly updated collection of ideas and assignments. You'll find simple ways to teach with new media, excite your students with activities, and join an ongoing conversation about teaching. Go to **macmillanhighered.com/litbits**.

- **Package one of our best-selling brief handbooks at a discount.** Do you need a pocket-sized handbook for your course? Package *Easy Writer* by Andrea Lunsford or *A Pocket Style Manual* by Diana Hacker and Nancy Sommers with this text at a 20% discount. We also offer *Writer's Help 2.0*, our powerful online handbook, as a package option for only $10 when packaged with any of our texts. For more information, go to **macmillanhighered.com /easywriter/catalog**, **macmillanhighered.com/pocket/catalog**, or **writershelp .bedfordstmartins.com/ebooks/helphandbook**.

- **Teach longer works at a nice price.** Volumes in our literary reprints series— Case Studies in Contemporary Criticism and Critical Controversy, the Bedford Shakespeare series, Bedford College Editions, Bedford Cultural Editions, and the Bedford Series in History and Culture—can be shrink-wrapped with *Literature: The Human Experience*. For a complete list of available titles, visit **macmillanhighered.com/literaryreprints/catalog**.

- **TradeUp** *and save 50%.* Add more value and choice to your students' learning experiences by packaging their Bedford/St. Martin's textbook with one of a thousand titles from our sister publishers such as Farrar, Straus and Giroux and St. Martin's Press—at a discount of 50% off the regular price. To learn more, visit **macmillanhighered.com/catalog/discipline/TradeUp**.

CONTENTS

PREFACE FOR INSTRUCTORS   iv

INTRODUCTION   1

RESPONDING TO LITERATURE   2

EMILY DICKINSON, THERE IS NO FRIGATE LIKE A BOOK   2
WHY WE READ LITERATURE   2
READING ACTIVELY AND CRITICALLY   4
READING FICTION   5
  The Methods of Fiction   6
    Tone   6
    Plot   6
    Characterization   7
    Setting   8
    Point of View   8
    Irony   8
    Theme   9
  Questions for Exploring Fiction   9
READING POETRY   10

WALT WHITMAN, WHEN I HEARD THE LEARN'D ASTRONOMER   10
  Word Choice   11
  Figurative Language   11
    Metaphor   12
    Simile   12
    Personification   12
    Allusion   12
    Symbols   13
  The Music of Poetry   13
  Questions for Exploring Poetry   15
READING DRAMA   16
  Stages and Staging   17
  The Elements of Drama   20
    Characters   20
    Dramatic Irony   21

xi

Plot and Conflict   21
Questions for Exploring Drama   22

READING NONFICTION   23
Types of Nonfiction   24
Narrative Nonfiction   24
Descriptive Nonfiction   24
Expository Nonfiction   24
Argumentative Nonfiction   24
Analyzing Nonfiction   25
The Thesis   25
Structure and Detail   25
Style and Tone   26
Questions for Exploring Nonfiction   29

WRITING ABOUT LITERATURE   30

RESPONDING TO YOUR READING   30
Annotating While You Read   30
WILLIAM SHAKESPEARE, SONNET 29   31
THOMAS HARDY, THE MAN HE KILLED   32
Freewriting   34
Keeping a Journal   36
Exploring and Planning   37
Thinking Critically   37
Asking Good Questions   37
Establishing a Working Thesis   38
Gathering Information   38
Organizing Information   39
DRAFTING THE ESSAY   41
Opening with an Argument   41
Supporting Your Thesis   42
REVISING THE ESSAY   43
Editing Your Draft   44
Selecting Strong Verbs   44
Eliminating Unnecessary Modifiers   45
Grammatical Connections   46
Proofreading Your Draft   47
SOME COMMON WRITING ASSIGNMENTS   47
Explication   48
Analysis   51
Comparison and Contrast   57

THE RESEARCH PAPER   60
AN ANNOTATED STUDENT RESEARCH PAPER   61
SOME MATTERS OF FORM AND DOCUMENTATION   69
  Titles   69
  Quotations   69
    Brackets and Ellipses   70
    Quotation Marks and Other Punctuation   70
  Documentation   71
    Documenting Online Sources   72
A CHECKLIST FOR WRITING ABOUT LITERATURE   73

INNOCENCE AND EXPERIENCE   74

QUESTIONS FOR THINKING AND WRITING   76

FICTION   77

NATHANIEL HAWTHORNE (1804–1864)
  YOUNG GOODMAN BROWN   77

NAGUIB MAHFOUZ (1911–2006)
  HALF A DAY   88

JOHN UPDIKE (1932–2009)
  A & P   92

TONI CADE BAMBARA (1939–1995)
  THE LESSON   98

JAMAICA KINCAID (B. 1949)
  GIRL   105

DANIEL OROZCO (B. 1942)
  ORIENTATION   107

CAMDEN JOY (B. 1964)
  DUM DUM BOYS   113

CONNECTING STORIES: CRUSHES   125

  JAMES JOYCE (1882–1941)
    ARABY   125

  RIVKA GALCHEN (B. 1976)
    WILD BERRY BLUE   130

CASE STUDY IN ARGUMENT

FINDING GRACE IN FLANNERY O'CONNOR   141

FLANNERY O'CONNOR (1925–1964)
    A GOOD MAN IS HARD TO FIND   141
    from MYSTERY AND MANNERS   153

BOB DOWELL (B. 1932)
    from THE MOMENT OF GRACE IN THE FICTION OF FLANNERY
    O'CONNOR   155

HALLMAN B. BRYANT (B. 1936)
    READING THE MAP IN "A GOOD MAN IS HARD TO FIND"   157

MICHAEL CLARK (1946–1999)
    FLANNERY O'CONNOR'S "A GOOD MAN IS HARD TO FIND":
    THE MOMENT OF GRACE   163

POETRY   167

JONATHAN SWIFT (1667–1745)
    STELLA'S BIRTH-DAY   167

WILLIAM BLAKE (1757–1827)
    THE CHIMNEY SWEEPER (SONGS OF INNOCENCE)   168
    THE CHIMNEY SWEEPER (SONGS OF EXPERIENCE)   169
    THE LAMB   170
    THE SHEPHERD   170
    THE GARDEN OF LOVE   171
    LONDON   171
    THE TYGER   172

ROBERT BROWNING (1812–1889)
    MY LAST DUCHESS   173

EMILY DICKINSON (1830–1886)
    I FELT A FUNERAL, IN MY BRAIN   175

THOMAS HARDY (1840–1928)
    MEN WHO MARCH AWAY   175

GERARD MANLEY HOPKINS (1844–1889)
    SPRING AND FALL   176

A. E. HOUSMAN (1859–1936)
    WHEN I WAS ONE-AND-TWENTY   177

ROBERT FROST (1874–1963)
    THE ROAD NOT TAKEN   178
    BIRCHES   178

E. E. CUMMINGS (1894–1962)
    IN JUST-   180

STEVIE SMITH (1902–1971)
NOT WAVING BUT DROWNING   180
TO CARRY THE CHILD   181

COUNTEE CULLEN (1903–1946)
INCIDENT   182

DYLAN THOMAS (1914–1953)
FERN HILL   183

LAWRENCE FERLINGHETTI (B. 1919)
CONSTANTLY RISKING ABSURDITY   185

PHILIP LARKIN (1922–1985)
A STUDY OF READING HABITS   186
THIS BE THE VERSE   187

AUDRE LORDE (1934–1992)
HANGING FIRE   187

ALICIA OSTRIKER (B. 1937)
THE DOGS AT LIVE OAK BEACH, SANTA CRUZ   189

JEAN NORDHAUS (B. 1939)
A DANDELION FOR MY MOTHER   189

LOUISE GLÜCK (B. 1943)
THE SCHOOL CHILDREN   190
THE MYTH OF INNOCENCE   190

ALAN FELDMAN (B. 1945)
MY CENTURY   192

SANDRA CISNEROS (B. 1954)
MY WICKED WICKED WAYS   194

SANDRA M. CASTILLO (B. 1962)
CHRISTMAS, 1970   195

SPENCER REECE (B. 1963)
THE MANHATTAN PROJECT   196

EVELYN LAU (B. 1971)
SOLIPSISM   197

CONNECTING POEMS:
VOICES OF EXPERIENCE   199

LANGSTON HUGHES (1902–1967)
MOTHER TO SON   199

PETER MEINKE (B. 1932)
ADVICE TO MY SON   200

ROBERT MEZEY (B. 1935)
MY MOTHER   201

GARY SOTO (B. 1952)
    BEHIND GRANDMA'S HOUSE   203

**CONNECTING POEMS:
HAPPY HOLIDAYS**   204

W. S. MERWIN (B. 1927)
    THANKS   204

CARL DENNIS (B. 1939)
    THANKSGIVING LETTER FROM HARRY   205

SHEILA ORTIZ TAYLOR (B. 1939)
    THE WAY BACK   207

JAMES WELCH (1940–2003)
    CHRISTMAS COMES TO MOCCASIN FLAT   210

MAGGIE NELSON (B. 1973)
    THANKSGIVING   211

DRAMA   213

HENRIK IBSEN (1828–1906)
    A DOLL'S HOUSE   213

SUZAN-LORI PARKS (B. 1963)
    FATHER COMES HOME FROM THE WARS   270

NONFICTION   284

LANGSTON HUGHES (1902–1967)
    SALVATION   284

JUDITH ORTIZ COFER (B. 1952)
    AMERICAN HISTORY   287

BRIAN DOYLE (B. 1956)
    POP ART   294

ALLIE BROSH (B. 1985)
    THIS IS WHY I'LL NEVER BE AN ADULT   296

**CONNECTING NONFICTION:
GRADUATING**   304

DAVID SEDARIS (B. 1956)
    WHAT I LEARNED   304

DAVID FOSTER WALLACE (1962–2008)
    COMMENCEMENT SPEECH, KENYON COLLEGE   309

FURTHER QUESTIONS FOR THINKING AND WRITING   315

CONFORMITY AND REBELLION 316

QUESTIONS FOR THINKING AND WRITING 318

FICTION 319

HERMAN MELVILLE (1819–1891)
BARTLEBY, THE SCRIVENER 319

FRANZ KAFKA (1883–1924)
A HUNGER ARTIST 347

RALPH ELLISON (1914–1994)
BATTLE ROYAL 355

SHIRLEY JACKSON (1919–1965)
THE LOTTERY 367

HARLAN ELLISON® (B. 1934)
"REPENT, HARLEQUIN!" SAID THE TICKTOCKMAN 374

AMY TAN (B. 1952)
TWO KINDS 384

JENNIFER EGAN (B. 1962)
SAFARI 393

CONNECTING STORIES: REBELLIOUS IMAGINATIONS 407

JAMES THURBER (1894–1961)
THE SECRET LIFE OF WALTER MITTY 407

GEORGE SAUNDERS (B. 1958)
THE END OF FIRPO IN THE WORLD 411

POETRY 416

JOHN DONNE (1572–1631)
HOLY SONNETS: "IF POISONOUS MINERALS, AND IF THAT TREE" 416

RICHARD CRASHAW (1613–1649)
BUT MEN LOVED DARKNESS RATHER THAN LIGHT 417

WILLIAM WORDSWORTH (1770–1850)
THE WORLD IS TOO MUCH WITH US 417

ALFRED, LORD TENNYSON (1809–1892)
ULYSSES 418

EMILY DICKINSON (1830–1886)
MUCH MADNESS IS DIVINEST SENSE 420
SHE ROSE TO HIS REQUIREMENT 421

WILLIAM BUTLER YEATS (1865–1939)
EASTER 1916   422
THE SECOND COMING   424

CARL SANDBURG (1878–1967)
I AM THE PEOPLE, THE MOB   425

WALLACE STEVENS (1879–1955)
PETER QUINCE AT THE CLAVIER   426

CLAUDE MCKAY (1890–1948)
IF WE MUST DIE   429

LANGSTON HUGHES (1902–1967)
HARLEM   429

W. H. AUDEN (1907–1973)
THE UNKNOWN CITIZEN   430

DUDLEY RANDALL (1914–2000)
BALLAD OF BIRMINGHAM   431

GWENDOLYN BROOKS (1917–2000)
WE REAL COOL   432

DONALD DAVIE (1922–1995)
THE NONCONFORMIST   432

PHILIP LEVINE (B. 1928–2015)
WHAT WORK IS   433

MARGE PIERCY (B. 1936)
THE MARKET ECONOMY   435

CAROLYN FORCHÉ (B. 1950)
THE COLONEL   436

NATASHA TRETHEWEY (B. 1966)
FLOUNDER   437

CONNECTING POEMS: REVOLUTIONARY THINKING   438

WILLIAM BUTLER YEATS (1865–1939)
THE GREAT DAY   438

ROBERT FROST (1874–1963)
A SEMI-REVOLUTION   439

NIKKI GIOVANNI (B. 1943)
DREAMS   439

CONNECTING POEMS: REVISING AMERICA 440

Walt Whitman (1819–1892)
One Song, America, Before I Go 440

Langston Hughes (1902–1967)
I, Too 441

Allen Ginsberg (1926–1997)
A Supermarket in California 442

Shirley Geok-Lin Lim (b. 1944)
Learning to Love America 443

CONNECTING POEMS: SOLDIERS' PROTESTS 444

Thomas Hardy (1840–1928)
The Man He Killed 445

Wilfred Owen (1893–1918)
Dulce et Decorum Est 445

Hanan Mikha'il 'Ashrawi (b. 1946)
Night Patrol 446

Kevin C. Powers (b. 1980)
Letter Composed During a Lull in the Fighting 448

DRAMA 450

Sophocles (496?–406 bce)
Antigonê 450

NONFICTION 481

Jonathan Swift (1667–1745)
A Modest Proposal 481

Jamaica Kincaid (b. 1949)
On Seeing England for the First Time 489

CONNECTING NONFICTION: WEIGHING BELIEF 498

E. L. Doctorow (b. 1931–2015)
Why We Are Infidels 498

Salman Rushdie (b. 1947)
"Imagine There's No Heaven" 501

CASE STUDY IN ARGUMENT

MAKING CHANGE 506

BILL MCKIBBEN (B. 1960)
A CALL TO ARMS: AN INVITATION TO DEMAND ACTION
ON CLIMATE CHANGE 506

REBECCA SOLNIT (B. 1961)
REVOLUTIONS PER MINUTE 510

MALCOLM GLADWELL (B. 1963)
SMALL CHANGE: WHY THE REVOLUTION WILL
NOT BE TWEETED 513

CLAY SHIRKY (B. 1964)
THE POLITICAL POWER OF SOCIAL MEDIA 522

FURTHER QUESTIONS FOR THINKING AND WRITING 533

CULTURE AND IDENTITY 534

QUESTIONS FOR THINKING AND WRITING 536

FICTION 537

LU XUN (1881–1936)
DIARY OF A MADMAN 537

CHARLOTTE PERKINS GILMAN (1860–1935)
THE YELLOW WALLPAPER 548

JAMES BALDWIN (1924–1987)
SONNY'S BLUES 561

ALICE WALKER (B. 1944)
EVERYDAY USE 586

SHERMAN ALEXIE (B. 1966)
WAR DANCES 594

EDWIDGE DANTICAT (B. 1969)
THE BOOK OF THE DEAD 614

CONNECTING STORIES: INSIDERS AND OUTCASTS 623

WILLIAM FAULKNER (1897–1962)
A ROSE FOR EMILY 623

HA JIN (B. 1956)
THE BRIDEGROOM 630

POETRY 646

JONATHAN SWIFT (1667–1745)
  MARKET WOMEN'S CRIES 646

EMILY DICKINSON (1830–1886)
  I'M NOBODY! WHO ARE YOU? 648

JAMES WELDON JOHNSON (1871–1938)
  A POET TO HIS BABY SON 648

PAUL LAURENCE DUNBAR (1872–1906)
  WE WEAR THE MASK 650

GEORGIA DOUGLAS JOHNSON (1880–1966)
  OLD BLACK MEN 650

T. S. ELIOT (1888–1965)
  THE LOVE SONG OF J. ALFRED PRUFROCK 651

E. E. CUMMINGS (1894–1962)
  THE CAMBRIDGE LADIES WHO LIVE IN FURNISHED SOULS 655

HOWARD NEMEROV (1920–1991)
  MONEY 656

ETHERIDGE KNIGHT (1931–1991)
  HARD ROCK RETURNS TO PRISON FROM THE HOSPITAL
    FOR THE CRIMINAL INSANE 658

MARGE PIERCY (B. 1936)
  BARBIE DOLL 659

KAY RYAN (B. 1945)
  ALL SHALL BE RESTORED 660

JUAN FELIPE HERRERA (B. 1948)
  187 REASONS MEXICANOS CAN'T CROSS
    THE BORDER (REMIX) 661

MAGGIE ANDERSON (B. 1948)
  LONG STORY 666

GREGORY DJANIKIAN (B. 1949)
  SAILING TO AMERICA 669

JUDITH ORTIZ COFER (B. 1952)
  LATIN WOMEN PRAY 670

LOUISE ERDRICH (B. 1954)
  DEAR JOHN WAYNE 671

MARILYN CHIN (B. 1955)
  HOW I GOT THAT NAME 672

JOSHUA CLOVER (B. 1962)
  THE NEVADA GLASSWORKS 675

TASLIMA NASRIN (B. 1962)
  THINGS CHEAPLY HAD   677

OMAR PÉREZ (B. 1964)
  CONTRIBUTIONS TO A RUDIMENTARY CONCEPT OF NATION   678

CHRIS ABANI (B. 1966)
  BLUE   679

KEVIN YOUNG (B. 1970)
  NEGATIVE   680

TERRANCE HAYES (B. 1971)
  ROOT   681

ALEXANDRA TEAGUE (B. 1974)
  ADJECTIVES OF ORDER   683

TISHANI DOSHI (B. 1975)
  THE IMMIGRANT'S SONG   683
  LAMENT—I   685

CONNECTING POEMS: POETIC IDENTITIES   686

WALT WHITMAN (1819–1892)
  from SONG OF MYSELF   686

FRANK O'HARA (1926–1966)
  MY HEART   690

BILLY COLLINS (B. 1941)
  MONDAY   691

CARL PHILLIPS (B. 1959)
  BLUE   692

TIMOTHY YU (B. 1974)
  CHINESE SILENCE NO. 22   694

CONNECTING POEMS: WORKING MOTHERS   696

TESS GALLAGHER (B. 1943)
  I STOP WRITING THE POEM   696

JULIA ALVAREZ (B. 1950)
  WOMAN'S WORK   697

RITA DOVE (B. 1952)
  MY MOTHER ENTERS THE WORK FORCE   698

DEBORAH GARRISON (B. 1965)
  SESTINA FOR THE WORKING MOTHER   699

CONNECTING POEMS: AMERICA THROUGH IMMIGRANTS' EYES 701

PHILLIS WHEATLEY (1753–1784)
ON BEING BROUGHT FROM AFRICA TO AMERICA 702

EMMA LAZARUS (1849–1887)
THE NEW COLOSSUS 702

LÉOPOLD SÉDAR SENGHOR (1906–2001)
TO NEW YORK 703

KOFI AWOONOR (1935–2013)
AMERICA 705

RICHARD BLANCO (B. 1968)
AMÉRICA 707

DRAMA 710

CASE STUDY IN ARGUMENT

REVIEWING AN AMERICAN CLASSIC: *A RAISIN IN THE SUN* 710

LORRAINE HANSBERRY (1930–1965)
A RAISIN IN THE SUN 710

LLOYD W. BROWN (B. 1938)
LORRAINE HANSBERRY AS IRONIST: A REAPPRAISAL OF *A RAISIN IN THE SUN* 782

MARGARET B. WILKERSON (B. ?)
A RAISIN IN THE SUN: ANNIVERSARY OF AN AMERICAN CLASSIC 788

ROBIN BERNSTEIN (B. 1969)
INVENTING A FISHBOWL: WHITE SUPREMACY AND THE CRITICAL RECEPTION OF LORRAINE HANSBERRY'S *A RAISIN IN THE SUN* 799

MARILYN STASIO (B. 1940)
VARIETY REVIEW OF *A RAISIN IN THE SUN* 810

DAVID HENRY HWANG (B. 1957)
TRYING TO FIND CHINATOWN 812

NONFICTION 819

VIRGINIA WOOLF (1882–1941)
WHAT IF SHAKESPEARE HAD HAD A SISTER? 819

GEORGE ORWELL (1903–1950)
  SHOOTING AN ELEPHANT 827

SABRINA JONES (B. 1960)
  LITTLE HOUSE IN THE BIG CITY 833

EULA BISS (B. 1977)
  TIME AND DISTANCE OVERCOME 844

**CONNECTING NONFICTION:
FITTING IN** 849

BHARATI MUKHERJEE (B. 1940)
  TWO WAYS TO BELONG IN AMERICA 849

LACY M. JOHNSON (B. 1978)
  WHITE TRASH PRIMER 852

FURTHER QUESTIONS FOR THINKING AND WRITING 857

LOVE AND HATE 858

QUESTIONS FOR THINKING AND WRITING 860

FICTION 861

KATE CHOPIN (1851–1904)
  THE STORM 861

ZORA NEALE HURSTON (1891–1960)
  SWEAT 866

RAYMOND CARVER (1938–1988)
  WHAT WE TALK ABOUT WHEN WE TALK ABOUT LOVE 876

JOYCE CAROL OATES (B. 1938)
  WHERE ARE YOU GOING, WHERE HAVE YOU BEEN? 886

LYDIA MILLET (B. 1968)
  LOVE IN INFANT MONKEYS 900

JUNOT DÍAZ (B. 1968)
  DROWN 906

CHIMAMANDA NGOZI ADICHIE (B. 1977)
  MY AMERICAN JON 915

CONNECTING STORIES: HAVING IT ALL   923

ERNEST HEMINGWAY (1899–1961)
  HILLS LIKE WHITE ELEPHANTS   923

DAVID FOSTER WALLACE (1962–2008)
  GOOD PEOPLE   927

POETRY   933

SAPPHO (CA. 610–CA. 580 BCE)
  WITH HIS VENOM   933

CATULLUS (CA. 84–CA. 54 BCE)
  85   933

WILLIAM SHAKESPEARE (1564–1616)
  SONNET 18 "SHALL I COMPARE THEE TO A SUMMER'S DAY?"   934
  SONNET 29 "WHEN, IN DISGRACE WITH FORTUNE
    AND MEN'S EYES"   934
  SONNET 64 "WHEN I HAVE SEEN BY TIME'S FELL HAND DEFAC'D"   935
  SONNET 116, "LET ME NOT TO THE MARRIAGE OF TRUE MINDS"   936
  SONNET 130 "MY MISTRESS' EYES ARE NOTHING LIKE THE SUN"   936

JOHN DONNE (1572–1631)
  THE FLEA   937
  A VALEDICTION: FORBIDDING MOURNING   938

BEN JONSON (1572–1637)
  SONG, TO CELIA   940

ROBERT HERRICK (1591–1674)
  TO THE VIRGINS, TO MAKE MUCH OF TIME   940

ANNE BRADSTREET (CA. 1612–1672)
  TO MY DEAR AND LOVING HUSBAND   941

WILLIAM BLAKE (1757–1827)
  A POISON TREE   941

ROBERT BURNS (1759–1796)
  A RED, RED ROSE   942

MATTHEW ARNOLD (1822–1888)
  DOVER BEACH   943

ROBERT FROST (1874–1963)
  FIRE AND ICE   944

DOROTHY PARKER (1893–1967)
  ONE PERFECT ROSE   944

THEODORE ROETHKE (1908–1963)
  I KNEW A WOMAN   944

ELIZABETH BISHOP (1911–1979)
ONE ART   946

JOHN FREDERICK NIMS (1913–1999)
LOVE POEM   946

LISEL MUELLER (B. 1924)
HAPPY AND UNHAPPY FAMILIES I   947

CAROLYN KIZER (B. 1925–2014)
BITCH   948
AFTERNOON HAPPINESS   949

GALWAY KINNELL (B. 1927–2014)
AFTER MAKING LOVE WE HEAR FOOTSTEPS   951

ADRIENNE RICH (1929–2012)
LIVING IN SIN   952

SYLVIA PLATH (1932–1963)
DADDY   953

LUCILLE CLIFTON (B. 1936–2010)
THERE IS A GIRL INSIDE   956

SEAMUS HEANEY (B. 1939–2013)
VALEDICTION   957

BILLY COLLINS (B. 1941)
SONNET   958

SHARON OLDS (B. 1942)
SEX WITHOUT LOVE   958

WYATT PRUNTY (B. 1947)
LEARNING THE BICYCLE   959

ADRIAN BLEVINS (B. 1964)
CASE AGAINST APRIL   960

DAISY FRIED (B. 1967)
ECONO MOTEL, OCEAN CITY   962

CONNECTING POEMS: LOOKING BACK ON LOVE   963

SIR THOMAS WYATT (1503–1542)
THEY FLEE FROM ME   963

LADY MARY WROTH (CA. 1587–CA. 1651)
"COME DARKEST NIGHT, BECOMING SORROW BEST"   964

SHARON OLDS (B. 1942)
MY FATHER'S DIARY   965

DEAN YOUNG (B. 1955)
WINGED PURPOSES   966

CONNECTING POEMS: REMEMBERING FATHERS 968

THEODORE ROETHKE (1908–1963)
MY PAPA'S WALTZ 968

ROBERT HAYDEN (1913–1980)
THOSE WINTER SUNDAYS 969

LI-YOUNG LEE (B. 1957)
EATING ALONE 970

CONNECTING POEMS: LOVE STINKS 972

CATULLUS (CA. 84–CA. 54 BCE)
70 972

APHRA BEHN (1640–1689)
LOVE IN FANTASTIQUE TRIUMPH SATT 972

EDNA ST. VINCENT MILLAY (1892–1950)
I KNOW I AM BUT SUMMER TO YOUR HEART (SONNET XXVII) 973

FAIZ AHMED FAIZ (1911–1984)
BE NEAR ME 974

ANDREA HOLLANDER (B. 1947)
BETRAYAL 975

CASE STUDY IN ARGUMENT

SEDUCTIVE REASONING 977

ANDREW MARVELL (1621–1678)
TO HIS COY MISTRESS 977

A. D. HOPE (1907–2000)
HIS COY MISTRESS TO MR. MARVELL 978

PETER DEVRIES (1910–1993)
TO HIS IMPORTUNATE MISTRESS (ANDREW MARVELL UPDATED) 981

ANNIE FINCH (B. 1956)
COY MISTRESS 982

DRAMA 984

WILLIAM SHAKESPEARE (1564–1616)
OTHELLO 984

SUSAN GLASPELL (1882–1948)
TRIFLES 1073

LYNN NOTTAGE (B. 1964)
POOF! 1087

NONFICTION 1095

PAUL (D. CA. 64 CE)
1 CORINTHIANS 13 1095

MAXINE HONG KINGSTON (B. 1940)
NO NAME WOMAN 1097

GRACE TALUSAN (B. 1972)
MY FATHER'S NOOSE 1107

SONYA CHUNG (B. 1973)
GETTING IT RIGHT 1109

CONNECTING NONFICTION: LOOKING FOR LOVE IN ALL THE WRONG PLACES 1111

DAGOBERTO GILB (B. 1950)
I KNEW SHE WAS BEAUTIFUL 1111

PABLO PIÑERO STILLMANN (B. 1982)
LIFE, LOVE, HAPPINESS: A FOUND ESSAY FROM THE TWITTERVERSE 1119

FURTHER QUESTIONS FOR THINKING AND WRITING 1121

LIFE AND DEATH 1122

QUESTIONS FOR THINKING AND WRITING 1124

FICTION 1126

EDGAR ALLAN POE (1809–1849)
THE CASK OF AMONTILLADO 1126

LEO TOLSTOY (1828–1910)
THE DEATH OF IVÁN ILÝICH 1132

KATE CHOPIN (1850–1904)
THE STORY OF AN HOUR 1174

TIM O'BRIEN (B. 1946)
THE THINGS THEY CARRIED 1177

HELENA MARÍA VIRAMONTES (B. 1954)
THE MOTHS 1191

SAM LIPSYTE (B. 1968)
THE NATURALS 1196

CONNECTING STORIES:
MOURNING RITUALS 1209

LESLIE MARMON SILKO (B. 1948)
THE MAN TO SEND RAIN CLOUDS 1209
ALLEGRA GOODMAN (B. 1967)
APPLE CAKE 1213

CONNECTING STORIES:
BETWEEN LIFE AND DEATH 1227

KATHERINE ANNE PORTER (1890–1980)
THE JILTING OF GRANNY WEATHERALL 1227
TOBIAS WOLFF (B. 1945)
BULLET IN THE BRAIN 1234

POETRY 1239

ANONYMOUS
EDWARD 1239

WILLIAM SHAKESPEARE (1564–1616)
SONNET 73 "THAT TIME OF YEAR THOU MAYST IN ME BEHOLD" 1241
FEAR NO MORE THE HEAT O' THE SUN 1242

JOHN DONNE (1572–1631)
DEATH, BE NOT PROUD 1243

JONATHAN SWIFT (1667–1745)
A SATIRICAL ELEGY ON THE DEATH OF A LATE
FAMOUS GENERAL 1243

PERCY BYSSHE SHELLEY (1792–1822)
OZYMANDIAS 1245

JOHN KEATS (1795–1821)
ODE ON A GRECIAN URN 1245

EMILY DICKINSON (1830–1886)
AFTER GREAT PAIN, A FORMAL FEELING COMES 1247
I HEARD A FLY BUZZ—WHEN I DIED 1248
APPARENTLY WITH NO SURPRISE 1248

CASE STUDY IN WORDS AND IMAGES

POEMS ABOUT PAINTINGS   1249

W. H. AUDEN (1907–1973)
MUSÉE DES BEAUX ARTS   1249

PIETER BRUEGHEL THE ELDER (C. 1525–1569)
LANDSCAPE WITH THE FALL OF ICARUS   1250

LAWRENCE FERLINGHETTI (B. 1919)
IN GOYA'S GREATEST SCENES   1251

FRANCISCO DE GOYA (1746–1828)
THE THIRD OF MAY, 1808, MADRID   1252

ANNE SEXTON (1928–1974)
THE STARRY NIGHT   1253

VINCENT VAN GOGH (1853–1890)
THE STARRY NIGHT   1254

DONALD FINKEL (1929–2008)
THE GREAT WAVE: HOKUSAI   1255

KATSUSHIKA HOKUSAI (1760–1849)
THE GREAT WAVE OFF KANAGAWA   1256

EMILY DICKINSON (1830–1886)
BECAUSE I COULD NOT STOP FOR DEATH   1257

GERARD MANLEY HOPKINS (1844–1889)
GOD'S GRANDEUR   1257

A. E. HOUSMAN (1859–1936)
TO AN ATHLETE DYING YOUNG   1258

WILLIAM BUTLER YEATS (1865–1939)
SAILING TO BYZANTIUM   1259

EDWIN ARLINGTON ROBINSON (1869–1935)
RICHARD CORY   1261

ROBERT FROST (1874–1963)
AFTER APPLE-PICKING   1261
'OUT, OUT—'   1262
NOTHING GOLD CAN STAY   1263
STOPPING BY WOODS ON A SNOWY EVENING   1264
DESIGN   1265

PABLO NERUDA (1904–1973)
THE DEAD WOMAN   1265

CZESŁAW MIŁOSZ (1911–2004)
A SONG ON THE END OF THE WORLD   1266

DYLAN THOMAS (1914–1953)
DO NOT GO GENTLE INTO THAT GOOD NIGHT   1267

DONALD HALL (B. 1928)
AFFIRMATION   1268

MARVIN KLOTZ (1930–2014)
REQUIEM   1270

MARY OLIVER (B. 1935)
WHEN DEATH COMES   1270

ALICIA OSTRIKER (B. 1937)
DAFFODILS   1272

SEAMUS HEANEY (B. 1939)
MID-TERM BREAK   1273

JANE KENYON (1947–1995)
LET EVENING COME   1275

YUSEF KOMUNYAKAA (B. 1947)
FACING IT   1276

VICTOR HERNÁNDEZ CRUZ (B. 1949)
PROBLEMS WITH HURRICANES   1277

MARK HALLIDAY (B. 1949)
CHICKEN SALAD   1278

MARIE HOWE (B. 1950)
WHAT THE LIVING DO   1279

MARK TURPIN (B. 1953)
THE MAN WHO BUILT THIS HOUSE   1280

DILRUBA AHMED (B. 1973)
SNAKE OIL, SNAKE BITE   1281

CONNECTING POEMS:
ANIMAL FATES   1282

ELIZABETH BISHOP (1911–1979)
THE FISH   1282

WILLIAM STAFFORD (1914–1995)
TRAVELING THROUGH THE DARK   1285

JOHN UPDIKE (1932–2009)
DOG'S DEATH   1286

WILLIAM GREENWAY (B. 1947)
PIT PONY   1287

CONNECTING POEMS:
SEIZING THE DAY 1289

RAINER MARIA RILKE (1875–1926)
ARCHAIC TORSO OF APOLLO 1289

JAMES WRIGHT (1927–1980)
LYING IN A HAMMOCK AT WILLIAM DUFFY'S FARM IN PINE ISLAND,
MINNESOTA 1290

BILLY COLLINS (B. 1941)
THE SANDHILL CRANES OF NEBRASKA 1291

BARBARA RAS (B. 1949)
YOU CAN'T HAVE IT ALL 1292

TONY HOAGLAND (B. 1953)
I HAVE NEWS FOR YOU 1294

DRAMA 1296

EDWARD ALBEE (B. 1928)
THE SANDBOX 1296

NONFICTION 1303

JOHN DONNE (1572–1631)
MEDITATION XVII, *from* DEVOTIONS UPON
EMERGENT OCCASIONS 1303

E. B. WHITE (1899–1985)
ONCE MORE TO THE LAKE 1305

JILL CHRISTMAN (B. 1969)
THE SLOTH 1311

JOHN JEREMIAH SULLIVAN (B. 1974)
FEET IN SMOKE 1312

CONNECTING NONFICTION:
MISSING MOTHERS 1319

JONATHAN LETHEM (B. 1964)
13, 1977, 21 1319

RUTH MARGALIT (B. 1983)
THE UNMOTHERED 1325

FURTHER QUESTIONS FOR THINKING AND WRITING 1331

APPENDIXES 1333

GLOSSARY OF CRITICAL APPROACHES 1334

Introduction 1334

Deconstruction 1336

Ethical Criticism 1337

Feminist Criticism 1337

Formalist Criticism 1338

Marxist Criticism 1338

New Historical Criticism 1339

Postcolonial Criticism 1340

Psychoanalytic Criticism 1340

Reader-Response Criticism 1341

BIOGRAPHICAL NOTES ON THE AUTHORS 1343

GLOSSARY OF LITERARY TERMS 1418

ACKNOWLEDGMENTS 1429

INDEX OF AUTHORS AND TITLES 1439

ALTERNATE CONTENTS

Arranged by genre and alphabetically by the author's last name.

FICTION

CHIMAMANDA NGOZI ADICHIE (B. 1977)
MY AMERICAN JON   915

SHERMAN ALEXIE (B. 1966)
WAR DANCES   594

JAMES BALDWIN (1924–1987)
SONNY'S BLUES   561

TONI CADE BAMBARA (1939–1995)
THE LESSON   98

RAYMOND CARVER (1938–1988)
WHAT WE TALK ABOUT WHEN WE TALK ABOUT LOVE   876

KATE CHOPIN (1851–1904)
THE STORM   861
THE STORY OF AN HOUR   1174

EDWIDGE DANTICAT (B. 1969)
THE BOOK OF THE DEAD   614

JUNOT DÍAZ (B. 1968)
DROWN   906

JENNIFER EGAN (B. 1962)
SAFARI   393

HARLAN ELLISON® (B. 1934)
"REPENT, HARLEQUIN!" SAID THE TICKTOCKMAN   374

RALPH ELLISON (1914–1994)
BATTLE ROYAL   355

WILLIAM FAULKNER (1897–1962)
A ROSE FOR EMILY   623

RIVKA GALCHEN (B. 1976)
WILD BERRY BLUE   130

CHARLOTTE PERKINS GILMAN (1860–1935)
THE YELLOW WALLPAPER   548

ALLEGRA GOODMAN (B. 1967)
APPLE CAKE   1213

NATHANIEL HAWTHORNE (1804–1864)
YOUNG GOODMAN BROWN 77

ERNEST HEMINGWAY (1899–1961)
HILLS LIKE WHITE ELEPHANTS 923

ZORA NEALE HURSTON (1891–1960)
SWEAT 866

SHIRLEY JACKSON (1919–1965)
THE LOTTERY 367

HA JIN (B. 1956)
THE BRIDEGROOM 630

CAMDEN JOY (B. 1964)
DUM DUM BOYS 113

JAMES JOYCE (1882–1941)
ARABY 125

FRANZ KAFKA (1883–1924)
A HUNGER ARTIST 347

JAMAICA KINCAID (B. 1949)
GIRL 105

SAM LIPSYTE (B. 1968)
THE NATURALS 1196

NAGUIB MAHFOUZ (1911–2006)
HALF A DAY 88

HERMAN MELVILLE (1819–1891)
BARTLEBY, THE SCRIVENER 319

LYDIA MILLET (B. 1968)
LOVE IN INFANT MONKEYS 900

JOYCE CAROL OATES (B. 1938)
WHERE ARE YOU GOING, WHERE HAVE YOU BEEN? 886

TIM O'BRIEN (B. 1946)
THE THINGS THEY CARRIED 1177

FLANNERY O'CONNOR (1925–1964)
A GOOD MAN IS HARD TO FIND 141

DANIEL OROZCO (B. 1942)
ORIENTATION 107

EDGAR ALLAN POE (1809–1849)
THE CASK OF AMONTILLADO 1126

KATHERINE ANNE PORTER (1890–1980)
THE JILTING OF GRANNY WEATHERALL 1227

GEORGE SAUNDERS (B. 1958)
THE END OF FIRPO IN THE WORLD 411

LESLIE MARMON SILKO (B. 1948)
THE MAN TO SEND RAIN CLOUDS   1209

AMY TAN (B. 1952)
TWO KINDS   384

JAMES THURBER (1984–1961)
THE SECRET LIFE OF WALTER MITTY   407

LEO TOLSTOY (1828–1910)
THE DEATH OF IVÁN ILÝICH   1132

JOHN UPDIKE (1932–2009)
A & P   92

HELENA MARÍA VIRAMONTES (B. 1954)
THE MOTHS   1191

ALICE WALKER (B. 1944)
EVERYDAY USE   586

DAVID FOSTER WALLACE (1962–2008)
GOOD PEOPLE   927

TOBIAS WOLFF (B. 1945)
BULLET IN THE BRAIN   1234

LU XUN (1881–1936)
DIARY OF A MADMAN   537

POETRY

CHRIS ABANI (B. 1966)
BLUE   679

DILRUBA AHMED (B. 1973)
SNAKE OIL, SNAKE BITE   1282

JULIA ALVAREZ (B. 1950)
WOMAN'S WORK   697

MAGGIE ANDERSON (B. 1948)
LONG STORY   666

ANONYMOUS
EDWARD   1239

MATTHEW ARNOLD (1822–1888)
DOVER BEACH   943

HANAN MIKHA'IL 'ASHRAWI (B. 1946)
NIGHT PATROL   446

W. H. AUDEN (1907–1973)
THE UNKNOWN CITIZEN   430
MUSÉE DES BEAUX ARTS   1249

KOFI AWOONOR (1935–2013)
AMERICA 705

APHRA BEHN (1640–1689)
LOVE IN FANTASTIQUE TRIUMPH SATT 972

ELIZABETH BISHOP (1911–1979)
ONE ART 946
THE FISH 1282

WILLIAM BLAKE (1757–1827)
THE CHIMNEY SWEEPER (SONGS OF INNOCENCE) 168
THE CHIMNEY SWEEPER (SONGS OF EXPERIENCE) 169
THE LAMB 170
THE SHEPHERD 170
THE GARDEN OF LOVE 171
LONDON 171
THE TYGER 172
A POISON TREE 941

RICHARD BLANCO (B. 1968)
AMÉRICA 707

ADRIAN BLEVINS (B. 1964)
CASE AGAINST APRIL 960

ANNE BRADSTREET (CA. 1612–1672)
TO MY DEAR AND LOVING HUSBAND 941

GWENDOLYN BROOKS (1917–2000)
WE REAL COOL 432

ROBERT BROWNING (1812–1889)
MY LAST DUCHESS 173

ROBERT BURNS (1759–1796)
A RED, RED ROSE 942

SANDRA M. CASTILLO (B. 1962)
CHRISTMAS, 1970 195

CATULLUS (CA. 84–CA. 54 BCE)
85 933
70 972

MARILYN CHIN (B. 1955)
HOW I GOT THAT NAME 672

SANDRA CISNEROS (B. 1954)
MY WICKED WICKED WAYS 194

LUCILLE CLIFTON (B. 1936–2010)
THERE IS A GIRL INSIDE 956

JOSHUA CLOVER (B. 1962)
THE NEVADA GLASSWORKS 675

JUDITH ORTIZ COFER (B. 1952)
LATIN WOMEN PRAY   670

BILLY COLLINS (B. 1941)
MONDAY   691
SONNET   958
THE SANDHILL CRANES OF NEBRASKA   1291

RICHARD CRASHAW (1613–1649)
BUT MEN LOVED DARKNESS RATHER THAN LIGHT   417

VICTOR HERNÁNDEZ CRUZ (B. 1949)
PROBLEMS WITH HURRICANES   1277

COUNTEE CULLEN (1903–1946)
INCIDENT   182

E. E. CUMMINGS (1894–1962)
IN JUST-   180
THE CAMBRIDGE LADIES WHO LIVE IN FURNISHED SOULS   655

DONALD DAVIE (1922–1995)
THE NONCONFORMIST   432

CARL DENNIS (B. 1939)
THANKSGIVING LETTER FROM HARRY   205

PETER DEVRIES (1910–1993)
TO HIS IMPORTUNATE MISTRESS (ANDREW MARVELL UPDATED)   981

EMILY DICKINSON (1830–1886)
THERE IS NO FRIGATE LIKE A BOOK   2
I FELT A FUNERAL, IN MY BRAIN   175
MUCH MADNESS IS DIVINEST SENSE   420
SHE ROSE TO HIS REQUIREMENT   421
I'M NOBODY! WHO ARE YOU?   648
AFTER GREAT PAIN, A FORMAL FEELING COMES   1247
I HEARD A FLY BUZZ—WHEN I DIED   1248
APPARENTLY WITH NO SURPRISE   1248
BECAUSE I COULD NOT STOP FOR DEATH   1257

GREGORY DJANIKIAN (B. 1949)
SAILING TO AMERICA   669

JOHN DONNE (1572–1631)
HOLY SONNETS: "IF POISONOUS MINERALS, AND IF THAT TREE"   416
THE FLEA   937
A VALEDICTION: FORBIDDING MOURNING   938
DEATH, BE NOT PROUD   1243

TISHANI DOSHI (B. 1975)
THE IMMIGRANT'S SONG   683
LAMENT—I   685

Rita Dove (b. 1952)
My Mother Enters the Work Force   698

Paul Laurence Dunbar (1872–1906)
We Wear the Mask   650

T. S. Eliot (1888–1965)
The Love Song of J. Alfred Prufrock   651

Louise Erdrich (b. 1954)
Dear John Wayne   671

Faiz Ahmed Faiz (1911–1984)
Be Near Me   974

Alan Feldman (b. 1945)
My Century   192

Lawrence Ferlinghetti (b. 1919)
Constantly Risking Absurdity   185
In Goya's Greatest Scenes   1251

Annie Finch (b. 1956)
Coy Mistress   982

Donald Finkel (1929–2008)
The Great Wave: Hokusai   1255

Carolyn Forché (b. 1950)
The Colonel   436

Daisy Fried (b. 1967)
Econo Motel, Ocean City   962

Robert Frost (1874–1963)
The Road Not Taken   178
Birches   178
A Semi-Revolution   439
Fire and Ice   944
After Apple-Picking   1261
'Out, Out—'   1262
Nothing Gold Can Stay   1263
Stopping by Woods on a Snowy Evening   1264
Design   1265

Tess Gallagher (b. 1943)
I Stop Writing the Poem   696

Deborah Garrison (b. 1965)
Sestina for the Working Mother   699

Allen Ginsberg (1926–1997)
A Supermarket in California   442

Nikki Giovanni (b. 1943)
Dreams   439

LOUISE GLÜCK (B. 1943)
  THE SCHOOL CHILDREN 190
  THE MYTH OF INNOCENCE 190

WILLIAM GREENWAY (B. 1947)
  PIT PONY 1287

DONALD HALL (B. 1928)
  AFFIRMATION 1268

MARK HALLIDAY (B. 1949)
  CHICKEN SALAD 1278

THOMAS HARDY (1840–1928)
  MEN WHO MARCH AWAY 175
  THE MAN HE KILLED 445

ROBERT HAYDEN (1913–1980)
  THOSE WINTER SUNDAYS 969

TERRANCE HAYES (B. 1971)
  ROOT 681

SEAMUS HEANEY (B. 1939–2013)
  VALEDICTION 957
  MID-TERM BREAK 1273

JUAN FELIPE HERRERA (B. 1948)
  187 REASONS MEXICANOS CAN'T CROSS THE BORDER (REMIX) 661

ROBERT HERRICK (1591–1674)
  TO THE VIRGINS, TO MAKE MUCH OF TIME 940

TONY HOAGLAND (B. 1953)
  I HAVE NEWS FOR YOU 1294

ANDREA HOLLANDER (B. 1947)
  BETRAYAL 975

A. D. HOPE (1907–2000)
  HIS COY MISTRESS TO MR. MARVELL 978

GERARD MANLEY HOPKINS (1844–1889)
  SPRING AND FALL 176
  GOD'S GRANDEUR 1257

A. E. HOUSMAN (1859–1936)
  WHEN I WAS ONE-AND-TWENTY 177
  TO AN ATHLETE DYING YOUNG 1258

MARIE HOWE (B. 1950)
  WHAT THE LIVING DO 1279

LANGSTON HUGHES (1902–1967)
  MOTHER TO SON 199
  HARLEM 429
  I, TOO 441

GEORGIA DOUGLAS JOHNSON (1880–1966)
OLD BLACK MEN   650

JAMES WELDON JOHNSON (1871–1938)
A POET TO HIS BABY SON   648

BEN JONSON (1572–1637)
SONG, TO CELIA   940

JOHN KEATS (1795–1821)
ODE ON A GRECIAN URN   1245

JANE KENYON (1947–1995)
LET EVENING COME   1275

GALWAY KINNELL (B. 1927–2014)
AFTER MAKING LOVE WE HEAR FOOTSTEPS   951

CAROLYN KIZER (B. 1925–2014)
BITCH   948
AFTERNOON HAPPINESS   949

MARVIN KLOTZ (1930–2014)
REQUIEM   1270

ETHERIDGE KNIGHT (1931–1991)
HARD ROCK RETURNS TO PRISON FROM THE HOSPITAL
   FOR THE CRIMINAL INSANE   658

YUSEF KOMUNYAKAA (B. 1947)
FACING IT   1276

PHILIP LARKIN (1922–1985)
A STUDY OF READING HABITS   186
THIS BE THE VERSE   187

EVELYN LAU (B. 1971)
SOLIPSISM   197

EMMA LAZARUS (1849–1887)
THE NEW COLOSSUS   702

LI-YOUNG LEE (B. 1957)
EATING ALONE   970

PHILIP LEVINE (B. 1928–2015)
WHAT WORK IS   433

SHIRLEY GEOK-LIN LIM (B. 1944)
LEARNING TO LOVE AMERICA   443

AUDRE LORDE (1934–1992)
HANGING FIRE   187

ANDREW MARVELL (1621–1678)
TO HIS COY MISTRESS   977

CLAUDE MCKAY (1890–1948)
IF WE MUST DIE   429

PETER MEINKE (B. 1932)
ADVICE TO MY SON   200

W. S. MERWIN (B. 1927)
THANKS   204

ROBERT MEZEY (B. 1935)
MY MOTHER   201

EDNA ST. VINCENT MILLAY (1892–1950)
I KNOW I AM BUT SUMMER TO YOUR HEART (SONNET XXVII)   973

CZESŁAW MIŁOSZ (1911–2004)
A SONG ON THE END OF THE WORLD   1266

LISEL MUELLER (B. 1924)
HAPPY AND UNHAPPY FAMILIES I   947

TASLIMA NASRIN (B. 1962)
THINGS CHEAPLY HAD   677

MAGGIE NELSON (B. 1973)
THANKSGIVING   211

HOWARD NEMEROV (1920–1991)
MONEY   656

PABLO NERUDA (1904–1973)
THE DEAD WOMAN   1265

JOHN FREDERICK NIMS (1913–1999)
LOVE POEM   946

JEAN NORDHAUS (B. 1939)
A DANDELION FOR MY MOTHER   189

FRANK O'HARA (1926–1966)
MY HEART   690

SHARON OLDS (B. 1942)
SEX WITHOUT LOVE   958
MY FATHER'S DIARY   965

MARY OLIVER (B. 1935)
WHEN DEATH COMES   1270

ALICIA OSTRIKER (B. 1937)
THE DOGS AT LIVE OAK BEACH, SANTA CRUZ   189
DAFFODILS   1272

WILFRED OWEN (1893–1918)
DULCE ET DECORUM EST   445

DOROTHY PARKER (1893–1967)
ONE PERFECT ROSE   944

OMAR PÉREZ (B. 1964)
CONTRIBUTIONS TO A RUDIMENTARY CONCEPT OF NATION 678

CARL PHILLIPS (B. 1959)
BLUE 692

MARGE PIERCY (B. 1936)
THE MARKET ECONOMY 435
BARBIE DOLL 659

SYLVIA PLATH (1932–1963)
DADDY 953

KEVIN C. POWERS (B. 1980)
LETTER COMPOSED DURING A LULL IN THE FIGHTING 448

WYATT PRUNTY (B. 1947)
LEARNING THE BICYCLE 959

DUDLEY RANDALL (1914–2000)
BALLAD OF BIRMINGHAM 431

BARBARA RAS (B. 1949)
YOU CAN'T HAVE IT ALL 1292

SPENCER REECE (B. 1963)
THE MANHATTAN PROJECT 196

ADRIENNE RICH (1929–2012)
LIVING IN SIN 952

RAINER MARIA RILKE (1875–1926)
ARCHAIC TORSO OF APOLLO 1289

EDWIN ARLINGTON ROBINSON (1869–1935)
RICHARD CORY 1261

THEODORE ROETHKE (1908–1963)
I KNEW A WOMAN 944
MY PAPA'S WALTZ 968

KAY RYAN (B. 1945)
ALL SHALL BE RESTORED 660

CARL SANDBURG (1878–1967)
I AM THE PEOPLE, THE MOB 425

SAPPHO (CA. 610–CA. 580 BCE)
WITH HIS VENOM 933

LÉOPOLD SÉDAR SENGHOR (1906–2001)
TO NEW YORK 703

ANNE SEXTON (1928–1974)
THE STARRY NIGHT 1253

WILLIAM SHAKESPEARE (1564–1616)
SONNET 18 "SHALL I COMPARE THEE TO A SUMMER'S DAY?" 934

SONNET 29 "WHEN, IN DISGRACE WITH FORTUNE AND MEN'S EYES"   934

SONNET 64 "WHEN I HAVE SEEN BY TIME'S FELL HAND DEFAC'D"   935

SONNET 116, "LET ME NOT TO THE MARRIAGE OF TRUE MINDS"   936

SONNET 130 "MY MISTRESS' EYES ARE NOTHING LIKE THE SUN"   936

SONNET 73 "THAT TIME OF YEAR THOU MAYST IN ME BEHOLD"   1241

FEAR NO MORE THE HEAT O' THE SUN   1242

PERCY BYSSHE SHELLEY (1792–1822)

OZYMANDIAS   1245

STEVIE SMITH (1902–1971)

NOT WAVING BUT DROWNING   180

TO CARRY THE CHILD   181

GARY SOTO (B. 1952)

BEHIND GRANDMA'S HOUSE   203

WILLIAM STAFFORD (1914–1995)

TRAVELING THROUGH THE DARK   1285

WALLACE STEVENS (1879–1955)

PETER QUINCE AT THE CLAVIER   426

JONATHAN SWIFT (1667–1745)

STELLA'S BIRTH-DAY   167

MARKET WOMEN'S CRIES   646

A SATIRICAL ELEGY ON THE DEATH OF A LATE FAMOUS GENERAL   1243

SHEILA ORTIZ TAYLOR (B. 1939)

THE WAY BACK   207

ALEXANDRA TEAGUE (B. 1974)

ADJECTIVES OF ORDER   683

ALFRED, LORD TENNYSON (1809–1892)

ULYSSES   418

DYLAN THOMAS (1914–1953)

FERN HILL   183

DO NOT GO GENTLE INTO THAT GOOD NIGHT   1267

NATASHA TRETHEWEY (B. 1966)

FLOUNDER   437

MARK TURPIN (B. 1953)

THE MAN WHO BUILT THIS HOUSE   1280

JOHN UPDIKE (1932–2009)

DOG'S DEATH   1286

JAMES WELCH (1940–2003)

CHRISTMAS COMES TO MOCCASIN FLAT   210

PHILLIS WHEATLEY (1753–1784)

ON BEING BROUGHT FROM AFRICA TO AMERICA   702

WALT WHITMAN (1819–1892)

WHEN I HEARD THE LEARN'D ASTRONOMER 10

ONE SONG, AMERICA, BEFORE I GO 440

from SONG OF MYSELF 686

WILLIAM WORDSWORTH (1770–1850)

THE WORLD IS TOO MUCH WITH US 417

JAMES WRIGHT (1927–1980)

LYING IN A HAMMOCK AT WILLIAM DUFFY'S FARM IN PINE

ISLAND, MINNESOTA 1290

LADY MARY WROTH (CA. 1587–CA. 1651)

"COME DARKEST NIGHT, BECOMING SORROW BEST" 964

SIR THOMAS WYATT (1503–1542)

THEY FLEE FROM ME 963

WILLIAM BUTLER YEATS (1865–1939)

EASTER 1916 422

THE SECOND COMING 424

THE GREAT DAY 438

SAILING TO BYZANTIUM 1259

DEAN YOUNG (B. 1955)

WINGED PURPOSES 966

KEVIN YOUNG (B. 1970)

NEGATIVE 680

TIMOTHY YU (B. 1974)

CHINESE SILENCE NO. 22 694

DRAMA

EDWARD ALBEE (B. 1928)

THE SANDBOX 1296

SUSAN GLASPELL (1882–1948)

TRIFLES 1073

LORRAINE HANSBERRY (1930–1965)

A RAISIN IN THE SUN 710

DAVID HENRY HWANG (B. 1957)

TRYING TO FIND CHINATOWN 812

HENRIK IBSEN (1828–1906)

A DOLL'S HOUSE 213

LYNN NOTTAGE (B. 1964)

POOF! 1087

SUZAN-LORI PARKS (B. 1963)

FATHER COMES HOME FROM THE WARS 270

WILLIAM SHAKESPEARE (1564–1616)
  OTHELLO 984

SOPHOCLES (496?–406 BCE)
  ANTIGONÊ 450

NONFICTION

ROBIN BERNSTEIN (B. 1969)
  INVENTING A FISHBOWL: WHITE SUPREMACY AND THE CRITICAL
    RECEPTION OF LORRAINE HANSBERRY'S *A RAISIN IN THE SUN* 799

EULA BISS (B. 1977)
  TIME AND DISTANCE OVERCOME 844

ALLIE BROSH (B. 1985)
  THIS IS WHY I'LL NEVER BE AN ADULT 296

LLOYD W. BROWN (B. 1938)
  LORRAINE HANSBERRY AS IRONIST: A REAPPRAISAL OF *A RAISIN IN
    THE SUN* 782

HALLMAN B. BRYANT (B. 1936)
  READING THE MAP IN "A GOOD MAN IS HARD TO FIND" 157

JILL CHRISTMAN (B. 1969)
  THE SLOTH 1311

SONYA CHUNG (B. 1973)
  GETTING IT RIGHT 1109

MICHAEL CLARK (1946–1999)
  FLANNERY O'CONNOR'S "A GOOD MAN IS HARD TO FIND": THE
    MOMENT OF GRACE 163

JUDITH ORTIZ COFER (B. 1952)
  AMERICAN HISTORY 287

E. L. DOCTOROW (1931–2015)
  WHY WE ARE INFIDELS 498

JOHN DONNE (1572–1631)
  MEDITATION XVII, *from* DEVOTIONS UPON EMERGENT
    OCCASIONS 1303

BOB DOWELL (B. 1932)
  from THE MOMENT OF GRACE IN THE FICTION OF FLANNERY
    O'CONNOR 155

BRIAN DOYLE (B. 1956)
  POP ART 294

DAGOBERTO GILB (B. 1950)
  I KNEW SHE WAS BEAUTIFUL 1111

MALCOLM GLADWELL (B. 1963)
SMALL CHANGE: WHY THE REVOLUTION WILL NOT BE TWEETED 513

LANGSTON HUGHES (1902–1967)
SALVATION 284

LACY M. JOHNSON (B. 1978)
WHITE TRASH PRIMER 852

SABRINA JONES (B. 1960)
LITTLE HOUSE IN THE BIG CITY 833

JAMAICA KINCAID (B. 1949)
ON SEEING ENGLAND FOR THE FIRST TIME 489

MAXINE HONG KINGSTON (B. 1940)
NO NAME WOMAN 1097

JONATHAN LETHEM (B. 1964)
13, 1977, 21 1319

RUTH MARGALIT (B. 1983)
THE UNMOTHERED 1325

BILL MCKIBBEN (B. 1960)
A CALL TO ARMS: AN INVITATION TO DEMAND ACTION ON CLIMATE
CHANGE 506

BHARATI MUKHERJEE (B. 1940)
TWO WAYS TO BELONG IN AMERICA 849

GEORGE ORWELL (1903–1950)
SHOOTING AN ELEPHANT 827

PAUL (D. CA. 64 CE)
1 CORINTHIANS 13 1095

SALMAN RUSHDIE (B. 1947)
"IMAGINE THERE'S NO HEAVEN" 501

DAVID SEDARIS (B. 1956)
WHAT I LEARNED 304

CLAY SHIRKY (B. 1964)
THE POLITICAL POWER OF SOCIAL MEDIA 522

REBECCA SOLNIT (B. 1961)
REVOLUTIONS PER MINUTE 510

MARILYN STASIO (B. 1940)
VARIETY REVIEW OF *A RAISIN IN THE SUN* 810

PABLO PIÑERO STILLMANN (B. 1982)
LIFE, LOVE, HAPPINESS: A FOUND ESSAY FROM THE
TWITTERVERSE 1119

JOHN JEREMIAH SULLIVAN (B. 1974)
FEET IN SMOKE 1312

JONATHAN SWIFT (1667–1745)
A MODEST PROPOSAL   481

GRACE TALUSAN (B. 1972)
MY FATHER'S NOOSE   1107

DAVID FOSTER WALLACE (1962–2008)
COMMENCEMENT SPEECH, KENYON COLLEGE   309

E. B. WHITE (1899–1985)
ONCE MORE TO THE LAKE   1305

MARGARET WILKERSON (B. ?)
A RAISIN IN THE SUN: ANNIVERSARY OF AN AMERICAN CLASSIC   788

VIRGINIA WOOLF (1882–1941)
WHAT IF SHAKESPEARE HAD HAD A SISTER?   819

ART

RIZA 'ABBASI (1565–1635)
TWO LOVERS   858

PIETER BRUEGHEL THE ELDER (1525–1569)
LANDSCAPE WITH THE FALL OF ICARUS   1250

GAETANO CHIERICI (1838–1920)
THE VETERAN   74

VINCENT VAN GOGH (1853–1890)
THE STARRY NIGHT   1254

FRANCISCO DE GOYA (1746–1828)
THE THIRD OF MAY, 1808, MADRID   1252

KATSUSHIKA HOKUSAI (1760–1849)
THE GREAT WAVE OFF KANAGAWA   1256

GUSTAV KLIMT (1862–1918)
DEATH AND LIFE   1122

JACOB LAWRENCE (1917–2000)
THIS IS HARLEM   534

RENÉ MAGRITTE (1898–1967)
GOLCONDE   316

INTRODUCTION

Responding to Literature

There is no Frigate like a Book
To take us Lands away
Nor any Coursers like a Page
Of prancing poetry—

This Traverse may the poorest take
Without oppress of Toll—
How frugal is the Chariot
That bears the Human soul.
    —Emily Dickinson (ca. 1873)

WHY WE READ LITERATURE

The epigraph from poet Emily Dickinson promotes reading as an escape, a way for us to take a vacation from our lives. If we think about our experiences with literature—and with other forms of entertainment, such as movies and TV shows—that probably sounds about right. Most of us have enjoyed forgetting about the cares of the world with a page-turning thriller or a tear-jerking melodrama. But literature can also help us get closer to life, to understand it in a new way when we get back from our literary journey. We understand what Dickinson means because we can connect to it—we think about our experiences as readers and that helps us understand the poem while, at the same time, the poem clarifies something about how reading makes us feel. The best literature helps us to understand ourselves, one another, and our world in new ways and to make connections that had never occurred to us or that we might have sensed but were unable to express.

Of course, you may not feel this way about reading the kind of literature you expect to find in a textbook. It may be that opening a textbook signals to you that the fun is over. And certainly reading and responding to serious literature requires concentrated attention and is not relaxing in the way that kicking back and watching a TV show might be. But what you may not realize is that you likely respond critically to literature without even realizing that you are doing so. Inevitably, when you encounter any kind of literature, you distinguish good from evil, right from wrong—and you do so based on your own experiences and knowledge of the world. When writers convey cultural ideas about the nature of love, of duty, of heroism—sometimes broadly, sometimes with subtlety—you agree or disagree, are moved or are not. You may not now be moved by the same literature that entranced you when you were a child, or you may have come to appreciate that literature in a fuller, more nuanced way. But you may be surprised, when you turn your attention to "serious" literature, to find how much these works have in common with the books, movies, and TV shows you have turned to for entertainment. Some "popular" authors—Janet Evanovich, Lee Child, John Grisham, Dorothy Sayers, and others—who write spy novels and detective fiction are routinely read in college courses that celebrate literature. Their exciting and suspenseful novels are often made into films, but so, too, are the classic works of William Shakespeare, Jane Austen, Edith Wharton, F. Scott Fitzgerald, and Ernest Hemingway.

Serious literature, no less than popular literature, embodies thrilling adventure. Serious literature is replete with monsters (consider the Old English epic *Beowulf*), ghosts (at the outset of Shakespeare's *Hamlet* and in the middle of *Macbeth*), witches, supernatural spirits, magical transformations, unspeakably brutal wars, terrible murders, and bloody vengeance. Given the close ties between popular and serious literature, scholars, teachers, and readers frequently debate what should be included in textbooks like this one, what literature best represents the "literary canon." Here things get a bit murky. *Canon* is derived from the Latin word meaning "measuring line or rule" and is used in religious discourse to signify "sacred writings admitted to the catalog according to the rule." Early theologians decided which books were the authentic word of God and which were not. But, much like today's literary scholars, they did not always agree. Although it attempts to establish the body of literature that humans need to study and master, the literary canon changes in response to political and social changes. Further, a literary canon is bound to reflect the cultural tradition that produces it. The literary canon of China will differ markedly from the literary canon of the United States. And both will change with the eruptions of history and the demands of fashion.

For example, although American literary history is replete with women writers, they have often been undervalued by the literary canon's guardians. But a century of political struggle—which led, first, to enfranchising women as voters and, later, to a feminist movement that demanded equality for women and their works—has allowed some women authors to gain entry to the canon, forever changing it. Writers like Kate Chopin and Charlotte Perkins Gilman are now routinely included in university courses and women writers are broadly represented in this anthology. Further, the political struggles of Native American, African American, Latino/a, and Asian American citizens have drawn considerable attention to a large and diverse body of writing that was often overlooked by critics who prized European authors. Skillful literary artists from these groups are also represented here.

You might reasonably ask, What difference does broadening the literary canon make? Consider: if you love books and movies, then you know how influential they can be and you'll probably agree that what we read makes a tremendous difference to the world we live in. You learn a great deal about your society from reading—what it values, what it condemns, how it expects you to behave, what constitutes success both economically and morally, what it sees as the very nature of good and evil. If your reading were limited to, say, European works and you were embedded in a non-European social group, you might not discover yourself or your peers in the books you read. Thus, schools and anthologies that project a narrow literary canon would present a world foreign to your experience. The resulting sense of anomie—a rootless lack of purpose, identity, and values—could be terribly damaging. At the same time, ignorance of your neighbors' lifestyles could also seriously impair your life by giving you a skewed, incomplete vision of the world. Conversely, reading widely could help you avoid the baleful consequences of racism, hypernationalism, and ignorance.

The stories, poems, plays, and essays in this textbook have been selected from a diverse array of important authors, some of them very popular, others often most appreciated by scholars and critics. Some of these writers have been read and studied in schools and colleges for centuries while others, especially from historically underrepresented groups, may be entirely new to you. We hope that you enjoy reading the works by the authors and thinkers in this book. We also hope that you find surprising commonalities among these very different writers and between them and you. The units are organized around universal themes and are designed to help you connect your own life and the things you are reading to the many literary traditions that join us to each other, to our collective history, and to the world at large. The literature in this volume will take you out of your comfort zone to "lands away" while giving you new tools for understanding yourself and your immediate world. The only "toll" required is an open mind and an attentive eye.

READING ACTIVELY AND CRITICALLY

In a well-ordered universe, you would enjoy all your reading—and your delight would derive from your complete absorption in and understanding of what you read. But just as sports require physical conditioning in order for you to perform at your best, you may need to build up your stamina as an effective reader. First of all, pay attention to *how* you read. Can you read fifty pages in one sitting, or do you find your mind wandering after a page or two? If you fall into the latter category, don't worry—we all succumb to the allure of distractions once in a while. But it is up to you to train yourself not to let it diminish your reading experience. If you feel your attention beginning to wander, stop and look back to the place in the text where you began to drift. When you come back to your reading, commit yourself to reading another portion of the passage that's longer than the last one you read. You can hold yourself accountable by writing a short summary—from memory—of what you've read every few sentences, paragraphs, or pages. When you deliberately "train" your mind in this way, your ability to focus and concentrate—and think—will be enhanced, and you will be a better reader for your efforts.

Equally important to reading actively is paying attention to *what* you read. It can be easy to get bogged down by the sheer volume of words on a page, but you can help make sense of them by keeping a pencil in hand and interacting with the page. Mark words you don't recognize and look them up in the dictionary. Note when you feel a protest rising in your throat. Jot down places where the text reminds you of something in your own life or in another work of art—any kind of connection. Active reading takes you beyond the role of an observer, removed and separate from the things you read, and makes you a participant in a conversation with the author or even with the characters. So don't be shy—speak up!

Beyond being an active reader of literature, you must also become a critical reader. Beyond simply perceiving the words on the page, critical reading invites you to question those words in profound, meaningful ways. When we ask you to read critically, we ask that you use the complex set of experiences that define you as a human being—as well as a sense of the cultural imperatives among which you live—to analyze the work you encounter. As a critical reader, you learn to address your biases, enlarge your universe, and test your comfortable convictions. Thus, when you adopt a critical position toward a piece of literature, you need to test and question that position. Ask, What perspective does the author have that led him or her to write this work? What social, cultural, or historical conditions influenced the production of the work? What other ways might the author have presented the ideas or subjects of the work? Are the author's values different from my own? How do my views and experiences affect whether I like or dislike the work? Such questions are stepping stones toward being able to write about literature meaningfully and compellingly (a process that is discussed in greater detail on pp. 30–73).

READING FICTION

Fiction creates imaginary worlds by telling stories written in *prose* (ordinary, unrhymed language), about realistic characters, set in physical environments, and with sustained attention to descriptive detail.

Works of fiction *narrate*, or tell, stories. Of course, narrative is not specific to fiction or to any other literary genre: telling stories pervades almost every aspect of our daily lives. We learn very early on how to recognize and tell stories, and we rely heavily on narrative to organize and make sense of our experience. For example, when we study history, we mostly study stories of various events. Likewise, an astronomer's account of the universe's origins may take the shape of a narrative. Even in our sleep, we tell ourselves stories in the form of dreams. It is impossible to imagine our lives without these narratives; in fact, every culture uses them to order and make sense of lived experience. Narrative fiction is not meant to recount actual events, of course, though it may refer to real events or real persons. Rather than relate actual experiences, fiction uses narrative to shape imaginary ones.

Works of fiction, however, cannot be reduced to a listing of their narrative events any more than paintings can be replaced by diagrams. Such summaries diminish a work's realism, which is produced by careful description of characters, settings, and actions, as well as its depths of meaning. For example, the emotional impact of James Joyce's "Araby" cannot be captured by summarizing its simple plot. Without suspending critical judgment, readers of fiction have to be willing to suspend disbelief, that is, to enter the imaginary world of the novel or short story.

The Methods of Fiction

In order to examine the methods of fiction—tone, setting, plot, theme, characterization, point of view, and irony—let us look more closely at James Joyce's "Araby" (p. 125).

TONE   One of the things most readers first respond to in a short story is its *tone*. Because it is like a *mood*, tone is difficult to talk about. It can be defined as an author's implicit attitude toward the characters, places, and events in the story and toward the reader of the work. Tone depends for its substance on delicate emotional responses to language and situation. Notice how a distinct tone is established in the language of the opening lines of "Araby":

> North Richmond Street, being blind, was a quiet street except at the hour when the Christian Brothers' School set the boys free. An uninhabited house of two storeys stood at the blind end, detached from its neighbours in a square ground. The other houses of the street, conscious of decent lives within them, gazed at one another with brown imperturbable faces.

Is this scene cheerful? Vital and active? Should we expect this story to celebrate the joys of growing up in Dublin? Negative responses to these questions arise from the tone of the opening description. Notice, for example, that the dead-end street is "blind"; that the school is said to "set the boys free," which makes it sound like a prison; that the uninhabited house is "detached from its neighbours"; and that the other houses, personified, gaze at one another with "brown imperturbable faces"—*brown* being a nondescript color and *imperturbable* reinforcing the still, lifeless, somber quality of the passage as a whole.

PLOT   Through the series of events that make up a story's *plot*, an author presents us with a carefully created fictional world. In "Araby," the plot, or the arrangement of a connected sequence of narrative events, can be simply stated. A young boy who lives in a drab but respectable neighborhood develops a crush on his playmate's sister. She asks him if he intends to go to a charity fair that she cannot attend. He resolves to go and purchase a gift for her. He is tormented by the late and drunken arrival of his uncle, who has promised him the money he needs. When the boy finally arrives at the bazaar, he is disappointed by the difference between his expectation and the actuality of the almost deserted fair. He perceives some minor events, overhears some minor conversation, and the climax occurs when he confronts the darkened fair and the banal expression of sexual attraction between two gentlemen and a young woman. This sequence of events prompts the boy to see himself "as a creature driven and derided by vanity."

CHARACTERIZATION One of the obvious differences between short stories and novels is that story writers develop *characters* rapidly and limit the number of developed characters. Many stories have only one fleshed-out, or *round*, character; the other characters are frequently two-dimensional, or *flat*. Rarely does a short story have more than three developed characters.

One feature that distinguishes "Araby" is its *characterization*, or the process by which the characters are rendered to make them seem real to the reader. Characterization, however, cannot easily be separated from the other elements of fiction; that is, it depends heavily on tone, plot, theme, setting, and so on. It is part of the boy's character, for example, that he lives in a brown imperturbable house on North Richmond Street, that he does the things he does (which constitute the plot of the story), and that he learns about what he does (which is the theme). Much of this characterization in "Araby" emerges from Joyce's rich *style*, or the way he uses language and images. Consider how the boy's character is revealed in the following paragraph:

> Her image accompanied me even in places the most hostile to romance. On Saturday evenings when my aunt went marketing I had to go to carry some of the parcels. We walked through the flaring streets, jostled by drunken men and bargaining women, amid the curses of labourers, the shrill litanies of shop-boys who stood on guard by the barrels of pigs' cheeks, the nasal chanting of street-singers, who sang a *come-all-you* about O'Donovan Rossa, or a ballad about the troubles in our native land. These noises converged in a single sensation of life for me: I imagined that I bore my chalice safely through a throng of foes. Her name sprang to my lips at moments in strange prayers and praises which I myself did not understand. My eyes were often full of tears (I could not tell why) and at times a flood from my heart seemed to pour itself out into my bosom. I thought little of the future. I did not know whether I would ever speak to her or not or, if I spoke to her, how I could tell her of my confused adoration. But my body was like a harp and her words and gestures were like fingers running upon the wires.

In this passage, character is revealed through *diction*, or choice of words. By using the words *litanies*, *prayers*, and *adoration*, the narrator draws heavily from the distinctive vocabulary of the Roman Catholic Church. (The reference to the harp also reinforces the religious tone of the passage.) *Chalice* and *throng of foes* are related to this tradition as well; a chalice is a cup for the consecrated wine of the Eucharist, and throngs of foes often confronted the Christian martyrs whose deeds are immortalized in religious literature. At the same time, however, these last two phrases call up the world of chivalric romance, which is alluded to in the first line of the paragraph. The narrator's diction casts his awakening sexuality in the mold of high romance on the one hand and Christian devotion on the other. This sense of holy chivalry (reinforced by the earlier reference to the priest who owned a chivalric novel) stands in sharp contrast to the humdrum experience of carrying groceries home from the market.

SETTING Unlike novels, short stories usually work themselves out in a restricted geographical *setting*—in a single place and within a short period of time. Any consideration of setting should include the historical time when a story takes place and the social situation set in the story, as well as the physical location of the events. In "Araby," the dreary details of Dublin are significantly described in the story's very first lines.

POINT OF VIEW A character's or narrator's diction raises important questions about who is narrating the story. What is the narrator like? Is he reliable or unreliable? How can we judge? These questions help us distinguish another element of fiction, *point of view.* "Araby" is a *first-person narrative*; that is, the story is told from the perspective of a narrator who speaks in the first person. Most of the time, first-person narrators use the singular (*I, my*); in "A Rose for Emily" (p. 623), however, Faulkner's narrator uses the first person plural (*we, our*).

Third-person point of view—in which the narrator does not appear as a character in the story—is the most common perspective used to tell stories. Using third-person point of view, a narrator tells a story from the outside, referring to the characters as *she, he,* and *they.* A narrator who knows everything, can tell us what the characters are thinking, and can move around in space and time at will is an *omniscient narrator.* Alternatively, a narrator who chooses to focus on the thoughts, feelings, and actions of a single character is called a *limited omniscient narrator.* Generally, the brevity of the short story makes the first-person or limited omniscient narrations the most frequently used points of view for these works, while the lengthy and comparatively complex narrative of novels is more suited to the omniscient point of view.

A less frequently employed point of view is that of the second person, in which the author addresses the action to a character identified as *you.* For example, "You ask the clerk for change; he gives you four quarters. You go outside and wait for the bus." Although it evokes a rare intimacy with the reader, second-person point of view is difficult to sustain even in a short story.

IRONY Authors' decisions about point of view create powerful narrative effects. Throughout "Araby," we sense a gap between the boy's sensibility and that of the more mature narrator, who refers at various times to his "innumerable follies" and "foolish blood." That is, we see the events of "Araby" from the boy's perspective, even though the language is that of an adult. The gap between the boy's knowledge and the narrator's creates *irony.*

There may be more than one level of irony at work in a story. When the narrator calls himself "a creature driven and derided by vanity," whose eyes "burned with anguish and anger," this overstatement is known as *verbal irony.* Some critics have maintained that the romanticized language of the story's conclusion itself invites an ironic reading—that is, we readers may know something about the narrator that he does not know himself—that he idealizes disenchantment as fervently as the boy idealized romance and religion. In short, Joyce may be using *dramatic irony,* encouraging the reader to see things about the first-person narrator that he does not see about himself. Both kinds of irony hinge on differing levels of knowledge and the author's skillful manipulation of narrative perspective.

THEME *Theme* is an underlying idea, a statement that a work makes about its subject. This tiny stretch of experience out of the boy's life introduces him to an awareness of the differences between imagination and reality, between his romantic infatuation and the vulgar reality all about him. The theme of "Araby" emerges from the drab setting and mundane events of the story as a general statement about an intensely idealized and childish love, the shattering recognition of the false sentimentality that occasions it, and the enveloping vulgarity of adult life. By detailing a few events from one boy's life, the story illuminates the painful loss of innocence we all endure. In this case, the *protagonist*, or main character, experiences what Joyce called an *epiphany*, or sudden flash of recognition, that signals the awareness of a set of moral complexities in a world that once seemed uncomplicated and predictable.

We often speak of tone, setting, plot, theme, characterization, and point of view as separate aspects of a story in order to break down a complex narrative into more manageable parts. But this analytic process of identifying various elements is something we have done to the story: the story (if it is a good one) is an integrated whole. The more closely we examine the separate elements, the clearer it becomes that each is integrally related to the others.

In "Araby," Joyce employs the methods of fiction to create a world based on 1895 Dublin and Irish middle-class society. The success or failure of the story depends on Joyce's ability to render that world convincingly and our willingness to enter it imaginatively. We must not refuse to engage that world because the characters do not act as we would have them act or because the events never actually happened. Novelist Henry James urged that readers allow the author to have his or her *donnée*, or "given." When we grant this, the act of reading fiction provides us with much more pleasure and emotional insight.

Here are some questions to ask as you set out to read or write about fiction. Your answers to these questions will help you brainstorm and develop the ideas that form your response to a story.

QUESTIONS FOR EXPLORING FICTION

1. WHAT IS THE TONE OF THE STORY? Does the tone change with the story's events or remain fixed? How does the tone contribute to the effect of the story?

2. WHAT IS THE PLOT OF THE STORY? Does the sequence of events that make up the plot emerge logically from the nature of the characters and circumstances? Or does the plot rely on coincidence and arbitrary events?

3. WHO ARE THE PRINCIPAL CHARACTERS IN THE STORY? What functions do the minor characters serve? Do any characters change during the course of the story? How and why?

4. WHAT IS THE SETTING OF THE STORY? Does it play an important role, or is it simply the place and time where things happen? How would some other setting affect the story?

5. FROM WHAT POINT OF VIEW IS THE NARRATOR TELLING THE STORY? Do you trust him or her?

6. WHAT IS THE THEME OF THE STORY?

7. DO YOU FIND AMBIGUITIES IN THE STORY? Does that ambiguity result in confusion, or does it add to the story's complexity?

8. DOES THE STORY SEEM TO SUPPORT OR CONFLICT WITH YOUR OWN POLITICAL AND MORAL POSITIONS?

9. WHEN WAS THE STORY WRITTEN? Draw on your knowledge of history and contemporary events as you read the story. Does the story clarify, enhance, or contradict your understanding of history?

10. CAN YOU CONNECT THE STORY TO ANYTHING ELSE YOU HAVE READ OR SEEN?

READING POETRY

Reading poetry is unlike the other reading you do. To appreciate the sounds and meaning of a poem, it is best to start by reading it aloud. Some poems are straightforward, requiring little analysis; others are more dense and complex. Try reading the poem "When I Heard the Learn'd Astronomer" (1865) by Walt Whitman out loud.

> When I heard the learn'd astronomer,
> When the proofs, the figures, were ranged in columns before me,
> When I was shown the charts and diagrams, to add, divide, and measure them,
> When I sitting heard the astronomer where he lectured with much
>   applause in the lecture-room,
> How soon unaccountable I became tired and sick,
> Till rising and gliding out I wander'd off by myself,
> In the mystical moist night-air, and from time to time,
> Look'd up in perfect silence at the stars.

Whitman's distinction between mind (intellectual knowledge) and heart (emotion and feelings) is an old but a useful one. Compelled to analyze, dissect, categorize, and classify, the poem's narrator finally yearns for the simple pleasure of unanalytical enjoyment—to look up "in perfect silence at the stars." You may very well enjoy a poem without recognizing its patterns of imagery or the intricate way its author weaves together the past and the present. But understanding the elements of poetry will allow you to use analysis to enhance your emotional response to a poem—and thereby deepen the pleasure a poem can give you.

Poems have to be read with great intensity but without any sense of urgency. Reading with a relaxed but complete mindfulness, try to slow down, pay attention, and allow the language of the poem to work.

Word Choice

Once you have listened to the poem, what should you pay attention to next? Start with the words that make up the poem. *Where* a poem takes the reader is inseparable from *how* it takes the reader. Poets pay especially close attention to diction, or their choice of words; every word in a poem counts. In your everyday reading, you encounter unfamiliar words and phrases, and figure out their meanings from the contexts in which they occur. Reading poetry requires even more scrupulous attention to unusual words and phrases. Here, again, making connections will help you get the most out of your reading. Look for words or images that repeat or change as a poem continues. Finding patterns can be the first step in developing an interpretive reading of a poem.

Critics often describe poetry as "heightened language," meaning that the poet strives for precision and richness in the words he or she uses. For the poet, "precision" and "richness" are not contradictory. Words have dictionary, or *denotative*, meanings as well as associative, or *connotative*, meanings; they also have histories and relationships with other words. The English language is rich in synonyms—words whose denotative meanings are roughly the same but whose connotations vary widely (*excite, stimulate, titillate, inflame*; *poor, impoverished, indigent, destitute*). Many words are identical in sound and often in spelling but differ in meaning (*forepaws, four paws*; *lie* ["recline"], *lie* ["fib"]). The meanings of words have changed over time, and the poet may deliberately select a word whose older meaning adds a dimension to the poem.

Figurative Language

Figurative language is the general term we use to describe the many devices of language that allow us to speak nonliterally in order to achieve some special effect. Figurative language makes a comparison between the thing being written about and something else that allows the reader to better picture or understand it. When Robert Burns compares his love to a red rose in his poem "A Red, Red Rose" (p. 942), he abandons literal language because the emotional energy of his thoughts can be expressed more effectively in figurative language.

Figurative language allows us—and the poet—to use *imagery* to transcend both the confinement of the literal and the vagueness of the abstract. The world is revealed to us through our senses—sight, sound, taste, touch, and smell. Through imagery, the poet creates a recognizable world by drawing on this fund of common experiences. The difference between good and bad poetry often turns on the skill with which imagery (or other figurative language) is used. Bad poetry is often bad because the imagery is stale ("golden sunset," "the smiling sun," "the rolling sea") or so skimpy that the poem dissolves into vague and meaningless abstraction.

Consider these familiar old sayings: "The grass is always greener on the other side of the fence"; "A bird in the hand is worth two in the bush"; "The early bird catches the worm." Although these sayings make literal sense (the grass you see from a distance looks greener than the grass under your feet), their meaning to a native speaker of English is clearly not literal. When we use them, we are making general and highly abstract observations about human attitudes and behavior. Yet these generalizations and abstractions are embodied in *concrete* imagery. Try to explain what any of these expressions mean and you will quickly discover that you are using many more words and much vaguer language than the expression itself uses. This is precisely what happens when you try to paraphrase or put into your own words the language of a poem. Like poetry, these sayings rely on the figurative use of language.

METAPHOR   Because poetry is an intense and heightened use of language, it relies on more frequent and original use of figurative language than does ordinary speech. One of the most common figurative devices, *metaphor*, in which one thing is compared to something else, occurs frequently in everyday language. "School is a rat race," or "That issue is a minefield for the mayor," we say, and the meaning is vividly clear. When W. H. Auden, commenting on the death of William Butler Yeats, says, "Let the Irish vessel lie/Emptied of his poetry," he pays a complex tribute to the great Irish poet with a metaphor that compels readers to confront not only the loss of a man but also the loss of his poetic voice.

SIMILE   *Simile* is closely related to metaphor. But where metaphor says that one thing *is* another, simile says that one thing *is like* another, as in Robert Burns's "O My Luve's like a red, red rose" and Frost's "life is too much like a pathless wood" (p. 179). The distinction between simile and metaphor, while easy enough to make technically, is often difficult to distinguish in terms of effect. Frost establishes a comparison between life and a pathless wood and keeps the two even more fully separated by adding the qualifier "too much." Burns's simile maintains the same separation and, in addition, because it occurs in the opening line of the poem, eliminates any possible confusion the reader might experience if the line were "O My Luve is a red, red rose." You can test the difference in effect by changing a metaphor into a simile or a simile into a metaphor to see if the meaning is in any way altered.

PERSONIFICATION   *Personification*, another device of figurative language, attributes human qualities to things or ideas. Personification can make an abstract thing more understandable in terms of human form, emotion, or action. For example, when John Donne, in his poem "Death, Be Not Proud" (p. 1243), exclaims "Death, thou shalt die," he transforms the abstraction of death into a human adversary (while also creating a memorable *paradox*).

ALLUSION   *Allusion* to other literary works, persons, places, or events enables poets to call up associations and contexts that complicate and enrich their poems. Whether these allusions are obvious or subtle, they draw on knowledge shared by the poet and the reader. In T. S. Eliot's dense and difficult "The Love Song of J. Alfred Prufrock" (p. 651), the speaker says at one point, "I have seen my head (grown slightly bald) brought in upon a platter." A reader familiar with the New Testament might recognize this allusion to John the Baptist's decapitation and better understand Prufrock's sense of spiritual desolation. The association Eliot makes brings an added, intensified layer of meaning to the work.

SYMBOLS   A *symbol*, in its broadest sense, is anything that stands for something else. In this sense, most words are symbolic: the word *tree* stands for an object in the real world. When we speak of a symbol in a literary work, however, we mean something more precise. In poetry, a symbol is an object or event that suggests more than itself. It is one of the most common and powerful devices available to the poet, for it allows him or her to convey economically and simply a wide range of meanings.

It is useful to distinguish between two kinds of symbols: *public symbols* and *contextual symbols*. Public symbols are those objects or events that history has invested with rich meanings and associations—for example, national flags or religious objects such as a cross. Yeats uses such a symbol in his poem "Sailing to Byzantium" (p. 1259), drawing on the celebrated and enduring art of the ancient Byzantine Empire as a symbol of timelessness.

In contrast to public symbols, contextual symbols are objects or events that are symbolic by virtue of the poet's handling of them in a particular work—that is, by virtue of the context. Consider, for example, the opening lines of Robert Frost's "After Apple-Picking" (p. 1261).

> My long two-pointed ladder's sticking through a tree
> Toward heaven still,
> And there's a barrel that I didn't fill
> Beside it, and there may be two or three
> Apples I didn't pick upon some bough.

The apple tree is a literal tree, but it also symbolizes the speaker's life, with a wide range of possible meanings (do the few unpicked apples symbolize the dreams that even the fullest life cannot satisfy?). Contextual symbols tend to present more interpretive difficulties than public symbols do because recognizing them depends on a sensitivity to everything else in the poem.

The Music of Poetry

A number of terms describe the various sound patterns that project the *music* of poetry. Of these, *rhyme*—the repetition of the final stressed vowel sound and any sounds following—is the best known: *brow, now; debate, relate;* and so on. *Alliteration,* or the repetition of a consonant sound, usually at the beginning of words in close proximity, is also common: "*besiege* thy *brow.*" Alliteration is frequently used to underscore key words and ideas.

Rhythm, created by the relationship between stressed and unstressed syllables, is another way poets can convey meaning. The pattern formed when the lines of a poem follow a recurrent or similar rhythm is the poem's *meter*. The smallest repeated unit in this pattern is called a *foot*. Looking, for example, at the first line of one of Shakespeare's sonnets, we see that the foot consists of an *iamb*—an unstressed syllable followed by a stressed one:

When forty winters shall besiege thy brow.

Because the line consists of five iambs, or sets of unstressed syllables followed by stressed ones, it is called *iambic pentameter*. (If the line had four iambic feet, it would be in iambic tetrameter; if six, iambic hexameter; and so on.)

Other metrical feet include the *trochee, anapest, dactyl,* and *spondee* (all of which are defined in the "Glossary of Literary Terms"); but such terms are the tools of literary study and not its object. Perhaps the most important thing to remember about meter is that it should not be mistaken for the actual rhythm of the poem. Instead, it is best thought of as a kind of ideal rhythm that the poem can play against. Meter suggests certain patterns that invite expectations that may or may not be satisfied. Much of the poet's art consists of crafting variations of sound and rhythm to create specific effects.

Some of these effects are illustrated nicely in the following passage from Alexander Pope's "An Essay on Criticism," in which the definitions of bad and good *verse* are ingeniously supported by the music of the lines.

These[1] equal syllables alone require,
Though oft the ear the open vowels tire;
While expletives their feeble aid do join;
And ten low words oft creep in one dull line;
While they ring round the same unvaried chimes,
With sure returns of still expected rhymes;
Where'er you find "the cooling western breeze,"
In the next line, it "whispers through the trees";
If crystal streams "with pleasing murmurs creep,"
The reader's threatened (not in vain) with "sleep";
Then, at the last and only couplet fraught
With some unmeaning thing they call a thought,
A needless Alexandrine[2] ends the song
That, like a wounded snake, drags its slow length along.

. . . . .

True ease in writing comes from art, not chance,
As those move easiest who have learned to dance.
'Tis not enough no harshness gives offense,
The sound must seem an echo to the sense:

[1] Bad poets.
[2] Twelve-syllable line or a line with six rhythmic feet. As in Pope's example, *alexandrines* often follow lines of pentameter, or lines with five metrical feet.

Soft is the strain when Zephyr gently blows,
And the smooth stream in smoother numbers flows;
But when loud surges lash the sounding shore,
The hoarse, rough verse should like the torrent roar:
When Ajax[3] strives some rock's vast weight to throw,
The line too labors, and the words move slow;
Not so, when swift Camilla[4] scours the plain,
Flies o'er the unbending corn, and skims along the main.

When the speaker condemns the use of ten monosyllables, the line contains ten monosyllables: "And ten low words oft creep in one dull line." When he speaks of the wind, the line is rich in hissing sounds that imitate that wind. When he speaks of Ajax striving, clusters of consonants and stressed syllables combine to slow the line; when he speaks of Camilla's swiftness, the final consonants and initial sounds form liaisons that can be pronounced swiftly.

Analysis of this sort can illuminate and enrich our understanding of poetry, but it does not exhaust the significance of a poem. As the poet Dylan Thomas once remarked,

You can tear a poem apart to see what makes it technically tick and say to yourself when the works are laid out before you—the vowels, the consonants, the rhymes, and rhythms—"Yes, this is it. This is why the poem moves me so. It is because of the craftsmanship." But you're back where you began. The best craftsmanship always leaves holes and gaps in the works of the poem so that something that is not in the poem can creep, crawl, flash, or thunder in.

A truly fine poem not only repays attention to its formal features but also points beyond its technique to something more sensuous and less domesticated.

Here are some questions to ask when you face the task of reading and writing about poetry.

QUESTIONS FOR EXPLORING POETRY

1. WHO IS THE SPEAKER? What does the poem reveal about the speaker's character? Do you think you can trust this speaker? In some poems the speaker may be nothing more than a voice meditating on a theme, while in others the speaker takes on a specific personality.

2. IS THE SPEAKER ADDRESSING A PARTICULAR PERSON? If so, who is that person, and why is the speaker interested in him or her?

3. DOES THE POEM HAVE A SETTING? Is the poem occasioned by a particular event?

4. IS THE THEME OF THE POEM STATED DIRECTLY OR INDIRECTLY? From what particular lines or words can you identify the theme of the poem?

[3] A Greek warrior celebrated for his strength.
[4] A swift-footed queen in Virgil's *Aeneid*.

5. FROM WHAT PERSPECTIVE IS THE SPEAKER DESCRIBING SPECIFIC EVENTS? Is the speaker recounting events of the past or events that are occurring in the present? If past events are being recalled, what present meaning do they have for the speaker?

6. DOES A CLOSE EXAMINATION OF THE FIGURATIVE LANGUAGE OF THE POEM REVEAL ANY PATTERNS? See p. 11 and "Glossary of Literary Terms."

7. WHAT IS THE STRUCTURE OF THE POEM? Since narrative poems—those that tell stories—reveal a high degree of selectivity, it is useful to ask why the poet has focused on particular details and left out others. Analyzing the structure of a nonnarrative or lyric poem can be more difficult because it does not contain an obvious series of chronologically related events. The structure of the poem will be revealed through an analysis of patterns of images that embody the theme.

8. WHAT DO SOUND AND METER (SEE "GLOSSARY OF LITERARY TERMS") CONTRIBUTE TO THE POEM?

9. WHAT WAS YOUR RESPONSE TO THE POEM ON FIRST READING? Did your response change after study of the poem or class discussions about it?

READING DRAMA

Drama is fundamentally different from other literary forms. Unlike fiction, for example, most plays are designed to be performed in public and not read in private. The public nature of drama is reflected in the words we use to discuss it. The word *drama* itself is derived from the Greek word for "action, deed, or performance," and *theater* derives from the Greek word for "sight or contemplation." By their nature, plays are more spectacular than poems or works of fiction. Directors and their staffs pay great attention to costumes, set design, lights, and stage movement; the reader, who doesn't experience these elements, must imagine the action on the basis of words alone. Dramatists use words as starting points for, rather than realizations of, their artistic visions.

Although plays typically lack narration and description—they are designed to show, not tell—they can be considered in terms of setting, plot, theme, characterization, and irony. Indeed, these notions are even more important in drama than in fiction, where narrative style and point of view carry great weight, or in poetry, where diction and imagery are central.

As much as possible, the way to read a play is to imagine that you are its director. In this role you must visualize yourself creating the set and the lighting. You will envision people dressed so that their clothes give support to their words. You will think about timing (how long between events and speeches) and blocking (how the characters move as they interact on stage). Perhaps the best way to confront the literature of the stage, to respond most fully to what is there, is to attempt to produce some scenes either in class or after class. If possible, attend the plays or the rehearsals of plays in production on campus. Nothing will provide better insight into the complexities of the theater than attending a rehearsal where the problems are encountered and solved.

As you read any of the opening speeches of any of the plays in this anthology, imagine yourself the director and make decisions. How should the lines be spoken (quietly, angrily, haltingly)? What should the characters do as they speak (remain stationary, look in some direction, traverse the stage)? How should the stage be lit (partially, brightly, in some color that contributes to the mood of the dialogue and action)? What should the characters who are not speaking do? What possibilities exist for conveying appropriate signals solely through gesture and facial expression—signals not contained in the words you read?

Stages and Staging

Although staging is more important to spectators than to readers, some knowledge of staging history can enrich your reading of a play. For example, it helps to know that in the Theatre of Dionysus in Athens (below), there was no scene shifting. In Sophocles' *Antigonê* (p. 450), which was staged in an open-air amphitheater seating about 14,000 people, actors entered from the *skene*, or a fixed-stage house, which might have had painted panels to suggest a scene. Important events, especially violent ones, occur offstage, and the audience learns of these events from a messenger, who comes onstage to describe them. This convention was partly a matter of taste, but the conditions of the Greek stage also prevented Sophocles from moving the action to another scene. Later dramatists, writing for a more flexible stage and a more intimate theater, exploited the dramatic possibilities of such violence.

The vast outdoor theater imposed restrictions on acting style. Facial expressions played no role in the actor's craft; in fact, the actors wore large masks, which were probably equipped with some sort of megaphone to amplify speech.

© Corbis.

Illustration of the Theatre of Dionysus in Athens.

As a result, it was difficult to modulate speech to create subtle effects, and the speeches were probably delivered in formal, declamatory style. In addition to these limitations, the Athenian government made available only three principal actors, all male, as the cast (excluding the *chorus*, a group of citizens that commented on the action and characters) for each play. Consequently, there were never more than three players onstage at once, and the roles were designed so that each actor could take several parts, each signified by a different mask.

Shakespeare's stage was altogether different from Sophocles'. Although both theaters were open-air, the enclosure around the Elizabethan stage was much smaller than the Greek amphitheater, and the theater's capacity was limited to between 2,000 and 3,000 spectators. As in classical drama, men played all the roles, but they no longer wore masks. The stage protruded into the audience, allowing for more intimacy and a greater range of speech, gesture, and expression. Even so, and despite Hamlet's advice to the troupe "to hold as 't were, the mirror up to nature," Shakespearean *tragedy* did not lend itself to a modern realistic style. Those great speeches are written in verse; they are frequently meant to augment the meager set design with verbal imagery; and they are much denser in texture, image, and import than is ordinary speech. Most of the important action was played out on the uncurtained main platform, jutting into the audience and surrounded on three sides by spectators. The swiftly moving scenes followed each other without interruption, doubtless using different areas of the stage to signify different locations. There was some sort of terrace or balcony one story above the main stage, and there was an area at the back of the main protruding stage that could be curtained off when not

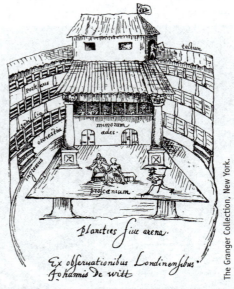

London: Swan Theatre. Johannes De Witt's
drawing of the Swan Theatre, London, c. 1596.

© Corbis.

Hypothetical reconstruction of the interior of the Globe Theatre in the days of Shakespeare.

in use. Although Shakespeare's plays are usually divided into five separate acts in printed versions, they were played straight through, without intermission, much like a modern motion picture. These characteristics distinguish the Shakespearean stage from the familiar realism of most contemporary theater.

Much current theater uses a *box stage*—essentially a box with one wall removed so that the audience can see into the playing area. The box stage lends itself to realistic settings. It can easily be furnished to look like a room; or, if outdoor scenes are required, painted backdrops and angled sets provide perspective. Shortly after the introduction of the box stage, the possibilities for scenic design produced great set designers and increasingly sophisticated stage machinery. These new possibilities, in turn, freed the dramatist from the physical limitations imposed by earlier stages.

By the late nineteenth century, the versatility of the box stage enabled playwrights such as Henrik Ibsen to write detailed stage settings for the various locations in which the drama unfolds. Further, the furnishing of the stage in Ibsen's plays sometimes functions symbolically to visually reinforce the claustrophobic quality of the bourgeois life depicted in his plays. Later dramatists have relied on realistic settings to convey meaning and to serve symbolic functions. The modern production may take place in a theater that is simply a large empty room (with provisions for technical flexibility in the matter of lighting) that can be rearranged to suit the requirements of specific productions. This ideal of a "theater space" that can be freely manipulated has become increasingly attractive since it frees the dramatist and the performance from limitations built into permanent stage design.

© Corbis.

Spectators at a seventeenth-century French box stage.

The Elements of Drama

CHARACTERS Plays usually consist of narratives with plots, settings, themes, characters, and irony, and most plays have no narrators as such. In Greek drama, the chorus functions as a kind of narrator. In Shakespearean drama, the *soliloquy*, in which an actor speaks thoughts aloud, allows the audience to hear what a character is thinking. But in most plays, the story unfolds before our eyes without the intervention of an authorial voice or point of view.

Without a narrator to tell us what a character is thinking, we usually infer a character's thoughts by his or her actions and demeanor, and by *dialogue*, or the words a character speaks to others. Characterization, in plays as in fiction, is a process by which the author establishes the personality of a character, revealed through what the particular character does and says, and by what other characters say. The main character, the hero or *protagonist*, is the center of our attention. He or she is often opposed by another major character, the *antagonist*, whose opposition creates the central conflict of the drama. The protagonist and the antagonist, as well as other characters of major significance in the drama, have a vital interest in the outcome of the action, and grow and develop as the action progresses and are therefore described as *rounded* characters. Those characters who are peripheral to the action, who often supply the kind of exposition a third-person narrator does in fiction, are minor, or *flat*, characters.

DRAMATIC IRONY *Dramatic irony* allows the audience to know more than the characters do about their own circumstances by letting the audience hear more than the characters hear. Shakespeare's *Othello* (p. 984) provides an excellent illustration of the uses of dramatic irony. At the end of act II, Cassio, who has lost his position as Othello's lieutenant, asks Iago for advice on how to regain favor. Iago, who, unknown to Cassio, had engineered Cassio's disgrace, advises him to ask Desdemona, Othello's adored wife, to intervene. Actually this is good advice; ordinarily the tactic would succeed, so much does Othello love his wife and wish to please her. But Iago explains, in a soliloquy to the audience, that he is laying groundwork for the ruin of all the objects of his envy and hatred—Cassio, Desdemona, and Othello:

> . . . for while this honest fool
> Plies Desdemona to repair his fortunes,
> And she for him pleads strongly to the Moor,
> I'll pour this pestilence into his ear
> That she repeals him for her body's lust;
> And, by how much she strives to do him good,
> She shall undo her credit with the Moor.
> So will I turn her virtue into pitch,
> And out of her goodness make the net
> That shall enmesh them all.

Of course, Desdemona, Cassio, and Othello are ignorant of Iago's enmity. Worse, all of them consider Iago a loyal friend. But the audience knows Iago's design, and that knowledge provides the chilling dramatic irony of act III, scene 3.

All the emotional tautness in the audience results from irony, from knowing what the victims do not know. But dramatic irony is the special tool of the dramatist, well suited to produce an electric tension in a live audience that watches and overhears the action onstage.

PLOT AND CONFLICT Plays often portray oppositions between characters or groups or even between two aspects of a character's personality. This opposition often takes the form of a *conflict* that drives the plot. In *Othello*, for example, a variety of conflicts shapes the action of the play. Most obviously, Iago's scheming puts Othello in conflict with Cassio, and turns him against Desdemona. But conflicts can be less literal: Othello and Desdemona's marriage puts them at odds with Venetian society, raising larger questions about race and culture. And conflicts can be within a single character: Othello's jealousy triggers conflicting emotions about himself and about his wife.

Understanding the methods of drama can help us analyze a play and its various effects. But such analysis only gestures at the emotional experience produced by successful drama. More than other forms of literature, plays give physical expression to the social and psychological conflicts that define us individually and collectively. As in *Othello*, a play may torment its audience by imposing on admirable characters unfair circumstances that will result in tragic deaths. Or, as in Susan Glaspell's *Trifles* (p. 1073), a play may mock prevalent attitudes and compel an audience to reexamine its values. By giving expression to human impulses and conflicts, plays enact our most persistent concerns with the greatest possible intensity.

A traditional and still useful way of looking at the plot of a play is to see it in five parts: exposition, rising action, climax, falling action, and denouement. *Exposition* provides the audience with information about background matters important to the play. The first part of the plot also includes *rising action*, as the plot progresses toward complexity and conflict, which reaches a crisis, or *climax*, of some sort. This is the turning point of the play, when the protagonist must act decisively or make a critical choice from which there is no turning back. This in turn leads to the *falling action*, as the protagonist confronts the inexorable consequences of his or her act or decision. The play ends with the *denouement* (French for "untying or unraveling"), with the conflict resolved or the mystery solved. Although this template cannot be applied to every play, it comes close enough in describing the structure of many plays to make it a useful tool for analyzing much drama.

Here are some more specific questions to ask when you begin to read or write about drama. Write out your answers to check your understanding of a play or to begin collecting ideas for an essay assignment.

QUESTIONS FOR EXPLORING DRAMA

1. HOW DOES THE PLAY BEGIN? Is the exposition presented dramatically as characters interact, novelistically through long speeches that convey a lot of information, or through some device such as a messenger who delivers long letters or lengthy reports?

2. HOW DOES THE INFORMATION CONVEYED IN EXPOSITION ESTABLISH THE BASIS FOR DRAMATIC IRONY? Does the audience know more than the characters do? How does that irony create tension in the audience?

3. WHO ARE THE PRINCIPAL CHARACTERS? How are the distinctive qualities of each dramatically conveyed? How do they change as the play proceeds? Are they sympathetic? What function do the minor characters serve?

4. WHERE IS THE PLAY SET? Why does it matter that it is set there? Does the setting play a significant role in the drama, or is it merely a place, any place?

5. WHAT IS THE CENTRAL CONFLICT IN THE PLAY? Is the central conflict between characters, between groups, or even between two parts of a character's personality? How is it resolved? Is the resolution satisfying?

6. WHAT IS THE CONTEXT FOR THE PLAY? Do you need to know the historical circumstances out of which the play emerged or something of the life of the author to appreciate the play fully? If so, how does the information enhance your understanding?

7. WHAT VISUAL AND AUDITORY ELEMENTS OF THE PLAY EFFECT YOUR RESPONSE TO THE PLAY? Since plays are usually written to be performed rather than read, place yourself in the position of the director and the actors to respond to this aspect of drama if you are reading a text.

8. WHAT IS THE PLAY'S THEME? How does the dramatic action embody that theme?

9. HOW DOES THE PLAY END? How does the ending connect to the beginning—or any other specific points—of the play?

10. HAS THE PLAY BEEN MADE INTO A FILM? In the adaptation, what has been added and what has been deleted? How does this production compare with your reading of the play?

READING NONFICTION

Essays differ from fiction in that they generally do not create imaginary worlds inhabited by fictional characters. For instance, Langston Hughes describes the real-life experience of attending his Auntie Reed's church as an adolescent in "Salvation" (p. 284), just as George Orwell recounts his own experience of shooting an elephant in Burma in "Shooting an Elephant" (p. 827). And although we cannot independently verify these personal experiences, both works exhibit the formal nonfictional qualities of essays rather than the imagined worlds of short stories.

Writers turn to the essay form when they wish to confront their readers directly with an idea, a problem (often with a proposed solution), an illuminating experience, an important definition, or some flaw (or virtue) in the social system. Usually, the essay is relatively short, and almost always embodies the writer's personal viewpoint. And although the essay may share many elements with other literary forms, it generally speaks with the voice of a real person about the real world. The term *essay* derives from the French verb *essayer*—"try, attempt." That verb, in turn, derives from the Latin verb *exigere*—"weigh out, examine."

While the French term calls attention to the personal perspective that characterizes the essay, the Latin verb suggests that an essay can not only examine personal experiences but can also explore and clarify ideas by arguing for or against a position.

As you read an essay, you need to ask yourself, What is the central argument or idea? Sometimes the answer is obvious, sometimes less so. In some cases, essays do not argue for one thing in particular, but rather meditate on human experience and address the inner lives of their readers. John Donne's "Meditation XVII" (p. 1303), for example, does not attack or justify anything. Rather, it reminds us to be aware of our mortality and thereby to alter our interactions with or perceptions of the people around us.

Types of Nonfiction

If you have taken a composition course, you may have read and written narrative, descriptive, expository, and argumentative essays. While reviewing the characteristics of each of these types, keep in mind that in the real world, authors of essays are more interested in effectiveness than in purity of form, and frequently combine features of different formal types.

NARRATIVE NONFICTION Narrative essays recount a sequence of related events and are often autobiographical. But those events are chosen because they suggest or illustrate some larger insight or problem. In "Shooting an Elephant" (p. 827), for example, George Orwell narrates an episode from his life that led him to an important insight about imperialism. In Maxine Hong Kingston's "No Name Woman" (p. 1097) the narrator's reflections on the significance of her aunt's suicide in China many years ago, a tragic family secret that still haunts her, powerfully illustrate the deep connection between past and present and the troubling idea that family and culture can oppress. In these narrative essays, the writers discover in their own experiences the evidence for generalizations about themselves and their societies.

DESCRIPTIVE NONFICTION Descriptive essays depict sensory observations in words. They evoke in the reader's imagination the sights and sounds, perhaps even the smells, that transport the reader to such places as George Orwell's Burma. The descriptive essay, like the narrative essay, often addresses complex issues that trouble our lives, but it does so by appealing primarily to sensory awareness—sight, sound, touch, taste, smell—rather than to intellect. The power of description is so great that narrative and expository essays often use lengthy descriptive passages to communicate forcefully.

EXPOSITORY NONFICTION Expository essays attempt to explain and elucidate, to organize and provide information. Often they embody an extended definition of a complex conception such as love or patriotism; other times, they describe a process—how to do something. This book's coverage of essays, for example, is clearly not narrative because it doesn't depend for its form on a chronological sequence of meaningful events. It is not descriptive in the pure sense of that type because it does not depend on conveying sensory impressions. It is, in fact, expository. It acquaints its readers with the techniques and types of essays and provides some tips to help students read essays both analytically and pleasurably. Many of these approaches involve making some kind of connection. You may recognize a number of rhetorical strategies from writing courses you may have taken. We *classify* essays by type; we *compare and contrast* them; we use *definition*; we give *examples* to make a point; we imply that there is a *cause-and-effect* relationship between what readers bring to an essay and the pleasure they derive from it. Similarly, the essayists represented in this book use a variety of such rhetorical strategies to achieve their aims.

ARGUMENTATIVE NONFICTION   Although Orwell's "Shooting an Elephant" can be categorized as a narrative essay, we might reasonably assert that it is also argumentative because it is designed to convince readers that imperialism is as destructive to the oppressors as to the oppressed. The argumentative essay wishes to persuade its readers. Thus, it usually deals with controversial ideas, marshals arguments and evidence to support a view, and anticipates and answers opposing arguments. Jonathan Swift accomplishes all these ends in "A Modest Proposal" (p. 481), with an approach complicated by his reliance on irony and satire.

Analyzing Nonfiction

THE THESIS   The best way to begin analyzing an essay is to ask, What is the point of this piece of writing—what is the author trying to show, attack, defend, or prove? If you can answer that question satisfactorily and succinctly, then the analysis of the essay's elements (i.e., its rhetorical strategies, structure, style, tone, and language) becomes easier. E. L. Doctorow's "Why We Are Infidels" (p. 498), for example, projects a clear thesis. On the other hand, a much more complex and ambitious essay, such as Virginia Woolf's "What If Shakespeare Had Had a Sister?" (p. 819), does not yield up its thesis quite so easily. We might say that Woolf's examination of the historical record leads her to argue that women did not write during the Elizabethan period because literary talent could not flourish in a social system that made women the ill-educated property of men. This formulation of the essay's thesis, as you will see when you read the essay, leaves a good deal out— notably the exhortation to action with which Woolf concludes the piece.

STRUCTURE AND DETAIL   Read carefully the first and last paragraphs of a number of essays. Note the writers' strategy for engaging you at the outset with an irresistible proposition:

> In Moulmein, in lower Burma, I was hated by large numbers of people—the only time in my life that I have been important enough for this to happen to me.

> If I speak in the tongues of men and of angels, but have not love, I am a noisy gong or a clanging cymbal.

> I was saved from sin when I was going on thirteen.

These opening sentences are startling, hooking readers so that they will eagerly read on to find out what it was that made Orwell so hated in Burma, why love is so important to Paul, how Langston Hughes was saved from sin. You will find that the opening lines of most well-wrought essays instantly capture your attention.

Endings, too, are critical. And if you examine the concluding lines of any of the essays in this collection, you will find forceful assertions that sharply focus the matter that precedes them. Essayists, unsurprisingly, systematically use gripping beginnings and forceful endings.

What come between those beginnings and endings are often abstract issues—the nature of love, the inevitability of death, the evils of imperialism. Though such abstractions do significantly influence our lives, as subject matter for reading they seem impersonal and distant. Reading about great ideas becomes a sort of academic task, relegated to some intellectual sphere, separate from the pain and passion of our own humanity. The accomplished essay writer, however, entices us to confront such issues by converting abstract ideas into concrete and illustrative detail.

STYLE AND TONE The word *style* refers to all the writing skills that contribute to the effect of any piece of literature. And *tone*—the attitude conveyed by the language a writer chooses—is a particularly significant aspect of writing style. As an illustration of the effect of tone, consider these opening lines of two essays— Jonathan Swift's "A Modest Proposal" and Langston Hughes's "Salvation":

> It is a melancholy object to those who walk through this great town or travel in the country, when they see the streets, the roads, and cabin doors, crowded with beggars of the female sex, followed by three, four, or six children, all in rags and importuning every passenger for an alms. These mothers, instead of being able to work for their honest livelihood, are forced to employ all their time in strolling to beg sustenance for their helpless infants, who, as they grow up, either turn thieves for want of work, or leave their dear native country to fight for the Pretender in Spain, or sell themselves to the Barbados.

> I was saved from sin when I was going on thirteen. But not really saved. It happened like this. There was a big revival at my Auntie Reed's church. Every night for weeks there had been much preaching, singing, praying, and shouting, and some very hardened sinners had been brought to Christ, and the membership of the church had grown by leaps and bounds. Then just before the revival ended, they held a special meeting for children, "to bring the young lambs to the fold."

Both accounts use provocative openings, immediately hooking the reader. Swift's tone, however, is formal; consider the complexity of his syntax ("It is a melancholy object to those who walk through this great town or travel in the country, when they see the streets, the roads, and cabin doors, crowded with beggars of the female sex, followed by three, four, or six children, all in rags and importuning every passenger for an alms") and the sophistication of his diction ("melancholy," "employ," "sustenance").

Hughes's tone, in his first-person account, is personal and informal. He uses colloquial diction ("It happened like this," "leaps and bounds") and a sardonic wit ("some very hardened sinners had been brought to Christ"). Although a reminiscing adult describes the event, the writer creates the voice of a child by using simple grammar and a child's vocabulary.

The tone a writer creates contributes substantially to the message he or she conveys. Jonathan Swift might have written a sound, academic essay about the economic diseases of Ireland and how to cure them—but his invention of the speaker of "A Modest Proposal," who ironically and sardonically proposes the establishment of a human-baby meat-exporting industry, jars the readers in ways no scholarly essay could. The high seriousness of Donne's tone in "Meditation XVII" perfectly suits his contemplation of the relationship among the living, the dying, and the dead.

Style is a more difficult quality to define than tone is. Dictionaries define *style* as both "a manner of expression in language" and "excellence in expression." Certainly it is easier to distinguish between various *manners* of expression than it is to describe just what constitutes *excellence* in expression. For example, the manners of expression of John Donne in "Meditation XVII" (p. 1303) and of Judith Ortiz Cofer in "American History" (p. 287) clearly differ. The first muses about death, God, alienation, and community in a style characterized by formality and complex extended images. The second uses the conversational style of a memoirist to evoke a particular moment in her life that has larger resonance in the story of twentieth-century America. Although Cofer considers some of the same broad themes that Donne does, her perspective, focus, and conclusions are entirely different, and this difference is reflected in the tone and style of the piece.

Despite their vast differences, we can describe the excellence of each style. Donne, an Anglican priest, meditates on the community of all living humans and the promise of eternal life in the face of physical death. He evokes a remarkable image when he states that "all mankind is of one author." Not so remarkable, you might argue; God is often called the "author of mankind." But why? This image is powerful not just because it is an apt metaphor but because it is an apt metaphor that famously appears in the opening lines of the Gospel according to John in the Bible, which tells us that "[i]n the beginning was the Word, . . . and the Word was God." Donne develops this idea, further insisting on the intimate relationship among all people because humankind "is one volume." Then he extends this metaphor by arguing that "when one man dies, one chapter is not torn out of the book, but translated into a better language." The vivid image is further extended. "God," Donne tells us, "employs several translators; some pieces are translated by age, some by sickness, some by war, some by justice." By alluding to the actual making of a book by the bookbinder, Donne elaborates on the central image and reestablishes the idea of community: "God's hand is in every translation, and his hand shall bind up all our scattered leaves again for that library where every book shall lie open to one another." Donne alludes to the Bible repeatedly throughout the essay, adding layers to the significance of the "holy book" image and further demonstrating his own faith by showing the depths of his biblical knowledge. The complexity and aptness of Donne's figurative characterization of death is a remarkable stylistic achievement, and one need not share his beliefs to be impressed by his mastery of his medium.

By contrast, Judith Ortiz Cofer's very specific examination of some apparently irreparable rifts in the "human volume" opens with a reference to *Ripley's Believe It or Not*, hardly an exalted cultural allusion and one whose words suggest anything but faith. While Donne argues—in language some readers might find alienating—that we are all connected by God, Cofer attempts a more earthly connection, using everyday language and popular references that she expects contemporary American readers to recognize and grasp immediately. For many of her readers, the Kennedy assassination became the ultimate where-were-you-when-you-heard moment, and the emotional resonance of the reference is as historically specific as Donne's references are not. While Donne's imagery seems intended to convey timeless religious truths, Cofer's brings to mind worldly divisions: even their shared grief over President Kennedy cannot bridge the various cultural divides between the young narrator and her neighbors. Her Catholicism implicitly separates her from white Protestant America and connects her to the martyred Kennedy, yet teenage heartache is more meaningful to the narrator than the death of Kennedy or any comfort or meaning that faith might provide. Indeed, looking toward heaven for answers is registered as a kind of denial in Cofer's essay: even as the girl looks up into the falling snow, she cannot keep from her mind the knowledge that it will get dirty the minute it touches her urban backyard. The "veil" of snow evokes nuns or even the Virgin Mary's traditional cloak, but Cofer tells us, once one looks around and sees the whole picture, one cannot avoid noticing the dirt of urban life turning that white snow grey. Although these essays have some surprising connections—like many essayists, both authors are struggling with questions about their mortality and their place in the world—their larger points, and thus their styles, are starkly different. Particularly in their uses of allusion—the kinds of works they refer to and why—the two pieces could hardly have less in common. Yet what they do share is that the style of each is ideally suited to its subject matter and position, and reinforces some larger truth about each piece. These writers exhibit distinctive manners of expression and distinctive varieties of excellence; in short, they have distinctive styles.

Your principal concern, when reading an essay, must always be to discover its central thesis. What does the writer wish you to understand about his or her experience, the world, or yourself? Once you have understood the essay's thesis, you can enhance your understanding by examining the means the author used to convey it and, perhaps, recognize techniques that will enhance the quality of your own writing. To that end, you ought to examine the essay's structure and the rhetorical strategies that shape it. How does it begin and end? What type is it—narrative, descriptive, expository, argumentative? How do rhetorical strategies—definition, cause and effect, classification, exemplification, comparison and contrast—function to serve the author's purposes? Then analyze the sources of the essay's effectiveness by closely analyzing the language of the essay. Watch the author energize abstract ideas with details and moving experience; consider the uses of figurative language—the metaphors and similes that create both physical and emotional landscapes in the prose; respond to the tone of voice and the stylistic choices that create it. When you have done all this successfully, when you have discovered not only *what* the author has said but also *how* the author moved you to his or her point of view—then you will have understood the essay.

Here are some questions to ask when you face the task of reading and writing about essays.

QUESTIONS FOR EXPLORING NONFICTION

1. WHAT IS THE AUTHOR'S THESIS? What evidence or arguments does the author advance to support the thesis? Is the thesis convincing? If not, why not? Does the author rely on any basic but unstated assumptions?

2. WHAT IS THE AUTHOR'S TONE? Select for analysis a passage you consider illustrative of the author's tone. Does the author maintain that tone consistently throughout the essay?

3. HOW WOULD YOU CHARACTERIZE THE AUTHOR'S STYLE? For example, are the syntax, length of sentences, and diction elevated and formal or familiar and informal?

4. WHAT RHETORICAL STRATEGIES DOES THE AUTHOR USE? For example, can you identify the effective use of narration, description, classification, comparison and contrast, analogy, cause and effect, or definition? Note that one of these rhetorical strategies may constitute the unifying idea of the essay or the means of structuring it.

5. WHAT ARE THE MAJOR DIVISIONS IN THE ESSAY? How are they set off? Are the transitions between the divisions effective and easy to follow?

6. HOW DOES THE AUTHOR BEGIN THE ESSAY? Does the opening paragraph effectively gain the reader's attention? Does it clearly state the essay's thesis? If it does not, at what point do the author's thesis and purpose become clear? How does the essay's concluding paragraph connect to the opening paragraph?

WRITING ABOUT LITERATURE

If reading literature offers a way to listen to the surprisingly alive voices of the past, writing about literature affords the opportunity to respond to these voices. Depending on how complicated the piece is or how foreign its world is to your own experiences, your initial responses might be just a jumble of vague impressions. Classroom discussion can help to clarify your thoughts, but the best ideas do not usually come together until you sit down and write. The act of composition often generates a line of thinking. Writing about literature is an invitation to organize your impressions and to check those impressions against the work that prompted them. When you accept this invitation, you undertake a process that helps make sense of the literary work and helps you understand your reactions to it. It is important to remember that your reactions can take the form of arguments—arguments about a work and arguments with it, or arguments with what you take a writer to be saying about the world. Such thoughts can sometimes be difficult to formulate, so the opportunity to write them down and see where they take you is especially valuable.

RESPONDING TO YOUR READING

As you know from experience, complete essays do not pop into your head immediately after you read a work of literature. The process starts with an impression here, a fragment there, or a question about something that catches your attention, which is why it is important to read actively and annotate while you read.

Annotating While You Read

Each of the discussions of the four literary genres concludes with "Questions for Exploring," a series of questions that you might bring to the reading of any text. As an active and critical reader, you must attempt to answer those questions as you read—and note your responses as you do. Look at the considerations we raise for readers of poetry (pp. 15–16). We asked some students to apply this questioning and annotating technique to Shakespeare's Sonnet 29, a moderately difficult poem. Here is a composite of what they produced:

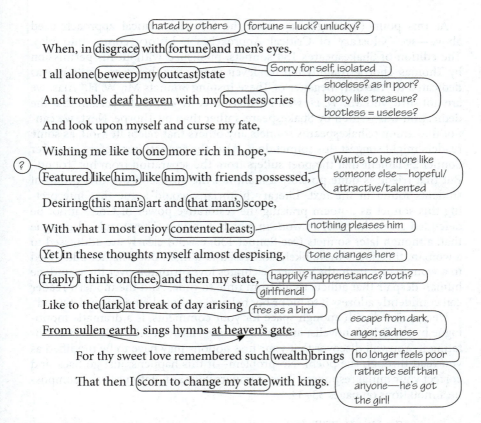

When, in disgrace with fortune and men's eyes,

I all alone beweep my outcast state

And trouble deaf heaven with my bootless cries

And look upon myself and curse my fate,

Wishing me like to one more rich in hope,

Featured like him, like him with friends possessed,

Desiring this man's art and that man's scope,

With what I most enjoy contented least;

Yet in these thoughts myself almost despising,

Haply I think on thee, and then my state,

Like to the lark at break of day arising

From sullen earth, sings hymns at heaven's gate;

For thy sweet love remembered such wealth brings

That then I scorn to change my state with kings.

Annotations (handwritten): hated by others; fortune = luck? unlucky?; Sorry for self, isolated; shoeless? as in poor? booty like treasure? bootless = useless?; Wants to be more like someone else—hopeful/attractive/talented; nothing pleases him; tone changes here; happily? happenstance? both?; girlfriend!; free as a bird; escape from dark, anger, sadness; no longer feels poor; rather be self than anyone—he's got the girl!

All in all, the annotations to this sonnet are quite good. The students grasped the poet's design, largely overcame the difficulties created by somewhat archaic language, and recognized the poet's aim to both flatter his love and express the saving grace that love provides.

But curious things happen with language. The deconstructionist critics (see "Glossary of Critical Approaches," p. 1334) have argued that because each reader brings a different set of experiences and assumptions to texts, it is difficult (some say impossible) to confidently understand any text. Put another way, different readers will interpret the same text in vastly different ways. For example, some readers, at the crucial moment when the poet remarks, "Haply I think on thee" (l. 10), might interpret the pronoun not as an *allusion* to a friend or lover but as an allusion to God. In this interpretation the sonnet resolves, not with the saving grace of a love that sets all things right, but with the ineffable saving grace of God that, with the promise of heaven, makes human pain and misery insignificant. Is such a religious reading of the poem simply wrong? And if so, what evidence could we use to show that it is wrong? Are the students who agree that the poet's girlfriend is the agent of his lifted spirits quite right? These are difficult questions, not the least because Shakespeare's sonnets seriously trouble scholars to this day.

At this point (moving away from the formalist critical approach used above—see "Glossary of Critical Approaches"), history comes into play. The edition of Shakespeare's 154 sonnets, published without his permission by Thomas Thorpe roughly ten to eleven years after they were written, was dedicated to "the only Begetter of These Insuing Sonnets Mr. W. H." Alas, we are not sure who Mr. W. H. was. Furthermore, we cannot be certain that the dedication was written by Shakespeare, rather than by Thorpe. Next, we cannot find among Shakespeare's sonnets any others that celebrate God, as some readers might suggest this sonnet does. Also, the sonnets just before and after Sonnet 29 lament that the poet suffers from the separation from his "friend." But that friend is quite possibly a man, not the girlfriend our first group of students found in the text. Literary historians would argue that interpreting this sonnet as a poem praising the restorative power of God cannot be defended given the body of work in which it resides. They would also argue that, although later sonnets (see Sonnet 130, p. 936) clearly are addressed to a woman, this one is more likely addressed to a man. But whether addressed to a woman or a man, the sonnet celebrates love's triumph over the mundane human despair that afflicts us all from time to time. And the modern reader can confidently address it to his or her beloved without being misunderstood.

Here, printed with enough space for your comments, is a dramatic monologue by the British novelist and poet Thomas Hardy (1840–1928). Try annotating it. You will discover that your first notions may have to be modified as you read through the poem. No problem—if this happens, just go back and correct your initial responses. Then compare your annotations to the composite annotations on pages 33–34.

The Man He Killed

"Had he and I but met

By some old ancient inn,

We should have sat us down to wet

Right many a nipperkin!

"But ranged as infantry,

And staring face to face,

I shot at him as he at me,

And killed him in his place.

"I shot him dead because—

Because he was my foe,

Just so: my foe of course he was:

　That's clear enough; although

"He thought he'd 'list, perhaps,

Off-hand-like—just as I—,

Was out of work—had sold his traps—

　No other reason why.

"Yes; quaint and curious war is!

　You shoot a fellow down

You'd treat, if met where any bar is,

　Or help to half-a-crown."

The Man He Killed

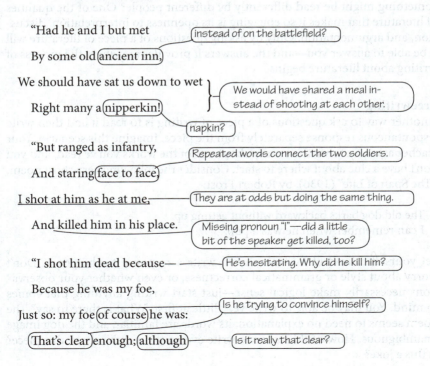

"Had he and I but met ⟮instead of on the battlefield?⟯

By some old ⟮ancient inn,⟯

We should have sat us down to wet ⟯ We would have shared a meal instead of shooting at each other.

Right many a ⟮nipperkin!⟯ ⟮napkin?⟯

"But ranged as infantry, ⟮Repeated words connect the two soldiers.⟯

And staring ⟮face to face⟯

I shot at him as he at me,— ⟮They are at odds but doing the same thing.⟯

And killed him in his place. ⟮Missing pronoun "I"—did a little bit of the speaker get killed, too?⟯

"I shot him dead because— ⟮He's hesitating. Why did he kill him?⟯

Because he was my foe,

Just so: my foe ⟮of course⟯ he was: ⟮Is he trying to convince himself?⟯

⟮That's clear⟯ enough; ⟮although⟯ ⟮Is it really that clear?⟯

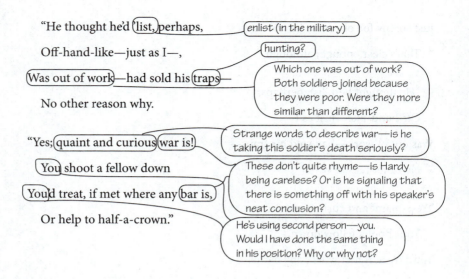

"He thought he'd list, perhaps, — enlist (in the military)

Off-hand-like—just as I—, — hunting?

Was out of work—had sold his traps— — Which one was out of work? Both soldiers joined because they were poor. Were they more similar than different?

No other reason why.

"Yes; quaint and curious war is! — Strange words to describe war—is he taking this soldier's death seriously?

You shoot a fellow down — These don't quite rhyme—is Hardy being careless? Or is he signaling that there is something off with his speaker's neat conclusion?

You'd treat, if met where any bar is,

Or help to half-a-crown." — He's using second person—you. Would I have done the same thing in his position? Why or why not?

Observe how these composite annotations engage with the poem and ask questions of Hardy's poetic structure and language. How do your own annotations compare to these composite annotations? Was there a certain point that you interpreted differently than the composite showed? Can you see how something might be read differently by different people? One of the qualities of literature that makes it so engaging is its openness to interpretation, discussion, and argumentation. Only by asking questions of a piece of literature will it be able to answer you—and the answers it provides are where the process of writing about literature begins.

Freewriting

Another way to ask questions of a piece of writing is to read it and then write a spontaneous response separately from the piece. Imagine this scenario. Your teacher asks you to write an essay about one of the works you've read, and you don't have a clue about where to start. Consider the following very short poem, "The Span of Life" (1936), by Robert Frost:

The old dog barks backward without getting up.
I can remember when he was a pup.

Set yourself a limit of five minutes to write a response to the poem. Don't worry about style or grammatical correctness, or even whether your observations necessarily make logical sense—just start writing anything that comes to mind. You may be able to write very little at first. What is there to say? The poem seems to need no explanation; its words are familiar, and the dog image unambiguous. How could someone write even a short essay about this piece? Is this a joke?

The purpose of this practice—called *freewriting*—is to force yourself to respond to a piece of writing, even when you think you might not have anything to say. By writing spontaneously and continuously for a certain amount of time, even when writing about a two-line poem, you have to look very closely at the piece—and in doing so, hitherto-unrealized connections can often work their way to the surface of your mind.

If we look again closely at "The Span of Life," we may observe more than we did on an initial reading. First, the title seems awfully grand for this tiny poem. Somehow, these two lines and sixteen words are to make a poetic statement about the nature of life itself. Perhaps we had better look at the lines and words carefully. As a first step, let's scan the poem:

The old dog barks backward without getting up.

I can remember when he was a pup.

Now, speak the poem aloud. Note that the first half of line 1 seems to move slowly, while line 2 seems to prance. That series of four stressed syllables in line 1 "slows" the line. Further, it seems that the words are hard to say quickly—perhaps because the last letter of each stressed syllable has to be finished before you can speak the first letter of the following word: "old *dog* barks *backward without*." The *meter* and the sound patterns that describe the dog, old and tired as he is, contribute to the lethargy described in line 1. But is this poem about a mere dog's life or, perhaps, life in general?

In the second line, the lilting *anapestic meter* dances across the page. (An *anapest* is a metrical foot consisting of two unaccented syllables followed by an accented syllable. See *Meter* in the "Glossary of Literary Terms.") The final *n* of "can" slides easily into the initial *r* of "remember"; the easy movements between words and in the sound sequences that follow all contribute to the quickness of the line. Thus, the joyful playfulness of a puppy, suggested by the bounding anapestic meter, is reinforced by the sound patterns embodied in the words chosen to evoke the old dog's youth. Since the title of the poem invites the reader to generalize, we could assume that human life spans, like the old dog's, move from the energetic exuberance of youth to the fatigued immobility of advanced age.

Now the title makes sense—and the *poetic* quality of the sixteen-word *couplet* (two consecutive rhyming lines) emerges from the rhythm and the sounds that reinforce the meaning of the words.

Reread your five-minute freewrite. Did you note any of these matters? Did you wonder about the poem's title? Do you have an alternative reading to suggest? After this discussion, could you now write a short essay on Frost's poem? These first jottings do not require that you bring any special knowledge to this poem, just that you attend to what's there on the page—a puzzling title, an unusual variation of metrical patterns, and the sounds that embody the poem.

Writing about literature challenges you to teach yourself. Every element in a literary work has been deliberately put there by the author—the description of the *setting*, the events that form the *plot*, the *dialogue*, the *imagery*. E. M. Forster, a literary critic and novelist, had one of his characters say, "only connect." This notion is a good one to follow when trying to write an essay that analyzes literature. Does what you are reading remind you of anything in your own life? Of anything else you have read? When you slow down and read even more carefully, you will notice connections between words and images that can help you find the key to interpreting the work of literature at hand. Readers experience a mysterious intellectual and emotional event as a result of the writer's purposeful manipulation of language. When you write about what you've read, you confront not only your response to a work but also the elements within the work that cause your response.

Think about a short story or novel that you have read or a movie you have seen recently. Did you like or dislike the story? Try to list the reasons for your general reaction and evaluation: the characters were interesting or dull and lifeless; the ending satisfied expectations or, perhaps, was surprising; the story was easy to understand; it offered new insights about people, or places, or a different society; you couldn't wait to see what would happen next (or found the story so boring that you had trouble finishing it). Your personal impressions, as you jot them down, represent your response to the work.

When you write about literature, you begin with your response to the work. Then you need to consider the writer's purpose. This is not easy; in fact, some critics argue that the reader can never fully recover the writer's purpose. But you can explore the text, try to discover how the plot, setting, *characterizations*—the very words (sometimes *symbolic*)—all conspire to generate the *theme*, and, finally, work on your feelings so that you have some response.

To write about literature is, in one way or another, an attempt to discover and describe how the writer's art created the reader's response. In other words, whatever your assignment, the fundamental task is to answer two questions: How do I respond to this piece? How has the author brought about my response?

Keeping a Journal

Your instructor may require you to keep a journal—a day-by-day account of your reactions to and reflections on your reading. Even if a journal is not required, you might want to keep one for a variety of reasons. From a purely practical perspective, writing in a journal regularly is excellent practice at conquering the blank page and generating ideas. You need not construct grammatical sentences, write cohesive paragraphs, develop your ideas, or even make sense. In a journal you are free to comment on only one aspect of a work or on a personal recollection that something in the work triggered. You are recording your reactions, ideas, feelings, questions. Jotting down personal connections—for example, if a character reminds you of a friend or teacher—can be helpful even if they don't make it in into your essay. If you are conscientious about keeping your journal, you may come to find writing in it a pleasant activity.

A journal's helpfulness extends beyond its use as a place for reflection. When the time comes to write a full-length essay for your class, the journal can provide many possible topics. Use your journal to express in writing the pleasure (or pain) of each reading assignment. Jot down unfamiliar words (which you should then, of course, look up in your dictionary). Note your reactions to characters—that some are nasty, others too saintly, some realistically rendered, still others unbelievable. Some of your journal entries may be confessions of confusion, posing open-ended questions about a reading. Others may be a record of personal feelings and recollections triggered by a work; thinking critically about such reactions might generate an essay that examines the conflict between your own moral values and those embodied in a particular work.

Finally, remember that—unless your instructor has specific guidelines for journal keeping—your journal will be the one place where you can write as much or as little as you please, as often or infrequently as you wish, with care and deliberation or careless speed. Its only purpose is to serve your needs. But if you write fairly regularly, you will probably be surprised not only at how much easier the act of writing becomes but also at how many ideas suddenly pop into your head in the act of writing. Henry Adams was surely right when he observed, "The habit of expression leads to the search for something to express."

Exploring and Planning

THINKING CRITICALLY Thinking critically about literature doesn't mean being critical of literature, that is, thinking about it negatively. Instead it means thinking like a literary critic, thinking about what lies beneath the obvious surface of a work of literature. Critical thinking more generally means not simply accepting everything you see or hear or read; thinking critically about literature means not taking literary works at face value. Instead, you should question everything: what the author seems to want to do, how she or he goes about doing it, what she or he seems to assume, what he or she concludes, and whether the work has a *point of view* or message. Ask yourself whether the work succeeds or does something else, what the effects are of how the author crafted the piece, and whether you agree with his or her assumptions and conclusions. Certainly judgment is involved: you will sometimes end up concluding that an author has succeeded or failed or even said something with which you cannot agree. The claim you end up making about a particular work of literature depends on this process of identifying what a work of literature does and how it does it and then thinking critically about those things.

ASKING GOOD QUESTIONS Often the best ideas for paper topics begin as questions (possibly from a freewrite) or as responses (perhaps from a journal) that can be turned into questions. In reading James Joyce's "Araby" (p. 125), for example, you may notice that the *narrator* makes a big deal out of carrying the groceries home. This observation can be converted into a question: Why the big deal about carrying the groceries home? Or, to focus the question a bit, Why and how does the boy idealize these everyday situations? Note that these questions do not lead to a single irrefutable answer. When you write responses to literature, your goal is to pose a good question, answer it clearly, and support the answer with evidence from the work.

While it is important to clear up basic questions—for example, what a word or phrase means, or who did what, or how the characters are related to one another—successful papers usually take up questions that are less easily settled; in other words, they make a claim that can be argued and supported. For example, you would probably not want to ask whether it was a mistake for Shakespeare's Othello to trust Iago, or whether the *tragedy* could have been avoided if he had acted otherwise. Questions such as these do not lend themselves to sustained discussion. Questions of personal taste are not immediately useful for the same reason; if you say you like a particular work, there is little anyone can say to the contrary. Sometimes such assertions can be usefully converted, especially if you begin to ask why you like or dislike a work. In general, however, you should strive to explore open-ended interpretative and thematic questions rather than rehash the facts or declare personal preferences.

ESTABLISHING A WORKING THESIS   Early in the writing process, as you gather ideas about what to write, you should formulate a tentative *working thesis* that states your topic and the point or argument you wish to make about the topic. Although your working thesis will probably change as you collect information, articulating it will help you focus your thoughts and further research. Make your working thesis as specific as possible to limit your topic and keep the scope of the essay manageable. Consider the audience appeal of your working thesis as well.

A *thesis* states the main claim you'll make in your final essay. In your opening paragraph, a clear thesis statement should both state the claim you intend to make and prepare your reader for what follows. The thesis statement should be accompanied by some indication of the *scope* of your argument—the several issues you intend to explore.

For example, generating ideas for an essay about *Othello*, you may be struck by a line Othello utters before the Duke in act I: "Rude I am in my speech, / and little blessed with the soft phrase of peace." Despite this line, you notice that Othello's speech is admirably measured and eloquent. Is he being falsely modest? Is he tailoring his rhetoric to his noble audience? Is there a genuine note of insecurity being sounded? Whatever your preliminary answer, it is the beginning of your working thesis. The next step is to reexamine Othello's speeches to see if you can find evidence to support and refine the claim of your working thesis.

GATHERING INFORMATION   Once you have chosen your topic and articulated a working thesis, consider what additional information you will need to explore the issue. This may mean identifying examples from the text of the literary work you are analyzing to support your thesis or gathering information from other sources. The library is likely to be the principal source of additional information, though online research is becoming increasingly reliable.

If you use an electronic source, it is often a simple matter to print online information. If you use print sources in a library, you will need to make a photocopy or take notes. In any case, be sure to indicate on your printout or your note cards the exact publication and location information for all your sources so that you can properly document your sources in the final essay. Even if you are using just one source, you will need to provide information crediting that source in your list of works cited. For more information about documenting sources and creating a Works Cited page, see page 71.

ORGANIZING INFORMATION Writing an essay would be a much quicker and more straightforward process if you could somehow magically know what you wanted to write about before you began your research and then whipped up a succinct thesis followed by a structured outline in which arguments I, II, and III were supported by points A, B, and C. In the real world, writers research a preliminary topic and then impose order on the information they have amassed. Think about how best to group or organize your points so that they will be persuasive to your readers.

One general approach to organizing an essay requires you to complete this statement: "My claim in this essay is X. To demonstrate X, I will support it with arguments A, B, and C." In an essay on *Othello*, for example, you might write, "My claim in this essay is that Othello's fall is a logical consequence of his situation and his character. To demonstrate this thesis, I will examine his age and race, his military life, and his inexperience with European women."

Once you've nailed down the thesis and scope of the essay, you can, in your draft, add layers to support your claim:

> Many writers have argued that the rapid fall of the noble Moor Othello is unbelievable. But consider his situation. He is a black man in a white country; he is much older than his beautiful wife. As a military man, he self-consciously lacks social grace. And his inexperience with European women contributes to the emotional insecurity that finally destroys him.

Where you cite other writers' arguments—as in the first sentence—you must offer documentation for your sources.

The next several paragraphs would follow the organization set up by the opening. First might be a paragraph on Othello's race and age and the attitudes toward him established in act I, followed by a paragraph on Othello's self-conscious unfamiliarity with the behavior of European women. The next paragraph might argue that he sees himself as unappealing to women from his adopted city. Each of these assertions should be supported with dialogue from the play. A conclusion would follow: Othello was never quite as noble as some have suggested and, under the circumstances, was doomed from the start.

One of the intellectual hurdles you'll face as a student of literature is learning to distinguish between a *summary* that recounts events and details and an *analysis* that interprets what events and details might mean. Of course an analysis should provide enough plot summary so that your reader has the context to understand what you are talking about. In fact, if you are confused about the plot of a literary work—what happened, in what order—then writing a summary may help to clear up your confusion. Moreover, writing a summary is often a first step to writing an analysis and offering an interpretation. As you describe what happens in a work of literature, you begin to ask questions about why those events happened. In choosing the details and events to include in your summary, you are making decisions about which details and events are worth attending to when you try to ascribe meaning to them in the context of analysis and interpretation.

The following summary of Shakespeare's *Othello* reduces the play to its major plot elements. Notice that it does not interpret or make arguments about the play, focusing on particular details and explaining what they mean. (Notice also that it is narrated in the present tense, a conventional practice when you summarize.) This is in contrast to the later analysis of *Othello* in this chapter that answers questions of why things happened in the play and what these events might mean to us as readers.

A Summary of *Othello*

Set in Venice and then Cyprus, *Othello* opens with a scene of the villainous Iago and his henchman Roderigo hatching a vengeful plot against Iago's commanding general Othello, who has passed him over to promote the handsome Michael Cassio to be his Lieutenant. Iago first tries to undermine Othello by anonymously revealing to the father of Othello's new wife that his daughter is now married to a person of a different race (Othello is a Moor—an African). The father, a nobleman named Brabantio, is appalled that his daughter, Desdemona, is married to a Moor, but when he takes his argument to the Duke of Venice, the Duke, who desires Othello's services to protect Venice from an invasion from Cyprus, judges that Othello and Desdemona truly love each other, and approves their wedding. Thwarted in his first attempts at vengeance, Iago contrives to draw Cassio into a drunken street brawl that leads to Othello stripping Cassio of his new rank.

Iago then advances his vengeance by leading Othello to believe Desdemona has betrayed him with Cassio. Exploiting his loving wife Emilia, Iago uses a handkerchief that Emilia obtains from Desdemona to fool Othello into believing Desdemona is involved with Cassio. Succumbing to Iago's lies, Othello grows mad with jealousy and asks Iago to help him kill Cassio and Desdemona. Iago continues to weave a series of lies and schemes that ultimately trick Othello into murdering his guiltless wife Desdemona. Believing himself a cuckold, Othello ignores Desdemona's protestations of innocence and strangles her in her bed. Then he discovers through Emilia how he has been duped by Iago. Confronted with Iago's betrayal and the enormity of his own crime against an innocent woman who loved him, Othello chooses to commit suicide rather than try to exculpate himself and live knowing his folly. Iago's vengeance is complete, but his crimes, which include the murder of Roderigo and Emilia, have come to light and he is arrested. Still he vows neither to repent nor ever to speak again of his crimes, even in the face of torture and death.

DRAFTING THE ESSAY

It is important to start writing even if you are unsure about the exact shape or direction of your argument since frequently your ideas develop and become more focused as you proceed. In working through a draft essay on *Othello*, you may initially find yourself interested in, on the one hand, how eloquent you found Othello's address to the court of the Duke of Venice and, on the other hand, his self-characterization as plainspoken, even ill-spoken. Does Othello really believe he is a "rude" speaker? Is he perhaps manipulating his audience? But as you write your first draft and your thoughts evolve, you may find yourself moving from a thesis that Othello has crafty control of his language to something quite different. Keep writing and stay flexible. A first draft does not have to be perfect. It's a stage for making discoveries and clarifying your ideas.

Opening with an Argument

Once the draft is done and you have a clear idea of your thesis and the passages in the work that best support it, you can begin to shape and refine the essay. In doing so, pay special attention to the introductory paragraph, which should introduce the topic and lead directly to a clear, arguable thesis. While there is no surefire formula for a first paragraph, some strategies are better than others. Avoid the following types of opening sentences:

> Ever since the dawn of time, people have been fascinated by the fall of great men.

> Insecurity is a feeling that can prove harmful in even the most accomplished people.

This kind of throat-clearing generalization is common and even helpful at the draft stage, but it gets the essay off to a slow start. If the working thesis is that Othello is undone not only by treachery but also because of the insecurities that lurk beneath his formidable bearing, a direct approach is more effective:

> In Othello's first speech at the court of the Duke, he presents him-self as a simple soldier awkwardly attempting to explain how he won the hand of the beautiful Desdemona. In fact his "rude" words are highly elo-quent, and a reader may judge that the proud general is using false mod-esty to advance his case. Such a judgment ignores a more central issue than Othello's pride and eloquence. His words hint at the insecurities—as a military man short on civilian social graces, an older man with a young wife, a black African in a white European culture—that will cloud his judgment and ultimately prove his undoing.

Note that this opening paragraph introduces the topic and moves directly toward an explicit and arguable claim. By doing so, it lets the reader—and the writer—know where the essay is going. That is, once a clear thesis is in place, both writer and reader can use it as a road map for the rest of the essay.

Supporting Your Thesis

The body of the essay will be devoted to supporting the thesis. The best way to establish a claim is to cite and analyze carefully selected passages from the text that relate directly to it. The following paragraph focuses on lines that support our sample claim directly:

> As indicated by the preceding examples, numerous passages reveal Othello's various insecurities. But in the following passage, his language manifests them all:

> Haply, for I am black,
>
> And have not those soft parts of conversation
>
> That chamberers have, or for I am decline'd,
>
> Into the vale of years—yet that's not much— (3.3 263–66)

Here Othello catalogs his self-perceived flaws: His Africanness ("for I am black"), his rough manners ("I...have not those soft parts of conversation"), and his age ("declin'd / Into the vale of years"). He is now tormented by the very qualities and achievements that once set him proudly apart from others in European culture.

The first part of the paragraph tells the reader what to look for in the cited lines, and the subsequent analysis underscores their relevance to the overall argument clearly and convincingly.

If you offer a claim, support it with an analysis of the relevant passages, and consider different interpretations of those passages, you have completed the main task in much writing about literature. Concluding paragraphs can move toward closure by reviewing the claim and its significance, which you should be careful not to overstate. In the essay on *Othello*, for example, it would not be effective to conclude with a sweeping claim that the Moor's insecurities represent Shakespeare's indictment of European culture in his era. Your readers will find your claims more convincing if you do not exaggerate their importance.

REVISING THE ESSAY

After you've completed your draft, it is time to look at the essay more critically, paying special attention to revision. Revision involves taking a fresh look at your essay's thesis and support, as well as its organization and language. Reading your essay aloud, or asking someone else to read it, will help you catch many problems. Revision is most effective if begun well before the paper is due. Start writing early so that you have time to review your decisions, ask for feedback from others, and revise accordingly. Because you cannot always anticipate audience reaction, a preliminary reading of your writing by a friend, a teaching assistant, a tutor, or an instructor can highlight the areas that need attention or additional revision.

The basic guidelines for good style are not mysterious; in fact, you use them every day in conversation. In conversation and in writing, we all rely heavily on cooperation to make sense of exchanges, and a polished practical style makes cooperation easier. Writers develop such a style by acknowledging that readers expect the same things that listeners expect in conversation: clarity, relevance, and proportion. If you listen to someone who is not clear, who cannot stay on the topic, or who offers too much or too little information, you will quickly lose interest in the conversation. Writers, too, need to be clear, stay on the topic, and give information appropriately. In fact, this attention to audience and appropriateness may be even more important in writing than in conversation because writing does not permit the nonverbal communication and immediate feedback that are part of conversation. As writers, we have to anticipate the absent reader's response; in effect, we have to imagine both halves of a virtual conversation.

Begin by evaluating your essay's thesis. Is it clear? Vagueness or tentativeness here may mean problems later in the essay, so make sure your thesis is crystal clear. Second, is the evidence you present relevant to each major point? While it is tempting and sometimes productive to go off on tangents while drafting a paper, in the final essay if the evidence doesn't fit the claim, tinker with the claim, or go back to the early exploratory writing you did and to your sources to look for better evidence. Are there any points that need to be clarified? Check all your quotations, paraphrases, and summaries for their citations and for accuracy.

Next, can you tighten the organization of your draft? Are your claims and evidence unified? Put yourself in your reader's place, and clarify ambiguities. Each detail or piece of evidence in a paragraph should relate back to the claim it supports in the topic sentence of that paragraph. At the same time, avoid oversupporting some points with too much discussion or detail.

Finally, ask yourself if the general proportions of your essay are suitable. A five-page paper should not use three of those pages to introduce the topic or recount a work's plot. If the essay is too short, the trouble might be an unarguable thesis or insufficient evidence. If it is running too long, eliminate or compress the parts that do not bear directly on the main claim, or limit the claim to something more manageable.

Editing Your Draft

After you have evaluated and revised your draft and determined the format for your paper, you are ready to edit it carefully, paying close attention to each sentence and paragraph. These guidelines will help you focus on some common trouble spots.

SELECTING STRONG VERBS Careful selection of lively, active verbs will make your writing more interesting to your audience. Consider the main verb in the following sentence:

> Three conflicts, all of which play crucial roles in the plot, are evident in
>
> Othello.

The core assertion of this sentence is that "[t]hree conflicts . . . are evident." Notice that nothing actually happens in this sentence. To stir things up, borrow the verb *play* from another part of the sentence:

Three conflicts play crucial roles in the plot of *Othello*.

The revision is better, but the sentence can be made even more concise using *drive*:

Three conflicts drive the plot of *Othello*.

The revised sentence more clearly gets to the point, an effect that is rarely lost on an audience. It also permits a more direct move to the topic—namely, the conflicts. Finally, in an economical seven words rather than a verbose fifteen, it neither belabors nor omits anything of importance in the first sentence.

Writing that relies too heavily on *be* verbs often produces wordiness and unnecessary abstraction:

There was opposition to interracial marriage among most of the citizens

of Venice.

Deleting the *be* verb (*was*) and converting the abstract noun *opposition* into a verb make the sentence more active:

Most Venetians opposed interracial marriage.

This clearer sentence lets the verb do the major work. Of course, a good verb does not always present itself as an abstract noun in an early draft. Sometimes you'll need to consult a thesaurus or a dictionary to find just the right word.

Search your draft for weak verbs and insignificant words and for sentences that begin *There is, There are, It is*. Often, a few words later, a *that, which,* or *who* will appear. Overuse of *There is* and *There are* produces sentences that bury the action. Edit these sentences by deleting the weak verb constructions and replacing them with strong, precise verbs. For example, change "*There is* a destiny *that* controls the fate of Sam*" to "Destiny controls Sam's fate."*

Finally, check your draft for passive constructions (the ball *was thrown*), and replace them when possible with active verbs. Passive sentences are often wordier and dull the action of a sentence. For example, change "The essay was read by the class" to "The class read the essay."

ELIMINATING UNNECESSARY MODIFIERS When choosing or revising a verb, you are also choosing the sentence elements that necessarily accompany it. These other sentence elements are called *complements* because they complete the meaning of the verb. In the following sentences the complements are underlined:

Iago betrays Othello.

The boy idealized his situation.

Iago cannot just betray; he has to betray something. Likewise, *his situation* completes the meaning of the verb *idealized*. Almost everything else added to these sentences will be *modifiers*—additional elements that will modify, rather than complete, the meaning of the sentences. A writer can add any number of modifiers to a sentence:

> Iago betrayed Othello <u>cold-bloodedly</u>, <u>with a malignity beyond measure,</u> <u>a malignity that Coleridge characterized as "motiveless."</u>

From a grammatical standpoint, these modifiers are optional; without them the sentence still expresses a complete thought. Unnecessary modifiers can make your writing heavy and murky:

> Basically, the Greeks invented <u>a rather innovative and distinctive form</u> <u>of government known as</u> democracy.

Eliminating the modifiers and making a few other snips result in the following:

> The Greeks invented democracy.

The clearer sentence does not lose much in the way of content. Of course, being able to eliminate modifiers does not mean that you should; sometimes modifiers are the most significant parts of a sentence. You can always use modifiers for nuance or emphasis, but you must ruthlessly trim unnecessary modifiers from wordy, unclear sentences.

GRAMMATICAL CONNECTIONS Make sure your sentences and paragraphs are firmly linked by using explicit transitional phrases such as *however*, *although*, *likewise*, *for example*, *therefore*, and so on. Note in this sample opening paragraph how the underlined transitional phrases indicate the relationships between the sentences:

> In his speech before the Duke's court, Othello speaks disarmingly to the assembled nobles. He flatteringly describes his audience as being potent, grave, and reverend. He modestly describes himself as being a blunt-spoken soldier hardly qualified to talk of anything but the wars that he has seen and fought. <u>However</u>, Othello's modesty is belied by the deeds of which he speaks. <u>In particular</u> he boldly admits to having won both the love of Desdemona and many battles, dating from when he

was but a child. The court is looking for a conqueror, and in his guise of modesty Othello presents himself as that man.

The appearance of *however* halfway through the paragraph signals the contrast between Othello's professed modesty and his powerful deeds. The transitional phrase *in particular* in the next sentence signals that we are narrowing the preceding point and focusing our discussion. Experienced readers look for such transitional phrases that suggest an interpretive path through an argument.

Note that the third sentence of the paragraph repeats a key word from the second one (*describes*); so does the first and fourth sentence (*speaks*). The repetition helps keep the spotlight on Othello's rhetoric, an important notion in the paragraph. Note also the use of *modestly* and *modesty*. By repeating key terms, sometimes with slight variation, you can powerfully illuminate the main idea of a paragraph.

After checking for explicit connections within paragraphs, make sure that the progression of ideas from one paragraph to another is clear. Here again, transitional phrases are useful. A simple transition such as *nevertheless, furthermore,* or *on the other hand* is often adequate. Sometimes the entire opening sentence of a paragraph may provide the transition, including key words, pronouns, or other references to the previous paragraph.

Proofreading Your Draft

Print out, type, or (if your instructor allows it) neatly write in ink the final copy of your essay for submission to your instructor, taking care to follow any special instructions about format that you have been given. Don't rush; be meticulous. When you have finished, proofread the final copy carefully, looking for spelling or punctuation errors, omitted words, disagreement between subjects and verbs or between pronouns and antecedents, and typographical errors that will detract from the essay you have worked hard to write.

For additional advice on checking your use of sources and documenting in your final essay, see "Some Matters of Form and Documentation" (p. 69). Finally, use "A Checklist for Writing about Literature" (p. 73) to help with a quick review of your final draft.

SOME COMMON WRITING ASSIGNMENTS

A writing assignment for a literature course may require any of a variety of kinds of writing. You might be called on to compare and contrast literary works, to analyze the language of a work, to discuss the interaction of a work's parts, to discuss a work's theme, or to articulate your own responses to the work. Sometimes an instructor may ask simply that you write an essay on one of the pieces you have read. This type of assignment requires you to create your own boundaries—to find a specific focus that both suits the piece you choose and is manageable within a paper of the assigned length. Sometimes you may be asked to simply summarize a complex literary work. The summary of *Othello* (pp. 40–41) would be adequate if the assignment was this straightforward. Other times, you may be asked to respond creatively, to come up with original work that reimagines a poem or story from your own point of view and in your own words. However, in many literature courses, assigned essays tend to fall into one of three modes—explication, analysis, and comparison and contrast—or some combination of these. Familiarity with these three kinds of writing about literature will help you not only with full-length essay assignments but also with exams and other in-class writing.

Explication

In an explication essay, you examine a work in much detail. Line by line, *stanza by stanza*, scene by scene, you explain each part as fully as you can and show how the author's techniques produce your response. An *explication* is essentially a demonstration of your thorough understanding of a work.

Here is a sample essay that explicates a relatively difficult poem, Dylan Thomas's "Do Not Go Gentle into That Good Night" (p. 1267).

> Dylan Thomas's villanelle "Do Not Go Gentle into That Good Night" is addressed to his aged father. The poem is remarkable in a number of ways, most notably in that contrary to most common poetic treatments of the inevitability of death, which argue for serenity or celebrate the peace that death provides, this poem urges resistance and rage in the face of death.
>
> It justifies that unusual attitude by describing the rage and resistance to death of four kinds of men, who each can summon up the image of a complete and satisfying life that is denied to him by death.
>
> The first tercet of the intricately rhymed villanelle opens with an arresting line. The adjective *gentle* appears where we would expect the adverb *gently*. The strange diction suggests that *gentle* may describe both the going (i.e., gently dying) and the person (i.e., gentleman) who confronts death. Further, the speaker characterizes "night," here clearly a figure for death, as "good." Yet in the next line, the speaker urges that the aged should violently resist death, characterized as the "close of day" and "the dying of the light." In effect, the first three lines argue that however good death may be, the aged should refuse to die gently, should passionately rave and rage against death.

In the second tercet, the speaker turns to a description of the way the first of four types of men confronts death (which is figuratively defined throughout the poem as "that good night" and "the dying of the light"). These are the "wise men," the scholars, the philosophers, those who understand the inevitability of death, men who "know dark is right." But they do not acquiesce in death "because their words had forked no lightning," because their published wisdom failed to bring them to that sense of completeness and fulfillment that can accept death. Therefore, wise as they are, they reject the theoretical "rightness" of death and refuse to "go gentle."

The second sort of men—"good men," the moralists, the social reformers, those who attempt to better the world through action as the wise men attempt to better it through "words"—also rage against death. Their deeds are, after all, "frail." With sea imagery, the speaker suggests that these men might have accomplished fine and fertile things—their deeds "might have danced in a green bay." But with the "last wave" gone, they see only the frailty, the impermanence of their acts, and so they, too, rage against the death that deprives them of the opportunity to leave a meaningful legacy.

The "wild men," the poets who "sang" the loveliness and vitality of nature, also learn as they approach death that the sensuous joys of human existence wane. As the life-giving sun moves toward dusk, as death approaches, their singing turns to grieving, and they refuse to surrender gently, to leave willingly the warmth, pleasure, and beauty that life can give.

Finally, with a pun suggestive of death, the "grave men," those who go through life with such high seriousness as never to experience gaiety and pleasure, see all the joyous possibilities that they were blind to in life. And they, too, rage against the dying of a light that they had never properly seen before.

The speaker then calls on his aged father to join these men raging against death. Only in this final stanza do we discover that the entire poem is addressed to the speaker's father and that, despite the generalized statements about old age and the focus on types of men, the poem is a personal lyric. The edge of death becomes a "sad height," the summit of wisdom and experience old age attains includes the sad knowledge of life's failure to satisfy the vision we all pursue. The depth and complexity of the speaker's sadness is startlingly given in the second line, when he calls on his father to both curse and bless him. These opposites richly suggest several related possibilities: "Curse me for not living up to your expectations. Curse me for remaining alive as you die. Bless me with forgiveness for my failings. Bless me for teaching you to rage against death." And the curses and blessings are contained in the "fierce tears"—fierce because you will burn and rave and rage against death.

As the poem closes by bringing together the two powerful refrains, the speaker himself seems to rage because his father's death will cut off a relationship that is incomplete.

This explication deals with the entire poem by coming to grips with each element in it.

You can learn a great deal about the technique of drama by selecting a short, self-contained scene and writing a careful description of it. The length of plays will probably require that you focus on a single segment—a scene, for example—rather than the entire play. This method of explication will force you to confront every speech and stage direction and to come to some conclusion regarding its function. Why is the set furnished as it is? Why does a character speak the words he or she does or remain silent? What do we learn of characters from the interchanges among them? Assume that everything that occurs in the play, whether on the printed page or on the stage, is put there for a purpose. Seek to discover the purpose, and you will, at the same time, discover the distinctive nature of drama.

Fiction, too, can be treated effectively in a formal explication. As with drama, it will be necessary to limit the text: you will not be able to explicate a ten-page story in a 1,000-word essay. Choose a key passage—a half page that reflects the form and content of the overall story, if possible. Often the first half page of a story, where the author, like the playwright, must supply information to the reader, will make a fine text for an explication. Although the explication will deal principally with only an excerpt, feel free to range across the story and show how the introductory material foreshadows what is to come. Or perhaps you can explicate the climax of the story—the half page that most pointedly establishes the story's theme—and subject it to a close line-by-line reading that illuminates the whole story.

Analysis

Breaking down a literary work into its elements is only the first step in literary analysis. When you are assigned an analysis essay, you are expected to focus on one of the elements that contributes to the complex compound of a work. This process requires you to extricate the element you plan to explore from the other elements that you can identify, to study this element—not only in isolation but also in relation to the other elements and the work as a whole—and, using the insights you have gained from your special perspective, to make an informed statement about it.

This process may sound complicated, but if you approach it methodically, each stage follows naturally from the stage that precedes it. If, for example, you are to write an analysis essay on characterization in *Othello*, you would begin by thinking about each character in the play. You would then select the character whose development you would like to explore and reread carefully those speeches that help to establish his or her substance. Exploring a character's development in this way involves a good deal of explication: in order to identify the "building blocks" that Shakespeare uses to create a three-dimensional role, you must comb very carefully through that character's speeches and actions. You must also be sensitive to the ways in which other characters respond to these speeches and actions. When you have completed this investigation, you will probably have a good understanding of why you intuitively responded to the character as you did when you first read the play. You will also probably be prepared to make a statement about the character's development: "From a realistic perspective, it is hard to believe that a man of Othello's position could be so gullible; however, Shakespeare develops the role with such craft that we accept the Moor as flesh and blood." At this point, you have moved from the broad *subject* of "characterization in *Othello*" to a thesis, a statement that you must prove. As you formulate your thesis, think of it as a position that you intend to *argue* for with a reader you need to persuade. This approach is useful in any essay that requires a thesis, where you move beyond simple explication and commit yourself to a stand. Note that our sample thesis is *argumentative* on two counts; "characterization in *Othello*" is not remotely argumentative. Further, you have more than enough material to write a well-documented essay of 1,000 words supporting your proposition; you cannot write a well-documented 1,000-word essay on the general subject of characterization in *Othello* without being superficial.

You may be one among the many writers who have trouble finding a starting point. For example, you have been assigned an analysis essay on a very broad subject, such as imagery in love poetry. A few poems come to mind, but you don't know where to begin. You read these poems and underline all the images that you can find. You look at these images over and over, finding no relation among them. You read some more poems, again underlining the images, but you still do not have even the germ of a thesis.

The technique of freewriting might help to overcome your block. You have read and reread the poems you intend to write about. Now, put the assignment temporarily out of your mind, and start writing about one or two of the poems without organizing your ideas, without trying to reach a point. Write down what you like about a poem, what you dislike about it, what sort of person the speaker is, which images seemed striking to you—anything at all about the work. If you do this for perhaps ten minutes, you will probably discover that you are voicing opinions. Pick one that interests you or seems the most promising to explore.

The basic form of the analysis assignment has a few variations. Your instructor might narrow the subject in a specific assignment: analyze the development of Othello's character in act I. This sort of assignment limits the amount of text you will have to study, but the process from this point on is no different from the process you would employ to address a broader subject. Sometimes instructors will supply you with a thesis, and you will have to work backward from the thesis to find supporting material. Again, careful analysis of the text is required. The problem you will have to address when writing an analytical essay remains the same regardless of the literary genre you are asked to discuss. You must find an arguable thesis that deals with the sources of your response to the work.

Suppose your instructor has made the following assignment: write an analysis of Harlan Ellison's story "'Repent, Harlequin!' Said the Ticktockman" (p. 374), in which you discuss the theme of the story in terms of the characters and the setting. Now consider the following opening (taken from a student paper):

> "'Repent, Harlequin!' Said the Ticktockman" is a story depicting a society in which time governs one's life. The setting is the United States, the time approximately 2400 CE somewhere in the heart of the country. Business deals, work shifts, and school lessons are started and finished with exacting precision. Tardiness is intolerable as this would hinder the system. In a society of order, precision, and punctuality, there is no room for likes, dislikes, scruples, or morals. Thus, personalities in people no longer exist. As these "personless" people know no good or bad, they very happily follow in the course of activities that their society has dictated.

At the outset, can you locate a thesis statement? The only sentences that would seem to qualify are the last three in the paragraph. But notice that, although those sentences are not unreasonable responses to the story, they do not establish a thesis that is *responsive to the assignment*. Because the assignment calls for a discussion of theme in terms of character and setting, a thesis statement should argue how character and setting embody the theme. Here is another opening paragraph on the same assignment (also taken from a student paper):

> Harlan Ellison's "'Repent, Harlequin!' Said the Ticktockman" opens with a quotation from Thoreau's essay "Civil Disobedience," which establishes the story's theme. Thoreau's observations about three varieties of men—those who serve the state as machines, those who serve it with their heads, and those who serve it with their consciences—are dramatized in Ellison's story, which takes place about 400 years in the future in a setting characterized by machinelike order. The interaction among the three characters, each of whom represents one of Thoreau's types, results in a telling restatement of his observation that "heroes, patriots, martyrs, reformers in the great sense, and men . . . necessarily resist [the state] and . . . are commonly treated as enemies by it."

Compare these two opening paragraphs sentence by sentence for their responsiveness to the assignment. The first sentence of the first opening does not refer to the theme of the story (or to its setting or characterization). In the second sentence, the discussion of the setting ignores the most important aspect—that the story is set in a machine- and time-dominated future. The last three sentences deal obliquely with character, but they are imprecise and do not establish a thesis. The second opening, on the other hand, immediately states the theme of the story. It goes on to emphasize the relevant aspects of the futuristic setting and then refers to the three characters who animate the story in terms of their reactions to the setting. The last sentence addresses the assignment directly and also serves as a thesis statement for the paper. It states the proposition that will be developed and supported in the rest of the paper. The reader of the second opening will expect the next paragraph of the paper to discuss the setting of the story and subsequent paragraphs to discuss the response to the setting of the three principal characters.

The middles of essays are largely determined by their opening paragraphs. However long the middle of any essay may be, each of its paragraphs ought to be responsive to some explicit statement made at the beginning of the essay.

Note that it is practically impossible to predict what the paragraph following the first opening will address. Here is the first half of that next paragraph as the first student wrote it:

> The Harlequin is a man in the society with no sense of time. His having a personality enables him to have a sense of moral values and a mind of his own. The Harlequin thinks that it is obscene and wrong to let time totally govern the lives of people. So he sets out to disrupt the time schedule with ridiculous antics such as showering people with jelly beans to try to break up the military fashion in which they are used to doing things.

The paragraph then goes on to discuss the Ticktockman, the capture and brainwashing of the Harlequin, and the resulting lateness of the Ticktockman.

Note that nothing in the opening of this student's paper prepared readers for the introduction of the Harlequin. In fact, the opening concluded rather inaccurately that the people within the story "happily follow in the course of activities that their society has dictated." Hence, the description of the Harlequin in the second paragraph is wholly unexpected. Further, because the student has not dealt with the theme of the story (as the assignment asked), the comments about the Harlequin's antics remain disconnected from any clear purpose. They are essentially devoted to what teachers constantly warn against: a mere plot summary. The student has obviously begun to write before analyzing the story sufficiently to understand its theme. With further thought, the student would have perceived that the central thematic issue is resistance to an oppressive state—the issue stated in the epigraph from Thoreau. On the other hand, because the second opening makes that thematic point clearly, we can expect it to be followed by a discussion of the environment (that is, the setting) in which the action occurs. Here is such a paragraph taken from the second student's paper:

> Ellison creates a society that reflects one possible future development of the modern American passion for productivity and efficiency. The setting is in perfect keeping with the time-conscious people who inhabit the city. It is pictured as a neat, colorless, and mechanized city. No mention is made of nature: grass, flowers, trees, and birds do not appear. The buildings are in a "Mondrian arrangement," stark and geometrical. The cold steel sidewalks, slowstrips, and expresstrips move with precision.

Like a chorus line, people move in unison to board the movers without a wasted motion. Doors close silently and lock themselves automatically. An ideal efficiency so dominates the social system that any "wasted time" is deducted from the life of an inefficient citizen.

Once the setting has been established, the writer turns to the characters, linking those characters to thematic considerations, beginning with a short transitional paragraph that shapes the remainder of the middle of the essay:

Into this smoothly functioning but coldly mechanized society, Ellison introduces three characters: Pretty Alice, one of Thoreau's machinelike creatures; the Ticktockman, one of those who "serve the state chiefly with their heads, and, as they rarely make any moral distinctions, they are as likely to serve the Devil, without intending it, as God"; and Everett C. Marm, the Harlequin, whose conscience forces him to resist the oppressive state.

Following a logical organization, the essay then includes a paragraph devoted to each of the three characters:

Pretty Alice is, probably, very pretty. (Everett didn't fall in love with her brains.) In the brief section in which we meet her, we find her hopelessly ordinary in her attitudes. She is upset that Marm finds it necessary to go about "annoying people." She finds him ridiculous and wishes only that he would stay home, as other people do. Clearly, she has no understanding of what Everett is struggling against. Though her anger finally leads her to betray him, Everett himself can't believe that she has done so. His own loyal and understanding nature colors his view of her so thoroughly that he cannot imagine the treachery that must have been so simple and satisfying for Pretty Alice, whose only desire is to be like everybody else.

The Ticktockman is more complex. He sees himself as a servant of the state, and he performs his duties with resolution and competence.

He skillfully supports a System he has never questioned. The System
exists; it must be good. His conscience is simply not involved in the
performance of his duty. He is one of those who follow orders and expect
others to follow orders. As a result, the behavior of the Harlequin is more
than just an irritant or a rebellion against authority. It is unnerving. The
Ticktockman wishes to understand that behavior, and with Everett's time-
card in his hand, he muses that he has the name of *"what* he is, not *who*
he is. . . . Before I can exercise proper revocation, I have to know *who*
this *what* is."* And when he confronts Everett, he does not just liquidate
him. He insists that Everett repent. He tries to convince Everett that the
System is sound, and when he cannot win the argument, he dutifully
reconditions Everett, since he is, after all, more interested in justifying
the System than in destroying its enemies. It is easy to see this man as a
competent servant of the devil who thinks he is serving God.

But only Everett C. Marm truly serves the state because his conscience requires him to resist. He is certainly not physically heroic. His very
name suggests weak conformity. Though he loves his Pretty Alice, he cannot resign from the rebellious campaign on which his conscience insists.
So without violence, and mainly with the weapon of laughter, he attacks
the mechanical precision of the System and succeeds in breaking it down
simply by making people late. He is himself, as Pretty Alice points out,
always late, and the delays that his antics produce seriously threaten the
well-being of the smooth but mindless System he hates. He is captured and
refuses, even then, to submit, and so his personality is destroyed by the
authorities that fear him. The Ticktockman is too strong for him.

An appropriate ending emerges naturally from this student's treatment of
the assignment. Having established that the story presents characters who deal
in different ways with the oppressive quality of life in a time- and machine-
obsessed society, the student concludes with a comment on the author's criticisms of such a society:

Harlequin is defeated, but Ellison, finally, leaves us with an optimistic note. The idea of rebellion against the System will linger in the minds of others. There will be more Harlequins and more disruption of this System. Many rebels will be defeated, but any System that suppresses individualism will give birth to resistance. And Harlequin's defeat is by no means total. The story ends with the Ticktockman himself arriving for work three minutes late.

Comparison and Contrast

An essay in comparison and contrast shows how two works are similar to and different from each other. It almost always starts with a recognition of similarities, often of subject matter. Sometimes you may be asked to connect what you have read with something in your own life, creating an original comparison, for example, between Peter Meinke's "Advice to My Son" (p. 200) and advice you have been given by an adult in your own life. Most comparison-and-contrast assignments involve two works of the same genre. While it is possible to compare *any* two works, the best comparison-and-contrast essays emerge from the analysis of two works similar enough to illuminate each other. Two works about love, or death, or conformity, or innocence, or identity give you something to begin with. The groupings in this book will suggest some ways you might read certain works together. For example, both Emily Dickinson's "Apparently with no surprise" (p. 1248) and Robert Frost's "Design" (p. 1265) are about death, and they both use remarkably similar events as the occasion for their poems. Starting with these similarities, you would soon find yourself noting the contrasts (in tone, for example, and theme) between nineteenth-century and twentieth-century views of the nature of God.

Before you begin writing a comparison-and-contrast essay, it is especially important to have clearly in mind the points of comparison and contrast you wish to discuss and the order in which you can most effectively discuss them. You will need to give careful thought to the best way to organize your paper, jotting down the plan your comparison will follow. As a general rule, it is best to avoid dividing the essay into separate discussions of each work. That method tends to produce two separate, loosely joined analysis essays. The successful comparison-and-contrast essay treats some point of similarity or contrast between the two works, then moves on to succeeding points, and ends with an evaluation of the comparative merits of the works.

Like any essay that goes beyond simple explication, a comparison-and-contrast essay requires a strong thesis statement. However, a comparison-and-contrast thesis is generally not difficult to formulate: you must identify the works under consideration and state clearly your reasons for making the comparison.

Here is a student paper that compares and contrasts Dylan Thomas's "Do Not Go Gentle into That Good Night" with the poetic response it triggered from a poet with different views:

Dylan Thomas's "Do Not Go Gentle into That Good Night" and Catherine Davis's "After a Time" demand comparison: Davis's poem was written in deliberate response to Thomas's. Davis assumes the reader's familiarity with "Do Not Go Gentle," which she uses to articulate her contrasting ideas. "After a Time," although it is a literary work in its own right, might even be thought of as serious parody—perhaps the greatest compliment one writer can pay another.

"Do Not Go Gentle into That Good Night" was written by a young man of thirty-eight who addresses it to his old and ailing father. Perhaps because Thomas had very little of his own self-destructive life left as he was composing this piece, he seems to have more insight into the subject of death than most people his age. He advocates raging and fighting against it, not giving in and accepting it.

"After a Time" was written by Davis at about the same age and is addressed to no one in particular. Davis has a different philosophy about death. She "answers" Thomas's poem and presents her differing views using the same poetic form—a villanelle. Evidently, she felt it necessary to present a contrasting point of view eight years after Thomas's death.

While "Do Not Go Gentle" protests and rages against death, Davis's poem suggests a quiet resignation and acquiescence. She seems to feel that raging against death is useless and profitless. She argues that we will eventually become tame, anyway, after the raging is done.

Thomas talks about different types of men and why they rage against death. "Wise men" desire immortality. They rage against death occurring before they've made their mark on history. "Good men" lament the frailty of their deeds. Given more time, they might have accomplished great things. "Wild men" regret their constant hedonistic pursuits. With more time they could prove their worth. "Grave men" are quite the opposite and regret they never took time for the pleasures in life. Now it is too late. They rage against death because they are not ready for it.

His father's death is painful to Thomas because he sees himself lying in that bed; his father's dying reminds him of his own inevitable death. The passion of the last stanza, in which the poet asks his father to bless and curse him, suggests that he has doubts about his relationship with his father. He may feel that he has not been a good enough son. He put off doing things with and for his father because he always felt there would be time later. Now time has run out and he feels cheated.

Catherine Davis advocates a calm submission, a peaceful acquiescence. She feels raging is useless and says that those of us who rage will finally "go tame / When what we have we can no longer use." When she says "One more thing lost is one thing less to lose," the reader can come to terms with the loss of different aspects of the mind and body, such as strength, eyesight, hearing, and intellect. Once one of these is lost, it's one thing less to worry about losing. After a time, everything will be lost, and we'll accept that, too, because we'll be ready for it.

Thomas's imagery is vivid and powerful. His various men not only rage and rave, they *burn*. Their words "forked no lightning," their deeds might have "danced in a green bay," they "sang the sun in flight," and they see that "blind eyes could blaze like meteors." Davis's images are quiet and generally abstract, without much sensory suggestiveness, as in "things lost," a "reassuring ruse," and "all losses are the same." Her most powerful image—"And we go stripped at last the way we came"—makes its point with none of the excitement of Thomas's rage. And yet, I prefer the quiet intelligence of Davis to the high energy of Thomas.

"And we go stripped at last the way we came" can give strange comfort and solace to those of us who always envied those in high places. People are not all created equal at birth, not by a long shot. But we will all be equal when we die. All wealth, power, and trappings will be left behind, and we will all ultimately be equal. So why rage? It won't do us any good.

THE RESEARCH PAPER

Research papers depend on secondary sources (the primary source is, of course, the work, the historical event, or the literary theory you are studying). Research assignments send you to the library, to the Web, or to any source of information that bears on your project. Whether you are researching to discover the varied responses to a work, to gain some insight into the author's life and times, or to identify relevant critical principles, you will synthesize what you have read *about* the work into a well-organized paper and provide *proper documentation.* But a research paper is not a mindless recitation of what your secondary sources have said. Nor does it require you to suspend your own critical judgment. By the time you settle into writing your paper, you will have learned some things you didn't know before. You have earned—and ought to exercise—the right to make your own claims based on other arguments you have read and the information you have synthesized. An assigned research topic will probably ask you to come to some conclusions. If you choose your own topic, you must discover in your research support for a clear, focused thesis before you begin to write.

Here is a sample student research paper that illustrates the technique. The marginal notes call attention to some of the details that make this a successful effort. In general, notice that the author has done research, but the paper is not weighed down with it. The opening paragraph provides a historical context for the subject of the paper, Kate Chopin's short story "The Storm" (p. 861). The writer has a point of view about the story, or thesis, stated in the second paragraph. While that thesis is developed throughout, the writer makes interesting observations on such matters as the relationship of other Chopin works to the story, the names of characters, local color, and a notable change in American moral attitudes. Note how the writer concludes with two paragraphs that resolve the issues raised in the opening two paragraphs.

The sample paper employs the Modern Language Association's (MLA) standard documentation and footnote form. The section that follows the research paper provides further samples that will help you manage formal matters and documentation. It concludes with a checklist that you might want to consult both before you begin writing your paper and before you submit your final draft.

AN ANNOTATED STUDENT RESEARCH PAPER

Lagos 1

Krissa Lagos

Professor Richard Abcarian

English 255

Sex and Sensibility

in Kate Chopin's "The Storm"

Kate Chopin's openly erotic depictions of marital

infidelity in her literary works separate her from all other

American female writers of her time. The adulterous affair of a

strong independent woman depicted in her novel *The Awakening*

(1899) created a public scandal. And, though she "never flouted

convention as strongly as did her fictitious heroine, she did

exhibit an individuality and strength remarkable for upper-

middle-class women of the time" (Moon). Her honest and direct

portrayal of the sexuality of her female characters was rejected

until well into the 1900s, when the minds of readers caught

up to her advanced thinking (Skaggs 5). Works such as "The

Storm"—once shunned (especially by the male community)

because of their focus on sexual exploration—are now celebrated

as serious literature. In fact, when Chopin wrote "The Storm"

in 1898, she knew that no magazine would ever publish such

an uninhibited and uncritical account of an adulterous encoun-

ter, and so never attempted to have it published (Toth 206).

Annotations (right margin):

Writer's name and page number.

Use MLA standard style or follow instructor's criteria.

Center title.

First paragraph establishes context.

Documents an Internet source with no page number (see Works Cited).

Documents a book in Works Cited and gives page number.

States the elements of the paper's thesis.

In "The Storm," Chopin utilizes the irony characteristic of her writing to give the story a light, easy feel. She also uses diction and imagery to draw the reader into the emotions of her characters. She ignores the usual implications of unfaithfulness to a spouse, and instead focuses on the pleasure inspired by the instant gratification of physical desire.

Provides important context for the story's events.

"The Storm" is in fact a sequel to another short story, "At the 'Cadian Ball." In the first tale, which takes place in Louisiana, a favorite setting for Chopin,[1] a farmer named Bobinôt is captivated with spirited, Spanish-blooded Calixta. Calixta, however, has her eyes on a handsome local planter, Alcée Laballière, who is charmed by her attractive features and openly sexual attitude. At the end of the night, however, Clarisse, a woman who is Alcée's social equal (and also happens to be his cousin), suddenly appears and agrees to marry him. Calixta, deserted by Alcée, is "deemed lucky to get anyone, even stodgy Bobinôt" (Ewell 77).

Discusses the significance of setting.

By setting "The Storm" in Louisiana, Chopin is able to take advantage of the unstable, muggy weather of the region to help build up to the story's climax. The events of the tale occur because of the weather: the storm strands Bobinôt and his son Bibi at a store while wife and mother Calixta is at home, and Alcée is driven into Bobinôt and Calixta's house by the approaching rain. More subtle events, nearly all of which carry sensual undercurrents, are also inspired by the weather conditions.

Uses concrete examples to bolster assertions.

Lagos 3

For instance, when Calixta is first mentioned, she is sewing, and Chopin immediately introduces an indirect sexual undertone to her movements: ". . . she felt very warm and often stopped to mop her face on which the perspiration gathered in beads. She unfastened her white sacque at the throat" (Chopin, "The Storm" 861). Except for what follows, there would be no reason at all to interpret this minor event. However, when Alcée arrives, the loosened collar eventually leads to more than one would imagine possible. First, Calixta is driven into his arms by the lightning crashing all around the house. Alcée attempts to ease her fears while at the same time fighting the desire for her that has been reawakened by contact with her body. Her unbuttoned collar is part of what defeats his battle against his desires:

> He pushed her hair back from her face that was warm and steaming. Her lips were as red and moist as pomegranate seed. Her white neck and a glimpse of her full firm bosom disturbed him powerfully. As she glanced up at him the fear in her liquid blue eyes had given place to a drowsy gleam that unconsciously betrayed a sensuous desire. (Chopin, "The Storm" 863)

Obviously the sole reason for Calixta and Alcée succumbing to their passions is not that she unbuttoned her shirt collar. However, the accumulation of this and other details—their shared climax with the storm, the correspondence between them lying contented afterward while the storm departs softly—make

Ellipses indicate omission in a direct quote.

Identifies the specific work from the Works Cited list when there is more than one work by the same author.

Shows how Chopin uses details to advance the plot.

this story a powerful work of art. Chopin crafts her sentences to enhance her narrative's power.

The French Louisiana setting of "The Storm" is typical of many of her writings (Ewell 52). The detailed local color is reflected by the French names of the characters. Calixta, Bobinôt, and Bibi speak the 'Cadian dialect of Louisiana, which in Calixta's case occasionally includes a small smattering of French (Ewell 77). Alcée, in contrast, speaks impeccable English, reflective of his better education. Chopin inserts a significant detail at the beginning of the story when Bobinôt purchases "a can of shrimps, of which Calixta was very fond" (Chopin, "The Storm" 861). The small gesture reveals Bobinôt's affectionate appreciation of his wife.

In "The Storm," Chopin conveys the theme of autonomy, something familiar to her female characters, especially in "The Story of an Hour."[2] Both Calixta and Clarisse are happiest in "The Storm" when they are separated from their husbands and free to do as they wish.

> As for Clarisse, she was charmed upon receiving her husband's letter. She and the babies were doing well. The society was agreeable; many of her old friends seemed to restore the pleasant liberty of her maiden days. Devoted as she was to her husband, their intimate conjugal life was something which she was more than willing to forego for a while. (Chopin, "The Storm" 865)

Discusses Chopin's view of the rights of women.

Therefore Clarisse, though far from the actual storm, benefits from its effects. She feels unfettered, pleased at being given space for the first time since she has been married to Alcée. For Calixta, the short time she spends with Alcée during the storm is enough to make her lift "her pretty chin in the air" and laugh with delight (Chopin, "The Storm" 864).

    In "At the 'Cadian Ball," the two couples are paired together at the end of the night due to Alcée's notion of honor and propriety (Ewell 77). As Chopin explains in "The Storm," he never intended to marry Calixta, but he did want more from her than what he took in the story's prequel at the ball: "If she was not an immaculate dove in those days, she was still inviolate; a passionate creature whose very defenselessness had made her defense, against which his honor forbade him to prevail" (Chopin, "The Storm" 863). When the ball ended, only Calixta was left unsatisfied, but by the time "The Storm" takes place, only Bobinôt is still utterly content.

    The fact that Calixta is now married somehow frees Alcée from his previous restraints, and he is able to satisfy his craving for her at last. As a result, Alcée is also more content with his wife away, which leads him to write the letter to her urging her to prolong her stay in Biloxi. Bobinôt is the most easily pleased of all. He reaches home cringing at what his wife will say to Bibi and him when she notices how dirty they are. Luckily for the father and son, she is still glowing from her brief interlude with Alcée, and "they laughed much and so loud that anyone might have heard them as far away as Laballière's" (Chopin, "The Storm" 864).

Earlier story is used to establish Alcée's character.

Chopin's irony shines through "The Storm" in many parts of the story. One of these moments occurs when she addresses the issue of natural right while Calixta and Alcée are making love: "Her firm, elastic flesh that was knowing for the first time its birthright, was like a creamy lily that the sun invites to contribute its breath and perfume to the undying life of the world" (Chopin, "The Storm" 863). Chopin goes further than condoning the affair between Calixta and Alcée by describing it as something completely natural, an event that was meant to occur.

What would have been most shocking to audiences in the nineteenth century was the fact that when the storm ended, there were no repercussions. Alcée "turned and smiled" at Calixta "with a beaming face" and rode away, Calixta showed "nothing but satisfaction" when her husband and son returned home, Bobinôt and Bibi "began to relax and enjoy themselves" when they saw that Calixta was in good spirits, and Clarisse stayed in Biloxi, enjoying herself. For such severe sins to be committed and go unpunished was unheard of in Chopin's time, and "even today some readers find that conclusion unforgivable" (Skaggs 62).

In truth, this very conclusion elevates "The Storm" to the high level it resides on. Through adultery, deception, and self-indulgence, the characters achieve happiness, a surprise ending that Chopin adopted from Guy de Maupassant.[3] This ironic twist makes the story a unique departure from the norm, even today, and "The Storm" ends on a comic note, the reader left as contented as the story's characters.

Asserts the proven thesis stated in the second paragraph.

Notes

[1]Chopin set many of her stories in the Cane River country of Louisiana; her husband, Oscar, was raised in Louisiana, and they lived there together for twelve years (Toth 92).

[2]In Chopin's "The Story of an Hour," the main character discovers that she prizes individual freedom over all else—even the life and love of her husband.

[3]Guy de Maupassant (1850–1893) was a French writer whose short stories often featured surprise endings.

Works Cited

Abcarian, Richard, Marvin Klotz, and Samuel Cohen, eds.
    Literature: The Human Experience. 12th ed. Boston:
    Bedford. 2016. Print.

Chopin, Kate. "At the 'Cadian Ball." *The Complete Works of Kate
    Chopin*. Ed. Per Seyersted. Baton Rouge: Louisiana State
    UP, 1969. 219–27. Print.

---. "The Storm." Abcarian, Klotz, and Cohen 861–65. Print.

Ewell, Barbara C. *Kate Chopin*. New York: Ungar, 1986. Print.

Moon, Jennifer. "ClassicNote on Kate Chopin." *GradeSaver*.
    ClassicNotes by GradeSaver. GradeSaver LLC, n.d. Web.
    30 Mar. 2000.

Skaggs, Peggy. *Kate Chopin*. New York: Twayne, 1985. Print.

Toth, Emily. *Unveiling Kate Chopin*. Jackson: UP of Mississippi,
    1999. Print.

SOME MATTERS OF FORM AND DOCUMENTATION

After you have worked hard to draft, revise, and edit an essay, check to be sure you have documented your sources accurately and fairly. A consistent, well-documented essay allows readers to focus on your argument rather than on your document.

Titles

When included in the body of your essay, the first word and all main words of titles are capitalized. Ordinarily (unless they are the first or last word), articles (*a*, *an*, and *the*), prepositions (*in*, *on*, *of*, *with*, *about*, and so on), conjunctions (*and*, *but*, *or*, and so on), and the *to* in an infinitive ("A Good Man Is Hard to Find") are not capitalized.

The titles of short stories, poems, articles, essays, songs, episodes of television programs, and parts of larger collections are enclosed in quotation marks.

The titles of plays, books, movies, periodicals, operas, television series, recordings, paintings, and newspapers are italicized. If your word-processing program does not produce italic type that is easily distinguishable from non-italic type, use underlining.

The title you give your essay is neither placed in quotation marks nor italicized. However, the title of a literary work used as a part of your title would be either placed in quotation marks or italicized, depending on the type of work it is.

Quotations

Quotation marks indicate that you are transcribing someone else's words; those words must, therefore, appear *exactly* as they do in your source.

As a general rule, quotations of not more than four lines of prose or two lines of poetry are placed between quotation marks and incorporated into your own text:

> Near the end of "Young Goodman Brown," the narrator asks, "Had Good-
>
> man Brown fallen asleep in the forest and only dreamed a wild dream
>
> of a witch-meeting?" (000).

If you are quoting two or three lines of verse in your text, indicate the division between lines with a slash. Leave a space before and after the slash:

> Prufrock hears the dilettantish talk in a room where "the women come
>
> and go / Talking of Michelangelo."

Longer quotations are indented ten spaces from the left margin and are double-spaced. They are not enclosed in quotation marks, since the indention signals a quotation.

BRACKETS AND ELLIPSES   If you insert anything into a quotation—even a word—the inserted material must be placed within brackets. If you wish to omit some material from a passage in quotation marks, the omission must be indicated with ellipsis points—three equally spaced periods. When an ellipsis occurs between complete sentences or at the end of a sentence, a fourth period, indicating the end of the sentence, should be inserted.

Here is an example of a full quotation from an original source:

> As one critic puts it, "Richard Wright, like Dostoevsky before him, sends
>
> his hero underground to discover the truth about the upper world, a
>
> world that has forced him to confess to a crime he has not committed."

Here is the quotation with insertion and omissions:

> As one critic puts it, "Richard Wright . . . sends his hero [Fred Daniels]
>
> underground to discover the truth about the upper world. . . ."

Use a full line of spaced periods to indicate the omission of a line or more of poetry:

> For I have known them all already, known them all—
>
> Have known the evenings, mornings, afternoons,
>
> I have measured out my life with coffee spoons;
>
> . . . .
>
> And I have known the eyes already, known them all—
>
> The eyes that fix you in a formulated phrase.

QUOTATION MARKS AND OTHER PUNCTUATION   Periods and commas are placed *inside* quotation marks:

> In "The Lesson," the narrator describes Miss Moore as someone "who
>
> always looked like she was going to church, though she never did."

Other punctuation marks such as colons or semicolons go outside the concluding quotation marks unless they are part of the material being quoted:

> Bartleby repeatedly insists that he "would prefer not to"; eventually
>
> these words become haunting.

For poetry quotations, provide the line number or numbers in parentheses immediately following the quotation:

With ironic detachment, Prufrock declares that he is "no prophet" (653).

Documentation

You must acknowledge sources for the ideas you paraphrase or summarize and material you quote. Such acknowledgments are extremely important, for even an unintentional failure to give formal credit to others for their words or ideas can leave you open to an accusation of *plagiarism*—that is, the presentation of someone else's ideas as your own.

In the body of your essay, use parenthetical citations to document those works that you quote, paraphrase, or summarize. A list of your sources should be the last page of your essay, the Works Cited page. If you use other kinds of sources not listed here, consult the *MLA Handbook for Writers of Research Papers*, Seventh Edition (2009), or online at www.mla.org/style.

This whimsical paragraph demonstrates the use of parenthetical citations.

Leslie Fiedler's view of the relationship between Jim and Huck (669–70) uses a method often discussed by other critics (Abcarian, Klotz, and Cohen 6–9). Cooper's 1971 study (180) raises similar issues, although such methods are not useful when dealing with such a line as "North Richmond Street, being blind, was a quiet street except at the hour when the Christian Brothers' School set the boys free" (Joyce, "Araby" 125). But when Joyce refers to the weather (*Dubliners* 224), the issue becomes clouded.

The first citation gives only the page reference, which is all that is necessary because the author's name is given in the text and only one work by that author appears in the list of works cited. The second citation gives the editors' names and thus identifies the work being cited. It then indicates the appropriate pages. The third citation, because the author's name is mentioned in the text, gives only a page reference. The fourth citation must provide the author's name *and* the work cited, because two works by the same author appear in the list of works cited. The last citation, because it refers to an author with two works in the list of works cited, gives the name of the work and the page where the reference can be found.

In short, your parenthetical acknowledgment should contain (1) the *minimum* information required to lead the reader to the appropriate work in the list of works cited and (2) the location within the work to which you refer. Citations give credit whenever it is due and enable your reader to go directly to your sources as quickly and easily as possible.

Works Cited

Abcarian, Richard, Marvin Klotz, and Samuel Cohen, eds. *Literature: The*

    Human Experience. 12th ed. Boston: Bedford. 2016. Print.

Cooper, Wendy. *Hair, Sex, Society, Symbolism.* New York: Stein, 1971.

    Print.

Fiedler, Leslie. "Come Back to the Raft Ag'in, Huck Honey." *Partisan*

    Review 15 (1948): 664–71. Print.

Joyce, James. "Araby." Abcarian, Klotz, and Cohen 125–29.

---. *Dubliners.* Eds. Robert Scholes and A. Walton Litz. New York:

    Penguin, 1976. Print.

The first of these citations is for this book. Note that the first editor's name is presented surname first, but the second and subsequent names are presented with the surname last. The second entry illustrates the form for citing a book with one author. The third gives the form for an article published in a periodical (note that the title of the article is in quotes and the title of the journal is italicized). The fourth entry shows how to cite a work included in an anthology. The fifth citation, because it is by the same author as the fourth, begins with three hyphens in place of the author's name.

DOCUMENTING ONLINE SOURCES Until recently, there were few standards governing the citation of electronic sources. However, it has become increasingly common to employ at least some online tools while conducting research. The form suggested below will probably serve for most citations to online books, articles, databases, and other kinds of sites. Keep in mind, however, that if it does not, you will have to decide for yourself the best way to include additional information. The most important thing is that you accurately cite every single source you consult whether that source is a Web site or a more traditional source like a book or an encyclopedia.

1. Author's name
2. Title of the work in quotation marks
3. Title of the Web site (italicized)
4. Sponsor or publisher
5. Date of publication or most recent update

6. Medium of publication

7. Date of access

O'Rourke, Megan. "A Pessimist in Flower." *Slate*. Washington Post. Newsweek Interactive Co. LLC, 18 Jan. 2007. Web. 9 Mar. 2015.

A Checklist for Writing about Literature

1. Is my essay clearly responsive to the assignment?

2. Does my essay put forward a clearly defined thesis at the outset?

3. Does each paragraph have an identifiable topic sentence?

4. Have I marshaled my paragraphs logically and provided appropriate transitions?

5. Do I support my assertions with evidence?

6. Have I used direct quotations appropriately, and have I transcribed them accurately?

7. Do I document the sources of other people's ideas and the direct quotations I use? Is the documentation in appropriate form?

8. Have I written syntactically correct sentences (no run-ons and no fragments except by design)?

9. Have I eliminated as many passive constructions and forms of the verb *to be* as possible?

10. Have I avoided long sequences (say, three or more) of prepositional phrases?

11. Can I feel good about this essay? Does it embody serious thinking in attractive form (free of typos and other errors)? Can I put my name on the essay with pride?

INNOCENCE AND EXPERIENCE

The Veteran, 1878 (oil on canvas). Gaetano Chierici (1838–1920)/Private Collection.

Humans strive to give order and meaning to their lives, to reduce the mystery and unpredictability that constantly threaten them. Life is infinitely more complex and surprising than we imagine, and the categories we establish to give it order and meaning are, for the most part, "a momentary stay against confusion" to borrow Robert Frost's description of poetry. At any time the equilibrium of our lives, the comfortable image of ourselves and the world around us, may be disrupted by something new, forcing us into painful reevaluation. These disruptions create pain, anxiety, and terror but also wisdom and awareness.

The works in this section deal generally with the movement of a central character from moral simplicities and certainties into a more complex and problematic world. Though these works frequently deal with awareness, even wisdom, their central figures rarely act decisively. The main character or protagonist is more often a passive figure who learns the difference between the ideal world he or she imagines and the injurious real world. If the protagonist survives the ordeal, he or she often becomes a better human—better able to wrest some satisfaction from a bleak and threatening world. Many of the works here deal with the passage from childhood to adulthood, the time that certainty gives way to uncertainty.

Almost universally, innocence is associated with childhood and youth, as experience is with age. We teach the young about an ideal world, without explaining that it has not yet been and may never be achieved. As innocents, children are terribly vulnerable to falsehood, to intrusive sexuality, and to the machinations of the wicked, who often triumph.

But the terms *innocence* and *experience* range widely in meaning, and that range is reflected here. Innocence may be social—the innocence of Brown in Nathaniel Hawthorne's "Young Goodman Brown." Or innocence may be seen as the child's ignorance of his or her own mortality, as in Gerard Manley Hopkins's "Spring and Fall" and Dylan Thomas's "Fern Hill." In such works as Nathaniel Hawthorne's "Young Goodman Brown" and Robert Browning's "My Last Duchess," one discovers the tragic consequences of an innocence that is blind.

The contrast between what we thought in our youth and what we have come to know, painfully, as adults stands as an emblem of the passage from innocence to experience. Yet all of us remain, to one degree or another, innocent throughout life, since we never—except with death—stop learning from experience. Looked at in this way, experience is the ceaseless assault life makes on our innocence, moving us to a greater wisdom about ourselves and the world around us.

QUESTIONS FOR THINKING AND WRITING

As you read the selections in this section, consider the following questions. You may want to write out your thoughts informally in a journal or notebook as a way of preparing to respond to the selections, or you may wish to make one of these questions the basis for a formal essay.

1. Innocence is often associated with childhood; responsibility, with adulthood. Were you happier or more contented as a preteen than you are now? Why? Which particular aspects of your childhood do you remember with pleasure? Which with pain? Do you look forward to the future with pleasurable anticipation or with dread? Why?

2. Do you know any adults who seem to be innocents? On what do you base your judgment? Do you know any preteens who seem to be particularly "adult" in their behavior (beyond politeness and good manners—they may, for example, have to cope with severe family difficulties)? On what do you base your judgment?

3. Have you spent your life under the authority of others, such as parents, teachers, and employers? How do you deal with authorities you resent? Do you look forward to exercising authority over others (your own children, your own students, employees under your supervision)? How will your experiences affect your behavior as an authority figure?

4. How does the growth from innocence to experience affect one's sexual behavior? Social behavior? Political behavior?

FICTION

NATHANIEL HAWTHORNE   (1804–1864)

YOUNG GOODMAN BROWN   1846

Young Goodman[1] Brown came forth at sunset into the street at Salem village; but put his head back, after crossing the threshold, to exchange a parting kiss with his young wife. And Faith, as the wife was aptly named, thrust her own pretty head into the street, letting the wind play with the pink ribbons of her cap while she called to Goodman Brown.

"Dearest heart," whispered she, softly and rather sadly, when her lips were close to his ear, "prithee put off your journey until sunrise and sleep in your own bed to-night. A lone woman is troubled with such dreams and such thoughts that she's afeared of herself sometimes. Pray tarry with me this night, dear husband, of all nights in the year."

"My love and my Faith," replied young Goodman Brown, "of all nights in the year, this one night must I tarry away from thee. My journey, as thou callest it, forth and back again, must needs be done 'twixt now and sunrise. What, my sweet, pretty wife, dost thou doubt me already, and we but three months married?"

"Then God bless you!" said Faith, with the pink ribbons; "and may you find all well when you come back."

"Amen!" cried Goodman Brown. "Say thy prayers, dear Faith, and go to bed   5 at dusk, and no harm will come to thee."

So they parted; and the young man pursued his way until, being about to turn the corner by the meeting-house, he looked back and saw the head of Faith still peeping after him with a melancholy air, in spite of her pink ribbons.

"Poor little Faith!" thought he, for his heart smote him. "What a wretch am I to leave her on such an errand! She talks of dreams, too. Methought as she spoke there was trouble in her face, as if a dream had warned her what work is to be done to-night. But no, no; 'twould kill her to think it. Well, she's a blessed angel on earth; and after this one night I'll cling to her skirts and follow her to heaven."

---

[1] Equivalent to *Mr.*, a title given to a man below the rank of gentleman.

With this excellent resolve for the future, Goodman Brown felt himself justified in making more haste on his present evil purpose. He had taken a dreary road, darkened by all the gloomiest trees of the forest, which barely stood aside to let the narrow path creep through, and closed immediately behind. It was all as lonely as could be; and there is this peculiarity in such a solitude, that the traveller knows not who may be concealed by the innumerable trunks and the thick boughs overhead; so that with lonely footsteps he may yet be passing through an unseen multitude.

"There may be a devilish Indian behind every tree," said Goodman Brown to himself; and he glanced fearfully behind him as he added, "What if the devil himself should be at my very elbow!"

His head being turned back, he passed a crook of the road, and, looking 10 forward again, beheld the figure of a man, in grave and decent attire, seated at the foot of an old tree. He arose at Goodman Brown's approach and walked onward side by side with him.

"You are late, Goodman Brown," said he. "The clock of the Old South[2] was striking as I came through Boston, and that is full fifteen minutes agone."

"Faith kept me back a while," replied the young man, with a tremor in his voice, caused by the sudden appearance of his companion, though not wholly unexpected.

It was now deep dusk in the forest, and deepest in that part of it where these two were journeying. As nearly as could be discerned, the second traveller was about fifty years old, apparently in the same rank of life as Goodman Brown, and bearing a considerable resemblance to him, though perhaps more in expression than features. Still they might have been taken for father and son. And yet, though the elder person was as simply clad as the younger, and as simple in manner too, he had an indescribable air of one who knew the world, and who would not have felt abashed at the governor's dinner table or in King William's[3] court, were it possible that his affairs should call him thither. But the only thing about him that could be fixed upon as remarkable was his staff, which bore the likeness of a great black snake, so curiously wrought that it might almost be seen to twist and wriggle itself like a living serpent. This, of course, must have been an ocular deception, assisted by the uncertain light.

"Come, Goodman Brown," cried his fellow-traveller, "this is a dull pace for the beginning of a journey. Take my staff, if you are so soon weary."

"Friend," said the other, exchanging his slow pace for a full stop, "having 15 kept covenant by meeting thee here, it is my purpose now to return whence I came. I have scruples touching the matter thou wot'st of."

"Sayest thou so?" replied he of the serpent, smiling apart. "Let us walk on, nevertheless, reasoning as we go; and if I convince thee not thou shalt turn back. We are but a little way in the forest yet."

---

[2] A church in Boston.
[3] Ruler of England from 1689 to 1702.

"Too far! too far!" exclaimed the goodman, unconsciously resuming his walk. "My father never went into the woods on such an errand, nor his father before him. We have been a race of honest men and good Christians since the days of the martyrs;[4] and shall I be the first of the name of Brown that ever took this path and kept—"

"Such company, thou wouldst say," observed the elder person, interpreting his pause. "Well said, Goodman Brown! I have been as well acquainted with your family as with ever a one among the Puritans; and that's no trifle to say. I helped your grandfather, the constable, when he lashed the Quaker woman so smartly through the streets of Salem; and it was I that brought your father a pitch-pine knot, kindled at my own hearth, to set fire to an Indian village, in King Philip's war.[5] They were my good friends, both; and many a pleasant walk have we had along this path, and returned merrily after midnight. I would fain be friends with you for their sake."

"If it be as thou sayest," replied Goodman Brown, "I marvel they never spoke of these matters; or, verily, I marvel not, seeing that the least rumor of the sort would have driven them from New England. We are a people of prayer, and good works to boot, and abide no such wickedness."

"Wickedness or not," said the traveller, with the twisted staff, "I have a very general acquaintance here in New England. The deacons of many a church have drunk the communion wine with me; the selectmen of divers towns make me their chairman; and a majority of the Great and General Court[6] are firm supporters of my interest. The governor and I, too—But these are state secrets." 20

"Can this be so?" cried Goodman Brown, with a stare of amazement at his undisturbed companion. "Howbeit, I have nothing to do with the governor and council; they have their own ways, and are no rule for a simple husbandman[7] like me. But, were I to go on with thee, how should I meet the eye of that good old man, our minister, at Salem village? Oh, his voice would make me tremble both Sabbath day and lecture day."

Thus far the elder traveller had listened with due gravity; but now burst into a fit of irrepressible mirth, shaking himself so violently that his snake-like staff actually seemed to wriggle in sympathy.

"Ha! ha! ha!" shouted he again and again; then composing himself, "Well, go on, Goodman Brown, go on; but, prithee, don't kill me with laughing."

"Well, then, to end the matter at once," said Goodman Brown, considerably nettled, "there is my wife, Faith. It would break her dear little heart; and I'd rather break my own."

---

[4] A reference to the persecution of Protestants in England (1553–1558) by the Catholic monarch Mary Tudor.

[5] War waged (1675–1676) against the colonists of New England by the Indian chief Metacomet, also known as "King Philip."

[6] The Puritan legislature.

[7] An ordinary person.

"Nay, if that be the case," answered the other, "e'en go thy ways, Goodman 25
Brown. I would not for twenty old women like the one hobbling before us that
Faith should come to any harm."

As he spoke he pointed his staff at a female figure on the path, in whom Goodman Brown recognized a very pious and exemplary dame, who had taught him
his catechism in youth, and was still his moral and spiritual adviser, jointly with
the minister and Deacon Gookin.

"A marvel, truly, that Goody[8] Cloyse should be so far in the wilderness at
nightfall," said he. "But with your leave, friend, I shall take a cut through the
woods until we have left this Christian woman behind. Being a stranger to you,
she might ask whom I was consorting with and whither I was going."

"Be it so," said his fellow-traveller. "Betake you to the woods, and let me keep
the path."

Accordingly the young man turned aside, but took care to watch his companion, who advanced softly along the road until he had come within a staff's
length of the old dame. She, meanwhile, was making the best of her way, with
singular speed for so aged a woman, and mumbling some indistinct words—a
prayer, doubtless—as she went. The traveller put forth his staff and touched
her withered neck with what seemed the serpent's tail.

"The devil!" screamed the pious old lady.   30

"Then Goody Cloyse knows her old friend?" observed the traveller, con-
fronting her and leaning on his writhing stick.

"Ah, forsooth, and is it your worship indeed?" cried the good dame. "Yea,
truly is it, and in the very image of my old gossip, Goodman Brown, the grandfather of the silly fellow that now is. But—would your worship believe it?—my
broomstick hath strangely disappeared, stolen, as I suspect, by that unhanged
witch, Goody Cory, and that, too, when I was all anointed with the juice of
smallage and cinquefoil and wolf's bane—"[9]

"Mingled with fine wheat and the fat of a new-born babe," said the shape of
old Goodman Brown.

"Ah, your worship knows the recipe," cried the old lady, cackling aloud. "So,
as I was saying, being all ready for the meeting, and no horse to ride on, I made
up my mind to foot it; for they tell me there is a nice young man to be taken
into communion to-night. But now your good worship will lend me your arm,
and we shall be there in a twinkling."

"That can hardly be," answered her friend. "I may not spare you my arm, 35
Goody Cloyse; but here is my staff, if you will."

So saying, he threw it down at her feet, where, perhaps, it assumed life, being
one of the rods which its owner had formerly lent to the Egyptian magi.[10] Of
this fact, however, Goodman Brown could not take cognizance. He had cast
up his eyes in astonishment, and, looking down again, beheld neither Goody

---

[8] A polite title for a wife of humble rank.
[9] All these plants were associated with magic and witchcraft.
[10] Allusion to the biblical magicians who turned their rods into serpents (Exodus 7:11–12).

Cloyse nor the serpentine staff, but his fellow-traveller alone, who waited for him as calmly as if nothing had happened.

"That old woman taught me my catechism," said the young man; and there was a world of meaning in this simple comment.

They continued to walk onward, while the elder traveller exhorted his companion to make good speed and persevere in the path, discoursing so aptly that his arguments seemed rather to spring up in the bosom of his auditor than to be suggested by himself. As they went, he plucked a branch of maple to serve for a walking stick, and began to strip it of the twigs and little boughs, which were wet with evening dew. The moment his fingers touched them they became strangely withered and dried up as with a week's sunshine. Thus the pair proceeded, at a good free pace, until suddenly, in a gloomy hollow of the road, Goodman Brown sat himself down on the stump of a tree and refused to go any farther.

"Friend," said he, stubbornly, "my mind is made up. Not another step will I budge on this errand. What if a wretched old woman do choose to go to the devil when I thought she was going to heaven: is that any reason why I should quit my dear Faith and go after her?"

"You will think better of this by and by," said his acquaintance, composedly. 40 "Sit here and rest yourself a while; and when you feel like moving again, there is my staff to help you along."

Without more words, he threw his companion the maple stick, and was as speedily out of sight as if he had vanished into the deepening gloom. The young man sat a few moments by the roadside, applauding himself greatly, and thinking with how clear a conscience he should meet the minister in his morning walk, nor shrink from the eye of good old Deacon Gookin. And what calm sleep would be his that very night, which was to have been spent so wickedly, but so purely and sweetly now, in the arms of Faith! Amidst these pleasant and praiseworthy meditations, Goodman Brown heard the tramp of horses along the road, and deemed it advisable to conceal himself within the verge of the forest, conscious of the guilty purpose that had brought him thither, though now so happily turned from it.

On came the hoof tramps and the voices of the riders, two grave old voices, conversing soberly as they drew near. These mingled sounds appeared to pass along the road, within a few yards of the young man's hiding-place; but, owing doubtless to the depth of the gloom at that particular spot, neither the travellers nor their steeds were visible. Though their figures brushed the small boughs by the wayside, it could not be seen that they intercepted, even for a moment, the faint gleam from the strip of bright sky athwart which they must have passed. Goodman Brown alternately crouched and stood on tiptoe, pulling aside the branches and thrusting forth his head as far as he durst without discerning so much as a shadow. It vexed him the more, because he could have sworn, were such a thing possible, that he recognized the voices of the minister and Deacon Gookin, jogging along quietly, as they were wont to do, when bound to some ordination or ecclesiastical council. While yet within hearing, one of the riders stopped to pluck a switch.

"Of the two, reverend sir," said the voice like the deacon's, "I had rather miss an ordination dinner than to-night's meeting. They tell me that some of our community are to be here from Falmouth[11] and beyond, and others from Connecticut and Rhode Island, besides several of the Indian powwows,[12] who, after their fashion, know almost as much deviltry as the best of us. Moreover, there is a goodly young woman to be taken into communion."

"Mighty well, Deacon Gookin!" replied the solemn old tones of the minister. "Spur up, or we shall be late. Nothing can be done, you know, until I get on the ground."

The hoofs clattered again; and the voices, talking so strangely in the empty air, passed on through the forest, where no church had ever been gathered, nor solitary Christian prayed. Whither, then, could these holy men be journeying so deep into the heathen wilderness? Young Goodman Brown caught hold of a tree for support, being ready to sink down on the ground, faint and overburdened with the heavy sickness of his heart. He looked up to the sky, doubting whether there really was a heaven above him. Yet there was the blue arch, and the stars brightening in it. 45

"With heaven above and Faith below, I will yet stand firm against the devil!" cried Goodman Brown.

While he still gazed upward into the deep arch of the firmament and had lifted his hands to pray, a cloud, though no wind was stirring, hurried across the zenith and hid the brightening stars. The blue sky was still visible, except directly overhead, where this black mass of cloud was sweeping swiftly northward. Aloft in the air, as if from the depths of the cloud, came a confused and doubtful sound of voices. Once the listener fancied that he could distinguish the accents of towns-people of his own, men and women, both pious and ungodly, many of whom he had met at the communion table, and had seen others rioting at the tavern. The next moment, so indistinct were the sounds, he doubted whether he had heard aught but the murmur of the old forest, whispering without a wind. Then came a stronger swell of those familiar tones, heard daily in the sunshine at Salem village, but never until now from a cloud of night. There was one voice, of a young woman, uttering lamentations, yet with an uncertain sorrow, and entreating for some favor, which, perhaps, it would grieve her to obtain; and all the unseen multitude, both saints and sinners, seemed to encourage her onward.

"Faith!" shouted Goodman Brown, in a voice of agony and desperation; and the echoes of the forest mocked him, crying, "Faith! Faith!" as if bewildered wretches were seeking her all through the wilderness.

The cry of grief, rage, and terror was yet piercing the night, when the unhappy husband held his breath for a response. There was a scream, drowned immediately in a louder murmur of voices, fading into far-off laughter, as the

[11] A town near Salem, Massachusetts.
[12] Medicine men.

dark cloud swept away, leaving the clear and silent sky above Goodman Brown. But something fluttered lightly down through the air and caught on the branch of a tree. The young man seized it, and beheld a pink ribbon.

"My Faith is gone!" cried he, after one stupefied moment. "There is no good on earth; and sin is but a name. Come, devil; for to thee is this world given." 50

And, maddened with despair, so that he laughed loud and long, did Goodman Brown grasp his staff and set forth again, at such a rate that he seemed to fly along the forest path rather than to walk or run. The road grew wilder and drearier and more faintly traced, and vanished at length, leaving him in the heart of the dark wilderness, still rushing onward with the instinct that guides mortal man to evil. The whole forest was peopled with frightful sounds—the creaking of the trees, the howling of wild beasts, and the yell of Indians; while sometimes the wind tolled like a distant church bell, and sometimes gave a broad roar around the traveller, as if all Nature were laughing him to scorn. But he was himself the chief horror of the scene, and shrank not from its other horrors.

"Ha! ha! ha!" roared Goodman Brown when the wind laughed at him. "Let us hear which will laugh loudest. Think not to frighten me with your deviltry. Come witch, come wizard, come Indian powwow, come devil himself, and here comes Goodman Brown. You may as well fear him as he fears you."

In truth, all through the haunted forest there could be nothing more frightful than the figure of Goodman Brown. On he flew among the black pines, brandishing his staff with frenzied gestures, now giving vent to an inspiration of horrid blasphemy, and now shouting forth such laughter as set all the echoes of the forest laughing like demons around him. The fiend in his own shape is less hideous than when he rages in the breast of man. Thus sped the demoniac on his course, until, quivering among the trees, he saw a red light before him, as when the felled trunks and branches of a clearing have been set on fire, and throw up their lurid blaze against the sky, at the hour of midnight. He paused, in a lull of the tempest that had driven him onward, and heard the swell of what seemed a hymn, rolling solemnly from a distance with the weight of many voices. He knew the tune; it was a familiar one in the choir of the village meeting-house. The verse died heavily away, and was lengthened by a chorus, not of human voices, but of all the sounds of the benighted wilderness pealing in awful harmony together. Goodman Brown cried out, and his cry was lost to his own ear by its unison with the cry of the desert.

In the interval of silence he stole forward until the light glared full upon his eyes. At one extremity of an open space, hemmed in by the dark wall of the forest, arose a rock, bearing some rude, natural resemblance either to an altar or a pulpit, and surrounded by four blazing pines, their tops aflame, their stems untouched, like candles at an evening meeting. The mass of foliage that had overgrown the summit of the rock was all on fire, blazing high into the night and fitfully illuminating the whole field. Each pendent twig and leafy festoon was in a blaze. As the red light arose and fell, a numerous congregation alternately shone forth, then disappeared in shadow, and again grew, as it were, out of the darkness, peopling the heart of the solitary woods at once.

"A grave and dark-clad company," quoth Goodman Brown.   55

In truth they were such. Among them, quivering to and fro between gloom and splendor, appeared faces that would be seen next day at the council board of the province, and others which, Sabbath after Sabbath, looked devoutly heavenward, and benignantly over the crowded pews, from the holiest pulpits in the land. Some affirm that the lady of the governor was there. At least there were high dames well known to her, and wives of honored husbands, and widows, a great multitude, and ancient maidens, all of excellent repute, and fair young girls, who trembled lest their mothers should espy them. Either the sudden gleams of light flashing over the obscure field bedazzled Goodman Brown, or he recognized a score of the church members of Salem village famous for their especial sanctity. Good old Deacon Gookin had arrived, and waited at the skirts of that venerable saint, his revered pastor. But, irreverently consorting with these grave, reputable, and pious people, these elders of the church, these chaste dames and dewy virgins, there were men of dissolute lives and women of spotted fame, wretches given over to all mean and filthy vice, and suspected even of horrid crimes. It was strange to see that the good shrank not from the wicked, nor were the sinners abashed by the saints. Scattered also among their pale-faced enemies were the Indian priests, or powwows, who had often scared their native forest with more hideous incantations than any known to English witchcraft.

"But where is Faith?" thought Goodman Brown; and, as hope came into his heart, he trembled.

Another verse of the hymn arose, a slow and mournful strain, such as the pious love, but joined to words which expressed all that our nature can conceive of sin, and darkly hinted at far more. Unfathomable to mere mortals is the lore of fiends. Verse after verse was sung; and still the chorus of the desert swelled between like the deepest tone of a mighty organ; and with the final peal of that dreadful anthem there came a sound, as if the roaring wind, the rushing streams, the howling beasts, and every other voice of the unconcerted wilderness were mingling and according with the voice of guilty man in homage to the prince of all. The four blazing pines threw up a loftier flame, and obscurely discovered shapes and visages of horror on the smoke wreaths above the impious assembly. At the same moment the fire on the rock shot redly forth and formed a glowing arch above its base, where now appeared a figure. With reverence be it spoken, the figure bore no slight similitude, both in garb and manner, to some grave divine of the New England churches.

"Bring forth the converts!" cried a voice that echoed through the field and rolled into the forest.

At the word, Goodman Brown stepped forth from the shadow of the trees   60 and approached the congregation, with whom he felt a loathful brotherhood by the sympathy of all that was wicked in his heart. He could have well-nigh sworn that the shape of his own dead father beckoned him to advance, looking downward from a smoke wreath, while a woman, with dim features of despair, threw out her hand to warn him back. Was it his mother? But he had no power to retreat one step, nor to resist, even in thought, when the minister and good old Deacon Gookin seized his arms and led him to the blazing rock. Thither came also the slender form of a veiled female, led between Goody Cloyse, that pious teacher of the catechism, and Martha Carrier,[13] who had received the devil's promise to be queen of hell. A rampant hag was she. And there stood the proselytes beneath the canopy of fire.

"Welcome, my children," said the dark figure, "to the communion of your race. Ye have found thus young your nature and your destiny. My children, look behind you!"

They turned; and flashing forth, as it were, in a sheet of flame, the fiend worshippers were seen; the smile of welcome gleamed darkly on every visage.

"There," resumed the sable form, "are all whom ye have reverenced from youth. Ye deemed them holier than yourselves, and shrank from your own sin, contrasting it with their lives of righteousness and prayerful aspirations heavenward. Yet here are they all in my worshipping assembly. This night it shall be granted you to know their secret deeds: how hoary-bearded elders of the church have whispered wanton words to the young maids of their households; how many a woman, eager for widows' weeds, has given her husband a drink at bedtime and let him sleep his last sleep in her bosom; how beardless youths have made haste to inherit their fathers' wealth; and how fair damsels—blush not, sweet ones—have dug little graves in the garden, and bidden me, the sole guest, to an infant's funeral. By the sympathy of your human hearts for sin ye shall scent out all the places—whether in church, bed-chamber, street, field, or forest—where crime has been committed, and shall exult to behold the whole earth one stain of guilt, one mighty blood spot. Far more than this. It shall be yours to penetrate, in every bosom, the deep mystery of sin, the fountain of all wicked arts, and which inexhaustibly supplies more evil impulses than human power—than my power at its utmost—can make manifest in deeds. And now, my children, look upon each other."

They did so; and, by the blaze of the hell-kindled torches, the wretched man beheld his Faith, and the wife her husband, trembling before that unhallowed altar.

"Lo, there ye stand, my children," said the figure, in a deep and solemn tone, almost sad with its despairing awfulness, as if his once angelic nature could yet mourn for our miserable race. "Depending upon one another's hearts, ye had still hoped that virtue were not all a dream. Now are ye undeceived. Evil is the nature of mankind. Evil must be your only happiness. Welcome again, my children, to the communion of your race."

"Welcome," repeated the fiend worshippers, in one cry of despair and triumph.

[13] One of the women hanged in Salem in 1697 for witchcraft.

And there they stood, the only pair, as it seemed, who were yet hesitating on the verge of wickedness in this dark world. A basin was hollowed, naturally, in the rock. Did it contain water, reddened by the lurid light? or was it blood? or, perchance, a liquid flame? Herein did the shape of evil dip his hand and prepare to lay the mark of baptism upon their foreheads, that they might be partakers of the mystery of sin, more conscious of the secret guilt of others, both in deed and thought, than they could now be of their own. The husband cast one look at his pale wife, and Faith at him. What polluted wretches would the next glance show them to each other, shuddering alike at what they disclosed and what they saw!

"Faith! Faith!" cried the husband, "look up to heaven, and resist the wicked one."

Whether Faith obeyed he knew not. Hardly had he spoken when he found himself amid calm night and solitude, listening to a roar of the wind which died heavily away through the forest. He staggered against the rock, and felt it chill and damp; while a hanging twig, that had been all on fire, besprinkled his cheek with the coldest dew.

The next morning young Goodman Brown came slowly into the street of 70 Salem village, staring around him like a bewildered man. The good old minister was taking a walk along the graveyard to get an appetite for breakfast and meditate his sermon, and bestowed a blessing, as he passed, on Goodman Brown. He shrank from the venerable saint as if to avoid an anathema. Old Deacon Gookin was at domestic worship, and the holy words of his prayer were heard through the open window. "What God doth the wizard pray to?" quoth Goodman Brown. Goody Cloyse, that excellent old Christian, stood in the early sunshine at her own lattice, catechizing a little girl who had brought her a pint of morning's milk. Goodman Brown snatched away the child as from the grasp of the fiend himself. Turning the corner by the meeting-house, he spied the head of Faith, with the pink ribbons, gazing anxiously forth, and bursting into such joy at sight of him that she skipped along the street and almost kissed her husband before the whole village. But Goodman Brown looked sternly and sadly into her face, and passed on without a greeting.

Had Goodman Brown fallen asleep in the forest and only dreamed a wild dream of a witch-meeting?

Be it so if you will; but, alas! it was a dream of evil omen for young Goodman Brown. A stern, a sad, a darkly meditative, a distrustful, if not a desperate man did he become from the night of that fearful dream. On the Sabbath day, when the congregation were singing a holy psalm, he could not listen because an anthem of sin rushed loudly upon his ear and drowned all the blessed strain. When the minister spoke from the pulpit with power and fervid eloquence, and, with his hand on the open Bible, of the sacred truths of our religion, and of saint-like lives and triumphant deaths, and of future bliss or misery unutterable, then did Goodman Brown turn pale, dreading lest the roof should thunder down upon the gray blasphemer and his hearers. Often, awakening suddenly at midnight, he shrank from the bosom of Faith; and at morning or eventide, when the family knelt down at prayer, he scowled and muttered to himself, and gazed sternly at his wife, and turned away. And when he had lived long, and was borne to his grave a hoary corpse, followed by Faith, an aged woman, and children and grandchildren, a goodly procession, besides neighbors not a few, they carved no hopeful verse upon his tombstone, for his dying hour was gloom.

FOR ANALYSIS

1. At the end of the story, the **narrator** asks, "Had Goodman Brown fallen asleep in the forest and only dreamed a wild dream of a witch-meeting?" Why, instead of answering the question, does he say, "Be it so if you will"?

2. Examine the seemingly supernatural events Brown experiences as he penetrates ever deeper into the forest. Can the reader determine whether those events are really taking place? If not, what purpose does the **ambiguity** serve?

3. What attitude does this story express toward the church of Puritan New England?

4. What elements of the story can be described as **allegorical** or **symbolic**?

5. What is the "guilty purpose" (para. 41) that has drawn Brown to the forest?

MAKING ARGUMENTS

1. Write an essay in which you argue for or against the proposition that the "truth" Brown discovers during his night in the forest justifies his gloom and withdrawal.

2. Ignore the narrator's suggestion not to worry about the nature of what happened to Young Goodman Brown in the forest. Instead, worry, and make an argument for one side or the other.

WRITING TOPIC

Write out a paraphrase of Satan's sermon.

MAKING CONNECTIONS

1. Both this story and Herman Melville's "Bartleby, the Scrivener" (p. 319) deal with **protagonists** who withdraw from life. What similarities and differences do you find in the reasons for their withdrawal, the ways in which they withdraw, and the consequences of their withdrawal?

2. Both Hawthorne's "Young Goodman Brown" and Ralph Ellison's "'Repent, Harlequin!' Said the Ticktockman" (p. 374) rely on fantasy. What advantages does the use of fantasy give the authors?

NAGUIB MAHFOUZ (1911–2006)

HALF A DAY 1989

I proceeded alongside my father, clutching his right hand, running to keep up with the long strides he was taking. All my clothes were new: the black shoes, the green school uniform, and the red tarboosh.[1] My delight in my new clothes, however, was not altogether unmarred, for this was no feast day but the day on which I was to be cast into school for the first time.

My mother stood at the window watching our progress, and I would turn toward her from time to time, as though appealing for help. We walked along a street lined with gardens; on both sides were extensive fields planted with crops, prickly pears, henna trees, and a few date palms.

"Why school?" I challenged my father openly. "I shall never do anything to annoy you."

"I'm not punishing you," he said, laughing. "School's not a punishment. It's the factory that makes useful men out of boys. Don't you want to be like your father and brothers?"

I was not convinced. I did not believe there was really any good to be had 5 in tearing me away from the intimacy of my home and throwing me into this building that stood at the end of the road like some huge, high-walled fortress, exceedingly stern and grim.

When we arrived at the gate we could see the courtyard, vast and crammed full of boys and girls. "Go in by yourself," said my father, "and join them. Put a smile on your face and be a good example to others."

I hesitated and clung to his hand, but he gently pushed me from him. "Be a man," he said. "Today you truly begin life. You will find me waiting for you when it's time to leave."

I took a few steps, then stopped and looked but saw nothing. Then the faces of boys and girls came into view. I did not know a single one of them, and none of them knew me. I felt I was a stranger who had lost his way. But glances of curiosity were directed toward me, and one boy approached and asked, "Who brought you?"

"My father," I whispered.

"My father's dead," he said quite simply. 10

I did not know what to say. The gate was closed, letting out a pitiable screech. Some of the children burst into tears. The bell rang. A lady came along, followed by a group of men. The men began sorting us into ranks. We were formed into an intricate pattern in the great courtyard surrounded on three

---

[1] A brimless felt hat similar to a fez worn by Muslim men.

sides by high buildings of several floors; from each floor we were overlooked by a long balcony roofed in wood.

"This is your new home," said the woman. "Here too there are mothers and fathers. Here there is everything that is enjoyable and beneficial to knowledge and religion. Dry your tears and face life joyfully."

We submitted to the facts, and this submission brought a sort of contentment. Living beings were drawn to other living beings, and from the first moments my heart made friends with such boys as were to be my friends and fell in love with such girls as I was to be in love with, so that it seemed my misgivings had had no basis. I had never imagined school would have this rich variety. We played all sorts of different games: swings, the vaulting horse, ball games. In the music room we chanted our first songs. We also had our first introduction to language. We saw a globe of the Earth, which revolved and showed the various continents and countries. We started learning the numbers. The story of the Creator of the universe was read to us, we were told of His present world and of His Hereafter, and we heard examples of what He said. We ate delicious food, took a little nap, and woke up to go on with friendship and love, play and learning.

As our path revealed itself to us, however, we did not find it as totally sweet and unclouded as we had presumed. Dust-laden winds and unexpected accidents came about suddenly, so we had to be watchful, at the ready, and very patient. It was not all a matter of playing and fooling around. Rivalries could bring about pain and hatred or give rise to fighting. And while the lady would sometimes smile, she would often scowl and scold. Even more frequently she would resort to physical punishment.

In addition, the time for changing one's mind was over and gone and there 15 was no question of ever returning to the paradise of home. Nothing lay ahead of us but exertion, struggle, and perseverance. Those who were able took advantage of the opportunities for success and happiness that presented themselves amid the worries.

The bell rang announcing the passing of the day and the end of work. The throngs of children rushed toward the gate, which was opened again. I bade farewell to friends and sweethearts and passed through the gate. I peered around but found no trace of my father, who had promised to be there. I stepped aside to wait. When I had waited for a long time without avail, I decided to return home on my own. After I had taken a few steps, a middle-aged man passed by, and I realized at once that I knew him. He came toward me, smiling, and shook me by the hand, saying, "It's a long time since we last met—how are you?"

With a nod of my head, I agreed with him and in turn asked, "And you, how are you?"

"As you can see, not all that good, the Almighty be praised!"

Again he shook me by the hand and went off. I proceeded a few steps, then came to a startled halt. Good Lord! Where was the street lined with gardens? Where had it disappeared to? When did all these vehicles invade it? And when did all these hordes of humanity come to rest upon its surface? How did these hills of refuse come to cover its sides? And where were the fields that bordered it? High buildings had taken over, the street surged with children, and disturbing noises shook the air. At various points stood conjurers showing off their tricks and making snakes appear from baskets. Then there was a band announcing the opening of a circus, with clowns and weight lifters walking in front. A line of trucks carrying central security troops crawled majestically by. The siren of a fire engine shrieked, and it was not clear how the vehicle would cleave its way to reach the blazing fire. A battle raged between a taxi driver and his passenger, while the passenger's wife called out for help and no one answered. Good God! I was in a daze. My head spun. I almost went crazy. How could all this have happened in half a day, between early morning and sunset? I would find the answer at home with my father. But where was my home? I could see only tall buildings and hordes of people. I hastened on to the crossroads between the gardens and Abu Khoda. I had to cross Abu Khoda to reach my house, but the stream of cars would not let up. The fire engine's siren was shrieking at full pitch as it moved at a snail's pace, and I said to myself, "Let the fire take its pleasure in what it consumes." Extremely irritated, I wondered when I would be able to cross. I stood there a long time, until the young lad employed at the ironing shop on the corner came up to me. He stretched out his arm and said gallantly, "Grandpa, let me take you across."

FOR ANALYSIS

1. What is significant about this day for the **narrator**?

2. What ages are the different male **characters**? Why are their ages important to the story?

3. How would you describe the differences in the **setting** and **mood** of the story at its beginning and at its end? Why do you think the author might have decided to have the story begin and end this way?

MAKING ARGUMENTS

1. While this story is about several things, it is certainly about education. Outline the arguments on both sides of the question, Is this story pro-education or anti-education? (You can also include a third outline that combines both sides of the argument.)

2. "Half a Day" could be read as a timeless story about life or as a story whose setting and historical details are central to its meaning. Find some information about its author, his concerns, and the time and place where he lived and wrote; with that information, make the argument for the story being the latter kind.

WRITING TOPICS

1. This story is narrated by a very young boy, so his knowledge of the world and ability to form judgments about it is limited. When writing this kind of story, authors have to strike a balance between the child's innocence and their own (and their readers') experience, providing material for advanced reflection without ascribing perceptions and thoughts to someone too young to have them. Argue that Mahfouz succeeds or fails here by describing his attempt to do so.

2. Imagine this experience as an essay or sermon. What might it look like? What kinds of ideas, lessons, or truths might it contain? Rewrite this story as an essay or sermon, or an outline of it.

MAKING CONNECTIONS

1. Both "Half a Day" and Toni Cade Bambara's "The Lesson" (p. 98) are in some ways about school, yet both stories are about much more than that. How do the other things that the stories are about appear? What are those things?

2. Though "Half a Day" and Daniel Orozco's "Orientation" (p. 107) have very different settings and are about characters of different ages, how are the stories similar? How are they different?

JOHN UPDIKE (1932–2009)

A & P 1961

In walks these three girls in nothing but bathing suits. I'm in the third check-out slot, with my back to the door, so I don't see them until they're over by the bread. The one that caught my eye first was the one in the plaid green two-piece. She was a chunky kid, with a good tan and a sweet broad soft-looking can with those two crescents of white just under it, where the sun never seems to hit, at the top of the backs of her legs. I stood there with my hand on a box of HiHo crackers trying to remember if I rang it up or not. I ring it up again and the customer starts giving me hell. She's one of these cash-register-watchers, a witch about fifty with rouge on her cheekbones and no eyebrows, and I know it made her day to trip me up. She'd been watching cash registers for fifty years and probably never seen a mistake before.

By the time I got her feathers smoothed and her goodies into a bag—she gives me a little snort in passing, if she'd been born at the right time they would have burned her over in Salem—by the time I get her on her way the girls had circled around the bread and were coming back, without a pushcart, back my way along the counters, in the aisle between the checkouts and the Special bins. They didn't even have shoes on. There was this chunky one, with the two-piece—it was bright green and the seams on the bra were still sharp and her belly was still pretty pale so I guessed she just got it (the suit)—there was this one, with one of those chubby berry-faces, the lips all bunched together under her nose, this one, and a tall one, with black hair that hadn't quite frizzed right, and one of these sunburns right across under the eyes, and a chin that was too long—you know, the kind of girl other girls think is very "striking" and "attractive" but never quite makes it, as they very well know, which is why they like her so much—and then the third one, that wasn't quite so tall. She was the queen. She kind of led them, the other two peeking around and making their shoulders round. She didn't look around, not this queen, she just walked straight on slowly, on these long white prima-donna legs. She came down a little hard on her heels, as if she didn't walk in her bare feet that much, putting down her heels and then letting the weight move along to her toes as if she was testing the floor with every step, putting a little deliberate extra action into it. You never know for sure how girls' minds work (do you really think it's a mind in there or just a little buzz like a bee in a glass jar?) but you got the idea she had talked the other two into coming in here with her, and now she was show-ing them how to do it, walk slow and hold yourself straight.

She had on a kind of dirty-pink—beige maybe, I don't know—bathing suit with a little nubble all over it, and what got me, the straps were down. They were off her shoulders looped loose around the cool tops of her arms, and I guess as a result the suit had slipped a little on her, so all around the top of the cloth there was this shining rim. If it hadn't been there you wouldn't have known there could have been anything whiter than those shoulders. With the straps pushed off, there was nothing between the top of the suit and the top of her head except just *her*, this clean bare plane of the top of her chest down from the shoulder bones like a dented sheet of metal tilted in the light. I mean, it was more than pretty.

She had sort of oaky hair that the sun and salt had bleached, done up in a bun that was unravelling, and a kind of prim face. Walking into the A & P with your straps down, I suppose it's the only kind of face you *can* have. She held her head so high her neck, coming up out of those white shoulders, looked kind of stretched, but I didn't mind. The longer her neck was, the more of her there was.

She must have felt in the corner of her eye me and over my shoulder Stoke- 5 sie in the second slot watching, but she didn't tip. Not this queen. She kept her eyes moving across the racks, and stopped, and turned so slow it made my stomach rub the inside of my apron, and buzzed to the other two, who kind of huddled against her for relief, and then they all three of them went up the cat-and-dog-food-breakfast-cereal-macaroni-rice-raisins-seasonings-spreads-spaghetti-soft-drinks-crackers-and-cookies aisle. From the third slot I look straight up this aisle to the meat counter, and I watched them all the way. The fat one with the tan sort of fumbled with the cookies, but on second thought she put the package back. The sheep pushing their carts down the aisle—the girls were walking against the usual traffic (not that we have one-way signs or anything)—were pretty hilarious. You could see them, when Queenie's white shoulders dawned on them, kind of jerk, or hop, or hiccup, but their eyes snapped back to their own baskets and on they pushed. I bet you could set off dynamite in an A & P and the people would by and large keep reaching and checking oatmeal off their lists and muttering "Let me see, there was a third thing, began with A, asparagus, no, ah, yes, applesauce!" or whatever it is they do mutter. But there was no doubt, this jiggled them. A few houseslaves in pin curlers even looked around after pushing their carts past to make sure what they had seen was correct.

You know, it's one thing to have a girl in a bathing suit down on the beach, where what with the glare nobody can look at each other much anyway, and another thing in the cool of the A & P, under the fluorescent lights, against all those stacked packages, with her feet paddling along naked over our check-board green-and-cream rubber-tile floor.

"Oh Daddy," Stokesie said beside me. "I feel so faint."

"Darling," I said. "Hold me tight." Stokesie's married, with two babies chalked up on his fuselage already, but as far as I can tell that's the only difference. He's twenty-two, and I was nineteen this April.

"Is it done?" he asks, the responsible married man finding his voice. I forgot to say he thinks he's going to be manager some sunny day, maybe in 1990 when it's called the Great Alexandrov and Petrooshki Tea Company or something.

What he meant was, our town is five miles from a beach, with a big summer 10
colony out on the Point, but we're right in the middle of town, and the women
generally put on a shirt or shorts or something before they get out of the car into
the street. And anyway these are usually women with six children and varicose
veins mapping their legs and nobody, including them, could care less. As I say,
we're right in the middle of town, and if you stand at our front doors you can
see two banks and the Congregational church and the newspaper store and three
real-estate offices and about twenty-seven old freeloaders tearing up Central
Street because the sewer broke again. It's not as if we're on the Cape; we're north of
Boston and there's people in this town haven't seen the ocean for twenty years.

The girls had reached the meat counter and were asking McMahon something. He pointed, they pointed, and they shuffled out of sight behind a pyra-
mid of Diet Delight peaches. All that was left for us to see was old McMahon
patting his mouth and looking after them sizing up their joints. Poor kids,
I began to feel sorry for them, they couldn't help it.

Now here comes the sad part of the story, at least my family says it's sad, but
I don't think it's so sad myself. The store's pretty empty, it being Thursday afternoon, so there was nothing much to do except lean on the register and wait for
the girls to show up again. The whole store was like a pinball machine and I
didn't know which tunnel they'd come out of. After a while they come around
out of the far aisle, around the light bulbs, records at discount of the Caribbean
Six or Tony Martin Sings or some such gunk you wonder they waste the wax
on, sixpacks of candy bars, and plastic toys done up in cellophane that fall apart
when a kid looks at them anyway. Around they come, Queenie still leading the
way, and holding a little gray jar in her hand. Slots Three through Seven are
unmanned and I could see her wondering between Stokes and me, but Stokesie
with his usual luck draws an old party in baggy gray pants who stumbles up with
four giant cans of pineapple juice (what do these bums *do* with all that pineapple
juice? I've often asked myself) so the girls come to me. Queenie puts down the
jar and I take it into my fingers icy cold. Kingfish Fancy Herring Snacks in Pure
Sour Cream: 49¢. Now her hands are empty, not a ring or a bracelet, bare as God
made them, and I wonder where the money's coming from. Still with that prim
look she lifts a folded dollar bill out of the hollow at the center of her nubbled
pink top. The jar went heavy in my hand. Really, I thought that was so cute.

Then everybody's luck begins to run out. Lengel comes in from haggling
with a truck full of cabbages on the lot and is about to scuttle into that door
marked MANAGER behind which he hides all day when the girls touch his
eye. Lengel's pretty dreary, teaches Sunday school and the rest, but he doesn't
miss that much. He comes over and says, "Girls, this isn't the beach."

Queenie blushes, though maybe it's just a brush of sunburn I was noticing
for the first time, now that she was so close. "My mother asked me to pick up
a jar of herring snacks." Her voice kind of startled me, the way voices do when
you see the people first, coming out so flat and dumb yet kind of tony, too, the
way it ticked over "pick up" and "snacks." All of a sudden I slid right down her
voice into her living room. Her father and the other men were standing around

in ice-cream coats and bow ties and the women were in sandals picking up herring snacks on toothpicks off a big glass plate and they were all holding drinks the color of water with olives and sprigs of mint in them. When my parents have somebody over they get lemonade and if it's a real racy affair Schlitz in tall glasses with "They'll Do It Every Time" cartoons stencilled on.

"That's all right," Lengel said. "But this isn't the beach." His repeating this 15 struck me as funny, as if it had just occurred to him, and he had been thinking all these years the A & P was a great big sand dune and he was the head lifeguard. He didn't like my smiling—as I say he doesn't miss much—but he concentrates on giving the girls that sad Sunday-school–superintendent stare.

Queenie's blush is no sunburn now, and the plump one in plaid, that I liked better from the back—a really sweet can—pipes up, "We weren't doing any shopping. We just came in for the one thing."

"That makes no difference," Lengel tells her, and I could see from the way his eyes went that he hadn't noticed she was wearing a two-piece before. "We want you decently dressed when you come in here."

"We *are* decent," Queenie says suddenly, her lower lip pushing, getting sore now that she remembers her place, a place from which the crowd that runs the A & P must look pretty crummy. Fancy Herring Snacks flashed in her very blue eyes.

"Girls, I don't want to argue with you. After this come in here with your shoulders covered. It's our policy." He turns his back. That's policy for you. Policy is what the kingpins want. What the others want is juvenile delinquency.

All this while, the customers had been showing up with their carts but, you 20 know, sheep, seeing a scene, they had all bunched up on Stokesie, who shook open a paper bag as gently as peeling a peach, not wanting to miss a word. I could feel in the silence everybody getting nervous, most of all Lengel, who asks me, "Sammy, have you rung up their purchase?"

I thought and said "No" but it wasn't about that I was thinking. I go through the punches, 4, 9, groc, tot—it's more complicated than you think, and after you do it often enough, it begins to make a little song, that you hear words to, in my case "Hello (*bing*) there, you (*gung*) hap-py *pee*-pul (*splat*)!"—the *splat* being the drawer flying out. I uncrease the bill, tenderly as you may imagine, it just having come from between the two smoothest scoops of vanilla I had ever known were there, and pass a half and a penny into her narrow pink palm, and nestle the herrings in a bag and twist its neck and hand it over, all the time thinking.

The girls, and who'd blame them, are in a hurry to get out, so I say "I quit" to Lengel [loud] enough for them to hear, hoping they'll stop and watch me, their unsuspected hero. They keep right on going, into the electric eye; the door flies open and they flicker across the lot to their car, Queenie and Plaid and Big Tall Goony-Goony (not that as raw material she was so bad), leaving me with Lengel and a kink in his eyebrow.

"Did you say something, Sammy?"

"I said I quit."

"I thought you did." 25

"You didn't have to embarrass them."

"It was they who were embarrassing us."

I started to say something that came out "Fiddle-de-doo." It's a saying of my grandmother's, and I know she would have been pleased.

"I don't think you know what you're saying," Lengel said.

"I know you don't," I said. "But I do." I pull the bow at the back of my apron 30 and start shrugging it off my shoulders. A couple customers that had been heading for my slot begin to knock against each other, like scared pigs in a chute.

Lengel sighs and begins to look very patient and old and gray. He's been a friend of my parents for years. "Sammy, you don't want to do this to your Mom and Dad," he tells me. It's true, I don't. But it seems to me that once you begin a gesture it's fatal not to go through with it. I fold the apron, "Sammy" stitched in red on the pocket, and put it on the counter, and drop the bow tie on top of it. The bow tie is theirs, if you've ever wondered. "You'll feel this for the rest of your life," Lengel says, and I know that's true, too, but remembering how he made that pretty girl blush makes me so scrunchy inside I punch the No Sale tab and the machine whirs "pee-pul" and the drawer splats out. One advantage to this scene taking place in summer, I can follow this up with a clean exit, there's no fumbling around getting your coat and galoshes, I just saunter into the electric eye in my white shirt that my mother ironed the night before, and the door heaves itself open, and outside the sunshine is skating around on the asphalt.

I look around for my girls, but they're gone, of course. There wasn't anybody but some young married screaming with her children about some candy they didn't get by the door of a powder-blue Falcon station wagon. Looking back in the big windows, over the bags of peat moss and aluminum lawn furniture stacked on the pavement, I could see Lengel in my place in the slot, checking the sheep through. His face was dark gray and his back stiff, as if he'd just had an injection of iron, and my stomach kind of fell as I felt how hard the world was going to be to me hereafter.

FOR ANALYSIS

1. Describe Sammy's voice as he tells the story. How does Updike's choice to have him **narrate** help us get a sense of Sammy as a **character**? Is he understandable? Is he likable? Can readers sympathize with him?

2. What about "Queenie" is most attractive to Sammy? Is it just her appearance? What else figures in?

3. At the very end of the story, Updike has Sammy describe his customers **figuratively** as pigs and sheep. Why do you think he does this? What does this choice reveal about Sammy's attitude toward them, and toward the adult ways of living he is on the verge of?

4. Sammy describes his quitting as a gesture. For whom is the gesture made—for one audience, or for multiple audiences? What does it say to each audience?

MAKING ARGUMENTS

Take up the proposition that Sammy's gesture is futile and empty. Make an argument supporting or refuting this claim.

WRITING TOPIC

Retell the story with Lengel as **narrator**, showing how that change might affect **point of view**, voice, and meaning.

MAKING CONNECTIONS

1. Compare the connections made between work and identity in "A & P" and in Daniel Orozco's "Orientation" (p. 107).

2. Reread the passage in which Sammy imagines the scene in "Queenie's" parents' living room. Compare to the passage in Toni Cade Bambara's "The Lesson" (p. 98) in which Miss Moore asks about the children's desks at home. What does each moment say about the pictures of the social divisions embedded in each story?

TONI CADE BAMBARA   (1939–1995)

THE LESSON   1972

Back in the days when everyone was old and stupid or young and foolish and me and Sugar were the only ones just right, this lady moved on our block with nappy hair and proper speech and no makeup. And quite naturally we laughed at her, laughed the way we did at the junk man who went about his business like he was some big-time president and his sorry-ass horse his secretary. And we kinda hated her too, hated the way we did the winos who cluttered up our parks and pissed on our handball walls and stank up our hallways and stairs so you couldn't halfway play hide-and-seek without a goddamn gas mask. Miss Moore was her name. The only woman on the block with no first name. And she was black as hell, cept for her feet, which were fish-white and spooky. And she was always planning these boring-ass things for us to do, us being my cousin, mostly, who lived on the block cause we all moved North the same time and to the same apartment then spread out gradual to breathe. And our parents would yank our heads into some kinda shape and crisp up our clothes so we'd be presentable for travel with Miss Moore, who always looked like she was going to church, though she never did. Which is just one of the things the grownups talked about when they talked behind her back like a dog. But when she came calling with some sachet she'd sewed up or some gingerbread she'd made or some book, why then they'd all be too embarrassed to turn her down and we'd get handed over all spruced up. She'd been to college and said it was only right that she should take responsibility for the young ones' education, and she not even related by marriage or blood. So they'd go for it. Specially Aunt Gretchen. She was the main gofer in the family. You got some old dumb shit foolishness you want somebody to go for, you send for Aunt Gretchen. She been screwed into the go-along for so long, it's a blood-deep natural thing with her. Which is how she got saddled with me and Sugar and Junior in the first place while our mothers were in a la-de-da apartment up the block having a good ole time.

So this one day Miss Moore rounds us all up at the mailbox and it's puredee hot and she's knockin herself out about arithmetic. And school suppose to let up in summer I heard, but she don't never let up. And the starch in my pinafore scratching the shit outta me and I'm really hating this nappy-head bitch and her goddamn college degree. I'd much rather go to the pool or to the show where it's cool. So me and Sugar leaning on the mailbox being surly, which is a Miss Moore word. And Flyboy checking out what everybody brought for lunch. And Fat Butt already wasting his peanut-butter-and-jelly sandwich like the pig he is. And Junebug punchin on Q.T.'s arm for potato chips. And Rosie Giraffe shifting from one hip to the other waiting for somebody to step on her foot or ask her if she from Georgia so she can kick ass, preferably Mercedes'. And Miss Moore asking us do we know what money is, like we a bunch of retards. I mean real money, she say, like it's only poker chips or monopoly papers we lay on the grocer. So right away I'm tired of this and say so. And would much rather snatch Sugar and go to the Sunset and terrorize the West Indian kids and take their hair ribbons and their money too. And Miss Moore files that remark away for next week's lesson on brotherhood, I can tell. And finally I say we oughta get to the subway cause it's cooler and besides we might meet some cute boys. Sugar done swiped her mama's lipstick, so we ready.

So we heading down the street and she's boring us silly about what things cost and what our parents make and how much goes for rent and how money ain't divided up right in this country. And then she gets to the part about we all poor and live in the slums, which I don't feature. And I'm ready to speak on that, but she steps out in the street and hails two cabs just like that. Then she hustles half the crew in with her and hands me a five-dollar bill and tells me to calculate 10 percent tip for the driver. And we're off. Me and Sugar and Junebug and Flyboy hangin out the window and hollering to everybody, putting lipstick on each other cause Flyboy a faggot anyway, and making farts with our sweaty armpits. But I'm mostly trying to figure how to spend this money. But they all fascinated with the meter ticking and Junebug starts laying bets as to how much it'll read when Flyboy can't hold his breath no more. Then Sugar lays bets as to how much it'll be when we get there. So I'm stuck. Don't nobody want to go for my plan, which is to jump out at the next light and run off to the first bar-b-que we can find. Then the driver tells us to get the hell out cause we there already. And the meter reads eighty-five cents. And I'm stalling to figure out the tip and Sugar say give him a dime. And I decide he don't need it bad as I do, so later for him. But then he tries to take off with Junebug foot still in the door so we talk about his mama something ferocious. Then we check out that we on Fifth Avenue and everybody dressed up in stockings. One lady in a fur coat, hot as it is. White folks crazy.

"This is the place," Miss Moore say, presenting it to us in the voice she uses at the museum. "Let's look in the windows before we go in."

"Can we steal?" Sugar asks very serious like she's getting the ground rules 5 squared away before she plays. "I beg your pardon," say Miss Moore, and we fall out. So she leads us around the windows of the toy store and me and Sugar screamin, "This is mine, that's mine, I gotta have that, that was made for me, I was born for that," till Big Butt drowns us out.

"Hey, I'm goin to buy that there."

"That there? You don't even know what it is, stupid."

"I do so," he say punchin on Rosie Giraffe. "It's a microscope."

"Whatcha gonna do with a microscope, fool?"

"Look at things." 10

"Like what, Ronald?" ask Miss Moore. And Big Butt ain't got the first notion. So here go Miss Moore gabbing about the thousands of bacteria in a drop of water and the somethinorother in a speck of blood and the million and one living things in the air around us is invisible to the naked eye. And what she say that for? Junebug go to town on that "naked" and we rolling. Then Miss Moore ask what it cost. So we all jam into the window smudgin it up and the price tag say $300. So then she ask how long'd take for Big Butt and Junebug to save up their allowances. "Too long," I say. "Yeh," adds Sugar, "outgrown it by that time." And Miss Moore say no, you never outgrow learning instruments. "Why, even medical students and interns and," blah, blah, blah. And we ready to choke Big Butt for bringing it up in the first damn place.

"This here costs four hundred eighty dollars," say Rosie Giraffe. So we pile up all over her to see what she pointin out. My eyes tell me it's a chunk of glass cracked with something heavy, and different-color inks dripped into the splits, then the whole thing put into a oven or something. But for $480 it don't make sense.

"That's a paperweight made of semi-precious stones fused together under tremendous pressure," she explains slowly, with her hands doing the mining and all the factory work.

"So what's a paperweight?" asks Rosie Giraffe.

"To weigh paper with, dumbbell," say Flyboy, the wise man from the East. 15

"Not exactly," say Miss Moore, which is what she say when you warm or way off too. "It's to weigh paper down so it won't scatter and make your desk untidy." So right away me and Sugar curtsy to each other and then to Mercedes who is more the tidy type.

"We don't keep paper on top of the desk in my class," say Junebug, figuring Miss Moore crazy or lyin one.

"At home, then," she say. "Don't you have a calendar and pencil case and a blotter and a letter-opener on your desk at home where you do your homework?" And she know damn well what our homes look like cause she nosys around in them every chance she gets.

"I don't even have a desk," say Junebug. "Do we?"

"No. And I don't get no homework neither," says Big Butt. 20

"And I don't even have a home," say Flyboy like he do at school to keep the white folks off his back and sorry for him. Send this poor kid to camp posters, is his specialty.

"I do," says Mercedes. "I have a box of stationery on my desk and a picture of my cat. My godmother bought the stationery and the desk. There's a big rose on each sheet and the envelopes smell like roses."

"Who wants to know about your smelly-ass stationery," say Rosie Giraffe fore I can get my two cents in.

"It's important to have a work area all your own so that . . ."

"Will you look at this sailboat, please," say Flyboy, cuttin her off and pointin 25 to the thing like it was his. So once again we tumble all over each other to gaze at this magnificent thing in the toy store which is just big enough to maybe sail two kittens across the pond if you strap them to the posts tight. We all start reciting the price tag like we in assembly. "Handcrafted sailboat of fiberglass at one thousand one hundred ninety-five dollars."

"Unbelievable," I hear myself say and am really stunned. I read it again for myself just in case the group recitation put me in a trance. Same thing. For some reason this pisses me off. We look at Miss Moore and she lookin at us, waiting for I dunno what.

"Who'd pay all that when you can buy a sailboat set for a quarter at Pop's, a tube of glue for a dime, and a ball of string for eight cents? It must have a motor and a whole lot else besides," I say. "My sailboat cost me about fifty cents."

"But will it take water?" say Mercedes with her smart ass.

"Took mine to Alley Pond Park once," say Flyboy. "String broke. Lost it. Pity."

"Sailed mine in Central Park and it keeled over and sank. Had to ask my 30 father for another dollar."

"And you got the strap," laugh Big Butt. "The jerk didn't even have a string on it. My old man wailed on his behind."

Little Q.T. was staring hard at the sailboat and you could see he wanted it bad. But he too little and somebody'd just take it from him. So what the hell. "This boat for kids, Miss Moore?"

"Parents silly to buy something like that just to get all broke up," say Rosie Giraffe.

"That much money it should last forever," I figure.

"My father'd buy it for me if I wanted it." 35

"Your father, my ass," say Rosie Giraffe getting a chance to finally push Mercedes.

"Must be rich people shop here," say Q.T.

"You are a very bright boy," say Flyboy. "What was your first clue?" And he rap him on the head with the back of his knuckles, since Q.T. the only one he could get away with. Though Q.T. liable to come up behind you years later and get his licks in when you half expect it.

"What I want to know is," I says to Miss Moore though I never talk to her, I wouldn't give the bitch that satisfaction, "is how much a real boat costs? I figure a thousand'd get you a yacht any day."

"Why don't you check that out," she says, "and report back to the group?" 40 Which really pains my ass. If you gonna mess up a perfectly good swim day least you could do is have some answers. "Let's go in," she say like she got something up her sleeve. Only she don't lead the way. So me and Sugar turn the corner to where the entrance is, but when we get there I kinda hang back. Not that I'm scared, what's there to be afraid of, just a toy store. But I feel funny, shame. But what I got to be shamed about? Got as much right to go in as anybody. But somehow I can't seem to get hold of the door, so I step away for Sugar to lead. But she hangs back too. And I look at her and she looks at me and this is ridiculous. I mean, damn, I have never ever been shy about doing nothing or going nowhere. But then Mercedes steps up and then Rosie Giraffe and Big Butt crowd in behind and shove, and next thing we all stuffed into the doorway with only Mercedes squeezing past us, smoothing out her jumper and walking right down the aisle. Then the rest of us tumble in like a glued-together jigsaw done all wrong. And people lookin at us. And it's like the time me and Sugar crashed into the Catholic church on a dare. But once we got in there and everything so hushed and holy and the candles and the bowin and the handkerchiefs on all the drooping heads, I just couldn't go through with the plan. Which was for me to run up to the altar and do a tap dance while Sugar played the nose flute and messed around in the holy water. And Sugar kept givin me the elbow. Then later teased me so bad I tied her up in the shower and turned it on and locked her in. And she'd be there till this day if Aunt Gretchen hadn't finally figured I was lyin about the boarder takin a shower.

Same thing in the store. We all walkin on tiptoe and hardly touchin the games and puzzles and things. And I watched Miss Moore who is steady watchin us like she waitin for a sign. Like Mama Drewery watches the sky and sniffs the air and takes note of just how much slant is in the bird formation. Then me and Sugar bump smack into each other, so busy gazing at the toys, 'specially the sailboat. But we don't laugh and go into our fat-lady bump-stomach routine. We just stare at that price tag. Then Sugar run a finger over the whole boat. And I'm jealous and want to hit her. Maybe not her, but I sure want to punch somebody in the mouth.

"Watcha bring us here for, Miss Moore?"

"You sound angry, Sylvia. Are you mad about something?" Givin me one of them grins like she tellin a grown-up joke that never turns out to be funny. And she's lookin very closely at me like maybe she planning to do my portrait from memory. I'm mad, but I won't give her that satisfaction. So I slouch around the store bein very bored and say, "Let's go."

Me and Sugar at the back of the train watchin the tracks whizzin by large then small then gettin gobbled up in the dark. I'm thinkin about this tricky toy I saw in the store. A clown that somersaults on a bar then does chin-ups just cause you yank lightly at his leg. Cost $35. I could see me askin my mother for a $35 birthday clown. "You wanna who that costs what?" she'd say, cocking her head to the side to get a better view of the hole in my head. Thirty-five dollars could buy new bunk beds for Junior and Gretchen's boy. Thirty-five dollars and the whole household could go visit Granddaddy Nelson in the country. Thirty-five dollars would pay for the rent and the piano bill too. Who are these people that spend that much for performing clowns and $1000 for toy sailboats? What kinda work they do and how they live and how come we ain't in on it? Where we are is who we are, Miss Moore always pointin out. But it don't necessarily have to be that way, she always adds then waits for somebody to say that poor people have to wake up and demand their share of the pie and don't none of us know what kind of pie she talking about in the first damn place. But she ain't so smart cause I still got her four dollars from the taxi and she sure ain't gettin it. Messin up my day with this shit. Sugar nudges me in my pocket and winks.

Miss Moore lines us up in front of the mailbox where we started from, seem like years ago, and I got a headache for thinkin so hard. And we lean all over each other 45 so we can hold up under the draggy-ass lecture she always finishes us off with at the end before we thank her for borin us to tears. But she just looks at us like she readin tea leaves. Finally she say, "Well, what did you think of F.A.O. Schwarz?"

Rosie Giraffe mumbles, "White folks crazy."

"I'd like to go there again when I get my birthday money," says Mercedes, and we shove her out the pack so she has to lean on the mailbox by herself.

"I'd like a shower. Tiring day," say Flyboy.

Then Sugar surprises me by sayin, "You know, Miss Moore, I don't think all of us here put together eat in a year what that sailboat costs." And Miss Moore lights up like somebody goosed her. "And?" she say, urging Sugar on. Only I'm standin on her foot so she don't continue.

"Imagine for a minute what kind of society it is in which some people can 50 spend on a toy what it would cost to feed a family of six or seven. What do you think?"

"I think," say Sugar pushing me off her feet like she never done before, cause I whip her ass in a minute, "that this is not much of a democracy if you ask me. Equal chance to pursue happiness means an equal crack at the dough, don't it?" Miss Moore is besides herself and I am disgusted with Sugar's treachery. So I stand on her foot one more time to see if she'll shove me. She shuts up, and Miss Moore looks at me, sorrowfully I'm thinkin. And somethin weird is goin on, I can feel it in my chest.

"Anybody else learn anything today?" lookin dead at me. I walk away and Sugar has to run to catch up and don't even seem to notice when I shrug her arm off my shoulder.

"Well, we got four dollars anyway," she says.

"Uh hunh."

"We could go to Hascombs and get half a chocolate layer and then go to the 55 Sunset and still have plenty money for potato chips and ice cream sodas."

"Un hunh."

"Race you to Hascombs," she say.

We start down the block and she gets ahead which is O.K. by me cause I'm going to the West End and then over to the Drive to think this day through. She can run if she want to and even run faster. But ain't nobody gonna beat me at nuthin.

FOR ANALYSIS

1. What are Sylvia's outstanding traits? How are they reflected in her language and in her description of her neighborhood?

2. How is Sylvia's **character** revealed through her relationship with Sugar?

3. Describe the lesson Miss Moore tries to teach the children by taking them to visit F.A.O. Schwarz.

4. How is Sylvia's assessment of Miss Moore at the beginning of the story borne out by the ending?

5. What evidence is there that Sylvia has been changed by the visit to F.A.O. Schwarz?

MAKING ARGUMENTS

Write an essay arguing for or against the proposition that "The Lesson" ends optimistically.

WRITING TOPIC

In your opinion, is Sylvia a reliable or unreliable **narrator**? Why or why not?

MAKING CONNECTIONS

1. Compare and contrast the use of the **first-person narrator** in this story with that in Updike's "A & P" (p. 92).

2. In "Commencement Speech, Kenyon College" (p. 309), David Foster Wallace implies that an individual's moral sense can come not as much from his religion or her upbringing but from a conscious effort to step outside of oneself and empathize, to think about how it feels to be other kinds of people. Sylvia's moral sense is likewise awakened in "The Lesson." Though Wallace's speech is about something else entirely, can we use it to help us think about Sylvia's sense of right and wrong? Where does it come from? How is it awakened? Do you have any sense if this awakening is temporary or longer-lasting?

JAMAICA KINCAID (B. 1949)

GIRL (1983)

Wash the white clothes on Monday and put them on the stone heap; wash the color clothes on Tuesday and put them on the clothesline to dry; don't walk barehead in the hot sun; cook pumpkin fritters in very hot sweet oil; soak your little clothes right after you take them off; when buying cotton to make yourself a nice blouse, be sure that it doesn't have gum on it, because that way it won't hold up well after a wash; soak salt fish overnight before you cook it; is it true that you sing benna[1] in Sunday school?; always eat your food in such a way that it won't turn someone else's stomach; on Sundays try to walk like a lady and not like the slut you are so bent on becoming; don't sing benna in Sunday school; you mustn't speak to wharf-rat boys, not even to give directions; don't eat fruits on the street—flies will follow you; *but I don't sing benna on Sundays at all and never in Sunday school*; this is how to sew on a button; this is how to make a button-hole for the button you have just sewed on; this is how to hem a dress when you see the hem coming down and so to prevent yourself from looking like the slut I know you are so bent on becoming; this is how you iron your father's khaki shirt so that it doesn't have a crease; this is how you iron your father's khaki pants so that they don't have a crease; this is how you grow okra—far from the house, because okra tree harbors red ants; when you are growing dasheen,[2] make sure it gets plenty of water or else it makes your throat itch when you are eating it; this is how you sweep a corner; this is how you sweep a whole house; this is how you sweep a yard; this is how you smile to someone you don't like too much; this is how you set a table for dinner with an important guest; this is how you smile to someone you don't like at all; this is how you smile to someone you like completely; this is how you set a table for tea; this is how you set a table for dinner; this is how you set a table for lunch; this is how you set a table for breakfast; this is how to behave in the presence of men who don't know you very well, and this way they won't recognize immediately the slut I have warned you against becoming; be sure to wash every day, even if it is with your own spit; don't squat down to play marbles—you are not a boy, you know; don't pick people's flowers—you might catch something; don't throw stones at blackbirds, because it might not be a blackbird at all; this is how to make a bread pudding; this is how to make doukona;[3] this is how to make pepper pot; this is how to make a good medicine for a cold; this is how to make a good medicine to

[1] Calypso music.
[2] Taro root.
[3] Spicy plantain pudding.

throw away a child before it even becomes a child; this is how to catch a fish; this is how to throw back a fish you don't like, and that way something bad won't fall on you; this is how to bully a man; this is how a man bullies you; this is how to love a man, and if this doesn't work there are other ways, and if they don't work don't feel too bad about giving up; this is how to spit up in the air if you feel like it, and this is how to move quick so that it doesn't fall on you;   40 this is how to make ends meet; always squeeze bread to make sure it's fresh; *but what if the baker won't let me feel the bread?*; you mean to say that after all you are really going to be the kind of woman who the baker won't let near the bread?

FOR ANALYSIS

1. What does the title of this piece suggest?

2. Who is the speaker? To whom is she speaking?

3. What kind of "girl" is the advice intended to produce?

4. What is the speaker's biggest fear?

5. Are the girl's two responses spoken aloud to the speaker, or are they only the girl's thoughts? Explain.

6. What do the girl's two responses suggest about her relationship to the speaker?

MAKING ARGUMENTS

Try to imagine Kincaid writing "Girl" as a more traditional story, with **exposition** and **plot** and **dialogue**. Then argue that the traditional version would be either more or less effective than the way she actually chose to write it.

WRITING TOPICS

1. List the advice you received from your parents and other elders, and write a paragraph in imitation of Kincaid's piece.

2. Examine the details that constitute the advice in this story. What kind of society and culture do these details seem to suggest?

MAKING CONNECTIONS

1. Compare the girl in this story with Sylvia, the **narrator** of Bambara's "The Lesson" (p. 98).

2. Describe the speaker in this story, and then compare the speaker with the father in Peter Meinke's poem "Advice to My Son" (p. 200). How do they differ? Do they share any qualities?

DANIEL OROZCO   (B. 1942)

ORIENTATION   1998

Those are the offices and these are the cubicles. That's my cubicle there, and this is your cubicle. This is your phone. Never answer your phone. Let the Voicemail System answer it. This is your Voicemail System Manual. There are no personal phone calls allowed. We do, however, allow for emergencies. If you must make an emergency phone call, ask your supervisor first. If you can't find your supervisor, ask Phillip Spiers, who sits over there. He'll check with Clarissa Nicks, who sits over there. If you make an emergency phone call without asking, you may be let go.

These are your IN and OUT boxes. All the forms in your IN box must be logged in by the date shown in the upper left-hand corner, initialed by you in the upper right-hand corner, and distributed to the Processing Analyst whose name is numerically coded in the lower left-hand corner. The lower right-hand corner is left blank. Here's your Processing Analyst Numerical Code Index. And here's your Forms Processing Procedures Manual.

You must pace your work. What do I mean? I'm glad you asked that. We pace our work according to the eight-hour workday. If you have twelve hours of work in your IN box, for example, you must compress that work into the eight-hour day. If you have one hour of work in your IN box, you must expand that work to fill the eight-hour day. That was a good question. Feel free to ask questions. Ask too many questions, however, and you may be let go.

That is our receptionist. She is a temp. We go through receptionists here. They quit with alarming frequency. Be polite and civil to the temps. Learn their names, and invite them to lunch occasionally. But don't get close to them, as it only makes it more difficult when they leave. And they always leave. You can be sure of that.

The men's room is over there. The women's room is over there. John LaFountaine, who sits over there, uses the women's room occasionally. He says it is accidental. We know better, but we let it pass. John LaFountaine is harmless, his forays into the forbidden territory of the women's room simply a benign thrill, a faint blip on the dull flat line of his life. 5

Russell Nash, who sits in the cubicle to your left, is in love with Amanda Pierce, who sits in the cubicle to your right. They ride the same bus together after work. For Amanda Pierce, it is just a tedious bus ride made less tedious by the idle nattering of Russell Nash. But for Russell Nash, it is the highlight of his day. It is the highlight of his life. Russell Nash has put on forty pounds, and grows fatter with each passing month, nibbling on chips and cookies while peeking glumly over the partitions at Amanda Pierce, and gorging himself at home on cold pizza and ice cream while watching adult videos on TV.

Amanda Pierce, in the cubicle to your right, has a six-year-old son named Jamie, who is autistic. Her cubicle is plastered from top to bottom with the boy's crayon artwork—sheet after sheet of precisely drawn concentric circles and ellipses, in black and yellow. She rotates them every other Friday. Be sure to comment on them. Amanda Pierce also has a husband, who is a lawyer. He subjects her to an escalating array of painful and humiliating sex games, to which Amanda Pierce reluctantly submits. She comes to work exhausted and freshly wounded each morning, wincing from the abrasions on her breasts, or the bruises on her abdomen, or the second-degree burns on the backs of her thighs.

But we're not supposed to know any of this. Do not let on. If you let on, you may be let go.

Amanda Pierce, who tolerates Russell Nash, is in love with Albert Bosch, whose office is over there. Albert Bosch, who only dimly registers Amanda Pierce's existence, has eyes only for Ellie Tapper, who sits over there. Ellie Tapper, who hates Albert Bosch, would walk through fire for Curtis Lance. But Curtis Lance hates Ellie Tapper. Isn't the world a funny place? Not in the ha-ha sense, of course.

Anika Bloom sits in that cubicle. Last year, while reviewing quarterly reports 10 in a meeting with Barry Hacker, Anika Bloom's left palm began to bleed. She fell into a trance, stared into her hand, and told Barry Hacker when and how his wife would die. We laughed it off. She was, after all, a new employee. But Barry Hacker's wife is dead. So unless you want to know exactly when and how you'll die, never talk to Anika Bloom.

Colin Heavey sits in that cubicle over there. He was new once, just like you. We warned him about Anika Bloom. But at last year's Christmas Potluck, he felt sorry for her when he saw that no one was talking to her. Colin Heavey brought her a drink. He hasn't been himself since. Colin Heavey is doomed. There's nothing he can do about it, and we are powerless to help him. Stay away from Colin Heavey. Never give any of your work to him. If he asks to do something, tell him you have to check with me. If he asks again, tell him I haven't gotten back to you.

This is the Fire Exit. There are several on this floor, and they are marked accordingly. We have a Floor Evacuation Review every three months, and an Escape Route Quiz once a month. We have our Biannual Fire Drill twice a year, and our Annual Earthquake Drill once a year. These are precautions only. These things never happen.

For your information, we have a comprehensive health plan. Any catastrophic illness, any unforeseen tragedy is completely covered. All dependents are completely covered. Larry Bagdikian, who sits over there, has six daughters. If anything were to happen to any of his girls, or to all of them, if all six were to simultaneously fall victim to illness or injury—stricken with a hideous degenerative muscle disease or some rare toxic blood disorder, sprayed with semiautomatic gunfire while on a class field trip, or attacked in their bunk beds by some prowling nocturnal lunatic—if any of this were to pass, Larry's girls would all be taken care of. Larry Bagdikian would not have to pay one dime. He would have nothing to worry about.

We also have a generous vacation and sick leave policy. We have an excellent disability insurance plan. We have a stable and profitable pension fund. We get group discounts for the symphony, and block seating at the ballpark. We get commuter ticket books for the bridge. We have Direct Deposit. We are all members of Costco.

This is our kitchenette. And this, this is our Mr. Coffee. We have a coffee 15 pool, into which we each pay two dollars a week for coffee, filters, sugar, and CoffeeMate. If you prefer Cremora or half-and-half to CoffeeMate, there is a special pool for three dollars a week. If you prefer Sweet'n Low to sugar, there is a special pool for two-fifty a week. We do not do decaf. You are allowed to join the coffee pool of your choice, but you are not allowed to touch the Mr. Coffee.

This is the microwave oven. You are allowed to *heat* food in the microwave oven. You are not, however, allowed to *cook* food in the microwave oven.

We get one hour for lunch. We also get one fifteen-minute break in the morning, and one fifteen-minute break in the afternoon. Always take your breaks. If you skip a break, it is gone forever. For your information, your break is a privilege, not a right. If you abuse the break policy, we are authorized to rescind your breaks. Lunch, however, is a right, not a privilege. If you abuse the lunch policy, our hands will be tied, and we will be forced to look the other way. We will not enjoy that.

This is the refrigerator. You may put your lunch in it. Barry Hacker, who sits over there, steals food from this refrigerator. His petty theft is an outlet for his grief. Last New Year's Eve, while kissing his wife, a blood vessel burst in her brain. Barry Hacker's wife was two months pregnant at the time, and lingered in a coma for half a year before dying. It was a tragic loss for Barry Hacker. He hasn't been himself since. Barry Hacker's wife was a beautiful woman. She was also completely covered. Barry Hacker did not have to pay one dime. But his dead wife haunts him. She haunts all of us. We have seen her, reflected in the monitors of our computers, moving past our cubicles. We have seen the dim shadow of her face in our photocopies. She pencils herself in in the receptionist's appointment book, with the notation: To see Barry Hacker. She has left messages in the receptionist's Voicemail box, messages garbled by the electronic chirrups and buzzes in the phone line, her voice echoing from an immense distance within the ambient hum. But the voice is hers. And beneath her voice, beneath the tidal *whoosh* of static and hiss, the gurgling and crying of a baby can be heard.

In any case, if you bring a lunch, put a little something extra in the bag for Barry Hacker. We have four Barrys in this office. Isn't that a coincidence?

This is Matthew Payne's office. He is our Unit Manager, and his door is 20 always closed. We have never seen him, and you will never see him. But he is here. You can be sure of that. He is all around us.

This is the Custodian's Closet. You have no business in the Custodian's Closet.

And this, this is our Supplies Cabinet. If you need supplies, see Curtis Lance. He will log you in on the Supplies Cabinet Authorization Log, then give you a Supplies Authorization Slip. Present your pink copy of the Supplies Authorization Slip to Ellie Tapper. She will log you in on the Supplies Cabinet Key Log, then give you the key. Because the Supplies Cabinet is located outside the Unit Manager's office, you must be very quiet. Gather your supplies quietly. The Supplies Cabinet is divided into four sections. Section One contains letterhead stationery, blank paper and envelopes, memo and note pads, and so on. Section Two contains pens and pencils and typewriter and printer ribbons, and the like. In Section Three we have erasers, correction fluids, transparent tapes, glue sticks, et cetera. And in Section Four we have paper clips and push pins and scissors and razor blades. And here are the spare blades for the shredder. Do not touch the shredder, which is located over there. The shredder is of no concern to you.

Gwendolyn Stich sits in that office there. She is crazy about penguins, and collects penguin knickknacks: penguin posters and coffee mugs and stationery, penguin stuffed animals, penguin jewelry, penguin sweaters and T-shirts and socks. She has a pair of penguin fuzzy slippers she wears when working late at the office. She has a tape cassette of penguin sounds which she listens to for relaxation. Her favorite colors are black and white. She has personalized license plates that read PEN GWEN. Every morning, she passes through all the cubicles to wish each of us a *good* morning. She brings Danish on Wednesdays for Hump Day morning break, and doughnuts on Fridays for TGIF afternoon break. She organizes the Annual Christmas Potluck, and is in charge of the Birthday List. Gwendolyn Stich's door is always open to all of us. She will always lend an ear, and put in a good word for you; she will always give you a hand, or the shirt off her back, or a shoulder to cry on. Because her door is always open, she hides and cries in a stall in the women's room. And John LaFountaine—who, enthralled when a woman enters, sits quietly in his stall with his knees to his chest—John LaFountaine has heard her vomiting in there. We have come upon Gwendolyn Stich huddled in the stairwell, shivering in the updraft, sipping a Diet Mr. Pibb and hugging her knees. She does not let any of this interfere with her work. If it interfered with her work, she might have to be let go.

Kevin Howard sits in that cubicle over there. He is a serial killer, the one they call the Carpet Cutter, responsible for the mutilations across town. We're not supposed to know that, so do not let on. Don't worry. His compulsion inflicts itself on strangers only, and the routine established is elaborate and unwavering. The victim must be a white male, a young adult no older than thirty, heavyset, with dark hair and eyes, and the like. The victim must be chosen at random, before sunset, from a public place; the victim is followed home, and must put up a struggle; et cetera. The carnage inflicted is precise: the angle and direction of the incisions; the layering of skin and muscle tissue; the rearrangement of the visceral organs; and so on. Kevin Howard does not let any of this interfere with his work. He is, in fact, our fastest typist. He types as if he were on fire. He has a secret crush on Gwendolyn Stich, and leaves a red-foil-wrapped Hershey's Kiss on her desk every afternoon. But he hates Anika Bloom, and keeps well away from her. In his presence, she has uncontrollable fits of shaking and trembling. Her left palm does not stop bleeding.

In any case, when Kevin Howard gets caught, act surprised. Say that he 25 seemed like a nice person, a bit of a loner, perhaps, but always quiet and polite.

This is the photocopier room. And this, this is our view. It faces southwest. West is down there, toward the water. North is back there. Because we are on the seventeenth floor, we are afforded a magnificent view. Isn't it beautiful? It overlooks the park, where the tops of those trees are. You can see a segment of the bay between those two buildings there. You can see the sun set in the gap between those two buildings over there. You can see this building reflected in the glass panels of that building across the way. There. See? That's you, waving. And look there. There's Anika Bloom in the kitchenette, waving back.

Enjoy this view while photocopying. If you have problems with the photocopier, see Russell Nash. If you have any questions, ask your supervisor. If you can't find your supervisor, ask Phillip Spiers. He sits over there. He'll check with Clarissa Nicks. She sits over there. If you can't find them, feel free to ask me. That's my cubicle. I sit in there.

FOR ANALYSIS

1. Who is the **narrator** in "Orientation"? What do you know about this person? What do you not know? Why do you think Orozco tells us what he does—and, omits what he does—about the narrator's identity?

2. What kind of workplace is this? What sort of work do the employees do there? How do they seem to feel about their work? How do you know?

3. How is this story structured? What can you say about the **plot**? Does a storyline develop from beginning to end? What drives the story along?

4. How would you describe the **tone** of "Orientation"? Is it uniform, or varied? If varied, between what tones does it move, and to what effect?

5. What **themes** arise in this story? Are they specific to the story's setting, or might they be more widely applied? If so, how?

MAKING ARGUMENTS

Starting from one of two propositions—that you never want to work in an office or that you would like to end up in a career in which you work in an office—argue that reading "Orientation" either confirms your desire or makes you question it (and not just for you, but for anyone who shares your inclination/disinclination).

WRITING TOPICS

1. Describe your feelings about a workplace in which you have been employed. (If you have never worked, describe a place that embodies your ideas about what a workplace might be like—the good things and the things you fear or wish to avoid.) How do your feelings about this real or imagined workplace connect to your ideas about what work should be like? How do you think people should feel about the place in which they spend a significant chunk of their waking hours?

2. Write a short piece in which you orient your readers to a place or situation and tell them what they need to know about it and how to act there. What are the difficulties of such an approach? What does it allow you to do?

MAKING CONNECTIONS

1. Compare and contrast "Orientation" to Hawthorne's "Young Goodman Brown" (p. 77) in terms of their commitment to representing reality. How does each draw a picture of life as it really is, or seems to be? How does each diverge from that kind of picture?

2. Read "Orientation" against Kincaid's "Girl" (p. 105) for the way both speak in imperatives. What kinds of things are their **narrators** telling their audience to do? What effects do they achieve by addressing their audience in this way?

CAMDEN JOY (B. 1964)

DUM DUM BOYS 2002

The thing I remember about Cameron—he would start smiling as soon as you'd start talking to him. Can't remember a single conversation we ever had, just remember him smiling. Don't think he knew he was smiling, it just happened, he couldn't help it, couldn't help but trust you, couldn't help but smile at you just for talking to him, watching you with his perfectly round blue-grey eyes, eyes the color of the Civil War, and when you got mid-sentence those eyes would open wider, momentarily surprised, then go back to watching, patiently waiting out your sarcasm with a disarming smile, slim good looks, a little stoned, leaning back, waiting on you to make him laugh, to earn that smile of his, to send his mouth open with laughter, his mouth with those perfect teeth.

Cameron and I first met when we were thirteen, and he alone remained as my comrade from junior high into high school, whereas my other pals of that time were lost along the way to the marching band or the swim team or the yearbook committee or the drama club. Together Cameron and I avoided the lure of school-sponsored activities. "You're running," we'd smirk at some former friend whom we'd catch training for a track and field event. They'd glance up dazed, their expression flushed, looking near death, sweat-covered, short of breath, their bodies ruddy, almost naked in those trim jerseys and gym shorts. Cameron and I would be warmly dressed as usual, long pants, trench coats preserving a pasty pallor. "What are you running *from*?" He and I distrusted the sudden crop of boring new pals one found following such pursuits. We were the only guys who by ninth grade had advanced to spray painting punk rock graffiti, gouging "Flipper" or "Nervous Gender" into the lacquered tops of school desks while our former buddies were still carving nonsense like "REO Speedwagon" or "Boston" or "The Wall." Eventually we met others who sympathized with our graffiti, who also lacked affiliations with any extra-curricular projects, and these became our new friends.

Cameron wrote a song on the guitar I lent him, the beat-up tomato-red Fender Duo-Sonic I bought off the dentist's son for $25. You can hear that model of guitar a lot nowadays, a toy-sized treble-rich guitar with no sustain. I let that guitar of mine go for almost nothing; starved for cash and desperate to get out of my hometown I, against my better judgment, hauled the Duo-Sonic into the music store, where they pointed at this and that defect and—positive that I was fencing stolen goods—said they could only offer me $60 for it. I took their money, then later heard that the Duo-Sonic was in their window— "a classic antique"—wearing a $490 price tag.

I attempted to teach Cameron to play that guitar in my parent's garage after school, weekdays, tried to turn him into a band member, but frankly he wasn't

113

very adept. His interest in guitar technique was quashed after meeting Greg of the Circle Jerks. Greg told him about the "Magic Chord," told him that you need just two fingers, that you finger the roots of the bar chord, pluck those strings together very fast, turn the amplifier to full distortion, and everyone will feel you're plenty talented. Greg had Cameron convinced that the rest of the guitar—the other four strings, the pick-up switches and bass/treble knobs—were made for wussy jazz and that no one who played rock and roll should touch them.

So Cameron wrote a song, sorta like you'd imagine, a fast distorted 4/4 hard- core basher which was played on only two strings, with Cameron just shifting the Magic Chord up and down the frets every half-measure. The song had no melody, no words, no title; we covered it, my band, long after Cameron stopped showing up for our garage rehearsals, and we dubbed it "Cameron's Song" in his honor but I doubt he ever came and saw us and I'm not certain, even if he had, whether he would have recognized the piece.

The thing I remember about giving him guitar lessons is Cameron smiling at me the whole time, nodding enthusiastically with a short "Okay, okay" each time I'd show him something.

"You want to hold your pick—"

"Okay, okay."

"Like this."

"Okay, okay."

We'd take our fake identification cards and together go to shows at the Starwood or the Whisky or the Cuckoo's Nest where the headliners dressed as we dressed, plain jeans, normal tee shirts, short hair, where the singers couldn't be heard above the instruments though they screamed themselves hoarse trying, their bent-up mouths appearing like dark wounds gashed into their pallid faces, features in terrific pain, the musicians brazenly using made-up names like "Jello" and "Smear," "Zoom" and "Crash." Our favorite singer was named Dinah Cancer, our favorite bassist Derf Scratch, our favorite drummer D.J. Bonebrake. Occasionally, Cameron and I would come out having favored different folks on the bill—he'd generally enjoy no-nonsense barrage, I'd prefer stronger melodies, better words. But still, we went to the gigs together, endured them all the way through, and to my mind that was the important part, the part that truly made us friends.

My mother calls and I'm immediately suspicious. I haven't been home in some time, and I know she's anxious to see me, to draw me back any way she can, to position me there, a permanent cushion between her and my little sister. But this time she doesn't sound that way at all; she just isn't sure I've seen the news. It has been drizzling in my hometown for weeks and now the storms are intensifying. Flash flood warnings have closed down most of the local campgrounds, including one located just a quarter-mile from my parent's house, the house I grew up in. In recent years, maybe due to the campground's proximity to freight tracks and the main highway, this particular site has housed a steady flow of unpaying inhabitants—drifters and runaways, migrant workers and homeless, their belongings in milk-crates, their tents improvised out of painter's tarps, their laundry draped like Christmas ornaments over the oleander. This campground straddles a dry creekbed, a broad sand ditch lined with pepper trees where my friends and I would hunt for fossils on summer afternoons.

A few weeks each winter the creekbed fills to capacity with roiling waters, the overflow from mountain dams located high over us in the Condor Sanctuary, rushing thousands of feet down, racing and scurrying and taking along gnarled husks of fallen oak and trunks of pine, turning the logs over and over in haste, momentum growing, a crashing river hiding within its foam so many half-visible scraps of weighty things that standing on the bank you might glimpse the top of a stove or a closet full of clothes or a sheared-off car door drifting by, strewn with uprooted tumbleweeds and greasewood.

Mom explains that the sheriff scoured the campground after the flash flood warning and removed all the transients, hauling them to higher ground, to safety. But the sheriff had inadvertently missed an occupant, some deranged man, a homeless guy, who drowned soon after in the middle of the night when the river burst its banks, water inundating the site with such force that trash cans and picnic tables were picked up and carried nearly ten miles downstream, washed almost to the beach.

In the obituary my mother was surprised to read that the dead man had actu- 15 ally been quite young, was a recent graduate from our local high school. She thought I might have known him because we were the same age, graduated the same year. His name sounds familiar to her. Didn't you know some boy, she asks, named Cam-something, whose last name was Joyce?

Cameron was the kind of kid who reassured parents, easy-going, amiable, even ingenuous, and mean to no one but himself. It used to offend me when I read of people being warned against punk's amorality and anti-ethics because though I often considered myself passionately bankrupt of values, devoutly bored with manners, wonderfully unimpressed with most any grown-up, still this did not seem true of Cameron, who was another kind of punk altogether, irregular, inconsistent, unreliable, yes, but shy too, always kind, civilized.

I would laugh at those anguished predictions about kids my age when I thought of Cameron, riding his quietly pleasant Vespa scooter around the sun-drenched valley, overdressed in his fishtail Union Jack parka with the fur-lined hood.

Tell Cameron not to do something and he wouldn't, whereas most of the rest of us would out of spite. They'd tell us not to skateboard over the pads in front of the automatic doors at the grocery store, they'd tell us time and again, not realizing the more they told us the more fun it was; but Cameron wouldn't do it, they asked him not to and he abruptly lost interest in it.

And yet Cameron was more complicated than that too, for he came along with us when we sourly stalked the school halls, my few friends and me, and any people we passed whom we didn't like we would nod at, declare "After the revolution . . .", and then draw a finger across our throat. And we liked almost none of them, not teachers, not students, and gradually we amassed detailed plans to kill most every one of them.

Leaning on our favorite wall of combination lockers, close to the edge of 20 campus, some of us crouched, positioned so that the wall supported only our heads, others standing, one knee bent, we would proudly pass around well-worn copies of berserk books whose scenarios fit us more comfortably than high school, although I must point out that in this Cameron was not one of us, he never ascribed to these bibles of ours. Cameron's rebel status—the reason he sought the company of petty thieves, liars, and braggarts like us—was more intuitive, less thought-out; he did not internalize, the way some of us did, the distant romance of anomie-struck youth in holy literature; Cameron in a sense wrote his own story, which he kept to himself and told none of us, and he shrugged away the books and essays we'd offer while smiling patiently, tall and lean, seldom speaking, eventually pushing off from our favorite wall, waving a small "so long" at us without pulling his hands from the deep pockets of his parka, and then putt-putt-putting away on his polite white Vespa.

We would drive long distances together, all of us, in order to see any showings of *A Clockwork Orange* or *Quadrophenia*, films we knew every line of dialogue from. One of us would usually have stolen a half-gallon of alcohol from the back of some parent's liquor cabinet, that untouched chardonnay from Christmas long ago, that cognac which a grown-up was reserving for a special occasion, that fancy malt-something which adults keep for later, and we'd pass it back and forth during the film, sloppy and more alive there than anywhere, each of us Alex and each of us Jimmy, cocky, defiant, sexy, intoxicated, dismissive of authority. It seemed to us these films alone appreciated us. *Never Grow Old*, they insisted, for once mature you would be Jimmy, heartbroken over his return to Brighton, or Alex, helpless in the hands of well-meaning, bungling adults.

Stretched out in the theater darkness, warm in the bath of flickering light, I grew bold enough to reflect on how we boys turned out this way, our hearts like onions, like stones, and why so lost, why so lonely, got far enough in contemplating these concerns to recognize that such musings should proceed no further if I wanted us still to retain our camaraderie. So I would simply stop, suddenly and completely, and seek to forget that I had ever raised such imponderables, and maybe ask for the bottle to be passed down my way once more, and work to be drawn back again into the movie.

I tell my Mom that it's too bad about Cameron but that I'm doing fine and no, I won't be coming back for the memorial service. After that, weeks follow when I cannot quell my thoughts of Cameron. I am summoned home every few minutes by one memory or another. Every time I step into a hot bath I anticipate drowning. I begin to recognize Cameron's mannerisms in most everyone around me, every coat I see is a parka, every motorcycle a Vespa. At the video store, I linger over A Clockwork Orange, *finally decide to rent it, find I can't watch it anymore. The front window of my neighborhood record store advertises expensive digital remasterings from many of the bands we used to see, reissues of Twisted Roots and the B-People and Middle Class. And one night, digging through my drawers looking for a set of thumbtacks, I uncover instead the receipt for the Duo-Sonic,*

the guitar I sold after Cameron gave up on it, and the receipt is just a piece of
paper with a date and "$60.00" written on it but it holds my attention for an
hour until I sigh, pack my bags. Finally, I drive home.

I remember being with Cameron the first time he did black beauties. He
swallowed three, then insisted I haul him over to the Arastradero, this all-ages
disco at a nearby strip mall. There was no liquor allowed inside so Cameron
and I first sat out on the concrete block at the head of our parking space, me
drinking a shoplifted forty-ounce bumper of beer, Cameron jiggling a foot,
sharing very little of what he was experiencing. We were sixteen. Once inside,
I danced with this college student to one lame new wave hit after another—
"One Step Beyond" then "Planet Claire" then "Pump it Up." I felt like a goddamn martyr, faking my pleasure at these songs solely to have this girl come
out to the car with me. I looked across at Cameron, who sat beside the dance
floor, nervously tapping on a tabletop, utterly enraptured by the sight of the
Arastradero's rotating mirrored ball. "I got a bottle in the car," I told the girl,
and impulsively I grabbed her hand. "Let's go outside!"

Just then the start of "Heart of Glass" blasted onto the sound system.   25

"No way!" she shook me off. "And miss *this* song?"

She started her wiggling again so I just walked off, dragged Cameron out
with me. He revealed that he was seeing spiderweb bridges and stalactites,
asked me whether he was hallucinating, softly requested that we listen to some
soothing Muzak on the car radio. We drove to get chili at Bob's Big Boy. Cameron had his teeth gritted, no appetite. He set about methodically crunching
the crackers with the tips of his thumbs. He did this for some time, silent, suddenly stopped, looked up, squinted, tried to focus on me.

"I got our band name," he whispered. He couldn't stop blinking. "It's real
good."

We were forever working to name our band, spent more time on that than
rehearsing. I wasn't even sure that there was any band to name, but still I was
interested.

He had this clammy look about him, very pale, sort of stuck. "Memorial   30
Garage," he spoke thickly, wiped his nose, gazed off.

"You alright?"

He shuddered, didn't respond.

"You gonna be sick?"

He shook his head, leaned two slender fingers into his pale neck to check his
own pulse.

"Okay," I sighed. "Memorial Garage. Do you think maybe you can explain   35
it?"

He clamped shut his eyes, opened them, once more shook his head. "Just
Memorial Garage. That's all." I saw that he had started to cry. "Really you fucking gotta trust me on this, man."

My sister wears a Walkman to the dinner table, my dad asks for the pepper to
please be passed, my mom says she fluffed my pillows and my old room is ready.
My dad tells me my sister quit eighth grade flag football, my mom says my sister

should be able to do whatever she wants, the Walkman plays Alice in Chains. I can make out the high-end rattle of the percussion leaking out the headphones across the table, can't distinguish the band's voices from its instruments. My dad says of course of course and that's not what he meant, my mom asks who wants another helping of squash, my sister loudly announces she has to go use the phone right now. My dad frowns at my mom, my mom shrugs, they look at me. Alice in Chains ends, Primus starts. I ask if there's some reason they're both looking at me, and they go back to their plates.

Once I'm gone I can speak up, I can notice how everything they say misfires, bounces off, I can pinpoint unhealthy patterns, sour dynamics, but when I'm in it, when I'm at their dinner table, everything is a haze, familiar, aching, confused, I can be no one but their disappointing son, I can do nothing else but choke out the few lines I have recited my entire life and shake my head at how little I feel, how little I comprehend this act called dinner with my family.

I wonder what the hell they are doing wrong because I personally can't think of a thing and yet the fact is that Cameron went mad for drugs the same way I went mad for girls, the fact is that whether or not it was his and my parents—he and I both went mad. I have to question what else they could have done, what could have been lacking, for when we were small boys our folks were the sort who always endeavored to comfort us, to encourage us, they raised us to appreciate sunsets and exercise, they gave us a chance at churchliness, moved us to suburbs close to the beach (they proudly told us this was once an "alluvial flood plain"), they made us camp out in the backyard to show us meteor showers and point out the North Star, bought us paint sets and bicycles and magazine subscriptions, they taught us to recognize good kite-flying weather and to say thanks and stop at stop signs and read newspapers and enjoy public television, and they worked hard at their jobs—perhaps a little too absent, a little too preoccupied, this is true, but still they worked hard nonetheless.

But maybe there was something murderous about this work ethic of theirs, 40 *maybe that was the source of the problem, for I think of how they would read our adolescent Christmas lists like aggrieved parents reading a ransom note, too proud to admit that they could not afford our teenage demands, confident that they could completely buy us back if they only drove themselves harder, removed themselves a little more, stayed late at work for enough nights. And then something happened where they began to work so hard at times we hardly saw them, and it felt as if we were being purposely kept out of their sight, as if we had already in fact been kidnapped, and our parents confirmed this for they began to behave as if they, in turn, were already set on being blackmailed. All I know is, despite the attention lavished on our early upbringings, by the time we were as old as my little sister we wanted none of it, all any of us hoped for was an early death, a violent early death. Out of all of us happily only one got what he'd hoped for; sadly, that was Cameron.*

Cameron barely graduated, he was forever skipping school to cruise around on his Vespa or hitch-hike down to L.A. I think it can be accurately claimed that as his friends we had more to do with his graduating than he ever did, for I believe that he got out of high school mainly due to the gullibility of teachers who believed the stories we fed them, the endless excuses we gave as to why Cameron didn't show up today or yesterday or the day before or last week either for this or that class. The example I remember is Mrs. Constantine, our literature teacher.

Ever the punk rebel, Cameron had taken to wearing exceedingly normal polo shirts and cardigan sweaters to high school and so we, in turn, took to telling Mrs. Constantine that Cameron's frequent absences were the fault of the school golf team.

"I had never before heard that Cameron golfed with our golf team," she informed us skeptically.

"Of course. Why do you think he wears those dorky polo shirts and stupid cardigans all the time?"

Mrs. Constantine considered this. "I suppose," she said. "I might have heard of 45 it if he were the type of boy who talks. Still, I should have seen his name on these lists that are circulated around, that have the names of all the golfers on them."

"Well naturally. But remember it's Cameron, after all. He doesn't want anyone to find out. You know how he is. He does everything he can to keep it a secret. 'L' Angelo Mysterioso,' all that."

Mrs. Constantine nodded, made a gesture to indicate the secret was safe with her because her lips were locked and she had tossed away the key, and then excused many of Cameron Joyce's absences in her ledger as "Necessary for School Business."

Cameron often took far too many uppers and then requested a lift to the disco. One time he was near to overdosing at the Arastradero on a handful of cross-tops. Two beautiful college girls kept checking us out. Eventually they came over and, with no other prelude, just liking the looks of us I guess, asked for Cameron and I to take them home. We drove them to their condo, followed them inside, watched the girls unceremoniously shrug out of their clothes.

"Oh," said Cameron. "Christ." He was suddenly moving away. He had that clammy look and he was staggering back and back, one hand darting behind him, unsuccessfully groping about for a chair, and then he quietly sank to the carpet, a pile of slouched limbs.

One of the girls giggled. 50

"Should we be worried?" they asked.

"Nope," I said, untangling Cameron's spindly arms and legs, smoothing him out so that he looked a bit more presentable laying there passed out cold on the condo's floor. "He's like this all the time."

"We should maybe call an ambulance though?"

"Amphetamines," I explained. "He'll wake up, he'll be fine." I made sure his breath was visible in a compact mirror and then I shed my own clothes.

The ice cream parlor closes at eight-thirty so we have to hurry. The dishwasher 55 *is quickly filled, my sister is dragged from the telephone, my dad from the computer. My mom, dad sit in the front of the car like always, my sister, me in back. The town goes by the window and nothing appears any different. My sister and I ignore each other. It's been four hours since I got home. We have yet to speak. Her Walkman and headphones rest in her lap, a threat.*

At the ice cream counter my parents pretend to be newlyweds. My dad croons along with the music on the loudspeaker, my mom giggles, takes his hand, rests a cheek on his shoulder. My sister and I take our cones, move outside. She leans on the car, notices me watching a homeless guy approach. He is having a tough time of it, stumbling, dropping things.

Fuck, she laughs, indicating the homeless guy. It's the first word she's directed towards me. Who's this loser? I laugh with her, nod. Her eyes connect with mine, share something. Too weird, wheezes an unfamiliar voice. It's you, hey man. The homeless guy is speaking. He croaks my name a few times. My sister rolls her eyes, stamps her feet, recrosses her arms, licks her cone. Figures, she snorts.

The homeless guy wants me to shake his hand. How have you been, he asks, you heard what happened to our friend? Yeah, I reply. I can't recall this guy's name, but I briefly give him my hand. He looks like someone I might have hated in high school, probably someone we'd planned on killing after the revolution. Yeah, I say again, too bad. Could be it's better off, the guy shrugs, he wasn't well, you knew that. Yeah, I say, guess I did.

I think of the party I heard about where, after a few drinks, Cameron made everyone whisper because he insisted the government was listening. Everyone assumed he was joking but they indulged him anyway. A few days later, he attacked a group of Asians on the street, claiming that they had placed electrodes in his brain, that they were monitoring his thoughts for the CIA. No one told me what happened to him subsequently; I caught rumors he'd disappeared somewhere across the country, in Boston or New York, I heard that he was calling himself "Camden Joy," writing on some city's walls or some crazy thing, and I kept setting his smile against East Coast backdrops, I'd imagine him smiling as the New Yorkers spoke, smiling like he couldn't help it, couldn't help but trust them, leaning back, just watching, hands deep in his parka, smiling. I always figured I'd find him eventually, I'd imagine these elaborate schemes in which I'd smoke him out, make him reveal himself, like maybe I'd write under that name "Camden Joy" and he'd track me down as a result, schemes like that, which were far-fetched and spooky in a way I knew he'd like, and then after finding me we'd shake our heads over our impossible past, disputing it like an amnesiac might if awakening to a hoax, we'd mock memories of "the good old days," and he'd smile and smile.

Hey man, you really gotta come out and see us, the homeless guy is saying to me. 60
I would, I say, but I'm just visiting, I'm leaving soon. Come out to the campground first, the guy encourages me, it's where him and me are staying. You and who, I ask. Him and me, the guy says. I got Camden out there. What, I ask. I got Camden with me out there, he says, man, they cremated his ass, don't you know. I got what's left of him out there with me. You should really see him before you go. I'll try, I say. I'm pressed for time, you understand. The guy fidgets for a long time, studying me. You haven't changed, man, he informs me at last, not at all, and he staggers off.

Cameron and my other friends and I remained close for a long while, for no other reason than that we simply dreaded explaining ourselves to anyone who didn't already get us, who didn't admire the complex hail of references which comprised our daily chit-chat.

Inevitably, Sex and Drugs got in the way of this friendship, for the intensity and immediacy of their sensate gratification so dwarfed the ordinary pleasure of our camaraderie as to make us entirely question the depth and commitment of our feelings towards one another, made us ask whether we truly knew each other, if we were ever even friends at all or just neighbor boys who had a few tastes in common, similar jokes and mannerisms, liked a couple of the same LPs and movies, nothing more.

What were such similarities in the face of Girls, who quickly meant everything to me, or Speed, which began to mean everything to Cameron? It grew crucial that we dismiss the friendship to pursue these bigger joys, and Cameron accepted—just as I was made to grasp and grudgingly admit—that he would have to make himself better understood in order to obtain access to these higher pleasures, and he began to hang out with agitated speed-freaks who endlessly described things they witnessed which were utterly invisible to the rest of us, and I began devoting myself to girls whom I respected solely for the tautness of their trim calves and the willingness in their open smiles. These were, in some ways, our uneasy attempts to apply for membership to new circles, signaling our willingness to be cheaply belittled and lamely categorized by these new so-called pals so that we might be allowed to drop a hungry hand into their grab-bag and come away having scored some of their goodies.

I stride down our block of tract homes and across the kiddie park, skirting the shopping center the whole while, then continue over the highway, down and up a tall cement embankment, wading through a field of knee-high green brush, across the railroad tracks, down a row of ditches which irrigate a field of baby's breath. Wild anise sprouts everywhere underfoot like weeds, encouraged by the winter's rains, the gentle morning breezes rippling its feathery leaves, the reek of licorice pouring from its sticky, cane-like stalk.

So you came, the homeless guy calls out, I knew you would. Well hey there, 65 *I say, I was just taking a walk. This is incredibly close to where my parents live, actually. The guy ignores me. I knew you would come, he repeats. We always figured if anyone got to be a household word, it'd be you. But then, you're not a household word, he mumbles dismally, not even you.*

Not even me, I agree.

What's the point anyways, he says. Right? You heard Susan Lucci on the radio the other night. No, I reply. Well, he discloses, I got a radio, I got me Camden's radio set-up . . . Wanna see Camden? Not really, I tell him. You came all this way, he mutters. Wanna see where he lived?

Yeah, I concede, okay.

The guy motions for me to follow, starts across the campsite. Watch the poison oak, he declares. Leaves don't turn red till summer. The guy leads me around barbecue pits, sacks of trash. So, he says, Susan Lucci has had no easy time of it. And you think, if not Susan Lucci, you know, then who. Because what she deserves . . . that's some incredible talent. And that Emmys thing is so screwed. Too weird. Breaks your heart. Oh, I drily put in, absolutely. You don't care for Susan Lucci, he notices. Okay well, you will. I didn't once upon a time either.

He points to the top of a eucalyptus tree. That's it, he says simply. About nine 70
feet up, three branches diverge off the frame of the main trunk. A piece of ply-
wood rests between the limbs.

Cameron lived there, I ask.

Camden, he corrects me, yeah. He hasn't been Cameron since high school. But
you know, the guy goes on, Camden always kept talking about you. What did he
say, I ask, do you remember? No, he says, you couldn't always hear him real good.
What's funny, I say, is I can't even remember anything we talked about, just him
smiling all the time, you know? Right, the guy says, I know. I hadn't seen him, I
say, in a long time. You kinda—the guy gesticulates frustratedly—we couldn't
find you, right after Camden got picked up for going off on those Jap dudes.

I got real busy, I acknowledge. My career just . . . It took off.

Fine, he says.

I always heard Cameron went to New York City, I say. Sometimes I'd go there, 75
I'd look all over for handwriting on the walls. The guy shakes his head, points up
again at the plywood. He came home, he says. He was at the emergency room,
they were calling him psychotic and all this, got him down on this cot, KO'd him
with Thorazine. I met him up there at the crisis center, they were doing him up
with four and a half milligrams of Haldol three times a day. We just took off
together, man, it was getting wicked.

The crisis center was in town here?

Near here, he nods, yeah. So we've been here now, this is our third springtime.
The state pays us general relief. Were you here that night, I ask, the night the cops
came to get everyone out of the way of the water. Sure, he says. Well, I ask, where
was . . . why didn't you take Cameron with you?

Well, he says, the difference there was, Camden didn't like the cops and so he
went and hid in the river bottom, soon as they showed up. And the stupid fucks,
they never even saw him down there.

We smile at each other, proud of our friend's ability to confound the law.

You know how he was, the guy murmurs, and we smile again. 80

Yeah, I admit, I know how he was. I begin to climb the eucalyptus.

Be careful, the guy warns me. Camden used to fall from there all the time. Yes,
I think to myself, I can see why, because only two sides of the plywood have any
sort of branch support, the other two open into thin air. None of his belongings
are up here, just this bare plywood placed in the trees. Is this all there was, I ask.
No, the guy replies, I took everything else, his books and shit I got down here
with me. You wanna see them? You still gotta come down and see Camden, man.
Can't believe you haven't even seen Camden.

I'm not really interested, I say. I am laying flat, my belly against the plywood,
gazing off through the acrid haze of fried burgers and fast-food neon, and sud-
denly I jerk at the sight of something. Did you know, I start to ask, then stop. It's
just a coincidence, it's gotta be. What, the guy asks. Well you can see, from this
perch here, you look right at my parent's garage. Yeah, concurs the guy, where you
guys used to rehearse. Exactly, I say. Yeah, he continues, I was aware of that, Cam-
den did that on purpose. He did, I say. The guy shrugs. I couldn't tell you why.

I have my fingers interlaced, palms down, my head on my hands. So, I think to myself, Cameron was home all this time, delusional in the arms of his euca-lyptus, conversing with his memories and watching that stupid garage. I shut my eyes against the sunshine and remember the winter weather, the way it hits here and holds on. I picture this board wobbling in a thundershower, Cameron unable to make out the sounds of the highway or the freight trains when above them both is the storm whistling through the treetops, breaking branches in the black-ness, shaking loose water and leaves with a high, relentless whoosh. As a child, I remember falling asleep to the rain pelting our roof, and in my mind the source of the storm was a face as big as the sky, a face with its mouth stuck open, howling, and the face was gruesomely contorted, and it never ran out of breath.

I feel those childhood storms howling in the pit of my stomach right now, week- 85 *long storms which seemed never to go away. And every fear ever imagined sings in my bones, there is the fear of being locked up in my room too long alone, the fear of being devoured by the storm, the dwarfed feeling of being left behind, insignificant, a trifling speck of humanity. I know that as a boy, laying in bed, eyes closed, I regu-larly fell asleep to this feeling, this absolute certainty that I had been forgotten.*

I feel the abrupt shudder of plywood beneath me. Hey, the homeless guy says, shaking the tree. Hey. You been up there long enough. Come down now and see him. You gotta see Camden, man. You haven't seen him yet.

In a minute, I say sleepily. Just give me half a minute. I'll be down.

FOR ANALYSIS

1. At what time(s) is the story set?

2. What do you think the "childhood storms" (para. 85) stand for?

3. On his return home, the narrator asks himself, "I wonder what the hell they are doing wrong" (para. 39). Who is the "they" he refers to? Why does he ask this ques-tion? Does he answer it?

MAKING ARGUMENTS

1. The **narrator** says that the appeal of the books he and his high school friends read was due to "the distant romance of anomie-struck youth in holy literature" (para. 20). How would you argue that "Dum Dum Boys" belongs in this category? How would you argue that it does not?

2. The author often writes about music in his fiction, and has also written rock criti-cism. Read up on punk music and make the argument that the kind of music the boys listen to is important to the story.

WRITING TOPICS

1. Reflect on the significance of the moment when the narrator hears that Cameron has renamed himself. What is the effect of the particular name the author chooses to give him? Why do you think it is important to the story? (Refer to the author's biogra-phy to help you think about this.)

2. Describe the structure of the story by first annotating it (if you haven't already) and then by thinking about how it's put together. What kinds of sections are there? How does each kind differ? How are they arranged? What are the effects of this structure, and why do you think Joy chose it?

MAKING CONNECTIONS

1. "Dum-Dum Boys" and Updike's "A & P" (p. 92) both feature young men who are drawn to young women. How might this attraction to girls be said to also be in part about other things?

2. Naguib Mahfouz tells a story of innocence's loss in "Half a Day" (p. 88) as experienced by a very young boy whose real awakening to life's realities lies ahead of him. From what temporal perspective does Joy's narrator see innocence's loss? How does this difference in perspective effect what the stories are able to see and say?

CONNECTING STORIES: CRUSHES

Crush is a funny word. Its literal meaning is "romantic attraction that is somewhere short of love"—something short-lived and superficial. But buried in the word's etymology is a somewhat contradictory sense of intensity, of something pressing or grinding (and even a sense of violence if you consider the word's original meaning, which included a loud crashing or cracking sound). As you read these stories, look for the ways in which a crush, while it lasts only a brief while and then is gone, can also be intense and even overwhelming. One of the reasons crushes are rich subjects for literature is that as powerful infatuations they contain contradiction, expressing something of life's deepest feelings as well as life's mutability—the quick-changing quality that often drives artists to try to capture lost, fleeting moments. In the following stories, James Joyce and Rivka Galchen manage to capture two similar— and similarly lost—moments, but in very different ways.

JAMES JOYCE (1882-1941)

ARABY 1914

North Richmond Street, being blind, was a quiet street except at the hour when the Christian Brothers' School set the boys free. An uninhabited house of two storeys stood at the blind end, detached from its neighbours in a square ground. The other houses of the street, conscious of decent lives within them, gazed at one another with brown imperturbable faces.

The former tenant of our house, a priest, had died in the back drawing-room. Air, musty from having been long enclosed, hung in all the rooms, and the waste room behind the kitchen was littered with old useless papers. Among these I found a few paper-covered books, the pages of which were curled and damp: *The Abbot*, by Walter Scott, *The Devout Communicant* and *The Memoirs of Vidocq*. I liked the last best because its leaves were yellow. The wild garden behind the house contained a central apple-tree and a few straggling bushes under one of which I found the late tenant's rusty bicycle pump. He had been a very charitable priest; in his will he had left all his money to institutions and the furniture of his house to his sister.

When the short days of winter came dusk fell before we had well eaten our dinners. When we met in the street the houses had grown sombre. The space of sky above us was the colour of ever-changing violet and towards it the lamps of the street lifted their feeble lanterns. The cold air stung us and we played till our bodies glowed. Our shouts echoed in the silent street. The career of our play brought us through the dark muddy lanes behind the houses where we ran the gauntlet of the rough tribes from the cottages, to the back doors of the dark dripping gardens where odours arose from the ashpits, to the dark odorous stables where a coachman smoothed and combed the horse or shook music from the buckled harness. When we returned to the street, light from the kitchen windows had filled the areas. If my uncle was seen turning the corner we hid in the shadow until we had seen him safely housed. Or if Mangan's sister came out on the doorstep to call her brother in to his tea we watched her from our shadow peer up and down the street. We waited to see whether she would remain or go in and, if she remained, we left our shadow and walked up to Mangan's steps resignedly. She was waiting for us, her figure defined by the light from the half-opened door. Her brother always teased her before he obeyed and I stood by the railings looking at her. Her dress swung as she moved her body and the soft rope of her hair tossed from side to side.

Every morning I lay on the floor in the front parlour watching her door. The blind was pulled down to within an inch of the sash so that I could not be seen. When she came out on the doorstep my heart leaped. I ran to the hall, seized my books and followed her. I kept her brown figure always in my eye and, when we came near the point at which our ways diverged, I quickened my pace and passed her. This happened morning after morning. I had never spoken to her, except for a few casual words, and yet her name was like a summons to all my foolish blood.

Her image accompanied me even in places the most hostile to romance. On ₅ Saturday evenings when my aunt went marketing I had to go to carry some of the parcels. We walked through the flaring streets, jostled by drunken men and bargaining women, amid the curses of labourers, the shrill litanies of shop-boys who stood on guard by the barrels of pigs' cheeks, the nasal chanting of street-singers, who sang a *come-all-you*[1] about O'Donovan Rossa, or a ballad about the troubles in our native land. These noises converged in a single sensation of life for me: I imagined that I bore my chalice safely through a throng of foes. Her name sprang to my lips at moments in strange prayers and praises which I myself did not understand. My eyes were often full of tears (I could not tell why) and at times a flood from my heart seemed to pour itself out into my bosom. I thought little of the future. I did not know whether I would ever speak to her or not or, if I spoke to her, how I could tell her of my confused adoration. But my body was like a harp and her words and gestures were like fingers running upon the wires.

One evening I went into the back drawing-room in which the priest had died. It was a dark rainy evening and there was no sound in the house. Through one of the broken panes I heard the rain impinge upon the earth, the fine incessant needles of water playing in the sodden beds. Some distant lamp or lighted window gleamed below me. I was thankful that I could see so little. All my senses seemed to desire to veil themselves and, feeling that I was about to slip from them, I pressed the palms of my hands together until they trembled, murmuring: *"O love! O love!"* many times.

---

[1] A street ballad beginning with these words. This one is about Jeremiah Donovan, a nineteenth-century Irish nationalist popularly known as O'Donovan Rossa.

At last she spoke to me. When she addressed the first words to me I was so confused that I did not know what to answer. She asked me was I going to *Araby*. I forgot whether I answered yes or no. It would be a splendid bazaar, she said she would love to go.

"And why can't you?" I asked.

While she spoke she turned a silver bracelet round and round her wrist. She could not go, she said, because there would be a retreat that week in her convent. Her brother and two other boys were fighting for their caps and I was alone at the railings. She held one of the spikes, bowing her head towards me. The light from the lamp opposite our door caught the white curve of her neck, lit up her hair that rested there and, falling, lit up the hand upon the railing. It fell over one side of her dress and caught the white border of a petticoat, just visible as she stood at ease.

"It's well for you," she said.   10

"If I go," I said, "I will bring you something."

What innumerable follies laid waste my waking and sleeping thoughts after that evening! I wished to annihilate the tedious intervening days. I chafed against the work of school. At night in my bedroom and by day in the classroom her image came between me and the page I strove to read. The syllables of the word *Araby* were called to me through the silence in which my soul luxuriated and cast an Eastern enchantment over me. I asked for leave to go to the bazaar on Saturday night. My aunt was surprised and hoped it was not some Freemason affair. I answered few questions in class. I watched my master's face pass from amiability to sternness; he hoped I was not beginning to idle. I could not call my wandering thoughts together. I had hardly any patience with the serious work of life which, now that it stood between me and my desire, seemed to me child's play, ugly monotonous child's play.

On Saturday morning I reminded my uncle that I wished to go to the bazaar in the evening. He was fussing at the hallstand, looking for the hat-brush, and answered me curtly:

"Yes, boy, I know."

As he was in the hall I could not go into the front parlour and lie at the win-   15
dow. I left the house in bad humour and walked slowly towards the school. The air was pitilessly raw and already my heart misgave me.

When I came home to dinner my uncle had not yet been home. Still it was early. I sat staring at the clock for some time and, when its ticking began to irritate me, I left the room. I mounted the staircase and gained the upper part of the house. The high cold empty gloomy rooms liberated me and I went from room to room singing. From the front window I saw my companions playing below in the street. Their cries reached me weakened and indistinct and, leaning my forehead against the cool glass, I looked over at the dark house where she lived. I may have stood there for an hour, seeing nothing but the brown-clad figure cast by my imagination, touched discreetly by the lamplight at the curved neck, at the hand upon the railings and at the border below the dress.

When I came downstairs again I found Mrs. Mercer sitting at the fire. She was an old garrulous woman, a pawnbroker's widow, who collected used stamps for some pious purpose. I had to endure the gossip of the tea-table. The meal was prolonged beyond an hour and still my uncle did not come. Mrs. Mercer stood up to go: she was sorry she couldn't wait any longer, but it was after eight o'clock and she did not like to be out late, as the night air was bad for her. When she had gone I began to walk up and down the room, clenching my fists. My aunt said:

"I'm afraid you may put off your bazaar for this night of Our Lord."

At nine o'clock I heard my uncle's latchkey in the hall door. I heard him talking to himself and heard the hallstand rocking when it had received the weight of his overcoat. I could interpret these signs. When he was midway through his dinner I asked him to give me the money to go to the bazaar. He had forgotten.

"The people are in bed and after their first sleep now," he said. 20

I did not smile. My aunt said to him energetically:

"Can't you give him the money and let him go? You've kept him late enough as it is."

My uncle said he was very sorry he had forgotten. He said he believed in the old saying: "All work and no play makes Jack a dull boy." He asked me where I was going and, when I had told him a second time he asked me did I know *The Arab's Farewell to His Steed.* When I left the kitchen he was about to recite the opening lines of the piece to my aunt.

I held a florin tightly in my hand as I strode down Buckingham Street towards the station. The sight of the streets thronged with buyers and glaring with gas recalled to me the purpose of my journey. I took my seat in a third-class carriage of a deserted train. After an intolerable delay the train moved out of the station slowly. It crept onward among ruinous houses and over the twinkling river. At Westland Row Station a crowd of people pressed to the carriage doors; but the porters moved them back, saying that it was a special train for the bazaar. I remained alone in the bare carriage. In a few minutes the train drew up beside an improvised wooden platform. I passed out on to the road and saw by the lighted dial of a clock that it was ten minutes to ten. In front of me was a large building which displayed the magical name.

I could not find any sixpenny entrance and, fearing that the bazaar would be 25 closed, I passed in quickly through a turnstile, handing a shilling to a weary-looking man. I found myself in a big hall girdled at half its height by a gallery. Nearly all the stalls were closed and the greater part of the hall was in darkness. I recognised a silence like that which pervades a church after a service. I walked into the centre of the bazaar timidly. A few people were gathered about the stalls which were still open. Before a curtain, over which the words *Café Chantant* were written in coloured lamps, two men were counting money on a salver. I listened to the fall of the coins.

Remembering with difficulty why I had come I went over to one of the stalls and examined porcelain vases and flowered tea-sets. At the door of the stall a

young lady was talking and laughing with two young gentlemen. I remarked
their English accents and listened vaguely to their conversation.

"O, I never said such a thing!"

"O, but you did!"

"O, but I didn't!"

"Didn't she say that?"

"Yes. I heard her."

"O, there's a . . . fib!"

Observing me the young lady came over and asked me did I wish to buy
anything. The tone of her voice was not encouraging; she seemed to have
spoken to me out of a sense of duty. I looked humbly at the great jars that
stood like Eastern guards at either side of the dark entrance to the stall and
murmured:

"No, thank you."

The young lady changed the position of one of the vases and went back to   35
the two young men. They began to talk of the same subject. Once or twice the
young lady glanced at me over her shoulder.

I lingered before her stall, though I knew my stay was useless, to make
my interest in her wares seem the more real. Then I turned away slowly and
walked down the middle of the bazaar. I allowed the two pennies to fall against
the sixpence in my pocket. I heard a voice call from one end of the gallery that
the light was out. The upper part of the hall was now completely dark.

Gazing up into the darkness I saw myself as a creature driven and derided by
vanity; and my eyes burned with anguish and anger.

FOR ANALYSIS

1. Reread the opening paragraph. How does it set the **tone** for the story?

2. Why does the **dialogue** the **narrator** overhears at the bazaar trigger the climax of
the story and the insight described in the final paragraph?

MAKING ARGUMENTS

Make an argument that in the end the narrator is either too hard on himself or not
hard enough (or at least not appropriately hard). That is, either argue that he is just
another human, with all of our failings, or else that he is a special case.

WRITING TOPICS

1. Write a page describing a romantic infatuation you experienced when you were
younger that blinded you to the reality of the person you adored.

2. Analyze the **imagery** of light and vision in this story.

30

WILD BERRY BLUE   2008

This is a story about my love for Roy, though first I have to say a few words about my dad, who was there with me at the McDonald's every Saturday letting his little girl—I was maybe eight—swig his extra half-and-halfs, stack the shells into messy towers. My dad drank from his bottomless cup of coffee and read the paper while I dipped my McDonaldland cookies in milk and pretended to read the paper. He wore gauzy plaid button-ups with pearline snaps. He had girlish wrists, a broad forehead like a Roman, an absolutely terrifying sneeze.

"How's the coffee?" I'd ask.

"Not good, not bad. How's the milk?"

"Terrific," I'd say. Or maybe, "Exquisite."

My mom was at home cleaning the house; our job there at the McDonald's 5
was to be out of her way.

And that's how it always was on Saturdays. We were Jews, we had our rituals. That's how I think about it. Despite the occasional guiltless cheeseburger, despite being secular Israelis living in the wilds of Oklahoma, the ineluctable Jew part in us still snuck out, like an inherited tic, indulging in habits of repetition. Our form of *davenning*. Our little Shabbat.

Many of the people who worked at the McDonald's were former patients of my dad's: mostly drug addicts and alcoholics in rehab programs. McDonald's hired people no one else would hire; I think it was a policy. And my dad, in effect, was the McDonald's–Psychiatric Institute liaison. The McDonald's manager, a deeply Christian man, would regularly come over and say hello to us, and thank my dad for many things. Once he thanked him for, as a Jew, having kept safe the word of God during all the dark years.

"I'm not sure I've done so much," my dad had answered, not seriously.

"But it's been living there in you," the manager said earnestly. He was basically a nice man, admirably tolerant of the accompanying dramas of his work force, dramas I picked up on peripherally. Absenteeism, petty theft, a worker OD-ing in the bathroom. I had no idea what that meant, to OD, but it sounded spooky. "They slip out from under their own control," I heard the manager say one time, and the phrase stuck with me. I pictured one half of a person lifting up a velvet rope and fleeing the other half.

Sometimes, dipping my McDonaldland cookies—Fryguy, Grimace—I'd hold 10
a cookie in the milk too long and it would saturate and crumble to the bottom of the carton. There, it was something mealy, vulgar. Horrible. I'd lose my appetite. Though the surface of the milk often remained pristine I could feel the cookie's presence down below, lurking. Like some ancient bottom-dwelling fish with both eyes on one side of his head.

I'd tip the carton back in order to see what I dreaded seeing, just to feel that queasiness, and also the pre-queasiness of knowing the main queasiness was coming, the anticipatory ill.

Beautiful/Horrible—I had a running mental list. Cleaning lint from the screen of the dryer—beautiful. Bright glare on glass—horrible. Mealworms—also horrible. The stubbles of shaved hair in a woman's armpit—beautiful.

The Saturday I was to meet Roy, after dropping a cookie in the milk, I looked up at my dad. "Cookie," I squeaked, turning a sour face at the carton.

He pulled out his worn leather wallet, with its inexplicable rust stain ring on the front. He gave me a dollar. My mom never gave me money and my dad always gave me more than I needed. (He also called me the Queen of Sheba sometimes, like when I'd stand up on a dining room chair to see how things looked from there.) The torn corner of the bill he gave me was held on with yellowed Scotch tape. Someone had written over the treasury seal in blue pen, "I love Becky!!!"

I go up to the counter with the Becky dollar to buy my replacement milk, and 15 what I see is a tattoo, most of which I can't see. A starched white long-sleeve shirt covers most of it. But a little blue-black lattice of it I can see—a fragment like ancient elaborate metalwork, that creeps down all the way, past the wrist, to the back of the hand, kinking up and over a very plump vein. The vein is so distended I imagine laying my cheek on it in order to feel the blood pulse and flow, to maybe even hear it. Beautiful. So beautiful. I don't know why but I'm certain this tattoo reaches all the way up to his shoulder. His skin is deeply tanned but the webbing between his fingers sooty pale.

This beautiful feeling. I haven't had it about a person before. Not in this way.

In a trembling moment I shift my gaze up to the engraved nametag. There's a yellow M emblem, then *Roy.*

I place my dollar down on the counter. I put it down like it's a password I'm unsure of, one told to me by an unreliable source. "Milk," I say, quietly.

Roy, whose face I finally look at, is staring off, up, over past my head, like a bored lifeguard. He hasn't heard or noticed me, little me, the only person in line. Roy is biting his lower lip and one of his teeth, one of the canines, is much whiter than the others. Along his cheekbones his skin looks dry and chalky. His eyes are blue, with beautiful bruisy eyelids.

I try again, a little bit louder. "Milk." 20

Still he doesn't hear me; I begin to feel as if maybe I am going to cry because of these accumulated moments of being nothing. That's what it feels like standing so close to this type of beauty—like being nothing.

Resolving to give up if I'm not noticed soon I make one last effort and, leaning over on my tiptoes, I push the dollar further along the counter, far enough that it tickles Roy's thigh, which is leaned up against the counter's edge.

He looks down at me, startled, then laughs abruptly. "Hi little sexy," he says. Then he laughs again, too loud, and the other cashier, who has one arm shrunken and paralyzed, turns and looks and then looks away again.

Suddenly these few seconds are everything that has ever happened to me.

My milk somehow purchased I go back to the table wondering if I am green, 25 or emitting a high-pitched whistling sound, or dead.

I realize back at the table that it's not actually the first time I've seen Roy. With great concentration, I dip my Hamburglar cookie into the cool milk. I think that maybe I've seen Roy—that coarse blond hair—every Saturday, for all my Saturdays. I take a bite from my cookie. I have definitely seen him before. Just somehow not in this way.

My dad appears to be safely immersed in whatever is on the other side of the crossword puzzle and bridge commentary page. I feel—a whole birch tree pressing against my inner walls, its leaves reaching to the top of my throat— the awful sense of wanting some other life. I have thought certain boys in my classes have pretty faces, but I have never before felt like laying my head down on the vein of a man's wrist. (I still think about that vein sometimes.) Almost frantically I wonder if Roy can see me there at my table, there with my dad, where I've been seemingly all my Saturdays.

Attempting to rein in my anxiety I try and think: What makes me feel this way? Possessed like this? Is it a smell in the air? It just smells like beefy grease. Which is pleasant enough but nothing new. A little mustard. A small vapor of disinfectant. I wonder obscurely if Roy is Jewish, as if that might make normal this spiraling fated feeling I have. As if really what's struck me is just an unobvious family resemblance. But I know that we're the only Jews in town.

Esther married the gentile king, I think, in a desperate absurd flash.

Since a part of me wants to stay forever I finish my cookies quickly. 30

"Let's go," I say.

"Already?"

"Can't we just leave? Let's leave."

There's the Medieval Fair, I think to myself in consolation all Sunday. It's two weekends away, a Saturday. You're always happy at the Medieval Fair, I say to myself, as I fail to enjoy sorting my stamps, fail to stand expectantly, joyfully, on the dining room chair. Instead I fantasize about running the French fry fryer in the back of McDonald's. I imagine myself learning to construct Happy Meal boxes in a breath, to fold the papers around the hamburgers *just so*. I envision a stool set out for me to climb atop so that I can reach the apple fritter dispenser; Roy spots me, making sure I don't fall. And I get a tattoo. Of a bird, or a fish, or a ring of birds and fish, around my ankle.

But there is no happiness in these daydreams. Just an overcrowded and 35 feverish empty.

At school on Monday I sit dejectedly in the third row of Mrs. Brown's class, because that is where we are on the weekly seating chart rotation. I suffer through exercises in long division, through bits about Magellan. Since I'm not in the front I'm able to mark most of my time drawing a tremendous maze, one that stretches to the outer edges of the notebook paper. This while the teacher reads to us from something about a girl and her horse. Something. A horse. Who cares! Who cares about a horse! I think, filled, suddenly, with unexpected rage. That extra white tooth. The creeping chain of the tattoo. I try so hard to be dedicated to my maze, pressing my pencil sharply into the paper as if to hold down my focus better.

All superfluous, even my sprawling maze, superfluous. A flurry of pencil shavings from the sharpener—they come out as if in a breath—distracts me. A sudden phantom pain near my elbow consumes my attention.

I crumple up my maze dramatically; do a basketball throw to the wastebasket like the boys do. I miss of course but no one seems to notice, which is the nature of my life at school, where I am only noticed in bland embarrassing ways, like when a substitute teacher can't pronounce my last name. The joylessness of my basketball toss—it makes me look over at my once-crush Josh Deere and feel sad for him, for the smallness of his life.

One day, I think, it will be Saturday again.

But time seemed to move so slowly. I'd lost my appetite for certain details 40 of life.

"Do you know about that guy at McDonald's with the one really white tooth?" I brave this question to my dad. This during a commercial break from *Kojak*.

"Roy's a recovering heroin addict," my dad says, turning to stare at me. He always said things to me other people wouldn't have said to kids. He'd already told me about the Oedipus complex and I had stared dully back at him. He would defend General Rommel to me, though I had no idea who General Rommel was. He'd make complex points about the straits of Bosporus. It was as if he couldn't distinguish ages.

So he said that to me, about Roy, which obviously he shouldn't have said. (Here, years later, I still think about the mystery of that plump vein, which seems a contradiction. Which occasionally makes me wonder if there were two Roys.)

"I don't know what the story with the tooth is," my dad adds. "Maybe it's false?" And then it's back to the mystery of *Kojak*.

I wander into the kitchen feeling unfulfilled and so start interrogating my 45 mom about my Purim costume for the carnival that is still two Sundays, eons, away. The Purim carnival is in Tulsa, over an hour's driving distance; I don't know the kids there, and my costume never measures up. "And the crown," I remind her hollowly. I'm not quite bold enough to bring up that she could buy me one of the beautiful ribbon crowns sold at the Medieval Fair, which we'll be at the day before. "I don't want," I mumble mostly to myself, "one of those paper crowns that everyone has."

Thursday night I am at the Skaggs Alpha Beta grocery with my mom. I am lingering amid all the sugar cereals I know will never come home with me. It's only every minute or so that I am thinking about Roy's hand, about how he called me sexy.

Then I see Roy. He has no cart, no basket. He's holding a gallon of milk and a supersized bag of Twizzlers and he is reaching for, I can't quite see—a big oversized box that looks to be Honeycomb. A beautiful assemblage. Beautiful.

I turn away from Roy but stand still. I feel my whole body, even my ears, blushing. The backs of my hands feel itchy the way they always do in spring. Seeking release I touch the cool metal shelving, run my fingers up and over the plastic slipcovers, over the price labels, hearing every nothing behind me. The price labels make a sandy sliding sound when I push them. He's a monster, Roy. Not looking at him, just feeling that power he has over me, a monster.

My mom in lace-up sandals cruises by the aisle with our shopping cart, unveiling to me my ridiculousness. Able now to turn around I see that Roy is gone. I run after my mom and when finally we're in the car again, back door closed on the groceries—I see celery stalks innocently sticking out of a brown paper bag when I turn around—I feel great relief.

I decide to wash my feet in the sink, this always makes me happy. On my dad's 50 shaving mirror in the bathroom, old Scotch tape holding it in place, is a yellowed bit of paper, torn from a magazine. For years it's been there, inscrutable, and suddenly I feel certain that it carries a secret. About love maybe. About the possessed feeling I have because of Roy.

It says *And human speech is but a cracked kettle upon which we tap crude rhythms for bears to dance to, while we long to make music that—*

Next to the scrap is a sticker of mine, of a green apple.

I look again at the quote: the bears, the kettle.

Silly, I decide. It's all very silly. I start to dry my feet with a towel.

For the impending McDonald's Saturday I resolve to walk right past my 55 tattooed crush. I'll have nothing to do with him, with his hi little sexys. This denouncement is actually extraordinarily painful since Roy alone is now my whole world. Everything that came before—my coin collection in the Tupperware, the corrugated cardboard trim on school bulletin boards, the terror of the fire pole—now revealed supremely childish and vain. Without even deciding to, I have left all that and now must leave Roy too. I commit to enduring the burden of the universe alone. The universe with its mysterious General Rommels, its heady straits of Bosporus. I resolve to suffer.

Saturday comes again. My mom has already taken the burner covers off the stove and set them in the sink. I'm anxious, like branches shaking in wind, and I'm trying the think-about-the-Medieval-Fair trick. I picture the ducks at the duck pond, the way they waddle right up and snatch the bread slice right out of my hand. I focus on the fair—knowing that time will move forward in that way, eventually waddle forward to the next weekend.

Buckling myself into the front seat of our yellow Pinto I put an imitation Life Saver under my tongue, a blue one. When my dad walks in front of the car on the way to the driver's side, I notice that he has slouchy shoulders. Horrible. Not his shoulders, but my noticing them.

"I love you," I say to my dad. He laughs and says that's good. I sit there hating myself a little.

I concentrate on my candy, on letting it be there, letting it do its exquisitely slow melt under my tongue. Beautiful. I keep that same candy the whole car ride over, through stop signs, waiting for a kid on a Bigwheel to cross, past the Conoco, with patience during the long wait for the final left turn. In my pocket I have more candies. Most of a roll of wild berry. When I move my tongue just a tiny bit, the flavor, the sugary slur, assaults my sensations. I choke on a little bit of saliva.

When we enter I sense Roy at our left; I walk on the far side of my dad, hoping   60
to hide in his shadow. In a hoarse whisper I tell my dad that I'll go save our table and that he should order me the milk and the cookies.

"Okay," he whispers back, winking, as if this is some spy game I am playing.

At the table I stare straight ahead at the molded plastic bench, summoning all my meager power to keep from looking feverishly around. I think I sense Roy's blond hair off in the distance to my left. I glimpse to the side, but see just a potted plant.

"How's the coffee?" I ask after my dad has settled in across from me.

He shrugs his ritual shrug but no words except the question of how is your milk. Is he mad at me? As I begin dipping my cookies with a kind of anguish, I answer that the milk is delicious.

Why do we say these little things? I wonder. Why do I always want the   65
McDonaldland butter cookies and never the chocolate chip? It seems creepy to me suddenly, all the habits and ways of the heart I have that I didn't choose for myself.

I throw back three half-and-halfs.

"Will you get me some more half-and-halfs?" my dad asks.

He asks nicely. And he is really reading the paper while I am not. Of course I'm going to go get creamers. I'm a kid, I remember. He's my dad. All this comes quickly into focus, lines sharp, like feeling the edges of a sticker on paper.

"I don't feel well," I try.

"Really?"   70

"I mean I feel fine," I say getting out of the chair.

Roy. Taking a wild berry candy from my pocket I resolve again to focus on a candy under my tongue instead of on him. I head first toward the back wall, darting betwixt and between the tables with their attached swiveling chairs. This is the shiniest cleanest place in town, that's what McDonald's was like back then. Even the corners and crevices are clean. It's strange to me in that way. Our house—even after my mom cleans, it's all still in disarray. I'll unfold a blanket and there'll be a stray sock inside. Behind the toilet there's blue lint. That's what makes a home, I think, its special type of mess.

And then I'm at the front counter. I don't look up.

I stand off to the side since I'm not really ordering anything, just asking for a favor, not paying for milk but asking for creamers. Waiting to be noticed, I stare down at the brushed steel counter with its flattering hazy reflection and then it appears, he appears. I see first his palm, reflected in the steel. Then I see his knuckles, the hairs on the back of his hand, the lattice tattoo, the starched shirt cuff that is the beginning of hiding all the rest of the tattoo that I can't see.

Beautiful.

A part of me decides I am taking him back into my heart. Even if no room will be left for anything else.

Roy notices me. He leans way down, eyes level with my sweaty curls stuck against my forehead, at the place where I know I have my birthmark—a dark brown mole there above my left eyebrow—and he says, his teeth showing, his strange glowing white canine showing—"D'ya need something?" He taps my nose with his finger.

That candy—I had forgotten about it, and I move my tongue and the flavor—it all comes rushing out, overwhelming, and I drool a little bit as I blurt out, "I'm going to the Medieval Fair next weekend." I wipe my wet lips with the back of my hand and see the wild-berry blue saliva staining there.

"Cool," he says, straightening up, and he interlaces his fingers and pushes them outward and they crack deliciously, and I think about macadamias. I think I see him noticing the blue smeared on my right hand. He then says to me: "I love those puppets they sell there—those real plain wood ones."

I just stare at Roy's blue eyes. I love blue eyes. Still to this day I am always telling myself that I don't like them, that I find them lifeless and dull and that I prefer brown eyes, like mine, like my parents', but it's a lie. It's a whole other wilder type of love that I feel for these blue-eyed people of the world. So I look up at him, at those blue eyes, and I'm thinking about those plain wooden puppets—this is all half a second—then the doors open behind me and that invasive heat enters and the world sinks down, mud and mush and the paste left behind by cookies.

"Oh," I say. "Half-and-half."

He reaches into a tray of much-melted ice and bobbing creamers and he hands three to me. My palm burns where he touched me and my vision is blurry; only the grooves on the half-and-half container keep me from vanishing.

"Are you going to the fair?" I brave. Heat in my face again, the feeling just before a terrible rash. I'm already leaving the counter so as not to see those awful blue eyes and I hear, "Ah I'm workin'" and I don't even turn around.

I read the back of my dad's newspaper. They have found more fossils at the Spiro mounds. There's no explanation for how I feel.

How can I describe the days of the next week? I'd hope to see Roy when I ran out to check the mail. I'd go drink from the hose in our front yard thinking he might walk or drive by, even though I had no reason to believe he might ever come to our neighborhood. I got detention for not turning in my book report of *The Yellow Wallpaper*. I found myself rummaging around in my father's briefcase, as if Roy's files—I imagined the yellow Confidential envelope from Clue—might somehow be there. Maybe I don't need to explain this because who hasn't been overtaken by this monstrous shade of love? I remember walking home from school very slowly, anxiously, as if through foreign, unpredictable terrain. I wanted to buy Roy a puppet at the Medieval Fair. One of the wooden ones like he'd mentioned. Only in that thought could I rest. All the clutter of my mind was waiting to come closer to that moment of purchasing a puppet.

So I did manage to wake up in the mornings. I did try to go to sleep at night. Though my heart seemed to be racing to its own obscure rhythm, private even from me.

Friday night before the fair, hopeless for sleep—my bedroom seemed alien and lurksome—I pulled my maze workbook from the shelf and went into the brightly lit bathroom. I turned on the overhead fan so that it would become noisy enough to overwhelm the sound in my mind of Roy cracking his knuckles, again and again. The whirring fan noise—it was like a quiet. I sat in the empty tub, set the maze book on the rounded ledge and purposely began on a difficult page. I worked cautiously, tracing ahead with my finger before setting pen to paper. This was pleasing, though out of the corner of my eye I saw the yellowed magazine fragment—*cracked kettle*—and it was like a ghost in the room with me, though its message, I felt sure—almost too sure considering that I didn't understand it—had nothing to do with me.

In the morning my mom found me there in the tub, like some passed-out drunk, my maze book open on my small chest. I felt like crying, didn't even know why. I must have fallen asleep there. I reached up to my face, wondering if something had gone wrong with it.

"Do you have a fever?" my mom asked.

It must have seemed like there had to be an explanation. When she left, 90 assured, somewhat, I tried out those words—*Human speech is like a cracked kettle*—like they were the coded answer to a riddle.

I was always that kind of kid who crawled into bed with her parents, who felt safe only with them. If my mom came into my classroom because I had forgotten my lunch at home, I wasn't ashamed like other kids were, but proud. For a few years of my life, up until then, my desires hadn't chased away from me. I wanted to fall asleep on the sofa while my dad watched *The Twilight Zone* and so I did. I wanted couscous with butter and so I had some. Yes, sometimes shopping with my mom I coveted a pair of overalls or a frosted cookie, but the want would be faint and fade as soon as we'd walked away.

I had always loved the Medieval Fair. A woman would dress up in an elaborate mermaid costume and sit under the bridge that spanned the artificial pond. I thought she was beautiful. People tossed quarters down at her. She'd flap her tail, wave coyly. It wasn't until years later that I realized that she was considered trashy.

Further on there was a stacked hay maze that had already become too easy by late elementary school but I liked looking at it from a distance, from up on the small knoll. I think every turn you might take was fine. Whichever way you went you still made it out. I remember it being upsetting, being spat out so soon.

We had left the house uncleaned when we went to the fair that Saturday. I was thinking about the wooden puppet but I felt obligated to hope for a crown; that's what I was supposed to be pining for. I imagined that my mom would think to buy me a crown for my Queen Esther costume. But maybe, I hoped, she would forget all about the crown. It wasn't unlikely. What seemed like the world to me often revealed itself, through her eyes, to be nothing.

We saw the dress-up beggar with the prosthetic nose and warts. We crossed the bridge, saw the mermaid. A pale teenage boy in stonewashed jeans and a tank top leaned against the bridge's railing, smoking, and looking down at her. Two corseted women farther along sang bawdy ballads in the shade of a willow and while we listened a slouchy man went by with a gigantic foam mallet. The whole world, it seemed, was laughing or fighting or crying or unfolding chairs or blending smoothies and this would go on until time immemorial. Vendors sold wooden flutes, Jacob's ladders. The smell of funnel cakes and sour mystery saturated the air. In an open field two ponies and three sheep were there for the petting and the overseer held a baby pig in his hands. We ate fresh ears of boiled corn, smothered with butter and cracked pepper. My mom didn't mention the price. That really did make it feel like a day in some other me's life.

But I felt so unsettled. Roy's tooth in my mind as I bit into the corn, Roy's fingers on my palm as I thrummed my hand along a low wooden fence. I had so little of Roy and yet he had all of me and the feeling ran deep, deep to the most ancient parts of me. So deep that in some way I felt that my love for Roy shamed my people, whoever my people were, whomever I was queen of, people I had never met, nervous people and sad people and dead people, all clambering for air and space inside of me. I didn't even know what I wanted from Roy. I still don't. All my life love has felt like a croquet mallet to the head. Something absurd, ready for violence. Love.

I remember once years later, in a love fit, stealing cherry Luden's cough drops from a convenience store. I had the money to pay for them but I stole them instead. I wanted a cheap childish cherry flavor on my tongue when I saw my love, who of course isn't my love anymore. That painful pathetic euphoria. Low-quality cough drops. That's how I felt looking around anxiously for the wooden puppet stand, how I felt looking twice at every blond man who passed, wondering if he might somehow be Roy, there for me, even though he'd said he wouldn't be there. Thinking about that puppet for Roy eclipsed all other thoughts, put a slithery veil over the whole day. How much would the puppet cost? I didn't have my own pocket money, an allowance or savings or anything like that. I wasn't in the habit of asking for things. I never asked for toys. I never asked for sugar cereals. I felt to do so was wrong. I had almost cried that one day just whispering to myself about the crown. But all I wanted was that puppet because that puppet was going to solve everything.

At the puppet stand I lingered. I was hoping that one of my parents would take notice of the puppets, pick one up. My dad, standing a few paces away, stood out from the crowd in his button-up shirt. He looked weak, sunbeaten. My mom was at my side, her arms crossed across an emergency orange tank top. It struck me, maybe for the first time, that they came to this fair just for me.

"I've never wanted anything this much in my whole life," I confessed in a rush, my hand on the unfinished wood of one of the puppets. "I want this more than a crown."

My mom laughed at me, or at the puppet. "But it's so ugly," she said, in Hebrew. 100

"That's not true," I whispered furiously, feeling as if everything had fallen silent, as if the ground beneath me was shifting. The vendor must surely have understood my mom, by her tone alone. I looked over at him: a fat bearded man talking to a long-haired barefoot princess. He held an end of her dusty hair distractedly; his other hand he had inside the collar of his shirt. He was sweating.

"*Drek.*" My mom shrugged. Junk.

"Grouch," I broke out, like a tree root heaving through soil. "You don't like anything," I almost screamed, there in the bright sun. "You never like anything at all." My mother turned her back to me. I sensed the ugly vendor turn our way.

"I'll get it for you," my dad said, suddenly right with us. There followed an awkward argument between my parents, which seemed only to heighten my dad's pleasure in taking out his rust-stained wallet, in standing his ground, in being, irrevocably, on my side.

His alliance struck me as misguided, pathetic, even childish. I felt like a vil- 105 lain. We bought the puppet.

That dumb puppet—I carried it around in its wrinkly green plastic bag. For some reason I found myself haunted by the word *leprosy*. When we watched the minstrel show in the little outdoor amphitheater I tried to forget the green bag under the bench. We only made it a few steps before my mom noticed it was gone. She went back and fetched it.

At home I noticed that the wood of one of the hands of the puppet was cracked. That wasn't the only reason I couldn't give the puppet to Roy. Looking at that mute piece of wood I saw something. A part of me that I'd never chosen, that I would never control. I went to the bathroom, turned on the loud fan, and cried, feeling angry, useless, silly. An image of Roy came to my mind, particularly of that tooth. I felt my love falling off, dissolving.

He was my first love, my first love in the way that first loves are usually second or third or fourth loves. I still think about a stranger in a green jacket across from me at the waiting room at the DMV. About a blue-eyed man with a singed earlobe whom I saw at a Baskin-Robbins with his daughter. My first that kind of love. I never got over him. I never get over anyone.

FOR ANALYSIS

1. How old is the **narrator** when the events in the story occur? How old is she when she tells this story about them? Is there a difference between how she felt at the time these events happened and how she feels about them at the time she tells the story?

2. From where does Galchen get the title for her story? What resonance does it have?

MAKING ARGUMENTS

In paragraph 55, the narrator resolves to live the rest of her life alone rather than live with the "possessed feeling" she has because of her crush (para. 50). Does the story support or refute the idea that she would be better off alone?

WRITING TOPICS

1. Write about a memory of your early years. What details stand out—what sensory images, what facts about place and time, what sense of your feelings and thoughts? Are there connections between this memory and how you think of yourself now?

2. Have you ever been to a fair—a county or state fair, a Medieval or Renaissance festival? If so, write an account of it that tries to capture the experience. If not, imagine what the experience might be like. What aspects of the experience stand out? What makes it different from regular daily life? How is it similar?

MAKING CONNECTIONS

1. Compare the **tone** in "Araby" and "Wild Berry Blue." How would you characterize each in terms of humor? What does the use or lack of humor tell us about the way each story handles the significance that the adult **narrator** attaches to childhood experience?

2. Carefully examine the language of paragraph 5 of "Araby" (p. 126). What **stylistic** devices allow the narrator to transform a simple shopping trip into a chivalric romance? Can you find a passage in "Wild Berry Blue" in which Galchen uses style to transform her equally everyday setting and situation into something seemingly more significant or more grand?

3. Compare the endings of these two stories. How do the two narrators think of themselves? How do you think these pictures of their past selves relate to their sense of themselves in the present?

CASE STUDY IN ARGUMENT

FINDING GRACE IN FLANNERY O'CONNOR

The fiction of Flannery O'Connor has become famous to readers for the darkness of its vision, for its vivid picture of the Southern grotesque, for its sharp humor, and for its unyielding religious undergirding. Her fiction has also become famous to critics not only for its excellence and power but also for the critical conundrums it introduces. Those who try to teach or write about O'Connor's work find very quickly that there are tensions in her work that translate into tensions between different arguments about exactly what the work is up to. Readers and critics are further vexed by the fact that O'Connor often offered her own interpretations of her stories (see her comments from *Mystery and Manners* about "A Good Man Is Hard to Find" on p. 153), though this did not always go over smoothly, as the essays in this casebook from Bob Dowell, Hallman B. Bryant, and Michael Clark will attest.

As you read "A Good Man Is Hard to Find," keep in mind the fact that these long-running arguments over O'Connor's stories exist, and that in thinking further after your first reading, you will be well-served to keep your mind open to the possibility of multiple interpretations—and to laughing at what might seem at first like some pretty dark stuff.

FLANNERY O'CONNOR (1925–1964)

A GOOD MAN IS HARD TO FIND 1953

The grandmother didn't want to go to Florida. She wanted to visit some of her connections in east Tennessee and she was seizing at every chance to change Bailey's mind. Bailey was the son she lived with, her only boy. He was sitting on the edge of his chair at the table, bent over the orange sports section of the *Journal*. "Now look here, Bailey," she said, "see here, read this," and she stood with one hand on her thin hip and the other rattling the newspaper at his bald head. "Here this fellow that calls himself The Misfit is aloose from the Federal Pen and headed toward Florida and you read here what it says he did to these people. Just you read it. I wouldn't take my children in any direction with a criminal like that aloose in it. I couldn't answer to my conscience if I did."

Bailey didn't look up from his reading so she wheeled around then and faced the children's mother, a young woman in slacks, whose face was as broad and innocent as a cabbage and was tied around with a green headkerchief that had two points on the top like a rabbit's ears. She was sitting on the sofa, feeding the baby his apricots out of a jar. "The children have been to Florida before," the old lady said. "You all ought to take them somewhere else for a change so they would see different parts of the world and be broad. They never have been to east Tennessee."

The children's mother didn't seem to hear her but the eight-year-old boy, John Wesley, a stocky child with glasses, said, "If you don't want to go to Florida, why dontcha stay at home?" He and the little girl, June Star, were reading the funny papers on the floor.

"She wouldn't stay at home to be queen for a day," June Star said without raising her yellow head.

"Yes and what would you do if this fellow, The Misfit, caught you?" the 5 grandmother asked.

"I'd smack his face," John Wesley said.

"She wouldn't stay at home for a million bucks," June Star said. "Afraid she'd miss something. She has to go everywhere we go."

"All right, Miss," the grandmother said. "Just remember that the next time you want me to curl your hair."

June Star said her hair was naturally curly.

The next morning the grandmother was the first one in the car, ready to go. 10 She had her big black valise that looked like the head of a hippopotamus in one corner, and underneath it she was hiding a basket with Pitty Sing, the cat, in it. She didn't intend for the cat to be left alone in the house for three days because he would miss her too much and she was afraid he might brush against one of the gas burners and accidentally asphyxiate himself. Her son, Bailey, didn't like to arrive at a motel with a cat.

She sat in the middle of the back seat with John Wesley and June Star on either side of her. Bailey and the children's mother and the baby sat in front and they left Atlanta at eight forty-five with the mileage on the car at 55890. The grandmother wrote this down because she thought it would be interesting to say how many miles they had been when they got back. It took them twenty minutes to reach the outskirts of the city.

The old lady settled herself comfortably, removing her white cotton gloves and putting them up with her purse on the shelf in front of the back window. The children's mother still had on slacks and still had her head tied up in a green kerchief, but the grandmother had on a navy blue straw sailor hat with a bunch of white violets on the brim and a navy blue dress with a small white dot in the print. Her collars and cuffs were white organdy trimmed with lace and at her neckline she had pinned a purple spray of cloth violets containing a sachet. In case of an accident, anyone seeing her dead on the highway would know at once that she was a lady.

She said she thought it was going to be a good day for driving, neither too hot nor too cold, and she cautioned Bailey that the speed limit was fifty-five miles an hour and that the patrolmen hid themselves behind billboards and small clumps of trees and sped out after you before you had a chance to slow down. She pointed out interesting details of the scenery: Stone Mountain; the blue granite that in some places came up to both sides of the highway; the brilliant red clay banks slightly streaked with purple; and the various crops that made rows of green lace-work on the ground. The trees were full of silver-white sunlight and the meanest of them sparkled. The children were reading comic magazines and their mother had gone back to sleep.

"Let's go through Georgia fast so we won't have to look at it much," John Wesley said.

"If I were a little boy," said the grandmother, "I wouldn't talk about my native state that way. Tennessee has the mountains and Georgia has the hills." 15

"Tennessee is just a hillbilly dumping ground," John Wesley said, "and Georgia is a lousy state too."

"You said it," June Star said.

"In my time," said the grandmother, folding her thin veined fingers, "children were more respectful of their native states and their parents and everything else. People did right then. Oh look at the cute little pickaninny!" she said and pointed to a Negro child standing in the door of a shack. "Wouldn't that make a picture, now?" she asked and they all turned and looked at the little Negro out of the back window. He waved.

"He didn't have any britches on," June Star said.

"He probably didn't have any," the grandmother explained. "Little niggers in 20 the country don't have things like we do. If I could paint, I'd paint that picture," she said.

The children exchanged comic books.

The grandmother offered to hold the baby and the children's mother passed him over the front seat to her. She set him on her knee and bounced him and told him about the things they were passing. She rolled her eyes and screwed up her mouth and stuck her leathery thin face into his smooth bland one. Occasionally he gave her a faraway smile. They passed a large cotton field with five or six graves fenced in the middle of it, like a small island. "Look at the graveyard!" the grandmother said, pointing it out. "That was the old family burying ground. That belonged to the plantation."

"Where's the plantation?" John Wesley asked.

"Gone With the Wind," said the grandmother. "Ha. Ha."

When the children finished all the comic books they had brought, they 25 opened the lunch and ate it. The grandmother ate a peanut butter sandwich and an olive and would not let the children throw the box and the paper napkins out the window. When there was nothing else to do they played a game by choosing a cloud and making the other two guess what shape it suggested. John Wesley took one the shape of a cow and June Star guessed a cow and John Wesley said, no, an automobile, and June Star said he didn't play fair, and they began to slap each other over the grandmother.

The grandmother said she would tell them a story if they would keep quiet. When she told a story, she rolled her eyes and waved her head and was very dramatic. She said once when she was a maiden lady she had been courted by a Mr. Edgar Atkins Teagarden from Jasper, Georgia. She said he was a very good-looking man and a gentleman and that he brought her a watermelon every Saturday afternoon with his initials cut in it, E.A.T. Well, one Saturday, she said, Mr. Teagarden brought the watermelon and there was nobody at home and he left it on the front porch and returned in his buggy to Jasper, but she never got the watermelon, she said, because a nigger boy ate it when he saw the initials, E.A.T.! This story tickled John Wesley's funny bone and he giggled and giggled but June Star didn't think it was any good. She said she wouldn't marry a man that just brought her a watermelon on Saturday. The grandmother said she would have done well to marry Mr. Teagarden because he was a gentleman and had bought Coca-Cola stock when it first came out and that he had died only a few years ago, a very wealthy man.

They stopped at The Tower for barbecued sandwiches. The Tower was a part stucco and part wood filling station and dance hall set in a clearing outside of Timothy. A fat man named Red Sammy Butts ran it and there were signs stuck here and there on the building and for miles up and down the highway saying, TRY RED SAMMY'S FAMOUS BARBECUE. NONE LIKE FAMOUS RED SAMMY'S! RED SAM! THE FAT BOY WITH THE HAPPY LAUGH. A VETERAN! RED SAMMY'S YOUR MAN!

Red Sammy was lying on the bare ground outside The Tower with his head under a truck while a gray monkey about a foot high, chained to a small chinaberry tree, chattered nearby. The monkey sprang back into the tree and got on the highest limb as soon as he saw the children jump out of the car and run toward him.

Inside, The Tower was a long dark room with a counter at one end and tables at the other and dancing space in the middle. They all sat down at a board table next to the nickelodeon and Red Sam's wife, a tall burnt-brown woman with hair and eyes lighter than her skin, came and took their order. The children's mother put a dime in the machine and played "The Tennessee Waltz," and the grandmother said that tune always made her want to dance. She asked Bailey if he would like to dance but he only glared at her. He didn't have a naturally sunny disposition like she did and trips made him nervous. The grandmother's brown eyes were very bright. She swayed her head from side to side and pretended she was dancing in her chair. June Star said play something she could tap to so the children's mother put in another dime and played a fast number and June Star stepped out onto the dance floor and did her tap routine.

"Ain't she cute?" Red Sam's wife said, leaning over the counter. "Would you 30 like to come be my little girl?"

"No I certainly wouldn't," June Star said. "I wouldn't live in a broken-down place like this for a million bucks!" and she ran back to the table.

"Ain't she cute?" the woman repeated, stretching her mouth politely.

"Aren't you ashamed?" hissed the grandmother.

Red Sam came in and told his wife to quit lounging on the counter and hurry up with these people's order. His khaki trousers reached just to his hip bones and his stomach hung over them like a sack of meal swaying under his shirt. He came over and sat down at a table nearby and let out a combination sigh and yodel. "You can't win," he said. "You can't win," and he wiped his sweating red face off with a gray handkerchief. "These days you don't know who to trust," he said. "Ain't that the truth?"

"People are certainly not nice like they used to be," said the grandmother.   35

"Two fellers come in here last week," Red Sammy said, "driving a Chrysler. It was a old beat-up car but it was a good one and these boys looked all right to me. Said they worked at the mill and you know I let them fellers charge the gas they bought? Now why did I do that?"

"Because you're a good man!" the grandmother said at once.

"Yes'm, I suppose so," Red Sam said as if he were struck with this answer.

His wife brought the orders, carrying the five plates all at once without a tray, two in each hand and one balanced on her arm. "It isn't a soul in this green world of God's that you can trust," she said. "And I don't count nobody out of that, not nobody," she repeated, looking at Red Sammy.

"Did you read about that criminal, The Misfit, that's escaped?" asked the   40 grandmother.

"I wouldn't be a bit surprised if he didn't attack this place right here," said the woman. "If he hears about it being here, I wouldn't be none surprised to see him. If he hears it's two cent in the cash register, I wouldn't be a tall surprised if he. . . ."

"That'll do," Red Sam said. "Go bring these people their Co'-Colas," and the woman went off to get the rest of the order.

"A good man is hard to find," Red Sammy said. "Everything is getting terrible. I remember the day you could go off and leave your screen door unlatched. Not no more."

He and the grandmother discussed better times. The old lady said that in her opinion Europe was entirely to blame for the way things were now. She said the way Europe acted you would think we were made of money and Red Sam said it was no use talking about it, she was exactly right. The children ran outside into the white sunlight and looked at the monkey in the lacy chinaberry tree. He was busy catching fleas on himself and biting each one carefully between his teeth as if it were a delicacy.

They drove off again into the hot afternoon. The grandmother took cat naps   45 and woke up every few minutes with her own snoring. Outside of Toombsboro she woke up and recalled an old plantation that she had visited in this neighborhood once when she was a young lady. She said the house had six white columns across the front and that there was an avenue of oaks leading up to it and two little wooden trellis arbors on either side in front where you sat down with your suitor after a stroll in the garden. She recalled exactly which road to turn off to get to it. She knew that Bailey would not be willing to lose any time looking at an old house, but the more she talked about it, the more she wanted to see it once again and find out if the little twin arbors were still standing. "There was a secret panel in this house," she said craftily, not telling the truth but wishing that she were, "and the story went that all the family silver was hidden in it when Sherman[1] came through but it was never found. . . ."

"Hey!" John Wesley said. "Let's go see it! We'll find it! We'll poke all the woodwork and find it! Who lives there? Where do you turn off at? Hey Pop, can't we turn off there?"

"We never have seen a house with a secret panel!" June Star shrieked. "Let's go to the house with the secret panel! Hey Pop, can't we go see the house with the secret panel!"

"It's not far from here, I know," the grandmother said. "It won't take over twenty minutes."

Bailey was looking straight ahead. His jaw was as rigid as a horseshoe. "No," he said.

The children began to yell and scream that they wanted to see the house   50
with the secret panel. John Wesley kicked the back of the front seat and June Star hung over her mother's shoulder and whined desperately into her ear that they never had any fun even on their vacation, that they could never do what THEY wanted to do. The baby began to scream and John Wesley kicked the back of the seat so hard that his father could feel the blows in his kidney.

"All right!" he shouted and drew the car to a stop at the side of the road. "Will you all shut up? Will you all just shut up for one second? If you don't shut up, we won't go anywhere."

"It would be very educational for them," the grandmother murmured.

"All right," Bailey said, "but get this: this is the only time we're going to stop for anything like this. This is the one and only time."

"The dirt road that you have to turn down is about a mile back," the grand-mother directed. "I marked it when we passed."

"A dirt road," Bailey groaned.   55

After they had turned around and were headed toward the dirt road, the grandmother recalled other points about the house, the beautiful glass over the front doorway and the candle-lamp in the hall. John Wesley said that the secret panel was probably in the fireplace.

"You can't go inside this house," Bailey said. "You don't know who lives there."

"While you all talk to the people in front, I'll run around behind and get in a window," John Wesley suggested.

"We'll all stay in the car," his mother said.

They turned onto the dirt road and the car raced roughly along in a swirl   60
of pink dust. The grandmother recalled the times when there were no paved roads and thirty miles was a day's journey. The dirt road was hilly and there were sudden washes in it and sharp curves on dangerous embankments. All at once they would be on a hill, looking down over the blue tops of trees for miles around, then the next minute, they would be in a red depression with the dust-coated trees looking down on them.

[1] William Tecumseh Sherman (1820–1891) was a Union Army general during the American Civil War.

"This place had better turn up in a minute," Bailey said, "or I'm going to turn around."

The road looked as if no one had traveled on it for months.

"It's not much farther," the grandmother said and just as she said it, a horrible thought came to her. The thought was so embarrassing that she turned red in the face and her eyes dilated and her feet jumped up, upsetting her valise in the corner. The instant the valise moved, the newspaper top she had over the basket under it rose with a snarl and Pitty Sing, the cat, sprang onto Bailey's shoulder.

The children were thrown to the floor and their mother, clutching the baby, was thrown out the door onto the ground; the old lady was thrown into the front seat. The car turned over once and landed right-side-up in a gulch off the side of the road. Bailey remained in the driver's seat with the cat—gray-striped with a broad white face and an orange nose—clinging to his neck like a caterpillar.

As soon as the children saw they could move their arms and legs, they 65 scrambled out of the car, shouting, "We've had an ACCIDENT!" The grandmother was curled up under the dashboard, hoping she was injured so that Bailey's wrath would not come down on her all at once. The horrible thought she had before the accident was that the house she had remembered so vividly was not in Georgia but in Tennessee.

Bailey removed the cat from his neck with both hands and flung it out the window against the side of a pine tree. Then he got out of the car and started looking for the children's mother. She was sitting against the side of the red gutted ditch, holding the screaming baby, but she only had a cut down her face and a broken shoulder. "We've had an ACCIDENT!" the children screamed in a frenzy of delight.

"But nobody's killed," June Star said with disappointment as the grandmother limped out of the car, her hat still pinned to her head but the broken front brim standing up at a jaunty angle and the violet spray hanging off the side. They all sat down in the ditch, except the children, to recover from the shock. They were all shaking.

"Maybe a car will come along," said the children's mother hoarsely.

"I believe I have injured an organ," said the grandmother, pressing her side, but no one answered her. Bailey's teeth were clattering. He had on a yellow sport shirt with bright blue parrots designed in it and his face was as yellow as the shirt. The grandmother decided that she would not mention that the house was in Tennessee.

The road was about ten feet above and they could see only the tops of the trees 70 on the other side of it. Behind the ditch they were sitting in there were more woods, tall and dark and deep. In a few minutes they saw a car some distance away on top of a hill, coming slowly as if the occupants were watching them. The grandmother stood up and waved both arms dramatically to attract their attention. The car continued to come on slowly, disappeared around a bend and appeared again, moving even slower, on top of the hill they had gone over. It was a big black battered hearse-like automobile. There were three men in it.

It came to a stop just over them and for some minutes, the driver looked down with a steady expressionless gaze to where they were sitting, and didn't speak. Then he turned his head and muttered something to the other two and they got out. One was a fat boy in black trousers and a red sweat shirt with a silver stallion embossed on the front of it. He moved around on the right side of them and stood staring, his mouth partly open in a kind of loose grin. The other had on khaki pants and a blue striped coat and a gray hat pulled down very low, hiding most of his face. He came around slowly on the left side. Neither spoke.

The driver got out of the car and stood by the side of it, looking down at them. He was an older man than the other two. His hair was just beginning to gray and he wore silver-rimmed spectacles that gave him a scholarly look. He had a long creased face and didn't have on any shirt or undershirt. He had on blue jeans that were too tight for him and was holding a black hat and a gun. The two boys also had guns.

"We've had an ACCIDENT!" the children screamed.

The grandmother had the peculiar feeling that the bespectacled man was someone she knew. His face was as familiar to her as if she had known him all her life but she could not recall who he was. He moved away from the car and began to come down the embankment, placing his feet carefully so that he wouldn't slip. He had on tan and white shoes and no socks, and his ankles were red and thin. "Good afternoon," he said. "I see you all had you a little spill."

"We turned over twice!" said the grandmother.   75

"Oncet," he corrected. "We seen it happen. Try their car and see will it run, Hiram," he said quietly to the boy with the gray hat.

"What you got that gun for?" John Wesley asked. "Whatcha gonna do with that gun?"

"Lady," the man said to the children's mother, "would you mind calling them children to sit down by you? Children make me nervous. I want all you all to sit down right together there where you're at."

"What are you telling US what to do for?" June Star asked.

Behind them the line of woods gaped like a dark open mouth. "Come here,"   80
said their mother.

"Look here now," Bailey said suddenly, "we're in a predicament! We're in...."

The grandmother shrieked. She scrambled to her feet and stood staring. "You're The Misfit!" she said. "I recognized you at once!"

"Yes'm," the man said, smiling slightly as if he were pleased in spite of himself to be known, "but it would have been better for all of you, lady, if you hadn't of reckernized me."

Bailey turned his head sharply and said something to his mother that shocked even the children. The old lady began to cry and The Misfit reddened.

"Lady," he said, "don't you get upset. Sometimes a man says things he don't   85
mean. I don't reckon he meant to talk to you thataway."

"You wouldn't shoot a lady, would you?" the grandmother said and removed a clean handkerchief from her cuff and began to slap at her eyes with it.

The Misfit pointed the toe of his shoe into the ground and made a little hole and then covered it up again. "I would hate to have to," he said.

"Listen," the grandmother almost screamed, "I know you're a good man. You don't look a bit like you have common blood. I know you must come from nice people!"

"Yes mam," he said, "finest people in the world." When he smiled he showed a row of strong white teeth. "God never made a finer woman than my mother and my daddy's heart was pure gold," he said. The boy with the red sweat shirt had come around behind them and was standing with his gun at his hip. The Misfit squatted down on the ground. "Watch them children, Bobby Lee," he said. "You know they make me nervous." He looked at the six of them huddled together in front of him and he seemed to be embarrassed as if he couldn't think of anything to say. "Ain't a cloud in the sky," he remarked, looking up at it. "Don't see no sun but don't see no cloud neither."

"Yes, it's a beautiful day," said the grandmother. "Listen," she said, "you 90 shouldn't call yourself The Misfit because I know you're a good man at heart. I can just look at you and tell."

"Hush!" Bailey yelled. "Hush! Everybody shut up and let me handle this!" He was squatting in the position of a runner about to sprint forward but he didn't move.

"I pre-chate that, lady," The Misfit said and drew a little circle in the ground with the butt of his gun.

"It'll take a half a hour to fix this here car," Hiram called, looking over the raised hood of it.

"Well, first you and Bobby Lee get him and that little boy to step over yonder with you," The Misfit said, pointing to Bailey and John Wesley. "The boys want to ast you something," he said to Bailey. "Would you mind stepping back in them woods there with them?"

"Listen," Bailey began, "we're in a terrible predicament! Nobody realizes 95 what this is," and his voice cracked. His eyes were as blue and intense as the parrots in his shirt and he remained perfectly still.

The grandmother reached up to adjust her hat brim as if she were going to the woods with him but it came off in her hand. She stood staring at it and after a second she let it fall to the ground. Hiram pulled Bailey up by the arm as if he were assisting an old man. John Wesley caught hold of his father's hand and Bobby Lee followed. They went off toward the woods and just as they reached the dark edge, Bailey turned and supporting himself against a gray naked pine trunk, he shouted, "I'll be back in a minute, Mamma, wait on me!"

"Come back this instant!" his mother shrilled but they all disappeared into the woods.

"Bailey Boy!" the grandmother called in a tragic voice but she found she was looking at The Misfit squatting on the ground in front of her. "I just know you're a good man," she said desperately. "You're not a bit common!"

"Nome, I ain't a good man," The Misfit said after a second as if he had considered her statement carefully, "but I ain't the worst in the world neither. My daddy said I was a different breed of dog from my brothers and sisters. 'You know,' Daddy said, 'it's some that can live their whole life out without asking about it and it's others has to know why it is, and this boy is one of the latters. He's going to be into everything!'" He put on his black hat and looked up suddenly and then away deep into the woods as if he were embarrassed again. "I'm sorry I don't have on a shirt before you ladies," he said, hunching his shoulders slightly. "We buried our clothes that we had on when we escaped and we're just making do until we can get better. We borrowed these from some folks we met," he explained.

"That's perfectly all right," the grandmother said. "Maybe Bailey has an extra 100 shirt in his suitcase."

"I'll look and see terrectly," The Misfit said.

"Where are they taking him?" the children's mother screamed.

"Daddy was a card himself," The Misfit said. "You couldn't put anything over on him. He never got in trouble with the Authorities though. Just had the knack of handling them."

"You could be honest too if you'd only try," said the grandmother. "Think how wonderful it would be to settle down and live a comfortable life and not have to think about somebody chasing you all the time."

The Misfit kept scratching in the ground with the butt of his gun as if he 105 were thinking about it. "Yes'm, somebody is always after you," he murmured.

The grandmother noticed how thin his shoulder blades were just behind his hat because she was standing up looking down on him. "Do you ever pray?" she asked.

He shook his head. All she saw was the black hat wiggle between his shoulder blades. "Nome," he said.

There was a pistol shot from the woods, followed closely by another. Then silence. The old lady's head jerked around. She could hear the wind move through the tree tops like a long satisfied insuck of breath. "Bailey Boy!" she called.

"I was a gospel singer for a while," The Misfit said. "I been most everything. Been in the arm service, both land and sea, at home and abroad, been twict married, been an undertaker, been with the railroads, plowed Mother Earth, been in a tornado, seen a man burnt alive oncet," and he looked up at the children's mother and the little girl who were sitting close together, their faces white and their eyes glassy; "I even seen a woman flogged," he said.

"Pray, pray," the grandmother began, "pray, pray. . . ." 110

"I never was a bad boy that I remember of," The Misfit said in an almost dreamy voice, "but somewheres along the line I done something wrong and got sent to the penitentiary. I was buried alive," and he looked up and held her attention to him by a steady stare.

"That's when you should have started to pray," she said. "What did you do to get sent to the penitentiary that first time?"

"Turn to the right, it was a wall," The Misfit said, looking up again at the cloudless sky. "Turn to the left, it was a wall. Look up it was a ceiling, look down it was a floor. I forget what I done, lady. I set there and set there, trying to remember what it was I done and I ain't recalled it to this day. Oncet in a while, I would think it was coming to me, but it never come."

"Maybe they put you in by mistake," the old lady said vaguely.

"Nome," he said. "It wasn't no mistake. They had the papers on me." 115

"You must have stolen something," she said.

The Misfit sneered slightly. "Nobody had nothing I wanted," he said. "It was a head-doctor at the penitentiary said what I had done was kill my daddy but I known that for a lie. My daddy died in nineteen ought nineteen of the epidemic flu and I never had a thing to do with it. He was buried in the Mount Hopewell Baptist churchyard and you can see for yourself."

"If you would pray," the old lady said, "Jesus would help you."

"That's right," The Misfit said.

"Well then, why don't you pray?" she asked trembling with delight suddenly. 120

"I don't want no hep," he said. "I'm doing all right by myself."

Bobby Lee and Hiram came ambling back from the woods. Bobby Lee was dragging a yellow shirt with bright blue parrots in it.

"Throw me that shirt, Bobby Lee," The Misfit said. The shirt came flying at him and landed on his shoulder and he put it on. The grandmother couldn't name what the shirt reminded her of. "No, lady," The Misfit said while he was buttoning it up, "I found out the crime don't matter. You can do one thing or you can do another, kill a man or take a tire off his car, because sooner or later you're going to forget what it was you done and just be punished for it."

The children's mother had begun to make heaving noises as if she couldn't get her breath. "Lady," he asked, "would you and that little girl like to step off yonder with Bobby Lee and Hiram and join your husband?"

"Yes, thank you," the mother said faintly. Her left arm dangled helplessly and 125 she was holding the baby, who had gone to sleep, in the other. "Hep that lady up, Hiram," The Misfit said as she struggled to climb out of the ditch, "and Bobby Lee, you hold onto that little girl's hand."

"I don't want to hold hands with him," June Star said. "He reminds me of a pig."

The fat boy blushed and laughed and caught her by the arm and pulled her off into the woods after Hiram and her mother.

Alone with The Misfit, the grandmother found that she had lost her voice. There was not a cloud in the sky nor any sun. There was nothing around her but woods. She wanted to tell him that he must pray. She opened and closed her mouth several times before anything came out. Finally she found herself saying, "Jesus, Jesus," meaning Jesus will help you, but the way she was saying it, it sounded as if she might be cursing.

"Yes'm," The Misfit said as if he agreed. "Jesus thown everything off balance. It was the same case with Him as with me except He hadn't committed any crime and they could prove I had committed one because they had the papers on me. Of course," he said, "they never shown me my papers. That's why I sign myself now. I said long ago, you get your signature and sign everything you do and keep a copy of it. Then you'll know what you done and you can hold up the crime to the punishment and see do they match and in the end you'll have something to prove you ain't been treated right. I call myself The Misfit," he said, "because I can't make what all I done wrong fit what all I gone through in punishment."

There was a piercing scream from the woods, followed closely by a pis- 130 tol report. "Does it seem right to you, lady, that one is punished a heap and another ain't punished at all?"

"Jesus!" the old lady cried. "You've got good blood! I know you wouldn't shoot a lady! I know you come from nice people! Pray! Jesus, you ought not to shoot a lady. I'll give you all the money I've got!"

"Lady," The Misfit said, looking beyond her far into the woods, "there never was a body that give the undertaker a tip."

There were two more pistol reports and the grandmother raised her head like a parched old turkey hen crying for water and called, "Bailey Boy, Bailey Boy!" as if her heart would break.

"Jesus was the only One that ever raised the dead," The Misfit continued, "and He shouldn't have done it. He thown everything off balance. If He did what He said, then it's nothing for you to do but thow away everything and follow Him, and if He didn't, then it's nothing for you to do but enjoy the few minutes you got left the best way you can—by killing somebody or burning down his house or doing some other meanness to him. No pleasure but meanness," he said and his voice had become almost a snarl.

"Maybe He didn't raise the dead," the old lady mumbled, not knowing what 135 she was saying and feeling so dizzy that she sank down in the ditch with her legs twisted under her.

"I wasn't there so I can't say He didn't," The Misfit said. "I wisht I had of been there," he said, hitting the ground with his fist. "It ain't right I wasn't there because if I had of been there I would of known. Listen lady," he said in a high voice, "if I had of been there I would of known and I wouldn't be like I am now." His voice seemed about to crack and the grandmother's head cleared for an instant. She saw the man's face twisted close to her own as if he were going to cry and she murmured, "Why you're one of my babies. You're one of my own children!" She reached out and touched him on the shoulder. The Misfit sprang back as if a snake had bitten him and shot her three times through the chest. Then he put his gun down on the ground and took off his glasses and began to clean them.

Hiram and Bobby Lee returned from the woods and stood over the ditch, looking down at the grandmother who half sat and half lay in a puddle of blood with her legs crossed under her like a child's and her face smiling up at the cloudless sky.

Without his glasses, The Misfit's eyes were red-rimmed and pale and defenseless-looking. "Take her off and thow her where you thown the others," he said, picking up the cat that was rubbing itself against his leg.

"She was a talker, wasn't she?" Bobby Lee said, sliding down the ditch with a yodel.

"She would of been a good woman," The Misfit said, "if it had been some- 140 body there to shoot her every minute of her life."

"Some fun!" Bobby Lee said.

"Shut up, Bobby Lee," The Misfit said. "It's no real pleasure in life."

FOR ANALYSIS

1. From whose **point of view** is the story told—that is, through whose eyes do we see events unfold? What is the effect of O'Connor's choice of **narrator**?

2. How would you describe the **tone** of this story? Is it uniform, or does it vary? How? Why do you think O'Connor uses tone the way she does?

3. With whom do you identify in this story? One character, or more, or none? How do you think identification works in this story?

4. Describe this story's **setting**. Does it inform the **mood** or tone of the story? How?

WRITING TOPICS

1. Compare and contrast The Misfit and the grandmother. Do they come to seem more different or more alike over the course of the story? In what ways?

2. The story's last line is The Misfit's: he says, "It's no real pleasure in life" (para. 142). While "A Good Man Is Hard to Find" is a sad, violent story, there is pleasure in reading it. Write about some of these pleasures. How do you reconcile them with the story's darkness?

MAKING CONNECTIONS

1. Hawthorne's "Young Goodman Brown" (p. 77) and "A Good Man Is Hard to Find" are both in part about religious belief, though they are of course very different stories. In what do the main characters—Brown, The Misfit, and the grandmother—believe, and not believe?

2. An important line in Bambara's "The Lesson" (p. 98) comes near the end: " 'Anybody else learn anything today?' " (para. 52). "The Lesson" is more obviously a story of education, but in what way is "A Good Man Is Hard to Find" also one? What character learns a lesson in the story? What is the lesson? "The Lesson" ends with the **narrator** reflecting on the impact of her lesson. What is the impact of the lesson in O'Connor's story?

FROM MYSTERY AND MANNERS 1963

It is true that the old lady is a hypocritical old soul; her wits are no match for the Misfit's, nor is her capacity for grace equal to his; yet I think the unprejudiced reader will feel that the Grandmother has a special kind of triumph in this story which instinctively we do not allow to someone altogether bad.

I often ask myself what makes a story work and what makes it hold up as a story, and I have decided that it is probably some action, some gesture of a character that is unlike any other in the story, one which indicates where the real heart of the story lies. This would have to be an action or a gesture which was both totally right and totally unexpected; it would have to be one that was both in character and beyond character; it would have to suggest both the world and eternity. The action or gesture I'm talking about would have to be on the anagogical level, that is, the level which has to do with the Divine life and our participation in it. It would be a gesture that transcended any neat allegory that might have been intended or any pat moral categories a reader could make. It would be a gesture which somehow made contact with mystery.

There is a point in this story where such a gesture occurs. The Grandmother is at last alone, facing the Misfit. Her head clears for an instant and she realizes, even in her limited way, that she is responsible for the man before her and joined to him by ties of kinship which have their roots deep in the mystery she has been merely prattling about so far. And at this point, she does the right thing, she makes the right gesture.

I find that students are often puzzled by what she says and does here, but I think myself that if I took out this gesture and what she says with it, I would have no story. What was left would not be worth your attention. Our age not only does not have a very sharp eye for the almost imperceptible intrusions of grace, it no longer has much feeling for the nature of the violences which precede and follow them. The devil's greatest wile, Baudelaire has said, is to convince us that he does not exist.

I suppose the reasons for the use of so much violence in modern fiction will differ with each writer who uses it, but in my own stories I have found that violence is strangely capable of returning my characters to reality and preparing them to accept their moment of grace. Their heads are so hard that almost nothing else will do the work. This idea, that reality is something to which we must be returned at considerable cost, is one which is seldom understood by the casual reader, but it is one which is implicit in the Christian view of the world. 5

I don't want to equate the Misfit with the devil. I prefer to think that, however unlikely this may seem, the old lady's gesture, like the mustard-seed, will grow to be a great crow-filled tree in the Misfit's heart and will be enough of a pain to him there to turn him into the prophet he was meant to become. But that's another story.

This story has been called grotesque, but I prefer to call it literal. A good story is literal in the same sense that a child's drawing is literal. When a child draws, he doesn't intend to distort but to set down exactly what he sees, and as his gaze is direct, he sees the lines that create motion. Now the lines of motion that interest the writer are usually invisible. They are lines of spiritual motion. And in this story you should be on the lookout for such things as the action of grace in the Grandmother's soul, and not for the dead bodies.

MAKING CONNECTIONS

1. How do you understand O'Connor's description of the grandmother's "gesture" as being about grace? Does your interpretation of the story change if you read it as being about a literal moment of salvation?

2. Do you read the story differently than O'Connor does? Is her interpretation helpful? What does it mean about how literature works that a reader can disagree with a writer about her own work?

BOB DOWELL   (B. 1932)

FROM THE MOMENT OF GRACE
IN THE FICTION OF FLANNERY
O'CONNOR   1965

Flannery O'Connor revealed, on more than one occasion, her concern about the public's misconstruing of the meaning of her fiction. She was perturbed by certain critics placing her in the School of Southern Degeneracy, and she was insulted by others placing her in the Southern Gothic School. "Degeneracy," she said, "at least can be taken in a moral sense," for it suggests a standard to degenerate from; but "the Gothic is a degeneracy which is not recognized as such" (L).

In a lecture entitled "Some Aspects of the Grotesque in Southern Literature,"[1] delivered at East Texas State University in the fall of 1962, Miss O'Connor seemed to answer misdirected criticism of her fiction by giving a general explanation of what she was attempting as a writer. Although in this lecture Miss O'Connor generally speaks collectively of Southern writers, she seems to be primarily explaining her own "poetics." Commenting on her grotesque characters, she concludes that the public views these protagonists as freaks and, "with its clinical bias invariably approaches them from the standpoint of abnormal psychology" (L). Such a view obviously annoys the author, for her own view of man is unmistakably theological, and in commenting on the milieu from which her characters are drawn she says that "in the South the general conception of man is still, in the main, theological" (L). The South is hardly Christ-centered, she explains, but "it is most certainly Christ-haunted" (L). Needless to say, psychological explanations for the compulsions of her characters will hardly suffice.

A perusal of Miss O'Connor's fiction will reveal that Christ-haunted figures furnish the author her principal subject matter. Through the conflicts, often violent ones, of these protagonists who oscillate between belief and unbelief, between self-will and submission, the author presents her view of reality. This

---

[1] References to this lecture are indicated in the text as follows: (L).

grotesque drama that she presents takes place in a discernible theological framework in which there is an implicit acceptance of the concept of a created universe, "with all that implies of human limitations and human obligations to an all-powerful Creator" (L). Such a view heightens man's every action, for his every action is seen "under the aspect of eternity" (L). Thus, Miss O'Connor's fiction is primarily concerned with man's life-and-death spiritual struggle. The protagonist, rebelling against belief, forces a crisis that reveals to him his haughty and willful misconception of reality, at which time he experiences what Miss O'Connor has called his "moment of grace." Without exception this moment comes at great price.

The grandmother in "A Good Man Is Hard to Find" experiences her moment of grace only seconds before the Misfit murders her by firing three bullets through her chest. "A Good Man Is Hard to Find" was my introduction to Flannery O'Connor, and I must admit that after considerable reflection on the story, I was still somewhat puzzled by the whole thing and particularly by the grandmother's final remark to the Misfit. As if confessing, she says, "Why you're one of my babies. You're one of my own children" [para. 136]. Upon being questioned about this passage, Miss O'Connor explained that this was the grandmother's "moment of grace."

Such an explanation makes sense only in a theological framework. The Mis- 5
fit's meanness is the result of his inability to believe. If Christ does exist and can raise the dead, says the Misfit, "then it's nothing for you to do but throw away everything and follow Him, and if He didn't, then it's nothing for you to do but enjoy the few minutes you got left the best way you can—by killing somebody or burning down his house or doing some other meanness to him. No pleasure but meanness" [para. 134]. Because he cannot believe, the Misfit commits himself to evil. The grandmother recognizes him as one of her own children because she suddenly realizes that her superficial commitment to good has been meaningless because she lived without faith, that is to say without Christ. By rejecting Christ, man usurps that place for himself, thereby committing the final disobedience to his Creator. In the O'Connor world whether one commits himself to evil deeds or good deeds makes little difference ultimately, for without Christ one's actions only lead to evil.

"A Good Man Is Hard to Find" dramatizes this theological view. Although it is the Misfit who has the grandmother's family killed and then kills the grandmother himself, it is the grandmother who causes the wreck that places the family at the mercy of the Misfit. It is also the grandmother who identifies the Misfit, thus causing him to deem it necessary to do away with the family for his own safety. [. . .]

Though willing to exploit his unwilling antics, Miss O'Connor never loses sight of man as a created being whose soul is precious to his Creator. Despite his ignorance, his rebelliousness, and his tendency toward evil, man still realizes his fullest potential by participating in a supernatural relation with his Creator. This depends upon his recognition of the existence of evil, of his own tendency toward evil, and his ability to triumph over evil through grace, a supernatural gift from God which comes only with man's full realization of his lost condition and his dependence on Christ. With this realization, which constitutes his moment of grace, man's salvation is begun; he can then begin to fulfill the purpose of his existence, which is to reflect the goodness of his Creator and to share the happiness of heaven with Him. This is Miss O'Connor's view of ultimate reality. [. . .]

Miss O'Connor sought to give new life to what she believed to be significant religious truths that were once a living reality but which the modern mind has tended to either distort or reject. Her stories, which are in a sense grotesque parables, dramatize the existence of evil. Satan's greatest triumph, her works seem to suggest, lies in the fact that he has convinced the world that he does not exist. But for Miss O'Connor he does exist. The backwoods fanatics who either believe he exists or at least are preoccupied with the possibility of his existence may seem ludicrously grotesque to most readers. Yet Miss O'Connor gives serious treatment to these grotesques because their concerns are her concerns. In their defense, she has publicly stated that "their fanaticism is a reproach, not simply an eccentricity. Those who, like Amos or Jeremiah, embrace a neglected truth will be seen to be the most grotesque of all" (L). The conflict between grace and evil in the lives of her characters reflects for the author the most significant drama in the realm of human experience.

MAKING CONNECTIONS

1. With his "Thus" (para. 3), Dowell makes a claim about O'Connor's fiction. Do you find the evidence that leads up to it convincing? What assumptions about what a story means or is concerned with underlie his claim? What differing assumptions might undermine his claim?

2. Dowell cites O'Connor's distinction between theological and psychological explanations for her **characters'** motivations. Reflect on this distinction. Do you think it is helpful? What psychological motivations would you ascribe to the characters in "A Good Man Is Hard to Find"?

HALLMAN B. BRYANT (B. 1936)

READING THE MAP IN "A GOOD MAN IS HARD TO FIND" 1981

Flannery O'Connor, remarking on her most famous short story, "A Good Man Is Hard to Find," issues several caveats to critics. She allows that "a certain amount of what is the significance of this" kind of investigation has to go on in teaching and in literary analysis, but she cautions against reducing a story to "a problem to be solved" so that it becomes "something which you evaporate to get Instant Enlightenment."

Without evaporating too much I will try to shed light on the significance of some small details in "A Good Man Is Hard to Find." Although I do not think an analysis of O'Connor's use of place names in the story will create instant enlightenment, I believe that the towns alluded to along the route which the family travels were chosen for two reasons: first, and most obviously, to foreshadow; and second, to augment the theme of the story. Furthermore, because the numerous places mentioned in the story can actually be found on the map, with only one important exception, it is thus possible to estimate within a few miles the physical distance that the family travels.

The first thing one notices about "A Good Man Is Hard to Find" is that it is set in a real place—in the state of Georgia. The opening scene describes an Atlanta family quarreling about their vacation plans. The grandmother is opposed to going to Florida ostensibly because a convict "that calls himself The Misfit is aloose from the Federal pen and headed toward Florida." (Apparently the Federal penitentiary from which The Misfit has escaped is the one in Atlanta, although it is not specified in the story.) Regardless of the threat posed by The Misfit, the family heads south for Florida instead of east Tennessee where the grandmother had tried to persuade them to take her. We are told that the family left Atlanta at 8:35 in the morning with the mileage on the car at 55890, a fact recorded by the grandmother because she "thought it would be interesting to say how many miles they had been when they got back." From this point on one can literally follow the journey of the family with a road map and take the mileage they put on their car before the wreck and the subsequent meeting with The Misfit and his henchmen.

One odd fact about their route emerges immediately to anyone familiar with Atlanta and its environs. Although the family lives in Atlanta and is headed south, we are told that they pass Stone Mountain along the way. This natural phenomenon and tourist attraction is about fifteen or sixteen miles from Atlanta on the northeast side of the city. At the time the story was written, one had to follow U.S. 78 North to get to Stone Mountain, a highly unlikely road to take out of Atlanta if one is going to Florida.[1]

---

[1] The detour by Stone Mountain was probably due to O'Connor's uncertainty about its exact location; she simply found it a convenient allusion since Stone Mountain was for years Georgia's most famous tourist attraction, but perhaps there is more than meets the eye. In 1915 a project was begun by the United Daughters of the Confederacy which called for Robert E. Lee and his lieutenants to be carved in heroic scale on the vertical face of the mountain. Ironically, the artist commissioned for the job was a Yankee sculptor named Gutzon Borglum who blasted and chiseled on the mountain until 1928 when funds and patience ran out. After expenditure of hundreds of thousands of dollars in a vain effort to impose the heroes of the "Lost Cause" on the side of the mountain, the project was dropped. The scarred carvings, empty catwalks and scaffolds were reminders of a long series of errors and frustrations of the U.D.C. ladies who dreamed of keeping the past alive with a memorial that would be "the perpetuation of a vision." (See *The Story of Stone Mountain* by Willard Neal [Atlanta: Neal and Rogers, 1963], 23–33). Flannery O'Connor was amused by the quixotic qualities of the U.D.C., and Stone Mountain would evoke for Georgians of O'Connor's generation the folly of a sentimental project—a project almost as futile as the grandmother's in the story, whose fascination with past grandeur is congruent with that of the U.D.C.'s and has equally unfortunate results.

Although one of the children urges his father to "go through Georgia fast 5 so we won't have to look at it much," there nevertheless are some interesting details of scenery along the roadside, and the grandmother tells us about many of the things they pass by. She notices "a cute little pickaninny" standing in the door of a shanty that she fancies would make a nice study for a sentimental painting, but the same subject disgusts her granddaughter June Star, who comments acidly, "He didn't have any britches on." More significantly, the grandmother points out a graveyard with five or six graves fenced off in the middle of a large cotton field, which is a rather obvious foreshadowing of the fate that will befall the family.

When the grandmother can no longer hold the children's attention with roadside attractions, she tells them a story of one of her girlhood suitors, Mr. Edgar Atkins Teagarden, who was from Jasper, Georgia, a small north Georgia town located in Pickens County and approximately fifty or sixty miles from the Tennessee state line. Although we are not told just where the grandmother is from, only that she has "connections in east Tennessee," it seems that to be consistent with her tale of Mr. Teagarden's courtship, she would have to have lived somewhere near Jasper, since he drove to her house by buggy every Saturday and gave her a watermelon monogrammed with his initials, E. A. T.

The family's journey is interrupted by a stop for a lunch of barbecued sandwiches at a café called The Tower which is located in "a clearing outside of Timothy." For economic effect this is one of the great scenes in all of Flannery O'Connor's fiction; yet here one cannot plot the location of the place on the map for there is no town of Timothy in Georgia. (If there is, it is such a small community it is not listed in the state atlas.) Since the other references to places in the story are to actual localities in the state, why does she create a fictitious name at this point? My theory is that in this scene, which has strong moral intention, O'Connor selects the name Timothy for the ironic effect it would produce. The allusion here is not geographical but Biblical, and the Timothy alluded to is almost certainly the book in the New Testament which bears the same name. Usually referred to as the Pastoral Letters, this gospel purports to be letters from Paul addressed to his disciples and through them to the Christian community at large. More than any other writing in the New Testament, the letters to Timothy are concerned with Christian orthodoxy. In this gospel Paul deals essentially with three topics: the opposition of false doctrine; the organization of the church and establishment of ecclesiastical regulations; and exhortations which indicate how to be a good citizen and Christian.

It seems to me that the concerns expressed by Paul in his letter to Timothy are very germane to the concerns expressed by Flannery O'Connor in "A Good Man Is Hard to Find," especially the concern with heretics and the advice on how to be a good Christian. One has only to set the family of six from Atlanta and Red Sammy and his wife (as well as The Misfit)—all of whom Flannery O'Connor considers heretics—against certain passages from Timothy to see that O'Connor's allusion ironically tells us just where these modern-day people are in error. For example, these verses seem to apply especially to Bailey. "He [the husband] must manage his own family well and see that his children obey him with proper respect" (I Tim. 3:4–5).

Also the author of the epistle commands good Christians to keep the faith and avoid "vain discussions" and concern with trivial matters and endless wrangling about genealogies (I Tim. 6:3–10). Further, he admonishes women "to dress modestly, with decency and propriety" and "to learn in quietness and full submission . . . and be silent" (I Tim. 2:9–12). This instruction seems to bear most directly on the grandmother, who is vain about her Old South heritage and certainly conscious of her social standing and what is required to be a lady. This is best brought out in her selection of attire for the trip. She is turned out in white gloves, black purse, a navy blue straw sailor hat with white violets on the brim, a navy blue polka dot dress with collar and cuffs of white organdy trimmed with lace, and on her neck she has pinned a purple spray of cloth violets containing a sachet. Her costume has been prepared so that, in the event of an accident, "anyone seeing her dead on the highway would know at once that she was a lady."

The grandmother's superficial conception of values is ironically under- 10 scored in the vain discussions with her grandchildren about what kind of conduct was once expected from children and her trivial remarks about plantation days and old suitors. Nowhere are her ideas more tellingly satirized than in her conversation with Red Sammy in the café where both complain of misplaced trust in their fellow man, which the grandmother sees as an indication of the general lack of manners in the modern world. She tells Red Sammy, "People are certainly not nice like they used to be." Of course, both Red Sammy and the grandmother are conceited enough to think that they are just as good as they ought to be. When Red Sammy complains of a recent theft of some gasoline by men driving a Chrysler and asks in a puzzled way why he had trusted them, he is quickly told by the grandmother that it was "because you're a good man," to which he candidly assents, "Yes'm, I suppose so."

The grandmother's inability to "learn in quietness" is tragically the cause of the deaths of the entire family. Shortly after Bailey overturns the car in a ditch, they are approached by a bespectacled man who the grandmother feels is "someone she knew" and soon she recognizes the stranger as The Misfit whose picture she has seen, and she blurts out this fact, saying, "You're The Misfit . . . I recognized you at once," to which he replies, "but it would have been better for all of you, lady, if you hadn't of reckernized me."

It is generally agreed that in the traumatic moments that follow in which the grandmother witnesses the deaths of her family and anticipates her own she does learn a lesson she has not heeded previously during her life. This lesson is the central message which Paul attempts to convey to Christians through Timothy and that is, "There is one God and one mediator between God and men, the Lord Jesus Christ, who gave himself to save mankind" (I Tim. 2:5). The evidence for assuming that she has come to a belated awareness that her faith has been misplaced in the pursuit of social graces and a concern with manners is limited to The Misfit's remark, "She would of been a good woman . . . if it had been somebody there to shoot her every minute of her life." Furthermore, in death she appears like a child, and her face is "smiling up at the cloudless sky," suggesting that she has found grace at last.

Another passage from Timothy seems especially applicable at this point: "The Spirit clearly says that in later times some will abandon the faith and follow deceiving spirits and things taught by demons. Such teachings come through hypocritical liars, whose consciences have been seared as with hot iron" (I Tim. 4:1–12). Although the whole cast of characters in the story has abandoned the faith and followed the wrong paths, the indictment of these lines would apply most forcibly to The Misfit who wears glasses and has a scholarly look. He has indeed been taught by demons, and from the Christian point of view that O'Connor takes in "A Good Man Is Hard to Find" he is a hypocritical liar who has no faith in a moral purpose in the universe and teaches that "it's nothing for you to do but enjoy the few minutes you got left the best way you can—by killing somebody or burning down his house or doing some other meanness to him." Thus, according to the ethics of this teacher, goodness is a matter of sadistic gratification. "No pleasure but meanness," he says, indicating how completely his conscience has been seared and his vision warped by his hedonistic atheism.

The numerous ways in which the content of this book of the New Testament dovetails with the characters and the theme of "A Good Man Is Hard to Find" could not be a complete accident. It cannot be demonstrated that Flannery O'Connor conceived of the moral of her story in terms of this specific book, but she made no bones about the fact that she wrote "from the standpoint of Christian orthodoxy";[2] and there is no doubt that Paul wrote from a similar standpoint, and his letter to Timothy has the same hortatory, moralizing tone that we find just below the surface in "A Good Man Is Hard to Find." Thus, it seems likely that she put the town of Timothy on the map because she wanted the reader to pick up the allusion and perhaps [review] the contents of the New Testament, but more probably she saw the parallel between her modern-day characters who have left the main road of Christian faith and Paul's warning to the church when he feared it was in danger off into the byways of heresy.

Just as the name of the town where the family stops for lunch is carefully 15 chosen, so is the name of Red Sammy's café. In Christian iconography towers are ambivalent symbols, that is, they speak *in bono* or *in malo*, to use the vocabulary of medieval exegetes, and can represent either good or evil qualities. For example, the Tower of Babel is symbolic of man's pride and stands for misbegotten human enterprises. The fate of the tower and its architects shows the consequences of overconfidence in the pursuit of fanciful ideas. (Interestingly enough, Nimrod, who began the construction of the tower, was also a

---

[2] *The Habit of Being: Letters of Flannery O'Connor*, ed. Sally Fitzgerald (New York: Farrar, 1979), 196.

mighty hunter, and like Red Sammy, a keeper of wild game, if Red Sammy's monkey can be called wild.)

As well as its nugatory meaning, the tower is a traditional symbol of the Virgin Mary and is a token of her purity and powers of transformation. Mary as the "refugee of sinners" according to Catholic doctrine is appropriately represented by the tower, a place associated with safety and sanctuary.

Outside of its Christian meaning the tower in arcane lore is a portent of disaster. In the sixteenth enigma of the Tarot pack of cards, catastrophe is indicated by the image of a tower struck by lightning. Whether O'Connor knew this fact about the meaning of the tower is uncertain, but she could not have been unaware of the former implications of the tower as a symbol, versed as she was in Biblical and church lore. It is appropriate that the conceited owner of this barbecue palace should have called it The Tower; it is ironic that this tower has no capacity to transform or give refuge.

Leaving Timothy and The Tower behind, both in the Biblical and geographical sense, the family [resume] their trip and we are told that just beyond Toombsboro, Georgia, the grandmother awakens from a nap with the recollection, mistaken as it turns out, that there is an old plantation nearby which she had visited as a girl; she even thinks she remembers the road to take to get there and tells Bailey, "It's not far from here, I know. . . . It wouldn't take over twenty minutes." As it so happens there is a Toomsboro (spelled without the "b") on the map and it is only twenty-three miles south of Milledgeville, Flannery O'Connor's home. She surely knew the place and chose to mention it because the name has an ominous ring, and it also would have been a logical terminus for the family's trip in terms of the time and distance they have traveled since leaving Atlanta in the morning. In fact, if one follows the usual route from Atlanta to Milledgeville (Georgia Highway 212), the distance is 93 miles, and if one adds to this the 23 miles further to Toomsboro, plus the estimated 15 or so miles that the detour to the plantation takes, then it can be calculated that the family has come a total of 130 miles. Considering the conditions of Georgia roads in the late 1940s, one had to drive under 50 m.p.h. to keep from knocking the wheels out of line from the numerous potholes that Governor Talmadge's highway people never patched. Thus, if one assumes that Bailey has averaged around 45 m.p.h. and takes account of the lunch stop, they have been on the road four or five hours and their meeting with The Misfit occurs in the early afternoon of a cloudless day with the mileage on the car standing at about 56020 on the meter. Sadly enough, the grandmother will be forever unaware of this "interesting fact," but we as readers should have a better understanding of how carefully O'Connor has used realistic detail for symbolic effects.

In the course of this story, the family's trip takes them from their complacent and smug living room to a confrontation with ultimate evil and ultimate reality as well. They are not prepared for the meeting because, like the heretics who concerned Paul in his epistle to Timothy, they have been occupied with the trivial things and involved in quarrels; and, like the builders of the Tower of Babel, they are preoccupied with vain enterprises.

Flannery O'Connor saw herself as a prophetic writer and her authorial strat- 20 egy was to shock; her fiction is intended as a rebuke to rationalistic, materialistic, and humanistic thought—the heresies of the twentieth century. She believed that people in the modern world were not following the true path and had to be made to see their condition for what it was—a wandering by the wayside. In "A Good Man Is Hard to Find" the family's wayward lives are given direction in their final moments, and from O'Connor's point of view they are at last on the right road.

MAKING CONNECTIONS

1. Bryant's "Reading the Map in 'A Good Man Is Hard to Find'" argues not simply for the significance of the journey taken in the story but for the significance of the place names, real and imagined. Compare his account of the story as meticulously constructed so as to imbed this significance to O'Connor's own account of a writer's activity as about discovering meaning as she goes along. Are these two kinds of journeys—one carefully planned, with a road atlas, the other a journey of discovery—reconcilable? If so, how?

2. Bryant takes "A Good Man Is Hard to Find" very seriously both as a carefully constructed narrative and as a spiritual and moral tale. Do you think it is possible to appreciate the story without reading it in this way? Why or why not?

MICHAEL CLARK   (1946–1999)

FLANNERY O'CONNOR'S "A GOOD MAN IS HARD TO FIND": THE MOMENT OF GRACE   1991

"A Good Man Is Hard to Find" is one of Flannery O'Connor's most discussed and most problematic short stories. The major difficulty involves the story's climax. Should the grandmother's final act—her touching of The Misfit—be taken as a token of true, divine grace and spiritual insight? Or should the story be interpreted strictly as a naturalistic document? Perhaps the grandmother achieves no spiritual insight. One can find critics on both sides of the argument. Since the issue is central to O'Connor's work at large, it is worth further examination. While this question may ultimately be impossible to resolve with certainty, further light can be shed upon this critical gesture.

In *Mystery and Manners*, O'Connor asserts that the grandmother's final act is a "moment of grace." Critics, though, have not been convinced. While acknowledging Flannery O'Connor's reading, Madison Jones prefers to stress the "realistic explanation" of grace—a "naturalistic" grace which may be "spelled in lower case letters." Stanley Renner is also uncomfortable with the "religious" explanation and describes "the vague touch" on the Misfit's shoulder as "a parental blessing" or "the ceremonial dubbing of knighthood." Thus the grandmother's response not so much reflects divine grace as it "touches her almost instinctive springs of sympathy and human kinship." Leon Driskell and Joan Brittain seem to see the grandmother's final act not as a transcendent spiritual experience but as a "gesture of kinship," which comes from one whose "revelation, though limited, is adequate." And most recently, Kathleen Ochshorn has entered the fray in a most unequivocal manner, insisting that in "A Good Man Is Hard to Find" "a world of propriety and illusion is laid low by wrath, not redeemed by grace." Rather than seeing the grandmother's final act as an embodiment of spirituality, Ochshorn asserts that the touch expresses the grandmother's "final hope that her noblesse can alter her fate," an interpretation that renders the grandmother's final gesture as mundane, selfish, and in every sense unredeeming. These critical responses—especially Ochshorn's—are symptomatic of the reluctance to read the story in light of O'Connor's religious beliefs.

Should O'Connor's interpretation of the story be judged as wrong? Critics have an excellent authority for a subversive reading in D. H. Lawrence's well-known dictum: trust the tale, not the teller of the tale. Unless the tale itself can guide us in our interpretation, we are threatened with being like the people in Plato's cave, very inadequate interpreters of shadows on the wall. But there is another piece of evidence in the story which has been overlooked and which strengthens O'Connor's claim that the tale should be read in a theological context.

In an indispensable article several years ago, Hallman Bryant noted that there is no Timothy, Georgia, the setting for the encounter with Red Sammy. He argues persuasively that O'Connor is alluding to "the book in the New Testament which bears the same name"—that is, Paul's Epistle to Timothy. The evidence that Bryant presents leaves no doubt that O'Connor did indeed have the Bible in mind. As Bryant notes, several of Paul's teachings are especially germane to the story: the role of the husband (a negative judgment of Bailey, the grandmother's son), for example, and strictures against hypocrisy and false religion (which are useful correctives to the family's, especially the grandmother's, attitudes). However, Bryant glosses O'Connor's story only with reference to a single book of the Bible, Timothy I. But Timothy II can help explain the crux of the story, the touching of The Misfit; it provides a subtext for the central and problematic episode of O'Connor's story, the grandmother's moment of grace.

In his Second Epistle, Paul stresses to Timothy that true grace is associated 5 with the charismatic tradition of the "laying on of hands":

I keep the memory of thy tears, and long to see thee again, so as to have my fill of joy when I receive fresh proof of thy sincere faith. That faith dwelt in thy grandmother Lois, and in thy mother, Eunice, before thee; I am fully persuaded that it dwells in thee too. That is why I would remind thee to fan the flame of that special grace which God kindled in thee, when my hands were laid upon thee.

True faith dwelt in Timothy's mother and grandmother and in Timothy too after Paul's hands were laid upon him. When the grandmother of the story touches The Misfit, she replicates Paul's laying on of hands at the very moment she loses her artificiality and realizes that she and The Misfit are spiritual kin. Both events emphasize the grace which accompanies charismatic physical contact. Those critics who argue for a "realistic" interpretation of the story must ultimately acknowledge and account for O'Connor's biblical allusions. The details of the story, particularly the allusion to Timothy, emphasize that the grandmother has undergone a personal experience that is significantly different from her normally artificial and spiritually dead self. Aside from whether God exists, such moments are real, and they have *de facto* been defined through history as "religious."

In a newly discovered and just recently published letter, O'Connor (in referring to *The Violent Bear It Away*) states the issue clearly and definitively: The novel "can only be understood in religious terms." The same is true of "A Good Man Is Hard to Find." God's grace is not limited by one's religious orientation. Even the most tough-minded critic will acknowledge that all human beings—even the self-satisfied grandmother—have the potential to experience epiphanies, moments of psychological clarity, that could save them from the sour and life-denying restrictions that human beings may labor under. These are moments (from the clarifying moment of the ordinary life to the trance of the mystic) that historically we have come to define as religious.

In *Mystery and Manners*, O'Connor tells us quite directly that the inescapable threat of death shatters the grandmother's complaisance and makes her look at the essential: "violence is strangely capable of returning my characters to reality and preparing them to accept their moment of grace." Life is full of such moments—though perhaps rarely on the crucial life-and-death plane of the grandmother's experience. O'Connor believed that such moments come from God. Theology and art are not mutually exclusive. As O'Connor wrote in *Mystery and Manners*, "In the greatest fiction, the writer's moral sense coincides with his dramatic sense."

MAKING ARGUMENTS

1. People, love 'em or hate 'em: argue for or against the claim that O'Connor is a misanthrope.

2. Does authorial intent matter? Argue for or against the claim that O'Connor's stories must be read according to what she says is their intended meaning.

3. Can literature make religion "believable"? Can it create belief, or bolster it? Make an argument about literature and religious belief.

MAKING CONNECTIONS

1. What is the "further light" (para. 1) that Clark claims he sheds here? Do you find his argument persuasive?

2. Clark somewhat quickly raises and dismisses what he calls "subversive readings" in his third paragraph. What is his argument against them? Does it convince you? Regardless of where you stand, make a counterargument that agrees with Lawrence's dictum, "trust the tale, not the teller of the tale," without merely nodding to Lawrence's "authority."

POETRY

JONATHAN SWIFT   (1667–1745)

STELLA'S BIRTH-DAY   1724–25

As when a beauteous nymph decays,
We say she's past her dancing days;
So poets lose their feet by time,
And can no longer dance in rhyme.
Your annual bard had rather chose
To celebrate your birth in prose:
Yet merry folks, who want by chance
A pair to make a country dance,
Call the old housekeeper, and get her
To fill a place for want of better:　　　　　　　10
While Sheridan is off the hooks,
And friend Delany at his books,
That Stella may avoid disgrace,
Once more the Dean supplies their place.

Beauty and wit, too sad a truth!
Have always been confined to youth;
The god of wit and beauty's queen,
He twenty-one and she fifteen,
No poet ever sweetly sung,
Unless he were, like Phoebus, young;　　　　　　20
Nor ever nymph inspired to rhyme,
Unless, like Venus, in her prime.
At fifty-six, if this be true,
Am I a poet fit for you?
Or, at the age of forty-three,
Are you a subject fit for me?
Adieu! bright wit, and radiant eyes!
You must be grave and I be wise.
Our fate in vain we would oppose:
But I'll be still your friend in prose:　　　　　　30
Esteem and friendship to express,
Will not require poetic dress;

And if the Muse deny her aid
To have them sung, they may be said.

But, Stella, say, what evil tongue
Reports you are no longer young;
That Time sits with his scythe to mow
Where erst sat Cupid with his bow;
That half your locks are turn'd to gray?
I'll ne'er believe a word they say.   40
'Tis true, but let it not be known,
My eyes are somewhat dimmish grown;
For nature, always in the right,
To your decays adapts my sight;
And wrinkles undistinguished pass,
For I'm ashamed to use a glass:
And till I see them with these eyes,
Whoever says you have them, lies.

No length of time can make you quit
Honour and virtue, sense and wit;   50
Thus you may still be young to me,
While I can better hear than see.
O ne'er may Fortune show her spite,
To make me deaf, and mend my sight!

FOR ANALYSIS

1. What does this poem seem to be saying about aging? How does it correspond to
what you think broader cultural attitudes toward aging are?

2. What kind of a birthday poem is this? What do you think Swift is trying to say to Stella?

WRITING TOPIC

Swift, best known as a prose **satirist**, also wrote political pamphlets and poetry. The
choice of poetry over **prose** is mentioned in the poem itself. Why does Swift say he
wrote this birthday message in poetry? How does he use the various techniques and
methods of poetry to do things prose might not be able to?

WILLIAM BLAKE   (1757–1827)

THE CHIMNEY SWEEPER   1789

(SONGS OF INNOCENCE)

When my mother died I was very young,
And my Father sold me while yet my tongue
Could scarcely cry "'weep! 'weep! 'weep! 'weep!"
So your chimneys I sweep, and in soot I sleep.

There's little Tom Dacre, who cried when his head,
That curled like a lamb's back, was shaved: so I said,
"Hush, Tom! never mind it, for when your head's bare
You know that the soot cannot spoil your white hair."

And so he was quiet and that very night
As Tom was a-sleeping, he had such a sight!   10
That thousands of sweepers, Dick, Joe, Ned, and Jack,
Were all of them locked up in coffins of black.

And by came an Angel who had a bright key,
And he opened the coffins and set them all free;
Then down a green plain leaping, laughing, they run,
And wash in a river, and shine in the Sun.

Then naked and white, all their bags left behind,
They rise upon clouds and sport in the wind;
And the Angel told Tom, if he'd be a good boy,
He'd have God for his father, and never want joy.   20

And so Tom awoke; and we rose in the dark,
And got with our bags and our brushes to work.
Though the morning was cold, Tom was happy and warm;
So if all do their duty they need not fear harm.

THE CHIMNEY SWEEPER   1794

(SONGS OF EXPERIENCE)

A little black thing among the snow,
Crying "'weep! 'weep!" in notes of woe!
"Where are thy father and mother? say?"
"They are both gone up to the church to pray.

Because I was happy upon the heath,
And smil'd among the winter's snow,
They clothed me in the clothes of death,
And taught me to sing the notes of woe.

And because I am happy and dance and sing,
They think they have done me no injury,   10
And are gone to praise God and his Priest and King,
Who make up a heaven of our misery."

MAKING CONNECTIONS

How would you characterize this poem's view of religion? How does it compare to the view implied in the *Songs of Innocence* poem of the same name? How does it inform the poem's larger reflection on the lives of the chimney sweeps?

THE LAMB   1789

Little Lamb, who made thee?
  Dost thou know who made thee?
Gave thee life, and bid thee feed
By the stream and o'er the mead;
Gave thee clothing of delight,
Softest clothing, wooly, bright;
Gave thee such a tender voice,
Making all the vales rejoice?
  Little Lamb, who made thee?
  Dost thou know who made thee?   10

Little Lamb, I'll tell thee,
  Little Lamb, I'll tell thee:
He is callèd by thy name,
For he calls himself a Lamb.
He is meek, and he is mild;
He became a little child.
I a child, and thou a lamb,
We are callèd by his name.
  Little Lamb, God bless thee!
  Little Lamb, God bless thee!   20

THE SHEPHERD   1789

How sweet is the shepherd's sweet lot!
From the morn to the evening he strays;
He shall follow his sheep all the day,
And his tongue shall be filled with praise.

For he hears the lambs' innocent call,
And he hears the ewes' tender reply;
He is watchful while they are in peace,
For they know when their shepherd is nigh.

THE GARDEN OF LOVE   1793

I went to the Garden of Love,
And saw what I never had seen:
A Chapel was built in the midst,
Where I used to play on the green.

And the gates of this Chapel were shut,
And "Thou shalt not" writ over the door;
So I turn'd to the Garden of Love,
That so many sweet flowers bore,

And I saw it was filled with graves,
And tomb-stones where flowers should be: 10
And Priests in black gowns were walking their rounds,
And binding with briars my joys & desires.

FOR ANALYSIS

1. What meanings does the word *love* have in this poem?
2. What is Blake's judgment on established religion?
3. Explain the meaning of *Chapel* (l. 3) and *briars* (l. 12).

MAKING ARGUMENTS

It has been argued, contrary to most readings of the poem, that there is some ironic distance between the speaker and the poet. How might you make this argument? Where might the poem allow the reader to critique the speaker?

WRITING TOPIC

Read the definition of **irony** in "Glossary of Literary Terms." Write an essay in which you distinguish between the types of irony used in the second "The Chimney Sweeper" and "The Garden of Love."

LONDON   1794

I wander through each chartered[1] street,
Near where the chartered Thames does flow
And mark in every face I meet
Marks of weakness, marks of woe.

London
[1] Preempted by the state and leased out under royal patent.

In every cry of every man,
In every infant's cry of fear,
In every voice, in every ban,
The mind-forged manacles I hear:

How the chimney-sweeper's cry
Every blackening church appalls,   10
And the hapless soldier's sigh
Runs in blood down palace-walls.

But most, through midnight streets I hear
How the youthful harlot's curse
Blasts the new-born infant's tear,
And blights with plagues the marriage-hearse.

THE TYGER   1794

Tyger! Tyger! burning bright
In the forests of the night,
What immortal hand or eye
Could frame thy fearful symmetry?

In what distant deeps or skies
Burnt the fire of thine eyes?
On what wings dare he aspire?
What the hand dare seize the fire?

And what shoulder, & what art,
Could twist the sinews of thy heart?   10
And when thy heart began to beat,
What dread hand? & what dread feet?

What the hammer? what the chain?
In what furnace was thy brain?
What the anvil? what dread grasp
Dare its deadly terrors clasp?

When the stars threw down their spears,
And water'd heaven with their tears,
Did he smile his work to see?
Did he who made the Lamb make thee?   20

Tyger! Tyger! burning bright
In the forests of the night,

What immortal hand or eye
Dare frame thy fearful symmetry?

ROBERT BROWNING   (1812–1889)

MY LAST DUCHESS   1842

FERRARA

That's my last Duchess painted on the wall,
Looking as if she were alive. I call
That piece a wonder, now: Frà Pandolf's[1] hands
Worked busily a day, and there she stands.
Will't please you sit and look at her? I said
"Frà Pandolf" by design, for never read
Strangers like you that pictured countenance,
The depth and passion of its earnest glance,
But to myself they turned (since none puts by
The curtain I have drawn for you, but I)   10
And seemed as they would ask me, if they durst,
How such a glance came there; so, not the first
Are you to turn and ask thus. Sir, 'twas not
Her husband's presence only, called that spot
Of joy into the Duchess' cheek: perhaps
Frà Pandolf chanced to say "Her mantle laps
Over my lady's wrist too much," or "Paint
Must never hope to reproduce the faint
Half-flush that dies along her throat": such stuff
Was courtesy, she thought, and cause enough   20
For calling up that spot of joy. She had
A heart—how shall I say?—too soon made glad,
Too easily impressed; she liked whate'er
She looked on, and her looks went everywhere.
Sir, 'twas all one! My favor at her breast,
The dropping of the daylight in the West,
The bough of cherries some officious fool
Broke in the orchard for her, the white mule
She rode with round the terrace—all and each
Would draw from her alike the approving speech,   30
Or blush, at least. She thanked men—good! but thanked

My Last Duchess
  [1] Frà Pandolf and Claus of Innsbruck (who is mentioned in the last line) are fictitious artists.

Somehow—I know not how—as if she ranked
My gift of a nine-hundred-years-old name
With anybody's gift. Who'd stoop to blame
This sort of trifling? Even had you skill
In speech—which I have not—to make your will
Quite clear to such an one, and say, "Just this
Or that in you disgusts me; here you miss,
Or there exceed the mark"—and if she let
Herself be lessoned° so, nor plainly set   taught 40
Her wits to yours, forsooth, and made excuse,
—E'en then would be some stooping; and I choose
Never to stoop. Oh sir, she smiled, no doubt,
Whene'er I passed her; but who passed without
Much the same smile? This grew; I gave commands;
Then all smiles stopped together. There she stands
As if alive. Will't please you rise? We'll meet
The company below, then. I repeat,
The Count your master's known munificence°   generosity
Is ample warrant that no just pretense   50
Of mine for dowry will be disallowed;
Though his fair daughter's self, as I avowed
At starting, is my object. Nay, we'll go
Together down, sir. Notice Neptune, though,
Taming a sea-horse, thought a rarity,
Which Claus of Innsbruck cast in bronze for me!

FOR ANALYSIS

1. To whom is the duke speaking, and what is the occasion?

2. What does a comparison between the duke's feelings about his artwork and his
feelings about his last duchess reveal about his **character**?

3. Does this poem rely on **irony**? Explain.

MAKING ARGUMENTS

Write an essay in which you argue that the reader either is or is not meant to sympathize with the duke's **characterization** of his wife.

WRITING TOPIC

Browning is said to have meant that the "commands" of line 45 are that the duchess
be executed or sent to a convent. Write a poem, short piece of prose, or journal entry,
from her **point of view**, addressing the painting of the portrait and her relationship
with the speaker.

EMILY DICKINSON   (1830–1886)

I FELT A FUNERAL, IN MY BRAIN   1861

I felt a Funeral, in my Brain,
And Mourners to and fro
Kept treading—treading—till it seemed
That Sense was breaking through—

And when they all were seated,
A Service, like a Drum—
Kept beating—beating—till I thought
My Mind was going numb—

And then I heard them lift a Box
And creak across my Soul   10
With those same Boots of Lead, again,
Then Space—began to toll,

As all the Heavens were a Bell,
And Being, but an Ear,
And I, and Silence, some strange Race
Wrecked, solitary, here—

And then a Plank in Reason, broke,
And I dropped down, and down—
And hit a World, at every plunge,
And Finished knowing—then—   20

THOMAS HARDY   (1840–1928)

MEN WHO MARCH AWAY   1914

What of the faith and fire within us
Men who march away
Ere the barn-cocks say
Night is growing gray,
Leaving all that here can win us;
What of the faith and fire within us
Men who march away?
Is it a purblind prank, O think you,
Friend with the musing eye,
Who watch us stepping by   10
With doubt and dolorous sigh?
Can much pondering so hoodwink you!

Is it a purblind prank, O think you,
Friend with the musing eye?
Nay. We well see what we are doing,
Though some may not see—
Dalliers as they be—
England's need are we;
Her distress would leave us rueing:
Nay. We well see what we are doing,
Though some may not see!   20
In our heart of hearts believing
Victory crowns the just,
And that braggarts must
Surely bite the dust,
Press we to the field ungrieving,
In our heart of hearts believing
Victory crowns the just.
Hence the faith and fire within us
Men who march away
Ere the barn-cocks say   30
Night is growing gray,
Leaving all that here can win us;
Hence the faith and fire within us
Men who march away.

FOR ANALYSIS

1. What question does the speaker ask at the beginning of "Men Who March Away"?
How does the poem answer it?

2. Some versions of this poem bear the subtitle "Song of the Soldiers." What kind of a
song is this? Does *of* mean "about" or "for"?

WRITING TOPIC

Compose a companion piece, in poetry or **prose**, written by the "friend with the musing eye" (l. 9). What does this "friend" think of what he sees? Does she or he agree or
disagree with the speaker?

GERARD MANLEY HOPKINS   (1844–1889)

SPRING AND FALL   1880

TO A YOUNG CHILD

Márgarét, áre you gríeving
Over Goldengrove unleaving?°   losing leaves
Leáves, líke the things of man, you
With your fresh thoughts care for, can you?

Áh! ás the heart grows older
It will come to such sights colder
By and by, nor spare a sigh
Though worlds of wanwood leafmeal[1] lie;
And yet you wíll weep and know why.
Now no matter, child, the name:
Sórrow's spríngs áre the same.
Nor mouth had, no nor mind, expressed
What heart heard of, ghost° guessed: soul
It ís the blight man was born for,
It is Margaret you mourn for.

10

FOR ANALYSIS

1. In this poem Margaret grieves over the passing of spring and the coming of fall. What does the coming of fall **symbolize**?

2. Why, when Margaret grows older, will she not sigh over the coming of fall?

3. What are "Sórrow's spríngs" (l. 11)?

A. E. HOUSMAN (1859–1936)

WHEN I WAS ONE-AND-TWENTY   1896

When I was one-and-twenty
   I heard a wise man say,
"Give crowns and pounds and guineas
   But not your heart away;
Give pearls away and rubies
   But keep your fancy free."
But I was one-and-twenty,
   No use to talk to me.

When I was one-and-twenty
   I heard him say again,
"The heart out of the bosom
   Was never given in vain;
'Tis paid with sighs a plenty
   And sold for endless rue."
And I am two-and-twenty,
   And oh, 'tis true, 'tis true.

10

Spring and Fall
  [1] Pale woods littered with mouldering leaves.

ROBERT FROST   (1874–1963)

THE ROAD NOT TAKEN   1915

Two roads diverged in a yellow wood,
And sorry I could not travel both
And be one traveler, long I stood
And looked down one as far as I could
To where it bent in the undergrowth;

Then took the other, as just as fair,
And having perhaps the better claim,
Because it was grassy and wanted wear;
Though as for that the passing there
Had worn them really about the same,   10

And both that morning equally lay
In leaves no step had trodden black.
Oh, I kept the first for another day!
Yet knowing how way leads on to way,
I doubted if I should ever come back.

I shall be telling this with a sigh
Somewhere ages and ages hence:
Two roads diverged in a wood, and I—
I took the one less traveled by,
And that has made all the difference.   20

BIRCHES   1916

When I see birches bend to left and right
Across the lines of straighter darker trees,
I like to think some boy's been swinging them.
But swinging doesn't bend them down to stay
As ice-storms do. Often you must have seen them
Loaded with ice a sunny winter morning
After a rain. They click upon themselves
As the breeze rises, and turn many-colored
As the stir cracks and crazes their enamel.
Soon the sun's warmth makes them shed crystal shells   10
Shattering and avalanching on the snow-crust—
Such heaps of broken glass to sweep away
You'd think the inner dome of heaven had fallen.
They are dragged to the withered bracken by the load,

And they seem not to break; though once they are bowed
So low for long, they never right themselves:
You may see their trunks arching in the woods
Years afterwards, trailing their leaves on the ground
Like girls on hands and knees that throw their hair
Before them over their heads to dry in the sun.   20
But I was going to say when Truth broke in
With all her matter-of-fact about the ice-storm
I should prefer to have some boy bend them
As he went out and in to fetch the cows—
Some boy too far from town to learn baseball,
Whose only play was what he found himself,
Summer or winter, and could play alone.
One by one he subdued his father's trees
By riding them down over and over again
Until he took the stiffness out of them,   30
And not one but hung limp, not one was left
For him to conquer. He learned all there was
To learn about not launching out too soon
And so not carrying the tree away
Clear to the ground. He always kept his poise
To the top branches, climbing carefully
With the same pains you use to fill a cup
Up to the brim, and even above the brim.
Then he flung outward, feet first, with a swish,
Kicking his way down through the air to the ground.   40
So was I once myself a swinger of birches.
And so I dream of going back to be.
It's when I'm weary of considerations,
And life is too much like a pathless wood
Where your face burns and tickles with the cobwebs
Broken across it, and one eye is weeping
From a twig's having lashed across it open.
I'd like to get away from earth awhile
And then come back to it and begin over.
May no fate willfully misunderstand me   50
And half grant what I wish and snatch me away
Not to return. Earth's the right place for love:
I don't know where it's likely to go better.
I'd like to go by climbing a birch tree,
And climb black branches up a snow-white trunk
Toward heaven, till the tree could bear no more,
But dipped its top and set me down again.
That would be good both going and coming back.
One could do worse than be a swinger of birches.

E. E. CUMMINGS   (1894–1962)

IN JUST-   1923

in Just-
spring   when the world is mud-
luscious the little
lame balloonman

whistles   far   and wee

and eddieandbill come
running from marbles and
piracies and it's
spring

when the world is puddle-wonderful   10

the queer
old balloonman whistles
far   and   wee
and bettyandisbel come dancing

from hop-scotch and jump-rope and

it's
spring
and
   the

      goat-footed

balloonMan   whistles   20
far
and
wee

STEVIE SMITH   (1902–1971)

NOT WAVING BUT DROWNING   1957

Nobody heard him, the dead man,
But still he lay moaning:
I was much further out than you thought
And not waving but drowning.

Poor chap, he always loved larking
And now he's dead
It must have been too cold for him his heart gave way,
They said.

Oh, no no no, it was too cold always
(Still the dead one lay moaning)   10
I was much too far out all my life
And not waving but drowning.

FOR ANALYSIS

1. Explain the **paradox** in the first and last **stanzas**, where the speaker describes someone dead as moaning. Who do you suppose the *you* of line 3 is? The *They* of line 8?

2. Explain the meaning of line 7. Can it be interpreted in more than one way?

3. Explain the meanings of *drowning*.

4. The only thing we learn about the dead man is that "he always loved larking" (l. 5). Why is this detail significant? What kind of man do you think he was?

5. Does the speaker know more about the dead man than the man's friends do? Explain.

MAKING ARGUMENTS

Stevie Smith suffered from depression; this poem was reportedly written during an especially bad stretch in her life. Make an argument either that the poem must be read with this biographical information in mind or that it should not. Do you read the poem differently in light of this information? Does this information alter your experience of the poem negatively?

WRITING TOPICS

1. Write an essay describing how you or someone you know suffered the experience of "not waving but drowning."

2. Write an essay describing how you came to the realization that someone close to you was not the person you thought he or she was.

TO CARRY THE CHILD   1966

To carry the child into adult life
Is good? I say it is not,
To carry the child into adult life
Is to be handicapped.

The child in adult life is defenceless
And if he is grown-up, knows it,

And the grown-up looks at the childish part
And despises it.

The child, too, despises the clever grown-up,
The man-of-the-world, the frozen,   10
For the child has the tears alive on his cheek
And the man has none of them.

As the child has colours, and the man sees no
Colours or anything,
Being easy only in things of the mind,
The child is easy in feeling.

Easy in feeling, easily excessive
And in excess powerful,
For instance, if you do not speak to the child
He will make trouble.   20

You would say a man had the upper hand
Of the child, if a child survive,
But I say the child has fingers of strength
To strangle the man alive.

Oh! it is not happy, it is never happy,
To carry the child into adulthood,
Let the children lie down before full growth
And die in their infanthood
And be guilty of no man's blood.

But oh the poor child, the poor child, what can he do,   30
Trapped in a grown-up carapace,
But peer outside of his prison room
With the eye of an anarchist?

COUNTEE CULLEN   (1903–1946)

INCIDENT   1925

Once riding in old Baltimore,
　　Heart-filled, head-filled with glee,
I saw a Baltimorean
　　Keep looking straight at me.

Now I was eight and very small,
   And he was no whit bigger,
And so I smiled, but he poked out
   His tongue and called me, "Nigger."

I saw the whole of Baltimore
   From May until December: 10
Of all the things that happened there
   That's all that I remember.

DYLAN THOMAS   (1914–1953)

FERN HILL   1946

Now as I was young and easy under the apple boughs
About the lilting house and happy as the grass was green,
     The night above the dingle° starry,   small wooded valley
       Time let me hail and climb
     Golden in the heydays of his eyes,
And honored among wagons I was prince of the apple towns
And once below a time I lordly had the trees and leaves
       Trail with daisies and barley
     Down the rivers of the windfall light.

And as I was green and carefree, famous among the barns   10
About the happy yard and singing as the farm was home,
     In the sun that is young once only,
       Time let me play and be
     Golden in the mercy of his means,
And green and golden I was huntsman and herdsman, the calves
Sang to my horn, the foxes on the hills barked clear and cold,
       And the sabbath rang slowly
     In the pebbles of the holy streams.

All the sun long it was running, it was lovely, the hay
Fields high as the house, the tunes from the chimneys, it was air   20
     And playing, lovely and watery
       And fire green as grass.
     And nightly under the simple stars
As I rode to sleep the owls were bearing the farm away,
All the moon long I heard, blessed among stables, the nightjars[1]

---

[1] Nightjars are nocturnal birds.

Flying with the ricks, and the horses
Flashing into the dark.

And then to awake, and the farm, like a wanderer white
With the dew, come back, the cock on his shoulder: it was all
Shining, it was Adam and maiden, 30
The sky gathered again
And the sun grew round that very day.
So it must have been after the birth of the simple light
In the first, spinning place, the spellbound horses walking warm
Out of the whinnying green stable
On to the fields of praise.

And honored among foxes and pheasants by the gay house
Under the new made clouds and happy as the heart was long,
In the sun born over and over,
I ran my heedless ways, 40
My wishes raced through the house high hay
And nothing I cared, at my sky blue trades, that time allows
In all his tuneful turning so few and such morning songs
Before the children green and golden
Follow him out of grace.

Nothing I cared, in the lamb white days, that time would take me
Up to the swallow thronged loft by the shadow of my hand,
In the moon that is always rising,
Nor that riding to sleep
I should hear him fly with the high fields 50
And wake to the farm forever fled from the childless land.
Oh as I was young and easy in the mercy of his means,
Time held me green and dying
Though I sang in my chains like the sea.

FOR ANALYSIS

1. What emotional impact does the color **imagery** in the poem provide?

2. Trace the behavior of "time" in the poem.

3. Fairy tales often begin with the words "once upon a time." Why does Thomas alter that formula in line 7?

4. Explain the **paradox** in line 53.

MAKING ARGUMENTS

Make an argument about **style**, answering the question of whether longer or shorter is better in poetry, as illustrated by this poem and Housman's "When I Was One-and-Twenty" (p. 177).

WRITING TOPICS

1. Lines 17–18, 30, and 45–46 incorporate religious language and biblical **allusion**. How do those allusions clarify the poet's vision of his childhood?

2. Compare this poem with either Hopkins's "Spring and Fall" (p. 176) or Housman's "When I Was One-and-Twenty" (p. 177).

LAWRENCE FERLINGHETTI   (B. 1919)

CONSTANTLY RISKING ABSURDITY   1958

Constantly risking absurdity
                              and death
              whenever he performs
                      above the heads
                              of his audience
       the poet like an acrobat
                      climbs on rime
                      to a high wire of his own making
and balancing on eyebeams
                      above a sea of faces   10
          paces his way
                      to the other side of day
performing entrechats[1]
                      and sleight-of-foot tricks
and other high theatrics
                      and all without mistaking
          any thing
                      for what it may not be

       For he's the super realist
                      who must perforce perceive   20
          taut truth
                      before the taking of each stance or step
in his supposed advance
                      toward that still higher perch
where Beauty stands and waits
                      with gravity
                      to start her death-defying leap

Constantly Risking Absurdity
[1] In ballet, a leap straight upward in which the legs are repeatedly crossed or heels struck together.

And he
    a little charleychaplin[2] man
                who may or may not catch   30
      her fair eternal form
             spreadeagled in the empty air
      of existence

PHILIP LARKIN   (1922-1985)

A STUDY OF READING HABITS   1960

When getting my nose in a book
Cured most things short of school,
It was worth ruining my eyes
To know I could still keep cool,
And deal out the old right hook
To dirty dogs twice my size.

Later, with inch-thick specs,
Evil was just my lark:
Me and my cloak and fangs
Had ripping times in the dark.   10
The women I clubbed with sex!
I broke them up like meringues.

Don't read much now: the dude
Who lets the girl down before
The hero arrives, the chap
Who's yellow and keeps the store,
Seem far too familiar. Get stewed:
Books are a load of crap.

FOR ANALYSIS

1. What different sorts of books did the speaker read as a schoolchild (stanza 1)?

2. How might reading cure "most things short of school" (l. 2)?

3. Describe the change in the speaker's reading habits revealed in the second **stanza**.

4. Explain why the speaker asserts that he doesn't read much now (l. 13). What experiences led him to the conclusion that "[b]ooks are a load of crap" (l. 18)?

Constantly Risking Absurdity
  [2] Charles Spencer Chaplin (1889–1977) was cinema's most celebrated comedian of the silent-film era. His trademark was the mustachioed Little Tramp, whose pathos and comedy were accompanied by extraordinary acrobatic skills.

WRITING TOPIC

Describe the poem's metrical pattern and its **rhyme** scheme. See **ballad** in the "Glossary of Literary Terms," read some ballads in this book, and argue for or against the proposition that this poem is a modern ballad.

THIS BE THE VERSE   1974

They fuck you up, your mum and dad.
   They may not mean to, but they do.
They fill you with the faults they had
   And add some extra, just for you.

But they were fucked up in their turn
   By fools in old-style hats and coats,
Who half the time were soppy-stern
   And half at one another's throats.

Man hands on misery to man.
   It deepens like a coastal shelf.
Get out as early as you can,   10
   And don't have any kids yourself.

AUDRE LORDE   (1934–1992)

HANGING FIRE   1978

I am fourteen
and my skin has betrayed me
the boy I cannot live without
still sucks his thumb
in secret
how come my knees are
always so ashy
what if I die
before morning
and momma's in the bedroom   10
with the door closed.

I have to learn how to dance
in time for the next party
my room is too small for me

suppose I die before graduation
they will sing sad melodies
but finally
tell the truth about me
There is nothing I want to do
and too much   20
that has to be done
and momma's in the bedroom
with the door closed.

Nobody even stops to think
about my side of it
I should have been on Math Team
my marks were better than his
why do I have to be
the one
wearing braces   30
I have nothing to wear tomorrow
will I live long enough
to grow up
and momma's in the bedroom
with the door closed.

FOR ANALYSIS

1. How do you think the speaker's skin has "betrayed" her (l. 2)?

2. What does the expression *hang fire* mean? In what ways is the speaker hanging fire?

MAKING ARGUMENTS

What is "the truth" (l. 18) about the speaker? Is it something specific alluded to in the poem? Is it something specific unnamed in the poem? Or, is it something general to speakers like her or to everyone? Make an argument for one of these options.

WRITING TOPICS

1. Look up the origins of the phrase used in the poem's title. Where does it come from? Is there anything about this original meaning that might add to the poem's meaning?

2. Analyze the structure of the poem—how it is divided into parts, how certain lines and images and feelings are repeated. How does the structure enrich the poem's meaning?

MAKING CONNECTIONS

Compare the speaker's repeated statements about her fear of death in "Hanging Fire" to Margaret in Hopkins's "Spring and Fall" (p. 176). What is different about the attitudes expressed—toward life, toward death, toward growing up—in these two poems?

ALICIA OSTRIKER (B. 1937)

THE DOGS AT LIVE OAK BEACH,
SANTA CRUZ 1998

As if there could be a world
Of absolute innocence
In which we forget ourselves

The owners throw sticks
And half-bald tennis balls
Toward the surf
And the happy dogs leap after them
As if catapulted—

Black dogs, tan dogs,
Tubes of glorious muscle—   10

Pursuing pleasure
More than obedience
They race, skid to a halt in the wet sand,
Sometimes they'll plunge straight into
The foaming breakers

Like diving birds, letting the green turbulence
Toss them, until they snap and sink

Teeth into floating wood
Then bound back to their owners
Shining wet, with passionate speed   20
For nothing,
For absolutely nothing but joy.

JEAN NORDHAUS (B. 1939)

A DANDELION FOR MY MOTHER 2006

How I loved those spiky suns,
rooted stubborn as childhood
in the grass, tough as the farmer's
big-headed children—the mats
of yellow hair, the bowl-cut fringe.
How sturdy they were and how

slowly they turned themselves
into galaxies, domes of ghost stars
barely visible by day, pale
cerebrums clinging to life   10
on tough green stems.   Like you.
Like you, In the end.   If you were here,
I'd pluck this trembling globe to show
how beautiful a thing can be
a breath will tear away.

LOUISE GLÜCK   (B. 1943)

THE SCHOOL CHILDREN   1975

The children go forward with their little satchels.
And all morning the mothers have labored
to gather the late apples, red and gold,
like words of another language.

And on the other shore
are those who wait behind great desks
to receive these offerings.

How orderly they are—the nails
on which the children hang
their overcoats of blue or yellow wool.   10

And the teachers shall instruct them in silence
and the mothers shall scour the orchards for a way out,
drawing to themselves the gray limbs of the fruit trees
bearing so little ammunition.

THE MYTH OF INNOCENCE   2006

One summer she goes into the field as usual
stopping for a bit at the pool where she often
looks at herself, to see
if she detects any changes. She sees
the same person, the horrible mantle
of daughterliness still clinging to her.

The sun seems, in the water, very close.
That's my uncle spying again, she thinks—

everything in nature is in some way her relative.
I am never alone, she thinks,   10
turning the thought into a prayer.
Then death appears, like the answer to a prayer.

No one understands anymore
how beautiful he was. But Persephone remembers.
Also that he embraced her, right there,
with her uncle watching. She remembers
sunlight flashing on his bare arms.

This is the last moment she remembers clearly.
Then the dark god bore her away.

She also remembers, less clearly,   20
the chilling insight that from this moment
she couldn't live without him again.

The girl who disappears from the pool
will never return. A woman will return,
looking for the girl she was.

She stands by the pool saying, from time to time,
I was abducted, but it sounds
wrong to her, nothing like what she felt.
Then she says, *I was not abducted*.   30
Then she says, *I offered myself, I wanted
to escape my body*. Even, sometimes,
I willed this. But ignorance

cannot will knowledge. Ignorance
wills something imagined, which it believes exists.

All the different nouns—
she says them in rotation.
Death, husband, god, stranger.
Everything sounds so simple, so conventional.
I must have been, she thinks, a simple girl.

She can't remember herself as that person   40
but she keeps thinking the pool will remember
and explain to her the meaning of her prayer
so she can understand
whether it was answered or not.

FOR ANALYSIS

1. If you are not familiar with the story of Persephone, read up on it. Reread "The Myth of Innocence" in light of Persephone's tale.

2. To what thing or things does the title of the poem refer?

3. Of what was the speaker innocent? What has experience taught her?

WRITING TOPIC

Glück writes, "But ignorance / cannot will knowledge. Ignorance / wills something imagined, which it believes exists" (ll. 32–34). Write a reflection on a moment in your own life when you wanted to experience something and found when you did that it was not what you thought it would be.

ALAN FELDMAN   (B. 1945)

MY CENTURY   2001

The year I was born the atomic bomb went off.
Here I'd just begun, and someone
found the switch to turn off the world.

In the furnace-light, in the central solar fire
of that heat lamp, the future got very finite,
and it was possible to imagine time-travelers

failing to arrive, because there was no future.
Inside the great dark clock in the hall,
heavy brass cylinders descended.

Tick-tock, the chimes changed their tune   10
one phrase at a time. The bomb became
a film star, its glamorous globe of smoke

searing the faces of men in beach chairs.
Someone threw up every day at school.
No time to worry about collective death,

when life itself was permeated by ordeals.
And so we grew up, beneath an umbrella of acceptance.
In bio we learned there were particles

cruising through us like whales through archipelagoes,
and in civics that if Hitler had gotten the bomb   20
he'd have used it on the inferior races,

and all this time love was etching its scars
on our skins like maps. The heavens
remained pure, except for little white slits

on the perfect blue skin that planes cut
in the icy upper air, like needles sewing.
From one, a tiny seed might fall

that would make a sun on earth.
And so the century passed, with me still in it,
books waiting on the shelves to become cinders,   30

what we felt locked up inside, waiting to be read,
down the long corridor of time. I was born
the year the bomb exploded. Twice

whole cities were charred like cities in the Bible,
but we didn't look back. We went on thinking
we could go on, our shapes the same,

darkened now against a background lit by fire.
Forgive me for doubting you're there,
Citizens, on your holodecks with earth wallpaper—

a shadow-toned ancestor with poorly pressed pants,   40
protected like a child from knowing the future.

FOR ANALYSIS

1. What kinds of **images** appear in this poem? Natural? Man-made? Large? Small?
Why do you think Feldman chose the combination of images that he did?

2. What sense of time does this poem have? What might it be trying to express?

3. What is this poem's central **paradox**? Where is it first named?

MAKING ARGUMENTS

Alan Feldman was born in 1945, the year the atomic bomb was used, and this poem
was written in 2001. Does the future look as fragile to people born fifty years later than
Feldman? How would you argue that it does? How would you argue that it does not?

WRITING TOPIC

Find a significant historical event that occurred in the year of your birth. In a poem, a
short story, or an essay, reflect on the event's significance to you, or to humankind, or
simply to the people to whom it happened.

SANDRA CISNEROS (B. 1954)

MY WICKED WICKED WAYS 1987

This is my father.
See? He is young.
He looks like Errol Flynn.[1]

He is wearing a hat
that tips over one eye,
a suit that fits him good,
and baggy pants.

He is also wearing
those awful shoes,
the two-toned ones   10
my mother hates.

Here is my mother.
She is not crying.
She cannot look into the lens
because the sun is bright.
The woman,
the one my father knows,
is not here.
She does not come till later.

My mother will get very mad.   20
Her face will turn red
and she will throw one shoe.
My father will say nothing.
After a while everyone
will forget it.
Years and years will pass.
My mother will stop mentioning it.

This is me she is carrying.
I am a baby.
She does not know   30
I will turn out bad.

---

[1] Errol Flynn (1909–1959) was a handsome leading man in many Hollywood movies during the 1930s and 1940s.

FOR ANALYSIS

1. Why does the speaker tell us that her mother "is not crying" (l. 13)?
2. What will the speaker's mother "get very mad" about (l. 20)?
3. What is the connection between the last four lines and the rest of the poem?

WRITING TOPIC

Discuss the meaning of the final line of the poem. What does the speaker mean by *bad*?

SANDRA M. CASTILLO (B. 1962)

CHRISTMAS, 1970   2002

We assemble the silver tree,
our translated lives,
its luminous branches,
numbered to fit into its body.
place its metallic roots
to decorate our first Christmas.
Mother finds herself
opening, closing the Red Cross box
she will carry into 1976
like an unwanted door prize,   10
a timepiece, a stubborn fact,
an emblem of exile measuring our days,
marked by the moment of our departure,
our lives no longer arranged.

Somewhere,
there is a photograph,
a Polaroid Mother cannot remember was ever taken:
I am sitting under Tia Tere's Christmas tree,
her first apartment in this, our new world:
my sisters by my side,   20
I wear a white dress, black boots,
an eight-year-old's resignation;
Mae and Mitzy, age four,
wear red and white snowflake sweaters and identical smiles,
on this, our first Christmas,
away from ourselves.

The future unreal, unmade,
Mother will cry into the new year

with Lidia and Emerito,
our elderly downstairs neighbors,   30
who realize what we are too young to understand:
Even a map cannot show you
the way back to a place
that no longer exists.

FOR ANALYSIS

1. How is the tree described in "Christmas, 1970"? Why do you think it is described in this way?

2. This poem includes a number of details about time, such as dates and ages and references to the past and the future, and about place, such as the different **settings** and the mention of a map. How do place and time intersect in this poem? Why are they important?

3. How does Castillo use verb tense in this poem? How does it change? What do you think it means that it does?

WRITING TOPIC

Recall a significant moment from your childhood when you were "too young to understand" something. What makes you able to understand it now?

SPENCER REECE   (B. 1963)

THE MANHATTAN PROJECT   2011

First, J. Robert Oppenheimer wrote his paper on dwarf stars—"What happens to a massive star that burns out?" he asked. His calculations suggested that instead of collapsing it would contract indefinitely, under the force of its own gravity. The bright star would disappear but it would still be there, where there had been brilliance there would be a blank. Soon after, workers built Oak Ridge, the accumulation of Cemesto hutments not placed on any map. They built a church, a school, a bowling alley. From all over, families drove through the muddy ruts. The ground swelled about the ruts like flesh stitched by sutures. My father, a child, watched the loads on the tops of their cars tip. Gates let everyone in and out with a pass. Forbidden to tell anyone they were there, my father's family 10 moved in, quietly, behind the chain-link fence. Niels Bohr said, "This bomb might be our great hope." My father watched his parents eat breakfast: his father opened his newspaper across the plate of bacon and eggs, his mother smoked Camel straights, the ash from her cigarette cometing across the back of the obituaries. They spoke little. Increasingly the mother drank Wild Turkey with her women friends from the bowling league. Generators from the Y-12 plant droned their ambition. There were no birds. General Leslie Groves marched the board-walks, yelled, his boots pressed the slates and the mud bubbled up like viscera. My father watched his father enter the plant. My shy father went to the library, which was a trailer with a circus tent painted on the side. There he read the defi-nition of "uranium" which was worn to a blur. My father read one Hardy Boys 20 mystery after another. It was August 1945. The librarian smiled sympathetically at the 12-year-old boy. "Time to go home," the librarian said. They named the bomb Little Boy. It weighed 9,700 pounds. It was the size of a go-kart. On the battle cruiser *Augusta*, President Truman said, "This is the greatest thing in his-tory." That evening, my father's parents mentioned Japanese cities. Everyone was quiet. It was the quiet of the exhausted and the innocent. The quietness inside my father was building and would come to define him. I was wrong to judge it. Speak, Father, and I will listen. And if you do not wish to speak, then I will listen to that.

FOR ANALYSIS

1. Who were J. Robert Oppenheimer, Niels Bohr, and Leslie Groves? Why are they in this poem? What is the effect of having real people in a poem?

2. How would you describe the form of this poem in terms of **rhythm**, **rhyme**, and the shape of the lines? Does it look or sound like a poem? What makes it a poem?

3. Why do you think Reece mentions the name of the bomb?

MAKING ARGUMENTS

Is the speaker wrong to judge his father? Are we as readers wrong to judge the Man-hattan Project or the U.S. government? Construct an argument about one or all of these questions on the evidence in this poem and on your knowledge of the history.

WRITING TOPIC

Write a short essay in which you compare "The Manhattan Project" to Feldman's "My Century" (p. 192). How do the different poems treat what is almost the same subject?

EVELYN LAU   (B. 1971)

SOLIPSISM   1994

I spend days at the gym enclosed by four mirrors,
a silver pole balanced on my shoulders.
I slide keys out of the machines, slot them lower
to lift my weights with increased strain,
to pump the last reps in my personal program.

I watch on television a show that is being taped
in the studio across the hall. It is shown simultaneously

in the green room but will not be broadcast publicly
until next week. I feel very special
yet out of step with the rest of the viewing world.   10

In aerobics class we lie on our backs and pump our hips
repetitively towards the ceiling. Soon lovers will come
to smother us with their bodies, pumping equally.
Now there are only our midriffs rising and lowering,
our shapes contained in lycra and cotton.

I break cold medication out of its blister wrap
in the green room, I swallow sedatives in soothing colours.
The makeup person touches my face with gentle fingers.
She covers me in a smock the colour of roses
and together we watch the changes in the mirror.   20

The faces around me are glazed with perspiration,
their bodies are lovely and plain by turns.
I take my position at the exercise bar between two bodies.
I resume the process of making myself perfect
as they both are, yet not like them, uniquely myself.

I see my body in four funhouse mirrors.
It is shaped exactly like an upended couch.
The gym is a marvel of bodies in motion,
lineups are polite at the popular machines,
active minds are occupied with weight goals, diet instructions.   30

The audience would wave if the camera glanced their way.
It would stampede to the nearest exit in case of fire
or planted bomb, crushing members of its own sex and race.
I am very calm. I have rehearsed my instructions,
not once do I stray from the script or structure.

Journalists declare there are weather and wars
happening outside the fitness-club doors,
but I hear only music and the splash of water fountains.
I only notice how others have tied back their hair.
Rarely do I look outside, for something other or more.   40

FOR ANALYSIS

1. Look up *solipsism* in the dictionary. Is it an appropriate title for this poem?
Explain.

2. Consider the first three lines of the last **stanza**. How do they relate to the central
issue of this poem?

3. How might you define *perfect* as it is used in line 24? Can the speaker make herself perfect in the fitness club? Explain.

MAKING ARGUMENTS

Who is the speaker in this poem? Is she actually a television personality? Make an argument for who she is based on your reading of the poem.

WRITING TOPICS

1. Describe the circumstances that would allow you to feel that nothing exists or is real but yourself.

2. Using someone you know—or know of—as a model, describe the behavior of a solipsistic person. Do you believe that solipsism is a desirable or an undesirable trait? Explain.

CONNECTING POEMS:
VOICES OF EXPERIENCE

The poems in this unit explore the role parents, or parental figures, play in guiding children through the innocence of childhood into the world of experience. The poems also address the contradictions and inconsistencies inherent in this role and in the world of human experience. As you read, pay attention not only to the ways the experienced try to guide the innocent—and the difficulties they have doing it—but also to the texture of their voices. How have the poets personalized these voices? How does the way they speak relate to what they have to say? What do the innocent have to say about the advice they are being given, and how does the way the poets have them express their thoughts relate to how we hear them?

LANGSTON HUGHES   (1902–1967)

MOTHER TO SON   1926

Well, son, I'll tell you:
Life for me ain't been no crystal stair.
It's had tacks in it,
And splinters,
And boards torn up,
And places with no carpet on the floor—
Bare.
But all the time
I'se been a-climbin' on,

And reachin' landin's,   10
And turnin' corners,
And sometimes goin' in the dark
Where there ain't been no light.
So boy, don't you turn back.
Don't you set down on the steps
'Cause you finds it's kinder hard.
Don't you fall now—
For I'se still goin', honey,
I'se still climbin',
And life for me ain't been no crystal stair.   20

FOR ANALYSIS

1. What are the two kinds of stairs in this poem? What do they stand for?

2. Analyze the structure of the poem. What are the functions of the various instances of repetition?

MAKING ARGUMENTS

Over the years, readers have argued about the use of African American vernacular in literature. What do you think about it? Make an argument for or against its use.

WRITING TOPIC

Write a poem, "Son to Mother," in response to Hughes's poem. It should be about the same topic but have a different **point of view**, perhaps with a different **tone** or sense.

PETER MEINKE   (B. 1932)

ADVICE TO MY SON   1965

—FOR TIM

The trick is, to live your days
as if each one may be your last
(for they go fast, and young men lose their lives
in strange and unimaginable ways)
but at the same time, plan long range
(for they go slow: if you survive
the shattered windshield and the bursting shell
you will arrive
at our approximation here below
of heaven or hell).   10

To be specific, between the peony and the rose
plant squash and spinach, turnips and tomatoes;
beauty is nectar
and nectar, in a desert, saves—
but the stomach craves stronger sustenance
than the honied vine.
Therefore, marry a pretty girl
after seeing her mother;
speak truth to one man,
work with another;   20
and always serve bread with your wine.

But, son,
always serve wine.

FOR ANALYSIS

1. Explain how the advice of lines 17–21 is logically related to the preceding lines.

2. What do the final two lines tell the reader about the speaker?

MAKING ARGUMENTS

"Advice to my Son" could be read as one in a long line of poems about seizing the day
and/or "plan[ning] long range," in the poem's words (l. 5). Does it make more sense to
read the poem as an act of giving sensible advice or as a commentary on the long history of poems mentioned above? Make an argument one way or the other.

WRITING TOPIC

The advice of the first **stanza** seems contradictory. In what ways does the second
stanza attempt to resolve the contradiction or explain the "trick" (l. 1)? What do the
various plants and the bread and wine **symbolize**?

ROBERT MEZEY (B. 1935)

MY MOTHER 1970

My mother writes from Trenton,
a comedian to the bone
but underneath, serious
and all heart. "Honey," she says,
"be a mensch[1] and Mary too,
it's no good to worry, you

My Mother
  [1] A person of integrity and honor.

are doing the best you can
your Dad and everyone
thinks you turned out very well
as long as you pay your bills   10
nobody can say a word
you can tell them to drop dead
so save a dollar it can't
hurt—remember Frank you went
to highschool with? he still lives
with his wife's mother, his wife
works while he writes his books and
did he ever sell a one
the four kids run around naked
36 and he's never had,   20
you'll forgive my expression
even a pot to piss in
or a window to throw it,
such a smart boy he couldn't
read the footprints on the wall
honey you think you know all
the answers you don't, please try
to put some money away
believe me it wouldn't hurt
artist shmartist life's too short   30
for that kind of, forgive me,
horseshit, I know what you want
better than you, all that counts
is to make a good living
and the best of everything,
as Sholem Aleichem[2] said
he was a great writer did
you ever read his books dear,
you should make what he makes a year
anyway he says some place   40
Poverty is no disgrace
but it's no honor either
that's what I say,
                    love,
                        Mother"

---

[2] Pen name of the Jewish author Sholem Naumovich Rabinovich (1859–1916).

BEHIND GRANDMA'S HOUSE   1985

At ten I wanted fame. I had a comb
And two Coke bottles, a tube of Bryl-creem.
I borrowed a dog, one with
Mismatched eyes and a happy tongue,
And wanted to prove I was tough
In the alley, kicking over trash cans,
A dull chime of tuna cans falling.
I hurled light bulbs like grenades
And men teachers held their heads,
Fingers of blood lengthening   10
On the ground. I flicked rocks at cats,
Their goofy faces spurred with foxtails.
I kicked fences. I shooed pigeons.
I broke a branch from a flowering peach
And frightened ants with a stream of piss.
I said "Shit," "Fuck you," and "No way
Daddy-O" to an imaginary priest
Until grandma came into the alley,
Her apron flapping in a breeze,
Her hair mussed, and said, "Let me help you,"   20
And punched me between the eyes.

FOR ANALYSIS

1. What word appears more than any other in this poem? What might it mean that it appears so often?

2. Who gets the "last word" in this poem? Of what does this last word consist?

3. What is the actual last word in the poem? Is there a pun involved?

MAKING ARGUMENTS

Argue with "Behind Grandma's House" by focusing not on the act that ends the poem but at the activity prior to the poem that consists of the ten years of the speaker's life up to that moment. Instead of looking at the punch that may have straightened him out, what acts or conditions might have inclined him to act the way he does in the poem?

WRITING TOPIC

Describe the effect of the poem's account of the speaker's actions. What feeling comes across from the **rhythms** and sounds and **images**? What moral judgment do you make of the actions they describe? Do these two sets of reactions go together? If not, what is the effect of their being seemingly mismatched?

MAKING CONNECTIONS

1. Compare the **tone** of the advice given in Meinke's "Advice to My Son" (p. 200) with that given in Mezey's "My Mother" (p. 201).

2. While only one of these poems is explicitly about school, all are in some way about education. How is each of these about teaching and learning? Is there only one way to teach?

3. The voices of experience in two of these poems are explicitly ethnic. What effects do the poems get from quoting, directly or indirectly, the ethnic **dialects** of their experienced voices?

CONNECTING POEMS: HAPPY HOLIDAYS

For the most part, we think of holidays as times of celebration and reflection, as times to remind ourselves of what's important and to be thankful for what we have. While this aspect of holidays serves an important function, one of literature's important functions has been to make us think beyond the accepted, obvious meanings of the things we do and say—of the rituals, practices, and values of the groups and cultures to which we belong—and give us the opportunity to examine them and what they say about our lives more openly and critically. When reading these poems, pay attention to the ways in which they play on the tension between what's supposed to be happening and other things that take on importance or demand attention—yours or the speaker's.

W. S. MERWIN (B. 1927)

THANKS   1988

Listen
with the night falling we are saying thank you
we are stopping on the bridges to bow from the railings
we are running out of the glass rooms
with our mouths full of food to look at the sky
and say thank you
we are standing by the water thanking it
smiling by the windows looking out
in our directions

back from a series of hospitals back from a mugging   10
after funerals we are saying thank you
after the news of the dead
whether or not we knew them we are saying thank you

over telephones we are saying thank you
in doorways and in the backs of cars and in elevators

remembering wars and the police at the door
and the beatings on stairs we are saying thank you
in the banks we are saying thank you
in the faces of the officials and the rich
and of all who will never change   20
we go on saying thank you thank you

with the animals dying around us
our lost feelings we are saying thank you
with the forests falling faster than the minutes
of our lives we are saying thank you
with the words going out like cells of a brain
with the cities growing over us
we are saying thank you faster and faster
with nobody listening we are saying thank you
we are saying thank you and waving   30
dark though it is

FOR ANALYSIS

1. What types of things are "we" thankful for? What kind of people are "we" in this poem?

2. What kinds of events are occurring in the background of the poem as thanks are being given? How does the nature of these events change over the course of the poem? To what effect?

3. What effect is saying "thank you" supposed to have here? Does it work?

MAKING ARGUMENTS

If you were to write a longer paper arguing that "Thanks" is a poem about a particular modern social problem or set of problems, what would you argue it is? Use outside sources to support your claim, if needed.

WRITING TOPIC

Reflect on the act of giving thanks. Can we give thanks for other people's good fortune? Is the act of giving thanks for one's own good fortune selfish?

CARL DENNIS (B. 1939)

THANKSGIVING LETTER
FROM HARRY 2007

I guess I have to begin by admitting
I'm thankful today I don't reside in a country
My country has chosen to liberate,
That Bridgeport's my home, not Baghdad.

Thankful my chances are good, when I leave
For the Super Duper, that I'll be returning.
And I'm thankful my TV set is still broken.
No point in wasting energy feeling shame
For the havoc inflicted on others in my name
When I need all the strength I can muster   10
To teach my eighth-grade class in the low-rent district.
There, at least, I don't feel powerless.
There my choices can make some difference.

This month I'd like to believe I've widened
My students' choice of vocation, though the odds
My history lessons on working the land
Will inspire any of them to farm
Are almost as small as the odds
One will become a monk or nun
Trained in the Buddhist practice
We studied last month in the unit on India.   20
The point is to get them suspecting the world
They know first hand isn't the only world.

As for the calling of soldier, if it comes up in class,
It's not because I feel obliged to include it,
As you, as a writer, may feel obliged.
A student may happen to introduce it,
As a girl did yesterday when she read her essay
About her older brother, Ramon,
Listed as "missing in action" three years ago,   30
And about her dad, who won't agree with her mom
And the social worker on how small the odds are
That Ramon's alive, a prisoner in the mountains.

I didn't allow the discussion that followed
More time than I allowed for the other essays.
And I wouldn't take sides: not with the group
That thought the father, having grieved enough,
Ought to move on to the life still left him;
Not with the group that was glad he hadn't made do
With the next-to-nothing the world's provided,   40
That instead he's invested his trust in a story
That saves the world from shameful failure.

Let me know of any recent attempts on your part
To save our fellow-citizens from themselves.
In the meantime, if you want to borrow Ramon

For a narrative of your own, remember that any scene
Where he appears under guard in a mountain village
Should be confined to the realm of longing. There
His captors may leave him when they move on.
There his wounds may be healed,   50
His health restored. A total recovery
Except for a lingering fog of forgetfulness
A father dreams he can burn away.

SHEILA ORTIZ TAYLOR   (B. 1939)

THE WAY BACK   1989

FOR UNCLE JIM

They stand in this Christmas snapshot
poised like adagio dancers
facing each other
their arms draped around
their matching bones
brother and sister
while behind them
out of focus
the family
spins   10

Around these two
youngest of thirteen
held now for eternity
in this moment before their
twin feet slide them out
in a celestial tango
a silence gathers

We see their handsome faces
Indian bones in glinting cheeks
their raven hair, gray-streaked   20
their eyes as deep and dark as wells
holding a history of careless loss
land, lovers, mothers, maps

The way back is a land
more innocent than this

He joined the navy
She married a judge
They both baked bread in institutional ovens
He wrote long letters home
and sent his mother silk pillows   30
embroidered with military targets

He baked bread while
his eight brothers lost fingers
toes, knees, elbows
He could almost hear the bullets
thud into dough
and the sound made him rise
growing from uniform to uniform
until they had to declare peace

Home again   40
he folded away his whites
kissed his sisters
and told his brothers
he was going to become
a hairdresser
news that made their wounds ache
more than seemed possible
Finally he followed them to work at Lockheed
learned to drill holes in himself
discovered insomnia   50
married a beautician named Molly
whose hair he dyed green every Christmas

He loved all holidays
Life needed themes
spelled out in sparkles, sprinkles
cutouts, paste-ups
but most of all
in costume.

Halloweens found brother and sister
on their knees   60
before bolts of cloth
and wimpling tissue
pins in their mouths
blue chalk on their hands
for years
artists of the self

You can see it here
in this snapshot
white polyester pants belling out
around white cowboy boots   70
red western shirts
tailored close to the rib
Indian silver at the waist
twins in spirit
if not by birth
holding each other
in a light embrace
their grace
not lost

And yet   80
the way back is a land
more innocent than this
The time came round
when neighbors
preferring razor blades to invention
would not let their children
trick or treat
where a grown man
put costumes on.

That Christmas night
very late   90
he backed his throbbing
Continental
into the dark garage
that shut down tight behind him
crawled into the backseat
bearing a bottle of champagne
one glass
a photograph

FOR ANALYSIS

1. How would you characterize the poem's **tone**? Does it match the holiday setting of
the photograph with which it opens?

2. How is the brother different than the other male children in the family? How does
the world around him react to this difference? What feelings does the poem convey
about this difference?

3. Compare this poem's use of the photograph to Castillo's in "Christmas, 1970"
(p. 195). Is the speaker in "The Way Back" in the snapshot? Does it matter?

MAKING ARGUMENTS

While the life story of the brother in this poem is pretty clear, Taylor is never explicit about his sexual orientation or about his death—and it is possible to imagine a very different poem in which these things are made clear. Make an argument claiming that Taylor's strategy either strengthens or weakens the poem, based on (1) how you think poetry should work and (2) a close reading of the techniques used in the poem.

WRITING TOPIC

What do you think happens at the end of this poem? Write one more **stanza** that makes this explicit. Do you think your stanza improves on the poem?

JAMES WELCH   (1940–2003)

CHRISTMAS COMES TO MOCCASIN FLAT   1976

Christmas comes like this: Wise men
unhurried, candles bought on credit (poor price
for calves), warriors face down in wine sleep.
Winds cheat to pull heat from smoke.

Friends sit in chinked cabins, stare out
plastic windows and wait for commodities.
Charlie Blackbird, twenty miles from church
and bar, stabs his fire with flint.

When drunks drain radiators for love
or need, chiefs eat snow and talk of change,   10
an urge to laugh pounding their ribs.
Elk play games in high country.

Medicine Woman, clay pipe and twist tobacco,
calls each blizzard by name and predicts
five o'clock by spitting at her television.
Children lean into her breath to beg a story:

Something about honor and passion,
warriors back with meat and song,
a peculiar evening star, quick vision of birth.
Blackbird feeds his fire. Outside, a quick 30 below.   20

FOR ANALYSIS

1. What kind of place is Moccasin Flat?
2. Welch's poem relies heavily on **irony**. How does he use it? To what effect?

3. Compare this poem's invocation of Christmas to that in Taylor's "The Way Back" (p. 207). How does each use the association with the holiday?

MAKING ARGUMENTS

Behind Welch's poem lies an implicit critique of the treatment of Native Americans by the U.S. government. Make that critique into an explicit argument by reading up on Native American history, outlining the ways in which the men and women in this poem live lives shaped by that history. If you disagree with this premise, make a counterargument, either against that interpretation of the past or against the idea that the past can shape the present in this way.

WRITING TOPIC

Welch's poem refers to stereotypes of Native American life. Create a list of elements or **images** in this poem that are other than you expect them to be. What is the effect of all this unmet expectation?

MAGGIE NELSON (B. 1973)

THANKSGIVING   2008

Can beauty save us? Yesterday
I looked at the river and a sliver
of moon and knew the answer;

today I fell asleep in a spot of sun
behind a Vermont barn, woke to
darkness, a thin whistle of wind

and the answer changed. Inside the barn
the boys build bongs out of
copper piping, electrical tape, and

jars. All of the children here have   10
leaky brown eyes, and a certain precision
of gesture. Even the maple syrup

tastes like liquor. After dinner
I sit the cutest little boy on my knee
and read him a book about the history of cod

absentmindedly explaining overfishing,
the slave trade. People for rum? he asks,
incredulously. Yes, I nod. People for rum.

FOR ANALYSIS

1. What purpose does the little boy's incredulity serve at the end of the poem?

2. How is this a Thanksgiving poem? Aside from the speaker's story seeming to happen on the day, what is the connection of the poem to the day?

3. "Can beauty save us?" is a question that has been answered in the affirmative by a long line of poems throughout history. How does Nelson's evocation of that history work here?

MAKING ARGUMENTS

Thanksgiving is a holiday that, like Columbus Day, has been challenged as a whitewashing of America's early history. How would you construct an argument that this challenge to the usual, traditional sense of Thanksgiving is central to this poem's meaning? How would you construct an argument that it is irrelevant?

WRITING TOPIC

Research the history of your favorite holiday and write a short account of a little-known or often overlooked historical aspect of it. Does this aspect make you think differently about the holiday?

DRAMA

HENRIK IBSEN   (1828–1906)

A DOLL'S HOUSE[1]   1879

CHARACTERS

Torvald Helmer, a lawyer
Nora, his wife
Dr. Rank
Mrs. Linde
Krogstad

The Helmers' three small
   children
Anne, the children's nurse
A Maid
A Porter

ACT I

Scene

A room furnished comfortably and tastefully, but not extravagantly. At the back, a door to the right leads to the entrance hall, another to the left leads to Helmer's study. Between the doors stands a piano. In the middle of the left-hand wall is a door, and beyond it a window. Near the window are a round table, armchairs and a small sofa. In the right-hand wall, at the farther end, another door; and on the same side, nearer the footlights, a stove, two easy chairs and a rocking-chair; between the stove and the door, a small table. Engravings on the walls; a cabinet with china and other small objects; a small bookcase with well-bound books. The floors are carpeted, and a fire burns in the stove. It is winter.

A bell rings in the hall; shortly afterwards the door is heard to open. Enter Nora, humming a tune and in high spirits. She is in outdoor dress and carries a number of parcels; these she lays on the table to the right. She leaves the outer door open after her, and through it is seen a Porter who is carrying a Christmas tree and a basket, which he gives to the Maid who has opened the door.

Nora. Hide the Christmas tree carefully, Helen. Be sure the children do not see it till this evening, when it is dressed. *(To the Porter, taking out her purse.)* How much?
Porter. Sixpence.

---

[1] Translated by R. Farquharson Sharp.

Nora. There is a shilling. No, keep the change. (*The Porter thanks her, and goes out. Nora shuts the door. She is laughing to herself, as she takes off her hat and coat. She takes a packet of macaroons from her pocket and eats one or two; then goes cautiously to her husband's door and listens.*) Yes, he is in.

(*Still humming, she goes to the table on the right.*)

Helmer (*calls out from his room*). Is that my little lark twittering out there?
Nora (*busy opening some of the parcels*). Yes, it is!
Helmer. Is it my little squirrel bustling about?
Nora. Yes!
Helmer. When did my squirrel come home?
Nora. Just now. (*Puts the bag of macaroons into her pocket and wipes her mouth.*) Come in here, Torvald, and see what I have bought.
Helmer. Don't disturb me. (*A little later, he opens the door and looks into the room, pen in hand.*) Bought, did you say? All these things? Has my little spendthrift been wasting money again?
Nora. Yes, but, Torvald, this year we really can let ourselves go a little. This is the first Christmas that we have not needed to economise.
Helmer. Still, you know, we can't spend money recklessly.
Nora. Yes, Torvald, we may be a wee bit more reckless now, mayn't we? Just a tiny wee bit! You are going to have a big salary and earn lots and lots of money.
Helmer. Yes, after the New Year; but then it will be a whole quarter before the salary is due.
Nora. Pooh! we can borrow till then.
Helmer. Nora! (*Goes up to her and takes her playfully by the ear.*) The same little featherhead! Suppose, now, that I borrowed fifty pounds to-day, and you spent it all in the Christmas week, and then on New Year's Eve a slate fell on my head and killed me, and——
Nora (*putting her hands over his mouth*). Oh! don't say such horrid things.
Helmer. Still, suppose that happened,—what then?
Nora. If that were to happen, I don't suppose I should care whether I owed money or not.
Helmer. Yes, but what about the people who had lent it?
Nora. They? Who would bother about them? I should not know who they were.
Helmer. That is like a woman! But seriously, Nora, you know what I think about that. No debt, no borrowing. There can be no freedom or beauty about a home life that depends on borrowing and debt. We two have kept bravely on the straight road so far, and we will go on the same way for the short time longer that there need be any struggle.
Nora (*moving towards the stove*). As you please, Torvald.
Helmer (*following her*). Come, come, my little skylark must not droop her wings. What is this! Is my little squirrel out of temper? (*Taking out his purse.*) Nora, what do you think I have got here?
Nora (*turning round quickly*). Money!

Helmer. There you are. *(Gives her some money.)* Do you think I don't know what a lot is wanted for house-keeping at Christmas-time?

Nora *(counting)*. Ten shillings—a pound—two pounds! Thank you, thank you, Torvald; that will keep me going for a long time.

Helmer. Indeed it must.

Nora. Yes, yes, it will. But come here and let me show you what I have bought. And all so cheap! Look, here is a new suit for Ivar, and a sword; and a horse and a trumpet for Bob; and a doll and dolly's bedstead for Emmy,—they are very plain, but anyway she will soon break them in pieces. And here are dress-lengths and handkerchiefs for the maids; old Anne ought really to have something better.

Helmer. And what is in this parcel?

Nora *(crying out)*. No, no! you mustn't see that till this evening.

Helmer. Very well. But now tell me something reasonable that you would particularly like to have.

Nora. No, I really can't think of anything—unless, Torvald——

Helmer. Well?

Nora *(playing with his coat buttons, and without raising her eyes to his)*. If you really want to give me something, you might—you might——

Helmer. Well, out with it!

Nora *(speaking quickly)*. You might give me money, Torvald. Only just as much as you can afford; and then one of these days I will buy something with it.

Helmer. But, Nora——

Nora. Oh, do! dear Torvald; please, please do! Then I will wrap it up in beautiful gilt paper and hang it on the Christmas tree. Wouldn't that be fun?

Helmer. What are little people called that are always wasting money?

Nora. Spendthrifts—I know. Let us do as you suggest, Torvald, and then I shall have time to think what I am most in want of. That is a very sensible plan, isn't it?

Helmer *(smiling)*. Indeed it is—that is to say, if you were really to save out of the money I give you, and then really buy something for yourself. But if you spend it all on the housekeeping and any number of unnecessary things, then I merely have to pay up again.

Nora. Oh but, Torvald——

Helmer. You can't deny it, my dear little Nora. *(Puts his arm round her waist.)* It's a sweet little spendthrift, but she uses up a deal of money. One would hardly believe how expensive such little persons are!

Nora. It's a shame to say that. I do really save all I can.

Helmer *(laughing)*. That's very true,—all you can. But you can't save anything!

Nora *(smiling quietly and happily)*. You haven't any idea how many expenses we skylarks and squirrels have, Torvald.

Helmer. You are an odd little soul. Very like your father. You always find some new way of wheedling money out of me, and, as soon as you have got it, it seems to melt in your hands. You never know where it has gone. Still, one must take you as you are. It is in the blood; for indeed it is true that you can inherit these things, Nora.

Nora. Ah, I wish I had inherited many of papa's qualities.

Helmer. And I would not wish you to be anything but just what you are, my sweet little skylark. But, do you know, it strikes me that you are looking rather—what shall I say—rather uneasy to-day?

Nora. Do I?

Helmer. You do, really. Look straight at me.

Nora *(looks at him).* Well?

Helmer *(wagging his finger at her).* Hasn't Miss Sweet-Tooth been breaking rules in town to-day?

Nora. No; what makes you think that?

Helmer. Hasn't she paid a visit to the confectioner's?

Nora. No, I assure you, Torvald——

Helmer. Not been nibbling sweets?

Nora. No, certainly not.

Helmer. Not even taken a bite at a macaroon or two?

Nora. No, Torvald, I assure you really——

Helmer. There, there, of course I was only joking.

Nora *(going to the table on the right).* I should not think of going against your wishes.

Helmer. No, I am sure of that! Besides, you gave me your word——*(Going up to her.)* Keep your little Christmas secrets to yourself, my darling. They will all be revealed to-night when the Christmas tree is lit, no doubt.

Nora. Did you remember to invite Doctor Rank?

Helmer. No. But there is no need; as a matter of course he will come to dinner with us. However, I will ask him, when he comes in this morning. I have ordered some good wine. Nora, you can't think how I am looking forward to this evening.

Nora. So am I! And how the children will enjoy themselves, Torvald!

Helmer. It is splendid to feel that one has a perfectly safe appointment, and a big enough income. It's delightful to think of, isn't it?

Nora. It's wonderful!

Helmer. Do you remember last Christmas? For a full three weeks beforehand you shut yourself up every evening till long after midnight, making ornaments for the Christmas tree and all the other fine things that were to be a surprise to us. It was the dullest three weeks I ever spent!

Nora. I didn't find it dull.

Helmer *(smiling).* But there was precious little result, Nora.

Nora. Oh, you shouldn't tease me about that again. How could I help the cat's going in and tearing everything to pieces?

Helmer. Of course you couldn't, poor little girl. You had the best of intentions to please us all, and that's the main thing. But it is a good thing that our hard times are over.

Nora. Yes, it is really wonderful.

Helmer. This time I needn't sit here and be dull all alone, and you needn't ruin your dear eyes and your pretty little hands——

Nora *(clapping her hands).* No, Torvald, I needn't any longer, need I! It's wonderfully lovely to hear you say so! *(Taking his arm.)* Now I will tell you how I have been thinking we ought to arrange things, Torvald. As soon as Christmas is over——(*A bell rings in the hall.*) There's the bell. (*She tidies the room a little.*) There's someone at the door. What a nuisance!

Helmer. If it is a caller, remember I am not at home.

Maid (*in the doorway*). A lady to see you, ma'am,—a stranger.

Nora. Ask her to come in.

Maid (*to Helmer*). The doctor came at the same time, sir.

Helmer. Did he go straight into my room?

Maid. Yes, sir.

(*Helmer goes into his room. The Maid ushers in Mrs. Linde, who is in traveling dress, and shuts the door.*)

Mrs. Linde (*in a dejected and timid voice*). How do you do, Nora?

Nora (*doubtfully*). How do you do——

Mrs. Linde. You don't recognise me, I suppose.

Nora. No, I don't know—yes, to be sure, I seem to——(*Suddenly.*) Yes! Christine! Is it really you?

Mrs. Linde. Yes, it is I.

Nora. Christine! To think of my not recognising you! And yet how could I——(*In a gentle voice.*) How you have altered, Christine!

Mrs. Linde. Yes, I have indeed. In nine, ten long years——

Nora. Is it so long since we met? I suppose it is. The last eight years have been a happy time for me, I can tell you. And so now you have come into the town, and have taken this long journey in winter—that was plucky of you.

Mrs. Linde. I arrived by steamer this morning.

Nora. To have some fun at Christmas-time, of course. How delightful! We will have such fun together! But take off your things. You are not cold, I hope. (*Helps her.*) Now we will sit down by the stove, and be cosy. No, take this arm-chair; I will sit here in the rocking-chair. (*Takes her hands.*) Now you look like your old self again; it was only the first moment——You are a little paler, Christine, and perhaps a little thinner.

Mrs. Linde. And much, much older, Nora.

Nora. Perhaps a little older; very, very little; certainly not much. (*Stops suddenly and speaks seriously.*) What a thoughtless creature I am, chattering away like this. My poor, dear Christine, do forgive me.

Mrs. Linde. What do you mean, Nora?

Nora (*gently*). Poor Christine, you are a widow.

Mrs. Linde. Yes; it is three years ago now.

Nora. Yes, I knew; I saw it in the papers. I assure you, Christine, I meant ever so often to write to you at the time, but I always put it off and something always prevented me.

Mrs. Linde. I quite understand, dear.

Nora. It was very bad of me, Christine. Poor thing, how you must have suffered. And he left you nothing?

Mrs. Linde. No.

Nora. And no children?

Mrs. Linde. No.

Nora. Nothing at all, then?

Mrs. Linde. Not even any sorrow or grief to live upon.

Nora (*looking incredulously at her*). But, Christine, is that possible?

Mrs. Linde (*smiles sadly and strokes her hair*). It sometimes happens, Nora.

Nora. So you are quite alone. How dreadfully sad that must be. I have three lovely children. You can't see them just now, for they are out with their nurse. But now you must tell me all about it.

Mrs. Linde. No, no; I want to hear you.

Nora. No, you must begin. I mustn't be selfish to-day, to-day I must only think of your affairs. But there is one thing I must tell you. Do you know we have just had a great piece of good luck?

Mrs. Linde. No, what is it?

Nora. Just fancy, my husband has been made manager of the Bank!

Mrs. Linde. Your husband? What good luck!

Nora. Yes, tremendous! A barrister's profession is such an uncertain thing, especially if he won't undertake unsavoury cases; and naturally Torvald has never been willing to do that, and I quite agree with him. You may imagine how pleased we are! He is to take up his work in the Bank at the New Year, and then he will have a big salary and lots of commissions. For the future we can live quite differently—we can do just as we like. I feel so relieved and so happy, Christine! It will be splendid to have heaps of money and not need to have any anxiety, won't it?

Mrs. Linde. Yes, anyhow I think it would be delightful to have what one needs.

Nora. No, not only what one needs, but heaps and heaps of money.

Mrs. Linde (*smiling*). Nora, Nora, haven't you learnt sense yet? In our schooldays you were a great spendthrift.

Nora (*laughing*). Yes, that is what Torvald says now. (*Wags her finger at her.*) But "Nora, Nora" is not so silly as you think. We have not been in a position for me to waste money. We have both had to work.

Mrs. Linde. You too?

Nora. Yes; odds and ends, needlework, crochet-work, embroidery, and that kind of thing. (*Dropping her voice.*) And other things as well. You know Torvald left his office when we were married? There was no prospect of promotion there, and he had to try and earn more than before. But during the first year he over-worked himself dreadfully. You see, he had to make money every way he could, and he worked early and late; but he couldn't stand it, and fell dreadfully ill, and the doctors said it was necessary for him to go south.

Mrs. Linde. You spent a whole year in Italy, didn't you?

Nora. Yes. It was no easy matter to get away, I can tell you. It was just after Ivar was born; but naturally we had to go. It was a wonderfully beautiful journey, and it saved Torvald's life. But it cost a tremendous lot of money, Christine.

Mrs. Linde. So I should think.

Nora. It cost about two hundred and fifty pounds. That's a lot, isn't it?

Mrs. Linde. Yes, and in emergencies like that it is lucky to have the money.

Nora. I ought to tell you that we had it from papa.

Mrs. Linde. Oh, I see. It was just about that time that he died, wasn't it?

Nora. Yes; and, just think of it, I couldn't go and nurse him. I was expecting little Ivar's birth every day and I had my poor sick Torvald to look after. My dear, kind father—I never saw him again, Christine. That was the saddest time I have known since our marriage.

Mrs. Linde. And your husband came back quite well?

Nora. As sound as a bell!

Mrs. Linde. But—the doctor?

Nora. What doctor?

Mrs. Linde. I thought your maid said the gentleman who arrived here just as I did was the doctor?

Nora. Yes, that was Doctor Rank, but he doesn't come here professionally. He is our greatest friend, and comes in at least once every day. No, Torvald has not had an hour's illness since then, and our children are strong and healthy and so am I. (*Jumps up and claps her hands.*) Christine! Christine! it's good to be alive and happy!——But how horrid of me; I am talking of nothing but my own affairs. (*Sits on a stool near her, and rests her arms on her knees.*) You mustn't be angry with me. Tell me, is it really true that you did not love your husband? Why did you marry him?

Mrs. Linde. My mother was alive then, and was bedridden and helpless, and I had to provide for my two younger brothers; so I did not think I was justified in refusing his offer.

Nora. No, perhaps you were quite right. He was rich at that time, then?

Mrs. Linde. I believe he was quite well off. But his business was a precarious one; and, when he died, it all went to pieces and there was nothing left.

Nora. And then?——

Mrs. Linde. Well, I had to turn my hand to anything I could find—first a small shop, then a small school, and so on. The last three years have seemed like one long working-day, with no rest. Now it is at an end, Nora. My poor mother needs me no more, for she is gone; and the boys do not need me either; they have got situations and can shift for themselves.

Nora. What a relief you must feel it——

Mrs. Linde. No, indeed; I only feel my life unspeakably empty. No one to live for any more. (*Gets up restlessly.*) That was why I could not stand the life in my little backwater any longer. I hope it may be easier here to find something which will busy me and occupy my thoughts. If only I could have the good luck to get some regular work—office work of some kind——

Nora. But, Christine, that is so frightfully tiring, and you look tired out now. You had far better go away to some watering-place.

Mrs. Linde (*walking to the window*). I have no father to give me money for a journey, Nora.

Nora (*rising*). Oh, don't be angry with me.

Mrs. Linde (*going up to her*). It is you that must not be angry with me, dear. The worst of a position like mine is that it makes one so bitter. No one to work for, and yet obliged to be always on the look-out for chances. One must live, and so one becomes selfish. When you told me of the happy turn your fortunes have taken—you will hardly believe it—I was delighted not so much on your account as on my own.

Nora. How do you mean?—Oh, I understand. You mean that perhaps Torvald could get you something to do.

Mrs. Linde. Yes, that was what I was thinking of.

Nora. He must, Christine. Just leave it to me; I will broach the subject very cleverly—I will think of something that will please him very much. It will make me so happy to be of some use to you.

Mrs. Linde. How kind you are, Nora, to be so anxious to help me! It is doubly kind in you, for you know so little of the burdens and troubles of life.

Nora. I——? I know so little of them?

Mrs. Linde (smiling). My dear! Small household cares and that sort of thing!—You are a child, Nora.

Nora (tosses her head and crosses the stage). You ought not to be so superior.

Mrs. Linde. No?

Nora. You are just like the others. They all think that I am incapable of anything really serious——

Mrs. Linde. Come, come——

Nora. —that I have gone through nothing in this world of cares.

Mrs. Linde. But, my dear Nora, you have just told me all your troubles.

Nora. Pooh!—those were trifles. (Lowering her voice.) I have not told you the important thing.

Mrs. Linde. The important thing? What do you mean?

Nora. You look down upon me altogether, Christine—but you ought not to. You are proud, aren't you, of having worked so hard and so long for your mother?

Mrs. Linde. Indeed, I don't look down on any one. But it is true that I am both proud and glad to think that I was privileged to make the end of my mother's life almost free from care.

Nora. And you are proud to think of what you have done for your brothers.

Mrs. Linde. I think I have the right to be.

Nora. I think so, too. But now, listen to this; I too have something to be proud and glad of.

Mrs. Linde. I have no doubt you have. But what do you refer to?

Nora. Speak low. Suppose Torvald were to hear! He mustn't on any account—no one in the world must know, Christine, except you.

Mrs. Linde. But what is it?

Nora. Come here. (Pulls her down on the sofa beside her.) Now I will show you that I too have something to be proud and glad of. It was I who saved Torvald's life.

Mrs. Linde. "Saved"? How?

Nora. I told you about our trip to Italy. Torvald would never have recovered if he had not gone there——

Mrs. Linde. Yes, but your father gave you the necessary funds.

Nora (smiling). Yes, that is what Torvald and all the others think, but——

Mrs. Linde. But——

Nora. Papa didn't give us a shilling. It was I who procured the money.

Mrs. Linde. You? All that large sum?

Nora. Two hundred and fifty pounds. What do you think of that?

Mrs. Linde. But, Nora, how could you possibly do it? Did you win a prize in the Lottery?

Nora (contemptuously). In the Lottery? There would have been no credit in that.

Mrs. Linde. But where did you get it from, then?

Nora (humming and smiling with an air of mystery). Hm, hm! Aha!

Mrs. Linde. Because you couldn't have borrowed it.

Nora. Couldn't I? Why not?

Mrs. Linde. No, a wife cannot borrow without her husband's consent.

Nora (tossing her head). Oh, if it is a wife who has any head for business—a wife who has the wit to be a little bit clever——

Mrs. Linde. I don't understand it at all, Nora.

Nora. There is no need you should. I never said I had borrowed the money. I may have got it some other way. (Lies back on the sofa.) Perhaps I got it from some other admirer. When anyone is as attractive as I am——

Mrs. Linde. You are a mad creature.

Nora. Now, you know you're full of curiosity, Christine.

Mrs. Linde. Listen to me, Nora dear. Haven't you been a little bit imprudent?

Nora (sits up straight). Is it imprudent to save your husband's life?

Mrs. Linde. It seems to me imprudent, without his knowledge, to——

Nora. But it was absolutely necessary that he should not know! My goodness, can't you understand that? It was necessary he should have no idea what a dangerous condition he was in. It was to me that the doctors came and said that his life was in danger, and that the only thing to save him was to live in the south. Do you suppose I didn't try, first of all, to get what I wanted as if it were for myself? I told him how much I should love to travel abroad like other young wives; I tried tears and entreaties with him; I told him that he ought to remember the condition I was in, and that he ought to be kind and indulgent to me; I even hinted that he might raise a loan. That nearly made him angry, Christine. He said I was thoughtless, and that it was his duty as my husband not to indulge me in my whims and caprices—as I believe he called them. Very well I thought, you must be saved—and that was how I came to devise a way out of the difficulty——

Mrs. Linde. And did your husband never get to know from your father that the money had not come from him?

Nora. No, never. Papa died just at that time. I had meant to let him into the secret and beg him never to reveal it. But he was so ill then—alas, there never was any need to tell him.

Mrs. Linde. And since then have you never told your secret to your husband?

Nora. Good Heavens, no! How could you think so? A man who has such strong opinions about these things! And besides, how painful and humiliating it would be for Torvald, with his manly independence, to know that he owed me anything! It would upset our mutual relations altogether; our beautiful happy home would no longer be what it is now.

Mrs. Linde. Do you mean never to tell him about it?

Nora *(meditatively, and with a half smile).* Yes—some day, perhaps, after many years, when I am no longer as nice-looking as I am now. Don't laugh at me! I mean, of course, when Torvald is no longer as devoted to me as he is now; when my dancing and dressing-up and reciting have palled on him; then it may be a good thing to have something in reserve——*(Breaking off.)* What nonsense! That time will never come. Now, what do you think of my great secret, Christine? Do you still think I am of no use? I can tell you, too, that this affair has caused me a lot of worry. It has been by no means easy for me to meet my engagements punctually. I may tell you that there is something that is called, in business, quarterly interest, and another thing called payment in instalments, and it is always so dreadfully difficult to manage them. I have had to save a little here and there, where I could, you understand. I have not been able to put aside much from my housekeeping money, for Torvald must have a good table. I couldn't let my children be shabbily dressed; I have felt obliged to use up all he gave me for them, the sweet little darlings!

Mrs. Linde. So it has all had to come out of your own necessaries of life, poor Nora?

Nora. Of course. Besides, I was the one responsible for it. Whenever Torvald has given me money for new dresses and such things, I have never spent more than half of it; I have always bought the simplest and cheapest things. Thank Heaven, any clothes look well on me, and so Torvald has never noticed it. But it was often very hard on me, Christine—because it is delightful to be really well dressed, isn't it?

Mrs. Linde. Quite so.

Nora. Well, then I have found other ways of earning money. Last winter I was lucky enough to get a lot of copying to do; so I locked myself up and sat writing every evening until quite late at night. Many a time I was desperately tired; but all the same it was a tremendous pleasure to sit there working and earning money. It was like being a man.

Mrs. Linde. How much have you been able to pay off in that way?

Nora. I can't tell you exactly. You see, it is very difficult to keep an account of a business matter of that kind. I only know that I have paid every penny that I could scrape together. Many a time I was at my wits' end. *(Smiles.)* Then I used to sit here and imagine that a rich old gentleman had fallen in love with me——

Mrs. Linde. What! Who was it?

Nora. Be quiet!—that he had died; and that when his will was opened it contained, written in big letters, the instruction: "The lovely Mrs. Nora Helmer is to have all I possess paid over to her at once in cash."

Mrs. Linde. But, my dear Nora—who could the man be?

Nora. Good gracious, can't you understand? There was no old gentleman at all; it was only something that I used to sit here and imagine, when I couldn't think of any way of procuring money. But it's all the same now; the tiresome old person can stay where he is, as far as I am concerned; I don't care about him or his will either, for I am free from care now. *(Jumps up.)* My goodness, it's delightful to think of, Christine! Free from care! To be able to be free from care, quite free from care; to be able to play and romp with the children; to be able to keep the house beautifully and have everything just as Torvald likes it! And, think of it, soon the spring will come and the big blue sky! Perhaps we shall be able to take a little trip—perhaps I shall see the sea again! Oh, it's a wonderful thing to be alive and be happy. (*A bell is heard in the hall.*)

Mrs. Linde (*rising*). There is the bell; perhaps I had better go.

Nora. No, don't go; no one will come in here; it is sure to be for Torvald.

Servant (*at the hall door*). Excuse me, ma'am—there is a gentleman to see the master, and as the doctor is with him——

Nora. Who is it?

Krogstad (*at the door*). It is I, Mrs. Helmer. (*Mrs. Linde starts, trembles, and turns to the window.*)

Nora (*takes a step towards him, and speaks in a strained, low voice*). You? What is it? What do you want to see my husband about?

Krogstad. Bank business—in a way. I have a small post in the Bank, and I hear your husband is to be our chief now——

Nora. Then it is——

Krogstad. Nothing but dry business matters, Mrs. Helmer; absolutely nothing else.

Nora. Be so good as to go into the study, then. (*She bows indifferently to him and shuts the door into the hall; then comes back and makes up the fire in the stove.*)

Mrs. Linde. Nora—who was that man?

Nora. A lawyer, of the name of Krogstad.

Mrs. Linde. Then it really was he.

Nora. Do you know the man?

Mrs. Linde. I used to—many years ago. At one time he was a solicitor's clerk in our town.

Nora. Yes, he was.

Mrs. Linde. He is greatly altered.

Nora. He made a very unhappy marriage.

Mrs. Linde. He is a widower now, isn't he?

Nora. With several children. There now, it is burning up.

(*Shuts the door of the stove and moves the rocking-chair aside.*)

Mrs. Linde. They say he carries on various kinds of business.

Nora. Really! Perhaps he does; I don't know anything about it. But don't let us think of business; it is so tiresome.

Doctor Rank (*comes out of Helmer's study. Before he shuts the door he calls to him*). No, my dear fellow, I won't disturb you; I would rather go in to your wife for a little while. (*Shuts the door and sees Mrs. Linde.*) I beg your pardon; I am afraid I am disturbing you too.

Nora. No, not at all. (*Introducing him.*) Doctor Rank, Mrs. Linde.

Rank. I have often heard Mrs. Linde's name mentioned here. I think I passed you on the stairs when I arrived, Mrs. Linde?

Mrs. Linde. Yes, I go up very slowly; I can't manage stairs well.

Rank. Ah! some slight internal weakness?

Mrs. Linde. No, the fact is I have been overworking myself.

Rank. Nothing more than that? Then I suppose you have come to town to amuse yourself with our entertainments?

Mrs. Linde. I have come to look for work.

Rank. Is that a good cure for overwork?

Mrs. Linde. One must live, Doctor Rank.

Rank. Yes, the general opinion seems to be that it is necessary.

Nora. Look here, Doctor Rank—you know you want to live.

Rank. Certainly. However wretched I may feel, I want to prolong the agony as long as possible. All my patients are like that. And so are those who are morally diseased; one of them, and a bad case too, is at this very moment with Helmer——

Mrs. Linde (sadly). Ah!

Nora. Whom do you mean?

Rank. A lawyer of the name of Krogstad, a fellow you don't know at all. He suffers from a diseased moral character, Mrs. Helmer; but even he began talking of its being highly important that he should live.

Nora. Did he? What did he want to speak to Torvald about?

Rank. I have no idea; I only heard that it was something about the Bank.

Nora. I didn't know this—what's his name—Krogstad had anything to do with the Bank.

Rank. Yes, he has some sort of appointment there. (To Mrs. Linde.) I don't know whether you find also in your part of the world that there are certain people who go zealously snuffing about to smell out moral corruption, and, as soon as they have found some, put the person concerned into some lucrative position where they can keep their eye on him. Healthy natures are left out in the cold.

Mrs. Linde. Still I think the sick are those who most need taking care of.

Rank (shrugging his shoulders). Yes, there you are. That is the sentiment that is turning Society into a sickhouse.

(Nora, who has been absorbed in her thoughts, breaks out into smothered laughter and claps her hands.)

Rank. Why do you laugh at that? Have you any notion what Society really is?

Nora. What do I care about tiresome Society? I am laughing at something quite different, something extremely amusing. Tell me, Doctor Rank, are all the people who are employed in the Bank dependent on Torvald now?

Rank. Is that what you find so extremely amusing?

Nora (smiling and humming). That's my affair! (Walking about the room.) It's perfectly glorious to think that we have—that Torvald has so much power over so many people. (Takes the packet from her pocket.) Doctor Rank, what do you say to a macaroon?

Rank. What, macaroons? I thought they were forbidden here.

Nora. Yes, but these are some Christine gave me.

Mrs. Linde. What! I?—

Nora. Oh, well, don't be alarmed! You couldn't know that Torvald had forbidden them. I must tell you that he is afraid they will spoil my teeth. But, bah!—once in a way——That's so, isn't it, Doctor Rank? By your leave? (*Puts a macaroon into his mouth.*) You must have one too, Christine. And I shall have one, just a little one—or at most two. (*Walking about.*) I am tremendously happy. There is just one thing in the world now that I should dearly love to do.

Rank. Well, what is that?

Nora. It's something I should dearly love to say, if Torvald could hear me.

Rank. Well, why can't you say it?

Nora. No, I daren't; it's so shocking.

Mrs. Linde. Shocking?

Rank. Well, I should not advise you to say it. Still, with us you might. What is it you would so much like to say if Torvald could hear you?

Nora. I should just love to say—Well, I'm damned!

Rank. Are you mad?

Mrs. Linde. Nora, dear——!

Rank. Say it, here he is!

Nora (*hiding the packet*). Hush! Hush! Hush!

(*Helmer comes out of his room, with his coat over his arm and his hat in his hand.*)

Nora. Well, Torvald dear, have you got rid of him?

Helmer. Yes, he has just gone.

Nora. Let me introduce you—this is Christine, who has come to town.

Helmer. Christine——? Excuse me, but I don't know——

Nora. Mrs. Linde, dear; Christine Linde.

Helmer. Of course. A school friend of my wife's, I presume?

Mrs. Linde. Yes, we have known each other since then.

Nora. And just think, she has taken a long journey in order to see you.

Helmer. What do you mean?

Mrs. Linde. No, really, I——

Nora. Christine is tremendously clever at book-keeping, and she is frightfully anxious to work under some clever man, so as to perfect herself——

Helmer. Very sensible, Mrs. Linde.

Nora. And when she heard you had been appointed manager of the Bank—the news was telegraphed, you know—she travelled here as quick as she could. Torvald, I am sure you will be able to do something for Christine, for my sake, won't you?

Helmer. Well, it is not altogether impossible. I presume you are a widow, Mrs. Linde?

Mrs. Linde. Yes.

Helmer. And have had some experience of book-keeping?

Mrs. Linde. Yes, a fair amount.

Helmer. Ah! well, it's very likely I may be able to find something for you——

Nora (*clapping her hands*). What did I tell you? What did I tell you?

Helmer. You have just come at a fortunate moment, Mrs. Linde.

Mrs. Linde. How am I to thank you?

Helmer. There is no need. (*Puts on his coat.*) But to-day you must excuse me——

Rank. Wait a minute; I will come with you.

(*Brings his fur coat from the hall and warms it at the fire.*)

Nora. Don't be long away, Torvald dear.

Helmer. About an hour, not more.

Nora. Are you going too, Christine?

Mrs. Linde (*putting on her cloak*). Yes, I must go and look for a room.

Helmer. Oh, well then, we can walk down the street together.

Nora (*helping her*). What a pity it is we are so short of space here; I am afraid it is impossible for us——

Mrs. Linde. Please don't think of it! Good-bye, Nora dear, and many thanks.

Nora. Good-bye for the present. Of course you will come back this evening. And you too, Dr. Rank. What do you say? If you are well enough? Oh, you must be! Wrap yourself up well.

(*They go to the door all talking together. Children's voices are heard on the staircase.*)

Nora. There they are. There they are! (*She runs to open the door. The Nurse comes in with the children.*) Come in! Come in! (*Stoops and kisses them.*) Oh, you sweet blessings! Look at them, Christine! Aren't they darlings?

Rank. Don't let us stand here in the draught.

Helmer. Come along, Mrs. Linde; the place will only be bearable for a mother now!

(*Rank, Helmer, and Mrs. Linde go downstairs. The Nurse comes forward with the children; Nora shuts the hall door.*)

Nora. How fresh and well you look! Such red cheeks!—like apples and roses. (*The children all talk at once while she speaks to them.*) Have you had great fun? That's splendid! What, you pulled both Emmy and Bob along on the sledge?—both at once?—that *was* good. You are a clever boy, Ivar. Let me take her for a little, Anne. My sweet little baby doll! (*Takes the baby from the Maid and dances it up and down.*) Yes, yes, mother will dance with Bob too. What! Have you been snowballing? I wish I had been there too! No, no, I will take their things off, Anne; please let me do it, it is such fun. Go in now, you look half frozen. There is some hot coffee for you on the stove.

(*The Nurse goes into the room on the left. Nora takes off the children's things and throws them about, while they all talk to her at once.*)

Nora. Really! Did a big dog run after you? But it didn't bite you? No, dogs don't bite nice little dolly children. You mustn't look at the parcels, Ivar. What are they? Ah, I daresay you would like to know. No, no—it's something nasty! Come, let us have a game! What shall we play at? Hide and Seek? Yes, we'll play Hide and Seek. Bob shall hide first. Must I hide? Very well, I'll hide first.

(She and the children laugh and shout, and romp in and out of the room; at last Nora hides under the table, the children rush in and look for her, but do not see her; they hear her smothered laughter, run to the table, lift up the cloth and find her. Shouts of laughter. She crawls forward and pretends to frighten them. Fresh laughter. Meanwhile there has been a knock at the hall door, but none of them has noticed it. The door is half opened, and Krogstad appears. He waits a little; the game goes on.)

Krogstad. Excuse me, Mrs. Helmer.

Nora *(with a stifled cry, turns round and gets up on to her knees).* Ah! what do you want?

Krogstad. Excuse me, the outer door was ajar; I suppose someone forgot to shut it.

Nora *(rising).* My husband is out, Mr. Krogstad.

Krogstad. I know that.

Nora. What do you want here, then?

Krogstad. A word with you.

Nora. With me?—*(to the children, gently.)* Go in to nurse. What? No, the strange man won't do mother any harm. When he has gone we will have another game. *(She takes the children into the room on the left, and shuts the door after them.)* You want to speak to me?

Krogstad. Yes, I do.

Nora. To-day? It is not the first of the month yet.

Krogstad. No, it is Christmas Eve, and it will depend on yourself what sort of a Christmas you will spend.

Nora. What do you want? To-day it is absolutely impossible for me——

Krogstad. We won't talk about that till later on. This is something different. I presume you can give me a moment?

Nora. Yes—yes, I can—although——

Krogstad. Good. I was in Olsen's Restaurant and saw your husband going down the street——

Nora. Yes?

Krogstad. With a lady.

Nora. What then?

Krogstad. May I make so bold as to ask if it was a Mrs. Linde?

Nora. It was.

Krogstad. Just arrived in town?

Nora. Yes, to-day.

Krogstad. She is a great friend of yours, isn't she?

Nora. She is. But I don't see——

Krogstad. I knew her too, once upon a time.

Nora. I am aware of that.

Krogstad. Are you? So you know all about it; I thought as much. Then I can ask you, without beating about the bush—is Mrs. Linde to have an appointment in the Bank?

Nora. What right have you to question me, Mr. Krogstad?—You, one of my husband's subordinates! But since you ask, you shall know. Yes, Mrs. Linde *is* to have an appointment. And it was I who pleaded her cause, Mr. Krogstad, let me tell you that.

Krogstad. I was right in what I thought, then.

Nora (*walking up and down the stage*). Sometimes one has a tiny little bit of influence, I should hope. Because one is a woman, it does not necessarily follow that——. When anyone is in a subordinate position, Mr. Krogstad, they should really be careful to avoid offending anyone who—who——

Krogstad. Who has influence?

Nora. Exactly.

Krogstad (*changing his tone*). Mrs. Helmer, you will be so good as to use your influence on my behalf.

Nora. What? What do you mean?

Krogstad. You will be so kind as to see that I am allowed to keep my subordinate position in the Bank.

Nora. What do you mean by that? Who proposes to take your post away from you?

Krogstad. Oh, there is no necessity to keep up the pretence of ignorance. I can quite understand that your friend is not very anxious to expose herself to the chance of rubbing shoulders with me; and I quite understand, too, whom I have to thank for being turned off.

Nora. But I assure you——

Krogstad. Very likely; but, to come to the point, the time has come when I should advise you to use your influence to prevent that.

Nora. But, Mr. Krogstad, I *have* no influence.

Krogstad. Haven't you? I thought you said yourself just now——

Nora. Naturally I did not mean you to put that construction on it. I! What should make you think I have any influence of that kind with my husband?

Krogstad. Oh, I have known your husband from our student days. I don't suppose he is any more unassailable than other husbands.

Nora. If you speak slightingly of my husband, I shall turn you out of the house.

Krogstad. You are bold, Mrs. Helmer.

Nora. I am not afraid of you any longer. As soon as the New Year comes, I shall in a very short time be free of the whole thing.

Krogstad (*controlling himself*). Listen to me, Mrs. Helmer. If necessary, I am prepared to fight for my small post in the Bank as if I were fighting for my life.

Nora. So it seems.

Krogstad. It is not only for the sake of the money; indeed, that weighs least with me in the matter. There is another reason—well, I may as well tell you. My position is this. I daresay you know, like everybody else, that once, many years ago, I was guilty of an indiscretion.

Nora. I think I have heard something of the kind.

Krogstad. The matter never came into court; but every way seemed to be closed to me after that. So I took to the business that you know of. I had to do something; and, honestly, I don't think I've been one of the worst. But now I must cut myself free from all that. My sons are growing up; for their sake I must try and win back as much respect as I can in the town. This post in the Bank was like the first step up for me—and now your husband is going to kick me downstairs again into the mud.

Nora. But you must believe me, Mr. Krogstad; it is not in my power to help you at all.

Krogstad. Then it is because you haven't the will; but I have means to compel you.

Nora. You don't mean that you will tell my husband that I owe you money?

Krogstad. Hm!—suppose I were to tell him?

Nora. It would be perfectly infamous of you. (*Sobbing.*) To think of his learning my secret, which has been my joy and pride, in such an ugly, clumsy way—that he should learn it from you! And it would put me in a horribly disagreeable position——

Krogstad. Only disagreeable?

Nora (*impetuously*). Well, do it, then!—and it will be the worse for you. My husband will see for himself what a blackguard you are, and you certainly won't keep your post then.

Krogstad. I asked you if it was only a disagreeable scene at home that you were afraid of?

Nora. If my husband does get to know of it, of course he will at once pay you what is still owing, and we shall have nothing more to do with you.

Krogstad (*coming a step nearer*). Listen to me, Mrs. Helmer. Either you have a very bad memory or you know very little of business. I shall be obliged to remind you of a few details.

Nora. What do you mean?

Krogstad. When your husband was ill, you came to me to borrow two hundred and fifty pounds.

Nora. I didn't know anyone else to go to.

Krogstad. I promised to get you that amount——

Nora. Yes, and you did so.

Krogstad. I promised to get you that amount, on certain conditions. Your mind was so taken up with your husband's illness, and you were so anxious to get the money for your journey, that you seem to have paid no attention to the conditions of our bargain. Therefore it will not be amiss if I remind you of them. Now, I promised to get the money on the security of a bond which I signed.

Nora. Yes, and which I signed.

Krogstad. Good. But below your signature there were a few lines constituting your father a surety for the money; those lines your father should have signed.

Nora. Should? He did sign them.

Krogstad. I had left the date blank; that is to say your father should himself have inserted the date on which he signed the paper. Do you remember that?

Nora. Yes, I think I remember——

Krogstad. Then I gave you the bond to send by post to your father. Is that not so?

Nora. Yes.

Krogstad. And you naturally did so at once, because five or six days afterwards you brought me the bond with your father's signature. And then I gave you the money.

Nora. Well, haven't I been paying it off regularly?

Krogstad. Fairly so, yes. But—to come back to the matter in hand—that must have been a very trying time for you, Mrs. Helmer?

Nora. It was, indeed.

Krogstad. Your father was very ill, wasn't he?

Nora. He was very near his end.

Krogstad. And died soon afterwards?

Nora. Yes.

Krogstad. Tell me, Mrs. Helmer, can you by any chance remember what day your father died?—on what day of the month, I mean.

Nora. Papa died on the 29th of September.

Krogstad. That is correct; I have ascertained it for myself. And, as that is so, there is a discrepancy *(taking a paper from his pocket)* which I cannot account for.

Nora. What discrepancy? I don't know——

Krogstad. The discrepancy consists, Mrs. Helmer, in the fact that your father signed this bond three days after his death.

Nora. What do you mean? I don't understand——

Krogstad. Your father died on the 29th of September. But, look here; your father has dated his signature the 2nd of October. It is a discrepancy, isn't it? *(Nora is silent.)* Can you explain it to me? *(Nora is still silent.)* It is a remarkable thing, too, that the words "2nd of October," as well as the year, are not written in your father's handwriting but in one that I think I know. Well, of course it can be explained; your father may have forgotten to date his signature, and someone else may have dated it haphazard before they knew of his death. There is no harm in that. It all depends on the signature of the name; and *that* is genuine, I suppose, Mrs. Helmer? It was your father himself who signed his name here?

Nora *(after a short pause, throws her head up and looks defiantly at him).* No, it was not. It was I that wrote papa's name.

Krogstad. Are you aware that is a dangerous confession?

Nora. In what way? You shall have your money soon.

Krogstad. Let me ask you a question; why did you not send the paper to your father?

Nora. It was impossible; papa was so ill. If I had asked him for his signature, I should have had to tell him what the money was to be used for; and when he was so ill himself I couldn't tell him that my husband's life was in danger—it was impossible.

Krogstad. It would have been better for you if you had given up your trip abroad.

Nora. No, that was impossible. That trip was to save my husband's life; I couldn't give that up.

Krogstad. But did it never occur to you that you were committing a fraud on me?

Nora. I couldn't take that into account; I didn't trouble myself about you at all. I couldn't bear you, because you put so many heartless difficulties in my way, although you knew what a dangerous condition my husband was in.

Krogstad. Mrs. Helmer, you evidently do not realise clearly what it is that you have been guilty of. But I can assure you that my one false step, which lost me all my reputation, was nothing more or nothing worse than what you have done.

Nora. You? Do you ask me to believe that you were brave enough to run a risk to save your wife's life?

Krogstad. The law cares nothing about motives.

Nora. Then it must be a very foolish law.

Krogstad. Foolish or not, it is the law by which you will be judged, if I produce this paper in court.

Nora. I don't believe it. Is a daughter not to be allowed to spare her dying father anxiety and care? Is a wife not to be allowed to save her husband's life? I don't know much about law; but I am certain that there must be laws permitting such things as that. Have you no knowledge of such laws—you who are a lawyer? You must be a very poor lawyer, Mr. Krogstad.

Krogstad. Maybe. But matters of business—such business as you and I have had together—do you think I don't understand that? Very well. Do as you please. But let me tell you this—if I lose my position a second time, you shall lose yours with me.

(He bows, and goes out through the hall.)

Nora *(appears buried in thought for a short time, then tosses her head).* Nonsense! Trying to frighten me like that—I am not so silly as he thinks. *(Begins to busy herself putting the children's things in order.)* And yet——? No, it's impossible! I did it for love's sake.

The Children *(in the doorway on the left).* Mother, the stranger man has gone out through the gate.

Nora. Yes, dears, I know. But don't tell anyone about the stranger man. Do you hear? Not even papa.

Children. No, mother; but will you come and play again?

Nora. No, no,—not now.

Children. But, mother, you promised us.

Nora. Yes, but I can't now. Run away in; I have such a lot to do. Run away in, my sweet little darlings. *(She gets them into the room by degrees and shuts the door on them; then sits down on the sofa, takes up a piece of needlework and sews a few stitches, but soon stops.)* No! *(Throws down the work, gets up, goes to the hall door and calls out.)* Helen! bring the tree in. *(Goes to the table on the left, opens a drawer, and stops again.)* No, no! it is quite impossible!

Maid (*coming in with the tree*). Where shall I put it, ma'am?

Nora. Here, in the middle of the floor.

Maid. Shall I get you anything else?

Nora. No, thank you. I have all I want.

(*Exit Maid.*)

Nora (*begins dressing the tree*). A candle here—and flowers here——. The horrible man! It's all nonsense—there's nothing wrong. The tree shall be splendid! I will do everything I can think of to please you, Torvald!—I will sing for you, dance for you—(*Helmer comes in with some papers under his arm.*) Oh! are you back already?

Helmer. Yes. Has anyone been here?

Nora. Here? No.

Helmer. That is strange. I saw Krogstad going out of the gate.

Nora. Did you? Oh yes, I forgot, Krogstad was here for a moment.

Helmer. Nora, I can see from your manner that he has been here begging you to say a good word for him.

Nora. Yes.

Helmer. And you were to appear to do it of your own accord; you were to conceal from me the fact of his having been here; didn't he beg that of you too?

Nora. Yes, Torvald, but——

Helmer. Nora, Nora, and you would be a party to that sort of thing? To have any talk with a man like that, and give him any sort of promise? And to tell me a lie into the bargain?

Nora. A lie——?

Helmer. Didn't you tell me no one had been here? (*Shakes his finger at her.*) My little song-bird must never do that again. A song-bird must have a clean beak to chirp with—no false notes! (*Puts his arm round her waist.*) That is so, isn't it? Yes, I am sure it is. (*Lets her go.*) We will say no more about it. (*Sits down by the stove.*) How warm and snug it is here!

(*Turns over his papers.*)

Nora (*after a short pause, during which she busies herself with the Christmas tree*). Torvald!

Helmer. Yes.

Nora. I am looking forward tremendously to the fancy dress ball at the Stenborgs' the day after to-morrow.

Helmer. And I am tremendously curious to see what you are going to surprise me with.

Nora. It was very silly of me to want to do that.

Helmer. What do you mean?

Nora. I can't hit upon anything that will do; everything I think of seems so silly and insignificant.

Helmer. Does my little Nora acknowledge that at last?

Nora (*standing behind his chair with her arms on the back of it*). Are you very busy, Torvald?

Helmer. Well——

Nora. What are all those papers?

Helmer. Bank business.

Nora. Already?

Helmer. I have got authority from the retiring manager to undertake the necessary changes in the staff and in the rearrangement of the work; and I must make use of the Christmas week for that, so as to have everything in order for the new year.

Nora. Then that was why this poor Krogstad——

Helmer. Hm!

Nora *(leans against the back of his chair and strokes his hair).* If you hadn't been so busy I should have asked you a tremendously big favour, Torvald.

Helmer. What is that? Tell me.

Nora. There is no one has such good taste as you. And I do so want to look nice at the fancy-dress ball. Torvald, couldn't you take me in hand and decide what I shall go as, and what sort of a dress I shall wear?

Helmer. Aha! so my obstinate little woman is obliged to get someone to come to her rescue?

Nora. Yes, Torvald, I can't get along a bit without your help.

Helmer. Very well, I will think it over, we shall manage to hit upon something.

Nora. That *is* nice of you. *(Goes to the Christmas tree. A short pause.)* How pretty the red flowers look——. But, tell me, was it really something very bad that this Krogstad was guilty of?

Helmer. He forged someone's name. Have you any idea what that means?

Nora. Isn't it possible that he was driven to do it by necessity?

Helmer. Yes; or, as in so many cases, by imprudence. I am not so heartless as to condemn a man altogether because of a single false step of that kind.

Nora. No you wouldn't, would you, Torvald?

Helmer. Many a man has been able to retrieve his character, if he has openly confessed his fault and taken his punishment.

Nora. Punishment——?

Helmer. But Krogstad did nothing of that sort; he got himself out of it by a cunning trick, and that is why he has gone under altogether.

Nora. But do you think it would——?

Helmer. Just think how a guilty man like that has to lie and play the hypocrite with everyone, how he has to wear a mask in the presence of those near and dear to him, even before his own wife and children. And about the children—that is the most terrible part of it all, Nora.

Nora. How?

Helmer. Because such an atmosphere of lies infects and poisons the whole life of a home. Each breath the children take in such a house is full of the germs of evil.

Nora *(coming nearer him).* Are you sure of that?

Helmer. My dear, I have often seen it in the course of my life as a lawyer. Almost everyone who has gone to the bad early in life has had a deceitful mother.

Nora. Why do you only say—mother?

Helmer. It seems most commonly to be the mother's influence, though naturally a bad father's would have the same result. Every lawyer is familiar with the fact. This Krogstad, now, has been persistently poisoning his own children with lies and dissimulation; that is why I say he has lost all moral character. (*Holds out his hands to her.*) That is why my sweet little Nora must promise me not to plead his cause. Give me your hand on it. Come, come, what is this? Give me your hand. There now, that's settled. I assure you it would be quite impossible for me to work with him; I literally feel physically ill when I am in the company of such people.

Nora (*takes her hand out of his and goes to the opposite side of the Christmas tree*). How hot it is in here; and I have such a lot to do.

Helmer (*getting up and putting his papers in order*). Yes, and I must try and read through some of these before dinner; and I must think about your costume, too. And it is just possible I may have something ready in gold paper to hang up on the tree. (*Puts his hand on her head.*) My precious little singing-bird!

(*He goes into his room and shuts the door after him.*)

Nora (*after a pause, whispers*). No, no—it isn't true. It's impossible; it must be impossible.

(*The Nurse opens the door on the left.*)

Nurse. The little ones are begging so hard to be allowed to come in to mamma.

Nora. No, no, no! Don't let them come in to me! You stay with them, Anne.

Nurse. Very well, ma'am.

(*Shuts the door.*)

Nora (*pale with terror*). Deprave my little children? Poison my home? (*A short pause. Then she tosses her head.*) It's not true. It can't possibly be true.

ACT II

The Same Scene

The Christmas tree is in the corner by the piano, stripped of its ornaments and with burnt-down candle-ends on its dishevelled branches. Nora's cloak and hat are lying on the sofa. She is alone in the room, walking about uneasily. She stops by the sofa and takes up her cloak.

Nora (*drops the cloak*). Someone is coming now! (*Goes to the door and listens.*) No—it is no one. Of course, no one will come to-day, Christmas Day—nor to-morrow either. But, perhaps—(*Opens the door and looks out*). No, nothing in the letter-box; it is quite empty. (*Comes forward.*) What rubbish! of course he can't be in earnest about it. Such a thing couldn't happen; it is impossible—I have three little children.

(*Enter the Nurse from the room on the left, carrying a big cardboard box.*)

Nurse. At last I have found the box with the fancy dress.

Nora. Thanks; put it on the table.

Nurse (doing so). But it is very much in want of mending.

Nora. I should like to tear it into a hundred thousand pieces.

Nurse. What an idea! It can easily be put in order—just a little patience.

Nora. Yes, I will go and get Mrs. Linde to come and help me with it.

Nurse. What, out again? In this horrible weather? You will catch cold, ma'am, and make yourself ill.

Nora. Well, worse than that might happen. How are the children?

Nurse. The poor little souls are playing with their Christmas presents, but——

Nora. Do they ask much for me?

Nurse. You see, they are so accustomed to have their mamma with them.

Nora. Yes, but, nurse, I shall not be able to be so much with them now as I was before.

Nurse. Oh well, young children easily get accustomed to anything.

Nora. Do you think so? Do you think they would forget their mother if she went away altogether?

Nurse. Good heavens!—went away altogether?

Nora. Nurse, I want you to tell me something I have often wondered about—how could you have the heart to put your own child out among strangers?

Nurse. I was obliged to, if I wanted to be little Nora's nurse.

Nora. Yes, but how could you be willing to do it?

Nurse. What, when I was going to get such a good place by it? A poor girl who has got into trouble should be glad to. Besides, that wicked man didn't do a single thing for me.

Nora. But I suppose your daughter has quite forgotten you.

Nurse. No, indeed she hasn't. She wrote to me when she was confirmed, and when she was married.

Nora (putting her arms round her neck). Dear old Anne, you were a good mother to me when I was little.

Nurse. Little Nora, poor dear, had no other mother but me.

Nora. And if my little ones had no other mother, I am sure you would——What nonsense I am talking! (Opens the box.) Go in to them. Now I must——. You will see to-morrow how charming I shall look.

Nurse. I am sure there will be no one at the ball so charming as you, ma'am.

(Goes into the room on the left.)

Nora (begins to unpack the box, but soon pushes it away from her). If only I dared go out. If only no one would come. If only I could be sure nothing would happen here in the meantime. Stuff and nonsense! No one will come. Only I mustn't think about it. I will brush my muff. What lovely, lovely gloves! Out of my thoughts, out of my thoughts! One, two, three, four, five, six——(Screams.) Ah! there is someone coming——

(Makes a movement towards the door, but stands irresolute. Enter Mrs. Linde from the hall, where she has taken off her cloak and hat.)

Nora. Oh, it's you, Christine. There is no one else out there, is there? How good of you to come!

Mrs. Linde. I heard you were up asking for me.

Nora. Yes, I was passing by. As a matter of fact, it is something you could help me with. Let us sit down here on the sofa. Look here. To-morrow evening there is to be a fancy-dress ball at the Stenborgs', who live above us; and Torvald wants me to go as a Neapolitan fisher-girl, and dance the Tarantella that I learnt at Capri.

Mrs. Linde. I see; you are going to keep up the character.

Nora. Yes, Torvald wants me to. Look, here is the dress; Torvald had it made for me there, but now it is all so torn, and I haven't any idea——

Mrs. Linde. We will easily put that right. It is only some of the trimming come unsewn here and there. Needle and thread? Now then, that's all we want.

Nora. It *is* nice of you.

Mrs. Linde *(sewing).* So you are going to be dressed up to-morrow, Nora. I will tell you what—I shall come in for a moment and see you in your fine feathers. But I have completely forgotten to thank you for a delightful evening yesterday.

Nora *(gets up, and crosses the stage).* Well I don't think yesterday was as pleasant as usual. You ought to have come to town a little earlier, Christine. Certainly Torvald does understand how to make a house dainty and attractive.

Mrs. Linde. And so do you, it seems to me; you are not your father's daughter for nothing. But tell me, is Doctor Rank always as depressed as he was yesterday?

Nora. No; yesterday it was very noticeable. I must tell you that he suffers from a very dangerous disease. He has consumption of the spine, poor creature. His father was a horrible man who committed all sorts of excesses; and that is why his son was sickly from childhood, do you understand?

Mrs. Linde *(dropping her sewing).* But, my dearest Nora, how do you know anything about such things?

Nora *(walking about).* Pooh! When you have three children, you get visits now and then from—from married women, who know something of medical matters, and they talk about one thing and another.

Mrs. Linde *(goes on sewing. A short silence).* Does Doctor Rank come here every day?

Nora. Every day regularly. He is Torvald's most intimate friend, and a great friend of mine too. He is just like one of the family.

Mrs. Linde. But tell me this—is he perfectly sincere? I mean, isn't he the kind of man that is very anxious to make himself agreeable?

Nora. Not in the least. What makes you think that?

Mrs. Linde. When you introduced him to me yesterday, he declared he had often heard my name mentioned in this house; but afterwards I noticed that your husband hadn't the slightest idea who I was. So how could Doctor Rank——?

Nora. That is quite right, Christine. Torvald is so absurdly fond of me that he wants me absolutely to himself, as he says. At first he used to seem almost jealous if I mentioned any of the dear folk at home, so naturally I gave up doing so. But I often talk about such things with Doctor Rank, because he likes hearing about them.

Mrs. Linde. Listen to me, Nora. You are still very like a child in many things, and I am older than you in many ways and have a little more experience. Let me tell you this—you ought to make an end of it with Doctor Rank.

Nora. What ought I to make an end of?

Mrs. Linde. Of two things, I think. Yesterday you talked some nonsense about a rich admirer who was to leave you money——

Nora. An admirer who doesn't exist, unfortunately! But what then?

Mrs. Linde. Is Doctor Rank a man of means?

Nora. Yes, he is.

Mrs. Linde. And has no one to provide for?

Nora. No, no one; but——

Mrs. Linde. And comes here every day?

Nora. Yes, I told you so.

Mrs. Linde. But how can this well-bred man be so tactless?

Nora. I don't understand you at all.

Mrs. Linde. Don't prevaricate, Nora. Do you suppose I don't guess who lent you the two hundred and fifty pounds?

Nora. Are you out of your senses? How can you think of such a thing! A friend of ours, who comes here every day! Do you realise what a horribly painful position that would be?

Mrs. Linde. Then it really isn't he?

Nora. No, certainly not. It would never have entered into my head for a moment. Besides, he had no money to lend then; he came into his money afterwards.

Mrs. Linde. Well, I think that was lucky for you, my dear Nora.

Nora. No, it would never have come into my head to ask Doctor Rank. Although I am quite sure that if I had asked him——

Mrs. Linde. But of course you won't.

Nora. Of course not. I have no reason to think it could possibly be necessary. But I am quite sure that if I told Doctor Rank——

Mrs. Linde. Behind your husband's back?

Nora. I must make an end of it with the other one, and that will be behind his back too. I *must* make an end of it with him.

Mrs. Linde. Yes, that is what I told you yesterday, but——

Nora (*walking up and down*). A man can put a thing like that straight much easier than a woman——

Mrs. Linde. One's husband, yes.

Nora. Nonsense! (*Standing still.*) When you pay off a debt you get your bond back, don't you?

Mrs. Linde. Yes, as a matter of course.

Nora. And can tear it into a hundred thousand pieces, and burn it up—the nasty dirty paper!

Mrs. Linde (*looks hard at her, lays down her sewing and gets up slowly*). Nora, you are concealing something from me.

Nora. Do I look as if I were?

Mrs. Linde. Something has happened to you since yesterday morning. Nora, what is it?

Nora (*going nearer to her*). Christine! (*Listens.*) Hush! there's Torvald come home. Do you mind going in to the children for the present? Torvald can't bear to see dressmaking going on. Let Anne help you.

Mrs. Linde (*gathering some of the things together*). Certainly—but I am not going away from here till we have had it out with one another.

(*She goes into the room on the left, as Helmer comes in from the hall.*)

Nora (*going up to Helmer*). I have wanted you so much, Torvald dear.

Helmer. Was that the dressmaker?

Nora. No, it was Christine; she is helping me to put my dress in order. You will see I shall look quite smart.

Helmer. Wasn't that a happy thought of mine, now?

Nora. Splendid! But don't you think it is nice of me, too, to do as you wish?

Helmer. Nice?—because you do as your husband wishes? Well, well, you little rogue, I am sure you did not mean it in that way. But I am not going to disturb you; you will want to be trying on your dress, I expect.

Nora. I suppose you are going to work.

Helmer. Yes. (*Shows her a bundle of papers.*) Look at that. I have just been into the bank.

(*Turns to go into his room.*)

Nora. Torvald.

Helmer. Yes.

Nora. If your little squirrel were to ask you for something very, very prettily——?

Helmer. What then?

Nora. Would you do it?

Helmer. I should like to hear what it is, first.

Nora. Your squirrel would run about and do all her tricks if you would be nice, and do what she wants.

Helmer. Speak plainly.

Nora. Your skylark would chirp about in every room, with her song rising and falling——

Helmer. Well, my skylark does that anyhow.

Nora. I would play the fairy and dance for you in the moonlight, Torvald.

Helmer. Nora—you surely don't mean that request you made of me this morning?

Nora (*going near him*). Yes, Torvald, I beg you so earnestly——

Helmer. Have you really the courage to open up that question again?

Nora. Yes, dear, you *must* do as I ask; you *must* let Krogstad keep his post in the Bank.

Helmer. My dear Nora, it is his post that I have arranged Mrs. Linde shall have.

Nora. Yes, you have been awfully kind about that; but you could just as well dismiss some other clerk instead of Krogstad.

Helmer. This simply incredible obstinacy! Because you chose to give him a thoughtless promise that you would speak for him, I am expected to——

Nora. That isn't the reason, Torvald. It is for your own sake. This fellow writes in the most scurrilous newspapers; you have told me so yourself. He can do you an unspeakable amount of harm. I am frightened to death of him——

Helmer. Ah, I understand; it is recollections of the past that scare you.

Nora. What do you mean?

Helmer. Naturally you are thinking of your father.

Nora. Yes—yes, of course. Just recall to your mind what these malicious creatures wrote in the papers about papa, and how horribly they slandered him. I believe they would have procured his dismissal if the Department had not sent you over to inquire into it, and if you had not been so kindly disposed and helpful to him.

Helmer. My little Nora, there is an important difference between your father and me. Your father's reputation as a public official was not above suspicion. Mine is, and I hope it will continue to be so, as long as I hold my office.

Nora. You never can tell what mischief these men may contrive. We ought to be so well off, so snug and happy here in our peaceful home, and have no cares— you and I and the children, Torvald! That is why I beg of you so earnestly——

Helmer. And it is just by interceding for him that you make it impossible for me to keep him. It is already known at the Bank that I mean to dismiss Krogstad. Is it to get about now that the new manager has changed his mind at his wife's bidding——

Nora. And what if it did?

Helmer. Of course!—if only this obstinate little person can get her way! Do you suppose I am going to make myself ridiculous before my whole staff, to let people think that I am a man to be swayed by all sorts of outside influence? I should very soon feel the consequences of it, I can tell you! And besides, there is one thing that makes it quite impossible for me to have Krogstad in the Bank as long as I am manager.

Nora. Whatever is that?

Helmer. His moral failings I might perhaps have overlooked, if necessary——

Nora. Yes, you could—couldn't you?

Helmer. And I hear he is a good worker, too. But I knew him when we were boys. It was one of those rash friendships that so often prove an incubus in after life. I may as well tell you plainly, we were once on very intimate terms with one another. But this tactless fellow lays no restraint on himself when other people are present. On the contrary, he thinks it gives him the right to adopt a familiar tone with me, and every minute it is "I say, Helmer, old fellow!" and that sort of thing. I assure you it is extremely painful for me. He would make my position in the Bank intolerable.

Nora. Torvald, I don't believe you mean that.

Helmer. Don't you? Why not?

Nora. Because it is such a narrow-minded way of looking at things.

Helmer. What are you saying? Narrow-minded? Do you think I am narrow-minded?

Nora. No, just the opposite, dear—and it is exactly for that reason.

Helmer. It's the same thing. You say my point of view is narrow-minded, so I must be so too. Narrow-minded! Very well—I must put an end to this. (*Goes to the hall-door and calls.*) Helen!

Nora. What are you going to do?

Helmer (*looking among his papers*). Settle it. (*Enter Maid.*) Look here; take this letter and go downstairs with it at once. Find a messenger and tell him to deliver it, and be quick. The address is on it, and here is the money.

Maid. Very well, sir. (*Exit with the letter.*)

Helmer (*putting his papers together*). Now then, little Miss Obstinate.

Nora (*breathlessly*). Torvald—what was that letter?

Helmer. Krogstad's dismissal.

Nora. Call her back, Torvald! There is still time. Oh Torvald, call her back! Do it for my sake—for your own sake—for the children's sake! Do you hear me, Torvald? Call her back! You don't know what that letter can bring upon us.

Helmer. It's too late.

Nora. Yes, it's too late.

Helmer. My dear Nora, I can forgive the anxiety you are in, although really it is an insult to me. It is, indeed. Isn't it an insult to think that I should be afraid of a starving quill-driver's vengeance? But I forgive you nevertheless, because it is such eloquent witness to your great love for me. (*Takes her in his arms.*) And that is as it should be, my darling Nora. Come what will, you may be sure I shall have both courage and strength if they be needed. You will see I am man enough to take everything upon myself.

Nora (*in a horror-stricken voice*). What do you mean by that?

Helmer. Everything, I say——

Nora (*recovering herself*). You will never have to do that.

Helmer. That's right. Well, we will share it, Nora, as man and wife should. That is how it shall be. (*Caressing her.*) Are you content now? There! there!—not these frightened dove's eyes! The whole thing is only the wildest fancy!—Now, you must go and play through the Tarantella and practise with your tambourine. I shall go into the inner office and shut the door, and I shall hear nothing; you can make as much noise as you please. (*Turns back at the door.*) And when Rank comes, tell him where he will find me.

(*Nods to her, takes his papers and goes into his room, and shuts the door after him.*)

Nora (*bewildered with anxiety, stands as if rooted to the spot, and whispers*). He was capable of doing it. He will do it. He will do it in spite of everything.—No, not that! Never, never! Anything rather than that! Oh, for some help, some way out of it! *(The door-bell rings.)* Doctor Rank! Anything rather than that—anything, whatever it is!

(She puts her hands over her face, pulls herself together, goes to the door and opens it. Rank is standing without, hanging up his coat. During the following dialogue it begins to grow dark.)

Nora. Good-day, Doctor Rank. I knew your ring. But you mustn't go in to Torvald now; I think he is busy with something.

Rank. And you?

Nora *(brings him in and shuts the door after him).* Oh, you know very well I always have time for you.

Rank. Thank you. I shall make use of as much of it as I can.

Nora. What do you mean by that? As much of it as you can?

Rank. Well, does that alarm you?

Nora. It was such a strange way of putting it. Is anything likely to happen?

Rank. Nothing but what I have long been prepared for. But certainly didn't expect it to happen so soon.

Nora *(gripping him by the arm).* What have you found out? Doctor Rank, you must tell me.

Rank *(sitting down by the stove).* It is all up with me. And it can't be helped.

Nora *(with a sigh of relief).* Is it about yourself?

Rank. Who else? It is no use lying to one's self. I am the most wretched of all my patients, Mrs. Helmer. Lately I have been taking stock of my internal economy. Bankrupt! Probably within a month I shall lie rotting in the churchyard.

Nora. What an ugly thing to say!

Rank. The thing itself is cursedly ugly, and the worst of it is that I shall have to face so much more that is ugly before that. I shall only make one more examination of myself; when I have done that, I shall know pretty certainly when it will be that the horrors of dissolution will begin. There is something I want to tell you. Helmer's refined nature gives him an unconquerable disgust at everything that is ugly; I won't have him in my sick-room.

Nora. Oh, but, Doctor Rank——

Rank. I won't have him there. Not on any account. I bar my door to him. As soon as I am quite certain that the worst has come, I shall send you my card with a black cross on it, and then you will know that the loathsome end has begun.

Nora. You are quite absurd to-day. And I wanted you so much to be in a really good humour.

Rank. With death stalking beside me?—To have to pay this penalty for another man's sin! Is there any justice in that? And in every single family, in one way or another, some such inexorable retribution is being exacted——

Nora *(putting her hands over her ears).* Rubbish! Do talk of something cheerful.

Rank. Oh, it's a mere laughing matter, the whole thing. My poor innocent spine has to suffer for my father's youthful amusements.

Nora (*sitting at the table on the left*). I suppose you mean that he was too partial to asparagus and pâté de foie gras, don't you.

Rank. Yes, and to truffles.

Nora. Truffles, yes. And oysters too, I suppose?

Rank. Oysters, of course, that goes without saying.

Nora. And heaps of port and champagne. It is sad that all these nice things should take their revenge on our bones.

Rank. Especially that they should revenge themselves on the unlucky bones of those who have not had the satisfaction of enjoying them.

Nora. Yes, that's the saddest part of it all.

Rank (*with a searching look at her*). Hm!——

Nora (*after a short pause*). Why did you smile?

Rank. No, it was you that laughed.

Nora. No, it was you that smiled, Doctor Rank!

Rank (*rising*). You are a greater rascal than I thought.

Nora. I am in a silly mood to-day.

Rank. So it seems.

Nora (*putting her hands on his shoulders*). Dear, dear Doctor Rank, death mustn't take you away from Torvald and me.

Rank. It is a loss you would easily recover from. Those who are gone are soon forgotten.

Nora (*looking at him anxiously*). Do you believe that?

Rank. People form new ties, and then——

Nora. Who will form new ties?

Rank. Both you and Helmer, when I am gone. You yourself are already on the high road to it, I think. What did that Mrs. Linde want here last night?

Nora. Oho!—you don't mean to say you are jealous of poor Christine?

Rank. Yes, I am. She will be my successor in this house. When I am done for, this woman will—

Nora. Hush! don't speak so loud. She is in that room.

Rank. To-day again. There, you see.

Nora. She has only come to sew my dress for me. Bless my soul, how unreasonable you are! (*Sits down on the sofa.*) Be nice now, Doctor Rank, and tomorrow you will see how beautifully I shall dance, and you can imagine I am doing it all for you—and for Torvald too, of course. (*Takes various things out of the box.*) Doctor Rank, come and sit down here, and I will show you something.

Rank (*sitting down*). What is it?

Nora. Just look at those!

Rank. Silk stockings.

Nora. Flesh-coloured. Aren't they lovely? It is so dark here now, but to-morrow—. No, no, no! you must only look at the feet. Oh well, you may have leave to look at the legs too.

Rank. Hm!—

Nora. Why are you looking so critical? Don't you think they will fit me?

Rank. I have no means of forming an opinion about that.

Nora (*looks at him for a moment*). For shame! (*Hits him lightly on the ear with the stockings.*) That's to punish you. (*Folds them up again.*)

Rank. And what other nice things am I to be allowed to see?

Nora. Not a single thing more, for being so naughty. (*She looks among the things, humming to herself.*)

Rank (*after a short silence*). When I am sitting here, talking to you as intimately as this, I cannot imagine for a moment what would have become of me if I had never come into this house.

Nora (*smiling*). I believe you do feel thoroughly at home with us.

Rank (*in a lower voice, looking straight in front of him*). And to be obliged to leave it all——

Nora. Nonsense, you are not going to leave it.

Rank (*as before*). And not be able to leave behind one the slightest token of one's gratitude, scarcely even a fleeting regret—nothing but an empty place which the first comer can fill as well as any other.

Nora. And if I asked you now for a—? No!

Rank. For what?

Nora. For a big proof of your friendship——

Rank. Yes, yes!

Nora. I mean a tremendously big favour——

Rank. Would you really make me so happy for once?

Nora. Ah, but you don't know what it is yet.

Rank. No—but tell me.

Nora. I really can't, Doctor Rank. It is something out of all reason; it means advice, and help, and a favour——

Rank. The bigger a thing it is the better. I can't conceive what it is you mean. Do tell me. Haven't I your confidence?

Nora. More than anyone else. I know you are my truest and best friend, and so I will tell you what it is. Well, Doctor Rank, it is something you must help me to prevent. You know how devotedly, how inexpressibly deeply Torvald loves me; he would never for a moment hesitate to give his life for me.

Rank (*leaning towards her*). Nora—do you think he is the only one——?

Nora (*with a slight start*). The only one—?

Rank. The only one who would gladly give his life for your sake.

Nora (*sadly*). Is that it?

Rank. I was determined you should know it before I went away, and there will never be a better opportunity than this. Now you know it, Nora. And now you know, too, that you can trust me as you would trust no one else.

Nora (*rises, deliberately and quietly*). Let me pass.

Rank (*makes room for her to pass him, but sits still*). Nora!

Nora (*at the hall door*). Helen, bring in the lamp. (*Goes over to the stove.*) Dear Doctor Rank, that was really horrid of you.

Rank. To have loved you as much as anyone else does? Was that horrid?

Nora. No, but to go and tell me so. There was really no need——

Rank. What do you mean? Did you know—? *(Maid enters with lamp, puts it down on the table, and goes out.)* Nora—Mrs. Helmer—tell me, had you any idea of this?

Nora. Oh, how do I know whether I had or whether I hadn't? I really can't tell you— To think you could be so clumsy, Doctor Rank! We were getting on so nicely.

Rank. Well, at all events you know now that you can command me, body and soul. So won't you speak out?

Nora *(looking at him).* After what happened?

Rank. I beg you to let me know what it is.

Nora. I can't tell you anything now.

Rank. Yes, yes. You mustn't punish me in that way. Let me have permission to do for you whatever a man may do.

Nora. You can do nothing for me now. Besides, I really don't need any help at all. You will find that the whole thing is merely fancy on my part. It really is so—of course it is! *(Sits down in the rocking-chair, and looks at him with a smile.)* You are a nice sort of man, Doctor Rank!—don't you feel ashamed of yourself, now the lamp has come?

Rank. Not a bit. But perhaps I had better go—forever?

Nora. No, indeed, you shall not. Of course you must come here just as before. You know very well Torvald can't do without you.

Rank. Yes, but you?

Nora. Oh, I am always tremendously pleased when you come.

Rank. It is just that, that put me on the wrong track. You are a riddle to me. I have often thought that you would almost as soon be in my company as in Helmer's.

Nora. Yes—you see there are some people one loves best, and others whom one would almost always rather have as companions.

Rank. Yes, there is something in that.

Nora. When I was at home, of course I loved papa best. But I always thought it tremendous fun if I could steal down into the maids' room, because they never moralised at all, and talked to each other about such entertaining things.

Rank. I see—it is *their* place I have taken.

Nora *(jumping up and going to him).* Oh, dear, nice Doctor Rank, I never meant that at all. But surely you can understand that being with Torvald is a little like being with papa——

(Enter Maid from the hall.)

Maid. If you please, ma'am. *(Whispers and hands her a card.)*

Nora *(glancing at the card).* Oh! *(Puts it in her pocket.)*

Rank. Is there anything wrong?

Nora. No, no, not in the least. It is only something—it is my new dress——

Rank. What? Your dress is lying there.

Nora. Oh, yes, that one; but this is another. I ordered it. Torvald mustn't know about it——

Rank. Oho! Then that was the great secret.

Nora. Of course. Just go in to him; he is sitting in the inner room. Keep him as long as——

Rank. Make your mind easy; I won't let him escape. *(Goes into Helmer's room.)*

Nora *(to the Maid).* And he is standing waiting in the kitchen?

Maid. Yes; he came up the back stairs.

Nora. But didn't you tell him no one was in?

Maid. Yes, but it was no good.

Nora. He won't go away?

Maid. No; he says he won't until he has seen you, ma'am.

Nora. Well, let him come in—but quietly. Helen, you mustn't say anything about it to anyone. It is a surprise for my husband.

Maid. Yes ma'am, I quite understand.   *(Exit.)*

Nora. This dreadful thing is going to happen! It will happen in spite of me! No, no, no, it can't happen—it shan't happen!

(She bolts the door of Helmer's room. The Maid opens the hall door for Krogstad and shuts it after him. He is wearing a fur coat, high boots, and a fur cap.)

Nora *(advancing towards him).* Speak low—my husband is at home.

Krogstad. No matter about that.

Nora. What do you want of me?

Krogstad. An explanation of something.

Nora. Make haste then. What is it?

Krogstad. You know, I suppose, that I have got my dismissal.

Nora. I couldn't prevent it, Mr. Krogstad. I fought as hard as I could on your side, but it was no good.

Krogstad. Does your husband love you so little, then? He knows what I can expose you to, and yet he ventures——

Nora. How can you suppose that he has any knowledge of the sort?

Krogstad. I didn't suppose so at all. It would not be the least like our dear Torvald Helmer to show so much courage——

Nora. Mr. Krogstad, a little respect for my husband, please.

Krogstad. Certainly—all the respect he deserves. But since you have kept the matter so carefully to yourself, I make bold to suppose that you have a little clearer idea, than you had yesterday, of what it actually is that you have done?

Nora. More than you could ever teach me.

Krogstad. Yes, such a bad lawyer as I am.

Nora. What is it you want of me?

Krogstad. Only to see how you were, Mrs. Helmer. I have been thinking about you all day long. A mere cashier, a quill-driver, a—well, a man like me—even he has a little of what is called feeling, you know.

Nora. Show it, then; think of my little children.

Krogstad. Have you and your husband thought of mine? But never mind about that. I only wanted to tell you that you need not take this matter too seriously. In the first place there will be no accusation made on my part.

Nora. No, of course not; I was sure of that.

Krogstad. The whole thing can be arranged amicably; there is no reason why anyone should know anything about it. It will remain a secret between us three.

Nora. My husband must never get to know anything about it.

Krogstad. How will you be able to prevent it? Am I to understand that you can pay the balance that is owing?

Nora. No, not just at present.

Krogstad. Or perhaps that you have some expedient for raising the money soon?

Nora. No expedient that I mean to make use of.

Krogstad. Well, in any case, it would have been of no use to you now. If you stood there with ever so much money in your hand, I would never part with your bond.

Nora. Tell me what purpose you mean to put it to.

Krogstad. I shall only preserve it—keep it in my possession. No one who is not concerned in the matter shall have the slightest hint of it. So that if the thought of it has driven you to any desperate resolution——

Nora. It has.

Krogstad. If you had it in your mind to run away from your home——

Nora. I had.

Krogstad. Or even something worse——

Nora. How could you know that?

Krogstad. Give up the idea.

Nora. How did you know I had thought of *that*?

Krogstad. Most of us think of that at first. I did, too—but I hadn't the courage.

Nora (*faintly*). No more had I.

Krogstad (*in a tone of relief*). No, that's it, isn't it—you hadn't the courage either?

Nora. No, I haven't—I haven't.

Krogstad. Besides, it would have been a great piece of folly. Once the first storm at home is over—. I have a letter for your husband in my pocket.

Nora. Telling him everything?

Krogstad. In as lenient a manner as I possibly could.

Nora (*quickly*). He mustn't get the letter. Tear it up. I will find some means of getting money.

Krogstad. Excuse me, Mrs. Helmer, but I think I told you just now——

Nora. I am not speaking of what I owe you. Tell me what sum you are asking my husband for, and I will get the money.

Krogstad. I am not asking your husband for a penny.

Nora. What do you want, then?

Krogstad. I will tell you. I want to rehabilitate myself, Mrs. Helmer; I want to get on; and in that your husband must help me. For the last year and a half I have not had a hand in anything dishonourable, and all that time I have been struggling in most restricted circumstances. I was content to work my way up step by step. Now I am turned out, and I am not going to be satisfied with merely being taken into favour again. I want to get on, I tell you. I want to get into the Bank again, in a higher position. Your husband must make a place for me——

Nora. That he will never do!

Krogstad. He will; I know him; he dare not protest. And as soon as I am in there again with him, then you will see! Within a year I shall be the manager's right hand. It will be Nils Krogstad and not Torvald Helmer who manages the Bank.

Nora. That's a thing you will never see!

Krogstad. Do you mean that you will——?

Nora. I have courage enough for it now.

Krogstad. Oh, you can't frighten me. A fine, spoilt lady like you——

Nora. You will see, you will see.

Krogstad. Under the ice, perhaps? Down into the cold, coal-black water? And then, in the spring, to float up to the surface, all horrible and unrecognisable, with your hair fallen out——

Nora. You can't frighten me.

Krogstad. Nor you me. People don't do such things, Mrs. Helmer. Besides, what use would it be? I should have him completely in my power all the same.

Nora. Afterwards? When I am no longer——

Krogstad. Have you forgotten that it is I who have the keeping of your reputation? *(Nora stands speechlessly looking at him.)* Well, now, I have warned you. Do not do anything foolish. When Helmer has had my letter, I shall expect a message from him. And be sure you remember that it is your husband himself who has forced me into such ways as this again. I will never forgive him for that. Good-bye, Mrs. Helmer. *(Exit through the hall.)*

Nora *(goes to the hall door, opens it slightly and listens).* He is going. He is not putting the letter in the box. Oh no, no! that's impossible! *(Opens the door by degrees.)* He is going. He is standing outside. He is not going downstairs. Is he hesitating? Can he——

(A letter drops into the box; then Krogstad's footsteps are heard, till they die away as he goes downstairs. Nora utters a stifled cry and runs across the room to the table by the sofa. A short pause.)

Nora. In the letter-box. *(Steals across to the hall door.)* There it lies—Torvald, Torvald, there is no hope for us now!

(Mrs. Linde comes in from the room on the left carrying the dress.)

Mrs. Linde. There, I can't see anything more to mend now. Would you like to try it on——?

Nora *(in a hoarse whisper).* Christine, come here.

Mrs. Linde *(throwing the dress down on the sofa).* What is the matter with you? You look so agitated!

Nora. Come here. Do you see that letter? There look—you can see it through the glass in the letter-box.

Mrs. Linde. Yes, I see it.

Nora. That letter is from Krogstad.

Mrs. Linde. Nora—it was Krogstad who lent you the money!

Nora. Yes, and now Torvald will know all about it.

Mrs. Linde. Believe me, Nora, that's the best thing for both of you.

Nora. You don't know all. I forged a name.

Mrs. Linde. Good heavens——!

Nora. I only want to say this to you, Christine—you must be my witness.

Mrs. Linde. Your witness? What do you mean? What am I to—?

Nora. If I should go out of my mind—and it might easily happen——

Mrs. Linde. Nora!

Nora. Or if anything else should happen to me—anything, for instance, that might prevent my being here—

Mrs. Linde. Nora! Nora! you are quite out of your mind.

Nora. And if it should happen that there were someone who wanted to take all the responsibility, all the blame, you understand——

Mrs. Linde. Yes, yes—but how can you suppose—?

Nora. Then you must be my witness, that it is not true, Christine. I am not out of my mind at all; I am in my right senses now, and I tell you no one else has known anything about it; I, and I alone, did the whole thing. Remember that.

Mrs. Linde. I will, indeed. But I don't understand all this.

Nora. How should you understand it? A wonderful thing is going to happen.

Mrs. Linde. A wonderful thing?

Nora. Yes, a wonderful thing!—But it is so terrible, Christine; it *mustn't* happen, not for all the world.

Mrs. Linde. I will go at once and see Krogstad.

Nora. Don't go to him; he will do you some harm.

Mrs. Linde. There was a time when he would gladly do anything for my sake.

Nora. He?

Mrs. Linde. Where does he live?

Nora. How should I know—? Yes *(feeling in her pocket)* here is his card. But the letter, the letter——!

Helmer *(calls from his room, knocking at the door).* Nora!

Nora *(cries out anxiously).* Oh, what's that? What do you want?

Helmer. Don't be so frightened. We are not coming in; you have locked the door. Are you trying on your dress?

Nora. Yes, that's it. I look so nice, Torvald.

Mrs. Linde *(who has read the card).* I see he lives at the corner here.

Nora. Yes, but it's no use. It is hopeless. The letter is lying there in the box.

Mrs. Linde. And your husband keeps the key?

Nora. Yes, always.

Mrs. Linde. Krogstad must ask for his letter back unread, he must find some pretence——

Nora. But it is just at this time that Torvald generally——

Mrs. Linde. You must delay him. Go in to him in the meantime. I will come back as soon as I can.

(She goes out hurriedly through the hall door.)

Nora *(goes to Helmer's door, opens it and peeps in)*. Torvald!

Helmer *(from the inner room)*. Well? May I venture at last to come into my own room again? Come along, Rank, now you will see— *(Halting in the doorway.)* But what is this?

Nora. What is what, dear?

Helmer. Rank led me to expect a splendid transformation.

Rank *(in the doorway)*. I understood so, but evidently I was mistaken.

Nora. Yes, nobody is to have the chance of admiring me in my dress until tomorrow.

Helmer. But, my dear Nora, you look so worn out. Have you been practising too much?

Nora. No, I have not practised at all.

Helmer. But you will need to—

Nora. Yes, indeed I shall, Torvald. But I can't get on a bit without you to help me; I have absolutely forgotten the whole thing.

Helmer. Oh, we will soon work it up again.

Nora. Yes, help me, Torvald. Promise that you will! I am so nervous about it—all the people—. You must give yourself up to me entirely this evening. Not the tiniest bit of business—you mustn't even take a pen in your hand. Will you promise, Torvald dear?

Helmer. I promise. This evening I will be wholly and absolutely at your service, you helpless little mortal. Ah, by the way, first of all I will just——

(Goes towards the hall door.)

Nora. What are you going to do there?

Helmer. Only see if any letters have come.

Nora. No, no! don't do that, Torvald!

Helmer. Why not?

Nora. Torvald, please don't. There is nothing there.

Helmer. Well, let me look. *(Turns to go to the letter-box. Nora at the piano, plays the first bars of the Tarantella. Helmer stops in the doorway.)* Aha!

Nora. I can't dance to-morrow if I don't practise with you.

Helmer *(going up to her)*. Are you really so afraid of it, dear?

Nora. Yes, so dreadfully afraid of it. Let me practise at once; there is time now, before we go to dinner. Sit down and play for me, Torvald dear; criticise me, and correct me as you play.

Helmer. With great pleasure, if you wish me to.

(Sits down at the piano.)

Nora (*takes out of the box a tambourine and a long variegated shawl. She hastily drapes the shawl round her. Then she springs to the front of the stage and calls out*). Now play for me! I am going to dance!

(*Helmer plays and Nora dances. Rank stands by the piano behind Helmer and looks on.*)

Helmer (*as he plays*). Slower, slower!

Nora. I can't do it any other way.

Helmer. Not so violently, Nora!

Nora. This is the way.

Helmer (*stops playing*). No, no—that is not a bit right.

Nora (*laughing and swinging the tambourine*). Didn't I tell you so?

Rank. Let me play for her.

Helmer (*getting up*). Yes, do. I can correct her better then.

(*Rank sits down at the piano and plays. Nora dances more and more wildly. Helmer has taken up a position beside the stove, and during her dance gives her frequent instructions. She does not seem to hear him; her hair comes down and falls over her shoulders; she pays no attention to it, but goes on dancing. Enter Mrs. Linde.*)

Mrs. Linde (*standing as if spell-bound in the doorway*). Oh!——

Nora (*as she dances*). Such fun, Christine!

Helmer. My dear darling Nora, you are dancing as if your life depended on it.

Nora. So it does.

Helmer. Stop, Rank; this is sheer madness. Stop, I tell you! (*Rank stops playing, and Nora suddenly stands still. Helmer goes up to her.*) I could never have believed it. You have forgotten everything I taught you.

Nora (*throwing away the tambourine*). There, you see.

Helmer. You will want a lot of coaching.

Nora. Yes, you see how much I need it. You must coach me up to the last minute. Promise me that, Torvald!

Helmer. You can depend on me.

Nora. You must not think of anything but me, either to-day or to-morrow; you mustn't open a single letter—not even open the letter-box——

Helmer. Ah, you are still afraid of that fellow——

Nora. Yes, indeed I am.

Helmer. Nora, I can tell from your looks that there is a letter from him lying there.

Nora. I don't know; I think there is; but you must not read anything of that kind now. Nothing horrid must come between us till this is all over.

Rank (*whispers to Helmer*). You mustn't contradict her.

Helmer (*taking her in his arms*). The child shall have her way. But to-morrow night, after you have danced——

Nora. Then you will be free.

(*The Maid appears in the doorway to the right.*)

Maid. Dinner is served, ma'am.

Nora. We will have champagne, Helen.

Maid. Very good, ma'am.   (*Exit.*)

Helmer. Hullo!—are we going to have a banquet?

Nora. Yes, a champagne banquet till the small hours. (*Calls out.*) And a few maca-roons, Helen—lots, just for once!

Helmer. Come, come, don't be so wild and nervous. Be my own little skylark, as you used.

Nora. Yes, dear, I will. But go in now and you too, Doctor Rank. Christine, you must help me to do up my hair.

Rank (*whispers to Helmer as they go out*). I suppose there is nothing—she is not expecting anything?

Helmer. Far from it, my dear fellow; it is simply nothing more than this childish nervousness I was telling you of.

(*They go into the right-hand room.*)

Nora. Well!

Mrs. Linde. Gone out of town.

Nora. I could tell from your face.

Mrs. Linde. He is coming home to-morrow evening. I wrote a note for him.

Nora. You should have let it alone; you must prevent nothing. After all, it is splen-did to be waiting for a wonderful thing to happen.

Mrs. Linde. What is it that you are waiting for?

Nora. Oh, you wouldn't understand. Go in to them, I will come in a moment. (*Mrs. Linde goes into the dining-room. Nora stands still for a little while, as if to compose herself. Then she looks at her watch.*) Five o'clock. Seven hours till midnight. Then the Tarantella will be over. Twenty-four and seven? Thirty-one hours to live.

Helmer (*from the doorway on the right*). Where's my little skylark?

Nora (*going to him with her arms outstretched*). Here she is!

ACT III

The Same Scene

The table has been placed in the middle of the stage, with chairs round it. A lamp is burning on the table. The door into the hall stands open. Dance music is heard in the room above. Mrs. Linde is sitting at the table idly turning over the leaves of a book; she tries to read, but does not seem able to collect her thoughts. Every now and then she listens intently for a sound at the outer door.

Mrs. Linde (*looking at her watch*). Not yet—and the time is nearly up. If only he does not—. (*Listens again.*) Ah, there he is. (*Goes into the hall and opens the outer door carefully. Light footsteps are heard on the stairs. She whispers.*) Come in. There is no one here.

Krogstad (*in the doorway*). I found a note from you at home. What does this mean?

Mrs. Linde. It is absolutely necessary that I should have a talk with you.

Krogstad. Really? And is it absolutely necessary that it should be here?

Mrs. Linde. It is impossible where I live; there is no private entrance to my rooms. Come in; we are quite alone. The maid is asleep, and the Helmers are at the dance upstairs.

Krogstad (*coming into the room*). Are the Helmers really at a dance to-night?

Mrs. Linde. Yes, why not?

Krogstad. Certainly—why not?

Mrs. Linde. Now, Nils, let us have a talk.

Krogstad. Can we two have anything to talk about?

Mrs. Linde. We have a great deal to talk about.

Krogstad. I shouldn't have thought so.

Mrs. Linde. No, you have never properly understood me.

Krogstad. Was there anything else to understand except what was obvious to all the world—a heartless woman jilts a man when a more lucrative chance turns up?

Mrs. Linde. Do you believe I am as absolutely heartless as all that? And do you believe that I did it with a light heart?

Krogstad. Didn't you?

Mrs. Linde. Nils, did you really think that?

Krogstad. If it were as you say, why did you write to me as you did at the time?

Mrs. Linde. I could do nothing else. As I had to break with you, it was my duty also to put an end to all that you felt for me.

Krogstad (*wringing his hands*). So that was it. And all this—only for the sake of money!

Mrs. Linde. You must not forget that I had a helpless mother and two little brothers. We couldn't wait for you, Nils; your prospects seemed hopeless then.

Krogstad. That may be so, but you had no right to throw me over for anyone else's sake.

Mrs. Linde. Indeed I don't know. Many a time did I ask myself if I had the right to do it.

Krogstad (*more gently*). When I lost you, it was as if all the solid ground went from under my feet. Look at me now—I am a shipwrecked man clinging to a bit of wreckage.

Mrs. Linde. But help may be near.

Krogstad. It *was* near; but then you came and stood in my way.

Mrs. Linde. Unintentionally, Nils. It was only to-day that I learnt it was your place I was going to take in the Bank.

Krogstad. I believe you, if you say so. But now that you know it, are you not going to give it up to me?

Mrs. Linde. No, because that would not benefit you in the least.

Krogstad. Oh, benefit, benefit—I would have done it whether or no.

Mrs. Linde. I have learnt to act prudently. Life, and hard, bitter necessity have taught me that.

Krogstad. And life has taught me not to believe in fine speeches.

Mrs. Linde. Then life has taught you something very reasonable. But deeds you must believe in?

Krogstad. What do you mean by that?

Mrs. Linde. You said you were like a shipwrecked man clinging to some wreckage.

Krogstad. I had good reason to say so.

Mrs. Linde. Well, I am like a shipwrecked woman clinging to some wreckage—no one to mourn for, no one to care for.

Krogstad. It was your own choice.

Mrs. Linde. There was no other choice—then.

Krogstad. Well, what now?

Mrs. Linde. Nils, how would it be if we two shipwrecked people could join forces?

Krogstad. What are you saying?

Mrs. Linde. Two on the same piece of wreckage would stand a better chance than each on their own.

Krogstad. Christine!

Mrs. Linde. What do you suppose brought me to town?

Krogstad. Do you mean that you gave me a thought?

Mrs. Linde. I could not endure life without work. All my life, as long as I can remember, I have worked, and it has been my greatest and only pleasure. But now I am quite alone in the world—my life is so dreadfully empty and I feel so forsaken. There is not the least pleasure in working for one's self. Nils, give me someone and something to work for.

Krogstad. I don't trust that. It is nothing but a woman's overstrained sense of generosity that prompts you to make such an offer of yourself.

Mrs. Linde. Have you ever noticed anything of the sort in me?

Krogstad. Could you really do it? Tell me—do you know all about my past life?

Mrs. Linde. Yes.

Krogstad. And do you know what they think of me here?

Mrs. Linde. You seemed to me to imply that with me you might have been quite another man.

Krogstad. I am certain of it.

Mrs. Linde. Is it too late now?

Krogstad. Christine, are you saying this deliberately? Yes, I am sure you are. I see it in your face. Have you really the courage then—?

Mrs. Linde. I want to be a mother to someone, and your children need a mother. We two need each other. Nils, I have faith in your real character—I can dare anything together with you.

Krogstad (*grasps her hands*). Thanks, thanks, Christine! Now I shall find a way to clear myself in the eyes of the world. Ah, but I forgot——

Mrs. Linde (*listening*). Hush! The Tarantella! Go, go!

Krogstad. Why? What is it?

Mrs. Linde. Do you hear them up there? When that is over, we may expect them back.

Krogstad. Yes, yes—I will go. But it is all no use. Of course you are not aware what steps I have taken in the matter of the Helmers.

Mrs. Linde. Yes, I know all about that.

Krogstad. And in spite of that have you the courage to—?

Mrs. Linde. I understand very well to what lengths a man like you might be driven by despair.

Krogstad. If I could only undo what I have done!

Mrs. Linde. You cannot. Your letter is lying in the letter-box now.

Krogstad. Are you sure of that?

Mrs. Linde. Quite sure, but——

Krogstad (*with a searching look at her*). Is that what it all means?—that you want to save your friend at my cost? Tell me frankly. Is that it?

Mrs. Linde. Nils, a woman who has once sold herself for another's sake, doesn't do it a second time.

Krogstad. I will ask for my letter back.

Mrs. Linde. No, no.

Krogstad. Yes, of course I will. I will wait here till Helmer comes; I will tell him he must give me my letter back—that it only concerns my dismissal—that he is not to read it——

Mrs. Linde. No, Nils, you must not recall your letter.

Krogstad. But, tell me, wasn't it for that very purpose that you asked me to meet you here?

Mrs. Linde. In my first moment of fright, it was. But twenty-four hours have elapsed since then, and in that time I have witnessed incredible things in this house. Helmer must know all about it. This unhappy secret must be disclosed; they must have a complete understanding between them, which is impossible with all this concealment and falsehood going on.

Krogstad. Very well, if you will take the responsibility. But there is one thing I can do in any case, and I shall do it at once.

Mrs. Linde (*listening*). You must be quick and go! The dance is over; we are not safe a moment longer.

Krogstad. I will wait for you below.

Mrs. Linde. Yes, do. You must see me back to my door.

Krogstad. I have never had such an amazing piece of good fortune in my life.

(*Goes out through the outer door. The door between the room and the hall remains open.*)

Mrs. Linde (*tidying up the room and laying her hat and cloak ready*). What a difference! what a difference! Someone to work for and live for—a home to bring comfort into. That I will do, indeed. I wish they would be quick and come— (*Listens.*) Ah, there they are now. I must put on my things.

(*Takes up her hat and cloak. Helmer's and Nora's voices are heard outside; a key is turned, and Helmer brings Nora almost by force into the hall. She is in an Italian costume with a large black shawl round her; he is in evening dress and a black domino² which is flying open.)*

Nora *(hanging back in the doorway, and struggling with him).* No, no, no!—don't take me in. I want to go upstairs again; I don't want to leave so early.

Helmer. But, my dearest Nora——

Nora. Please, Torvald dear—please, *please*—only an hour more.

Helmer. Not a single minute, my sweet Nora. You know that was our agreement. Come along into the room; you are catching cold standing there.

(He brings her gently into the room, in spite of her resistance.)

Mrs. Linde. Good evening.

Nora. Christine!

Helmer. You here, so late, Mrs. Linde?

Mrs. Linde. Yes, you must excuse me; I was so anxious to see Nora in her dress.

Nora. Have you been sitting here waiting for me?

Mrs. Linde. Yes, unfortunately I came too late, you had already gone upstairs; and I thought I couldn't go away again without having seen you.

Helmer *(taking off Nora's shawl).* Yes, take a good look at her. I think she is worth looking at. Isn't she charming, Mrs. Linde?

Mrs. Linde. Yes, indeed she is.

Helmer. Doesn't she look remarkably pretty? Everyone thought so at the dance. But she is terribly self-willed, this sweet little person. What are we to do with her? You will hardly believe that I had almost to bring her away by force.

Nora. Torvald, you will repent not having let me stay, even if it were only for half an hour.

Helmer. Listen to her, Mrs. Linde! She had danced her Tarantella, and it had been a tremendous success, as it deserved—although possibly the performance was a trifle too realistic—a little more so, I mean, than was strictly compatible with the limitations of art. But never mind about that! The chief thing is, she had made a success—she had made a tremendous success. Do you think I was going to let her remain there after that, and spoil the effect? No indeed! I took my charming little Capri maiden—my capricious little Capri maiden, I should say—on my arm; took one quick turn round the room; a curtsey on either side, and, as they say in novels, the beautiful apparition disappeared. An exit ought always to be effective, Mrs. Linde; but that is what I cannot make Nora understand. Pooh! this room is hot. *(Throws his domino on a chair and opens the door of his room.)* Hullo! it's dark in here. Oh, of course—excuse me——.

(He goes in and lights some candles.)

---

² A long, loose, hooded cloak.

Nora *(in a hurried and breathless whisper).* Well?

Mrs. Linde *(in a low voice).* I have had a talk with him.

Nora. Yes, and——

Mrs. Linde. Nora, you must tell your husband all about it.

Nora *(in an expressionless voice).* I knew it.

Mrs. Linde. You have nothing to be afraid of as far as Krogstad is concerned; but you must tell him.

Nora. I won't tell him.

Mrs. Linde. Then the letter will.

Nora. Thank you, Christine. Now I know what I must do. Hush——!

Helmer *(coming in again).* Well, Mrs. Linde, have you admired her?

Mrs. Linde. Yes, and now I will say good-night.

Helmer. What, already? Is this yours, this knitting?

Mrs. Linde *(taking it).* Yes, thank you, I have very nearly forgotten it.

Helmer. So you knit?

Mrs. Linde. Of course.

Helmer. Do you know, you ought to embroider.

Mrs. Linde. Really? Why?

Helmer. Yes, it's far more becoming. Let me show you. You hold the embroidery thus in your left hand, and use the needle with the right—like this—with a long, easy sweep. Do you see?

Mrs. Linde. Yes, perhaps——

Helmer. But in the case of knitting—that can never be anything but ungraceful; look here—the arms close together, the knitting-needles going up and down—it has a sort of Chinese effect—. That was really excellent champagne they gave us.

Mrs. Linde. Well,—good-night, Nora, and don't be self-willed any more.

Helmer. That's right, Mrs. Linde.

Mrs. Linde. Good-night, Mr. Helmer.

Helmer *(accompanying her to the door).* Good-night, good-night. I hope you will get home all right. I should be very happy to—but you haven't any great distance to go. Good-night, good-night. *(She goes out; he shuts the door after her, and comes in again.)* Ah!—at last we have got rid of her. She is a frightful bore, that woman.

Nora. Aren't you very tired, Torvald?

Helmer. No, not in the least.

Nora. Nor sleepy?

Helmer. Not a bit. On the contrary, I feel extraordinarily lively. And you?—you really look both tired and sleepy.

Nora. Yes, I am very tired. I want to go to sleep at once.

Helmer. There, you see it was quite right of me not to let you stay there any longer.

Nora. Everything you do is quite right, Torvald.

Helmer *(kissing her on the forehead).* Now my little skylark is speaking reasonably. Did you notice what good spirits Rank was in this evening?

Nora. Really? Was he? I didn't speak to him at all.

Helmer. And I very little, but I have not for a long time seen him in such good form. (*Looks for a while at her and then goes nearer to her.*) It is delightful to be at home by ourselves again, to be all alone with you—you fascinating, charming little darling!

Nora. Don't look at me like that, Torvald.

Helmer. Why shouldn't I look at my dearest treasure?—at all the beauty that is mine, all my very own?

Nora (*going to the other side of the table*). You mustn't say things like that to me to-night.

Helmer (*following her*). You have still got the Tarantella in your blood, I see. And it makes you more captivating than ever. Listen—the guests are beginning to go now. (*In a lower voice.*) Nora—soon the whole house will be quiet.

Nora. Yes, I hope so.

Helmer. Yes, my own darling Nora. Do you know, when I am out at a party with you like this, why I speak so little to you, keep away from you, and only send a stolen glance in your direction now and then?—do you know why I do that? It is because I make believe to myself that we are secretly in love, and you are my secretly promised bride, and that no one suspects there is anything between us.

Nora. Yes, yes—I know very well your thoughts are with me all the time.

Helmer. And when we are leaving, and I am putting the shawl over your beautiful young shoulders—on your lovely neck—then I imagine that you are my young bride and that we have just come from the wedding, and I am bringing you for the first time into our home—to be alone with you for the first time—quite alone with my shy little darling! All this evening I have longed for nothing but you. When I watched the seductive figures of the Tarantella, my blood was on fire; I could endure it no longer, and that was why I brought you down so early——

Nora. Go away, Torvald! You must let me go. I won't——

Helmer. What's that? You're joking, my little Nora! You won't—you won't? Am I not your husband—?

(*A knock is heard at the outer door.*)

Nora (*starting*). Did you hear——?

Helmer (*going into the hall*). Who is it?

Rank (*outside*). It is I. May I come in for a moment?

Helmer (*in a fretful whisper*). Oh, what does he want now? (*Aloud.*) Wait a minute? (*Unlocks the door.*) Come, that's kind of you not to pass by our door.

Rank. I thought I heard your voice, and felt as if I should like to look in. (*With a swift glance round.*) Ah, yes!—these dear familiar rooms. You are very happy and cosy in here, you two.

Helmer. It seems to me that you looked after yourself pretty well upstairs too.

Rank. Excellently. Why shouldn't I? Why shouldn't one enjoy everything in this world?—at any rate as much as one can, and as long as one can. The wine was capital——

Helmer. Especially the champagne.

Rank. So you noticed that too? It is almost incredible how much I managed to put away!

Nora. Torvald drank a great deal of champagne to-night, too.

Rank. Did he?

Nora. Yes, and he is always in such good spirits afterwards.

Rank. Well, why should one not enjoy a merry evening after a well-spent day?

Helmer. Well spent? I am afraid I can't take credit for that.

Rank (*clapping him on the back*). But I can, you know!

Nora. Doctor Rank, you must have been occupied with some scientific investigation to-day.

Rank. Exactly.

Helmer. Just listen—little Nora talking about scientific investigations!

Nora. And may I congratulate you on the result?

Rank. Indeed you may.

Nora. Was it favourable, then?

Rank. The best possible, for both doctor and patient—certainty.

Nora (*quickly and searchingly*). Certainty?

Rank. Absolute certainty. So wasn't I entitled to make a merry evening of it after that?

Nora. Yes, you certainly were, Doctor Rank.

Helmer. I think so too, so long as you don't have to pay for it in the morning.

Rank. Oh well, one can't have anything in this life without paying for it.

Nora. Doctor Rank—are you fond of fancy-dress balls?

Rank. Yes, if there is a fine lot of pretty costumes.

Nora. Tell me—what shall we two wear at the next?

Helmer. Little featherbrain!—are you thinking of the next already?

Rank. We two? Yes, I can tell you. You shall go as a good fairy——

Helmer. Yes, but what do you suggest as an appropriate costume for that?

Rank. Let your wife go dressed just as she is in everyday life.

Helmer. That was really very prettily turned. But can't you tell us what you will be?

Rank. Yes, my dear friend, I have quite made up my mind about that.

Helmer. Well?

Rank. At the next fancy dress ball I shall be invisible.

Helmer. That's a good joke!

Rank. There is a big black hat—have you never heard of hats that make you invisible? If you put one on, no one can see you.

Helmer (*suppressing a smile*). Yes, you are quite right.

Rank. But I am clean forgetting what I came for. Helmer, give me a cigar—one of the dark Havanas.

Helmer. With the greatest pleasure.

(*Offers him his case.*)

Rank (*takes a cigar and cuts off the end*). Thanks.

Nora (*striking a match*). Let me give you a light.

Rank. Thank you. *(She holds the match for him to light his cigar.)* And now good-bye!

Helmer. Good-bye, good-bye, dear old man!

Nora. Sleep well, Doctor Rank.

Rank. Thank you for that wish.

Nora. Wish me the same.

Rank. You? Well, if you want me to—sleep well! And thanks for the light.

(He nods to them both and goes out.)

Helmer *(in a subdued voice).* He has drunk more than he ought.

Nora *(absently).* Maybe. *(Helmer takes a bunch of keys out of his pocket and goes into the hall.)* Torvald! what are you going to do there?

Helmer. Empty the letter-box; it is quite full; there will be no room to put the newspaper in to-morrow morning.

Nora. Are you going to work to-night?

Helmer. You know quite well I'm not. What is this? Some one has been at the lock.

Nora. At the lock—?

Helmer. Yes, someone has. What can it mean? I should never have thought the maid—. Here is a broken hairpin. Nora, it is one of yours.

Nora *(quickly).* Then it must have been the children—

Helmer. Then you must get them out of those ways. There, at last I have got it open. *(Takes out the contents of the letter-box, and calls to the kitchen.)* Helen!—Helen, put out the light over the front door. *(Goes back into the room and shuts the door into the hall. He holds out his hand full of letters.)* Look at that—look what a heap of them there are. *(Turning them over.)* What on earth is that?

Nora *(at the window).* The letter—No! Torvald, no!

Helmer. Two cards—of Rank's.

Nora. Of Doctor Rank's?

Helmer *(looking at them).* Doctor Rank. They were on the top. He must have put them in when he went out.

Nora. Is there anything written on them?

Helmer. There is a black cross over the name. Look there—what an uncomfortable idea! It looks as if he were announcing his own death.

Nora. It is just what he is doing.

Helmer. What? Do you know anything about it? Has he said anything to you?

Nora. Yes. He told me that when the cards came it would be his leave-taking from us. He means to shut himself up and die.

Helmer. My poor old friend. Certainly I knew we should not have him very long with us. But so soon! And so he hides himself away like a wounded animal.

Nora. If it has to happen, it is best it should be without a word—don't you think so, Torvald?

Helmer *(walking up and down).* He had so grown into our lives. I can't think of him as having gone out of them. He, with his sufferings and his loneliness, was like a cloudy background to our sunlit happiness. Well, perhaps it is best so. For him, anyway. *(Standing still.)* And perhaps for us too, Nora. We two are thrown quite upon each other now. *(Puts his arms round her.)* My darling wife, I don't feel as if I could hold you tight enough. Do you know, Nora, I have often wished that you might be threatened by some great danger, so that I might risk my life's blood, and everything, for your sake.

Nora *(disengages herself, and says firmly and decidedly).* Now you must read your letters, Torvald.

Helmer. No, no; not to-night. I want to be with you, my darling wife.

Nora. With the thought of your friend's death——

Helmer. You are right, it has affected us both. Something ugly has come between us—the thought of the horrors of death. We must try and rid our minds of that. Until then—we will each go to our own room.

Nora *(hanging on his neck).* Good-night, Torvald—Good-night!

Helmer *(kissing her on the forehead).* Good-night, my little singing-bird. Sleep sound, Nora. Now I will read my letters through.

(He takes his letters and goes into his room, shutting the door after him.)

Nora *(gropes distractedly about, seizes Helmer's domino, throws it round her, while she says in quick, hoarse, spasmodic whispers).*   Never to see him again. Never! Never! *(Puts her shawl over her head.)* Never to see my children again either— never again. Never! Never!—Ah! the icy, black water—the unfathomable depths—If only it were over! He has got it now—now he is reading it. Good-bye, Torvald and my children!

(She is about to rush out through the hall, when Helmer opens his door hurriedly and stands with an open letter in his hand.)

Helmer. Nora!

Nora. Ah!——

Helmer. What is this? Do you know what is in this letter?

Nora. Yes, I know. Let me go! Let me get out!

Helmer *(holding her back).* Where are you going?

Nora *(trying to get free).* You shan't save me, Torvald!

Helmer *(reeling).* True? Is this true, what I read here? Horrible! No, no—it is impossible that it can be true.

Nora. It is true. I have loved you above everything else in the world.

Helmer. Oh, don't let us have any silly excuses.

Nora *(taking a step towards him).* Torvald——!

Helmer. Miserable creature—what have you done?

Nora. Let me go. You shall not suffer for my sake. You shall not take it upon yourself.

Helmer. No tragedy airs, please. *(Locks the hall door.)* Here you shall stay and give me an explanation. Do you understand what you have done? Answer me! Do you understand what you have done?

Nora (*looks steadily at him and says with a growing look of coldness in her face*). Yes, now I am beginning to understand thoroughly.

Helmer (*walking about the room*). What a horrible awakening! All these eight years—she who was my joy and pride—a hypocrite, a liar—worse, worse—a criminal! The unutterable ugliness of it all! For shame! For shame! (*Nora is silent and looks steadily at him. He stops in front of her.*) I ought to have suspected that something of the sort would happen. I ought to have foreseen it. All your father's want of principle—be silent!—all your father's want of principle has come out in you. No religion, no morality, no sense of duty—. How I am punished for having winked at what he did! I did it for your sake, and this is how you repay me.

Nora. Yes, that's just it.

Helmer. Now you have destroyed all my happiness. You have ruined all my future. It is horrible to think of! I am in the power of an unscrupulous man; he can do what he likes with me, ask anything he likes of me, give me any orders he pleases—I dare not refuse. And I must sink to such miserable depths because of a thoughtless woman!

Nora. When I am out of the way, you will be free.

Helmer. No fine speeches, please. Your father had always plenty of those ready, too. What good would it be to me if you were out of the way, as you say? Not the slightest. He can make the affair known everywhere; and if he does, I may be falsely suspected of having been a party to your criminal action. Very likely people will think I was behind it all—that it was I who prompted you! And I have to thank you for all this—you whom I have cherished during the whole of our married life. Do you understand now what it is you have done for me?

Nora (*coldly and quietly*). Yes.

Helmer. It is so incredible that I can't take it in. But we must come to some understanding. Take off that shawl. Take it off, I tell you. I must try and appease him some way or another. The matter must be hushed up at any cost. And as for you and me, it must appear as if everything between us were just as before—but naturally only in the eyes of the world. You will still remain in my house, that is a matter of course. But I shall not allow you to bring up the children; I dare not trust them to you. To think that I should be obliged to say so to one whom I have loved so dearly, and whom I still——. No, that is all over. From this moment happiness is not the question; all that concerns us is to save the remains, the fragments, the appearance——

(*A ring is heard at the front-door bell.*)

Helmer (*with a start*). What is that? So late! Can the worst——? Can he——? Hide yourself, Nora. Say you are ill.

(*Nora stands motionless. Helmer goes and unlocks the hall door.*)

Maid (*half-dressed, comes to the door*). A letter for the mistress.

Helmer. Give it to me. (*Takes the letter, and shuts the door.*) Yes, it is from him. You shall not have it; I will read it myself.

Nora. Yes, read it.

Helmer (*standing by the lamp*). I scarcely have the courage to do it. It may mean ruin for both of us. No, I must know. (*Tears open the letter, runs his eye over a few lines, looks at a paper enclosed and gives a shout of joy.*) Nora! (*She looks at him questioningly.*) Nora!—No, I must read it once again——. Yes, it is true! I am saved! Nora, I am saved!

Nora. And I?

Helmer. You too, of course; we are both saved, both you and I. Look, he sends you your bond back. He says he regrets and repents—that a happy change in his life—never mind what he says! We are saved, Nora! No one can do anything to you. Oh, Nora, Nora!—no, first I must destroy these hateful things. Let me see——. (*Takes a look at the bond.*) No, no, I won't look at it. The whole thing shall be nothing but a bad dream to me. (*Tears up the bond and both letters, throws them all into the stove, and watches them burn.*) There—now it doesn't exist any longer. He says that since Christmas Eve you——. These must have been three dreadful days for you, Nora.

Nora. I have fought a hard fight these three days.

Helmer. And suffered agonies, and seen no way out but——. No, we won't call any of the horrors to mind. We will only shout with joy, and keep saying, "It's all over! It's all over!" Listen to me, Nora. You don't seem to realise that it is all over. What is this?—such a cold, set face! My poor little Nora, I quite understand; you don't feel as if you could believe that I have forgiven you. But it is true, Nora, I swear it; I have forgiven you everything. I know that what you did, you did out of love for me.

Nora. That is true.

Helmer. You have loved me as a wife ought to love her husband. Only you had not sufficient knowledge to judge of the means you used. But do you suppose you are any the less dear to me, because you don't understand how to act on your own responsibility? No, no; only lean on me; I will advise you and direct you. I should not be a man if this womanly helplessness did not just give you a double attractiveness in my eyes. You must not think any more about the hard things I said in my first moment of consternation, when I thought everything was going to overwhelm me. I have forgiven you, Nora; I swear to you I have forgiven you.

(*She goes out through the door to the right.*)

Helmer. No, don't go——. (*Looks in.*) What are you doing in there?

Nora (*from within*). Taking off my fancy dress.

Helmer (*standing at the open door*). Yes, do. Try and calm yourself, and make your mind easy again, my frightened little singing-bird. Be at rest, and feel secure; I have broad wings to shelter you under. (*Walks up and down by the door.*) How warm and cosy our home is, Nora. Here is shelter for you; here I will protect you like a hunted dove that I have saved from a hawk's claws. I will bring peace to your poor beating heart. It will come, little by little, Nora, believe me.

To-morrow morning you will look upon it all quite differently; soon everything will be just as it was before. Very soon you won't need me to assure you that I have forgiven you; you will yourself feel the certainty that I have done so. Can you suppose I should ever think of such a thing as repudiating you, or even reproaching you? You have no idea what a true man's heart is like, Nora. There is something so indescribably sweet and satisfying, to a man, in the knowledge that he has forgiven his wife—forgiven her freely, and with all his heart. It seems as if that had made her, as it were, doubly his own; he has given her a new life, so to speak; and she has in a way become both wife and child to him. So you shall be for me after this, my little scared, helpless darling. Have no anxiety about anything, Nora; only be frank and open with me, and I will serve as will and conscience both to you——. What is this? Not gone to bed? Have you changed your things?

Nora (*in everyday dress*). Yes, Torvald, I have changed my things now.

Helmer. But what for?—so late as this.

Nora. I shall not sleep to-night.

Helmer. But, my dear Nora——

Nora (*looking at her watch*). It is not so very late. Sit down here, Torvald. You and I have much to say to one another.

(*She sits down at one side of the table.*)

Helmer. Nora—what is this?—this cold, set face?

Nora. Sit down. It will take some time; I have a lot to talk over with you.

Helmer (*sits down at the opposite side of the table*). You alarm me, Nora!—and I don't understand you.

Nora. No, that is just it. You don't understand me, and I have never understood you either—before to-night. No, you mustn't interrupt me. You must simply listen to what I say. Torvald, this is a settling of accounts.

Helmer. What do you mean by that?

Nora (*after a short silence*). Isn't there one thing that strikes you as strange in our sitting here like this?

Helmer. What is that?

Nora. We have been married now eight years. Does it not occur to you that this is the first time we two, you and I, husband and wife, have had a serious conversation?

Helmer. What do you mean by serious?

Nora. In all these eight years—longer than that—from the very beginning of our acquaintance, we have never exchanged a word on any serious subject.

Helmer. Was it likely that I would be continually and for ever telling you about worries that you could not help me to bear?

Nora. I am not speaking about business matters. I say that we have never sat down in earnest together to try and get at the bottom of anything.

Helmer. But, dearest Nora, would it have been any good to you?

Nora. That is just it; you have never understood me. I have been greatly wronged, Torvald—first by papa and then by you.

Helmer. What! By us two—by us two, who have loved you better than anyone else in the world?

Nora (*shaking her head*). You have never loved me. You have only thought it pleasant to be in love with me.

Helmer. Nora, what do I hear you saying?

Nora. It is perfectly true, Torvald. When I was at home with papa, he told me his opinion about everything, and so I had the same opinions; and if I differed from him I concealed the fact, because he would not have liked it. He called me his doll-child, and he played with me just as I used to play with my dolls. And when I came to live with you——

Helmer. What sort of an expression is that to use about our marriage?

Nora (*undisturbed*). I mean that I was simply transferred from papa's hands into yours. You arranged everything according to your own taste, and so I got the same tastes as you—or else I pretended to, I am really not quite sure which—I think sometimes the one and sometimes the other. When I look back on it, it seems to me as if I had been living here like a poor woman—just from hand to mouth. I have existed merely to perform tricks for you, Torvald. But you would have it so. You and papa have committed a great sin against me. It is your fault that I have made nothing of my life.

Helmer. How unreasonable and how ungrateful you are, Nora! Have you not been happy here?

Nora. No, I have never been happy. I thought I was, but it has never really been so.

Helmer. Not—not happy!

Nora. No, only merry. And you have always been so kind to me. But our home has been nothing but a playroom. I have been your doll-wife, just as at home I was papa's doll-child; and here the children have been my dolls. I thought it great fun when you played with me, just as they thought it great fun when I played with them. That is what our marriage has been, Torvald.

Helmer. There is some truth in what you say—exaggerated and strained as your view of it is. But for the future it shall be different. Playtime shall be over, and lesson-time shall begin.

Nora. Whose lessons? Mine, or the children's?

Helmer. Both your and the children's, my darling Nora.

Nora. Alas, Torvald, you are not the man to educate me into being a proper wife for you.

Helmer. And you can say that!

Nora. And I—how am I fitted to bring up the children?

Helmer. Nora!

Nora. Didn't you say so yourself a little while ago—that you dare not trust me to bring them up?

Helmer. In a moment of anger! Why do you pay any heed to that?

Nora. Indeed, you were perfectly right. I am not fit for the task. There is another task I must undertake first. I must try and educate myself—you are not the man to help me in that. I must do that for myself. And that is why I am going to leave you now.

Helmer (*springing up*). What do you say?

Nora. I must stand quite alone, if I am to understand myself and everything about me. It is for that reason that I cannot remain with you any longer.

Helmer. Nora! Nora!

Nora. I am going away from here now, at once. I am sure Christine will take me in for the night——

Helmer. You are out of your mind! I won't allow it! I forbid you!

Nora. It is no use forbidding me anything any longer. I will take with me what belongs to myself. I will take nothing from you, either now or later.

Helmer. What sort of madness is this!

Nora. To-morrow I shall go home—I mean, to my old home. It will be easiest for me to find something to do there.

Helmer. You blind, foolish woman!

Nora. I must try and get some sense, Torvald.

Helmer. To desert your home, your husband and your children! And you don't consider what people will say!

Nora. I cannot consider that at all. I only know that it is necessary for me.

Helmer. It's shocking. This is how you would neglect your most sacred duties.

Nora. What do you consider my most sacred duties?

Helmer. Do I need to tell you that? Are they not your duties to your husband and your children?

Nora. I have other duties just as sacred.

Helmer. That you have not. What duties could those be?

Nora. Duties to myself.

Helmer. Before all else, you are a wife and a mother.

Nora. I don't believe that any longer. I believe that before all else I am a reasonable human being, just as you are—or, at all events, that I must try and become one. I know quite well, Torvald, that most people would think you right, and that views of that kind are to be found in books; but I can no longer content myself with what most people say, or with what is found in books. I must think over things for myself and get to understand them.

Helmer. Can you not understand your place in your own home? Have you not a reliable guide in such matters as that?—have you no religion?

Nora. I am afraid, Torvald, I do not exactly know what religion is.

Helmer. What are you saying?

Nora. I know nothing but what the clergyman said, when I went to be confirmed. He told us that religion was this, and that, and the other. When I am away from all this, and am alone, I will look into that matter too. I will see if what the clergyman said is true, or at all events if it is true for me.

Helmer. This is unheard of in a girl of your age! But if religion cannot lead you aright, let me try and awaken your conscience. I suppose you have some moral sense? Or—answer me—am I to think you have none?

Nora. I assure you, Torvald, that is not an easy question to answer. I really don't know. The thing perplexes me altogether. I only know that you and I look at it in quite another light. I am learning, too, that the law is quite another thing from what I supposed; but I find it impossible to convince myself that the law is right. According to it a woman has no right to spare her old dying father, or to save her husband's life. I can't believe that.

Helmer. You talk like a child. You don't understand the conditions of the world in which you live.

Nora. No, I don't. But now I am going to try. I am going to see if I can make out who is right, the world or I.

Helmer. You are ill, Nora; you are delirious; I almost think you are out of your mind.

Nora. I have never felt my mind so clear and certain as to-night.

Helmer. And is it with a clear and certain mind that you forsake your husband and your children?

Nora. Yes, it is.

Helmer. Then there is only one possible explanation.

Nora. What is that?

Helmer. You do not love me any more.

Nora. No, that is just it.

Helmer. Nora!—and you can say that?

Nora. It gives me great pain, Torvald, for you have always been so kind to me, but I cannot help it. I do not love you any more.

Helmer (regaining his composure). Is that a clear and certain conviction too?

Nora. Yes, absolutely clear and certain. That is the reason why I will not stay here any longer.

Helmer. And can you tell me what I have done to forfeit your love?

Nora. Yes, indeed I can. It was to-night, when the wonderful thing did not happen; then I saw you were not the man I had thought you.

Helmer. Explain yourself better—I don't understand you.

Nora. I have waited so patiently for eight years; for, goodness knows, I knew very well that wonderful things don't happen every day. Then this horrible misfortune came upon me; and then I felt quite certain that the wonderful thing was going to happen at last. When Krogstad's letter was lying out there, never for a moment did I imagine that you would consent to accept this man's conditions. I was so absolutely certain that you would say to him: Publish the thing to the whole world. And when that was done——

Helmer. Yes, what then?—when I had exposed my wife to shame and disgrace?

Nora. When that was done, I was so absolutely certain, you would come forward and take everything upon yourself, and say: I am the guilty one.

Helmer. Nora——!

Nora. You mean that I would never have accepted such a sacrifice on your part? No, of course not. But what would my assurances have been worth against yours? That was the wonderful thing which I hoped for and feared; and it was to prevent that, that I wanted to kill myself.

Helmer. I would gladly work night and day for you, Nora—bear sorrow and want for your sake. But no man would sacrifice his honour for the one he loves.

Nora. It is a thing hundreds of thousands of women have done.

Helmer. Oh, you think and talk like a heedless child.

Nora. Maybe. But you neither think nor talk like the man I could bind myself to. As soon as your fear was over—and it was not fear for what threatened me, but for what might happen to you—when the whole thing was past, as far as you were concerned it was exactly as if nothing at all had happened. Exactly as before, I was your little skylark, your doll, which you would in future treat with doubly gentle care, because it was so brittle and fragile. *(Getting up.)* Torvald—it was then it dawned upon me that for eight years I had been living here with a strange man, and had borne him three children——. Oh, I can't bear to think of it! I could tear myself into little bits!

Helmer *(sadly).* I see, I see. An abyss has opened between us—there is no denying it. But, Nora, would it not be possible to fill it up?

Nora. As I am now, I am no wife for you.

Helmer. I have it in me to become a different man.

Nora. Perhaps—if your doll is taken away from you.

Helmer. But to part!—to part from you! No, no, Nora, I can't understand that idea.

Nora *(going out to the right).* That makes it all the more certain that it must be done.

(She comes back with her cloak and hat and a small bag which she puts on a chair by the table.)

Helmer. Nora, Nora, not now! Wait till to-morrow.

Nora *(putting on her cloak).* I cannot spend the night in a strange man's room.

Helmer. But can't we live here like brother and sister——?

Nora *(putting on her hat).* You know very well that would not last long. *(Puts the shawl round her.)* Good-bye, Torvald. I won't see the little ones. I know they are in better hands than mine. As I am now, I can be of no use to them.

Helmer. But some day, Nora—some day?

Nora. How can I tell? I have no idea what is going to become of me.

Helmer. But you are my wife, whatever becomes of you.

Nora. Listen, Torvald. I have heard that when a wife deserts her husband's house, as I am doing now, he is legally freed from all obligations towards her. In any case I set you free from all your obligations. You are not to feel yourself bound in the slightest way, any more than I shall. There must be perfect freedom on both sides. See here is your ring back. Give me mine.

Helmer. That too?

Nora. That too.

Helmer. Here it is.

Nora. That's right. Now it is all over. I have put the keys here. The maids know all about everything in the house—better than I do. To-morrow, after I have left her, Christine will come here and pack up my own things that I brought with me from home. I will have them sent after me.

Helmer. All over! All over!—Nora, shall you never think of me again?

Nora. I know I shall often think of you and the children and this house.

Helmer. May I write to you, Nora?

Nora. No—never. You must not do that.

Helmer. But at least let me send you——

Nora. Nothing—nothing——

Helmer. Let me help you if you are in want.

Nora. No. I can receive nothing from a stranger.

Helmer. Nora—can I never be anything more than a stranger to you?

Nora (taking her bag). Ah, Torvald, the most wonderful thing of all would have to happen.

Helmer. Tell me what that would be!

Nora. Both you and I would have to be so changed that——. Oh, Torvald, I don't believe any longer in wonderful things happening.

Helmer. But I will believe in it. Tell me? So changed that——?

Nora. That our life together would be a real wedlock. Good-bye.

(She goes out through the hall.)

Helmer (sinks down on a chair at the door and buries his face in his hands). Nora! Nora! (Looks round, and rises.) Empty. She is gone. (A hope flashes across his mind.) The most wonderful thing of all——?

(The sound of a door shutting is heard from below.)

FOR ANALYSIS

1. What evidence can you find to support the interpretation that this play is not only about the Helmers' marriage but also about the institution of marriage itself?

2. What does the first meeting between Nora and Mrs. Linde tell us about Nora's character?

3. On a number of occasions, Nora recalls her father. What relevance do these recollections have to the development of the **theme**?

4. Is Krogstad presented as a conventional villain, or are we meant to sympathize with him? Explain.

5. What function does Dr. Rank serve in the play?

6. Examine the stage directions at the beginning of each act. In what ways do they contribute to and reflect the developing action?

7. Acts I and II contain early **dialogues** between Nora and Torvald. What changes in Nora does a comparison between the two dialogues reveal?

8. At what point in the action does Nora begin to understand the truth of her situation and take responsibility for her life?

9. Summarize the various arguments Torvald uses in his attempt to persuade Nora not to leave.

10. Is the feminist theme of the play weakened by Ibsen's failure to suggest how Nora could conceivably make it on her own in such a patriarchal society? Explain.

MAKING ARGUMENTS

A Doll's House aroused great controversy in its time. Today, we like to think society has evolved beyond such prejudices. Do you think this play, if it first appeared now, would arouse no controversy? Would some still find it objectionable? Support your argument with reference both to the text and also to the current state of gender relations, legal and social, in the Western world.

WRITING TOPICS

1. Does the fact that Nora abandons her children undermine her otherwise heroic decision to walk out on a hollow marriage? For an 1880 German production, Ibsen— in response to public demand—provided an alternate ending in which Nora, after struggling with her conscience, decides that she cannot abandon her children. Do you think this is a better ending than the original one?

2. How does the **subplot** involving the relationship between Mrs. Linde and Krogstad add force to the main **plot** of *A Doll's House*?

3. When you were younger, did you ever defy social pressure because the cost of conforming was too high? Describe the source of the pressure, the issues at stake, and the consequences of your refusal. Since then, have you had second thoughts about your actions? Would you act the same way now that you are older?

4. Write a brief description of a marriage you are familiar with that endured only out of inertia, economic pressure, or fear.

MAKING CONNECTIONS

Compare the attitudes toward women revealed in this play with those in Susan Glaspell's *Trifles* (p. 1078) and Lorraine Hansberry's *A Raisin in the Sun* (p. 710).

SUZAN-LORI PARKS   (B. 1963)

FATHER COMES HOME FROM THE WARS[1]   2006

FATHER COMES HOME FROM THE WARS (PART 1)

Father. Hi honey, Im home.
Mother. Yr home.
Father. Yes.
Mother. I wasnt expecting you. Ever.
Father. Should I go back out and come back in again?
Mother. Please.

He goes back out and comes back in again.

Mother. Once more.
Father. Yr kidding.
Mother. Please.

He goes back out and comes back in again.

Mother. Yr home.
Father. Yes.
Mother. Let me get a good look at you.
Father. I'll just turn around.
Mother. Please.

He turns around once. Counterclockwise,

Mother. They should of sent a letter. A letter saying you were coming home. Or at least a telephone call. That is the least they could do. Give a woman and her family and her friends and neighbors a chance to get ready. A chance to spruce things up. Put new ribbons in the hair of the dog. Get the oil changed. Have everything running. Smoothly. And bake a cake of course. Hang

Father. They sent a letter saying I was coming or at least they telephoned. Maybe you didnt open the letter. I dont blame you. It could have been bad news. I see yr unopened envelopes piled up. I dont blame you. I dont blame you at all. They called several times. Maybe you were out. Maybe you were screwing the yard man. If you had known I was coming you woulda put new ribbons

---

[1] The following twelve plays are from *365 Days/365 Plays* by Suzan-Lori Parks.

Mother (cont). streamers. Tell the yard man to—tidy up his act. Oh God. Long story. Oh God. Long story. Oh God. Long story. I woulda invited the neighbors over. Had everyone on the block jump out from their hiding places from behind the brand-new furniture with the plastic still on it and say—WHAT? Say: "Welcome Home" of course. And then after a few slices of cake and a few drinks theyd all get the nerve to say what theyre really thinking. For now itll stay unthought and unsaid. Well. You came home. All in one piece looks like. We're lucky. I guess. We're lucky, right? Hhhhh.

Father (cont). in the hair of the dog, got the oil changed, baked a cake and invited all the neighbors over so they could jump out of their various hiding places behind the brand-new furniture purchased with the blood of some people I used to know— and some blood of some people I used to kill. Oh God. Long story. Oh God. Long story. And theyd shout at me—WHAT? "Welcome Home" of course. And then after a few slices of cake and a few drinks theyd get the nerve to tell me what they really think: "Murderer, baby killer, racist, government pawn, ultimate patsy, stooge, fall guy, camp follower, dumbass, dope fiend, loser." Hhhhh.

Mother
Father

(Rest)

Mother. I cant understand a word yr saying.
Father. I dont speak English anymore.
Mother. I dont blame you. SIT DOWN, I'LL FIX YOU SOMETHING.

He sits. She takes a heavy frying pan and holds it over his head. Almost murder. She lowers the pan.

Mother
Father

(Rest)

He sits. Again she raises the frying pan and holds it over his head. Almost murder. She lowers the pan.

Father. Where are the children?
Mother. What children?

Sound of the wind and the rain.

FATHER COMES HOME FROM THE WARS (PART 2)

A Family (Mother, Father, Children) sitting. Neatly dressed. They're posing for a family portrait. Painter walks in.

Painter. Lets take up where we left off yesterday, shall we?
Mother. Thatll do nicely.

Painter paints. Children fidget. Mother eyes them or slaps them on their hands and they do their best to keep still. Painter paints. Soldier Man arrives, dressed in battle dress. It does not matter from what war; the Trojan war, WWI, American Civil, Iran-Iraq, Napoleonic, Spanish Civil, Crimean, Zulu, ANC against the Powers that Were, whatever, the Chinese-Tibetan conflict, the War of the Worlds, whatever, it does not matter. Soldier Man taps the Father of the Family on the shoulder, relieving him from duty. The Father was only a father figure, and, very graciously bows, clicks his heels and leaves. The Family does not flinch. The Painter continues to paint. After posing for awhile with his Family, Soldier Man wanders away. He puts on a record. Opera. A Puccini aria. He starts moving around.

Soldier Man. Lets have a sing-along, shall we?

He reaches out to the Family. They cringe and shrink from his touch. He can live with it. He dances around. Its clear that he's missing an eye, a leg, an arm—he sings and dances, quite beautifully, though, all the same. The Family watches him, with mounting horror, spoiling the portrait. The Painter turns to the audience:

Painter. Oh, this will never do!

The Family snaps back into polite alignment. The Painter continues painting. The Soldier Man's hearing is now gone too. He turns up the record player and continues singing and dancing as the Family, very bravely, you understand, holds very very still.

FATHER COMES HOME FROM THE WARS (PART 3)

Father, surrounded by his Soldiers, stands at the door. The Family is at dinner.

Father. Hi, honey, Im home.

The Family stares.

1st Soldier. When you hear the word "war" what comes to mind?
Father. Dont start that talk here. Im home.
2nd Soldier. You dont mind if we wait here do you?
Father. Do what you gotta do. Im home.

Father sits in his easy chair. His Soldiers wait.

Father. Come on, Junior. Lets watch some game shows.

Mother. Yr not hungry?

Sister. Mother and me made a welcome home pie for you. See the writing: "Welcome home from the wars, Father!"

(Rest)

Yr not even looking.

Father. All I wanna do is watch some goddamn game shows.

Junior. All thats on is war movies.

Father. Fine.

Mother. Who are yr friends, honey?

Father. Turn up the volume, Junior.

Junior. Im gonna be a soldier just like yr a soldier, right, Pop?

Father

Father

Father. You betcha.

Junior turns up the volume and the Soldiers in the doorway make loud war sounds. Father leans back and relaxes.

FATHER COMES HOME FROM THE WARS (PART 4)

A man, the Father, comes in wearing army fatigues.

Father. Hello? Im home. Made it home in one piece! Anybody home?

He looks for the Family, finds no one. Even goes looking offstage. No one. He spies a note.

Father. "Gone to the store. Back soon. Love, Family."

(Rest)

Thats nice.

(Rest)

Gives me plenty of time to change.

He opens his pack. Changes into an army-issued business suit. Complete with army-issued shoes and socks, a necktie, and a pipe and tobacco.

Father. Army issue. Could be worse. Made in a country I cant even pronounce. Could be worse. I got a full suit. Some guys just get the jacket or just the shoes. Some guys dont got a need for the shoes, cause they dont got feet. There was a guy I knew, he used to be 6´4″: Save that story. Dont tell the kids. Dont tell the missus. Not suitable. Tell the soldiers at the VA hospital when you go in for yr shots. Right. Some lost their feet or their arms. Or their minds. Or they house. Or they wife and kids. Put that in yr army-issue pipe and smoke it. Leave yr edge at the door. Think: "Peace." Think: "Lucky You." Think: "Same Old Same Old." Sit in my favorite chair. Watch my army-issue tv. All I need is an army-issue dog. "Gone to the store. Back soon." I'll wait.

(Rest)

Im a lucky man.

FATHER COMES HOME FROM THE WARS (PART 5)

Cocktails before dinner. Very stylish. The den of an early 1960s home. Sophisticated but not over-the-top. Joe and Lovey (husband and wife) are the center of attention.

Joe. Crawling. For miles.
Host. Yr exaggerating.
Hostess. Let him tell his story.
Host. Just as long as you dont exaggerate.
Hostess. He loves tales, he hates tall tales.

Joe gives Lovey's hand a squeeze. Too hard.

Lovey. Its not a tall tale. Its the facts.
Host. Miles?
Joe. Scout's honor.

After a beat. The girls laugh in a stylish upscale manner.

Next Door Neighbor. Crawling for miles in the dirt? Go on—
Joe. In the sand.
Host. Tall tale.
Lovey. Not at all. He had so much sand in his boots. There was barely any room for his feet!

More stylish laughter.

Joe. I had sand in my mouth too. And every other uniform I saw—
Next Door Neighbor. Had the enemy in it.
Lovey. Worse.
Joe. Had a dead man in it.

Joe
Joe

(Rest)

A Kitchen Servant appears and whispers to the Host.

Host. The cook is making yr favorite dish, Joe. He wants to know how you like yr meat.

Joe. Raw.

Host. You mean rare.

Joe. 1 mean raw. With the skin of the animal still on it. Right, Lovey?

He hugs Lovey too hard.

Lovey. Joe's such a kidder.

Host
Joe

Host. How about well-done, Joe?

Joe. How about well-done, Sam?

Lovey. Yr home now, Joe.

Hostess. How about well-done, Joe?

Joe. Well-done it is. Im home now. After all.

Host. 3 cheers for Joe.

They toast Joe.

FATHER COMES HOME FROM THE WARS (PART 6)

The same people—minus Joe. All are many years older.

Host. 3 cheers for Joe. Come on.

They toast Joe.

Lovey. They wanted me to testify against him.

Hostess. No!

Lovey. They wanted me to say he beat me.

Next Door Neighbor. And after all he's done for this country.

Lovey
Host
Hostess
Next Door Neighbor

(Rest)

Host. Good old Joe!

(Rest)

Next Door Neighbor. Lovey, how about I sit on the picnic bench and you do for me what you do for Joe? Whaddayathink?
Lovey. I dont think so, K?
Next Door Neighbor. Dont hurt to ask, does it?

(Rest)

Hostess. Does Joe like it better at the Front?
Host. Its where he can be himself with no pretense.
Lovey. He writes to me every day. I have a whole room full of letters and theyre all love letters. And sometimes, when he writes about something—Top Secret—you know something he knows but that he's not supposed to know, something he knows that he's not supposed to say he knows, the censors crop it out. And—

Lovey
Lovey

Hostess. Well at least he doesnt come home with blood on his clothes anymore.
Host. Thats something.
Lovey. He doesnt come home at all.

They raise their glasses and laugh politely.

MOTHER COMES HOME FROM THE WARS

A Man looks up at the sky. A Woman enters.

Man. Yr back.
Woman. I got in last night.
Man. I heard they freed you.
Woman. Ive been doing interviews nonstop. The National Publisher wants to buy rights to my story.
Man. The National Publisher?
Woman. That means big money.
Man. Wow.
Woman. There was a picture of me on the front page of the paper.
Man. I missed it.
Woman. Ive got a copy for you.
Man. Thanks.

Woman
Man

Woman. Hon?
Man. What.
Woman. What are you looking at?
Man. God.
Woman. Youll go blind.

The Man lowers his head—he wears black spectacles.

Woman. Yr blind already.
Man. Yep.

The Man lifts his glasses and smiles.

Man. Just kidding.
Woman. Yr such a joker. I could have you shot. I had a lot of men shot. They were
   all just like you. Just like you but—
Man. Foreign.
Woman. Just like you but foreign. Yes.

Man
Woman

Man. Welcome home, hon.

They embrace. We can see that their embrace, while warm and passionate, causes
them both excruciating pain.

PLAYING CHOPSTICKS (FATHER COMES
HOME FROM THE WARS, PART 7)

A Soldier Dad in an army uniform, like he's just come in from jungle combat.
He's still got a camouflage suit on, and dark paint covers his face. Maybe even jungle
twigs and branches stick out of his helmet and clothing. He sits on a campstool, a Kid
sits with him. The Soldier Dad is teaching the Kid to use chopsticks. They are moving
a mountain of rice into another pile, far across the other side of the stage, making
another, hopefully identical mountain. The Soldier Dad is great with chopsticks. The
Kid is hopeless. Somewhere offstage someone plays the piano. Theyre playing "Chop-
sticks" over and over.

Soldier Dad. You wanted yr dad to bring you back something from over there. I
   brought you something, right?

Kid. Right.
(Rest)
Whats "gonorrhea"?

(Rest)

Soldier Dad. Thats something for adults, Kid. Lets stick to our chopsticks.
Kid. I heard Mom telling Grandmom that you brought her some "gonorrhea" home from the war.

Soldier Dad
Soldier Dad

Soldier Dad. I brought you something nice and yr acting like you dont like it, Kid. Here. Watch Dad do it.

Soldier Dad effortlessly picks up a piece of rice and walks over to the other side of the stage where he arranges it carefully on the pile.

Soldier Dad. The idea is to pick up the rice with the chopsticks, carry it over here and put the rice down. And put it down in such a way as we remake the rice mountain over here.
Kid. Right.
Soldier Dad. Its good practice.
Kid. For what?

Soldier Dad
Kid

Soldier Dad smacks Kid upside the head. The move comes so fast and seemingly out of nowhere. Like a flash flood. The Kid's head snaps horribly back, but then, just as quickly, the Soldier Dad's anger is spent. The Kid doesnt cry or anything.

Soldier Dad. Try it again. Go on. You gotta learn it.

The Kid tries moving the rice with the chopsticks again.

Soldier Dad. Not much better. Ok, a little better, but, watch.

Soldier Dad moves several pieces of rice, all one at a time, very quickly and with great fanfare, talking as he moves them.

Soldier Dad. Soldier Dad can move them quick. Soldier Dad can hold the chopsticks in his right hand and move rice, and he can hold them in his left hand too.

Makes no difference. Soldier Dad can hold the sticks behind his back, he doesnt have to look, its just that easy. And every piece of rice gets put in its place!

The Kid watches with mounting awe and mounting anger. Offstage the piano playing gets louder.

Soldier Dad (*Yelling to the offstage piano*). CUT THAT OUT, HUH? HOW AM I SUPPOSED TO FUCKING THINK WITH YOU FUCKING, FUCKING THAT MUSIC UP??!!

The music stops.

Kid
Soldier Dad

Kid. You want me to try it again?
Soldier Dad. Yr mother used to be a concert pianist.
Kid. You want me to try it again?
Soldier Dad. Yeah. Go ahead.

The Kid tries moving the rice again. He's much better this time—like a miracle happened—and now he's actually pretty good.

Soldier Dad. Wow! Great job, Kid.
Kid. Thanks.
Soldier Dad. Chip off the old block after all. I was worried. I'd been away for so long and you—you couldnt do the rice thing.
(*Rest*)
It was the only thing I brought you back and you couldnt do it and I was worried. But you can do it. My Kid's my Kid! Good. So lets get to work, huh?

The music starts up again and the Kid and Soldier Dad get back to work. Each is amazing at moving the rice. And they are enjoying themselves. It is horrible to see them enjoying themselves doing such a pointless task. But they are building a monument together—and this monument will be a fortress against the future pain. And the music, playing all the while, seeps into the walls of the fortress, seeps in and holds it like stone.

FATHER COMES HOME FROM THE WARS (PART 8)

Mother stares out toward the audience into space. Father enters dragging an enormous bloody sword.

Father. Im home.
Mother. At last.

Father. Yes

(Rest)

Mother. Where were you?
Father. The wars.
Mother. And then?
Father. Lost.
Mother. Oh.
Father. Where are the children?
Mother. Grown up and moved away.
Father. Oh.

Sounds of the sea in the near distance

FATHER COMES HOME FROM THE WARS (PART 9)

Several Fathers, men in army suits or uniforms, are sitting in a row: a Soldier, a Sailor, a Janitor with a broom, a Security Guard with a badge and a gun, a Mechanic with an oily rag and a wrench, a Businessman with a suit and a briefcase, maybe an Astronaut even. They are all young-looking: fresh-faced, and firm-limbed; but very, very old-acting in the most typical of ways: forgetful, passive, paranoid, sad, weak, infirm, angry. The Mechanic wipes his head. The Security Guard peers worriedly at the audience. The Janitor sweeps. The Businessman opens his briefcase, realizes its empty, and closes it. The Soldier and Sailor are having a conversation:

Soldier. "Father's Home—Comes from the Wars."
Sailor. You got the title wrong.
Soldier. Did not.
Sailor. Did too.
Soldier. You got water in yr ears. You wanna step outside?
Sailor. You got the title wrong. Im just trying to—
Soldier. What the hell is it, then?
Sailor. I dont know. But "Father's Home—Comes from the Wars" it aint.

(Rest)

Janitor. They put me in the doghouse. Thats not a lie. Do you know how hard it was? A man my size, living in a house so small. And in the backyard.
Mechanic. Least they didnt put you on the junk pile. Thats where they put me. Cause I'd cost them an arm and a leg to fix. So they junked me. After that, I turned to junk. Drugs, you know. Thats what I did. Lots of drugs. What else could I do?
Security Guard. Look! The war!

They strain their necks downstage to get a better look.

Businessman. Its something, isnt it?
Soldier. Its bloody.
Businessman. Cant have a war without blood.
Janitor. Why have a war at all?
Businessman. Clean-up. Theres money in the clean-up.
Sailor. Its closer than it was yesterday. I can feel the heat from the fire on my face.

They all lean in their chairs slightly, like heliotropism, when flowers crane and strain and turn beautifully toward the sun. Theres the sound of a high-pitched whine underneath, like the barely audible (but sustained) screeching of fingernails on a blackboard. The lights grow very bright and then pop out.

SWEET (FATHER COMES HOME FROM THE WARS, PART 10)

A Man eats slowly, but like an animal. A Woman watches.

Woman. Yr home.
Man. I know.

His plate is empty. The Woman piles more food onto his plate.

Man. Im home but I still got the taste for killing, you know?
Woman. Lemmie put some sugar on. It tastes like shit without sugar.

She pours a lot of sugar on his food. He continues eating. At last his plate is empty. He puts his knife in its sheath.

Man. Im gonna go out for awhile.
Woman. Where to?
Man. Nowhere special. I'll just, you know—
Woman. Walk around.
Man. Yeah.

(Rest)

Woman. Just smell them before you cut them, ok?
Man. Have I ever killed one of our own?
Woman. No, but—
Man. Yr talking to me like I killed one of our own.
Woman. You never done nothing like that—its just—l worry.

Man. If you kept them in the house you wouldnt have no worries.
Woman. Theyre grown. And the house is small.
Man. So I'll get us a bigger house. WHEN I GET A BIGGER JOB!
(Rest)
In the meantime, I gotta go out.

Woman
Man

(Rest)

Man. Itll wear off in awhile. The taste for it.
Woman. Lets hope.

He goes. She frets, then cleans up the dishes. A Young Man enters.

Junior. Hey Mom. Wheres Pop?—
Woman. Out bowling—with his bowling buddies, Junior.
Junior. Sweet. Im history, K?
Woman. Oh no yr not.
Junior. Come on, I did my homework. And my chores.
Woman. One step out there and yr grounded, mister.
Junior. You cant ground me, Ive served my country.
(Rest)
Later. K, Mom?

He kisses her and goes. As soon as he has cleared the stage, Sister comes on.

Sister. Wheres Junior and Pop?
Woman. Out and about.
Sister. Im—
Woman. Dont—
Sister. Hey—
Woman. Sure. Yr history. I know. Whatever. Sweet.

Sister
Woman

Sister goes. The Woman very meticulously cleans up the dishes and sits. Then she quickly gets up, puts on a coat and hat and hurries out the door. The house is empty. No foul play will happen to any of them, although, of course, they may cause foul play to others, and, of course, none of them will ever ever return.

FATHER COMES HOME FROM THE WARS (PART 11: HIS ETERNAL RETURN—A PLAY FOR MY FATHER)

During this play we hear a war news-in-brief soundtrack, laced with military band music thats played at a slower than normal speed. The action is as follows: A never-ending loop of action—Servicemen walk downstage together. All wear military uniforms from the same side of the same war, but not necessarily the same branch of Service. They stand upstage and walk very vibrantly and heroically downstage. Theyre returning home as heroes. As they reach centerstage, 5 women, their Service-wives, stand up from the audience, and run toward the men. Just as the Servicemen reach the downstage edge, the Servicewives meet them. The Servicemen pick up their Servicewives, twirling them around very joyfully. Before each Wife returns to the ground a Child comes onstage and, racing toward its respective Mother and Father, jumps for joy. This action repeats. New Servicemen walk downstage, new Wives leap up from the audience and rush into their arms, new Children run in to cheer. The action repeats eternally. Long after the audience has emptied of Women; long after the Men have grown out of the desire to be hugged and kissed and welcomed; long after the Children have become less cheerful and more sensible and have taken up trades, like accounting or teaching or real estate or politics; long after the Childrens Children have outgrown joy and have all grown-up and moved away. Forever.

FOR ANALYSIS

1. Would you describe these short plays as realistic or unrealistic? How does their realism or irrealism serve their subject?

2. It is typical to think of soldiers who make it back from wars, and the families to whom they return, as lucky. Is that how these short plays present this situation? How else do they portray these soldiers and their families?

MAKING ARGUMENTS

Characterize the stance these different *Father Comes Home from the Wars* plays have toward war. Are they prowar? Antiwar? Prosoldier? Antisoldier? Make your argument with support from specific moments in the plays.

WRITING TOPIC

In *Father Comes Home from the Wars (Part 4)*, Father says, "Save that story. Dont tell the kids. Dont tell the missus. Not suitable" (p. 274). What kind of story is Father not telling? How does Parks herself do the same thing and to what effect?

MAKING CONNECTIONS

1. Compare Parks's techniques for reflecting on war to those employed by Wilfred Owen in "Dulce et Decorum Est" (p. 445). Do they have similar things to say? How does the way they say them affect their meaning?

2. Compare the depictions of Father by Parks to one of the fathers in "Connecting Poems: Remembering Fathers" (p. 968) in "Love and Hate." Based on the settings, what are fathers "supposed" to be? How, in these works, do they really behave?

NONFICTION

LANGSTON HUGHES (1902–1967)

SALVATION 1940

I was saved from sin when I was going on thirteen. But not really saved. It happened like this. There was a big revival at my Auntie Reed's church. Every night for weeks there had been much preaching, singing, praying, and shouting, and some very hardened sinners had been brought to Christ, and the membership of the church had grown by leaps and bounds. Then just before the revival ended, they held a special meeting for children, "to bring the young lambs to the fold." My aunt spoke of it for days ahead. That night I was escorted to the front row and placed on the mourners' bench with all the other young sinners, who had not yet been brought to Jesus.

My aunt told me that when you were saved you saw a light, and something happened to you inside! And Jesus came into your life! And God was with you from then on! She said you could see and hear and feel Jesus in your soul. I believed her. I had heard a great many old people say the same thing and it seemed to me they ought to know. So I sat there calmly in the hot, crowded church, waiting for Jesus to come to me.

The preacher preached a wonderful rhythmical sermon, all moans and shouts and lonely cries and dire pictures of hell, and then he sang a song about the ninety and nine safe in the fold, but one little lamb was left out in the cold. Then he said: "Won't you come? Won't you come to Jesus? Young lambs, won't you come?" And he held out his arms to all us young sinners there on the mourners' bench. And the little girls cried. And some of them jumped up and went to Jesus right away. But most of us just sat there.

A great many old people came and knelt around us and prayed, old women with jet-black faces and braided hair, old men with work-gnarled hands. And the church sang a song about the lower lights are burning, some poor sinners to be saved. And the whole building rocked with prayer and song.

Still I kept waiting to *see* Jesus.

Finally all the young people had gone to the altar and were saved, but one boy and me. He was a rounder's son named Westley. Westley and I were

5

surrounded by sisters and deacons praying. It was very hot in the church, and getting late now. Finally Westley said to me in a whisper: "God damn! I'm tired o' sitting here. Let's get up and be saved." So he got up and was saved.

Then I was left all alone on the mourners' bench. My aunt came and knelt at my knees and cried, while prayers and song swirled all around me in the little church. The whole congregation prayed for me alone, in a mighty wail of moans and voices. And I kept waiting serenely for Jesus, waiting, waiting—but he didn't come. I wanted to see him, but nothing happened to me. Nothing! I wanted something to happen to me, but nothing happened.

I heard the songs and the minister saying: "Why don't you come? My dear child, why don't you come to Jesus? Jesus is waiting for you. He wants you. Why don't you come? Sister Reed, what is this child's name?"

"Langston," my aunt sobbed.

"Langston, why don't you come? Why don't you come and be saved? Oh, 10 Lamb of God! Why don't you come?"

Now it was really getting late. I began to be ashamed of myself, holding everything up so long. I began to wonder what God thought about Westley, who certainly hadn't seen Jesus either, but who was now sitting proudly on the platform, swinging his knickerbockered legs and grinning down at me, surrounded by deacons and old women on their knees praying. God had not struck Westley dead for taking his name in vain or for lying in the temple. So I decided that maybe to save further trouble, I'd better lie, too, and say that Jesus had come, and get up and be saved.

So I got up.

Suddenly the whole room broke into a sea of shouting, as they saw me rise. Waves of rejoicing swept the place. Women leaped in the air. My aunt threw her arms around me. The minister took me by the hand and led me to the platform.

When things quieted down, in a hushed silence, punctuated by a few ecstatic "Amens," all the new young lambs were blessed in the name of God. Then joyous singing filled the room.

That night, for the last time in my life but one—for I was a big boy twelve 15 years old—I cried. I cried, in bed alone, and couldn't stop. I buried my head under the quilts, but my aunt heard me. She woke up and told my uncle I was crying because the Holy Ghost had come into my life, and because I had seen Jesus. But I was really crying because I couldn't bear to tell her that I had lied, that I had deceived everybody in the church, that I hadn't seen Jesus, and that now I didn't believe there was a Jesus any more, since he didn't come to help me.

FOR ANALYSIS

1. Is the **tone** of this essay comic or serious or both? Explain.
2. What role does Westley (para. 6) play in the narrative?
3. Can the word *salvation* as Hughes uses it be construed in more than one way? Explain.

4. Discuss how the **point of view** of a **narrator** who looks back on a childhood experience helps define the meaning of the experience.

MAKING ARGUMENTS

How would you argue that young Langston did the right thing in "Salvation"? What points would you use to argue that he did the wrong thing?

WRITING TOPIC

Describe an experience in which public pressure forced you either to express an opinion or a belief that you didn't really hold or to act in a way you otherwise would not have.

MAKING CONNECTIONS

1. Compare and contrast Hughes's loss of **innocence** with that of Sylvia in Bambara's "The Lesson" (p. 98).

2. Compare and contrast the **narrator's** attitude toward adult authority in this story with Sylvia's in Bambara's "The Lesson" (p. 98).

JUDITH ORTIZ COFER (B. 1952)

AMERICAN HISTORY 1993

I once read in a *Ripley's Believe It or Not* column that Paterson, New Jersey, is the place where the Straight and Narrow (streets) intersect. The Puerto Rican tenement known as El Building was one block up from Straight. It was, in fact, the corner of Straight and Market; not "at" the corner, but *the* corner. At almost any hour of the day, El Building was like a monstrous jukebox, blasting out *salsas* from open windows as the residents, mostly new immigrants just up from the island, tried to drown out whatever they were currently enduring with loud music. But the day President Kennedy was shot, there was a profound silence in El Building, even the abusive tongues of viragoes, the cursing of the unemployed, and the screeching of small children had been somehow muted. President Kennedy was a saint to these people. In fact, soon his photograph would be hung alongside the Sacred Heart and over the spiritist altars that many women kept in their apartments. He would become part of the hierarchy of martyrs they prayed to for favors that only one who had died for a cause would understand.

On the day that President Kennedy was shot, my ninth grade class had been out in the fenced playground of Public School Number 13. We had been given "free" exercise time and had been ordered by our P.E. teacher, Mr. DePalma, to "keep moving." That meant that the girls should jump rope and the boys toss basketballs through a hoop at the far end of the yard. He in the meantime would "keep an eye" on us from just inside the building.

It was a cold gray day in Paterson. The kind that warns of early snow. I was miserable, since I had forgotten my gloves and my knuckles were turning red and raw from the jump rope. I was also taking a lot of abuse from the black girls for not turning the rope hard and fast enough for them.

"Hey, Skinny Bones, pump it, girl. Ain't you got no energy today?" Gail, the biggest of the black girls who had the other end of the rope yelled, "Didn't you eat your rice and beans and pork chops for breakfast today?"

The other girls picked up the "pork chop" and made it into a refrain: "pork 5 chop, pork chop, did you eat your pork chop?" They entered the double ropes in pairs and exited without tripping or missing a beat. I felt a burning on my cheeks, and then my glasses fogged up so that I could not manage to coordinate the jump rope with Gail. The chill was doing to me what it always did, entering my bones, making me cry, humiliating me. I hated the city, especially in winter. I hated Public School Number 13. I hated my skinny flat-chested body, and I envied the black girls who could jump rope so fast that their legs became a blur. They always seemed to be warm while I froze.

There was only one source of beauty and light for me that school year. The only thing I had anticipated at the start of the semester. That was seeing Eugene. In August, Eugene and his family had moved into the only house on the block that had a yard and trees. I could see his place from my window in El Building. In fact, if I sat on the fire escape I was literally suspended above Eugene's backyard. It was my favorite spot to read my library books in the summer. Until that August the house had been occupied by an old Jewish couple. Over the years I had become part of their family, without their knowing it, of course. I had a view of their kitchen and their backyard, and though I could not hear what they said, I knew when they were arguing, when one of them was sick, and many other things. I knew all this by watching them at mealtimes. I could see their kitchen table, the sink and the stove. During good times, he sat at the table and read his newspapers while she fixed the meals. If they argued, he would leave and the old woman would sit and stare at nothing for a long time. When one of them was sick, the other would come and get things from the kitchen and carry them out on a tray. The old man had died in June. The last week of school I had not seen him at the table at all. Then one day I saw that there was a crowd in the kitchen. The old woman had finally emerged from the house on the arm of a stocky middle-aged woman whom I had seen there a few times before, maybe her daughter. Then a man had carried out suitcases. The house had stood empty for weeks. I had had to resist the temptation to climb down into the yard and water the flowers the old lady had taken such good care of.

By the time Eugene's family moved in, the yard was a tangled mass of weeds. The father had spent several days mowing, and when he finished, I didn't see the red, yellow, and purple clusters that meant flowers to me from where I sat. I didn't see this family sit down at the kitchen table together. It was just the mother, a red-headed tall woman who wore a white uniform—a nurse's, I guessed it was; the father was gone before I got up in the morning and was never there at dinner time. I only saw him on weekends when they sometimes sat on lawn chairs under the oak tree, each hidden behind a section of the newspaper; and there was Eugene. He was tall and blond, and he wore glasses. I liked him right away because he sat at the kitchen table and read books for hours. That summer, before we had even spoken one word to each other, I kept him company on my fire escape.

Once school started I looked for him in all my classes, but P.S. 13 was a huge, overpopulated place and it took me days and many discreet questions to discover that Eugene was in honors classes for all his subjects; classes that were not open to me because English was not my first language, though I was a straight A student. After much maneuvering I managed "to run into him" in the hallway where his locker was—on the other side of the building from mine—and in study hall at the library, where he first seemed to notice me but did not speak; and finally, on the way home after school one day when I decided to approach him directly, though my stomach was doing somersaults.

I was ready for rejection, snobbery, the worst. But when I came up to him, practically panting in my nervousness, and blurted out: "You're Eugene. Right?" He smiled, pushed his glasses up on his nose, and nodded. I saw then that he was blushing deeply. Eugene liked me, but he was shy. I did most of the talking that day. He nodded and smiled a lot. In the weeks that followed, we walked home together. He would linger at the corner of El Building for a few minutes then walk down to his two-story house. It was not until Eugene moved into that house that I noticed that El Building blocked most of the sun and that the only spot that got a little sunlight during the day was the tiny square of earth the old woman had planted with flowers.

I did not tell Eugene that I could see inside his kitchen from my bedroom.   10
I felt dishonest, but I liked my secret sharing of his evenings, especially now that I knew what he was reading, since we chose our books together at the school library.

One day my mother came into my room as I was sitting on the windowsill staring out. In her abrupt way she said: "Elena, you are acting 'moony.'" *Enamorada* was what she really said—that is, like a girl stupidly infatuated. Since I had turned fourteen and started menstruating my mother had been more vigilant than ever. She acted as if I was going to go crazy or explode or something if she didn't watch me and nag me all the time about being a señorita now. She kept talking about virtue, morality, and other subjects that did not interest me in the least. My mother was unhappy in Paterson, but my father had a good job at the blue jeans factory in Passaic, and soon, he kept assuring us, we would be moving to our own house there. Every Sunday we drove out to the suburbs of Paterson, Clifton, and Passaic, out to where people mowed grass on Sundays in the summer and where children made snowmen in the winter from pure white snow, not like the gray slush of Paterson, which seemed to fall from the sky in that hue. I had learned to listen to my parents' dreams, which were spoken in Spanish, as fairy tales, like the stories about life in the island paradise of Puerto Rico before I was born. I had been to the Island once as a little girl, to grandmother's funeral, and all I remembered was wailing women in black, my mother becoming hysterical and being given a pill that made her sleep two days, and me feeling lost in a crowd of strangers all claiming to be my aunts, uncles, and cousins. I had actually been glad to return to the city. We had not been back there since then, though my parents talked constantly about buying a house on the beach someday, retiring on the island—that was a common topic among the residents of El Building. As for me, I was going to go to college and become a teacher.

But after meeting Eugene I began to think of the present more than of the future. What I wanted now was to enter that house I had watched for so many years. I wanted to see the other rooms where the old people had lived and where the boy I liked spent his time. Most of all, I wanted to sit at the kitchen table with Eugene like two adults, like the old man and his wife had done, maybe drink some coffee and talk about books. I had started reading *Gone with the Wind.* I was enthralled by it, with the daring and the passion of the beautiful girl living in a mansion, and with her devoted parents and the slaves who did everything for them. I didn't believe such a world had ever really existed, and I wanted to ask Eugene some questions, since he and his parents, he had told me, had come up from Georgia, the same place where the novel was set. His father worked for a company that had transferred him to Paterson. His mother was very unhappy, Eugene said, in his beautiful voice that rose and fell over words in a strange, lilting way. The kids at school called him the Hick and made fun of the way he talked. I knew I was his only friend so far, and I liked that, though I felt sad for him sometimes. Skinny Bones and the Hick, was what they called us at school when we were seen together.

The day Mr. DePalma came out into the cold and asked us to line up in front of him was the day that President Kennedy was shot. Mr. DePalma, a short, muscular man with slicked-down black hair, was the science teacher, P.E. coach, and disciplinarian at P.S. 13. He was the teacher to whose homeroom you got assigned if you were a troublemaker, and the man called out to break up playground fights, and to escort violently angry teenagers to the office. And Mr. DePalma was the man who called your parents in for "a conference."

That day, he stood in front of two rows of mostly black and Puerto Rican kids, brittle from their efforts to "keep moving" on a November day that was turning bitter cold. Mr. DePalma, to our complete shock, was crying. Not just silent adult tears, but really sobbing. There were a few titters from the back of the line where I stood, shivering.

"Listen," Mr. DePalma raised his arms over his head as if he were about to 15 conduct an orchestra. His voice broke, and he covered his face with his hands. His barrel chest was heaving. Someone giggled behind me.

"Listen," he repeated, "something awful has happened." A strange gurgling came from his throat, and he turned around and spit on the cement behind him.

"Gross," someone said, and there was a lot of laughter.

"The president is dead, you idiots. I should have known that wouldn't mean anything to a bunch of losers like you kids. Go home." He was shrieking now. No one moved for a minute or two, but then a big girl let out a "yeah!" and ran to get her books piled up with the others against the brick wall of the school building. The others followed in a mad scramble to get to their things before somebody caught on. It was still an hour to the dismissal bell.

A little scared, I headed for El Building. There was an eerie feeling on the streets. I looked into Mario's drugstore, a favorite hangout for the high school crowd, but there were only a couple of old Jewish men at the soda bar, talking with the short order cook in tones that sounded almost angry, but they were keeping their voices low. Even the traffic on one of the busiest intersections in Paterson—Straight Street and Park Avenue—seemed to be moving slower. There were no horns blasting that day. At El Building, the usual little group of unemployed men were not hanging out on the front stoop, making it difficult for women to enter the front door. No music spilled out from open doors in the hallway. When I walked into our apartment, I found my mother sitting in front of the grainy picture of the television set.

She looked up at me with a tear-streaked face and just said: "Dios mío," turn- 20 ing back to the set as if it were pulling at her eyes. I went into my room.

Though I wanted to feel the right thing about President Kennedy's death, I could not fight the feeling of elation that stirred in my chest. Today was the day I was to visit Eugene in his house. He had asked me to come over after school to study for an American history test with him. We had also planned to walk to the public library together. I looked down into his yard. The oak tree was bare of leaves, and the ground looked gray with ice. The light through the large kitchen window of his house told me that El Building blocked the sun to such an extent that they had to turn lights on in the middle of the day. I felt ashamed about it. But the white kitchen table with the lamp hanging just above it looked cozy and inviting. I would soon sit there, across from Eugene, and I would tell him about my perch just above his house. Maybe I would.

In the next thirty minutes I changed clothes, put on a little pink lipstick, and got my books together. Then I went in to tell my mother that I was going to a friend's house to study. I did not expect her reaction.

"You are going out *today*?" The way she said "today" sounded as if a storm warning had been issued. It was said in utter disbelief. Before I could answer, she came toward me and held my elbows as I clutched my books.

"*Hija*, the president has been killed. We must show respect. He was a great man. Come to church with me tonight."

She tried to embrace me, but my books were in the way. My first impulse 25 was to comfort her, she seemed so distraught, but I had to meet Eugene in fifteen minutes.

"I have a test to study for, Mama. I will be home by eight."

"You are forgetting who you are, *Niña*. I have seen you staring down at that boy's house. You are heading for humiliation and pain." My mother said this in Spanish and in a resigned tone that surprised me, as if she had no intention of stopping me from "heading for humiliation and pain." I started for the door. She sat in front of the TV, holding a white handkerchief to her face.

I walked out to the street and around the chain-link fence that separated El Building from Eugene's house. The yard was neatly edged around the little walk that led to the door. It always amazed me how Paterson, the inner core of the city, had no apparent logic to its architecture. Small, neat, single residences like this one could be found right next to huge, dilapidated apartment buildings like El Building. My guess was that the little houses had been there first, then the immigrants had come in droves, and the monstrosities had been raised for them—the Italians, the Irish, the Jews, and now us, the Puerto Ricans, and the blacks. The door was painted a deep green: *verde*, the color of hope. I had heard my mother say it: *Verde-Esperanza*.

I knocked softly. A few suspenseful moments later the door opened just a crack. The red, swollen face of a woman appeared. She had a halo of red hair floating over a delicate ivory face—the face of a doll—with freckles on the nose. Her smudged eye makeup made her look unreal to me, like a mannequin seen through a warped store window.

"What do you want?" Her voice was tiny and sweet-sounding, like a little 30 girl's, but her tone was not friendly.

"I'm Eugene's friend. He asked me over. To study." I thrust out my books, a silly gesture that embarrassed me almost immediately.

"You live there?" She pointed up to El Building, which looked particularly ugly, like a gray prison with its many dirty windows and rusty fire escapes. The woman had stepped halfway out, and I could see that she wore a white nurse's uniform with "St. Joseph's Hospital" on the name tag.

"Yes. I do."

She looked intently at me for a couple of heartbeats, then said as if to herself, "I don't know how you people do it." Then directly to me: "Listen. Honey. Eugene doesn't want to study with you. He is a smart boy. Doesn't need help. You understand me. I am truly sorry if he told you you could come over. He cannot study with you. It's nothing personal. You understand? We won't be in this place much longer, no need for him to get close to people—it'll just make it harder for him later. Run back home now."

I couldn't move. I just stood there in shock at hearing these things said to me 35 in such a honey-drenched voice. I had never heard an accent like hers except for Eugene's softer version. It was as if she were singing me a little song.

"What's wrong? Didn't you hear what I said?" She seemed very angry, and I finally snapped out of my trance. I turned away from the green door and heard her close it gently.

Our apartment was empty when I got home. My mother was in someone else's kitchen, seeking the solace she needed. Father would come in from his late shift at midnight. I would hear them talking softly in the kitchen for hours that night. They would not discuss their dreams for the future, or life in Puerto Rico, as they often did; that night they would talk sadly about the young widow and her two children, as if they were family. For the next few days, we would observe *luto* in our apartment; that is, we would practice restraint and silence—no loud music or laughter. Some of the women of El Building would wear black for weeks.

That night, I lay in my bed, trying to feel the right thing for our dead president. But the tears that came up from a deep source inside me were strictly for me. When my mother came to the door, I pretended to be sleeping. Sometime during the night, I saw from my bed the streetlight come on. It had a pink halo around it. I went to my window and pressed my face to the cool glass. Looking up at the light I could see the white snow falling like a lace veil over its face. I did not look down to see it turning gray as it touched the ground below.

FOR ANALYSIS

1. Suggest a reason why the **narrator** spies on the neighbors.

2. Why does Elena's mother warn her that "[y]ou are forgetting who you are" and that "[y]ou are heading for humiliation and pain" (para. 27)?

3. What does Eugene's mother reveal when she says, "I don't know how you people do it" (para. 34)? Why does she refuse to let Elena study with Eugene?

4. How would you describe the **tone** of this essay? Is it bitter? Belligerent? Argumentative? Accepting? Explain.

5. Discuss the implications of the essay's title.

MAKING ARGUMENTS

While we have to assume that Kennedy's assassination and the author's experience at her friend's door did occur on the same day, the essay capitalizes on this fact, putting the events next to each other. It does so, however, not by drawing explicit connections but by leaving that work to the reader. Make the argument that this method is effective; alternatively, argue that spelling things out would be more effective.

WRITING TOPIC

Explain which event—President Kennedy's death or Eugene's mother's remarks—more significantly shapes the **narrator's** view of American history.

BRIAN DOYLE (B. 1956)

POP ART 2001

In nine years I have been graced with three children and here is what I have learned about them. They are engines of incalculable joy and agonizing despair. They are comedy machines. Their language is their own and the order of their new halting words has never been heard before in the whole history of the world. They are headlong and hilarious. Their hearts are enormous and sensitive beyond calculation by man or machine. Their pride is vast. They are cruel, and move in herds and gaggles and mobs, and woe unto the silent one, the one who looks funny, the one who speaks awkwardly, the fat one, for she will be shouldered aside, he will never get the ball, she will never be asked to jump rope, he will not be invited to the pool party, she will weep with confusion and rage, he will lash out with sharp small fists. Yet they are endlessly kind, kind by nature, and among them there is often an artless democracy, a linking of arms against the vast puzzle of the long people. They search for rules and rank, for what is allowed and what is forbidden, and poke the rules to see which bends and which is steel, for they wish to know their place in the world, where they might walk, what they may wear, which shows are allowed, how far they can go, who they are. They rise early in excitement and return reluctantly to barracks at night for fear of missing a shred of the daily circus. They eat nothing to speak of but grow at stunning rates that produce mostly leg. They are absorbed by dogs and toast. Mud and jelly accrue to them. They are at war with wasps. They eat no green things. Once they learn sarcasm they use it with abandon, slashing here and there without control and wreaking havoc. When they weep they weep utterly from the marrows of their lonely bones. They will not speak of death but when it comes, a dark hooded hawk on the fence, they face it without fear. They are new creatures hourly, and what you think you know of them is already lost in the river. Their hearts are dense books no one can read. They speak many languages of the body. To them you are a stone who has always been and will always be. When they are ill they shrivel. To father them is not a brief noun but an endless verb that exhausts, enrages, edifies, elevates, educates; I am a thinner and grayer man than I was; and closer to joy. They frighten me, for they will make a new world on the bowed back of the one I love; but they delight me, for to have loved them is to have tasted the furious love the Maker has for what He made, and fathers still, and always will.

FOR ANALYSIS

1. Why do you think Doyle chose "Pop Art" as his title?

2. Describe the **tone** of "Pop Art." Does it have only one, or is it varied? Can you chart its changes? What effect do these changes have?

MAKING ARGUMENTS

The final sentence of "Pop Art," in referring to "the Maker," brings up religion, a topic that had not been previously raised. Make an argument about this move; regardless of your own religious beliefs, do you think it is successful? Do you think it is detrimental? Do you think it has little impact either way on the essay?

WRITING TOPICS

1. "Pop Art" first appeared in a creative nonfiction venue called *Brevity*. Write an essay in which you describe the effects "Pop Art" makes with its brevity. Can you imagine it longer? How would it change?

2. Write your own short piece, modeled on Doyle's, in which you list descriptions of something or someone in a way that adds up to more than a roster of characteristics and reveals the nature of the subject.

MAKING CONNECTIONS

1. In "Those Winter Sundays," Robert Hayden writes, "What did I know, what did I know / of love's austere and lonely offices?" (p. 970). In what ways could "Pop Art" be seen as a response to Hayden's speaker's innocence of fathering?

2. Both "Pop Art" and Galway Kinnell's "After Making Love We Hear Footsteps" (p. 951) examine the relationship between parents and children in ways that move beyond the stereotypical and expected. How does each look at parenthood?

ALLIE BROSH (B. 1985)

THIS IS WHY I'LL NEVER
BE AN ADULT   2010

I have repeatedly discovered that it is important for me not to surpass my capacity for responsibility. Over the years, this capacity has grown, but the results of exceeding it have not changed.

Normally, my capacity is exceeded gradually, through the accumulation of simple daily tasks.

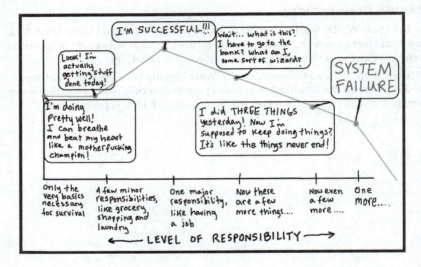

But a few times a year, I spontaneously decide that I'm ready to be a *real* adult. I don't know why I decide this; it always ends terribly for me. But I do it anyway. I sit myself down and tell myself how I'm going to start cleaning the house every day and paying my bills on time and replying to emails before my inbox reaches quadruple digits. Schedules are drafted. Day planners are purchased. I stock up on fancy food because I'm also planning on morphing into a master chef and actually cooking instead of just eating nachos for dinner every night. I prepare for my new life as an adult like some people prepare for the apocalypse.

The first day or two of my plans usually goes okay.

For a little while, I actually feel grown-up and responsible. I strut around 5
with my head held high, looking the other responsible people in the eye with
that knowing glance that says, *I understand. I'm responsible now too. Just look
at my groceries.*

At some point, I start feeling self-congratulatory.

This is a mistake.

I begin to feel like I've accomplished my goals. It's like I think that adulthood is something that can be earned like a trophy in one monumental burst
of effort.

What usually ends up happening is that I completely wear myself out. Thinking that I've earned it, I give myself permission to slack off for a while and recover. Since I've exceeded my capacity for responsibility in such a dramatic fashion, I end up needing to take more recovery time than usual. This is when the guilt spiral starts.

The longer I procrastinate on returning phone calls and emails, the more guilty I feel about it. The guilt I feel causes me to avoid the issue further, which only leads to more guilt and more procrastination. It gets to the point where I don't email someone for fear of reminding them that they emailed me and thus giving them a reason to be disappointed in me.

Then the guilt from my ignored responsibilities grows so large that merely carrying it around with me feels like a huge responsibility. It takes up a sizable portion of my capacity, leaving me almost completely useless for anything other than consuming nachos and surfing the Internet like an attention-deficient squirrel on PCP.

10

At some point in this endlessly spiraling disaster, I am forced to throw all of my energy into trying to be an adult again, just to dig myself out of the pit I've fallen into. The problem is that I enter this round of attempted adulthood already burnt out from the last round. I can't not fail.

It always ends the same way. Slumped and haggard, I contemplate the seemingly endless tasks ahead of me.

And then I rebel.

FOR ANALYSIS

1. Why will the author never be an adult? Do you agree with her prediction? What definition of *adult* is she working with?

2. What kind of memoir is this? Success story? Growing up story? Tale of personal struggles overcome (or not overcome)?

3. Why do you think Brosh draws herself the way she does? What is the effect of this portrayal?

MAKING ARGUMENTS

1. How does Brosh describe her behavior on the Internet? From this start and with evidence, make the argument that the Internet has negative effects on our behavior.

2. Make the counterargument that the Internet has positive effects on our behavior, marshaling evidence (including, perhaps, that this piece first appeared on Brosh's blog).

WRITING TOPIC

Imagine yourself in twenty years. Will there be a specific moment on which you can look back and say, "That's when I became an adult"? Or, if you already consider yourself one, do you have such a moment? If so, describe it; if not, then why not? Will you never become one? Do you believe such moments exist?

MAKING CONNECTIONS

1. Compare "This Is Why I'll Never Be an Adult" to the poems in the "Connecting Poems: Voices of Experience" cluster. What advice might Brosh give a young person? Would she have any?

2. Compare this piece to any other thing you've read so far this semester. Are there things Brosh does with her drawings that other authors are not able to do merely with text?

The college experience is a significant stage in the passage from adolescence to adulthood, from school to work, from dependence to independence, and from innocence to experience. College is also the place where students learn to think in new and different ways about the world in which they live. No matter what students learn, the college experience is part of the process through which they discover who they are and their place in the world. While you read the selections in this unit, pay attention to the ways the movement from teenage innocence to adult experience is connected with the education that college offers—not just about the world, but about the students themselves. Also look for the ways in which the essays reveal that the college experience is sometimes about learning that the world is a bigger, more complicated place than students thought it was. Finally, keep an eye out for the ways that the essays themselves acknowledge how the form on which they are based—the commencement address—is supposed to function, and what that function means.

DAVID SEDARIS   (B. 1956)

WHAT I LEARNED
AND WHAT I SAID AT PRINCETON   2006

It's been interesting to walk around campus this afternoon, as when *I* went to Princeton things were completely different. This chapel, for instance—I remember when it was just a clearing, cordoned off with sharp sticks. Prayer was compulsory back then, and you couldn't just fake it by moving your lips; you had to know the words, and really mean them. I'm dating myself, but this was before Jesus Christ. We worshipped a God named Sashatiba, who had five eyes, including one right here, on the Adam's apple. None of us ever met him, but word had it that he might appear at any moment, so we were always at the ready. *Whatever you do, don't look at his neck,* I used to tell myself

It's funny now, but I thought about it a lot. Some people thought about it a little too much, and it really affected their academic performance. Again, I date myself, but back then we were on a pass-fail system. If you passed, you got to live, and if you failed you were burned alive on a pyre that's now the Transgender Studies Building. Following the first grading period, the air was so thick with smoke you could barely find your way across campus. There were those who said that it smelled like meat, no different from a barbecue, but I could tell the difference. I mean, really. Since when do you grill hair? Or those ugly, chunky shoes we all used to wear?

It kept you on your toes, though, I'll say that much. If I'd been burned alive because of bad grades, my parents would have killed me, especially my father, who meant well but was just a little too gung ho for my taste. He had the whole outfit: Princeton breastplate, Princeton nightcap; he even got the velvet cape with the tiger head hanging like a rucksack from between the shoulder blades. In those days, the mascot was a sabretooth, so you can imagine how silly it looked, and how painful it was to sit down. Then, there was his wagon, completely covered with decals and bumper stickers: "I hold my horses for Ivy league schools," "My son was accepted at the best university in the United States and all I got was a bill for a hundred and sixty-eight thousand dollars." On and on, which was just so . . . *wrong.*

One of the things they did back then was start you off with a modesty seminar, an eight-hour session that all the freshmen had to sit through. It might be different today, but in my time it took the form of a role-playing exercise, my classmates and I pretending to be graduates, and the teacher assuming the part of an average citizen: the soldier, the bloodletter, the whore with a heart of gold.

"Tell me, young man. Did you attend a university of higher learning?" 5

To anyone holding a tool or a weapon, we were trained to respond, "What? Me go to college?" If, on the other hand, the character held a degree, you were allowed to say, "Sort of," or, sometimes, "I think so."

"So where do you sort of think you went?"

And it was the next bit that you had to get just right. Inflection was everything, and it took the foreign students forever to master it.

"Where do you sort of think you went?"

And we'd say, "Umm, Princeton?"—as if it were an oral exam, and we 10 weren't quite sure that this was the correct answer.

"Princeton, my goodness," the teacher would say. "That must have been quite something!"

You had to let him get it out, but once he started in on how brilliant and committed you must be it was time to hold up your hands, saying, "Oh, it isn't that hard to get into."

Then he'd say, "Really? But I heard—"

"Wrong," you'd tell him. "You heard wrong. It's not that great of a school."

This was the way it had to be done— you had to play it down, which wasn't 15 easy when your dad was out there, reading your acceptance letter into a bullhorn.

I needed to temper my dad's enthusiasm a bit, and so I announced that I would be majoring in patricide. The Princeton program was very strong back then, the best in the country, but it wasn't the sort of thing your father could get too worked up about. Or, at least, most fathers wouldn't. Mine was over the moon. "Killed by a Princeton graduate!" he said. "And my own son, no less."

My mom was actually jealous. "So what's wrong with matricide?" she asked. "What, I'm not good enough to murder?"

They started bickering, so in order to make peace I promised to consider a double major.

"And how much more is that going to cost us?" they said.

Those last few months at home were pretty tough, but then I started my freshman year, and got caught up in the life of the mind. My idol-worship class was the best, but my dad didn't get it. "What the hell does that have to do with patricide?" he asked.

And I said, "Umm. *Everything?*"

He didn't understand that it's all connected, that one subject leads to another and forms a kind of chain that raises its head and nods like a cobra when you're sucking on a bong after three days of no sleep. On acid it's even wilder, and appears to eat things. But, not having gone to college, my dad had no concept of a well-rounded liberal-arts education. He thought that all my classes should be murder-related, with no lunch breaks or anything. Fortunately, it doesn't work that way.

In truth, I had no idea what I wanted to study, so for the first few years I took everything that came my way. I enjoyed pillaging and astrology, but the thing that ultimately stuck was comparative literature. There wasn't much of it to compare back then, no more than a handful of epic poems and one novel about a lady detective, but that's part of what I liked about it. The field was new, and full of possibilities, but try telling that to my parents.

"You mean you *won't* be killing us?" my mother said. "But I told everyone you were going for that double major."

Dad followed his "I'm so disappointed" speech with a lecture on career opportunities. "You're going to study literature and get a job doing *what*?" he said. "*Literaturizing*?"

We spent my entire vacation arguing; then, just before I went back to school, my father approached me in my bedroom. "Promise me you'll keep an open mind," he said. And, as he left, he slipped an engraved dagger into my book bag.

I had many fine teachers during my years at Princeton, but the one I think of most often was my fortune-telling professor—a complete hag with wild gray hair, warts the size of new potatoes, the whole nine yards. She taught us to forecast the weather up to two weeks in advance, but ask her for anything weightier and you were likely to be disappointed.

The alchemy majors wanted to know how much money they'd be making after graduation. "Just give us an approximate figure," they'd say, and the professor would shake her head and cover her crystal ball with a little cozy given to her by one of her previous classes. When it came to our futures, she drew the line, no matter how hard we begged—and, I mean, we really tried. I was as let down as the next guy, but, in retrospect, I can see that she acted in our best interests. Look at yourself on the day that you graduated from college, then look at yourself today. I did that recently, and it was, like, "What the hell happened?"

The answer, of course, is life. What the hag chose not to foretell—and what we, in our certainty, could not have fathomed—is that stuff comes up. Weird doors open. People fall into things. Maybe the engineering whiz will wind up brewing cider, not because he has to but because he finds it challenging. Who knows? Maybe the athlete will bring peace to all nations, or the class moron will go on to become the President of the United States—though that's more likely to happen at Harvard or Yale, schools that will pretty much let in anybody.

There were those who left Princeton and soared like arrows into the bosoms 30 of power and finance, but I was not one of them. My path was a winding one, with plenty of obstacles along the way. When school was finished, I went back home, an Ivy League graduate with four years' worth of dirty laundry and his whole life ahead of him. "What are you going to do now?" my parents asked.

And I said, "Well, I was thinking of washing some of these underpants."

That took six months. Then I moved on to the shirts.

"Now what?" my parents asked.

And, when I told them I didn't know, they lost what little patience they had left. "What kind of a community-college answer is that?" my mother said. "You went to the best school there is—how can you not know something?"

And I said, "I don't know." 35

In time, my father stopped wearing his Princeton gear. My mother stopped talking about my "potential," and she and my dad got themselves a brown-and-white puppy. In terms of intelligence, it was just average, but they couldn't see that at all. "Aren't you just the smartest dog in the world?" they'd ask, and the puppy would shake their hands just like I used to do.

My first alumni weekend cheered me up a bit. It was nice to know that I wasn't the only unemployed graduate in the world, but the warm feeling evaporated when I got back home and saw that my parents had given the dog my bedroom. In place of the Princeton pennant they'd bought for my first birthday was a banner reading, "Westminster or bust."

I could see which way the wind was blowing, and so I left, and moved to the city, where a former classmate, a philosophy major, got me a job on his rag-picking crew. When the industry moved overseas—this the doing of *another* former classmate—I stayed put, and eventually found work skinning hides for a ratcatcher, a thin, serious man with the longest beard I had ever seen.

At night, I read and reread the handful of books I'd taken with me when I left home, and eventually, out of boredom as much as anything else, I started to write myself. It wasn't much, at first: character sketches, accounts of my day, parodies of articles in the alumni newsletter. Then, in time, I became more ambitious, and began crafting little stories about my family. I read one of them out loud to the ratcatcher, who'd never laughed at anything but roared at the description of my mother and her puppy. "My mom was just the same," he said. "I graduated from Brown, and two weeks later she was raising falcons on my top bunk!" The story about my dad defecating in his neighbor's well pleased my boss so much that he asked for a copy, and sent it to his own father.

This gave me the confidence to continue, and in time I completed an entire 40 book, which was subsequently published. I presented a first edition to my parents, who started with the story about our neighbor's well, and then got up to close the drapes. Fifty pages later, they were boarding up the door and looking for ways to disguise themselves. Other people had loved my writing, but these two didn't get it at all. "What's wrong?" I asked.

My father adjusted his makeshift turban, and sketched a mustache on my mother's upper lip. "What's wrong?" he said. "I'll tell you what's wrong: you're killing us."

"But I thought that's what you wanted?"

"We did," my mother wept, "but not this way."

It hadn't occurred to me until that moment, but I seemed to have come full circle. What started as a dodge had inadvertently become my life's work, an irony I never could have appreciated had my extraordinary parents not put me through Princeton.

FOR ANALYSIS

1. Do you think this essay was delivered at a real commencement? Why or why not?

2. What do you think the author's attitude is about elitism in higher education? Does he endorse his mother's implicit view of the difference between Ivy League schools such as Princeton and community colleges?

3. Can you isolate serious moments among this essay's general silliness? How do they function? What do they say?

MAKING ARGUMENTS

Write a letter to the editor of the Princeton student newspaper in which you argue either that Sedaris's speech was the most inappropriate commencement address you have ever heard or that it was great and you loved it. Base your arguments both on a close reading of the text and on your ideas about what a commencement speech should or should not be.

WRITING TOPIC

Pick a form of ceremonial address—a graduation address, a wedding toast, a retirement speech—and write a **parody** of it. Think about what the different aspects of the address are supposed to do and how each might be subverted not just to be funny but to make a point.

DAVID FOSTER WALLACE (1962–2008)

COMMENCEMENT SPEECH, KENYON COLLEGE[1] 2005

There are these two young fish swimming along, and they happen to meet an older fish swimming the other way, who nods at them and says, "Morning, boys, how's the water?" And the two young fish swim on for a bit, and then eventually one of them looks over at the other and goes, "What the hell is water?"

If at this moment, you're worried that I plan to present myself here as the wise old fish explaining what water is to you younger fish, please don't be. I am not the wise old fish. The immediate point of the fish story is that the most obvious, ubiquitous, important realities are often the ones that are the hardest to see and talk about. Stated as an English sentence, of course, this is just a banal platitude—but the fact is that, in the day-to-day trenches of adult existence, banal platitudes can have life-or-death importance. That may sound like hyperbole, or abstract nonsense.

A huge percentage of the stuff that I tend to be automatically certain of is, it turns out, totally wrong and deluded. Here's one example of the utter wrongness of something I tend to be automatically sure of: everything in my own immediate experience supports my deep belief that I am the absolute center of the universe, the realest, most vivid, and important person in existence. We rarely talk about this sort of natural, basic self-centeredness, because it's so socially repulsive, but it's pretty much the same for all of us, deep down. It is our default-setting, hard-wired into our boards at birth. Think about it: there is no experience you've had that you were not at the absolute center of. The world as you experience it is right there in front of you, or behind you, to the left or right of you, on your TV, or your monitor, or whatever. Other people's thoughts and feelings have to be communicated to you somehow, but your own are so immediate, urgent, *real*—you get the idea. But please don't worry that I'm getting ready to preach to you about compassion or other-directedness or the so-called virtues. This is not a matter of virtue—it's a matter of my choosing to do the work of somehow altering or getting free of my natural, hard-wired default-setting, which is to be deeply and literally self-centered, and to see and interpret everything through this lens of self.

People who can adjust their natural default-setting this way are often described as being "well adjusted," which I suggest to you is not an accidental term.

Given the triumphal academic setting here, an obvious question is how much of this work of adjusting our default-setting involves actual knowledge or intellect. This question gets tricky. Probably the most dangerous thing about college education, at least in my own case, is that it enables my tendency to

---

[1] Adapted from a commencement speech given by David Foster Wallace to the 2005 graduating class at Kenyon College.

over-intellectualize stuff, to get lost in abstract arguments inside my head instead of simply paying attention to what's going on right in front of me. Paying attention to what's going on inside me. As I'm sure you guys know by now, it is extremely difficult to stay alert and attentive instead of getting hypnotized by the constant monologue inside your own head. Twenty years after my own graduation, I have come gradually to understand that the liberal-arts cliché about "teaching you how to think" is actually shorthand for a much deeper, more serious idea: "learning how to think" really means learning how to exercise some control over how and what you think. It means being conscious and aware enough to choose what you pay attention to and to choose how you construct meaning from experience. Because if you cannot exercise this kind of choice in adult life, you will be totally hosed. Think of the old cliché about "the mind being an excellent servant but a terrible master." This, like many clichés, so lame and unexciting on the surface, actually expresses a great and terrible truth. It is not the least bit coincidental that adults who commit suicide with firearms almost always shoot themselves in the head. And the truth is that most of these suicides are actually dead long before they pull the trigger. And I submit that this is what the real, no-bull-value of your liberal-arts education is supposed to be about: how to keep from going through your comfortable, prosperous, respectable adult life dead, unconscious, a slave to your head and to your natural default-setting of being uniquely, completely, imperially alone, day in and day out.

That may sound like hyperbole, or abstract nonsense. So let's get concrete. The plain fact is that you graduating seniors do not yet have any clue what "day in, day out" really means. There happen to be whole large parts of adult American life that nobody talks about in commencement speeches. One such part involves boredom, routine, and petty frustration. The parents and older folks here will know all too well what I'm talking about.

By way of example, let's say it's an average day, and you get up in the morning, go to your challenging job, and you work hard for nine or ten hours, and at the end of the day you're tired, and you're stressed out, and all you want is to go home and have a good supper and maybe unwind for a couple of hours and then hit the rack early because you have to get up the next day and do it all again. But then you remember there's no food at home—you haven't had time to shop this week, because of your challenging job—and so now after work you have to get in your car and drive to the supermarket. It's the end of the workday, and the traffic's very bad, so getting to the store takes way longer than it should, and when you finally get there the supermarket is very crowded, because of course it's the time of day when all the other people with jobs also try to squeeze in some grocery shopping, and the store's hideously, fluorescently lit, and infused with soul-killing Muzak or corporate pop, and it's pretty much the last place you want to be, but you can't just get in and quickly out: you have to wander all over the huge, overlit store's crowded aisles to find the stuff you want, and you have to maneuver your junky cart through all these other tired, hurried people with carts, and of course there are also the glacially slow old people and the spacey people and the ADHD kids who all block the aisle and you have to grit your teeth and try to be polite as you ask them to let you by, and eventually, finally, you get all your supper supplies, except now it turns out there aren't enough checkout lanes open even though it's the end-of-the-day-rush, so the checkout line is incredibly long, which is stupid and infuriating, but you can't take your fury out on the frantic lady working the register.

Anyway, you finally get to the checkout line's front, and pay for your food, and wait to get your check or card authenticated by a machine, and then get told to "Have a nice day" in a voice that is the absolute voice of *death*, and then you have to take your creepy flimsy plastic bags of groceries in your cart through the crowded, bumpy, littery parking lot, and try to load the bags in your car in such a way that everything doesn't fall out of the bags and roll around in the trunk on the way home, and then you have to drive all the way home through slow, heavy, SUV-intensive rush-hour traffic, etcetera, etcetera.

The point is that petty, frustrating crap like this is exactly where the work of choosing comes in. Because the traffic jams and crowded aisles and long checkout lines give me time to think, and if I don't make a conscious decision about how to think and what to pay attention to, I'm going to be pissed and miserable every time I have to food-shop, because my natural default-setting is the certainty that situations like this are really all about *me*, about my hungriness and my fatigue and my desire to just get home, and it's going to seem, for all the world, like everybody else is just *in my way*, and who are all these people in my way? And look at how repulsive most of them are and how stupid and cow-like and dead-eyed and nonhuman they seem here in the checkout line, or at how annoying and rude it is that people are talking loudly on cell phones in the middle of the line, and look at how deeply unfair this is: I've worked really hard all day and I'm starved and tired and I can't even get home to eat and unwind because of all these stupid g-d- *people*.

Or, of course, if I'm in a more socially conscious form of my default-setting, I can spend time in the end-of-the-day traffic jam being angry and disgusted at all the huge, stupid, lane-blocking SUVs and Hummers and V-12 pickup trucks burning their wasteful, selfish, forty-gallon tanks of gas, and I can dwell on the fact that the patriotic or religious bumper stickers always seem to be on the biggest, most disgustingly selfish vehicles driven by the ugliest, most inconsiderate and aggressive drivers, who are usually talking on cell phones as they cut people off in order to get just twenty stupid feet ahead in a traffic jam, and I can think about how our children's children will despise us for wasting all the future's fuel and probably screwing up the climate, and how spoiled and stupid and disgusting we all are, and how it all just *sucks*, and so on and so forth. . . .

Look, if I choose to think this way, fine, lots of us do—except that thinking this way tends to be so easy and automatic it doesn't *have* to be a choice. Thinking this way is my natural default-setting. It's the automatic, unconscious way that I experience the boring, frustrating, crowded parts of adult life when I'm operating on the automatic, unconscious belief that I am the center of the world and that my immediate needs and feelings are what should determine the world's priorities. The thing is that there are obviously different ways to think about these kinds of situations. In this traffic, all these vehicles stuck and idling in my way: it's not impossible that some of these people in SUVs have been in horrible auto accidents in the past and now find driving so traumatic that their therapist has all but ordered them to get a huge, heavy SUV so they can feel safe enough to drive; or that the Hummer that just cut me off is maybe being driven by a father whose little child is hurt or sick in the seat next to him, and he's trying to rush to the hospital, and he's in a way bigger, more legitimate hurry than I am—it is actually *I* who am in *his* way. Or I can choose to force myself to consider the likelihood that everyone else in the supermarket's checkout line is just as bored and frustrated as I am, and that some of these people probably have much harder, more tedious or painful lives than I do, overall.

Again, please don't think that I'm giving you moral advice, or that I'm saying you're "supposed to" think this way, or that anyone expects you to just automatically do it, because it's hard, it takes will and mental effort, and if you're like me, some days you won't be able to do it, or you just flat-out won't want to. But most days, if you're aware enough to give yourself a choice, you can choose to look differently at this fat, dead-eyed, over-made-up lady who just screamed at her little child in the checkout line—maybe she's not usually like this; maybe she's been up three straight nights holding the hand of her husband who's dying of bone cancer, or maybe this very lady is the low-wage clerk at the Motor Vehicles Department, who just yesterday helped your spouse resolve a nightmarish red-tape problem through some small act of bureaucratic kindness. Of course, none of this is likely, but it's also not impossible—it just depends on what you want to consider. If you're automatically sure that you know what reality is and who and what is really important—if you want to operate on your default-setting—then you, like me, will not consider possibilities that aren't pointless and annoying. But if you've really learned how to think, how to pay attention, then you will know you have other options. It will actually be within your power to experience a crowded, loud, slow, consumer-hell-type situation as not only meaningful but sacred, on fire with the same force that lit the stars—compassion, love, the subsurface unity of all things. Not that that mystical stuff's necessarily true: the only thing that's capital-T True is that you get to *decide* how you're going to try to see it. You get to consciously decide what has meaning and what doesn't. You get to decide what to worship. . . .

Because here's something else that's true. In the day-to-day trenches of adult life, there is actually no such thing as atheism. There is no such thing as not worshipping. Everybody worships. The only choice we get is *what* to worship. And an outstanding reason for choosing some sort of God or spiritual-type thing to worship—be it J.C. or Allah, be it Yahweh or the Wiccan mother-goddess or the Four Noble Truths or some infrangible set of ethical principles—is that pretty much anything else you worship will eat you alive. If you worship money and things—if they are where you tap real meaning in life—then you will never have enough. Never feel you have enough. It's the truth. Worship your own body and beauty and sexual allure and you will always feel ugly, and when time and age start showing, you will die a million deaths before they finally plant you. On one level, we all know this stuff already—it's been codified as myths, proverbs, clichés, bromides, epigrams, parables: the skeleton of every great story. The trick is keeping the truth up front in daily consciousness. Worship power—you will feel weak and afraid, and you will need ever more power over others to keep the fear at bay. Worship your intellect, being seen as smart—you will end up feeling stupid, a fraud, always on the verge of being found out. And so on.

Look, the insidious thing about these forms of worship is not that they're evil or sinful; it is that they are *unconscious*. They are default-settings. They're the kind of worship you just gradually slip into, day after day, getting more and more selective about what you see and how you measure value without ever being fully aware that that's what you're doing. And the world will not discourage you from operating on your default-settings, because the world of men and money and power hums along quite nicely on the fuel of fear and contempt and frustration and craving and the worship of self. Our own present culture has harnessed these forces in ways that have yielded extraordinary wealth and comfort and personal freedom. The freedom to be lords of our own tiny skull-sized kingdoms, alone at the center of all creation. This kind of freedom has much to recommend it. But of course there are all different kinds of freedom, and the kind that is most precious you will not hear much talked about in the great outside world of winning and achieving and displaying. The really important kind of freedom involves attention, and awareness, and discipline, and effort, and being able truly to care about other people and to sacrifice for them, over and over, in myriad petty little unsexy ways, every day. That is real freedom. The alternative is unconsciousness, the default-setting, the "rat race"—the constant gnawing sense of having had and lost some infinite thing.

I know that this stuff probably doesn't sound fun and breezy or grandly 15 inspirational. What it is, so far as I can see, is the truth with a whole lot of rhetorical bullshit pared away. Obviously, you can think of it whatever you wish. But please don't dismiss it as some finger-wagging Dr. Laura sermon. None of this is about morality, or religion, or dogma, or big fancy questions of life after death. The capital-T Truth is about life *before* death. It is about making it to thirty, or maybe fifty, without wanting to shoot yourself in the head. It is about simple awareness—awareness of what is so real and essential, so hidden in plain sight all around us, that we have to keep reminding ourselves, over and over: "This is water, this is water."

It is unimaginably hard to do this, to stay conscious and alive, day in and day out.

FOR ANALYSIS

1. What does Wallace mean when he says, "This is water" (para. 15)?

2. "That may sound like hyperbole, or abstract nonsense," Wallace comments on something he's said, "So let's get concrete" (para. 6). What are Wallace's **abstractions**? How does he use the **concrete** to anchor them?

MAKING ARGUMENTS

At the end of his address, Wallace talks about the difficulty not just of remaining mindful of the world and the people around us but of staying alive. He says these two sentences after talking about suicide. Wallace took his life in 2008 after a lifelong struggle with depression. Make an argument about whether this fact changes how you read his speech.

WRITING TOPIC

Write your own reflection on an everyday event, like Wallace's on the checkout line (or the traffic jam). Try to make a more general statement based on these reflections.

MAKING CONNECTIONS

1. Wallace writes, "A huge percentage of the stuff that I tend to be automatically certain of is, it turns out, totally wrong and deluded" (para. 3). Education, especially higher education, is often thought of as the way people prepare themselves for careers by mastering particular thinking skills and bodies of knowledge. How do Wallace and Sedaris challenge this idea?

2. Which view of higher education appeals to you more? Why?

3. Compare Wallace's writing style to Sedaris's. Both have been praised as stylists, but they write very differently. How do they write? Think about different elements of writing—**diction**, sentence structure, voice—and different adjectives used to describe writing—flowery, spare, hard-edged, sophisticated, showy, smug, generous. Do you like one's **style** more? Why?

FURTHER QUESTIONS
FOR THINKING AND WRITING

1. How do the works in this section illustrate Thomas Gray's well-known observation that "where ignorance is bliss, / 'Tis folly to be wise"? **Writing Topic:** Use Gray's observation as the basis for an analysis of Toni Cade Bambara's "The Lesson."

2. In poems such as William Blake's "The Garden of Love," Robert Frost's "Birches," and Stevie Smith's "To Carry the Child," growing up is seen as a growing away from a kind of truth and reality; in other poems, such as Gerard Manley Hopkins's "Spring and Fall" and Dylan Thomas's "Fern Hill," growing up is seen as growing into truth and reality. Do these two groups of poems embody contradictory and mutually exclusive conceptions of childhood? Explain. **Writing Topic:** Select one poem from each of these two groups, and contrast the conception of childhood embodied in each.

3. Eighteenth-century novelist Henry Fielding wrote: "Oh Innocence, how glorious and happy a portion art thou to the breast that possesses thee! Thou fearest neither the eyes nor the tongues of men. Truth, the most powerful of all things, is thy strongest friend; and the brighter the light is in which thou art displayed, the more it discovers thy transcendent beauties." Which works in this section support this assessment of innocence? Which works contradict it? How would you characterize the relationship between "truth" and "innocence" in the fiction, drama, and essays presented here? **Writing Topic:** Use this observation as the basis for an analysis of Nathaniel Hawthorne's "Young Goodman Brown" or Toni Cade Bambara's "The Lesson."

4. James Joyce's "Araby" and Rivka Galchen's "Wild Berry Blue" deal with some aspect of sexuality as a force that moves the **protagonist** from innocence toward experience. How does the recognition of sexuality function in each of the stories? **Writing Topic:** Discuss the relationship between sexuality and innocence in these stories.

5. Which poems in this section depend largely on **irony** for their force? Why do you think irony is a useful device in literature that portrays innocence and experience? **Writing Topic:** Analyze the function of irony in Blake's "The Garden of Love" and Spencer Reece's "The Manhattan Project."

6. Some authors treat the passage from innocence to experience as **comedy**, while others treat it more seriously, even as **tragedy**. Do you find one or the other treatment more satisfying? Explain. **Writing Topic:** Select one short story, and show how the author achieves either a comic or a serious tone.

CONFORMITY AND REBELLION

Golconde, 1953, by René Magritte (1898–1967).

The works in this section, "Conformity and Rebellion," feature a clash between two well-articulated positions in which a rebel, on principle, confronts and struggles with established authority. Central in these works are powerful external forces—the state, the church, tradition—which sometimes can be obeyed only at the expense of conscience and humanity. At the most general level, these works confront the ages-old dilemma that the very organizations men and women establish to protect and nurture the individual often demand—on pain of economic ruin, social ostracism, even spiritual or physical death—that individuals violate their most deeply cherished beliefs. In these works, some individuals refuse such a demand and translate their awareness of a hostile social order into action against it. In " 'Repent, Harlequin!' Said the Ticktockman," Everett C. Marm disrupts a system he doesn't believe in. On a different note, in Melville's "Bartleby, the Scrivener" the crisis arises out of the protagonist's passive refusal to conform to the expectations of society.

Many of the works in this section, particularly the poems, do not treat the theme of conformity and rebellion quite so explicitly and dramatically. Some, like Emily Dickinson's "She rose to His Requirement," reveal the painful injustice of certain traditional values; others, like W. H. Auden's "The Unknown Citizen," tell us that the price exacted for total conformity to the industrial superstate is spiritual death. In "Easter 1916," William Butler Yeats meditates on the awesome meaning of the lives and deaths of political revolutionaries, and in "Harlem," Langston Hughes warns that an inflexible and constricting social order will generate explosion.

While in many of the works the individual is caught up in a crisis that forces him or her into rebellion, in other works the focus may be on the individual's failure to move from awareness into action. For example, the portrait of Auden's unknown citizen affirms the necessity for rebellion by rendering so effectively the hollow life of mindless conformity.

Although diverse in treatment and technique, all the works in this section are about individuals struggling with complex sets of external forces that regulate and define their lives. As social beings, these individuals may recognize that they must be controlled for some larger good; yet they are aware that established social power is often abusive. The institution at its best can act as a conserving force, keeping in check the individual's disruptive impulse to abandon and destroy, without cause, old ways and ideas. At its worst, the power of social institutions is self-serving. It is up to the individual to judge whether power is being abused. Because the power of the individual is often negligible beside that of abusive social forces, it is not surprising that many artists find a fundamental human dignity in the resistance of the individual to organized society.

QUESTIONS FOR THINKING AND WRITING

Before you begin reading the selections in "Conformity and Rebellion," consider the following questions. Then write out your thoughts informally in a reading journal, if you are keeping one, as a way of preparing to respond to the selections. Or you may wish to make your response to one of these questions the basis for a formal essay.

1. How do you define *conformity*? What forms of rebellion are possible for a person in your situation? Do you perceive yourself as a conformist? A rebel? Some combination of the two? Explain.

2. How do you define *sanity*? Based on your definition, do you know an insane person? What form does that insanity take? Do you agree or disagree with Emily Dickinson's assertion that "Much Madness is divinest Sense"? Explain.

3. Discuss this proposition: governments routinely engage in behavior for which an individual would be imprisoned or institutionalized.

4. Freewrite an extended response to each of the following questions: Is war sane? Should one obey an "unjust" law? Should one be guided absolutely by religious principles?

FICTION

HERMAN MELVILLE (1819–1891)

BARTLEBY, THE SCRIVENER 1853

A STORY OF WALL STREET

I am a rather elderly man. The nature of my avocations, for the last thirty years, has brought me into more than ordinary contact with what would seem an interesting and somewhat singular set of men, of whom, as yet, nothing, that I know of, has ever been written—I mean, the law-copyists, or scriveners. I have known very many of them, professionally and privately, and, if I pleased, could relate divers histories, at which good-natured gentlemen might smile, and sentimental souls might weep. But I waive the biographies of all other scriveners, for a few passages in the life of Bartleby, who was a scrivener, the strangest I ever saw, or heard of. While, of other law-copyists, I might write the complete life, of Bartleby nothing of that sort can be done. I believe that no materials exist for a full and satisfactory biography of this man. It is an irreparable loss to literature. Bartleby was one of those beings of whom nothing is ascertainable, except from the original sources, and, in his case, those are very small. What my own astonished eyes saw of Bartleby, *that* is all I know of him, except, indeed, one vague report, which will appear in the sequel.

Ere introducing the scrivener, as he first appeared to me, it is fit I make some mention of myself, my employees, my business, my chambers, and general surroundings; because some such description is indispensable to an adequate understanding of the chief character about to be presented. Imprimis: I am a man who, from his youth upwards, has been filled with a profound conviction that the easiest way of life is the best. Hence, though I belong to a profession proverbially energetic and nervous, even to turbulence, at times, yet nothing of that sort have I ever suffered to invade my peace. I am one of those unambitious lawyers who never addresses a jury, or in any way draws down public applause; but, in the cool tranquillity of a snug retreat, do a snug business among rich men's bonds, and mortgages, and title-deeds. All who know me, consider me an eminently *safe* man. The late John Jacob

Astor,[1] a personage little given to poetic enthusiasm, had no hesitation in pronouncing my first grand point to be prudence; my next, method. I do not speak it in vanity, but simply record the fact, that I was not unemployed in my profession by the late John Jacob Astor; a name which, I admit, I love to repeat; for it hath a rounded and orbicular sound to it, and rings like unto bullion. I will freely add, that I was not insensible to the late John Jacob Astor's good opinion.

Some time prior to the period at which this little history begins, my avocations had been largely increased. The good old office, now extinct in the State of New York, of a Master in Chancery,[2] had been conferred upon me. It was not a very arduous office, but very pleasantly remunerative. I seldom lose my temper; much more seldom indulge in dangerous indignation at wrongs and outrages; but, I must be permitted to be rash here, and declare that I consider the sudden and violent abrogation of the office of Master in Chancery, by the new Constitution, as a—premature act; inasmuch as I had counted upon a lifelease of the profits, whereas I only received those of a few short years. But this is by the way.

My chambers were up stairs, at No. —— Wall Street. At one end, they looked upon the white wall of the interior of a spacious sky-light shaft, penetrating the building from top to bottom.

This view might have been considered rather tame than otherwise, deficient in what landscape painters call "life." But, if so, the view from the other end of my chambers offered, at least, a contrast, if nothing more. In that direction, my windows commanded an unobstructed view of a lofty brick wall, black by age and everlasting shade; which wall required no spyglass to bring out its lurking beauties, but, for the benefit of all near-sighted spectators, was pushed up to within ten feet of my window panes. Owing to the great height of the surrounding buildings, and my chambers being on the second floor, the interval between this wall and mine not a little resembled a huge square cistern.

At the period just preceding the advent of Bartleby, I had two persons as copyists in my employment, and a promising lad as an office-boy. First, Turkey; second, Nippers; third, Ginger Nut. These may seem names, the like of which are not usually found in the Directory. In truth, they were nicknames, mutually conferred upon each other by my three clerks, and were deemed expressive of their respective persons or characters. Turkey was a short, pursy Englishman, of about my own age—that is, somewhere not far from sixty. In the morning, one might say, his face was of a fine florid hue, but after twelve o'clock, meridian—his dinner hour—it blazed like a grate full of Christmas coals; and continued blazing—but, as it were, with a gradual wane—till six o'clock P.M., or thereabouts; after which, I saw no more of the proprietor of the face, which, gaining its meridian with the sun, seemed to set with it, to rise, culminate, and decline the following day, with the like regularity and undiminished glory.

[1] A poor immigrant from Germany who became one of the great business tycoons of the nineteenth century.
[2] Courts of Chancery often adjudicated business disputes.

There are many singular coincidences I have known in the course of my life, not the least among which was the fact, that, exactly when Turkey displayed his fullest beams from his red and radiant countenance, just then, too, at that critical moment, began the daily period when I considered his business capacities as seriously disturbed for the remainder of the twenty-four hours. Not that he was absolutely idle, or averse to business, then; far from it. The difficulty was, he was apt to be altogether too energetic. There was a strange, inflamed, flurried, flighty recklessness of activity about him. He would be incautious in dipping his pen into his inkstand. All his blots upon my documents were dropped there after twelve o'clock meridian. Indeed, not only would he be reckless, and sadly given to making blots in the afternoon, but, some days, he went further, and was rather noisy. At such times, too, his face flamed with augmented blazonry, as if cannel coal had been heaped on anthracite. He made an unpleasant racket with his chair; spilled his sand-box; in mending his pens, impatiently split them all to pieces, and threw them on the floor in a sudden passion; stood up, and leaned over his table, boxing his papers about in a most indecorous manner, very sad to behold in an elderly man like him. Nevertheless, as he was in many ways a most valuable person to me, and all the time before twelve o'clock meridian, was the quickest, steadiest creature, too, accomplishing a great deal of work in a style not easily to be matched—for these reasons, I was willing to overlook his eccentricities, though, indeed, occasionally, I remonstrated with him. I did this very gently, however, because, though the civilest, nay, the blandest and most reverential of men in the morning, yet, in the afternoon, he was disposed, upon provocation, to be slightly rash with his tongue—in fact, insolent. Now, valuing his morning services as I did, and resolved not to lose them—yet, at the same time, made uncomfortable by his inflamed ways after twelve o'clock—and being a man of peace, unwilling by my admonitions to call forth unseemly retorts from him, I took upon me, one Saturday noon (he was always worse on Saturdays) to hint to him, very kindly, that, perhaps, now that he was growing old, it might be well to abridge his labors; in short, he need not come to my chambers after twelve o'clock, but, dinner over, had best go home to his lodgings, and rest himself till tea-time. But no; he insisted upon his afternoon devotions. His countenance became intolerably fervid, as he oratorically assured me—gesticulating with a long ruler at the other end of the room—that if his services in the morning were useful, how indispensable, then, in the afternoon?

"With submission, sir," said Turkey, on this occasion, "I consider myself your right-hand man. In the morning I but marshal and deploy my columns; but in the afternoon I put myself at their head, and gallantly charge the foe, thus"—and he made a violent thrust with the ruler.

"But the blots, Turkey," intimated I.

"True; but, with submission, sir, behold these hairs! I am getting old. Surely, sir, a blot or two of a warm afternoon is not to be severely urged against gray hairs. Old age—even if it blot the page—is honorable. With submission, sir, we *both* are getting old."

This appeal to my fellow-feeling was hardly to be resisted. At all events, 10 I saw that go he would not. So, I made up my mind to let him stay, resolving, nevertheless, to see to it that, during the afternoon, he had to do with my less important papers.

Nippers, the second on my list, was a whiskered, sallow, and, upon the whole, rather piratical-looking young man, of about five and twenty. I always deemed him the victim of two evil powers—ambition and indigestion. The ambition was evinced by a certain impatience of the duties of a mere copyist, an unwarrantable usurpation of strictly professional affairs, such as the original drawing up of legal documents. The indigestion seemed betokened in an occasional nervous testiness and grinning irritability, causing the teeth to audibly grind together over mistakes committed in copying; unnecessary maledictions, hissed, rather than spoken, in the heat of business; and especially by a continual discontent with the height of the table where he worked. Though of a very ingenious, mechanical turn, Nippers could never get this table to suit him. He put chips under it, blocks of various sorts, bits of pasteboard, and at last went so far as to attempt an exquisite adjustment, by final pieces of folded blotting-paper. But no invention would answer. If, for the sake of easing his back, he brought the table-lid at a sharp angle well up towards his chin, and wrote there like a man using the steep roof of a Dutch house for his desk, then he declared that it stopped the circulation in his arms. If now he lowered the table to his waistbands, and stooped over it in writing, then there was a sore aching in his back. In short, the truth of the matter was, Nippers knew not what he wanted. Or, if he wanted anything, it was to be rid of a scrivener's table altogether. Among the manifestations of his diseased ambition was a fondness he had for receiving visits from certain ambiguous-looking fellows in seedy coats, whom he called his clients. Indeed, I was aware that not only was he, at times, considerable of a ward-politician, but he occasionally did a little business at the Justices' courts, and was not unknown on the steps of the Tombs.[3] I have good reason to believe, however, that one individual who called upon him at my chambers, and who, with a grand air, he insisted was his client, was no other than a dun, and the alleged title-deed, a bill. But, with all his failings, and the annoyances he caused me, Nippers, like his compatriot Turkey, was a very useful man to me; wrote a neat, swift hand; and, when he chose, was not deficient in a gentlemanly sort of deportment. Added to this, he always dressed in a gentlemanly sort of way; and so, incidentally, reflected credit upon my chambers. Whereas, with respect to Turkey, I had much ado to keep him from being a reproach to me. His clothes were apt to look oily, and smell of eating houses. He wore his pantaloons very loose and baggy in summer. His coats were execrable, his hat not to be handled. But while the hat was a thing of indifference to me, inasmuch as his natural civility and deference, as a dependent Englishman, always led him to doff it the moment he entered the room, yet his coat was another matter. Concerning his coats,

[3] A prison in New York City.

I reasoned with him; but with no effect. The truth was, I suppose, that a man with so small an income could not afford to sport such a lustrous face and a lustrous coat at one and the same time. As Nippers once observed, Turkey's money went chiefly for red ink. One winter day, I presented Turkey with a highly respectable-looking coat of my own—a padded gray coat, of a most comfortable warmth, and which buttoned straight up from the knee to the neck. I thought Turkey would appreciate the favor, and abate his rashness and obstreperousness of afternoons. But no; I verily believe that buttoning himself up in so downy and blanket-like a coat had a pernicious effect upon him— upon the same principle that too much oats are bad for horses. In fact, precisely as a rash, restive horse is said to feel his oats, so Turkey felt his coat. It made him insolent. He was a man whom prosperity harmed.

Though, concerning the self-indulgent habits of Turkey, I had my own private surmises, yet, touching Nippers, I was well persuaded that, whatever might be his faults in other respects, he was, at least, a temperate young man. But, indeed, nature herself seemed to have been his vintner, and, at his birth, charged him so thoroughly with an irritable, brandy-like disposition, that all subsequent potations were needless. When I consider how, amid the stillness of my chambers, Nippers would sometimes impatiently rise from his seat, and stooping over his table, spread his arms wide apart, seize the whole desk, and move it, and jerk it, with a grim, grinding motion on the floor, as if the table were a perverse voluntary agent and vexing him, I plainly perceive that, for Nippers, brandy-and-water were altogether superfluous.

It was fortunate for me that, owing to its peculiar cause—indigestion—the irritability and consequent nervousness of Nippers were mainly observable in the morning, while in the afternoon he was comparatively mild. So that, Turkey's paroxysms only coming on about twelve o'clock, I never had to do with their eccentricities at one time. Their fits relieved each other, like guards. When Nippers's was on, Turkey's was off; and *vice versa*. This was a good natural arrangement, under the circumstances.

Ginger Nut, the third on my list, was a lad, some twelve years old. His father was a car-man, ambitious of seeing his son on the bench instead of a cart, before he died. So he sent him to my office, as student at law, errand-boy, cleaner and sweeper, at the rate of one dollar a week. He had a little desk to himself; but he did not use it much. Upon inspection, the drawer exhibited a great array of shells of various sorts of nuts. Indeed, to this quick-witted youth, the whole noble science of the law was contained in a nutshell. Not the least among the employments of Ginger Nut, as well as one which he discharged with the most alacrity, was his duty as cake and apple purveyor for Turkey and Nippers. Copying law-papers being proverbially a dry, husky sort of business, my two scriveners were fain to moisten their mouths very often with Spitzenbergs,[4] to be had at the numerous stalls nigh the Custom House and Post Office. Also, they sent Ginger Nut very frequently for that peculiar

---

[4] A variety of apple.

cake—small, flat, round, and very spicy—after which he had been named by them. Of a cold morning, when business was but dull, Turkey would gobble up scores of these cakes, as if they were mere wafers—indeed, they sell them at the rate of six or eight for a penny—the scrape of his pen blending with the crunching of the crisp particles in his mouth. Rashest of all the fiery afternoon blunders and flurried rashnesses of Turkey, was his once moistening a ginger-cake between his lips, and clapping it on to a mortgage, for a seal. I came within an ace of dismissing him then. But he mollified me by making an oriental bow, and saying—

"With submission, sir, it was generous of me to find you in stationery on my own account." 15

Now my original business—that of a conveyancer and title hunter, and drawer-up of recondite documents of all sorts—was considerably increased by receiving the master's office. There was now great work for scriveners. Not only must I push the clerks already with me, but I must have additional help.

In answer to my advertisement, a motionless young man one morning stood upon my office threshold, the door being open, for it was summer. I can see that figure now—pallidly neat, pitiably respectable, incurably forlorn! It was Bartleby.

After a few words touching his qualifications, I engaged him, glad to have among my corps of copyists a man of so singularly sedate an aspect, which I thought might operate beneficially upon the flighty temper of Turkey, and the fiery one of Nippers.

I should have stated before that ground-glass folding-doors divided my premises into two parts, one of which was occupied by my scriveners, the other by myself. According to my humor, I threw open these doors, or closed them. I resolved to assign Bartleby a corner by the folding-doors, but on my side of them, so as to have this quiet man within easy call, in case any trifling thing was to be done. I placed his desk close up to a small side-window in that part of the room, a window which originally had afforded a lateral view of certain grimy backyards and bricks, but which, owing to subsequent erections, commanded at present no view at all, though it gave some light. Within three feet of the panes was a wall, and the light came down from far above, between two lofty buildings, as from a very small opening in a dome. Still further to a satisfactory arrangement, I procured a high green folding screen, which might entirely isolate Bartleby from my sight, though not remove him from my voice. And thus, in a manner, privacy and society were conjoined.

At first, Bartleby did an extraordinary quantity of writing. As if long famishing for something to copy, he seemed to gorge himself on my documents. There was no pause for digestion. He ran a day and night line, copying by sun-light and by candle-light. I should have been quite delighted with his application, had he been cheerfully industrious. But he wrote on silently, palely, mechanically. 20

It is, of course, an indispensable part of a scrivener's business to verify the accuracy of his copy, word by word. Where there are two or more scriveners in an office, they assist each other in this examination, one reading from the copy, the other holding the original. It is a very dull, wearisome, and lethargic affair. I can readily imagine that, to some sanguine temperaments, it would be altogether intolerable. For example, I cannot credit that the mettlesome poet, Byron, would have contentedly sat down with Bartleby to examine a law document of, say five hundred pages, closely written in a crimpy hand.

Now and then, in the haste of business, it had been my habit to assist in comparing some brief document myself, calling Turkey or Nippers for this purpose. One object I had, in placing Bartleby so handy to me behind the screen, was to avail myself of his services on such trivial occasions. It was on the third day, I think, of his being with me, and before any necessity had arisen for having his own writing examined, that, being much hurried to complete a small affair I had in hand, I abruptly called to Bartleby. In my haste and natural expectancy of instant compliance, I sat with my head bent over the original on my desk, and my right hand sideways, and somewhat nervously extended with the copy, so that, immediately upon emerging from his retreat, Bartleby might snatch it and proceed to business without the least delay.

In this very attitude did I sit when I called to him, rapidly stating what it was I wanted him to do—namely, to examine a small paper with me. Imagine my surprise, nay, my consternation, when, without moving from his privacy, Bartleby, in a singularly mild, firm voice, replied, "I would prefer not to."

I sat awhile in perfect silence, rallying my stunned faculties. Immediately it occurred to me that my ears had deceived me, or Bartleby had entirely misunderstood my meaning. I repeated my request in the clearest tone I could assume; but in quite as clear a one came the previous reply, "I would prefer not to."

"Prefer not to," echoed I, rising in high excitement, and crossing the room 25 with a stride. "What do you mean? Are you moon-struck? I want you to help me compare this sheet here—take it," and I thrust it towards him.

"I would prefer not to," said he.

I looked at him steadfastly. His face was leanly composed; his gray eye dimly calm. Not a wrinkle of agitation rippled him. Had there been the least uneasiness, anger, impatience, or impertinence in his manner; in other words, had there been any thing ordinarily human about him, doubtless I should have violently dismissed him from the premises. But as it was, I should have as soon thought of turning my pale plaster-of-paris bust of Cicero out of doors. I stood gazing at him awhile, as he went on with his own writing, and then reseated myself at my desk. This is very strange, thought I. What had one best do? But my business hurried me. I concluded to forget the matter for the present, reserving it for my future leisure. So calling Nippers from the other room, the paper was speedily examined.

A few days after this, Bartleby concluded four lengthy documents, being quadruplicates of a week's testimony taken before me in my High Court of Chancery. It became necessary to examine them. It was an important suit, and great accuracy was imperative. Having all things arranged, I called Turkey, Nippers, and Ginger Nut from the next room, meaning to place the four copies in the hands of my four clerks, while I should read from the original. Accordingly, Turkey, Nippers, and Ginger Nut had taken their seats in a row, each with his document in his hand, when I called to Bartleby to join this interesting group.

"Bartleby! quick, I am waiting."

I heard a slow scrape of his chair legs on the uncarpeted floor, and soon he 30 appeared standing at the entrance of his hermitage.

"What is wanted?" said he, mildly.

"The copies, the copies," said I, hurriedly. "We are going to examine them. There—" and I held towards him the fourth quadruplicate.

"I would prefer not to," he said, and gently disappeared behind the screen.

For a few moments I was turned into a pillar of salt, standing at the head of my seated column of clerks. Recovering myself, I advanced towards the screen, and demanded the reason for such extraordinary conduct.

"*Why* do you refuse?" 35

"I would prefer not to."

With any other man I should have flown outright into a dreadful passion, scorned all further words, and thrust him ignominiously from my presence. But there was something about Bartleby that not only strangely disarmed me, but in a wonderful manner, touched and disconcerted me. I began to reason with him.

"These are your own copies we are about to examine. It is labor saving to you, because one examination will answer for your four papers. It is common usage. Every copyist is bound to help examine his copy. Is it not so? Will you not speak? Answer!"

"I prefer not to," he replied in a flutelike tone. It seemed to me that, while I had been addressing him, he carefully revolved every statement that I made; fully comprehended the meaning; could not gainsay the irresistible conclusion; but, at the same time, some paramount consideration prevailed with him to reply as he did.

"You are decided, then, not to comply with my request—a request made 40 according to common usage and common sense?"

He briefly gave me to understand, that on that point my judgment was sound. Yes: his decision was irreversible.

It is not seldom the case that, when a man is browbeaten in some unprecedented and violently unreasonable way, he begins to stagger in his own plainest faith. He begins, as it were, vaguely to surmise that, wonderful as it may be, all the justice and all the reason is on the other side. Accordingly, if any disinterested persons are present, he turns to them for some reinforcement of his own faltering mind.

"Turkey," said I, "what do you think of this? Am I not right?"

"With submission, sir," said Turkey, in his blandest tone, "I think that you are."

"Nippers," said I, "what do *you* think of it?" 45

"I think I should kick him out of the office."

(The reader, of nice perceptions, will here perceive that, it being morning, Turkey's answer is couched in polite and tranquil terms, but Nippers replies in ill-tempered ones. Or, to repeat a previous sentence, Nippers's ugly mood was on duty, and Turkey's off.)

"Ginger Nut," said I, willing to enlist the smallest suffrage in my behalf, "what do *you* think of it?"

"I think, sir, he's a little *luny*," replied Ginger Nut, with a grin.

"You hear what they say," said I, turning towards the screen, "come forth and 50 do your duty."

But he vouchsafed no reply. I pondered a moment in sore perplexity. But once more business hurried me. I determined again to postpone the consideration of this dilemma to my future leisure. With a little trouble we made out to examine the papers without Bartleby, though at every page or two Turkey deferentially dropped his opinion, that this proceeding was quite out of the common; while Nippers, twitching in his chair with a dyspeptic nervousness, ground out, between his set teeth, occasional hissing maledictions against the stubborn oaf behind the screen. And for his (Nippers's) part, this was the first and the last time he would do another man's business without pay.

Meanwhile Bartleby sat in his hermitage, oblivious to everything but his own peculiar business there.

Some days passed, the scrivener being employed upon another lengthy work. His late remarkable conduct led me to regard his ways narrowly. I observed that he never went to dinner; indeed, that he never went anywhere. As yet I had never, of my personal knowledge, known him to be outside of my office. He was a perpetual sentry in the corner. At about eleven o'clock though, in the morning, I noticed that Ginger Nut would advance towards the opening in Bartleby's screen, as if silently beckoned thither by a gesture invisible to me where I sat. The boy would then leave the office, jingling a few pence, and reappear with a handful of ginger-nuts, which he delivered in the hermitage, receiving two of the cakes for his trouble.

He lives, then, on ginger-nuts, thought I; never eats a dinner, properly speaking; he must be a vegetarian, then; but no; he never eats even vegetables; he eats nothing but ginger-nuts. My mind then ran on in reveries concerning the probable effects upon the human constitution of living entirely on ginger-nuts. Ginger-nuts are so called, because they contain ginger as one of their peculiar constituents, and the final flavoring one. Now, what was ginger? A hot, spicy thing. Was Bartleby hot and spicy? Not at all. Ginger, then, had no effect upon Bartleby. Probably he preferred it should have none.

Nothing so aggravates an earnest person as a passive resistance. If the indi- 55 vidual so resisted be of a not inhumane temper, and the resisting one perfectly harmless in his passivity, then, in the better moods of the former, he will endeavor charitably to construe to his imagination what proves impossible to be solved by his judgment. Even so, for the most part, I regarded Bartleby and his ways. Poor fellow! thought I, he means no mischief; it is plain he intends no insolence; his aspect sufficiently evinces that his eccentricities are involuntary. He is useful to me. I can get along with him. If I turn him away, the chances are he will fall in with some less-indulgent employer, and then he will be rudely treated, and perhaps driven forth miserably to starve. Yes. Here I can cheaply purchase a delicious self-approval. To befriend Bartleby; to humor him in his strange willfulness, will cost me little or nothing, while I lay up in my soul what will eventually prove a sweet morsel for my conscience. But this mood was not invariable with me. The passiveness of Bartleby sometimes irritated me. I felt strangely goaded on to encounter him in new opposition—to elicit some angry spark from him answerable to my own. But, indeed, I might as well have essayed to strike fire with my knuckles against a bit of Windsor soap. But one afternoon the evil impulse in me mastered me, and the following little scene ensued:

"Bartleby," said I, "when those papers are all copied, I will compare them with you."

"I would prefer not to."

"How? Surely you do not mean to persist in that mulish vagary?"

No answer.

I threw open the folding-doors near by, and, turning upon Turkey and Nippers, exclaimed:

"Bartleby a second time says, he won't examine his papers. What do you think of it, Turkey?"

It was afternoon, be it remembered. Turkey sat glowing like a brass boiler; his bald head steaming; his hands reeling among his blotted papers.

"Think of it?" roared Turkey; "I think I'll just step behind his screen, and black his eyes for him!"

So saying, Turkey rose to his feet and threw his arms into a pugilistic position. He was hurrying away to make good his promise, when I detained him, alarmed at the effect of incautiously rousing Turkey's combativeness after dinner.

"Sit down, Turkey," said I, "and hear what Nippers has to say. What do you think of it, Nippers? Would I not be justified in immediately dismissing Bartleby?"

"Excuse me, that is for you to decide, sir. I think his conduct quite unusual, and, indeed, unjust, as regards Turkey and myself. But it may only be a passing whim."

"Ah," exclaimed I, "you have strangely changed your mind, then—you speak very gently of him now."

"All beer," cried Turkey; "gentleness is effects of beer—Nippers and I dined together to-day. You see how gentle I am, sir. Shall I go and black his eyes?"

"You refer to Bartleby, I suppose. No, not to-day, Turkey," I replied; "pray, put up your fists."

I closed the doors, and again advanced towards Bartleby. I felt additional incentives tempting me to my fate. I burned to be rebelled against again. I remembered that Bartleby never left the office.

"Bartleby," said I, "Ginger Nut is away; just step around to the post office, won't you? (it was but a three minutes' walk), and see if there is anything for me."

"I would prefer not to."

"You *will* not?"

"I *prefer* not."

I staggered to my desk, and sat there in a deep study. My blind inveteracy 75 returned. Was there any other thing in which I could procure myself to be ignominiously repulsed by this lean, penniless wight?—my hired clerk? What added thing is there, perfectly reasonable, that he will be sure to refuse to do? "Bartleby!"

No answer.

"Bartleby," in a louder tone.

No answer.

"Bartleby," I roared.

Like a very ghost, agreeably to the laws of magical invocation, at the third 80 summons, he appeared at the entrance of his hermitage.

"Go to the next room, and tell Nippers to come to me."

"I prefer not to," he respectfully and slowly said and mildly disappeared.

"Very good, Bartleby," said I, in a quiet sort of serenely-severe, self-possessed tone, intimating the unalterable purpose of some terrible retribution very close at hand. At the moment I half intended something of the kind. But upon the whole, as it was drawing towards my dinner-hour, I thought it best to put on my hat and walk home for the day, suffering much from perplexity and distress of mind.

Shall I acknowledge it? The conclusion of this whole business was, that it soon became a fixed fact of my chambers, that a pale young scrivener, by the name of Bartleby, had a desk there; that he copied for me at the usual rate of four cents a folio (one hundred words); but he was permanently exempt from examining the work done by him, that duty being transferred to Turkey and Nippers, out of compliment, doubtless, to their superior acuteness; moreover, said Bartleby was never, on any account, to be dispatched on the most trivial errand of any sort; and that even if entreated to take upon him such a matter, it was generally understood that he would "prefer not to"—in other words, he would refuse point blank.

As days passed on, I became considerably reconciled to Bartleby. His steadi- 85 ness, his freedom from all dissipation, his incessant industry (except when he chose to throw himself into a standing revery behind his screen), his great stillness, his unalterableness of demeanor under all circumstances, made him a valuable acquisition. One prime thing was this—*he was always there*—first in the morning, continually through the day, and the last at night. I had a singular confidence in his honesty. I felt my most precious papers perfectly safe in his hands. Sometimes, to be sure, I could not, for the very soul of me, avoid falling into sudden spasmodic passions with him. For it was exceeding difficult to bear in mind all the time those strange peculiarities, privileges, and unheard of exemptions, forming the tacit stipulations on Bartleby's part under which he remained in my office. Now and then, in the eagerness of dispatching pressing business, I would inadvertently summon Bartleby, in a short, rapid tone, to put his finger, say, on the incipient tie of a bit of red tape with which I was about compressing some papers. Of course, from behind the screen the usual answer, "I prefer not to," was sure to come; and then, how could a human creature, with the common infirmities of our nature, refrain from bitterly exclaiming upon such perverseness—such unreasonableness? However, every added repulse of this sort which I received only tended to lessen the probability of my repeating the inadvertence.

Here it must be said, that according to the custom of most legal gentlemen occupying chambers in densely-populated law buildings, there were several keys to my door. One was kept by a woman residing in the attic, which person weekly scrubbed and daily swept and dusted my apartments. Another was kept by Turkey for convenience sake. The third I sometimes carried in my own pocket. The fourth I knew not who had.

Now, one Sunday morning I happened to go to Trinity Church, to hear a celebrated preacher, and finding myself rather early on the ground I thought I would walk round to my chambers for a while. Luckily I had my key with me; but upon applying it to the lock, I found it resisted by something inserted from the inside. Quite surprised, I called out; when to my consternation a key was turned from within; and thrusting his lean visage at me, and holding the door ajar, the apparition of Bartleby appeared, in his shirt sleeves, and otherwise in a strangely tattered *déshabillé*, saying quietly that he was sorry, but he was deeply engaged just then, and—preferred not admitting me at present. In a brief word or two, he moreover added, that perhaps I had better walk around the block two or three times, and by that time he would probably have concluded his affairs.

Now, the utterly unsurmised appearance of Bartleby, tenanting my law-chambers of a Sunday morning, with his cadaverously gentlemanly *nonchalance*, yet withal firm and self-possessed, had such a strange effect upon me, that incontinently I slunk away from my own door, and did as desired. But not without sundry twinges of impotent rebellion against the mild effrontery of this unaccountable scrivener. Indeed, it was his wonderful mildness chiefly, which not only disarmed me, but unmanned me as it were. For I consider that one, for the time, is somehow unmanned when he tranquilly permits his hired clerk to dictate to him, and order him away from his own premises. Furthermore, I was full of uneasiness as to what Bartleby could possibly be doing in my office in his shirt sleeves, and in an otherwise dismantled condition of a Sunday morning. Was anything amiss going on? Nay, that was out of the question. It was not to be thought of for a moment that Bartleby was an immoral person. But what could he be doing there?—copying? Nay again, whatever might be his eccentricities, Bartleby was an eminently decorous person. He would be the last man to sit down to his desk in any state approaching to nudity. Besides, it was Sunday; and there was something about Bartleby that forbade the supposition that he would by any secular occupation violate the proprieties of the day.

Nevertheless, my mind was not pacified; and full of a restless curiosity, at last I returned to the door. Without hindrance I inserted my key, opened it, and entered. Bartleby was not to be seen. I looked round anxiously, peeped behind his screen; but it was very plain that he was gone. Upon more closely examining the place, I surmised that for an indefinite period Bartleby must have eaten, dressed, and slept in my office, and that, too, without plate, mirror, or bed. The cushioned seat of a rickety old sofa in one corner bore the faint impress of a lean, reclining form. Rolled away under his desk, I found a blanket; under the empty grate, a blacking box and brush; on a chair, a tin basin, with soap and a ragged towel; in a newspaper a few crumbs of ginger-nuts and a morsel of cheese. Yes, thought I, it is evident enough that Bartleby has been making his home here, keeping bachelor's hall all by himself. Immediately then the thought came sweeping across me, what miserable friendlessness and loneliness are here revealed! His poverty is great; but his solitude, how horrible! Think of it. Of a Sunday, Wall Street is deserted as Petra;[5] and every night of every day it is an emptiness. This building, too, which of week-days hums with industry and life, at nightfall echoes with sheer vacancy, and all through Sunday is forlorn. And here Bartleby makes his home; sole spectator of a solitude which he has seen all populous—a sort of innocent and transformed Marius brooding among the ruins of Carthage![6]

For the first time in my life a feeling of over-powering stinging melancholy 90 seized me. Before, I had never experienced aught but a not unpleasing sadness. The bond of a common humanity now drew me irresistibly to gloom. A fraternal melancholy! For both I and Bartleby were sons of Adam. I remembered the bright silks and sparkling faces I had seen that day, in gala trim, swan-like sailing down the Mississippi of Broadway; and I contrasted them with the pallid copyist, and thought to myself, Ah, happiness courts the light, so we deem the world is gay; but misery hides aloof, so we deem that misery there is none. These sad fancyings—chimeras, doubtless, of a sick and silly brain—led on to other and more special thoughts, concerning the eccentricities of Bartleby. Presentiments of strange discoveries hovered round me. The scrivener's pale form appeared to me laid out, among uncaring strangers, in its shivering winding sheet.

Suddenly I was attracted by Bartleby's closed desk, the key in open sight left in the lock.

I mean no mischief, seek the gratification of no heartless curiosity, thought I; besides, the desk is mine, and its contents, too, so I will make bold to look within. Everything was methodically arranged, the papers smoothly placed. The pigeon holes were deep, and removing the files of documents, I groped into their recesses. Presently I felt something there, and dragged it out. It was an old bandanna handkerchief, heavy and knotted. I opened it, and saw it was a saving's bank.

I now recalled all the quiet mysteries which I had noted in the man. I remembered that he never spoke but to answer; that, though at intervals he had considerable time to himself, yet I had never seen him reading—no, not even a newspaper; that for long periods he would stand looking out, at his pale window behind the screen, upon the dead brick wall; I was quite sure he never visited any refectory or eating house; while his pale face clearly indicated that he never drank beer like Turkey; or tea and coffee even, like other men; that

[5] A city in Palestine found by explorers in 1812. It had been deserted and lost for centuries.
[6] Gaius Marius (155–86 BCE), a plebeian general who was forced to flee from Rome. Nineteenth-century democratic literature sometimes pictured him old and alone among the ruins of Carthage.

he never went anywhere in particular that I could learn; never went out for a walk, unless, indeed, that was the case at present; that he had declined telling who he was, or whence he came, or whether he had any relatives in the world; that though so thin and pale, he never complained of ill health. And more than all, I remembered a certain unconscious air of pallid—how shall I call it?—of pallid haughtiness, say, or rather an austere reserve about him, which had positively awed me into my tame compliance with his eccentricities, when I had feared to ask him to do the slightest incidental thing for me, even though I might know, from his long-continued motionlessness, that behind his screen he must be standing in one of those dead-wall reveries of his.

Revolving all these things, and coupling them with the recently discovered fact, that he made my office his constant abiding place and home, and not forgetful of his morbid moodiness; revolving all these things, a prudential feeling began to steal over me. My first emotions had been those of pure melancholy and sincerest pity; but just in proportion as the forlornness of Bartleby grew and grew to my imagination, did that same melancholy merge into fear, that pity into repulsion. So true it is, and so terrible, too, that up to a certain point the thought or sight of misery enlists our best affections; but, in certain special cases, beyond that point it does not. They err who would assert that invariably this is owing to the inherent selfishness of the human heart. It rather proceeds from a certain hopelessness of remedying excessive and organic ill. To a sensitive being, pity is not seldom pain. And when at last it is perceived that such pity cannot lead to effectual succor, common sense bids the soul be rid of it. What I saw that morning persuaded me that the scrivener was the victim of innate and incurable disorder. I might give alms to his body; but his body did not pain him; it was his soul that suffered, and his soul I could not reach.

I did not accomplish the purpose of going to Trinity Church that morning. Somehow, the things I had seen disqualified me for the time from church-going. I walked homeward, thinking what I would do with Bartleby. Finally, I resolved upon this—I would put certain calm questions to him the next morning, touching his history, etc., and if he declined to answer them openly and unreservedly (and I supposed he would prefer not), then to give him a twenty dollar bill over and above whatever I might owe him, and tell him his services were no longer required; but that if in any other way I could assist him, I would be happy to do so, especially if he desired to return to his native place, wherever that might be, I would willingly help to defray the expenses. Moreover, if, after reaching home, he found himself at any time in want of aid, a letter from him would be sure of a reply.

The next morning came.

"Bartleby," said I, gently calling to him behind his screen.

No reply.

"Bartleby," said I, in a still gentler tone, "come here; I am not going to ask you to do anything you would prefer not to do—I simply wish to speak to you."

Upon this he noiselessly slid into view. 100

"Will you tell me, Bartleby, where you were born?"

"I would prefer not to."

"Will you tell me *anything* about yourself?"

"I would prefer not to."

"But what reasonable objection can you have to speak to me? I feel friendly 105
towards you."

He did not look at me while I spoke, but kept his glance fixed upon my bust
of Cicero, which, as I then sat, was directly behind me, some six inches above
my head.

"What is your answer, Bartleby," said I, after waiting a considerable time for
a reply, during which his countenance remained immovable, only there was
the faintest conceivable tremor of the white attenuated mouth.

"At present I prefer to give no answer," he said, and retired into his hermitage.

It was rather weak in me I confess, but his manner, on this occasion,
nettled me. Not only did there seem to lurk in it a certain calm disdain, but his
perverseness seemed ungrateful, considering the undeniable good usage and
indulgence he had received from me.

Again I sat ruminating what I should do. Mortified as I was at his behavior, 110
and resolved as I had been to dismiss him when I entered my office, nevertheless I strangely felt something superstitious knocking at my heart, and forbidding me to carry out my purpose, and denouncing me for a villain if I dared
to breathe one bitter word against this forlornest of mankind. At last, familiarly drawing my chair behind his screen, I sat down and said: "Bartleby, never
mind, then, about revealing your history; but let me entreat you, as a friend, to
comply as far as may be with the usages of this office. Say now, you will help
to examine papers tomorrow or next day: in short, say now, that in a day or
two you will begin to be a little reasonable—say so, Bartleby."

"At present I would prefer not to be a little reasonable," was his mildly cadaverous reply.

Just then the folding-doors opened, and Nippers approached. He seemed
suffering from an unusually bad night's rest, induced by severer indigestion
than common. He overheard those final words of Bartleby.

"*Prefer not*, eh?" gritted Nippers—"I'd *prefer* him, if I were you, sir," addressing me—"I'd *prefer* him; I'd give him preferences, the stubborn mule! What is
it, sir, pray, that he *prefers* not to do now?"

Bartleby moved not a limb.

"Mr. Nippers," said I, "I'd prefer that you would withdraw for the present." 115

Somehow, of late, I had got into the way of involuntarily using this word "prefer" upon all sorts of not exactly suitable occasions. And I trembled to think that
my contact with the scrivener had already and seriously affected me in a mental
way. And what further and deeper aberration might it not yet produce? This
apprehension had not been without efficacy in determining me to summary
measures.

As Nippers, looking very sour and sulky, was departing, Turkey blandly and
deferentially approached.

"With submission, sir," said he, "yesterday I was thinking about Bartleby here, and I think that if he would but prefer to take a quart of good ale every day, it would do much towards mending him, and enabling him to assist in examining his papers."

"So you have got the word, too," said I, slightly excited.

"With submission, what word, sir," asked Turkey, respectfully crowding himself into the contracted space behind the screen, and by so doing, making me jostle the scrivener. "What word, sir?" 120

"I would prefer to be left alone here," said Bartleby, as if offended at being mobbed in his privacy.

"*That's* the word, Turkey," said I—"*that's* it."

"Oh, *prefer*? oh yes—queer word. I never use it myself. But, sir, as I was saying, if he would but prefer—"

"Turkey," interrupted I, "you will please withdraw."

"Oh certainly, sir, if you prefer that I should." 125

As he opened the folding-door to retire, Nippers at his desk caught a glimpse of me, and asked whether I would prefer to have a certain paper copied on blue paper or white. He did not in the least roguishly accent the word prefer. It was plain that it involuntarily rolled from his tongue. I thought to myself, surely I must get rid of a demented man, who already has in some degree turned the tongues, if not the heads of myself and clerks. But I thought it prudent not to break the dismission at once.

The next day I noticed that Bartleby did nothing but stand at his window in his dead-wall revery. Upon asking him why he did not write, he said that he had decided upon doing no more writing.

"Why, how now? What next?" exclaimed I, "do no more writing?"

"No more."

"And what is the reason?" 130

"Do you not see the reason for yourself?" he indifferently replied.

I looked steadfastly at him, and perceived that his eyes looked dull and glazed. Instantly it occurred to me, that his unexampled diligence in copying by his dim window for the first few weeks of his stay with me might have temporarily impaired his vision.

I was touched. I said something in condolence with him. I hinted that of course he did wisely in abstaining from writing for a while; and urged him to embrace that opportunity of taking wholesome exercise in the open air. This, however, he did not do. A few days after this, my other clerks being absent, and being in a great hurry to dispatch certain letters by the mail, I thought that, having nothing else earthly to do, Bartleby would surely be less inflexible than usual, and carry these letters to the post office. But he blankly declined. So, much to my inconvenience, I went myself.

Still added days went by. Whether Bartleby's eyes improved or not, I could not say. To all appearance, I thought they did. But when I asked him if they did, he vouchsafed no answer. At all events, he would do no copying. At last, in reply to my urgings, he informed me that he had permanently given up copying.

"What!" exclaimed I; "suppose your eyes should get entirely well—better 135
than ever before—would you not copy then?"

"I have given up copying," he answered, and slid aside.

He remained as ever, a fixture in my chamber. Nay—if that were possible—
he became still more of a fixture than before. What was to be done? He would
do nothing in the office; why should he stay there? In plain fact, he had now
become a millstone to me, not only useless as a necklace, but afflictive to bear.
Yet I was sorry for him. I speak less than truth when I say that, on his own
account, he occasioned me uneasiness. If he would but have named a single relative or friend, I would instantly have written, and urged their taking the poor
fellow away to some convenient retreat. But he seemed alone, absolutely alone
in the universe. A bit of wreck in the mid-Atlantic. At length, necessities connected with my business tyrannized over all other considerations. Decently as
I could, I told Bartleby that in six days time he must unconditionally leave the
office. I warned him to take measures, in the interval, for procuring some other
abode. I offered to assist him in this endeavor, if he himself would but take the
first step towards a removal. "And when you finally quit me, Bartleby," added I,
"I shall see that you go not away entirely unprovided. Six days from this hour,
remember."

At the expiration of that period, I peeped behind the screen, and lo! Bartleby
was there.

I buttoned up my coat, balanced myself; advanced slowly towards him,
touched his shoulder, and said, "The time has come; you must quit this place; I
am sorry for you; here is money; but you must go."

"I would prefer not," he replied, with his back still towards me. 140

"You *must*."

He remained silent.

Now I had an unbounded confidence in this man's common honesty. He
had frequently restored to me sixpences and shillings carelessly dropped upon
the floor, for I am apt to be very reckless in such shirt-button affairs. The proceeding, then, which followed will not be deemed extraordinary.

"Bartleby," said I, "I owe you twelve dollars on account; here are thirty-two, the
odd twenty are yours—Will you take it?" and I handed the bills towards him.

But he made no motion. 145

"I will leave them here, then," putting them under a weight on the table.
Then taking my hat and cane and going to the door, I tranquilly turned and
added—"After you have removed your things from these offices, Bartleby,
you will of course lock the door—since every one is now gone for the day but
you—and if you please, slip your key underneath the mat, so that I may have
it in the morning. I shall not see you again; so good-by to you. If, hereafter, in
your new place of abode, I can be of any service to you, do not fail to advise me
by letter. Good-by, Bartleby, and fare you well."

But he answered not a word; like the last column of some ruined temple, he
remained standing mute and solitary in the middle of the otherwise deserted
room.

As I walked home in a pensive mood, my vanity got the better of my pity. I could not but highly plume myself on my masterly management in getting rid of Bartleby. Masterly I call it, and such it must appear to any dispassionate thinker. The beauty of my procedure seemed to consist in its perfect quietness. There was no vulgar bullying, no bravado of any sort, no choleric hectoring, and striding to and fro across the apartment, jerking out vehement commands for Bartleby to bundle himself off with his beggarly traps. Nothing of the kind. Without loudly bidding Bartleby depart—as an inferior genius might have done—I *assumed* the ground that depart he must; and upon that assumption built all I had to say. The more I thought over my procedure, the more I was charmed with it. Nevertheless, next morning, upon awakening, I had my doubts—I had somehow slept off the fumes of vanity. One of the coolest and wisest hours a man has, is just after he awakes in the morning. My procedure seemed as sagacious as ever— but only in theory. How it would prove in practice—there was the rub. It was truly a beautiful thought to have assumed Bartleby's departure; but, after all, that assumption was simply my own, and none of Bartleby's. The great point was, not whether I had assumed that he would quit me, but whether he would prefer to do so. He was more a man of preferences than assumptions.

After breakfast, I walked down town, arguing the probabilities *pro* and *con*. One moment I thought it would prove a miserable failure, and Bartleby would be found all alive at my office as usual; the next moment it seemed certain that I should find his chair empty. And so I kept veering about. At the corner of Broadway and Canal Street, I saw quite an excited group of people standing in earnest conversation.

"I'll take odds he doesn't," said a voice as I passed.   150

"Doesn't go?—done!" said I; "put up your money."

I was instinctively putting my hand in my pocket to produce my own, when I remembered that this was an election day. The words I had overheard bore no reference to Bartleby, but to the success or non-success of some candidate for the mayoralty. In my intent frame of mind, I had, as it were, imagined that all Broadway shared in my excitement, and were debating the same question with me. I passed on, very thankful that the uproar of the street screened my momentary absent-mindedness.

As I had intended, I was earlier than usual at my office door. I stood listening for a moment. All was still. He must be gone. I tried the knob. The door was locked. Yes, my procedure had worked to a charm; he indeed must be vanished. Yet a certain melancholy mixed with this: I was almost sorry for my brilliant success. I was fumbling under the door mat for the key, which Bartleby was to have left there for me, when accidentally my knee knocked against a panel, producing a summoning sound, and in response a voice came to me from within—"Not yet; I am occupied."

It was Bartleby.

I was thunderstruck. For an instant I stood like the man who, pipe in mouth,   155
was killed one cloudless afternoon long ago in Virginia, by summer lightning;

at his own warm open window he was killed, and remained leaning out there upon the dreamy afternoon, till some one touched him, when he fell.

"Not gone!" I murmured at last. But again obeying that wondrous ascendancy which the inscrutable scrivener had over me, and from which ascendancy, for all my chafing, I could not completely escape, I slowly went down stairs and out into the street, and while walking round the block, considered what I should next do in this unheard-of perplexity. Turn the man out by an actual thrusting I could not; to drive him away by calling him hard names would not do; calling in the police was an unpleasant idea; and yet, permit him to enjoy his cadaverous triumph over me—this, too, I could not think of. What was to be done? or, if nothing could be done, was there anything further that I could *assume* in the matter? Yes, as before I had prospectively assumed that Bartleby would depart, so now I might retrospectively assume that departed he was. In the legitimate carrying out of this assumption, I might enter my office in a great hurry, and pretending not to see Bartleby at all, walk straight against him as if he were air. Such a proceeding would in a singular degree have the appearance of a home-thrust. It was hardly possible that Bartleby could withstand such an application of the doctrine of assumption. But upon second thoughts the success of the plan seemed rather dubious. I resolved to argue the matter over with him again.

"Bartleby," said I, entering the office, with a quietly severe expression, "I am seriously displeased. I am pained, Bartleby. I had thought better of you. I had imagined you of such a gentlemanly organization, that in any delicate dilemma a slight hint would suffice—in short, an assumption. But it appears I am deceived. Why," I added, unaffectedly starting, "you have not even touched that money yet," pointing to it, just where I had left it the evening previous.

He answered nothing.

"Will you, or will you not, quit me?" I now demanded in a sudden passion, advancing close to him.

"I would prefer *not* to quit you," he replied, gently emphasizing the *not*. 160

"What earthly right have you to stay here? Do you pay any rent? Do you pay my taxes? Or is this property yours?"

He answered nothing.

"Are you ready to go on and write now? Are your eyes recovered? Could you copy a small paper for me this morning? or help examine a few lines? or step round to the post office? In a word, will you do anything at all, to give a coloring to your refusal to depart the premises?"

He silently retired into his hermitage.

I was now in such a state of nervous resentment that I thought it but pru- 165 dent to check myself at present from further demonstrations. Bartleby and I were alone. I remembered the tragedy of the unfortunate Adams and the still more unfortunate Colt in the solitary office of the latter; and how poor Colt, being dreadfully incensed by Adams, and imprudently permitting himself to get wildly excited, was at unawares hurried into his fatal act—an act which certainly no man could possibly deplore more than the actor himself.[7] Often it had occurred to me in my ponderings upon the subject that had that altercation taken place in the public street, or at a private residence, it would not have terminated as it did. It was the circumstance of being alone in a solitary office, up stairs, of a building entirely unhallowed by humanizing domestic associations—an uncarpeted office, doubtless, of a dusty, haggard sort of appearance—this it must have been, which greatly helped to enhance the irritable desperation of the hapless Colt.

But when this old Adam of resentment rose in me and tempted me concerning Bartleby, I grappled him and threw him. How? Why, simply by recalling the divine injunction: "A new commandment give I unto you, that ye love one another." Yes, this it was that saved me. Aside from higher considerations, charity often operates as a vastly wise and prudent principle—a great safeguard to its possessor. Men have committed murder for jealousy's sake, and anger's sake, and hatred's sake, and selfishness' sake, and spiritual pride's sake; but no man, that ever I heard of, ever committed a diabolical murder for sweet charity's sake. Mere self-interest, then, if no better motive can be enlisted, should, especially with high-tempered men, prompt all beings to charity and philanthropy. At any rate, upon the occasion in question, I strove to drown my exasperated feelings towards the scrivener by benevolently construing his conduct. Poor fellow, poor fellow! thought I, he don't mean anything; and besides, he has seen hard times, and ought to be indulged.

I endeavored, also, immediately to occupy myself, and at the same time to comfort my despondency. I tried to fancy, that in the course of the morning, at such time as might prove agreeable to him, Bartleby, of his own free accord, would emerge from his hermitage and take up some decided line of march in the direction of the door. But no. Half-past twelve o'clock came; Turkey began to glow in the face, overturn his inkstand, and become generally obstreperous; Nippers abated down into quietude and courtesy; Ginger Nut munched his noon apple; and Bartleby remained standing at his window in one of his profoundest dead-wall reveries. Will it be credited? Ought I to acknowledge it? That afternoon I left the office without saying one further word to him.

Some days now passed, during which, at leisure intervals I looked a little into "Edwards on the Will," and "Priestley on Necessity."[8] Under the circumstances, those books induced a salutary feeling. Gradually I slid into the persuasion that these troubles of mine, touching the scrivener, had been all predestinated from eternity, and Bartleby was billeted upon me for some mysterious purpose of an all-wise Providence, which it was not for a mere mortal like me to fathom. Yes, Bartleby, stay there behind your screen, thought I; I shall persecute you no more; you are harmless and noiseless as any of these old chairs; in short, I never feel so private as when I know you are here. At last I see it, I feel it; I penetrate

---

[7] A sensational 1841 homicide case in which John C. Colt murdered printer Samuel Adams in a fit of passion.

[8] Jonathan Edwards (1703–1758), American theologian, and Joseph Priestley (1733–1804), English clergyman and chemist, both held that a person's life was predetermined.

to the predestinated purpose of my life. I am content. Others may have loftier parts to enact; but my mission in this world, Bartleby, is to furnish you with office-room for such period as you may see fit to remain.

I believe that this wise and blessed frame of mind would have continued with me, had it not been for the unsolicited and uncharitable remarks obtruded upon me by my professional friends who visited the rooms. But thus it often is, that the constant friction of illiberal minds wears out at last the best resolves of the more generous. Though to be sure, when I reflected upon it, it was not strange that people entering my office should be struck by the peculiar aspect of the unaccountable Bartleby, and so be tempted to throw out some sinister observations concerning him. Sometimes an attorney, having business with me, and calling at my office, and finding no one but the scrivener there, would undertake to obtain some sort of precise information from him touching my whereabouts; but without heeding his idle talk, Bartleby would remain standing immovable in the middle of the room. So after contemplating him in that position for a time, the attorney would depart, no wiser than he came.

Also, when a reference was going on, and the room full of lawyers and witnesses, and business driving fast, some deeply-occupied legal gentleman present, seeing Bartleby wholly unemployed, would request him to run round to his (the legal gentleman's) office and fetch some papers for him. Thereupon, Bartleby would tranquilly decline, and yet remain idle as before. Then the lawyer would give a great stare, and turn to me. And what could I say? At last I was made aware that all through the circle of my professional acquaintance, a whisper of wonder was running round, having reference to the strange creature I kept at my office. This worried me very much. And as the idea came upon me of his possibly turning out a long-lived man, and keep occupying my chambers, and denying my authority; and perplexing my visitors; and scandalizing my professional reputation; and casting a general gloom over the premises; keeping soul and body together to the last upon his savings (for doubtless he spent but half a dime a day), and in the end perhaps outlive me, and claim possession of my office by right of his perpetual occupancy: as all these dark anticipations crowded upon me more and more, and my friends continually intruded their relentless remarks upon the apparition in my room; a great change was wrought in me. I resolved to gather all my faculties together, and forever rid me of this intolerable incubus.

Ere revolving any complicated project, however, adapted to this end, I first simply suggested to Bartleby the propriety of his permanent departure. In a calm and serious tone, I commended the idea to his careful and mature consideration. But, having taken three days to meditate upon it, he apprised me, that his original determination remained the same; in short, that he still preferred to abide with me.

What shall I do? I now said to myself, buttoning up my coat to the last button. What shall I do? what ought I to do? what does conscience say I *should* do with this man, or, rather, ghost. Rid myself of him, I must; go, he shall. But how? You will not thrust him, the poor, pale, passive mortal—you will not thrust such a

170

helpless creature out of your door? you will not dishonor yourself by such cruelty? No, I will not, I cannot do that. Rather would I let him live and die here,
and then mason up his remains in the wall. What, then, will you do? For all your
coaxing, he will not budge. Bribes he leaves under your own paper-weight on
your table; in short, it is quite plain that he prefers to cling to you.

Then something severe, something unusual must be done. What! surely
you will not have him collared by a constable, and commit his innocent pallor to the common jail? And upon what ground could you procure such a
thing to be done?—a vagrant, is he? What! he a vagrant, a wanderer, who
refuses to budge? It is because he will *not* be a vagrant, then, that you seek to
count him *as* a vagrant. That is too absurd. No visible means of support: there
I have him. Wrong again: for indubitably he *does* support himself, and that
is the only unanswerable proof that any man can show of his possessing the
means so to do. No more, then. Since he will not quit me, I must quit him. I
will change my offices; I will move elsewhere, and give him fair notice, that if
I find him in my new premises I will then proceed against him as a common
trespasser.

Acting accordingly, next day I thus addressed him: "I find these chambers
too far from the City Hall; the air is unwholesome. In a word, I propose to
remove my offices next week, and shall no longer require your services. I tell
you this now, in order that you may seek another place."

He made no reply, and nothing more was said. 175

On the appointed day I engaged carts and men, proceeded to my chambers,
and, having but little furniture, everything was removed in a few hours. Throughout, the scrivener remained standing behind the screen, which I directed to be
removed the last thing. It was withdrawn; and, being folded up like a huge folio,
left him the motionless occupant of a naked room. I stood in the entry watching
him a moment, while something from within me upbraided me.

I re-entered, with my hand in my pocket—and—and my heart in my mouth.

"Good-by, Bartleby; I am going—good-by, and God some way bless you;
and take that," slipping something in his hand. But it dropped upon the floor,
and then—strange to say—I tore myself from him whom I had so longed to be
rid of.

Established in my new quarters, for a day or two I kept the door locked, and
started at every footfall in the passages. When I returned to my rooms, after
any little absence, I would pause at the threshold for an instant, and attentively
listen, ere applying my key. But these fears were needless. Bartleby never came
nigh me.

I thought all was going well, when a perturbed-looking stranger visited 180
me, inquiring whether I was the person who had recently occupied rooms at
No. —— Wall Street.

Full of forebodings, I replied that I was.

"Then, sir," said the stranger, who proved a lawyer, "you are responsible for
the man you left there. He refuses to do any copying; he refuses to do anything;
he says he prefers not to; and he refuses to quit the premises."

"I am very sorry, sir," said I, with assumed tranquillity, but an inward tremor, "but, really, the man you allude to is nothing to me—he is no relation or apprentice of mine, that you should hold me responsible for him."

"In mercy's name, who is he?"

"I certainly cannot inform you. I know nothing about him. Formerly I   185 employed him as a copyist; but he has done nothing for me now for some time past."

"I shall settle him, then—good morning, sir."

Several days passed, and I heard nothing more; and, though I often felt a charitable prompting to call at the place and see poor Bartleby, yet a certain squeamishness, of I know not what, withheld me.

All is over with him, by this time, thought I, at last, when, through another week, no further intelligence reached me. But, coming to my room the day after, I found several persons waiting at my door in a high state of nervous excitement.

"That's the man—here he comes," cried the foremost one, whom I recognized as the lawyer who had previously called upon me alone.

"You must take him away, sir, at once," cried a portly person among them,   190 advancing upon me, and whom I knew to be the landlord of No. ——— Wall Street. "These gentlemen, my tenants, cannot stand it any longer; Mr. B———," pointing to the lawyer, "has turned him out of his room, and he now persists in haunting the building generally, sitting upon the banisters of the stairs by day, and sleeping in the entry by night. Everybody is concerned; clients are leaving the offices; some fears are entertained of a mob; something you must do, and that without delay."

Aghast at this torrent, I fell back before it, and would fain have locked myself in my new quarters. In vain I persisted that Bartleby was nothing to me—no more than to any one else. In vain—I was the last person known to have anything to do with him, and they held me to the terrible account. Fearful, then, of being exposed in the papers (as one person present obscurely threatened), I considered the matter, and, at length, said, that if the lawyer would give me a confidential interview with the scrivener, in his (the lawyer's) own room, I would, that afternoon, strive my best to rid them of the nuisance they complained of.

Going up stairs to my old haunt, there was Bartleby silently sitting upon the banister at the landing.

"What are you doing here, Bartleby?" said I.

"Sitting upon the banister," he mildly replied.

I motioned him into the lawyer's room, who then left us.   195

"Bartleby," said I, "are you aware that you are the cause of great tribulation to me, by persisting in occupying the entry after being dismissed from the office?"

No answer.

"Now one of two things must take place. Either you must do something, or something must be done to you. Now what sort of business would you like to engage in? Would you like to re-engage in copying for some one?"

"No; I would prefer not to make any change."

"Would you like a clerkship in a dry-goods store?" 200

"There is too much confinement about that. No, I would not like a clerkship; but I am not particular."

"Too much confinement," I cried, "why, you keep yourself confined all the time!"

"I would prefer not to take a clerkship," he rejoined, as if to settle that little item at once.

"How would a bar-tender's business suit you? There is no trying of the eye-sight in that."

"I would not like it at all; though, as I said before, I am not particular." 205

His unwonted wordiness inspirited me. I returned to the charge.

"Well, then, would you like to travel through the country collecting bills for the merchants? That would improve your health."

"No, I would prefer to be doing something else."

"How, then, would going as a companion to Europe, to entertain some young gentleman with your conversation—how would that suit you?"

"Not at all. It does not strike me that there is anything definite about that. I 210 like to be stationary. But I am not particular."

"Stationary you shall be, then," I cried, now losing all patience, and, for the first time in all my exasperating connection with him, fairly flying into a passion. "If you do not go away from these premises before night, I shall feel bound—indeed, I *am* bound—to—to—to quit the premises myself!" I rather absurdly concluded, knowing not with what possible threat to try to frighten his immobility into compliance. Despairing of all further efforts, I was precipi-tately leaving him, when a final thought occurred to me—one which had not been wholly unindulged before.

"Bartleby," said I, in the kindest tone I could assume under such excit-ing circumstances, "will you go home with me now—not to my office, but my dwelling—and remain there till we can conclude upon some convenient arrangement for you at our leisure? Come, let us start now, right away."

"No: at present I would prefer not to make any change at all."

I answered nothing; but, effectually dodging every one by the sudden-ness and rapidity of my flight, rushed from the building, ran up Wall Street towards Broadway, and, jumping into the first omnibus, was soon removed from pursuit. As soon as tranquillity returned, I distinctly perceived that I had now done all that I possibly could, both in respect to the demands of the landlord and his tenants, and with regard to my own desire and sense of duty, to benefit Bartleby, and shield him from rude persecution. I now strove to be entirely care-free and quiescent; and my conscience justified me in the attempt; though, indeed, it was not so successful as I could have wished. So fearful was I of being again hunted out by the incensed landlord and his exas-perated tenants, that, surrendering my business to Nippers, for a few days, I drove about the upper part of the town and through the suburbs, in my rocka-way; crossed over to Jersey City and Hoboken, and paid fugitive visits to Man-hattanville and Astoria. In fact, I almost lived in my rockaway for the time.

When again I entered my office, lo, a note from the landlord lay upon the desk. I opened it with trembling hands. It informed me that the writer had sent to the police, and had Bartleby removed to the Tombs as a vagrant. Moreover, since I knew more about him than any one else, he wished me to appear at that place, and make a suitable statement of the facts. These tidings had a conflicting effect upon me. At first I was indignant; but, at last, almost approved. The landlord's energetic, summary disposition, had led him to adopt a procedure which I do not think I would have decided upon myself; and yet, as a last resort, under such peculiar circumstances, it seemed the only plan. 215

As I afterwards learned, the poor scrivener, when told that he must be conducted to the Tombs, offered not the slightest obstacle, but, in his pale, unmoving way, silently acquiesced.

Some of the compassionate and curious by-standers joined the party; and headed by one of the constables arm in arm with Bartleby, the silent procession filed its way through all the noise, and heat, and joy of the roaring thoroughfares at noon.

The same day I received the note, I went to the Tombs, or, to speak more properly, the Halls of Justice. Seeking the right officer, I stated the purpose of my call, and was informed that the individual I described was, indeed, within. I then assured the functionary that Bartleby was a perfectly honest man, and greatly to be compassionated, however unaccountably eccentric. I narrated all I knew, and closed by suggesting the idea of letting him remain in as indulgent confinement as possible, till something less harsh might be done— though, indeed, I hardly knew what. At all events, if nothing else could be decided upon, the alms-house must receive him. I then begged to have an interview.

Being under no disgraceful charge, and quite serene and harmless in all his ways, they had permitted him freely to wander about the prison, and, especially, in the inclosed grass-platted yards thereof. And so I found him there, standing all alone in the quietest of the yards, his face towards a high wall, while all around, from the narrow slits of the jail windows, I thought I saw peering out upon him the eyes of murderers and thieves.

"Bartleby!" 220

"I know you," he said, without looking round—"and I want nothing to say to you."

"It was not I that brought you here, Bartleby," said I, keenly pained at his implied suspicion. "And to you, this should not be so vile a place. Nothing reproachful attaches to you by being here. And see, it is not so sad a place as one might think. Look, there is the sky, and here is the grass."

"I know where I am," he replied, but would say nothing more, and so I left him.

As I entered the corridor again, a broad meat-like man, in an apron, accosted me, and, jerking his thumb over his shoulder, said—"Is that your friend?"

"Yes." 225

"Does he want to starve? If he does, let him live on the prison fare, that's all."

"Who are you?" asked I, not knowing what to make of such an unofficially speaking person in such a place.

"I am the grub-man. Such gentlemen as have friends here, hire me to provide them with something good to eat."

"Is this so?" said I, turning to the turnkey.

He said it was.

"Well, then," said I, slipping some silver into the grub-man's hands (for so they called him), "I want you to give particular attention to my friend there; let him have the best dinner you can get. And you must be as polite to him as possible."

"Introduce me, will you?" said the grub-man, looking at me with an expression which seemed to say he was all impatience for an opportunity to give a specimen of his breeding.

Thinking it would prove of benefit to the scrivener, I acquiesced; and, asking the grub-man his name, went up with him to Bartleby.

"Bartleby, this is a friend; you will find him very useful to you."

"Your sarvant, sir, your sarvant," said the grub-man, making a low salutation behind his apron. "Hope you find it pleasant here, sir; nice grounds—cool apartments—hope you'll stay with us some time—try to make it agreeable. What will you have for dinner to-day?"

"I prefer not to dine to-day," said Bartleby, turning away. "It would disagree with me; I am unused to dinners." So saying, he slowly moved to the other side of the inclosure, and took up a position fronting the deadwall.

"How's this?" said the grub-man, addressing me with a stare of astonishment. "He's odd, ain't he?"

"I think he is a little deranged," said I, sadly.

"Deranged? deranged is it? Well, now, upon my word, I thought that friend of yourn was a gentleman forger; they are always pale and genteel-like, them forgers. I can't help pity 'em—can't help it, sir. Did you know Monroe Edwards?" he added, touchingly, and paused. Then, laying his hand piteously on my shoulder, sighed, "he died of consumption at Sing-Sing.[9] So you weren't acquainted with Monroe?"

"No, I was never socially acquainted with any forgers. But I cannot stop longer. Look to my friend yonder. You will not lose by it. I will see you again."

Some few days after this, I again obtained admission to the Tombs, and went through the corridors in quest of Bartleby; but without finding him.

"I saw him coming from his cell not long ago," said a turnkey, "may be he's gone to loiter in the yards."

So I went in that direction.

"Are you looking for the silent man?" said another turnkey, passing me. "Yonder he lies—sleeping in the yard there. 'Tis not twenty minutes since I saw him lie down."

The yard was entirely quiet. It was not accessible to the common prisoners. The surrounding walls of amazing thickness, kept off all sounds behind them.

[9] The state prison near Ossining, New York.

The Egyptian character of the masonry weighed upon me with its gloom. But a soft imprisoned turf grew under foot. The heart of the eternal pyramids, it seemed, wherein, by some strange magic, through the clefts, grass-seed, dropped by birds, had sprung.

Strangely huddled at the base of the wall, his knees drawn up, and lying on his side, his head touching the cold stones, I saw the wasted Bartleby. But nothing stirred. I paused; then went close up to him; stooped over, and saw that his dim eyes were open; otherwise he seemed profoundly sleeping. Something prompted me to touch him. I felt his hand, when a tingling shiver ran up my arm and down my spine to my feet.

The round face of the grub-man peered upon me now. "His dinner is ready. Won't he dine to-day, either? Or does he live without dining?"

"Lives without dining," said I, and closed the eyes.

"Eh!—He's asleep, ain't he?"

"With kings and counselors," murmured I.

250

There would seem little need for proceeding further in this history. Imagination will readily supply the meagre recital of poor Bartleby's interment. But, ere parting with the reader, let me say, that if this little narrative has sufficiently interested him, to awaken curiosity as to who Bartleby was, and what manner of life he led prior to the present narrator's making his acquaintance, I can only reply, that in such curiosity I fully share, but am wholly unable to gratify it. Yet here I hardly know whether I should divulge one little item of rumor, which came to my ear a few months after the scrivener's decease. Upon what basis it rested, I could never ascertain; and hence, how true it is I cannot now tell. But, inasmuch as this vague report has not been without a certain suggestive interest to me, however said, it may prove the same with some others; and so I will briefly mention it. The report was this: that Bartleby had been a subordinate clerk in the Dead Letter[10] Office at Washington, from which he had been suddenly removed by a change in the administration. When I think over this rumor, hardly can I express the emotions which seize me. Dead letters! does it not sound like dead men? Conceive a man by nature and misfortune prone to a pallid hopelessness, can any business seem more fitted to heighten it than that of continually handling these dead letters, and assorting them for the flames? For by the cartload they are annually burned. Some times from out the folded paper the pale clerk takes a ring—the finger it was meant for, perhaps, moulders in the grave; a bank-note sent in swiftest charity—he whom it would relieve, nor eats nor hungers any more; pardon for those who died despairing; hope for those who died unhoping; good tidings for those who died stifled by unrelieved calamities. On errands of life, these letters speed to death.

Ah, Bartleby! Ah, humanity!

---

[10] A letter that is undeliverable and unreturnable.

FOR ANALYSIS

1. List a half dozen adjectives that describe the **narrator**. Would the narrator agree that these adjectives are accurate?

2. What is it about Bartleby that so intrigues and fascinates the narrator? Why does the narrator continue to feel a moral obligation to an employee who refuses to work and curtly rejects kind offers of help?

3. What thematic function do Turkey and Nippers serve?

4. As the narrator congratulates himself on the cleverness of his scheme to dismiss Bartleby, he becomes fascinated with his "assumptions" about how Bartleby will behave. Examine the passage (paras. 149–56), and show how it advances the narrator's growing awareness of what Bartleby represents.

5. Readers differ as to whether this is the story of Bartleby or the lawyer-narrator. What is your view?

6. Would it be fair to describe Bartleby as a rebel without a cause, as a young man who refuses to participate in a comfortable and well-ordered business world but fails to offer any alternative way of life? Write a paragraph or two explaining why or why not.

MAKING ARGUMENTS

Commentators on Occupy Wall Street (OWS) have discussed the movement's connections to Melville's "Bartleby, the Scrivener." Do a little reading on OWS and argue for or against those connections.

WRITING TOPICS

1. About midway through the story (paras. 87–94), the **narrator** discovers that Bartleby has been living in the law offices, and he is profoundly moved when his eyes fall on the scrivener's worldly possessions. Reread those paragraphs, and write an analysis showing how they describe the narrator's growing awareness of who Bartleby is.

2. With his final utterance, "Ah, Bartleby! Ah, humanity!" the narrator apparently penetrates the mystery of the silent scrivener. The comment suggests that the narrator sees Bartleby as a representative of humanity. In what sense might the narrator have come to see Bartleby in this light?

3. Why does Melville allow the narrator (and the reader) to discover so little about Bartleby and the causes of his behavior? All we learn of Bartleby's past is told in the next-to-last paragraph. What clues does this paragraph give us to the narrator's fascination with Bartleby?

MAKING CONNECTIONS

Compare and contrast Bartleby's rebellion to that of the **protagonist** in Updike's "A & P" (p. 92). What do we know about the motivations of each? How do we know what we know? How do the stories seem to want us to feel about each of these acts of rebellion and the protagonists who commit them?

FRANZ KAFKA   (1883–1924)

A HUNGER ARTIST[1]   1924

During these last decades the interest in professional fasting has markedly diminished. It used to pay very well to stage such great performances under one's own management, but today that is quite impossible. We live in a different world now. At one time the whole town took a lively interest in the hunger artist; from day to day of his fast the excitement mounted; everybody wanted to see him at least once a day; there were people who bought season tickets for the last few days and sat from morning till night in front of his small barred cage; even in the nighttime there were visiting hours, when the whole effect was heightened by torch flares; on fine days the cage was set out in the open air, and then it was the children's special treat to see the hunger artist; for their elders he was often just a joke that happened to be in fashion, but the children stood open-mouthed, holding each other's hands for greater security, marveling at him as he sat there pallid in black tights, with his ribs sticking out so prominently, not even on a seat but down among straw on the ground, sometimes giving a courteous nod, answering questions with a constrained smile, or perhaps stretching an arm through the bars so that one might feel how thin it was, and then again withdrawing deep into himself, paying no attention to anyone or anything, not even to the all-important striking of the clock that was the only piece of furniture in his cage, but merely staring into vacancy with half shut eyes, now and then taking a sip from a tiny glass of water to moisten his lips.

Besides casual onlookers there were also relays of permanent watchers selected by the public, usually butchers, strangely enough, and it was their task to watch the hunger artist day and night, three of them at a time, in case he should have some secret recourse to nourishment. This was nothing but a formality, instituted to reassure the masses, for the initiates knew well enough that during his fast the artist would never in any circumstances, not even under forcible compulsion, swallow the smallest morsel of food; the honor of his profession forbade it. Not every watcher, of course, was capable of understanding this; there were often groups of night watchers who were very lax in carrying out their duties and deliberately huddled together in a retired corner to play cards with great absorption, obviously intending to give the hunger artist the chance of a little refreshment, which they supposed he could draw from some private hoard. Nothing annoyed the artist more than such watchers; they made him miserable; they made his fast seem unendurable; sometimes he mastered his feebleness sufficiently to sing during their watch for as long as he could keep

---

[1] Translated by Edwin and Willa Muir.

going, to show them how unjust their suspicions were. But that was of little use; they only wondered at his cleverness in being able to fill his mouth even while singing. Much more to his taste were the watchers who sat close up to the bars, who were not content with the dim night lighting of the hall but focused him in the full glare of the electric pocket torch given them by the impresario. The harsh light did not trouble him at all, in any case he could never sleep properly, and he could always drowse a little, whatever the light, at any hour, even when the hall was thronged with noisy onlookers. He was quite happy at the prospect of spending a sleepless night with such watchers; he was ready to exchange jokes with them, to tell them stories out of his nomadic life, anything at all to keep them awake and demonstrate to them again that he had no eatables in his cage and that he was fasting as not one of them could fast. But his happiest moment was when the morning came and an enormous breakfast was brought them, at his expense, on which they flung themselves with the keen appetite of healthy men after a weary night of wakefulness. Of course there were people who argued that this breakfast was an unfair attempt to bribe the watchers, but that was going rather too far, and when they were invited to take on a night's vigil without a breakfast, merely for the sake of the cause, they made themselves scarce, although they stuck stubbornly to their suspicions.

Such suspicions, anyhow, were a necessary accompaniment to the profession of fasting. No one could possibly watch the hunger artist continuously, day and night, and so no one could produce first-hand evidence that the fast had really been rigorous and continuous; only the artist himself could know that, he was therefore bound to be the sole completely satisfied spectator of his own fast. Yet for other reasons he was never satisfied; it was not perhaps mere fasting that had brought him to such skeleton thinness that many people had regretfully to keep away from his exhibitions, because the sight of him was too much for them, perhaps it was dissatisfaction with himself that had worn him down. For he alone knew, what no other initiate knew, how easy it was to fast. It was the easiest thing in the world. He made no secret of this, yet people did not believe him, at the best they set him down as modest; most of them, however, thought he was out for publicity or else was some kind of cheat who found it easy to fast because he had discovered a way of making it easy, and then had the impudence to admit the fact, more or less. He had to put up with all that, and in the course of time had got used to it, but his inner dissatisfaction always rankled, and never yet, after any term of fasting—this must be granted to his credit—had he left the cage of his own free will. The longest period of fasting was fixed by his impresario at forty days, beyond that term he was not allowed to go, not even in great cities, and there was good reason for it, too. Experience had proved that for about forty days the interest of the public could be stimulated by a steadily increasing pressure of advertisement, but after that the town began to lose interest, sympathetic support began notably to fall off; there were of course local variations as between one town and another or one country and another, but as a general rule forty days marked the limit. So on the fortieth day the flower bedecked cage was opened, enthusiastic spectators filled the hall, a military band played, two doctors entered the cage to measure the results of the fast, which were announced through a megaphone, and finally two young ladies appeared, blissful at having been selected for the honor, to help the hunger artist down the few steps leading to a small table on which was spread a carefully chosen invalid repast. And at this very moment the artist always turned stubborn. True, he would entrust his bony arms to the outstretched helping hands of the ladies bending over him, but stand up he would not. Why stop fasting at this particular moment, after forty days of it? He had held out for a long time, an illimitably long time; why stop now, when he was in his best fasting form, or rather, not yet quite in his best fasting form? Why should he be cheated of the fame he would get for fasting longer, for being not only the record hunger artist of all time, which presumably he was already, but for beating his own record by a performance beyond human imagination, since he felt that there were no limits to his capacity for fasting? His public pretended to admire him so much, why should it have so little patience with him; if he could endure fasting longer, why shouldn't the public endure it? Besides, he was tired, he was comfortable sitting in the straw, and now he was supposed to lift himself to his full height and go down to a meal the very thought of which gave him a nausea that only the presence of the ladies kept him from betraying, and even that with an effort. And he looked up into the eyes of the ladies who were apparently so friendly and in reality so cruel, and shook his head, which felt too heavy on its strengthless neck. But then there happened yet again what always happened. The impresario came forward, without a word—for the band made speech impossible—lifted his arms in the air above the artist, as if inviting Heaven to look down upon its creature here in the straw, this suffering martyr, which indeed he was, although in quite another sense; grasped him round the emaciated waist, with exaggerated caution, so that the frail condition he was in might be appreciated; and committed him to the care of the blenching ladies, not without secretly giving him a shaking so that his legs and body tottered and swayed. The artist now submitted completely; his head lolled on his breast as if it had landed there by chance; his body was hollowed out; his legs in a spasm of self-preservation clung close to each other at the knees, yet scraped on the ground as if it were not really solid ground, as if they were only trying to find solid ground; and the whole weight of his body, a feather-weight after all, relapsed onto one of the ladies, who, looking round for help and panting a little—this post of honor was not at all what she had expected it to be—first stretched her neck as far as she could to keep her face at least free from contact with the artist, when finding this impossible, and her more fortunate companion not coming to her aid but merely holding extended on her own trembling hand the little bunch of knucklebones that was the artist's, to the great delight of the spectators burst into tears and had to be replaced by an attendant who had long been stationed in readiness. Then came the food, a little of which the impresario managed to get between the artist's lips, while he sat in a kind of half-fainting trance, to the accompaniment of cheerful patter designed to distract the public's attention from the artist's condition; after that a toast was drunk to the public, supposedly prompted by a whisper from the artist in the impresario's ear; the band confirmed it with a mighty flourish, the spectators melted away, and no one had any cause to be dissatisfied with the proceedings, no one except the hunger artist himself, he only, as always.

So he lived for many years, with small regular intervals of recuperation, in visible glory, honored by the world, yet in spite of that troubled in spirit, and all the more troubled because no one would take his trouble seriously. What comfort could he possibly need? What more could he possibly wish for? And if some good-natured person, feeling sorry for him, tried to console him by pointing out that his melancholy was probably caused by fasting; it could happen, especially when he had been fasting for some time, that he reacted with an outburst of fury and to the general alarm began to shake the bars of his cage like a wild animal. Yet the impresario had a way of punishing these outbreaks which he rather enjoyed putting into operation. He would apologize publicly for the artist's behavior, which was only to be excused, he admitted, because of the irritability caused by fasting; a condition hardly to be understood by well-fed people; then by natural transition he went on to mention the artist's equally incomprehensible boast that he could fast for much longer than he was doing; he praised the high ambition, the good will, the great self-denial undoubtedly implicit in such a statement; and then quite simply countered it by bringing out photographs, which were also on sale to the public, showing the artist on the fortieth day of a fast lying in bed almost dead from exhaustion. This perversion of the truth, familiar to the artist though it was, always unnerved him afresh and proved too much for him. What was a consequence of the premature ending of his fast was here presented as the cause of it! To fight against this lack of understanding, against a whole world of nonunderstanding, was impossible. Time and again in good faith he stood by the bars listening to the impresario, but as soon as the photographs appeared he always let go and sank with a groan back on to his straw, and the reassured public could once more come close and gaze at him.

A few years later when the witnesses of such scenes called them to mind, 5 they often failed to understand themselves at all. For meanwhile the aforementioned change in public interest had set in; it seemed to happen almost overnight; there may have been profound causes for it, but who was going to bother about that; at any rate the pampered hunger artist suddenly found himself deserted one fine day by the amusement seekers, who were streaming past him to other more favored attractions. For the last time the impresario hurried him over half Europe to discover whether the old interest might still survive here and there; all in vain; everywhere, as if by secret agreement, a positive revulsion from professional fasting was in evidence. Of course it could not really have sprung up so suddenly as all that, and many premonitory symptoms which had not been sufficiently remarked or suppressed during the rush and glitter of success now came retrospectively to mind, but it was now too late to take any countermeasures. Fasting would surely come into fashion again at some future date, yet that was no comfort for those living in the present. What, then, was the hunger artist to do? He had been applauded by thousands in his time and could hardly come down to showing himself in a street booth at village fairs, and as for adopting another profession, he was not only too old for that but too frantically devoted to fasting. So he took leave of the impresario, his partner in an unparalleled career, and hired himself to a large circus; in order to spare his own feelings he avoided reading the conditions of his contract.

A large circus with its enormous traffic in replacing and recruiting men, animals, and apparatus can always find a use for people at any time, even for a hunger artist, provided of course that he does not ask too much, and in this particular case anyhow it was not only the artist who was taken on but his famous and long-known name as well, indeed considering the peculiar nature of his performance, which was not impaired by advancing age, it could not be objected that there was an artist past his prime, no longer at the height of his professional skill, seeking a refuge in some quiet corner of a circus; on the contrary, the hunger artist averred that he could fast as well as ever, which was entirely credible; he even alleged that if he were allowed to fast as he liked, and this was at once promised him without more ado, he could astound the world by establishing a record never yet achieved, a statement which certainly provoked a smile among the other professionals, since it left out of account the change in public opinion, which the hunger artist in his zeal conveniently forgot.

He had not, however, actually lost his sense of the real situation and took it as a matter of course that he and his cage should be stationed, not in the middle of the ring as a main attraction, but outside, near the animal cages, on a site that was after all easily accessible. Large and gaily painted placards made a frame for the cage and announced what was to be seen inside it. When the public came thronging out in the intervals to see the animals, they could hardly avoid passing the hunger artist's cage and stopping there for a moment; perhaps they might even have stayed longer had not those pressing behind them in the narrow gangway, who did not understand why they should be held up on their way toward the excitements of the menagerie, made it impossible for anyone to stand gazing quietly for any length of time. And that was the reason why the hunger artist, who had of course been looking forward to these visiting hours as the main achievement of his life, began instead to shrink from them. At first he could hardly wait for the intervals; it was exhilarating to watch the crowds come streaming his way, until only too soon—not even the most obstinate self-deception, clung to almost consciously, could hold out against the fact—the conviction was borne in upon him that these people, most of them, to judge from their actions, again and again, without exception, were all on their way to the menagerie. And the first sight of them from the distance remained the best. For when they reached his cage he was at once deafened by the storm of shouting and abuse that arose from the two contending factions, which renewed themselves continuously, of those who wanted to stop and stare at him—he soon began to dislike them more than the others—not out of real interest but only out of obstinate self-assertiveness, and those who wanted to go straight on to the animals. When the first great rush was past, the stragglers came along, and these, whom nothing could have prevented from stopping to look at him as long as they had breath, raced past with long strides, hardly even glancing at him, in their haste to get to the menagerie in time. And all too rarely did it happen that he had a stroke of luck, when some father of a family fetched up before him with his children, pointed a finger at the hunger artist, and explained at length what the phenomenon meant, telling stories of earlier years when he himself had watched similar but much more thrilling performances, and the children, still rather uncomprehending, since neither inside nor outside school had they been sufficiently prepared for this lesson—what did they care about fasting?—yet showed by the brightness of their intent eyes that new and better times might be coming. Perhaps, said the hunger artist to himself many a time, things would be a little better if his cage were set not quite so near the menagerie. That made it too easy for people to make their choice, to say nothing of what he suffered from the stench of the menagerie, the animals' restlessness by night, the carrying past of raw lumps of flesh for the beasts of prey, the roaring at feeding times, which depressed him continually. But he did not dare to lodge a complaint with the management; after all, he had the animals to thank for the troops of people who passed his cage, among whom there might always be one here and there to take an interest in him, and who could tell where they might seclude him if he called attention to his existence and thereby to the fact that, strictly speaking, he was only an impediment on the way to the menagerie.

A small impediment, to be sure, one that grew steadily less. People grew familiar with the strange idea that they could be expected, in times like these, to take an interest in a hunger artist, and with this familiarity the verdict went out against him. He might fast as much as he could, and he did so; but nothing could save him now, people passed him by. Just try to explain to anyone the art of fasting! Anyone who has no feeling for it cannot be made to understand it. The fine placards grew dirty and illegible, they were torn down; the little notice board telling the number of fast days achieved, which at first was changed carefully every day, had long stayed at the same figure, for after the first few weeks even this small task seemed pointless to the staff; and so the artist simply fasted on and on, as he had once dreamed of doing, and it was no trouble to him, just as he had always foretold, but no one counted the days, no one, not even the artist himself, knew what records he was already breaking, and his heart grew heavy. And when once in a time some leisurely passerby stopped, made merry over the old figure on the board, and spoke of swindling, that was in its way the stupidest lie ever invented by indifference and inborn malice, since it was not the hunger artist who was cheating; he was working honestly, but the world was cheating him of his reward.

Many more days went by, however, and that too came to an end. An overseer's eye fell on the cage one day and asked the attendants why this perfectly good cage should be left standing there unused with dirty straw inside it; nobody knew, until one man, helped out by the notice board, remembered about the hunger artist. They poked into the straw with sticks and found him in it. "Are you still fasting?" asked the overseer. "When on earth do you mean to stop?" "Forgive me, everybody," whispered the hunger artist; only the overseer, who had his ear to the bars, understood him. "Of course," said the overseer, and tapped his forehead with a finger to let the attendants know what state the man was in, "we forgive you." "I always wanted you to admire my fasting," said the hunger artist. "We do admire it," said the overseer, affably. "But you shouldn't admire it," said the hunger artist. "Well, then we don't admire it," said the overseer, "but why shouldn't we admire it?" "Because I have to fast, I can't help it," said the hunger artist. "What a fellow you are," said the overseer, "and why can't you help it?" "Because," said the hunger artist, lifting his head a little and speaking, with his lips pursed, as if for a kiss, right into the overseer's ear, so that no syllable might be lost, "because I couldn't find the food I liked. If I had found it, believe me, I should have made no fuss and stuffed myself like you or anyone else." These were his last words, but in his dimming eyes remained the firm though no longer proud persuasion that he was still continuing to fast.

"Well, clear this out now!" said the overseer, and they buried the hunger art- 10 ist, straw and all. Into the cage they put a young panther. Even the most insensitive felt it refreshing to see this wild creature leaping around the cage that had so long been dreary. The panther was all right. The food he liked was brought him without hesitation by the attendants; he seemed not even to miss his freedom; his noble body, furnished almost to the bursting point with all that it needed, seemed to carry freedom around with it too; somewhere in his jaws it seemed to lurk; and the joy of life streamed with such ardent passion from his throat that for the onlookers it was not easy to stand the shock of it. But they braced themselves, crowded round the cage, and did not want ever to move away.

FOR ANALYSIS

1. Many readers interpret this story as a parable of the artist in the modern world, while others see it as a religious parable. What evidence do you find in the story to support either interpretation?

2. Suggest reasons for Kafka's selection of an expert in fasting (rather than a priest or a singer, for example) as the central figure in the story.

3. How does Kafka manage to achieve such a bizarre, dreamlike effect with dry and factual **prose**?

4. Since his greatest achievements involve inwardness and withdrawal, why does the hunger artist nevertheless seem to need an audience?

MAKING ARGUMENTS

Should the hunger artist be admired for his passionate and single-minded devotion to his art or condemned for his withdrawal from humanity and his sickness of will? Why? Be sure to discuss the significance of the panther put in the cage after the artist's death.

WRITING TOPIC

In an essay, compare the hunger artist with Melville's Bartleby. Discuss the origins, rationale, consequences, and significance of their behavior.

MAKING CONNECTIONS

1. Compare this story with Hawthorne's "Young Goodman Brown" (p. 77) and Melville's "Bartleby, the Scrivener" (p. 319). What similarities do the central figures in the three stories share? What differences do you find? How does the alienation of each of the central figures contribute to each story's **theme**?

2. Describe feelings of isolation and alienation that you have experienced. What caused those feelings? How did you cope with them? How, finally, do you differ from the hunger artist?

RALPH ELLISON (1914–1994)

BATTLE ROYAL 1952

It goes a long way back, some twenty years. All my life I had been looking for something, and everywhere I turned someone tried to tell me what it was. I accepted their answers too, though they were often in contradiction and even self-contradictory. I was naive. I was looking for myself and asking everyone except myself questions which I, and only I, could answer. It took me a long time and much painful boomeranging of my expectations to achieve a realization everyone else appears to have been born with: that I am nobody but myself. But first I had to discover that I am an invisible man!

And yet I am no freak of nature, nor of history. I was in the cards, other things having been equal (or unequal) eighty-five years ago. I am not ashamed of my grandparents for having been slaves. I am only ashamed of myself for having at one time been ashamed. About eighty-five years ago they were told that they were free, united with others of our country in everything pertaining to the common good, and, in everything social, separate like the fingers of the hand. And they believed it. They exulted in it. They stayed in their place, worked hard, and brought up my father to do the same. But my grandfather is the one. He was an odd old guy, my grandfather, and I am told I take after him. It was he who caused the trouble. On his deathbed he called my father to him and said, "Son, after I'm gone I want you to keep up the good fight. I never told you, but our life is a war and I have been a traitor all my born days, a spy in the enemy's country ever since I give up my gun back in the Reconstruction. Live with your head in the lion's mouth. I want you to overcome 'em with yeses, undermine 'em with grins, agree 'em to death and destruction, let 'em swoller you till they vomit or bust wide open." They thought the old man had gone out of his mind. He had been the meekest of men. The younger children were rushed from the room, the shades drawn, and the flame of the lamp turned so low that it sputtered on the wick like the old man's breathing. "Learn it to the younguns," he whispered fiercely; then he died.

But my folks were more alarmed over his last words than over his dying. It was as though he had not died at all, his words caused so much anxiety. I was warned emphatically to forget what he had said and, indeed, this is the first time it has been mentioned outside the family circle. It had a tremendous effect upon me, however. I could never be sure of what he meant. Grandfather had been a quiet old man who never made any trouble, yet on his deathbed he had called himself a traitor and a spy, and he had spoken of his meekness as a dangerous activity. It became a constant puzzle which lay unanswered in the back of my mind. And whenever things went well for me I remembered my grandfather and felt guilty and uncomfortable. It was as though I was carrying out his advice in spite of myself. And to make it worse, everyone loved me for it. I was praised by the most lily-white men of the town. I was considered an example of desirable conduct—just as my grandfather had been. And what puzzled me was that the old man had defined it as *treachery*. When I was praised for my conduct I felt a guilt that in some way I was doing something that was really against the wishes of the white folks, that if they had understood they would have desired me to act just the opposite, that I should have been sulky and mean, and that that really would have been what they wanted, even though they were fooled and thought they wanted me to act as I did. It made me afraid that some day they would look upon me as a traitor and I would be lost. Still I was more afraid to act any other way because they didn't like that at all. The old man's words were like a curse. On my graduation day I delivered an oration in which I showed that humility was the secret, indeed, the very essence of progress. (Not that I believed this—how could I, remembering my grandfather?—I only believed that it worked.) It was a great success. Everyone praised me and I was invited to give the speech at a gathering of the town's leading white citizens. It was a triumph for our whole community.

It was in the main ballroom of the leading hotel. When I got there I discovered that it was on the occasion of a smoker, and I was told that since I was to be there anyway I might as well take part in the battle royal to be fought by some of my schoolmates as part of the entertainment. The battle royal came first.

All of the town's big shots were there in their tuxedoes, wolfing down the buffet foods, drinking beer and whiskey and smoking black cigars. It was a large room with a high ceiling. Chairs were arranged in neat rows around three sides of a portable boxing ring. The fourth side was clear, revealing a gleaming space of polished floor. I had some misgivings over the battle royal, by the way. Not from a distaste for fighting, but because I didn't care too much for the other fellows who were to take part. They were tough guys who seemed to have no grandfather's curse worrying their minds. No one could mistake their toughness. And besides, I suspected that fighting a battle royal might detract from the dignity of my speech. In those pre-invisible days I visualized myself as a potential Booker T. Washington. But the other fellows didn't care too much for me either, and there were nine of them. I felt superior to them in my way, and I didn't like the manner in which we were all crowded together into the servants' elevator. Nor did they like my being there. In fact, as the warmly lighted floors flashed past the elevator we had words over the fact that I, by taking part in the fight, had knocked one of their friends out of a night's work.

We were led out of the elevator through a rococo hall into an anteroom and told to get into our fighting togs. Each of us was issued a pair of boxing gloves and ushered out into the big mirrored hall, which we entered looking cautiously about us and whispering, lest we might accidentally be heard above the noise of the room. It was foggy with cigar smoke. And already the whiskey was taking effect. I was shocked to see some of the most important men of the town quite tipsy. They were all there—bankers, lawyers, judges, doctors, fire chiefs, teachers, merchants. Even one of the more fashionable pastors. Something we could not see was going on up front. A clarinet was vibrating sensuously and the men were standing up and moving eagerly forward. We were a small tight group, clustered together, our bare upper bodies touching and shining with anticipatory sweat; while up front the big shots were becoming increasingly excited over something we still could not see. Suddenly I heard the school superintendent, who had told me to come, yell, "Bring up the shines, gentlemen! Bring up the little shines!"

We were rushed up to the front of the ballroom, where it smelled even more strongly of tobacco and whiskey. Then we were pushed into place. I almost wet my pants. A sea of faces, some hostile, some amused, ringed around us, and in the center, facing us, stood a magnificent blonde—stark naked. There was dead silence. I felt a blast of cold air chill me. I tried to back away, but they were behind me and around me. Some of the boys stood with lowered heads, trembling. I felt a wave of irrational guilt and fear. My teeth chattered, my skin turned to goose flesh, my knees knocked. Yet I was strongly attracted and looked in spite of myself. Had the price of looking been blindness, I would have looked. The hair was yellow like that of a circus kewpie doll, the face heavily powdered and rouged, as though to form an abstract mask, the eyes hollow and smeared a cool blue, the color of a baboon's butt. I felt a desire to spit upon her as my eyes brushed slowly over her body. Her breasts were firm and round as the domes of East Indian temples, and I stood so close as to see the fine skin texture and beads of pearly perspiration glistening like dew around the pink and erected buds of her nipples. I wanted at one and the same time to run from the room, to sink through the floor, or go to her and cover her from my eyes and the eyes of the others with my body; to feel the soft thighs, to caress her and destroy her, to love her and murder her, to hide from her, and yet to stroke where below the small American flag tattooed upon her belly her thighs formed a capital V. I had a notion that of all in the room she saw only me with her impersonal eyes.

And then she began to dance, a slow sensuous movement; the smoke of a hundred cigars clinging to her like the thinnest of veils. She seemed like a fair bird-girl girdled in veils calling to me from the angry surface of some gray and threatening sea. I was transported. Then I became aware of the clarinet playing and the big shots yelling at us. Some threatened us if we looked and others if we did not. On my right I saw one boy faint. And now a man grabbed a silver pitcher from a table and stepped close as he dashed ice water upon him and stood him up and forced two of us to support him as his head hung and moans issued from his thick bluish lips. Another boy began to plead to go home. He was the largest of the group, wearing dark red fighting trunks much too small to conceal the erection which projected from him as though in answer to the insinuating low-registered moaning of the clarinet. He tried to hide himself with his boxing gloves.

And all the while the blonde continued dancing, smiling faintly at the big shots who watched her with fascination, and faintly smiling at our fear.

I noticed a certain merchant who followed her hungrily, his lips loose and drooling. He was a large man who wore diamond studs in a shirtfront which swelled with the ample paunch underneath, and each time the blonde swayed her undulating hips he ran his hand through the thin hair of his bald head and, with his arms upheld, his posture clumsy like that of an intoxicated panda, wound his belly in a slow and obscene grind. This creature was completely hypnotized. The music had quickened. As the dancer flung herself about with a detached expression on her face, the men began reaching out to touch her. I could see their beefy fingers sink into her soft flesh. Some of the others tried to stop them and she began to move around the floor in graceful circles, as they gave chase, slipping and sliding over the polished floor. It was mad. Chairs went crashing, drinks were spilt, as they ran laughing and howling after her. They caught her just as she reached a door, raised her from the floor, and tossed her as college boys are tossed at a hazing, and above her red fixed-smiling lips I saw the terror and disgust in her eyes, almost like my own terror and that which I saw in some of the other boys. As I watched, they tossed her twice and her soft breasts seemed to flatten against the air and her legs flung wildly as she spun. Some of the more sober ones helped her to escape. And I started off the floor, heading for the anteroom with the rest of the boys.

Some were still crying and in hysteria. But as we tried to leave we were 10 stopped and ordered to get into the ring. There was nothing to do but what we were told. All ten of us climbed under the ropes and allowed ourselves to be blindfolded with broad bands of white cloth. One of the men seemed to feel a bit sympathetic and tried to cheer us up as we stood with our backs against the ropes. Some of us tried to grin. "See that boy over there?" one of the men said. "I want you to run across at the bell and give it to him right in the belly. If you don't get him, I'm going to get you. I don't like his looks." Each of us was told the same. The blindfolds were put on. Yet even then I had been going over my speech. In my mind each word was as bright as flame. I felt the cloth pressed into place, and frowned so that it would be loosened when I relaxed.

But now I felt a sudden fit of blind terror. I was unused to darkness. It was as though I had suddenly found myself in a dark room filled with poisonous cottonmouths. I could hear the bleary voices yelling insistently for the battle royal to begin.

"Get going in there!"

"Let me at that big nigger!"

I strained to pick up the school superintendent's voice, as though to squeeze some security out of that slightly more familiar sound.

"Let me at those black sonsabitches!" someone yelled. 15

"No, Jackson, no!" another voice yelled. "Here, somebody, help me hold Jack."

"I want to get at that ginger-colored nigger. Tear him limb from limb," the first voice yelled.

I stood against the ropes trembling. For in those days I was what they called ginger-colored, and he sounded as though he might crunch me between his teeth like a crisp ginger cookie.

Quite a struggle was going on. Chairs were being kicked about and I could hear voices grunting as with a terrific effort. I wanted to see, to see more desperately than ever before. But the blindfold was as tight as a thick skin-puckering scab and when I raised my gloved hands to push the layers of white aside a voice yelled, "Oh, no you don't, black bastard! Leave that alone!"

"Ring the bell before Jackson kills him a coon!" someone boomed in the 20 sudden silence. And I heard the bell clang and the sound of the feet scuffling forward.

A glove smacked against my head. I pivoted, striking out stiffly as someone went past, and felt the jar ripple along the length of my arm to my shoulder. Then it seemed as though all nine of the boys had turned upon me at once. Blows pounded me from all sides while I struck out as best I could. So many blows landed upon me that I wondered if I were not the only blindfolded fighter in the ring, or if the man called Jackson hadn't succeeded in getting me after all.

Blindfolded, I could no longer control my motions. I had no dignity. I stumbled about like a baby or a drunken man. The smoke had become thicker and with each new blow it seemed to sear and further restrict my lungs. My saliva became like hot bitter glue. A glove connected with my head, filling my mouth with warm blood. It was everywhere. I could not tell if the moisture I felt upon my body was sweat or blood. A blow landed hard against the nape of my neck. I felt myself going over, my head hitting the floor. Streaks of blue light filled the black world behind the blindfold. I lay prone, pretending that I was knocked out, but felt myself seized by hands and yanked to my feet. "Get going, black boy! Mix it up!" My arms were like lead, my head smarting from blows. I managed to feel my way to the ropes and held on, trying to catch my breath. A glove landed in my mid-section and I went over again, feeling as though the smoke had become a knife jabbed into my guts. Pushed this way and that by the legs milling around me, I finally pulled erect and discovered that I could see the black, sweat-washed forms weaving in the smoky-blue atmosphere like drunken dancers weaving to the rapid drum-like thuds of blows.

Everyone fought hysterically. It was complete anarchy. Everybody fought everybody else. No group fought together for long. Two, three, four, fought one, then turned to fight each other, were themselves attacked. Blows landed below the belt and in the kidney, with the gloves open as well as closed, and with my eye partly opened now there was not so much terror. I moved carefully, avoiding blows, although not too many to attract attention, fighting from group to group. The boys groped about like blind, cautious crabs crouching to protect their mid-sections, their heads pulled in short against their shoulders, their arms stretched nervously before them, with their fists testing the smoke-filled air like the knobbed feelers of hypersensitive snails. In one corner I glimpsed a boy violently punching the air and heard him scream in pain as he smashed his hand against a ring post. For a second I saw him bent over holding his hand, then going down as a blow caught his unprotected head. I played one group against the other, slipping in and throwing a punch then stepping out of range while pushing the others into the melee to take the blows blindly aimed at me. The smoke was agonizing and there were no rounds, no bells at three minute intervals to relieve our exhaustion. The room spun round me, a swirl of lights, smoke, sweating bodies surrounded by tense white faces. I bled from both nose and mouth, the blood spattering upon my chest.

The men kept yelling, "Slug him, black boy! Knock his guts out!"

"Uppercut him! Kill him! Kill that big boy!"   25

Taking a fake fall, I saw a boy going down heavily beside me as though we were felled by a single blow, saw a sneaker-clad foot shoot into his groin as the two who had knocked him down stumbled upon him. I rolled out of range, feeling a twinge of nausea.

The harder we fought the more threatening the men became. And yet, I had begun to worry about my speech again. How would it go? Would they recognize my ability? What would they give me?

I was fighting automatically and suddenly I noticed that one after another of the boys was leaving the ring. I was surprised, filled with panic, as though I had been left alone with an unknown danger. Then I understood. The boys had arranged it among themselves. It was the custom for the two men left in the ring to slug it out for the winner's prize. I discovered this too late. When the bell sounded two men in tuxedoes leaped into the ring and removed the blindfold. I found myself facing Tatlock, the biggest of the gang. I felt sick at my stomach. Hardly had the bell stopped ringing in my ears than it clanged again and I saw him moving swiftly toward me. Thinking of nothing else to do I hit him smash on the nose. He kept coming, bringing the rank sharp violence of stale sweat. His face was a black blank of a face, only his eyes alive—with hate of me and aglow with a feverish terror from what had happened to us all. I became anxious. I wanted to deliver my speech and he came at me as though he meant to beat it out of me. I smashed him again and again, taking his blows as they came. Then on a sudden impulse I struck him lightly and as we clinched, I whispered, "Fake like I knocked you out, you can have the prize."

"I'll break your behind," he whispered hoarsely.

"For *them*?"   30

"For *me*, sonofabitch!"

They were yelling for us to break it up and Tatlock spun me half around with a blow, and as a joggled camera sweeps in a reeling scene, I saw the howling red faces crouching tense beneath the cloud of blue-gray smoke. For a moment the world wavered, unraveled, flowed, then my head cleared and Tatlock bounced before me. That fluttering shadow before my eyes was his jabbing left hand. Then falling forward, my head against his damp shoulder, I whispered,

"I'll make it five dollars more."

"Go to hell!"

But his muscles relaxed a trifle beneath my pressure and I breathed, "Seven!"   35

"Give it to your ma," he said, ripping me beneath the heart.

And while I still held him I butted him and moved away. I felt myself bombarded with punches. I fought back with hopeless desperation. I wanted to deliver my speech more than anything else in the world, because I felt that only these men could judge truly my ability, and now this stupid clown was ruining my chances. I began fighting carefully now, moving in to punch him and out again with my greater speed. A lucky blow to his chin and I had him going too—until I heard a loud voice yell, "I got my money on the big boy."

Hearing this, I almost dropped my guard. I was confused: Should I try to win against the voice out there? Would not this go against my speech, and was not this a moment for humility, for nonresistance? A blow to my head as I danced about sent my right eye popping like a jack-in-the-box and settled my dilemma. The room went red as I fell. It was a dream fall, my body languid and fastidious as to where to land, until the floor became impatient and smashed up to meet me. A moment later I came to. An hypnotic voice said FIVE emphatically. And I lay there, hazily watching a dark red spot of my own blood shaping itself into a butterfly, glistening and soaking into the soiled gray world of the canvas.

When the voice drawled TEN I was lifted up and dragged to a chair. I sat dazed. My eye pained and swelled with each throb of my pounding heart and I wondered if now I would be allowed to speak. I was wringing wet, my mouth still bleeding. We were grouped along the wall now. The other boys ignored me as they congratulated Tatlock and speculated as to how much they would be paid. One boy whimpered over his smashed hand. Looking up front, I saw attendants in white jackets rolling the portable ring away and placing a small square rug in the vacant space surrounded by chairs. Perhaps, I thought, I will stand on the rug to deliver my speech.

Then the M.C. called to us, "Come on up here boys and get your money." 40

We ran forward to where the men laughed and talked in their chairs, waiting. Everyone seemed friendly now.

"There it is on the rug," the man said. I saw the rug covered with coins of all dimensions and a few crumpled bills. But what excited me, scattered here and there, were the gold pieces.

"Boys, it's all yours," the man said. "You get all you grab."

"That's right, Sambo," a blond man said, winking at me confidentially.

I trembled with excitement, forgetting my pain. I would get the gold and the 45 bills, I thought. I would use both hands. I would throw my body against the boys nearest me to block them from the gold.

"Get down around the rug now," the man commanded, "and don't anyone touch it until I give the signal."

"This ought to be good," I heard.

As told, we got around the square rug on our knees. Slowly the man raised his freckled hand as we followed it upward with our eyes.

I heard, "These niggers look like they're about to pray!"

Then, "Ready," the man said. "Go!" 50

I lunged for a yellow coin lying on the blue design of the carpet, touching it and sending a surprised shriek to join those rising around me. I tried frantically to remove my hand but could not let go. A hot, violent force tore through my body, shaking me like a wet rat. The rug was electrified. The hair bristled up on my head as I shook myself free. My muscles jumped, my nerves jangled, writhed. But I saw that this was not stopping the other boys. Laughing in fear and embarrassment, some were holding back and scooping up the coins knocked off by the painful contortions of the others. The men roared above us as we struggled.

"Pick it up, goddamnit, pick it up!" someone called like a bass-voiced parrot. "Go on, get it!"

I crawled rapidly around the floor, picking up the coins, trying to avoid the coppers and to get greenbacks and the gold. Ignoring the shock by laughing, as I brushed the coins off quickly, I discovered that I could contain the electricity—a contradiction, but it works. Then the men began to push us onto the rug. Laughing embarrassedly, we struggled out of their hands and kept after the coins. We were all wet and slippery and hard to hold. Suddenly I saw a boy lifted into the air, glistening with sweat like a circus seal, and dropped, his wet back landing flush upon the charged rug, heard him yell and saw him literally dance upon his back, his elbows beating a frenzied tatoo upon the floor, his muscles twitching like the flesh of a horse stung by many flies. When he finally rolled off, his face was gray and no one stopped him when he ran from the floor amid booming laughter.

"Get the money," the M.C. called. "That's good hard American cash!"

And we snatched and grabbed, snatched and grabbed. I was careful not to   55 come too close to the rug now, and when I felt the hot whiskey breath descend upon me like a cloud of foul air I reached out and grabbed the leg of a chair. It was occupied and I held on desperately.

"Leggo, nigger! Leggo!"

The huge face wavered down to mine as he tried to push me free. But my body was slippery and he was too drunk. It was Mr. Colcord, who owned a chain of movie houses and "entertainment palaces." Each time he grabbed me I slipped out of his hands. It became a real struggle. I feared the rug more than I did the drunk, so I held on, surprising myself for a moment by trying to topple *him* upon the rug. It was such an enormous idea that I found myself actually carrying it out. I tried not to be obvious, yet when I grabbed his leg, trying to tumble him out of the chair, he raised up roaring with laughter, and, looking at me with soberness dead in the eye, kicked me viciously in the chest. The chair leg flew out of my hand. I felt myself going and rolled. It was as though I had rolled through a bed of hot coals. It seemed a whole century would pass before I would roll free, a century in which I was seared through the deepest levels of my body to the fearful breath within me and the breath seared and heated to the point of explosion. It'll all be over in a flash, I thought as I rolled clear. It'll all be over in a flash.

But not yet, the men on the other side were waiting, red faces swollen as though from apoplexy as they bent forward in their chairs. Seeing their fingers coming toward me I rolled away as a fumbled football rolls off the receiver's fingertips, back into the coals. That time I luckily sent the rug sliding out of place and heard the coins ringing against the floor and the boys scuffling to pick them up and the M.C. calling, "All right, boys, that's all. Go get dressed and get your money."

I was limp as a dish rag. My back felt as though it had been beaten with wires.

When we had dressed the M.C. came in and gave us each five dollars, except Tatlock, who got ten for being last in the ring. Then he told us to leave. I was not to get a chance to deliver my speech, I thought. I was going out into the dim alley in despair when I was stopped and told to go back. I returned to the ballroom, where the men were pushing back their chairs and gathering in groups to talk.

The M.C. knocked on a table for quiet. "Gentlemen," he said, "we almost forgot an important part of the program. A most serious part, gentlemen. This boy was brought here to deliver a speech which he made at his graduation yesterday. . . ."

"Bravo!"

"I'm told that he is the smartest boy we've got out there in Greenwood. I'm told that he knows more big words than a pocket-sized dictionary."

Much applause and laughter.

"So now, gentlemen, I want you to give him your attention."

There was still laughter as I faced them, my mouth dry, my eye throbbing. I began slowly, but evidently my throat was tense, because they began shouting, "Louder! Louder!"

"We of the younger generation extol the wisdom of that great leader and educator," I shouted, "who first spoke these flaming words of wisdom: 'A ship lost at sea for many days suddenly sighted a friendly vessel. From the mast of the unfortunate vessel was seen a signal: "Water, water; we die of thirst!" The answer from the friendly vessel came back: "Cast down your bucket where you are." The captain of the distressed vessel, at last heeding the injunction, cast down his bucket, and it came up full of fresh sparkling water from the mouth of the Amazon River.' And like him I say, and in his words, 'To those of my race who depend upon bettering their condition in a foreign land, or who underestimate the importance of cultivating friendly relations with the Southern white man, who is his next-door neighbor, I would say: "Cast down your bucket where you are"—cast it down in making friends in every manly way of the people of all races by whom we are surrounded. . . .'"

I spoke automatically and with such fervor that I did not realize that the men were still talking and laughing until my dry mouth, filling up with blood from the cut, almost strangled me. I coughed, wanting to stop and go to one of the tall brass, sand-filled spittoons to relieve myself, but a few of the men, especially the superintendent, were listening and I was afraid. So I gulped it down, blood, saliva, and all, and continued. (What powers of endurance I had during those days! What enthusiasm! What a belief in the rightness of things!) I spoke even louder in spite of the pain. But still they talked and still they laughed, as though deaf with cotton in dirty ears. So I spoke with greater emotional emphasis. I closed my ears and swallowed blood until I was nauseated.

The speech seemed a hundred times as long as before, but I could not leave out a single word. All had to be said, each memorized nuance considered, rendered. Nor was that all. Whenever I uttered a word of three or more syllables a group of voices would yell for me to repeat it. I used the phrase "social responsibility" and they yelled:

"What's the word you say, boy?"

"Social responsibility," I said. 70

"What?"

"Social . . ."

"Louder."

". . . responsibility."

"More!" 75

"Respon—"

"Repeat!"

"—sibility."

The room filled with the uproar of laughter until, no doubt, distracted by having to gulp down my blood, I made a mistake and yelled a phrase I had often seen denounced in newspaper editorials, heard debated in private.

"Social . . ." 80

"What?" they yelled.

". . . equality—"

The laughter hung smokelike in the sudden stillness. I opened my eyes, puzzled. Sounds of displeasure filled the room. The M.C. rushed forward. They shouted hostile phrases at me. But I did not understand.

A small dry mustached man in the front row blared out, "Say that slowly, son!"

"What sir?" 85

"What you just said!"

"Social responsibility, sir," I said.

"You weren't being smart, were you, boy?" he said, not unkindly.

"No, sir!"

"You sure that about 'equality' was a mistake?" 90

"Oh, yes, sir," I said. "I was swallowing blood."

"Well, you had better speak more slowly so we can understand. We mean to do right by you, but you've got to know your place at all times. All right, now, go on with your speech."

I was afraid. I wanted to leave but I wanted also to speak and I was afraid they'd snatch me down.

"Thank you, sir," I said, beginning where I had left off, and having them ignore me as before.

Yet when I finished there was a thunderous applause. I was surprised to see 95 the superintendent come forth with a package wrapped in white tissue paper, and, gesturing for quiet, address the men.

"Gentlemen, you see that I did not overpraise this boy. He makes a good speech and some day he'll lead his people in the proper paths. And I don't have to tell you that that is important in these days and times. This is a good, smart boy, and so to encourage him in the right direction, in the name of the Board of Education I wish to present him a prize in the form of this . . ."

He paused, removing the tissue paper and revealing a gleaming calfskin brief case.

". . . in the form of this first-class article from Shad Whitmore's shop."

"Boy," he said, addressing me, "take this prize and keep it well. Consider it a badge of office. Prize it. Keep developing as you are and some day it will be filled with important papers that will help shape the destiny of your people."

I was so moved that I could hardly express my thanks. A rope of bloody 100 saliva forming a shape like an undiscovered continent drooled upon the leather and I wiped it quickly away. I felt an importance that I had never dreamed.

"Open it and see what's inside," I was told.

My fingers a-tremble, I complied, smelling the fresh leather and finding an official-looking document inside. It was a scholarship to the state college for Negroes. My eyes filled with tears and I ran awkwardly off the floor.

I was overjoyed; I did not even mind when I discovered that the gold pieces I had scrambled for were brass pocket tokens advertising a certain make of automobile.

When I reached home everyone was excited. Next day the neighbors came to congratulate me. I even felt safe from grandfather, whose deathbed curse usually spoiled my triumphs. I stood beneath his photograph with my brief case in hand and smiled triumphantly into his stolid black peasant's face. It was a face that fascinated me. The eyes seemed to follow everywhere I went.

That night I dreamed I was at a circus with him and that he refused to 105 laugh at the clowns no matter what they did. Then later he told me to open my brief case and read what was inside and I did, finding an official envelope stamped with the state seal; and inside the envelope I found another and another, endlessly, and I thought I would fall of weariness. "Them's years," he said. "Now open that one." And I did and in it I found an engraved document containing a short message in letters of gold. "Read it," my grandfather said. "Out loud."

"To Whom It May Concern," I intoned. "Keep This Nigger-Boy Running."

I awoke with the old man's laughter ringing in my ears.

(It was a dream I was to remember and dream again for many years after. But at the time I had no insight into its meaning. First I had to attend college.)

For Analysis

1. What phrase does the **narrator** inadvertently utter, causing the room to go quiet? Why does it have such an effect?

2. Why is it significant that the naked woman in the story is white?

3. The meaning of the grandfather's last words, recounted at the story's opening, are ambiguous; the narrator even says, "I could never be sure of what he meant" (para. 3). Does the meaning become clearer by the end of the story? What do you think it is, and how is it revealed?

MAKING ARGUMENTS

Construct two arguments—one for and one against the plan of action urged on the narrator's father by his grandfather. Was it good advice? Has it been followed? Has it worked?

WRITING TOPICS

1. Write about the **symbolism** in "Battle Royal." For what might the different objects and different activities stand? How do they fit together? Why do you think Ellison has his **protagonist** see and experience these symbolic things?

2. Write a reflective personal essay on invisibility. Possible topics for this essay include ways in which you are invisible, ways in which other people you know or see are invisible, and ways in which you are guilty of not seeing others.

MAKING CONNECTIONS

1. There is much more action in "Battle Royal" than in Bambara's "The Lesson" (p. 98). It is more obvious, then, that Bambara's story is about what its main **character** sees and what she learns from it. How, in spite of Ellison's story's differences, is it like Bambara's? Does the main character learn a lesson? How? What is it?

2. Read "Battle Royal" in the context of the connections unit "Voices of Experience" (p. 199). What voices of experience speak in this story, including but not limited to the grandfather? What advice do they give? How is it taken? To which of the poems in "Voices of Experience" is "Battle Royal" most similar? To which is it most different?

SHIRLEY JACKSON (1919–1965)

THE LOTTERY 1948

The morning of June 27th was clear and sunny, with the fresh warmth of a full-summer day; the flowers were blossoming profusely and the grass was richly green. The people of the village began to gather in the square, between the post office and the bank, around ten o'clock; in some towns there were so many people that the lottery took two days and had to be started on June 26th, but in this village, where there were only about three hundred people, the whole lottery took less than two hours, so it could begin at ten o'clock in the morning and still be through in time to allow the villagers to get home for noon dinner.

The children assembled first, of course. School was recently over for the summer, and the feeling of liberty sat uneasily on most of them; they tended to gather together quietly for a while before they broke into boisterous play, and their talk was still of the classroom and the teacher, of books and reprimands. Bobby Martin had already stuffed his pockets full of stones, and the other boys soon followed his example, selecting the smoothest and roundest stones; Bobby and Harry Jones and Dickie Delacroix—the villagers pronounced his name "Dellacroy"—eventually made a great pile of stones in one corner of the square and guarded it against the raids of the other boys. The girls stood aside, talking among themselves, looking over their shoulders at the boys, and the very small children rolled in the dust or clung to the hands of their older brothers or sisters.

Soon the men began to gather, surveying their own children, speaking of planting and rain, tractors and taxes. They stood together, away from the pile of stones in the corner, and their jokes were quiet and they smiled rather than laughed. The women, wearing faded house dresses and sweaters, came shortly after their menfolk. They greeted one another and exchanged bits of gossip as they went to join their husbands. Soon the women, standing by their husbands, began to call to their children, and the children came reluctantly, having to be called four or five times. Bobby Martin ducked under his mother's grasping hand and ran, laughingly, back to the pile of stones. His father spoke up sharply, and Bobby came quickly and took his place, between his father and his oldest brother.

The lottery was conducted—as were the square dances, the teenage club, the Halloween program—by Mr. Summers, who had time and energy to devote to civic activities. He was a round-faced, jovial man and he ran the coal business, and people were sorry for him, because he had no children and his wife was a scold. When he arrived in the square, carrying the black wooden box, there was a murmur of conversation among the villagers, and he waved and called

367

"Little late today, folks." The postmaster, Mr. Graves, followed him, carrying a three-legged stool, and the stool was put in the center of the square and Mr. Summers set the black box down on it. The villagers kept their distance, leaving a space between themselves and the stool, and when Mr. Summers said, "Some of you fellows want to give me a hand?" there was a hesitation before two men, Mr. Martin and his oldest son, Baxter, came forward to hold the box steady on the stool while Mr. Summers stirred up the papers inside it.

The original paraphernalia for the lottery had been lost long ago, and the 5 black box now resting on the stool had been put into use even before Old Man Warner, the oldest man in town, was born. Mr. Summers spoke frequently to the villagers about making a new box, but no one liked to upset even as much tradition as was represented by the black box. There was a story that the present box had been made with some pieces of the box that had preceded it, the one that had been constructed when the first people settled down to make a village here. Every year, after the lottery, Mr. Summers began talking about a new box, but every year the subject was allowed to fade off without anything's being done. The black box grew shabbier each year; by now it was no longer completely black but splintered badly along one side to show the original wood color, and in some places faded and stained.

Mr. Martin and his oldest son, Baxter, held the black box securely on the stool until Mr. Summers had stirred the papers thoroughly with his hand. Because so much of the ritual had been forgotten or discarded, Mr. Summers had been successful in having slips of paper substituted for the chips of wood that had been used for generations. Chips of wood, Mr. Summers had argued, had been all very well when the village was tiny, but now that the population was more than three hundred and likely to keep on growing, it was necessary to use something that would fit more easily into the black box. The night before the lottery, Mr. Summers and Mr. Graves made up the slips of paper and put them in the box, and it was then taken to the safe of Mr. Summers's coal company and locked up until Mr. Summers was ready to take it to the square the next morning. The rest of the year, the box was put away, sometimes one place, sometimes another; it had spent one year in Mr. Graves's barn and another year underfoot in the post office, and sometimes it was set on a shelf in the Martin grocery and left there.

There was a great deal of fussing to be done before Mr. Summers declared the lottery open. There were the lists to make up—of heads of families, heads of households in each family, members of each household in each family. There was the proper swearing-in of Mr. Summers by the postmaster, as the official of the lottery; at one time, some people remembered, there had been a recital of some sort, performed by the official of the lottery, a perfunctory, tuneless chant that had been rattled off duly each year; some people believed that the official of the lottery used to stand just so when he said or sang it, others believed that he was supposed to walk among the people, but years and years ago this part of the ritual had been allowed to lapse. There had been, also, a ritual salute, which the official of the lottery had had to use in addressing each person who came up to draw from the box, but this also had changed with time, until now it was felt necessary only for the official to speak to each person approaching. Mr. Summers was very good at all this; in his clean white shirt and blue jeans, with one hand resting carelessly on the black box, he seemed very proper and important as he talked interminably to Mr. Graves and the Martins.

Just as Mr. Summers finally left off talking and turned to the assembled villagers, Mrs. Hutchinson came hurriedly along the path to the square, her sweater thrown over her shoulders, and slid into place in the back of the crowd. "Clean forgot what day it was," she said to Mrs. Delacroix, who stood next to her, and they both laughed softly. "Thought my old man was out back stacking wood," Mrs. Hutchinson went on, "and then I looked out the window and the kids were gone, and then I remembered it was the twenty-seventh and came a-running." She dried her hands on her apron, and Mrs. Delacroix said, "You're in time, though. They're still talking away up there."

Mrs. Hutchinson craned her neck to see through the crowd and found her husband and children standing near the front. She tapped Mrs. Delacroix on the arm as a farewell and began to make her way through the crowd. The people separated good-humoredly to let her through; two or three people said, in voices just loud enough to be heard across the crowd, "Here comes your Missus, Hutchinson," and "Bill, she made it after all." Mrs. Hutchinson reached her husband, and Mr. Summers, who had been waiting, said cheerfully, "Thought we were going to have to get on without you, Tessie." Mrs. Hutchinson said, grinning, "Wouldn't have me leave m'dishes in the sink, now, would you, Joe?" and soft laughter ran through the crowd as the people stirred back into position after Mrs. Hutchinson's arrival.

"Well, now," Mr. Summers said soberly, "guess we better get started, get this 10 over with, so's we can go back to work. Anybody ain't here?"

"Dunbar," several people said. "Dunbar, Dunbar."

Mr. Summers consulted his list. "Clyde Dunbar," he said. "That's right. He's broke his leg, hasn't he? Who's drawing for him?"

"Me, I guess," a woman said, and Mr. Summers turned to look at her. "Wife draws for her husband," Mr. Summers said. "Don't you have a grown boy to do it for you, Janey?" Although Mr. Summers and everyone else in the village knew the answer perfectly well, it was the business of the official of the lottery to ask such questions formally. Mr. Summers waited with an expression of polite interest while Mrs. Dunbar answered.

"Horace's not but sixteen yet," Mrs. Dunbar said regretfully. "Guess I gotta fill in for the old man this year."

"Right," Mr. Summers said. He made a note on the list he was holding. Then 15 he asked, "Watson boy drawing this year?"

A tall boy in the crowd raised his hand. "Here," he said. "I'm drawing for m'mother and me." He blinked his eyes nervously and ducked his head as several voices in the crowd said things like "Good fellow, Jack," and "Glad to see your mother's got a man to do it."

"Well," Mr. Summers said, "guess that's everyone. Old Man Warner make it?"

"Here," a voice said, and Mr. Summers nodded.

A sudden hush fell on the crowd as Mr. Summers cleared his throat and looked at the list. "All ready?" he called. "Now, I'll read the names—heads of families first—and the men come up and take a paper out of the box. Keep the paper folded in your hand without looking at it until everyone has had a turn. Everything clear?"

The people had done it so many times that they only half listened to the directions; most of them were quiet, wetting their lips, not looking around. Then Mr. Summers raised one hand high and said, "Adams." A man disengaged himself from the crowd and came forward. "Hi, Steve," Mr. Summers said, and Mr. Adams said, "Hi, Joe." They grinned at one another humorlessly and nervously. Then Mr. Adams reached into the black box and took out a folded paper. He held it firmly by one corner as he turned and went hastily back to his place in the crowd, where he stood a little apart from his family, not looking down at his hand.

"Allen." Mr. Summers said. "Anderson. . . . Betham."

"Seems like there's no time at all between lotteries any more," Mrs. Delacroix said to Mrs. Graves in the back row. "Seems like we got through the last one only last week."

"Time sure goes fast," Mrs. Graves said.

"Clark. . . . Delacroix."

"There goes my old man," Mrs. Delacroix said. She held her breath while her husband went forward.

"Dunbar," Mr. Summers said, and Mrs. Dunbar went steadily to the box while one of the women said, "Go on, Janey," and another said, "There she goes."

"We're next," Mrs. Graves said. She watched while Mr. Graves came around from the side of the box, greeted Mr. Summers gravely, and selected a slip of paper from the box. By now, all through the crowd there were men holding the small folded papers in their large hands, turning them over and over nervously. Mrs. Dunbar and her two sons stood together, Mrs. Dunbar holding the slip of paper.

"Harburt. . . . Hutchinson."

"Get up there, Bill," Mrs. Hutchinson said, and the people near her laughed.

"Jones."

"They do say," Mr. Adams said to Old Man Warner, who stood next to him, "that over in the north village they're talking of giving up the lottery."

Old Man Warner snorted. "Pack of crazy fools," he said. "Listening to the young folks, nothing's good enough for *them*. Next thing you know, they'll be wanting to go back to living in caves, nobody work any more, live *that* way for a while. Used to be a saying about 'Lottery in June, corn be heavy soon.' First thing you know, we'd all be eating stewed chickweed and acorns. There's *always* been a lottery," he added petulantly. "Bad enough to see young Joe Summers up there joking with everybody."

"Some places have already quit lotteries," Mrs. Adams said.

"Nothing but trouble in *that*," Old Man Warner said stoutly. "Pack of young fools."

₂₀

₂₅

₃₀

"Martin." And Bobby Martin watched his father go forward. "Overdyke. . . . 35
Percy."

"I wish they'd hurry," Mrs. Dunbar said to her older son. "I wish they'd hurry."

"They're almost through," her son said.

"You get ready to run tell Dad," Mrs. Dunbar said.

Mr. Summers called his own name and then stepped forward precisely and selected a slip from the box. Then he called, "Warner."

"Seventy-seventh year I been in the lottery," Old Man Warner said as he 40 went through the crowd. "Seventy-seventh time."

"Watson." The tall boy came awkwardly through the crowd. Someone said, "Don't be nervous, Jack," and Mr. Summers said, "Take your time, son."

"Zanini."

After that, there was a long pause, a breathless pause, until Mr. Summers, holding his slip of paper in the air, said, "All right fellows." For a minute, no one moved, and then all the slips of paper were opened. Suddenly, all the women began to speak at once, saying, "Who is it?" "Who's got it?" "Is it the Dunbars?" "Is it the Watsons?" Then the voices began to say, "It's Hutchinson. It's Bill," "Bill Hutchinson's got it."

"Go tell your father," Mrs. Dunbar said to her older son.

People began to look around to see the Hutchinsons. Bill Hutchinson 45 was standing quiet, staring down at the paper in his hand. Suddenly, Tessie Hutchinson shouted to Mr. Summers, "You didn't give him time enough to take any paper he wanted. I saw you. It wasn't fair!"

"Be a good sport, Tessie," Mrs. Delacroix called, and Mrs. Graves said, "All of us took the same chance."

"Shut up, Tessie," Bill Hutchinson said.

"Well, everyone," Mr. Summers said, "That was done pretty fast, and now we've got to be hurrying a little more to get it done in time." He consulted his next list. "Bill," he said, "you draw for the Hutchinson family. You got any other households in the Hutchinsons?"

"There's Don and Eva," Mrs. Hutchinson yelled. "Make *them* take their chance!"

"Daughters draw with their husbands' families, Tessie," Mr. Summers said 50 gently. "You know that as well as anyone else."

"It wasn't *fair*," Tessie said.

"I guess not, Joe," Bill Hutchinson said regretfully. "My daughter draws with her husband's family, that's only fair. And I've got no other family except the kids."

"Then, as far as drawing for families is concerned, it's you," Mr. Summers said in explanation, "and as far as drawing for households is concerned, that's you, too. Right?"

"Right," Bill Hutchinson said.

"How many kids, Bill?" Mr. Summers asked formally. 55

"Three," Bill Hutchinson said. "There's Bill, Jr., and Nancy, and little Dave. And Tessie and me."

"All right then," Mr. Summers said. "Harry, you got their tickets back?"

Mr. Graves nodded and held up the slips of paper. "Put them in the box, then," Mr. Summers directed. "Take Bill's and put it in."

"I think we ought to start over," Mrs. Hutchinson said, as quietly as she could. "I tell you it wasn't *fair*. You didn't give him time enough to choose. *Every*body saw that."

Mr. Graves had selected the five slips and put them in the box, and he 60 dropped all the papers but those onto the ground, where the breeze caught them and lifted them off.

"Listen, everybody," Mrs. Hutchinson was saying to the people around her.

"Ready, Bill?" Mr. Summers asked, and Bill Hutchinson, with one quick glance around at his wife and children, nodded.

"Remember," Mr. Summers said, "take the slips and keep them folded until each person has taken one. Harry, you help little Dave." Mr. Graves took the hand of the little boy, who came willingly with him up to the box. "Take a paper out of the box, Davy," Mr. Summers said. Davy put his hand into the box and laughed. "Take just *one* paper," Mr. Summers said. "Harry, you hold it for him." Mr. Graves took the child's hand and removed the folded paper from the tight fist and held it while little Dave stood next to him and looked up at him wonderingly.

"Nancy next," Mr. Summers said. Nancy was twelve, and her school friends breathed heavily as she went forward, switching her skirt, and took a slip daintily from the box. "Bill, Jr.," Mr. Summers said, and Billy, his face red and his feet over-large, nearly knocked the box over as he got a paper out. "Tessie," Mr. Summers said. She hesitated for a minute, looking around defiantly, and then set her lips and went up to the box. She snatched a paper out and held it behind her.

"Bill," Mr. Summers said, and Bill Hutchinson reached into the box and felt 65 around, bringing his hand out at last with the slip of paper in it.

The crowd was quiet. A girl whispered, "I hope it's not Nancy," and the sound of the whisper reached the edges of the crowd.

"It's not the way it used to be," Old Man Warner said clearly. "People ain't the way they used to be."

"All right," Mr. Summers said. "Open the papers. Harry, you open little Dave's."

Mr. Graves opened the slip of paper and there was a general sigh through the crowd as he held it up and everyone could see that it was blank. Nancy and Bill, Jr., opened theirs at the same time, and both beamed and laughed, turning around to the crowd and holding their slips of paper above their heads.

"Tessie," Mr. Summers said. There was a pause, and then Mr. Summers looked 70 at Bill Hutchinson, and Bill unfolded his paper and showed it. It was blank.

"It's Tessie," Mr. Summers said, and his voice was hushed. "Show us her paper, Bill."

Bill Hutchinson went over to his wife and forced the slip of paper out of her hand. It had a black spot on it, the black spot Mr. Summers had made the night before with the heavy pencil in the coal-company office. Bill Hutchinson held it up, and there was a stir in the crowd.

"All right, folks," Mr. Summers said. "Let's finish quickly."

Although the villagers had forgotten the ritual and lost the original black box, they still remembered to use stones. The pile of stones the boys had made earlier was ready; there were stones on the ground with the blowing scraps of paper that had come out of the box. Mrs. Delacroix selected a stone so large she had to pick it up with both hands and turned to Mrs. Dunbar. "Come on," she said. "Hurry up."

Mrs. Dunbar had small stones in both hands, and she said, gasping for 75 breath, "I can't run at all. You'll have to go ahead and I'll catch up with you."

The children had stones already, and someone gave little Davy Hutchinson a few pebbles.

Tessie Hutchinson was in the center of a cleared space by now, and she held her hands out desperately as the villagers moved in on her. "It isn't fair," she said. A stone hit her on the side of the head.

Old Man Warner was saying, "Come on, come on, everyone." Steve Adams was in the front of the crowd of villagers, with Mrs. Graves beside him.

"It isn't fair, it isn't right," Mrs. Hutchinson screamed, and then they were upon her.

FOR ANALYSIS

1. What evidence in the story suggests that the lottery is a ritualistic ceremony?

2. Does the straightforward narrative **style** describing the holiday atmosphere diminish or intensify the horror of the story's conclusion? Explain.

3. Might the story be a comment on religious orthodoxy? Explain.

MAKING ARGUMENTS

After the 1948 publication of "The Lottery," Jackson and the *New Yorker*, which published it, received hundreds of negative letters, often angry ones. Make an argument for the importance to this reaction of the historical climate in which "The Lottery" was written and read, in particular the Cold War; make reference to historical evidence as well as to textual evidence.

WRITING TOPICS

1. Explain the purpose of the lottery, and identify contemporary rituals that exhibit similar purposes.

2. Magic and religion differ because magicians can compel change whereas priests can only ask for change. Comment on this distinction. Can you identify magical elements in religion?

MAKING CONNECTIONS

Compare this story with Leslie Marmon Silko's "The Man to Send Rain Clouds" (p. 1209). What similarities do you find? What differences?

HARLAN ELLISON® (B. 1934)

"REPENT, HARLEQUIN!" SAID THE TICKTOCKMAN 1965

There are always those who ask, what is it all about? For those who need to ask, for those who need points sharply made, who need to know "where it's at," this:

> The mass of men serve the state thus, not as men mainly, but as machines, with their bodies. They are the standing army, and the militia, jailors, constables, posse comitatus, etc. In most cases there is no free exercise whatever of the judgment or of the moral sense; but they put themselves on a level with wood and earth and stones; and wooden men can perhaps be manufactured that will serve the purpose as well. Such command no more respect than men of straw or a lump of dirt. They have the same sort of worth only as horses and dogs. Yet such as these even are commonly esteemed good citizens. Others—as most legislators, politicians, lawyers, ministers, and officeholders—serve the state chiefly with their heads; and, as they rarely make any moral distinctions, they are as likely to serve the Devil, without intending it, as God. A very few, as heroes, patriots, martyrs, reformers in the great sense, and men, serve the state with their consciences also, and so necessarily resist it for the most part; and they are commonly treated as enemies by it.

Henry David Thoreau
CIVIL DISOBEDIENCE

That is the heart of it. Now begin in the middle, and later learn the beginning; the end will take care of itself.

But because it was the very world it was, the very world they had allowed it to *become*, for months his activities did not come to the alarmed attention of The Ones Who Kept The Machine Functioning Smoothly, the ones who poured the very best butter over the cams and mainsprings of the culture. Not until it had become obvious that somehow, someway, he had become a notoriety, a celebrity, perhaps even a hero for (what Officialdom inescapably tagged) "an emotionally disturbed segment of the populace," did they turn it over to the Ticktockman and his legal machinery. But by then, because it was the very world it was, and they had no way to predict he would happen—possibly a strain of disease long-defunct, now, suddenly, reborn in a system where immunity had been forgotten, had lapsed—he had been allowed to become too real. Now he had form and substance.

He had become a *personality*, something they had filtered out of the system many decades before. But there it was, and there *he* was, a very definitely imposing personality. In certain circles—middle-class circles—it was thought disgusting. Vulgar ostentation. Anarchistic. Shameful. In others, there was only sniggering: those strata where thought is subjugated to form and ritual, niceties, proprieties. But down below, ah, down below, where the people always needed their saints and sinners, their bread and circuses, their heroes and villains, he was considered a Bolivar; a Napoleon; a Robin Hood; a Dick Bong (Ace of Aces); a Jesus; a Jomo Kenyatta.

And at the top—where, like socially-attuned Shipwreck Kellys, every tremor 5 and vibration threatening to dislodge the wealthy, powerful and titled from their flagpoles—he was considered a menace; a heretic; a rebel; a disgrace; a peril. He was known down the line, to the very heartmeat core, but the important reactions were high above and far below. At the very top, at the very bottom.

So his file was turned over, along with his time-card and his cardioplate, to the office of the Ticktockman.

The Ticktockman: very much over six feet tall, often silent, a soft purring man when things went timewise. The Ticktockman.

Even in the cubicles of the hierarchy, where fear was generated, seldom suffered, he was called the Ticktockman. But no one called him that to his mask.

You don't call a man a hated name, not when that man, behind his mask, is capable of revoking the minutes, the hours, the days and nights, the years of your life. He was called the Master Timekeeper to his mask. It was safer that way.

"This is *what* he is," said the Ticktockman with genuine softness, "but not 10 *who* he is. This time-card I'm holding in my left hand has a name on it, but it is the name of *what* he is, not *who* he is. The cardioplate here in my right hand is also named, but not *whom* named, merely *what* named. Before I can exercise proper revocation, I have to know *who* this *what* is."

To his staff, all the ferrets, all the loggers, all the finks, all the commex, even the mineez, he said, "Who is this Harlequin?"

He was not purring smoothly. Timewise, it was jangle.

However, it *was* the longest speech they had ever heard him utter at one time, the staff, the ferrets, the loggers, the finks, the commex, but not the mineez, who usually weren't around to know, in any case. But even they scurried to find out.

Who is the Harlequin?

High above the third level of the city, he crouched on the humming 15 aluminum-frame platform of the air-boat (foof! air-boat, indeed! swizzleskid is what it was, with a tow-rack jerry-rigged) and he stared down at the neat Mondrian arrangement of the buildings.

Somewhere nearby, he could hear the metronomic left-right-left of the 2:47 PM shift, entering the Timkin roller-bearing plant in their sneakers. A minute later, precisely, he heard the softer right-left-right of the 5:00 AM formation, going home.

An elfin grin spread across his tanned features, and his dimples appeared for a moment. Then, scratching at his thatch of auburn hair, he shrugged within his motley, as though girding himself for what came next, and threw the joystick forward, and bent into the wind as the air-boat dropped. He skimmed over a slidewalk, purposely dropping a few feet to crease the tassels of the ladies of fashion, and—inserting thumbs in large ears—he stuck out his tongue, rolled his eyes, and went wugga-wugga-wugga. It was a minor diversion. One pedestrian skittered and tumbled, sending parcels everywhichway, another wet herself, a third keeled slantwise and the walk was stopped automatically by the servitors till she could be resuscitated. It was a minor diversion.

Then he swirled away on a vagrant breeze, and was gone. Hi-ho. As he rounded the cornice of the Time-Motion Study Building, he saw the shift, just boarding the slidewalk. With practiced motion and an absolute conservation of movement, they sidestepped up onto the slow-strip and (in a chorus line reminiscent of a Busby Berkeley film of the antediluvian 1930s) advanced across the strips ostrich-walking till they were lined up on the expresstrip.

Once more, in anticipation, the elfin grin spread, and there was a tooth missing back there on the left side. He dipped, skimmed, and swooped over them; and then, scrunching about on the air-boat, he released the holding pins that fastened shut the ends of the home-made pouring troughs that kept his cargo from dumping prematurely. And as he pulled the trough-pins, the air-boat slid over the factory workers and one hundred and fifty thousand dollars' worth of jelly beans cascaded down on the expresstrip.

Jelly beans! Millions and billions of purples and yellows and greens and 20 licorice and grape and raspberry and mint and round and smooth and crunchy outside and soft-mealy inside and sugary and bouncing jouncing tumbling clittering clattering skittering fell on the heads and shoulders and hardhats and carapaces of the Timkin workers, tinkling on the slidewalk and bouncing away and rolling about underfoot and filling the sky on their way down with all the colors of joy and childhood and holidays, coming down in a steady rain, a solid wash, a torrent of color and sweetness out of the sky from above, and entering a universe of sanity and metronomic order with quite-mad coocoo newness. Jelly beans!

The shift workers howled and laughed and were pelted, and broke ranks, and the jelly beans managed to work their way into the mechanism of the slidewalks after which there was a hideous scraping as the sound of a million fingernails rasped down a quarter of a million blackboards, followed by a coughing and a sputtering, and then the slidewalks all stopped and everyone was dumped thisawayandthataway in a jackstraw tumble, still laughing and popping little jelly bean eggs of childish color into their mouths. It was a holiday, and a jollity, an absolute insanity, a giggle. But . . .

The shift was delayed seven minutes.

They did not get home for seven minutes.

The master schedule was thrown off by seven minutes.

Quotas were delayed by inoperative slidewalks for seven minutes. 25

He had tapped the first domino in the line, and one after another, like chik chik chik, the others had fallen.

The System had been seven minutes' worth of disrupted. It was a tiny matter, one hardly worthy of note, but in a society where the single driving force was order and unity and equality and promptness and clocklike precision and attention to the clock, reverence of the gods of the passage of time, it was a disaster of major importance.

So he was ordered to appear before the Ticktockman. It was broadcast across every channel of the communications web. He was ordered to be *there* at 7:00 dammit on time. And they waited, and they waited, but he didn't show up till almost ten-thirty, at which time he merely sang a little song about moonlight in a place no one had ever heard of, called Vermont, and vanished again. But they had all been waiting since seven, and it wrecked *hell* with their schedules. So the question remained: Who is the Harlequin?

But the *unasked* question (more important of the two) was: how did we get *into* this position, where a laughing, irresponsible japer of jabberwocky and jive could disrupt our entire economic and cultural life with a hundred and fifty thousand dollars' worth of jelly beans . . .

Jelly for God's sake *beans*! This is madness! Where did he get the money to 30 buy a hundred and fifty thousand dollars' worth of jelly beans? (They knew it would have cost that much, because they had a team of Situation Analysts pulled off another assignment, and rushed to the slidewalk scene to sweep up and count the candies, and produce findings, which disrupted *their* schedules and threw their entire branch at least a day behind.) Jelly beans! Jelly . . . *beans*? Now wait a second—a second accounted for—no one has manufactured jelly beans for over a hundred years. Where did he get jelly beans?

That's another good question. More than likely it will never be answered to your complete satisfaction. But then, how many questions ever are?

The middle you know. Here is the beginning. How it starts:

A DESK PAD. DAY FOR DAY, AND TURN EACH DAY. 9:00—OPEN THE MAIL. 9:45—APPOINTMENT WITH PLANNING COMMISSION BOARD. 10:30—DISCUSS INSTALLATION PROGRESS CHARTS WITH J.L. 11:45— PRAY FOR RAIN. 12:00—LUNCH. *AND SO IT GOES.*

"I'm sorry, Miss Grant, but the time for interviews was set at 2:30, and it's almost five now. I'm sorry you're late, but those are the rules. You'll have to wait till next year to submit application for this college again." *And so it goes.*

The 10:10 local stops at Cresthaven, Galesville, Tonawanda Junction, Selby, and 35 Farnhurst, but not at Indiana City, Lucasville and Colton, except on Sunday. The 10:35 express stops at Galesville, Selby, and Indiana City, except on Sundays & Holidays, at which time it stops at . . . *and so it goes.*

"I couldn't wait, Fred. I had to be at Pierre Cartain's by 3:00, and you said you'd meet me under the clock in the terminal at 2:45, and you weren't there, so I had to go on. You're always late, Fred. If you'd been there, we could have sewed it up together, but as it was, well, I took the order alone . . ." *And so it goes.*

Dear Mr. and Mrs. Atterley: In reference to your son Gerold's constant tardiness, I am afraid we will have to suspend him from school unless some more reliable method can be instituted guaranteeing he will arrive at his classes on time. Granted he is an exemplary student, and his marks are high, his constant flouting of the schedules of this school makes it impractical to maintain him in a system where the other children seem capable of getting where they are supposed to be on time *and so it goes*.

YOU CANNOT VOTE UNLESS YOU APPEAR AT 8:45 AM.

"I don't care if the script is *good*, I need it Thursday!"

CHECK-OUT TIME IS 2:00 PM.   40

"You got here late. The job's taken. Sorry."

YOUR SALARY HAS BEEN DOCKED FOR TWENTY MINUTES TIME LOST.

"God, what time is it, I've gotta run!"

And so it goes. And so it goes. And so it goes. And so it goes goes goes goes goes tick tock tick tock tick tock and one day we no longer let time serve us, we serve time and we are slaves of the schedule, worshippers of the sun's passing, bound into a life predicated on restrictions because the system will not function if we don't keep the schedule tight.

Until it becomes more than a minor inconvenience to be late. It becomes a   45
sin. Then a crime. Then a crime punishable by this:

> **EFFECTIVE 15 JULY 2389 12:00:00 midnight, the office of the Master Timekeeper will require all citizens to submit their time-cards and cardioplates for processing. In accordance with Statute 555-7-SGH-999 governing the revocation of time per capita, all cardioplates will be keyed to the individual holder and—**

What they had done was devise a method of curtailing the amount of life a person could have. If he was ten minutes late, he lost ten minutes of his life. An hour was proportionately worth more revocation. If someone was consistently tardy, he might find himself, on a Sunday night, receiving a communiqué from the Master Timekeeper that his time had run out, and he would be "turned off" at high noon on Monday, please straighten your affairs, sir, madame, or bisex.

And so, by this simple scientific expedient (utilizing a scientific process held dearly secret by the Ticktockman's office) the System was maintained. It was the only expedient thing to do. It was, after all, patriotic. The schedules had to be met. After all, there *was* a war on!

But, wasn't there always?

"Now that is really disgusting," the Harlequin said, when Pretty Alice 50
showed him the wanted poster. "Disgusting and *highly* improbable. After all,
this isn't the Day of the Desperado. A *wanted* poster!"

"You know," Pretty Alice noted, "you speak with a great deal of inflection."

"I'm sorry," said the Harlequin, humbly.

"No need to be sorry. You're always saying 'I'm sorry.' You have such massive
guilt, Everett, it's really very sad."

"I'm sorry," he said again, then pursed his lips so the dimples appeared
momentarily. He hadn't wanted to say that at all. "I have to go out again. I have
to *do* something."

Pretty Alice slammed her coffee-bulb down on the counter. "Oh for God's 55
sake, Everett, can't you stay home just *one* night! Must you always be out in that
ghastly clown suit, running around an*noy*ing people?"

"I'm—" He stopped, and clapped the jester's hat onto his auburn thatch with
a tiny tinkling of bells. He rose, rinsed out his coffee-bulb at the spray, and put
it into the dryer for a moment. "I have to go."

She didn't answer. The faxbox was purring, and she pulled a sheet out,
read it, threw it toward him on the counter. "It's about you. Of course. You're
ridiculous."

He read it quickly. It said the Ticktockman was trying to locate him. He
didn't care, he was going out to be late again. At the door, dredging for an exit
line, he hurled back petulantly, "Well, *you* speak with inflection, *too*!"

Pretty Alice rolled her pretty eyes heavenward. "You're ridiculous."

The Harlequin stalked out, slamming the door, which sighed shut softly, and 60
locked itself.

There was a gentle knock, and Pretty Alice got up with an exhalation of exasperated breath, and opened the door. He stood there. "I'll be back about ten-
thirty, okay?"

She pulled a rueful face. "Why do you tell me that? Why? You *know* you'll be
late! You *know* it! You're *always* late, so why do you tell me these dumb things?"
She closed the door.

On the other side, the Harlequin nodded to himself. *She's right. She's always
right. I'll be late. I'm always late. Why do I tell her these dumb things?*

He shrugged again, and went off to be late once more.

He had fired off the firecracker rockets that said: I will attend the 115th 65
annual International Medical Association Invocation at 8:00 PM precisely. I do
hope you will all be able to join me.

The words had burned in the sky, and of course the authorities were there,
lying in wait for him. They assumed, naturally, that he would be late. He
arrived twenty minutes early, while they were setting up the spiderwebs to trap
and hold him. Blowing a large bullhorn, he frightened and unnerved them so,
their own moisturized encirclement webs sucked closed, and they were hauled
up, kicking and shrieking, high above the amphitheater's floor. The Harlequin
laughed and laughed, and apologized profusely. The physicians, gathered in

solemn conclave, roared with laughter, and accepted the Harlequin's apologies with exaggerated bowing and posturing, and a merry time was had by all, who thought the Harlequin was a regular foofaraw in fancy pants; all, that is, but the authorities, who had been sent out by the office of the Ticktockman; they hung there like so much dockside cargo, hauled up above the floor of the amphitheater in a most unseemly fashion.

(In another part of the same city where the Harlequin carried on his "activities," totally unrelated in every way to what concerns us here, save that it illustrates the Ticktockman's power and import, a man named Marshall Delahanty received his turn-off notice from the Ticktockman's office. His wife received the notification from the gray-suited minee who delivered it, with the traditional "look of sorrow" plastered hideously across his face. She knew what it was, even without unsealing it. It was a billet-doux of immediate recognition to everyone these days. She gasped, and held it as though it were a glass slide tinged with botulism, and prayed it was not for her. Let it be for Marsh, she thought, brutally, realistically, or one of the kids, but not for me, please dear God, not for me. And then she opened it, and it *was* for Marsh, and she was at one and the same time horrified and relieved. The next trooper in the line had caught the bullet. "Marshall," she screamed, "Marshall! Termination, Marshall! OhmiGod, Marshall, whattl we do, whattl we do, Marshall omigodmarshall . . ." and in their home that night was the sound of tearing paper and fear, and the stink of madness went up the flue and there was nothing, absolutely nothing they could do about it.

(But Marshall Delahanty tried to run. And early the next day, when turn-off time came, he was deep in the Canadian forest two hundred miles away, and the office of the Ticktockman blanked his cardioplate, and Marshall Delahanty keeled over, running, and his heart stopped, and the blood dried up on its way to his brain, and he was dead that's all. One light went out on the sector map in the office of the Master Timekeeper, while notification was entered for fax reproduction, and Georgette Delahanty's name was entered on the dole roles till she could remarry. Which is the end of the footnote, and all the point that need be made, except don't laugh, because that is what would happen to the Harlequin if ever the Ticktockman found out his real name. It isn't funny.)

The shopping level of the city was thronged with the Thursday-colors of the buyers. Women in canary yellow chitons and men in pseudo-Tyrolean outfits that were jade and leather and fit very tightly, save for the balloon pants.

When the Harlequin appeared on the still-being-constructed shell of the new Efficiency Shopping Center, his bullhorn to his elfishly-laughing lips, everyone pointed and stared, and he berated them:

"Why let them order you about? Why let them tell you to hurry and scurry like ants or maggots? Take your time! Saunter a while! Enjoy the sunshine, enjoy the breeze, let life carry you at your own pace! Don't be slaves of time, it's a helluva way to die, slowly, by degrees . . . down with the Ticktockman!"

Who's the nut? most of the shoppers wanted to know. Who's the nut oh wow I'm gonna be late I gotta run . . .

And the construction gang on the Shopping Center received an urgent order from the office of the Master Timekeeper that the dangerous criminal known as the Harlequin was atop their spire, and their aid was urgently needed in apprehending him. The work crew said no, they would lose time on their construction schedule, but the Ticktockman managed to pull the proper threads of governmental webbing, and they were told to cease work and catch that nitwit up there on the spire; up there with the bullhorn. So a dozen and more burly workers began climbing into their construction platforms, releasing the a-grav plates, and rising toward the Harlequin.

After the debacle (in which, through the Harlequin's attention to personal safety, no one was seriously injured), the workers tried to reassemble, and assault him again, but it was too late. He had vanished. It had attracted quite a crowd, however, and the shopping cycle was thrown off by hours, simply hours. The purchasing needs of the system were therefore falling behind, and so measures were taken to accelerate the cycle for the rest of the day, but it got bogged down and speeded up and they sold too many float-valves and not nearly enough wegglers, which meant that the popli ratio was off, which made it necessary to rush cases and cases of spoiling Smash-O to stores that usually needed a case only every three or four hours. The shipments were bollixed, the transshipments were misrouted, and in the end, even the swizzleskid industries felt it.

"Don't come back till you have him!" the Ticktockman said, very quietly, very sincerely, extremely dangerously. 75

They used dogs. They used probes. They used cardioplate crossoffs. They used teepers. They used bribery. They used stiktytes. They used intimidation. They used torment. They used torture. They used finks. They used cops. They used search&seizure. They used fallaron. They used betterment incentive. They used fingerprints. They used the Bertillon system. They used cunning. They used guile. They used treachery. They used Raoul Mitgong, but he didn't help much. They used applied physics. They used techniques of criminology.

And what the hell: they caught him.

After all, his name was Everett C. Marm, and he wasn't much to begin with, except a man who had no sense of time.

"Repent, Harlequin!" said the Ticktockman.

"Get stuffed!" the Harlequin replied, sneering. 80

"You've been late a total of sixty-three years, five months, three weeks, two days, twelve hours, forty-one minutes, fifty-nine seconds, point oh three six one one one microseconds. You've used up everything you can, and more. I'm going to turn you off."

"Scare someone else. I'd rather be dead than live in a dumb world with a bogeyman like you."

"It's my job."

"You're full of it. You're a tyrant. You have no right to order people around and kill them if they show up late."

"You can't adjust. You can't fit in." 85

"Unstrap me, and I'll fit my fist into your mouth."

"You're a nonconformist."

"That didn't used to be a felony."

"It is now. Live in the world around you."

"I hate it. It's a terrible world." 90

"Not everyone thinks so. Most people enjoy order."

"I don't, and most of the people I know don't."

"That's not true. How do you think we caught you?"

"I'm not interested."

"A girl named Pretty Alice told us who you were." 95

"That's a lie."

"It's true. You unnerve her. She wants to belong; she wants to conform; I'm going to turn you off."

"Then do it already, and stop arguing with me."

"I'm not going to turn you off."

"You're an idiot!" 100

"Repent, Harlequin!" said the Ticktockman.

"Get stuffed."

So they sent him to Coventry. And in Coventry they worked him over. It was just like what they did to Winston Smith in NINETEEN EIGHTY-FOUR, which was a book none of them knew about, but the techniques are really quite ancient, and so they did it to Everett C. Marm; and one day, quite a long time later, the Harlequin appeared on the communications web, appearing elfin and dimpled and bright-eyed, and not at all brainwashed, and he said he had been wrong, that it was a good, a very good thing indeed, to belong, to be right on time hip-ho and away we go, and everyone stared up at him on the public screens that covered an entire city block, and they said to themselves, well, you see, he was just a nut after all, and if that's the way the system is run, then let's do it that way, because it doesn't pay to fight city hall, or in this case, the Ticktockman. So Everett C. Marm was destroyed, which was a loss, because of what Thoreau said earlier, but you can't make an omelet without breaking a few eggs, and in every revolution a few die who shouldn't, but they have to, because that's the way it happens, and if you make only a little change, then it seems to be worthwhile. Or, to make the point lucidly:

"Uh, excuse me, sir, I, uh, don't know how to uh, to uh, tell you this, but you were three minutes late. The schedule is a little, uh, bit off."

He grinned sheepishly. 105

"That's ridiculous!" murmured the Ticktockman behind his mask. "Check your watch." And then he went into his office, going *mrmee, mrmee, mrmee, mrmee*.

FOR ANALYSIS

1. What are the **connotations** of the names *Harlequin* and *Everett C. Marm*? Is the contrast between the names similar to that between, say, *Superman* and *Clark Kent*?

2. What is it about his society that drives Everett C. Marm to rebel?

3. What is Pretty Alice's role in the story?

MAKING ARGUMENTS

Carefully read the passage (para. 1) taken from Thoreau's "Civil Disobedience." Write an essay explaining why you do or do not agree (in whole or in part) with Thoreau's view of "the state" and with his classification of citizens as those who serve the state with their "bodies," those who serve it with their "heads," and those who serve it with their "consciences." In which group would you place Everett C. Marm?

WRITING TOPICS

1. Explain the final section of the story (paras. 104–6). Has the Ticktockman triumphed?

2. Characterize Pretty Alice. Why does she turn Everett in?

MAKING CONNECTIONS

1. Compare the statement this story makes about the human spirit with that made in Updike's "A & P" (p. 92). Do Everett C. Marm and Sammy share any attributes?

2. Compare Everett C. Marm and the narrator in Ellison's "Battle Royal" (p. 355) as rebels. Who is more successful as a rebel? As a conformist? Will the narrator of "Battle Royal" grow up to be like the Harlequin?

TWO KINDS 1989

My mother believed you could be anything you wanted to be in America. You could open a restaurant. You could work for the government and get good retirement. You could buy a house with almost no money down. You could become rich. You could become instantly famous.

"Of course you can be prodigy, too," my mother told me when I was nine. "You can be best anything. What does Auntie Lindo know? Her daughter, she is only best tricky."

America was where all my mother's hopes lay. She had come here in 1949 after losing everything in China: her mother and father, her family home, her first husband, and two daughters, twin baby girls. But she never looked back with regret. There were so many ways for things to get better.

We didn't immediately pick the right kind of prodigy. At first my mother thought I could be a Chinese Shirley Temple. We'd watch Shirley's old movies on TV as though they were training films. My mother would poke my arm and say, *"Ni kan"*—You watch. And I would see Shirley tapping her feet, or singing a sailor song, or pursing her lips into a very round O while saying, "Oh my goodness."

"*Ni kan,*" said my mother as Shirley's eyes flooded with tears. "You already 5 know how. Don't need talent for crying!"

Soon after my mother got this idea about Shirley Temple, she took me to a beauty training school in the Mission district and put me in the hands of a student who could barely hold the scissors without shaking. Instead of getting big fat curls, I emerged with an uneven mass of crinkly black fuzz. My mother dragged me off to the bathroom and tried to wet down my hair.

"You look like Negro Chinese," she lamented, as if I had done this on purpose.

The instructor of the beauty training school had to lop off these soggy clumps to make my hair even again. "Peter Pan is very popular these days," the instructor assured my mother. I now had hair the length of a boy's, with straight-across bangs that hung at a slant two inches above my eyebrows. I liked the haircut and it made me actually look forward to my future fame.

In fact, in the beginning, I was just as excited as my mother, maybe even more so. I pictured this prodigy part of me as many different images, trying each one on for size. I was a dainty ballerina girl standing by the curtains, waiting to hear the right music that would send me floating on my tiptoes. I was like the Christ child lifted out of the straw manger, crying with holy indignity. I was Cinderella stepping from her pumpkin carriage with sparkly cartoon music filling the air.

In all of my imaginings, I was filled with a sense that I would soon become 10 *perfect*. My mother and father would adore me. I would be beyond reproach. I would never feel the need to sulk for anything.

But sometimes the prodigy in me became impatient. "If you don't hurry up and get me out of here, I'm disappearing for good," it warned. "And then you'll always be nothing."

Every night after dinner, my mother and I would sit at the Formica kitchen table. She would present new tests, taking her examples from stories of amazing children she had read in *Ripley's Believe It or Not*, or *Good Housekeeping*, *Reader's Digest*, and a dozen other magazines she kept in a pile in our bathroom. My mother got these magazines from people whose houses she cleaned. And since she cleaned many houses each week, we had a great assortment. She would look through them all, searching for stories about remarkable children.

The first night she brought out a story about a three-year-old boy who knew the capitals of all the states and even of most of the European countries. A teacher was quoted as saying the little boy could also pronounce the names of the foreign cities correctly.

"What's the capital of Finland?" my mother asked me, looking at the magazine story.

All I knew was the capital of California, because Sacramento was the name 15 of the street we lived on in Chinatown. "Nairobi!" I guessed, saying the most foreign word I could think of. She checked to see if that was possibly one way to pronounce "Helsinki" before showing me the answer.

The tests got harder—multiplying numbers in my head, finding the queen of hearts in a deck of cards, trying to stand on my head without using my hands, predicting the daily temperatures in Los Angeles, New York, and London.

One night I had to look at a page from the Bible for three minutes and then report everything I could remember. "Now Jehoshaphat had riches and honor in abundance and . . . that's all I remember, Ma," I said.

And after seeing my mother's disappointed face once again, something inside of me began to die. I hated the tests, the raised hopes and failed expectations. Before going to bed that night, I looked in the mirror above the bathroom sink and when I saw only my face staring back—and that it would always be this ordinary face—I began to cry. Such a sad, ugly girl! I made high-pitched noises like a crazed animal, trying to scratch out the face in the mirror.

And then I saw what seemed to be the prodigy side of me—because I had never seen that face before. I looked at my reflection, blinking so I could see more clearly. The girl staring back at me was angry, powerful. This girl and I were the same. I had new thoughts, willful thoughts, or rather thoughts filled with lots of won'ts. I won't let her change me, I promised myself. I won't be what I'm not.

So now on nights when my mother presented her tests, I performed listlessly, 20 my head propped on one arm. I pretended to be bored. And I was. I got so bored I started counting the bellows of the foghorns out on the bay while my mother drilled me in other areas. The sound was comforting and reminded me of the cow jumping over the moon. And the next day, I played a game with myself, seeing if my mother would give up on me before eight bellows. After a while I usually counted only one, maybe two bellows at most. At last she was beginning to give up hope.

Two or three months had gone by without any mention of my being a prodigy again. And then one day my mother was watching *The Ed Sullivan Show* on TV. The TV was old and the sound kept shorting out. Every time my mother got halfway up from the sofa to adjust the set, the sound would come back on and Ed would be talking. As soon as she sat down, Ed would go silent again. She got up, the TV broke into loud piano music. She sat down. Silence. Up and down, back and forth, quiet and loud. It was like a stiff embraceless dance between her and the TV set. Finally she stood by the set with her hand on the sound dial.

She seemed entranced by the music, a little frenzied piano piece with this mesmerizing quality, sort of quick passages and then teasing lilting ones before it returned to the quick playful parts.

"*Ni kan*," my mother said, calling me over with hurried hand gestures, "Look here."

I could see why my mother was fascinated by the music. It was being pounded out by a little Chinese girl, about nine years old, with a Peter Pan haircut. The girl had the sauciness of a Shirley Temple. She was proudly modest like a proper Chinese child. And she also did a fancy sweep of a curtsy, so that the fluffy skirt of her white dress cascaded slowly to the floor like the petals of a large carnation.

In spite of these warning signs, I wasn't worried. Our family had no piano 25 and we couldn't afford to buy one, let alone reams of sheet music and piano lessons. So I could be generous in my comments when my mother bad-mouthed the little girl on TV.

"Play note right, but doesn't sound good! No singing sound," complained my mother.

"What are you picking on her for?" I said carelessly. "She's pretty good. Maybe she's not the best, but she's trying hard." I knew almost immediately I would be sorry I said that.

"Just like you," she said. "Not the best. Because you not trying." She gave a little huff as she let go of the sound dial and sat down on the sofa.

The little Chinese girl sat down also to play an encore of "Anitra's Dance" by Grieg.[1] I remember the song, because later on I had to learn how to play it.

Three days after watching *The Ed Sullivan Show*, my mother told me what my 30 schedule would be for piano lessons and piano practice. She had talked to Mr. Chong, who lived on the first floor of our apartment building. Mr. Chong was a retired piano teacher, and my mother had traded housecleaning services for

---

[1] From Edvard Grieg's (1843–1907) incidental music composed for Henrik Ibsen's play *Peer Gynt*.

weekly lessons and a piano for me to practice on every day, two hours a day, from four until six.

When my mother told me this, I felt as though I had been sent to hell. I whined and then kicked my foot a little when I couldn't stand it anymore.

"Why don't you like me the way I am? I'm *not* a genius! I can't play the piano. And even if I could, I wouldn't go on TV if you paid me a million dollars!" I cried.

My mother slapped me. "Who ask you be genius?" she shouted. "Only ask you be your best. For you sake. You think I want you be genius? Hnnh! What for! Who ask you!"

"So ungrateful," I heard her mutter in Chinese. "If she had as much talent as she has temper, she would be famous now."

Mr. Chong, whom I secretly nicknamed Old Chong, was very strange, 35 always tapping his fingers to the silent music of an invisible orchestra. He looked ancient in my eyes. He had lost most of the hair on top of his head and he wore thick glasses and had eyes that always looked tired and sleepy. But he must have been younger than I thought, since he lived with his mother and was not yet married.

I met Old Lady Chong once and that was enough. She had this peculiar smell like a baby that had done something in its pants. And her fingers felt like a dead person's, like an old peach I once found in the back of the refrigerator; the skin just slid off the meat when I picked it up.

I soon found out why Old Chong had retired from teaching piano. He was deaf. "Like Beethoven!" he shouted to me. "We're both listening only in our head!" And he would start to conduct his frantic silent sonatas.

Our lessons went like this. He would open the book and point to different things, explaining their purpose: "Key! Treble! Bass! No sharps or flats! So this is C major! Listen now and play after me!"

And then he would play the C scale a few times, a simple chord, and then, as if inspired by an old unreachable itch, he would gradually add more notes and running trills and a pounding bass until the music was really something quite grand.

I would play after him, the simple scale, the simple chord, and then I just 40 played some nonsense that sounded like a cat running up and down on top of garbage cans. Old Chong smiled and applauded and then said, "Very good! But now you must learn to keep time!"

So that's how I discovered that Old Chong's eyes were too slow to keep up with the wrong notes I was playing. He went through the motions in half-time. To help me keep rhythm, he stood behind me, pushing down on my right shoulder for every beat. He balanced pennies on top of my wrists so I would keep them still as I slowly played scales and arpeggios. He had me curve my hand around an apple and keep that shape when playing chords. He marched stiffly to show me how to make each finger dance up and down, staccato like an obedient little soldier.

He taught me all these things, and that was how I also learned I could be lazy and get away with mistakes, lots of mistakes. If I hit the wrong notes because

I hadn't practiced enough, I never corrected myself. I just kept playing in rhythm. And Old Chong kept conducting his own private reverie.

So maybe I never really gave myself a fair chance. I did pick up the basics pretty quickly, and I might have become a good pianist at that young age. But I was so determined not to try, not to be anybody different that I learned to play only the most ear-splitting preludes, the most discordant hymns.

Over the next year, I practiced like this, dutifully in my own way. And then one day I heard my mother and her friend Lindo Jong both talking in a loud bragging tone of voice so others could hear. It was after church, and I was leaning against the brick wall wearing a dress with stiff white petticoats. Auntie Lindo's daughter, Waverly, who was about my age, was standing farther down the wall about five feet away. We had grown up together and shared all the closeness of two sisters squabbling over crayons and dolls. In other words, for the most part, we hated each other. I thought she was snotty. Waverly Jong had gained a certain amount of fame as "Chinatown's Littlest Chinese Chess Champion."

"She bring home too many trophy," lamented Auntie Lindo that Sunday. "All 45 day she play chess. All day I have no time do nothing but dust off her winnings." She threw a scolding look at Waverly, who pretended not to see her.

"You lucky you don't have this problem," said Auntie Lindo with a sigh to my mother.

And my mother squared her shoulders and bragged: "Our problem worser than yours. If we ask Jing-mei wash dish, she hear nothing but music. It's like you can't stop this natural talent."

And right then I was determined to put a stop to her foolish pride.

A few weeks later, Old Chong and my mother conspired to have me play in a talent show which would be held in the church hall. By then, my parents had saved up enough to buy me a secondhand piano, a black Wurlitzer spinet with a scarred bench. It was the showpiece of our living room.

For the talent show, I was to play a piece called "Pleading Child" from 50 Schumann's *Scenes from Childhood*. It was a simple, moody piece that sounded more difficult than it was. I was supposed to memorize the whole thing, playing the repeat parts twice to make the piece sound longer. But I dawdled over it, playing a few bars and then cheating, looking up to see what notes followed. I never really listened to what I was playing. I daydreamed about being somewhere else, about being someone else.

The part I liked to practice best was the fancy curtsy: right foot out, touch the rose on the carpet with a pointed foot, sweep to the side, left leg bends, look up, and smile.

My parents invited all the couples from the Joy Luck Club to witness my debut. Auntie Lindo and Uncle Tin were there. Waverly and her two older brothers had also come. The first two rows were filled with children both younger and older than I was. The littlest ones got to go first. They recited simple nursery rhymes, squawked out tunes on miniature violins, twirled Hula Hoops, pranced in pink ballet tutus, and when they bowed or curtsied, the audience would sigh in unison, "Awww," and then clap enthusiastically.

When my turn came, I was very confident. I remember my childish excitement. It was as if I knew, without a doubt, that the prodigy side of me really did exist. I had no fear whatsoever, no nervousness. I remember thinking to myself, This is it! This is it! I looked out over the audience, at my mother's blank face, my father's yawn, Auntie Lindo's stiff-lipped smile, Waverly's sulky expression. I had on a white dress, layered with sheets of lace, and a pink bow in my Peter Pan haircut. As I sat down, I envisioned people jumping to their feet and Ed Sullivan rushing up to introduce me to everyone on TV.

And I started to play. It was so beautiful. I was so caught up in how lovely I looked that at first I didn't worry how I would sound. So it was a surprise to me when I hit the first wrong note and I realized something didn't sound quite right. And then I hit another and another followed that. A chill started at the top of my head and began to trickle down. Yet I couldn't stop playing, as though my hands were bewitched. I kept thinking my fingers would adjust themselves back, like a train switching to the right track. I played this strange jumble through two repeats, the sour notes staying with me all the way to the end.

When I stood up, I discovered my legs were shaking. Maybe I had just been 55 nervous and the audience, like Old Chong, had seen me go through the right motions and had not heard anything wrong at all. I swept my right foot out, went down on my knee, looked up and smiled. The room was quiet, except for Old Chong, who was beaming and shouting, "Bravo! Bravo! Well done!" But then I saw my mother's face, her stricken face. The audience clapped weakly, and as I walked back to my chair, with my whole face quivering as I tried not to cry, I heard a little boy whisper loudly to his mother, "That was awful," and the mother whispered, "Well, she certainly tried."

And now I realized how many people were in the audience, the whole world, it seemed. I was aware of eyes burning into my back. I felt the shame of my mother and father as they sat stiffly throughout the rest of the show.

We could have escaped during intermission. Pride and some strange sense of honor must have anchored my parents to their chairs. And so we watched it all: the eighteen-year-old boy with a fake moustache who did a magic show and juggled flaming hoops while riding a unicycle. The breasted girl with white makeup who sang an aria from *Madama Butterfly* and got an honorable mention. And the eleven-year-old boy who won first prize playing a tricky violin song that sounded like a busy bee.

After the show, the Hsus, the Jongs, and the St. Clairs from the Joy Luck Club came up to my mother and father.

"Lots of talented kids," Auntie Lindo said vaguely, smiling broadly.

"That was somethin' else," my father said, and I wondered if he was referring 60 to me in a humorous way, or whether he even remembered what I had done.

Waverly looked at me and shrugged her shoulders. "You aren't a genius like me," she said matter-of-factly. And if I hadn't felt so bad, I would have pulled her braids and punched her stomach.

But my mother's expression was what devastated me: a quiet, blank look that said she had lost everything. I felt the same way, and it seemed as if everybody were now coming up, like gawkers at the scene of an accident, to see what parts were actually missing. When we got on the bus to go home, my father was humming the busy-bee tune and my mother was silent. I kept thinking she wanted to wait until we got home before shouting at me. But when my father unlocked the door to our apartment, my mother walked in and then went to the back, into the bedroom. No accusations. No blame. And in a way, I felt disappointed. I had been waiting for her to start shouting, so I could shout back and cry and blame her for all my misery.

I assumed my talent-show fiasco meant I never had to play the piano again. But two days later, after school, my mother came out of the kitchen and saw me watching TV.

"Four clock," she reminded me as if it were any other day. I was stunned, as though she were asking me to go through the talent-show torture again. I wedged myself more tightly in front of the TV.

"Turn off TV," she called from the kitchen five minutes later. 65

I didn't budge. And then I decided. I didn't have to do what my mother said anymore. I wasn't her slave. This wasn't China. I had listened to her before, and look what happened. She was the stupid one.

She came out of the kitchen and stood in the arched entryway of the living room. "Four clock," she said once again, louder.

"I'm not going to play anymore," I said nonchalantly. "Why should I? I'm not a genius."

She stood in front of the TV. I saw her chest was heaving up and down in an angry way.

"No!" I said, and I now felt stronger, as if my true self had finally emerged. 70 So this was what had been inside me all along.

"No! I won't!" I screamed.

She yanked me by the arm, pulled me off the floor, snapped off the TV. She was frighteningly strong, half pulling, half carrying me toward the piano as I kicked the throw rugs under my feet. She lifted me up and onto the hard bench. I was sobbing by now, looking at her bitterly. Her chest was heaving even more and her mouth was open, smiling crazily as if she were pleased that I was crying.

"You want me to be someone that I'm not!" I sobbed. "I'll never be the kind of daughter you want me to be!"

"Only two kinds of daughters," she shouted in Chinese. "Those who are obedient and those who follow their own mind! Only one kind of daughter can live in this house. Obedient daughter!"

"Then I wish I weren't your daughter. I wish you weren't my mother," I 75 shouted. As I said these things I got scared. It felt like worms and toads and slimy things crawling out of my chest, but it also felt good, as if this awful side of me had surfaced, at last.

"Too late change this," said my mother shrilly.

And I could sense her anger rising to its breaking point. I wanted to see it spill over. And that's when I remembered the babies she had lost in China, the ones we never talked about. "Then I wish I'd never been born!" I shouted. "I wish I were dead! Like them."

It was as if I had said the magic words. Alakazam!—and her face went blank, her mouth closed, her arms went slack, and she backed out of the room, stunned, as if she were blowing away like a small brown leaf, thin, brittle, lifeless.

It was not the only disappointment my mother felt in me. In the years that followed, I failed her so many times, each time asserting my own will, my right to fall short of expectations. I didn't get straight As. I didn't become class president. I didn't get into Stanford. I dropped out of college.

For unlike my mother, I did not believe I could be anything I wanted to be. I 80 could only be me.

And for all those years, we never talked about the disaster at the recital or my terrible accusations afterward at the piano bench. All that remained unchecked, like a betrayal that was now unspeakable. So I never found a way to ask her why she had hoped for something so large that failure was inevitable.

And even worse, I never asked her about what frightened me the most: Why had she given up hope?

For after our struggle at the piano, she never mentioned my playing again. The lessons stopped. The lid to the piano was closed, shutting out the dust, my misery, and her dreams.

So she surprised me. A few years ago, she offered to give me the piano, for my thirtieth birthday. I had not played in all those years. I saw the offer as a sign of forgiveness, a tremendous burden removed.

"Are you sure?" I asked shyly. "I mean, won't you and Dad miss it?" 85

"No, this your piano," she said firmly. "Always your piano. You only one can play."

"Well, I probably can't play anymore," I said. "It's been years."

"You pick up fast," said my mother, as if she knew this was certain. "You have natural talent. You could been genius if you want to."

"No I couldn't."

"You just not trying," said my mother. And she was neither angry nor sad. She 90 said it as if to announce a fact that could never be disproved. "Take it," she said.

But I didn't at first. It was enough that she had offered it to me. And after that, every time I saw it in my parents' living room, standing in front of the bay windows, it made me feel proud, as if it were a shiny trophy that I had won back.

Last week I sent a tuner over to my parents' apartment and had the piano reconditioned, for purely sentimental reasons. My mother had died a few months before and I had been getting things in order for my father, a little bit at a time. I put the jewelry in special silk pouches. The sweaters she had knitted in yellow, pink, bright orange—all the colors I hated—I put those in moth-proof boxes. I found some old Chinese silk dresses, the kind with little slits up the sides. I rubbed the old silk against my skin, then wrapped them in tissue and decided to take them home with me.

After I had the piano tuned, I opened the lid and touched the keys. It sounded even richer than I remembered. Really, it was a very good piano. Inside the bench were the same exercise notes with handwritten scales, the same second-hand music books with their covers held together with yellow tape.

I opened up the Schumann book to the dark little piece I had played at the recital. It was on the left-hand page, "Pleading Child." It looked more difficult than I remembered. I played a few bars, surprised at how easily the notes came back to me.

And for the first time, or so it seemed, I noticed the piece on the right-hand side. It was called "Perfectly Contented." I tried to play this one as well. It had a lighter melody but the same flowing rhythm and turned out to be quite easy. "Pleading Child" was shorter but slower; "Perfectly Contented" was longer, but faster. And after I played them both a few times, I realized they were two halves of the same song. 95

FOR ANALYSIS

1. Do you think the **conflict** between the mother and daughter is unique to this family? To Asian American families? To any group of families? Why or why not?

2. What does the mother want for her daughter? What does the daughter want for herself?

3. What is the significance of the story's last paragraph?

MAKING ARGUMENTS

Using evidence from the story as well as drawing on your own experience, support or refute the notion that children should be allowed to choose their own paths.

WRITING TOPIC

Describe the similarities or the differences between the mother's attempt to influence her daughter's life and your own family's attempt to influence yours.

MAKING CONNECTIONS

Several of the stories in "Conformity and Rebellion" are driven by tensions between parents and children. Compare "Two Kinds" with stories from elsewhere in this anthology, such as William Faulkner's "A Rose for Emily" (p. 623) or Alice Walker's "Everyday Use" (p. 586). Each of these stories deals with a different culture. What significant similarities do you find among them? What substantive differences?

JENNIFER EGAN (B. 1962)

SAFARI 2010

"**R**emember, Charlie? In Hawaii? When we went to the beach at night and it started to rain?" Rolph is talking to his older sister, Charlene, who despises her real name. But because they're crouched around a bonfire with the other people on the safari, and because Rolph doesn't speak up all that often, and because their father, Lou, sitting behind them on a camp chair, is a record producer whose personal life is of general interest, those near enough to hear are listening closely. "Remember? How Mom and Dad stayed at the table for one more drink—"

"Impossible," their father interjects, with a wink at the elderly bird-watching ladies to his left. Both women wear their binoculars even in the dark, as if hoping to spot birds in the firelit tree overhead.

"Remember, Charlie? How the beach was still warm, and that crazy wind was blowing?"

But Charlie is focussed on her father's legs, which have intertwined behind her with those of his girlfriend, Mindy. Soon Lou and Mindy will bid the group good night and retreat to their tent, where they'll make love on one of its narrow rickety cots, or possibly on the ground. From the adjacent tent, which she and Rolph share, Charlie, who is fourteen, can hear them—not sounds, exactly, but movement. Rolph, at eleven, is too young to notice.

Charlie throws back her head, startling her father. Lou is in his late thir- 5 ties, his square-jawed surfer's face gone a little draggy under the eyes. "You were married to Mom on that trip," she informs him, her voice distorted by the arching of her neck, which is encircled by a puka-shell choker.

"Yes, Charlie," Lou says. "I'm aware of that."

The bird-watching ladies trade a sad smile. Lou is one of those men whose restless charm has generated a contrail of personal upheaval that is practically visible behind him: two failed marriages and two more kids back home in L.A., who were too young to bring on this three-week safari. The safari is a new business venture of Lou's old Army buddy Ramsey, with whom he drank and misbehaved, having barely avoided Korea almost twenty years ago.

Rolph pulls at his sister's shoulder. He wants her to remember, to feel it all again: the wind, the endless black ocean, the two of them peering into the dark as if awaiting a signal from their distant, grownup lives. "Remember, Charlie?"

"Yeah," Charlie says, narrowing her eyes. "I do remember that."

The Samburu warriors have arrived—four of them, two holding drums, and 10 a child in the shadows minding a yellow long-horned cow. They came yesterday, too, after the morning game run, when Lou and Mindy were "napping."

That was when Charlie exchanged shy glances with the most beautiful warrior, who has scar-tissue designs coiled like railroad tracks over the rigorous architecture of his chest and shoulders and back.

Charlie stands up and moves closer to the warriors: a slender girl in shorts and a raw-cotton shirt with small round buttons made of wood. Her teeth are slightly crooked. When the drummers pat their drums, Charlie's warrior and the other one begin to sing: guttural noises pried from their abdomens. She sways in front of them. During her ten days in Africa, she has begun to act differently—like one of the girls who intimidate her back home. In a cinder-block town that the group visited a few days ago, she drank a muddy-looking concoction in a bar and wound up trading away her silver butterfly earrings (a birthday gift from her father) in a hut belonging to a very young woman whose breasts were leaking milk. She was late returning to the jeeps; Albert, who works for Ramsey, had to go and find her. "Prepare yourself," he warned. "Your dad is having kittens." Charlie didn't care then, and doesn't now; there's a charge for her in simply commanding the fickle beam of her father's attention, feeling his disquiet as she dances, alone, by the fire.

Lou lets go of Mindy's hand and sits up straight. He has an urge to grab his daughter's skinny arm and yank her away from the warriors, but does no such thing, of course. That would be letting her win.

The warrior smiles at Charlie. He's nineteen, and has lived away from his village since he was ten. But he has sung for enough American tourists to recognize that, in her world, Charlie is a child.

"Son," Lou says, into Rolph's ear, "let's take a walk."

The boy rises from the dust and walks with his father away from the fire. Twelve tents, each sleeping two safari guests, form a circle around it, along with three outhouses and a shower stall, where water warmed on the fire is released from a sack with a rope pull. Out of view are some smaller tents for the staff, and then the black, muttering expanse of the bush, where they've been cautioned never to go.

"Your sister's acting nuts," Lou says, striding into the dark.

"Why?" Rolph asks. He hasn't noticed anything nutty in Charlie's behavior. But his father hears the question differently.

"Women are crazy," he says. "You could spend a goddam lifetime trying to figure out why."

"Mom's not."

"True," Lou reflects, calmer now. "In fact, your mother's not crazy enough."

The singing and drumbeats fall suddenly away, leaving Lou and Rolph alone under a sharp moon.

"What about Mindy?" Rolph asks. "Is she crazy?"

"Good question," Lou says. "What do you think?"

"She likes to read. She brought a lot of books."

"Did she?"

"I like her," Rolph says. "But I don't know if she's crazy. Or what the right amount is."

Lou puts his arm around Rolph. If he were an introspective man, he would have understood years ago that his son is the one person in the world who has the power to soothe him. And that, although he expects Rolph to resemble him, what he most enjoys in his son is the many ways in which he is different: quiet, reflective, attuned to the natural world and the pain of others.

"Who cares," Lou says. "Right?"

"Right," Rolph says, and the women fall away like the drumbeats, leaving him and his father together, an invincible unit amid the burbling, whispering bush. The sky is crammed with stars. Rolph closes his eyes and opens them again. He is in Africa with his father. He thinks, I'll remember this night for the rest of my life. And he's right.

When they finally return to camp, the warriors have gone. Only a few die-   30 hards from the Phoenix faction (as Lou calls the safari members who hail from there) are still sitting by the fire, comparing the day's animal sightings. Rolph creeps into his tent, pulls off his pants, and climbs onto his cot in a T-shirt and underwear. He assumes that Charlie is asleep. When she speaks, he can hear in her voice that she's been crying.

"Where did you go?" she says.

"What on earth have you got in that backpack?"

It's Cora, Lou's travel agent. She hates Mindy, but Mindy doesn't take it per-sonally—it's structural hatred, a term she coined herself and is finding highly useful on this trip. A single woman in her forties who wears high-collared shirts to conceal the thready sinews of her neck will structurally despise the twenty-three-year-old girlfriend of a powerful male who not only employs said middle-aged female but is paying her way on this trip.

"Anthropology books," Mindy tells Cora. "I'm in the Ph.D. program at Berkeley."

"Why don't you read them?"   35

"Carsick," Mindy says, which is plausible, God knows, in the shudder-ing jeeps, though untrue. She isn't sure why she hasn't cracked her Boas or Malinowski or Julian Jaynes, but assumes that she must be acquiring knowl-edge in other ways that will prove equally fruitful. In bold moments, fuelled by the boiled black coffee that is served each morning in the meal tent, Mindy has even wondered whether her insights on the links between social struc-ture and emotional response amount to more than a rehash of Lévi-Strauss—a refinement, a contemporary application. She's only in her second year of coursework.

Their jeep is the last in a line of five, nosing along a dirt road through grassland whose apparent brown masks a wide internal spectrum of color: purples, greens, reds. Albert, the surly Englishman who is Ramsey's second-in-command, is driving. Mindy has managed to avoid Albert's jeep for sev-eral days, but he has developed a reputation for discovering the best animals, so although there's no game run today—they're relocating to the hills, where they'll spend the night in a hotel for the first time this trip—the children begged to ride with him. And keeping Lou's children happy, or as close to happy as is structurally possible, is part of Mindy's job.

Structural resentment: The adolescent daughter of a twice-divorced male will be unable to tolerate the presence of his new girlfriend, and will do everything in her limited power to distract him from said girlfriend's presence, her own nascent sexuality being her chief weapon.

Structural affection: A twice-divorced male's preadolescent son (and favorite child) will embrace and accept his father's new girlfriend because he hasn't yet learned to separate his father's loves and desires from his own. In a sense, he, too, will love and desire her, and she will feel maternal toward him, though she isn't old enough to be his mother.

Structural incompatibility: A powerful twice-divorced male will be unable to acknowledge, much less sanction, the ambitions of a much younger female mate. By definition, their relationship will be temporary. 40

Structural desire: The much younger temporary female mate of a powerful male will be inexorably drawn to the single male within range who disdains her mate's power.

Albert drives with one elbow out the window. He has been a largely silent presence on this safari, eating quickly in the meal tent, providing terse answers to people's questions ("Where do you live?" "Mombasa." "How long have you been in Africa?" "Eight years." "What brought you here?" "This and that."). He rarely joins the group around the fire after dinner. On a trip to the outhouse one night, Mindy glimpsed him at the other fire, near the staff tents, drinking a beer and laughing with the Kikuyu drivers. With the tour group, he rarely smiles. Whenever his eyes happen to graze Mindy's, she senses that he feels shame on her behalf: because of her prettiness; because she sleeps with Lou; because she keeps telling herself that this trip constitutes anthropological research into group dynamics and ethnographic enclaves, when really what she's after is luxury, adventure, and a break from her four insomniac roommates.

Next to Albert, in the shotgun seat, Chronos is ranting about animals. He's the bassist for the Mat Hatters, one of the groups that Lou produces, and has come on the trip as Lou's guest, along with the Hatters' guitarist and a girlfriend each. These four are locked in a visceral animal-sighting competition. (*Structural fixation:* A collective, contextually induced obsession that becomes a temporary locus of greed, competition, and envy.) They challenge one another nightly over who saw more and at what range, invoking witnesses from their respective jeeps and promising definitive proof when they develop their film, back home.

Behind Albert sits Cora, the travel agent, and beside her, gazing out his window, is Dean, a blond actor whose genius for stating the obvious—"It's hot," or "The sun is setting," or "There aren't many trees"—is a staple source of amusement for Mindy. Dean is starring in a movie whose soundtrack Lou is helping to create; the presumption seems to be that its release will bring Dean immediate and stratospheric fame. In the seat behind him, Rolph and Charlie are showing their *Mad* magazine to Mildred, one of the bird-watching ladies. She or her companion, Fiona, can usually be found near Lou, who flirts with them tirelessly and needles them to take him bird-watching. His indulgence of these women in their seventies (strangers to him before this trip) intrigues Mindy; she can find no structural reason for it.

In the last row, beside Mindy, Lou opens the large aluminum case where his new camera is partitioned in its foam padding, like a dismantled rifle, and thrusts his torso from the open roof, ignoring the rule to stay seated while the jeep is moving. Albert swerves suddenly, and Lou is knocked back down, camera smacking his forehead. He swears at Albert, but the words are lost in the jeep's wobbly jostle through tall grass. After a minute or two of chaotic driving, they emerge a few feet from a pride of lions. Everyone gawks in startled silence—it's the closest they've been to any animal on this trip. The motor is still running, Albert's hand tentatively on the wheel, but the lions appear so relaxed, so indifferent, that he kills the engine. In the ticking motor silence they can hear the lions breathe: two females, one male, three cubs. The cubs and one of the females are gorging on a bloody zebra carcass. The others are dozing.

"They're eating," Dean says.

Chronos's hands shake as he spools film into his camera. "Fuck," he keeps muttering. "Fuck."

Albert lights a cigarette—forbidden in the brush—and waits, as indifferent to the scene as if he had paused outside a rest room.

"Can we stand?" the children ask. "Is it safe?"

"I'm sure as hell going to," Lou says.

Lou, Charlie, Rolph, Chronos, and Dean all climb onto their seats and jam their upper halves through the open roof. Mindy is now effectively alone inside the jeep with Albert, Cora, and Mildred, who peers at the lions through her bird-watching binoculars.

"How did you know?" Mindy asks, after a silence.

Albert swivels around to look at her down the length of the jeep. He has unruly hair and a soft brown mustache. There is a suggestion of humor in his face. "Just a guess."

"From half a mile away?"

"He probably has a sixth sense," Cora says, "after so many years here."

Albert turns back around and blows smoke through his open window.

"Did you see something?" Mindy says, persisting.

She doesn't expect Albert to turn again, but he does, leaning over the back of his seat, his eyes meeting hers between the children's bare legs. Mindy feels a jolt of attraction roughly akin to having someone seize her intestines and twist. She understands now that it's mutual; she sees this in Albert's face.

"Broken bushes," he says. "Like something got chased. It could have been nothing."

Cora, sensing her exclusion, sighs wearily. "Can someone come down so I can look, too?" she calls to those above the roof.

"Coming," Lou says, but Chronos is faster, ducking back into the front seat and then leaning out his window. Cora rises in her big print skirt. Mindy's face pounds with blood. Her own window, like Albert's, is on the jeep's left side, facing away from the lions. Mindy watches him wet his fingers and snuff out his cigarette. They sit in silence, hands dangling separately from their windows, a warm breeze stirring the hair on their arms, ignoring the most spectacular animal sighting of the safari.

"You're driving me crazy," Albert says, very softly. The sound seems to travel out his window and back in through Mindy's, like one of those whispering tubes. "You must know that."

"I didn't," she murmurs back.

"Well, you are."

"My hands are tied."   65

"Forever?"

She smiles. "Please. An interlude."

"Then?"

"Grad school. Berkeley."

Albert chuckles. Mindy isn't sure what the chuckle means—is it funny that 70
she's in graduate school, or that Berkeley and Mombasa, where he lives, are irreconcilable locations?

"Chronos, you crazy fuck, get back in here."

It's Lou's voice, from overhead. But Mindy feels sluggish, almost drugged, and reacts only when she hears the change in Albert's voice. "No," he hisses. "No! Back in the jeep."

Chronos is skulking among the lions, holding his camera close to the faces of the sleeping male and female, taking pictures.

"Walk backward," Albert says, with hushed urgency. "Backward, Chronos, gently."

Movement comes from a direction that no one is expecting: the lion- 75
ess gnawing at the zebra. She vaults at Chronos in an agile, gravity-defying spring that anyone with a house cat would recognize. She lands on his head, flattening him instantly. There are screams, a gunshot, and those overhead tumble back into their seats so violently that at first Mindy thinks they've been shot. But it's the lioness; Albert has killed her with a rifle he'd secreted somewhere, maybe under his seat. The other lions have scattered; all that's left is the zebra carcass and the body of the lioness, Chronos's legs splayed beneath her.

Albert, Lou, Dean, and Cora bolt from the jeep. Mindy starts to follow, but Lou pushes her back, and she realizes that he wants her to stay with his children. She leans over the back of their seat and puts an arm around each of them. As they stare through the open windows, a wave of nausea rolls through Mindy; she feels in danger of passing out. Mildred is still in her spot beside the children, and it occurs to Mindy, vaguely, that the elderly bird-watcher was inside the jeep the whole time that she and Albert were talking.

"Is Chronos dead?" Rolph asks flatly.

"I'm sure he's not," Mindy says.

"Why isn't he moving?"

"The lion is on top of him. See, they're pulling her off. He's probably fine 80 under there."

"There's blood on the lion's mouth," Charlie says.

"That's from the zebra. Remember, she was eating the zebra?" It takes enormous effort to keep her teeth from chattering, but Mindy knows that she must hide her terror from the children—her belief that whatever turns out to have happened is her fault.

They wait in pulsing isolation, surrounded by the hot, blank day. Mildred rests a knobby hand on Mindy's shoulder, and Mindy feels her eyes fill with tears. "He'll be fine," the old woman says gently. "You watch."

By the time the group assembles in the bar of the mountain hotel after dinner, everyone seems to have gained something. Chronos has won a blistering victory over his bandmate and both girlfriends, at the cost of thirty-two stitches on his left cheek that you could argue are also a gain (he's a rock star, after all) and several huge antibiotic pills administered by an English surgeon with hooded eyes and beery breath—an old friend of Albert's, whom he unearthed in a cinder-block town about an hour away from the lions.

Albert has gained the status of a hero, though you wouldn't know it to look 85 at him. He gulps a bourbon and mutters his responses to the giddy queries of the Phoenix faction. No one has yet confronted him on the damning basics: Why were you in the bush? How did you get so close to the lions? Why didn't you stop Chronos from getting out of the jeep? But Albert knows that Ramsey, his boss, will ask these questions, and that they will likely lead to his being fired: the latest in a series of failures brought on by what his mother, back in Minehead, calls his "self-destructive tendencies."

The passengers in Albert's jeep have gained a story that they'll tell for the rest of their lives. They are witnesses, to be questioned endlessly about what they saw and heard and felt. A gang of children, including Rolph, Charlie, a set of eight-year-old twin boys from Phoenix, and Louise, a chubby twelve-year-old, leave the bar and stampede along a slatted path to a blind beside a watering hole: a wooden hut full of long benches with a slot they can peek through, invisible to the animals. It's dark inside. They rush to the slot, but no animals are drinking at the moment.

"Did you actually see the lion?" Louise asks, with wonder.

"Lion*ess*," Rolph says. "There were two, plus a lion. And three cubs."

"She means the one that got shot," Charlie says, impatiently. "Obviously we saw it. We were inches away!"

"Feet," Rolph says, correcting her. 90

"Feet are *made* out of inches," Charlie says. "We saw everything."

Rolph has already started to hate these conversations—the panting excitement behind them, the way Charlie seems to revel in it. A thought has been troubling him. "I wonder what will happen to the cubs," he says. "The lioness who got shot must have been their mom—she was eating with them."

"Not necessarily," Charlie says.

"But if she was."

"Maybe the dad will take care of them," Charlie says, doubtfully. The other 95 children are quiet, considering the question.

"Lions tend to raise their cubs communally"—a voice comes from the far end of the blind. Mildred and Fiona were already there or have just arrived; being old and female, they're easily missed. "The pride will likely take care of them," Fiona says, "even if the one killed was their mother."

"Which it might not have been," Charlie adds.

"Which it might not have been," Mildred agrees.

It doesn't occur to the children to ask Mildred, who was also in the jeep, what she saw.

"I'm going back," Rolph tells his sister. 100

He follows the path up to the hotel. His father and Mindy are still in the smoky bar; the strange, celebratory feeling unnerves Rolph. His mind bends again and again to the jeep, but his memories are a muddle: the lioness springing; a jerk of impact from the gun; Chronos moaning during the drive to the doctor, blood collecting in an actual puddle under his head on the floor of the jeep, like in a comic book. All of it is suffused with the feel of Mindy holding him from behind, her cheek against his head, her smell: not bready, like his mom's, but salty, bitter almost—a smell that seems akin to that of the lions themselves.

He stands by his father, who pauses in the middle of an Army story he's telling with Ramsey. "You tired, son?"

"Want me to walk you upstairs?" Mindy asks, and Rolph nods: he does want that.

The blue, mosquito-y night pushes in from the hotel windows. Outside the bar, Rolph is suddenly less tired. Mindy collects her key from the front desk, then says, "Let's go out on the porch."

They step outside. Dark as it is, the silhouettes of mountains against the sky 105 are even darker. Rolph can dimly hear the voices of the other children, down in the blind. He's relieved to have escaped them. He stands with Mindy at the edge of the porch and looks at the mountains. Rolph senses her waiting for something and he waits, too, his heart stamping.

There is a cough farther down the porch. Rolph sees the orange tip of a cigarette move in the dark, and Albert comes toward them with a creak of boots. "Hello there," he says to Rolph. He doesn't speak to Mindy, and Rolph decides that the one hello must be for both of them.

"Hello," he greets Albert.

"What are you up to?" Albert asks.

Rolph turns to Mindy. "What are we up to?"

"Enjoying the night," she says, still facing the mountains, but her voice is 110 tense. "We should go up," she tells Rolph, and walks abruptly back inside. Rolph is troubled by her rudeness. "Are you coming?" he asks Albert.

"Why not?"

As the three of them ascend the stairs, Rolph feels an odd pressure to make conversation. "Is your room up here, too?" he asks.

"Down the hall," Albert says. "Room 3."

Mindy unlocks the door to Rolph's room and steps in, leaving Albert in the hall. Rolph is suddenly angry with her.

"Want to see my room?" he asks Albert. "Mine and Charlie's?" 115

Mindy emits a single syllable of laughter—the way his mother laughs when things have annoyed her to the point of absurdity. Albert steps into his room. It's plain, with wooden furniture and dusty flowered curtains, but after ten nights in tents it feels lavish.

"Very nice," Albert says. Mindy crosses her arms and stares out the window. There is a feeling in the room that Rolph can't identify. He's angry with Mindy and thinks that Albert must be, too. *Women are crazy.* Mindy's body is slender and elastic; she could slip through a keyhole, or under a door. Her thin purple sweater rises and falls quickly as she breathes. Rolph is surprised by how angry he is.

Albert taps a cigarette from his pack, but doesn't light it. It is unfiltered, tobacco emerging from both ends. "Well," he says. "Good night, you two."

Rolph had imagined Mindy tucking him into bed, her arm around him as it was in the jeep. Now this seems out of the question. He can't change into his pajamas with Mindy there; he doesn't even want her to *see* his pajamas, which have small blue elves all over them. "I'm fine," he tells her, hearing the coldness in his voice. "You can go back."

"O.K.," she says. She turns down his bed, plumps the pillow, adjusts the open 120
window. Rolph senses her finding reasons not to leave the room.

"Your dad and I will be just next door," Mindy says. "You know that, right?"

"Duh," he mutters. Then, chastened, he says, "I know."

Five days later, they take a long, very old train overnight to Mombasa. Every few minutes, it slows down just enough for people to leap from the doors, bundles clutched to their chests, and for others to scramble on. Lou's group and the Phoenix faction install themselves in the cramped bar car, which they share with African men in suits and bowler hats. Charlie is allowed to drink one beer, but she sneaks two more with the help of handsome Dean, who stands beside her narrow barstool. "You're sunburned," he says, pressing a finger to Charlie's cheek. "The African sun is strong."

"True," Charlie says, grinning as she swigs her beer. Now that Mindy has pointed out Dean's platitudes, Charlie finds him hilarious.

"You have to wear sunscreen," he says. 125

"I know—I did."

"Once isn't enough. You have to reapply."

Charlie catches Mindy's eye and succumbs to giggles. Her father moves close. "What's so funny?"

"Life," Charlie says, leaning against him.

"*Life!*" Lou snorts. "How old are you?" 130

He hugs her to him. When Charlie was little, he did this all the time, but as she grows older it happens less. Her father is warm, almost hot, his heartbeat like someone banging on a heavy door.

"Ow," Lou says. "Your quill is stabbing me." It's a black-and-white porcupine quill—she found it in the hills and uses it to pin up her long hair. Her father slides it out, and the tangled golden mass of Charlie's hair collapses onto her shoulders like a shattered window. She's aware of Dean watching.

"I like this," Lou says, squinting at the quill's translucent point. "It's a dangerous weapon."

"Weapons are necessary," Dean says.

By the next afternoon, the safari-goers have settled into a hotel a half hour 135
up the coast from Mombasa. On a white beach traversed by knobby-chested men selling beads and gourds, Mildred and Fiona gamely appear in floral-print swimsuits, binoculars still at their necks. The livid Medusa tattoo on Chronos's chest is less startling than his small potbelly—a disillusioning trait he shares with a number of the men, though not Lou, who is lean, a little ropy, tanned from occasional surfing. He walks toward the cream-colored sea with his arm around Mindy, who looks even better than expected (and expectations were high) in her sparkling blue bikini.

After a swim, Lou goes in search of spears and snorkeling gear, resisting the temptation to follow Mindy back to their room, though clearly she'd like him to. She's gone bananas in the sack since they left the tents—hungry for it now, pawing Lou's clothes off at odd moments, ready to start again when he's barely finished. He feels tenderly toward Mindy, now that the trip is winding down. She's studying at Berkeley, and Lou has never travelled for a woman. It's doubtful that he'll lay eyes on her again.

Rolph and Charlie are reading in the sand under a palm tree when Lou gets back with the snorkeling equipment, but Rolph puts aside "The Hobbit" without protest and stands. Charlie ignores them, and Lou wonders momentarily if he should have included her. He and Rolph walk to the edge of the sea and pull on their masks and flippers, hanging their spears from belts at their sides. Rolph looks thin; he needs more exercise. He's timid in the water. His mother is a reader and a gardener, and Lou is constantly having to fight her influence. He wishes that Rolph could live with him, but his lawyer just shakes his head whenever he mentions it. The fish are beautiful, easy targets, nibbling at coral. Lou has speared seven by the time he realizes that Rolph hasn't killed a single one.

"What's the problem, son?" he asks, when they surface.

"I just like watching them," Rolph says.

They've drifted toward a spit of rocks extending into the sea. Carefully they 140
climb from the water. The tide pools throng with starfish and urchins and sea cucumbers; Rolph crouches, poring over them. Lou's fish hang from a netted bag at his waist. From the beach, Mindy is watching them through Fiona's binoculars. She waves, and Lou and Rolph wave back.

"Dad," Rolph asks, lifting a tiny green crab from a tide pool, "what do you think about Mindy?"

"Mindy's great. Why?"

The crab splays its little claws; Lou notes with approval that his son knows how to hold it safely. Rolph squints up at him. "You know. Is she the right amount of crazy?"

Lou gives a hoot of laughter. He'd forgotten the earlier conversation, but Rolph forgets nothing—a quality that delights his father. "She's crazy enough. But crazy isn't everything."

"I think she's rude," Rolph says.   145

"Rude to *you*?"

"No. To Albert."

Lou turns to his son, cocking his head. "Albert?"

Rolph releases the crab and begins to tell the story. He remembers each thing—the porch, the stairs, "Room 3"—realizing as he speaks how much he has wanted to tell his father this, as punishment to Mindy. Lou listens keenly, without interrupting. But as Rolph goes on he senses the story landing heavily, in a way he doesn't understand. When he finishes talking, his father takes a long breath and lets it out. He looks back at the beach. It's nearly sunset, and people are shaking the fine white sand from their towels and packing up for the day. The hotel has a disco, and the group plans to go dancing there after dinner.

"When exactly did this happen?" Lou asks.   150

"The same day as the lions—that night." Rolph waits a moment, then asks, "Why do you think she was rude like that?"

"Women are cunts," his father says. "That's why."

Rolph gapes at him. His father is angry, a muscle jumping in his jaw, and without warning Rolph is angry, too: assailed by a deep, sickening rage that stirs in him very occasionally—most often when he and Charlie come back from a riotous weekend around their father's pool, rock stars jamming on the roof, guacamole and big pots of chili, to find their mother alone in her bungalow, drinking peppermint tea. Rage at this man who casts everyone aside.

"They are not—" He can't make himself repeat the word.

"They are," Lou says tightly. "Pretty soon you'll know it for sure."   155

Rolph turns away from his father. There is nowhere to go, so he jumps into the sea and begins slowly paddling his way back toward the shore. The sun is low, the water choppy and full of shadows. Rolph imagines sharks just under his feet, but he doesn't turn or look back. He keeps swimming toward that white sand, knowing instinctively that his struggle to stay afloat is the most exquisite torture he can concoct for his father—knowing also that, if he sinks, Lou will jump in instantly and save him.

That night, Rolph and Charlie are allowed to have wine at dinner. Rolph dislikes the sour taste, but enjoys the swimmy blur it makes of his surroundings: the giant beaklike flowers all over the dining room; his father's speared fish cooked by the chef with olives and tomatoes; Mindy in a shimmery green dress. His father's arm is around her. He isn't angry anymore, so neither is Rolph.

Lou has spent the past hour in bed, fucking Mindy senseless. Now he keeps one hand on her slim thigh, reaching under her hem, waiting for that cloudy look she gets. Lou is a man who cannot tolerate defeat—can't *perceive* it as anything but a spur to his own inevitable victory. He doesn't give a shit about Albert—Albert is invisible, Albert is nothing. (In fact, Albert has left the group and returned to his Mombasa apartment.) What matters now is that *Mindy* understand this.

He refills Mildred's and Fiona's wineglasses until their cheeks are patchy and flushed. "You still haven't taken me bird-watching," he chides them. "I keep asking, but it never happens."

"We could go tomorrow," Mildred says. "There are some coastal birds we're 160 hoping to see."

"Is that a promise?"

"A solemn promise."

"Come on," Charlie whispers to Rolph. "Let's go outside."

They slip from the crowded dining room and skitter onto the silvery beach. The palm trees make a slapping, rainy sound, but the air is dry.

"It's like Hawaii," Rolph says, wanting it to be true. The ingredients are there: 165 the dark, the beach, his sister. But it doesn't feel the same.

"Without the rain," Charlie says.

"Without Mom," Rolph says.

"I think Dad's going to marry Mindy," Charlie says.

"No way! He doesn't love her."

"So? He can still marry her." 170

They sink onto the sand, still faintly warm, radiating a lunar glow. The ghost sea tumbles against it.

"She's not so bad," Charlie says.

"I don't like her. And why are you the world's expert?"

Charlie shrugs. "I know Dad."

Charlie doesn't yet know herself. Four years from now, at eighteen, she'll join 175 a cult across the Mexican border whose charismatic leader promotes a diet of raw eggs; she'll nearly die from salmonella poisoning before Lou rescues her. A cocaine habit will require partial reconstruction of her nose, changing her appearance, and a series of feckless, domineering men will leave her solitary in her late twenties, trying to broker peace between Rolph and Lou, who will have stopped speaking.

But Charlie *does* know her father. He'll marry Mindy because that's what winning means, and because Mindy's eagerness to finish this odd episode and return to her studies will last until precisely the moment when she unlocks the door to her Berkeley apartment and walks into the smell of simmering lentils: one of the cheap stews that she and her roommates survive on. She'll collapse onto the swaybacked couch they found on the sidewalk and unpack her many books, realizing that in the weeks of lugging them through Africa she has read virtually nothing. And when the phone rings her heart will flip.

Structural dissatisfaction: Returning to circumstances that once pleased you, after having experienced a more thrilling or opulent way of life, and finding that you can no longer tolerate them.

Suddenly, Rolph and Charlie are galloping up the beach, drawn by the pulse of light and music from the open-air disco. They run barefoot into the crowd, trailing powdery sand onto a translucent dance floor overlaid on lozenges of flashing color. The shuddering bass line seems to interfere with Rolph's heartbeat.

"C'mon," Charlie says. "Let's dance."

She begins to undulate in front of him—the way the new Charlie is planning 180 to dance when she gets home. But Rolph is embarrassed; he can't dance that way. The rest of the group surrounds them. Louise, the twelve-year-old, is dancing with Dean, the actor. Ramsey flings his arms around one of the Phoenix-faction moms. Lou and Mindy dance close together, their whole bodies touching, but Mindy is thinking of Albert, as she will, periodically, after marrying Lou and having two daughters, Lou's fifth and sixth children, in quick succession, as if sprinting against the inevitable drift of his attention. On paper he'll be penniless, and Mindy will end up working as a travel agent to support her little girls. For a time, her life will be joyless; the girls will seem to cry too much, and she'll think longingly of this trip to Africa as the last perfect moment of her life, when she still had a choice, when she was free and unencumbered. She'll dream senselessly, futilely, of Albert, wondering what he is doing at particular moments, and how her life would have turned out if she'd run away with him as he suggested, half joking, when she visited him in Room 3. Later, of course, she'll recognize "Albert" as nothing more than a focus of regret for her own immaturity and disastrous choices. When both her children are in high school, she'll finally resume her studies, complete her Ph.D. at U.C.L.A., and begin an academic career at forty-five, spending long periods doing social-structures field work in the Brazilian rain forest. Her youngest daughter will go to work for Lou, become his protégée, and inherit his business.

"Look," Charlie tells Rolph, over the music. "The bird-watchers are watching us."

Mildred and Fiona are sitting on chairs beside the dance floor, waving in their long print dresses. It's the first time the children have seen them without binoculars.

"Maybe we remind them of birds," Charlie says.

"Or maybe when there are no birds they watch people," Rolph says.

"Come on, Rolphus," Charlie says. "Dance with me."

She takes hold of his hands. As they move together, Rolph feels his self- 185 consciousness miraculously fade, as if he were growing up right there on the dance floor, becoming a boy who dances with girls like his sister. Charlie feels it, too. In fact, this particular memory is one she'll return to again and again, for the rest of her life, long after Rolph has shot himself in the head in their father's house at twenty-eight: her brother as a boy, hair slicked flat, eyes sparkling, shyly learning to dance. But the woman who remembers won't be Charlie; after Rolph dies, she'll revert to her real name—Charlene—unlatching herself forever from the girl who danced with her brother in Africa. Charlene will cut her hair short and go to law school. When she gives birth to a son, she'll want to name him Rolph, but her parents will still be too shattered for her to do this. So she'll call him that privately, just in her mind, and years later she'll stand with her mother among a crowd of cheering parents beside a field, watching him play, a dreamy look on his face as he glances at the sky.

"Charlie!" Rolph says. "Guess what I just figured out."

Charlie leans toward her brother, who is grinning with his news. He cups both hands into her hair to be heard above the thudding beat. His warm, sweet breath fills her ear.

"I don't think those ladies were ever watching birds," Rolph says.

FOR ANALYSIS

1. When is "Safari" set? Does everything that we learn happens to these **characters** happen to them there and then?

2. What is the significance of Mindy's field of study to the story? How does Egan use it to tell the story?

3. Do you think it matters that the **setting** of the story is a safari? If so, why? If not, why not?

MAKING ARGUMENTS

1. Egan's use of the flash-forward is key to this story. Describing how she uses it, argue for or against its effectiveness.

2. In her deployment of the analytic tool of structure, Egan violates the often-violated "show, don't tell" rule that some writing teachers try to enforce. Make an argument that criticizes or defends Egan's use of this idea/device. How does it work in the story? How does it tell rather than show? Can its function be so easily categorized?

WRITING TOPICS

1. Pick another story you've read in this book that focuses on young **characters**. Imagine it uses the same kind of flash-forwards that Egan uses here. How might the story be expanded or changed by including glimpses into the characters' future?

2. With whom do you identify most in "Safari"? Why do you think that is? Does it have to do with things that Mindy might call "structural"?

MAKING CONNECTIONS

1. Compare "Safari" to a story of your choice from the "Innocence and Experience" chapter. How could the other work be read through the lens of Mindy's ideas about structural emotions? How do **characters** or speakers in the other story lose their innocence about the structures that effect how we feel and live?

2. Compare this story to Ostriker's "The Dogs at Live Oak Beach, Santa Cruz" (p. 189) or another work that includes animals. How do both authors use animals to tell their story?

The stories in this cluster share protagonists whose imaginations rebel against the realities of their lives. These lives are as different as the ways that they escape them through imagination. Despite these differences, however, these stories have much in common. As you read these two tales of secret lives, watch for the parallels between both the two lives and the two imaginations. Also note the effect that reading these stories has on you—how they jump back and forth between reality and imagination and how it feels to make that jump with them.

JAMES THURBER (1894–1961)

THE SECRET LIFE OF WALTER MITTY 1939

"We're going through!" The Commander's voice was like thin ice breaking. He wore his full-dress uniform, with the heavily braided white cap pulled down rakishly over one cold gray eye. "We can't make it, sir. It's spoiling for a hurricane, if you ask me." "I'm not asking you, Lieutenant Berg," said the Commander. "Throw on the power lights! Rev her up to 8,500! We're going through!" The pounding of the cylinders increased: ta-pocketa-pocketa-pocketa-*pocketa-pocketa*. The Commander stared at the ice forming on the pilot window. He walked over and twisted a row of complicated dials. "Switch on No. 8 auxiliary!" he shouted. "Switch on No. 8 auxiliary!" repeated Lieutenant Berg. "Full strength in No. 3 turret!" shouted the Commander. "Full strength in No. 3 turret!" The crew, bending to their various tasks in the huge, hurtling eight-engined Navy hydroplane, looked at each other and grinned. "The Old Man'll get us through," they said to one another. "The Old Man ain't afraid of Hell!" . . .

"Not so fast! You're driving too fast!" said Mrs. Mitty. "What are you driving so fast for?"

"Hmm?" said Walter Mitty. He looked at his wife, in the seat beside him, with shocked astonishment. She seemed grossly unfamiliar, like a strange woman who had yelled at him in a crowd. "You were up to fifty-five," she said. "You know I don't like to go more than forty. You were up to fifty-five." Walter Mitty drove on toward Waterbury in silence, the roaring of the SN202 through the worst storm in twenty years of Navy flying fading in the remote, intimate airways of his mind. "You're tensed up again," said Mrs. Mitty. "It's one of your days. I wish you'd let Dr. Renshaw look you over."

Walter Mitty stopped the car in front of the building where his wife went to have her hair done. "Remember to get those overshoes while I'm having my hair done," she said. "I don't need overshoes," said Mitty. She put her mirror back into her bag. "We've been all through that," she said, getting out of the car. "You're not a young man any longer." He raced the engine a little. "Why don't you wear your gloves? Have you lost your gloves?" Walter Mitty reached in a pocket and brought out the gloves. He put them on, but after she had turned and gone into the building and he had driven on to a red light, he took them off again. "Pick it up, brother!" snapped a cop as the light changed, and Mitty hastily pulled on his gloves and lurched ahead. He drove around the streets aimlessly for a time, and then he drove past the hospital on his way to the parking lot.

 . . . "It's the millionaire banker, Wellington McMillan," said the pretty nurse. ⁵ "Yes?" said Walter Mitty, removing his gloves slowly. "Who has the case?" "Dr. Renshaw and Dr. Benbow, but there are two specialists here, Dr. Remington from New York and Dr. Pritchard-Mitford from London. He flew over." A door opened down a long, cool corridor and Dr. Renshaw came out. He looked distraught and haggard. "Hello, Mitty," he said. "We're having the devil's own time with McMillan, the millionaire banker and close personal friend of Roosevelt. Obstreosis of the ductal tract. Tertiary. Wish you'd take a look at him." "Glad to," said Mitty.

In the operating room there were whispered introductions: "Dr. Remington, Dr. Mitty. Dr. Pritchard-Mitford, Dr. Mitty." "I've read your book on streptothricosis," said Pritchard-Mitford, shaking hands. "A brilliant performance, sir." "Thank you," said Walter Mitty. "Didn't know you were in the States, Mitty," grumbled Remington. "Coals to Newcastle, bringing Mitford and me up here for a tertiary." "You are very kind," said Mitty. A huge, complicated machine, connected to the operating table, with many tubes and wires, began at this moment to go pocketa-pocketa-pocketa. "The new anaesthetizer is giving way!" shouted an interne. "There is no one in the East who knows how to fix it!" "Quiet, man!" said Mitty, in a low, cool voice. He sprang to the machine, which was now going pocketa-pocketa-queep-pocketa-queep. He began fingering delicately a row of glistening dials. "Give me a fountain pen!" he snapped. Someone handed him a fountain pen. He pulled a faulty piston out of the machine and inserted the pen in its place. "That will hold for ten minutes," he said. "Get on with the operation." A nurse hurried over and whispered to Renshaw, and Mitty saw the man turn pale. "Coreopsis has set in," said Renshaw nervously. "If you would take over, Mitty?" Mitty looked at him and at the craven figure of Benbow, who drank, and at the grave, uncertain faces of the two great specialists. "If you wish," he said. They slipped a white gown on him; he adjusted a mask and drew on thin gloves; nurses handed him shining . . .

"Back it up, Mac! Look out for that Buick!" Walter Mitty jammed on the brakes. "Wrong lane, Mac," said the parking-lot attendant, looking at Mitty closely. "Gee. Yeh," muttered Mitty. He began cautiously to back out of the lane marked "Exit Only." "Leave her sit there," said the attendant. "I'll put her away." Mitty got out of the car. "Hey, better leave the key." "Oh," said Mitty, handing the man the ignition key. The attendant vaulted into the car, backed it up with insolent skill, and put it where it belonged.

They're so damn cocky, thought Walter Mitty, walking along Main Street; they think they know everything. Once he had tried to take his chains off, outside New Milford, and he had got them wound around the axles. A man had had to come out in a wrecking car and unwind them, a young, grinning garageman. Since then Mrs. Mitty always made him drive to a garage to have the chains taken off. The next time, he thought, I'll wear my right arm in a sling; they won't grin at me then. I'll have my right arm in a sling and they'll see I couldn't possibly take the chains off myself. He kicked at the slush on the sidewalk. "Overshoes," he said to himself, and he began looking for a shoe store.

When he came out into the street again, with the overshoes in a box under his arm, Walter Mitty began to wonder what the other thing was his wife had told him to get. She had told him, twice, before they set out from their house for Waterbury. In a way he hated these weekly trips to town—he was always getting something wrong. Kleenex, he thought, Squibb's, razor blades? No. Toothpaste, toothbrush, bicarbonate, carborundum, initiative and referendum? He gave it up. But she would remember it. "Where's the what's-its-name?" she would ask. "Don't tell me you forgot the what's-its-name." A newsboy went by shouting something about the Waterbury trial.

. . . "Perhaps this will refresh your memory." The District Attorney suddenly 10 thrust a heavy automatic at the quiet figure on the witness stand. "Have you ever seen this before?" Walter Mitty took the gun and examined it expertly. "This is my Webley-Vickers 50.80," he said calmly. An excited buzz ran around the courtroom. The Judge rapped for order. "You are a crack shot with any sort of firearms, I believe?" said the District Attorney, insinuatingly. "Objection!" shouted Mitty's attorney. "We have shown that the defendant could not have fired the shot. We have shown that he wore his right arm in a sling on the night of the fourteenth of July." Walter Mitty raised his hand briefly and the bickering attorneys were stilled. "With any known make of gun," he said evenly, "I could have killed Gregory Fitzhurst at three hundred feet with my left hand." Pandemonium broke loose in the courtroom. A woman's scream rose above the bedlam and suddenly a lovely, dark-haired girl was in Walter Mitty's arms. The District Attorney struck at her savagely. Without rising from his chair, Mitty let the man have it on the point of the chin. "You miserable cur!" . . .

"Puppy biscuit," said Walter Mitty. He stopped walking and the buildings of Waterbury rose up out of the misty courtroom and surrounded him again. A woman who was passing laughed. "He said 'Puppy biscuit,'" she said to her companion. "That man said 'Puppy biscuit' to himself." Walter Mitty hurried on. He went into an A. & P., not the first one he came to but a smaller one farther up the street. "I want some biscuit for small, young dogs," he said to the clerk. "Any special brand, sir?" The greatest pistol shot in the world thought a moment. "It says 'Puppies Bark for It' on the box," said Walter Mitty.

His wife would be through at the hairdresser's in fifteen minutes, Mitty saw in looking at his watch, unless they had trouble drying it; sometimes they had trouble drying it. She didn't like to get to the hotel first; she would want him to be there waiting for her as usual. He found a big leather chair in the lobby, facing a window, and he put the overshoes and the puppy biscuit on the floor beside it. He picked up an old copy of *Liberty* and sank down into the chair. "Can Germany Conquer the World Through the Air?" Walter Mitty looked at the pictures of bombing planes and of ruined streets.

. . . "The cannonading has got the wind up in young Raleigh, sir," said the sergeant. Captain Mitty looked up at him through tousled hair. "Get him to bed," he said wearily. "With the others. I'll fly alone." "But you can't, sir," said the sergeant anxiously. "It takes two men to handle that bomber and the Archies are pounding hell out of the air. Von Richtman's circus is between here and Saulier." "Somebody's got to get that ammunition dump," said Mitty. "I'm going over. Spot of brandy?" He poured a drink for the sergeant and one for himself. War thundered and whined around the dugout and battered at the door. There was a rending of wood and splinters flew through the room. "A bit of a near thing," said Captain Mitty carelessly. "The box barrage is closing in," said the sergeant. "We only live once, Sergeant," said Mitty, with his faint, fleeting smile. "Or do we?" He poured another brandy and tossed it off. "I never see a man could hold his brandy like you, sir," said the sergeant. "Begging your pardon, sir." Captain Mitty stood up and strapped on his huge Webley-Vickers automatic. "It's forty kilometres through hell, sir," said the sergeant. Mitty finished one last brandy. "After all," he said softly, "what isn't?" The pounding of the cannon increased; there was the rat-tat-tatting of machine guns, and from somewhere came the menacing pocketa-pocketa-pocketa of the new flame-throwers. Walter Mitty walked to the door of the dugout humming "Auprès de Ma Blonde." He turned and waved to the sergeant. "Cheerio!" he said. . . .

Something struck his shoulder. "I've been looking all over this hotel for you," said Mrs. Mitty. "Why do you have to hide in this old chair? How did you expect me to find you?" "Things close in," said Walter Mitty vaguely. "What?" Mrs. Mitty said. "Did you get the what's-its-name? The puppy biscuit? What's in that box?" "Overshoes," said Mitty. "Couldn't you have put them on in the store?" "I was thinking," said Walter Mitty. "Does it ever occur to you that I am sometimes thinking?" She looked at him. "I'm going to take your temperature when I get you home," she said.

They went out through the revolving doors that made a faintly derisive 15 whistling sound when you pushed them. It was two blocks to the parking lot. At the drugstore on the corner she said, "Wait here for me. I forgot something. I won't be a minute." She was more than a minute. Walter Mitty lighted a cigarette. It began to rain, rain with sleet in it. He stood up against the wall of the drugstore, smoking. . . . He put his shoulders back and his heels together. "To hell with the handkerchief," said Walter Mitty scornfully. He took one last drag on his cigarette and snapped it away. Then, with that faint, fleeting smile playing about his lips, he faced the firing squad; erect and motionless, proud and disdainful, Walter Mitty the Undefeated, inscrutable to the last.

FOR ANALYSIS

1. What is Mitty's secret life?

2. Describe Mitty's relationship with his wife.

3. How is **irony** an important device in this story?

MAKING ARGUMENTS

1. Argue that this story is either a tragedy or a comedy, using evidence from the text.

2. Is Mitty simply a daydreamer, or is he suffering from a more serious condition? Line up the evidence for each side of this argument.

WRITING TOPICS

1. Thurber's story continues to be widely read seventy-five years after it was published. What do you think has made it so timeless?

2. Write your own "Secret Life" story. What might you daydream about? What about your daily life makes you feel as Mitty does in his?

GEORGE SAUNDERS (B. 1958)

THE END OF FIRPO IN THE WORLD 1998

The boy on the bike flew by the Chink's house, and the squatty-body's house, and the house where the dead guy had rotted for five days, remembering that the Chink had once called him nasty, and the squatty-body had once called the cops when he'd hit her cat with a lug nut on a string, and the chick in the dead guy's house had once asked if he, Cody, ever brushed his teeth. Someday when he'd completed the invention of his special miniaturizing ray he would shrink their houses and flush them down the shitter while in tiny voices all three begged for some sophisticated mercy, but he would only say, Sophisticated? When were you ever sophisticated to me? And from the toilet bowl they would say, Well yes, you're right, we were pretty mean, flush us down, we deserve it; but no, at the last minute he would pluck them out and place them in his lunchbox so he could send them on secret missions such as putting hideous boogers of assassination in Lester Finn's thermos if Lester Finn ever again asked him in Civics why his rear smelled like hot cotton with additional crap cling-ons.

It was a beautiful, sunny day and the aerobics class at the Rec had let out and cars were streaming out of the parking lot with sun glinting off their hoods, and he rode along on the sidewalk, racing the cars as they passed.

Here was the low-hanging willow where you had to duck down, here was the place with the tilty sidewalk square that served as a ramp when you jerked hard on the handlebars, which he did, and the crowd went wild, and the announcers in the booth above the willow shook their heads and said, Wow, he takes that jump like there's no tomorrow while them other racers fret about it like tiny crying babies!

Were the Dalmeyers home?

Their gray car was still in the driveway.   5

He would need to make another lap.

Yesterday he had picked up a bright-red goalie pad and all three Dalmeyers had screamed at him, Not that pad Cody you dick, we never use those pads in the driveway because they get scuffed, you rectum, those are only for ice, were you born a rectal shitbrain or did you take special rectal shitbrain lessons, in rectal shitbrain lessons did they teach you how to ruin everybody's things?

Well yes, he had ruined a few Dalmeyer things in his life, he had yes pounded a railroad spike in a good new volleyball, he had yes secretly scraped a ski with a nail, he had yes given the Dalmeyer dog Rudy a cut on its leg with a shovel, but that had been an accident, he'd thrown the shovel at a rosebush and stupid Rudy had walked in front of it.

And the Dalmeyers had snatched away the goalie pad and paraded around the driveway making the nosehole sound, and when he tried to laugh to show he was a good sport he made the nosehole sound for real, and they totally cracked up, and Zane Dalmeyer said why didn't he take his trademark nose-hole sound on Broadway so thousands could crap their pants laughing? And Eric Dalmeyer said hey if only he had like fifty different-sized noseholes that each made a different sound then he could play songs. And they laughed so hard at the idea of him playing songs on Broadway on his fifty different-sized noseholes that they fell to the driveway thrashing their idiotic Dalmeyer limbs, even Ginnie, the baby Dalmeyer, and ha ha ha that had been a laugh, that had been so funny he had almost gone around one two three four and smashed their cranial cavities with his off-brand gym shoes, which were another puzzling dilemmoid, because why did he have Arroes when every single Dalmeyer, even Ginnie, had the Nikes with the lights in the heel that lit up?

Fewer cars were coming by now from the Rec; the ones that did were going 10 faster, and he no longer tried to race them.

Oh, it would be revenge, sweet revenge, when he stuck the lozenge stolen from wood shop up the Dalmeyers' water hose, and the next time they turned the hose on it exploded, and all the Dalmeyers, even Dad Dalmeyer, stood around in their nice tan pants puzzling over it like them guys on "Nova." And the Dalmeyers were so stupid they would conclude that it had been a miracle, and would call some guys from a science lab to confirm the miracle, and one of the lab guys would flip the wooden lozenge into the air and say to Dad Dalmeyer, You know what, a very clever Einstein lives in your neighborhood and I suggest that in the future you lock this hose up, because in all probability this guy cannot be stopped. And he, Cody, would give the lab guy a wink and later, when they were walking away, the lab guy would say, Look, why not come live with us in the experimental space above our lab and help us discover some amazing compounds with the same science brain that thought up this brilliant lozenge, because, frankly, when we lab guys were your age, no way, this lozenge concept was totally beyond us, we were just playing with baby toys and doing baby math, but you, you're really something scientifically special.

And when the Dalmeyers came for a lab tour with a school group they would approach him with their big confident underwater watches and say wow oh boy had they ever missed the boat in terms of him, sorry, they were so very sorry, what was this beaker for, how did this burner work, was it really true that he had built a whole entire *T. Rex* from scratch and energized it by taming the miraculous power of cosmic thunder? And down in the basement the *T. Rex* would rear up its ugly head and want to have a Dalmeyer snack, but using his special system of codes, pounding on a heat pipe a different number of times for each alphabet letter, he would tell the *T. Rex*, No no no, don't eat a single Dalmeyer, although why not lift Eric Dalmeyer up just for the fun of it on the tip of your tremendous green snout and give him a lesson in what kind of power those crushing jaws would have if he, Cody, pounded out on the heat pipe Kill Kill Kill.

Pedalling wildly now, he passed into the strange and dangerous zone of three consecutive MonteVistas, and inside of each lived an old wop in a dago tee, and sometimes in the creepy trees there were menacing gorillas he took pot-shots at from bikeback, but not today, he was too busy with revenge to think about monkeys, and then he was out, into the light, coasting into a happier zone of forthright and elephantine BuenoVerdes that sat very honestly with the big open eyes that were their second-story windows, and in his mind as he passed he said hello HELLO to the two elephants and they in turn said to him in kind Dumbo voices hey Cody HEY CODY.

The block was shaped something like South America and as he took the tight turn that was Cape Horn he looked across The Field to his small yellow house, which was neither MonteVista nor BuenoVerde, but predated the subdivision and smelled like cat pee and hamburger blood and had recently been christened by Ma's boyfriend Daryl, that dick, The House of FIRPO, FIRPO being the word Daryl used to describe anything he, Cody, did that was bad or dorky. Some-times Mom and Daryl tried to pretend FIRPO was a lovey-dovey term by tou-sling his hair when they said it but other times they gave him a poke or pinch and sometimes when they thought he couldn't hear they whispered very darkly and meanly to one another FIRP attack in progress and he would go to his room and make the nosehole sound in his closet, after which they would come in and fine him a quarter for each nosehole sound they thought they had heard him make, which was often many, many more than he had actually really made.

Sometimes at night in his room Mom babied him by stroking his big wide head and saying he didn't have to pay all the quarters he owed for making the nosehole sound, but other times she said if he didn't knock it off and lose a few pounds how was he ever going to get a date in junior high, because who wanted to date a big chubby nosehole snorter, and then he couldn't help it, it made him nervous to think of junior high, and he made the nosehole sound and she said, Very funny I hope you're amusing your own self because you're not amusing my ass one bit.

The Dalmeyer house now came into sight.

The Dalmeyer car was gone.

It was Go Time.

The decisive butt-kicking he was about to give the Dalmeyer hose would constitute the end of FIRPO in the world, and all, including Ma, would have to bow down before him, saying, Wow wow wow, do we ever stand corrected in terms of you, how could someone FIRPO hatch and execute such a daring manly plan?

The crowd was on its feet now, screaming his name, and he passed the Chink's 20 house again, here was the driveway down which he must turn to cross the street to the Dalmeyers', but then oh crap he was going too fast and missed it, and the announcers in the booth above the willow gasped in pleasure at his sudden decisive decision to swerve across the newly sodded lawn of the squatty-body's house. His bike made a trough in the sod and went HUMPF over the curb, and as the white car struck him the boy and the bike flew together in a high comic arc across the street and impacted the oak on the opposite side with such violence that the bike wrapped around the tree and the boy flew back into the street.

Arghh arghh Daryl will be pissed and say Cody why are you bleeding like a stuck pig you little shit. There was something red wrong with his Arroes. At Payless when they bought the Arroes Mom said, If you squirm once more you're gonna be facedown on this carpet with my hand whacking your big fat ass. Daryl will say I buy you a good bike and what do you do, you ruin it. Ma will come up with a dish towel and start swiping at the blood and Daryl will say don't ruin that dish towel, he made his bed let him sleep in it, I'll hose him off in the yard, a little shivering won't kill him, he did the crime let him do the time. Or Ma might throw a fit like the night he slipped and fell in the school play, and Ms. Phillips said, Tell your mother, Cody, how you came to slip and fall during the school play so that everyone in the auditorium was looking at you instead of Julia who was at that time speaking her most important line.

And Mom said, Cody are you deaf?

And Ms. Phillips said, He slipped because when I told him stay out of that mopped spot did he do it? No, he did not, he walked right through it on purpose and then down he went.

Which is exactly what he does at home, Mom said. Sometimes I think he's wired wrong.

And Ms. Phillips said, Well, today, Cody, you learned a valuable lesson 25 which is if someone tells you don't do something, don't do it, because maybe that someone knows something you don't from having lived a longer time than you.

And Daryl said, Or maybe he liked falling on his butt in front of all his friends.

Now a white-haired stickman with no shirt was bending over him, touch touch touching him all over, like looking to see if he was wearing a bulletproof vest, doing some very nervous mouthbreathing, with a silver cross hanging down, and around his nipples were sprigs of white hair.

Oh boy, oh God, said the stickman. Say something, pal, can you talk?

And he tried to talk but nothing came and tried to move but nothing moved.

Oh God, said the stickman, don't go, pal, please say something, stay here 30 with me now, we'll get through this.

What crazy teeth. What a stickman. The stickman's hands flipped around like nervous old-lady hands in movies where the river is rising and the men are away. What a Holy Roller. What a FIRPO. A Holy Roller FIRPO stickman with hairy nips and plus his breath smelled like coffee.

Listen, God loves you, said the stickman. You're going, O.K., I see you're going, but look, please don't go without knowing you are beautiful and loved. O.K.? Do you hear me? You are good, do you know that? God loves you. God loves you. He sent His son to die for you.

Oh the freaking FIRPO, why couldn't he just shut up? If the stickman thought he, Cody, was good he must be FIRPO because he, Cody, wasn't good, he was FIRPO, Mom had said so and Daryl had said so and even Mr. Dean in Science had told him to stop lying the time he tried to tell about seeing the falling star. The announcers in the booth above the willow began weeping as he sat on Mom's lap and said he was very sorry for having been such a FIRPO son and Mom said, Oh thank you, thank you, Cody, for finally admitting it, that makes it nice, and her smile was so sweet he closed his eyes and felt a certain urge to sort of shake things out and oh Christ dance.

You are beautiful, beautiful, the stickman kept saying, long after the boy had stopped thrashing, God loves you, you are beautiful in His sight.

FOR ANALYSIS

1. What are the two meanings of the title in the story?

2. Cody's mother says that he is "wired wrong" (para. 24). Do you agree? How would you describe him?

3. What do the Dalmeyers represent to Cody and to the story?

MAKING ARGUMENTS

When the story first appeared in the *New Yorker*, under the title it said "Cody's last stand." From the observation that this line is an intentional echo of Custer's last stand, make the argument that this echo can help readers understand the story better.

WRITING TOPICS

1. Annotate Saunders's story, marking where the **third-person narration** uses free indirect discourse (FID)—that is, where the narrator's words seem like they could come from Cody's mouth. Analyze Saunders's use of FID and its effectiveness.

2. How do you take the last line of the story? How do Cody or the story feel about religion? Describe what you think the fact that the story ends as it does means in terms of religion.

MAKING CONNECTIONS

1. Compare the rebellions of the **protagonists** in Thurber's and Saunders's stories. What is the nature of each? Is there a way to judge whether each succeeds?

2. Compare the circumstances that define the lives of each of these protagonists, and their reactions to them. How are they similar? How are they different? How generalizable are both their circumstances and their reactions?

POETRY

JOHN DONNE (1572-1631)

HOLY SONNETS: "IF POISONOUS MINERALS, AND IF THAT TREE" 1609

If poisonous minerals, and if that tree
Whose fruit threw death on else immortal us,
If lecherous goats, if serpents envious
Cannot be damn'd, alas, why should I be?
Why should intent or reason, born in me,
Make sins, else equal, in me more heinous?
And mercy being easy, and glorious
To God, in his stern wrath why threatens he?
But who am I, that dare dispute with thee,
O God? Oh, of thine only worthy blood   10
And my tears, make a heavenly Lethean flood,
And drown in it my sins' black memory.
That thou remember them, some claim as debt;
I think it mercy, if thou wilt forget.

FOR ANALYSIS

1. What is a "Lethean flood" (l. 11)? What does the speaker want it to wash away?

2. Does this poem express one **mood**, or does it shift between moods? If it shifts, to what effect does it do so, and what it is it trying to express with this shift?

MAKING ARGUMENTS

Make the argument that Donne's **sonnet** is less an entreaty to be forgiven than a questioning of God. Be careful to engage with counterarguments, since your reading will be one contrary to the way many other people read this poem.

WRITING TOPIC

The ideas of damnation and mercy have motivated an endless number of poems. What makes this one stand out? What makes it seem so personal?

RICHARD CRASHAW   (1613–1649)

BUT MEN LOVED DARKNESS
RATHER THAN LIGHT   1646

The world's light shines, shine as it will,
The world will love its darkness still.
I doubt though when the world's in hell,
It will not love its darkness half so well.

FOR ANALYSIS

1. Would you characterize this poem as complicated or simple? Think in terms of
rhyme, **rhythm**, **diction**, and **imagery**. How does the complexity—or simplicity—of
its form relate to its subject and meaning?

2. What is the biblical **allusion** that Crashaw makes here? Use a search engine to find
it. Does knowing the lines to which the poem refers help you to better understand it?

WRITING TOPIC

While Crashaw was writing out of a specifically religious worldview, it's not hard to
imagine a way in which this poem could be read more broadly if the idea of hell is not
taken literally. To what other situations or phenomena or ideas could this poem apply?

WILLIAM WORDSWORTH   (1770–1850)

THE WORLD IS
TOO MUCH WITH US   1807

The world is too much with us; late and soon,
Getting and spending, we lay waste our powers;
Little we see in Nature that is ours;
We have given our hearts away, a sordid boon!
This Sea that bares her bosom to the moon,
The winds that will be howling at all hours,
And are up-gathered now like sleeping flowers,
For this, for everything, we are out of tune;
It moves us not.—Great God! I'd rather be
A Pagan suckled in a creed outworn;   10
So might I, standing on this pleasant lea,
Have glimpses that would make me less forlorn;
Have sight of Proteus rising from the sea;
Or hear old Triton blow his wreathèd horn.[1]

[1] Proteus and Triton are both figures from Greek mythology. Proteus had the power to assume different forms; Triton was often represented blowing on a conch shell.

FOR ANALYSIS

1. What does "world" mean in line 1?

2. What does Wordsworth complain of in the first four lines?

3. In lines 4–8 Wordsworth tells us what we have lost; in the concluding lines he suggests a remedy. What is that remedy? What do Proteus and Triton **symbolize**?

MAKING ARGUMENTS

Relying on a little research to establish some key differences between Western life in 1807, the year of this poem's appearance, and today, argue that the world is still too much with us, is with us to a greater degree, or is less with us.

WRITING TOPIC

In what ways does Wordsworth's use of **images** both define what we have lost and suggest a remedy for this loss?

ALFRED, LORD TENNYSON   (1809–1892)

ULYSSES[1]   1833

It little profits that an idle king,
By this still hearth, among these barren crags,
Matched with an agéd wife, I mete and dole
Unequal laws unto a savage race,
That hoard, and sleep, and feed, and know not me.

    I cannot rest from travel; I will drink
Life to the lees. All times I have enjoyed
Greatly, have suffered greatly, both with those
That loved me, and alone; on shore, and when
Through scudding drifts the rainy Hyades[2]   10
Vexed the dim sea. I am become a name;
For always roaming with a hungry heart
Much have I seen and known—cities of men
And manners, climates, councils, governments,
Myself not least, but honored of them all—
And drunk delight of battle with my peers,
Far on the ringing plains of windy Troy.
I am a part of all that I have met;

---

[1] Ulysses, according to Greek legend, was the king of Ithaca and a hero of the Trojan War. Tennyson represents him as eager to resume the life of travel and adventure.
[2] A group of stars in the constellation Taurus. According to Greek mythology, the rising of these stars with the sun foretold rain.

Yet all experience is an arch wherethrough
Gleams that untraveled world whose margin fades   20
Forever and forever when I move.
How dull it is to pause, to make an end,
To rust unburnished, not to shine in use!
As though to breathe were life. Life piled on life
Were all too little, and of one to me
Little remains; but every hour is saved
From that eternal silence, something more,
A bringer of new things; and vile it were
For some three suns to store and hoard myself,
And this gray spirit yearning in desire   30
To follow knowledge like a sinking star,
Beyond the utmost bound of human thought.

    This is my son, mine own Telemachus,
To whom I leave the scepter and the isle—
Well-loved of me, discerning to fulfill
This labor, by slow prudence to make mild
A rugged people, and through soft degrees
Subdue them to the useful and the good.
Most blameless is he, centered in the sphere
Of common duties, decent not to fail   40
In offices of tenderness, and pay
Meet° adoration to my household gods,   proper
When I am gone. He works his work, I mine.

    There lies the port; the vessel puffs her sail;
There gloom the dark, broad seas. My mariners,
Souls that have toiled, and wrought, and thought with me—
That ever with a frolic welcome took
The thunder and the sunshine, and opposed
Free hearts, free foreheads—you and I are old;
Old age hath yet his honor and his toil.   50
Death closes all; but something ere the end,
Some work of noble note, may yet be done,
Not unbecoming men that strove with Gods.
The lights begin to twinkle from the rocks;
The long day wanes; the slow moon climbs; the deep
Moans round with many voices. Come, my friends,
'Tis not too late to seek a newer world.
Push off, and sitting well in order smite
The sounding furrows; for my purpose holds
To sail beyond the sunset, and the baths   60
Of all the western stars, until I die.

It may be that the gulfs will wash us down;
It may be we shall touch the Happy Isles,[3]
And see the great Achilles, whom we knew.
Though much is taken, much abides; and though
We are not now that strength which in old days
Moved earth and heaven, that which we are, we are—
One equal temper of heroic hearts,
Made weak by time and fate, but strong in will
To strive, to seek, to find, and not to yield.   70

FOR ANALYSIS

1. Is Ulysses' desire to abdicate his duties as king irresponsible?

2. Contrast Ulysses with his son Telemachus (see ll. 33–43). Is Telemachus admirable?

3. At the conclusion of the poem, Ulysses is determined not to yield. Yield to what?

MAKING ARGUMENTS

While many readers have for years seen Tennyson as identifying with and being sympathetic toward the speaker in this poem, others have detected an ironic distance between the poet and the hero. Make an argument defending the traditional reading of the poem, or make an argument for a reading in which Ulysses is at least as much an object of criticism as an object of sympathy.

EMILY DICKINSON (1830–1886)

MUCH MADNESS IS DIVINEST SENSE— 1862

Much Madness is divinest Sense—
To a discerning Eye—
Much Sense—the starkest Madness—
'Tis the Majority
In this, as All, prevail—
Assent—and you are sane—
Demur—you're straightway dangerous—
And handled with a Chain—

Ulysses
[3] The Islands of the Blessed (also Elysium), thought to be in the far western oceans, where those favored by the gods, such as Achilles, enjoyed life after death.

SHE ROSE TO HIS REQUIREMENT   CA. 1863

She rose to His Requirement—dropt
The Playthings of Her Life
To take the honorable Work
Of Woman, and of Wife—

If ought° She missed in Her new Day,   anything
Of Amplitude, or Awe—
Or first Prospective—Or the Gold
In using, wear away,

It lay unmentioned—as the Sea
Develope Pearl, and Weed,   10
But only to Himself—be known
The Fathoms they abide—

FOR ANALYSIS

1. What are the "Playthings" referred to in line 2?

2. Why does the poet refer to both "Woman" and "Wife" in line 4, since a wife is also a woman?

3. Look up the words *amplitude*, *awe*, and *prospective* in your dictionary, and consider how these words help you to understand the woman's losses.

4. What does "It" in the third **stanza** refer to?

5. Why is the sea **image** at the end of the poem appropriate? What does the contrast between "Pearl" and "Weed" suggest?

6. The last word of the poem, *abide*, has several meanings. Which of them are relevant to the meaning of the poem?

MAKING ARGUMENTS

Make the contrarian argument that Dickinson's stance on marriage, while informed by observation of the institution in her historical moment, is not based on firsthand knowledge, since she never married. Be creative if you want, but be sure to stick to the text—while also bringing in any outside knowledge or logical arguments you think might support your case.

WRITING TOPIC

Write an essay describing a woman you know who gave up an important part of herself to be a wife.

MAKING CONNECTIONS .

Compare and contrast the attitudes toward marriage in this poem with those in Glück's "The Myth of Innocence" (p. 190).

WILLIAM BUTLER YEATS (1865–1939)

EASTER 1916[1] 1916

I have met them at close of day
Coming with vivid faces
From counter or desk among grey
Eighteenth-century houses.
I have passed with a nod of the head
Or polite meaningless words,
Or have lingered awhile and said
Polite meaningless words,
And thought before I had done
Of a mocking tale or a gibe   10
To please a companion
Around the fire at the club,
Being certain that they and I
But lived where motley is worn:
All changed, changed utterly:
A terrible beauty is born.

That woman's days were spent
In ignorant good-will,
Her nights in argument
Until her voice grew shrill.   20
What voice more sweet than hers
When, young and beautiful,
She rode to harriers?[2]
This man had kept a school
And rode our wingèd horse;[3]
This other his helper and friend
Was coming into his force;
He might have won fame in the end,
So sensitive his nature seemed,
So daring and sweet his thought.   30
This other man I had dreamed
A drunken, vainglorious lout.

---

[1] On Easter Monday in 1916, a group of Irish nationalists seized key points in Ireland, including the Dublin Post Office, from which they proclaimed an independent Irish Republic. At first, most of the Irish were indifferent to the nationalists' futile yet heroic gesture, but as the rebellion was crushed and the leaders executed, they became heroes in the eyes of their fellow citizens. Some of those leaders are alluded to in the second stanza and are named in lines 75 and 76.

[2] In the aristocratic sport of hare hunting, a "pack of harriers" refers to the hounds as well as the persons following the chase.

[3] In Greek mythology, a winged horse is associated with poetic inspiration.

422

He had done most bitter wrong
To some who are near my heart,
Yet I number him in the song;
He, too, has resigned his part
In the casual comedy;
He, too, has been changed in his turn,
Transformed utterly:
A terrible beauty is born.   40

Hearts with one purpose alone
Through summer and winter seem
Enchanted to a stone
To trouble the living stream.
The horse that comes from the road,
The rider, the birds that range
From cloud to tumbling cloud,
Minute by minute they change;
A shadow of cloud on the stream
Changes minute by minute;   50
A horse-hoof slides on the brim,
And a horse plashes within it;
The long-legged moor-hens dive,
And hens to moor-cocks call;
Minute by minute they live:
The stone's in the midst of all.

Too long a sacrifice
Can make a stone of the heart.
O when may it suffice?
That is Heaven's part, our part   60
To murmur name upon name,
As a mother names her child
When sleep at last has come
On limbs that had run wild.
What is it but nightfall?
No, no, not night but death;
Was it needless death after all?
For England may keep faith
For all that is done and said.
We know their dream; enough   70
To know they dreamed and are dead;
And what if excess of love
Bewildered them till they died?
I write it out in a verse—
MacDonagh and MacBride

And Connolly and Pearse[4]
Now and in time to be,
Wherever green is worn,
Are changed, changed utterly:
A terrible beauty is born.   80

FOR ANALYSIS

1. What is "changed utterly"? In what sense can beauty be "terrible" (ll. 15–16)?

2. Who or what does "they" in line 55 refer to? What does the "stone" in lines 43 and 56 **symbolize**? What is Yeats contrasting?

3. How does the poet answer the question he asks in line 67?

MAKING ARGUMENTS

Is Yeats convinced that these sacrifices were worthwhile in the end? While many read the poem as ultimately ambivalent, reject that conclusion for the sake of argument. How would you argue that Yeats is ambivalent? How would you argue that he is not?

WRITING TOPIC

In the first **stanza**, the attitude of the poet toward the people he is describing is indifferent, even contemptuous. How is that attitude modified in the rest of the poem?

THE SECOND COMING[1]   1921

Turning and turning in the widening gyre°   spiral
The falcon cannot hear the falconer;
Things fall apart; the center cannot hold;
Mere anarchy is loosed upon the world,
The blood-dimmed tide is loosed, and everywhere
The ceremony of innocence is drowned;
The best lack all conviction, while the worst
Are full of passionate intensity.

Surely some revelation is at hand;
Surely the Second Coming is at hand;   10
The Second Coming! Hardly are those words out

Easter 1916
   [4] Thomas MacDonagh, John MacBride, James Connolly, and Patrick Pearse, shot by a firing squad at Kilmainham Jail in Dublin following the Easter Rising.

The Second Coming
   [1] The New Testament (Matthew 24:29–44) describes the Second Coming of Christ as following a period of tribulation to judge the living and the dead and to inaugurate the millennium.

When a vast image out of *Spiritus Mundi*[2]
Troubles my sight: somewhere in sands of the desert
A shape with lion body and the head of a man,
A gaze blank and pitiless as the sun,
Is moving its slow thighs, while all about it
Reel shadows of the indignant desert birds.
The darkness drops again; but now I know
That twenty centuries of stony sleep
Were vexed to nightmare by a rocking cradle,   20
And what rough beast, its hour come round at last,
Slouches towards Bethlehem to be born?

CARL SANDBURG   (1878–1967)

I AM THE PEOPLE, THE MOB   1916

I am the people—the mob—the crowd—the mass.
Do you know that all the great work of the world is done through me?
I am the workingman, the inventor, the maker of the world's food and clothes.
I am the audience that witnesses history. The Napoleons come from me
      and the Lincolns. They die. And then I send forth more Napoleons
      and Lincolns.
I am the seed ground. I am a prairie that will stand for much plowing.
      Terrible storms pass over me. I forget. The best of me is sucked
      out and wasted. I forget. Everything but Death comes to me and
      makes me work and give up what I have. And I forget.   10
Sometimes I growl, shake myself and spatter a few red drops for history to
      remember. Then—I forget.
When I, the People, learn to remember, when I, the People, use the lessons
      of yesterday and no longer forget who robbed me last year, who
      played me for a fool—then there will be no speaker in all the
      world say the name: "The People," with any fleck of a sneer in
      his voice or any far-off smile of derision.
The mob—the crowd—the mass—will arrive then.

FOR ANALYSIS

1. Describe the speaker in this poem. Who is speaking? What is the effect of having this kind of speaker?

2. How does the poem change in the last of the lines that begins "I am"?

The Second Coming
  [2] The Soul or Spirit of the Universe, which Yeats believed constituted a fund of racial images and memories.

MAKING ARGUMENTS

To whom do you think Sandburg was addressing this poem? Is his speaker talking to itself—to "the mob"—or to people of a different social class? Make an argument for one or the other, or both, with reference to specific moments in the poem.

WRITING TOPIC

What political beliefs does this poem implicitly champion? Try to construct a **concrete** political platform out of the more **abstract** ideas expressed here.

WALLACE STEVENS   (1879–1955)

PETER QUINCE AT THE CLAVIER[1]   1915

I

Just as my fingers on these keys
Make music, so the self-same sounds
On my spirit make a music too.

Music is feeling then, not sound;
And thus it is that what I feel,
Here in this room, desiring you,

Thinking of your blue-shadowed silk,
Is music. It is like the strain
Waked in the elders by Susanna:[2]

Of a green evening, clear and warm,   10
She bathed in her still garden, while
The red-eyed elders, watching, felt

The basses of their being throb
In witching chords, and their thin blood
Pulse pizzicati° of Hosanna.   a pizzicato note or passage

Peter Quince at the Clavier
   [1] Peter Quince is a character from William Shakespeare's *A Midsummer Night's Dream*. He is the playwright and stage manager of "The Most Lamentable Comedy and Most Cruel Death of Pyramus and Thisbe," a comical amateur play performed at Theseus and Hippolyta's wedding. He is the speaker in Stevens's poem.
   [2] In the book of Daniel in the Bible, two village elders spy on a young Hebrew wife named Susanna while she bathes in the garden spring. The elders threaten to accuse her of committing adultery unless she makes love to them. She refuses and they accuse her of infidelity, tarnishing her reputation. However, a cross-examination of the elders later reveals that they fabricated the story, after which the elders are put to death.

II

In the green water, clear and warm,
Susanna lay.
She searched
The touch of springs,
And found   20
Concealed imaginings.
She sighed
For so much melody.

Upon the bank she stood
In the cool
Of spent emotions.
She felt, among the leaves,
The dew
Of old devotions.

She walked upon the grass,   30
Still quavering.
The winds were like her maids,
On timid feet,
Fetching her woven scarves,
Yet wavering.

A breath upon her hand
Muted the night.
She turned—
A cymbal crashed,
And roaring horns.   40

III

Soon, with a noise like tambourines,
Came her attendant Byzantines.

They wondered why Susanna cried
Against the elders by her side:

And as they whispered, the refrain
Was like a willow swept by rain.

Anon, their lamps' uplifted flame
Revealed Susanna and her shame.

And then the simpering Byzantines,
Fled, with a noise like tambourines.   50

IV

Beauty is momentary in the mind—
The fitful tracing of a portal;
But in the flesh it is immortal.

The body dies; the body's beauty lives.
So evenings die, in their green going,
A wave, interminably flowing.
So gardens die, their meek breath scenting
The cowl° of Winter, done repenting.   a hood or long hooded cloak
So maidens die, to the auroral
Celebration of a maiden's choral.   60

Susanna's music touched the bawdy strings
Of those white elders; but, escaping,
Left only Death's ironic scraping.
Now, in its immortality, it plays
On the clear viol° of her memory,   a bowed, stringed instrument
And makes a constant sacrament of praise.

FOR ANALYSIS

1. Who is this poem's speaker? What is he or she doing? How does this inform the poem's meaning?

2. Who is Susanna? What is she doing? How important is her identity to the poem?

3. What things are compared in "Peter Quince at the Clavier"?

4. Section IV begins: "Beauty is momentary in the mind— / The fitful tracing of a portal; / But in the flesh it is immortal" (11. 51–53). What does this mean? How does this idea relate to the poem as a whole?

MAKING ARGUMENTS

Is poetry the same thing as music? What does this poem have to say on the matter? Make an argument answering these questions.

WRITING TOPIC

Describe the poem's music, section by section. How does Stevens use the poet's tools to create and vary the sound of the lines? How do the sections differ from one another? How do these differences relate to the poem's meanings?

MAKING CONNECTIONS

1. Connect "Peter Quince at the Clavier" to another art—painting.

2. Read Stevens's poem with Blake's "The Garden of Love" (p. 171). What are the points of connection? Are these gardens similar? How about what happens in them?

CLAUDE McKAY   (1890–1948)

IF WE MUST DIE   1922

If we must die, let it not be like hogs
Hunted and penned in an inglorious spot,
While round us bark the mad and hungry dogs,
Making their mock at our accursèd lot.
If we must die, O let us nobly die,
So that our precious blood may not be shed
In vain; then even the monsters we defy
Shall be constrained to honor us though dead!
O kinsmen! we must meet the common foe!
Though far outnumbered let us show us brave,   10
And for their thousand blows deal one deathblow!
What though before us lies the open grave?
Like men we'll face the murderous, cowardly pack,
Pressed to the wall, dying, but fighting back!

LANGSTON HUGHES   (1902–1967)

HARLEM   1951

What happens to a dream deferred?

    Does it dry up
    like a raisin in the sun?
    Or fester like a sore—
    And then run?
    Does it stink like rotten meat?
    Or crust and sugar over—
    like a syrupy sweet?

    Maybe it just sags
    like a heavy load.   10

Or does it explode?

W. H. AUDEN (1907–1973)

THE UNKNOWN CITIZEN 1940

(TO JS/07/M/378

THIS MARBLE MONUMENT

IS ERECTED BY THE STATE)

He was found by the Bureau of Statistics to be
One against whom there was no official complaint,
And all the reports on his conduct agree
That, in the modern sense of an old-fashioned word, he was a saint,
For in everything he did he served the Greater Community.
Except for the War till the day he retired
He worked in a factory and never got fired,
But satisfied his employers, Fudge Motors Inc.
Yet he wasn't a scab or odd in his views,
For his Union reports that he paid his dues,   10
(Our report on his Union shows it was sound)
And our Social Psychology workers found
That he was popular with his mates and liked a drink.
The Press are convinced that he bought a paper every day
And that his reactions to advertisements were normal in every way.
Policies taken out in his name prove that he was fully insured,
And his Health-card shows he was once in hospital but left it cured.
Both Producers Research and High-Grade Living declare
He was fully sensible to the advantages of the Installment Plan
And had everything necessary to the Modern Man,   20
A phonograph, radio, a car and a frigidaire.
Our researchers into Public Opinion are content
That he held the proper opinions for the time of year;
When there was peace, he was for peace; when there was war, he went.
He was married and added five children to the population,
Which our Eugenist says was the right number for a parent of his generation,
And our teachers report that he never interfered with their education.
Was he free? Was he happy? The question is absurd:
Had anything been wrong, we should certainly have heard.

DUDLEY RANDALL (1914–2000)

BALLAD OF BIRMINGHAM 1969

(ON THE BOMBING OF A CHURCH IN BIRMINGHAM, ALABAMA, 1963)[1]

"Mother dear, may I go downtown
Instead of out to play,
And march the streets of Birmingham
In a Freedom March today?"

"No, baby, no, you may not go,
For the dogs are fierce and wild,
And clubs and hoses, guns and jails
Aren't good for a little child."

"But, mother, I won't be alone.
Other children will go with me,   10
And march the streets of Birmingham
To make our country free."

"No, baby, no, you may not go,
For I fear those guns will fire.
But you may go to church instead
And sing in the children's choir."

She has combed and brushed her night-dark hair,
And bathed rose petal sweet.
And drawn white gloves on her small brown hands,
And white shoes on her feet.   20

The mother smiled to know her child
Was in the sacred place,
But that smile was the last smile
To come upon her face.

For when she heard the explosion,
Her eyes grew wet and wild.
She raced through the streets of Birmingham
Calling for her child.

---

[1] This poem commemorates the murder of four young African American girls when a bomb was thrown into the Sixteenth Street Baptist Church in 1963, one of the early and most traumatic events in the modern civil rights movement.

431

She clawed through bits of glass and brick,
Then lifted out a shoe.   30
"Oh, here's the shoe my baby wore,
But, baby, where are you?"

GWENDOLYN BROOKS   (1917–2000)

WE REAL COOL   1959

THE POOL PLAYERS
SEVEN AT THE GOLDEN SHOVEL.

We real cool. We
Left school. We

Lurk late. We
Strike straight. We

Sing sin. We
Thin gin. We

Jazz June. We
Die soon.

DONALD DAVIE   (1922–1995)

THE NONCONFORMIST   1985

X, whom society's most mild command,
For instance evening dress, infuriates,
In art is seen confusingly to stand
For disciplined conformity, with Yeats.

Taxed to explain what this resentment is
He feels for small proprieties, it comes,
He likes to think, from old enormities
And keeps the faith with famous martyrdoms.

Yet it is likely, if indeed the crimes
His fathers suffered rankle in his blood,   10
That he find least excusable the times
When they acceded, not when they withstood.

How else explain this bloody-minded bent
To kick against the prickings of the norm;
When to conform is easy, to dissent;
And when it is most difficult, conform?

FOR ANALYSIS

1. Reread the poem's final two lines. What is noteworthy about the word order in this sentence? How does it affect you as you read it? How does it relate to the lines' meaning?

2. What is the speaker's attitude toward X?

3. How would you characterize the range of conformities that are resisted in this poem?

MAKING ARGUMENTS

Davie has described his religious upbringing outside the Church of England (as a Baptist) as making him feel both set apart and very aware of his heritage. Do a little reading on Davie and make the argument that the feelings and experiences of his poem's "X" reflect Davie's own.

WRITING TOPIC

How do you feel about dissent? Do you think American society is hostile or hospitable to it? Discuss with concrete contemporary and/or historical examples.

PHILIP LEVINE (1928–2015)

WHAT WORK IS 1991

We stand in the rain in a long line
waiting at Ford Highland Park. For work.
You know what work is—if you're
old enough to read this you know what
work is, although you may not do it.
Forget you. This is about waiting,
shifting from one foot to another.
Feeling the light rain falling like mist
into your hair, blurring your vision
until you think you see your own brother   10
ahead of you, maybe ten places.
You rub your glasses with your fingers,
and of course it's someone else's brother,
narrower across the shoulders than
yours but with the same sad slouch, the grin
that does not hide the stubbornness,

the sad refusal to give in to
rain, to the hours wasted waiting,
to the knowledge that somewhere ahead
a man is waiting who will say, "No,   20
we're not hiring today," for any
reason he wants. You love your brother,
now suddenly you can hardly stand
the love flooding you for your brother,
who's not beside you or behind or
ahead because he's home trying to
sleep off a miserable night shift
at Cadillac so he can get up
before noon to study his German.
Works eight hours a night so he can sing   30
Wagner, the opera you hate most,
the worst music ever invented.
How long has it been since you told him
you loved him, held his wide shoulders,
opened your eyes wide and said those words,
and maybe kissed his cheek? You've never
done something so simple, so obvious,
not because you're too young or too dumb,
not because you're jealous or even mean
or incapable of crying in   40
the presence of another man, no,
just because you don't know what work is.

FOR ANALYSIS

1. What is the poem's **tone**? Is it simple or complicated? Does it evoke one feeling or many?

2. Does the poem supply the definition it promises in its title?

MAKING ARGUMENTS

Argue for the importance of lines 30–32 to the poem—while they might seem tangential to the poem, make and support the claim that they are central to it.

WRITING TOPICS

1. Who is the "you" addressed in this poem? What is the speaker's attitude toward this "you"? Write an essay in which you analyze Levine's use of the second-person point of view in this poem.

2. Write a poem that at first seems to be about a sibling (or another close family member or a friend) but is really as much about you as it is about them.

MARGE PIERCY   (B. 1936)

THE MARKET ECONOMY   1973

Suppose some peddler offered
you can have a color TV
but your baby will be
born with a crooked spine;
you can have polyvinyl cups
and wash and wear
suits but it will cost
you your left lung
rotted with cancer; suppose
somebody offered you   10
a frozen precooked dinner
every night for ten years
but at the end
your colon dies
and then you do,
slowly and with much pain.
You get a house in the suburbs
but you work in a new plastics
factory and die at fifty-one
when your kidneys turn off.   20
But where else will you
work? where else can
you rent but Smog City?
The only houses for sale
are under the yellow sky.
You've been out of work for
a year and they're hiring
at the plastics factory.
Don't read the fine
print, there isn't any.   30

FOR ANALYSIS

1. Characterize the **tone** of this poem.

2. Would this still be a poem if it were printed as a paragraph? Compare this poem
with Carolyn Forché's "The Colonel" (p. 436), which is written as a paragraph. Which
do you find more "poetic"? Explain.

3. What is meant by the last two lines of the poem?

MAKING ARGUMENTS

Regardless of your own politics, how would you make the argument that "the market"
isn't to blame for the ills Piercy's poem enumerates? What would you propose as an
alternative cause?

CAROLYN FORCHÉ (B. 1950)

THE COLONEL 1981

What you have heard is true. I was in his house. His wife carried a tray of coffee and sugar. His daughter filed her nails, his son went out for the night. There were daily papers, pet dogs, a pistol on the cushion beside him. The moon swung bare on its black cord over the house. On the television was a cop show. It was in English. Broken bottles were embedded in the walls round the house to scoop the kneecaps from a man's legs or cut his hands to lace. On the windows there were gratings like those in liquor stores. We had dinner, rack of lamb, good wine, a gold bell was on the table for calling the maid. The maid brought green mangoes, salt, a type of bread. I was asked how I enjoyed the country. There was a brief commercial in Spanish. His wife took everything 10
away. There was some talk then of how difficult it had become to govern. The parrot said hello on the terrace. The colonel told it to shut up, and pushed himself from the table. My friend said to me with his eyes: say nothing. The colonel returned with a sack used to bring groceries home. He spilled many human ears on the table. They were like dried peach halves. There is no other way to say this. He took one of them in his hands, shook it in our faces, dropped it into a water glass. It came alive there. I am tired of fooling around he said. As for the rights of anyone, tell your people they can go fuck themselves. He swept the ears to the floor with his arm and held the last of his wine in the air. Something for your poetry, no? he said. Some of the ears on the floor caught this scrap of 20
his voice. Some of the ears on the floor were pressed to the ground.

FOR ANALYSIS

1. What is the occasion of this poem? Where is it set? How would you characterize the colonel's family?

2. In line 11 the speaker recounts, "There was some talk then of how difficult it had become to govern." Can you suggest why it had become difficult to govern? How does the colonel respond to these difficulties?

3. What does the last sentence suggest?

4. This piece is printed as if it were **prose**. Does it have any of the formal characteristics of a poem?

MAKING ARGUMENTS

Poems have often traditionally been classified as public or private. Is "The Colonel" a public poem or a private poem? Make the argument that the idea of a "poetry of witness," a phrase that appeared in the subtitle of Forché's 1993 international anthology *Against Forgetting*, provides a way out of this problem of classification.

NATASHA TRETHEWEY (B. 1966)

FLOUNDER 2000

Here, she said, *put this on your head.*
She handed me a hat.
You 'bout as white as your dad,
and you gone stay like that.

Aunt Sugar rolled her nylons down
around each bony ankle,
and I rolled down my white knee socks
letting my thin legs dangle,

circling them just above water
and silver backs of minnows   10
flitting here then there between
the sun spots and the shadows.

This is how you hold the pole
to cast the line out straight.
Now put that worm on your hook,
throw it out and wait.

She sat spitting tobacco juice
into a coffee cup.
Hunkered down when she felt the bite,
jerked the pole straight up   20

reeling and tugging hard at the fish
that wriggled and tried to fight back.
A flounder, she said, *and you can tell*
'cause one of its sides is black.

The other side is white, she said.
It landed with a thump.
I stood there watching that fish flip-flop,
switch sides with every jump.

FOR ANALYSIS

1. Why does Aunt Sugar want the speaker to put a hat on? Why is it important to her?

2. What is the most important physical characteristic of the flounder? What is the most important action it takes?

3. What kind of sentence does Aunt Sugar address the speaker with in lines 1, 15, and 16? Why might that be important for the poem's depiction of their relationship and of what the aunt has to say to the speaker?

MAKING ARGUMENTS

"Flounder" is pretty clear on the speaker's parents' racial identity—one is white, the other black. But what about Aunt Sugar? What things about her, from the way she talks to the attitudes you would have to assume, make the argument that she is white? What things would you have to assume if she is black?

WRITING TOPIC

Animals are used in literature for as many different reasons as there are different kinds of animals on the planet. Most animal appearances in stories and poems are motivated by something other than a desire to focus on the animals themselves; more often, they are there in the service of a **plot** or as **metaphorical** illustrations about people. Do you think the way we use animals in imaginative literature is significant? What does it mean to you about our relation to the nonhuman animal world?

CONNECTING POEMS: REVOLUTIONARY THINKING

"Hurrah for revolution and more cannon-shot!" So begins William Butler Yeats's "The Great Day." In this beginning line—and the title—we hear both the anger some poets have felt about revolution and the energy it can take to oppose popular support of the idea. Throughout history, there has been a romantic attraction to revolution, as there has been to armed struggle. In Yeats's mock cheer, and ironic "Great," readers encounter a poet challenging that romantic attitude. As you read the poems in this unit, think about the different things revolutions can do, the different ways they can end, and especially the different things they can mean—to revolutionaries, to those in power, and to those who engage in revolutionary thinking.

WILLIAM BUTLER YEATS   (1865–1939)

THE GREAT DAY   1939

Hurrah for revolution and more cannon-shot!
A beggar upon horseback lashes a beggar on foot.
Hurrah for revolution and cannon come again!
The beggars have changed places, but the lash goes on.

ROBERT FROST (1874–1963)

A SEMI-REVOLUTION 1942

I advocate a semi-revolution.
The trouble with a total revolution
(Ask any reputable Rosicrucian)[1]
Is that it brings the same class up on top.
Executives of skillful execution
Will therefore plan to go half-way and stop.
Yes, revolutions are the only salves,
But they're one thing that should be done by halves.

NIKKI GIOVANNI (B. 1943)

DREAMS 1968

i used to dream militant
dreams of taking
over america to show
these white folks how it should be
done
i used to dream radical dreams
of blowing everyone away with my perceptive powers
of correct analysis
i even used to think i'd be the one
to stop the riot and negotiate the peace   10
then i awoke and dug
that if i dreamed natural
dreams of being a natural
woman doing what a woman
does when she's natural
i would have a revolution

MAKING ARGUMENTS

Which of these arguments about revolution do you think is closest to correct or to
what you think? Identify the central argument each poem makes about revolution as
we traditionally think of it, then make your own argument for which way of "revolutionary thinking" is ultimately most accurate or helpful or congenial to you.

A Semi-Revolution
[1] Rosicrucians are members of a society professing mystic religious principles and a belief in occult
knowledge and powers. William Butler Yeats was a member of this group (see his poem "The Great
Day" on page 438).

MAKING CONNECTIONS

1. All of these poems make skillful use of **tone**, often hiding **irony** not too far beneath what seem at first straightforward statements. In what ways do these different poems manipulate tone, and to what effect?

2. When we think of revolutions, we often think of action—of warfare—but, as the unit title suggests, these poems instead focus on thinking *about* revolutions. Why is thinking—or to use Giovanni's phrase "militant dream[ing]" (above)—so important to revolutions? What kind of revolution is Giovanni imagining in her poem?

CONNECTING POEMS: REVISING AMERICA

The poems in this section are all about America the nation and America the idea. None of them celebrates the nation—in its present or in its past—in an uncritical way, but neither do any of them condemn it wholesale. As you read these poems, written in a number of different places and times, pay attention to how they are in some ways quite similar and how in others they diverge in what they have to say about the American present, the American past, and American identity—and in the way they say those things. Also look for connections between what they have to say and how that message is presented through form.

WALT WHITMAN   (1819–1892)

ONE SONG, AMERICA, BEFORE I GO   1872

One song, America, before I go,
I'd sing, o'er all the rest, with trumpet sound,
For thee—the Future.

I'd sow a seed for thee of endless Nationality;
I'd fashion thy Ensemble, including Body and Soul;
I'd show, away ahead, thy real Union, and how it may be accomplish'd.

(The paths to the House I seek to make,
But leave to those to come, the House itself.)

Belief I sing—and Preparation;
As Life and Nature are not great with reference to the Present only,   10
But greater still from what is yet to come,
Out of that formula for Thee I sing.

FOR ANALYSIS

1. In his poem "America," Whitman **parodies** the patriotic song "My Country 'Tis of Thee" to draw attention to some less positive aspects of American history. What kind of song of America does Whitman sing here?

2. Why is the future important here? What is Whitman saying about the present and past of America?

MAKING ARGUMENTS

Imagine Whitman as a contemporary of yours, writing poetry about America today. Make an argument for what sort of opinions he would hold, what kinds of policies he would support or oppose, even what political party he would identify with.

LANGSTON HUGHES   (1902–1967)

I, TOO   1926

I, too, sing America.

I am the darker brother.
They send me to eat in the kitchen
When company comes,
But I laugh,
And eat well,
And grow strong.

Tomorrow,
I'll be at the table
When company comes.   10
Nobody'll dare
Say to me,
"Eat in the kitchen,"
Then.

Besides,
They'll see how beautiful I am
And be ashamed—

I, too, am America.

FOR ANALYSIS

1. The title "I, Too" alludes to Walt Whitman's "I Hear America Singing" (you may find it helpful to look at Whitman's poem online). Why does Hughes add the word "too"? How does it respond to the Whitman poem to which it **alludes**?

2. How does this poem's last line relate to the first? What does the difference express?

MAKING ARGUMENTS

Think about the "they" in "I, Too." Who are "they" in relation to the speaker? Who are they in relation to the audience? Make an argument about the identity of "they," about the identity of the audience, and about how the poem wants its readers to feel about this group.

ALLEN GINSBERG (1926–1997)

A SUPERMARKET IN CALIFORNIA   1955

What thoughts I have of you tonight, Walt Whitman, for I walked down the sidestreets under the trees with a headache self-conscious looking at the full moon.

In my hungry fatigue, and shopping for images, I went into the neon fruit supermarket, dreaming of your enumerations!

What peaches and what penumbras! Whole families shopping at night! Aisles full of husbands! Wives in the avocados, babies in the tomatoes! —and you, Garcia Lorca, what were you doing down by the watermelons?

I saw you, Walt Whitman, childless, lonely old grubber, poking among the meats in the refrigerator and eyeing the grocery boys.   10

I heard you asking questions of each: Who killed the pork chops? What price bananas? Are you my Angel?

I wandered in and out of the brilliant stacks of cans following you, and followed in my imagination by the store detective.

We strode down the open corridors together in our solitary fancy tasting artichokes, possessing every frozen delicacy, and never passing the cashier.

Where are we going, Walt Whitman? The doors close in a hour. Which way does your beard point tonight?

(I touch your book and dream of our odyssey in the supermarket and   20 feel absurd.)

Will we walk all night through solitary streets? The trees add shade to shade, lights out in the houses, we'll both be lonely.

Will we stroll dreaming of the lost America of love past blue automobiles in driveways, home to our silent cottage?

Ah, dear father, graybeard, lonely old courage-teacher, what America did you have when Charon quit poling his ferry and you got out on a smoking bank and stood watching the boat disappear on the black waters of Lethe?

FOR ANALYSIS

1. Why does the speaker address Whitman? What is the poem's relation to him?

2. How does the speaker feel about contemporary America? How does he feel about the America of the past?

MAKING ARGUMENTS

Imagine an argument between you and Ginsberg over whether America is really lost, or still lost. How would you make an argument against the poem's idea of a lost America? Think in terms of the poem and your understanding of both the country's past and present.

SHIRLEY GEOK-LIN LIM (B. 1944)

LEARNING TO LOVE AMERICA 1998

because it has no pure products

because the Pacific Ocean sweeps along the coastline
because the water of the ocean is cold
and because land is better than ocean

because I say we rather than they

because I live in California
I have eaten fresh artichokes
and jacaranda bloom in April and May

because my senses have caught up with my body
my breath with the air it swallows   10
my hunger with my mouth

because I walk barefoot in my house

because I have nursed my son at my breast
because he is a strong American boy
because I have seen his eyes redden when he is asked who he is
because he answers I don't know

because to have a son is to have a country
because my son will bury me here
because countries are in our blood and we bleed them

because it is late and too late to change my mind   20
because it is time.

FOR ANALYSIS

1. The first line of William Carlos Williams's "To Elsie" refers to "The pure products of America." What about this line might have made Lim want to invoke it in the first line of her poem?

2. What do the words that follow the repeated "because" explain? Of what are they the cause?

MAKING ARGUMENTS

Make an argument about line 19 in "Learning to Love America." Are our countries in our blood? What does it mean to say this? Is it a good thing? A bad thing? Both?

MAKING CONNECTIONS

1. Each of the poems in this section refers to other, earlier creative works. Are there any parallels in the way they make these references? Why do you think they make them? What's the connection between poetic **allusion** and the way these poems view America?

2. Many of these poems reflect on America not simply in general but in relation to personal identity. What are the connections between them in regard to the way national identity takes shape? What kinds of identity are implicitly and explicitly considered?

3. What role does love play in these poems? What kinds of love are represented? How are they treated? How does their treatment relate to their poem's **themes**?

4. Each of these poems is in some way about process—about being in the middle of something happening, becoming, or being undertaken. Why is this shared trait significant? How are these poems about a process or processes?

CONNECTING POEMS: SOLDIERS' PROTESTS

War is many things to many people; however, it is rarely described as "quaint and curious," as the speaker in Hardy's "The Man He Killed" (below) says it is. Hardy's speaker arrives at this conclusion as he confronts the realization, after shooting someone, that his victim was probably just a regular guy like he is, someone he'd loan a little money to or buy a drink for. As you read the poems in this unit, think about the different voices in them and the different realizations they have about war and the people who fight and die in them. Think also about the times and places these poets wrote from—England before and after the Great War (what we now call World War I), the Middle East in the late 1980s, the United States during the Iraq War—and about what changes and what stays the same, across place and time, in these war poems.

THOMAS HARDY (1840–1928)

THE MAN HE KILLED   1902

"Had he and I but met
    By some old ancient inn,
We should have sat us down to wet
    Right many a nipperkin!

"But ranged as infantry,
    And staring face to face,
I shot at him as he at me,
    And killed him in his place.

"I shot him dead because—
    Because he was my foe,   10
Just so: my foe of course he was:
    That's clear enough; although

"He thought he'd 'list, perhaps,
    Off-hand-like—just as I—
Was out of work—had sold his traps—
    No other reason why.

"Yes; quaint and curious war is!
    You shoot a fellow down
You'd treat, if met where any bar is,
    Or help to half-a-crown."   20

WILFRED OWEN (1893–1918)

DULCE ET DECORUM EST   1920

Bent double, like old beggars under sacks,
Knock-kneed, coughing like hags, we cursed through sludge,
Till on the haunting flares we turned our backs,
And towards our distant rest began to trudge.
Men marched asleep. Many had lost their boots,
But limped on, blood-shod. All went lame, all blind;
Drunk with fatigue; deaf even to the hoots
Of gas-shells dropping softly behind.

Gas! GAS! Quick, boys!—An ecstasy of fumbling,
Fitting the clumsy helmets just in time,   10
But someone still was yelling out and stumbling
And flound'ring like a man in fire or lime.—
Dim through the misty panes and thick green light,
As under a green sea, I saw him drowning.
In all my dreams before my helpless sight
He plunges at me, guttering, choking, drowning.

If in some smothering dreams, you too could pace
Behind the wagon that we flung him in,
And watch the white eyes writhing in his face,
His hanging face, like a devil's sick of sin,   20
If you could hear, at every jolt, the blood
Come gargling from the froth-corrupted lungs
Bitter as the cud
Of vile, incurable sores on innocent tongues,—
My friend, you would not tell with such high zest
To children ardent for some desperate glory,
The old lie: *Dulce et decorum est*
Pro patria mori.[1]

HANAN MIKHA'IL 'ASHRAWI   (B. 1946)

NIGHT PATROL   1988

(AN ISRAELI SOLDIER ON THE WEST BANK)

It's not the sudden hail
of stones, nor the mocking of
their jeers, but this deliberate
quiet in their eyes that
threatens to wipe itself
around my well-armed uniformed
presence and drag me into
depths of confrontation I
never dared to probe.

Their stares bounce off stone,
walls and amateur barricades, and   10

Dulce et Decorum Est
  [1] A quotation from the Latin poet Horace, "It is sweet and fitting to die for one's country."

I'm forced to listen
to the echo of my own
gun fire and tear gas
grenades in the midst of
a deafening silence which
I could almost touch, almost
But not quite.
I refuse to be made
into a figment of my   20
own imagination. I catch
myself, at times, glimpsing
glimpsing the child I
was in one of them. That
same old recklessness, a daredevil
stance, a secret wisdom only
youth can impart as it hurtles
towards adulthood. Then I
begin to take substance before
my very eyes, and   30
shrink back in terror—as
an organism on its long
evolutionary trek recoils at the
touch of a human hand.

If I should once, just
once, grasp the elusive
end of the thread which
ties my being here with
their being there, I
could unravel the beginning . . . no,   40
no, it was not an act
of will that brought me
here, and I shall wrap myself in
fabric woven by hands
other than mine, perhaps
lie down and take a nap.

Should I admit then into
my hapless dreams a thousand
eyes, a thousand hands, and allow
unknowingly the night's   50
silence to conceal me, I
would have done no
more or less than what
thousands have done before, turning

over in sleep clutching my
cocoon of army issue blankets,
and hope for a different posting
in the morning.

FOR ANALYSIS

1. Why do the children from the West Bank hurl stones at the soldier?

2. This Palestinian poet speaks with the voice of an Israeli soldier. In the first **stanza**, how would "this deliberate / quiet in their eyes" drag the soldier into "depths of confrontation I / never dared to probe"? How does this confrontation differ from the "hail of stones"? How would you characterize the "depths of confrontation"? Why had the speaker "never dared to probe" such a confrontation?

3. In the second stanza, what is the consequence for the speaker when he perceives himself "glimpsing the child I / was in one of them"?

4. Why does the speaker "hope for a different posting / in the morning"?

MAKING ARGUMENTS

"Night Patrol" was published in 1988. Almost three decades later, the situation in the Middle East remains unsettled. Doing enough research to feel informed, make an argument about whether this poem might be different if written today. Is Israel's well-being still threatened in the same way that this soldier's is? Are the parties involved any closer to being able to "grasp the elusive end of the thread" (ll. 36–37) that ties them together?

WRITING TOPIC

Evaluate the character of the Israeli soldier on night patrol. Is he a good person or an evil one? A true patriot or a troubled one? What human and moral imperatives embody his consciousness?

KEVIN C. POWERS   (B. 1980)

LETTER COMPOSED DURING A LULL IN THE FIGHTING   2009

I tell her I love her like not killing
or ten minutes of sleep
beneath the low rooftop wall
on which my rifle rests.

I tell her in a letter that will stink,
when she opens it,
of bolt oil and burned powder
and the things it says.

I tell her how Pvt. Bartle says, offhand,
that war is just us
making little pieces of metal
pass through each other.

10

FOR ANALYSIS

1. List the **images** in this poem, then list the **metaphors**. How do they interact? Does one kind of element illuminate the other? What is the effect of the intermingling of the two?

2. What things do you think the letter says?

MAKING ARGUMENTS

Powers's way of describing war is similar to that employed by Kurt Vonnegut in his novel *Slaughterhouse-Five*, when he imagines a movie about World War II seen by a character who sees it backward: "The Germans had miraculous devices of their own, which were long steel tubes. They used them to suck more fragments from the crewmen and planes." Make an argument about this connection. What is the effect of each? How does reading lines 10–12 of this poem and this short passage from Vonnegut make you think and feel?

MAKING CONNECTIONS

1. Compare the different effects achieved by the choice of **persona** in these four poems. Hardy's, for example, is entirely within quotation marks, a speech delivered by someone—the "He" of the title—while Owen's poem ranges from first-person plural to first-person singular to second-person **point of view**. How do these choices help shape the effects of these poems?

2. What do these poems have to say about the reasons for war? Which seem unconcerned with this question or seem to think it doesn't matter? Which seem more concerned with the reasons why individuals become soldiers than the reasons why nations enter armed conflict? Do you think poetry may be more suited to exploring the former concern? Why?

3. None of these poems seems interested in defending the old idea that, to paraphrase Owen quoting Horace, it is sweet and proper to die for one's country. Are there any voices within the poems who say that, or who might say that? Are there voices who actually believe it or might say it without believing it?

DRAMA

SOPHOCLES (496?–406 BCE)

ANTIGONÊ[1] CA. 441 BCE

CHARACTERS

Antigonê	Teiresias
Ismenê	A Sentry
Eurydicê	A Messenger
Creon	Chorus
Haimon	

Scene

Before the Palace of Creon, King of Thebes. A central double door, and two lateral doors. A platform extends the length of the facade, and from this platform three steps lead down into the "orchestra," or chorus-ground.

Time

Dawn of the day after the repulse of the Argive army from the assault on Thebes.

PROLOGUE

(Antigonê and Ismenê enter from the central door of the Palace.)

Antigonê. Ismenê, dear sister,
    You would think that we had already suffered enough
    For the curse on Oedipus:[2]
    I cannot imagine any grief

---

[1] An English version by Dudley Fitts and Robert Fitzgerald.   [2] Oedipus, a former king of Thebes, unwittingly killed his father and married his own mother, Iocastê. By her he had four children, the sisters Antigonê and Ismenê and the brothers Polyneicês and Eteoclês. When Oedipus realized what he had done, he blinded himself and left Thebes. Eteoclês drove Polyneicês out of Thebes after a quarrel, but Polyneicês returned with an army and laid siege to Thebes. In the ensuing struggle, the brothers killed each other. Creon became king and, as a punishment, decreed that Polyneicês be denied the rites of burial.

That you and I have not gone through. And now—
Have they told you of the new decree of our King Creon?
Ismenê. I have heard nothing: I know
That two sisters lost two brothers, a double death
In a single hour; and I know that the Argive army
Fled in the night; but beyond this, nothing.   10
Antigonê. I thought so. And that is why I wanted you
To come out here with me. There is something we must do.
Ismenê. Why do you speak so strangely?
Antigonê. Listen, Ismenê:
Creon buried our brother Eteoclês
With military honors, gave him a soldier's funeral,
And it was right that he should; but Polyneicês,
Who fought as bravely and died as miserably,—
They say that Creon has sworn
No one shall bury him, no one mourn for him,   20
But his body must lie in the fields, a sweet treasure
For carrion birds to find as they search for food.
That is what they say, and our good Creon is coming here
To announce it publicly; and the penalty—
Stoning to death in the public square.
                                   There it is,
And now you can prove what you are:
A true sister, or a traitor to your family.
Ismenê. Antigonê, you are mad! What could I possibly do?
Antigonê. You must decide whether you will help me or not.
Ismenê. I do not understand you. Help you in what?   30
Antigonê. Ismenê, I am going to bury him. Will you come?
Ismenê. Bury him! You have just said the new law forbids it.
Antigonê. He is my brother. And he is your brother, too.
Ismenê. But think of the danger! Think what Creon will do!
Antigonê. Creon is not strong enough to stand in my way.
Ismenê. Ah sister!
Oedipus died, everyone hating him
For what his own search brought to light, his eyes
Ripped out by his own hand; and Iocastê died,
His mother and wife at once: she twisted the cords   40
That strangled her life; and our two brothers died,
Each killed by the other's sword. And we are left:
But oh, Antigonê,
Think how much more terrible than these
Our own death would be if we should go against Creon
And do what he has forbidden! We are only women,
We cannot fight with men, Antigonê!
The law is strong, we must give in to the law

In this thing, and in worse. I beg the Dead
To forgive me, but I am helpless: I must yield   50
To those in authority. And I think it is dangerous business
To be always meddling.

Antigonê.   If that is what you think,
I should not want you, even if you asked to come.
You have made your choice, you can be what you want to be.
But I will bury him; and if I must die,
I say that this crime is holy: I shall lie down
With him in death, and I shall be as dear
To him as he to me.
                              It is the dead,
Not the living, who make the longest demands:
We die for ever . . .
                              You may do as you like,   60
Since apparently the laws of the gods mean nothing to you.

Ismenê. They mean a great deal to me; but I have no strength
To break laws that were made for the public good.

Antigonê. That must be your excuse, I suppose. But as for me,
I will bury the brother I love.

Ismenê.   Antigonê,
I am so afraid for you!

Antigonê. You need not be:
You have yourself to consider, after all.

Ismenê. But no one must hear of this, you must tell no one!
I will keep it a secret, I promise!

Antigonê.   Oh tell it! Tell everyone!
Think how they'll hate you when it all comes out   70
If they learn that you knew about it all the time!

Ismenê. So fiery! You should be cold with fear.

Antigonê. Perhaps. But I am doing only what I must.

Ismenê. But can you do it? I say that you cannot.

Antigonê. Very well: when my strength gives out, I shall do no more.

Ismenê. Impossible things should not be tried at all.

Antigonê. Go away, Ismenê:
I shall be hating you soon, and the dead will too,
For your words are hateful. Leave me my foolish plan:
I am not afraid of the danger; if it means death,   80
It will not be the worst of deaths—death without honor.

Ismenê. Go then, if you feel you must.
You are unwise,
But a loyal friend indeed to those who love you.

(Exit into the Palace. Antigonê goes off, L. Enter the Chorus.)

PÁRODOS[3]

Chorus. Now the long blade of the sun, lying   *(Strophe 1)*
    Level east to west, touches with glory
    Thebes of the Seven Gates. Open, unlidded
    Eye of golden day! O marching light
    Across the eddy and rush of Dircê's stream,[4]
    Striking the white shields of the enemy
    Thrown headlong backward from the blaze of morning!
Choragos.[5] Polyneicês their commander
    Roused them with windy phrases,
    He the wild eagle screaming   10
    Insults above our land,
    His wings their shields of snow,
    His crest their marshalled helms.

Chorus. Against our seven gates in a yawning ring   *(Antistrophe 1)*
    The famished spears came onward in the night;
    But before his jaws were sated with our blood,
    Or pinefire took the garland of our towers,
    He was thrown back; and as he turned, great Thebes—
    No tender victim for his noisy power—
    Rose like a dragon behind him, shouting war.   20
Choragos. For God hates utterly
    The bray of bragging tongues;
    And when he beheld their smiling,
    Their swagger of golden helms,
    The frown of his thunder blasted
    Their first man from our walls.

Chorus. We heard his shout of triumph high in the air   *(Strophe 2)*
    Turn to a scream; far out in a flaming arc
    He fell with his windy torch, and the earth struck him.
    And others storming in fury no less than his   30
    Found shock of death in the dusty joy of battle.
Choragos. Seven captains at seven gates
    Yielded their clanging arms to the god
    That bends the battle-line and breaks it.
    These two only, brothers in blood,

---

[3] The Párodos is the *ode* sung by the Chorus as it entered the theater and moved down the aisles to the playing area. The *strophe*, in Greek tragedy, is the unit of verse the Chorus chanted as it moved to the left in a dance rhythm. The Chorus sang the *antistrophe* as it moved to the right, and the *epode* while standing still.   [4] A stream near Thebes.   [5] Choragos is the leader of the Chorus.

Face to face in matchless rage,
Mirroring each the other's death,
Clashed in long combat.

Chorus. But now in the beautiful morning of victory   *(Antistrophe 2)*
Let Thebes of the many chariots sing for joy!   40
With hearts for dancing we'll take leave of war:
Our temples shall be sweet with hymns of praise,
And the long night shall echo with our chorus.

SCENE 1

Choragos. But now at last our new King is coming:
Creon of Thebes, Menoikeus' son.
In this auspicious dawn of his reign
What are the new complexities
That shifting Fate has woven for him?
What is his counsel? Why has he summoned
The old men to hear him?

(Enter Creon from the Palace, C. He addresses the Chorus from the top step.)

Creon. Gentlemen: I have the honor to inform you that our Ship of State, which recent storms have threatened to destroy, has come safely to harbor at last, guided by the merciful wisdom of Heaven. I have summoned you here 10 this morning because I know that I can depend upon you: your devotion to King Laïos was absolute; you never hesitated in your duty to our late ruler Oedipus; and when Oedipus died, your loyalty was transferred to his children. Unfortunately, as you know, his two sons, the princes Eteoclês and Polyneicês, have killed each other in battle; and I, as the next in blood, have succeeded to the full power of the throne.

I am aware, of course, that no Ruler can expect complete loyalty from his subjects until he has been tested in office. Nevertheless, I say to you at the very outset that I have nothing but contempt for the kind of Governor who is afraid, for whatever reason, to follow the course that he knows is best for 20 the State; and as for the man who sets private friendship above the public welfare,—I have no use for him, either. I call God to witness that if I saw my country headed for ruin, I should not be afraid to speak out plainly; and I need hardly remind you that I would never have any dealings with an enemy of the people. No one values friendship more highly than I; but we must remember that friends made at the risk of wrecking our Ship are not real friends at all.

These are my principles, at any rate, and that is why I have made the following decision concerning the sons of Oedipus: Eteoclês, who died as a man should die, fighting for his country, is to be buried with full military honors, with all the 30 ceremony that is usual when the greatest heroes die; but his brother Polyneicês, who broke his exile to come back with fire and sword against his native city and the shrines of his fathers' gods, whose one idea was to spill the blood of his blood and sell his own people into slavery—Polyneicês, I say, is to have no burial: no man is to touch him or say the least prayer for him; he shall lie on the plain, unburied; and the birds and the scavenging dogs can do with him whatever they like.

This is my command, and you can see the wisdom behind it. As long as I am King, no traitor is going to be honored with the loyal man. But whoever shows by word and deed that he is on the side of the State,—he shall have my respect 40 while he is living and my reverence when he is dead.

Choragos. If that is your will, Creon, son of Menoikeus,
You have the right to enforce it: we are yours.
Creon. That is my will. Take care that you do your part.
Choragos. We are old men: let the younger ones carry it out.
Creon. I do not mean that: the sentries have been appointed.
Choragos. Then what is it that you would have us do?
Creon. You will give no support to whoever breaks this law.
Choragos. Only a crazy man is in love with death!
Creon. And death it is; yet money talks, and the wisest
Have sometimes been known to count a few coins too many. 50

(Enter Sentry from L.)

Sentry. I'll not say that I'm out of breath from running, King, because every time I stopped to think about what I have to tell you, I felt like going back. And all the time a voice kept saying, "You fool, don't you know you're walking straight into trouble?"; and then another voice: "Yes, but if you let somebody else get the news to Creon first, it will be even worse than that for you!" But good sense won out, at least I hope it was good sense, and here I am with a story that makes no sense at all; but I'll tell it anyhow, because, as they say, what's going to happen's going to happen, and—
Creon. Come to the point. What have you to say? 60
Sentry. I did not do it. I did not see who did it. You must not punish me for what someone else has done.
Creon. A comprehensive defense! More effective, perhaps,
If I knew its purpose. Come: what is it?
Sentry. A dreadful thing . . . I don't know how to put it—
Creon. Out with it!
Sentry.   Well, then;
The dead man—
                    Polyneicês—

(Pause. The Sentry is overcome, fumbles for words. Creon waits impassively.)

out there—   70
                                    someone,—
New dust on the slimy flesh!

(Pause. No sign from Creon.)

Someone has given it burial that way, and
Gone . . .

(Long pause. Creon finally speaks with deadly control.)

Creon. And the man who dared do this?
Sentry.   I swear I
Do not know! You must believe me!
                                         Listen:
The ground was dry, not a sign of digging, no,
Not a wheel track in the dust, no trace of anyone.   80
It was when they relieved us this morning: and one of them,
The corporal, pointed to it.
                              There it was,
The strangest—
          Look:
The body, just mounded over with light dust: you see?
Not buried really, but as if they'd covered it
Just enough for the ghost's peace. And no sign
Of dogs or any wild animal that had been there.

And then what a scene there was! Every man of us   90
Accusing the other: we all proved the other man did it,
We all had proof that we could not have done it.
We were ready to take hot iron in our hands,
Walk through fire, swear by all the gods,
It was not I!
I do not know who it was, but it was not I!

(Creon's rage has been mounting steadily, but the Sentry is too intent upon his story to notice it.)

And then, when this came to nothing, someone said
A thing that silenced us and made us stare
Down at the ground: you had to be told the news,
And one of us had to do it! We threw the dice,   90
And the bad luck fell to me. So here I am,
No happier to be here than you are to have me:
Nobody likes the man who brings bad news.

Choragos. I have been wondering, King: can it be that the gods have done this?
Creon (*furiously*). Stop!

> Must you doddering wrecks
> Go out of your heads entirely? "The gods!"
> Intolerable!
> The gods favor this corpse? Why? How had he served them?
> Tried to loot their temples, burn their images,   100
> Yes, and the whole State, and its laws with it!
> Is it your senile opinion that the gods love to honor bad men?
> A pious thought—
>   No, from the very beginning
> There have been those who have whispered together,
> Stiff-necked anarchists, putting their heads together,
> Scheming against me in alleys. These are the men,
> And they have bribed my own guard to do this thing.
> (*Sententiously.*) Money!
> There's nothing in the world so demoralizing as money.   110
> Down go your cities,
> Homes gone, men gone, honest hearts corrupted,
> Crookedness of all kinds, and all for money!
> (*To Sentry.*)   But you—!
> I swear by God and by the throne of God,
> The man who has done this thing shall pay for it!
> Find that man, bring him here to me, or your death
> Will be the least of your problems: I'll string you up
> Alive, and there will be certain ways to make you
> Discover your employer before you die;   120
> And the process may teach you a lesson you seem to have missed:
> The dearest profit is sometimes all too dear:
> That depends on the source. Do you understand me?
> A fortune won is often misfortune.

Sentry. King, may I speak?
Creon.   Your very voice distresses me.
Sentry. Are you sure that it is my voice, and not your conscience?
Creon. By God, he wants to analyze me now!
Sentry. It is not what I say, but what has been done, that hurts you.
Creon. You talk too much.   130
Sentry.   Maybe; but I've done nothing.
Creon. Sold your soul for some silver: that's all you've done.
Sentry. How dreadful it is when the right judge judges wrong!
Creon. Your figures of speech

> May entertain you now; but unless you bring me the man,
> You will get little profit from them in the end.

(*Exit Creon into the Palace.*)

Sentry. "Bring me the man"—!
    I'd like nothing better than bringing him the man!
    But bring him or not, you have seen the last of me here.
    At any rate, I am safe!   140

(Exit Sentry.)

ODE I

Chorus. Numberless are the world's wonders, but none   *(Strophe 1)*
    More wonderful than man; the stormgray sea
    Yields to his prows, the huge crests bear him high;
    Earth, holy and inexhaustible, is graven
    With shining furrows where his plows have gone
    Year after year, the timeless labor of stallions.

    The lightboned birds and beasts that cling to cover,   *(Antistrophe 1)*
    The lithe fish lighting their reaches of dim water,
    All are taken, tamed in the net of his mind;
    The lion on the hill, the wild horse windy-maned,   10
    Resign to him; and his blunt yoke has broken
    The sultry shoulders of the mountain bull.

    Words also, and thought as rapid as air,   *(Strophe 2)*
    He fashions to his good use; statecraft is his,
    And his the skill that deflects the arrows of snow,
    The spears of winter rain: from every wind
    He has made himself secure—from all but one:
    In the late wind of death he cannot stand.

    O clear intelligence, force beyond all measure!   *(Antistrophe 2)*
    O fate of man, working both good and evil!   20
    When the laws are kept, how proudly his city stands!
    When the laws are broken, what of his city then?
    Never may the anarchic man find rest at my hearth,
    Never be it said that my thoughts are his thoughts.

SCENE 2

(Re-enter Sentry leading Antigonê.)

Choragos. What does this mean? Surely this captive woman
    Is the Princess, Antigonê. Why should she be taken?
Sentry. Here is the one who did it! We caught her
    In the very act of burying him.—Where is Creon?

Choragos. Just coming from the house.

(Enter Creon, C.)

Creon.	What has happened?

  Why have you come back so soon?

Sentry *(expansively).*	O King,

  A man should never be too sure of anything:
  I would have sworn
  That you'd not see me here again: your anger
  Frightened me so, and the things you threatened me with;   10
  But how could I tell then
  That I'd be able to solve the case so soon?
  No dice-throwing this time: I was only too glad to come!

  Here is this woman. She is the guilty one:
  We found her trying to bury him.
  Take her, then; question her; judge her as you will.
  I am through with the whole thing now, and glad of it.

Creon. But this is Antigonê! Why have you brought her here?

Sentry. She was burying him, I tell you!

Creon *(severely).*	Is this the truth?

Sentry. I saw her with my own eyes. Can I say more?   20

Creon. The details: come, tell me quickly!

Sentry.	It was like this:

  After those terrible threats of yours, King,
  We went back and brushed the dust away from the body.
  The flesh was soft by now, and stinking,
  So we sat on a hill to windward and kept guard.
  No napping this time! We kept each other awake.
  But nothing happened until the white round sun
  Whirled in the center of the round sky over us:
  Then, suddenly,
  A storm of dust roared up from the earth, and the sky   30
  Went out, the plain vanished with all its trees
  In the stinging dark. We closed our eyes and endured it.
  The whirlwind lasted a long time, but it passed;
  And then we looked, and there was Antigonê!
  I have seen
  A mother bird come back to a stripped nest, heard
  Her crying bitterly a broken note or two
  For the young ones stolen. Just so, when this girl
  Found the bare corpse, and all her love's work wasted,
  She wept, and cried on heaven to damn the hands   40
  That had done this thing.

	And then she brought more dust

And sprinkled wine three times for her brother's ghost.
We ran and took her at once. She was not afraid,
Not even when we charged her with what she had done.
She denied nothing.
                And this was a comfort to me,
And some uneasiness: for it is a good thing
To escape from death, but it is no great pleasure
To bring death to a friend.
                Yet I always say
There is nothing so comfortable as your own safe skin!
Creon (*slowly, dangerously*). And you, Antigonê,   50
You with your head hanging,—do you confess this thing?
Antigonê. I do. I deny nothing.
Creon (*to Sentry*).   You may go.

(Exit Sentry.)

(To Antigonê.) Tell me, tell me briefly:
Had you heard my proclamation touching this matter?
Antigonê. It was public. Could I help hearing it?
Creon. And yet you dared defy the law.
Antigonê.   I dared.
It was not God's proclamation. That final Justice
That rules the world below makes no such laws.

Your edict, King, was strong,
But all your strength is weakness itself against   60
The immortal unrecorded laws of God.
They are not merely now: they were, and shall be,
Operative for ever, beyond man utterly.

I knew I must die, even without your decree:
I am only mortal. And if I must die
Now, before it is my time to die,
Surely this is no hardship: can anyone
Living, as I live, with evil all about me,
Think Death less than a friend? This death of mine
Is of no importance; but if I had left my brother   70
Lying in death unburied, I should have suffered.
Now I do not.
           You smile at me. Ah Creon,
Think me a fool, if you like; but it may well be
That a fool convicts me of folly.
Choragos. Like father, like daughter: both headstrong, deaf to reason!
She has never learned to yield.

Creon. She has much to learn.
The inflexible heart breaks first, the toughest iron
Cracks first, and the wildest horses bend their necks
At the pull of the smallest curb.
Pride? In a slave?
This girl is guilty of a double insolence, 80
Breaking the given laws and boasting of it.
Who is the man here,
She or I, if this crime goes unpunished?
Sister's child, or more than sister's child,
Or closer yet in blood—she and her sister
Win bitter death for this!
(To servants.) Go, some of you,
Arrest Ismenê. I accuse her equally.
Bring her: you will find her sniffling in the house there.

Her mind's a traitor: crimes kept in the dark
Cry for light, and the guardian brain shudders; 90
But how much worse than this
Is brazen boasting of barefaced anarchy!
Antigonê. Creon, what more do you want than my death?
Creon. Nothing.
That gives me everything.
Antigonê. Then I beg you: kill me.
This talking is a great weariness: your words
Are distasteful to me, and I am sure that mine
Seem so to you. And yet they should not seem so:
I should have praise and honor for what I have done.
All these men here would praise me
Were their lips not frozen shut with fear of you. 100
(Bitterly.) Ah the good fortune of kings,
Licensed to say and do whatever they please!
Creon. You are alone here in that opinion.
Antigonê. No, they are with me. But they keep their tongues in leash.
Creon. Maybe. But you are guilty, and they are not.
Antigonê. There is no guilt in reverence for the dead.
Creon. But Eteoclês—was he not your brother too?
Antigonê. My brother too.
Creon. And you insult his memory?
Antigonê *(softly).* The dead man would not say that I insult it.
Creon. He would: for you honor a traitor as much as him. 110
Antigonê. His own brother, traitor or not, and equal in blood.
Creon. He made war on his country. Eteoclês defended it.
Antigonê. Nevertheless, there are honors due all the dead.
Creon. But not the same for the wicked as for the just.

Antigonê. Ah Creon, Creon,
　　Which of us can say what the gods hold wicked?
Creon. An enemy is an enemy, even dead.
Antigonê. It is my nature to join in love, not hate.
Creon (*finally losing patience*). Go join them, then; if you must have your
　　　love,
　　Find it in hell!   120
Choragos. But see, Ismenê comes:

(*Enter Ismenê, guarded.*)

　　Those tears are sisterly, the cloud
　　That shadows her eyes rains down gentle sorrow.
Creon. You too, Ismenê,
　　Snake in my ordered house, sucking my blood
　　Stealthily—and all the time I never knew
　　That these two sisters were aiming at my throne!
　　　　　　　　　　　　　　　　　　　　　　　　　Ismenê,
　　Do you confess your share in this crime, or deny it?
　　Answer me.
Ismenê. Yes, if she will let me say so. I am guilty.   130
Antigonê (*coldly*). No, Ismenê. You have no right to say so.
　　You would not help me, and I will not have you help me.
Ismenê. But now I know what you meant; and I am here
　　To join you, to take my share of punishment.
Antigonê. The dead man and the gods who rule the dead
　　Know whose act this was. Words are not friends.
Ismenê. Do you refuse me, Antigonê? I want to die with you:
　　I too have a duty that I must discharge to the dead.
Antigonê. You shall not lessen my death by sharing it.
Ismenê. What do I care for life when you are dead?   140
Antigonê. Ask Creon. You're always hanging on his opinions.
Ismenê. You are laughing at me. Why, Antigonê?
Antigonê. It's a joyless laughter, Ismenê.
Ismenê.　　　　　　　　　　　　　But can I do nothing?
Antigonê. Yes. Save yourself. I shall not envy you.
　　There are those who will praise you; I shall have honor, too.
Ismenê. But we are equally guilty!
Antigonê.　　　　　　　　　　　No more, Ismenê.
　　You are alive, but I belong to Death.
Creon (*to the Chorus*). Gentlemen, I beg you to observe these girls:
　　One has just now lost her mind; the other,
　　It seems, has never had a mind at all.   150
Ismenê. Grief teaches the steadiest minds to waver, King.
Creon. Yours certainly did, when you assumed guilt with the guilty!

Ismenê. But how could I go on living without her?
Creon.   You are.
   She is already dead.
Ismenê.   But your own son's bride!
Creon. There are places enough for him to push his plow.
   I want no wicked women for my sons!
Ismenê. O dearest Haimon, how your father wrongs you!
Creon. I've had enough of your childish talk of marriage!
Choragos. Do you really intend to steal this girl from your son?
Creon. No; Death will do that for me.
Choragos.   Then she must die?   160
Creon (*ironically*). You dazzle me.
                              —But enough of this talk!
   (*To Guards.*) You there, take them away and guard them well:
   For they are but women, and even brave men run
   When they see Death coming.

(*Exeunt Ismenê, Antigonê, and Guards.*)

ODE II

Chorus. Fortunate is the man who has never tasted   (*Strophe 1*)
      God's vengeance!
   Where once the anger of heaven has struck, that house is shaken
   For ever: damnation rises behind each child
   Like a wave cresting out of the black northeast,
   When the long darkness under sea roars up
   And bursts drumming death upon the windwhipped sand.

   I have seen this gathering sorrow from time long past   (*Antistrophe I*)
   Loom upon Oedipus' children: generation from generation
   Takes the compulsive rage of the enemy god.
   So lately this last flower of Oedipus' line   10
   Drank the sunlight! but now a passionate word
   And a handful of dust have closed up all its beauty.

      What mortal arrogance   (*Strophe 2*)
      Transcends the wrath of Zeus?
   Sleep cannot lull him, nor the effortless long months
   Of the timeless gods: but he is young for ever,
   And his house is the shining day of high Olympos.
      And that is and shall be,
      And all the past, is his.
   No pride on earth is free of the curse of heaven,   20

The straying dreams of men   *(Antistrophe 2)*
   May bring them ghosts of joy:
But as they drowse, the waking embers burn them;
Or they walk with fixed eyes, as blind men walk.
But the ancient wisdom speaks for our own time:
    Fate works most for woe
    With Folly's fairest show.
Man's little pleasure is the spring of sorrow.

SCENE 3

Choragos. But here is Haimon, King, the last of all your sons.
   Is it grief for Antigonê that brings him here,
   And bitterness at being robbed of his bride?

(Enter Haimon.)

Creon. We shall soon see, and no need of diviners,
                               —Son,
   You have heard my final judgment on that girl:
   Have you come here hating me, or have you come
   With deference and with love, whatever I do?
Haimon. I am your son, father. You are my guide.
   You make things clear for me, and I obey you.
   No marriage means more to me than your continuing wisdom.   10
Creon. Good. That is the way to behave: subordinate
   Everything else, my son, to your father's will.
   This is what a man prays for, that he may get
   Sons attentive and dutiful in his house,
   Each one hating his father's enemies,
   Honoring his father's friends. But if his sons
   Fail him, if they turn out unprofitably,
   What has he fathered but trouble for himself
   And amusement for the malicious?
                      So you are right
   Not to lose your head over this woman.   20
   Your pleasure with her would soon grow cold, Haimon,
   And then you'd have a hellcat in bed and elsewhere.
   Let her find her husband in Hell!
   Of all the people in this city, only she
   Has had contempt for my law and broken it.

   Do you want me to show myself weak before the people?
   Or to break my sworn word? No, and I will not.

The woman dies.
I suppose she'll plead "family ties." Well, let her.
If I permit my own family to rebel,   30
How shall I earn the world's obedience?
Show me the man who keeps his house in hand,
He's fit for public authority.

                        I'll have no dealings
With law-breakers, critics of the government:
Whoever is chosen to govern should be obeyed—
Must be obeyed, in all things, great and small,
Just and unjust! O Haimon,
The man who knows how to obey, and that man only,
Knows how to give commands when the time comes.
You can depend on him, no matter how fast   40
The spears come: he's a good soldier, he'll stick it out.
Anarchy, anarchy! Show me a greater evil!
This is why cities tumble and the great houses rain down,
This is what scatters armies!

No, no: good lives are made so by discipline.
We keep the laws then, and the lawmakers,
And no woman shall seduce us. If we must lose,
Let's lose to a man, at least! Is a woman stronger than we?
Choragos. Unless time has rusted my wits,
    What you say, King, is said with point and dignity.   50
Haimon (*boyishly earnest*). Father:
    Reason is God's crowning gift to man, and you are right
To warn me against losing mine. I cannot say—
I hope that I shall never want to say!—that you
Have reasoned badly. Yet there are other men
Who can reason, too; and their opinions might be helpful.
You are not in a position to know everything
That people say or do, or what they feel:
Your temper terrifies them—everyone
Will tell you only what you like to hear.   60
But I, at any rate, can listen; and I have heard them
Muttering and whispering in the dark about this girl.
They say no woman has ever, so unreasonably,
Died so shameful a death for a generous act:
"She covered her brother's body. Is this indecent?
She kept him from dogs and vultures. Is this a crime?
Death?—She should have all the honor that we can give her!"

This is the way they talk out there in the city.

You must believe me:
Nothing is closer to me than your happiness.   70
What could be closer? Must not any son
Value his father's fortune as his father does his?
I beg you, do not be unchangeable:
Do not believe that you alone can be right.
The man who thinks that,
The man who maintains that only he has the power
To reason correctly, the gift to speak, the soul—
A man like that, when you know him, turns out empty.
It is not reason never to yield to reason!

In flood time you can see how some trees bend   80
And because they bend, even their twigs are safe,
While stubborn trees are torn up, roots and all.
And the same thing happens in sailing:
Make your sheet fast, never slacken—and over you go,
Head over heels and under: and there's your voyage.
Forget you are angry! Let yourself be moved!
I know I am young; but please let me say this:
The ideal condition
Would be, I admit, that men should be right by instinct;
But since we are all too likely to go astray,   90
The reasonable thing is to learn from those who can teach.

Choragos. You will do well to listen to him, King,
If what he says is sensible. And you, Haimon,
Must listen to your father.—Both speak well.

Creon. You consider it right for a man of my years and experience
To go to school to a boy?

Haimon.   It is not right
If I am wrong. But if I am young, and right,
What does my age matter?

Creon. You think it right to stand up for an anarchist?

Haimon. Not at all. I pay no respect to criminals.   100

Creon. Then she is not a criminal?

Haimon. The City would deny it, to a man.

Creon. And the City proposes to teach me how to rule?

Haimon. Ah. Who is it that's talking like a boy now?

Creon. My voice is the one voice giving orders in this City!

Haimon. It is no City if it takes orders from one voice.

Creon. The State is the King!

Haimon.   Yes, if the State is a desert.

(Pause.)

Creon. This boy, it seems, has sold out to a woman.

Haimon. If you are a woman: my concern is only for you.
Creon. So? Your "concern"! In a public brawl with your father!   110
Haimon. How about you, in a public brawl with justice?
Creon. With justice, when all that I do is within my rights?
Haimon. You have no right to trample on God's right.
Creon (completely out of control).   Fool, adolescent fool! Taken in by a
    woman!
Haimon. You'll never see me taken in by anything vile.
Creon. Every word you say is for her!
Haimon (quietly, darkly).   And for you.
    And for me. And for the gods under the earth.
Creon. You'll never marry her while she lives.
Haimon. Then she must die.—But her death will cause another.
Creon. Another?   120
    Have you lost your senses? Is this an open threat?
Haimon. There is no threat in speaking to emptiness.
Creon. I swear you'll regret this superior tone of yours!
    You are the empty one!
Haimon.   If you were not my father,
    I'd say you were perverse.
Creon. You girlstruck fool, don't play at words with me!
Haimon. I am sorry. You prefer silence.
Creon.   Now, by God—!
    I swear, by all the gods in heaven above us,
    You'll watch it, I swear you shall!
    (To the servants.)   Bring her out!
    Bring the woman out! Let her die before his eyes!   130
    Here, this instant, with her bridegroom beside her!
Haimon. Not here, no; she will not die here, King.
    And you will never see my face again.
    Go on raving as long as you've a friend to endure you.

(Exit Haimon.)

Choragos. Gone, gone.
    Creon, a young man in a rage is dangerous!
Creon. Let him do, or dream to do, more than a man can.
    He shall not save these girls from death.
Choragos.   These girls?
    You have sentenced them both?
Creon.   No, you are right.
    I will not kill the one whose hands are clean.   140
Choragos. But Antigonê?
Creon (somberly).   I will carry her far away
    Out there in the wilderness, and lock her
    Living in a vault of stone. She shall have food,

As the custom is, to absolve the State of her death.
And there let her pray to the gods of hell:
They are her only gods:
Perhaps they will show her an escape from death,
Or she may learn
though late,
That piety shown the dead is pity in vain.   150

(Exit Creon.)

ODE III

Chorus. Love, unconquerable   *(Strophe)*
Waster of rich men, keeper
Of warm lights and all-night vigil
In the soft face of a girl:
Sea-wanderer, forest-visitor!
Even the pure Immortals cannot escape you,
And mortal man, in his one day's dusk,
Trembles before your glory.

Surely you swerve upon ruin   *(Antistrophe)*
The just man's consenting heart,   10
As here you have made bright anger
Strike between father and son—
And none had conquered but Love!
A girl's glance working the will of heaven:
Pleasure to her alone who mocks us,
Merciless Aphroditê.[6]

SCENE 4

Choragos *(as Antigonê enters guarded).* But I can no longer stand in awe
of this,
Nor, seeing what I see, keep back my tears.
Here is Antigonê, passing to that chamber
Where all find sleep at last.

Antigonê. Look upon me, friends, and pity me   *(Strophe 1)*
Turning back at the night's edge to say
Good-by to the sun that shines for me no longer;

[6] Aphroditê is the goddess of love.

Now sleepy Death
Summons me down to Acheron,[7] that cold shore:
There is no bridesong there, nor any music.   10
Chorus. Yet not unpraised, not without a kind of honor,
You walk at last into the underworld;
Untouched by sickness, broken by no sword.
What woman has ever found your way to death?
Antigonê. How often I have heard the story of Niobê,[8]   *(Antistrophe 1)*
Tantalos' wretched daughter, how the stone
Clung fast about her, ivy-close: and they say
The rain falls endlessly
And sifting soft snow; her tears are never done.
I feel the loneliness of her death in mine.   20
Chorus. But she was born of heaven, and you
Are woman, woman-born. If her death is yours,
A mortal woman's, is this not for you
Glory in our world and in the world beyond?

Antigonê. You laugh at me. Ah, friends, friends,   *(Strophe 2)*
Can you not wait until I am dead? O Thebes,
O men many-charioted, in love with Fortune,
Dear springs of Dircê, sacred Theban grove,
Be witnesses for me, denied all pity,
Unjustly judged! and think a word of love   30
For her whose path turns
Under dark earth, where there are no more tears.
Chorus. You have passed beyond human daring and come at last
Into a place of stone where Justice sits.
I cannot tell
What shape of your father's guilt appears in this.

Antigonê. You have touched it at last: that bridal bed   *(Antistrophe 2)*
Unspeakable, horror of son and mother mingling:
Their crime, infection of all our family!
O Oedipus, father and brother!   40
Your marriage strikes from the grave to murder mine.
I have been a stranger here in my own land:
All my life
The blasphemy of my birth has followed me.
Chorus. Reverence is a virtue, but strength

---

[7] A river of Hades.   [8] Niobê married an ancestor of Oedipus named Amphion. Her fourteen children were killed by Apollo and Artemis after Niobê boasted to their mother, Leto, that her children were superior to them. She wept incessantly and was finally transformed into a rock on Mt. Sipylos, whose streams are her tears.

Lives in established law: that must prevail.
You have made your choice,
Your death is the doing of your conscious hand.

Antigonê. Then let me go, since all your words are bitter,   *(Epode)*
And the very light of the sun is cold to me.   50
Lead me to my vigil, where I must have
Neither love nor lamentation; no song, but silence.

(Creon interrupts impatiently.)

Creon. If dirges and planned lamentations could put off death,
Men would be singing for ever.
(To the servants.)   Take her, go!
You know your orders: take her to the vault
And leave her alone there. And if she lives or dies,
That's her affair, not ours: our hands are clean.
Antigonê. O tomb, vaulted bride-bed in eternal rock,
Soon I shall be with my own again
Where Persephonê[9] welcomes the thin ghosts underground: 60
And I shall see my father again, and you, mother,
And dearest Polyneicês—
                              dearest indeed
To me, since it was my hand
That washed him clean and poured the ritual wine:
And my reward is death before my time!

And yet, as men's hearts know, I have done no wrong,
I have not sinned before God. Or if I have,
I shall know the truth in death. But if the guilt
Lies upon Creon who judged me, then, I pray,
May his punishment equal my own.
Choragos.   O passionate heart,   70
Unyielding, tormented still by the same winds!
Creon. Her guards shall have good cause to regret their delaying.
Antigonê. Ah! That voice is like the voice of death!
Creon. I can give you no reason to think you are mistaken.
Antigonê. Thebes, and you my fathers' gods,
And rulers of Thebes, you see me now, the last
Unhappy daughter of a line of kings,
Your kings, led away to death. You will remember
What things I suffer, and at what men's hands,

[9] Queen of Hades.

Because I would not transgress the laws of heaven.   80
(To the guards, simply.) Come: let us wait no longer.

(Exit Antigonê, L., guarded.)

ODE IV

Chorus. All Danaê's[10] beauty was locked away   *(Strophe 1)*
In a brazen cell where the sunlight could not come:
A small room, still as any grave, enclosed her.
Yet she was a princess too,
And Zeus in a rain of gold poured love upon her.
O child, child,
No power in wealth or war
Or tough sea-blackened ships
Can prevail against untiring Destiny!

And Dryas' son[11] also, that furious king,   *(Antistrophe 1)* 10
Bore the god's prisoning anger for his pride:
Sealed up by Dionysos in deaf stone,
His madness died among echoes.
So at the last he learned what dreadful power
His tongue had mocked:
For he had profaned the revels,
And fired the wrath of the nine
Implacable Sisters[12] that love the sound of the flute.

And old men tell a half-remembered tale   *(Strophe 2)*
Of horror where a dark ledge splits the sea   20
And a double surf beats on the gray shores:
How a king's new woman,[13] sick
With hatred for the queen he had imprisoned,
Ripped out his two sons' eyes with her bloody hands
While grinning Arês[14] watched the shuttle plunge
Four times: four blind wounds crying for revenge,

Crying, tears and blood mingled.—Piteously born,   *(Antistrophe 2)*
Those sons whose mother was of heavenly birth!

---

[10] Though Danaê, a beautiful princess of Argos, was confined by her father, Zeus visited her in the form of a shower of gold, and she gave birth to Perseus as a result.   [11] Lycurgus, king of Thrace, who was driven mad by Dionysos, the god of wine.   [12] The Muses.   [13] The ode alludes to a story indicating the uselessness of high birth against implacable fate. The king's new woman is Eidothea, the second wife of King Phineus. Though Cleopatra, his first wife, was the daughter of Boreas, the north wind, and Phineus himself was descended from kings, Eidothea, out of hatred for Cleopatra, blinded her two sons.   [14] The god of war.

Her father was the god of the North Wind
And she was cradled by gales,   30
She raced with young colts on the glittering hills
And walked untrammeled in the open light:
But in her marriage deathless Fate found means
To build a tomb like yours for all her joy.

SCENE 5

(Enter blind Teiresias, led by a boy. The opening speeches of Teiresias should be in singsong contrast to the realistic lines of Creon.)

Teiresias. This is the way the blind man comes, Princes, Princes,
   Lock-step, two heads lit by the eyes of one.
Creon. What new thing have you to tell us, old Teiresias?
Teiresias. I have much to tell you: listen to the prophet, Creon.
Creon. I am not aware that I have ever failed to listen.
Teiresias. Then you have done wisely, King, and ruled well.
Creon. I admit my debt to you. But what have you to say?
Teiresias. This, Creon: you stand once more on the edge of fate.
Creon. What do you mean? Your words are a kind of dread.
Teiresias. Listen, Creon: 10
   I was sitting in my chair of augury, at the place
   Where the birds gather about me. They were all a-chatter,
   As is their habit, when suddenly I heard
   A strange note in their jangling, a scream, a
   Whirring fury; I knew that they were fighting,
   Tearing each other, dying
   In a whirlwind of wings clashing. And I was afraid.
   I began the rites of burnt-offering at the altar,
   But Hephaistos[15] failed me: instead of bright flame,
   There was only the sputtering slime of the fat thigh-flesh   20
   Melting: the entrails dissolved in gray smoke;
   The bare bone burst from the welter. And no blaze!

   This was a sign from heaven. My boy described it,
   Seeing for me as I see for others.

   I tell you, Creon, you yourself have brought
   This new calamity upon us. Our hearths and altars
   Are stained with the corruption of dogs and carrion birds
   That glut themselves on the corpse of Oedipus' son.

---

[15] The god of fire.

The gods are deaf when we pray to them, their fire
Recoils from our offering, their birds of omen 30
Have no cry of comfort, for they are gorged
With the thick blood of the dead.

       O my son,
These are no trifles! Think: all men make mistakes,
But a good man yields when he knows his course is wrong,
And repairs the evil. The only crime is pride.

Give in to the dead man, then: do not fight with a corpse—
What glory is it to kill a man who is dead?
Think, I beg you:
It is for your own good that I speak as I do.
You should be able to yield for your own good. 40

Creon. It seems that prophets have made me their especial province.
All my life long
I have been a kind of butt for the dull arrows
Of doddering fortune-tellers!

      No, Teiresias:
If your birds—if the great eagles of God himself
Should carry him stinking bit by bit to heaven,
I would not yield. I am not afraid of pollution:
No man can defile the gods.

     Do what you will,
Go into business, make money, speculate
In India gold or that synthetic gold from Sardis, 50
Get rich otherwise than by my consent to bury him.
Teiresias, it is a sorry thing when a wise man
Sells his wisdom, lets out his words for hire!

Teiresias. Ah Creon! Is there no man left in the world—

Creon. To do what?—Come, let's have the aphorism!

Teiresias. No man who knows that wisdom outweighs any wealth?

Creon. As surely as bribes are baser than any baseness.

Teiresias. You are sick, Creon! You are deathly sick!

Creon. As you say: it is not my place to challenge a prophet.

Teiresias. Yet you have said my prophecy is for sale. 60

Creon. The generation of prophets has always loved gold.

Teiresias. The generation of kings has always loved brass.

Creon. You forget yourself! You are speaking to your King.

Teiresias. I know it. You are a king because of me.

Creon. You have a certain skill; but you have sold out.

Teiresias. King, you will drive me to words that—

Creon.   Say them, say them!
Only remember: I will not pay you for them.

Teiresias. No, you will find them too costly.

Creon.   No doubt. Speak:
    Whatever you say, you will not change my will.

Teiresias. Then take this, and take it to heart!   70
    The time is not far off when you shall pay back
    Corpse for corpse, flesh of your own flesh.
    You have thrust the child of this world into living night,
    You have kept from the gods below the child that is theirs:
    The one in a grave before her death, the other,
    Dead, denied the grave. This is your crime:
    And the Furies and the dark gods of Hell
    Are swift with terrible punishment for you.

    Do you want to buy me now, Creon?
                                  Not many days,
    And your house will be full of men and women weeping,   80
    And curses will be hurled at you from far
    Cities grieving for sons unburied, left to rot
    Before the walls of Thebes.
    These are my arrows, Creon: they are all for you.

    (To boy.) But come, child: lead me home.
    Let him waste his fine anger upon younger men.
    Maybe he will learn at last
    To control a wiser tongue in a better head.

(Exit Teiresias.)

Choragos. The old man has gone, King, but his words
    Remain to plague us. I am old, too,   90
    But I cannot remember that he was ever false.

Creon. That is true. . . . It troubles me.
    Oh it is hard to give in! but it is worse
    To risk everything for stubborn pride.

Choragos. Creon: take my advice.

Creon.   What shall I do?

Choragos. Go quickly: free Antigonê from her vault
    And build a tomb for the body of Polyneicês.

Creon. You would have me do this?

Choragos.   Creon, yes!
    And it must be done at once: God moves   100
    Swiftly to cancel the folly of stubborn men.

Creon. It is hard to deny the heart! But I
    Will do it: I will not fight with destiny.

Choragos. You must go yourself, you cannot leave it to others.

Creon. I will go
                    —Bring axes, servants:
Come with me to the tomb. I buried her, I
Will set her free.
                    Oh quickly!
My mind misgives—
The laws of the gods are mighty, and a man must serve them
To the last days of his life!

(Exit Creon.)

PAEAN[16]

Choragos. God of many names   *(Strophe 1)*
Chorus.   O Iacchos[17]
                              Son
of Kadmeian Sémelê
                    O born of the Thunder!
Guardian of the West
                    Regent
of Eleusis's plain
                    O Prince of maenad Thebes
and the Dragon Field by rippling Ismenos:[18]

Choragos. God of many names   *(Antistrophe 1)*
Chorus.   the flame of torches
flares on our hills
                    the nymphs of Iacchos
dance at the spring of Castalia:[19]
from the vine-close mountain
                    come ah come in ivy:
Evohé evohé! sings through the streets of Thebes   10

Choragos. God of many names   *(Strophe 2)*
Chorus.   Iacchos of Thebes
heavenly Child
                    of Sémelê bride of the Thunderer!
The shadow of plague is upon us:
                          come
with clement feet;
                    oh come from Parnasos

---

[16] A hymn.   [17] Iacchos is a name for Dionysos. His mother was Sémelê, daughter of Kadmos, the founder of Thebes. His father was Zeus. The Maenads were priestesses of Dionysos who cry "evohé evohé."   [18] A river of Thebes, sacred to Apollo. Dragon Field refers to the legend that the ancestors of Thebes sprang from the dragon's teeth sown by Kadmos.   [19] A spring on Mt. Parnasos.

down the long slopes
across the lamenting water

Choragos. Iô Fire! Chorister of the throbbing stars!   (*Antistrophe 2*)
O purest among the voices of the night!
Thou son of God, blaze for us!
Chorus. Come with choric rapture of circling Maenads
Who cry Iô Iacche!
God of many names!   20

EXODOS

(Enter Messenger, L.)

Messenger. Men of the line of Kadmos, you who live
Near Amphion's[20] citadel:
I cannot say
Of any condition of human life "This is fixed,
This is clearly good, or bad." Fate raises up,
And Fate casts down the happy and unhappy alike:
No man can foretell his Fate.
Take the case of Creon:
Creon was happy once, as I count happiness:
Victorious in battle, sole governor of the land,
Fortunate father of children nobly born.
And now it has all gone from him! Who can say   10
That a man is still alive when his life's joy fails?
He is a walking dead man. Grant him rich,
Let him live like a king in his great house:
If his pleasure is gone, I would not give
So much as the shadow of smoke for all he owns.
Choragos. Your words hint at sorrow: what is your news for us?
Messenger. They are dead. The living are guilty of their death.
Choragos. Who is guilty? Who is dead? Speak!
Messenger.   Haimon.
Haimon is dead; and the hand that killed him
Is his own hand.   20
Choragos. His father's? or his own?
Messenger. His own, driven mad by the murder his father had done.
Choragos. Teiresias, Teiresias, how clearly you saw it all!
Messenger. This is my news: you must draw what conclusions you can from it.
Choragos. But look: Eurydicê, our Queen:

---

[20] A child of Zeus and Antiope. He is noted for building the walls of Thebes by charming the stones into place with a lyre.

Has she overheard us?

(Enter Eurydicê from the Palace, C.)

Eurydicê. I have heard something, friends:
As I was unlocking the gate of Pallas'[21] shrine,
For I needed her help today, I heard a voice
Telling of some new sorrow. And I fainted   30
There at the temple with all my maidens about me.
But speak again: whatever it is, I can bear it:
Grief and I are no strangers.

Messenger.   Dearest lady,
I will tell you plainly all that I have seen.
I shall not try to comfort you: what is the use,
Since comfort could lie only in what is not true?
The truth is always best.
                               I went with Creon
To the outer plain where Polyneicês was lying,
No friend to pity him, his body shredded by dogs.
We made our prayers in that place to Hecatê[22]   40
And Pluto,[23] that they would be merciful. And we bathed
The corpse with holy water, and we brought
Fresh-broken branches to burn what was left of it,
And upon the urn we heaped up a towering barrow
Of the earth of his own land.
                               When we were done, we ran
To the vault where Antigonê lay on her couch of stone.
One of the servants had gone ahead,
And while he was yet far off he heard a voice
Grieving within the chamber, and he came back
And told Creon. And as the King went closer,   50
The air was full of wailing, the words lost,
And he begged us to make all haste. "Am I a prophet?"
He said, weeping, "And must I walk this road,
The saddest of all that I have gone before?
My son's voice calls me on. Oh quickly, quickly!
Look through the crevice there, and tell me
If it Haimon, or some deception of the gods!"

We obeyed; and in the cavern's farthest corner
We saw her lying:
She had made a noose of her fine linen veil   60

---

[21] Pallas Athene, goddess of wisdom.   [22] Hecatê is often identified with Persephone, a goddess of Hades; generally Hecatê is a goddess of sorcery and witchcraft.   [23] King of Hades and brother of Zeus and Poseidon.

And hanged herself. Haimon lay beside her,
His arms about her waist, lamenting her,
His love lost under ground, crying out
That his father had stolen her away from him.

When Creon saw him the tears rushed to his eyes
And he called to him: "What have you done, child? Speak to me.
What are you thinking that makes your eyes so strange?
O my son, my son, I come to you on my knees!"
But Haimon spat in his face. He said not a word,
Staring—
        And suddenly drew his sword   70
And lunged. Creon shrank back, the blade missed; and the boy,
Desperate against himself, drove it half its length
Into his own side, and fell. And as he died
He gathered Antigonê close in his arms again,
Choking, his blood bright red on her white cheek.
And now he lies dead with the dead, and she is his
At last, his bride in the houses of the dead.

(Exit Eurydicê into the Palace.)

Choragos. She has left us without a word. What can this mean?
Messenger. It troubles me, too; yet she knows what is best,
    Her grief is too great for public lamentation,   80
    And doubtless she has gone to her chamber to weep
    For her dead son, leading her maidens in his dirge.
Choragos. It may be so: but I fear this deep silence.

(Pause.)

Messenger. I will see what she is doing. I will go in.

(Exit Messenger into the Palace.)
(Enter Creon with attendants, bearing Haimon's body.)

Choragos. But here is the King himself: oh look at him,
    Bearing his own damnation in his arms.
Creon. Nothing you say can touch me any more.
    My own blind heart has brought me
    From darkness to final darkness. Here you see
    The father murdering, the murdered son—   90
    And all my civic wisdom!
    Haimon my son, so young to die,
    I was the fool, not you; and you died for me.
Choragos. That is the truth; but you were late in learning it.

Creon. This truth is hard to bear. Surely a god
    Has crushed me beneath the hugest weight of heaven,
    And driven me headlong a barbaric way
    To trample out the thing I held most dear.

    The pains that men will take to come to pain!

(Enter Messenger from the Palace.)

Messenger. The burden you carry in your hands is heavy,   100
    But it is not all: you will find more in your house.
Creon. What burden worse than this shall I find there?
Messenger. The Queen is dead.
Creon. O port of death, deaf world,
    Is there no pity for me? And you, Angel of evil,
    I was dead, and your words are death again.
    Is it true, boy? Can it be true?
    Is my wife dead? Has death bred death?
Messenger. You can see for yourself.

(The doors are opened, and the body of Eurydicê is disclosed within.)

Creon. Oh pity!   110
    All true, all true, and more than I can bear!
    O my wife, my son!
Messenger. She stood before the altar, and her heart
    Welcomed the knife her own hand guided,
    And a great cry burst from her lips for Megareus[24] dead,
    And for Haimon dead, her sons; and her last breath
    Was a curse for their father, the murderer of her sons,
    And she fell, and the dark flowed in through her closing eyes.
Creon. O God, I am sick with fear.
    Are there no swords here? Has no one a blow for me?   120
Messenger. Her curse is upon you for the deaths of both.
Creon. It is right that it should be. I alone am guilty.
    I know it, and I say it. Lead me in,
    Quickly, friends.
    I have neither life nor substance. Lead me in.
Choragos. You are right, if there can be right in so much wrong.
    The briefest way is best in a world of sorrow.
Creon. Let it come,
    Let death come quickly, and be kind to me.
    I would not ever see the sun again.   130
Choragos. All that will come when it will; but we, meanwhile,

---

[24] Son of Creon who was killed in the attack on Thebes.

Have much to do. Leave the future to itself.

Creon. All my heart was in that prayer!

Choragos. Then do not pray any more: the sky is deaf.

Creon. Lead me away. I have been rash and foolish.
I have killed my son and my wife.
I look for comfort; my comfort lies here dead.
Whatever my hands have touched has come to nothing.
Fate has brought all my pride to a thought of dust.

(As Creon is being led into the house, the Choragos advances and speaks directly to the audience.)

Choragos. There is no happiness where there is no wisdom; 140
No wisdom but in submission to the gods.
Big words are always punished,
And proud men in old age learn to be wise.

FOR ANALYSIS

1. Show how the Prologue establishes the **mood** and **theme** of the play. What does it reveal about the **characters** of the two sisters?

2. What evidence is there that Creon would treat Antigonê differently if she were a man?

3. Does the character of Antigonê change in the course of the play?

4. Does the action of the play prepare us for Creon's sudden realization that he has been wrong?

5. Is there any justification for Antigonê's cold refusal to allow Ismenê to share her martyrdom?

6. Speculate on why Sophocles never brings Haimon and Antigonê together.

7. How does the **chorus** contribute to the dramatic development and tension of the play?

8. Analyze the use of **dramatic irony** in the play.

MAKING ARGUMENTS

Critics are divided on the question of whether Antigonê or Creon is the **protagonist** of the play. How does the answer to this question affect one's interpretation of the play? How would you argue for one or the other?

WRITING TOPICS

1. Summarize the **theme** of this play in a brief paragraph.

2. Write a one-page essay using this play and Susan Glaspell's *Trifles* (p. 1073) as the basis for defining poetic drama on the one hand and realistic drama on the other.

MAKING CONNECTIONS

Compare the grounds on which Antigonê makes her argument with those on which Jonathan Swift bases his in "A Modest Proposal" (p. 481). How can you identify them? How do they use them to argue their points?

NONFICTION

JONATHAN SWIFT (1667–1745)

A MODEST PROPOSAL 1729

It is a melancholy object to those who walk through this great town[1] or travel in the country, when they see the streets, the roads, and cabin doors, crowded with beggars of the female sex, followed by three, four, or six children, all in rags and importuning every passenger for an alms. These mothers, instead of being able to work for their honest livelihood, are forced to employ all their time in strolling to beg sustenance for their helpless infants, who, as they grow up, either turn thieves for want of work, or leave their dear native country to fight for the Pretender in Spain, or sell themselves to the Barbados.[2]

I think it is agreed by all parties that this prodigious number of children in the arms, or on the backs, or at the heels of their mothers, and frequently of their fathers, is in the present deplorable state of the kingdom a very great additional grievance; and therefore whoever could find out a fair, cheap, and easy method of making these children sound, useful members of the commonwealth would deserve so well of the public as to have his statue set up for a preserver of the nation.

But my intention is very far from being confined to provide only for the children of professed beggars; it is of a much greater extent, and shall take in the whole number of infants at a certain age who are born of parents in effect as little able to support them as those who demand our charity in the streets.

As to my own part, having turned my thoughts for many years upon this important subject, and maturely weighed the several schemes of other projectors,[3] I have always found them grossly mistaken in their computation. It is true, a child just dropped from its dam may be supported by her milk for a solar year, with little other nourishment; at most not above the value of

---

[1] Dublin.

[2] Many Irish men joined the army of the exiled James Stuart (1688–1766), who laid claim to the British throne. Others exchanged their labor for passage to the British colony of Barbados, in the Caribbean.

[3] People with projects.

two shillings,[4] which the mother may certainly get, or the value in scraps, by her lawful occupation of begging; and it is exactly at one year that I propose to provide for them in such a manner as instead of being a charge upon their parents or the parish, or wanting food and raiment for the rest of their lives, they shall on the contrary contribute to the feeding, and partly to the clothing, of many thousands.

There is likewise another great advantage in my scheme, that it will prevent those voluntary abortions, and that horrid practice of women murdering their bastard children, alas, too frequent among us, sacrificing the poor innocent babes, I doubt, more to avoid the expense than the shame, which would move tears and pity in the most savage and inhuman breast.

The number of souls in this kingdom being usually reckoned one million and a half, of these I calculate there may be about two hundred thousand couples whose wives are breeders; from which number I subtract thirty thousand couples who are able to maintain their own children, although I apprehend there cannot be so many under the present distress of the kingdom; but this being granted, there will remain an hundred and seventy thousand breeders. I again subtract fifty thousand for those women who miscarry, or whose children die by accident or disease within the year. There only remain an hundred and twenty thousand children of poor parents annually born. The question therefore is, how this number shall be reared and provided for, which, as I have already said, under the present situation of affairs, is utterly impossible by all the methods hitherto proposed. For we can neither employ them in handicraft or agriculture; we neither build houses (I mean in the country) nor cultivate land. They can very seldom pick up a livelihood by stealing till they arrive at six years old except where they are of towardly parts;[5] although I confess they learn the rudiments much earlier, during which time they can however be looked upon only as probationers, as I have been informed by a principal gentleman in the country of Cavan, who protested to me that he never knew above one or two instances under the age of six, even in a part of the kingdom so renowned for the quickest proficiency in that art.

I am assured by our merchants that a boy or a girl before twelve years old is no salable commodity; and even when they come to this age they will not yield above three pounds, or three pounds and half a crown at most on the Exchange;[6] which cannot turn to account either to the parents or the kingdom, the charge of nutriment and rags having been at least four times that value.

I shall now therefore humbly propose my own thoughts, which I hope will not be liable to the least objection.

I have been assured by a very knowing American of my acquaintance in London, that a young healthy child well nursed is at a year old a most delicious,

[4] A shilling was worth about twenty-five cents.
[5] Able and eager to learn.
[6] A pound was twenty shillings; a crown, five shillings.

nourishing, and wholesome food, whether stewed, roasted, baked, or boiled; and I make no doubt that it will equally serve in a fricassee or a ragout.

I do therefore humbly offer it to public consideration that of the hundred 10 and twenty thousand children, already computed, twenty thousand may be reserved for breed, whereof only one fourth part to be males, which is more than we allow to sheep, black cattle, or swine; and my reason is that these children are seldom the fruits of marriage, a circumstance not much regarded by our savages, therefore one male will be sufficient to serve four females. That the remaining hundred thousand may at a year old be offered in sale to the persons of quality and fortune through the kingdom, always advising the mother to let them suck plentifully in the last month, so as to render them plump and fat for a good table. A child will make two dishes at an entertainment for friends; and when the family dines alone, the fore or hind quarter will make a reasonable dish, and seasoned with a little pepper or salt will be very good boiled on the fourth day, especially in winter.

I have reckoned upon a medium that a child just born will weigh twelve pounds, and in a solar year if tolerably nursed increaseth to twenty-eight pounds.

I grant this food will be somewhat dear, and therefore very proper for landlords, who, as they have already devoured most of the parents, seem to have the best title to the children.

Infant's flesh will be in season throughout the year, but more plentiful in March, and a little before and after. For we are told by a grave author, an eminent French physician,[7] that fish being a prolific diet, there are more children born in Roman Catholic countries about nine months after Lent than at any other season; therefore, reckoning a year after Lent, the markets will be more glutted than usual, because the number of popish infants is at least three to one in this kingdom; and therefore it will have one other collateral advantage, by lessening the number of Papists among us.

I have already computed the charge of nursing a beggar's child (in which list I reckon all cottagers, laborers, and four-fifths of the farmers) to be about two shillings per annum, rags included; and I believe no gentleman would repine to give ten shillings for the carcass of a good fat child, which, as I have said, will make four dishes of excellent nutritive meat, when he hath only some particular friend or his own family to dine with him. Thus the squire will learn to be a good landlord, and grow popular among the tenants; the mother will have eight shillings net profit, and be fit for work till she produces another child.

Those who are more thrifty (as I must confess the times require) may flay 15 the carcass; the skin of which artificially[8] dressed will make admirable gloves for ladies, and summer boots for fine gentlemen.

As to our city of Dublin, shambles[9] may be appointed for this purpose in the most convenient parts of it, and butchers we may be assured will not be

---

[7] François Rabelais, sixteenth-century French comic writer.
[8] Skillfully.
[9] Slaughterhouses.

wanting; although I rather recommend buying the children alive, and dressing them hot from the knife as we do roasting pigs.

A very worthy person, a true lover of his country, and whose virtues I highly esteem, was lately pleased in discoursing on this matter to offer a refinement upon my scheme. He said that many gentlemen of his kingdom, having of late destroyed their deer, he conceived that the want of venison might be well supplied by the bodies of young lads and maidens, not exceeding fourteen years of age nor under twelve, so great a number of both sexes in every country being now ready to starve for want of work or service; and these to be disposed of by their parents, if alive, or otherwise by their nearest relations. But with due deference to so excellent a friend and so deserving a patriot, I cannot be altogether in his sentiments; for as to the males, my American acquaintance assured me from frequent experience that their flesh was generally tough and lean, like that of our schoolboys, by continual exercise, and their taste disagreeable; and to fatten them would not answer the charge. Then as to the females; it would, I think with humble submission, be a loss to the public, because they soon would become breeders themselves; and besides, it is not improbable that some scrupulous people might be apt to censure such a practice (although indeed very unjustly) as a little bordering upon cruelty; which, I confess, hath always been with me the strongest objection against any project, how well soever intended.

But in order to justify my friend, he confessed that this expedient was put into his head by the famous Psalmanazar,[10] a native of the island Formosa, who came from thence to London above twenty years ago, and in conversation told my friend that in his country when any young person happened to be put to death, the executioner sold the carcass to persons of quality as a prime dainty; and that in his time the body of a plump girl of fifteen, who was crucified for an attempt to poison the emperor, was sold to his Imperial Majesty's prime minister of state, and other great mandarins of the court, in joints from the gibbet, at four hundred crowns. Neither indeed can I deny that if the same use were made of several plump young girls in this town, who without one single groat[11] to their fortunes cannot stir abroad without a chair,[12] and appear at the playhouse and assemblies in foreign fineries which they never will pay for, the kingdom would not be the worse.

Some persons of a desponding spirit are in great concern about the vast number of poor people who are aged, diseased, or maimed, and I have been desired to employ my thoughts what course may be taken to ease the nation of so grievous an encumbrance. But I am not in the least pain upon the matter, because it is very well known that they are every day dying and rotting by cold and famine, and filth and vermin, as fast as can be reasonably expected. And

---

[10] George Psalmanazar was a Frenchman who passed himself off as a native of Formosa (the former name for Taiwan).

[11] A coin worth about four cents.

[12] A sedan chair, an enclosed chair carried by poles on the front and back.

as to the younger laborers, they are now in almost as hopeful a condition. They cannot get work, and consequently pine away for want of nourishment to a degree that if any time they are accidently hired to common labor, they have not the strength to perform it; and thus the country and themselves are happily delivered from the evils to come.

I have too long digressed, and therefore I shall return to my subject. I think 20 the advantages by the proposal which I have made are obvious and many, as well as of the highest importance.

For first, I have already observed, it would greatly lessen the number of Papists, with whom we are yearly overrun, being the principal breeders of the nation as well as our most dangerous enemies; and who stay at home on purpose to deliver the kingdom to the Pretender, hoping to take their advantage by the absence of so many good Protestants, who have chose rather to leave their country than to stay at home and pay tithes against their conscience to an Episcopal curate.

Secondly, the poorer tenants will have something valuable of their own, which by law may be made liable to distress,[13] and help to pay their landlord's rent, their corn and cattle being already seized and money a thing unknown.

Thirdly, whereas the maintenance of a hundred thousand children, from two years old and upwards, cannot be computed at less than ten shillings a piece per annum, the nation's stock will be thereby increased fifty thousand pounds per annum, besides the profit of a new dish introduced to the tables of all gentlemen of fortune in the kingdom who have any refinement in taste. And all the money will circulate among ourselves, the goods being entirely of our own growth and manufacture.

Fourthly, the constant breeders, besides the gain of eight shillings sterling per annum by the sale of their children, will be rid of the charge of maintaining them after the first year.

Fifthly, this food would likewise bring great custom to taverns, where the 25 vintners will certainly be so prudent as to procure the best receipts[14] for dressing it to perfection, and consequently have their houses frequented by all the fine gentlemen, who justly value themselves upon their knowledge in good eating; and a skillful cook, who understands how to oblige his guests, will contrive to make it as expensive as they please.

Sixthly, this would be a great inducement to marriage, which all wise nations have either encouraged by rewards or enforced by laws and penalties. It would increase the care and tenderness of mothers towards their children, when they were sure of a settlement for life to the poor babes, provided in some sort by the public, to their annual profit instead of expense. We should see an honest emulation among the married women, which of them could bring the fattest child to the market. Men would become as fond of their wives during the time of their pregnancy as they are now of their mares in foal, their cows in calf, or

---

[13] Seizure for payment of debts.
[14] Recipes.

sows when they are ready to farrow; nor offer to beat or kick them (as is too frequent a practice) for fear of a miscarriage.

Many other advantages might be enumerated. For instance, the addition of some thousand carcasses in our exportation of barreled beef, the propagation of swine's flesh, and improvements in the art of making good bacon, so much wanted among us by the great destruction of pigs, too frequent at our tables, which are no way comparable in taste or magnificence to a well-grown, fat, yearling child, which roasted whole will make a considerable figure at a lord mayor's feast or any other public entertainment. But this and many others I omit, being studious of brevity.

Supposing that one thousand families in this city would be constant customers for infants' flesh, besides others who might have it at merry meetings, particularly weddings and christenings, I compute that Dublin would take off annually about twenty thousand carcasses, and the rest of the kingdom (where probably they will be sold somewhat cheaper) the remaining eighty thousand.

I can think of no one objection that will possibly be raised against this proposal unless it should be urged that the number of people will be thereby much lessened in the kingdom. This I freely own, and it was indeed one principal design in offering it to the world. I desire the reader will observe, that I calculate my remedy for this one individual kingdom of Ireland and for no other that ever was, is, or I think ever can be upon earth. Therefore let no man talk to me of other expedients: of taxing our absentees at five shillings a pound: of using neither clothes nor household furniture except what is of our own growth and manufacture: of utterly rejecting the materials and instruments that promote foreign luxury: of curing the expensiveness of pride, vanity, idleness, and gaming in our women: of introducing a vein of parsimony, prudence, and temperance: of learning to love our country, in the want of which we differ even from Laplanders and the inhabitants of Topinamboo:[15] of quitting our animosities and factions, nor acting any longer like the Jews, who were murdering one another at the very moment their city was taken:[16] of being a little cautious not to sell our country and conscience for nothing: of teaching landlords to have at least one degree of mercy toward their tenants: lastly, of putting a spirit of honesty, industry, and skill into our shopkeepers; who, if a resolution could now be taken to buy only our native goods, would immediately unite to cheat and exact upon us in the price, the measure, and the goodness, nor could ever yet be brought to make one fair proposal of just dealing, though often and earnestly invited to it.

Therefore, I repeat, let no man talk to me of these and the like expedients, 30 till he hath at least some glimpse of hope that there will be some hearty and sincere attempt to put them in practice.

---

[15] A district in Brazil, inhabited in Swift's day by primitive tribes.
[16] While the Roman emperor Titus laid siege to Jerusalem in A.D. 70, bloody fighting erupted among factions within the city.

But as to myself, having been wearied out for many years of offering vain, idle, visionary thoughts, and at length utterly despairing of success, I fortunately fell upon this proposal, which, as it is wholly new, so it hath something solid and real, of no expense and little trouble, full in our own power, and whereby we can incur no danger in disobliging England. For this kind of commodity will not bear exportation, the flesh being of too tender a consistence to admit a long continuance in salt, although perhaps I could name a country[17] which would be glad to eat up our whole nation without it.

After all, I am not so violently bent upon my own opinion as to reject any offer proposed by wise men, which shall be found equally innocent, cheap, easy, and effectual. But before something of that kind shall be advanced in contradiction to my scheme, and offering a better, I desire the author or authors will be pleased maturely to consider two points. First, as things now stand, how they will be able to find food and raiment for an hundred thousand useless mouths and backs. And secondly, there being a round million of creatures in human figure throughout this kingdom, whose sole subsistence put into a common stock would leave them in debt two millions of pounds sterling, adding those who are beggars by profession to the bulk of farmers, cottagers, and laborers, with their wives and children who are beggars in effect; I desire those politicians who dislike my overture, and may perhaps be so bold to attempt to answer, that they will first ask the parents of these mortals whether they would not at this day think it a great happiness to have been sold for food at a year old in this manner I prescribe, and thereby have avoided such a perpetual scene of misfortunes as they have since gone through by the oppression of landlords, the impossibility of paying rent without money or trade, the want of common sustenance, with neither house nor clothes to cover them from the inclemencies of the weather, and the most inevitable prospect of entailing the like or greater miseries upon their breed forever.

I profess, in the sincerity of my heart, that I have not the least personal interest in endeavoring to promote this necessary work, having no other motive than the public good of my country, by advancing our trade, providing for infants, relieving the poor, and giving some pleasure to the rich. I have no children by which I can propose to get a single penny; the youngest being nine years old, and my wife past childbearing.

FOR ANALYSIS

1. What kind of person is the speaker? What does his tone of voice reveal about who he is? Is his voice direct and transparent, or does it seem deliberately created to achieve a specific effect?

2. In what sense is the proposal "modest"?

3. Where are the major divisions of the essay? What function does each serve?

4. What function does paragraph 29 serve?

---

[17] England.

5. Explain what Swift means when he says in paragraph 20, "I have too long digressed."

6. Whom is Swift addressing in this essay?

MAKING ARGUMENTS

Rather than making your own argument, write a detailed description of the use of argument in "A Modest Proposal." Pay attention to the use of argument techniques both by the speaker (or "projector") and by Swift himself as author of the essay.

WRITING TOPICS

1. Some background information on Swift's life, as well as familiarity with his other works, would make it clear that in this essay he is being satiric. Without that background—that is, on the basis of this essay alone—would you conclude that Swift is writing **satire**? Explain.

2. In one brief paragraph, paraphrase the major arguments Swift uses to support his plan.

MAKING CONNECTIONS

Some other works in this anthology that use **satire** include e. e. cummings, "the Cambridge ladies who live in furnished souls" (p. 655); W. H. Auden, "The Unknown Citizen" (p. 430); and Harlan Ellison, " 'Repent, Harlequin!' Said the Ticktockman" (p. 374). Compare and contrast the use of satire in one of these works with Swift's use of satire.

JAMAICA KINCAID   (B. 1949)

ON SEEING ENGLAND
FOR THE FIRST TIME   1991

When I saw England for the first time, I was a child in school sitting at a desk. The England I was looking at was laid out on a map gently, beautifully, delicately, a very special jewel; it lay on a bed of sky blue—the background of the map—its yellow form mysterious, because though it looked like a leg of mutton, it could not really look like anything so familiar as a leg of mutton because it was England—with shadings of pink and green, unlike any shadings of pink and green I had seen before, squiggly veins of red running in every direction. England was a special jewel all right, and only special people got to wear it. The people who got to wear England were English people. They wore it well and they wore it everywhere: in jungles, in deserts, on plains, on top of the highest mountains, on all the oceans, on all the seas, in places where they were not welcome, in places they should not have been. When my teacher had pinned this map up on the blackboard, she said, "This is England"—and she said it with authority, seriousness, and adoration, and we all sat up. It was as if she had said, "This is Jerusalem, the place you will go to when you die but only if you have been good." We understood then—we were meant to understand then—that England was to be our source of myth and the source from which we got our sense of reality, our sense of what was meaningful, our sense of what was meaningless—and much about our own lives and much about the very idea of us headed that last list.

At the time I was a child sitting at my desk seeing England for the first time, I was already very familiar with the greatness of it. Each morning before I left for school, I ate a breakfast of half a grapefruit, an egg, bread and butter and a slice of cheese, and a cup of cocoa; or half a grapefruit, a bowl of oat porridge, bread and butter and a slice of cheese, and a cup of cocoa. The can of cocoa was often left on the table in front of me. It had written on it the name of the company, the year the company was established, and the words "Made in England." Those words, "Made in England," were written on the box the oats came in too. They would also have been written on the box the shoes I was wearing came in; a bolt of gray linen cloth lying on the shelf of a store from which my mother had bought three yards to make the uniform that I was wearing had written along its edge those three words. The shoes I wore were made in England; so were my socks and cotton undergarments and the satin ribbons I wore tied at the end of two plaits of my hair. My father, who might have sat next to me at breakfast, was a carpenter and cabinet maker. The shoes he wore to work would have been made in England, as were his khaki shirt and trousers, his underpants and undershirt, his socks and brown felt hat. Felt was not the proper material from which a hat that was expected to provide shade from the hot sun should be made, but my father must have seen and admired a picture of an Englishman wearing such a hat in England, and this picture that he saw must have been so compelling that it caused him to wear the wrong hat for a hot climate most of his long life. And this hat—a brown felt hat—became so central to his character that it was the first thing he put on in the morning as he stepped out of bed and the last thing he took off before he stepped back into bed at night. As we sat at breakfast a car might go by. The car, a Hillman or a Zephyr, was made in England. The very idea of the meal itself, breakfast, and its substantial quality and quantity was an idea from England; we somehow knew that in England they began the day with this meal called breakfast and a proper breakfast was a big breakfast. No one I knew liked eating so much food so early in the day; it made us feel sleepy, tired. But this breakfast business was Made in England like almost everything else that surrounded us, the exceptions being the sea, the sky, and the air we breathed.

At the time I saw this map—seeing England for the first time—I did not say to myself, "Ah, so that's what it looks like," because there was no longing in me to put a shape to those three words that ran through every part of my life, no matter how small; for me to have had such a longing would have meant that I lived in a certain atmosphere, an atmosphere in which those three words were felt as a burden. But I did not live in such an atmosphere. My father's brown felt hat would develop a hole in its crown, the lining would separate from the hat itself, and six weeks before he thought that he could not be seen wearing it—he was a very vain man—he would order another hat from England. And my mother taught me to eat my food in the English way: the knife in the right hand, the fork in the left, my elbows held still close to my side, the food carefully balanced on my fork and then brought up to my mouth. When I had finally mastered it, I overheard her saying to a friend, "Did you see how nicely she can eat?" But I knew then that I enjoyed my food more when I ate it with my bare hands, and I continued to do so when she wasn't looking. And when my teacher showed us the map, she asked us to study it carefully, because no test we would ever take would be complete without this statement: "Draw a map of England."

I did not know then that the statement "Draw a map of England" was something far worse than a declaration of war, for in fact a flat-out declaration of war would have put me on alert, and again in fact, there was no need for war—I had long ago been conquered. I did not know then that this statement was part of a process that would result in my erasure, not my physical erasure, but my erasure all the same. I did not know then that this statement was meant to make me feel in awe and small whenever I heard the word "England": awe at its existence, small because I was not from it. I did not know very much of anything then—certainly not what a blessing it was that I was unable to draw a map of England correctly.

After that there were many times of seeing England for the first time. I saw England in history. I knew the names of all the kings of England. I knew the 5 names of their children, their wives, their disappointments, their triumphs, the names of people who betrayed them, I knew the dates on which they were born and the dates they died. I knew their conquests and was made to feel glad if I figured in them; I knew their defeats. I knew the details of the year 1066 (the Battle of Hastings, the end of the reign of the Anglo-Saxon kings) before I knew the details of the year 1832 (the year slavery was abolished). It wasn't as bad as I make it sound now; it was worse. I did like so much hearing again and again how Alfred the Great, traveling in disguise, had been left to watch cakes, and because he wasn't used to this the cakes got burned, and Alfred burned his hands pulling them out of the fire, and the woman who had left him to watch the cakes screamed at him. I loved King Alfred. My grandfather was named after him; his son, my uncle, was named after King Alfred; my brother is named after King Alfred. And so there are three people in my family named after a man they have never met, a man who died over ten centuries ago. The first view I got of England then was not unlike the first view received by the person who named my grandfather.

This view, though—the naming of the kings, their deeds, their disappointments—was the vivid view, the forceful view. There were other views, subtler ones, softer, almost not there—but these were the ones that made the most lasting impression on me, these were the ones that made me really feel like nothing. "When morning touched the sky" was one phrase, for no morning touched the sky where I lived. The mornings where I lived came on abruptly, with a shock of heat and loud noises. "Evening approaches" was another, but the evenings where I lived did not approach; in fact, I had no evening—I had night and I had day and they came and went in a mechanical way: on, off; on, off. And then there were gentle mountains and low blue skies and moors over which people took walks for nothing but pleasure, when where I lived a walk was an act of labor, a burden, something only death or the automobile could relieve. And there were things that a small turn of a head could convey—entire worlds, whole lives would depend on this thing, a certain turn of a head. Everyday life could be quite tiring, more tiring than anything I was told not to do. I was told not to gossip, but they did that all the time. And they ate so much food, violating another of those rules they taught me: do not indulge in gluttony. And the foods they ate actually: if only sometime I could eat cold cuts after theater, cold cuts of lamb and mint sauce, and Yorkshire pudding and scones, and clotted cream, and sausages that came from upcountry (imagine, "up-country"). And having troubling thoughts at twilight, a good time to have troubling thoughts, apparently; and servants who stole and left in the middle of a crisis, who were born with a limp or some other kind of deformity, not nourished properly in their mother's womb (that last part I figured out for myself; the point was, oh to have an untrustworthy servant); and wonderful cobbled streets onto which solid front doors opened; and people whose eyes were blue and who had fair skins and who smelled only of lavender, or sometimes sweet pea or primrose. And those flowers with those names: delphiniums, foxgloves, tulips, daffodils, floribunda, peonies; in bloom, a striking display, being cut and placed in large glass bowls, crystal, decorating rooms so large twenty families the size of mine could fit in comfortably but used only for passing through. And the weather was so remarkable because the rain fell gently always, only occasionally in deep gusts, and it colored the air various shades of gray, each an appealing shade for a dress to be worn when a portrait was being painted; and when it rained at twilight, wonderful things happened: people bumped into each other unexpectedly and that would lead to all sorts of turns of events—a plot, the mere weather caused plots. I saw that people rushed: they rushed to catch trains, they rushed toward each other and away from each other; they rushed and rushed and rushed. That word: rushed! I did not know what it was to do that. It was too hot to do that, and so I came to envy people who would rush, even though it had no meaning to me to do such a thing. But there they are again. They loved their children; their children were sent to their own rooms as a punishment, rooms larger than my entire house. They were special, everything about them said so, even their clothes; their clothes rustled, swished, soothed. The world was theirs, not mine; everything told me so.

If now as I speak of all this I give the impression of someone on the outside looking in, nose pressed up against a glass window, that is wrong. My nose was pressed up against a glass window all right, but there was an iron vise at the back of my neck forcing my head to stay in place. To avert my gaze was to fall back into something from which I had been rescued, a hole filled with nothing, and that was the word for everything about me, nothing. The reality of my life was conquests, subjugation, humiliation, enforced amnesia. I was forced to forget. Just for instance, this: I lived in a part of St. John's, Antigua, called Ovals. Ovals was made up of five streets, each of them named after a famous English seaman—to be quite frank, an officially sanctioned criminal: Rodney Street (after George Rodney), Nelson Street (after Horatio Nelson), Drake Street (after Francis Drake), Hood Street, and Hawkins Street (after John Hawkins). But John Hawkins was knighted after a trip he made to Africa, opening up a new trade, the slave trade. He was then entitled to wear as his crest a Negro bound with a cord. Every single person living on Hawkins Street was descended from a slave. John Hawkins's ship, the one in which he transported the people he had bought and kidnapped, was called *The Jesus*. He later became the treasurer of the Royal Navy and rear admiral.

Again, the reality of my life, the life I led at the time I was being shown these views of England for the first time, for the second time, for the one-hundred-millionth time, was this: the sun shone with what sometimes seemed to be a deliberate cruelty; we must have done something to deserve that. My dresses did not rustle in the evening air as I strolled to the theater (I had no evening, I had no theater; my dresses were made of a cheap cotton, the weave of which would give way after not too many washings). I got up in the morning, I did my chores (fetched water from the public pipe for my mother, swept the yard). I washed myself, I went to a woman to have my hair combed freshly every day (because before we were allowed into our classroom our teachers would inspect us, and children who had not bathed that day, or had dirt under their fingernails, or whose hair had not been combed anew that day, might not be allowed to attend class). I ate that breakfast. I walked to school. At school we gathered in an auditorium and sang a hymn, "All Things Bright and Beautiful," and looking down on us as we sang were portraits of the Queen of England and her husband; they wore jewels and medals and they smiled. I was a Brownie. At each meeting we would form a little group around a flagpole, and after raising the Union Jack, we would say, "I promise to do my best, to do my duty to God and the Queen, to help other people every day and obey the scouts' law."

Who were these people and why had I never seen them, I mean really seen them, in the place where they lived? I had never been to England. No one I knew had ever been to England, or I should say, no one I knew had ever been and returned to tell me about it. All the people I knew who had gone to England had stayed there. Sometimes they left behind them their small children, never to see them again. England! I had seen England's representatives. I had seen the governor general at the public grounds at a ceremony celebrating the Queen's birthday. I had seen an old princess and I had seen a young princess. They had both been extremely not beautiful, but who of us would have told them that? I had never seen England, really seen it, I had only met a representative, seen a picture, read books, memorized its history. I had never set foot, my own foot, in it.

The space between the idea of something and its reality is always wide ₁₀ and deep and dark. The longer they are kept apart—idea of thing, reality of thing—the wider the width, the deeper the depth, the thicker and darker the darkness. This space starts out empty, there is nothing in it, but it rapidly becomes filled up with obsession or desire or hatred or love—sometimes all of these things, sometimes some of these things, sometimes only one of these things. The existence of the world as I came to know it was a result of this: idea of thing over here, reality of thing way, way over there. There was Christopher Columbus, an unlikable man, an unpleasant man, a liar (and so, of course, a thief) surrounded by maps and schemes and plans, and there was the reality on the other side of that width, that depth, that darkness. He became obsessed, he became filled with desire, the hatred came later, love was never a part of it. Eventually, his idea met the longed-for reality. That the idea of something and its reality are often two completely different things is something no one ever remembers; and so when they meet and find that they are not compatible, the weaker of the two, idea or reality, dies. That idea Christopher Columbus had was more powerful than the reality he met, and so the reality he met died.

And so finally, when I was a grown-up woman, the mother of two children, the wife of someone, a person who resides in a powerful country that takes up more than its fair share of a continent, the owner of a house with many rooms in it and of two automobiles, with the desire and will (which I very much act upon) to take from the world more than I give back to it, more than I deserve, more than I need, finally then, I saw England, the real England, not a picture, not a painting, not through a story in a book, but England, for the first time. In me, the space between the idea of it and its reality had become filled with hatred, and so when at last I saw it I wanted to take it into my hands and tear it into little pieces and then crumble it up as if it were clay, child's clay. That was impossible, and so I could only indulge in not-favorable opinions.

There were monuments everywhere; they commemorated victories, battles fought between them and the people who lived across the sea from them, all vile people, fought over which of them would have dominion over the people who looked like me. The monuments were useless to them now, people sat on them and ate their lunch. They were like markers on an old useless trail, like a piece of old string tied to a finger to jog the memory, like old decoration in an old house, dirty, useless, in the way. Their skins were so pale, it made them look so fragile, so weak, so ugly. What if I had the power to simply banish them from their land, send boat after boatload of them on a voyage that in fact had no destination, force them to live in a place where the sun's presence was a constant? This would rid them of their pale complexion and make them look more like me, make them look more like the people I love and treasure and hold dear, and more like the people who occupy the near and far reaches of my imagination, my history, my geography, and reduce them and everything they have ever known to figurines as evidence that I was in divine favor, what if all this was in my power? Could I resist it? No one ever has.

And they were rude, they were rude to each other. They didn't like each other very much. They didn't like each other in the way they didn't like me, and it occurred to me that their dislike for me was one of the few things they agreed on.

I was on a train in England with a friend, an English woman. Before we were in England she liked me very much. In England she didn't like me at all. She didn't like the claim I said I had on England, she didn't like the views I had of England. I didn't like England, she didn't like England, but she didn't like me not liking it too. She said, "I want to show you my England, I want to show you the England that I know and love." I had told her many times before that I knew England and I didn't want to love it anyway. She no longer lived in England; it was her own country, but it had not been kind to her, so she left. On the train, the conductor was rude to her; she asked something, and he responded in a rude way. She became ashamed. She was ashamed at the way he treated her; she was ashamed at the way he behaved. "This is the new England," she said. But I liked the conductor being rude; his behavior seemed quite appropriate. Earlier this had happened: we had gone to a store to buy a shirt for my husband; it was meant to be a special present, a special shirt to wear on special occasions. This was a store where the Prince of Wales has his shirts made, but the shirts sold in this store are beautiful all the same. I found a shirt I thought my husband would like and I wanted to buy him a tie to go with it. When I couldn't decide which one to choose, the salesman showed me a new set. He was very pleased with these, he said, because they bore the crest of the Prince of Wales, and the Prince of Wales had never allowed his crest to decorate an article of clothing before. There was something in the way he said it; his tone was slavish, reverential, awed. It made me feel angry; I wanted to hit him. I didn't do that. I said, my husband and I hate princes, my husband would never wear anything that had a prince's anything on it. My friend stiffened. The salesman stiffened. They both drew themselves in, away from me. My friend told me that the prince was a symbol of her Englishness, and I could see that I had caused offense. I looked at her. She was an English person, the sort of English person I used to know at home, the sort who was nobody in England but somebody when they came to live among the people like me. There were many people I could have seen England with; that I was seeing it with this particular person, a person who reminded me of the people who showed me England long ago as I sat in church or at my desk, made me feel silent and afraid, for I wondered if, all these years of our friendship, I had had a friend or had been in the thrall of a racial memory.

I went to Bath—we, my friend and I, did this, but though we were together, 15 I was no longer with her. The landscape was almost as familiar as my own hand, but I had never been in this place before, so how could that be again? And the streets of Bath were familiar, too, but I had never walked on them before. It was all those years of reading, starting with Roman Britain. Why did I have to know about Roman Britain? It was of no real use to me, a person living on a hot, drought-ridden island, and it is of no use to me now, and yet my head is filled with this nonsense, Roman Britain. In Bath, I drank tea in a room I had read about in a novel written in the eighteenth century. In this very same room, young women wearing those dresses that rustled and so on danced and flirted and sometimes disgraced themselves with young men, soldiers, sailors, who were on their way to Bristol or someplace like that, so many places like that where so many adventures, the outcome of which was not good for me, began. Bristol, England. A sentence that began "That night the ship sailed from Bristol, England" would end not so good for me. And then I was driving through the countryside in an English motorcar, on narrow winding roads, and they were so familiar, though I had never been on them before; and through little villages the names of which I somehow knew so well though I had never been there before. And the countryside did have all those hedges and hedges, fields hedged in. I was marveling at all the toil of it, the planting of the hedges to begin with and then the care of it, all that clipping, year after year of clipping, and I wondered at the lives of the people who would have to do this, because wherever I see and feel the hands that hold up the world, I see and feel myself and all the people who look like me. And I said, "Those hedges" and my friend said that someone, a woman named Mrs. Rothchild, worried that the hedges weren't being taken care of properly; the farmers couldn't afford or find the help to keep up the hedges, and often they replaced them with wire fencing. I might have said to that, well if Mrs. Rothchild doesn't like the wire fencing, why doesn't she take care of the hedges herself, but I didn't. And then in those fields that were now hemmed in by wire fencing that a privileged woman didn't like was planted a vile yellow flowering bush that produced an oil, and my friend said that Mrs. Rothchild didn't like this either; it ruined the English countryside, it ruined the traditional look of the English countryside.

It was not at that moment that I wished every sentence, everything I knew, that began with England would end with "and then it all died; we don't know how, it just all died." At that moment, I was thinking, who are these people who forced me to think of them all the time, who forced me to think that the world I knew was incomplete, or without substance, or did not measure up because it was not England; that I was incomplete, or without substance, and did not measure up because I was not English. Who were these people? The person sitting next to me couldn't give me a clue; no one person could. In any case, if I had said to her, I find England ugly, I hate England; the weather is like a jail sentence, the English are a very ugly people, the food in England is like a jail sentence, the hair of English people is so straight, so dead looking, the English have an unbearable smell so different from the smell of people I know, real people of course, she would have said that I was a person full of prejudice. Apart from the fact that it is I—that is, the people who look like me—who made her aware of the unpleasantness of such a thing, the idea of such a thing, prejudice, she would have been only partly right, sort of right: I may be capable of prejudice, but my prejudices have no weight to them, my prejudices have no force behind them, my prejudices remain opinions, my prejudices remain my personal opinion. And a great feeling of rage and disappointment came over me as I looked at England, my head full of personal opinions that could not have public, my public, approval. The people I come from are powerless to do evil on grand scale.

The moment I wished every sentence, everything I knew, that began with England would end with "and then it all died, we don't know how, it just all died" was when I saw the white cliffs of Dover. I had sung hymns and recited poems that were about a longing to see the white cliffs of Dover again. At the time I sang the hymns and recited the poems, I could really long to see them again because I had never seen them at all, nor had anyone around me at the time. But there we were, groups of people longing for something we had never seen. And so there they were, the white cliffs, but they were not that pearly majestic thing I used to sing about, that thing that created such a feeling in these people that when they died in the place where I lived they had themselves buried facing a direction that would allow them to see the white cliffs of Dover when they were resurrected, as surely they would be. The white cliffs of Dover, when finally I saw them, were cliffs, but they were not white; you would only call them that if the word "white" meant something special to you; they were dirty and they were steep; they were so steep, the correct height from which all my views of England, starting with the map before me in my classroom and ending with the trip I had just taken, should jump and die and disappear forever.

FOR ANALYSIS

1. How does the England that Kincaid reads about as a schoolgirl contrast to the Antigua she lived in?

2. Why does England, never seen by Kincaid until her adulthood, inspire such strong feelings in her? How does her essay convey the depth of these feelings?

3. Kincaid writes, "The space between the idea of something and its reality is always wide and deep and dark" (para. 10). How does the essay dramatize this idea? What

figurative language or other techniques does Kincaid use that represent the gap between the real and the idea of it?

MAKING ARGUMENTS

"What if I had the power to simply banish them from their land," Kincaid writes (para. 12). She ends this paragraph: "[W]hat if all this was in my power? Could I resist it? No one ever has." What exactly do you think Kincaid means by "all this"? Do you agree with her final statement? Make an argument agreeing or disagreeing, using not only the essay but historical evidence.

WRITING TOPIC

Name a place that you had a strong sense of without having visited it. If you have since been there, how was it similar or different? If not, how do you think it might be similar or different?

MAKING CONNECTIONS

1. Compare any of the poems in "Connecting Poems: Revising America" (p. 440) to "On Seeing England for the First Time." How is Kincaid's essay similarly interested in rethinking an **image** of a nation? How is it different in the object of its scrutiny not being the place where its author lives?

2. Compare Kincaid's use of the recalled-from-adulthood child's **point of view** to 'Ashrawi's use of the point of view of the child in the moment in "Night Patrol" (p. 446). What is gained or lost in terms of knowledge and immediacy in each case?

For much of human history, religious belief has been an inextricable and unexamined part of culture—it was unthinkable for individuals to doubt their culture's singular story of creation and divine involvement in daily life. In the modern world, it is much more possible to weigh belief—to choose to believe or not to believe, to adhere to one or a number of available religions, or to choose to disbelieve in any theological explanation whatsoever of existence.

The world has recently seen an upsurge in fundamentalism, in styles of religious belief that offer a return to the time before doubt. The two essays in this unit deal with this phenomenon in different ways, but both speak from outside fundamentalist religious belief, examining it in itself and in its (to them) unavoidable historical and social contexts. As you read Rushdie's and Doctorow's thoughts, "imagine" discussions of religious belief that avoid these framing issues. Is it possible to critically examine religion, or any system of belief or ostensible knowledge, without taking into account other, ever-changing elements of human experience?

E. L. DOCTOROW (B. 1931–2015)

WHY WE ARE INFIDELS 2003

We have lately been called infidels. Yet we are perhaps the most prayerful nation in the world. Both Tocqueville and Dickens[1] when they came over here to have a look at us were astonished at how much God there was in American society. True, the infidel is not necessarily a nonbeliever; he may also be a believer of the wrong stripe. But I think, given the variety of religious practice in our country, including that of Islam, that the term *infidel* as it has lately been applied to us probably does not refer to any particular religion we may as a nation subscribe to, but to the fact that we subscribe, within our population of three hundred million, to all of them.

Of course most of our religions, including Christianity, Judaism, Islam, Buddhism, landed here at different times from other parts of the world. They have been vulnerable as religions usually are to such denominational fracture as to offer a potential parishioner a virtual supermarket of spiritual choice. Some of our religions, Mormonism, Christian Science, Native American Anthropomorphism, were invented, or revealed, right here. And if we think even casually of

---

[1] Alexis de Tocqueville (1805–1859), an eminent French statesman who traveled to the United States in 1831 to study its prison system. His general observations on democratic government were recorded in *Democracy in America* (1835). The popular English novelist Charles Dickens (1812–1870) recorded his views of American life gathered during a trip in 1842.

the parade of creative and influential religionists on our shores[2]—from the colonists Anne Hutchinson and Roger Williams, George Fox, Jonathan Edwards, and Cotton Mather to our citizen evangelicals Aimee Semple McPherson, Billy Sunday, Father Divine, and Billy Graham, we notice immediately that we have left out the Adventists, the Millerites, the Shakers, Swedenborgians, and Perfectionists of the nineteenth century, to say nothing of the stadium-filling brides and grooms of the Reverend Moon's Unification Church, or the suicidal cultists of Jim Jones, or the unfortunate Branch Davidians of Waco, Texas, or the Heaven's Gate believers who castrated themselves and took their own lives in order to board the Hale-Bopp comet when it flew past in 1997.

One of the less scintillating debates among theologians is on the distinction between a religion and a cult. But all together, our religions or religious cults testify to the deeply serious American thirst for celestial connection. We want a spiritual release from the society we have made out of secular humanism.

That our God-soaked country is, as political science, secular, may be indicated by the fact that the word for the state of being of an infidel, *infidelity*, brings to our minds not a violation of faith in the true God but a violation of the marriage contract between ordinary mortals. Philandering husbands and adulterous wives may be viewed as immoral and looked upon with contempt or pity, but they are not usually regarded as infidels. The term however may be justly applied to all of us, including the most pious and monogamous among us, because of a major national sin committed over two hundred years ago when religion and the American state were rent asunder and all worship was consigned to private life. It was Jefferson who said, "Our civil rights have no dependence on our religious opinions, any more than our opinions in physics or geometry." And while it is precisely because of this principle of religious freedom that we enjoy such a continuous national uproar of praying and singing and studying and fasting and confessing and atoning and praising and preaching and dancing and dunking and vowing and quaking and shaking and abstaining and ordaining, a paradox arises from this expression of our religious democracy: if you have extracted the basic ethics of religious invention and found the mechanism for installing them in the statutes of the secular civil order, as we have with our Constitution and our Bill of Rights, but have consigned all the doctrine and rite and ritual, all the symbols and traditional practices to the precincts of private life, you are saying there is no one proven path to salvation, there are only traditions. If you relegate the old stories to the personal choices of private worship, you admit the ineffable[3] is ineffable, and in terms of a possible theological triumphalism everything is up for grabs.

Our pluralism has to be a profound offense to the fundamentalist who by 5 definition is an absolutist intolerant of all forms of belief but his own, all stories but his own. In our raucous democracy fundamentalist religious belief has

---

[2] Doctorow alludes to a number of persons and religious constructs in paragraph 2. Use a search engine to find information on those unfamiliar to you.

[3] Indescribable; too awesome to be spoken.

organized itself with political acumen to promulgate law that would undermine just those secular humanist principles that encourage it to flourish in freedom. Of course there has rarely been a period in our history when God has not been called upon to march. The abolitionists decried slavery as a sin against God. The South claimed biblical authority for its slaveholding. The civil disobedience of Dr. Martin Luther King Jr.'s civil rights movement drew its strength from prayer and the examples of Christian fortitude, while the Ku Klux Klan and other white supremacy groups invoked Jesus as a sponsor of their racism. But there is a crucial difference of emphasis between these traditional invocations and the politically astute and well-funded actions in recent years of the leaders of the movement known as the Christian Right, who do not call upon their faith to certify their politics as much as they call for a country that certifies their faith.

Fundamentalism really cannot help itself—it is absolutist and can compromise with nothing, not even democracy. It is not surprising that immediately after the Islamic fundamentalist attack on the World Trade Center and the Pentagon two prominent Christian fundamentalists were reported to have accounted it as justifiable punishment by God for our secularism, our civil libertarianism, our feminists, our gay and lesbian citizens, our abortion providers, and everything and everyone else which their fundamentalist belief condemns. In thus honoring the foreign killers of over three thousand Americans as agents of God's justice, they established their own consanguinity with the principle of righteous warfare in the name of all that is holy, and gave their pledge of allegiance to the theocratic ideal of government of whatever sacred text.

Not just on other shores are we considered a nation of infidels.

FOR ANALYSIS

1. In religious terms, what is an infidel?

2. What are religious fundamentalists? How would they respond to the presumptions of a religion different from their own?

3. What is the official relationship between religion and government in the United States? Do you approve or disapprove of that relationship? Explain.

4. Two American religious leaders asserted that the Islamic attackers who killed over 3,000 people on September 11, 2001, were used by God to punish the country for allowing behavior "which their fundamentalist belief condemns." How does Doctorow characterize this argument? How do you?

5. On what issues does the conflict between civil government and religious conviction often center? Describe the positions that animate such disagreements.

MAKING ARGUMENTS

If a majority of Americans voted to abolish the separation between church and state embedded in the Constitution, should the United States amend the Constitution to reflect that position and become a Protestant Christian theocratic state? Upon what assumptions does your position rest?

WRITING TOPICS

1. America's justification for its presence in the Middle East is that it wishes to bring "freedom and democracy" to Afghanistan, Iraq, and the entire region; what do you believe should be the response of the United States if one or more of these nations, in a fair and open election, chooses to have a theocratic authoritarian government?

2. Discuss Doctorow's view of the relationship between religion and politics in the modern world.

SALMAN RUSHDIE (B. 1947)

"IMAGINE THERE'S NO HEAVEN"[1] 1997
A LETTER TO THE SIX BILLIONTH WORLD CITIZEN

[Written for a UN-backed anthology of such letters]

Dear little Six Billionth Living Person,

As the newest member of a notoriously inquisitive species, you'll probably soon be asking the two sixty-four-thousand-dollar questions with which the other 5,999,999,999 of us have been wrestling for some time: How did we get here? And, now that we are here, how shall we live?

Oddly—as if six billion of us weren't enough to be going on with—it will almost certainly be suggested to you that the answer to the question of origins requires you to believe in the existence of a further, invisible, ineffable Being "somewhere up there," an omnipotent creator whom we poor limited creatures are unable even to perceive, much less to understand. That is, you will be strongly encouraged to imagine a heaven, with at least one god in residence. This sky-god, it's said, made the universe by churning its matter in a giant pot. Or, he danced. Or, he vomited Creation out of himself. Or, he simply called it into being, and lo, it Was. In some of the more interesting creation stories, the single mighty sky-god is subdivided into many lesser forces—junior deities, avatars, gigantic metamorphic "ancestors" whose adventures create the landscape, or the whimsical, wanton, meddling, cruel pantheons of the great polytheisms, whose wild doings will convince you that the real engine of creation was lust: for infinite power, for too easily broken human bodies, for clouds of glory. But it's only fair to add that there are also stories which offer the message that the primary creative impulse was, and is, love.

Many of these stories will strike you as extremely beautiful, and therefore seductive. Unfortunately, however, you will not be required to make a purely literary response to them. Only the stories of "dead" religions can be appreciated for their beauty. Living religions require much more of you. So you will be told that belief in "your" stories, and adherence to the rituals of worship that have grown up around them, must become a vital part of your life

---

[1] Rushdie takes his title from the first line of "Imagine," a song by John Lennon (1940–1980).

in the crowded world. They will be called the heart of your culture, even of your individual identity. It is possible that they may at some point come to feel inescapable, not in the way that the truth is inescapable but in the way that a jail is. They may at some point cease to feel like the texts in which human beings have tried to solve a great mystery and feel, instead, like the pretexts for other, properly anointed human beings to order you around. And it's time that human history is full of the public oppression wrought by the charioteers of the gods. In the opinion of religious people, however, the private comfort that religion brings more than compensates for the evil done in its name.

As human knowledge has grown, it has also become plain that every religious story ever told about how we got here is quite simply wrong. This, finally, is what all religions have in common. They didn't get it right. There was no celestial churning, no maker's dance, no vomiting of galaxies, no snake or kangaroo ancestors, no Valhalla, no Olympus, no six-day conjuring trick followed by a day of rest. Wrong, wrong, wrong. But here's something genuinely odd. The wrongness of the sacred tales hasn't lessened the zeal of the devout in the least. If anything, the sheer out-of-step zaniness of religion leads the religious to insist ever more stridently on the importance of blind faith.

As a result of this faith, by the way, it has proved impossible, in many parts 5 of the world, to prevent the human race's numbers from swelling alarmingly. Blame the overcrowded planet at least partly on the misguidedness of the race's spiritual guides. In your own lifetime, you may well witness the arrival of the nine billionth world citizen. If you're Indian (and there's a one in six chance that you are) you will be alive when, thanks to the failure of family-planning schemes in that poor, God-ridden land, its population surges past China's. And if too many people are being born as a result, in part, of religious strictures against birth control, then too many people are also dying because religious culture, by refusing to face the facts of human sexuality, also refuses to fight against the spread of sexually transmitted diseases.

There are those who say that the great wars of the new century will once again be wars of religion, jihads and crusades, as they were in the Middle Ages. I don't believe them, or not in the way they mean it. Take a look at the Muslim world, or rather the *Islamist* world, to use the word coined to describe Islam's present-day "political arm." The divisions between its great powers (Afghanistan versus Iran versus Iraq versus Saudi Arabia versus Syria versus Egypt) are what strike you most forcefully. There's very little resembling a common purpose. Even after the non-Islamic NATO fought a war for the Muslim Kosovar Albanians, the Muslim world was slow in coming forward with much-needed humanitarian aid.

The real wars of religion are the wars religions unleash against ordinary citizens within their "spheres of influence." They are wars of the godly against the largely defenseless—American fundamentalists against pro-choice doctors, Iranian mullahs against their country's Jewish minority, the Taliban against the people of Afghanistan, Hindu fundamentalists in Bombay against that city's increasingly fearful Muslims.

The victors in that war must not be the closed-minded, marching into battle with, as ever, God on their side. To choose unbelief is to choose mind over dogma, to trust in our humanity instead of all these dangerous divinities. So, how did we get here? Don't look for the answer in storybooks. Imperfect human knowledge may be a bumpy, potholed street, but it's the only road to wisdom worth taking. Virgil, who believed that the apiarist Aristaeus could spontaneously generate new bees from the rotting carcass of a cow, was closer to a truth about origins than all the revered old books.

The ancient wisdoms are modern nonsenses. Live in your own time, use what we know, and as you grow up, perhaps the human race will finally grow up with you and put aside childish things.

As the song says, "It's easy if you try."   10

As for morality, the second great question—how to live? What is right action, and what wrong?—it comes down to your willingness to think for yourself. Only you can decide if you want to be handed down the law by priests, and accept that good and evil are somehow external to ourselves. To my mind religion, even at its most sophisticated, essentially infantilizes our ethical selves by setting infallible moral Arbiters and irredeemably immoral Tempters above us; the eternal parents, good and bad, light and dark, of the supernatural realm.

How, then, are we to make ethical choices without a divine rulebook or judge? Is unbelief just the first step on the long slide into the brain-death of cultural relativism,[2] according to which many unbearable things—female circumcision, to name just one—can be excused on culturally specific grounds, and the universality of human rights, too, can be ignored? (This last piece of moral unmaking finds supporters in some of the world's most authoritarian regimes and also, unnervingly, on the op-ed pages of *The Daily Telegraph*.)

Well, no, it isn't, but the reasons for saying so aren't clear-cut. Only hard-line ideology is clear-cut. Freedom, which is the word I use for the secular-ethical position, is inevitably fuzzier. Yes, freedom is that space in which contradiction can reign, it is a never-ending debate. It is not in itself the answer to the question of morals but the conversation about that question.

And it is much more than mere relativism, because it is not merely a never-ending talk-shop, but a place in which choices are made, values defined and defended. Intellectual freedom, in European history, has mostly meant freedom from the restraints of the Church, not the State. This is the battle Voltaire[3] was fighting, and it's also what all six billion of us could do for ourselves, the revolution in which each of us could play our small, six-billionth part: once and for all we could refuse to allow priests, and the fictions on whose behalf they claim to speak, to be the policemen of our liberties and behavior. Once

[2] The view that truth is relative and may differ depending on the believer's situation, and that all beliefs are equally valid. Cultural relativism developed in the late nineteenth century as a backlash against the Western tendency to perceive culture as advancing from ignorant savagery to enlightened civilization.

[3] The pen name of François-Marie Arouet (1694–1778), author of *Candide* and a major antiecclesiastical writer of his time.

and for all we could put the stories back into the books, put the books back on the shelves, and see the world undogmatized and plain.

Imagine there's no heaven, my dear Six Billionth, and at once the sky's the 15 limit.

FOR ANALYSIS

1. Rushdie argues from the **point of view** of a "secular-ethical" humanist. How do his arguments differ from those a religious leader might put forward?

2. Using a search engine, try to identify the sources of the "creation stories" that Rushdie enumerates in paragraph 2.

3. At the end of paragraph 4, Rushdie speaks of "blind faith." How does blind faith differ from faith?

4. In paragraph 5, Rushdie argues that overpopulation and certain diseases are the direct result of religious strictures. Do you agree or disagree? Explain.

5. Since this essay was written in 1997, much has changed in the "Islamist world." Do you find Rushdie's assertions about the struggle among Islamic nations (paras. 6–7) convincing or misguided? Explain.

6. In Rushdie's world without religion, what will determine "right action" (para. 11)? Do you find Rushdie's position valid or foolish? Explain.

7. In paragraph 12, Rushdie alludes to the "brain-death of cultural relativism." What is cultural relativism? Why would the author characterize it as "brain-death"?

8. Rushdie promotes "freedom" (paras. 13–14) as the appropriate source of ethical choices and behavior. Do you find his argument convincing? Explain.

MAKING ARGUMENTS

Defend or rebut Rushdie's argument by examining the significance of religious principles as the source of rules that make social organization possible.

WRITING TOPICS

1. The essay embodies this seminal assertion: "To choose unbelief is to choose mind over dogma, to trust in our humanity instead of all these dangerous divinities" (para. 8). Defend or rebut this assertion.

2. Distinguish between what Rushdie calls "cultural relativism" and "freedom."

3. Hinduism, Jainism, Buddhism, Judaism, Christianity, Islam, Taoism, Shintoism, animism, Bahaism—these "great" religions—exist side by side throughout the world. And these religious structures are complicated by internal divisions. There are Reform, Conservative, and Orthodox Jews; Catholic and Protestant Christians; Orthodox Catholics (Russian, Greek, and others) and Roman Catholics. Protestants include Baptists, Methodists, Lutherans, Anglicans, Seventh-Day Adventists, and many other churches. Buddhism includes many competing congregations. Islam is divided (bitterly in some regions) into Sunni and Shiite congregations, with further prominent divisions within each group. In an essay, (1) suggest the conditions under which these disparate and competing systems might peacefully coexist, or (2) describe the likely outcome of the ultimate collision between such disparate worldviews.

MAKING CONNECTIONS

1. Compare and contrast Rushdie's and Doctorow's essays. Which do you find more stirring? More persuasive? Do they both advocate the same principles?

2. While both of these essays take a negative stance toward their shared subject, they adopt a variety of **tones** over the course of their arguments. Describe the tones adopted in each essay. How do Rushdie and Doctorow each use shifts in tone to help get across their messages?

3. If you do not agree with one or both of these essays, what would you say in defense of the thing they attack? Are Rushdie and Doctorow unreasonably harsh about religious belief? How so? What might you say, if writing your own essay, to counter their arguments?

CASE STUDY IN ARGUMENT

MAKING CHANGE

These four essays take on the subject of attempting to make social change through the mobilization of public opinion. Each writer has different ideas about what form such mobilization might take and how opinion, once mobilized, expresses itself and works for change. All four focus on moments when citizens desire a change in the status quo, but each of these essays has its own stance on these moments, its own attitude about what constitutes taking to the streets, and what defines success. As you read, note the differences not only in the opinions of these four writers but also in the ways in which they express those opinions—the way they do (or don't) issue their own invitations to take part in such movements, or to think critically about them.

BILL McKIBBEN   (B. 1960)

A CALL TO ARMS: AN INVITATION TO DEMAND ACTION ON CLIMATE CHANGE   2014

This is an invitation, an invitation to come to New York City. An invitation to anyone who'd like to prove to themselves, and to their children, that they give a damn about the biggest crisis our civilization has ever faced.

My guess is people will come by the tens of thousands, and it will be the largest demonstration yet of human resolve in the face of climate change. Sure, some of it will be exciting—who doesn't like the chance to march and sing and carry a clever sign through the canyons of Manhattan? But this is dead-serious business, a signal moment in the gathering fight of human beings to do something about global warming before it's too late to do anything but watch. You'll tell your grandchildren, assuming we win. So circle September 20th and 21st on your calendar, and then I'll explain.

Since Ban Ki-moon runs the United Nations, he's altogether aware that we're making no progress as a planet on slowing climate change. He presided over the collapse of global-climate talks at Copenhagen in 2009, and he knows the prospects are not much better for the "next Copenhagen" in Paris in December 2015. In order to spur those talks along, he's invited the world's leaders to New York in late September for a climate summit.

But the "world's leaders" haven't been leaders on climate change—at least not leaders enough. Like many of us, they've attended to the easy stuff, but they haven't set the world on a fundamentally new course. Barack Obama is the perfect example: Sure, he's imposed new mileage standards for cars, but he's also opened vast swaths of territory to oil drilling and coal mining, which will take us past Saudi Arabia and Russia as the world's biggest petro producer.

Like other world leaders, that is, he's tried, but not nearly hard enough. 5 Consider what he told *The New Yorker* in an interview earlier this year: "At the end of the day, we're part of a long-running story. We just try to get our paragraph right." And "I think we are fortunate at the moment that we do not face a crisis of the scale and scope that Lincoln or FDR faced."

We do, though; we face a crisis as great as any president has ever encountered. Here's how his paragraph looks so far: Since he took office, summer sea ice in the Arctic has mostly disappeared, and at the South Pole, scientists in May made clear that the process of massive melt is now fully under way, with 10 feet of sea-level rise in the offing. Scientists have discovered the depth of changes in ocean chemistry: that seawater is 30 percent more acidic than just four decades ago, and it's already causing trouble for creatures at the bottom of the marine food chain. America has weathered the hottest year in its history, 2012, which saw a drought so deep that the corn harvest largely failed. At the moment, one of the biggest states in Obama's union, California, is caught in a drought deeper than any time since Europeans arrived. Hell, a few blocks south of the U.N. buildings, Hurricane Sandy turned the Lower East Side of New York into a branch of the East River. And that's just the United States. The world's scientists earlier this spring issued a 32-volume report explaining exactly how much worse it's going to get, which is, to summarize, a lot worse even than they'd thought before. It's not that the scientists are alarmists—it's that the science is alarming. Here's how one Princeton scientist summarized the situation for reporters: "We're all sitting ducks."

The gap between "We're all sitting ducks" and "We do not face a crisis" is the gap between halfhearted action and the all-out effort that might make a difference. It's the gap between changing light bulbs and changing the system that's powering our destruction.

In a rational world, no one would need to march. In a rational world, policymakers would have heeded scientists when they first sounded the alarm 25 years ago. But in this world, reason, having won the argument, has so far lost the fight. The fossil-fuel industry, by virtue of being perhaps the richest enterprise in human history, has been able to delay effective action, almost to the point where it's too late.

So in this case taking to the streets is very much necessary. It's not all that's necessary—a sprawling fossil-fuel resistance works on a hundred fronts around the world, from putting up solar panels to forcing colleges to divest their oil stocks to electioneering for truly green candidates. And it's true that marching doesn't always work: At the onset of the war in Iraq, millions marched, to no immediate avail. But there are moments when it's been essential. This is how the Vietnam War was ended, and segregation too—or consider the nuclear-freeze campaign of the early 1980s, when half a million people gathered in New York's Central Park. The rally, and all the campaigning that led to it, set the mood for a planet—even, amazingly, in the Reagan era. By mid-decade, the conservative icon was proposing to Mikhail Gorbachev that they abolish nuclear weapons altogether.

The point is, sometimes you can grab the zeitgeist by the scruff of the neck and shake it a little. At the moment, the overwhelming sense around the world is nothing will happen in time. That's on the verge of becoming a self-fulfilling prophecy—indeed, as I've written in these pages, it's very clear that the fossil-fuel industry has five times as much carbon in its reserves as it would take to break the planet. On current trajectories, the industry will burn it, and governments will make only small whimpering noises about changing the speed at which it happens. A loud movement—one that gives our "leaders" permission to actually lead, and then scares them into doing so—is the only hope of upending that prophecy.

A loud movement is, of necessity, a big movement—and this fossil-fuel resistance draws from every corner of our society. It finds powerful leadership from the environmental-justice community, the poor people, often in communities of color, who have suffered most directly under the reign of fossil fuel. In this country they're survivors of Sandy and Katrina and the BP spill; they're the people whose kids troop off to kindergarten clutching asthma inhalers because they live next to oil refineries, and the people whose reservations become resource colonies. Overseas, they're the ones whose countries are simply disappearing.

Sometimes in the past, trade unionists have fought against environmentalists—but unions in health care, mass transit, higher education, domestic work, and building services are all beginning to organize for September, fully aware that there are no jobs on a dead planet. Energy-sector unions see the jobs potential in massive solar installation and a "just transition" off fossil fuels. Here's a banner I know you'll see in the streets of New York: CLIMATE/JOBS. TWO CRISES, ONE SOLUTION.

There will be clergy and laypeople from synagogues and churches and mosques, now rising in record numbers to say, "If the Bible means anything, it means that we need to care for the world God gave us." And there will, of course, be scientists, saying, "What exactly don't you understand about what we've been telling you for a quarter-century?"

And students will arrive from around the country, because who knows better how to cope with long bus rides and sleeping on floors—and who knows better that their very futures are at stake? They're near the front of this battle right now, getting arrested at Harvard and at Washington University as they fight for fossil-fuel divestment, and shaking up the establishment enough that Stanford, with its $18.7 billion endowment, just agreed to get rid of its coal stocks. Don't worry about "kids today." Kids today know how to organize at least as well as kids in the Sixties.

And then there will be those of us plain old middle-class Americans who may still benefit from our lives of cheap fossil fuel, but who just can't stand to watch the world drift into chaos. We look around and see that the price of solar panels has fallen 90 percent in a few decades; we understand that it won't be easy to shift our economy off coal and gas and oil, but we know that it will be easier than coping with temperatures that no human has ever seen. We may have different proposed solutions—carbon taxes! tidal power!—but we know that none of them will happen unless we open up some space. That's our job: opening up space for change on the scale that physics requires. No more fine words, no more nifty websites. Hard deeds. Now.

You can watch the endgame of the fossil-fuel era with a certain amount of hope. The pieces are in place for real, swift, sudden change, not just slow and grinding linear shifts: If Germany on a sunny day can generate half its power from solar panels, and Texas makes a third of its electricity from wind, then you know technology isn't an impossible obstacle anymore. The pieces are in place, but the pieces won't move themselves. That's where movements come in. They're not subtle; they can't manage all the details of this transition. But they can build up pressure on the system, enough, with luck, to blow out those bags of money that are blocking progress with the force of Typhoon Haiyan on a Filipino hut. Because if our resistance fails, there will be ever-stronger typhoons. The moment to salvage something of the Holocene is passing fast. But it hasn't passed yet, which is why September is so important.

Day to day this resistance is rightly scattered, local and focused on the more mundane: installing a new zoning code, putting in a solar farm, persuading the church board to sell its BP stock. But sometimes it needs to come together and show the world how big it's gotten. That next great moment is late September in New York. See you there.

FOR ANALYSIS

1. What are the effects of climate change that are already apparent? What steps does McKibben claim might avert climate change?

2. Why does McKibben argue that the fossil fuel industry bears much of the blame for the climate crisis?

3. Analyze McKibben's **style**. As he claims, these arguments are serious business; does McKibben's writing match the seriousness? Characterize his **tone** and **diction**, and what you imagine is the desired effect on readers.

WRITING TOPICS

1. Discuss taking to the streets as a political tactic. How does it work? Cite historical examples of successes and failures of street protest.

2. What role do governments play in the crisis, according to McKibben? How might they avert it?

MAKING ARGUMENTS

McKibben quotes Barack Obama saying, "I think we are fortunate at the moment that we do not face a crisis of the scale and scope that Lincoln or FDR faced" (para. 5). McKibben himself describes climate change as "the biggest crisis our civilization has ever faced" (para. 1). Construct an argument concerning the comparisons Obama suggests, making or refuting the claim that one or the other (or both) are bigger crises than climate change.

REBECCA SOLNIT (B. 1961)

REVOLUTIONS PER MINUTE 2008

When I was a young activist, the '60s were not yet far enough away, and people still talked about "after the revolution." They still believed in some sort of decisive event that would make everything different—an impossible event, because even a change in administration cannot bring a universal change of heart, and the process of changing imagination and culture is plodding, incremental, frustrating, comes complete with backlashes . . . and is wildly exciting if you slow down enough to see the broad spans of time across which change occurs. A lot of people then were waiting for the revolution; a lot of people now have lost faith that there will be one. The overthrow of the United States government seems extremely unlikely at the moment, but the transformation of everything within, around, and despite it has been under way for decades, including radical transformation in the governments of many other countries.

Sex before marriage. Bob and his boyfriend. Madame Speaker. Do those words make your hair stand on end or your eyes widen? Their flatness is the register of successful revolution. Many of the changes are so incremental that you adjust without realizing something has changed until suddenly one day you realize everything is different. I was reading something about food politics recently and thinking it was boring.

Then I realized that these were incredibly exciting ideas—about understanding where your food comes from and who grows it and what its impact on the planet and your body are. Fifteen or twenty years ago, hardly anyone thought about where coffee came from, or milk, or imagined fair-trade coffee. New terms like *food miles*, fairly new words like *organic, sustainable, non-GMO*, and reborn phenomena like farmers' markets are all the result of what it's fair to call the food revolution, and it has been so successful that ideas that were once startling and subversive have become familiar en route to becoming status quo. So my boredom was one register of victory.

Although we typically associate revolution with the sudden overthrow of a regime, the Industrial Revolution was an incremental change in everyday life and production that began a little over two centuries ago and never ended. It's a useful reminder of what else revolution is. Late in 2006, I had the pleasure and honor of meeting Grace Lee Boggs in Detroit, where she's lived and organized radical politics since the 1950s. Grace, who was born to Chinese immigrant parents in 1915, earned a PhD in philosophy in 1935, and married the African-American labor organizer Jimmy Boggs in the early 1950s, has lived long enough to see the whole idea of revolution change. She said to me, "In the first half of this century people never thought revolution involved transforming ourselves, that it required a two-sided transformation. They thought that all we had to do was transform the system, that all the problems were on the other side. It took the splitting of the atom and the Montgomery bus boycott to introduce us to a whole new way of thinking about revolution

510

as tied to evolution." In another interview, she expanded on this rejection of the idea that everything would change suddenly: "In revolutionary struggles throughout the twentieth century, we've seen that state power, viewed as a way to empower workers, ends up disempowering them. So we have to begin thinking differently. The old concept used to be: first we make the political revolution and then the cultural revolution. Now we have to think about how the cultural revolution can empower people differently."

The fantasy of a revolution is that it will make everything different—and regime-changing revolutions generally make a difference, sometimes a significantly positive one—but the making of differences in everyday practices is a more protracted and incremental and ultimately more revolutionary process. Last month, I was asked in public about where the antiglobalization movement now stood. I gulped a little. I'm a slow thinker—I like to have a month to a year to mull something over, which is why I'm a writer. My first thought was that there wasn't anything so dramatic and dynamic and visible as those ten thousand blockaders in the streets of Seattle on November 30 and December 1, 1999. Fortunately, I made the other person go first, and by the time her answer was complete, mine had grown to encompass how the very ideas around corporate globalization had spread, so that what was wild new thinking by radicals or revolutionaries in the streets in 1999 had become a reasonable position for many governments to take by 2003 or so—and even some of the Democratic presidential candidates by 2008.

In recent years, most Latin American nations have turned against the ideology of unfettered markets and trade pacts, and even in countries whose governments have not, most of the citizens have. Immanuel Wallerstein, the left-wing sociologist with a talent for prophecy, wrote an essay earlier this year headed "2008: The Demise of Neoliberal Globalization." In it he said, "The political balance is swinging back. Neoliberal globalization will be written about ten years from now as a cyclical swing in the history of the capitalist world-economy. The real question is not whether this phase is over but whether the swing back will be able, as in the past, to restore a state of relative equilibrium in the world-system. Or has too much damage been done?" Such critiques of globalization have ceased to be inflammatory or extraordinary as the global public has grown increasingly educated in economics and the sinister underside of all those free-trade treaties. Those of us who fought against them won some practical victories and a lot more in the realm of public imagination, but the position ceased to belong exclusively to us as it became a reasonable position for many to take. This is why we need training in slowness, and the long attention span that makes it possible to see the remarkable changes of our time.

There's also the widespread greening of the public imagination, with climate change having finally arrived on center stage. Cities and states across the country are now pushing to regulate emissions (and having to fight the Bush administration's EPA in order to do so). My own state is even looking at regulating commercial airplane emissions. The revolution is here, but it doesn't look like what people expected, and it isn't even visible to those who aren't practiced in the long view.

If the term *revolution* can be used to describe the Industrial Revolution, then perhaps we are launched upon something as profound—a backlash against the industrial revolution that brought us the acceleration of everyday life, the industrialization of time and space, the shrinkage of the contemplative time and space in which to understand ourselves and our lives. That is to say, the revolution is in part against the very speedup that has made us all busy, distracted, anxious, and unable even to perceive the tenor of our own times. So it is a revolution in perception and daily practice, as well as against the concrete institutions that spell the misery of everyday life for too many and the destruction of the Earth for us all.

It may never be finished, but the time to join it is now.

FOR ANALYSIS

1. What does Solnit use food politics as an example of?

2. What are the different kinds of revolution Solnit lists? What makes them different? Are they all equally important?

3. How would you characterize this essay in terms of the different modes of writing Solnit employs? Where does she describe, or explain, or tell a story, or exhort to action? How does she make it all fit together?

MAKING ARGUMENTS

Toward the end of her essay, Solnit writes, "The revolution is here, but it doesn't look like what people expected, and it isn't even visible to those who aren't practiced in the long view" (para. 7). Argue against Solnit here, in favor of the short view. Why might it be important to be impatient?

WRITING TOPICS

1. Solnit writes, "Many of the changes are so incremental that you adjust without realizing something has changed until suddenly one day you realize everything is different" (para. 2). Write about something that has changed in the world around you in your lifetime. Did you notice it happening?

2. Grace Lee Boggs is quoted as saying, "It took the splitting of the atom and the Montgomery bus boycott to introduce us to a whole new way of thinking about revolution as tied to evolution" (para. 4). How did these events lead to this way of thinking?

MALCOLM GLADWELL (B. 1963)

SMALL CHANGE: WHY THE REVOLUTION WILL NOT BE TWEETED 2010

At four-thirty in the afternoon on Monday, February 1, 1960, four college students sat down at the lunch counter at the Woolworth's in downtown Greensboro, North Carolina. They were freshmen at North Carolina A. & T., a black college a mile or so away.

"I'd like a cup of coffee, please," one of the four, Ezell Blair, said to the waitress.

"We don't serve Negroes here," she replied.

The Woolworth's lunch counter was a long L-shaped bar that could seat sixty-six people, with a standup snack bar at one end. The seats were for whites. The snack bar was for blacks. Another employee, a black woman who worked at the steam table, approached the students and tried to warn them away. "You're acting stupid, ignorant!" she said. They didn't move. Around five-thirty, the front doors to the store were locked. The four still didn't move. Finally, they left by a side door. Outside, a small crowd had gathered, including a photographer from the Greensboro *Record*. "I'll be back tomorrow with A. & T. College," one of the students said.

By next morning, the protest had grown to twenty-seven men and four 5 women, most from the same dormitory as the original four. The men were dressed in suits and ties. The students had brought their schoolwork, and studied as they sat at the counter. On Wednesday, students from Greensboro's "Negro" secondary school, Dudley High, joined in, and the number of protesters swelled to eighty. By Thursday, the protesters numbered three hundred, including three white women, from the Greensboro campus of the University of North Carolina. By Saturday, the sit-in had reached six hundred. People spilled out onto the street. White teenagers waved Confederate flags. Someone threw a firecracker. At noon, the A. & T. football team arrived. "Here comes the wrecking crew," one of the white students shouted.

By the following Monday, sit-ins had spread to Winston-Salem, twenty-five miles away, and Durham, fifty miles away. The day after that, students at Fayetteville State Teachers College and at Johnson C. Smith College, in Charlotte, joined in, followed on Wednesday by students at St. Augustine's College and Shaw University, in Raleigh. On Thursday and Friday, the protest crossed state lines, surfacing in Hampton and Portsmouth, Virginia, in Rock Hill, South Carolina, and in Chattanooga, Tennessee. By the end of the month, there were sit-ins throughout the South, as far west as Texas. "I asked every student I met what the first day of the sitdowns had been like on his campus," the political theorist Michael Walzer wrote in *Dissent*. "The answer was always the same: 'It was like a fever. Everyone wanted to go.'" Some seventy thousand students eventually took part. Thousands were arrested and untold thousands more radicalized. These events in the early sixties became a civil-rights war that engulfed the South for the rest of the decade—and it happened without e-mail, texting, Facebook, or Twitter.

The world, we are told, is in the midst of a revolution. The new tools of social media have reinvented social activism. With Facebook and Twitter and the like, the traditional relationship between political authority and popular will has been upended, making it easier for the powerless to collaborate, coordinate, and give voice to their concerns. When ten thousand protesters took to the streets in Moldova in the spring of 2009 to protest against their country's Communist government, the action was dubbed the Twitter Revolution, because of the means by which the demonstrators had been brought together. A few months after that, when student protests rocked Tehran, the State Department took the unusual step of asking Twitter to suspend scheduled maintenance of its Web site, because the Administration didn't want such a critical organizing tool out of service at the height of the demonstrations. "Without Twitter the people of Iran would not have felt empowered and confident to stand up for freedom and democracy," Mark Pfeifle, a former national-security adviser, later wrote, calling for Twitter to be nominated for the Nobel Peace Prize. Where activists were once defined by their causes, they are now defined by their tools. Facebook warriors go online to push for change. "You are the best hope for us all," James K. Glassman, a former senior State Department official, told a crowd of cyber activists at a recent conference sponsored by Facebook, A. T. & T., Howcast, MTV, and Google. Sites like Facebook, Glassman said, "give the U.S. a significant competitive advantage over terrorists. Some time ago, I said that Al Qaeda was 'eating our lunch on the Internet.' That is no longer the case. Al Qaeda is stuck in Web 1.0. The Internet is now about interactivity and conversation."

These are strong, and puzzling, claims. Why does it matter who is eating whose lunch on the Internet? Are people who log on to their Facebook page really the best hope for us all? As for Moldova's so-called Twitter Revolution, Evgeny Morozov, a scholar at Stanford who has been the most persistent of digital evangelism's critics, points out that Twitter had scant internal significance in Moldova, a country where very few Twitter accounts exist. Nor does it seem to have been a revolution, not least because the protests—as Anne Applebaum suggested in the *Washington Post*—may well have been a bit of stagecraft cooked up by the government. (In a country paranoid about Romanian revanchism,[1] the protesters flew a Romanian flag over the Parliament building.) In the Iranian case, meanwhile, the people tweeting about the demonstrations were almost all in the West. "It is time to get Twitter's role in the events in Iran right," Golnaz Esfandiari wrote, this past summer, in *Foreign Policy*. "Simply put: There was no Twitter Revolution inside Iran." The cadre of prominent bloggers, like Andrew Sullivan, who championed the role of social media in Iran,

---

[1] A political policy of a nation or an ethnic group, intended to regain lost territory or standing (from the French: *revanche*, "revenge").

Esfandiari continued, misunderstood the situation. "Western journalists who couldn't reach—or didn't bother reaching?—people on the ground in Iran simply scrolled through the English-language tweets post with tag #iranelection," she wrote. "Through it all, no one seemed to wonder why people trying to coordinate protests in Iran would be writing in any language other than Farsi."

Some of this grandiosity is to be expected. Innovators tend to be solipsists. They often want to cram every stray fact and experience into their new model. As the historian Robert Darnton has written, "The marvels of communication technology in the present have produced a false consciousness about the past—even a sense that communication has no history, or had nothing of importance to consider before the days of television and the Internet." But there is something else at work here, in the outsized enthusiasm for social media. Fifty years after one of the most extraordinary episodes of social upheaval in American history, we seem to have forgotten what activism is.

Greensboro in the early nineteen-sixties was the kind of place where racial 10 insubordination was routinely met with violence. The four students who first sat down at the lunch counter were terrified. "I suppose if anyone had come up behind me and yelled 'Boo,' I think I would have fallen off my seat," one of them said later. On the first day, the store manager notified the police chief, who immediately sent two officers to the store. On the third day, a gang of white toughs showed up at the lunch counter and stood ostentatiously behind the protesters, ominously muttering epithets such as "burr-head nigger." A local Ku Klux Klan leader made an appearance. On Saturday, as tensions grew, someone called in a bomb threat, and the entire store had to be evacuated.

The dangers were even clearer in the Mississippi Freedom Summer Project of 1964, another of the sentinel campaigns of the civil-rights movement. The Student Nonviolent Coordinating Committee recruited hundreds of Northern, largely white unpaid volunteers to run Freedom Schools, register black voters, and raise civil-rights awareness in the Deep South. "No one should go *anywhere* alone, but certainly not in an automobile and certainly not at night," they were instructed. Within days of arriving in Mississippi, three volunteers—Michael Schwerner, James Chaney, and Andrew Goodman—were kidnapped and killed, and, during the rest of the summer, thirty-seven black churches were set on fire and dozens of safe houses were bombed; volunteers were beaten, shot at, arrested, and trailed by pickup trucks full of armed men. A quarter of those in the program dropped out. Activism that challenges the status quo—that attacks deeply rooted problems—is not for the faint of heart.

What makes people capable of this kind of activism? The Stanford sociologist Doug McAdam compared the Freedom Summer dropouts with the participants who stayed, and discovered that the key difference wasn't, as might be expected, ideological fervor. "*All* of the applicants—participants and withdrawals alike—emerge as highly committed, articulate supporters of the goals and values of the summer program," he concluded. What mattered more was an applicant's degree of personal connection to the civil-rights movement. All the volunteers were required to provide a list of personal contacts—the people they wanted kept apprised of their activities—and participants were far more likely than dropouts to have close friends who were also going to Mississippi. High-risk activism, McAdam concluded, is a "strong-tie" phenomenon.

This pattern shows up again and again. One study of the Red Brigades, the Italian terrorist group of the nineteen-seventies, found that seventy percent of recruits had at least one good friend already in the organization. The same is true of the men who joined the mujahideen in Afghanistan. Even revolutionary actions that look spontaneous, like the demonstrations in East Germany that led to the fall of the Berlin Wall, are, at core, strong-tie phenomena. The opposition movement in East Germany consisted of several hundred groups, each with roughly a dozen members. Each group was in limited contact with the others: at the time, only thirteen percent of East Germans even had a phone. All they knew was that on Monday nights, outside St. Nicholas Church in downtown Leipzig, people gathered to voice their anger at the state. And the primary determinant of who showed up was "critical friends"—the more friends you had who were critical of the regime the more likely you were to join the protest.

So one crucial fact about the four freshmen at the Greensboro lunch counter—David Richmond, Franklin McCain, Ezell Blair, and Joseph McNeil—was their relationship with one another. McNeil was a roommate of Blair's in A. & T.'s Scott Hall dormitory. Richmond roomed with McCain one floor up, and Blair, Richmond, and McCain had all gone to Dudley High School. The four would smuggle beer into the dorm and talk late into the night in Blair and McNeil's room. They would all have remembered the murder of Emmett Till in 1955, the Montgomery bus boycott that same year, and the showdown in Little Rock in 1957. It was McNeil who brought up the idea of a sit-in at Woolworth's. They'd discussed it for nearly a month. Then McNeil came into the dorm room and asked the others if they were ready. There was a pause, and McCain said, in a way that works only with people who talk late into the night with one another, "Are you guys chicken or not?" Ezell Blair worked up the courage the next day to ask for a cup of coffee because he was flanked by his roommate and two good friends from high school.

The kind of activism associated with social media isn't like this at all. The [15] platforms of social media are built around weak ties. Twitter is a way of following (or being followed by) people you may never have met. Facebook is a tool for efficiently managing your acquaintances, for keeping up with the people you would not otherwise be able to stay in touch with. That's why you can have a thousand "friends" on Facebook, as you never could in real life.

This is in many ways a wonderful thing. There is strength in weak ties, as the sociologist Mark Granovetter has observed. Our acquaintances—not our friends—are our greatest source of new ideas and information. The Internet lets us exploit the power of these kinds of distant connections with marvellous efficiency. It's terrific at the diffusion of innovation, interdisciplinary collaboration, seamlessly matching up buyers and sellers, and the logistical functions of the dating world. But weak ties seldom lead to high-risk activism.

In a new book called *The Dragonfly Effect: Quick, Effective, and Powerful Ways to Use Social Media to Drive Social Change*, the business consultant Andy Smith and the Stanford Business School professor Jennifer Aaker tell the story of Sameer Bhatia, a young Silicon Valley entrepreneur who came down with acute myelogenous leukemia. It's a perfect illustration of social media's strengths. Bhatia needed a bone-marrow transplant, but he could not find a match among his relatives and friends. The odds were best with a donor of his ethnicity, and there were few South Asians in the national bone-marrow database. So Bhatia's business partner sent out an e-mail explaining Bhatia's plight to more than four hundred of their acquaintances, who forwarded the e-mail to their personal contacts; Facebook pages and You-Tube videos were devoted to the Help Sameer campaign. Eventually, nearly twenty-five thousand new people were registered in the bone-marrow database, and Bhatia found a match.

But how did the campaign get so many people to sign up? By not asking too much of them. That's the only way you can get someone you don't really know to do something on your behalf. You can get thousands of people to sign up for a donor registry, because doing so is pretty easy. You have to send in a cheek swab and—in the highly unlikely event that your bone marrow is a good match for someone in need—spend a few hours at the hospital. Donating bone marrow isn't a trivial matter. But it doesn't involve financial or personal risk; it doesn't mean spending a summer being chased by armed men in pickup trucks. It doesn't require that you confront socially entrenched norms and practices. In fact, it's the kind of commitment that will bring only social acknowledgment and praise.

The evangelists of social media don't understand this distinction; they seem to believe that a Facebook friend is the same as a real friend and that signing up for a donor registry in Silicon Valley today is activism in the same sense as sitting at a segregated lunch counter in Greensboro in 1960. "Social networks are particularly effective at increasing motivation," Aaker and Smith write. But that's not true. Social networks are effective at increasing *participation*—by lessening the level of motivation that participation requires. The Facebook page of the Save Darfur Coalition has 1,282,339 members, who have donated an average of nine cents apiece. The next biggest Darfur charity on Facebook has 22,073 members, who have donated an average of thirty-five cents. Help Save Darfur has 2,797 members, who have given, on average, fifteen cents. A spokesperson for the Save Darfur Coalition told *Newsweek*, "We wouldn't necessarily gauge someone's value to the advocacy movement based on what they've given. This is a powerful mechanism to engage this critical population. They inform their community, attend events, volunteer. It's not something you can measure by looking at a ledger." In other words, Facebook activism succeeds not by motivating people to make a real sacrifice but by motivating them to do the things that people do when they are not motivated enough to make a real sacrifice. We are a long way from the lunch counters of Greensboro.

*   *   *

The students who joined the sit-ins across the South during the winter of 20
1960 described the movement as a "fever." But the civil-rights movement was
more like a military campaign than like a contagion. In the late nineteen-fifties,
there had been sixteen sit-ins in various cities throughout the South, fifteen of
which were formally organized by civil-rights organizations like the NAACP
and CORE. Possible locations for activism were scouted. Plans were drawn
up. Movement activists held training sessions and retreats for would-be
protesters. The Greensboro Four were a product of this groundwork: all were
members of the NAACP Youth Council. They had close ties with the head of
the local NAACP chapter. They had been briefed on the earlier wave of sit-
ins in Durham, and had been part of a series of movement meetings in activist churches. When the sit-in movement spread from Greensboro throughout
the South, it did not spread indiscriminately. It spread to those cities which
had preexisting "movement centers"—a core of dedicated and trained activists
ready to turn the "fever" into action.

The civil-rights movement was high-risk activism. It was also, crucially, strategic activism: a challenge to the establishment mounted with precision and
discipline. The NAACP was a centralized organization, run from New York
according to highly formalized operating procedures. At the Southern Christian Leadership Conference, Martin Luther King, Jr., was the unquestioned
authority. At the center of the movement was the black church, which had,
as Aldon D. Morris points out in his superb 1984 study, "The Origins of the
Civil Rights Movement," a carefully demarcated division of labor, with various
standing committees and disciplined groups. "Each group was task-oriented
and coordinated its activities through authority structures," Morris writes.
"Individuals were held accountable for their assigned duties, and important
conflicts were resolved by the minister, who usually exercised ultimate authority over the congregation."

This is the second crucial distinction between traditional activism and its
online variant: social media are not about this kind of hierarchical organization. Facebook and the like are tools for building *networks*, which are the opposite, in structure and character, of hierarchies. Unlike hierarchies, with their
rules and procedures, networks aren't controlled by a single central authority.
Decisions are made through consensus, and the ties that bind people to the
group are loose.

This structure makes networks enormously resilient and adaptable in low-
risk situations. Wikipedia is a perfect example. It doesn't have an editor, sitting in New York, who directs and corrects each entry. The effort of putting
together each entry is self-organized. If every entry in Wikipedia were to be
erased tomorrow, the content would swiftly be restored, because that's what
happens when a network of thousands spontaneously devote their time to a
task.

There are many things, though, that networks don't do well. Car companies sensibly use a network to organize their hundreds of suppliers, but not
to design their cars. No one believes that the articulation of a coherent design

philosophy is best handled by a sprawling, leaderless organizational system. Because networks don't have a centralized leadership structure and clear lines of authority, they have real difficulty reaching consensus and setting goals. They can't think strategically; they are chronically prone to conflict and error. How do you make difficult choices about tactics or strategy or philosophical direction when everyone has an equal say?

The Palestine Liberation Organization originated as a network, and the 25 international-relations scholars Mette Eilstrup-Sangiovanni and Calvert Jones argue in a recent essay in *International Security* that this is why it ran into such trouble as it grew: "Structural features typical of networks—the absence of central authority, the unchecked autonomy of rival groups, and the inability to arbitrate quarrels through formal mechanisms—made the P.L.O. excessively vulnerable to outside manipulation and internal strife."

In Germany in the nineteen-seventies, they go on, "the far more unified and successful left-wing terrorists tended to organize hierarchically, with professional management and clear divisions of labor. They were concentrated geographically in universities, where they could establish central leadership, trust, and camaraderie through regular, face-to-face meetings." They seldom betrayed their comrades in arms during police interrogations. Their counterparts on the right were organized as decentralized networks, and had no such discipline. These groups were regularly infiltrated, and members, once arrested, easily gave up their comrades. Similarly, Al Qaeda was most dangerous when it was a unified hierarchy. Now that it has dissipated into a network, it has proved far less effective.

The drawbacks of networks scarcely matter if the network isn't interested in systemic change—if it just wants to frighten or humiliate or make a splash—or if it doesn't need to think strategically. But if you're taking on a powerful and organized establishment you have to be a hierarchy. The Montgomery bus boycott required the participation of tens of thousands of people who depended on public transit to get to and from work each day. It lasted a *year*. In order to persuade those people to stay true to the cause, the boycott's organizers tasked each local black church with maintaining morale, and put together a free alternative private carpool service, with forty-eight dispatchers and forty-two pickup stations. Even the White Citizens Council, King later said, conceded that the carpool system moved with "military precision." By the time King came to Birmingham, for the climactic showdown with Police Commissioner Eugene (Bull) Connor, he had a budget of a million dollars, and a hundred full-time staff members on the ground, divided into operational units. The operation itself was divided into steadily escalating phases, mapped out in advance. Support was maintained through consecutive mass meetings rotating from church to church around the city.

Boycotts and sit-ins and nonviolent confrontations—which were the weapons of choice for the civil-rights movement—are high-risk strategies. They leave little room for conflict and error. The moment even one protester deviates from the script and responds to provocation, the moral legitimacy of the entire protest is compromised. Enthusiasts for social media would no doubt have us believe that King's task in Birmingham would have been made infinitely easier had he been able to communicate with his followers through Facebook, and contented himself with tweets from a Birmingham jail. But networks are messy: think of the ceaseless pattern of correction and revision, amendment and debate, that characterizes Wikipedia. If Martin Luther King, Jr., had tried to do a wiki-boycott in Montgomery, he would have been steamrollered by the white power structure. And of what use would a digital communication tool be in a town where ninety-eight percent of the black community could be reached every Sunday morning at church? The things that King needed in Birmingham—discipline and strategy—were things that online social media cannot provide.

The bible of the social-media movement is Clay Shirky's *Here Comes Everybody*. Shirky, who teaches at New York University, sets out to demonstrate the organizing power of the Internet, and he begins with the story of Evan, who worked on Wall Street, and his friend Ivanna, after she left her smart phone, an expensive Sidekick, on the back seat of a New York City taxicab. The telephone company transferred the data on Ivanna's lost phone to a new phone, whereupon she and Evan discovered that the Sidekick was now in the hands of a teenager from Queens, who was using it to take photographs of herself and her friends.

When Evan e-mailed the teenager, Sasha, asking for the phone back, she 30 replied that his "white ass" didn't deserve to have it back. Miffed, he set up a Web page with her picture and a description of what had happened. He forwarded the link to his friends, and they forwarded it to their friends. Someone found the MySpace page of Sasha's boyfriend, and a link to it found its way onto the site. Someone found her address online and took a video of her home while driving by; Evan posted the video on the site. The story was picked up by the news filter Digg. Evan was now up to ten e-mails a minute. He created a bulletin board for his readers to share their stories, but it crashed under the weight of responses. Evan and Ivanna went to the police, but the police filed the report under "lost," rather than "stolen," which essentially closed the case. "By this point millions of readers were watching," Shirky writes, "and dozens of mainstream news outlets had covered the story." Bowing to the pressure, the NYPD reclassified the item as "stolen." Sasha was arrested, and Evan got his friend's Sidekick back.

Shirky's argument is that this is the kind of thing that could never have happened in the pre-Internet age—and he's right. Evan could never have tracked down Sasha. The story of the Sidekick would never have been publicized. An army of people could never have been assembled to wage this fight. The police wouldn't have bowed to the pressure of a lone person who had misplaced something as trivial as a cell phone. The story, to Shirky, illustrates "the ease and speed with which a group can be mobilized for the right kind of cause" in the Internet age.

Shirky considers this model of activism an upgrade. But it is simply a form of organizing which favors the weak-tie connections that give us access to information over the strong-tie connections that help us persevere in the face of danger. It shifts our energies from organizations that promote strategic and disciplined activity and toward those which promote resilience and adaptability. It makes it easier for activists to express themselves, and harder for that expression to have any impact. The instruments of social media are well suited to making the existing social order more efficient. They are not a natural enemy of the status quo. If you are of the opinion that all the world needs is a little buffing around the edges, this should not trouble you. But if you think that there are still lunch counters out there that need integrating it ought to give you pause.

Shirky ends the story of the lost Sidekick by asking, portentously, "What happens next?"—no doubt imagining future waves of digital protesters. But he has already answered the question. What happens next is more of the same. A networked, weak-tie world is good at things like helping Wall Streeters get phones back from teenage girls. *Viva la revolución.*

FOR ANALYSIS

1. Why does Gladwell begin with the story of the lunch counter sit-ins?

2. According to Gladwell, what is the difference between a strong tie and a weak tie? What is the significance of that difference for his argument?

3. How would you characterize Gladwell's **tone**? List word choices and descriptions that reveal his attitude toward his subject. Do you think his tone helps or hurts his argument?

MAKING ARGUMENTS

How would you refute Gladwell's argument? List your counterargument points, and try both to respond to his specific arguments and also to make your own.

WRITING TOPIC

Gladwell finds claims for the importance of the Internet to contemporary social movements "puzzling" (para. 8). How do you feel about it? Have you seen or participated in Internet-related activities that have had social or political effects? Were these positive effects? Write about your experience or observations, and reflect on your feelings about them.

CLAY SHIRKY (B. 1964)

THE POLITICAL POWER OF SOCIAL MEDIA 2011

On January 17, 2001, during the impeachment trial of Philippine President Joseph Estrada, loyalists in the Philippine Congress voted to set aside key evidence against him. Less than two hours after the decision was announced, thousands of Filipinos, angry that their corrupt president might be let off the hook, converged on Epifanio de los Santos Avenue, a major crossroads in Manila. The protest was arranged, in part, by forwarded text messages reading, "Go 2 EDSA. Wear blk." The crowd quickly swelled, and in the next few days, over a million people arrived, choking traffic in downtown Manila.

The public's ability to coordinate such a massive and rapid response—close to seven million text messages were sent that week—so alarmed the country's legislators that they reversed course and allowed the evidence to be presented. Estrada's fate was sealed; by January 20, he was gone. The event marked the first time that social media had helped force out a national leader. Estrada himself blamed "the text-messaging generation" for his downfall.

Since the rise of the Internet in the early 1990s, the world's networked population has grown from the low millions to the low billions. Over the same period, social media have become a fact of life for civil society worldwide, involving many actors—regular citizens, activists, nongovernmental organizations, telecommunications firms, software providers, governments. This raises an obvious question for the U.S. government: How does the ubiquity of social media affect U.S. interests, and how should U.S. policy respond to it?

As the communications landscape gets denser, more complex, and more participatory, the networked population is gaining greater access to information, more opportunities to engage in public speech, and an enhanced ability to undertake collective action. In the political arena, as the protests in Manila demonstrated, these increased freedoms can help loosely coordinated publics demand change.

The Philippine strategy has been adopted many times since. In some cases, 5 the protesters ultimately succeeded, as in Spain in 2004, when demonstrations organized by text messaging led to the quick ouster of Spanish Prime Minister José María Aznar, who had inaccurately blamed the Madrid transit bombings on Basque separatists. The Communist Party lost power in Moldova in 2009 when massive protests coordinated in part by text message, Facebook, and Twitter broke out after an obviously fraudulent election. Around the world, the Catholic Church has faced lawsuits over its harboring of child rapists, a process that started when *The Boston Globe*'s 2002 exposé of sexual abuse in the church went viral online in a matter of hours.

There are, however, many examples of the activists failing, as in Belarus in March 2006, when street protests (arranged in part by e-mail) against President Aleksandr Lukashenko's alleged vote rigging swelled, then faltered, leaving Lukashenko more determined than ever to control social media.

During the June 2009 uprising of the Green Movement in Iran, activists used every possible technological coordinating tool to protest the miscount of votes for Mir-Hossein Mousavi but were ultimately brought to heel by a violent crackdown. The Red Shirt uprising in Thailand in 2010 followed a similar but quicker path: protesters savvy with social media occupied downtown Bangkok until the Thai government dispersed the protesters, killing dozens.

The use of social media tools—text messaging, e-mail, photo sharing, social networking, and the like—does not have a single preordained outcome. Therefore, attempts to outline their effects on political action are too often reduced to dueling anecdotes. If you regard the failure of the Belarusian protests to oust Lukashenko as paradigmatic, you will regard the Moldovan experience as an outlier, and vice versa. Empirical work on the subject is also hard to come by, in part because these tools are so new and in part because relevant examples are so rare. The safest characterization of recent quantitative attempts to answer the question, Do digital tools enhance democracy? (such as those by Jacob Groshek and Philip Howard) is that these tools probably do not hurt in the short run and might help in the long run—and that they have the most dramatic effects in states where a public sphere already constrains the actions of the government.

Despite this mixed record, social media have become coordinating tools for nearly all of the world's political movements, just as most of the world's authoritarian governments (and, alarmingly, an increasing number of democratic ones) are trying to limit access to it. In response, the U.S. State Department has committed itself to "Internet freedom" as a specific policy aim. Arguing for the right of people to use the Internet freely is an appropriate policy for the United States, both because it aligns with the strategic goal of strengthening civil society worldwide and because it resonates with American beliefs about freedom of expression. But attempts to yoke the idea of Internet freedom to short-term goals—particularly ones that are country-specific or are intended to help particular dissident groups or encourage regime change—are likely to be ineffective on average. And when they fail, the consequences can be serious.

Although the story of Estrada's ouster and other similar events have led observers to focus on the power of mass protests to topple governments, the potential of social media lies mainly in their support of civil society and the public sphere—change measured in years and decades rather than weeks or months. The U.S. government should maintain Internet freedom as a goal to be pursued in a principled and regime-neutral fashion, not as a tool for effecting immediate policy aims country by country. It should likewise assume that progress will be incremental and, unsurprisingly, slowest in the most authoritarian regimes.

THE PERILS OF INTERNET FREEDOM

In January 2010, U.S. Secretary of State Hillary Clinton outlined how the United States would promote Internet freedom abroad. She emphasized several kinds of freedom, including the freedom to access information (such as the ability to use Wikipedia and Google inside Iran), the freedom of ordinary citizens to produce their own public media (such as the rights of Burmese activists to 10 blog), and the freedom of citizens to converse with one another (such as the Chinese public's capacity to use instant messaging without interference).

Most notably, Clinton announced funding for the development of tools designed to reopen access to the Internet in countries that restrict it. This "instrumental" approach to Internet freedom concentrates on preventing states from censoring outside Web sites, such as Google, YouTube, or that of *The New York Times*. It focuses only secondarily on public speech by citizens and least of all on private or social uses of digital media. According to this vision, Washington can and should deliver rapid, directed responses to censorship by authoritarian regimes.

The instrumental view is politically appealing, action-oriented, and almost certainly wrong. It overestimates the value of broadcast media while underestimating the value of media that allow citizens to communicate privately among themselves. It overestimates the value of access to information, particularly information hosted in the West, while underestimating the value of tools for local coordination. And it overestimates the importance of computers while underestimating the importance of simpler tools, such as cell phones.

The instrumental approach can also be dangerous. Consider the debacle around the proposed censorship-circumvention software known as Haystack, which, according to its developer, was meant to be a "one-to-one match for how the [Iranian] regime implements censorship." The tool was widely praised in Washington; the U.S. government even granted it an export license. But the program was never carefully vetted, and when security experts examined it, it turned out that it not only failed at its goal of hiding messages from governments but also made it, in the words of one analyst, "possible for an adversary to specifically pinpoint individual users." In contrast, one of the most successful anti-censorship software programs, Freegate, has received little support from the United States, partly because of ordinary bureaucratic delays and partly because the U.S. government is wary of damaging U.S.-Chinese relations: the tool was originally created by Falun Gong, the spiritual movement that the Chinese government has called "an evil cult." The challenges of Freegate and Haystack demonstrate how difficult it is to weaponize social media to pursue country-specific and near-term policy goals.

New media conducive to fostering participation can indeed increase the freedoms Clinton outlined, just as the printing press, the postal service, the telegraph, and the telephone did before. One complaint about the idea of new media as a political force is that most people simply use these tools for commerce, social life, or self-distraction, but this is common to all forms of media. Far more people in the 1500s were reading erotic novels than Martin Luther's "Ninety-five Theses," and far more people before the American Revolution were reading *Poor Richard's Almanack* than the work of the Committees of Correspondence. But those political works still had an enormous political effect.

Just as Luther adopted the newly practical printing press to protest against 15 the Catholic Church, and the American revolutionaries synchronized their beliefs using the postal service that Benjamin Franklin had designed, today's dissident movements will use any means possible to frame their views and coordinate their actions; it would be impossible to describe the Moldovan Communist Party's loss of Parliament after the 2009 elections without discussing the use of cell phones and online tools by its opponents to mobilize. Authoritarian governments stifle communication among their citizens because they fear, correctly, that a better-coordinated populace would constrain their ability to act without oversight.

Despite this basic truth—that communicative freedom is good for political freedom—the instrumental mode of Internet statecraft is still problematic. It is difficult for outsiders to understand the local conditions of dissent. External support runs the risk of tainting even peaceful opposition as being directed by foreign elements. Dissidents can be exposed by the unintended effects of novel tools. A government's demands for Internet freedom abroad can vary from country to country, depending on the importance of the relationship, leading to cynicism about its motives.

The more promising way to think about social media is as long-term tools that can strengthen civil society and the public sphere. In contrast to the instrumental view of Internet freedom, this can be called the "environmental" view. According to this conception, positive changes in the life of a country, including pro-democratic regime change, follow, rather than precede, the development of a strong public sphere. This is not to say that popular movements will not successfully use these tools to discipline or even oust their governments, but rather that U.S. attempts to direct such uses are likely to do more harm than good. Considered in this light, Internet freedom is a long game, to be conceived of and supported not as a separate agenda but merely as an important input to the more fundamental political freedoms.

THE THEATER OF COLLAPSE

Any discussion of political action in repressive regimes must take into account the astonishing fall of communism in 1989 in eastern Europe and the subsequent collapse of the Soviet Union in 1991. Throughout the Cold War, the United States invested in a variety of communications tools, including broadcasting the Voice of America radio station, hosting an American pavilion in Moscow (home of the famous Nixon-Khrushchev "kitchen debate"), and smuggling Xerox machines behind the Iron Curtain to aid the underground press, or samizdat. Yet despite this emphasis on communications, the end of the Cold War was triggered not by a defiant uprising of Voice of America listeners but by economic change. As the price of oil fell while that of wheat spiked, the Soviet model of selling expensive oil to buy cheap wheat stopped working. As a result, the Kremlin was forced to secure loans from the West, loans that would have been put at risk had the government intervened militarily in the affairs of non-Russian states. In 1989, one could argue, the ability of citizens to communicate, considered against the background of macroeconomic forces, was largely irrelevant.

But why, then, did the states behind the Iron Curtain not just let their people starve? After all, the old saying that every country is three meals away from revolution turned out to be sadly incorrect in the twentieth century; it is possible for leaders to survive even when millions die. Stalin did it in the 1930s, Mao did it in the 1960s, and Kim Jong Il has done it more than once in the last two decades. But the difference between those cases and the 1989 revolutions was that the leaders of East Germany, Czechoslovakia, and the rest faced civil societies strong enough to resist. The weekly demonstrations in East Germany, the Charter 77 civic movement in Czechoslovakia, and the Solidarity movement in Poland all provided visible governments in waiting.

The ability of these groups to create and disseminate literature and political documents, even with simple photocopiers, provided a visible alternative to the communist regimes. For large groups of citizens in these countries, the political and, even more important, economic bankruptcy of the government was no longer an open secret but a public fact. This made it difficult and then impossible for the regimes to order their troops to take on such large groups. 20

Thus, it was a shift in the balance of power between the state and civil society that led to the largely peaceful collapse of communist control. The state's ability to use violence had been weakened, and the civil society that would have borne the brunt of its violence had grown stronger. When civil society triumphed, many of the people who had articulated opposition to the communist regimes—such as Tadeusz Mazowiecki in Poland and Václav Havel in Czechoslovakia—became the new political leaders of those countries. Communications tools during the Cold War did not cause governments to collapse, but they helped the people take power from the state when it was weak.

The idea that media, from the Voice of America to samizdat, play a supporting role in social change by strengthening the public sphere echoes the historical role of the printing press. As the German philosopher Jürgen Habermas argued in his 1962 book, *The Structural Transformation of the Public Sphere*, the printing press helped democratize Europe by providing space for discussion and agreement among politically engaged citizens, often before the state had fully democratized, an argument extended by later scholars, such as Asa Briggs, Elizabeth Eisenstein, and Paul Starr.

Political freedom has to be accompanied by a civil society literate enough and densely connected enough to discuss the issues presented to the public. In a famous study of political opinion after the 1948 U.S. presidential election, the sociologists Elihu Katz and Paul Lazarsfeld discovered that mass media alone do not change people's minds; instead, there is a two-step process. Opinions are first transmitted by the media, and then they get echoed by friends, family members, and colleagues. It is in this second, social step that political opinions are formed. This is the step in which the Internet in general, and social media in particular, can make a difference. As with the printing press, the Internet spreads not just media consumption but media production as well—it allows people to privately and publicly articulate and debate a welter of conflicting views.

A slowly developing public sphere, where public opinion relies on both media and conversation, is the core of the environmental view of Internet freedom. As opposed to the self-aggrandizing view that the West holds the source code for democracy—and if it were only made accessible, the remaining autocratic states would crumble—the environmental view assumes that little political change happens without the dissemination and adoption of ideas and opinions in the public sphere. Access to information is far less important, politically, than access to conversation. Moreover, a public sphere is more likely to emerge in a society as a result of people's dissatisfaction with matters of economics or day-to-day governance than from their embrace of abstract political ideals.

To take a contemporary example, the Chinese government today is in more danger of being forced to adopt democratic norms by middle-class members of the ethnic Han majority demanding less corrupt local governments than it is by Uighurs or Tibetans demanding autonomy. Similarly, the One Million Signatures Campaign, an Iranian women's rights movement that focuses on the repeal of laws inimical to women, has been more successful in liberalizing the behavior of the Iranian government than the more confrontational Green Movement. 25

For optimistic observers of public demonstrations, this is weak tea, but both the empirical and the theoretical work suggest that protests, when effective, are the end of a long process, rather than a replacement for it. Any real commitment by the United States to improving political freedom worldwide should concentrate on that process—which can only occur when there is a strong public sphere.

THE CONSERVATIVE DILEMMA

Disciplined and coordinated groups, whether businesses or governments, have always had an advantage over undisciplined ones: they have an easier time engaging in collective action because they have an orderly way of directing the action of their members. Social media can compensate for the disadvantages of undisciplined groups by reducing the costs of coordination. The anti-Estrada movement in the Philippines used the ease of sending and forwarding text messages to organize a massive group with no need (and no time) for standard managerial control. As a result, larger, looser groups can now take on some kinds of coordinated action, such as protest movements and public media campaigns, that were previously reserved for formal organizations. For political movements, one of the main forms of coordination is what the military calls "shared awareness," the ability of each member of a group to not only understand the situation at hand but also understand that everyone else does, too. Social media increase shared awareness by propagating messages through social networks. The anti-Aznar protests in Spain gained momentum so quickly precisely because the millions of people spreading the message were not part of a hierarchical organization.

The Chinese anticorruption protests that broke out in the aftermath of the devastating May 2008 earthquake in Sichuan are another example of such ad hoc synchronization. The protesters were parents, particularly mothers, who had lost their only children in the collapse of shoddily built schools, the result of collusion between construction firms and the local government. Before the earthquake, corruption in the country's construction industry was an open secret. But when the schools collapsed, citizens began sharing documentation of the damage and of their protests through social media tools. The consequences of government corruption were made broadly visible, and it went from being an open secret to a public truth.

The Chinese government originally allowed reporting on the post-earthquake protests, but abruptly reversed itself in June. Security forces began arresting protesters and threatening journalists when it became clear that the protesters were demanding real local reform and not merely state reparations. From the government's perspective, the threat was not that citizens were aware of the corruption, which the state could do nothing about in the short run. Beijing was afraid of the possible effects if this awareness became shared: it would have to either enact reforms or respond in a way that would alarm more citizens. After all, the prevalence of camera phones has made it harder to carry out a widespread but undocumented crackdown.

This condition of shared awareness—which is increasingly evident in all 30 modern states—creates what is commonly called "the dictator's dilemma" but that might more accurately be described by the phrase coined by the media theorist Briggs: "the conservative dilemma," so named because it applies not only to autocrats but also to democratic governments and to religious and business leaders. The dilemma is created by new media that increase public access to speech or assembly; with the spread of such media, whether photocopiers or Web browsers, a state accustomed to having a monopoly on public speech finds itself called to account for anomalies between its view of events and the public's. The two responses to the conservative dilemma are censorship and propaganda. But neither of these is as effective a source of control as the enforced silence of the citizens. The state will censor critics or produce propaganda as it needs to, but both of those actions have higher costs than simply not having any critics to silence or reply to in the first place. But if a government were to shut down Internet access or ban cell phones, it would risk radicalizing otherwise pro-regime citizens or harming the economy.

The conservative dilemma exists in part because political speech and apolitical speech are not mutually exclusive. Many of the South Korean teenage girls who turned out in Seoul's Cheonggyecheon Park in 2008 to protest U.S. beef imports were radicalized in the discussion section of a Web site dedicated to Dong Bang Shin Ki, a South Korean boy band. DBSK is not a political group, and the protesters were not typical political actors. But that online community, with around 800,000 active members, amplified the second step of Katz and Lazarsfeld's two-step process by allowing members to form political opinions through conversation.

Popular culture also heightens the conservative dilemma by providing cover for more political uses of social media. Tools specifically designed for dissident use are politically easy for the state to shut down, whereas tools in broad use become much harder to censor without risking politicizing the larger group of otherwise apolitical actors. Ethan Zuckerman of Harvard's Berkman Center for Internet and Society calls this "the cute cat theory of digital activism." Specific tools designed to defeat state censorship (such as proxy servers) can be shut down with little political penalty, but broader tools that the larger population uses to, say, share pictures of cute cats are harder to shut down.

For these reasons, it makes more sense to invest in social media as general, rather than specifically political, tools to promote self-governance. The norm of free speech is inherently political and far from universally shared. To the degree that the United States makes free speech a first-order goal, it should expect that goal to work relatively well in democratic countries that are allies, less well in undemocratic countries that are allies, and least of all in undemocratic countries that are not allies. But nearly every country in the world desires economic growth. Since governments jeopardize that growth when they ban technologies that can be used for both political and economic coordination, the United States should rely on countries' economic incentives to allow widespread media use. In other words, the U.S. government should work for conditions that increase the conservative dilemma, appealing to states' self-interest rather than the contentious virtue of freedom, as a way to create or strengthen countries' public spheres.

SOCIAL MEDIA SKEPTICISM

There are, broadly speaking, two arguments against the idea that social media will make a difference in national politics. The first is that the tools are themselves ineffective, and the second is that they produce as much harm to democratization as good, because repressive governments are becoming better at using these tools to suppress dissent.

The critique of ineffectiveness, most recently offered by Malcolm Gladwell 35 in *The New Yorker*, concentrates on examples of what has been termed "slacktivism," whereby casual participants seek social change through low-cost activities, such as joining Facebook's "Save Darfur" group, that are long on bumper-sticker sentiment and short on any useful action. The critique is correct but not central to the question of social media's power; the fact that barely committed actors cannot click their way to a better world does not mean that committed actors cannot use social media effectively. Recent protest movements—including a movement against fundamentalist vigilantes in India in 2009, the beef protests in South Korea in 2008, and protests against education laws in Chile in 2006—have used social media not as a replacement for real-world action but as a way to coordinate it. As a result, all of those protests exposed participants to the threat of violence, and in some cases its actual use. In fact, the adoption of these tools (especially cell phones) as a way to coordinate and document real-world action is so ubiquitous that it will probably be a part of all future political movements.

This obviously does not mean that every political movement that uses these tools will succeed, because the state has not lost the power to react. This points to the second, and much more serious, critique of social media as tools for political improvement—namely, that the state is gaining increasingly sophisticated means of monitoring, interdicting, or co-opting these tools. The use of social media, the scholars Rebecca MacKinnon of the New America Foundation and Evgeny Morozov of the Open Society Institute have argued, is just as likely to strengthen authoritarian regimes as it is to weaken them. The

Chinese government has spent considerable effort perfecting several systems for controlling political threats from social media. The least important of these is its censorship and surveillance program. Increasingly, the government recognizes that threats to its legitimacy are coming from inside the state and that blocking the Web site of *The New York Times* does little to prevent grieving mothers from airing their complaints about corruption.

The Chinese system has evolved from a relatively simple filter of incoming Internet traffic in the mid-1990s to a sophisticated operation that not only limits outside information but also uses arguments about nationalism and public morals to encourage operators of Chinese Web services to censor their users and users to censor themselves. Because its goal is to prevent information from having politically synchronizing effects, the state does not need to censor the Internet comprehensively; rather, it just needs to minimize access to information.

Authoritarian states are increasingly shutting down their communications grids to deny dissidents the ability to coordinate in real time and broadcast documentation of an event. This strategy also activates the conservative dilemma, creating a short-term risk of alerting the population at large to political conflict. When the government of Bahrain banned Google Earth after an annotated map of the royal family's annexation of public land began circulating, the effect was to alert far more Bahrainis to the offending map than knew about it originally. So widely did the news spread that the government relented and reopened access after four days.

Such shutdowns become more problematic for governments if they are long-lived. When antigovernment protesters occupied Bangkok in the summer of 2010, their physical presence disrupted Bangkok's shopping district, but the state's reaction, cutting off significant parts of the Thai telecommunications infrastructure, affected people far from the capital. The approach creates an additional dilemma for the state—there can be no modern economy without working phones—and so its ability to shut down communications over large areas or long periods is constrained.

In the most extreme cases, the use of social media tools is a matter of life 40 and death, as with the proposed death sentence for the blogger Hossein Derakhshan in Iran (since commuted to 19 and a half years in prison) or the suspicious hanging death of Oleg Bebenin, the founder of the Belarusian opposition Web site Charter 97. Indeed, the best practical reason to think that social media can help bring political change is that both dissidents and governments think they can. All over the world, activists believe in the utility of these tools and take steps to use them accordingly. And the governments they contend with think social media tools are powerful, too, and are willing to harass, arrest, exile, or kill users in response. One way the United States can heighten the conservative dilemma without running afoul of as many political complications is to demand the release of citizens imprisoned for using media in these ways. Anything that constrains the worst threats of violence by the state against citizens using these tools also increases the conservative dilemma.

LOOKING AT THE LONG RUN

To the degree that the United States pursues Internet freedom as a tool of state-craft, it should de-emphasize anti-censorship tools, particularly those aimed at specific regimes, and increase its support for local public speech and assembly more generally. Access to information is not unimportant, of course, but it is not the primary way social media constrain autocratic rulers or benefit citizens of a democracy. Direct, U.S. government–sponsored support for specific tools or campaigns targeted at specific regimes risk creating backlash that a more patient and global application of principles will not.

This entails reordering the State Department's Internet freedom goals. Securing the freedom of personal and social communication among a state's population should be the highest priority, closely followed by securing individual citizens' ability to speak in public. This reordering would reflect the reality that it is a strong civil society—one in which citizens have freedom of assembly—rather than access to Google or YouTube, that does the most to force governments to serve their citizens.

As a practical example of this, the United States should be at least as worried about Egypt's recent controls on the mandatory licensing of group-oriented text-messaging services as it is about Egypt's attempts to add new restrictions on press freedom. The freedom of assembly that such text-messaging services support is as central to American democratic ideals as is freedom of the press. Similarly, South Korea's requirement that citizens register with their real names for certain Internet services is an attempt to reduce their ability to surprise the state with the kind of coordinated action that took place during the 2008 protest in Seoul. If the United States does not complain as directly about this policy as it does about Chinese censorship, it risks compromising its ability to argue for Internet freedom as a global ideal.

More difficult, but also essential, will be for the U.S. government to articulate a policy of engagement with the private companies and organizations that host the networked public sphere. Services based in the United States, such as Facebook, Twitter, Wikipedia, and YouTube, and those based overseas, such as QQ (a Chinese instant-messaging service), WikiLeaks (a repository of leaked documents whose servers are in Sweden), Tuenti (a Spanish social network), and Naver (a Korean one), are among the sites used most for political speech, conversation, and coordination. And the world's wireless carriers transmit text messages, photos, and videos from cell phones through those sites. How much can these entities be expected to support freedom of speech and assembly for their users?

The issue here is analogous to the questions about freedom of speech in the United States in private but commercial environments, such as those regarding what kind of protests can be conducted in shopping malls. For good or ill, the platforms supporting the networked public sphere are privately held and run; Clinton committed the United States to working with those companies, but it is unlikely that without some legal framework, as exists for real-world speech and action, moral suasion will be enough to convince commercial actors to support freedom of speech and assembly.

It would be nice to have a flexible set of short-term digital tactics that could be used against different regimes at different times. But the requirements of real-world statecraft mean that what is desirable may not be likely. Activists in both repressive and democratic regimes will use the Internet and related tools to try to effect change in their countries, but Washington's ability to shape or target these changes is limited. Instead, Washington should adopt a more general approach, promoting freedom of speech, freedom of the press, and freedom of assembly everywhere. And it should understand that progress will be slow. Only by switching from an instrumental to an environmental view of the effects of social media on the public sphere will the United States be able to take advantage of the long-term benefits these tools promise—even though that may mean accepting short-term disappointment.

FOR ANALYSIS

1. What is Internet freedom? Is there more than one kind?

2. What does Shirky mean by "instrumental"? Why is it a significant concept in this essay?

3. What is the public sphere and why does Shirky think it is so important?

MAKING ARGUMENTS

How would you describe Shirky's writing in paragraph 7 in the context of his larger argument? Is he pressing his claim? Exploring the issues? Refuting counterclaims? Do you find it effective?

WRITING TOPIC

Shirky writes, "One complaint about the idea of new media as a political force is that most people simply use these tools for commerce, social life, or self-distraction, but this is common to all forms of media. Far more people in the 1500s were reading erotic novels than Martin Luther's 'Ninety-five Theses,' and far more people before the American Revolution were reading *Poor Richard's Almanack* than the work of the Committees of Correspondence. But those political works still had an enormous political effect" (para. 14). Think about one or more other inventions, media, ideas—other "tools"—that have had different uses of varying significance. Do people think of them in terms of one use or the other? Are they overlooked because of their less significant use?

MAKING CONNECTIONS

1. Compare Gladwell's and Shirky's essays: what they argue and how. Compare **tone**, nuance, use of evidence, and use of rhetoric. Do you find one more convincing than the other? How much of that relies on your feelings about the issues and how much on the differences in the way the authors make their arguments about the issues?

2. Compare McKibben's and Solnit's essays. How do their views of what revolution is differ? Whose view do you find more accurate or useful? Can both be right, and important?

3. For all of the writers in this cluster, what drives change?

FURTHER QUESTIONS FOR THINKING AND WRITING

1. What support do the works in this section offer for Emily Dickinson's assertion that "Much Madness is divinest Sense"? **Writing Topic:** The central characters in Herman Melville's "Bartleby, the Scrivener" and Harlan Ellison's "'Repent, Harlequin!' Said the Ticktockman" are viewed by society as mad. How might it be argued that they exhibit "divinest sense"?

2. In a number of these works, a single individual rebels against society and suffers defeat or death. Are these works therefore pessimistic and despairing? If not, what is the purpose of the rebellions, and why do the authors choose to bring their characters to such ends? **Writing Topic:** Compare two works from this section that offer support for the idea that a single individual can have a decisive effect on society.

3. Examine some of the representatives of established order—the lawyer in "Bartleby, the Scrivener," the Ticktockman—and discuss what attitudes they share and how effectively they function as spokespeople for law and order. **Writing Topic:** Compare and evaluate the kinds of order that each represents.

4. William Butler Yeats's "Easter 1916" and Carolyn Forché's "The Colonel" are poems about political struggle against oppressive rulers. In what ways are the poems similar? In what ways are they different? **Writing Topic:** Select the poem that makes the most powerful and effective case on behalf of the oppressed, and write an argument defending your choice.

5. Most of us live out our lives in the ordinary and humdrum world that is rejected in poems such as William Wordsworth's "The World Is Too Much with Us" and W. H. Auden's "The Unknown Citizen." Can these poems be said to be calls to social irresponsibility? **Writing Topic:** Consider whether "we" in Wordsworth's poem and the unknown citizen are simply objects of scorn or whether they deserve sympathy and perhaps even respect.

6. Characters in two of the works in this section—the Harlequin in "'Repent, Harlequin!' Said the Ticktockman" and Bartleby in "Bartleby, the Scrivener"—are rebels. What similarities do you find between these rebels? **Writing Topic:** Explain how the attitudes and actions of these characters constitute an attack on the status quo.

7. Many works in this section deal explicitly with the relationship between individuals and religion. What similarities do you find among them? What differences? **Writing Topic:** Compare and contrast the way that relationship is perceived in Shirley Jackson's "The Lottery" and Salman Rushdie's "Imagine There's No Heaven."

CULTURE AND
IDENTITY

This Is Harlem (detail), 1943, by Jacob Lawrence.

Historically, a group of people bound together by kinship and geography will form a society that exhibits a *culture*—common language, behavioral rules, traditions, skills, mores, religion, and art that define the civilization of that group. Literary works, including folklore and myth, are inseparable from the particular human society from which they emerge.

Until relatively recently, with the invention of trains, automobiles, and airplanes, travel over long distances was difficult. Instant communication—the telephone, the Internet—is an innovation of our time. Originally, information about other societies could be heard only as far away as a human could shout. Letters helped transmit ideas and cultural values over time and distance, but no more quickly than a horse could gallop or a ship could sail. For thousands of years cultures lived in relative isolation from each other, and hence they tended to develop distinctive traits and values. Within China, for instance, there are numerous well-defined cultures: the Uighurs of the northwest, the coastal Chinese of Shanghai, the Tibetan mountain people, the Szechuanese of the southwest. They eat different foods; they practice different religions; they speak different dialects.

Though technological advances have made the world seem smaller and, generally, have ended the geographical isolation of various cultures, these advances have not diminished the powerful cultural distinctions that mark societies all over the world. In fact, modern communication and transport have sometimes served to bring cultures into conflict. The works in this section, varied as they are, share a preoccupation with the connection between culture and identity. Some, such as George Orwell's "Shooting an Elephant," examine the devastating consequences of cultural imperialism. Others, such as Louise Erdrich's "Dear John Wayne," focus on the way dominant cultural stereotypes distort and undermine the sense of self.

The works in this section demonstrate how powerfully culture shapes identity. They reveal the tension generated by interacting cultures, and offer insight into the conflicts that usually emerge. But these works also provide an opportunity for us to step outside the bounds and bonds of our own culture and to experience just how complex, diverse, and interesting the human condition can be.

QUESTIONS FOR THINKING AND WRITING

As you read the selections in this section, consider the questions that follow. You may want to write out your thoughts informally—in a journal, if you are keeping one—as a way of preparing to respond to the selections. Or you may wish to make one of these questions the basis for a formal essay.

1. What cultural tradition(s) do you come from? Describe this tradition as fully as you can. Do you feel that you live in or out of the cultural mainstream? Explain.

2. Except for Native Americans, the people of the United States descended from or arrived as citizens of foreign cultures. Is there, nonetheless, an American culture? Explain. The United States was once called a *cultural melting pot*. Now it is sometimes called a *cultural mosaic*. Which **metaphor** strikes you as more apt? Explain.

3. Do economic considerations affect culture? Aside from their wealth, are the rich different from the poor? Explain. Does education strengthen or weaken traditional culture? Explain.

4. What are some of the positive and negative associations you have with the values of the cultural tradition(s) you come from? Is the preservation of these values a good thing or a bad thing? Explain.

FICTION

LU XUN   (1881–1936)

DIARY OF A MADMAN[1]   1918

*T*here was once a pair of male siblings whose actual names I beg your indulgence to withhold. Suffice it to say that we three were boon companions during our school years. Subsequently, circumstances contrived to rend us asunder so that we were gradually bereft of knowledge regarding each other's activities.

Not too long ago, however, I chanced to hear that one of them had been hard afflicted with a dread disease. I obtained this intelligence at a time when I happened to be returning to my native haunts and, hence, made so bold as to detour somewhat from my normal course in order to visit them. I encountered but one of the siblings. He apprised me that it had been his younger brother who had suffered the dire illness. By now, however, he had long since become sound and fit again; in fact he had already repaired to other parts to await a substantive official appointment.[2]

The elder brother apologized for having needlessly put me to the inconvenience of this visitation, and concluding his disquisition with a hearty smile, showed me two volumes of diaries which, he assured me, would reveal the nature of his brother's disorder during those fearful days.

As to the lapsus calami *that occur in the course of the diaries, I have altered not a word. Nonetheless, I have changed all the names, despite the fact that their publication would be of no great consequence since they are all humble villagers unknown to the world at large.*

Recorded this 2nd day in the 7th year of the Republic.[3]

5

[1] Translated by William A. Lyell.

[2] When there were too many officials for the number of offices to be filled, a man might well be appointed to an office that already had an incumbent. The new appointee would proceed to his post and wait until said office was vacated. Sometimes there would be a number of such appointees waiting their turns. [Translator's note.]

[3] April 2, 1918. This introduction is written in classical Chinese, while the diary entries that follow are all in the colloquial language. [Translator's note.]

1

Moonlight's really nice tonight. Haven't seen it in over thirty years. Seeing it today, I feel like a new man. I know now that I've been completely out of things for the last three decades or more. But I've still got to be *very* careful. Otherwise, how do you explain those dirty looks the Zhao family's dog gave me?

I've got good reason for my fears.

2

No moonlight at all tonight—something's not quite right. When I made my way out the front gate this morning—ever so carefully—there was something funny about the way the Venerable Old Zhao looked at me: seemed as though he was afraid of me and yet, at the same time, looked as though he had it in for me. There were seven or eight other people who had their heads together whispering about me. They were afraid I'd see them too! All up and down the the street people acted the same way. The meanest looking one of all spread his lips out wide and actually *smiled* at me! A shiver ran from the top of my head clear down to the tips of my toes, for I realized that meant they already had their henchmen well deployed, and were ready to strike.

But I wasn't going to let that intimidate *me*. I kept right on walking. There was a group of children up ahead and they were talking about me too. The expressions in their eyes were just like the Venerable Old Zhao's, and their faces were iron gray. I wondered what grudge the children had against me that they were acting this way too. I couldn't contain myself any longer and shouted, "Tell me, tell me!" But they just ran away.

Let's see now, what grudge can there be between me and the Venerable Old Zhao, or the people on the street for that matter? The only thing I can think of is that twenty years ago I trampled the account books kept by Mr. Antiquity, and he was hopping mad about it too. Though the Venerable Old Zhao doesn't know him, he must have gotten wind of it somehow. Probably decided to right the injustice I had done Mr. Antiquity by getting all those people on the street to gang up on me. But the children? Back then they hadn't even come into the world yet. Why should they have given me those funny looks today? Seemed as though they were afraid of me and yet, at the same time, looked as though they would like to do me some harm. That really frightens me. Bewilders me. Hurts me.

I have it! Their fathers and mothers have *taught* them to be like that!

3

I can never get to sleep at night. You really have to study something before you can understand it.

Take all those people: some have worn the cangue on the district magistrate's order, some have had their faces slapped by the gentry, some have had their wives ravished by *yamen* clerks,[4] some have had their dads and moms dunned to death by creditors; and yet, right at the time when all those terrible things were taking place, the expressions on their faces were never as frightened, or as savage, as the ones they wore yesterday.

Strangest of all was that woman on the street. She slapped her son and said: "Damn it all, you've got me so riled up I could take a good bite right out of your hide!" She was talking to him, but she was looking at me! I tried, but couldn't conceal a shudder of fright. That's when that ghastly crew of people, with their green faces and protruding fangs, began to roar with laughter. Old Fifth Chen ran up, took me firmly in tow, and dragged me away.

When we got back, the people at home all pretended not to know me. The expressions in their eyes were just like all the others too. After he got me into the study, Old Fifth Chen bolted the door from the outside—just the way you would pen up a chicken or a duck! That made figuring out what was at the bottom of it all harder than ever.

A few days back one of our tenant farmers came in from Wolf Cub Village to report a famine. Told my elder brother the villagers had all ganged up on a "bad" man and beaten him to death. Even gouged out his heart and liver. Fried them up and ate them to bolster their own courage! When I tried to horn in on the conversation, Elder Brother and the tenant farmer both gave me sinister looks. I realized for the first time today that the expression in their eyes was just the same as what I saw in those people on the street.

As I think of it now, a shiver's running from the top of my head clear down to the tips of my toes.

If they're capable of eating people, then who's to say they won't eat *me*?

Don't you see? That woman's words about "taking a good bite," and the laughter of that ghastly crew with their green faces and protruding fangs, and the words of our tenant farmer a few days back—it's perfectly clear to me now that all that talk and all that laughter were really a set of secret signals. Those words were poison! That laughter, a knife! Their teeth are bared and waiting—white and razor sharp! Those people are cannibals!

As I see it myself, though I'm not what you'd call an evil man, still, ever since I trampled the Antiquity family's account books, it's hard to say *what* they'll do. They seem to have something in mind, but I can't begin to guess what. What's more, as soon as they turn against someone, they'll *say* he's evil anyway. I can still remember how it was when Elder Brother was teaching me composition. No matter how good a man was, if I could find a few things wrong with him he would approvingly underline my words; on the other hand, if I made a few allowances for a bad man, he'd say I was "an extraordinary student, an absolute genius." When all is said and done, how can I possibly guess what people like *that* have in mind, especially when they're getting ready for a cannibals' feast?

[4] The cangue was a split board, hinged at one end and locked at the other; holes were cut out to accommodate the prisoner's neck and wrists. *Yamen* was the term for local government offices. The petty clerks who worked in them were notorious for relying on their proximity to power in order to bully and abuse the common people. [Translator's note.]

You have to *really* go into something before you can understand it. I seemed to remember, though not too clearly, that from ancient times on people have often been eaten, and so I started leafing through a history book to look it up. There were no dates in this history, but scrawled this way and that across every page were the words BENEVOLENCE, RIGHTEOUSNESS, and MORALITY. Since I couldn't get to sleep anyway, I read that history very carefully for most of the night, and finally I began to make out what was written *between* the lines; the whole volume was filled with a single phrase: EAT PEOPLE!

The words written in the history book, the things the tenant farmer said—all of it began to stare at me with hideous eyes, began to snarl and growl at me from behind bared teeth!

Why sure, *I'm* a person too, and they want to eat *me*!

4

In the morning I sat in the study for a while, calm and collected. Old Fifth Chen brought in some food—vegetables and a steamed fish. The fish's eyes were white and hard. Its mouth was wide open, just like the mouths of those people who wanted to eat human flesh. After I'd taken a few bites, the meat felt so smooth and slippery in my mouth that I couldn't tell whether it was fish or human flesh. I vomited.

"Old Fifth," I said, "tell Elder Brother that it's absolutely stifling in here and that I'd like to take a walk in the garden." He left without answering, but sure enough, after a while the door opened. I didn't even budge—just sat there waiting to see what they'd do to me. I *knew* that they wouldn't be willing to set me loose.

Just as I expected! Elder Brother came in with an old man in tow and walked slowly toward me. There was a savage glint in the old man's eyes. He was afraid I'd see it and kept his head tilted toward the floor while stealing sidewise glances at me over the temples of his glasses. "You seem to be fine today," said Elder Brother.

"You bet!" I replied.

"I've asked Dr. He to come and examine your pulse today."

"He's welcome!" I said. But don't think for one moment that I didn't know the old geezer was an executioner in disguise! Taking my pulse was nothing but a ruse; he wanted to feel my flesh and decide if I was fat enough to butcher yet. He'd probably even get a share of the meat for his troubles. I wasn't a *bit* afraid. Even though I don't eat human flesh, I still have a lot more courage than those who do. I thrust both hands out to see how the old buzzard would make his move.[5] Sitting down, he closed his eyes and felt my pulse for a good long while. Then he froze. Just sat there without moving a muscle for another good long while. Finally he opened his spooky eyes and said: "Don't let your thoughts run away with you. Just convalesce in peace and quiet for a few days and you'll be all right."

---

[5] In Chinese medicine the pulse is taken at both wrists. [Translator's note.]

Don't let my thoughts run away with me? Convalesce in peace and quiet? If 30
I convalesce till I'm good and fat, they get more to eat, but what do *I* get out of
it? How can I possibly be *all right*? What a bunch! All they think about is eating human flesh, and then they go sneaking around, thinking up every which
way they can to camouflage their real intentions. They were comical enough
to crack *anybody* up. I couldn't hold it in any longer and let out a good loud
laugh. Now *that* really felt good. I knew in my heart of hearts that my laughter was *packed* with courage and righteousness. And do you know what? They
were so completely subdued by it that the old man and my elder brother both
went pale!

But the more *courage* I had, the more that made them want to eat me so
that they could get a little of it for free. The old man walked out. Before he had
taken many steps, he lowered his head and told Elder Brother, "To be eaten as
soon as possible!" He nodded understandingly. So, Elder Brother, you're in it
too! Although that discovery seemed unforeseen, it really wasn't, either. My
own elder brother had thrown in with the very people who wanted to eat me!

My elder brother is a cannibal!

I'm brother to a cannibal.

Even though I'm to be the victim of cannibalism, I'm *brother* to a cannibal
all the same!

5

During the past few days I've taken a step back in my thinking. Supposing 35
that old man wasn't an executioner in disguise but really was a doctor—well,
he'd still be a cannibal just the same. In *Medicinal . . . something or other*
by Li Shizhen, the grandfather of the doctor's trade, it says quite clearly
that human flesh can be eaten, so how can that old man say that *he's* not a
cannibal too?[6]

And as for my own elder brother, I'm not being the least bit unfair to him.
When he was explaining the classics to me, he said with his very own tongue
that it was all right to *exchange children and eat them*. And then there was
another time when he happened to start in on an evil man and said that not
only should the man be killed, but his *flesh should he eaten* and *his skin used as
a sleeping mat* as well.[7]

[6] *Taxonomy of Medicinal Herbs,* a gigantic work, was the most important pharmacopoeia in traditional China. Li Shizhen lived from 1518 to 1593. [Translator's note.]

[7] Both italicized expressions are from the *Zuozhuan* (Zuo Commentary [to the *Spring and Autumn
Annals*]), a historical work which dates from the third century B.C. In 448 B.C., an officer who was
exhorting his own side not to surrender is recorded as having said, "When the army of Chu besieged
the capital of Song [in 603 B.C.], the people exchanged their children and ate them, and used the bones
for fuel; and still they would not submit to a covenant at the foot of their walls. For us who have sustained no great loss, to do so is to cast our state away" (Legge 5.817). It is also recorded that in 551 B.C.
an officer boasting of his own prowess before his ruler, pointed to two men whom his ruler considered
brave and said, "As to those two, they are like beasts, whose flesh I will eat, and then sleep upon their
skins" (Legge 5.492). [Translator's note.]

When our tenant farmer came in from Wolf Cub Village a few days back and talked about eating a man's heart and liver, Elder Brother didn't seem to see anything out of the way in that either—just kept nodding his head. You can tell from that alone that his present way of thinking is every bit as malicious as it was when I was a child. If it's all right to exchange *children* and eat them, then *anyone* can be exchanged, anyone can be eaten. Back then I just took what he said as explanation of the classics and let it go at that, but now I realize that while he was explaining, the grease of human flesh was smeared all over his lips, and what's more, his mind was filled with plans for further cannibalism.

6

Pitch black out. Can't tell if it's day or night. The Zhao family's dog has started barking again.

Savage as a lion, timid as a rabbit, crafty as a fox . . .

7

I'm on to the way they operate. They'll never be willing to come straight out 40 and kill me. Besides, they wouldn't dare. They'd be afraid of all the bad luck it might bring down on them if they did. And so, they've gotten everyone into cahoots with them and have set traps all over the place so that I'll do *myself* in. When I think back on the looks of those men and women on the streets a few days ago, coupled with the things my elder brother's been up to recently, I can figure out eight or nine tenths of it. From their point of view, the best thing of all would be for me to take off my belt, fasten it around a beam, and hang myself. They wouldn't be guilty of murder, and yet they'd still get everything they're after. Why, they'd be so beside themselves with joy, they'd sob with laughter. Or if they couldn't get me to do that, maybe they could torment me until I died of fright and worry. Even though I'd come out a bit leaner that way, they'd still nod their heads in approval.

Their kind only know how to eat dead meat. I remember reading in a book somewhere about something called the *hai-yi-na*. Its general appearance is said to be hideous, and the expression in its eyes particularly ugly and malicious. Often eats carrion, too. Even chews the bones to a pulp and swallows them down. Just thinking about it's enough to frighten a man.

The *hai-yi-na* is kin to the wolf.[8] The wolf's a relative of the dog, and just a few days ago the Zhao family dog gave me a funny look. It's easy to see that he's in on it too. How did that old man expect to fool *me* by staring at the floor?

My elder brother's the most pathetic of the whole lot. Since he's a human being too, how can he manage to be so totally without qualms, and what's more, even gang up with them to eat me? Could it be that he's been used to

[8] Three Chinese characters are used here for phonetic value only—that is, *hai yi na* is a transliteration into Chinese of the English word "hyena." [Translator's note.]

this sort of thing all along and sees nothing wrong with it? Or could it be that he's lost all conscience and just goes ahead and does it even though he knows it's wrong?

If I'm going to curse cannibals, I'll have to start with him. And if I'm going to *convert* cannibals, I'll have to start with him too.

8

Actually, by now even they should long since have understood the truth of this . . . 45

Someone came in. Couldn't have been more than twenty or so. I wasn't able to make out what he looked like too clearly, but he was all smiles. He nodded at me. His smile didn't look like the real thing either. And so I asked him, "Is this business of eating people right?"

He just kept right on smiling and said, "Except perhaps in a famine year, how could anyone get eaten?" I knew right off that he was one of them—one of those monsters who devour people!

At that point my own courage increased a hundredfold and I asked him, "Is it right?"

"Why are you talking about this kind of thing anyway? You really know how to . . . uh . . . how to pull a fellow's leg. Nice weather we're having."

"The weather *is* nice. There's a nice moon out, too, but I *still* want to know if it's right." 50

He seemed quite put out with me and began to mumble, "It's not—"

"Not right? Then how come they're still eating people?"

"No one's eating anyone."

"No one's *eating* anyone? They're eating people in Wolf Cub Village this very minute. And it's written in all the books, too, written in bright red blood!"

His expression changed and his face went gray like a slab of iron. His eyes 55 started out from their sockets as he said, "Maybe they are, but it's always been that way, it's—"

"Just because it's always been that way, does that make it *right*?"

"I'm not going to discuss such things with you. If you insist on talking about that, then *you're* the one who's in the wrong!"

I leaped from my chair, opened my eyes, and looked around—but the fellow was nowhere to be seen. He was far younger than my elder brother, and yet he was actually one of them. It must be because his mom and dad taught him to be that way. And he's probably already passed it on to his own son. No wonder that even the children give me murderous looks.

9

They want to eat others and at the same time they're afraid that other people are going to eat them. That's why they're always watching each other with such suspicious looks in their eyes.

But all they'd have to do is give up that way of thinking, and then they could 60
travel about, work, eat, and sleep in perfect security. Think how happy they'd
feel! It's only a threshold, a pass. But what do they do instead? What is it that
these fathers, sons, brothers, husbands, wives, friends, teachers, students, enemies, and even people who don't know each other *really* do? Why they all join
together to hold each other back, and talk each other out of it!

That's it! They'd rather *die* than take that one little step.

10

I went to see Elder Brother bright and early. He was standing in the courtyard looking at the sky. I went up behind him so as to cut him off from the
door back into the house. In the calmest and friendliest of tones, I said, "Elder
Brother, there's something I'd like to tell you."

"Go right ahead." He immediately turned and nodded his head.

"It's only a few words, really, but it's hard to get them out. Elder Brother, way
back in the beginning, it's probably the case that primitive peoples *all* ate some
human flesh. But later on, because their ways of thinking changed, some gave up
the practice and tried their level best to improve themselves; they kept on changing until they became human beings, *real* human beings. But the others didn't;
they just kept right on with their cannibalism and stayed at that primitive level.

"You have the same sort of thing with evolution in the animal world. Some 65
reptiles, for instance, changed into fish, and then they evolved into birds, then
into apes, and then into human beings.[9] But the others didn't want to improve
themselves and just kept right on being reptiles down to this very day.

"Think how ashamed those primitive men who have remained cannibals
must feel when they stand before *real* human beings. They must feel even
more ashamed than reptiles do when confronted with their brethren who have
evolved into apes.

"There's an old story from ancient times about Yi Ya boiling his son and
serving him up to Jie Zhou. But if the truth be known, people have *always*
practiced cannibalism, all the way from the time when Pan Gu separated
heaven and earth down to Yi Ya's son, down to Xu Xilin, and on down to the
man they killed in Wolf Cub Village.[10] And just last year when they executed

[9] Darwin's theory of evolution was immensely important to Chinese intellectuals during Lu Xun's
lifetime and the common coin of much discourse. [Translator's note.]

[10] An early philosophical text, *Guan Zi*, reports that the famous cook, Yi Ya, boiled his son and
served him to his ruler, Duke Huan of Qi (685–643 B.C.), because the meat of a human infant was
one of the few delicacies the duke had never tasted. Jie and Zhou were the last evil rulers of the Shang
(1776–1122 B.C.) and Zhou (1122–221 B.C.) dynasties. The madman has mixed up some facts here.

Pan Gu (literally, Coiled-up Antiquity) was born out of an egg. As he stood up he separated heaven
and earth. The world, as we know it, was formed from his body.

Xu Xilin (1873–1907) was from Lu Xun's hometown, Shaoxing. After studies in Japan he returned
to China and served as head of the Anhui Police Academy. When a high Qing official, En Ming, participated in a graduation ceremony at the academy, Xu assassinated him, hoping that this spark would
touch off the revolution. After the assassination, he and some of his students at the academy occupied
the police armory and managed, for a while, to hold off En Ming's troops. When Xu was finally captured, En Ming's personal bodyguards dug out his heart and liver and ate them. [Translator's note.]

a criminal in town, there was even someone with T.B. who dunked a steamed bread roll in his blood and then licked it off.[11]

"When they decided to eat me, by yourself, of course, you couldn't do much to prevent it, but why did you have to go and *join* them? Cannibals are capable of anything! If they're capable of eating me, then they're capable of eating *you* too! Even within their own group, they think nothing of devouring each other. And yet all they'd have to do is turn back—*change*—and then everything would be fine. Even though people may say, 'It's always been like this,' we can still do our best to improve. And we can start today!

"You're going to tell me it can't be done! Elder Brother, I think you're very likely to say that. When that tenant wanted to reduce his rent the day before yesterday, wasn't it you who said it couldn't be done?"

At first he just stood there with a cold smile, but then his eyes took on a 70 murderous gleam. (I had exposed their innermost secrets.) His whole face had gone pale. Some people were standing outside the front gate. The Venerable Old Zhao and his dog were among them. Stealthily peering this way and that, they began to crowd through the open gate. Some I couldn't make out too well—their faces seemed covered with cloth. Some looked the same as ever—smiling green faces with protruding fangs. I could tell at a glance that they all belonged to the same gang, that they were all cannibals. But at the same time I also realized that they didn't all think the same way. Some thought *it's always been like this* and that they really should eat human flesh. Others knew they shouldn't but went right on doing it anyway, always on the lookout for fear someone might give them away. And since that's exactly what I had just done, I knew they must be furious. But they were all *smiling* at me—cold little smiles!

At this point Elder Brother suddenly took on an ugly look and barked, "Get out of here! All of you! What's so funny about a madman?"

Now I'm on to *another* of their tricks: not only are they unwilling to change, but they're already setting me up for their next cannibalistic feast by labeling me a "madman." That way, they'll be able to eat me without getting into the slightest trouble. Some people will even be grateful to them. Wasn't that the very trick used in the case that the tenant reported? Everybody ganged up on a "bad" man and ate him. It's the same old thing.

Old Fifth Chen came in and made straight for me, looking mad as could be. But he wasn't going to shut *me* up! I was going to tell that bunch of cannibals off, and no two ways about it!

"You can change! You can change from the bottom of your hearts! You ought to know that in the future they're not going to allow cannibalism in the world anymore. If you don't change, you're going to devour each other anyway. And even if a lot of you *are* left, a real human being's going to come along and eradicate the lot of you, just like a hunter getting rid of wolves—or reptiles!"

---

[11] A similar incident is the basis for Lu Xun's story "Medicine." Human blood was believed to be a cure for tuberculosis. [Translator's note.]

Old Fifth Chen chased them all out. I don't know where Elder Brother dis- 75
appeared to. Old Fifth talked me into going back to my room.

It was pitch black inside. The beams and rafters started trembling overhead.
They shook for a bit, and then they started getting bigger and bigger. They
piled themselves up into a great heap on top of my body!

The weight was incredibly heavy and I couldn't even budge—they were
trying to kill me! But I knew their weight was an illusion, and I struggled out
from under them, my body bathed in sweat. I was still going to have my say.
"Change this minute! Change from the bottom of your hearts! You ought
to know that in the future they're not going to allow cannibals in the world
anymore . . ."

11

The sun doesn't come out. The door doesn't open. It's two meals a day.

I picked up my chopsticks and that got me thinking about Elder Brother. I
realized that the reason for my younger sister's death lay entirely with him. I
can see her now—such a lovable and helpless little thing, only five at the time.
Mother couldn't stop crying, but *he* urged her to stop, probably because he'd
eaten sister's flesh himself and hearing mother cry over her like that shamed
him! But if he's still capable of feeling shame, then maybe . . .

Younger Sister was eaten by Elder Brother. I have no way of knowing 80
whether Mother knew about it or not.

I think she *did* know, but while she was crying she didn't say anything about
it. She probably thought it was all right, too. I can remember once when I was
four or five, I was sitting out in the courtyard taking in a cool breeze when
Elder Brother told me that when parents are ill, a son, in order to be counted
as a really good person, should slice off a piece of his own flesh, boil it, and let
them eat it.[12] At the time Mother didn't come out and say there was anything
wrong with that. But if it was all right to eat one piece, then there certainly
wouldn't be anything wrong with her eating the whole body. And yet when
I think back to the way she cried and cried that day, it's enough to break my
heart. It's all strange—very, very strange.

12

Can't think about it anymore. I just realized today that I too have muddled
around for a good many years in a place where they've been continually eating people for four thousand years. Younger Sister happened to die at just the
time when Elder Brother was in charge of the house. Who's to say he didn't slip
some of her meat into the food we ate?

Who's to say I didn't eat a few pieces of my younger sister's flesh without
knowing it? And now it's my turn . . .

---

[12] In traditional literature, stories about such gruesome acts of filial piety were not unusual.
[Translator's note.]

Although I wasn't aware of it in the beginning, now that I *know* I'm someone with four thousand years' experience of cannibalism behind me, how hard it is to look real human beings in the eye!

13

Maybe there are some children around who still haven't eaten human flesh. 85
  Save the children . . .

FOR ANALYSIS

1. How is this story framed? Why do you think the author chose to introduce the story in this way?

2. How would you describe the diarist's state of mind? Use words not found in the title. How does the author convey his state to us?

3. What might the cannibalism in this story be a **metaphor** for?

MAKING ARGUMENTS

Build an argument for reading this story as an **allegory**. What does it allegorize? How do you know? Build your argument on textual and historical evidence.

WRITING TOPICS

1. Like Swift's "A Modest Proposal" (p. 481), "Diary of a Madman" employs the figure of eating one's young. In what ways might one think that a society "eats" its young?

2. Lu Xun's creation of the diarist's voice is noteworthy in its effectiveness. Keep a log in which you track the subtle and not-so-subtle changes in that voice, noting not what the diarist sees but how he expresses it. Are there any observations you can make about the author's specific techniques? Any generalizations about his method?

MAKING CONNECTIONS

1. Read "Diary of a Madman" with Charlotte Perkins Gilman's "The Yellow Wallpaper" (p. 548). How are they similar? How do they differ? What do those differences mean for the way each story reads and for any greater significance you might find in them?

2. What connections can you draw between this story and Ha Jin's "The Bridegroom" (p. 630)? How might each be read as a commentary on its author's native culture?

CHARLOTTE PERKINS GILMAN (1860–1935)

THE YELLOW WALLPAPER   1892

It is very seldom that mere ordinary people like John and myself secure ancestral halls for the summer.

A colonial mansion, a hereditary estate, I would say a haunted house and reach the height of romantic felicity—but that would be asking too much of fate!

Still I will proudly declare that there is something queer about it.

Else, why should it be let so cheaply? And why have stood so long untenanted?

John laughs at me, of course, but one expects that.   5

John is practical in the extreme. He has no patience with faith, an intense horror of superstition, and he scoffs openly at any talk of things not to be felt and seen and put down in figures.

John is a physician, and *perhaps*—(I would not say it to a living soul, of course, but this is dead paper and a great relief to my mind)—*perhaps* that is one reason I do not get well faster.

You see, he does not believe I am sick! And what can one do?

If a physician of high standing, and one's own husband, assures friends and relatives that there is really nothing the matter with one but temporary nervous depression—a slight hysterical tendency—what is one to do?

My brother is also a physician, and also of high standing, and he says the   10
same thing.

So I take phosphates or phosphites—whichever it is, and tonics, and air and exercise, and journeys, and am absolutely forbidden to "work" until I am well again.

Personally, I disagree with their ideas.

Personally, I believe that congenial work, with excitement and change, would do me good.

But what is one to do?

I did write for a while in spite of them; but it *does* exhaust me a good deal—   15
having to be so sly about it, or else meet with heavy opposition.

I sometimes fancy that in my condition if I had less opposition and more society and stimulus—but John says the very worst thing I can do is to think about my condition, and I confess it always makes me feel bad.

So I will let it alone and talk about the house.

The most beautiful place! It is quite alone, standing well back from the road, quite three miles from the village. It makes me think of English places that you read about, for there are hedges and walls and gates that lock, and lots of separate little houses for the gardeners and people.

There is a *delicious* garden! I never saw such a garden—large and shady, full of box-bordered paths, and lined with long grape-covered arbors with seats under them.

There were greenhouses, too, but they are all broken now. 20

There was some legal trouble, I believe, something about the heirs and co-heirs; anyhow, the place has been empty for years.

That spoils my ghostliness, I am afraid, but I don't care—there is something strange about the house—I can feel it.

I even said so to John one moonlight evening, but he said what I felt was a draught, and shut the window.

I get unreasonably angry with John sometimes. I'm sure I never used to be so sensitive. I think it is due to this nervous condition.

But John says if I feel so I shall neglect proper self-control; so I take pains to 25 control myself—before him, at least, and that makes me very tired.

I don't like our room a bit. I wanted one downstairs that opened onto the piazza and had roses all over the window, and such pretty old-fashioned chintz hangings! But John would not hear of it.

He said there was only one window and not room for two beds, and no near room for him if he took another.

He is very careful and loving, and hardly lets me stir without special direction.

I have a schedule prescription for each hour in the day; he takes all care from me, and so I feel basely ungrateful not to value it more.

He said we came here solely on my account, that I was to have perfect rest 30 and all the air I could get. "Your exercise depends on your strength, my dear," said he, "and your food somewhat on your appetite; but air you can absorb all the time." So we took the nursery at the top of the house.

It is a big, airy room, the whole floor nearly, with windows that look all ways, and air and sunshine galore. It was a nursery first, and then playroom and gymnasium, I should judge, for the windows are barred for little children, and there are rings and things in the walls.

The paint and paper look as if a boys' school had used it. It is stripped off— the paper—in great patches all around the head of my bed, about as far as I can reach, and in a great place on the other side of the room low down. I never saw a worse paper in my life. One of those sprawling, flamboyant patterns committing every artistic sin.

It is dull enough to confuse the eye in following, pronounced enough constantly to irritate and provoke study, and when you follow the lame uncertain curves for a little distance they suddenly commit suicide—plunge off at outrageous angles, destroy themselves in unheard-of contradictions.

The color is repellent, almost revolting; a smouldering unclean yellow, strangely faded by the slow-turning sunlight. It is a dull yet lurid orange in some places, a sickly sulphur tint in others.

No wonder the children hated it! I should hate it myself if I had to live in this 35 room long.

There comes John, and I must put this away—he hates to have me write a word.

We have been here two weeks, and I haven't felt like writing before, since that first day.

I am sitting by the window now, up in this atrocious nursery, and there is nothing to hinder my writing as much as I please, save lack of strength.

John is away all day, and even some nights when his cases are serious.

I'm glad my case is not serious!   40

But these nervous troubles are dreadfully depressing.

John does not know how much I really suffer. He knows there is no reason to suffer, and that satisfies him.

Of course it is only nervousness. It does weigh on me so not to do my duty in any way!

I meant to be such a help to John, such a real rest and comfort, and here I am a comparative burden already!

Nobody would believe what an effort it is to do what little I am able—to   45 dress and entertain, and order things.

It is fortunate Mary is so good with the baby. Such a dear baby!

And yet I *cannot* be with him, it makes me so nervous.

I suppose John never was nervous in his life. He laughs at me so about this wallpaper!

At first he meant to repaper the room, but afterward he said that I was letting it get the better of me, and that nothing was worse for a nervous patient than to give way to such fancies.

He said that after the wallpaper was changed it would be the heavy bedstead,   50 and then the barred windows, and then that gate at the head of the stairs, and so on.

"You know the place is doing you good," he said, "and really, dear, I don't care to renovate the house just for a three months' rental."

"Then do let us go downstairs," I said. "There are such pretty rooms there."

Then he took me in his arms and called me a blessed little goose, and said he would go down to the cellar, if I wished, and have it whitewashed into the bargain.

But he is right enough about the beds and windows and things.

It is as airy and comfortable a room as anyone need wish, and, of course,   55 I would not be so silly as to make him uncomfortable just for a whim.

I'm really getting quite fond of the big room, all but that horrid paper.

Out of one window I can see the garden—those mysterious deep-shaded arbors, the riotous old-fashioned flowers, and bushes and gnarly trees.

Out of another I get a lovely view of the bay and a little private wharf belonging to the estate. There is a beautiful shaded lane that runs down there from the house. I always fancy I see people walking in these numerous paths and arbors, but John has cautioned me not to give way to fancy in the least. He says that with my imaginative power and habit of story-making, a nervous weakness like mine is sure to lead to all manner of excited fancies, and that I ought to use my will and good sense to check the tendency. So I try.

I think sometimes that if I were only well enough to write a little it would relieve the press of ideas and rest me.

But I find I get pretty tired when I try. 60

It is so discouraging not to have any advice and companionship about my work. When I get really well, John says we will ask Cousin Henry and Julia down for a long visit; but he says he would as soon put fireworks in my pillow-case as to let me have those stimulating people about now.

I wish I could get well faster.

But I must not think about that. This paper looks to me as if it *knew* what a vicious influence it had!

There is a recurrent spot where the pattern lolls like a broken neck and two bulbous eyes stare at you upside down.

I get positively angry with the impertinence of it and the everlastingness. 65 Up and down and sideways they crawl, and those absurd, unblinking eyes are everywhere. There is one place where two breadths didn't match, and the eyes go all up and down the line, one a little higher than the other.

I never saw so much expression in an inanimate thing before, and we all know how much expression they have! I used to lie awake as a child and get more entertainment and terror out of blank walls and plain furniture than most children could find in a toy-store.

I remember what a kindly wink the knobs of our big old bureau used to have, and there was one chair that always seemed like a strong friend.

I used to feel that if any of the other things looked too fierce I could always hop into that chair and be safe.

The furniture in this room is no worse than inharmonious, however, for we had to bring it all from downstairs. I suppose when this was used as a play-room they had to take the nursery things out, and no wonder! I never saw such ravages as the children have made here.

The wallpaper, as I said before, is torn off in spots, and it sticketh closer than 70 a brother—they must have had perseverance as well as hatred.

Then the floor is scratched and gouged and splintered, the plaster itself is dug out here and there, and this great heavy bed, which is all we found in the room, looks as if it had been through the wars.

But I don't mind it a bit—only the paper.

There comes John's sister. Such a dear girl as she is, and so careful of me! I must not let her find me writing.

She is a perfect and enthusiastic housekeeper, and hopes for no better profession. I verily believe she thinks it is the writing which made me sick!

But I can write when she is out, and see her a long way off from these 75 windows.

There is one that commands the road, a lovely shaded winding road, and one that just looks off over the country. A lovely country, too, full of great elms and velvet meadows.

This wallpaper has a kind of sub-pattern in a different shade, a particularly irritating one, for you can only see it in certain lights, and not clearly then.

But in the places where it isn't faded and where the sun is just so—I can see a strange, provoking, formless sort of figure that seems to skulk about behind that silly and conspicuous front design.

There's sister on the stairs!

Well, the Fourth of July is over! The people are all gone and I am tired out. 80 John thought it might do me good to see a little company, so we just had Mother and Nellie and the children down for a week.

Of course I didn't do a thing. Jennie sees to everything now.

But it tired me all the same.

John says if I don't pick up faster he shall send me to Weir Mitchell in the fall.

But I don't want to go there at all. I had a friend who was in his hands once, and she says he is just like John and my brother, only more so!

Besides, it is such an undertaking to go so far. 85

I don't feel as if it was worthwhile to turn my hand over for anything, and I'm getting dreadfully fretful and querulous.

I cry at nothing, and cry most of the time.

Of course I don't when John is here, or anybody else, but when I am alone.

And I am alone a good deal just now. John is kept in town very often by serious cases, and Jennie is good and lets me alone when I want her to.

So I walk a little in the garden or down that lovely lane, sit on the porch 90 under the roses, and lie down up here a good deal.

I'm getting really fond of the room in spite of the wallpaper. Perhaps *because* of the wallpaper.

It dwells in my mind so!

I lie here on this great immovable bed—it is nailed down, I believe—and follow that pattern about by the hour. It is as good as gymnastics, I assure you. I start, we'll say, at the bottom, down in the corner over there where it has not been touched, and I determine for the thousandth time that I *will* follow that pointless pattern to some sort of a conclusion.

I know a little of the principle of design, and I know this thing was not arranged on any laws of radiation, or alternation, or repetition, or symmetry, or anything else that I ever heard of.

It is repeated, of course, by the breadths, but not otherwise. 95

Looked at in one way, each breadth stands alone; the bloated curves and flourishes—a kind of "debased Romanesque" with delirium tremens—go waddling up and down in isolated columns of fatuity.

But, on the other hand, they connect diagonally, and the sprawling outlines run off in great slanting waves of optic horror, like a lot of wallowing seaweeds in full chase.

The whole thing goes horizontally, too, at least it seems so, and I exhaust myself in trying to distinguish the order of its going in that direction.

They have used a horizontal breadth for a frieze, and that adds wonderfully to the confusion.

There is one end of the room where it is almost intact, and there, when the 100
crosslights fade and the low sun shines directly upon it, I can almost fancy
radiation after all,—the interminable grotesque seems to form around a common center and rush off in headlong plunges of equal distraction.

It makes me tired to follow it. I will take a nap, I guess.

I don't know why I should write this.

I don't want to.

I don't feel able.

And I know John would think it absurd. But I *must* say what I feel and think 105
in some way—it is such a relief!

But the effort is getting to be greater than the relief.

Half the time now I am awfully lazy, and lie down ever so much. John says
I musn't lose my strength, and has me take cod liver oil and lots of tonics and
things, to say nothing of ale and wine and rare meat.

Dear John! He loves me very dearly, and hates to have me sick. I tried to
have a real earnest reasonable talk with him the other day, and tell him how
I wish he would let me go and make a visit to Cousin Henry and Julia.

But he said I wasn't able to go, nor able to stand it after I got there; and I did
not make out a very good case for myself, for I was crying before I had finished.

It is getting to be a great effort for me to think straight. Just this nervous 110
weakness, I suppose.

And dear John gathered me up in his arms, and just carried me upstairs and
laid me on the bed, and sat by me and read to me till it tired my head.

He said I was his darling and his comfort and all he had, and that I must take
care of myself for his sake, and keep well.

He says no one but myself can help me out of it, that I must use my will and
self-control and not let any silly fancies run away with me.

There's one comfort—the baby is well and happy, and does not have to
occupy this nursery with the horrid wallpaper.

If we had not used it, that blessed child would have! What a fortunate escape! 115
Why, I wouldn't have a child of mine, an impressionable little thing, live in
such a room for worlds.

I never thought of it before, but it is lucky that John kept me here after all;
I can stand it so much easier than a baby, you see.

Of course I never mention it to them any more—I am too wise—but I keep
watch of it all the same.

There are things in that wallpaper that nobody knows but me, or ever will.

Behind that outside pattern the dim shapes get clearer every day.

It is always the same shape, only very numerous. 120

And it is like a woman stooping down and creeping about behind that pattern. I don't like it a bit. I wonder—I begin to think—I wish John would take
me away from here!

It is so hard to talk with John about my case, because he is so wise, and
because he loves me so.

But I tried it last night.

It was moonlight. The moon shines in all around just as the sun does.

I hate to see it sometimes, it creeps so slowly, and always comes in by one 125
window or another.

John was asleep and I hated to waken him, so I kept still and watched the
moonlight on that undulating wallpaper till I felt creepy.

The faint figure behind seemed to shake the pattern, just as if she wanted to
get out.

I got up softly and went to feel and see if the paper *did* move, and when
I came back John was awake.

"What is it, little girl?" he said. "Don't go walking about like that—you'll get
cold."

I thought it was a good time to talk, so I told him that I really was not gain- 130
ing here, and that I wished he would take me away.

"Why, darling!" said he, "Our lease will be up in three weeks, and I can't see
how to leave before.

"The repairs are not done at home, and I cannot possibly leave town just
now. Of course if you were in any danger, I could and would, but you really
are better, dear, whether you can see it or not. I am a doctor, dear, and I know.
You are gaining flesh and color, your appetite is better, I feel really much easier
about you."

"I don't weigh a bit more," said I, "nor as much; and my appetite may be better in the evening when you are here but it is worse in the morning when you
are away!"

"Bless her little heart!" said he with a big hug, "She shall be as sick as she
pleases! But now let's improve the shining hours by going to sleep, and talk
about it in the morning!"

"And you won't go away?" I asked gloomily. 135

"Why, how can I, dear? It is only three weeks more and then we will take a
nice little trip of a few days while Jennie is getting the house ready. Really, dear,
you are better!"

"Better in body perhaps—" I began, and stopped short, for he sat up straight
and looked at me with such a stern, reproachful look that I could not say
another word.

"My darling," said he, "I beg of you, for my sake and for our child's sake, as
well as for your own, that you will never for one instant let that idea enter your
mind! There is nothing so dangerous, so fascinating, to a temperament like
yours. It is a false and foolish fancy. Can you trust me as a physician when I tell
you so?"

So of course I said no more on that score, and we went to sleep before
long. He thought I was asleep first, but I wasn't, and lay there for hours trying to decide whether that front pattern and the back pattern really did move
together or separately.

On a pattern like this, by daylight, there is a lack of sequence, a defiance of 140
law, that is a constant irritant to a normal mind.

The color is hideous enough, and unreliable enough, and infuriating enough, but the pattern is torturing.

You think you have mastered it, but just as you get well under way in following, it turns a back-somersault and there you are. It slaps you in the face, knocks you down, and tramples upon you. It is like a bad dream.

The outside pattern is a florid arabesque, reminding one of a fungus. If you can imagine a toadstool in joints, an interminable string of toadstools, budding and sprouting in endless convolutions—why, that is something like it.

That is, sometimes!

There is one marked peculiarity about this paper, a thing nobody seems to 145 notice but myself, and that is that it changes as the light changes.

When the sun shoots in through the east window—I always watch for that first long, straight ray—it changes so quickly that I never can quite believe it.

That is why I watch it always.

By moonlight—the moon shines in all night when there is a moon—I wouldn't know it was the same paper.

At night in any kind of light, in twilight, candlelight, lamplight, and worst of all by moonlight, it becomes bars! The outside pattern, I mean, and the woman behind it is as plain as can be.

I didn't realize for a long time what the thing was that showed behind, that 150 dim sub-pattern, but now I am quite sure it is a woman.

By daylight she is subdued, quiet. I fancy it is the pattern that keeps her so still. It is so puzzling. It keeps me quiet by the hour.

I lie down ever so much now. John says it is good for me, and to sleep all I can.

Indeed he started the habit by making me lie down for an hour after each meal.

It is a very bad habit, I am convinced, for you see, I don't sleep.

And that cultivates deceit, for I don't tell them I'm awake—oh, no! 155

The fact is I am getting a little afraid of John.

He seems very queer sometimes, and even Jennie has an inexplicable look.

It strikes me occasionally, just as a scientific hypothesis, that perhaps it is the paper!

I have watched John when he did not know I was looking, and come into the room suddenly on the most innocent excuses, and I've caught him several times looking at the paper! And Jennie too. I caught Jennie with her hand on it once.

She didn't know I was in the room, and when I asked her in a quiet, a very 160 quiet voice, with the most restrained manner possible, what she was doing with the paper—she turned around as if she had been caught stealing, and looked quite angry—asked me why I should frighten her so!

Then she said that the paper stained everything it touched, that she had found yellow smooches on all my clothes and John's and she wished we would be more careful!

Did not that sound innocent? But I know she was studying that pattern, and I am determined that nobody shall find it out but myself!

Life is very much more exciting now than it used to be. You see, I have something more to expect, to look forward to, to watch. I really do eat better, and am more quiet than I was.

John is so pleased to see me improve! He laughed a little the other day, and said I seemed to be flourishing in spite of my wallpaper.

I turned it off with a laugh. I had no intention of telling him it was *because* of the wallpaper—he would make fun of me. He might even want to take me away. 165

I don't want to leave now until I have found it out. There is a week more, and I think that will be enough.

I'm feeling so much better!

I don't sleep much at night, for it is so interesting to watch developments; but I sleep a good deal in the daytime.

In the daytime it is tiresome and perplexing.

There are always new shoots on the fungus, and new shades of yellow all over it. I cannot keep count of them, though I have tried conscientiously. 170

It is the strangest yellow, that wallpaper! It makes me think of all the yellow things I ever saw—not beautiful ones like buttercups, but old, foul, bad yellow things.

But there is something else about that paper—the smell! I noticed it the moment we came into the room, but with so much air and sun it was not bad. Now we have had a week of fog and rain, and whether the windows are open or not, the smell is here.

It creeps all over the house.

I find it hovering in the dining-room, skulking in the parlor, hiding in the hall, lying in wait for me on the stairs.

It gets into my hair. 175

Even when I go to ride, if I turn my head suddenly and surprise it—there is that smell!

Such a peculiar odor, too! I have spent hours in trying to analyze it, to find what it smelled like.

It is not bad—at first—and very gentle, but quite the subtlest, most enduring odor I ever met.

In this damp weather it is awful. I wake up in the night and find it hanging over me.

It used to disturb me at first. I thought seriously of burning the house—to reach the smell. 180

But now I am used to it. The only thing I can think of that it is like is the *color* of the paper! A yellow smell.

There is a very funny mark on this wall, low down, near the mopboard. A streak that runs round the room. It goes behind every piece of furniture, except the bed, a long, straight, even *smooch*, as if it had been rubbed over and over.

I wonder how it was done and who did it, and what they did it for. Round and round and round—round and round and round—it makes me dizzy!

I really have discovered something at last.

Through watching so much at night, when it changes so, I have finally found out. 185

The front pattern *does* move—and no wonder! The woman behind shakes it!

Sometimes I think there are a great many women behind, and sometimes only one, and she crawls around fast, and her crawling shakes it all over.

Then in the very bright spots she keeps still, and in the very shady spots she just takes hold of the bars and shakes them hard.

And she is all the time trying to climb through. But nobody could climb through that pattern—it strangles so; I think that is why it has so many heads.

They get through, and then the pattern strangles them off and turns them 190 upside down and makes their eyes white!

If those heads were covered or taken off it would not be half so bad.

I think that woman gets out in the daytime!

And I'll tell you why—privately—I've seen her!

I can see her out of every one of my windows!

It is the same woman, I know, for she is always creeping, and most women 195 do not creep by daylight.

I see her in that long shaded lane, creeping up and down. I see her in those dark grape arbors, creeping all around the garden.

I see her on that long road under the trees, creeping along, and when a carriage comes she hides under the blackberry vines.

I don't blame her a bit. It must be very humiliating to be caught creeping by daylight!

I always lock the door when I creep by daylight. I can't do it at night, for I know John would suspect something at once.

And John is so queer now that I don't want to irritate him. I wish he would 200 take another room! Besides, I don't want anybody to get that woman out at night but myself.

I often wonder if I could see her out of all the windows at once.

But, turn as fast as I can, I can only see out of one at one time.

And though I always see her, she *may* be able to creep faster than I can turn! I have watched her sometimes away off in the open country, creeping as fast as a cloud shadow in a high wind.

If only that top pattern could be gotten off from the under one! I mean to try it, little by little.

I have found out another funny thing, but I shan't tell it this time! It does not 205 do to trust people too much.

There are only two more days to get this paper off, and I believe John is beginning to notice. I don't like the look in his eyes.

And I hear him ask Jennie a lot of professional questions about me. She had a very good report to give.

She said I slept a good deal in the daytime.

John knows I don't sleep very well at night, for all I'm so quiet!

He asked me all sorts of questions, too, and pretended to be very loving and 210 kind.

As if I couldn't see through him!

Still, I don't wonder he acts so, sleeping under this paper for three months.

It only interests me, but I feel sure John and Jennie are secretly affected by it.

Hurrah! This is the last day, but it is enough. John is to stay in town over night, and won't be out until this evening.

Jennie wanted to sleep with me—the sly thing; but I told her I should 215 undoubtedly rest better for a night all alone.

That was clever, for really I wasn't alone a bit! As soon as it was moonlight and that poor thing began to crawl and shake the pattern, I got up and ran to help her.

I pulled and she shook. I shook and she pulled, and before morning we had peeled off yards of that paper.

A strip about as high as my head and half around the room.

And then when the sun came and that awful pattern began to laugh at me, I declared I would finish it to-day!

We go away to-morrow, and they are moving all my furniture down again to 220 leave things as they were before.

Jennie looked at the wall in amazement, but I told her merrily that I did it out of pure spite at the vicious thing.

She laughed and said she wouldn't mind doing it herself, but I must not get tired.

How she betrayed herself that time!

But I am here, and no person touches this paper but Me—not *alive!*

She tried to get me out of the room—it was too patent! But I said it was so 225 quiet and empty and clean now that I believed I would lie down again and sleep all I could, and not to wake me even for dinner—I would call when I woke.

So now she is gone, and the servants are gone, and the things are gone, and there is nothing left but that great bedstead nailed down, with the canvas mattress we found on it.

We shall sleep downstairs to-night, and take the boat home to-morrow.

I quite enjoy the room, now it is bare again.

How those children did tear about here!

This bedstead is fairly gnawed! 230

But I must get to work.

I have locked the door and thrown the key down into the front path.

I don't want to go out, and I don't want to have anybody come in, till John comes.

I want to astonish him.

I've got a rope up here that even Jennie did not find. If that woman does get 235 out, and tries to get away, I can tie her!

But I forgot I could not reach far without anything to stand on!

This bed will *not* move!

I tried to lift and push it until I was lame, and then I got so angry I bit off a little piece at one corner—but it hurt my teeth.

Then I peeled off all the paper I could reach standing on the floor. It sticks horribly and the pattern just enjoys it! All those strangled heads and bulbous eyes and waddling fungus growths just shriek with derision!

I am getting angry enough to do something desperate. To jump out of the 240
window would be admirable exercise, but the bars are too strong even to try.

Besides I wouldn't do it. Of course not. I know well enough that a step like
that is improper and might be misconstrued.

I don't like to *look* out of the windows even—there are so many of those
creeping women, and they creep so fast.

I wonder if they all come out of that wallpaper as I did?

But I am securely fastened now by my well-hidden rope—you don't get *me*
out in the road there!

I suppose I shall have to get back behind the pattern when it comes night, 245
and that is hard!

It is so pleasant to be out in this great room and creep around as I please!

I don't want to go outside. I won't, even if Jennie asks me to.

For outside you have to creep on the ground, and everything is green instead
of yellow.

But here I can creep smoothly on the floor, and my shoulder just fits in that
long smooch around the wall, so I cannot lose my way.

Why, there's John at the door! 250

It is no use, young man, you can't open it!

How he does call and pound!

Now he's crying to Jennie for an axe.

It would be a shame to break down that beautiful door!

"John, dear!" said I in the gentlest voice, "The key is down by the front steps, 255
under a plantain leaf!"

That silenced him for a few moments.

Then he said—very quietly indeed, "Open the door, my darling!"

"I can't," said I. "The key is down by the front door under a plantain leaf!"
And then I said it again, several times, very gently and slowly, and said it so
often that he had to go and see, and he got it of course, and came in. He stopped
short by the door.

"What is the matter?" he cried. "For God's sake, what are you doing!"

I kept on creeping just the same, but I looked at him over my shoulder. 260

"I've got out at last," said I, "in spite of you and Jane. And I've pulled off most
of the paper, so you can't put me back!"

Now why should that man have fainted? But he did, and right across my
path by the wall, so that I had to creep over him every time!

FOR ANALYSIS

1. Why have the **narrator** and her husband, John, rented the mansion?

2. In the opening paragraphs, what **tone** does the narrator's description of the mansion establish?

3. Describe the **character** of John. Does the narrator's view of him change in the course of the story? Explain.

4. After telling us that her husband, John, is a physician, the narrator adds that "*perhaps
that is one reason I do not get well faster*" (para. 7). What does she mean by this comment?

5. How does the narrator's description of what she sees in the outside world reflect her inner state?

6. Who is Jennie? What is her function in the story?

7. The narrator both accepts her husband's control over her and disobeys him by secretly continuing to write. What effect does writing have on her? Is her husband correct in his judgment that writing will hinder her recovery?

8. What evidence does the story provide to explain the narrator's present state?

9. In what ways does the wallpaper embody the **theme** of the story?

MAKING ARGUMENTS

Can it be argued that, on some level, the **narrator** refuses to recover? Explain the logic of your argument and state the evidence you would use. What would it mean for the story that she refused to recover?

WRITING TOPICS

1. Analyze the way **irony** is used in this story.

2. Write an essay in which you imaginatively reconstruct the early life of the **narrator**, including her marriage, to explain her illness.

3. Write an essay describing the aptness of wallpaper as a **symbol** for the life of the narrator.

4. In a paragraph, explain why we never learn the narrator's name.

MAKING CONNECTIONS

1. Compare the marriage relationship in this story with the marriage in Ibsen's play *A Doll's House* (p. 213).

2. Compare and contrast the **narrator** in this story with Emily Grierson in William Faulkner's story "A Rose for Emily" (p. 623) as examples of women wounded by a patriarchal society.

3. Compare the wallpaper in this story with the birdcage in Susan Glaspell's play *Trifles* (p. 1073) as **symbols**. In what ways are they similar? In what ways different? Which do you find more effective? Explain.

4. Considered as a horror story, in what ways is Gilman's narrative similar to Edgar Allan Poe's "The Cask of Amontillado" (p. 1126)? In what ways is it different?

JAMES BALDWIN (1924–1987)

SONNY'S BLUES 1957

I read about it in the paper, in the subway, on my way to work. I read it, and I couldn't believe it, and I read it again. Then perhaps I just stared at it, at the newsprint spelling out his name, spelling out the story. I stared at it in the swinging lights of the subway car, and in the faces and bodies of the people, and in my own face, trapped in the darkness which roared outside.

It was not to be believed and I kept telling myself that, as I walked from the subway station to the high school. And at the same time I couldn't doubt it. I was scared, scared for Sonny. He became real to me again. A great block of ice got settled in my belly and kept melting there slowly all day long, while I taught my classes algebra. It was a special kind of ice. It kept melting, sending trickles of ice water all up and down my veins, but it never got less. Sometimes it hardened and seemed to expand until I felt my guts were going to come spilling out or that I was going to choke or scream. This would always be at a moment when I was remembering some specific thing Sonny had once said or done.

When he was about as old as the boys in my classes his face had been bright and open, there was a lot of copper in it; and he'd had wonderfully direct brown eyes, and great gentleness and privacy. I wondered what he looked like now. He had been picked up, the evening before, in a raid on an apartment downtown, for peddling and using heroin.

I couldn't believe it: but what I mean by that is that I couldn't find any room for it anywhere inside me. I had kept it outside me for a long time. I hadn't wanted to know. I had had suspicions, but I didn't name them, I kept putting them away. I told myself that Sonny was wild, but he wasn't crazy. And he'd always been a good boy, he hadn't ever turned hard or evil or disrespectful, the way kids can, so quick, so quick, especially in Harlem. I didn't want to believe that I'd ever see my brother going down, coming to nothing, all that light in his face gone out, in the condition I'd already seen so many others. Yet it had happened and here I was, talking about algebra to a lot of boys who might, every one of them for all I knew, be popping off needles every time they went to the head. Maybe it did more for them than algebra could.

I was sure that the first time Sonny had ever had horse,[1] he couldn't have been much older than these boys were now. These boys, now, were living as we'd been living then, they were growing up with a rush and their heads bumped abruptly against the low ceiling of their actual possibilities. They were filled with rage. All they really knew were two darknesses, the darkness

[1] Heroin.

of their lives, which was now closing in on them, and the darkness of the movies, which had blinded them to that other darkness, and in which they now, vindictively, dreamed, at once more together than they were at any other time, and more alone.

When the last bell rang, the last class ended, I let out my breath. It seemed I'd been holding it for all that time. My clothes were wet—I may have looked as though I'd been sitting in a steam bath, all dressed up, all afternoon. I sat alone in the classroom a long time. I listened to the boys outside, downstairs, shouting and cursing and laughing. Their laughter struck me for perhaps the first time. It was not the joyous laughter which—God knows why—one associates with children. It was mocking and insular, its intent to denigrate. It was disenchanted, and in this, also, lay the authority of their curses. Perhaps I was listening to them because I was thinking about my brother and in them I heard my brother. And myself.

One boy was whistling a tune, at once very complicated and very simple, it seemed to be pouring out of him as though he were a bird, and it sounded very cool and moving through all that harsh, bright air, only just holding its own through all those other sounds.

I stood up and walked over to the window and looked down into the courtyard. It was the beginning of the spring and the sap was rising in the boys. A teacher passed through them every now and again, quickly, as though he or she couldn't wait to get out of that courtyard, to get those boys out of their sight and off their minds. I started collecting my stuff. I thought I'd better get home and talk to Isabel.

The courtyard was almost deserted by the time I got downstairs. I saw this boy standing in the shadow of a doorway, looking just like Sonny. I almost called his name. Then I saw that it wasn't Sonny, but somebody we used to know, a boy from around our block. He'd been Sonny's friend. He'd never been mine, having been too young for me, and, anyway, I'd never liked him. And now, even though he was a grown-up man, he still hung around that block, still spent hours on the street corners, was always high and raggy. I used to run into him from time to time and he'd often work around to asking me for a quarter or fifty cents. He always had some real good excuse, too, and I always gave it to him. I don't know why.

But now, abruptly, I hated him. I couldn't stand the way he looked at me, 10 partly like a dog, partly like a cunning child. I wanted to ask him what the hell he was doing in the school courtyard.

He sort of shuffled over to me, and he said, "I see you got the papers. So you already know about it."

"You mean about Sonny? Yes, I already know about it. How come they didn't get you?"

He grinned. It made him repulsive and it also brought to mind what he'd looked like as a kid. "I wasn't there. I stay away from them people."

"Good for you." I offered him a cigarette and I watched him through the smoke. "You come all the way down here just to tell me about Sonny?"

"That's right." He was sort of shaking his head and his eyes looked strange, 15 as though they were about to cross. The bright sun deadened his damp dark brown skin and it made his eyes look yellow and showed up the dirt in his kinked hair. He smelled funky. I moved a little away from him and I said, "Well, thanks. But I already know about it and I got to get home."

"I'll walk you a little ways," he said. We started walking. There were a couple of kids still loitering in the courtyard and one of them said goodnight to me and looked strangely at the boy beside me.

"What're you going to do?" he asked me. "I mean, about Sonny?"

"Look. I haven't seen Sonny for over a year, I'm not sure I'm going to do anything. Anyway, what the hell *can* I do?"

"That's right," he said quickly, "ain't nothing you can do. Can't much help old Sonny no more, I guess."

It was what I was thinking and so it seemed to me he had no right to say it. 20

"I'm surprised at Sonny, though," he went on—he had a funny way of talking, he looked straight ahead as though he were talking to himself—"I thought Sonny was a smart boy, I thought he was too smart to get hung."

"I guess he thought so too," I said sharply, "and that's how he got hung. And how about you? You're pretty goddamn smart, I bet."

Then he looked directly at me, just for a minute. "I ain't smart," he said. "If I was smart, I'd have reached for a pistol a long time ago."

"Look. Don't tell *me* your sad story, if it was up to me, I'd give you one." Then I felt guilty—guilty, probably, for never having supposed that the poor bastard *had* a story of his own, much less a sad one, and I asked, quickly, "What's going to happen to him now?"

He didn't answer this. He was off by himself some place. 25

"Funny thing," he said, and from his tone we might have been discussing the quickest way to get to Brooklyn, "when I saw the papers this morning, the first thing I asked myself was if I had anything to do with it. I felt sort of responsible."

I began to listen more carefully. The subway station was on the corner, just before us, and I stopped. He stopped, too. We were in front of a bar and he ducked slightly, peering in, but whoever he was looking for didn't seem to be there. The juke box was blasting away with something black and bouncy and I half watched the barmaid as she danced her way from the juke box to her place behind the bar. And I watched her face as she laughingly responded to something someone said to her, still keeping time to the music. When she smiled one saw the little girl, one sensed the doomed, still-struggling woman beneath the battered face of the semi-whore.

"I never *give* Sonny nothing," the boy said finally, "but a long time ago I come to school high and Sonny asked me how it felt." He paused, I couldn't bear to watch him, I watched the barmaid, and I listened to the music which seemed to be causing the pavement to shake. "I told him it felt great." The music stopped, the barmaid paused and watched the juke box until the music began again. "It did."

All this was carrying me some place I didn't want to go. I certainly didn't want to know how it felt. It filled everything, the people, the houses, the music, the dark, quicksilver barmaid, with menace; and this menace was their reality.

"What's going to happen to him now?" I asked again.   30

"They'll send him away some place and they'll try to cure him." He shook his head. "Maybe he'll even think he's kicked the habit. Then they'll let him loose"—he gestured, throwing his cigarette into the gutter. "That's all."

"What do you mean, that's *all*?"

But I knew what he meant.

"I *mean*, that's all." He turned his head and looked at me, pulling down the corners of his mouth. "Don't you know what I mean?" he asked, softly.

"How the hell *would* I know what you mean?" I almost whispered it, I don't   35 know why.

"That's right," he said to the air, "how would *he* know what I mean?" He turned toward me again, patient and calm, and yet I somehow felt him shaking, shaking as though he were going to fall apart. I felt that ice in my guts again, the dread I'd felt all afternoon; and again I watched the barmaid, moving about the bar, washing glasses, and singing. "Listen. They'll let him out and then it'll just start all over again. That's what I mean."

"You mean—they'll let him out. And then he'll just start working his way back in again. You mean he'll never kick the habit. Is that what you mean?"

"That's right," he said, cheerfully. "*You* see what I mean."

"Tell me," I said at last, "why does he want to die? He must want to die, he's killing himself, why does he want to die?"

He looked at me in surprise. He licked his lips. "He don't want to die. He   40 wants to live. Don't nobody want to die, ever."

Then I wanted to ask him—too many things. He could not have answered, or if he had, I could not have borne the answers. I started walking. "Well, I guess it's none of my business."

"It's going to be rough on old Sonny," he said. We reached the subway station. "This is your station?" he asked. I nodded. I took one step down. "Damn!" he said, suddenly. I looked up at him. He grinned again. "Damn it if I didn't leave all my money home. You ain't got a dollar on you, have you? Just for a couple of days, is all."

All at once something inside gave and threatened to come pouring out of me. I didn't hate him any more. I felt that in another moment I'd start crying like a child.

"Sure," I said. "Don't sweat." I looked in my wallet and didn't have a dollar, I only had a five. "Here," I said. "That hold you?"

He didn't look at it—he didn't want to look at it. A terrible, closed look came   45 over his face, as though he were keeping the number on the bill a secret from him and me. "Thanks," he said, and now he was dying to see me go. "Don't worry about Sonny. Maybe I'll write him or something."

"Sure," I said. "You do that. So long."

"Be seeing you," he said. I went on down the steps.

And I didn't write Sonny or send him anything for a long time. When I finally did, it was just after my little girl died, and he wrote me back a letter which made me feel like a bastard.

Here's what he said:

> Dear brother,
>
> You don't know how much I needed to hear from you. I wanted to write you many a time but I dug how much I must have hurt you and so I didn't write. But now I feel like a man who's been trying to climb up out of some deep, real deep and funky hole and just saw the sun up there, outside. I got to get outside.
>
> I can't tell you much about how I got here. I mean I don't know how to tell you. I guess I was afraid of something or I was trying to escape from something and you know I have never been very strong in the head (smile). I'm glad Mama and Daddy are dead and can't see what's happened to their son and I swear if I'd known what I was doing I would never have hurt you so, you and a lot of other fine people who were nice to me and who believed in me.
>
> I don't want you to think it had anything to do with me being a musician. It's more than that. Or maybe less than that. I can't get anything straight in my head down here and I try not to think about what's going to happen to me when I get outside again. Sometime I think I'm going to flip and never get outside and sometime I think I'll come straight back. I tell you one thing, though, I'd rather blow my brains out than go through this again. But that's what they all say, so they tell me. If I tell you when I'm coming to New York and if you could meet me, I sure would appreciate it. Give my love to Isabel and the kids and I was sure sorry to hear about little Gracie. I wish I could be like Mama and say the Lord's will be done, but I don't know it seems to me that trouble is the one thing that never does get stopped and I don't know what good it does to blame it on the Lord. But maybe it does some good if you believe it.
>
> Your brother,
> Sonny

Then I kept in constant touch with him and I sent him whatever I could and 50 I went to meet him when he came back to New York. When I saw him many things I thought I had forgotten came flooding back to me. This was because I had begun, finally, to wonder about Sonny, about the life that Sonny lived inside. This life, whatever it was, had made him older and thinner and it had deepened the distant stillness in which he had always moved. He looked very unlike my baby brother. Yet, when he smiled, when we shook hands, the baby brother I'd never known looked out from the depths of his private life, like an animal waiting to be coaxed into the light.

"How you been keeping?" he asked me.

"All right. And you?"

"Just fine." He was smiling all over his face. "It's good to see you again."

"It's good to see you."

The seven years' difference in our ages lay between us like a chasm: I won-   55
dered if these years would ever operate between us as a bridge. I was remembering, and it made it hard to catch my breath, that I had been there when he
was born; and I had heard the first words he had ever spoken. When he started
to walk, he walked from our mother straight to me. I caught him just before he
fell when he took the first steps he ever took in this world.

"How's Isabel?"

"Just fine. She's dying to see you."

"And the boys?"

"They're fine, too. They're anxious to see their uncle."

"Oh, come on. You know they don't remember me."   60

"Are you kidding? Of course they remember you."

He grinned again. We got into a taxi. We had a lot to say to each other, far
too much to know how to begin.

As the taxi began to move, I asked, "You still want to go to India?"

He laughed. "You still remember that. Hell, no. This place is Indian enough
for me."

"It used to belong to them," I said.   65

And he laughed again. "They damn sure knew what they were doing when
they got rid of it."

Years ago, when he was around fourteen, he'd been all hipped on the idea of
going to India. He read books about people sitting on rocks, naked, in all kinds
of weather, but mostly bad, naturally, and walking barefoot through hot coals
and arriving at wisdom. I used to say that it sounded to me as though they
were getting away from wisdom as fast as they could. I think he sort of looked
down on me for that.

"Do you mind," he asked, "if we have the driver drive alongside the park?
On the west side—I haven't seen the city in so long."

"Of course not," I said. I was afraid that I might sound as though I were
humoring him, but I hoped he wouldn't take it that way.

So we drove along, between the green of the park and the stony, lifeless   70
elegance of hotels and apartment buildings, toward the vivid, killing streets
of our childhood. These streets hadn't changed, though housing projects jut-
ted up out of them now like rocks in the middle of a boiling sea. Most of the
houses in which we had grown up had vanished, as had the stores from which
we had stolen, the basements in which we had first tried sex, the rooftops from
which we had hurled tin cans and bricks. But houses exactly like the houses of
our past yet dominated the landscape, boys exactly like the boys we once had
been found themselves smothering in these houses, came down into the streets
for light and air and found themselves encircled by disaster. Some escaped
the trap, most didn't. Those who got out always left something of themselves
behind, as some animals amputate a leg and leave it in the trap. It might be
said, perhaps, that I had escaped, after all, I was a school teacher; or that
Sonny had, he hadn't lived in Harlem for years. Yet, as the cab moved uptown
through streets which seemed, with a rush, to darken with dark people, and as

I covertly studied Sonny's face, it came to me that what we both were seeking through our separate cab windows was that part of ourselves which had been left behind. It's always at the hour of trouble and confrontation that the missing member aches.

We hit 110th Street and started rolling up Lenox Avenue. And I'd known this avenue all my life, but it seemed to me again, as it had seemed on the day I'd first heard about Sonny's trouble, filled with a hidden menace which was its very breath of life.

"We almost there," said Sonny.

"Almost." We were both too nervous to say anything more.

We live in a housing project. It hasn't been up long. A few days after it was up it seemed uninhabitably new, now, of course, it's already rundown. It looks like a parody of the good, clean, faceless life—God knows the people who live in it do their best to make it a parody. The beat-looking grass lying around isn't enough to make their lives green, the hedges will never hold out the streets, and they know it. The big windows fool no one, they aren't big enough to make space out of no space. They don't bother with the windows, they watch the TV screen instead. The playground is most popular with the children who don't play at jacks, or skip rope, or roller skate, or swing, and they can be found in it after dark. We moved in partly because it's not too far from where I teach, and partly for the kids; but it's really just like the houses in which Sonny and I grew up. The same things happen, they'll have the same things to remember. The moment Sonny and I started into the house I had the feeling that I was simply bringing him back into the danger he had almost died trying to escape.

Sonny has never been talkative. So I don't know why I was sure he'd be dying 75 to talk to me when supper was over the first night. Everything went fine, the oldest boy remembered him, and the youngest boy liked him, and Sonny had remembered to bring something for each of them; and Isabel, who is really much nicer than I am, more open and giving, had gone to a lot of trouble about dinner and was genuinely glad to see him. And she's always been able to tease Sonny in a way that I haven't. It was nice to see her face so vivid again and to hear her laugh and watch her make Sonny laugh. She wasn't, or, anyway, she didn't seem to be, at all uneasy or embarrassed. She chatted as though there were no subject which had to be avoided and she got Sonny past his first, faint stiffness. And thank God she was there, for I was filled with that icy dread again. Everything I did seemed awkward to me, and everything I said sounded freighted with hidden meaning. I was trying to remember everything I'd heard about dope addiction and I couldn't help watching Sonny for signs. I wasn't doing it out of malice. I was trying to find out something about my brother. I was dying to hear him tell me he was safe.

"Safe!" my father grunted, whenever Mama suggested trying to move to a neighborhood which might be safer for children. "Safe, hell! Ain't no place safe for kids, nor nobody."

He always went on like this, but he wasn't, ever, really as bad as he sounded, not even on weekends, when he got drunk. As a matter of fact, he was always on the lookout for "something a little better," but he died before he found it. He died suddenly, during a drunken weekend in the middle of the war, when Sonny was fifteen. He and Sonny hadn't ever got on too well. And this was partly because Sonny was the apple of his father's eye. It was because he loved Sonny so much and was frightened for him, that he was always fighting with him. It doesn't do any good to fight with Sonny. Sonny just moves back, inside himself, where he can't be reached. But the principal reason that they never hit it off is that they were so much alike. Daddy was big and rough and loud-talking, just the opposite of Sonny, but they both had—that same privacy.

Mama tried to tell me something about this, just after Daddy died. I was home on leave from the army.

This was the last time I ever saw my mother alive. Just the same, this picture gets all mixed up in my mind with pictures I had of her when she was younger. The way I always see her is the way she used to be on a Sunday afternoon, say, when the old folks were talking after the big Sunday dinner. I always see her wearing pale blue. She'd be sitting on the sofa. And my father would be sitting in the easy chair, not far from her. And the living room would be full of church folks and relatives. There they sit, in chairs all around the living room, and the night is creeping up outside, but nobody knows it yet. You can see the darkness growing against the windowpanes and you hear the street noises every now and again, or maybe the jangling beat of a tambourine from one of the churches close by, but it's real quiet in the room. For a moment nobody's talking, but every face looks darkening, like the sky outside. And my mother rocks a little from the waist, and my father's eyes are closed. Everyone is looking at something a child can't see. For a minute they've forgotten the children. Maybe a kid is lying on the rug, half asleep. Maybe somebody's got a kid in his lap and is absent-mindedly stroking the kid's head. Maybe there's a kid, quiet and big-eyed, curled up in a big chair in the corner. The silence, the darkness coming, and the darkness in the faces frighten the child obscurely. He hopes that the hand which strokes his forehead will never stop—will never die. He hopes that there will never come a time when the old folks won't be sitting around the living room, talking about where they've come from, and what they've seen, and what's happened to them and their kinfolk.

But something deep and watchful in the child knows that this is bound 80 to end, is already ending. In a moment someone will get up and turn on the light. Then the old folks will remember the children and they won't talk any more that day. And when light fills the room, the child is filled with darkness. He knows that every time this happens he's moved just a little closer to that darkness outside. The darkness outside is what the old folks have been talking about. It's what they've come from. It's what they endure. The child knows that they won't talk any more because if he knows too much about what's happened to *them*, he'll know too much too soon, about what's going to happen to *him*.

The last time I talked to my mother, I remember I was restless. I wanted to get out and see Isabel. We weren't married then and we had a lot to straighten out between us.

There Mama sat, in black, by the window. She was humming an old church song, *Lord, you brought me from a long ways off.* Sonny was out somewhere. Mama kept watching the streets.

"I don't know," she said, "if I'll ever see you again, after you go off from here. But I hope you'll remember the things I tried to teach you."

"Don't talk like that," I said, and smiled. "You'll be here a long time yet."

She smiled, too, but she said nothing. She was quiet for a long time. And 85 I said, "Mama, don't you worry about nothing. I'll be writing all the time, and you be getting the checks. . . ."

"I want to talk to you about your brother," she said, suddenly. "If anything happens to me he ain't going to have nobody to look out for him."

"Mama," I said, "ain't nothing going to happen to you *or* Sonny. Sonny's all right. He's a good boy and he's got good sense."

"It ain't a question of his being a good boy," Mama said, "nor of his having good sense. It ain't only the bad ones, nor yet the dumb ones that gets sucked under." She stopped, looking at me. "Your Daddy once had a brother," she said, and she smiled in a way that made me feel she was in pain. "You didn't never know that, did you?"

"No," I said, "I never knew that," and I watched her face.

"Oh, yes," she said, "your Daddy had a brother." She looked out of the win- 90 dow again. "I know you never saw your Daddy cry. But *I* did—many a time, through all these years."

I asked her, "What happened to his brother? How come nobody's ever talked about him?"

This was the first time I ever saw my mother look old.

"His brother got killed," she said, "when he was just a little younger than you are now. I knew him. He was a fine boy. He was maybe a little full of the devil, but he didn't mean nobody no harm."

Then she stopped and the room was silent, exactly as it had sometimes been on those Sunday afternoons. Mama kept looking out into the streets.

"He used to have a job in the mill," she said, "and, like all young folks, he 95 just liked to perform on Saturday nights. Saturday nights, him and your father would drift around to different places, go to dances and things like that, or just sit around with people they knew, and your father's brother would sing, he had a fine voice, and play along with himself on his guitar. Well, this particular Saturday night, him and your father was coming home from some place, and they were both a little drunk and there was a moon that night, it was bright like day. Your father's brother was feeling kind of good, and he was whistling to himself, and he had his guitar slung over his shoulder. They was coming down a hill and beneath them was a road that turned off from the highway. Well, your father's brother, being always kind of frisky, decided to run down this hill, and he did, with that guitar banging and clanging behind him, and he ran across the road, and he was making water behind a tree. And your father was sort of amused at him and he was still coming down the hill, kind of slow. Then he heard a car motor and that same minute his brother stepped from behind the tree, into the road, in the moonlight. And he started to cross the road. And your father started to run down the hill, he says he don't know why. This car was full of white men. They was all drunk, and when they seen your father's brother they let out a great whoop and holler and they aimed the car straight at him. They was having fun, they just wanted to scare him, the way they do sometimes, you know. But they was drunk. And I guess the boy, being drunk, too, and scared, kind of lost his head. By the time he jumped it was too late. Your father says he heard his brother scream when the car rolled over him, and he heard the wood of that guitar when it give, and he heard them strings go flying, and he heard them white men shouting, and the car kept on a-going and it ain't stopped till this day. And, time your father got down the hill, his brother weren't nothing but blood and pulp."

Tears were gleaming on my mother's face. There wasn't anything I could say.

"He never mentioned it," she said, "because I never let him mention it before you children. Your Daddy was like a crazy man that night and for many a night thereafter. He says he never in his life seen anything as dark as that road after the lights of that car had gone away. Weren't nothing, weren't nobody on that road, just your Daddy and his brother and that busted guitar. Oh, yes. Your Daddy never did really get right again. Till the day he died he weren't sure but that every white man he saw was the man that killed his brother."

She stopped and took out her handkerchief and dried her eyes and looked at me.

"I ain't telling you all this," she said, "to make you scared or bitter or to make you hate nobody. I'm telling you this because you got a brother. And the world ain't changed."

I guess I didn't want to believe this. I guess she saw this in my face. She 100 turned away from me, toward the window again, searching those streets.

"But I praise my Redeemer," she said at last, "that He called your Daddy home before me. I ain't saying it to throw no flowers at myself, but, I declare, it keeps me from feeling too cast down to know I helped your father get safely through this world. Your father always acted like he was the roughest, strongest man on earth. And everybody took him to be like that. But if he hadn't had me there—to see his tears!"

She was crying again. Still, I couldn't move. I said, "Lord, Lord, Mama, I didn't know it was like that."

"Oh, honey," she said, "there's a lot that you don't know. But you are going to find out." She stood up from the window and came over to me. "You got to hold on to your brother," she said, "and don't let him fall, no matter what it looks like is happening to him and no matter how evil you gets with him. You going to be evil with him many a time. But don't you forget what I told you, you hear?"

"I won't forget," I said. "Don't you worry, I won't forget. I won't let nothing happen to Sonny."

My mother smiled as though she was amused at something she saw in my 105 face. Then, "You may not be able to stop nothing from happening. But you got to let him know you's *there*."

Two days later I was married, and then I was gone. And I had a lot of things on my mind and I pretty well forgot my promise to Mama until I got shipped home on a special furlough for her funeral.

And, after the funeral, with just Sonny and me alone in the empty kitchen, I tried to find out something about him.

"What do you want to do?" I asked him.

"I'm going to be a musician," he said.

For he had graduated, in the time I had been away, from dancing to the juke 110 box to finding out who was playing what, and what they were doing with it, and he had bought himself a set of drums.

"You mean, you want to be a drummer?" I somehow had the feeling that being a drummer might be all right for other people but not for my brother Sonny.

"I don't think," he said, looking at me very gravely, "that I'll ever be a good drummer. But I think I can play a piano."

I frowned. I'd never played the role of the oldest brother quite so seriously before, had scarcely ever, in fact, *asked* Sonny a damn thing. I sensed myself in the presence of something I didn't really know how to handle, didn't understand. So I made my frown a little deeper as I asked: "What kind of musician do you want to be?"

He grinned. "How many kinds do you think there are?"

"Be *serious*," I said. 115

He laughed, throwing his head back, and then looked at me. "I *am* serious."

"Well, then, for Christ's sake, stop kidding around and answer a serious question. I mean, do you want to be a concert pianist, you want to play classical music and all that, or—or what?" Long before I finished he was laughing again. "For Christ's *sake*, Sonny!"

He sobered, but with difficulty. "I'm sorry. But you sound so—*scared!*" and he was off again.

"Well, you may think it's funny now, baby, but it's not going to be so funny when you have to make your living at it, let me tell you *that*." I was furious because I knew he was laughing at me and I didn't know why.

"No," he said, very sober now, and afraid, perhaps, that he'd hurt me, 120 "I don't want to be a classical pianist. That isn't what interests me. I mean"—he paused, looking hard at me, as though his eyes would help me to understand, and then gestured helplessly, as though perhaps his hand would help— "I mean, I'll have a lot of studying to do, and I'll have to study *everything*, but, I mean, I want to play *with*—jazz musicians." He stopped. "I want to play jazz," he said.

Well, the word had never before sounded as heavy, as real, as it sounded that afternoon in Sonny's mouth. I just looked at him and I was probably frowning a real frown by this time. I simply couldn't see why on earth he'd want to spend his time hanging around nightclubs, clowning around on bandstands, while people pushed each other around a dance floor. It seemed—beneath him, somehow. I had never thought about it before, had never been forced to, but I suppose I had always put jazz musicians in a class with what Daddy called "good-time people."

"Are you *serious*?"

"Hell, *yes*, I'm serious."

He looked more helpless than ever, and annoyed, and deeply hurt.

I suggested, helpfully: "You mean—like Louis Armstrong?"[2]   125

His face closed as though I'd struck him. "No. I'm not talking about none of that old-time, down home crap."

"Well, look, Sonny, I'm sorry, don't get mad. I just don't altogether get it, that's all. Name somebody—you know, a jazz musician you admire."

"Bird."

"Who?"

"Bird! Charlie Parker![3] Don't they teach you nothing in the goddamn army?"   130

I lit a cigarette. I was surprised and then a little amused to discover that I was trembling. "I've been out of touch," I said. "You'll have to be patient with me. Now. Who's this Parker character?"

"He's just one of the greatest jazz musicians alive," said Sonny, sullenly, his hands in his pockets, his back to me. "Maybe *the* greatest," he added, bitterly, "that's probably why *you* never heard of him."

"All right," I said, "I'm ignorant. I'm sorry. I'll go out and buy all the cat's records right away, all right?"

"It don't," said Sonny, with dignity, "make any difference to me. I don't care what you listen to. Don't do me no favors."

I was beginning to realize that I'd never seen him so upset before. With   135
another part of my mind I was thinking that this would probably turn out to be one of those things kids go through and that I shouldn't make it seem important by pushing it too hard. Still, I didn't think it would do any harm to ask: "Doesn't all this take a lot of time? Can you make a living at it?"

He turned back to me and half leaned, half sat, on the kitchen table. "Everything takes time," he said, "and—well, yes, sure, I can make a living at it. But what I don't seem to be able to make you understand is that it's the only thing I want to do."

"Well, Sonny," I said, gently, "you know people can't always do exactly what they *want* to do—"

"*No*, I don't know that," said Sonny, surprising me. "I think people *ought* to do what they want to do, what else are they alive for?"

"You getting to be a big boy," I said desperately, "it's time you started thinking about your future."

---

[2] Louis "Satchmo" Armstrong (1901–1971) played the trumpet and was one of the most innovative and influential figures in the history of jazz.

[3] Charlie "Bird" Parker (1920–1955), a seminal saxophonist, was one of the originators of the bebop style of jazz. Parker was also a heroin addict.

"I'm thinking about my future," said Sonny, grimly. "I think about it all the 140 time."

I gave up. I decided, if he didn't change his mind, that we could always talk about it later. "In the meantime," I said, "you got to finish school." We had already decided that he'd have to move in with Isabel and her folks. I knew this wasn't the ideal arrangement because Isabel's folks are inclined to be dicty[4] and they hadn't especially wanted Isabel to marry me. But I didn't know what else to do. "And we have to get you fixed up at Isabel's."

There was a long silence. He moved from the kitchen table to the window. "That's a terrible idea. You know it yourself."

"Do you have a *better* idea?"

He just walked up and down the kitchen for a minute. He was as tall as I was. He had started to shave. I suddenly had the feeling that I didn't know him at all.

He stopped at the kitchen table and picked up my cigarettes. Looking at me 145 with a kind of mocking, amused defiance, he put one between his lips. "You mind?"

"You smoking already?"

He lit the cigarette and nodded, watching me through the smoke. "I just wanted to see if I'd have the courage to smoke in front of you." He grinned and blew a great cloud of smoke to the ceiling. "It was easy." He looked at my face. "Come on, now. I bet you was smoking at my age, tell the truth."

I didn't say anything but the truth was on my face, and he laughed. But now there was something very strained in his laugh. "Sure. And I bet that ain't all you was doing."

He was frightening me a little. "Cut the crap," I said. "We already decided that you was going to go and live at Isabel's. Now what's got into you all of a sudden?"

"*You* decided it," he pointed out. "*I* didn't decide nothing." He stopped in 150 front of me, leaning against the stove, arms loosely folded. "Look, brother. I don't want to stay in Harlem no more, I really don't." He was very earnest. He looked at me, then over toward the kitchen window. There was something in his eyes I'd never seen before, some thoughtfulness, some worry all his own. He rubbed the muscle of one arm. "It's time I was getting out of here."

"Where do you want to *go*, Sonny?"

"I want to join the army. Or the navy, I don't care. If I say I'm old enough, they'll believe me."

Then I got mad. It was because I was so scared. "You must be crazy. You goddamn fool, what the hell do you want to go and join the *army* for?"

"I just told you. To get out of Harlem."

"Sonny, you haven't even finished *school*. And if you really want to be a 155 musician, how do you expect to study if you're in the *army*?"

He looked at me, trapped, and in anguish. "There's ways. I might be able to work out some kind of deal. Anyway, I'll have the G.I. Bill when I come out."

[4] Snobbish.

"*If* you come out." We stared at each other. "Sonny, please. Be reasonable. I know the setup is far from perfect. But we got to do the best we can."

"I ain't learning nothing in school," he said. "Even when I go." He turned away from me and opened the window and threw his cigarette out into the narrow alley. I watched his back. "At least, I ain't learning nothing you'd want me to learn." He slammed the window so hard I thought the glass would fly out, and turned back to me. "And I'm sick of the stink of these garbage cans!"

"Sonny," I said, "I know how you feel. But if you don't finish school now, you're going to be sorry later that you didn't." I grabbed him by the shoulders. "And you only got another year. It ain't so bad. And I'll come back and I swear I'll help you do *whatever* you want to do. Just try to put up with it till I come back. Will you please do that? For me?"

He didn't answer and he wouldn't look at me.   160

"Sonny. You hear me?"

He pulled away. "I hear you. But you never hear anything *I* say."

I didn't know what to say to that. He looked out of the window and then back at me. "OK," he said, and sighed. "I'll try."

Then I said, trying to cheer him up a little, "They got a piano at Isabel's. You can practice on it."

And as a matter of fact, it did cheer him up for a minute. "That's right,"   165
he said to himself. "I forgot that." His face relaxed a little. But the worry, the thoughtfulness, played on it still, the way shadows play on a face which is staring into the fire.

But I thought I'd never hear the end of that piano. At first, Isabel would write me, saying how nice it was that Sonny was so serious about his music and how, as soon as he came in from school, or wherever he had been when he was supposed to be at school, he went straight to that piano and stayed there until suppertime. And, after supper, he went back to that piano and stayed there until everybody went to bed. He was at the piano all day Saturday and all day Sunday. Then he bought a record player and started playing records. He'd play one record over and over again, all day long sometimes, and he'd improvise along with it on the piano. Or he'd play one section of the record, one chord, one change, one progression, then he'd do it on the piano. Then back to the record. Then back to the piano.

Well, I really don't know how they stood it. Isabel finally confessed that it wasn't like living with a person at all, it was like living with sound. And the sound didn't make any sense to her, didn't make any sense to any of them— naturally. They began, in a way, to be afflicted by this presence that was living in their home. It was as though Sonny were some sort of god, or monster. He moved in an atmosphere which wasn't like theirs at all. They fed him and he ate, he washed himself, he walked in and out of their door; he certainly wasn't nasty or unpleasant or rude, Sonny isn't any of those things; but it was as though he were all wrapped up in some cloud, some fire, some vision all his own; and there wasn't any way to reach him.

At the same time, he wasn't really a man yet, he was still a child, and they had to watch out for him in all kinds of ways. They certainly couldn't throw him out. Neither did they dare to make a great scene about that piano because even they dimly sensed, as I sensed, from so many thousands of miles away, that Sonny was at that piano playing for his life.

But he hadn't been going to school. One day a letter came from the school board and Isabel's mother got it—there had, apparently, been other letters but Sonny had torn them up. This day, when Sonny came in, Isabel's mother showed him the letter and asked where he'd been spending his time. And she finally got it out of him that he'd been down in Greenwich Village, with musicians and other characters, in a white girl's apartment. And this scared her and she started to scream at him and what came up, once she began—though she denies it to this day—was what sacrifices they were making to give Sonny a decent home and how little he appreciated it.

Sonny didn't play the piano that day. By evening, Isabel's mother had 170 calmed down but then there was the old man to deal with, and Isabel herself. Isabel says she did her best to be calm but she broke down and started crying. She says she just watched Sonny's face. She could tell, by watching him, what was happening with him. And what was happening was that they penetrated his cloud, they had reached him. Even if their fingers had been a thousand times more gentle than human fingers ever are, he could hardly help feeling that they had stripped him naked and were spitting on that nakedness. For he also had to see that his presence, that music, which was life or death to him, had been torture for them and that they had endured it, not at all for his sake, but only for mine. And Sonny couldn't take that. He can take it a little better today than he could then but he's still not very good at it and, frankly, I don't know anybody who is.

The silence of the next few days must have been louder than the sound of all the music ever played since time began. One morning, before she went to work, Isabel was in his room for something and she suddenly realized that all of his records were gone. And she knew for certain that he was gone. And he was. He went as far as the navy would carry him. He finally sent me a postcard from some place in Greece and that was the first I knew that Sonny was still alive. I didn't see him any more until we were both back in New York and the war had long been over.

He was a man by then, of course, but I wasn't willing to see it. He came by the house from time to time, but we fought almost every time we met. I didn't like the way he carried himself, loose and dreamlike all the time, and I didn't like his friends, and his music seemed to be merely an excuse for the life he led. It sounded just that weird and disordered.

Then we had a fight, a pretty awful fight, and I didn't see him for months. By and by I looked him up, where he was living, in a furnished room in the Village, and I tried to make it up. But there were lots of other people in the room and Sonny just lay on his bed, and he wouldn't come downstairs with me, and he treated these other people as though they were his family and

I weren't. So I got mad and then he got mad, and then I told him that he might just as well be dead as live the way he was living. Then he stood up and he told me not to worry about him any more in life, that he *was* dead as far as I was concerned. Then he pushed me to the door and the other people looked on as though nothing were happening, and he slammed the door behind me. I stood in the hallway, staring at the door. I heard somebody laugh in the room and then the tears came to my eyes. I started down the steps, whistling to keep from crying, I kept whistling to myself, *You going to need me, baby, one of these cold, rainy days.*

I read about Sonny's trouble in the spring. Little Grace died in the fall. She was a beautiful little girl. But she only lived a little over two years. She died of polio and she suffered. She had a slight fever for a couple of days, but it didn't seem like anything and we just kept her in bed. And we would certainly have called the doctor, but the fever dropped, she seemed to be all right. So we thought it had just been a cold. Then, one day, she was up, playing, Isabel was in the kitchen fixing lunch for the two boys when they'd come in from school, and she heard Grace fall down in the living room. When you have a lot of children you don't always start running when one of them falls, unless they start screaming or something. And, this time, Gracie was quiet. Yet, Isabel says that when she heard that *thump* and then that silence, something happened to her to make her afraid. And she ran to the living room and there was little Grace on the floor, all twisted up, and the reason she hadn't screamed was that she couldn't get her breath. And when she did scream, it was the worst sound, Isabel says, that she'd ever heard in all her life, and she still hears it sometimes in her dreams. Isabel will sometimes wake me up with a low, moaning, strangling sound and I have to be quick to awaken her and hold her to me and where Isabel is weeping against me seems a mortal wound.

I think I may have written Sonny the very day that little Grace was buried. I 175 was sitting in the living room in the dark, by myself, and I suddenly thought of Sonny. My trouble made his real.

One Saturday afternoon, when Sonny had been living with us, or, anyway, been in our house, for nearly two weeks, I found myself wandering aimlessly about the living room, drinking from a can of beer, and trying to work up courage to search Sonny's room. He was out, he was usually out whenever I was home, and Isabel had taken the children to see their grandparents. Suddenly I was standing still in front of the living room window, watching Seventh Avenue. The idea of searching Sonny's room made me still. I scarcely dared to admit to myself what I'd be searching for. I didn't know what I'd do if I found it. Or if I didn't.

On the sidewalk across from me, near the entrance to a barbecue joint, some people were holding an old-fashioned revival meeting. The barbecue cook, wearing a dirty white apron, his conked[5] hair reddish and metallic in

---

[5] Straightened and greased.

the pale sun, and a cigarette between his lips, stood in the doorway, watching them. Kids and older people paused in their errands and stood there, along with some older men and a couple of very tough-looking women who watched everything that happened on the avenue, as though they owned it, or were maybe owned by it. Well, they were watching this, too. The revival was being carried on by three sisters in black, and a brother. All they had were their voices and their Bibles and a tambourine. The brother was testifying and while he testified two of the sisters stood together, seeming to say, amen, and the third sister walked around with the tambourine outstretched and a couple of people dropped coins into it. Then the brother's testimony ended and the sister who had been taking up the collection dumped the coins into her palm and transferred them to the pocket of her long black robe. Then she raised both hands, striking the tambourine against the air, and then against one hand, and she started to sing. And the two other sisters and the brother joined in.

It was strange, suddenly, to watch, though I had been seeing these meetings all my life. So, of course, had everybody else down there. Yet, they paused and watched and listened and I stood still at the window. "*'Tis the old ship of Zion*," they sang, and the sister with the tambourine kept a steady, jangling beat, "*it has rescued many a thousand!*" Not a soul under the sound of their voices was hearing this song for the first time, not one of them had been rescued. Nor had they seen much in the way of rescue work being done around them. Neither did they especially believe in the holiness of the three sisters and the brother, they knew too much about them, knew where they lived, and how. The woman with the tambourine, whose voice dominated the air, whose face was bright with joy, was divided by very little from the woman who stood watching her, a cigarette between her heavy, chapped lips, her hair a cuckoo's nest, her face scarred and swollen from many beatings, and her black eyes glittering like coal. Perhaps they both knew this, which was why, when, as rarely, they addressed each other, they addressed each other as Sister. As the singing filled the air the watching, listening faces underwent a change, the eyes focusing on something within; the music seemed to soothe a poison out of them; and time seemed, nearly, to fall away from the sullen, belligerent, battered faces, as though they were fleeing back to their first condition, while dreaming of their last. The barbecue cook half shook his head and smiled, and dropped his cigarette and disappeared into his joint. A man fumbled in his pockets for change and stood holding it in his hand impatiently, as though he had just remembered a pressing appointment further up the avenue. He looked furious. Then I saw Sonny, standing on the edge of the crowd. He was carrying a wide, flat notebook with a green cover, and it made him look, from where I was standing, almost like a schoolboy. The coppery sun brought out the copper in his skin, he was very faintly smiling, standing very still. Then the singing stopped, the tambourine turned into a collection plate again. The furious man dropped in his coins and vanished, so did a couple of the women, and Sonny dropped some change in the plate, looking directly at the woman with a little smile. He started across the avenue, toward the house. He has a slow, loping walk, something like the way Harlem hipsters walk, only he's imposed on this his own half-beat. I had never really noticed it before.

I stayed at the window, both relieved and apprehensive. As Sonny disappeared from my sight, they began singing again. And they were still singing when his key turned in the lock.

"Hey," he said.

"Hey, yourself. You want some beer?"

"No. Well, maybe." But he came up to the window and stood beside me, looking out. "What a warm voice," he said.

They were singing *If I could only hear my mother pray again!*

"Yes," I said, "and she can sure beat that tambourine."

"But what a terrible song," he said, and laughed. He dropped his notebook on the sofa and disappeared into the kitchen. "Where's Isabel and the kids?"

"I think they went to see their grandparents. You hungry?"

"No." He came back into the living room with his can of beer. "You want to come some place with me tonight?"

I sensed, I don't know how, that I couldn't possibly say no. "Sure. Where?"

He sat down on the sofa and picked up his notebook and started leafing through it. "I'm going to sit in with some fellows in a joint in the Village."

"You mean, you're going to play, tonight?"

"That's right." He took a swallow of his beer and moved back to the window. He gave me a sidelong look. "If you can stand it."

"I'll try," I said.

He smiled to himself and we both watched as the meeting across the way broke up. The three sisters and the brother, heads bowed, were singing *God be with you till we meet again.* The faces around them were very quiet. Then the song ended. The small crowd dispersed. We watched the three women and the lone man walk slowly up the avenue.

"When she was singing before," said Sonny, abruptly, "her voice reminded me for a minute of what heroin feels like sometimes—when it's in your veins. It makes you feel sort of warm and cool at the same time. And distant. And—and sure." He sipped his beer, very deliberately not looking at me. I watched his face. "It makes you feel—in control. Sometimes you've got to have that feeling."

"Do you?" I sat down slowly in the easy chair.

"Sometimes." He went to the sofa and picked up his notebook again. "Some people do."

"In order," I asked, "to play?" And my voice was very ugly, full of contempt and anger.

"Well"—he looked at me with great, troubled eyes, as though, in fact, he hoped his eyes would tell me things he could never otherwise say—"they *think* so. And *if* they think so—!"

"And what do *you* think?" I asked.

He sat on the sofa and put his can of beer on the floor. "I don't know," he said, and I couldn't be sure if he were answering my question or pursuing his

180

185

190

195

200

thoughts. His face didn't tell me. "It's not so much to *play*. It's to *stand* it, to be able to make it at all. On any level." He frowned and smiled: "In order to keep from shaking to pieces."

"But these friends of yours," I said, "they seem to shake themselves to pieces pretty goddamn fast."

"Maybe." He played with the notebook. And something told me that I should curb my tongue, that Sonny was doing his best to talk, that I should listen. "But of course you only know the ones that've gone to pieces. Some don't—or at least they haven't *yet* and that's just about all *any* of us can say." He paused. "And then there are some who just live, really, in hell, and they know it and they see what's happening and they go right on. I don't know." He sighed, dropped the notebook, folded his arms. "Some guys, you can tell from the way they play, they on something *all* the time. And you can see that, well, it makes something real for them. But of course," he picked up his beer from the floor and sipped it and put the can down again, "they *want* to, too, you've got to see that. Even some of them that say they don't—*some*, not all."

"And what about you?" I asked—I couldn't help it. "What about you? Do *you* want to?"

He stood up and walked to the window and remained silent for a long time. Then he sighed. "Me," he said. Then: "While I was downstairs before, on my way here, listening to that woman sing, it struck me all of a sudden how much suffering she must have had to go through—to sing like that. It's *repulsive* to think you have to suffer that much."

I said: "But there's no way not to suffer—is there, Sonny?" 205

"I believe not," he said and smiled, "but that's never stopped anyone from trying." He looked at me. "Has it?" I realized, with this mocking look, that there stood between us, forever, beyond the power of time or forgiveness, the fact that I had held silence—so long!—when he had needed human speech to help him. He turned back to the window. "No, there's no way not to suffer. But you try all kinds of ways to keep from drowning in it, to keep on top of it, and to make it seem—well, like *you*. Like you did something, all right, and now you're suffering for it. You know?" I said nothing. "Well you know," he said, impatiently, "why *do* people suffer? Maybe it's better to do something to give it a reason, *any* reason."

"But we just agreed," I said, "that there's no way not to suffer. Isn't it better, then, just to—take it?"

"But nobody just takes it," Sonny cried, "that's what I'm telling you! *Everybody* tries not to. You're just hung up on the *way* some people try—it's not *your* way!"

The hair on my face began to itch, my face felt wet. "That's not true," I said, "that's not true. I don't give a damn what other people do, I don't even care how they suffer. I just care how *you* suffer." And he looked at me. "Please believe me," I said, "I don't want to see you—die—trying not to suffer."

"I won't," he said, flatly, "die trying not to suffer. At least, not any faster than 210 anybody else."

"But there's no need," I said, trying to laugh, "is there? in killing yourself."

I wanted to say more, but I couldn't. I wanted to talk about will power and how life could be—well, beautiful. I wanted to say that it was all within; but was it? or, rather, wasn't that exactly the trouble? And I wanted to promise that I would never fail him again. But it would all have sounded—empty words and lies.

So I made the promise to myself and prayed that I would keep it.

"It's terrible sometimes, inside," he said, "that's what's the trouble. You walk these streets, black and funky and cold, and there's not really a living ass to talk to, and there's nothing shaking, and there's no way of getting it out—that storm inside. You can't talk it and you can't make love with it, and when you finally try to get with it and play it, you realize *nobody's* listening. So *you've* got to listen. You got to find a way to listen."

And then he walked away from the window and sat on the sofa again, as though all the wind had suddenly been knocked out of him. "Sometimes you'll do *anything* to play, even cut your mother's throat." He laughed and looked at me. "Or your brother's." Then he sobered. "Or your own." Then: "Don't worry. I'm all right now and I think I'll *be* all right. But I can't forget—where I've been. I don't mean just the physical place I've been, I mean where I've *been*. And *what* I've been." 215

"What have you been, Sonny?" I asked.

He smiled—but sat sideways on the sofa, his elbow resting on the back, his fingers playing with his mouth and chin, not looking at me. "I've been something I didn't recognize, didn't know I could be. Didn't know anybody could be." He stopped, looking inward, looking helplessly young, looking old. "I'm not talking about it now because I feel *guilty* or anything like that—maybe it would be better if I did, I don't know. Anyway, I can't really talk about it. Not to you, not to anybody," and now he turned and faced me. "Sometimes, you know, and it was actually when I was most *out* of the world, I felt that I was in it, that I was *with* it, really, and I could play or I didn't really have to *play*, it just came out of me, it was there. And I don't know how I played, thinking about it now, but I know I did awful things, those times, sometimes, to people. Or it wasn't that I *did* anything to them—it was that they weren't real." He picked up the beer can; it was empty; he rolled it between his palms: "And other times—well, I needed a fix, I needed to find a place to lean, I needed to clear a space to *listen*—and I couldn't find it, and I—went crazy, I did terrible things to *me*, I was terrible *for* me." He began pressing the beer can between his hands, I watched the metal begin to give. It glittered, as he played with it like a knife, and I was afraid he would cut himself, but I said nothing. "Oh well. I can never tell you. I was all by myself at the bottom of something, stinking and sweating and crying and shaking, and I smelled it, you know? *my* stink, and I thought I'd die if I couldn't get away from it and yet, all the same, I knew that everything I was doing was just locking me in with it. And I didn't know," he paused, still flattening the beer can, "I didn't know, I still *don't* know, something kept telling me that maybe it was good to smell your own stink, but

I didn't think that *that* was what I'd been trying to do—and—who can stand it?" and he abruptly dropped the ruined beer can, looking at me with a small, still smile, and then rose, walking to the window as though it were the lodestone rock. I watched his face, he watched the avenue. "I couldn't tell you when Mama died—but the reason I wanted to leave Harlem so bad was to get away from drugs. And then, when I ran away, that's what I was running from—really. When I came back, nothing had changed, *I* hadn't changed, I was just—older." And he stopped, drumming with his fingers on the windowpane. The sun had vanished, soon darkness would fall. I watched his face. "It can come again," he said, almost as though speaking to himself. Then he turned to me. "It can come again," he repeated. "I just want you to know that."

"All right," I said, at last. "So it can come again. All right."

He smiled, but the smile was sorrowful. "I had to try to tell you," he said.

"Yes," I said. "I understand that." 220

"You're my brother," he said, looking straight at me, and not smiling at all.

"Yes," I repeated, "yes. I understand that."

He turned back to the window, looking out. "All that hatred down there," he said, "all that hatred and misery and love. It's a wonder it doesn't blow the avenue apart."

We went to the only nightclub on a short, dark street, downtown. We squeezed through the narrow, chattering, jampacked bar to the entrance of the big room, where the bandstand was. And we stood there for a moment, for the lights were very dim in this room and we couldn't see. Then, "Hello, boy," said the voice and an enormous black man, much older than Sonny or myself, erupted out of all that atmospheric lighting and put an arm around Sonny's shoulder. "I been sitting right here," he said, "waiting for you."

He had a big voice, too, and heads in the darkness turned toward us. 225

Sonny grinned and pulled a little away, and said, "Creole, this is my brother. I told you about him."

Creole shook my hand. "I'm glad to meet you, son," he said, and it was clear that he was glad to meet me *there*, for Sonny's sake. And he smiled, "You got a real musician in *your* family," and he took his arm from Sonny's shoulder and slapped him, lightly, affectionately, with the back of his hand.

"Well. Now I've heard it all," said a voice behind us. This was another musician, and a friend of Sonny's, a coal-black, cheerful-looking man, built close to the ground. He immediately began confiding to me, at the top of his lungs, the most terrible things about Sonny, his teeth gleaming like a lighthouse and his laugh coming up out of him like the beginning of an earthquake. And it turned out that everyone at the bar knew Sonny, or almost everyone; some were musicians, working there, or nearby, or not working, some were simply hangers-on, and some were there to hear Sonny play. I was introduced to all of them and they were all very polite to me. Yet, it was clear that, for them, I was only Sonny's brother. Here, I was in Sonny's world. Or, rather: his kingdom. Here, it was not even a question that his veins bore royal blood.

They were going to play soon and Creole installed me, by myself, at a table in a dark corner. Then I watched them, Creole, and the little black man, and Sonny, and the others, while they horsed around, standing just below the bandstand. The light from the bandstand spilled just a little short of them and, watching them laughing and gesturing and moving about, I had the feeling that they, nevertheless, were being most careful not to step into that circle of light too suddenly; that if they moved into the light too suddenly, without thinking, they would perish in flame. Then, while I watched, one of them, the small, black man, moved into the light and crossed the bandstand and started fooling around with his drums. Then—being funny and being, also, extremely ceremonious—Creole took Sonny by the arm and led him to the piano. A woman's voice called Sonny's name and a few hands started clapping. And Sonny, also being funny and being ceremonious, and so touched, I think, that he could have cried, but neither hiding it nor showing it, riding it like a man, grinned, and put both hands to his heart and bowed from the waist.

Creole then went to the bass fiddle and a lean, very bright-skinned brown 230
man jumped up on the bandstand and picked up his horn. So there they were, and the atmosphere on the bandstand and in the room began to change and tighten. Someone stepped up to the microphone and announced them. Then there were all kinds of murmurs. Some people at the bar shushed others. The waitress ran around, frantically getting in the last orders, guys and chicks got closer to each other, and the lights on the bandstand, on the quartet, turned to a kind of indigo. Then they all looked different there. Creole looked about him for the last time, as though he were making certain that all his chickens were in the coop, and then he—jumped and struck the fiddle. And there they were.

All I know about music is that not many people ever really hear it. And even then, on the rare occasions when something opens within, and the music enters, what we mainly hear, or hear corroborated, are personal, private, vanishing evocations. But the man who creates the music is hearing something else, is dealing with the roar rising from the void and imposing order on it as it hits the air. What is evoked in him, then, is of another order, more terrible because it has no words, and triumphant, too, for that same reason. And his triumph, when he triumphs, is ours. I just watched Sonny's face. His face was troubled, he was working hard, but he wasn't with it. And I had the feeling that, in a way, everyone on the bandstand was waiting for him, both waiting for him and pushing him along. But as I began to watch Creole, I realized that it was Creole who held them all back. He had them on a short rein. Up there, keeping the beat with his whole body, wailing on the fiddle, with his eyes half closed, he was listening to everything, but he was listening to Sonny. He was having a dialogue with Sonny. He wanted Sonny to leave the shoreline and strike out for the deep water. He was Sonny's witness that deep water and drowning were not the same thing—he had been there, and he knew. And he wanted Sonny to know. He was waiting for Sonny to do the things on the keys which would let Creole know that Sonny was in the water.

And, while Creole listened, Sonny moved, deep within, exactly like someone in torment. I had never before thought of how awful the relationship must be between the musician and his instrument. He has to fill it, this instrument, with the breath of life, his own. He has to make it do what he wants it to do. And a piano is just a piano. It's made out of so much wood and wires and little hammers and big ones, and ivory. While there's only so much you can do with it, the only way to find this out is to try; to try and make it do everything.

And Sonny hadn't been near a piano for over a year. And he wasn't on much better terms with his life, not the life that stretched before him now. He and the piano stammered, started one way, got scared, stopped; started another way, panicked, marked time, started again; then seemed to have found a direction, panicked again, got stuck. And the face I saw on Sonny I'd never seen before. Everything had been burned out of it, and, at the same time, things usually hidden were being burned in, by the fire and fury of the battle which was occurring in him up there.

Yet, watching Creole's face as they neared the end of the first set, I had the feeling that something had happened, something I hadn't heard. Then they finished, there was scattered applause, and then, without an instant's warning, Creole started into something else, it was almost sardonic, it was *Am I Blue*.[6] And, as though he commanded, Sonny began to play. Something began to happen. And Creole let out the reins. The dry, low, black man said something awful on the drums, Creole answered, and the drums talked back. Then the horn insisted, sweet and high, slightly detached perhaps, and Creole listened, commenting now and then, dry, and driving, beautiful and calm and old. Then they all came together again, and Sonny was part of the family again. I could tell this from his face. He seemed to have found, right there beneath his fingers, a damn brand-new piano. It seemed that he couldn't get over it. Then, for a while, just being happy with Sonny, they seemed to be agreeing with him that brand-new pianos certainly were a gas.

Then Creole stepped forward to remind them that what they were playing was the blues. He hit something in all of them, he hit something in me, myself, and the music tightened and deepened, apprehension began to beat the air. Creole began to tell us what the blues were all about. They were not about anything very new. He and his boys up there were keeping it new, at the risk of ruin, destruction, madness, and death, in order to find new ways to make us listen. For, while the tale of how we suffer, and how we are delighted, and how we may triumph is never new, it always must be heard. There isn't any other tale to tell, it's the only light we've got in all this darkness.

And this tale, according to that face, that body, those strong hands on those strings, has another aspect in every country, and a new depth in every generation. Listen, Creole seemed to be saying, listen. Now these are Sonny's blues. He made the little black man on the drums know it, and the bright, brown

---

[6] One of the standard tunes in the jazz/blues repertoire.

man on the horn. Creole wasn't trying any longer to get Sonny in the water. He was wishing him Godspeed. Then he stepped back, very slowly, filling the air with the immense suggestion that Sonny speak for himself.

Then they all gathered around Sonny and Sonny played. Every now and again one of them seemed to say, amen. Sonny's fingers filled the air with life, his life. But that life contained so many others. And Sonny went all the way back, he really began with the spare, flat statement of the opening phrase of the song. Then he began to make it his. It was very beautiful because it wasn't hurried and it was no longer a lament. I seemed to hear with what burning he had made it his, and what burning we had yet to make it ours, how we could cease lamenting. Freedom lurked around us and I understood, at last, that he could help us to be free if we would listen, that he would never be free until we did. Yet, there was no battle in his face now, I heard what he had gone through, and would continue to go through until he came to rest in earth. He had made it his: that long line, of which we knew only Mama and Daddy. And he was giving it back, as everything must be given back, so that, passing through death, it can live forever. I saw my mother's face again, and felt, for the first time, how the stones of the road she had walked on must have bruised her feet. I saw the moonlit road where my father's brother died. And it brought something else back to me, and carried me past it, I saw my little girl again and felt Isabel's tears again, and I felt my own tears begin to rise. And I was yet aware that this was only a moment, that the world waited outside, as hungry as a tiger, and that trouble stretched above us, longer than the sky.

Then it was over. Creole and Sonny let out their breath, both soaking wet, and grinning. There was a lot of applause and some of it was real. In the dark, the girl came by and I asked her to take drinks to the bandstand. There was a long pause, while they talked up there in the indigo light and after awhile I saw the girl put a Scotch and milk on top of the piano for Sonny. He didn't seem to notice it, but just before they started playing again, he sipped from it and looked toward me, and nodded. Then he put it back on top of the piano. For me, then, as they began to play again, it glowed and shook above my brother's head like the very cup of trembling.[7]

FOR ANALYSIS

1. Explain this story's title.

2. What is the relation between the opening events and the end of the story?

3. What function does the **narrator's** encounter with Sonny's friend at the beginning of the story (paras. 9–47) serve?

---

[7] See the Old Testament, Isaiah 51:17, 22–23: "Awake, awake, stand up, O Jerusalem, which hast drunk at the hand of the Lord the cup of his fury; thou hast drunken the dregs of the cup of trembling, and wrung them out. . . . Behold, I have taken out of thine hand the cup of trembling, even the dregs of the cup of my fury; thou shalt no more drink it again: But I will put it into the hand of them that afflict thee."

4. Does the story offer any explanation for Sonny's addiction? Explain.

5. What adjectives would you use to describe the narrator? Does he change in the course of the story? Explain.

6. What effects does Baldwin achieve by rearranging the order of events?

7. What does the final sentence mean?

MAKING ARGUMENTS

Make an argument about the relationship between suffering and creativity. Is there something inherent in suffering that enables artists to make great art? As evidence, use "Sonny's Blues" and any other artists or works of art with which you're familiar.

WRITING TOPICS

1. What does this story have to say about the sources of creativity?

2. Discuss the significance of the **narrator's** observations on the revival meeting (paras. 177–78) to the **theme** of the story.

MAKING CONNECTIONS

1. Compare and contrast the way racism is portrayed in this story with its portrayal in Bambara's "The Lesson" (p. 98).

2. Kafka's "A Hunger Artist" (p. 347) is also about an artist and the process of artistic creation. What similarities or differences do you find between Kafka's story and Baldwin's?

ALICE WALKER (B. 1944)

EVERYDAY USE   1973

FOR YOUR GRANDMAMA

I will wait for her in the yard that Maggie and I made so clean and wavy yesterday afternoon. A yard like this is more comfortable than most people know. It is not just a yard. It is like an extended living room. When the hard clay is swept clean as a floor and the fine sand around the edges lined with tiny, irregular grooves anyone can come and sit and look up into the elm tree and wait for the breezes that never come inside the house.

Maggie will be nervous until after her sister goes: she will stand hopelessly in corners homely and ashamed of the burn scars down her arms and legs, eyeing her sister with a mixture of envy and awe. She thinks her sister has held life always in the palm of one hand, that "no" is a word the world never learned to say to her.

You've no doubt seen those TV shows where the child who has "made it" is confronted, as a surprise, by her own mother and father, tottering in weakly from backstage. (A pleasant surprise, of course: What would they do if parent and child came on the show only to curse out and insult each other?) On TV mother and child embrace and smile into each other's faces. Sometimes the mother and father weep, the child wraps them in her arms and leans across the table to tell how she would not have made it without their help. I have seen these programs.

Sometimes I dream a dream in which Dee and I are suddenly brought together on a TV program of this sort. Out of a dark and soft-seated limousine I am ushered into a bright room filled with many people. There I meet a smiling, gray, sporty man like Johnny Carson who shakes my hand and tells me what a fine girl I have. Then we are on the stage and Dee is embracing me with tears in her eyes. She pins on my dress a large orchid, even though she has told me once that she thinks orchids are tacky flowers.

In real life I am a large, big-boned woman with rough, man-working hands. 5 In the winter I wear flannel nightgowns to bed and overalls during the day. I can kill and clean a hog as mercilessly as a man. My fat keeps me hot in zero weather. I can work outside all day, breaking ice to get water for washing. I can eat pork liver cooked over the open fire minutes after it comes steaming from the hog. One winter I knocked a bull calf straight in the brain between the eyes with a sledge hammer and had the meat hung up to chill before nightfall. But of course all this does not show on television. I am the way my daughter would want me to be: a hundred pounds lighter, my skin like an uncooked barley pancake. My hair glistens in the hot bright lights. Johnny Carson has much to do to keep up with my quick and witty tongue.

But that is a mistake. I know even before I wake up. Who ever knew a Johnson with a quick tongue? Who can even imagine me looking a strange white man in the eye? It seems to me I have talked to them always with one foot raised in flight, with my head turned in whichever way is farthest from them. Dee, though. She would always look anyone in the eye. Hesitation was no part of her nature.

"How do I look, Mama?" Maggie says, showing just enough of her thin body enveloped in pink skirt and red blouse for me to know she's there, almost hidden by the door.

"Come out into the yard," I say.

Have you ever seen a lame animal, perhaps a dog run over by some careless person rich enough to own a car, sidle up to someone who is ignorant enough to be kind to him? That is the way my Maggie walks. She has been like this, chin on chest, eyes on ground, feet in shuffle, ever since the fire that burned the other house to the ground.

Dee is lighter than Maggie, with nicer hair and a fuller figure. She's a woman now, though sometimes I forget. How long ago was it that the other house burned? Ten, twelve years? Sometimes I can still hear the flames and feel Maggie's arms sticking to me, her hair smoking and her dress falling off her in little black papery flakes. Her eyes seemed stretched open, blazed open by the flames reflected in them. And Dee. I see her standing off under the sweet gum tree she used to dig gum out of; a look of concentration on her face as she watched the last dingy gray board of the house fall in toward the red-hot brick chimney. Why don't you do a dance around the ashes? I'd wanted to ask her. She had hated the house that much.

I used to think she hated Maggie, too. But that was before we raised the money, the church and me, to send her to Augusta to school. She used to read to us without pity; forcing words, lies, other folks' habits, whole lives upon us two, sitting trapped and ignorant underneath her voice. She washed us in a river of make-believe, burned us with a lot of knowledge we didn't necessarily need to know. Pressed us to her with the serious way she read, to shove us away at just the moment, like dimwits, we seemed about to understand.

Dee wanted nice things. A yellow organdy dress to wear to her graduation from high school; black pumps to match a green suit she'd made from an old suit somebody gave me. She was determined to stare down any disaster in her efforts. Her eyelids would not flicker for minutes at a time. Often I fought off the temptation to shake her. At sixteen she had a style of her own: and knew what style was.

I never had an education myself. After second grade the school was closed down. Don't ask me why: in 1927 colored asked fewer questions than they do now. Sometimes Maggie reads to me. She stumbles along good-naturedly but can't see well. She knows she is not bright. Like good looks and money,

10

quickness passed her by. She will marry John Thomas (who has mossy teeth in an earnest face) and then I'll be free to sit here and I guess just sing church songs to myself. Although I never was a good singer. Never could carry a tune. I was always better at a man's job. I used to love to milk till I was hoofed in the side in '49. Cows are soothing and slow and don't bother you, unless you try to milk them the wrong way.

I have deliberately turned my back on the house. It is three rooms, just like the one that burned, except the roof is tin; they don't make shingle roofs any more. There are no real windows, just some holes cut in the sides, like the portholes in a ship, but not round and not square, with rawhide holding the shutters up on the outside. This house is in a pasture, too, like the other one. No doubt when Dee sees it she will want to tear it down. She wrote me once that no matter where we "choose" to live, she will manage to come see us. But she will never bring her friends. Maggie and I thought about this and Maggie asked me, "Mama, when did Dee ever *have* any friends?"

She had a few. Furtive boys in pink shirts hanging about on washday after 15 school. Nervous girls who never laughed. Impressed with her they worshiped the well-turned phrase, the cute shape, the scalding humor that erupted like bubbles in lye. She read to them.

When she was courting Jimmy T she didn't have much time to pay to us, but turned all her faultfinding power on him. He *flew* to marry a cheap gal from a family of ignorant flashy people. She hardly had time to recompose herself.

When she comes I will meet—but there they are!

Maggie attempts to make a dash for the house, in her shuffling way, but I stay her with my hand. "Come back here," I say. And she stops and tries to dig a well in the sand with her toe.

It is hard to see them clearly through the strong sun. But even the first glimpse of leg out of the car tells me it is Dee. Her feet were always neat-looking, as if God himself had shaped them with a certain style. From the other side of the car comes a short, stocky man. Hair is all over his head a foot long and hanging from his chin like a kinky mule tail. I hear Maggie suck in her breath. "Uhnnnh," is what it sounds like. Like when you see the wriggling end of a snake just in front of your foot on the road. "Uhnnnh."

Dee next. A dress down to the ground, in this hot weather. A dress so loud 20 it hurts my eyes. There are yellows and oranges enough to throw back the light of the sun. I feel my whole face warming from the heat waves it throws out. Earrings, too, gold and hanging down to her shoulders. Bracelets dangling and making noises when she moves her arm up to shake the folds of the dress out of her armpits. The dress is loose and flows, and as she walks closer, I like it. I hear Maggie go "Uhnnnh" again. It is her sister's hair. It stands straight up like the wool on a sheep. It is black as night and around the edges are two long pigtails that rope about like small lizards disappearing behind her ears.

"Wa-su-zo-Tean-o!" she says, coming on in that gliding way the dress makes her move. The short stocky fellow with the hair to his navel is all grinning and he follows up with "Asalamalakim, my mother and sister!" He moves to hug

Maggie but she falls back, right up against the back of my chair. I feel her trembling there and when I look up I see the perspiration falling off her chin.

"Don't get up," says Dee. Since I am stout it takes something of a push. You can see me trying to move a second or two before I make it. She turns, showing white heels through her sandals, and goes back to the car. Out she peeks next with a Polaroid. She stoops down quickly and lines up picture after picture of me sitting there in front of the house with Maggie cowering behind me. She never takes a shot without making sure the house is included. When a cow comes nibbling around the edge of the yard she snaps it and me and Maggie *and* the house. Then she puts the Polaroid in the back seat of the car, and comes up and kisses me on the forehead.

Meanwhile Asalamalakim is going through motions with Maggie's hand. Maggie's hand is as limp as a fish, and probably as cold, despite the sweat, and she keeps trying to pull it back. It looks like Asalamalakim wants to shake hands but wants to do it fancy. Or maybe he don't know how people shake hands. Anyhow, he soon gives up on Maggie.

"Well," I say. "Dee."

"No, Mama," she says. "Not 'Dee,' Wangero Leewanika Kemanjo!"   25

"What happened to 'Dee'?" I wanted to know.

"She's dead," Wangero said. "I couldn't bear it any longer being named after the people who oppress me."

"You know as well as me you was named after your aunt Dicie," I said. Dicie is my sister. She named Dee. We called her "Big Dee" after Dee was born.

"But who was *she* named after?" asked Wangero.

"I guess after Grandma Dee," I said.   30

"And who was she named after?" asked Wangero.

"Her mother," I said, and saw Wangero was getting tired. "That's about as far back as I can trace it," I said. Though, in fact, I probably could have carried it back beyond the Civil War through the branches.

"Well," said Asalamalakim, "there you are."

"Uhnnnh," I heard Maggie say.

"There I was not," I said, "before 'Dicie' cropped up in our family, so why   35
should I try to trace it that far back?"

He just stood there grinning, looking down on me like somebody inspecting a Model A car. Every once in a while he and Wangero sent eye signals over my head.

"How do you pronounce this name?" I asked.

"You don't have to call me by it if you don't want to," said Wangero.

"Why shouldn't I?" I asked. "If that's what you want us to call you, we'll call you."

"I know it might sound awkward at first," said Wangero.   40

"I'll get used to it," I said. "Ream it out again."

Well, soon we got the name out of the way. Asalamalakim had a name twice as long and three times as hard. After I tripped over it two or three times he told me to just call him Hakim-a-barber. I wanted to ask him was he a barber, but I didn't really think he was, so I didn't ask.

"You must belong to those beef-cattle peoples down the road," I said. They said "Asalamalakim" when they met you, too, but they didn't shake hands. Always too busy: feeding the cattle, fixing the fences, putting up salt-lick shelters, throwing down hay. When the white folks poisoned some of the herd the men stayed up all night with rifles in their hands. I walked a mile and a half just to see the sight.

Hakim-a-barber said, "I accept some of their doctrines, but farming and raising cattle is not my style." (They didn't tell me, and I didn't ask, whether Wangero [Dee] had really gone and married him.)

We sat down to eat and right away he said he didn't eat collards and pork was unclean. Wangero, though, went on through the chitlins and corn bread, the greens and everything else. She talked a blue streak over the sweet potatoes. Everything delighted her. Even the fact that we still used the benches her daddy made for the table when we couldn't afford to buy chairs. 45

"Oh, Mama!" she cried. Then turned to Hakim-a-barber. "I never knew how lovely these benches are. You can feel the rump prints," she said, running her hands underneath her and along the bench. Then she gave a sigh and her hand closed over Grandma Dee's butter dish. "That's it!" she said. "I knew there was something I wanted to ask you if I could have." She jumped up from the table and went over in the corner where the churn stood, the milk in its clabber by now. She looked at the churn and looked at it.

"This churn top is what I need," she said. "Didn't Uncle Buddy whittle it out of a tree you all used to have?"

"Yes," I said.

"Uh huh," she said happily. "And I want the dasher, too."

"Uncle Buddy whittle that, too?" asked the barber. 50

Dee (Wangero) looked up at me.

"Aunt Dee's first husband whittled the dash," said Maggie so low you almost couldn't hear her. "His name was Henry, but they called him Stash."

"Maggie's brain is like an elephant's," Wangero said, laughing. "I can use the churn top as a centerpiece for the alcove table," she said, sliding a plate over the churn, "and I'll think of something artistic to do with the dasher."

When she finished wrapping the dasher the handle stuck out. I took it for a moment in my hands. You didn't even have to look close to see where hands pushing the dasher up and down to make butter had left a kind of sink in the wood. In fact, there were a lot of small sinks; you could see where thumbs and fingers had sunk into the wood. It was beautiful light yellow wood, from a tree that grew in the yard where Big Dee and Stash had lived.

After dinner Dee (Wangero) went to the trunk at the foot of my bed and started rifling through it. Maggie hung back in the kitchen over the dishpan. Out came Wangero with two quilts. They had been pieced by Grandma Dee and then Big Dee and me had hung them on the quilt frames on the front porch and quilted them. One was in the Lone Star pattern. The other was Walk Around the Mountain. In both of them were scraps of dresses Grandma Dee had worn fifty and more years ago. Bits and pieces of Grandpa Jarrell's 55

Paisley shirts. And one teeny faded blue piece, about the size of a penny matchbox, that was from Great Grandpa Ezra's uniform that he wore in the Civil War.

"Mama," Wangero said sweet as a bird. "Can I have these old quilts?"

I heard something fall in the kitchen, and a minute later the kitchen door slammed.

"Why don't you take one or two of the others?" I asked. "These old things was just done by me and Big Dee from some tops your grandma pieced before she died."

"No," said Wangero. "I don't want those. They are stitched around the borders by machine."

"That'll make them last better," I said.   60

"That's not the point," said Wangero. "These are all pieces of dresses Grandma used to wear. She did all this stitching by hand. Imagine!" She held the quilts securely in her arms, stroking them.

"Some of the pieces, like those lavender ones, come from old clothes her mother handed down to her," I said, moving up to touch the quilts. Dee (Wangero) moved back just enough so that I couldn't reach the quilts. They already belonged to her.

"Imagine!" she breathed again, clutching them closely to her bosom.

"The truth is," I said, "I promised to give them quilts to Maggie, for when she marries John Thomas."

She gasped like a bee had stung her.   65

"Maggie can't appreciate these quilts!" she said. "She'd probably be backward enough to put them to everyday use."

"I reckon she would," I said. "God knows I been saving 'em for long enough with nobody using 'em. I hope she will!" I didn't want to bring up how I had offered Dee (Wangero) a quilt when she went away to college. Then she had told me they were old-fashioned, out of style.

"But they're *priceless!*" she was saying now, furiously; for she has a temper. "Maggie would put them on the bed and in five years they'd be in rags. Less than that!"

"She can always make some more," I said. "Maggie knows how to quilt."

Dee (Wangero) looked at me with hatred. "You just will not understand. The   70
point is these quilts, *these* quilts!"

"Well," I said, stumped. "What would *you* do with them?"

"Hang them," she said. As if that was the only thing you *could* do with quilts.

Maggie by now was standing in the door. I could almost hear the sound her feet made as they scraped over each other.

"She can have them, Mama," she said, like somebody used to never winning anything, or having anything reserved for her. "I can 'member Grandma Dee without the quilts."

I looked at her hard. She had filled her bottom lip with checkerberry snuff   75
and it gave her face a kind of dopey, hangdog look. It was Grandma Dee and Big Dee who taught her how to quilt herself. She stood there with her scarred

hands hidden in the folds of her skirt. She looked at her sister with something like fear but she wasn't mad at her. This was Maggie's portion. This was the way she knew God to work.

When I looked at her like that something hit me in the top of my head and ran down to the soles of my feet. Just like when I'm in church and the spirit of God touches me and I get happy and shout. I did something I never had done before: hugged Maggie to me, then dragged her on into the room, snatched the quilts out of Miss Wangero's hands and dumped them into Maggie's lap. Maggie just sat there on my bed with her mouth open.

"Take one or two of the others," I said to Dee.

But she turned without a word and went out to Hakim-a-barber.

"You just don't understand," she said, as Maggie and I came out to the car.

"What don't I understand?" I wanted to know.　　　　　　　　　　　80

"Your heritage," she said. And then she turned to Maggie, kissed her, and said, "You ought to try to make something of yourself, too, Maggie. It's really a new day for us. But from the way you and Mama still live you'd never know it."

She put on some sunglasses that hid everything above the tip of her nose and her chin.

Maggie smiled; maybe at the sunglasses. But a real smile, not scared. After we watched the car dust settle I asked Maggie to bring me a dip of snuff. And then the two of us sat there just enjoying, until it was time to go in the house and go to bed.

FOR ANALYSIS

1. What are the **narrator's** outstanding traits, her weaknesses, and her strengths?

2. How would you describe the narrator's feelings about her daughter Dee? About her daughter Maggie?

3. How would you describe the narrator's descriptions of herself? Are her actions consistent with the kind of person she says she is? Explain.

4. Why does the narrator recall the burning of the house? How does this event from the past help the reader understand the present action?

5. What are the sources of the story's humor?

6. What does Dee's boyfriend, Asalamalakim, represent?

7. Why does the narrator give the quilts to Maggie?

8. Explain the title. What is the meaning of the subtitle, "For Your Grandmama"?

MAKING ARGUMENTS

So much of "Everyday Use" is about the **narrator**, down to her **voice**—the way she describes what she sees and feels and thinks. Make an argument about Walker's choice to write in the first person, arguing either that she could or could not have achieved the same effects if she had written in the third person. How would Walker have let us see things from the narrator's **point of view**?

WRITING TOPICS

1. Analyze the opening two paragraphs of the story, showing how they set the **tone** and establish the tension of the story.

2. Write an essay analyzing the **conflict** in the story and the way it is resolved. Is the resolution satisfying? Explain.

MAKING CONNECTIONS

Compare Dee in this story and Miss Moore in Bambara's "The Lesson" (p. 98) as characters whose intellectual and educational superiority enables them to unsettle the tranquillity of those around them.

SHERMAN ALEXIE   (B. 1966)

WAR DANCES   2009

MY KAFKA BAGGAGE

A few years ago, after I returned home to Seattle from a trip to Los Angeles, I unpacked my bag and found a dead cockroach, shrouded by a dirty sock, in a corner. Shit, I thought. We're being invaded. So I threw the clothes, books, shoes, and toiletries back into the suitcase, carried it out to the driveway, and dumped the contents onto the pavement, ready to stomp on any other cockroach stowaways. But there was only the one cockroach, dead and stiff. As he lay on the pavement, I leaned closer to him. His legs were curled under his body. His head was tilted at a sad angle. Sad? Yes, sad. For who is lonelier than the cockroach without his tribe? I laughed at myself. I was feeling empathy for a dead cockroach. I wondered about its story. How had it got into my bag? And where? At the hotel in Los Angeles? In the airport baggage system? It hadn't originated in our house. We've kept those tiny bastards from our place for fifteen years. So where had this little vermin come from? Had he smelled something delicious in my bag—my musky deodorant or some crumb from a chocolate Power Bar—and climbed inside, only to be crushed by the shifts of fate and garment bags? As he died, did he feel fear? Isolation? Existential dread?

SYMPTOMS

Last summer, in reaction to various allergies I was suffering from, defensive mucus flooded my inner right ear and confused, frightened, and unmoored me. My allergies had never been this severe. I could barely hear a fucking thing with that side, so I had to turn my head in order to understand what my two sons, ages eight and ten, were saying.

"We're hungry," they said. "We keep telling you."

I was embarrassed.

"Mom would have fed us by now," they said.

Their mother had left for Italy with her mother two days before. My sons and I were going to enjoy a boys' week, filled with unwashed socks, REI rock-wall climbing, and ridiculous heaps of pasta.

"What are you going to cook?" my sons asked. "Why haven't you cooked yet?"

I'd been lying on the couch reading a book while they played and I hadn't realized that I'd gone partially deaf. So, for just, a moment, I could only weakly blame my allergies.

Then I recalled the man who went to the emergency room because he'd woken having lost most, if not all, of his hearing. The doctor peered into one

5

594

ear, saw an obstruction, reached in with small tweezers, and pulled out a cock-roach, then reached into the other ear and extracted a much larger cockroach. Did you know that ear wax is a delicacy for roaches?

I cooked dinner for my sons—overfed them out of guilt—and cleaned the 10 hell out of our home. Then I walked into the bathroom and stood before the mirror. I turned my head and body at weird angles and tried to see deeply into my congested ear; I sang hymns and prayed that I'd see a small angel trapped in the canal. I would free the poor thing, and she'd unfurl and pat dry her tiny wings, then fly to my lips and give me a sweet kiss for sheltering her metamorphosis.

When I woke at 3 A.M., completely deaf in my right ear, and positive that a damn swarm of locusts was wedged inside, I left a message for my doctor, and told him that I would be sitting outside his office when he reported for work.

This would be the first time I had been inside a health-care facility since my father's last surgery.

BLANKETS

After the surgeon had cut off my father's right foot—no, half of my father's right foot—and three toes from the left, I sat with him in the recovery room. It was more like a recovery hallway. There was no privacy, not even a thin cur-tain. I supposed this made it easier for the nurses to monitor the post-surgical patients, but, still, my father was exposed—his decades of poor health and worse decisions were illuminated—on white sheets in a white hallway under white lights.

"Are you O.K.?" I asked. It was a stupid question. Who could be O.K. after such a thing? Yesterday, my father had walked into the hospital. Yes, he'd shuffled while balancing on two canes, but that was still called walking. A few hours ago, my father still had both of his feet. They were black with rot and disease, but they were still, technically speaking, feet and toes. And, most important, those feet had belonged to my father. Now they were gone, sliced off. Where were they? What had the hospital done with the right foot and the toes from the left foot? Had they been thrown into the incinerator? Were their ashes already floating over the city?

"Doctor, I'm cold," my father said.   15

"Dad, it's me," I said.

"I know who you are. You're my son." But, given the blankness in my father's eyes, I assumed he was just guessing.

"Dad, you're in the hospital. You just had surgery."

"I know where I am. I'm cold."

"Do you want another blanket?" Stupid question. Of course, he wanted 20 another blanket. He probably wanted me to build a fucking campfire or drag in one of those giant heat blasters that N.F.L. football teams use on the sidelines.

I walked down the hallway—the recovery hallway—to the nurses' station. There were three women nurses there, two white and one black. I am Native American—Spokane and Coeur d'Alene Indian—and I thought my darker pigment might give me an edge with the black nurse, so I addressed her directly.

"My father is cold," I said. "Can I get another blanket?"

The nurse glanced up from her paperwork and regarded me. Her expression was neither compassionate nor callous.

"How can I help you, sir?" she asked.

"I'd like another blanket for my father. He's cold."   25

"I'll be with you in a moment, sir."

She looked back down at her paperwork. She made a few notes. Not knowing what else to do, I stood there and waited.

"Sir," the nurse said, "I'll be with you in a moment."

She was irritated. I understood. After all, how many thousands of times had she been asked for an extra blanket? She was a nurse, an educated woman, not a damn housekeeper. And it was never really about an extra blanket, was it? No, when people asked for an extra blanket they were asking for a time machine. My father, an alcoholic, diabetic Indian with terminally damaged kidneys, had just endured an incredibly expensive surgery for what? So that he could ride his motorized wheelchair to the bar and win bets by showing off his disfigured foot? Yes, she was a health-care worker and she didn't want to be cruel, but she believed that there came a point when doctors should stop rescuing people from their own self-destructive impulses. And I couldn't disagree with her, but I could ask for the most basic of comforts, couldn't I?

"My father," I said. "An extra blanket, please."   30

"Fine," she said. She got up and walked back to a linen closet, grabbed a white blanket, and handed it to me. "If you need anything else—"

I didn't wait around for the end of her sentence. With the blanket in hand, I walked back to my father. It was a thin blanket, laundered and sterilized a hundred times. In fact, it was too thin. It wasn't really a blanket. It was more like a large beach towel. Hell, it wasn't even good enough for that. It was more like the world's biggest coffee filter. Jesus, had health care finally come to this? Everybody was uninsured and unblanketed.

"Dad, I'm back."

He looked so small and pale lying in that hospital bed. How had this happened? For the first sixty-seven years of his life, my father had been a large and dark man. Now he was just another pale, sick drone in a hallway of pale, sick drones. A hive, I thought. This place is like a beehive with colony-collapse disorder.

"Dad, it's me."   35

"I'm cold."

"I have a blanket."

As I draped it over my father and tucked it around his body, I felt the first sting of grief. I'd read the hospital literature about this moment. There would come a time when roles would reverse and the adult child would become the caretaker of the ill parent. The circle of life. Such poetic bullshit.

"I can't get warm," my father said. "I'm freezing."

"I brought you a blanket, Dad. I put it on you."

"Get me another one. Please. I'm so cold. I need another blanket." 40

I knew that ten more of these cheap blankets wouldn't be enough. My father needed a real blanket, a good blanket.

I walked out of the recovery hallway and made my way through various doorways and other hallways, peering into rooms, looking at the patients and their families, searching for a particular kind of patient and family.

I walked through the E.R., through the cancer, heart and vascular, neuroscience, orthopedic, women's health, pediatric, and surgical wards. Nobody stopped me. My expression and posture were those of a man with a sick father, and so I belonged.

And then I saw him, another Native man, leaning against a wall near the 45 gift shop. Well, maybe he was Asian—lots of those in Seattle. He was a small man, pale brown, with muscular arms and a soft belly. Maybe he was Mexican, which is really a kind of Indian, too, but not the kind that I needed. It's hard to tell sometimes what people are. Even brown people guess at the identity of other brown people.

"Hey," I said.

"Hey," the other man said.

"You Indian?" I asked.

"Yeah."

"What tribe?" 50

"Lummi."

"I'm Spokane."

"My first wife was Spokane. I hated her."

"My first wife was Lummi. She hated me."

We laughed at the new jokes that instantly sounded old. 55

"Why are you in here?" I asked.

"My sister is having a baby," he said. "But don't worry, it's not mine."

"Ayyyyyy," I said and laughed.

"I don't even want to be here," the other Indian said. "But my dad started, like, this new Indian tradition. He says it's a thousand years old. But that's bullshit. He just made it up to impress himself. And the whole family goes along with it, even when we know it's bullshit. He's in the delivery room waving eagle feathers around. Jesus."

"What's the tradition?" 60

"Oh, he does a naming ceremony right in the hospital. It's supposed to protect the baby from all the technology and shit. Like hospitals are the big problem. You know how many babies died before we had good hospitals?"

"I don't know."

"Most of them. Well, shit, a lot of them, at least."

This guy was talking out of his ass. I liked him immediately.

"I mean," the guy said. "You should see my dad right now. He's pretending 65 to go into this, like, fucking trance, dancing around my sister in the bed, and he says he's trying to, you know, see into her womb, to see who the baby is, to see its true nature, so he can give it a name—a protective name—before it's born."

The guy laughed and threw his head back, banging it on the wall.

"I mean, come on, I'm a loser," he said and rubbed his sore skull. "My whole family is filled with losers."

The Indian world is filled with charlatans, men and women who pretend— hell, who might have come to believe—that they are holy. The year before, I went to a lecture at the University of Washington. An elderly Indian woman, a scholar, had come to orate on Indian sovereignty and literature. She kept arguing for some kind of separate indigenous literary identity, which was ironic considering that she was speaking English to a room full of white professors. But I wasn't angry with the woman, or even bored. No, I felt sorry for her. I realized that she was dying of nostalgia. She had taken nostalgia as her false idol—her thin blanket—and it was murdering her.

"Nostalgia," I said.

"What?" 70

"Your dad, he sounds like he's got a bad case of nostalgia."

"Yeah, I hear you catch that from fucking old high-school girlfriends," the man said. "What the hell you doing here, anyway?"

"My dad just got his feet cut off," I said.

"Diabetes?"

"And vodka."

"Vodka straight up or with a nostalgia chaser?" 75

"Both."

"Natural causes for an Indian."

"Yep."

There wasn't much to say after that. 80

"Well, I better get back," the man said. "Otherwise, my dad might wave an eagle feather and change my name."

"Hey, wait," I said.

"Yeah?"

"Can I ask you a favor?"

"What?" 85

"My dad, he's in the recovery room," I said. "Well, it's more like a hallway, and he's freezing, and they've only got these shitty little blankets, and I came looking for Indians in the hospital because I figured—well, I guessed if I found any Indians they might have some good blankets."

"So you want to borrow a blanket from us?" the man asked.

"Yeah."

"Because you thought Indians would just happen to have some extra blankets lying around?"

"Yeah." 90

"That's fucking ridiculous."

"I know."

"And it's racist."

"I know."

"You're stereotyping your own damn people."   95

"I know."

"But damn if we don't have a room full of Pendleton blankets. New ones. Jesus, you'd think my sister was having, like, a dozen babies."

Five minutes later, carrying a Pendleton Star blanket, the Indian man walked out of his sister's hospital room, accompanied by his father, who wore Levi's, a black T-shirt, and eagle feathers in his gray braids.

"We want to give your father this blanket," the old man said. "It was meant for my grandson, but I think it will be good for your father, too."

"Thank you."   100

"Let me bless it. I will sing a healing song for the blanket. And for your father."

I flinched. This old man wanted to sing a song? That was dangerous. The song could take two minutes or two hours. It was impossible to know. Hell, considering how desperate the old man was to be seen as holy, he might sing for a week. I couldn't let him begin his song without issuing a caveat.

"My dad," I said. "I really need to get back to him. He's really sick."

"Don't worry," the old man said, winking. "I'll sing one of my short ones."

Jesus, who'd ever heard of a self-aware fundamentalist? The son, perhaps   105 not the unbeliever he'd pretended to be, sang backup as his father launched into a radio-friendly honor song, just three and a half minutes, like any Top Forty rock song of the past fifty years. But here's the funny thing: the old man couldn't sing very well. If you had the balls to sing healing songs in hospital hallways, then you should have a great voice, right? But, no, this guy couldn't keep the tune; his voice cracked and wavered. Does a holy song lose its power if the singer is untalented?

"That is your father's song," the old man said when he finished. "I give it to him. I will never sing it again. It belongs to your father now."

Behind his back, the old man's son rolled his eyes and walked into his sister's room.

"O.K., thank you," I said. I felt like an ass, accepting the blanket and the old man's good wishes, and silently mocking them at the same time. But maybe the old man did have some power, some real medicine, because he peeked into my brain.

"It doesn't matter if you believe in the healing song," he said. "It only matters that the blanket heard."

"Where have you been?" my father asked when I returned. "I'm cold."   110

"I know, I know," I said. "I found you a blanket. A good one. It will keep you warm."

I draped the Star blanket over my father. He pulled the thick wool up to his chin. And then he began to sing. It was a healing song, not the same song that

I had just heard but a healing song nonetheless. My father could sing beautifully. I wondered if it was proper for a man to sing a healing song for himself. I wondered if my father needed help with the song. I hadn't sung for many years, not like that, but I joined him. I knew that this song would not bring back my father's feet. This song would not repair my father's bladder, kidneys, lungs, and heart. This song would not prevent my father from drinking a bottle of vodka as soon as he could sit up in bed. This song would not defeat death. No, I thought, this song is temporary, but right now temporary is good enough. And it was a good song. Our voices filled the recovery hallway. The sick and the healthy stopped to listen. The nurses, even the remote black one, unconsciously took a few steps toward us. She sighed and smiled. I smiled back. I knew what she was thinking. Sometimes, even after all these years, she could still be surprised by her work. She still marvelled at the infinite and ridiculous faith of other people.

DOCTOR'S OFFICE

I took my kids with me to my doctor, a handsome man—a reservist—who'd served in both Iraq wars. I told him that I couldn't hear because of my allergies. He said he would likely have to clear wax and mucus out of my ear, but when he scoped inside he discovered nothing.

"Nope, it's all dry in there," he said.

He led my sons and me to the audiologist in the other half of the building. 115
I was scared, but I wanted my children to remain calm, so I tried to stay measured. More than anything, I wanted my wife to materialize.

During the hearing test, I heard only thirty per cent of the clicks, bells, and words—I apparently had nerve- and bone-conductive deafness. My inner ear thumped and thumped.

How many cockroaches were in my head?

My doctor said, "We need an MRI of your ear and brain, and maybe we'll find out what's going on."

"Maybe"? That word terrified me.

What the fuck was wrong with my fucking head? Had my hydrocephalus 120
come back? Had my levees burst? Was I going to flood?

HYDROCEPHALUS

Merriam-Webster's dictionary defines "hydrocephalus" as "an abnormal increase in the amount of cerebrospinal fluid within the cranial cavity that is accompanied by expansion of the cerebral ventricles, enlargement of the skull and especially the forehead, and atrophy of the brain." I define "hydrocephalus" as "the obese, imperialistic water demon that nearly killed me when I was a baby."

In order to save my life, and stop the water demon, I had brain surgery in 1967, when I was six months old. I was supposed to die. Obviously, I didn't. I was supposed to be severely mentally disabled. I have only minor to moderate brain damage. I was supposed to have epileptic seizures. Those I did have, until I was seven years old. I was on phenobarbital, a major-league anti-seizure medication, for six years.

The side effects of phenobarbital—all of which I suffered to some degree or another as a child—are sleepwalking, agitation, confusion, depression, nightmares, hallucinations, insomnia, apnea, vomiting, constipation, dermatitis, fever, liver and bladder dysfunction, and psychiatric disturbance.

How do you like them cockroaches?

Now, as an adult, thirty-three years removed from phenobarbital, I still 125 suffer—to some degree or another—from sleepwalking, agitation, confusion, depression, nightmares, hallucinations, insomnia, bladder dysfunction, apnea, and dermatitis.

Is there such a disease as post-phenobarbital traumatic stress disorder?

Most hydrocephalics are shunted. A shunt is essentially brain plumbing that drains away excess cerebrospinal fluid. The shunts often fuck up and stop working. I know hydrocephalics who've had a hundred or more shunt revisions and repairs. That's more than a hundred brain surgeries. There are ten fingers on any surgeon's hands. There are two or three surgeons involved in any particular brain operation. That means that some hydrocephalics have had their brains fondled by three thousand fingers.

I'm lucky. I was shunted only temporarily. And I hadn't suffered any hydrocephalic symptoms since I was seven years old.

Until July, 2008, when, at the age of forty-one, I went deaf in my right ear.

CONVERSATION

Sitting in my car in the hospital parking garage, I called my brother-in-law, 130 who was babysitting my sons.

"Hey, it's me. I just got done with the MRI on my head."

My brother-in-law said something unintelligible. I realized that I was holding my cell to my bad ear, and I switched it to the good ear.

"The MRI dude didn't look happy," I said.

"That's not good," my brother-in-law said.

"No, it's not. But he's just a tech guy, right? He's not an expert on brains or 135 anything. He's just the photographer, really. And he doesn't know anything about ears or deafness or anything, I don't think. Ah, hell, I don't know what he knows. I just didn't like the look on his face when I was done."

"Maybe he just didn't like you."

"Well, I got worried when I told him I had hydrocephalus when I was a baby and he didn't seem to know what that was."

"Nobody knows what that is."

"That's the truth. Have you fed the boys dinner?'

"Yeah, but I was scrounging. There's not much here."   140

"I better go shopping."

"Are you sure? I can do it if you need me to. I can shop the shit out of Trader Joe's."

"No, it'll be good for me. I feel good. I fell asleep during the MRI. And I kept twitching, so we had to do it twice. Otherwise, I would've been done earlier."

"That's O.K. I'm O.K. The boys are O.K."

"You know, before you go in the MRI tube they ask you what kind of music 145
you want to listen to—jazz, classical, rock, or country—and I remembered how my dad spent a lot of time in MRI tubes near the end of his life. So I was wondering what kind of music he chose. I mean, he couldn't hear shit anyway by that time, but he still must have chosen something. And I wanted to choose the same thing he chose. So I picked country."

"Was it good country?"

"It was fucking Shania Twain and Faith Hill shit. I was hoping for George Jones or Loretta Lynn, or even some George Strait. Hell, I would've cried if they'd played Charley Pride or Freddy Fender."

"You wanted to hear the Alcoholic Indian Father Jukebox."

"Hey, that's my line. You can't quote me to me."

"Why not? You're always quoting you to you."   150

"Kiss my ass. So, hey, I'm O.K., I think. And I'm going to the store. I'll see you in a bit. You want anything?"

"Ah, man, I love Trader Joe's. But you know what's bad about them? You fall in love with something they have—they stock it for a year—and then it just disappears. They had those wontons I loved, and now they don't. I was willing to shop for you and the boys, but I don't want anything for me. I'm on a one-man hunger strike against them."

WORLD PHONE CONVERSATION, 3 A.M.

After I got home with yogurt and turkey dogs and Cinnamon Toast Crunch and my brother-in-law left, I watched George Romero's "Diary of the Dead," and laughed at myself for choosing a movie that featured dozens of zombies getting shot in the head.

When the movie was over, I called my wife, nine hours ahead in Italy.

"I should come home," she said.   155

"No, I'm O.K.," I said. "Come on, you're in Rome. What are you seeing today?"

"The Vatican."

"You can't leave now. You have to go and steal something. It will be revenge for every Indian. Or maybe you can plant an eagle feather and claim that you just discovered Italy."

"I'm worried."

"Yeah, Catholicism has always worried me."   160

"Stop being funny. I should see if I can get Mom and me on a flight tonight."

"No, no, listen, your mom is old. This might be her last adventure. It might be your last adventure with her. Stay there. Say hi to the Pope for me. Tell him I like his shoes."

That night, my sons climbed into bed with me. We all slept curled around one another like sled dogs in a snowstorm. I woke, hour by hour, and touched my head and neck to see if they had changed shape—to feel if antennae were growing. Some insects hear with their antennae. Maybe that was what was happening to me.

VALEDICTION

My father, a part-time blue-collar construction worker, died of full-time alcoholism in March, 2003. On his deathbed, he said to me, "Turn down that light, please."

"Which light?" I asked.   165

"The light on the ceiling."

"Dad, there's no light."

"It burns my skin, son. It's too bright. It hurts my eyes."

"Dad, I promise you there's no light."

"Don't lie to me, son. It's God passing judgment on earth."   170

"Dad, you've been an atheist since '79. Come on, you're just remembering your birth. On your last day, you're going back to your first."

"No, son, it's God telling me I'm doomed. He's using the brightest lights in the universe to show me the way to my flame-filled tomb."

"No, Dad, those lights were in your delivery room."

"If that's true, son, then turn down my mother's womb."

We buried my father in the tiny Catholic cemetery on our reservation.   175
Since I am named after him, I had to stare at a tombstone with my name on it.

BATTLE FATIGUE

Two months after my father's death, I began research on a book about our family's history with war. I had a cousin who served as a cook in the Gulf War, in 1990; I had another cousin who served in the Vietnam War as a cook; and my father's father, Adolph, served in the Second World War and was killed in action on Okinawa, on April 5, 1945.

During my research, I interviewed thirteen men who'd served with my cousin in Vietnam but could find only one surviving man who'd served with my grandfather. This is a partial transcript of that interview, recorded with a microphone and an iPod on January 14, 2008:

Me: Ah, yes, hello. I'm here in Livonia, Michigan, to interview—well, perhaps you should introduce yourself, please?

Leonard Elmore: What?

Me: Um, oh, I'm sorry, I was asking if you could perhaps introduce yourself. 180

L.E.: You're going to have to speak up. I think my hearing aid is going low on power or something.

Me: That is a fancy thing in your ear.

L.E.: Yeah, let me mess with it a bit. I got a remote control for it. I can listen to the TV, the stereo, and the telephone with this thing. It's fancy. It's one of them Bluetooth hearing aids. My grandson bought it for me. Wait, O.K., there we go. I can hear now. So, what were you asking?

Me: I was hoping you could introduce yourself into my recorder here.

L.E.: Sure, my name is Leonard Elmore. 185

Me: How old are you?

L.E.: I'm eighty-five and a half years old (*laughter*). My great-grandkids are always saying they're seven and a half or nine and a half or whatever. It just cracks me up to say the same thing at my age.

Me: So, that's funny, um, but I'm here to ask you some questions about my grandfather—

L.E.: Adolph. It's hard to forget a name like that. An Indian named Adolph, and there was that Nazi bastard named Adolph. Your grandfather caught plenty of grief over that. But we mostly called him Chief. Did you know that?

Me: I could have guessed. 190

L.E.: Yeah, nowadays I suppose it isn't a good thing to call an Indian Chief, but back then it was what we did. I served with a few Indians. They didn't segregate them Indians, you know, not like the black boys. I know you aren't supposed to call them boys anymore, but they were boys. All of us were boys, I guess. But the thing is, those Indian boys lived and slept and ate with us white boys. They were right there with us. But, anyway, we called all them Indians Chief. I bet you've been called Chief a few times yourself.

Me: Just once.

L.E.: Were you all right with it?

Me: I threw a basketball in the guy's face.

L.E. (*laughs*). 195

Me: We live in different times.

L.E.: Yes, we do. Yes, we do.

Me: So, perhaps you could, uh, tell me something about my grandfather.

L.E.: I can tell you how he died.

Me: Really? 200

L.E.: Yeah, it was on Okinawa, and we hit the beach, and, well, it's hard to talk about it. It was the worst thing—it was hell. No, that's not even a good way to describe it. I'm not a writer like you, I'm not a poet, so I don't have the word, but just think of it this way. That beach, that island, was filled with sons and fathers, men who loved and were loved, American and Japanese and Okinawan, and all of us were dying, were being killed by other sons and fathers who also loved and were loved.

Me: That sounds like poetry to me—tragic poetry.

L.E.: Well, anyway, it was like that. Fire everywhere. And two of our boys, Jonesy and O'Neal, went down, were wounded and in the open on the sand. And your grandfather—who was just this little man, barely over five feet tall and maybe a hundred and thirty pounds—he just ran out there and picked up those two guys, one on each shoulder, and carried them to cover. Hey, are you O.K., son?

Me: Yes, I'm sorry. But, well, the thing is, I knew my grandfather was a war hero—he won twelve medals—but I could never find out what he did to win the medals.

L.E.: I didn't know about any medals. I just know what I saw. Your grand- 205 father saved those two boys, but he got shot in the back doing it. And he lay there in the sand—I was lying right beside him—and he died.

Me: Did he say anything before he died?

L.E.: Hold on. I need to—

Me: Are you O.K.?

L.E.: It's just—I can't—

Me: I'm sorry. Is there something wrong? 210

L.E.: No, it's just—with your book and everything, I know you want something big here. I know you want something big from your grandfather. I know you're hoping he said something huge and poetic, and, honestly, I was thinking about lying to you. I was thinking about making up something as beautiful as I could. Something about love and forgiveness and courage and all that. But I couldn't think of anything good enough. And I didn't want to lie to you. So I have to be honest and say that your grandfather didn't say anything. He just died there in the sand. In silence.

ORPHANS

I could not sleep. I was scared that I would die if I slept. And I didn't want my sons to become orphans—partial orphans—as they slept. So I stayed awake and waited for dawn. Then, at 3 a.m., the phone rang.

"It's me," my wife said. "I don't care what you say. I'll be home in sixteen hours."

"Thank you," I said.

COFFEE-SHOP NEWS

While I waited for the results of the MRI, I asked my brother-in-law to watch 215 the boys again because I didn't want to get bad news in front of them.

Alone and haunted, I wandered the mall, tried on clothes, and waited for my cell phone to ring.

Two hours later, I wanted to murder everything, so I drove south to a coffee joint, a spotless place called Dirty Joe's. Yes, I was silly enough to think that I'd be calmer with a caffeinated drink.

As I sat outside in a wooden chair and sipped my coffee, I cursed the vague, rumbling, ringing noise in my ear. And yet when my cell phone rang I again held it to my deaf ear.

"Hello. Hello," I said and wondered if it was a prank call, then remembered and switched the phone to my left ear.

"Hello," my doctor said. "Are you there?   220

"Yes," I said. "So what's going on?"

"There are irregularities in your head."

"My head's always been irregular."

"It's good to have a sense of humor," the doctor said. "You have a small tumor that is called a meningioma. They grow in the meninges membranes that lie between your brain and your skull."

"Shit," I said. "I have cancer."   225

"Well," he said. "These kinds of tumors are usually non-cancerous. And they grow very slowly, so in six months or so we'll do another MRI. Don't worry. You're going to be O.K."

"What about my hearing?" I asked.

"We don't know what is causing the hearing loss, but you should start a course of prednisone, a steroid, just to go with the odds. Your deafness might lessen if left alone, but we've had success with the steroids in bringing back hearing. There are side effects, like insomnia, weight gain, night sweats, and depression."

"Oh, boy," I said. "Those side effects might make up most of my personality already. Will the 'roids also make me quick to pass judgment? And I've always wished I had a dozen more skin tags and moles."

The doctor chuckled. "You're a funny man."   230

I wanted to throw my phone into a wall, but I said goodbye instead and glared at the tumorless people and their pretty tumorless heads.

MENINGIOMA

Mayoclinic.com gave this definition of "meningioma": "a tumor that arises from the meninges—the membranes that surround your brain and spinal cord. The majority of meningioma cases are noncancerous (benign), though rarely a meningioma can be cancerous (malignant)."

It was a scary and yet strangely positive description. No one ever wants to read the word "malignant" unless you're reading a Charles Dickens novel about an evil landlord, but "benign" and "majority" are two words that go well together.

From the University of Washington Medical School Web site I learned that meningioma tumors "are usually benign, slow growing and do not spread into normal brain tissue. Typically, a meningioma grows inward causing pressure on the brain or spinal cord. It may grow outward toward the skull, causing it to thicken."

So, wait, what the fuck? A meningioma can cause pressure on the brain, and 235 spinal fluid? Oh, you mean just like fucking hydrocephalus? Just like the water demon that once tried to crush my brain and kill me? Armed with this new information—with these new questions—I called my doctor.

"Hey, you're O.K.," he said. "We're going to closely monitor you. And your meningioma is very small."

"O.K., but I just read—"

"Did you go on the Internet?"

"Yes."

"Which sites?" 240

"Mayo Clinic and the University of Washington."

"O.K., those are pretty good sites. Let me look at them."

I listened to my doctor type.

"O.K., those are accurate," he said.

"What do you mean by accurate?" I asked. "I mean, the whole pressure- 245 on-the-brain thing—that sounds like hydrocephalus."

"Well, there were some irregularities in your MRI that were the burr holes from your surgery, and there seems to be some scarring and perhaps you had an old concussion. But other than that it all looks fine."

"But what about me going deaf? Can't these tumors make you lose hearing?"

"Yes, but only if they're located near an auditory nerve. And your tumor is not."

"Can this tumor cause pressure on my brain?"

"It could, but yours is too small for that." 250

"So I'm supposed to trust you on the tumor thing when you can't figure out the hearing thing?"

"There is no physical correlation between your deafness and the tumor. Do the twenty-day treatment of prednisone, and the audiologist and I will examine your ear and your hearing then. If there's no improvement, we'll figure out other ways of treating you."

"But you won't be treating the tumor?"

"Like I said, we'll scan you again in six to nine months—"

"You said six before." 255

"O.K., in six months we'll take another MRI, and if it has grown significantly—or has changed shape or location or anything dramatic—then we'll talk about treatment options. But if you look on the Internet—and I know you're going to spend a lot of time obsessing about this, so I'll tell you what you'll find. About two per cent of the population live their whole lives with undetected meningiomas. The tumors can become quite large, without any side effects, and are found only at autopsies conducted for other reasons of death. Even when these kinds of tumors become invasive or dangerous, they are still rarely fatal. And your tumor, even if it grows fairly quickly, will not likely become an issue for many years, decades. So that's what I can tell you right now. How are you feeling?"

"Freaked and fucked,"

I wanted to feel reassured, but I had a brain tumor. How can one feel any optimism about being diagnosed with a brain tumor? Even if that brain tumor is neither cancerous nor interested in crushing one's brain?

DRUGSTORE INDIAN

In Bartell Drugs, I gave the pharmacist my prescription for prednisone.

"Is this your first fill with us?" she asked.   260

"No," I said. "And it won't be my last."

I felt like an ass, but she looked bored.

"It'll take thirty minutes," she said. "More or less. We'll page you over the speakers."

I don't think I'd ever felt weaker. Or more vulnerable. Or more absurd. I was the weak antelope in the herd—yeah, the mangy fucker with the big limp and a sign that read, "Eat Me! I'm a Gimp!"

So for thirty minutes I walked the store and found myself shoving more   265
and more useful shit into my shopping basket, as if I were filling my casket with things I'd need in the afterlife. I grabbed toothpaste, a Swiss Army knife, moisturizer, mouthwash, nonstick Band-Aids, antacid, protein bars, and extra razor blades. I grabbed pen and paper. And I also grabbed an ice scraper and sunscreen. Who can predict what kind of weather awaits us in Heaven?

This random shopping made me feel better for a few minutes, but then I stopped and walked to the toy aisle. My boys needed gifts, Lego cars or something, for a lift, a shot of capitalist joy. But the selection of proper toys is both an art and a science. I have been wrong as often as right and have heard the sad song of a disappointed son.

Shit, I knew that if I died my sons would survive, even thrive, because of their graceful mother.

I thought of my father's life. He had been just six when his father was killed in the Second World War. Then his mother, ill with tuberculosis, had died a few months later. Six years old and my father was cratered. In most ways, he never stopped being six. There was no religion, no magic, and no song or dance that could have helped my father.

I needed a drink of water, so I found the fountain and drank and drank until the pharmacist called my name.

"Have you taken these before?" she asked.   270

I said, "No, but they're going to kick my ass, aren't they?"

That made the pharmacist smile, so I felt sadly and briefly worthwhile. But another customer, some nosy hag, said, "You've got a lot of sleepless nights ahead of you."

I was shocked. I stammered, glared at her, and said, "Miss, how is this any of your business? Please, just fuck all the way off, O.K.?"

She had no idea what to say, so she just turned and walked away, and I pulled out my credit card and paid far too much for my goddam steroids, and forgot to bring the toys home to my boys.

EXIT INTERVIEW FOR MY FATHER

- True or False: When a reservation-raised Native American dies of alco- 275
holism, it should be considered death by natural causes.
- Do you understand the term "wanderlust," and, if you do, can you please
tell us, in twenty-five words or less, what place made you wanderlust the most?
- Did you, when drunk, ever get behind the tattered wheel of a '76 Ford
three-speed van and somehow drive your family a thousand miles on an
empty tank of gas?
- Is it true that the only literary term that has any real meaning in the Native
American world is "road movie"?
- How many times, during any of your road trips, did your children ask
you, "Are we there yet?"
- In twenty-five words or less, please define "there." 280
- Sir, in your thirty-nine years as a parent you broke your children's hearts,
collectively and individually, six hundred and twelve times, and you did this
without ever striking any human being in anger. Does this absence of physical
violence make you a better man than you might otherwise have been?
- Without using the words "man" or "good," can you please define what it
means to be a good man?
- Do you think you will see angels before you die? Do you think angels will
come to escort you to Heaven? As the angels are carrying you to Heaven, how
many times will you ask, "Are we there yet?"
- Your son distinctly remembers stopping once or twice a month at that
grocery store in Freeman, Washington, where you would buy him a red-white-
and-blue rocket Popsicle and purchase for yourself a pickled pig foot. Your son
distinctly remembers that the feet still had their toenails and little tufts of pig
fur. Could this be true? Did you actually eat such horrendous food?
- Your son has often made the joke that you were the only Indian of your 285
generation who went to Catholic school on purpose. This is, of course, a taste-
less joke that makes light of the forced incarceration and subsequent physical,
spiritual, cultural, and sexual abuse of tens of thousands of Native American
children in Catholic and Protestant boarding schools. In consideration of your
son's questionable judgment in telling jokes, do you think there should be any
moral limits placed on comedy?
- Your other son and your two daughters, all over thirty-six years of age,
still live in your house. Do you think that this is a lovely expression of tribal
culture? Or is it a symptom of extreme familial co-dependency? Or is it both
things at the same time?
- F. Scott Fitzgerald wrote that the sign of a superior mind "is the ability to
hold two opposing ideas at the same time." Do you believe this to be true? And
is it also true that you once said, "The only time white people tell the truth is
when they keep their mouths shut"?
- A poet once wrote, "Pain is never added to pain. It multiplies." Can you
tell us, in twenty-five words or less, exactly how much we all hate mathematical blackmail?

• Your son wrote this poem to explain one of the most significant nights in his life:

Mutually Assured Destruction

When I was nine, my father sliced his knee
With a chainsaw. But he let himself bleed
And finished cutting down one more tree
Before his boss drove him to EMERGENCY.

Late that night, stoned on morphine and beer,
My father needed my help to steer
His pickup into the woods. "Watch for deer,"
My father said. "Those things just appear

Like magic." It was an Indian summer
And we drove through warm rain and thunder,
Until we found that chainsaw, lying under
The fallen pine. Then I watched, with wonder,

As my father, shotgun-rich and impulse-poor,
Blasted that chainsaw dead. "What was that for?"
I asked. "Son," my father said. "Here's the score.
Once a thing tastes blood, it will come for more."

• Well, first of all, as you know, you did cut your knee with a chainsaw, but
in direct contradiction to your son's poem:

(a) You immediately went to the emergency room.

(b) Your boss called your wife, who drove you to the emergency room.

(c) You were given morphine, but even you were not stupid enough to drink alcohol while on serious narcotics.

(d) You and your son did not get into the pickup that night.

(e) And, even if you had driven the pickup, you were not injured seriously enough to need your son's help with the pedals and/or the steering wheel.

(f) You never in your life used the word "appear," and you certainly never used the phrase "like magic."

(g) You think that "Indian summer" is a questionable seasonal reference for an Indian poet to use.

(h) What the fuck is "warm rain and thunder"? Well, everybody knows what "warm rain" is, but what the fuck is "warm thunder"?

(i) You never went looking for that chainsaw, because it belonged to the Spokane Tribe of Indians, and what kind of freak would want to reclaim the chainsaw that had just cut the shit out of his knee?

(j) You also agree that the entire third stanza of this poem sounds like a Bruce Springsteen song, and not necessarily one of the great ones.

(k) And yet "shotgun-rich and impulse-poor" is one of the greatest descriptions your son has ever written and probably redeems the entire poem.

(l) You never owned a shotgun. You did own a few rifles in your youth, but did not own so much as a pellet gun during the last thirty years of your life.

(m) You never said, in any context, "Once a thing tastes blood, it will come for more."

(n) But, as you read it, you know that is absolutely true and does indeed sound suspiciously like your entire life philosophy.

(o) Other summations of your life philosophy include: "It's all wasted days and wasted nights." 305

(p) And: "If God really loved Indians, he would have made us white people."

(q) And: "Oscar Robertson should be the man on the N.B.A. logo. They only put Jerry West on there because he's a white guy."

(r) And: "A peanut-butter sandwich with onions—damn, that's the way to go."

(s) And: "Why eat a pomegranate when you can eat a plain old apple. Or a carrot. When it comes to fruit and vegetables, eat only the simple stuff."

(t) And: "If you really want a woman to love you, then you have to dance. 310 And if you don't want to dance, then you're going to have to work extra hard to make a woman love you forever, and you will always run the risk that she will leave you at any second for a man who knows how to tango."

(u) And: "I really miss those cafeterias they used to have at Kmart. I don't know why they stopped having those. If there is a Heaven, I firmly believe it's a Kmart cafeteria."

(v) And: "A father always knows what his sons are doing. For instance, boys, I knew you were sneaking that *Hustler* magazine out of my bedroom. You remember that one. Where actors who looked like Captain Kirk and Lieutenant Uhura were screwing on the bridge of the Enterprise. Yeah, that one. I know you kept borrowing it. I let you borrow it. Remember this: men and pornography are like plants and sunshine. To me, porn is photosynthesis."

(w) And: "Your mother is a better man than me. Mothers are almost always better men than men are."

REUNION

After she returned from Italy, my wife climbed into bed with me. I felt as if I hadn't slept comfortably in years.

I said, "There was a rumor that I'd grown a tumor, but I killed it with humor." 315

"How long have you been waiting to tell me that one?" she asked.

"Oh, probably since the first time some doctor put his fingers in my brain."

We made love. We fell asleep. But, agitated by the steroids, I woke at 2, 3, 4, and 5 A.M. The bed was killing my back, so I lay flat on the floor. I wasn't going to die anytime soon, at least not because of my little friend Tumor, but that didn't make me feel any more comfortable or comforted. I felt distant from the world—from my wife and my sons, from my mother and my siblings, from all my friends. I felt closest to those who'd always had fingers in their brains.

I didn't feel any closer to the world six months later, when another MRI revealed that my meningioma had not grown in size or changed its shape.

"You're looking good," my doctor said. "How's your hearing?"   320

"I think I've got about ninety per cent of it back."

"Well, then, the steroids worked. Good."

And I didn't feel any more intimate with the world nine months after that, when one more MRI made my doctor hypothesize that my meningioma might only be more scar tissue from the hydrocephalus.

"Frankly," he said, "your brain is beautiful."

"Thank you," I said, though it was the oddest compliment I'd ever received.   325

I wanted to call my father and tell him that a white man thought my brain was beautiful. But I couldn't tell him anything. He was dead. I told my wife and my sons that I was O.K. I told my mother and my siblings. I told my friends. But none of them laughed as hard about my beautiful brain as I knew my father—the drunk bastard—would have.

FOR ANALYSIS

1. Why do you think Alexie calls the first section of his story "My Kafka Baggage"?

2. Can you identify the main **plot** of this story? If so, what is it? If not, why?

3. When (in terms of events, not the calendar) does the main action in the story take place? Identify the other plotlines and describe their chronological relation to it.

4. What is the significance to the story of the ceremony that takes place in the hospital? How would you describe the **narrator's** reaction to it?

5. Why might it be important that three generations of the narrator's family are present in the story? How is this story not only about the narrator's relationship with his father but also about his relationship with his children?

6. What role does humor play in this story? Do you expect humor in a story about a subject such as this? What effects does it have on you as you read?

7. How does the narrator feel about his Native American heritage? Is there a simple answer to this question? Why or why not?

8. Reread the story's last sentence. What about the entire story does it capture?

MAKING ARGUMENTS

The first question in the "Exit Interview" section reads: "True or False: When a reservation-raised Native American dies of alcoholism, it should be considered death by natural causes." How do you think the **narrator** would answer this question? Outline an argument for his answer as well as an argument for the opposing claim. Which do you find more convincing? Why?

WRITING TOPIC

The penultimate section of the story is titled "Exit Interview for My Father." Write your own "exit interview" for either yourself or someone else—for example, a person you are close to, a public figure, or someone you see around town. Following this interview, reflect on what it means to look back on a life after its end, and also to do it by asking questions of the deceased.

MAKING CONNECTIONS

1. Perhaps the most important way cultural identity is formed is through family. Consider Alexie's story and Tan's "Two Kinds" (p. 384). How do each of the parents in these stories shape the cultural identity of the protagonists? How do each of the protagonists feel about this influence?

2. What is the importance of health in this story? Compare its meaning—what it represents to others, how it makes them think and feel—to its meaning in Nordhaus's "A Dandelion for My Mother" (p. 189). How does each writer use illness?

THE BOOK OF THE DEAD   1999

My father is gone. I am slouched in a cast-aluminum chair across from two men, one the manager of the hotel where we're staying and the other a policeman. They are waiting for me to explain what has become of him, my father.

The manager—"Mr. Flavio Salinas," the plaque on his office door reads—has the most striking pair of chartreuse eyes I have ever seen on a man with an island-Spanish lilt to his voice.

The officer is a baby-faced, short white Floridian with a pot belly.

"Where are you and your daddy from, Ms. Bienaimé?" he asks.

I answer "Haiti," even though I was born and raised in East Flatbush, Brook-   5
lyn, and have never visited my parents' birthplace. I do this because it is one more thing I have longed to have in common with my parents.

The officer plows forward. "You down here in Lakeland from Haiti?"

"We live in New York. We were on our way to Tampa."

I find Manager Salinas's office gaudy. The walls are covered with orange-and-green wallpaper, briefly interrupted by a giant gold-leaf-bordered print of a Victorian cottage that somehow resembles the building we're in. Patting his light-green tie, he whispers reassuringly, "Officer Bo and I will do the best we can to help you find your father."

We start out with a brief description: "Sixty-four, five feet eight inches, two hundred and twenty pounds, moonfaced, with thinning salt-and-pepper hair. Velvet-brown eyes—"

"Velvet-brown?" says Officer Bo.   10

"Deep brown—same color as his complexion."

My father has had partial frontal dentures for ten years, since he fell off his and my mother's bed when his prison nightmares began. I mention that, too. Just the dentures, not the nightmares. I also bring up the claw-shaped marks that run from his left ear down along his cheek to the corner of his mouth—the only visible reminder of the year he spent at Fort Dimanche, the Port-au-Prince prison ironically named after the Lord's Day.

"Does your daddy have any kind of mental illness, senility?" asks Officer Bo.

"No."

"Do you have any pictures of your daddy?"   15

I feel like less of a daughter because I'm not carrying a photograph in my wallet. I had hoped to take some pictures of him on our trip. At one of the rest stops I bought a disposable camera and pointed it at my father. No, no, he had protested, covering his face with both hands like a little boy protecting his cheeks from a slap. He did not want any more pictures taken of him for the rest of his life. He was feeling too ugly.

"That's too bad," says Officer Bo. "Does he speak English, your daddy? He can ask for directions, et cetera?"

"Yes."

"Is there anything that might make your father run away from you—particularly here in Lakeland?" Manager Salinas interjects. "Did you two have a fight?"

I had never tried to tell my father's story in words before now, but my first 20 sculpture of him was the reason for our trip: a two-foot-high mahogany figure of my father, naked, crouching on the floor, his back arched like the curve of a crescent moon, his downcast eyes fixed on his short stubby fingers and the wide palms of his hands. It was hardly revolutionary, minimalist at best, but it was my favorite of all my attempted representations of him. It was the way I had imagined him in prison.

The last time I had seen my father?

The previous night, before falling asleep. When we pulled into the pebbled driveway, densely lined with palm and banana trees, it was almost midnight. All the restaurants in the area were closed. There was nothing to do but shower and go to bed.

"It is like a paradise here," my father said when he saw the room. It had the same orange-and-green wallpaper as Salinas's office, and the plush green carpet matched the walls. "Look, Annie," he said, "it is like grass under our feet." He was always searching for a glimpse of paradise, my father.

He picked the bed closest to the bathroom, removed the top of his gray jogging suit, and unpacked his toiletries. Soon after, I heard him humming, as he always did, in the shower.

After he got into bed, I took a bath, pulled my hair back in a ponytail, and 25 checked on the sculpture—just felt it a little bit through the bubble padding and carton wrapping to make sure it wasn't broken. Then I slipped under the covers, closed my eyes, and tried to sleep.

I pictured the client to whom I was delivering the sculpture: Gabrielle Fonteneau, a young woman about my age, an actress on a nationally syndicated television series. My friend Jonas, the principal at the East Flatbush elementary school where I teach drawing to fifth graders, had shown her a picture of my "Father" sculpture, and, the way Jonas told it, Gabrielle Fonteneau had fallen in love with it and wished to offer it as a gift to her father on his birthday.

Since this was my first big sale, I wanted to make sure that the piece got there safely. Besides, I needed a weekend away, and both my mother and I figured that my father, who watched a lot of television, both in his barbershop and at home, would enjoy meeting Gabrielle, too. But when I woke up the next morning my father was gone.

I showered, put on my driving jeans and a T-shirt, and waited. I watched a half hour of midmorning local news, smoked three mentholated cigarettes even though we were in a nonsmoking room, and waited some more. By noon, four hours had gone by. And it was only then that I noticed that the car was still there but the sculpture was gone.

I decided to start looking for my father: in the east garden, the west garden, the dining room, the exercise room, and in the few guest rooms cracked open while the maid changed the sheets; in the little convenience store at the Amoco gas station nearby; even in the Salvation Army thrift shop that from a distance seemed to blend into the interstate. All that waiting and looking actually took six hours, and I felt guilty for having held back so long before going to the front desk to ask, "Have you seen my father?"

I feel Officer Bo's fingers gently stroking my wrist. Up close he smells like 30 fried eggs and gasoline, like breakfast at the Amoco. "I'll put the word out with the other boys," he says. "Salinas here will be in his office. Why don't you go back to your room in case he shows up there?"

I return to the room and lie in the unmade bed, jumping up when I hear the click from the electronic key in the door. It's only the housekeeper. I turn down the late-afternoon cleaning and call my mother at the beauty salon where she perms, presses, and braids hair, next door to my father's barbershop. But she isn't there. So I call my parents' house and leave the hotel number on their machine. "Please call me as soon as you can, Manman. It's about Papi."

Once, when I was twelve, I overheard my mother telling a young woman who was about to get married how she and my father had first met on the sidewalk in front of Fort Dimanche the evening that my father was released from jail. (At a dance, my father had fought with a soldier out of uniform who had him arrested and thrown in prison for a year.) That night, my mother was returning home from a sewing class when he stumbled out of the prison gates and collapsed into her arms, his face still bleeding from his last beating. They married and left for New York a year later. "We were like two seeds planted in a rock," my mother had told the young woman, "but somehow when our daughter, Annie, came we took root."

My mother soon calls me back, her voice staccato with worry.

"Where is Papi?"

"I lost him." 35

"How you lost him?"

"He got up before I did and disappeared."

"How long he been gone?"

"Eight hours," I say, almost not believing myself that it's been that long.

My mother is clicking her tongue and humming. I can see her sitting at 40 the kitchen table, her eyes closed, her fingers sliding up and down her flesh-colored stockinged legs.

"You call police?"

"Yes."

"What they say?"

"To wait, that he'll come back."

My mother is thumping her fingers against the phone's mouthpiece, which is 45 giving me a slight ache in my right ear.

"Tell me where you are," she says. "Two more hours and he's not there, call me, I come."

I dial Gabrielle Fonteneau's cellular-phone number. When she answers, her voice sounds just as it does on television, but more silken and seductive without the sitcom laugh track.

"To think," my father once said while watching her show, "Haitian-born actresses on American television."

"And one of them wants to buy my stuff," I'd added.

When she speaks, Gabrielle Fonteneau sounds as if she's in a place with cica- 50 das, waterfalls, palm trees, and citronella candles to keep the mosquitoes away. I realize that I, too, am in such a place, but I can't appreciate it.

"So nice of you to come all this way to deliver the sculpture," she says. "Jonas tell you why I like it so much? My papa was a journalist in Port-au-Prince. In 1975, he wrote a story criticizing the dictatorship, and he was arrested and put in jail."

"Fort Dimanche?"

"No, another one," she says. "Caserne. Papa kept track of days there by scrap-ing lines with his fingernails on the walls of his cell. One of the guards didn't like this, so he pulled out all his fingernails with pliers."

I think of the photo spread I saw in the *Haitian Times* of Gabrielle Fonteneau and her parents in their living room in Tampa. Her father was described as a lawyer, his daughter's manager; her mother a court stenogra-pher. There was no hint in that photograph of what had once happened to the father. Perhaps people don't see anything in my father's face, either, in spite of his scars.

"We celebrate his birthday on the day he was released from prison," she says. 55 "It's the hands I love so much in your sculpture. They're so strong."

I am drifting away from Gabrielle Fonteneau when I hear her say, "So when will you get here? You have instructions from Jonas, right? Maybe we can make you lunch. My mother makes great *lanbi*."

"I'll be there at twelve tomorrow," I say. "My father is with me. We are mak-ing a little weekend vacation of this."

My father loves museums. When he isn't working in his barbershop, he's often at the Brooklyn Museum. The ancient Egyptian rooms are his favorites.

"The Egyptians, they was like us," he likes to say. The Egyptians worshipped their gods in many forms and were often ruled by foreigners. The pharaohs were like the dictators he had fled. But what he admires most about the Egyptians is the way they mourned.

"Yes, they grieve," he'll say. He marvels at the mummification that went on 60 for weeks, resulting in bodies that survived thousands of years.

My whole adult life, I have struggled to find the proper manner of sculpting my father, a man who learned about art by standing with me most of the Saturday mornings of my childhood, mesmerized by the golden masks, the shawabtis, and Osiris, ruler of the underworld.

When my father finally appears in the hotel-room doorway, I am awed by him. Smiling, he looks like a much younger man, further bronzed after a long day at the beach.

"Annie, let your father talk to you." He walks over to my bed, bends down to unlace his sneakers. "*On ti koze*, a little chat."

"Where were you? Where is the sculpture, Papi?" I feel my eyes twitching, a nervous reaction I inherited from my mother.

"That's why we need to chat," he says. "I have objections with your statue."   65

He pulls off his sneakers and rubs his feet with both hands.

"I don't want you to sell that statue," he says. Then he picks up the phone and calls my mother.

"I know she called you," he says to her in Creole. "Her head is so hot. She panics so easily. I was just out walking, thinking."

I hear my mother lovingly scolding him and telling him not to leave me again. When he hangs up the phone, he picks up his sneakers and puts them back on.

"Where is the sculpture?" My eyes are twitching so hard now that I can   70 barely see.

"Let us go," he says. "I will take you to it."

As my father maneuvers the car out of the parking lot, I tell myself he might be ill, mentally ill, even though I have never detected anything wrong beyond his prison nightmares. I am trying to piece it together, this sudden yet familiar picture of a parent's vulnerability. When I was ten years old and my father had the chicken pox, I overheard him say to a friend on the phone, "The doctor tells me that at my age chicken pox can kill a man." This was the first time I realized that my father could die. I looked up the word "kill" in every dictionary and encyclopedia at school, trying to comprehend what it meant, that my father could be eradicated from my life.

My father stops the car on the side of the highway near a man-made lake, one of those artificial creations of the modern tropical city, with curved stone benches surrounding stagnant water. There is little light to see by except a half-moon. He heads toward one of the benches, and I sit down next to him, letting my hands dangle between my legs.

"Is this where the sculpture is?" I ask.

"In the water," he says.   75

"O.K.," I say. "But please know this about yourself. You are an especially harsh critic."

My father tries to smother a smile.

"Why?" I ask.

He scratches his chin. Anger is a wasted emotion, I've always thought. My parents got angry at unfair politics in New York or Port-au-Prince, but they never got angry at my grades—at all the B's I got in everything but art classes—or at my not eating vegetables or occasionally vomiting my daily spoonful of cod-liver oil. Ordinary anger, I thought, was a weakness. But now I am angry. I want to hit my father, beat the craziness out of his head.

"Annie," he says. "When I first saw your statue, I wanted to be buried with it,   80 to take it with me into the other world."

"Like the ancient Egyptians," I say. He smiles, grateful, I think, that I still recall his passions.

"Annie," he asks, "do you remember when I read to you from 'The Book of the Dead'?"

"Are you dying?" I say to my father. "Because I can only forgive you for this if you are. You can't take this back."

He is silent for a moment too long.

I think I hear crickets, though I cannot imagine where they might be. There is the highway, the cars racing by, the half-moon, the lake dug up from the depths of the ground, the allée of royal palms beyond. And there is me and my father.

"You remember the judgment of the dead," my father says, "when the heart of a person is put on a scale. If it is heavy, then this person cannot enter the other world."

It is a testament to my upbringing that I am not yelling at him.

"I don't deserve a statue," he says, even while looking like one: the Madonna of Humility, for example, contemplating her losses in the dust.

"Annie, your father was the hunter," he says. "He was not the prey."

"What are you saying?" I ask.

"We have a proverb," he says. "'One day for the hunter, one day for the prey.' Your father was the hunter. He was not the prey." Each word is hard-won as it leaves my father's mouth, balanced like those hearts on the Egyptian scale.

"Annie, when I saw your mother the first time, I was not just out of prison. I was a guard in the prison. One of the prisoners I was questioning had scratched me with a piece of tin. I went out to the street in a rage, blood all over my face. I was about to go back and do something bad, very bad. But instead comes your mother. I smash into her, and she asks me what I am doing there. I told her I was just let go from prison and she held my face and cried in my hair."

"And the nightmares, what are they?"

"Of what I, your father, did to others."

"Does Manman know?"

"I told her, Annie, before we married."

I am the one who drives back to the hotel. In the car, he says, "Annie, I am still your father, still your mother's husband. I would not do these things now."

When we g t back to the hotel room, I leave a message for Officer Bo, and another for M nager Salinas, telling them that I have found my father. He has slipped into the bathroom, and now he runs the shower at full force. When it seems that he is never coming out, I call my mother at home in Brooklyn.

"How do you love him?" I whisper into the phone.

My mother is tapping her fingers against the mouthpiece.

"I don't know, Annie," she whispers back, as though there is a chance that she might also be overheard by him. "I feel only that you and me, we saved him. When I met him, it made him stop hurting the people. This is how I see it. He was a seed thrown into a rock, and you and me, Annie, we helped push a flower out of a rock."

When I get up the next morning, my father is already dressed. He is sitting on the edge of his bed with his back to me, his head bowed, his face buried in his hands. If I were sculpting him, I would make him a praying mantis, crouching motionless, seeming to pray while waiting to strike.

With his back still turned, my father says, "Will you call those people and tell them you have it no more, the statue?"

"We were invited to lunch there. I believe we should go."

He raises his shoulders and shrugs. It is up to me.   105

The drive to Gabrielle Fonteneau's house seems longer than the twenty-four hours it took to drive from New York: the ocean, the palms along the road, the highway so imposingly neat. My father fills in the silence in the car by saying, "So now you know, Annie, why your mother and me, we have never returned home."

The Fonteneaus' house is made of bricks of white coral, on a cul-de-sac with a row of banyans separating the two sides of the street.

Silently, we get out of the car and follow a concrete path to the front door. Before we can knock, an older woman walks out. Like Gabrielle, she has stunning midnight-black eyes and skin the color of sorrel, with spiralling curls brushing the sides of her face. When Gabrielle's father joins her, I realize where Gabrielle Fonteneau gets her height. He is more than six feet tall.

Mr. Fonteneau extends his hands, first to my father and then to me. They're large, twice the size of my father's. The fingernails have grown back, thick, densely dark, as though the past had nestled itself there in black ink.

We move slowly through the living room, which has a cathedral ceiling and   110
walls covered with Haitian paintings—Obin, Hyppolite, Tiga, Duval-Carrié. Out on the back terrace, which towers over a nursery of orchids and red dracaenas, a table is set for lunch.

Mr. Fonteneau asks my father where his family is from in Haiti, and my father lies. In the past, I thought he always said a different province because he had lived in all those places, but I realize now that he says this to keep anyone from tracing him, even though twenty-six years and eighty more pounds shield him from the threat of immediate recognition.

When Gabrielle Fonteneau makes her entrance, in an off-the-shoulder ruby dress, my father and I stand up.

"Gabrielle," she says, when she shakes hands with my father, who blurts out spontaneously, "You are one of the flowers of Haiti."

Gabrielle Fonteneau tilts her head coyly.

"We eat now," Mrs. Fonteneau announces, leading me and my father to a   115
bathroom to wash up before the meal. Standing before a pink seashell-shaped sink, my father and I dip our hands under the faucet flow.

"Annie," my father says, "we always thought, your mother and me, that children could raise their parents higher. Look at what this girl has done for her parents."

During the meal of conch, plantains, and mushroom rice, Mr. Fonteneau tries to draw my father into conversation. He asks when my father was last in Haiti.

"Twenty-six years," my father replies.

"No going back for you?" asks Mrs. Fonteneau.

"I have not had the opportunity," my father says.   120

"We go back every year to a beautiful place overlooking the ocean in the mountains in Jacmel," says Mrs. Fonteneau.

"Have you ever been to Jacmel?" Gabrielle Fonteneau asks me.

I shake my head no.

"We are fortunate," Mrs. Fonteneau says, "that we have another place to go where we can say our rain is sweeter, our dust is lighter, our beach is prettier."

"So now we are tasting rain and weighing dust," Mr. Fonteneau says, and   125
laughs.

"There is nothing like drinking the sweet juice from a green coconut you fetched yourself from your own tree, or sinking your hand in sand from the beach in your own country," Mrs. Fonteneau says.

"When did you ever climb a coconut tree?" Mr. Fonteneau says, teasing his wife.

I am imagining what my father's nightmares might be. Maybe he dreams of dipping his hands in the sand on a beach in his own country and finds that what he comes up with is a fist full of blood.

After lunch, my father asks if he can have a closer look at the Fonteneaus' back-yard garden. While he's taking the tour, I confess to Gabrielle Fonteneau that I don't have the sculpture.

"My father threw it away," I say.   130

Gabrielle Fonteneau frowns.

"I don't know," she says. "Was there even a sculpture at all? I trust Jonas, but maybe you fooled him, too. Is this some scam, to get into our home?"

"There was a sculpture," I say. "Jonas will tell you that. My father just didn't like it, so he threw it away."

She raises her perfectly arched eyebrows, perhaps out of concern for my father's sanity or my own.

"I'm really disappointed," she says. "I wanted it for a reason. My father goes   135
home when he looks at a piece of art. He goes home deep inside himself. For a long time, he used to hide his fingers from people. It's like he was making a fist all the time. I wanted to give him this thing so that he knows we understand what happened to him."

"I am truly sorry," I say.

Over her shoulders, I see her parents guiding my father through rows of lemongrass. I want to promise her that I will make her another sculpture, one especially modelled on her father. But I don't know when I will be able to work on anything again. I have lost my subject, the father I loved as well as pitied.

In the garden, I watch my father snap a white orchid from its stem and hold it out toward Mrs. Fonteneau, who accepts it with a nod of thanks.

"I don't understand," Gabrielle Fonteneau says. "You did all this for nothing."

I wave to my father to signal that we should perhaps leave now, and he comes 140 toward me, the Fonteneaus trailing slowly behind him.

With each step he rubs the scars on the side of his face.

Perhaps the last person my father harmed had dreamed this moment into my father's future—his daughter seeing those marks, like chunks of warm plaster still clinging to a cast, and questioning him about them, giving him a chance to either lie or tell the truth. After all, we have the proverb, as my father would say: "Those who give the blows may try to forget, but those who carry the scars must remember."

FOR ANALYSIS

1. Why is the story titled "The Book of the Dead"?

2. How does Annie's family differ from the Fonteneau's? Why is this difference significant?

3. What does Annie discover about her father's past? How does she feel about it? Does knowing her father better mean the same thing when this is the kind of thing she learns about him?

MAKING ARGUMENTS

People often talk about the kind of violence that occurs during wartime or in failed or failing states in terms of trauma—the kinds of psychological damage that being the victim of that violence can cause. How is the damage the **narrator's** father has experienced both similar and different to that kind of trauma? Make an argument for or against considering the inner wounds of the perpetrators of violence in the same way that we consider those of their victims.

WRITING TOPICS

1. Write or outline a poem along the lines of one of the "Voices of Experience" cluster of poems (p. 199) in the "Innocence and Experience" chapter. What kind of advice might the **narrator's** father give her, if he could?

2. Imagine a sculpture that the narrator would make of her father at the end of this story, after what she has learned. What might it look like? How would it compare to the sculpture of him she brought with them on this trip?

MAKING CONNECTIONS

1. Compare "The Book of the Dead" to one or two of the poems from the cluster at the end of this section, "America through Immigrants' Eyes" (p. 701). How does this story play off of more typical or even stereotypical portrayals of immigrant experience?

2. Think about this story in light of the poems in the "Voices of Experience" cluster (p. 199) in the "Innocence and Experience" chapter. How does doing this make you think about the relationship between the **narrator** and her father?

William Faulkner's "A Rose for Emily" is a classic example of a story depicting the tension between the community and the individual—a conflict that animates so much fiction. Ha Jin's "The Bridegroom" is a contemporary example, one that equals Faulkner's in addressing the more universal question of the fate of the individual in a world organized by groups. As you read these two stories, think about how the manner of their telling implicates not just the characters on whom the stories focus but also the tellers themselves. Think also about the endings of these stories, which reveal much about the character of the people, the complex social issues of the settings, and the larger difficulties of the human experience.

WILLIAM FAULKNER (1897–1962)

A ROSE FOR EMILY 1931

I

When Miss Emily Grierson died, our whole town went to her funeral: the men through a sort of respectful affection for a fallen monument, the women mostly out of curiosity to see the inside of her house, which no one save an old manservant—a combined gardener and cook—had seen in at least ten years.

It was a big, squarish frame house that had once been white, decorated with cupolas and spires and scrolled balconies in the heavily lightsome style of the seventies, set on what had once been our most select street. But garages and cotton gins had encroached and obliterated even the august names of that neighborhood; only Miss Emily's house was left, lifting its stubborn and coquettish decay above the cotton wagons and the gasoline pumps—an eyesore among eyesores. And now Miss Emily had gone to join the representatives of those august names where they lay in the cedar-bemused cemetery among the ranked and anonymous graves of Union and Confederate soldiers who fell at the battle of Jefferson.

Alive, Miss Emily had been a tradition, a duty, and a care; a sort of hereditary obligation upon the town, dating from that day in 1894 when Colonel Sartoris, the mayor—he who fathered the edict that no Negro woman should appear on the streets without an apron—remitted her taxes, the dispensation dating from the death of her father on into perpetuity. Not that Miss Emily would have accepted charity. Colonel Sartoris invented an involved tale to the effect that Miss Emily's father had loaned money to the town, which the town, as a matter of business, preferred this way of repaying. Only a man of Colonel

Sartoris' generation and thought could have invented it, and only a woman could have believed it.

When the next generation, with its more modern ideas, became mayors and aldermen, this arrangement created some little dissatisfaction. On the first of the year they mailed her a tax notice. February came, and there was no reply. They wrote her a formal letter, asking her to call at the sheriff's office at her convenience. A week later the mayor wrote her himself, offering to call or to send his car for her, and received in reply a note on paper of an archaic shape, in a thin, flowing calligraphy in faded ink, to the effect that she no longer went out at all. The tax notice was also enclosed, without comment.

They called a special meeting of the Board of Aldermen. A deputation 5 waited upon her, knocked at the door through which no visitor had passed since she ceased giving china-painting lessons eight or ten years earlier. They were admitted by the old Negro into a dim hall from which a stairway mounted into still more shadow. It smelled of dust and disuse—a close, dank smell. The Negro led them into the parlor. It was furnished in heavy, leather-covered furniture. When the Negro opened the blinds of one window, they could see that the leather was cracked; and when they sat down, a faint dust rose sluggishly about their thighs, spinning with slow motions in the single sun-ray. On a tarnished gilt easel before the fireplace stood a crayon portrait of Miss Emily's father.

They rose when she entered—a small, fat woman in black, with a thin gold chain descending to her waist and vanishing into her belt, leaning on an ebony cane with a tarnished gold head. Her skeleton was small and spare; perhaps that was why what would have been merely plumpness in another was obesity in her. She looked bloated, like a body long submerged in motionless water, and of that pallid hue. Her eyes, lost in the fatty ridges of her face, looked like two small pieces of coal pressed into a lump of dough as they moved from one face to another while the visitors stated their errand.

She did not ask them to sit. She just stood in the door and listened quietly until the spokesman came to a stumbling halt. Then they could hear the invisible watch ticking at the end of the gold chain.

Her voice was dry and cold. "I have no taxes in Jefferson. Colonel Sartoris explained it to me. Perhaps one of you can gain access to the city records and satisfy yourselves."

"But we have. We are the city authorities, Miss Emily. Didn't you get a notice from the sheriff, signed by him?"

"I received a paper, yes," Miss Emily said. "Perhaps he considers himself the 10 sheriff . . . I have no taxes in Jefferson."

"But there is nothing on the books to show that, you see. We must go by the—"

"See Colonel Sartoris." (Colonel Sartoris had been dead almost ten years.) "I have no taxes in Jefferson. Tobe!" The Negro appeared. "Show these gentlemen out."

II

So she vanquished them, horse and foot, just as she had vanquished their fathers thirty years before about the smell. That was two years after her father's death and a short time after her sweetheart—the one we believed would marry her—had deserted her. After her father's death she went out very little; after her sweetheart went away, people hardly saw her at all. A few of the ladies had the temerity to call, but were not received, and the only sign of life about the place was the Negro man—a young man then—going in and out with a market basket.

"Just as if a man—any man—could keep a kitchen properly," the ladies said; so they were not surprised when the smell developed. It was another link between the gross, teeming world and the high and mighty Griersons.

A neighbor, a woman, complained to the mayor, Judge Stevens, eighty years 15 old.

"But what will you have me do about it, madam?" he said.

"Why, send her word to stop it," the woman said. "Isn't there a law?"

"I'm sure that won't be necessary," Judge Stevens said. "It's probably just a snake or a rat that nigger of hers killed in the yard. I'll speak to him about it."

The next day he received two more complaints, one from a man who came in diffident deprecation. "We really must do something about it, Judge. I'd be the last one in the world to bother Miss Emily, but we've got to do something." That night the Board of Aldermen met—three graybeards and one younger man, a member of the rising generation.

"It's simple enough," he said. "Send her word to have her place cleaned up. 20 Give her a certain time to do it in, and if she don't . . ."

"Dammit, sir," Judge Stevens said, "will you accuse a lady to her face of smelling bad?"

So the next night, after midnight, four men crossed Miss Emily's lawn and slunk about the house like burglars, sniffing along the base of the brickwork and at the cellar openings while one of them performed a regular sowing motion with his hand out of a sack slung from his shoulder. They broke open the cellar door and sprinkled lime there, and in all the outbuildings. As they recrossed the lawn, a window that had been dark was lighted and Miss Emily sat in it, the light behind her, and her upright torso motionless as that of an idol. They crept quietly across the lawn and into the shadow of the locusts that lined the street. After a week or two the smell went away.

That was when people had begun to feel really sorry for her. People in our town, remembering how old lady Wyatt, her great-aunt, had gone completely crazy at last, believed that the Griersons held themselves a little too high for what they really were. None of the young men were quite good enough for Miss Emily and such. We had long thought of them as a tableau, Miss Emily a slender figure in white in the background, her father a spraddled silhouette in the foreground, his back to her and clutching a horsewhip, the two of them framed by the back-flung front door. So when she got to be thirty and was still single, we were not pleased exactly, but vindicated; even with insanity in the family she wouldn't have turned down all of her chances if they had really materialized.

When her father died, it got about that the house was all that was left to her; and in a way, people were glad. At last they could pity Miss Emily. Being left alone, and a pauper, she had become humanized. Now she too would know the old thrill and the old despair of a penny more or less.

The day after his death all the ladies prepared to call at the house and offer 25 condolence and aid, as is our custom. Miss Emily met them at the door, dressed as usual and with no trace of grief on her face. She told them that her father was not dead. She did that for three days, with the ministers calling on her, and the doctors, trying to persuade her to let them dispose of the body. Just as they were about to resort to law and force, she broke down, and they buried her father quickly.

We did not say she was crazy then. We believed she had to do that. We remembered all the young men her father had driven away, and we knew that with nothing left, she would have to cling to that which had robbed her, as people will.

III

She was sick for a long time. When we saw her again, her hair was cut short, making her look like a girl, with a vague resemblance to those angels in colored church windows—sort of tragic and serene.

The town had just let the contracts for paving the sidewalks, and in the summer after her father's death they began the work. The construction company came with niggers and mules and machinery, and a foreman named Homer Barron, a Yankee—a big, dark, ready man, with a big voice and eyes lighter than his face. The little boys would follow in groups to hear him cuss the niggers, and the niggers singing in time to the rise and fall of picks. Pretty soon he knew everybody in town. Whenever you heard a lot of laughing anywhere about the square, Homer Barron would be in the center of the group. Presently we began to see him and Miss Emily on Sunday afternoons driving in the yellow-wheeled buggy and the matched team of bays from the livery stable.

At first we were glad that Miss Emily would have an interest, because the ladies all said, "Of course a Grierson would not think seriously of a Northerner, a day laborer." But there were still others, older people, who said that even grief could not cause a real lady to forget *noblesse oblige*—without calling it *noblesse oblige*. They just said, "Poor Emily. Her kinsfolk should come to her." She had some kin in Alabama; but years ago her father had fallen out with them over the estate of old lady Wyatt, the crazy woman, and there was no communication between the two families. They had not even been represented at the funeral.

And as soon as the old people said, "Poor Emily," the whispering began. 30 "Do you suppose it's really so?" they said to one another. "Of course it is.

What else could . . ." This behind their hands; rustling of craned silk and satin behind jalousies closed upon the sun of Sunday afternoon as the thin, swift clop-clop-clop of the matched team passed: "Poor Emily."

She carried her head high enough—even when we believed that she was fallen. It was as if she demanded more than ever the recognition of her dignity as the last Grierson; as if it had wanted that touch of earthiness to reaffirm her imperviousness. Like when she bought the rat poison, the arsenic. That was over a year after they had begun to say "Poor Emily," and while the two female cousins were visiting her.

"I want some poison," she said to the druggist. She was over thirty then, still a slight woman, though thinner than usual, with cold, haughty black eyes in a face the flesh of which was strained across the temples and about the eye-sockets as you imagine a lighthouse-keeper's face ought to look. "I want some poison," she said.

"Yes, Miss Emily. What kind? For rats and such? I'd recom—"

"I want the best you have. I don't care what kind."

The druggist named several. "They'll kill anything up to an elephant. But   35 what you want is—"

"Arsenic," Miss Emily said. "Is that a good one?"

"Is . . . arsenic? Yes, ma'am. But what you want—"

"I want arsenic."

The druggist looked down at her. She looked back at him, erect, her face like a strained flag. "Why, of course," the druggist said. "If that's what you want. But the law requires you to tell what you are going to use it for."

Miss Emily just stared at him, her head tilted back in order to look him eye   40 for eye, until he looked away and went and got the arsenic and wrapped it up. The Negro delivery boy brought her package; the druggist didn't come back. When she opened the package at home there was written on the box, under the skull and bones: "For rats."

IV

So the next day we all said, "She will kill herself"; and we said it would be the best thing. When she had first begun to be seen with Homer Barron, we had said, "She will marry him." Then we said, "She will persuade him yet," because Homer himself had remarked—he liked men, and it was known that he drank with the younger men in the Elks' Club—that he was not a marrying man. Later we said, "Poor Emily" behind the jalousies as they passed on Sunday afternoon in the glittering buggy, Miss Emily with her head high and Homer Barron with his hat cocked and a cigar in his teeth, reins and whip in a yellow glove.

Then some of the ladies began to say that it was a disgrace to the town and a bad example to the young people. The men did not want to interfere, but at last the ladies forced the Baptist minister—Miss Emily's people were Episcopal—to call upon her. He would never divulge what happened during that interview, but he refused to go back again. The next Sunday they again drove about the streets, and the following day the minister's wife wrote to Miss Emily's relations in Alabama.

So she had blood-kin under her roof again and we sat back to watch developments. At first nothing happened. Then we were sure that they were to be married. We learned that Miss Emily had been to the jeweler's and ordered a man's toilet set in silver, with the letters H.B. on each piece. Two days later we learned that she had bought a complete outfit of men's clothing, including a nightshirt, and we said, "They are married." We were really glad. We were glad because the two female cousins were even more Grierson than Miss Emily had ever been.

So we were not surprised when Homer Barron—the streets had been finished some time since—was gone. We were a little disappointed that there was not a public blowing-off, but we believed that he had gone on to prepare for Miss Emily's coming, or to give her a chance to get rid of the cousins. (By that time it was a cabal, and we were all Miss Emily's allies to help circumvent the cousins.) Sure enough, after another week they departed. And, as we had expected all along, within three days Homer Barron was back in town. A neighbor saw the Negro man admit him at the kitchen door at dusk one evening.

And that was the last we saw of Homer Barron. And of Miss Emily for some   45 time. The Negro man went in and out with the market basket, but the front door remained closed. Now and then we would see her at the window for a moment, as the men did that night when they sprinkled the lime, but for almost six months she did not appear on the streets. Then we knew that this was to be expected too; as if that quality of her father which had thwarted her woman's life so many times had been too virulent and too furious to die.

When we next saw Miss Emily, she had grown fat and her hair was turning gray. During the next few years it grew grayer and grayer until it attained an even pepper-and-salt iron-gray, when it ceased turning. Up to the day of her death at seventy-four it was still that vigorous iron-gray, like the hair of an active man.

From that time on her front door remained closed, save during a period of six or seven years, when she was about forty, during which she gave lessons in china-painting. She fitted up a studio in one of the downstairs rooms, where the daughters and granddaughters of Colonel Sartoris' contemporaries were sent to her with the same regularity and in the same spirit that they were sent to church on Sundays with a twenty-five-cent piece for the collection plate. Meanwhile her taxes had been remitted.

Then the newer generation became the backbone and the spirit of the town, and the painting pupils grew up and fell away and did not send their children to her with boxes of color and tedious brushes and pictures cut from the ladies' magazines. The front door closed upon the last one and remained closed for good. When the town got free postal delivery, Miss Emily alone refused to let them fasten the metal numbers above her door and attach a mailbox to it. She would not listen to them.

Daily, monthly, yearly we watched the Negro grow grayer and more stooped, going in and out with the market basket. Each December we sent her a tax notice, which would be returned by the post office a week later, unclaimed. Now and then we would see her in one of the downstairs windows—she had evidently shut up the top floor of the house—like the carven torso of an idol in a niche, looking or not looking at us, we could never tell which. Thus she passed from generation to generation—dear, inescapable, impervious, tranquil, and perverse.

And so she died. Fell ill in the house filled with dust and shadows, with only 50 a doddering Negro man to wait on her. We did not even know she was sick; we had long since given up trying to get any information from the Negro. He talked to no one, probably not even to her, for his voice had grown harsh and rusty, as if from disuse.

She died in one of the downstairs rooms, in a heavy walnut bed with a curtain, her gray head propped on a pillow yellow and moldy with age and lack of sunlight.

V

The Negro met the first of the ladies at the front door and let them in, with their hushed, sibilant voices and their quick, curious glances, and then he disappeared. He walked right through the house and out the back and was not seen again.

The two female cousins came at once. They held the funeral on the second day, with the town coming to look at Miss Emily beneath a mass of bought flowers, with the crayon face of her father musing profoundly above the bier and the ladies sibilant and macabre; and the very old men—some in their brushed Confederate uniforms—on the porch and the lawn, talking of Miss Emily as if she had been a contemporary of theirs, believing they had danced with her and courted her perhaps, confusing time with its mathematical progression, as the old do, to whom all the past is not a diminishing road but, instead, a huge meadow which no winter ever quite touches, divided from them now by the narrow bottle-neck of the most recent decade of years.

Already we knew that there was one room in that region above stairs which no one had seen in forty years, and which would have to be forced. They waited until Miss Emily was decently in the ground before they opened it.

The violence of breaking down the door seemed to fill this room with per- 55 vading dust. A thin, acrid pall as of the tomb seemed to lie everywhere upon this room decked and furnished as for a bridal: upon the valance curtains of faded rose color, upon the rose-shaded lights, upon the dressing table, upon the delicate array of crystal and the man's toilet things backed with tarnished silver, silver so tarnished that the monogram was obscured. Among them lay a collar and tie, as if they had just been removed, which, lifted, left upon the surface a pale crescent in the dust. Upon a chair hung the suit, carefully folded; beneath it the two mute shoes and the discarded socks.

The man himself lay in the bed.

For a long while we just stood there, looking down at the profound and fleshless grin. The body had apparently once lain in the attitude of an embrace, but now the long sleep that outlasts love, that conquers even the grimace of love, had cuckolded him. What was left of him, rotted beneath what was left of the nightshirt, had become inextricable from the bed in which he lay; and upon him and upon the pillow beside him lay that even coating of the patient and biding dust.

Then we noticed that in the second pillow was the indentation of a head. One of us lifted something from it, and leaning forward, that faint and invisible dust dry and acrid in the nostrils, we saw a long strand of iron-gray hair.

FOR ANALYSIS

1. Why does Faulkner title the narrative "A Rose for Emily"?

2. At the end of section II, the **narrator** says, "We remembered all the young men her father had driven away." What is the significance of this statement? How would you characterize Emily's relationship with her father? Her father's relationship with the town?

3. In section III, we learn that "the ladies all said, 'Of course a Grierson would not think seriously of a Northerner, a day laborer.'" Why not? What are Emily's alternatives?

4. What is the effect of the final paragraph?

5. Why does the narrator use the pronoun *we*? The narrator often speaks of "the town." What does "the town" signify?

6. Reread the description of Emily's house in paragraph 2. What does this description suggest?

7. What does the author accomplish by not presenting the story in chronological order?

MAKING ARGUMENTS

Write an essay arguing for or against the assertion that Emily's father determined the course of her life.

WRITING TOPIC

Write a brief essay discussing the role of time in this story. How does the town's response to the Griersons in general, and Emily in particular, change as time passes?

HA JIN (B. 1956)

THE BRIDEGROOM 1999

Before Beina's father died, I promised him that I'd take care of his daughter. He and I had been close friends for twenty years. He left his only child with me because my wife and I had no children of our own. It was easy to keep my word when Beina was still a teenager. As she grew older, it became more difficult, not because she was willful or troublesome but because no man was interested in her, a short, homely girl. When she turned twenty-three and still had no boyfriend, I began to worry. Where could I find her a husband? Timid and quiet, she didn't know how to get close to a man. I was afraid she'd become an old maid.

Then out of the blue Baowen Huang proposed to her. I found myself at a loss, because they'd hardly known each other. How could he be serious about his offer? I feared he might make a fool of Beina, so I insisted they get engaged if he meant business. He came to my home with two trussed-up capons, four cartons of Ginseng cigarettes, two bottles of Five Grains' Sap, and one tall tin of oolong tea. I was pleased, though not very impressed by his gifts.

Two months later they got married. My colleagues congratulated me, saying, "That was fast, Old Cheng."

What a relief to me. But to many young women in our sewing-machine factory, Beina's marriage was a slap in the face. They'd say, "A hen cooped up a peacock." Or, "A fool always lands in the arms of fortune." True, Baowen had been one of the most handsome unmarried men in the factory, and nobody had expected that Beina, stocky and stout, would win him. What's more, Baowen was good-natured and well educated—a middle-school graduate— and he didn't smoke or drink or gamble. He had fine manners and often smiled politely, showing his bright, straight teeth. In a way he resembled a woman, delicate, clear-skinned, and soft-spoken; he even could knit things out of wool. But no men dared bully him because he was skilled at martial arts. Three times in a row he had won the first prize for kung fu at our factory's annual sports meet. He was very good at the long sword and freestyle boxing. When he was in middle school, bigger boys had often picked on him, so his stepfather had sent him to the martial arts school in their hometown. A year later nobody would ever bug him again.

Sometimes I couldn't help wondering why Baowen had chosen Beina. 5 What in her had caught his heart? Did he really like her fleshy face, which often reminded me of a globefish? Although we had our doubts, my wife and I couldn't say anything negative about the marriage. Our only concern was that Baowen might be too good for our nominal daughter. Whenever I heard that somebody had divorced, I'd feel a sudden flutter of panic.

As the head of the Security Section in the factory, I had some pull and did what I could to help the young couple. Soon after their wedding I secured them a brand-new two-bedroom apartment, which angered some people waiting in line for housing. I wasn't daunted by their criticism. I'd do almost anything to make Beina's marriage stable, because I believed that if it survived the first two years, it might last decades—once Baowen became a father, it would be difficult for him to break loose.

But after they'd been married for eight months, Beina still wasn't pregnant. I was afraid that Baowen would soon grow tired of her and run after another woman, since many young women in the factory were still attracted to him. A brazen one even declared that she'd leave her door open for him all night long. Some of them frequently offered him movie tickets and meat coupons. It seemed that they were determined to wreck Beina's marriage. I hated them, and just the thought of them would give me an earache or a sour stomach. Fortunately, Baowen hadn't yet done anything outside the bounds of a decent husband.

One morning in early November, Beina stepped into my office. "Uncle," she said in a tearful voice, "Baowen didn't come home last night."

I tried to remain calm, though my head began to swim. "Do you know where he's been?" I asked.

"I don't know. I looked for him everywhere." She licked her cracked lips and 10 took off her green work cap, her hair in a huge bun.

"When did you see him last?"

"At dinner yesterday evening. He said he was going to see somebody. He has lots of buddies in town."

"Is that so?" I didn't know he had many friends. "Don't worry. Go back to your workshop and don't tell anybody about this. I'll call around and find him."

She dragged herself out of my office. She must have gained at least a dozen pounds since the wedding. Her blue dungarees had become so tight that they seemed about to burst. Viewed from behind, she looked like a giant turnip.

I called the Rainbow Movie Theater, Victory Park, and a few restaurants 15 in town. They all said they had not seen anyone matching Baowen's description. Before I could phone the city library, where Baowen sometimes spent his weekends, a call came in. It was from the city's Public Security Bureau. The man on the phone said they'd detained a worker of ours named Baowen Huang. He wouldn't tell me what had happened. He just said, "Indecent activity. Come as soon as you can."

It was a cold day. As I cycled toward downtown, the shrill north wind kept flipping up the front ends of my overcoat. My knees were sore, and I couldn't help shivering. Soon my asthma tightened my throat and I began moaning. I couldn't stop cursing Baowen. "I knew it. I just knew it," I said to myself. I had sensed that sooner or later he'd seek pleasure with another woman. Now he was in the police's hands, and the whole factory would talk about him. How could Beina take this blow?

At the Public Security Bureau I was surprised to see that about a dozen officials from other factories, schools, and companies were already there. I knew most of them, who were in charge of security affairs at their workplaces. A policewoman conducted us into a conference room upstairs, where green silk curtains hung in the windows. We sat down around a long mahogany table and waited to be briefed about the case. The glass tabletop was brand new, its edge still sharp. I saw worry and confusion on the other men's faces. I figured Baowen must have been involved in an organized crime—either an orgy or a gang rape. On second thought I felt he couldn't have been a rapist; by nature he was kindhearted, very gentle. I hoped this was not a political case, which would be absolutely unpardonable. Six or seven years ago a half-wit and a high school graduate had started an association in our city, named the China Liberation

Party, which had later recruited nine members. Although the sparrow is small it has a complete set of organs—their party elected a chairman, a secretary, and even a prime minister. But before they could print their manifesto, which expressed their intention to overthrow the government, the police rounded them up. Two of the top leaders were executed, and the rest of the members were jailed.

As I was wondering about the nature of Baowen's crime, a middle-aged man came in. He had a solemn face, and his eyes were half closed. He took off his dark blue tunic, hung it on the back of a chair, and sat down at the end of the table. I recognized him; he was Chief Miao of the Investigation Department. Wearing a sheepskin jerkin, he somehow reminded me of Genghis Khan, thick-boned and round-faced. His hooded eyes were shrewd, though they looked sleepy. Without any opening remarks he declared that we had a case of homosexuality on our hands. At that, the room turned noisy. We'd heard of the term but didn't know what it meant exactly. Seeing many of us puzzled, Chief Miao explained, "It's a social disease, like gambling, or prostitution, or syphilis." He kept on squirming as if itchy with hemorrhoids.

A young man from the city's Fifth Middle School raised his hand. He asked, "What do homosexuals do?"

Miao smiled and his eyes almost disappeared. He said, "People of the same 20 sex have a sexual relationship."

"Sodomy!" cried someone.

The room turned quiet for at least ten seconds. Then somebody asked what kind of crime this was.

Chief Miao explained, "Homosexuality originated from Western capitalism and bourgeois lifestyle. According to our law it's dealt with as a kind of hooliganism. Therefore, every one of the men we arrested will serve a sentence, from six months to five years, depending on the severity of his crime and his attitude toward it."

A truck blew its horn on the street and made my heart twinge. If Baowen went to prison, Beina would live like a widow, unless she divorced him. Why had he married her to begin with? Why did he ruin her this way?

What had happened was that a group of men, mostly clerks, artists, and 25 schoolteachers, had formed a club called Men's World, a salon of sorts. Every Thursday evening they'd met in a large room on the third floor of the office building of the Forestry Institute. Since the club admitted only men, the police suspected that it might be a secret association with a leaning toward violence, so they assigned two detectives to mix with the group. True, some of the men appeared to be intimate with each other in the club, but most of the time they talked about movies, books, and current events. Occasionally music was played, and they danced together. According to the detectives' account, it was a bizarre, emotional scene. A few men appeared in pairs, unashamed of necking and cuddling in the presence of others, and some would say with tears, "At last we men have a place for ourselves." A middle-aged painter wearing earrings exclaimed, "Now I feel alive! Only in here can I stop living in hypocrisy." Every week two or three new faces would show up. When the club grew close to the size of thirty men, the police took action and arrested them all.

After Chief Miao's briefing, we were allowed to meet with the criminals for fifteen minutes. A policeman led me into a small room in the basement and let me read Baowen's confession while he went to fetch him. I glanced through the four pages of interrogation notes, which stated that Baowen had been new to the club and that he'd joined them only twice, mainly because he was interested in their talks. Yet he didn't deny that he was a homosexual.

The room smelled of urine, since it was next to a bathroom. The policeman took Baowen in and ordered him to sit opposite me at the table. Baowen, in handcuffs, avoided looking at me. His face was bloated, covered with bruises. A broad welt left by a baton, about four inches long, slanted across his forehead. The collar of his jacket was torn open. Yet he didn't appear frightened. His calm manner angered me, though I felt sorry for him.

I kept a hard face, and said, "Baowen, do you know you committed a crime?"

"I didn't do anything. I just went there to listen to them talk."

"You mean you didn't do that thing with any man?" I wanted to make sure   30
so that I could help him.

He looked at me, then lowered his eyes, saying, "I might've done something, to be honest, but I didn't."

"What's that supposed to mean?"

"I—liked a man in the club, a lot. If he'd asked me, I might've agreed." His lips curled upward as if he prided himself on what he had said.

"You're sick!" I struck the table with my knuckles.

To my surprise, he said, "So? I'm a sick man. You think I don't know that?"   35

I was bewildered. He went on, "Years ago I tried everything to cure myself. I took a lot of herbs and boluses, and even ate baked scorpions, lizards, and toads. Nothing helped me. Still I'm fond of men. I don't know why I'm not interested in women. Whenever I'm with a woman my heart is as calm as a stone."

Outraged by his confession, I asked, "Then why did you marry my Beina? To make fun of her, eh? To throw mud in my face?"

"How could I be that mean? Before we got married, I told her I didn't like women and might not give her a baby."

"She believed you?"

"Yes. She said she wouldn't mind. She just wanted a husband."   40

"She's an idiot!" I unfolded my hanky and blew my clogged nose into it, then asked, "Why did you choose her if you had no feelings for her at all?"

"What was the difference? For me she was similar to other women."

"You're a scoundrel!"

"If I didn't marry her, who would? The marriage helped us both, covering me and saving face for her. Besides, we could have a good apartment—a home. You see, I tried living like a normal man. I've never been mean to Beina."

"But the marriage is a fake! You lied to your mother too, didn't you?"   45

"She wanted me to marry."

The policeman signaled that our meeting was over. In spite of my anger, I told Baowen that I'd see what I could do, and that he'd better cooperate with the police and show a sincere attitude.

What should I do? I was sick of him, but he belonged to my family, at least in name, and I was obligated to help him.

On the way home I pedaled slowly, my mind heavy with thoughts. Gradually I realized that I might be able to do something to prevent him from going to jail. There were two steps I could take: first, I would maintain that he had done nothing in the club, so as to isolate him from those real criminals; second, I would present him as a sick man, so that he might receive medical treatment instead of a prison term. Once he became a criminal, he'd be marked forever as an enemy of society, no longer redeemable. Even his children might suffer. I ought to save him.

Fortunately both the party secretary and the director of our factory were willing to accept Baowen as a sick man, particularly Secretary Zhu, who liked Baowen's kung-fu style and had once let him teach his youngest son how to use a three-section cudgel. Zhu suggested we make an effort to rescue Baowen from the police. He said to me in the men's room inside our office building, "Old Cheng, we must not let Baowen end up in prison." I was grateful for his words.

All of a sudden homosexuality became a popular topic in the factory. A few old workers said that some actors of the Beijing opera had slept together as lovers in the old days, because no women were allowed to perform in any troupe and the actors could spend time with men only. Secretary Zhu, who was well read, said that some emperors in the Han Dynasty had owned male lovers in addition to their large harems. Director Liu had heard that the last emperor, Puyi, had often ordered his eunuchs to suck his penis and caress his testicles. Someone even claimed that homosexuality was an upper-class thing, not something for ordinary people. All the talk sickened me. I felt ashamed of my nominal son-in-law. I wouldn't join them in talking and just listened, pretending I wasn't bothered.

As I expected, rumors went wild in the factory, especially in the foundry shop. Some people said Baowen was impotent. Some believed he was a hermaphrodite, otherwise his wife would've been pregnant long ago.

To console Beina, I went to see her one evening. She had a pleasant home, in which everything was in order. Two bookcases, filled with industrial manuals, biographies, novels, and medical books, stood against the whitewashed wall, on either side of the window. In one corner of the living room was a coat tree on which hung the red feather parka Baowen had bought her before their wedding, and in another corner sat a floor lamp. At the opposite end of the room two pots of blooming flowers, one of cyclamens and the other of Bengal roses, were placed on a pair of low stools kept at an equal distance from each other and from the walls on both sides. Near the inner wall, beside a yellow enamel spittoon, was a large sofa upholstered in orange imitation leather. A black-and-white TV perched on an oak chest against the outer wall.

I was impressed, especially by the floor inlaid with bricks and coated with bright red paint. Even my wife couldn't keep a home so neat. No doubt it was Baowen's work, because Beina couldn't be so tidy. Already the room showed the trace of her sloppy habits—in a corner were scattered an empty flour sack and a pile of soiled laundry. Sipping the tea she had poured me, I said, "Beina, I'm sorry about Baowen. I didn't know he was so bad."

"No, he's a good man." Her round eyes looked at me with a steady light.   55

"Why do you say that?"

"He's been good to me."

"But he can't be a good husband, can he?"

"What do you mean?"

I said bluntly, "He didn't go to bed with you very often, did he?"   60

"Oh, he can't do that because he practices kung fu. He said if he slept with a woman, all his many years' work would be gone. From the very beginning his master told him to avoid women."

"So you don't mind?" I was puzzled, saying to myself, What a stupid girl.

"Not really."

"But you two must've shared the bed a couple of times, haven't you?"

"No, we haven't."

"Really? Not even once?"   65

"No." She blushed a little and looked away, twisting her earlobe with her fingertips.

My head was reeling. After eight months' marriage she was still a virgin! And she didn't mind! I lifted the cup and took a large gulp of the jasmine tea.

A lull settled in. We both turned to watch the evening news; my numb mind couldn't take in what the anchorwoman said about a border skirmish between Vietnamese and Chinese troops.

A moment later I told Beina, "I'm sorry he has such a problem. If only we   70 had known."

"Don't feel so bad, Uncle. In fact he's better than a normal man."

"How so?"

"Most men can't stay away from pretty women, but Baowen just likes to have a few buddies. What's wrong with that? It's better this way, 'cause I don't have to worry about those shameless bitches in our factory. He won't bother to give them a look. He'll never have a lifestyle problem."

I almost laughed, wondering how I should explain to her that he could have a sexual relationship with a man and that he'd been detained precisely because of a lifestyle problem. On second thought I realized it might be better for her to continue to think that way. She didn't need more stress at the moment.

Then we talked about how to help Baowen. I told her to write a report,   75 emphasizing what a good, considerate husband he'd been. Of course she must not mention his celibacy in their marriage. Also, from now on, however vicious her fellow workers' remarks were, she should ignore them and never talk back, as if she'd heard nothing.

That night when I told my wife about Beina's silly notions, she smiled, saying, "Compared with most men, Baowen isn't too bad. Beina's not a fool."

I begged Chief Miao and a high-ranking officer to treat Baowen leniently and even gave each of them two bottles of brandy and a coupon for a Butterfly sewing machine. They seemed willing to help but wouldn't promise me anything. For days I was so anxious that my wife was afraid my ulcer might recur.

One morning the Public Security Bureau called, saying they had accepted our factory's proposal and would have Baowen transferred to the mental hospital in a western suburb, provided our factory agreed to pay for his hospitalization. I accepted the offer readily, feeling relieved. Later, I learned that there wasn't enough space in the city's prison for twenty-seven gay men, who couldn't be mixed with other inmates and had to be put in solitary cells. So only four of them were jailed; the rest were either hospitalized (if their work units agreed to pay for the medical expenses) or sent to some labor farms to be reformed. The two party members among them didn't go to jail, though they were expelled from the party, a very severe punishment that ended their political lives.

The moment I put down the phone, I hurried to the assembly shop and found Beina. She broke into tears at the good news. She ran back home and filled a duffel bag with Baowen's clothes. We met at my office, then together set out for the Public Security Bureau. I rode my bicycle while she sat behind me, embracing the duffel as if it were a baby. With a strong tailwind, the cycling was easy and fast, so we arrived before Baowen left for the hospital. He was waiting for a van in front of the police station, accompanied by two policemen.

The bruises on his face had healed, so he looked handsome again. He smiled 80 at us, and said rather secretively, "I want to ask you a favor." He rolled his eyes as the dark green van rounded the street corner, coming toward us.

"What?" I said.

"Don't let my mother know the truth. She's too old to take it. Don't tell her, please!"

"What should we say to her, then?" I asked.

"Just say I have a temporary mental disorder."

Beina couldn't hold back her tears anymore, saying loudly, "Don't worry. We 85 won't let her know. Take care of yourself and come back soon." She handed him the duffel, which he took without a word.

I nodded to assure him that I wouldn't reveal the truth. He smiled at her, then at me. For some reason his face turned rather sweet—charming and enticing, as though it were a mysterious female face. I blinked my eyes and wondered if he was really a man. It flashed through my mind that if he were a woman he could've been a beauty—tall, slim, muscular, and slightly languid.

My thoughts were cut short by a metallic screech as the van stopped in front of us. Baowen climbed into it; so did the policemen. I walked around the van, and shook his hand, saying that I'd visit him the next week and that meanwhile, if he needed anything, just to give me a ring.

We waved good-bye as the van drew away, its tire chains clattering and flinging up bits of snow. After a blasting toot, it turned left and disappeared from the icy street. I got on my bicycle as a gust of wind blew up and almost threw me down. Beina followed me for about twenty yards, then leaped on the carrier, and together we headed home. She was so heavy. Thank heaven, I was riding a Great Golden Deer, one of the sturdiest makes.

During the following week I heard from Baowen once. He said on the phone that he felt better now and less agitated. Indeed his voice sounded calm and smooth. He asked me to bring him a few books when I came, specifically his *Dictionary of Universal Knowledge*, which was a hefty, rare book translated from the Russian in the late fifties. I had no idea how he had come by it.

I went to see him on Thursday morning. The hospital was on a mountain, 90
six miles southwest of Muji City. As I was cycling on the asphalt road, a few tall smokestacks fumed lazily beyond the larch woods in the west. To my right the power lines along the roadside curved, heavy with fluffy snow, which would drop in little chunks whenever the wind blew across them. Now and then I overtook a horse cart loaded with earless sheaves of wheat, followed by one or two foals. After I pedaled across a stone bridge and turned into the mouth of a valley, a group of brick buildings emerged on a gentle slope, connected with one another by straight cement paths. Farther up the hill, past the buildings, there was a cow pen, in which about two dozen milk cows were grazing on dry grass while a few others huddled together to keep warm.

It was so peaceful here that if you hadn't known this was a mental hospital, you might have imagined it was a sanatorium for ranking officials. Entering Building 9, I was stopped by a guard, who then took me to Baowen's room on the ground floor. It happened that the doctor on duty, a tall fortyish man with tapering fingers, was making the morning rounds and examining Baowen. He shook hands with me and said that my son-in-law was doing fine. His surname was Mai; his whiskered face looked very intelligent. When he turned to give a male nurse instructions about Baowen's treatment, I noticed an enormous wart in his ear almost blocking the ear hole like a hearing aid. In a way he looked like a foreigner. I wondered if he had some Mongolian or Tibetan blood.

"We give him the electric bath," Doctor Mai said to me a moment later.

"What?" I asked, wincing.

"We treat him with the electric bath."

I turned to Baowen. "How is it?"   95

"It's good, really soothing." He smiled, but there was a churlish look in his eyes, and his mouth tightened.

The nurse was ready to take him for the treatment. Never having heard of such a bath, I asked Doctor Mai, "Can I see how it works?"

"All right, you may go with them."

Together we climbed the stairs to the second floor. There was another reason for me to join them. I wanted to find out whether Baowen was a normal man. The rumors in our factory had gotten on my nerves, particularly the one that said he had no penis—that was why he had always avoided bathing in the workers' bathhouse.

After taking off our shoes and putting on plastic slippers, we entered a small room that had pea green walls and a parquet floor. At its center lay a porcelain bathtub, as ghastly as an apparatus of torture. Affixed along the interior wall of the tub were rectangles of black perforated metal. Three thick rubber cords connected them to a tall machine standing by the wall. A control board full of buttons, gauges, and switches slanted atop the machine. The young nurse, burly and square-faced, turned on the faucet; steaming water began to tumble into the tub. Then he went over to operate the machine. He seemed good-natured; his name was Fuhai Dong. He said he came from the countryside, apparently of peasant stock, and had graduated from Jilin Nursing School.

Baowen smiled at me while unbuttoning his zebra-striped hospital robe. He looked fine now—all the bruises had disappeared from his face, which had become pinkish and smooth. I was scared by the tub. It seemed suitable for electrocuting a criminal. However sick I was, I wouldn't lie in it with my back resting against that metal groove. What if there was an electricity leak?

"Does it hurt?" I asked Baowen.

"No."

He went behind a khaki screen in a corner and began taking off his clothes. When the water half filled the tub, the nurse took a small bag of white powder out of a drawer, cut it open with scissors, and poured the stuff into the water. It must have been salt. He tucked up his shirtsleeves and bent double to agitate the solution with both hands, which were large and sinewy.

To my dismay, Baowen came out in a clean pair of shorts. Without hesitation he got into the tub and lay down, just as one would enter a lukewarm bathing pool. I was amazed. "Have you given him electricity yet?" I asked Nurse Dong.

"Yes, a little. I'll increase it by and by." He turned to the machine and adjusted a few buttons.

"You know," he said to me, "your son-in-law is a very good patient, always cooperative."

"He should be."

"That's why we give him the bath. Other patients get electric cuffs around their limbs or electric rods on their bodies. Some of them scream like animals every time. We have to tie them up."

"When will he be cured?"

"I'm not sure."

Baowen was noiseless in the electrified water, with his eyes shut and his head resting on a black rubber pad at the end of the tub. He looked fine, rather relaxed.

I drew up a chair and sat down. Baowen seemed reluctant to talk, concentrating on the treatment, so I remained silent, observing him. His body was wiry, his legs hairless, and the front of his shorts bulged quite a bit. He looked all right physically. Once in a while he breathed a feeble sigh.

As the nurse increased the electric current, Baowen began to squirm in the tub as if smarting from something. "Are you all right?" I asked, and dared not touch him.

"Yeah." 115

He kept his eyes shut. Glistening beads of sweat gathered on his forehead. He looked pale, his lips curling now and again as though he were thirsty.

Then the nurse gave him more electricity. Baowen began writhing and moaning a little. Obviously he was suffering. This bath couldn't be as soothing as he'd claimed. With a white towel Nurse Dong wiped the sweat off Baowen's face, and whispered, "I'll turn it down in a few minutes."

"No, give me more!" Baowen said resolutely without opening his eyes, his face twisted.

I felt as though he was ashamed of himself. Perhaps my presence made this section of the treatment more uncomfortable to him. His hands gripped the rim of the tub, the arched wrists trembling. For a good three minutes nobody said a word; the room was so quiet that its walls seemed to be ringing.

As the nurse gradually reduced the electricity, Baowen calmed down. His 120 toes stopped wiggling.

Not wanting to bother him further with my presence, I went out to look for Doctor Mai, to thank him and find out when Baowen could be cured. The doctor was not in his office, so I walked out of the building for a breath of air. The sun was high and the snow blazingly white. Once outside, I had to close my eyes for a minute to adjust them. I then sat down on a bench and lit a cigarette. A young woman in an ermine hat and army mittens passed by, holding an empty milk pail and humming the song "Comrade, Please Have a Cup of Tea." She looked handsome, and her crisp voice pleased me. I gazed at the pair of thick braids behind her, which swayed a little in the wind.

My heart was full of pity for Baowen. He was such a fine young man that he ought to be able to love a woman, have a family, and enjoy a normal life.

Twenty minutes later I rejoined him in his room. He looked tired, still shivering a little. He told me that as the electric currents increased, his skin had begun prickling as though stung by hundreds of mosquitoes. That was why he couldn't stay in the tub for longer than half an hour.

I felt for him, and said, "I'll tell our leaders how sincere your attitude is and how cooperative you are."

"Oh sure." He tilted his damp head. "Thanks for bringing the books." 125

"Do you need something else?"

"No." He sounded sad.

"Baowen, I hope you can come home before the New Year. Beina needs you."

"I know. I don't want to be locked up here forever."

I told him that Beina had written to his mother, saying he'd been away on 130 a business trip. Then the bell for lunch rang in the building, and outside the loudspeaker began broadcasting the fiery music of "March of the Volunteers."

Nurse Dong walked in with a pair of chopsticks and a plate containing two corn buns. He said cheerily to Baowen, "I'll bring you the dish in a minute. We have tofu stewed with sauerkraut today, also bean sprout soup."

I stood up and took my leave.

When I reported Baowen's condition to the factory leaders, they seemed impressed. The term "electric bath" must have given their imagination free rein. Secretary Zhu kept shaking his head, and said, "I'm sorry Baowen has to go through such a thing."

I didn't explain that the electric bath was a treatment less severe than the other kinds, nor did I describe what the bath was like. I just said, "They steep him in electrified water every day." Let the terror seize their brains, I thought, so that they might be more sympathetic to Baowen when he is discharged from the hospital.

It was mid-December, and Baowen had been in the hospital for a month already. For days Beina went on saying that she wanted to see how her husband was doing; she was eager to take him home before the New Year. Among her fellow workers rumors persisted. One said the electric bath had blistered Baowen; another claimed that his genitals had been shriveled up by the treatment; another added that he had become a vegetarian, nauseated at the mere sight of meat. The young woman who had once declared she'd leave her door open for him had just married and proudly told everybody she was pregnant. People began to be kind and considerate to Beina, treating her like an abused wife. The leaders of the assembly shop assigned her only the daytime shift. I was pleased that Finance still paid Baowen his wages as though he were on sick leave. Perhaps they did this because they didn't want to upset me.

On Saturday Beina and I went to the mental hospital. She couldn't pedal, and it was too far for me to carry her on my bicycle, so we took the bus. She had been there by herself two weeks ago to deliver some socks and a pair of woolen pajamas she'd knitted for Baowen.

We arrived at the hospital early in the afternoon. Baowen looked healthy, in good spirits. It seemed that the bath had helped him. He was happy to see Beina and even cuddled her in my presence. He gave her two toffees; knowing I disliked candies, he didn't give me one. He poured a large mug of malted milk for both of us, since there was only one mug in the room. I didn't touch the milk, unsure whether homosexuality was communicable. I was glad to see that he treated his wife well. He took a genuine interest in what she said about their comrades in our factory, and now and then laughed heartily. What a wonderful husband he could have been if he were not sick.

Having sat with the couple for a few minutes, I left so that they could be alone. I went to the nurses' office upstairs and found Fuhai Dong writing at a desk. The door was open, and I knocked on its frame. Startled, he closed his brown notebook and stood up.

"I didn't mean to scare you," I said.

"No, Uncle, I just didn't expect anyone to come up here."

I took a carton of Peony cigarettes out of my bag and put it on the desk, 140
saying, "I won't take too much of your time, young man. Please keep this as
a token of my regards." I didn't mean to bribe him. I was sincerely grateful to
him for treating Baowen well.

"Oh, don't give me this, please."

"You don't smoke?"

"I do. Tell you what, give it to Doctor Mai. He'll help Baowen more."

I was puzzled. Why didn't he want the top-quality cigarettes if he smoked?
Seeing that I was confused, he went on, "I'll be nice to Baowen without any gift
from you. He's a good man. It's the doctor's wheels that you should grease."

"I have another carton for him."   145

"One carton's nothing here. You should give him at least two."

I was moved by his words, thanked him, and said good-bye.

Doctor Mai happened to be in his office. When I walked in, he was reading
the current issue of *Women's Life*, whose back cover carried a large photo of
Madame Mao on trial—she wore black and stood, handcuffed, between two
young policewomen. Doctor Mai put the magazine aside and asked me to sit
down. In the room, tall shelves, loaded with books and files, lined the walls. A
smell of rotten fruit hung in there. He seemed pleased to see me.

After we exchanged a few words, I took out both cartons of cigarettes and
handed them to him. "This is just a small token of my gratitude, for the New
Year," I said.

He took the cigarettes and put them away under his desk. "Thanks a lot," he 150
whispered.

"Doctor Mai, do you think Baowen will be cured before the holiday?"
I asked.

"What did you say? Cured?" He looked surprised.

"Yes."

He shook his head slowly, then turned to check that the door was shut. He
motioned me to move closer. I pulled the chair forward a little and rested my
forearms on the edge of his Bakelite desktop.

"To be honest, there's no cure," he said.   155

"What?"

"Homosexuality isn't an illness, so it has no cure. Don't tell anyone I said
this."

"Then why torture Baowen like that?"

"The police sent him here and we couldn't refuse. Besides, we ought to make
him feel better and hopeful."

"So it isn't a disease?"   160

"Unfortunately no. Let me say this again: there's no cure for your son-in-law,
Old Cheng. It's not a disease. It's just a sexual preference; it may be congenital,
like being left-handed. Got it?"

"Then why give him the electric bath?" Still I wasn't convinced.

"Electrotherapy is prescribed by the book—a standard treatment required by
the Department of Public Health. I have no choice but to follow the regulations.

That's why I didn't give him any of those harsher treatments. The bath is very mild by comparison. You see, I've done everything in my power to help him. Let me tell you another fact: according to the statistics, so far electrotherapy has cured only one out of a thousand homosexuals. I bet cod liver oil, or chocolate, or fried pork, anything, could produce a better result. All right, enough of this. I've talked too much."

At last his words sank in. For a good while I sat there motionless with a numb mind. A flock of sparrows were flitting about in the naked branches outside the window, chasing the one that held a tiny ear of millet in its bill. Another of them dragged a yellow string tied around its leg, unable to fly as nimbly as the others. I rose to my feet and thanked the doctor for his candid words. He stubbed out his cigarette in the ashtray on the windowsill, and said, "I'll take special care of your son-in-law. Don't worry."

I rejoined Beina downstairs. Baowen looked quite cheerful, and it seemed 165 they'd had a good time. He said to me, "If I can't come home soon, don't try too hard to get me out. They won't keep me here forever."

"I'll see what I can do."

In my heart I was exasperated, because if Doctor Mai's words were true, there'd be little I could do for Baowen. If homosexuality wasn't a disease, why had he felt sick and tried to have himself cured? Had he been shamming? It was unlikely.

Beina had been busy cleaning their home since her last visit to the hospital. She bought two young drakes and planned to make drunk duck, a dish she said Baowen liked best. My heart was heavy. On the one hand, I'd have loved to have him back for the holiday; on the other hand, I was unsure what would happen if his condition hadn't improved. I dared not reveal my thoughts to anybody, not even to my wife, who had a big mouth. Because of her, the whole factory knew that Beina was still a virgin, and some people called her the Virgin Bride.

For days I pondered what to do. I was confused. Everybody thought homosexuality was a disease except for Doctor Mai, whose opinion I dared not mention to others. The factory leaders would be mad at me if they knew there was no cure for homosexuality. We had already spent over three thousand yuan on Baowen. I kept questioning in my mind, If homosexuality is a natural thing, then why are there men and women? Why can't two men get married and make a baby? Why didn't nature give men another hole? I was beset by doubts. If only I could have seen a trustworthy doctor for a second opinion. If only there were a knowledgeable, honest friend I could have talked with.

I hadn't yet made up my mind about what to do when Chief Miao called 170 from the Public Security Bureau five days before the holiday. He informed me that Baowen had repeated his crime, so the police had taken him out of the hospital and sent him to the prison in Tangyuan County. "This time he did it," said the chief.

"Impossible!" I cried.

"We have evidence and witnesses. He doesn't deny it himself."

"Oh." I didn't know how to continue.

"He has to be incarcerated now."

"Are you sure he's not a hermaphrodite?" I mentioned that as a last resort.   175

Miao chuckled dryly. "No, he's not. We had him checked. Physically he's a man, healthy and normal. Obviously it's a mental, moral disease, like an addiction to opium."

Putting down the phone, I felt dizzy, cursing Baowen for having totally ruined himself. What had happened was that he and Fuhai Dong had developed a relationship secretly. The nurse often gave him a double amount of meat or fish at dinner. Baowen, in return, unraveled his woolen pajamas and knitted Dong a pullover with the wool. One evening when they were lying in each other's arms in the nurses' office, an old cleaner passed by in the corridor and coughed. Fuhai Dong was terrified and convinced that the man had seen what they had been doing. For days, however hard Baowen tried to talk him out of his conviction, Dong wouldn't change his mind, blaming Baowen for having misled him. He said that the old cleaner often smiled at him meaningfully and would definitely turn them in. Finally Fuhai Dong went to the hospital leaders and confessed everything. So, unlike Baowen, who got three and a half years in jail, Nurse Dong was merely put on probation; if he worked harder and criticized himself well, he might keep his current job.

That evening I went to tell Beina about the new development. As I was talking, she sobbed continually. Although she'd been cleaning the apartment for several days, her home was in shambles, most of the flowers half-dead, and dishes and pots piled in the sink. Mopping her face with a pink towel, she asked me, "What should I tell my mother-in-law?"

"Tell her the truth."

She made no response. I said again, "You should consider a divorce."   180

"No!" Her sobbing turned into wailing. "He—he's my husband and I'm his wife. If I die my soul belongs to him. We've sworn never to leave each other. Let others say whatever they want, I know he's a good man."

"Then why did he go to bed with a guy?"

"He just wanted to have a good time. That was all. It's nothing like adultery or bigamy, is it?"

"But it's a crime that got him into jail," I said. Although in my heart I admitted that Baowen in every way was a good fellow except for his fondness for men, I had to be adamant about my position. I was in charge of security for our factory; if I had a criminal son-in-law, who would listen to me? Wouldn't I be removed from my office soon? If I lost my job, who could protect Beina? Sooner or later she would be laid off, since a criminal's wife was not supposed to have the same opportunities for employment as others. Beina remained silent; I asked again, "What are you going to do?"

"Wait for him."   185

I took a few spiced pumpkin seeds from a bowl, stood up, and went over to the window. Under the sill the radiator was hissing softly with a tiny steam leak. Outside, in the distance, firecrackers one after another scattered clusters of sparks into the indigo dusk. I turned around, and said, "He's not worth waiting for. You must divorce him."

"No, I won't," she moaned.

"Well, it's impossible for me to have a criminal as my son-in-law. I've been humiliated enough. If you want to wait for him, don't come to see me again." I put the pumpkin seeds back into the bowl, picked up my fur hat, and dragged myself out the door.

FOR ANALYSIS

1. Toward the end of the story, the **narrator** asks himself of Baowen, "If homosexuality wasn't a disease, why had he felt sick and tried to have himself cured?" (para. 167). What do you think is the story's answer to this question?

2. Why does the doctor continue Baowen's treatment if he knows homosexuality is not a disease that can be cured?

3. While this story is about a small number of **characters**, it is also about an entire society. What do the events in this story imply about life in China? Consider both the actions taken by and against Baowen and the actions taken by his wife and father-in-law. Consider also the attitudes and behaviors of "the people" generally, such as those of the factory workers and the bureaucrats.

MAKING ARGUMENTS

How would you argue that this story is critical of contemporary China? How would you make the counterargument? Use as evidence not only the support you find for each position in the story but also information you can gather about Chinese society, government, and so on.

WRITING TOPICS

1. While the story is called "The Bridegroom," it is really as much about the **narrator** as it is about Baowen. What kind of man is the narrator? How do you feel about him? Do your feelings about him change over the course of the story? How about at the end?

2. How would this story be different if it were narrated by Baowen? What would be gained, in terms of understanding the situation and the events? What would be lost?

MAKING CONNECTIONS

1. In spite of the very different **settings** and situations in "A Rose for Emily" (p. 623) and "The Bridegroom," what makes Miss Emily and Baowen similar?

2. At the center of both stories is the relation of the main **characters** to their societies. This is true beyond the title characters; for example, the relationship of the **narrator** of "The Bridegroom" to his society is very important to the story. Is there an analogous figure in "A Rose for Emily"?

3. Both stories feature judgmental narrating figures. Do the stories (or the authors) seem to agree entirely with these narrators' opinions? Do the stories present these judgments straight, or is there some **ironic** distance between what the narrators say and what you think the stories themselves say?

POETRY

JONATHAN SWIFT   (1667–1745)

MARKET WOMEN'S CRIES

APPLES

Come buy my fine wares,
Plums, apples and pears.
A hundred a penny,
In conscience too many:
Come, will you have any?
My children are seven,
I wish them in Heaven;
My husband's a sot,
With his pipe and his pot,
Not a farthen[1] will gain them,   10
And I must maintain them.

ONIONS

Come, follow me by the smell,
Here are delicate onions to sell;
I promise to use you well.
They make the blood warmer,
You'll feed like a farmer;
For this is every cook's opinion,
No savoury dish without an onion;
But, lest your kissing should be spoiled,
Your onions must be thoroughly boiled: 20
Or else you may spare
Your mistress a share,

---

[1] A former British monetary unit equal to one fourth of a penny.

The secret will never be known:
  She cannot discover
  The breath of her lover,
But think it as sweet as her own.

HERRINGS

  Be not sparing,
  Leave off swearing.
  Buy my herring
  Fresh from Malahide,
  Better never was tried.
Come, eat them with pure fresh butter and mustard,
Their bellies are soft, and as white as a custard.
Come, sixpence a dozen, to get me some bread,
Or, like my own herrings, I soon shall be dead.

    30

FOR ANALYSIS

1. What is the scene of this poem? Do you imagine it is a common one for poetry? Why or why not?

2. Are these the typical things you would expect someone selling items at a market to say? Do you think Swift ever heard any market women actually say them?

3. Characterize the movement in each of the three **stanzas** from their opening to their ending. How do they change? What are the effects?

MAKING ARGUMENTS

Imagine someone who is critical of Swift's poem for its emphasis on the unhappiness of these women. On what grounds might this critic make this argument? Why is this emphasis a problem? What alternative might Swift have pursued?

WRITING TOPICS

1. Imagine writing a modern "Market Women's Cries." Where would you set it? What would you have them selling? What would they say about their wares and their lives?

2. Think about the speakers in this poem in terms of their identity. How do you imagine they are seen—classified, evaluated—by others? How do you think they see themselves? What if anything does the poem have to say about their identity (or identities)?

MAKING CONNECTIONS

1. Compare this poem to Levine's "What Work Is" (p. 433). How does each poem see work? How does each connect it to other parts of life?

2. Both "Market Women's Cries" and Sandburg's "I Am the People, the Mob" (p. 425) are about regular people rather than kings, or knights, or princesses. How does each poem treat its subject? What does each have to say about everyday life?

EMILY DICKINSON   (1830–1886)

I'M NOBODY! WHO ARE YOU?   CA. 1861, 1891

I'm Nobody! Who are you?
Are you—Nobody—Too?
Then there's a pair of us!
Don't tell! they'd advertise—you know!

How dreary—to be—Somebody!
How public—like a Frog—
To tell one's name—the livelong June—
To an admiring Bog!

JAMES WELDON JOHNSON   (1871–1938)

A POET TO HIS BABY SON   1935

Tiny bit of humanity,
Blessed with your mother's face,
And cursed with your father's mind.

I say cursed with your father's mind,
Because you can lie so long and so quietly on your back,
Playing with the dimpled big toe of your left foot,
And looking away,
Through the ceiling of the room, and beyond.
Can it be that already you are thinking of being a poet?

Why don't you kick and howl,   10
And make the neighbors talk about
"That damned baby next door,"
And make up your mind forthwith
To grow up and be a banker
Or a politician or some other sort of go-getter
Or—?—whatever you decide upon,
Rid yourself of these incipient thoughts
About being a poet.

For poets no longer are makers of songs,
Chanters of the gold and purple harvest,   20

Sayers of the glories of earth and sky,
Of the sweet pain of love
And the keen joy of living;
No longer dreamers of the essential dreams,
And interpreters of the eternal truth,
Through the eternal beauty.
Poets these days are unfortunate fellows.
Baffled in trying to say old things in a new way
Or new things in an old language,
They talk abracadabra   30
In an unknown tongue,
Each one fashioning for himself
A wordy world of shadow problems,
And as a self-imagined Atlas,
Struggling under it with puny legs and arms,
Groaning out incoherent complaints at his load.

My son, this is no time nor place for a poet;
Grow up and join the big, busy crowd
That scrambles for what it thinks it wants
Out of this old world which is—as it is—   40
And, probably, always will be.

Take the advice of a father who knows:
You cannot begin too young
Not to be a poet.

FOR ANALYSIS

1. What is this poem's **tone**? Does it have more than one?

2. What did you expect the poem to be like based on the poem's title and opening lines? How did it meet or not meet your expectations?

3. Why does the speaker think his son shouldn't grow up to be a poet?

MAKING ARGUMENTS

You will hear people say the same things about poets and poetry today that Johnson wrote eighty years ago. Citing his specific claims about poetry in 1935 and applying them to the contemporary scene, argue for or against those claims, using as evidence contemporary poems in this book or that you know from elsewhere and any other support you think relevant.

WRITING TOPICS

1. Many poems are in part about poetry itself. What does this poem have to say specifically about poetry? Paraphrase its thoughts about the state of the genre.

2. "A Poet to His Baby Son" would not be what it is without the skillful use of **irony**. List the different ways and moments in which Johnson uses irony. What is the effect on you as you read? How is that effect different than it might be if Johnson's sentiments were expressed more directly?

PAUL LAURENCE DUNBAR   (1872–1906)

WE WEAR THE MASK   1896

We wear the mask that grins and lies,
It hides our cheeks and shades our eyes—
This debt we pay to human guile;
With torn and bleeding hearts we smile,
And mouth with myriad subtleties.

Why should the world be over-wise,
In counting all our tears and sighs?
Nay, let them only see us, while
        We wear the mask.

We smile, but, O great Christ, our cries   10
To thee from tortured souls arise.
We sing, but oh the clay is vile
Beneath our feet, and long the mile;
But let the world dream otherwise,
        We wear the mask!

GEORGIA DOUGLAS JOHNSON   (1880–1966)

OLD BLACK MEN   1922

They have dreamed as young men dream
        Of glory, love and power;
They have hoped as youth will hope
        Of life's sun-minted hour.

They have seen as other saw
        Their bubbles burst in air,
And they have learned to live it down
        As though they did not care.

T. S. ELIOT   (1888–1965)

THE LOVE SONG OF
J. ALFRED PRUFROCK 1917

S'io credessi che mia risposta fosse
a persona che mai tornasse al mondo,
questa fiamma staria senza più scosse.
Ma per ciò che giammai di questo fondo
non tornò vivo alcun, s'i'odo il vero,
senza tema d'infamia ti rispondo.[1]

Let us go then, you and I,
When the evening is spread out against the sky
Like a patient etherized upon a table;
Let us go, through certain half-deserted streets,
The muttering retreats
Of restless nights in one-night cheap hotels
And sawdust restaurants with oyster shells:
Streets that follow like a tedious argument
Of insidious intent
To lead you to an overwhelming question . . .   10
Oh, do not ask, "What is it?"
Let us go and make our visit.

In the room the women come and go
Talking of Michelangelo.

The yellow fog that rubs its back upon the windowpanes,
The yellow smoke that rubs its muzzle on the windowpanes
Licked its tongue into the corners of the evening,
Lingered upon the pools that stand in drains,
Let fall upon its back the soot that falls from chimneys,
Slipped by the terrace, made a sudden leap,   20
And seeing that it was a soft October night,
Curled once about the house, and fell asleep.

And indeed there will be time
For the yellow smoke that slides along the street,
Rubbing its back upon the windowpanes;

---

[1] From Dante, *Inferno*, XXVII, 61–66. The speaker is Guido da Montefeltro, who is imprisoned in a flame in the level of hell reserved for false counselors. He tells Dante and Virgil, "If I thought my answer were given to one who might return to the world, this flame would stay without further movement. But since from this depth none has ever returned alive, if what I hear is true, I answer you without fear of infamy."

There will be time, there will be time
To prepare a face to meet the faces that you meet;
There will be time to murder and create,
And time for all the works and days of hands
That lift and drop a question on your plate;   30
Time for you and time for me,
And time yet for a hundred indecisions,
And for a hundred visions and revisions,
Before the taking of a toast and tea.

In the room the women come and go
Talking of Michelangelo.

And indeed there will be time
To wonder, "Do I dare?" and, "Do I dare?"
Time to turn back and descend the stair,
With a bald spot in the middle of my hair—   40
(They will say: "How his hair is growing thin!")
My morning coat, my collar mounting firmly to the chin,
My necktie rich and modest, but asserted by a simple pin—
(They will say: "But how his arms and legs are thin!")
Do I dare
Disturb the universe?
In a minute there is time
For decisions and revisions which a minute will reverse.

For I have known them all already, known them all—
Have known the evenings, mornings, afternoons,
I have measured out my life with coffee spoons;   50
I know the voices dying with a dying fall
Beneath the music from a farther room.
    So how should I presume?

And I have known the eyes already, known them all—
The eyes that fix you in a formulated phrase,
And when I am formulated, sprawling on a pin,
When I am pinned and wriggling on the wall,
Then how should I begin
To spit out all the butt-ends of my days and ways?   60
    And how should I presume?

And I have known the arms already, known them all—
Arms that are braceleted and white and bare
(But in the lamplight, downed with light brown hair!)
Is it perfume from a dress

That makes me so digress?
Arms that lie along a table, or wrap about a shawl.
   And should I then presume?
   And how should I begin?

Shall I say, I have gone at dusk through narrow streets   70
And watched the smoke that rises from the pipes
Of lonely men in shirt-sleeves, leaning out of windows? . . .

I should have been a pair of ragged claws
Scuttling across the floors of silent seas.

And the afternoon, the evening, sleeps so peacefully!
Smoothed by long fingers,
Asleep . . . tired . . . or it malingers,
Stretched on the floor, here beside you and me.
Should I, after tea and cakes and ices,
Have the strength to force the moment to its crisis?   80
But though I have wept and fasted, wept and prayed,
Though I have seen my head (grown slightly bald) brought in upon a platter,[2]
I am no prophet—and here's no great matter;
I have seen the moment of my greatness flicker,
And I have seen the eternal Footman hold my coat, and snicker,
And in short, I was afraid.

And would it have been worth it, after all,
After the cups, the marmalade, the tea,
Among the porcelain, among some talk of you and me,
Would it have been worth while,   90
To have bitten off the matter with a smile,
To have squeezed the universe into a ball
To roll it toward some overwhelming question,
To say: "I am Lazarus,[3] come from the dead,
Come back to tell you all, I shall tell you all"—
If one, settling a pillow by her head,
   Should say: "That is not what I meant at all.
   That is not it, at all."

And would it have been worth it, after all,
Would it have been worth while,   100

---

[2] Like the head of John the Baptist. See Matthew 14:3–12.
[3] See John 11:1–14 and Luke 16:19–26.

After the sunsets and the dooryards and the sprinkled streets,
After the novels, after the teacups, after the skirts that trail along the floor—
And this, and so much more?—
It is impossible to say just what I mean!
But as if a magic lantern threw the nerves in patterns on a screen:
Would it have been worth while
If one, settling a pillow or throwing off a shawl,
And turning toward the window, should say:
    "That is not it at all,
    That is not what I meant, at all."   110

. . . . .

No! I am not Prince Hamlet, nor was meant to be;
Am an attendant lord, one that will do
To swell a progress,° start a scene or two,   state journey
Advise the prince; no doubt, an easy tool,
Deferential, glad to be of use,
Politic, cautious, and meticulous;
Full of high sentence,° but a bit obtuse;   sententiousness
At times, indeed, almost ridiculous—
Almost, at times, the Fool.

I grow old . . . I grow old . . .   120
I shall wear the bottoms of my trousers rolled.°   cuffed

Shall I part my hair behind? Do I dare to eat a peach?
I shall wear white flannel trousers, and walk upon the beach.
I have heard the mermaids singing, each to each.

I do not think that they will sing to me.

I have seen them riding seaward on the waves
Combing the white hair of the waves blown back
When the wind blows the water white and black.

We have lingered in the chambers of the sea
By sea-girls wreathed with seaweed red and brown   130
Till human voices wake us, and we drown.

FOR ANALYSIS

1. This poem may be understood as a **stream of consciousness** passing through the mind of Prufrock. The "you and I" of line 1 may be different aspects of his personality. Or perhaps the "you and I" is parallel to Guido da Montefeltro, who speaks the epigraph, and Dante, to whom he tells the story that resulted in his damnation—hence, "you" is the reader and "I" is Prufrock. The poem is disjointed because it proceeds by psychological rather than logical stages. To what social class does Prufrock belong? How does Prufrock respond to the attitudes and values of his class? Does he change in the course of the poem?

2. Line 92 provides a good example of literary **allusion** (see the last stanza of Marvell's "To His Coy Mistress," p. 977). How does an awareness of the allusion contribute to your response?

3. What might the song of the mermaids (l. 124) signify, and why does Prufrock think they will not sing to him (l. 125)?

4. T. S. Eliot once said that some poetry "can communicate without being understood." Is this such a poem?

MAKING ARGUMENTS

Upon the poem's publication, one reviewer wrote, "The fact that these things occurred to the mind of Mr. Eliot is surely of the very smallest importance to anyone, even to himself. They certainly have no relation to poetry." Regardless of whether you agree with this dismissive reviewer, construct an argument for the importance of the things that occurred to Eliot's mind. Make your argument in terms of this poem specifically but also as a defense of poetry in general.

WRITING TOPIC

What sort of man is J. Alfred Prufrock? How does the poet establish his characteristics?

E. E. CUMMINGS   (1894–1962)

THE CAMBRIDGE LADIES WHO LIVE IN FURNISHED SOULS   1923

the Cambridge ladies who live in furnished souls
are unbeautiful and have comfortable minds
(also, with the church's protestant blessings
daughters, unscented shapeless spirited)
they believe in Christ and Longfellow, both dead,
are invariably interested in so many things—
at the present writing one still finds
delighted fingers knitting for the is it Poles?
perhaps. While permanent faces coyly bandy
scandal of Mrs. N. and Professor D.   10
... the Cambridge ladies do not care, above
Cambridge if sometimes in its box of
sky lavender and cornerless, the
moon rattles like a fragment of angry candy

FOR ANALYSIS

1. What **images** does the poet use to describe "the Cambridge ladies"? What do the images suggest?

2. What is the effect of the interruption "is it" in line 8?

3. In the final lines, the moon seems to protest against the superficiality of these women. What is the effect of comparing the moon to a fragment of candy?

MAKING ARGUMENTS

Make an argument on behalf of the "Cambridge Ladies" from their **point of view**. What might they say in their own defense to the poem's criticisms—about how they live, how they act, how they got to be the way they are?

WRITING TOPIC

This poem **satirizes** the behavior of the Cambridge ladies. Does it imply how they should behave?

HOWARD NEMEROV (1920–1991)

MONEY 1977

an introductory lecture

This morning we shall spend a few minutes
Upon the study of symbolism, which is basic
To the nature of money. I show you this nickel.
Icons and cryptograms are written all over
The nickel: one side shows a hunchbacked bison
Bending his head and curling his tail to accommodate
The circular nature of money. Over him arches
UNITED STATES OF AMERICA, and, squinched in
Between that and his rump, E PLURIBUS UNUM,
A Roman reminiscence that appears to mean   10
An indeterminately large number of things
All of which are the same. Under the bison
A straight line giving him a ground to stand on
Reads FIVE CENTS. And on the other side of our nickel
There is the profile of a man with long hair
And a couple of feathers in the hair; we know
Somehow that he is an American Indian, and
He wears the number nineteen-thirty-six.
Right in front of his eyes the word LIBERTY, bent

To conform with the curve of the rim, appears   20
To be falling out of the sky ɣ first; the Indian
Keeps his eyes downcast and does not notice this;
To notice it, indeed, would be shortsighted of him.
So much for the iconography of one of our nickels,
Which is now becoming a rarity and something of
A collectors' item: for as a matter of fact
There is almost nothing you can buy with a nickel,
The representative American Indian was destroyed
A hundred years or so ago, and his descendants'
Relations with liberty are maintained with reservations,   30
Or primitive concentration camps; while the bison,
Except for a few examples kept in cages,
Is now extinct. Something like that, I think,
Is what Keats must have meant in his celebrated
Ode on a Grecian Urn.
                    Notice, in conclusion,
A number of circumstances sometimes overlooked
Even by experts: (*a*) Indian and bison,
Confined to obverse and reverse of the coin,
Can never see each other; (*b*) they are looking   40
In opposite directions, the bison past
The Indian's feathers, the Indian past
The bison's tail; (*c*) they are upside down
To one another; (*d*) the bison has a human face
Somewhat resembling that of Jupiter Ammon.
I hope that our studies today will have shown you
Something of the import of symbolism
With respect to the understanding of what is symbolized.

FOR ANALYSIS

1. What object is the poem's speaker describing? Why do you think Nemerov chose that object in particular?

2. What are the different ways in which **symbolism** is basic to the nature of money?

3. What is your "understanding of what is symbolized" (l. 48) in this poem?

MAKING ARGUMENTS

Regardless of your own feelings, argue against Nemerov's implicit reading of U.S. history. What would such an argument say about the history of European contact, settlement, and displacement? What would it say about the ideals enshrined on U.S. currency?

WRITING TOPIC

Find another everyday item that can be seen as a **symbol** of larger things and look at it in the way Nemerov's poem looks at the buffalo nickel. What do you see?

MAKING CONNECTIONS

Explain Nemerov's **allusion** to John Keats's "Ode on a Grecian Urn" (p. 1245). What is it that Keats "must have meant"?

ETHERIDGE KNIGHT   (1931–1991)

HARD ROCK RETURNS TO PRISON FROM THE HOSPITAL FOR THE CRIMINAL INSANE   1968

Hard Rock was "known not to take no shit
From nobody," and he had the scars to prove it:
Split purple lips, lumped ears, welts above
His yellow eyes, and one long scar that cut
Across his temple and plowed through a thick
Canopy of kinky hair.

The WORD was that Hard Rock wasn't a mean nigger
Anymore, that the doctors had bored a hole in his head,
Cut out part of his brain, and shot electricity
Through the rest. When they brought Hard Rock back,   10
Handcuffed and chained, he was turned loose,
Like a freshly gelded stallion, to try his new status.
And we all waited and watched, like Indians at a corral,
To see if the WORD was true.

As we waited we wrapped ourselves in the cloak
Of his exploits: "Man, the last time, it took eight
Screws to put him in the Hole." "Yeah, remember when he
Smacked the captain with his dinner tray?" "He set
The record for time in the Hole—67 straight days!"
"Ol Hard Rock! man, that's one crazy nigger."   20
And then the jewel of a myth that Hard Rock had once bit
A screw on the thumb and poisoned him with syphilitic spit.

The testing came, to see if Hard Rock was really tame.
A hillbilly called him a black son of a bitch
And didn't lose his teeth, a screw who knew Hard Rock
From before shook him down and barked in his face.
And Hard Rock did nothing. Just grinned and looked silly,
His eyes empty like knot holes in a fence.

And even after we discovered that it took Hard Rock
Exactly 3 minutes to tell you his first name,   30
We told ourselves that he had just wised up,
Was being cool; but we could not fool ourselves for long,
And we turned away, our eyes on the ground. Crushed.

He had been our Destroyer, the doer of things
We dreamed of doing but could not bring ourselves to do,
The fears of years, like a biting whip,
Had cut grooves too deeply across our backs.

MARGE PIERCY (B. 1936)

BARBIE DOLL 1973

This girlchild was born as usual
and presented dolls that did pee-pee
and miniature GE stoves and irons
and wee lipsticks the color of cherry candy.
Then in the magic of puberty, a classmate said:
You have a great big nose and fat legs.

She was healthy, tested intelligent,
possessed strong arms and back,
abundant sexual drive and manual dexterity.
She went to and fro apologizing.   10
Everyone saw a fat nose on thick legs.

She was advised to play coy,
exhorted to come on hearty,
exercise, diet, smile and wheedle.
Her good nature wore out
like a fan belt.
So she cut off her nose and her legs
and offered them up.

In the casket displayed on satin she lay
with the undertaker's cosmetics painted on,   20
a turned-up putty nose,
dressed in a pink and white nightie.
Doesn't she look pretty? everyone said.
Consummation at last.
To every woman a happy ending.

FOR ANALYSIS

1. In what way does this poem have a "happy ending" (l. 25)? Is it really happy?

2. List the characteristics attributed to the girl in the poem. Which are judged by others to be important? Which are judged unimportant? Why?

3. Why does the girl apologize? Should she?

WRITING TOPIC

Reflect on the turn in line 17. Why is this an unusual moment? What are its effects? Why do you think Piercy chooses to have something like this happen?

MAKING ARGUMENTS

People have long argued over what makes boys and girls conform to society's expectations. Some argue that the differences are genetic: that boys and girls are intrinsically different. Others argue that gendered behavior is socialized: that differences come not from nature but from nurture. Where do you stand on this argument? What evidence could you cite to support your position?

KAY RYAN (B. 1945)

ALL SHALL BE RESTORED 1996

The grains shall be collected
from the thousand shores
to which they found their way,
and the boulder restored,
and the boulder itself replaced
in the cliff, and likewise
the cliff shall rise
or subside until the plate of earth
is without fissure. Restoration
knows no half measure. It will   10
not stop when the treasured and lost
bronze horse remounts the steps.
Even this horse will founder backward
to coin, cannon, and domestic pots,
which themselves shall bubble and
drain back to green veins in stone.
And every word written shall lift off
letter by letter, the backward text
read ever briefer, ever more antic
in its effort to insist that nothing   20
shall be lost.

FOR ANALYSIS

1. What process is being reversed in lines 1–9? In lines 10–16? What kind of processes are these? Are they actually reversible?

2. What does the last sentence add to the poem's meaning? How is the last clause—"nothing shall be lost"—related to the poem's title?

3. Describe the **style** of the poem. What kind of voice does Ryan create? How does she do it?

WRITING TOPIC

One of the most important facts of human experience is that it ends—at least in the case of individual life. Many different aspects of human culture can be seen, in part, to be dealing with this eventuality: either accepting this natural process or working against it. What does "All Shall Be Restored" say about the way people deal with death?

MAKING ARGUMENTS

"All Shall Be Restored" focuses on loss. How would you make an argument that life is not a march from birth to death but rather a cycle? How, on the evidence of what you know about the natural world and the social world, could life be read not as tending inexorably toward loss but rather as a never-ending process of change?

JUAN FELIPE HERRERA   (B. 1948)

187 REASONS MEXICANOS CAN'T CROSS THE BORDER (REMIX)   1994

—Abutebaris modo subjunctivo denuo.[1]

Because Lou Dobbs has been misusing the subjunctive again
Because our suitcases are made with biodegradable maguey fibers
Because we still resemble La Malinche
Because multiplication is our favorite sport
Because we'll dig a tunnel to Seattle
Because Mexico needs us to keep the peso from sinking
Because the Berlin Wall is on the way through Veracruz
Because we just learned we are Huichol
Because someone made our IDs out of corn
Because our border thirst is insatiable   10
Because we're on peyote & Coca-Cola & Banamex
Because it's Indian land stolen from our mothers

[1] You've been misusing the subjunctive again.

Because we're too emotional when it comes to our mothers
Because we've been doing it for over five hundred years already
Because it's too easy to say "I am from here"
Because Latin American petrochemical juice flows first
Because what would we do in El Norte
Because Nahuatl, Mayan & Chicano will spread to Canada
Because Zedillo & Salinas & Fox are still on vacation
Because the World Bank needs our abuelita's account   20
Because the CIA trains better with brown targets
Because our accent is unable to hide U.S. colonialism
Because what will the Hispanik MBAs do
Because our voice resembles La Llorona's
Because we are still voting
Because the North is really South
Because we can read about it in an ethnic prison
Because Frida beat us to it
Because U.S. & European Corporations would rather visit us first
Because environmental U.S. industrial pollution suits our color   30
Because of a new form of Overnight Mayan Anarchy
Because there are enough farmworkers in California already
Because we're meant to usher a postmodern gloom into Mexico
Because Nabisco, Exxon, & Union Carbide gave us Mal de Ojo
Because every nacho chip can morph into a Mexican Wrestler
Because it's better to be rootless, unconscious, & rapeable
Because we're destined to have the "Go Back to Mexico" Blues
Because of Pancho Villa's hidden treasure in Chihuahua
Because of Bogart's hidden treasure in the Sierra Madre
Because we need more murals honoring our Indian Past   40
Because we are really dark French Creoles in a Cantínflas costume
Because of this Aztec reflex to sacrifice ourselves
Because we couldn't clean up hurricane Katrina
Because of this Spanish penchant to be polite and aggressive
Because we had a vision of Sor Juana in drag
Because we smell of tamales soaked in Tequila
Because we got hooked listening to Indian Jazz in Chiapas
Because we're still waiting to be cosmic
Because our passport says we're out of date
Because our organ donor got lost in a Bingo game   50
Because we got to learn English first & get in line & pay a little fee
Because we're understanding & appreciative of our Capitalist neighbors
Because our 500-year penance was not severe enough
Because we're still running from La Migra
Because we're still kissing the Pope's hand
Because we're still practicing to be Franciscan priests
Because they told us to sit & meditate & chant "Nosotros los Pobres"

Because of the word "Revolución" & the words "Viva Zapata"
Because we rely more on brujas than lawyers
Because we never finished our Ph.D. in Total United Service   60
Because our identity got mixed up with passion
Because we have visions instead of televisions
Because our huaraches are made with Goodyear & Uniroyal
Because the pesticides on our skin are still glowing
Because it's too easy to say "American Citizen" in cholo
Because you can't shrink-wrap enchiladas
Because a Spy in Spanish sounds too much like "Es Pie" in English
Because our comadres are an International Political Party
Because we believe in The Big Chingazo Theory of the Universe
Because we're still holding our breath in the Presidential Palace in   70
      Mexico City
Because every Mexican is a Living Theatre of Rebellion
Because Hollywood needs its subject matter in proper folkloric costume
Because the Grammys & iTunes are finally out in Spanish
Because the Right is writing an epic poem of apology for our proper edification
Because the Alamo really is pronounced "Alamadre"
Because the Mayan concept of zero means "U.S. Out of Mexico"
Because the oldest ceiba in Yucatán is prophetic
Because England is making plans
Because we can have Nicaragua, Honduras, & Panama anyway
Because 125 million Mexicans can be wrong   80
Because we'll smuggle an earthquake into New York
Because we'll organize like the Vietnamese in San José
Because we'll organize like the Mixtecos in Fresno
Because East L.A. is sinking
Because the Christian Coalition doesn't cater at César Chávez Parque
Because you can't make mace out of beans
Because the computers can't pronounce our names
Because the National Border Police are addicted to us
Because Africa will follow
Because we're still dressed in black rebozos   90
Because we might sing a corrido at any moment
Because our land grants are still up for grabs
Because our tattoos are indecipherable
Because people are hanging milagros on the 2,000 miles of border wire
Because we're locked into Magical Realism
Because Mexican dependence is a form of higher learning
Because making chilaquiles leads to plastic explosives
Because a simple Spanish Fly can mutate into a raging Bird Flu
Because we eat too many carbohydrates
Because we gave enough blood at the Smithfield, Inc., slaughterhouse in   100
      Tar Heel, North Carolina

Because a quinceañera will ruin the concept of American virginity
Because huevos rancheros are now being served at Taco Bell as Wavoritos
Because every Mexican grito undermines English intonation
Because the President has a Mexican maid
Because the Vice President has a Mexican maid
Because it's Rosa López's fault O.J. Simpson was guilty
Because Banda music will take over the White House
Because Aztec sexual aberrations are still in practice
Because our starvation & squalor isn't as glamorous as Somalia's
Because agribusiness will whack us anyway   110
Because the information superhighway is not for Chevys & Impalas
Because white men are paranoid of Frida's mustache
Because the term "mariachi" comes from the word "cucarachi"
Because picking grapes is not a British tradition
Because they are still showing *Zoot Suit* in prisons
Because Richie Valens is alive in West Liberty, Iowa
Because ? & the Mysterians cried 97 tears not 96
Because Hoosgow, Riata and Rodeo are Juzgado, Riata and Rodeo
Because Jackson Hole, Wyoming, will blow as soon as we hit Oceanside
Because U.S. narco-business needs us in Nogales   120
Because the term "Mexican" comes from "Mexicanto"
Because Mexican queers crossed already
Because Mexican lesbians wear Ben Davis pants & sombreros de palma to work
Because VFW halls aren't built to serve cabeza con tripas
Because the National Guard are going international
Because we still bury our feria in the backyard
Because we don't have international broncas for profit
Because we are in love with our sister Rigoberta Menchú
Because California is on the verge of becoming California
Because the PRI is a family affair   130
Because we may start a television series called *No Chingues Conmigo*
Because we are too sweet & obedient & confused & (still) full of rage
Because the CIA needs us in a Third World State of mind
Because brown is the color of the future
Because we turned Welfare into El Huero Fèlix
Because we know what the Jews have been through
Because we know what the Blacks have been through
Because the Irish became the San Patricio Corps at the Battle of Churubusco
Because of our taste for Yiddish gospel raps & tardeadas & salsa limericks
Because El Sistema Nos La Pela   140
Because you can take the boy outta Mexico but not outta the Boycott
Because the Truckers, Arkies and Okies enjoy our telenovelas
Because we'd rather shop at the flea market than Macy's
Because pan dulce feels sexual, especially conchas & the elotes
Because we'll Xerox tamales in order to survive

Because we'll export salsa to Russia & call it "Pikushki"
Because cilantro aromas follow us wherever we go
Because we'll unionize & sing *De Colores*
Because A Day Without a Mexican is a day away
Because we're in touch with our Boricua camaradas   150
Because we are the continental majority
Because we'll build a sweat lodge in front of Bank of America
Because we should wait for further instructions from Televisa
Because 125 million Mexicanos are potential Chicanos
Because we'll take over the Organic Foods business with a
        molcajete
Because 2,000 miles of maquiladoras want to promote us
Because the next Olympics will commemorate the Mexico City
        massacre of 1968
Because there is an Aztec temple beneath our Nopales
Because we know how to pronounce all the Japanese corporations
Because the Comadre network is more accurate than CNN   160
Because the Death Squads are having a hard time with Caló
Because the mayor of San Diego likes salsa medium-picante
Because the Navy, Army, Marines like us topless in Tijuana
Because when we see red, white & blue we just see red
Because when we see the numbers 187 we still see red
Because we need to pay a little extra fee to the Border
Because Mexican Human Rights sounds too Mexican
Because Chrysler is putting out a lowrider
Because they found a lost Chicano tribe in Utah
Because harina white flour bag suits don't cut it at graduation   170
Because we'll switch from AT&T & MCI to Y-que, y-que
Because our hand signs aren't registered
Because Freddy Fender wasn't Baldomar Huerta's real name
Because "lotto" is another Chicano word for "pronto"
Because we won't nationalize a State of Immigrant Paranoia
Because the depression of the '30s was our fault
Because "xenophobia" is a politically correct term
Because we shoulda learned from the Chinese Exclusion Act of 1882
Because we shoulda listened to the Federal Immigration Laws of
        1917, '21, '24 & '30
Because we lack a Nordic/Teutonic approach   180
Because Executive Order 9066 of 1942 shudda had us too
Because Operation Wetback took care of us in the '50s
Because Operation Clean Sweep picked up the loose ends in the '70s
Because one more operation will finish us off anyway
Because you can't deport 12 million migrantes in a Greyhound bus
Because we got this thing about walking out of everything
Because we have a heart that sings rancheras and feet that polka

FOR ANALYSIS

1. In 1994, California voters passed a ballot initiative called Proposition 187 that sought to deny "illegal aliens" a variety of social services guaranteed to legal residents, claiming that such services placed an undue financial burden on the state. The measure was later overturned by federal courts. Why do you think Herrera chose 187 for his title? How many lines are in the poem?

2. Repetition of a word or phrase at the beginning of a sentence, clause, or line of poetry is called *anaphora*. How does Herrera use anaphora, and to what effect?

MAKING ARGUMENTS

Immigration remains a major topic of argument in U.S. politics. Summarize the arguments on both sides—of those in favor of loosening rules against illegal immigrants and helping them achieve citizenship and of those in favor of making it harder to enter the country and increasing deportation.

WRITING TOPICS

1. Write a "because" list poem about some issue of interest to you and in which you dispute reasons or motivations.

2. Describe the complicated use of **irony** in "187 Reasons Mexicanos Can't Cross the Border."

MAKING CONNECTIONS

Compare the ways in which Louise Erdrich's "Dear John Wayne" (p. 671) and "187 Reasons Mexicanos Can't Cross the Border" are concerned not just with how minorities are seen by the majority culture but also how minorities see themselves.

MAGGIE ANDERSON   (B. 1948)

LONG STORY   1992

> *To speak in a flat voice*
> *Is all that I can do*
> —James Wright, "Speak"

I need to tell you that I live in a small town
in West Virginia you would not know about.
It is one of the places I think of as home.
When I go for a walk, I take my basset hound
whose sad eyes and ungainliness always draw
a crowd of children. She tolerates anything
that seems to be affection, so she lets the kids

put scarves and ski caps on her head
until she starts to resemble the women who have to dress
from rummage sales in poverty's mismatched polyester.   10

The dog and I trail the creek bank with the kids,
past clapboard row houses with Christmas seals
pasted to the windows as a decoration.
Inside, television glows around the vinyl chairs
and curled linoleum, and we watch someone old
perambulating to the kitchen on a shiny walker.
Up the hill in town, two stores have been
boarded up beside the youth center and miners
with amputated limbs are loitering outside
the Heart and Hand. They wear Cat diesel caps   20
and spit into the street. The wind
carries on, whining through the alleys,
rustling down the sidewalks, agitating
leaves, and circling the courthouse steps
past the toothless Field sisters who lean
against the flagpole holding paper bags
of chestnuts they bring to town to sell.

History is one long story of what happened to us,
and its rhythms are local dialect and anecdote.
In West Virginia a good story takes awhile,   30
and if it has people in it, you have to swear
that it is true. I tell the kids the one about
my Uncle Craig who saw the mountain move
so quickly and so certainly it made the sun
stand in a different aspect to his little town
until it rearranged itself and settled down again.
This was his favorite story. When he got old,
he mixed it up with baseball games, his shift boss
pushing scabs through a picket line, the Masons
in white aprons at a funeral, but he remembered   40
everything that ever happened, and he knew how far
he lived from anywhere you would have heard of.

Anything that happens here has a lot of versions,
how to get from here to Logan twenty different ways.
The kids tell me convoluted country stories
full of snuff and bracken, about how long
they sat quiet in the deer blind with their fathers
waiting for the ten-point buck that got away.
They like to talk about the weather,

how the wind we're walking in means rain,   50
how the flood pushed cattle fifteen miles downriver.

These kids know mines like they know hound dogs
and how the sirens blow when something's wrong.
They know the blast, and the stories, how
the grown-ups drop whatever they are doing
to get out there. Story is shaped
by sound, and it structures what we know.
They told me this, and three of them
swore it was true, so I'll tell you
even though I know you do not know   60
this place, or how tight and dark the hills
pull in around the river and the railroad.

I'll say it as the children spoke it,
in the flat voice of my people:
down in Boone County, they sealed up
forty miners in a fire. The men who had come
to help tried and tried to get down to them,
but it was a big fire and there was danger,
so they had to turn around
and shovel them back in. All night long   70
they stood outside with useless picks and axes
in their hands, just staring at the drift mouth.
Here's the thing: what the sound must have been,
all those fire trucks and ambulances, the sirens,
and the women crying and screaming out
the names of their buried ones, who must have
called back up to them from deep inside
the burning mountain, right up to the end.

For Analysis

1. The speaker says her uncle "knew how far / he lived from anywhere you would have heard of" (ll. 41–42). What does this fact mean to him, and to the speaker? How does the poem give a sense of this place, which most of the poem's readers will not know?

2. Do you think the voice the speaker uses in this poem remains uniform throughout? If not, when and how does it change, and why do you think the poet chose to have it change?

Making Arguments

This poem is about the hard life of a mining town. Make an argument about the otherwise absent "they" (l. 65) who employ these miners: are they responsible for the difficulty of these lives? In what ways might they be to blame? Alternatively, make a counterargument defending the mine owner/operator's role in the "history [...] of what happened to us" (l. 28).

WRITING TOPICS

1. Describe the feeling of the poem's last line and how Anderson achieves it.

2. List examples of ways in which Anderson creates the "flat voice" referred to at the beginning of the poem and again in line 64. What makes it flat? How would a different voice have changed the poem's effects?

GREGORY DJANIKIAN   (B. 1949)

SAILING TO AMERICA   1989

Alexandria, 1956

The rugs had been rolled up and islands of them
Floated in the centers of every room,
And now, on the bare wood floors,
My sister and I were skimming among them
In the boats we'd made from newspaper,
Sheets of them pinned to each other,
Dhows, gondolas, clippers, arks.
There was a mule outside on the street
Braying under a load of figs, though mostly
There was quiet, a wind from the desert   10
Was putting the city to sleep,
But we were too far adrift, the air
Was scurfy and wet, the currents tricking
Our bows against reef and coral
And hulls shearing under the weight of cargo.
"Ahoy and belay!" I called to my sister,
"Avast, avast!" she yelled back from her rigging,
And neither of us knew what we were saying
But the words came to us as from a movie,
Cinemascopic, American. "Richard Widmark,"   20
I said. "Clark Gable, Bogie," she said,
"Yo-ho-ho." We had passed Cyprus
And now there was Crete or Sardinia
Maybe something larger further off.
The horizon was everywhere I turned,
The waters were becoming turgid,

They were roiling, weeks had passed.
"America, America, land-ho!" I yelled directionless.
"Gibraltar," my sister said, "Heave to,"
And signalling a right, her arm straight out,   30
She turned and bravely set our course
North-by-northwest for the New World.
Did we arrive? Years later, yes.
By plane, suddenly. With suitcases
And something as hazy as a future.
The November sun was pale and far off,
The air was colder than we'd ever felt,
And already these were wonders to us
As much as snow would be or evergreens,
And it would take me a long time   40
Before I'd ever remember
Boats made of paper, islands of wool,
And my sister's voice, as in a fog,
Calling out the hazards,
Leading me on, getting us there.

JUDITH ORTIZ COFER (B. 1952)

LATIN WOMEN PRAY   1987

Latin women pray
In incense sweet churches
They pray in Spanish to an Anglo God
With a Jewish heritage.

And this Great White Father
Imperturbable in his marble pedestal
Looks down upon his brown daughters
Votive candles shining like lust
In his all seeing eyes
Unmoved by their persistent prayers.   10

Yet year after year
Before his image they kneel
Margarita Josefina Maria and Isabel
All fervently hoping
That if not omnipotent
At least he be bilingual.

LOUISE ERDRICH   (B. 1954)

DEAR JOHN WAYNE   1984

August and the drive-in picture is packed.
We lounge on the hood of the Pontiac
surrounded by the slow-burning spirals they sell
at the window, to vanquish the hordes of mosquitoes.
Nothing works. They break through the smoke screen for blood.

Always the lookout spots the Indians first,
spread north to south, barring progress.
The Sioux or some other Plains bunch
in spectacular columns, ICBM missiles,
feathers bristling in the meaningful sunset.   10

The drum breaks. There will be no parlance.
Only the arrows whining, a death-cloud of nerves
swarming down on the settlers
who die beautifully, tumbling like dust weeds
into the history that brought us all here
together: this wide screen beneath the sign of the bear.

The sky fills, acres of blue squint and eye
that the crowd cheers. His face moves over us,
a thick cloud of vengeance, pitted
like the land that was once flesh. Each rut,   20
each scar makes a promise: *It is
not over, this fight, not as long as you resist.*

Everything we see belongs to us.

A few laughing Indians fall over the hood
slipping in the hot spilled butter.
The eye sees a lot, John, but the heart is so blind.
Death makes us owners of nothing.
He smiles, a horizon of teeth
the credits reel over, and then the white fields
again blowing in the true-to-life dark.   30
The dark films over everything.
We get into the car
scratching our mosquito bites, speechless and small
as people are when the movie is done.
We are back in our skins.

How can we help but keep hearing his voice,
the flip side of the sound track, still playing:
Come on, boys, we got them
where we want them, drunk, running.
They'll give us what we want, what we need.   40
Even his disease was the idea of taking everything.
Those cells, burning, doubling, splitting out of their skins.

FOR ANALYSIS

1. Part of the power of "Dear John Wayne" lies in the difference between its two **settings**, or places. What are they? What are their differences, and why are they significant?

2. Describing the "Indians" in the movie, Erdrich calls them "The Sioux or some other Plains bunch" (l. 8). What **ironic** effect is intended by this last phrase? Note other places where Erdrich is being ironic. What are the effects there?

3. From its very title onward, Erdrich's poem is concerned with the question of audience. Who are the different audiences implied in this poem, intended and actual? Who are the different speakers? As a reader, which audience are you?

MAKING ARGUMENTS

Make an argument for the significance of the poem's last two lines. What is "his disease"? To what does "taking everything" refer? How does the rest of the poem resonate in the image of the last line?

WRITING TOPICS

1. Address the issue of this poem's complicated **tone**. What are its various **moods** and attitudes toward its subjects? When and how do they shift, and to what effect?

2. Draw a line down the middle of a piece of paper. In the left column, write down everything the white men in the poem see. In the right column, write down everything the Native Americans in the poem see. Compare the two columns in an essay that discusses the issue of power in seeing and being seen.

MARILYN CHIN   (B. 1955)

HOW I GOT THAT NAME   1994

AN ESSAY ON ASSIMILATION

I am Marilyn Mei Ling Chin.
Oh, how I love the resoluteness
of that first person singular
followed by that stalwart indicative

of "be," without the uncertain i-n-g
of "becoming." Of course,
the name had been changed
somewhere between Angel Island and the sea,
when my father the paperson
in the late 1950s   10
obsessed with a bombshell blonde
transliterated "Mei Ling" to "Marilyn."
And nobody dared question
his initial impulse—for we all know
lust drove men to greatness,
not goodness, not decency.
And there I was, a wayward pink baby,
named after some tragic white woman
swollen with gin and Nembutal.
My mother couldn't pronounce the "r."   20
She dubbed me "Numba one female offshoot"
for brevity: henceforth, she will live and die
in sublime ignorance, flanked
by loving children and the "kitchen deity."
While my father dithers,
a tomcat in Hong Kong trash—
a gambler, a petty thug,
who bought a chain of chopsuey joints
in Piss River, Oregon,
with bootlegged Gucci cash.   30
Nobody dared question his integrity given
his nice, devout daughters
and his bright, industrious sons
as if filial piety were the standard
by which all earthly men were measured.

Oh, how trustworthy our daughters,
how thrifty our sons!
How we've managed to fool the experts
in education, statistics and demography—
We're not very creative but not adverse to rote-learning.   40
Indeed, they can *use* us.
But the "Model Minority" is a tease.
We know you are watching now,
so we refuse to give you any!
Oh, bamboo shoots, bamboo shoots!
The further west we go, we'll hit east;
the deeper down we dig, we'll find China.
History has turned its stomach

on a black polluted beach—
where life doesn't hinge
on that red, red wheelbarrow,   50
but whether or not our new lover
in the final episode of "Santa Barbara"
will lean over a scented candle
and call us a "bitch."
Oh God, where have we gone wrong?
We have no inner resources!

Then, one redolent spring morning
the Great Patriarch Chin
peered down from his kiosk in heaven   60
and saw that his descendants were ugly.
One had a squarish head and a nose without a bridge.
Another's profile—long and knobbed as a gourd.
A third, the sad, brutish one
may never, never marry.
And I, his least favorite—
"not quite boiled, not quite cooked,"
a plump pomfret simmering in my juices—
too listless to fight for my people's destiny.
"To kill without resistance is not slaughter"   70
says the proverb. So, I wait for imminent death.
The fact that this death is also metaphorical
is testament to my lethargy.

So here lies Marilyn Mei Ling Chin,
married once, twice to so-and-so, a Lee and a Wong,
granddaughter of Jack "the patriarch"
and the brooding Suilin Fong,
daughter of the virtuous Yuet Kuen Wong
and G. G. Chin the infamous,
sister of a dozen, cousin of a million,   80
survived by everybody and forgotten by all.
She was neither black nor white,
neither cherished nor vanquished,
just another squatter in her own bamboo grove
minding her poetry—
when one day heaven was unmerciful,
and a chasm opened where she stood.
Like the jowls of a mighty white whale,
or the jaws of a metaphysical Godzilla,
it swallowed her whole.   90
She did not flinch nor writhe,
nor fret about the afterlife,

but stayed! Solid as wood, happily
a little gnawed, tattered, mesmerized
by all that was lavished upon her
and all that was taken away!

FOR ANALYSIS

1. Why does the speaker "love the resoluteness / of that first person singular / followed by that stalwart indicative / of 'be' " (ll. 2–5)?

2. Why is how the poet/**persona** got her name so important?

3. What is wrong, in the speaker's eyes, with being a "Model Minority" (l. 42)?

MAKING ARGUMENTS

There have been a number of different models for immigrants to the United States to follow—from the melting pot to multiculturalism. What are the arguments for the desirability of one over the other? Outline the arguments on each side of the spectrum from total assimilation to ethnic pride and preservation of culture of origin.

WRITING TOPICS

1. How is this poem, as its subtitle claims, "An essay on assimilation"? What was "lavished upon her" (l. 95) and what was "taken away" (l. 96)?

2. *Assimilation* is usually meant to indicate what happens to immigrants in a new land. Write about a situation in your life when you had to assimilate in a different sense—not as an international immigrant or a child of immigrants but as a person in a new place. What impact did the experience have on your sense of self?

JOSHUA CLOVER (B. 1962)

THE NEVADA GLASSWORKS   1997

Ka-Boom! They're making glass in Nevada!
Figure August, 1953,
mom's 13, it's hot as a simile.
Ker-Pow! Transmutation in Nevada!
Imagine mom: pre-postModern new teen,
innocent for Elvis, ditto "Korean
conflict," John Paul George Ringo Viet Nam.
Mom's 1 state west of the glassworks, she's
in a tree/K*I*S*S*I*N*G,
lurid cartoon-colored kisses. Ka-Blam!   10
They're blowing peacock-tinted New World glass
in southern Nevada, the alchemists
& architects of mom's duck-&-cover
adolescence, they're making Las Vegas
turn to gold—real neon gold—in the blast

furnace heat that reaches clear to Clover
Ranch in dry Central Valley: O the dust—
It is the Golden State! O the landscape—
dreaming of James Dean! O mom in a tree
close-range kissing as in Nevada just   20
now they're making crazy ground-zero shapes
of radiant see-through geography.
What timing! What kisses! What a fever
this day's become, humming hundred-degree
California afternoon that she's
sure she could never duplicate, *never*,
she feels transparent, gone—isn't this heat
suffocating—no, she forgot to breathe
for a flash while in the Nevada flats
factory glassblowers exhale . . . exhale . . .   30
a philosopher's stone, a crystal ball,
a spectacular machine. Hooray! Hats
off—they're making a window in the sand!
Mom's in the tree—picture this—all alone!
Unforgettable kisses, comic-book
mnemonic kisses. O something's coming
out of the ranch road heat mirage: That drone—
an engine? Mom quits practice & looks
east, cups an ear to the beloved humming,
the hazy gold dust kicked wildly west   40
ahead of something almost . . . in . . . sight. Vroom!
It's the Future, hot like nothing else, dressed
as sonic-boom Cadillac. O mom!
This land *is* your land/This land Amnesia—
they're dropping some new science out there,
a picture-perfect hole blown clear to Asia:
everything in the desert—Shazam!—turns
to glass, gold glass, a picture-window where
the bomb-dead kids are burned & burn & burn

FOR ANALYSIS

1. What exactly is happening in Nevada to make glass? What is the "new science" (l. 45)?

2. When Clover writes, "What timing!" (l. 23), to what is he referring? Why does the poem cut back and forth between Nevada and "1 state west" (l. 8)?

3. Identify Clover's **tone**. What is his attitude toward his subject? Is it directly stated? If not, how do you know what it is?

MAKING ARGUMENTS

Nuclear power—as energy source and as weapon—has been controversial for as long as it has existed. Outline the arguments for and against the use of this power, making reference to important historical moments.

WRITING TOPIC

Clover mixes various kinds of language and **imagery**. Catalog examples of one element—kinds of words, kind of images (remembering that images aren't necessarily only visual)—and group them into different types (for example, long complicated words and simple words). In an essay, consider how and why Clover uses the kinds of elements he does.

TASLIMA NASRIN   (B. 1962)

THINGS CHEAPLY HAD[1]   1991

In the market nothing can be had as cheap as women.
If they get a small bottle of *alta*[2] for their feet
       they spend three nights sleepless for sheer joy.
If they get a few bars of soap to scrub their skin
       and some scented oil for their hair
they become so submissive that they scoop out
       chunks of their flesh
to be sold in the flea market twice a week.
If they get a jewel for their nose
       they lick feet for seventy days or so,   10
a full three and a half months
       if it's a single striped sari.[3]

Even the mangy cur of the house barks now and then,
and over the mouths of women cheaply had
       there's a lock
a golden lock.

FOR ANALYSIS

1. Why is the lock in the final line of the poem "golden"?

2. What are the "things" of the title? Do they include more than the items the women "get"?

MAKING ARGUMENTS

While Nasrin's subject is the treatment of women in a male-dominated culture, her poem does not describe actual specific acts and effects of mistreatment but rather illustrates the situation through poetic **hyperbole**. Make an argument for one or the other side of this question: does her decision to write about this subject in this way result in a more powerful poem than being literal would have created?

---

[1] Translated from the Bengali by Carolyne Wright with Mohammad Nurul Huda and the author.

[2] *Alta*, or lac-dye, is a red liquid with which South Asian women decorate the borders of their feet on ceremonial occasions, such as weddings and dance performances. *Alta* is more in vogue among Hindus, but Bangladeshi women also use it, and it can be seen on the feet of Muslim heroines and harem women in Moghul miniature paintings. [Translator's note.]

[3] An outer garment worn chiefly by women of India and Pakistan, consisting of a length of cloth wrapped around the waist at one end and draped over the shoulder or head at the other.

OMAR PÉREZ   (B. 1964)

CONTRIBUTIONS TO A RUDIMENTARY CONCEPT OF NATION[1]   2007

On the volatile nights of a winter
nature corroborates with magnanimity
a Cuban is in training for amusement or amnesia,
so often and unfairly assumed as the same,
he brings candy to God, he cultivates the vernacular, he fights off
cirrhosis with fruit poached in syrup, he conducts business;
thus research has shown that The Cuban is resourceful.
In the weighty choreographies of a summer
nature authorizes already with suspicion
a Cuban meets the ocean with offerings and harpoons,   10
so often and unfairly assumed as the same,
he finger-counts the casualties, he commits an infraction
he slides his hands into his pockets, he avows and commits;
thus analysis has shown that The Cuban is inspired.
Let's attend the improbable territory
where with pasty mouths a Cuban and The Cuban engage in virile
conversation
we will learn there by what voyage, by what strange condition
by what exchange
we fall prey to so much ingenuity.   20

FOR ANALYSIS

1. What nation is the nation to which the title refers? Why is this important? Could it be any nation?

2. What stereotypes about the Cuban people does the poem allude to?

3. What is the difference between "a Cuban" and "The Cuban"?

MAKING ARGUMENTS

Although he did not know it until his mid-twenties, Pérez is the son of Che Guevara. Do a little research into Guevara and make an argument concerning the relevance of the poet's parentage to this poem. Does it change the way you read it? If so, how? If not, why not?

WRITING TOPICS

Pérez spent a year in an agricultural reeducation camp for signing a manifesto suggesting political changes in Cuba. Reread this poem and try to describe its politics. What does it say about Cuban nationhood and identity? What does it say about Cuban political history?

[1] Translated by Roberto Tejada.

678

CHRIS ABANI (B. 1966)

BLUE 2004

I

Africans in the hold fold themselves
to make room for hope. In the afternoon's
ferocity, tar, grouting the planks like the glue
of family, melts to the run of a child's licorice stick.

Wet decks crack, testing the wood's mettle.
Distilled from evaporating brine, salt
dusts the floor, tickling with the measure
into time and the thirst trapped below.

II

The captain's new cargo of Igbos disturbs him.
They stand, computing the swim back to land.   10
Haitians still say: *Igbo pend'c or'a ya!*
But we do not hang ourselves in cowardice.

III

Sold six times on the journey to the coast,
once for a gun, then cloth, then iron
manilas, her pride was masticated like husks
of chewing sticks, spat from morning-rank mouths.

Breaking loose, edge of handcuffs held high
like the blade of a vengeful axe, she runs
across the salt scratch of deck,
pain deeper than the blue inside a flame.   20

IV

The sound, like the break of bone
could have been the Captain's skull
or the musket shot dropping her
over the side, her chains wrapped
around his neck in dance.

FOR ANALYSIS

1. What is the **setting** of "Blue"?

2. Read the poem aloud to yourself. What patterns of sound do you notice (from listening to what you read and from feeling your face move as you read)?

3. Describe the poem's shifting focus. What is it at the start of the poem? What is it at the end? What are the effects of this shift?

MAKING ARGUMENTS

Make an argument for the significance of the poem's mention of the captain. Take into account the context, the history, and the different ethnicities and national origins of the poem's audience.

WRITING TOPIC

Abani's poem rests on his ability to put himself into the shoes of people whose lives were very different from his. Write or describe a poem of your own in which you try to do a similar thing (with different people). What are the difficulties of such a task? What are the possibilities?

MAKING CONNECTIONS

Compare this poem to McKay's "If We Must Die" (p. 429). What motivates the speaker in McKay's poem? What motivates the woman in "Blue"? What do they share despite the differences in their circumstances?

KEVIN YOUNG   (B. 1970)

NEGATIVE   2005

Wake to find everything black
what was white, all the vice
versa—white maids on TV, black

sitcoms that star white dwarfs
cute as pearl buttons, Black Presidents,
Black Houses, White Horse

candidates. All bleach burns
clothes black. Drive roads
white as you are, white songs

on the radio stolen by black bands   10
like secret pancake recipes, white back-up
singers, ball-players & boxers all

white as tar. Feathers on chickens
dark as everything, boiling in the pot
that called the kettle honky. Even

whites of the eye turn dark, pupils
clear & changing as a cat's.
Is this what we've wanted

& waited for? to see snow
covering everything black   20
as Christmas, dark pages written

white upon? All our eclipses bright,
dark stars shooting across pale
sky, glowing like ash in fire, shower

every skin. Only money keeps
green, still grows & burns like grass
under dark daylight.

TERRANCE HAYES   (B. 1971)

ROOT   2006

My parents would have had me believe
there was no such thing as race
there in the wild backyard, our knees black
with store-bought grass and dirt,
black as the soil of pastures or of orchards
grown above graves. We clawed free
the stones and filled their beds with soil
and covered the soil with sod
as if we owned the earth.
We worked into the edge of darkness   10
and rose in the edge of darkness
until everything came from the dirt.
We clawed free the moss and brambles,
the colonies of crab-weed, the thorns
patrolling stems and I liked it then:
the mute duty that tightened my parents'
backs as if they meant to work
the devil from his den. Rock and spore
and scraps of leaf; wild bouquets withered

in bags by the road, cast from the ground   20
we broke. We scrubbed the patio,
we raked the cross hatch of pine needles,
we soaked the ant-cathedrals in gas.
I found an axe blade beneath an untamed hedge,
its edge too dull to sever vine and half expected
to find a jawbone scabbed with mud,
because no one told me what happened
to the whites who'd owned the house.
No one spoke of the color that curled
around our tools or of the neighbors   30
who knew our name before we knew theirs.
Sometimes they were almost visible,
clean as fence posts in porch light;
their houses burning with wonder,
their hammocks drunk with wind.
When I dreamed, I dreamed of them
and believed they dreamed of us
and believed we were made of dirt or shadows:
something not held or given, irredeemable, inexact,
all of us asking what it means to be black . . .   40
I have never wanted another life, but I know the story
of pursuit: the dream of a gate standing open,
a grill and folding chairs, a new yard boxed in light.

FOR ANALYSIS

1. Does the speaker believe what his parents wanted him to believe? How do you know?

2. Who is "them" in line 36? Who is "us" in line 37? What is the nature of their relationship?

3. Describe the main action in this poem. Does its significance lie in what it is or in what it stands for? If the latter, why do you think Hayes chooses to dramatize his subject in this way?

MAKING ARGUMENTS

It has been argued that U.S. society is now "post-racial." Support or refute this claim, using as support a summary of what is meant by the claim, historical evidence, and evidence drawn from the contemporary scene.

WRITING TOPIC

Imaginative literature often works by indirection—by finding hidden, obscured, or circuitous routes to ideas rather than following well-worn, straight paths to the thing or idea or feeling it wants to represent. From the first line, "Root" works in this way. Write a description of the ways in which Hayes says things in ways other than straight out.

ALEXANDRA TEAGUE (B. 1974)

ADJECTIVES OF ORDER   2007

That summer, she had a student who was obsessed
with the order of adjectives. A soldier in the South
Vietnamese army, he had been taken prisoner when

Saigon fell. He wanted to know why the order
could not be altered. The sweltering city streets shook
with rockets and helicopters. The city sweltering

streets. On the dusty brown field of the chalkboard,
she wrote: *The mother took warm homemade bread
from the oven. City* is essential to *streets* as *homemade*

is essential to *bread*. He copied this down, but   10
he wanted to know if his brothers were *lost* before
older, if he worked security at a twenty-story modern

downtown bank or downtown twenty-story modern.
When he first arrived, he did not know enough English
to order a sandwich. He asked her to explain each part

of *Lovely big rectangular old red English Catholic
leather Bible*. Evaluation before size. Age before color.
Nationality before religion. Time before length. Adding

and, one could determine if two adjectives were equal.
After Saigon fell, he had survived nine long years   20
of torture. Nine *and* long. He knew no other way to say this.

TISHANI DOSHI (B. 1975)

THE IMMIGRANT'S SONG   2013

Let us not speak of those days
when coffee beans filled the morning
with hope, when our mothers' headscarves
hung like white flags on washing lines.
Let us not speak of the long arms of sky
that used to cradle us at dusk.
And the baobabs—let us not trace
the shape of their leaves in our dreams,

or yearn for the noise of those nameless birds
that sang and died in the church's eaves.   10
Let us not speak of men,
stolen from their beds at night.
Let us not say the word
                 disappeared.
Let us not remember the first smell of rain.
Instead, let us speak of our lives now—
the gates and bridges and stores.
And when we break bread
in cafés and at kitchen tables
with our new brothers,   20
let us not burden them with stories
of war or abandonment.
Let us not name our old friends
who are unravelling like fairy tales
in the forests of the dead.
Naming them will not bring them back.
Let us stay here, and wait for the future
to arrive, for grandchildren to speak
in forked tongues about the country
we once came from.   30
Tell us about it, they might ask.
And you might consider telling them
of the sky and the coffee beans,
the small white houses and dusty streets.
You might set your memory afloat
like a paper boat down a river.
You might pray that the paper
whispers your story to the water,
that the water sings it to the trees,
that the trees howl and howl   40
it to the leaves. If you keep still
and do not speak, you might hear
your whole life fill the world
until the wind is the only word.

FOR ANALYSIS

1. What is the situation the speaker recounts? Where is he now? Where has he come from? How specific can you be in your answers? Why is that, and what is the effect when reading the poem?

2. Note the repetition of the statements such as those in lines 1 and 5. Where else do statements of this kind appear? How do they change? What is their significance to the poem as a whole?

MAKING ARGUMENTS

Make an argument for the larger significance of the word *disappeared* in "The Immigrant's Song" (l. 14). What is its first, more obvious meaning? What else might it refer to?

WRITING TOPIC

Describe a number of alternative poems that could be written under the title "The Immigrant's Song." How could they differ in their attitudes about the lives immigrants lead and the ways they think about them?

LAMENT —I   2013

When I see the houses in this city,
the electric gates and uniformed men
employed to guard the riches of the rich,
the gilded columns and gardens,
the boats on water, I wonder,
how to describe my home to you:
the short, mud walls,
the whispering roof, the veranda
on which my whole family
used to spread sheets and sleep.   10

The year I came to find work in the city,
my wife painted our house white
so it would be brighter than the neighbours'.
I beat her for her foolishness.
The children are hungry, I said,
the cow is old,
the money collector is after my blood,
and you steal like a magpie—
half a month's wage—to decorate
your nest like a shiny jewel?   20

The monsoon finally arrived the year I left,
dripped through the thatch,
peeled paint off the walls.
The wells grew full and overflowed.
The farmers rejoiced in the fields.
My son sat with his mouth open
catching drops of water like a frog.
My wife clung to the walls and wept.

When I fall asleep on the pavements
in this city, I try to imagine my wife's skin   30
against mine, the kohl in her eyes,
the white walls, the whole village sky
bearing down upon us
with all the weight of the stars.
I think of returning to that life,
but mostly I try to remember
how the world was once.
I want to open my mouth like my son,
and swallow things whole—
feel water filling all the voids,   40
until I am shaped back into existence.

CONNECTING POEMS:
POETIC IDENTITIES

The poems in this unit are about the "self," but not just any self: they are about
the selves of poets. Because of this, they are about poetry and the writing of poetry,
of course, but they are also in some measure about the identities of people who
lived in particular places at particular times and dealt with the possibilities and
challenges presented by their circumstances, as all people do. As you read their
reflections on those circumstances and the ways in which these poets lived
within them, thought about them, and challenged them, note the different ways
in which each poet also reflects on how those external circumstances interact
with the singular circumstance of being someone who writes poetry.

WALT WHITMAN (1819–1892)

FROM SONG OF MYSELF 1855

1

I celebrate myself, and sing myself,
And what I assume you shall assume,
For every atom belonging to me as good belongs to you.

I loafe and invite my soul,
I lean and loafe at my ease observing a spear of summer grass.

My tongue, every atom of my blood, form'd from this soil, this air,
Born here of parents born here from parents the same, and their parents
          the same,
I, now thirty-seven years old in perfect health begin,
Hoping to cease not till death.

Creeds and schools in abeyance,   10
Retiring back a while sufficed at what they are, but never forgotten,
I harbor for good or bad, I permit to speak at every hazard,
Nature without check with original energy.

6

A child said *What is the grass?* fetching it to me with full hands;
How could I answer the child? I do not know what it is any more than he.

I guess it must be the flag of my disposition, out of hopeful green stuff woven.

Or I guess it is the handkerchief of the Lord,
A scented gift and remembrancer designedly dropt,
Bearing the owner's name someway in the corners, that we may see and
        remark, and say *Whose?*

Or I guess the grass is itself a child, the produced babe of the vegetation.   20

Or I guess it is a uniform hieroglyphic,
And it means, Sprouting alike in broad zones and narrow zones,
Growing among black folks as among white,
Kanuck, Tuckahoe, Congressman, Cuff, I give them the same, I receive them the
        same.

And now it seems to me the beautiful uncut hair of graves.

Tenderly will I use you curling grass,
It may be you transpire from the breasts of young men,
It may be if I had known them I would have loved them,
It may be you are from old people, or from offspring taken soon out of
        their mothers' laps,
And here you are the mothers' laps.   30

This grass is very dark to be from the white heads of old mothers,
Darker than the colorless beards of old men,
Dark to come from under the faint red roofs of mouths.

O I perceive after all so many uttering tongues,
And I perceive they do not come from the roofs of mouths for nothing.

I wish I could translate the hints about the dead young men and women,
And the hints about old men and mothers, and the offspring taken soon out
        of their laps.

What do you think has become of the young and old men?
And what do you think has become of the women and children?

They are alive and well somewhere,
The smallest sprout shows there is really no death,
And if ever there was it led forward life, and does not wait at the end to arrest it,
And ceas'd the moment life appear'd.

40

All goes onward and outward, nothing collapses,
And to die is different from what anyone supposed, and luckier.

50

There is that in me—I do not know what it is—but I know it is in me.

Wrench'd and sweaty—calm and cool then my body becomes,
I sleep—I sleep long.

I do not know it—it is without name—it is a word unsaid,
It is not in any dictionary, utterance, symbol.

50

Sometimes it swings on more than the earth I swing on,
To it the creation is the friend whose embracing awakes me.

Perhaps I might tell more. Outlines! I plead for my brothers and sisters.

Do you see O my brothers and sisters?
It is not chaos or death—it is form, union, plan—it is eternal life—it is Happiness.

51

The past and present wilt—I have fill'd them, emptied them.
And proceed to fill my next fold of the future.

Listener up there! what have you to confide to me?
Look in my face while I snuff the sidle of evening,
(Talk honestly, no one else hears you, and I stay only a minute longer.)

60

Do I contradict myself?
Very well then I contradict myself.
(I am large, I contain multitudes.)

I concentrate toward them that are nigh, I wait on the door-slab.

Who has done his day's work? who will soonest be through with his supper?
Who wishes to walk with me?

Will you speak before I am gone? will you prove already too late?

52

The spotted hawk swoops by and accuses me, he complains of my gab
    and my loitering.

I too am not a bit tamed, I too am untranslatable,
I sound my barbaric yawp over the roofs of the world.   70

The last scud of day holds back for me,
It flings my likeness after the rest and true as any on the shadowed wilds,
It coaxes me to the vapor and the dusk.

I depart as air, I shake my white locks at the runaway sun,
I effuse my flesh in eddies, and drift it in lacy jags.

I bequeath myself to the dirt to grow from the grass I love,
If you want me again look for me under your boot-soles.

You will hardly know who I am or what I mean,
But I shall be good health to you nevertheless,
And filter and fibre your blood.   80

Failing to fetch me at first keep encouraged,
Missing me one place search another,
I stop somewhere waiting for you.

FOR ANALYSIS

1. Who or what is the speaker of this poem? List the lines in which he seems to be an individual speaker. Then make a list of the lines in which he seems to be something more.

2. The poem from which these excerpts are drawn is part of a book, *Leaves of Grass*. Why does this poem pay so much attention to grass? What does it mean?

3. How does this poem "contain multitudes" (l. 63)?

MAKING ARGUMENTS

Some critics at the time *Leaves of Grass* was published (and since) have criticized it as self-involved. Make an argument, on the evidence of this excerpt from one of its poems, that refutes this criticism. How is it about more than the poet or speaker? How does it use this personal, singing-of-itself voice to be about more than the poet's interest in himself?

WRITING TOPICS

1. Whitman writes, "You will hardly know who I am or what I mean, / But I shall be good health to you nevertheless" (ll. 78–79). How might this poem be intended to be "good" for its readers?

2. "Song of Myself" achieves strong and varied effects. Reread the poem, and keep a log of your reactions—your emotional, intellectual, and hard-to-categorize responses—as you encounter the different parts of the poem. Then write a reflection on this log. Do you see any patterns? As you moved again through "Song of Myself," what did you notice about how it works as a poem and on you as a reader?

FRANK O'HARA   (1926–1966)

MY HEART   1970

I'm not going to cry all the time
nor shall I laugh all the time,
I don't prefer one "strain" to another.
I'd have the immediacy of a bad movie,
not just a sleeper, but also the big,
overproduced first-run kind. I want to be
at least as alive as the vulgar. And if
some aficionado of my mess says "That's
not like Frank!", all to the good! I
don't wear brown and grey suits all the time,   10
do I? No. I wear workshirts to the opera,
often. I want my feet to be bare,
I want my face to be shaven, and my heart—
you can't plan on the heart, but
the better part of it, my poetry, is open.

FOR ANALYSIS

1. What is this poem about—a person or his poetry? Why is it necessary to ask this question? What is the effect of O'Hara's writing the poem in such a way that the reader has to ask it?

2. How would you characterize the voice in this poem? What kinds of words and sentences does the speaker use? What are the effects?

3. What stands out about line 11? Why does it stand out? What effect does it have on you as you read?

MAKING ARGUMENTS

In lines 5 through 7, O'Hara assumes the distinction between "sleeper" movies and "the big, overproduced first-run kind" and refers to "the vulgar." Do some research into the distinction, important in the middle of the last century and still to some people today, between different "levels" of culture—highbrow, middlebrow, and low-brow—and make an argument for or against the usefulness of the concept. Base your argument on your understanding of the concept (and arguments against it) and on the evidence of contemporary popular culture.

WRITING TOPIC

List the different things the speaker wants. Can you divide the list up into categories? What does the divisibility of the list and the nature of the categories say about the poem?

BILLY COLLINS (B. 1941)

MONDAY 2005

The birds are in their trees,
the toast is in the toaster,
and the poets are at their windows.

They are at their windows
in every section of the tangerine of earth—
the Chinese poets looking up at the moon,
the American poets gazing out
at the pink and blue ribbons of sunrise.

The clerks are at their desks,
the miners are down in their mines, 10
and the poets are looking out their windows
maybe with a cigarette, a cup of tea,
and maybe a flannel shirt or bathrobe is involved.

The proofreaders are playing the ping-pong
game of proofreading,
glancing back and forth from page to page,
the chefs are dicing celery and potatoes,
and the poets are at their windows
because it is their job for which
they are paid nothing every Friday afternoon. 20

Which window it hardly seems to matter
though many have a favorite,
for there is always something to see—
a bird grasping a thin branch,
the headlights of a taxi rounding a corner,
those two boys in wool caps angling across the street.

The fishermen bob in their boats,
the linemen climb their round poles,
the barbers wait by their mirrors and chairs,
and the poets continue to stare 30
at the cracked birdbath or a limb knocked down by the wind.

By now, it should go without saying
that what the oven is to the baker
and the berry-stained blouse to the dry cleaner,
so the window is to the poet.

Just think—
before the invention of the window,
the poets would have had to put on a jacket
and a winter hat to go outside
or remain indoors with only a wall to stare at.   40

And when I say a wall,
I do not mean a wall with striped wallpaper
and a sketch of a cow in a frame.

I mean a cold wall of fieldstones,
the wall of the medieval sonnet,
the original woman's heart of stone,
the stone caught in the throat of her poet-lover.

FOR ANALYSIS

1. Who or what is the speaker of this poem? List the lines in which he seems to be an individual speaker. Then list the lines in which he seems to be something more.

2. What does this poem have to say about poetry writing as work? In what ways is it like the other kinds of occupations mentioned in the poem? In what ways is it unlike them?

3. How does the last **stanza** differ from those that precede it? What is the effect? Why do you think Collins chose to write the ending this way?

MAKING ARGUMENTS

Many readers love Billy Collins; a number of critics do not. People on both sides base their love or lack of love for his poetry on the same thing—his attention to the everyday and the clear way in which he expresses what he sees in his poetry. Where do you stand, on the evidence of this poem and what you think poetry can or should do and be?

WRITING TOPIC

Why do you think Collins chose the title he did? Use textual evidence to back up your opinion.

CARL PHILLIPS   (B. 1959)

BLUE   1992

As through marble or the lining of
certain fish split open and scooped
clean, this is the blue vein

that rides, where the flesh is even
whiter than the rest of her, the splayed
thighs mother forgets, busy struggling
for command over bones: her own,
those of the chaise longue, all
equally uncooperative, and there's
the wind, too. This is her hair, gone
from white to blue in the air.

This is the black, shot with blue, of my dark
daddy's knuckles, that do not change, ever.
Which is to say they are no more pale
in anger than at rest, or when, as
I imagine them now, they follow
the same two fingers he has always used
to make the rim of every empty blue
glass in the house sing.
Always, the same
blue-to-black sorrow
no black surface can entirely hide.

Under the night, somewhere
between the white that is nothing so much as
blue, and the black that is, finally; nothing,
I am the man neither of you remembers.
Shielding, in the half-dark,
the blue eyes I sometimes forget
I don't have. Pulling my own stoop-
shouldered kind of blues across paper.
Apparently misinformed about the rumored
stuff of dreams: everywhere I inquired,
I was told look for blue.

For Analysis

1. This poem is filled with **concrete** visual detail. Why is that appropriate for this poem?

2. Colors lend detail to **imagery** in poems, but they also connote a range of meanings. What are the dominant colors in this poem? What are their different **connotations**?

3. What is the **setting** of this poem in terms of the speaker's life? What time or times is he writing about? What time in his life is he writing from? What is the relation between these times, and what is the effect of putting them together in one poem?

Making Arguments

Research the blues as a musical form. What are its roots? Who are its foremost practitioners, historically and today? Regardless of your opinion, outline an argument you imagine might be made by people who believe that it is a musical form that can only really be played by people of the historical and ethnic background identical to those who originated it.

WRITING TOPIC

In what way is this poem a blues poem? (If you are unfamiliar with the blues as a musical genre, do a few minutes of research on it.) Think in terms of sounds and **rhythm** as well as content.

TIMOTHY YU   (B. 1974)

CHINESE SILENCE NO. 22   2011

AFTER BILLY COLLINS, "MONDAY"

The Italians are making their pasta,
the French are making things French,
and the Chinese cultivate their silence.

They cultivate silence
in every Chinatown on the persimmon of earth—
mute below the towers of Toronto,
silently sweeping the streets of Singapore
clear of noisy self-expression.

The Americans are in their sport utility vehicles,
the Canadians are behaving reasonably,   10
but the Chinese remain silent
maybe with a cup of tea or an opium pipe
and maybe a finger puzzle or water torture is involved.

Or maybe the Chinese are playing the Chinese
game of ping-pong,
the pock-pock of the ball against their tight-lipped mouths
as their chefs dice scallions and bean curd.
The Chinese are silent
because it is their job for which
I pay them what they got for building the railroads.   20

Which silence it is hardly seems to matter
though many have a favorite
out of the 100 different kinds—
the Silence of the Well-Adjusted Minority,
the Girlish Silence of Reluctant Acquiescence,
the Silence that by No Means Should Be Mistaken for Bitterness.

By now, it should go without saying
that what Crocodile Dundee is to the Australian
and Mel Gibson is to the Scot,
so is silence to the Chinese. 30

Just think—
before I invented the 100 Chinese silences,
the Chinese would have had to stay indoors
and gabble about civil war and revolution
or go outside and build a really loud wall.

And when I say a wall,
I do not mean a wall of thousands of miles
that is visible from the moon.

I mean a noisy wall of language
that dwarfs my medieval battlements 40
and paves the Pacific to lap
California's shores with its brick-hard words.

FOR ANALYSIS

1. What principle of selection governed Yu's choices for things he has "the Chinese" doing in this poem? What is the poem's attitude toward these things and toward the thing that unites them?

2. What does the "after" in the poem's subtitle mean? What is the relationship between Yu's poem and Collins's?

3. This poem is one of a series of 100 "Chinese Silence" poems. When Yu **alludes** to the series in the poem, what does he reveal about his view of himself as a poet?

4. How would you characterize the poem's voice? Is it straightforward, or **ironic**? Detached, or full of feeling?

MAKING ARGUMENTS

This and the other ninety-nine poems in this series have been published in a book called *100 Chinese Silences*. These poems are not only about Billy Collins's poems, but about poems written by many other poets. Make an argument in which you defend this practice against hypothetical criticism. How does Yu treat the work of other poets? What do you imagine his justification for this treatment is?

WRITING TOPIC

While we often think of poems as simply things to be studied, enjoyed quietly, or maybe shared—especially when we encounter them in class—"Chinese Silence No. 22" considers poetry as something with power in the real world. Reflect on how you think of poetry. Is it something that lives only on pages between covers, or is it something that can make real things happen?

MAKING CONNECTIONS

1. Many of these poems feature the first-person "I" point of view. What do these "I's" have in common? How do they differ?

2. These poems all address identity; many do so in part with references to the past. What roles does the past play in these poems? How do the poets connect the past to their present identities?

3. These poems are about not just personal identity, but the personal identity of poets. In this way, they are different from poems that are just about poetry; the poems in this unit are about poetry too, of course, but they also pay attention to the makers of poems. What different things do these poems say about poetic identity? Which seem similar, and which are more in contrast?

CONNECTING POEMS: WORKING MOTHERS

The kind of work people do is often partly determined by their gender. Particular jobs are often restricted to or almost always filled by either men or women, and particular kinds of uncompensated tasks, like housework, are too. The poems in this unit address work from the viewpoint of the women who do it or the daughters who watch them do it. As you read, notice the shared **point of view** but also the different situations in which these women find themselves. How does lifestyle—social class, typical experiences—help shape what these women see when they look at work?

TESS GALLAGHER   (B. 1943)

I STOP WRITING THE POEM   1992

to fold the clothes. No matter who lives
or who dies, I'm still a woman.
I'll always have plenty to do.
I bring the arms of his shirt
together. Nothing can stop
our tenderness. I'll get back
to the poem. I'll get back to being
a woman. But for now
there's a shirt, a giant shirt
in my hands, and somewhere a small girl   10
standing next to her mother
watching to see how it's done.

FOR ANALYSIS

1. Does the speaker stop writing the poem? Does the continuation of the title into the first line help answer this question?

2. How does the **enjambment**, or continuation, of the first and second lines help signal an important context for the poem's situation?

3. If the speaker is not being a poet or a woman at the end of the poem, what is she being?

MAKING ARGUMENTS

Research the division of labor in contemporary U.S. households. Make an argument claiming that the way things are is the way they ought to be or that they ought to be different. Use the evidence of the poem, of your research, and of any other support you think relevant.

WRITING TOPICS

1. Especially for a self-conscious poem, "I Stop Writing the Poem" is simple, relatively devoid of poetic devices. Reflect on why Gallagher chose to write the poem in this spare **style**.

2. The "it" in the last line refers to more than shirt folding; the poem is about more than poetry or laundry, and, though it alludes to a context, it does not explore it. Tell the story that you think lies behind this poem, and explain what the "it" of the last line might be.

JULIA ALVAREZ   (B. 1950)

WOMAN'S WORK   1996

Who says a woman's work isn't high art?
She'd challenge as she scrubbed the bathroom tiles.
Keep house as if the address were your heart.

We'd clean the whole upstairs before we'd start
downstairs, I'd sigh, hearing my friends outside.
Doing her woman's work was a hard art

to practice when the summer sun would bar
the floor I swept till she was satisfied.
She kept me prisoner in her housebound heart.

She'd shine the tines of forks, the wheels of carts,   10
cut lacy lattices for all her pies.
Her woman's work was nothing less than art.

And I, her masterpiece since I was smart,
was primed, praised, polished, scolded and advised
to keep a house much better than my heart.

I did not want to be her counterpart!
I struck out . . . but became my mother's child:
a woman working at home on her art,
housekeeping paper as if it were her heart.

FOR ANALYSIS

1. How is the speaker her mother's "masterpiece" (l. 13)?
2. To what does "housekeeping paper" (l. 19) refer?
3. Answer the first line's question as if it weren't rhetorical.

MAKING ARGUMENTS

In contemporary discussion of women's social roles, the phrase "having it all" is often used to discuss whether women can fulfill traditional roles while at the same time pursuing careers. Some believe it is impossible, others think it is a perfectly valid choice to stay home and take care of the family, while still others criticize the phrase and ask why it never is used with reference to men. Where does this poem come down on the question? Make an argument answering this question, with close reference to the text of the poem.

WRITING TOPICS

1. Write an account of Alvarez's use of repetition and **rhyme** in "Woman's Work." What effects does Alvarez achieve?
2. **Tone** in this poem is complicated and nuanced. Make a list of words that seem to have positive **connotations**. Then make a list of words that seem to have negative connotations. How do these words express how the speaker feels about the various subjects?

RITA DOVE   (B. 1952)

MY MOTHER ENTERS THE WORK FORCE   2000

The path to ABC Business School
was paid for by a lucky sign:
Alterations, Qualified Seamstress Inquire Within.
Tested on Sleeves, hers
never puckered—puffed or sleek,
Leg o' or Raglan—
they barely needed the damp cloth
to steam them perfect.

Those were the afternoons. Evenings
she took in piecework, the treadle machine

10

with its locomotive whir
traveling the lit path of the needle
through quicksand taffeta
or velvet deep as a forest.
And now and now sang the treadle,
I know, I know. . . .

And then it was day again, all morning
at the office machines, their clack and chatter
another journey—rougher,
that would go on forever   20
until she could break a hundred words
with no errors—ah, and then

no more postponed groceries,
and that blue pair of shoes!

FOR ANALYSIS

1. Dove's poem describes the mother's sewing work in great detail. What does the specific nature of this detail express about the daughter-speaker's attitude toward her mother's work?

2. How would you characterize the poem's overall **tone**? What about it informs the tone?

3. What is the treadle saying, and to whom?

MAKING ARGUMENTS

Make an argument about the poem's attitude concerning the event named in its title. How does it feel about it? How is this attitude conveyed in its **tone**?

WRITING TOPICS

1. Although the poem speaks very little about it, this mother and daughter are not as comfortable economically as they might be. How do we know this? What is the poem's attitude toward this situation?

2. Write a poem about work you have done, or work a parent or another relative or a friend has done. Describe that work in a way that reveals, without being explicit, your (or his or her) feelings about it.

DEBORAH GARRISON (B. 1965)

SESTINA FOR THE WORKING MOTHER   2007

No time for a sestina for the working mother.
Who has so much to do, from first thing in the morning
When she has to get herself dressed and the children
Too, when they tumble in the pillow pile rather than listening

To her exhortations about brushing teeth, making ready for the day;
They clamor with "up" hugs when she struggles out the door.

Every time, as if shot from a cannon when she shuts the door.
She stomps down the street in her city boots, slipping from mother
Mode into commuter trance, trees swaying at the corner of a new day
Nearly turned, her familiar bus stop cool and welcoming in the morning.   10
She hears her own heart here, though no one else is listening,
And if the bus is late she hears down the block the voices of her children

Bobbing under their oversized backpacks to greet other children
At their own bus stop. They too have come flying from the door,
Brave for the journey, and everyone is talking and no one is listening
As they head off to school. The noisy children of the working mother,
Waiting with their sitter for the bus, are healthy and happy this morning.
And that's the best way, the mother knows, for a day

To begin. The apprehension of what kind of day
It will be in the world of work, blissful without children,   20
Trembles in the anxious and pleasurable pulse of the morning;
It has tamped her down tight and lit her out the door
And away from what she might have been as a mother
At home, perhaps drinking coffee and listening

To NPR, what rapt and intelligent listening
She'd do at home. And volunteering, she thinks, for part of the day
At their school—she'd be a playground monitor, a PTA mother!
She'd see them straggle into the sunshine, her children
Bright in the slipstream, and she a gracious shadow at the school door;
She would not be separated from them for long by the morning.   30

But she has chosen her flight from them, on this and every morning.
She's now so far away she trusts someone else is listening
To their raised voices, applying a Band-Aid, opening the door
For them when the sunshine calls them out into the day.
At certain moments, head bent at her desk, she can see her children,
And feels the quick stab. She hasn't forgotten that she is their mother.
Every weekday morning, every working day,
She listens to her heart and the voices of her children.
Goodbye! they shout, and the door closes behind the working mother.

FOR ANALYSIS

1. *Sestina* is a highly structured traditional form of poetry. Can you guess what the "rules" are for a sestina by figuring out the structure of this one?

2. What is the effect of reading a sestina, or at least this sestina? Considering these effects, why do you think Garrison chose the sestina form for this poem? What about her poem's **themes** might be expressed by its form?

3. Is the speaker happy to be a working mother? Sad? Both?

MAKING ARGUMENTS

How would you construct an argument against Garrison's poem from a woman who made the opposite choice from the one the speaker mentions in line 31? What moments in the poem might that argument seize on? What would it do with them?

WRITING TOPICS

1. What function do lines 23–30 serve? How do they fit into the larger poem? What about the opening of the sixth stanza helps you understand its function and its fit?

2. The final stanza in a sestina, the *envoi*, is often used to comment on the rest of the poem. How does the envoi in "Sestina for the Working Mother" comment on the rest of it?

MAKING CONNECTIONS

1. Three of the four poems in this unit feature a speaker who might be understood to be a poet. How does each of these poems relate poetry to the other things—work, motherhood, and so on—that these poems are about? Is poetry work? Is it more or less than work?

2. All of these poems reflect on issues surrounding women working, sometimes explicitly. Though the first concern is often about social expectations—what work is "appropriate" for women and what isn't—in the background is the question of economics. Which of these poems makes economics a central concern? Which of these does not? Can you read the economics behind one or more that don't foreground it?

3. Address the role housework plays in these poems. Is it drudgery or an art? A necessity or a way to teach work habits?

CONNECTING POEMS: AMERICA THROUGH IMMIGRANTS' EYES

The poems in this section are about immigration to America, seen from a variety of angles and through a number of different lenses. The events about which these poets write occurred in the mid-eighteenth century, the late nineteenth century, the early twentieth century, and in our contemporary moments. The places of origin of the immigrants include Africa and Europe and the Americas. The motivation for coming to the United States vary as well: from the search for a better life, to the fleeing of a worsening one, to the absence of motivation that characterizes being stolen unwillingly from one's home. Despite these differences, there is much that unites these poems. As you read and notice all of these differences, keep an eye out for those connections.

PHILLIS WHEATLEY (1753–1784)

ON BEING BROUGHT FROM AFRICA TO AMERICA 1773

'Twas mercy brought me from my pagan land,
Taught my benighted soul to understand
That there's a God, that there's a Savior too:
Once I redemption neither sought nor knew.
Some view our sable race with scornful eye,
"Their color is a diabolic die.°"   dye
Remember, Christians, Negros, black as Cain,
May be refined, and join th' angelic train.

FOR ANALYSIS

1. Wheatley was brought from Senegal or Gambia to the United States and sold as a slave to the Wheatley family in Boston when she was seven or eight years old. What is your response to the poem's first three lines? Why?

2. Paraphrase "Negros, black as Cain, / May be refined, and join th' angelic train."

3. What historical conditions would perhaps account for the fame of the poet and the extraordinary contemporary wonder at her achievements?

4. Can you imagine an African American poet writing a similar poem in the twenty-first century? Explain.

MAKING ARGUMENTS

Imagine a response to Wheatley that takes issue with the sentiment expressed in the poem's first three lines. Use research into the history of slavery and the slave trade as well as any evidence you may find within the poem.

WRITING TOPIC

First write a review of this poem based on your perception of eighteenth-century society in Massachusetts; then write a twenty-first-century review.

EMMA LAZARUS (1849–1887)

THE NEW COLOSSUS[1] (1883)

Not like the brazen giant of Greek fame,[2]
With conquering limbs astride from land to land;
Here at our sea-washed, sunset gates shall stand

The New Colossus
[1] This poem was engraved on a bronze plaque and mounted inside the Statue of Liberty in 1903.
[2] The Colossus of Rhodes, one of the Seven Wonders of the Ancient World.

A mighty woman with a torch, whose flame
Is the imprisoned lightning, and her name
Mother of Exiles. From her beacon-hand
Glows world-wide welcome; her mild eyes command
The air-bridged harbor that twin cities frame.
"Keep, ancient lands, your storied pomp!" cries she
With silent lips. "Give me your tired, your poor,   10
Your huddled masses yearning to breathe free,
The wretched refuse of your teeming shore.
Send these, the homeless, tempest-tost to me,
I lift my lamp beside the golden door!"

FOR ANALYSIS

1. What was the Colossus of Rhodes? How does Lazarus describe it in the poem's
opening lines?

2. To what does "mighty woman with a torch" (l. 4) refer? To what other object in the
poem is it compared?

MAKING ARGUMENTS

Is the United States still a haven for exiles? Was it ever? Answer these questions, using
historical evidence to support your argument.

WRITING TOPICS

Write or imagine a similar poem about a major statue or monument. What could be
said about it? How might you say it?

LÉOPOLD SÉDAR SENGHOR   (1906–2001)

TO NEW YORK[1]   1998

(for jazz orchestra and trumpet solo)

New York! At first I was bewildered by your beauty,
Those huge, long-legged, golden girls.
So shy, at first, before your blue metallic eyes and icy smile,
So shy. And full of despair at the end of skyscraper streets
Raising my owl eyes at the eclipse of the sun.
Your light is sulphurous against the pale towers
Whose heads strike lightning into the sky,
Skyscrapers defying storms with their steel shoulders
And weathered skin of stone.
But two weeks on the naked sidewalks of Manhattan—   10

[1] Translated by Melvin Dixon.

At the end of the third week the fever
Overtakes you with a jaguar's leap
Two weeks without well water or pasture all birds of the air
Fall suddenly dead under the high, sooty terraces.
No laugh from a growing child, his hand in my cool hand.
No mother's breast, but nylon legs. Legs and breasts
Without smell or sweat. No tender word, and no lips,
Only artificial hearts paid for in cold cash
And not one book offering wisdom.
The painter's palette yields only coral crystals.   20
Sleepless nights, O nights of Manhattan!
Stirring with delusions while car horns blare the empty hours
And murky streams carry away hygenic loving
Like rivers overflowing with the corpses of babies.

II

Now is the time of signs and reckoning, New York!
Now is the time of manna and hyssop.
You have only to listen to God's trombones, to your heart
Beating to the rhythm of blood, your blood.
I saw Harlem teeming with sounds and ritual colors
And outrageous smells—   30
At teatime in the home of the drugstore-deliveryman
I saw the festival of Night begin at the retreat of day.
And I proclaim Night more truthful than the day.
It is the pure hour when God brings forth
Life immemorial in the streets,
All the amphibious elements shining like suns.
Harlem, Harlem! Now I've seen Harlem, Harlem!
A green breeze of corn rising from the pavements
Plowed by the Dan dancers' bare feet,
Hips rippling like silk and spearhead breasts,   40
Ballets of water lilies and fabulous masks
And mangoes of love rolling from the low houses
To the feet of police horses.
And along sidewalks I saw streams of white rum
And streams of black milk in the blue haze of cigars.
And at night I saw cotton flowers snow down
From the sky and the angels' wings and sorcerers' plumes.
Listen, New York! O listen to your bass male voice,
Your vibrant oboe voice, the muted anguish of your tears
Falling in great clots of blood,   50
Listen to the distant beating of your nocturnal heart,
The tom-tom's rhythm and blood, tom-tom blood and tom-tom.

III

New York! I say New York, let black blood flow into your blood.
Let it wash the rust from your steel joints, like an oil of life
Let it give your bridges the curve of hips and supple vines.
Now the ancient age returns, unity is restored,
The reconciliation of the Lion and Bull and Tree
Idea links to action, the ear to the heart, sign to meaning.
See your rivers stirring with musk alligators
And sea cows with mirage eyes. No need to invent the Sirens.   60
Just open your eyes to the April rainbow
And your eyes, especially your ears, to God
Who in one burst of saxophone laughter
Created heaven and earth in six days,
And on the seventh slept a deep Negro sleep.

FOR ANALYSIS

1. Why do you think Senghor describes New York as having "blue metallic eyes" and an "icy smile" (l. 3)? To what is this description contrasted?

2. How does the speaker feel about New York?

3. Why do you think Senghor divides the poem up as he does? What are the similarities and differences between the three sections? What is the significance of the movement from the first to the second to the third?

MAKING ARGUMENTS

Senghor was a champion of Négritude, which promoted a pan-African diasporic identity—that is, a belief that there was something essential about people of African descent, regardless of whether they lived in Africa or elsewhere, that united them. Later black writers claimed that this idea paradoxically promoted racism, since it still maintained that there were traits essential to different races. The movement was a response to colonialism and racism. How would you construct the arguments on both sides of this issue?

WRITING TOPIC

Senghor gives "To New York" faux instructions for instrumental arrangement. Describe the ways in which the poem is musical in the way that it is written and explain why music is important to it thematically.

KOFI AWOONOR   (1935–2013)

AMERICA   2014

A name only once
crammed into the child's fitful memory
in malnourished villages,

vast deliriums like the galloping foothills of the Colorado:
of Mohawks and the Chippewa,
horsey penny-movies
brought cheap at the tail of the war
to Africa. Where indeed is the Mississippi panorama
and the girl that played the piano and
kept her hand on her heart   10
as Flanagan drank a quart of moonshine
before the eyes of the town's gentlemen?
What happened to your locomotive in Winter, Walt,
and my ride across the prairies in the trail
of the stage-coach, the gold-rush and the Swanee River?
Where did they bury Geronimo,
heroic chieftain, lonely horseman of this apocalypse
who led his tribesmen across deserts of cholla
and emerald hills
in pursuit of despoilers,   20
half-starved immigrants
from a despoiled Europe?
What happened to Archibald's
soul's harvest on this raw earth
of raw hates?
To those that have none
a festival is preparing at graves' ends
where the mockingbird's hymn
closes evening of prayers
and supplication as   30
new winds blow from graves
flowered in multi-colored cemeteries even
where they say the races are intact.

FOR ANALYSIS

1. What is the **setting** of this poem? From whose **point of view** is it seen?

2. What history does the poem's speaker recount? What history is he or she part of?

MAKING ARGUMENTS

While U.S. influence around the globe has been economically and militarily significant, there are some who say its greatest influence has been cultural, in particular through the spread of its films around the world. How would you argue that that influence has been positive? Negative? Mixed?

WRITING TOPIC

Imagine going to a place you have heard and seen a lot about but never been to. How might it differ from what you expect?

Richard Blanco (b. 1968)

AMÉRICA 1998

I

Although Tía Miriam boasted she discovered
at least half a dozen uses for peanut butter—
topping for guava shells in syrup,
butter substitute for Cuban toast,
hair conditioner and relaxer—
Mamá never knew what to make
of the monthly five-pound jars
handed out by the immigration department
until my friend, Jeff, mentioned jelly.

II

There was always pork though,
for every birthday and wedding,
whole ones on Christmas and New Year's Eve,
even on Thanksgiving day—pork,   10
fried, broiled, or crispy skin roasted—
as well as cauldrons of black beans,
fried plantain chips, and *yuca con mojito.*
These items required a special visit
to Antonio's Mercado on the corner of Eighth Street
where men in *guayaberas* stood in senate
blaming Kennedy for everything—*"Ese hijo de puta!"*   20
the bile of Cuban coffee and cigar residue
filling the creases of their wrinkled lips;
clinging to one another's lies of lost wealth,
ashamed and empty as hollow trees.

III

By seven I had grown suspicious—we were still here.
Overheard conversations about returning
had grown wistful and less frequent.
I spoke English; my parents didn't.
We didn't live in a two-story house
with a maid or a wood-panel station wagon   30
nor vacation camping in Colorado.
None of the girls had hair of gold;
none of my brothers or cousins

were named Greg, Peter, or Marcia;
we were not the Brady Bunch.
None of the black and white characters
on Donna Reed or on the Dick Van Dyke Show
were named Guadalupe, Lázaro, or Mercedes.
Patty Duke's family wasn't like us either—
they didn't have pork on Thanksgiving,   40
they ate turkey with cranberry sauce;
they didn't have *yuca*, they had yams
like the dittos of Pilgrims I colored in class.

IV

A week before Thanksgiving
I explained to my *abuelita*
about the Indians and the Mayflower,
how Lincoln set the slaves free;
I explained to my parents about
the purple mountain's majesty,
"one if by land, two if by sea,"   50
the cherry tree, the tea party,
the amber waves of grain,
the "masses yearning to be free,"
liberty and justice for all, until
finally they agreed:
this Thanksgiving we would have turkey,
as well as pork.

V

Abuelita prepared the poor fowl
as if committing an act of treason,
faking her enthusiasm for my sake.
Mamá set a frozen pumpkin pie in the oven   60
and prepared candied yams following instructions
I translated from the marshmallow bag.
The table was arrayed with gladiolas,
the plattered turkey loomed at the center
on plastic silver from Woolworth's.
Everyone sat in green velvet chairs
we had upholstered with clear vinyl,
except Tío Carlos and Toti, seated
in the folding chairs from the Salvation Army.   70
I uttered a bilingual blessing

and the turkey was passed around
like a game of Russian Roulette.
"DRY," Tío Berto complained, and proceeded
to drown the lean slices with pork fat drippings
and cranberry jelly—*"esa mierda roja,"* he called it.
Faces fell when *Mamá* presented her ochre pie—
pumpkin was a home remedy for ulcers, not a dessert.
Tía María made three rounds of Cuban coffee
then *Abuelo* and Pepe cleared the living room furniture,   80
put on a Celia Cruz LP and the entire family
began to *merengue* over the linoleum of our apartment,
sweating rum and coffee until they remembered—
it was 1970 and 46 degrees—
in *América.*
After repositioning the furniture,
an appropriate darkness filled the room.
Tío Berto was the last to leave.

FOR ANALYSIS

1. What is the **setting** of this poem? Where is the speaker from? How do you know?

2. In what ways does television disappoint the speaker?

3. In what ways is this poem its own sort of "bilingual blessing" (l. 71) on the speaker's family's experience in America? In what ways is it not?

MAKING ARGUMENTS

Richard Blanco read a poem at President Barack Obama's second inauguration that he wrote for the occasion (as is the tradition). Look up that poem, read it, and construct an argument about the relationship between that poem and this one. Do they express identical sentiments or different ones? Are they written in the same ways? Relate your arguments about these issues to the circumstances under which they were written.

WRITING TOPICS

Blanco makes great use of food in describing the immigrant experience. In what other ways can writers use food to convey ideas about the way people in different circumstances live? Use your imagination and describe a poem using this strategy.

MAKING CONNECTIONS

1. Are all of these poems even about immigration? Which are not, and how do they compare to each other and to the "truer" immigration poems?

2. Compare the use of media in Awoonor's and Blanco's poems. How does each present media and their influence?

3. Compare these poems' views on immigration to the United States. Is there one experience or many?

DRAMA

CASE STUDY IN ARGUMENT

REVIEWING AN AMERICAN CLASSIC: *A RAISIN IN THE SUN*

Lorraine Hansberry's play appeared at a pivotal time in the history of race in the United States. The first play about an African American family to appear on Broadway, it tackled the very subjects that the civil rights movement was working to address. A central element of Hansberry's plot was in fact "ripped from the headlines" (as we say of contemporary crime dramas) of the legal struggles over segregation that preceded the Fair Housing Act. The play can tell us much about the state of racial thinking and politics at the time of its writing as well as today; there are some who would argue that not as much has changed as we might like to think. We can also learn a lot about those things by studying the way in which reviewers and critics at the time talked about it, and have since, and we can also profit by looking at the many rebirths of the play in film and television. As you read, track the kinds of arguments that have been made around this text, and think always about how they are made and what you think.

LORRAINE HANSBERRY (1930-1965)

A RAISIN IN THE SUN 1959

CHARACTERS (in order of appearance)

Ruth Younger
Walter Lee Younger, brother
Lena Younger, Mama
George Murchison
Karl Lindner
Moving Men

Travis Younger
Beneatha Younger
Joseph Asagai
Mrs. Johnson
Bobo

The action of the play is set in Chicago's Southside, sometime between World War II and the present.

ACT I

Scene 1. *(Friday morning.)*

The Younger living room would be a comfortable and well-ordered room if it were not for a number of indestructible contradictions to this state of being. Its furnishings are typical and undistinguished and their primary feature now is that they have clearly had to accommodate the living of too many people for too many years—and they are tired. Still, we can see that at some time, a time probably no longer remembered by the family (except perhaps for Mama), the furnishings of this room were actually selected with care and love and even hope—and brought to this apartment and arranged with taste and pride.

That was a long time ago. Now the once loved pattern of the couch upholstery has to fight to show itself from under acres of crocheted doilies and couch covers which have themselves finally come to be more important than the upholstery. And here a table or a chair has been moved to disguise the worn places in the carpet; but the carpet has fought back by showing its weariness, with depressing uniformity, elsewhere on its surface.

Weariness has, in fact, won in this room. Everything has been polished, washed, sat on, used, scrubbed too often. All pretenses but living itself have long since vanished from the very atmosphere of this room.

Moreover, a section of this room, for it is not really a room unto itself, though the landlord's lease would make it seem so, slopes backward to provide a small kitchen area, where the family prepares the meals that are eaten in the living room proper, which must also serve as dining room. The single window that has been provided for these "two" rooms is located in this kitchen area. The sole natural light the family may enjoy in the course of a day is only that which fights its way through this little window.

At left, a door leads to a bedroom which is shared by Mama and her daughter, Beneatha. At right, opposite, is a second room (which in the beginning of the life of this apartment was probably a breakfast room) which serves as a bedroom for Walter and his wife, Ruth.

Time: Sometime between World War II and the present.

Place: Chicago's Southside.

At Rise: It is morning dark in the living room. Travis is asleep on the make-down bed at center. An alarm clock sounds from within the bedroom at right, and presently Ruth enters from that room and closes the door behind her. She crosses sleepily toward the window. As she passes her sleeping son she reaches down and shakes him a little. At the window she raises the shade and a dusky Southside morning light comes in feebly. She fills a pot with water and puts it on to boil. She calls to the boy, between yawns, in a slightly muffled voice.

Ruth is about thirty. We can see that she was a pretty girl, even exceptionally so, but now it is apparent that life has been little that she expected, and disappointment has already begun to hang in her face. In a few years, before thirty-five even, she will be known among her people as a "settled woman."

She crosses to her son and gives him a good, final, rousing shake.

Ruth. Come on now, boy, it's seven thirty! *(Her son sits up at last, in a stupor of sleepiness.)* I say hurry up, Travis! You ain't the only person in the world got to use a bathroom! *(The child, a sturdy, handsome little boy of ten or eleven, drags himself out of the bed and almost blindly takes his towels and "today's clothes" from drawers and a closet and goes out to the bathroom, which is in an outside hall and which is shared by another family or families on the same floor. Ruth crosses to the bedroom door at right and opens it and calls in to her husband.)* Walter Lee! . . . It's after seven thirty! Lemme see you do some waking up in there now! *(She waits.)* You better get up from there, man! It's after seven thirty I tell you. *(She waits again.)* All right, you just go ahead and lay there and next thing you know Travis be finished and Mr. Johnson'll be in there and you'll be fussing and cussing round here like a madman! And be late too! *(She waits, at the end of patience.)* Walter Lee—it's time for you to GET UP!

She waits another second and then starts to go into the bedroom, but is apparently satisfied that her husband has begun to get up. She stops, pulls the door to, and returns to the kitchen area. She wipes her face with a moist cloth and runs her fingers through her sleep-disheveled hair in a vain effort and ties an apron around her housecoat. The bedroom door at right opens and her husband stands in the doorway in his pajamas, which are rumpled and mismated. He is a lean, intense young man in his middle thirties, inclined to quick nervous movements and erratic speech habits—and always in his voice there is a quality of indictment.

Walter. Is he out yet?

Ruth. What you mean *out?* He ain't hardly got in there good yet.

Walter *(wandering in, still more oriented to sleep than to a new day).* Well, what was you doing all that yelling for if I can't even get in there yet? *(Stopping and thinking.)* Check coming today?

Ruth. They *said* Saturday and this is just Friday and I hopes to God you ain't going to get up here first thing this morning and start talking to me 'bout no money— 'cause I 'bout don't want to hear it.

Walter. Something the matter with you this morning?

Ruth. No—I'm just sleepy as the devil. What kind of eggs you want?

Walter. Not scrambled. *(Ruth starts to scramble eggs.)* Paper come? *(Ruth points impatiently to the rolled up Tribune on the table, and he gets it and spreads it out and vaguely reads the front page.)* Set off another bomb yesterday.

Ruth *(maximum indifference).* Did they?

Walter *(looking up).* What's the matter with you?

Ruth. Ain't nothing the matter with me. And don't keep asking me that this morning.

Walter. Ain't nobody bothering you. *(Reading the news of the day absently again.)* Say Colonel McCormick is sick.

Ruth (*affecting tea-party interest*). Is he now? Poor thing.

Walter (*sighing and looking at his watch*). Oh, me. (*He waits.*) Now what is that boy doing in that bathroom all this time? He just going to have to start getting up earlier. I can't be being late to work on account of him fooling around in there.

Ruth (*turning on him*). Oh, no he ain't going to be getting up no earlier no such thing! It ain't his fault that he can't get to bed no earlier nights 'cause he got a bunch of crazy good-for-nothing clowns sitting up running their mouths in what is supposed to be his bedroom after ten o'clock at night . . .

Walter. That's what you mad about, ain't it? The things I want to talk about with my friends just couldn't be important in your mind, could they?

He rises and finds a cigarette in her handbag on the table and crosses to the little window and looks out, smoking and deeply enjoying this first one.

Ruth (*almost matter of factly, a complaint too automatic to deserve emphasis*). Why you always got to smoke before you eat in the morning?

Walter (*at the window*). Just look at 'em down there . . . Running and racing to work . . . (*He turns and faces his wife and watches her a moment at the stove, and then, suddenly.*) You look young this morning, baby.

Ruth (*indifferently*). Yeah?

Walter. Just for a second—stirring them eggs. Just for a second it was—you looked real young again. (*He reaches for her; she crosses away. Then, drily.*) It's gone now—you look like yourself again!

Ruth. Man, if you don't shut up and leave me alone.

Walter (*looking out to the street again*). First thing a man ought to learn in life is not to make love to no colored woman first thing in the morning. You all some eeeevil people at eight o'clock in the morning.

Travis appears in the hall doorway, almost fully dressed and quite wide awake now, his towels and pajamas across his shoulders. He opens the door and signals for his father to make the bathroom in a hurry.

Travis (*watching the bathroom*). Daddy, come on!

Walter gets his bathroom utensils and flies out to the bathroom.

Ruth. Sit down and have your breakfast, Travis.

Travis. Mama, this is Friday. (*Gleefully.*) Check coming tomorrow, huh?

Ruth. You get your mind off money and eat your breakfast.

Travis (*eating*). This is the morning we supposed to bring the fifty cents to school.

Ruth. Well, I ain't got no fifty cents this morning.

Travis. Teacher say we have to.

Ruth. I don't care what teacher say. I ain't got it. Eat your breakfast, Travis.

Travis. I *am* eating.

Ruth. Hush up now and just eat!

The boy gives her an exasperated look for her lack of understanding, and eats grudgingly.

Travis. You think Grandmama would have it?

Ruth. No! And I want you to stop asking your grandmother for money, you hear me?

Travis *(outraged).* Gaaaleee! I don't ask her, she just gimme it sometimes!

Ruth. Travis Willard Younger—I got too much on me this morning to be—

Travis. Maybe Daddy—

Ruth. *Travis!*

The boy hushes abruptly. They are both quiet and tense for several seconds.

Travis *(presently).* Could I maybe go carry some groceries in front of the supermarket for a little while after school then?

Ruth. Just hush, I said. *(Travis jabs his spoon into his cereal bowl viciously, and rests his head in anger upon his fists.)* If you through eating, you can get over there and make up your bed.

The boy obeys stiffly and crosses the room, almost mechanically, to the bed and more or less folds the bedding into a heap, then angrily gets his books and cap.

Travis *(sulking and standing apart from her unnaturally).* I'm gone.

Ruth *(looking up from the stove to inspect him automatically).* Come here. *(He crosses to her and she studies his head.)* If you don't take this comb and fix this here head, you better! *(Travis puts down his books with a great sigh of oppression, and crosses to the mirror. His mother mutters under her breath about his "slubbornness.")* 'Bout to march out of here with that head looking just like chickens slept in it! I just don't know where you get your slubborn ways . . . And get your jacket, too. Looks chilly out this morning.

Travis *(with conspicuously brushed hair and jacket).* I'm gone.

Ruth. Get carfare and milk money—*(Waving one finger.)*—and not a single penny for no caps, you hear me?

Travis *(with sullen politeness).* Yes'm.

He turns in outrage to leave. His mother watches after him as in his frustration he approaches the door almost comically. When she speaks to him, her voice has become a very gentle tease.

Ruth *(mocking; as she thinks he would say it).* Oh, Mama makes me so mad sometimes, I don't know what to do! *(She waits and continues to his back as he stands stock-still in front of the door.)* I wouldn't kiss that woman good-bye for nothing in this world this morning! *(The boy finally turns around and rolls his eyes at her, knowing the mood has changed and he is vindicated; he does not, however, move toward her yet.)* Not for nothing in this world! *(She finally laughs aloud at him and holds out her arms to him and we see that it is a way between them, very old* *and practiced. He crosses to her and allows her to embrace him warmly but keeps his face fixed with masculine rigidity. She holds him back from her presently and looks at him and runs her fingers over the features of his face. With utter gentleness—.)* Now—whose little old angry man are you?

Travis *(the masculinity and gruffness start to fade at last).* Aw gaalee—Mama . . .

Ruth *(mimicking).* Aw—gaaaaalleeeee, Mama! *(She pushes him, with rough playfulness and finality, toward the door.)* Get on out of here or you going to be late.

Travis *(in the face of love, new aggressiveness).* Mama, could I *please* go carry groceries?

Ruth. Honey, it's starting to get so cold evenings.

Walter *(coming in from the bathroom and drawing a make-believe gun from a make-believe holster and shooting at his son).* What is it he wants to do?

Ruth. Go carry groceries after school at the supermarket.

Walter. Well, let him go . . .

Travis *(quickly, to the ally).* I *have* to—she won't gimme the fifty cents . . .

Walter *(to his wife only).* Why not?

Ruth *(simply, and with flavor).* 'Cause we don't have it.

Walter *(to Ruth only).* What you tell the boy things like that for? *(Reaching down into his pants with a rather important gesture.)* Here, son—

He hands the boy the coin, but his eyes are directed to his wife's. Travis takes the money happily.

Travis. Thanks, Daddy.

He starts out. Ruth watches both of them with murder in her eyes. Walter stands and stares back at her with defiance, and suddenly reaches into his pocket again on an afterthought.

Walter *(without even looking at his son, still staring hard at his wife).* In fact, here's another fifty cents . . . Buy yourself some fruit today—or take a taxicab to school or something!

Travis. Whoopee—

He leaps up and clasps his father around the middle with his legs, and they face each other in mutual appreciation; slowly Walter Lee peeks around the boy to catch the violent rays from his wife's eyes and draws his head back as if shot.

Walter. You better get down now—and get to school, man.

Travis *(at the door).* O.K. Good-bye.

He exits.

Walter *(after him, pointing with pride).* That's *my* boy. *(She looks at him in disgust and turns back to her work.)* You know what I was thinking 'bout in the bathroom this morning?

Ruth. No.

Walter. How come you always try to be so pleasant!

Ruth. What is there to be pleasant 'bout!

Walter. You want to know what I was thinking 'bout in the bathroom or not!

Ruth. I know what you thinking 'bout.

Walter *(ignoring her).* 'Bout what me and Willy Harris was talking about last night.

Ruth *(immediately—a refrain).* Willy Harris is a good-for-nothing loudmouth.

Walter. Anybody who talks to me has got to be a good-for-nothing loudmouth, ain't he? And what you know about who is just a good-for-nothing loudmouth? Charlie Atkins was just a "good-for-nothing loudmouth" too, wasn't he! When he wanted me to go in the dry-cleaning business with him. And now—he's grossing a hundred thousand a year. A hundred thousand dollars a year! You still call *him* a loudmouth!

Ruth *(bitterly).* Oh, Walter Lee . . .

She folds her head on her arms over the table.

Walter *(rising and coming to her and standing over her).* You tired, ain't you? Tired of everything. Me, the boy, the way we live—this beat-up hole—everything. Ain't you? *(She doesn't look up, doesn't answer.)* So tired—moaning and groaning all the time, but you wouldn't do nothing to help, would you? You couldn't be on my side that long for nothing, could you?

Ruth. Walter, please leave me alone.

Walter. A man needs for a woman to back him up . . .

Ruth. Walter—

Walter. Mama would listen to you. You know she listen to you more than she do me and Bennie. She think more of you. All you have to do is just sit down with her when you drinking your coffee one morning and talking 'bout things like you do and—*(He sits down beside her and demonstrates graphically what he thinks her methods and tone should be.)*—you just sip your coffee, see, and say easy like that you been thinking 'bout that deal Walter Lee is so interested in, 'bout the store and all, and sip some more coffee, like what you saying ain't really that important to you—And the next thing you know, she be listening good and asking you questions and when I come home—I can tell her the details. This ain't no fly-by-night proposition, baby. I mean we figured it out, me and Willy and Bobo.

Ruth *(with a frown).* Bobo?

Walter. Yeah. You see, this little liquor store we got in mind cost seventy-five thousand and we figured the initial investment on the place be 'bout thirty thousand, see. That be ten thousand each. Course, there's a couple of hundred you got to pay so's you don't spend your life just waiting for them clowns to let your license get approved—

Ruth. You mean graft?

Walter *(frowning impatiently).* Don't call it that. See there, that just goes to show you what women understand about the world. Baby, don't *nothing* happen for you in the world 'less you pay *somebody* off!

Ruth. Walter, leave me alone! (*She raises her head and stares at him vigorously—then says, more quietly.*) Eat your eggs, they gonna be cold.

Walter (*straightening up from her and looking off*). That's it. There you are. Man say to his woman: I got me a dream. His woman say: Eat your eggs. (*Sadly, but gaining in power.*) Man say: I got to take hold of this here world, baby! And a woman will say: Eat your eggs and go to work. (*Passionately now.*) Man say: I got to change my life, I'm choking to death, baby! And his woman say— (*In utter anguish as he brings his fists down on his thighs.*)—Your eggs is getting cold!

Ruth (*softly*). Walter, that ain't none of our money.

Walter (*not listening at all or even looking at her*). This morning, I was lookin' in the mirror and thinking about it . . . I'm thirty-five years old; I been married eleven years and I got a boy who sleeps in the living room—(*Very, very quietly.*)—and all I got to give him is stories about how rich white people live . . .

Ruth. Eat your eggs, Walter.

Walter (*slams the table and jumps up*). —DAMN MY EGGS—DAMN ALL THE EGGS THAT EVER WAS!

Ruth. Then go to work.

Walter (*looking up at her*). See—I'm trying to talk to you 'bout myself—(*Shaking his head with the repetition.*)—and all you can say is eat them eggs and go to work.

Ruth (*wearily*). Honey, you never say nothing new. I listen to you every day, every night and every morning, and you never say nothing new. (*Shrugging.*) So you would rather *be* Mr. Arnold than be his chauffeur. So—I would *rather* be living in Buckingham Palace.

Walter. That is just what is wrong with the colored woman in this world . . . Don't understand about building their men up and making 'em feel like they somebody. Like they can do something.

Ruth (*drily, but to hurt*). There *are* colored men who do things.

Walter. No thanks to the colored woman.

Ruth. Well, being a colored woman, I guess I can't help myself none.

She rises and gets the ironing board and sets it up and attacks a huge pile of rough-dried clothes, sprinkling them in preparation for the ironing and then rolling them into tight fat balls.

Walter (*mumbling*). We one group of men tied to a race of women with small minds!

His sister Beneatha enters. She is about twenty, as slim and intense as her brother. She is not as pretty as her sister-in-law, but her lean, almost intellectual face has a handsomeness of its own. She wears a bright-red flannel nightie, and her thick hair stands wildly about her head. Her speech is a mixture of many things; it is different from the rest of the family's insofar as education has permeated her sense of English—and perhaps the Midwest rather than the South has finally—at last—won out in her inflection; but not altogether, because over all of it is a soft slurring and transformed use of vowels which is the decided influence of the Southside. She passes through the room without looking at either Ruth or Walter and goes to the outside door and looks, a little blindly, out to the bathroom. She sees that it has been lost to the Johnsons. She closes the door with a sleepy vengeance and crosses to the table and sits down a little defeated.

Beneatha. I am going to start timing those people.

Walter. You should get up earlier.

Beneatha *(her face in her hands. She is still fighting the urge to go back to bed).* Really—would you suggest dawn? Where's the paper?

Walter *(pushing the paper across the table to her as he studies her almost clinically, as though he has never seen her before).* You a horrible-looking chick at this hour.

Beneatha *(drily).* Good morning, everybody.

Walter *(senselessly).* How is school coming?

Beneatha *(in the same spirit).* Lovely. Lovely. And you know, biology is the greatest. *(Looking up at him.)* I dissected something that looked just like you yesterday.

Walter. I just wondered if you've made up your mind and everything.

Beneatha *(gaining in sharpness and impatience).* And what did I answer yesterday morning—and the day before that?

Ruth *(from the ironing board, like someone disinterested and old).* Don't be so nasty, Bennie.

Beneatha *(still to her brother).* And the day before that and the day before that!

Walter *(defensively).* I'm interested in you. Something wrong with that? Ain't many girls who decide—

Walter and Beneatha *(in unison).* —"to be a doctor."

Silence.

Walter. Have we figured out yet just exactly how much medical school is going to cost?

Ruth. Walter Lee, why don't you leave that girl alone and get out of here to work?

Beneatha *(exits to the bathroom and bangs on the door).* Come on out of there, please!

She comes back into the room.

Walter *(looking at his sister intently).* You know the check is coming tomorrow.

Beneatha *(turning on him with a sharpness all her own).* That money belongs to Mama, Walter, and it's for her to decide how she wants to use it. I don't care if she wants to buy a house or a rocket ship or just nail it up somewhere and look at it. It's hers. Not ours—*hers.*

Walter *(bitterly).* Now ain't that fine! You just got your mother's interest at heart, ain't you, girl? You such a nice girl—but if Mama got that money she can always take a few thousand and help you through school too—can't she?

Beneatha. I have never asked anyone around here to do anything for me!

Walter. No! And the line between asking and just accepting when the time comes is big and wide—ain't it!

Beneatha *(with fury).* What do you want from me, Brother—that I quit school or just drop dead, which!

Walter. I don't want nothing but for you to stop acting holy 'round here. Me and Ruth done made some sacrifices for you—why can't you do something for the family?

Ruth. Walter, don't be dragging me in it.

Walter. You are in it—Don't you get up and go work in somebody's kitchen for the last three years to help put clothes on her back?

Ruth. Oh, Walter—that's not fair . . .

Walter. It ain't that nobody expects you to get on your knees and say thank you, Brother; thank you, Ruth; thank you, Mama—and thank you, Travis, for wearing the same pair of shoes for two semesters—

Beneatha *(dropping to her knees).* Well—I *do*—all right?—thank everybody! And forgive me for ever wanting to be anything at all! *(Pursuing him on her knees across the floor.)* FORGIVE ME, FORGIVE ME, FORGIVE ME!

Ruth. Please stop it! Your mama'll hear you.

Walter. Who the hell told you you had to be a doctor? If you so crazy 'bout messing 'round with sick people—then go be a nurse like other women—or just get married and be quiet . . .

Beneatha. Well—you finally got it said . . . It took you three years but you finally got it said. Walter, give up; leave me alone—it's Mama's money.

Walter. *He was my father, too!*

Beneatha. So what? He was mine, too—and Travis's grandfather—but the insurance money belongs to Mama. Picking on me is not going to make her give it to you to invest in any liquor stores—*(Under breath, dropping into a chair.)*—and I for one say, God bless Mama for that!

Walter *(to Ruth).* See—did you hear? Did you hear!

Ruth. Honey, please go to work.

Walter. Nobody in this house is ever going to understand me.

Beneatha. Because you're a nut.

Walter. Who's a nut?

Beneatha. You—you are a nut. Thee is mad, boy.

Walter *(looking at his wife and his sister from the door, very sadly).* The world's most backward race of people, and that's a fact.

Beneatha *(turning slowly in her chair).* And then there are all those prophets who would lead us out of the wilderness—*(Walter slams out of the house.)*—into the swamps!

Ruth. Bennie, why you always gotta be pickin' on your brother? Can't you be a little sweeter sometimes? *(Door opens. Walter walks in. He fumbles with his cap, starts to speak, clears throat, looks everywhere but at Ruth. Finally:)*

Walter *(to Ruth).* I need some money for carfare.

Ruth *(looks at him, then warms; teasing, but tenderly).* Fifty cents? *(She goes to her bag and gets money.)* Here—take a taxi!

Walter exits. Mama enters. She is a woman in her early sixties, full-bodied and strong. She is one of those women of a certain grace and beauty who wear it so unobtrusively that it takes a while to notice. Her dark-brown face is surrounded by the total whiteness of her hair, and, being a woman who has adjusted to many things in life and overcome many more, her face is full of strength. She has, we can see, wit and faith of a kind that keep her eyes lit and full of interest and expectancy. She is, in a word, a beautiful woman. Her bearing is perhaps most like the noble bearing of the women of the Hereros of Southwest Africa—rather as if she imagines that as she walks she still bears a basket or a vessel upon her head. Her speech, on the other hand, is as careless as her carriage is precise—she is inclined to slur everything—but her voice is perhaps not so much quiet as simply soft.

Mama. Who that 'round here slamming doors at this hour?

She crosses through the room, goes to the window, opens it, and brings in a feeble little plant growing doggedly in a small pot on the window sill. She feels the dirt and puts it back out.

Ruth. That was Walter Lee. He and Bennie was at it again.

Mama. My children and they tempers. Lord, if this little old plant don't get more sun than it's been getting it ain't never going to see spring again. (*She turns from the window.*) What's the matter with you this morning, Ruth? You looks right peaked. You aiming to iron all them things? Leave some for me. I'll get to 'em this afternoon. Bennie honey, it's too drafty for you to be sitting 'round half dressed. Where's your robe?

Beneatha. In the cleaners.

Mama. Well, go get mine and put it on.

Beneatha. I'm not cold, Mama, honest.

Mama. I know—but you so thin . . .

Beneatha (*irritably*). Mama, I'm not cold.

Mama (*seeing the make-down bed as Travis has left it*). Lord have mercy, look at that poor bed. Bless his heart—he tries, don't he?

She moves to the bed Travis has sloppily made up.

Ruth. No—he don't half try at all 'cause he knows you going to come along behind him and fix everything. That's just how come he don't know how to do nothing right now—you done spoiled that boy so.

Mama (*folding bedding*). Well—he's a little boy. Ain't supposed to know 'bout housekeeping. My baby, that's what he is. What you fix for his breakfast this morning?

Ruth (*angrily*). I feed my son, Lena!

Mama. I ain't meddling—(*Under breath; busy-bodyish.*) I just noticed all last week he had cold cereal, and when it starts getting this chilly in the fall a child ought to have some hot grits or something when he goes out in the cold—

Ruth (*furious*). I gave him hot oats—is that all right!

Mama. I ain't meddling. (*Pause.*) Put a lot of nice butter on it? (*Ruth shoots her an angry look and does not reply.*) He likes lots of butter.

Ruth (exasperated). Lena—

Mama (to Beneatha. Mama is inclined to wander conversationally sometimes). What was you and your brother fussing 'bout this morning?

Beneatha. It's not important, Mama.

She gets up and goes to look out at the bathroom, which is apparently free, and she picks up her towels and rushes out.

Mama. What was they fighting about?

Ruth. Now you know as well as I do.

Mama (shaking her head). Brother still worrying hisself sick about that money?

Ruth. You know he is.

Mama. You had breakfast?

Ruth. Some coffee.

Mama. Girl, you better start eating and looking after yourself better. You almost thin as Travis.

Ruth. Lena—

Mama. Un-hunh?

Ruth. What are you going to do with it?

Mama. Now don't you start, child. It's too early in the morning to be talking about money. It ain't Christian.

Ruth. It's just that he got his heart set on that store—

Mama. You mean that liquor store that Willy Harris want him to invest in?

Ruth. Yes—

Mama. We ain't no business people, Ruth. We just plain working folks.

Ruth. Ain't nobody business people till they go into business. Walter Lee say colored people ain't never going to start getting ahead till they start gambling on some different kinds of things in the world—investments and things.

Mama. What done got into you, girl? Walter Lee done finally sold you on investing.

Ruth. No. Mama, something is happening between Walter and me. I don't know what it is—but he needs something—something I can't give him any more. He needs this chance, Lena.

Mama (frowning deeply). But liquor, honey—

Ruth. Well—like Walter say—I spec people going to always be drinking themselves some liquor.

Mama. Well—whether they drinks it or not ain't none of my business. But whether I go into business selling it to 'em *is*, and I don't want that on my ledger this late in life. (Stopping suddenly and studying her daughter-in-law.) Ruth Younger, what's the matter with you today? You look like you could fall over right there.

Ruth. I'm tired.

Mama. Then you better stay home from work today.

Ruth. I can't stay home. She'd be calling up the agency and screaming at them, "My girl didn't come in today—send me somebody! My girl didn't come in!" Oh, she just have a fit . . .

Mama. Well, let her have it. I'll just call her up and say you got the flu—

Ruth *(laughing).* Why the flu?

Mama. 'Cause it sounds respectable to 'em. Something white people get, too. They know 'bout the flu. Otherwise they think you been cut up or something when you tell 'em you sick.

Ruth. I got to go in. We need the money.

Mama. Somebody would of thought my children done all but starved to death the way they talk about money here late. Child, we got a great big old check coming tomorrow.

Ruth *(sincerely, but also self-righteously).* Now that's your money. It ain't got nothing to do with me. We all feel like that—Walter and Bennie and me—even Travis.

Mama *(thoughtfully, and suddenly very far away).* Ten thousand dollars—

Ruth. Sure is wonderful.

Mama. Ten thousand dollars.

Ruth. You know what you should do, Miss Lena? You should take yourself a trip somewhere. To Europe or South America or someplace—

Mama *(throwing up her hands at the thought).* Oh, child!

Ruth. I'm serious. Just pack up and leave! Go on away and enjoy yourself some. Forget about the family and have yourself a ball for once in your life—

Mama *(drily).* You sound like I'm just about ready to die. Who'd go with me? What I look like wandering 'round Europe by myself?

Ruth. Shoot—these here rich white women do it all the time. They don't think nothing of packing up they suitcases and piling on one of them big steamships and—swoosh!—they gone, child.

Mama. Something always told me I wasn't no rich white woman.

Ruth. Well—what are you going to do with it then?

Mama. I ain't rightly decided. *(Thinking. She speaks now with emphasis.)* Some of it got to be put away for Beneatha and her schoolin'—and ain't nothing going to touch that part of it. Nothing. *(She waits several seconds, trying to make up her mind about something, and looks at Ruth a little tentatively before going on.)* Been thinking that we maybe could meet the notes on a little old two-story somewhere, with a yard where Travis could play in the summertime, if we use part of the insurance for a down payment and everybody kind of pitch in. I could maybe take on a little day work again, few days a week—

Ruth *(studying her mother-in-law furtively and concentrating on her ironing, anxious to encourage without seeming to).* Well, Lord knows, we've put enough rent into this here rat trap to pay for four houses by now . . .

Mama *(looking up at the words "rat trap" and then looking around and leaning back and sighing—in a suddenly reflective mood—).* "Rat trap"—yes, that's all it is. *(Smiling.)* I remember just as well the day me and Big Walter moved in here. Hadn't been married but two weeks and wasn't planning on living here no more than a year. *(She shakes her head at the dissolved dream.)* We was going to set away, little by little, don't you know, and buy a little place out in Morgan Park. We had even picked out the house. *(Chuckling a little.)* Looks right dumpy today. But Lord, child, you should know all the dreams I had 'bout buying that house and fixing it up and making me a little garden in the back—*(She waits and stops smiling.)* And didn't none of it happen.

Dropping her hands in a futile gesture.

Ruth *(keeps her head down, ironing).* Yes, life can be a barrel of disappointments, sometimes.

Mama. Honey, Big Walter would come in here some nights back then and slump down on that couch there and just look at the rug, and look at me and look at the rug and then back at me—and I'd know he was down then . . . really down. *(After a second very long and thoughtful pause; she is seeing back to times that only she can see.)* And then, Lord, when I lost that baby—little Claude—I almost thought I was going to lose Big Walter too. Oh, that man grieved hisself! He was one man to love his children.

Ruth. Ain't nothin' can tear at you like losin' your baby.

Mama. I guess that's how come that man finally worked hisself to death like he done. Like he was fighting his own war with this here world that took his baby from him.

Ruth. He sure was a fine man, all right. I always liked Mr. Younger.

Mama. Crazy 'bout his children! God knows there was plenty wrong with Walter Younger—hard-headed, mean, kind of wild with women—plenty wrong with him. But he sure loved his children. Always wanted them to have something—be something. That's where Brother gets all these notions, I reckon. Big Walter used to say, he'd get right wet in the eyes sometimes, lean his head back with the water standing in his eyes and say, "Seem like God didn't see fit to give the black man nothing but dreams—but He did give us children to make them dreams seem worthwhile." *(She smiles.)* He could talk like that, don't you know.

Ruth. Yes, he sure could. He was a good man, Mr. Younger.

Mama. Yes, a fine man—just couldn't never catch up with his dreams, that's all.

Beneatha comes in, brushing her hair and looking up to the ceiling, where the sound of a vacuum cleaner has started up.

Beneatha. What could be so dirty on that woman's rugs that she has to vacuum them every single day?

Ruth. I wish certain young women 'round here who I could name would take inspiration about certain rugs in a certain apartment I could also mention.

Beneatha *(shrugging).* How much cleaning can a house need, for Christ's sakes.

Mama *(not liking the Lord's name used thus).* Bennie!

Ruth. Just listen to her—just listen!

Beneatha. Oh, God!

Mama. If you use the Lord's name just one more time—

Beneatha *(a bit of a whine).* Oh, Mama—

Ruth. Fresh—just fresh as salt, this girl!

Beneatha *(drily).* Well—if the salt loses its savor—

Mama. Now that will do. I just ain't going to have you 'round here reciting the scriptures in vain—you hear me?

Beneatha. How did I manage to get on everybody's wrong side by just walking into a room?

Ruth. If you weren't so fresh—

Beneatha. Ruth, I'm twenty years old.

Mama. What time you be home from school today?

Beneatha. Kind of late. *(With enthusiasm.)* Madeline is going to start my guitar lessons today.

Mama and Ruth look up with the same expression.

Mama. Your *what* kind of lessons?

Beneatha. Guitar.

Ruth. Oh, Father!

Mama. How come you done taken it in your mind to learn to play the guitar?

Beneatha. I just want to, that's all.

Mama *(smiling).* Lord, child, don't you know what to do with yourself? How long it going to be before you get tired of this now—like you got tired of that little play-acting group you joined last year? *(Looking at Ruth.)* And what was it the year before that?

Ruth. The horseback-riding club for which she bought that fifty-five-dollar riding habit that's been hanging in the closet ever since!

Mama *(to Beneatha).* Why you got to flit so from one thing to another, baby?

Beneatha *(sharply).* I just want to learn to play the guitar. Is there anything wrong with that?

Mama. Ain't nobody trying to stop you. I just wonders sometimes why you has to flit so from one thing to another all the time. You ain't never done nothing with all that camera equipment you brought home—

Beneatha. I don't flit! I—I experiment with different forms of expression—

Ruth. Like riding a horse?

Beneatha. —People have to express themselves one way or another.

Mama. What is it you want to express?

Beneatha *(angrily).* Me! *(Mama and Ruth look at each other and burst into raucous laughter.)* Don't worry—I don't expect you to understand.

Mama *(to change the subject).* Who you going out with tomorrow night?

Beneatha *(with displeasure).* George Murchison again.

Mama *(pleased).* Oh—you getting a little sweet on him?

Ruth. You ask me, this child ain't sweet on nobody but herself—*(Under breath.)* Express herself!

They laugh.

Beneatha. Oh—I like George all right, Mama. I mean I like him enough to go out with him and stuff, but—

Ruth *(for devilment).* What does *and stuff* mean?

Beneatha. Mind your own business.

Mama. Stop picking at her now, Ruth. *(She chuckles—then a suspicious sudden look at her daughter as she turns in her chair for emphasis.)* What DOES it mean?

Beneatha *(wearily).* Oh, I just mean I couldn't ever really be serious about George. He's—he's so shallow.

Ruth. Shallow—what do you mean he's shallow? He's *rich!*

Mama. Hush, Ruth.

Beneatha. I know he's rich. He knows he's rich, too.

Ruth. Well—what other qualities a man got to have to satisfy you, little girl?

Beneatha. You wouldn't even begin to understand. Anybody who married Walter could not possibly understand.

Mama *(outraged).* What kind of way is that to talk about your brother?

Beneatha. Brother is a flip—let's face it.

Mama *(to Ruth, helplessly).* What's a flip?

Ruth *(glad to add kindling).* She's saying he's crazy.

Beneatha. Not crazy. Brother isn't really crazy yet—he—he's an elaborate neurotic.

Mama. Hush your mouth!

Beneatha. As for George. Well. George looks good—he's got a beautiful car and he takes me to nice places and, as my sister-in-law says, he is probably the richest boy I will ever get to know and I even like him sometimes—but if the Youngers are sitting around waiting to see if their little Bennie is going to tie up the family with the Murchisons, they are wasting their time.

Ruth. You mean you wouldn't marry George Murchison if he asked you someday? That pretty, rich thing? Honey, I knew you was odd—

Beneatha. No I would not marry him if all I felt for him was what I feel now. Besides, George's family wouldn't really like it.

Mama. Why not?

Beneatha. Oh, Mama—The Murchisons are honest-to-God-real-*live*-rich colored people, and the only people in the world who are more snobbish than rich white people are rich colored people. I thought everybody knew that. I've met Mrs. Murchison. She's a scene!

Mama. You must not dislike people 'cause they well off, honey.

Beneatha. Why not? It makes just as much sense as disliking people 'cause they are poor, and lots of people do that.

Ruth *(a wisdom-of-the-ages manner. To Mama).* Well, she'll get over some of this—

Beneatha. Get over it? What are you talking about, Ruth? Listen, I'm going to be a doctor. I'm not worried about who I'm going to marry yet—if I ever get married.

Mama and Ruth. *If!*

Mama. Now, Bennie—

Beneatha. Oh, I probably will . . . but first I'm going to be a doctor, and George, for one, still thinks that's pretty funny. I couldn't be bothered with that. I am going to be a doctor and everybody around here better understand that!

Mama *(kindly).* 'Course you going to be a doctor, honey, God willing.

Beneatha *(drily).* God hasn't got a thing to do with it.

Mama. Beneatha—that just wasn't necessary.

Beneatha. Well—neither is God. I get sick of hearing about God.

Mama. Beneatha!

Beneatha. I mean it! I'm just tired of hearing about God all the time. What has He got to do with anything? Does He pay tuition?

Mama. You 'bout to get your fresh little jaw slapped!

Ruth. That's just what she needs, all right!

Beneatha. Why? Why can't I say what I want to around here, like everybody else?

Mama. It don't sound nice for a young girl to say things like that—you wasn't brought up that way. Me and your father went to trouble to get you and Brother to church every Sunday.

Beneatha. Mama, you don't understand. It's all a matter of ideas, and God is just one idea I don't accept. It's not important. I am not going out and be immoral or commit crimes because I don't believe in God. I don't even think about it. It's just that I get tired of Him getting credit for all the things the human race achieves through its own stubborn effort. There simply is no blasted God— there is only man and it is He who makes miracles!

Mama absorbs this speech, studies her daughter, and rises slowly and crosses to Beneatha and slaps her powerfully across the face. After, there is only silence and the daughter drops her eyes from her mother's face, and Mama is very tall before her.

Mama. Now—you say after me, in my mother's house there is still God. *(There is a long pause and Beneatha stares at the floor wordlessly. Mama repeats the phrase with precision and cool emotion.)* In my mother's house there is still God.

Beneatha. In my mother's house there is still God.

A long pause.

Mama *(walking away from Beneatha, too disturbed for triumphant posture. Stopping and turning back to her daughter).* There are some ideas we ain't going to have in this house. Not long as I am at the head of this family.

Beneatha. Yes, ma'am.

Mama walks out of the room.

Ruth *(almost gently, with profound understanding).* You think you a woman, Bennie—but you still a little girl. What you did was childish—so you got treated like a child.

Beneatha. I see. *(Quietly.)* I also see that everybody thinks it's all right for Mama to be a tyrant. But all the tyranny in the world will never put a God in the heavens!

She picks up her books and goes out. Pause.

Ruth (*goes to Mama's door*). She said she was sorry.

Mama (*coming out, going to her plant*). They frightens me, Ruth. My children.

Ruth. You got good children, Lena. They just a little off sometimes—but they're good.

Mama. No—there's something come down between me and them that don't let us understand each other and I don't know what it is. One done almost lost his mind thinking 'bout money all the time and the other done commence to talk about things I can't seem to understand in no form or fashion. What is it that's changing, Ruth?

Ruth (*soothingly, older than her years*). Now . . . you taking it all too seriously. You just got strong-willed children and it takes a strong woman like you to keep 'em in hand.

Mama (*looking at her plant and sprinkling a little water on it*). They spirited all right, my children. Got to admit they got spirit—Bennie and Walter. Like this little old plant that ain't never had enough sunshine or nothing—and look at it . . .

She has her back to Ruth, who has had to stop ironing and lean against something and put the back of her hand to her forehead.

Ruth (*trying to keep Mama from noticing*). You . . . sure . . . loves that little old thing, don't you? . . .

Mama. Well, I always wanted me a garden like I used to see sometimes at the back of the houses down home. This plant is close as I ever got to having one. (*She looks out of the window as she replaces the plant.*) Lord, ain't nothing as dreary as the view from this window on a dreary day, is there? Why ain't you singing this morning, Ruth? Sing that "No Ways Tired." That song always lifts me up so—(*She turns at last to see that Ruth has slipped quietly to the floor, in a state of semiconsciousness.*) Ruth! Ruth honey—what's the matter with you . . . Ruth!

Curtain.

Scene 2. (*The following morning.*)

It is the following morning; a Saturday morning, and house cleaning is in progress at the Youngers'. Furniture has been shoved hither and yon and Mama is giving the kitchen-area walls a washing down. Beneatha, in dungarees, with a handkerchief tied around her face, is spraying insecticide into the cracks in the walls. As they work, the radio is on and a Southside disk-jockey program is inappropriately filling the house with a rather exotic saxophone blues. Travis, the sole idle one, is leaning on his arms, looking out of the window.

Travis. Grandmama, that stuff Bennie is using smells awful. Can I go downstairs, please?

Mama. Did you get all them chores done already? I ain't seen you doing much.

Travis. Yes'm—finished early. Where did Mama go this morning?

Mama (*looking at Beneatha*). She had to go on a little errand.

The phone rings. Beneatha runs to answer it and reaches it before Walter, who has entered from bedroom.

Travis. Where?

Mama. To tend to her business.

Beneatha. Haylo . . . (*Disappointed.*) Yes, he is. (*She tosses the phone to Walter, who barely catches it.*) It's Willie Harris again.

Walter (*as privately as possible under Mama's gaze*). Hello, Willie. Did you get the papers from the lawyer? . . . No, not yet. I told you the mailman doesn't get here till ten-thirty . . . No, I'll come there . . . Yeah! Right away. (*He hangs up and goes for his coat.*)

Beneatha. Brother, where did Ruth go?

Walter (*as he exits*). How should I know!

Travis. Aw come on, Grandma. Can I go outside?

Mama. Oh, I guess so. You stay right in front of the house, though, and keep a good lookout for the postman.

Travis. Yes'm. (*He darts into bedroom for stickball and bat, reenters, and sees Beneatha on her knees spraying under sofa with behind upraised. He edges closer to the target, takes aim, and lets her have it. She screams.*) Leave them poor little cockroaches alone, they ain't bothering you none! (*He runs as she swings the spraygun at him viciously and playfully.*) Grandma! Grandma!

Mama. Look out there, girl, before you be spilling some of that stuff on that child!

Travis (*safely behind the bastion of Mama*). That's right—look out, now! (*He exits.*)

Beneatha (*drily*). I can't imagine that it would hurt him—it has never hurt the roaches.

Mama. Well, little boys' hides ain't as tough as Southside roaches. You better get over there behind the bureau. I seen one marching out of there like Napoleon yesterday.

Beneatha. There's really only one way to get rid of them, Mama—

Mama. How?

Beneatha. Set fire to this building! Mama, where did Ruth go?

Mama (*looking at her with meaning*). To the doctor, I think.

Beneatha. The doctor? What's the matter? (*They exchange glances.*) You don't think—

Mama (*with her sense of drama*). Now I ain't saying what I think. But I ain't never been wrong 'bout a woman neither.

The phone rings.

Beneatha (*at the phone*). Hay-lo . . . (*Pause, and a moment of recognition.*) Well—when did you get back! . . . And how was it? . . . Of course I've missed you—in my way . . . This morning? No . . . house cleaning and all that and Mama hates it if I let people come over when the house is like this . . . You *have*?

Well, that's different . . . What is it—Oh, what the hell, come on over . . . Right, see you then. *Arrivederci.*

She hangs up.

Mama (*who has listened vigorously, as is her habit*). Who is that you inviting over here with this house looking like this? You ain't got the pride you was born with!

Beneatha. Asagai doesn't care how houses look, Mama—he's an intellectual.

Mama. *Who?*

Beneatha. Asagai—Joseph Asagai. He's an African boy I met on campus. He's been studying in Canada all summer.

Mama. What's his name?

Beneatha. Asagai, Joseph. Ah-sah-guy . . . He's from Nigeria.

Mama. Oh, that's the little country that was founded by slaves way back . . .

Beneatha. No, Mama—that's Liberia.

Mama. I don't think I never met no African before.

Beneatha. Well, do me a favor and don't ask him a whole lot of ignorant questions about Africans. I mean, do they wear clothes and all that—

Mama. Well, now, I guess if you think we so ignorant 'round here maybe you shouldn't bring your friends here—

Beneatha. It's just that people ask such crazy things. All anyone seems to know about when it comes to Africa is Tarzan—

Mama (*indignantly*). Why should I know anything about Africa?

Beneatha. Why do you give money at church for the missionary work?

Mama. Well, that's to help save people.

Beneatha. You mean save them from *heathenism*—

Mama (*innocently*). Yes.

Beneatha. I'm afraid they need more salvation from the British and the French.

Ruth comes in forlornly and pulls off her coat with dejection. They both turn to look at her.

Ruth (*dispiritedly*). Well, I guess from all the happy faces—everybody knows.

Beneatha. You pregnant?

Mama. Lord have mercy, I sure hope it's a little old girl. Travis ought to have a sister.

Beneatha and Ruth give her a hopeless look for this grandmotherly enthusiasm.

Beneatha. How far along are you?

Ruth. Two months.

Beneatha. Did you mean to? I mean did you plan it or was it an accident?

Mama. What do you know about planning or not planning?

Beneatha. Oh, Mama.

Ruth (*wearily*). She's twenty years old, Lena.

Beneatha. Did you plan it, Ruth?

Ruth. Mind your own business.

Beneatha. It is my business—where is he going to live, on the *roof*? *(There is silence following the remark as the three women react to the sense of it.)* Gee—I didn't mean that, Ruth, honest. Gee, I don't feel like that at all. I—I think it is wonderful.

Ruth *(dully)*. Wonderful.

Beneatha. Yes—really.

Mama *(looking at Ruth, worried)*. Doctor say everything going to be all right?

Ruth *(far away)*. Yes—she says everything is going to be fine . . .

Mama *(immediately suspicious)*. "She"—What doctor you went to?

Ruth folds over, near hysteria.

Mama *(worriedly hovering over Ruth)*. Ruth honey—what's the matter with you— you sick?

Ruth has her fists clenched on her thighs and is fighting hard to suppress a scream that seems to be rising in her.

Beneatha. What's the matter with her, Mama?

Mama *(working her fingers in Ruth's shoulders to relax her)*. She be all right. Women gets right depressed sometimes when they get her way. *(Speaking softly, expertly, rapidly.)* Now you just relax. That's right . . . just lean back, don't think 'bout nothing at all . . . nothing at all—

Ruth. I'm all right . . .

The glassy-eyed look melts and then she collapses into a fit of heavy sobbing. The bell rings.

Beneatha. Oh, my God—that must be Asagai.

Mama *(to Ruth)*. Come on now, honey. You need to lie down and rest awhile . . . then have some nice hot food.

They exit, Ruth's weight on her mother-in-law. Beneatha, herself profoundly disturbed, opens the door to admit a rather dramatic-looking young man with a large package.

Asagai. Hello, Alaiyo—

Beneatha *(holding the door open and regarding him with pleasure)*. Hello . . . *(Long pause.)* Well—come in. And please excuse everything. My mother was very upset about my letting anyone come here with the place like this.

Asagai *(coming into the room)*. You look disturbed too . . . Is something wrong?

Beneatha *(still at the door, absently)*. Yes . . . we've all got acute ghetto-itus. *(She smiles and comes toward him, finding a cigarette and sitting.)* So—sit down! No!

Wait! (*She whips the spraygun off sofa where she had left it and puts the cushions back. At last perches on arm of sofa. He sits.*) So, how was Canada?

Asagai (*a sophisticate*). Canadian.

Beneatha (*looking at him*). Asagai, I'm very glad you are back.

Asagai (*looking back at her in turn*). Are you really?

Beneatha. Yes—very.

Asagai. Why?—you were quite glad when I went away. What happened?

Beneatha. You went away.

Asagai. Ahhhhhhhh.

Beneatha. Before—you wanted to be so serious before there was time.

Asagai. How much time must there be before one knows what one feels?

Beneatha (*stalling this particular conversation. Her hands pressed together, in a deliberately childish gesture*). What did you bring me?

Asagai (*handing her the package*). Open it and see.

Beneatha (*eagerly opening the package and drawing out some records and the colorful robes of a Nigerian woman*). Oh Asagai! . . . You got them for me! . . . How beautiful . . . and the records too! (*She lifts out the robes and runs to the mirror with them and holds the drapery up in front of herself.*)

Asagai (*coming to her at the mirror*). I shall have to teach you how to drape it properly. (*He flings the material about her for the moment and stands back to look at her.*) Ah—Oh-pay-gay-day, oh-gbah-mu-shay. (*A Yoruba exclamation for admiration.*) You wear it well . . . very well . . . mutilated hair and all.

Beneatha (*turning suddenly*). My hair—what's wrong with my hair?

Asagai (*shrugging*). Were you born with it like that?

Beneatha (*reaching up to touch it*). No . . . of course not.

She looks back to the mirror, disturbed.

Asagai (*smiling*). How then?

Beneatha. You know perfectly well how . . . as crinkly as yours . . . that's how.

Asagai. And it is ugly to you that way?

Beneatha (*quickly*). Oh, no—not ugly . . . (*More slowly, apologetically.*) But it's so hard to manage when it's, well—raw.

Asagai. And so to accommodate that—you mutilate it every week?

Beneatha. It's not mutilation!

Asagai (*laughing aloud at her seriousness*). Oh . . . please! I am only teasing you because you are so very serious about these things. (*He stands back from her and folds his arms across his chest as he watches her pulling at her hair and frowning in the mirror.*) Do you remember the first time you met me at school? . . . (*He laughs.*) You came up to me and you said—and I thought you were the most serious little thing I had ever seen—you said: (*He imitates her.*) "Mr. Asagai—I want very much to talk with you. About Africa. You see, Mr. Asagai, I am looking for my *identity!*"

He laughs.

Beneatha (*turning to him, not laughing*). Yes—

Her face is quizzical, profoundly disturbed.

Asagai (*still teasing and reaching out and taking her face in his hands and turning her profile to him*). Well . . . it is true that this is not so much a profile of a Hollywood queen as perhaps a queen of the Nile—(*A mock dismissal of the importance of the question.*) But what does it matter? Assimilationism is so popular in your country.

Beneatha (*wheeling, passionately, sharply*). I am not an assimilationist!

Asagai (*the protest hangs in the room for a moment and Asagai studies her, his laughter fading*). Such a serious one. (*There is a pause.*) So—you like the robes? You must take excellent care of them—they are from my sister's personal wardrobe.

Beneatha (*with incredulity*). You—you sent all the way home—for me?

Asagai (*with charm*). For you—I would do much more . . . Well, that is what I came for. I must go.

Beneatha. Will you call me Monday?

Asagai. Yes . . . We have a great deal to talk about. I mean about identity and time and all that.

Beneatha. Time?

Asagai. Yes. About how much time one needs to know what one feels.

Beneatha. You see! You never understood that there is more than one kind of feeling which can exist between a man and a woman—or, at least, there should be.

Asagai (*shaking his head negatively but gently*). No. Between a man and a woman there need be only one kind of feeling. I have that for you . . . Now even . . . right this moment . . .

Beneatha. I know—and by itself—it won't do. I can find that anywhere.

Asagai. For a woman it should be enough.

Beneatha. I know—because that's what it says in all the novels that men write. But it isn't. Go ahead and laugh—but I'm not interested in being someone's little episode in America or—(*With feminine vengeance.*)—one of them! (*Asagai has burst into laughter again.*) That's funny as hell, huh!

Asagai. It's just that every American girl I have known has said that to me. White—black—in this you are all the same. And the same speech, too!

Beneatha (*angrily*). Yuk, yuk, yuk!

Asagai. It's how you can be sure that the world's most liberated women are not liberated at all. You all talk about it too much!

Mama enters and is immediately all social charm because of the presence of a guest.

Beneatha. Oh—Mama—this is Mr. Asagai.

Mama. How do you do?

Asagai (*total politeness to an elder*). How do you do, Mrs. Younger. Please forgive me for coming at such an outrageous hour on a Saturday.

Mama. Well, you are quite welcome. I just hope you understand that our house don't always look like this. (*Chatterish.*) You must come again. I would love to hear all about—(*Not sure of the name.*)—your country. I think it's so sad the way our American Negroes don't know nothing about Africa 'cept Tarzan and all that. And all that money they pour into these churches when they ought to be helping you people over there drive out them French and Englishmen done taken away your land.

The mother flashes a slightly superior look at her daughter upon completion of the recitation.

Asagai (*taken aback by this sudden and acutely unrelated expression of sympathy*). Yes . . . yes . . .

Mama (*smiling at him suddenly and relaxing and looking him over*). How many miles is it from here to where you come from?

Asagai. Many thousands.

Mama (*looking at him as she would Walter*). I bet you don't half look after yourself, being away from your mama either. I spec you better come 'round here from time to time to get yourself some decent homecooked meals . . .

Asagai (*moved*). Thank you. Thank you very much. (*They are all quiet, then—*) Well . . . I must go. I will call you Monday, Alaiyo.

Mama. What's that he call you?

Asagai. Oh—"Alaiyo." I hope you don't mind. It is what you would call a nickname, I think. It is a Yoruba word. I am a Yoruba.

Mama (*looking at Beneatha*). I—I thought he was from—(*Uncertain.*)

Asagai (*understanding*). Nigeria is my country. Yoruba is my tribal origin—

Beneatha. You didn't tell us what Alaiyo means . . . for all I know, you might be calling me Little Idiot or something . . .

Asagai. Well . . . let me see . . . I do not know how just to explain it . . . The sense of a thing can be so different when it changes languages.

Beneatha. You're evading.

Asagai. No—really it is difficult . . . (*Thinking.*) It means . . . it means One for Whom Bread—Food—Is Not Enough. (*He looks at her.*) Is that all right?

Beneatha (*understanding, softly*). Thank you.

Mama (*looking from one to the other and not understanding any of it*). Well . . . that's nice . . . You must come see us again—Mr.—

Asagai. Ah-sah-guy . . .

Mama. Yes . . . Do come again.

Asagai. Good-bye.

He exits.

Mama (*after him*). Lord, that's a pretty thing just went out here! (*Insinuatingly, to her daughter.*) Yes, I guess I see why we done commence to get so interested in Africa 'round here. Missionaries my aunt Jenny!

She exits.

Beneatha. Oh, Mama! . . .

She picks up the Nigerian dress and holds it up to her in front of the mirror again. She sets the headdress on haphazardly and then notices her hair again and clutches at it and then replaces the headdress and frowns at herself. Then she starts to wriggle in front of the mirror as she thinks a Nigerian woman might. Travis enters and stands regarding her.

Travis. What's the matter, girl, you cracking up?
Beneatha. Shut up.

She pulls the headdress off and looks at herself in the mirror and clutches at her hair again and squinches her eyes as if trying to imagine something. Then, suddenly, she gets her raincoat and kerchief and hurriedly prepares for going out.

Mama *(coming back into the room).* She's resting now. Travis, baby, run next door and ask Miss Johnson to please let me have a little kitchen cleanser. This here can is empty as Jacob's kettle.
Travis. I just came in.
Mama. Do as you told. *(He exits and she looks at her daughter.)* Where you going?
Beneatha *(halting at the door).* To become a queen of the Nile!

She exits in a breathless blaze of glory. Ruth appears in the bedroom doorway.

Mama. Who told you to get up?
Ruth. Ain't nothing wrong with me to be lying in no bed for. Where did Bennie go?
Mama *(drumming her fingers).* Far as I could make out—to Egypt. *(Ruth just looks at her.)* What time is it getting to?
Ruth. Ten twenty. And the mailman going to ring that bell this morning just like he done every morning for the last umpteen years.

Travis comes in with the cleanser can.

Travis. She say to tell you that she don't have much.
Mama *(angrily).* Lord, some people I could name sure is tight-fisted! *(Directing her grandson.)* Mark two cans of cleanser on the list there. If she that hard up for kitchen cleanser, I sure don't want to forget to get her none!
Ruth. Lena—maybe the woman is just short on cleanser—
Mama *(not listening).* —Much baking powder as she done borrowed from me all these years, she could of done gone into the baking business!

The bell sounds suddenly and sharply and all three are stunned—serious and silent—midspeech. In spite of all the other conversations and distractions of the morning, this is what they have been waiting for, even Travis, who looks helplessly from his mother to his grandmother. Ruth is the first to come to life again.

Ruth *(to Travis).* Get down them steps, boy!

Travis snaps to life and flies out to get the mail.

Mama *(her eyes wide, her hand to her breast).* You mean it done really come?

Ruth *(excited).* Oh, Miss Lena!

Mama *(collecting herself).* Well . . . I don't know what we all so excited about 'round here for. We known it was coming for months.

Ruth. That's a whole lot different from having it come and being able to hold it in your hands . . . a piece of paper worth ten thousand dollars . . . *(Travis bursts back into the room. He holds the envelope high above his head, like a little dancer, his face is radiant and he is breathless. He moves to his grandmother with sudden slow ceremony and puts the envelope into her hands. She accepts it, and then merely holds it and looks at it.)* Come on! Open it . . . Lord have mercy, I wish Walter Lee was here!

Travis. Open it, Grandmama!

Mama *(staring at it).* Now you all be quiet. It's just a check.

Ruth. Open it . . .

Mama *(still staring at it).* Now don't act silly . . . We ain't never been no people to act silly 'bout no money—

Ruth *(swiftly).* We ain't never had none before—OPEN IT!

Mama finally makes a good strong tear and pulls out the thin blue slice of paper and inspects it closely. The boy and his mother study it raptly over Mama's shoulders.

Mama. *Travis! (She is counting off with doubt.)* Is that the right number of zeros?

Travis. Yes'm . . . ten thousand dollars. Gaalee, Grandmama, you rich.

Mama *(She holds the check away from her, still looking at it. Slowly her face sobers into a mask of unhappiness).* Ten thousand dollars. *(She hands it to Ruth.)* Put it away somewhere, Ruth. *(She does not look at Ruth; her eyes seem to be seeing something somewhere very far off.)* Ten thousand dollars they give you. Ten thousand dollars.

Travis *(to his mother, sincerely).* What's the matter with Grandmama—don't she want to be rich?

Ruth *(distractedly).* You go on out and play now, baby. *(Travis exits. Mama starts wiping dishes absently, humming intently to herself. Ruth turns to her, with kind exasperation.)* You've gone and got yourself upset.

Mama *(not looking at her).* I spec if it wasn't for you all . . . I would just put that money away or give it to the church or something.

Ruth. Now what kind of talk is that. Mr. Younger would just be plain mad if he could hear you talking foolish like that.

Mama (*stopping and staring off*). Yes . . . he sure would. (*Sighing.*) We got enough to do with that money, all right. (*She halts then, and turns and looks at her daughter-in-law hard; Ruth avoids her eyes and Mama wipes her hands with finality and starts to speak firmly to Ruth.*) Where did you go today, girl?

Ruth. To the doctor.

Mama (*impatiently*). Now, Ruth . . . you know better than that. Old Doctor Jones is strange enough in his way but there ain't nothing 'bout him make somebody slip and call him "she"—like you done this morning.

Ruth. Well, that's what happened—my tongue slipped.

Mama. You went to see that woman, didn't you?

Ruth (*defensively, giving herself away*). What woman you talking about?

Mama (*angrily*). That woman who—

Walter enters in great excitement.

Walter. Did it come?

Mama (*quietly*). Can't you give people a Christian greeting before you start asking about money?

Walter (*to Ruth*). Did it come? (*Ruth unfolds the check and lays it quietly before him, watching him intently with thoughts of her own. Walter sits down and grasps it close and counts off the zeros.*) Ten thousand dollars—(*He turns suddenly, frantically to his mother and draws some papers out of his breast pocket.*) Mama—look. Old Willy Harris put everything on paper—

Mama. Son—I think you ought to talk to your wife . . . I'll go on out and leave you alone if you want—

Walter. I can talk to her later—Mama, look—

Mama. Son—

Walter. WILL SOMEBODY PLEASE LISTEN TO ME TODAY!

Mama (*quietly*). I don't 'low no yellin' in this house, Walter Lee, and you know it—(*Walter stares at them in frustration and starts to speak several times.*) And there ain't going to be no investing in no liquor stores.

Walter. But, Mama, you ain't even looked at it.

Mama. I don't aim to have to speak on that again.

A long pause.

Walter. You ain't looked at it and you don't aim to have to speak on that again? You ain't even looked at it and *you* have decided—(*Crumpling his papers.*) Well, *you* tell that to my boy tonight when you put him to sleep on the living-room couch . . . (*Turning to Mama and speaking directly to her.*) Yeah—and tell it to my wife, Mama, tomorrow when she has to go out of here to look after somebody else's kids. And tell it to *me*, Mama, every time we need a new pair of curtains and I have to watch *you* go out and work in somebody's kitchen. Yeah, you tell me then!

Walter starts out.

Ruth. Where you going?

Walter. I'm going out!

Ruth. Where?

Walter. Just out of this house somewhere—

Ruth *(getting her coat).* I'll come too.

Walter. I don't want you to come!

Ruth. I got something to talk to you about, Walter.

Walter. That's too bad.

Mama *(still quietly).* Walter Lee—*(She waits and he finally turns and looks at her.)* Sit down.

Walter. I'm a grown man, Mama.

Mama. Ain't nobody said you wasn't grown. But you still in my house and my presence. And as long as you are—you'll talk to your wife civil. Now sit down.

Ruth *(suddenly).* Oh, let him go on out and drink himself to death! He makes me sick to my stomach! *(She flings her coat against him and exits to bedroom.)*

Walter *(violently flinging the coat after her).* And you turn mine too, baby! *(The door slams behind her.)* That was my biggest mistake—

Mama *(still quietly).* Walter, what is the matter with you?

Walter. Matter with me? Ain't nothing the matter with *me!*

Mama. Yes there is. Something eating you up like a crazy man. Something more than me not giving you this money. The past few years I been watching it happen to you. You get all nervous acting and kind of wild in the eyes—*(Walter jumps up impatiently at her words.)* I said sit there now, I'm talking to you!

Walter. Mama—I don't need no nagging at me today.

Mama. Seem like you getting to a place where you always tied up in some kind of knot about something. But if anybody ask you 'bout it you just yell at 'em and bust out the house and go out and drink somewheres. Walter Lee, people can't live with that. Ruth's a good, patient girl in her way—but you getting to be too much. Boy, don't make the mistake of driving that girl away from you.

Walter. Why—what she do for me?

Mama. She loves you.

Walter. Mama—I'm going out. I want to go off somewhere and be by myself for a while.

Mama. I'm sorry 'bout your liquor store, son. It just wasn't the thing for us to do. That's what I want to tell you about—

Walter. I got to go out, Mama—

He rises.

Mama. It's dangerous, son.

Walter. What's dangerous?

Mama. When a man goes outside his home to look for peace.

Walter (*beseechingly*). Then why can't there never be no peace in this house then?

Mama. You done found it in some other house?

Walter. No—there ain't no woman! Why do women always think there's a woman somewhere when a man gets restless. (*Picks up the check.*) Do you know what this money means to me? Do you know what this money can do for us? (*Puts it back.*) Mama—Mama—I want so many things . . .

Mama. Yes, son—

Walter. I want so many things that they are driving me kind of crazy . . . Mama—look at me.

Mama. I'm looking at you. You a good-looking boy. You got a job, a nice wife, a fine boy, and—

Walter. A job. (*Looks at her.*) Mama, a job? I open and close car doors all day long. I drive a man around in his limousine and I say, "Yes, sir; no, sir; very good, sir; shall I take the Drive, sir?" Mama, that ain't no kind of job . . . that ain't nothing at all. (*Very quietly.*) Mama, I don't know if I can make you understand.

Mama. Understand what, baby?

Walter (*quietly*). Sometimes it's like I can see the future stretched out in front of me—just plain as day. The future, Mama. Hanging over there at the edge of my days. Just waiting for me—a big, looming blank space—full of *nothing.* Just waiting for *me.* But it don't have to be. (*Pause. Kneeling beside her chair.*) Mama—sometimes when I'm downtown and I pass them cool, quiet-looking restaurants where them white boys are sitting back and talking 'bout things . . . sitting there turning deals worth millions of dollars . . . sometimes I see guys don't look much older than me—

Mama. Son—how come you talk so much 'bout money?

Walter (*with immense passion*). Because it is life, Mama!

Mama (*quietly*). Oh—(*Very quietly.*) So now it's life. Money is life. Once upon a time freedom used to be life—now it's money. I guess the world really do change . . .

Walter. No—it was always money, Mama. We just didn't know about it.

Mama. No . . . something has changed. (*She looks at him.*) You something new, boy. In my time we was worried about not being lynched and getting to the North if we could and how to stay alive and still have a pinch of dignity too . . . Now here come you and Beneatha—talking 'bout things we ain't never even thought about hardly, me and your daddy. You ain't satisfied or proud of nothing we done. I mean that you had a home; that we kept you out of trouble till you was grown; that you don't have to ride to work on the back of nobody's streetcar—You my children—but how different we done become.

Walter (*a long beat. He pats her hand and gets up*). You just don't understand, Mama, you just don't understand.

Mama. Son—do you know your wife is expecting another baby? (*Walter stands, stunned, and absorbs what his mother has said.*) That's what she wanted to talk to you about. (*Walter sinks down into a chair.*) This ain't for me to be telling—but you ought to know. (*She waits.*) I think Ruth is thinking 'bout getting rid of that child.

Walter (*slowly understanding*). —No—no—Ruth wouldn't do that.

Mama. When the world gets ugly enough—a woman will do anything for her family. *The part that's already living.*

Walter. You don't know Ruth, Mama, if you think she would do that.

Ruth opens the bedroom door and stands there a little limp.

Ruth *(beaten).* Yes I would too, Walter. *(Pause.)* I gave her a five-dollar down payment.

There is total silence as the man stares at his wife and the mother stares at her son.

Mama *(presently).* Well—*(Tightly.)* Well—son, I'm waiting to hear you say something . . . *(She waits.)* I'm waiting to hear how you be your father's son. Be the man he was . . . *(Pause. The silence shouts.)* Your wife say she going to destroy your child. And I'm waiting to hear you talk like him and say we a people who give children life, not who destroys them—*(She rises.)* I'm waiting to see you stand up and look like your daddy and say we done give up one baby to poverty and that we ain't going to give up nary another one . . . I'm waiting.

Walter. Ruth—*(He can say nothing.)*

Mama. If you a son of mine, tell her! *(Walter picks up his keys and his coat and walks out. She continues, bitterly.)* You . . . you are a disgrace to your father's memory. Somebody get me my hat!

Curtain.

ACT II

Scene 1.

Time: Later the same day.
    At rise: Ruth is ironing again. She has the radio going. Presently Beneatha's bedroom door opens and Ruth's mouth falls and she puts down the iron in fascination.

Ruth. What have we got on tonight!

Beneatha *(emerging grandly from the doorway so that we can see her thoroughly robed in the costume Asagai brought).* You are looking at what a well-dressed Nigerian woman wears—*(She parades for Ruth, her hair completely hidden by the headdress; she is coquettishly fanning herself with an ornate oriental fan, mistakenly more like Butterfly than any Nigerian that ever was.)* Isn't it beautiful? *(She promenades to the radio and, with an arrogant flourish, turns off the good loud blues that is playing.)* Enough of this assimilationist junk! *(Ruth follows her with her eyes as she goes to the phonograph and puts on a record and turns and waits ceremoniously for the music to come up. Then, with a shout—)* OCOMOGOSIAY!

Ruth jumps. The music comes up, a lovely Nigerian melody. Beneatha listens, enraptured, her eyes far way—"back to the past." She begins to dance. Ruth is dumbfounded.

Ruth. What kind of dance is that?

Beneatha. A folk dance.

Ruth *(Pearl Bailey).* What kind of folks do that, honey?

Beneatha. It's from Nigeria. It's a dance of welcome.

Ruth. Who you welcoming?

Beneatha. The men back to the village.

Ruth. Where they been?

Beneatha. How should I know—out hunting or something. Anyway, they are coming back now . . .

Ruth. Well, that's good.

Beneatha *(with the record).*

> Alundi, alundi
> Alundi alunya
> Jop pu a jeepua
> Ang gu soooooooooo
> Ai yai yae . . .
> Ayehaye—alundi . . .

Walter comes in during this performance; he has obviously been drinking. He leans against the door heavily and watches his sister, at first with distaste. Then his eyes look off—"back to the past"—as he lifts both his fists to the roof, screaming.

Walter. YEAH . . . AND ETHIOPIA STRETCH FORTH HER HANDS AGAIN! . . .

Ruth *(drily, looking at him).* Yes—and Africa sure is claiming her own tonight. *(She gives them both up and starts ironing again.)*

Walter *(all in a drunken, dramatic shout).* Shut up! . . . I'm diggin them drums . . . them drums move me! . . . *(He makes his weaving way to his wife's face and leans in close to her.)* In my *heart of hearts—(He thumps his chest.)*—I am much warrior!

Ruth *(without even looking up).* In your heart of hearts you are much drunkard.

Walter *(coming away from her and starting to wander around the room, shouting).* Me and Jomo . . . *(Intently, in his sister's face. She has stopped dancing to watch him in this unknown mood.)* That's my man, Kenyatta. *(Shouting and thumping his chest.)* FLAMING SPEAR! HOT DAMN! *(He is suddenly in possession of an imaginary spear and actively spearing enemies all over the room.)* OCOMOGOSIAY . . .

Beneatha *(to encourage Walter, thoroughly caught up with this side of him).* OCOMOGOSIAY, FLAMING SPEAR!

Walter. THE LION IS WAKING . . . OWIMOWEH!

He pulls his shirt open and leaps up on the table and gestures with his spear.

Beneatha. OWIMOWEH!

Walter (*on the table, very far gone, his eyes pure glass sheets. He sees what we cannot, that he is a leader of his people, a great chief, a descendant of Chaka, and that the hour to march has come*). Listen, my black brothers—

Beneatha. OCOMOGOSIAY!

Walter. —Do you hear the waters rushing against the shores of the coastlands—

Beneatha. OCOMOGOSIAY!

Walter. —Do you hear the screeching of the cocks in yonder hills beyond where the chiefs meet in council for the coming of the mighty war—

Beneatha. OCOMOGOSIAY!

And now the lighting shifts subtly to suggest the world of Walter's imagination, and the mood shifts from pure comedy. It is the inner Walter speaking: the Southside chauffeur has assumed an unexpected majesty.

Walter. —Do you hear the beating of the wings of the birds flying low over the mountains and the low places of our land—

Beneatha. OCOMOGOSIAY!

Walter. —Do you hear the singing of the women, singing the war songs of our fathers to the babies in the great houses? Singing the sweet war songs! (*The doorbell rings.*) OH, DO YOU HEAR, MY *BLACK* BROTHERS!

Beneatha (*completely gone*). We hear you, Flaming Spear—

Ruth shuts off the phonograph and opens the door. George Murchison enters.

Walter. Telling us to prepare for the GREATNESS OF THE TIME! (*Lights back to normal. He turns and sees George.*) Black Brother!

He extends his hand for the fraternal clasp.

George. Black Brother, hell!

Ruth (*having had enough, and embarrassed for the family*). Beneatha, you got company—what's the matter with you? Walter Lee Younger, get down off that table and stop acting like a fool . . .

Walter comes down off the table suddenly and makes a quick exit to the bathroom.

Ruth. He's had a little to drink . . . I don't know what her excuse is.

George (*to Beneatha*). Look honey, we're going to the theater—we're not going to be *in* it . . . so go change, huh?

Beneatha looks at him and slowly, ceremoniously, lifts her hands and pulls off the headdress. Her hair is close-cropped and unstraightened. George freezes mid-sentence and Ruth's eyes all but fall out of her head.

George. What in the name of—

Ruth *(touching Beneatha's hair).* Girl, you done lost your natural mind? Look at your head!

George. What have you done to your head—I mean your hair!

Beneatha. Nothing—except cut it off.

Ruth. Now that's the truth—it's what ain't been done to it! You expect this boy to go out with you with your head all nappy like that?

Beneatha *(looking at George).* That's up to George. If he's ashamed of his heritage—

George. Oh, don't be so proud of yourself, Bennie—just because you look eccentric.

Beneatha. How can something that's natural be eccentric?

George. That's what being eccentric means—being natural. Get dressed.

Beneatha. I don't like that, George.

Ruth. Why must you and your brother make an argument out of everything people say?

Beneatha. Because I hate assimilationist Negroes!

Ruth. Will somebody please tell me what assimila-whoever means!

George. Oh, it's just a college girl's way of calling people Uncle Toms—but that isn't what it means at all.

Ruth. Well, what does it mean?

Beneatha *(cutting George off and staring at him as she replies to Ruth).* It means someone who is willing to give up his own culture and submerge himself completely in the dominant, and in this case *oppressive* culture!

George. Oh, dear, dear, dear! Here we go! A lecture on the African past! On our Great West African Heritage! In one second we will hear all about the great Ashanti empires; the great Songhay civilizations; and the great sculpture of Bénin—and then some poetry in the Bantu—and the whole monologue will end with the word *heritage!* *(Nastily.)* Let's face it, baby, your heritage is nothing but a bunch of raggedy-assed spirituals and some grass huts!

Beneatha. GRASS HUTS! *(Ruth crosses to her and forcibly pushes her toward the bedroom.)* See there . . . you are standing there in your splendid ignorance talking about people who were the first to smelt iron on the face of the earth! *(Ruth is pushing her through the door.)* The Ashanti were performing surgical operations when the English—*(Ruth pulls the door to, with Beneatha on the other side, and smiles graciously at George. Beneatha opens the door and shouts the end of the sentence defiantly at George.)*—were still tattooing themselves with blue dragons! *(She goes back inside.)*

Ruth. Have a seat, George. *(They both sit. Ruth folds her hands rather primly on her lap, determined to demonstrate the civilization of the family.)* Warm, ain't it? I mean for September. *(Pause.)* Just like they always say about Chicago weather: if it's too hot or cold for you, just wait a minute and it'll change. *(She smiles happily at this cliché of clichés.)* Everybody say it's got to do with them bombs and things they keep setting off. *(Pause.)* Would you like a nice cold beer?

George. No, thank you. I don't care for beer. *(He looks at his watch.)* I hope she hurries up.

Ruth. What time is the show?

George. It's an eight-thirty curtain. That's just Chicago, though. In New York standard curtain time is eight–forty.

He is rather proud of this knowledge.

Ruth *(properly appreciating it).* You get to New York a lot?

George *(offhand).* Few times a year.

Ruth. Oh—that's nice. I've never been to New York.

Walter enters. We feel he has relieved himself, but the edge of unreality is still with him.

Walter. New York ain't got nothing Chicago ain't. Just a bunch of hustling people all squeezed up together—being "Eastern."

He turns his face into a screw of displeasure.

George. Oh—you've been?

Walter. *Plenty* of times.

Ruth *(shocked at the lie).* Walter Lee Younger!

Walter *(staring her down).* Plenty! *(Pause.)* What we got to drink in this house? Why don't you offer this man some refreshment. *(To George.)* They don't know how to entertain people in this house, man.

George. Thank you—I don't really care for anything.

Walter *(feeling his head; sobriety coming).* Where's Mama?

Ruth. She ain't come back yet.

Walter *(looking Murchison over from head to toe, scrutinizing his carefully casual tweed sports jacket over cashmere V-neck sweater over soft eyelet shirt and tie, and soft slacks, finished off with white buckskin shoes).* Why all you college boys wear them faggoty-looking white shoes?

Ruth. Walter Lee!

George Murchison ignores the remark.

Walter *(to Ruth).* Well, they look crazy as hell—white shoes, cold as it is.

Ruth *(crushed).* You have to excuse him—

Walter. No he don't! Excuse me for what? What you always excusing me for! I'll excuse myself when I needs to be excused! *(A pause.)* They look as funny as them black knee socks Beneatha wears out of here all the time.

Ruth. It's the college *style*, Walter.

Walter. Style, hell. She looks like she got burnt legs or something!

Ruth. Oh, Walter—

Walter *(an irritable mimic).* Oh, Walter! Oh, Walter! *(To Murchison.)* How's your old man making out? I understand you all going to buy that big hotel on the Drive? *(He finds a beer in the refrigerator, wanders over to Murchison,* *sipping and wiping his lips with the back of his hand, and straddling a chair backwards to talk to the other man.)* Shrewd move. Your old man is all right, man. *(Tapping his head and half winking for emphasis.)* I mean he knows how to operate. I mean he thinks *big*, you know what I mean, I mean for a *home*, you know? But I think he's kind of running out of ideas now. I'd like to talk to him. Listen, man, I got some plans that could turn this city upside down. I mean think like he does. *Big.* Invest big, gamble big, hell, lose *big* if you have to, you know what I mean. It's hard to find a man on this whole Southside who understands my kind of thinking—you dig? *(He scrutinizes Murchison again, drinks his beer, squints his eyes and leans in close, confidential, man to man.)* Me and you ought to sit down and talk sometimes, man. Man, I got me some ideas . . .

Murchison *(with boredom).* Yeah—sometimes we'll have to do that, Walter.

Walter *(understanding the indifference, and offended).* Yeah—well, when you get the time, man. I know you a busy little boy.

Ruth. Walter, please—

Walter *(bitterly, hurt).* I know ain't nothing in this world as busy as you colored college boys with your fraternity pins and white shoes . . .

Ruth *(covering her face with humiliation).* Oh, Walter Lee—

Walter. I see you all all the time—with the books tucked under your arms—going to your *(British A—a mimic.)* "clahsses." And for what! What the hell you learning over there? Filling up your heads—*(Counting off on his fingers.)*—with the sociology and the psychology—but they teaching you how to be a man? How to take over and run the world? They teaching you how to run a rubber plantation or a steel mill? Naw—just to talk proper and read books and wear them faggoty-looking white shoes . . .

George *(looking at him with distaste, a little above it all).* You're all wacked up with bitterness, man.

Walter *(intently, almost quietly, between the teeth, glaring at the boy).* And you—ain't you bitter, man? Ain't you just about had it yet? Don't you see no stars gleaming that you can't reach out and grab? You happy?—You contented son-of-a-bitch—you happy? You got it made? Bitter? Man, I'm a volcano. Bitter? Here I am a giant—surrounded by ants! Ants who can't even understand what it is the giant is talking about.

Ruth *(passionately and suddenly).* Oh, Walter—ain't you with nobody!

Walter *(violently).* No! 'Cause ain't nobody with me! Not even my own mother!

Ruth. Walter, that's a terrible thing to say!

Beneatha enters, dressed for the evening in a cocktail dress and earrings, hair natural.

George. Well—hey—*(Crosses to Beneatha; thoughtful, with emphasis, since this is a reversal.)* You look great!

Walter *(seeing his sister's hair for the first time).* What's the matter with your head?

Beneatha *(tired of the jokes now).* I cut it off, Brother.

Walter (*coming close to inspect it and walking around her*). Well, I'll be damned. So that's what they mean by the African bush . . .

Beneatha. Ha ha. Let's go, George.

George (*looking at her*). You know something? I like it. It's sharp. I mean it really is. (*Helps her into her wrap.*)

Ruth. Yes—I think so, too. (*She goes to the mirror and starts to clutch at her hair.*)

Walter. Oh no! You leave yours alone, baby. You might turn out to have a pin-shaped head or something!

Beneatha. See you all later.

Ruth. Have a nice time.

George. Thanks. Good night. (*Half out the door, he reopens it. To Walter.*) Good night, Prometheus!

Beneatha and George exit.

Walter (*to Ruth*). Who is Prometheus?

Ruth. I don't know. Don't worry about it.

Walter (*in fury, pointing after George*). See there—they get to a point where they can't insult you man to man—they got to go talk about something ain't nobody never heard of!

Ruth. How do you know it was an insult? (*To humor him.*) Maybe Prometheus is a nice fellow.

Walter. Prometheus! I bet there ain't even no such thing! I bet that simpleminded clown—

Ruth. Walter—

She stops what she is doing and looks at him.

Walter (*yelling*). Don't start!

Ruth. Start what?

Walter. Your nagging! Where was I? Who was I with? How much money did I spend?

Ruth (*plaintively*). Walter Lee—why don't we just try to talk about it . . .

Walter (*not listening*). I been out talking with people who understand me. People who care about the things I got on my mind.

Ruth (*wearily*). I guess that means people like Willy Harris.

Walter. Yes, people like Willy Harris.

Ruth (*with a sudden flash of impatience*). Why don't you all just hurry up and go into the banking business and stop talking about it!

Walter. Why? You want to know why? 'Cause we all tied up in a race of people that don't know how to do nothing but moan, pray, and have babies!

The line is too bitter even for him and he looks at her and sits down.

Ruth. Oh, Walter . . . (*Softly.*) Honey, why can't you stop fighting me?

Walter (*without thinking*). Who's fighting you? Who even cares about you?

This line begins the retardation of his mood.

Ruth. Well—(*She waits a long time, and then with resignation starts to put away her things.*) I guess I might as well go on to bed . . . (*More or less to herself.*) I don't know where we lost it . . . but we have . . . (*Then, to him.*) I—I'm sorry about this new baby, Walter. I guess maybe I better go on and do what I started . . . I guess I just didn't realize how bad things was with us . . . I guess I just didn't really real-ize—(*She starts out to the bedroom and stops.*) You want some hot milk?

Walter. Hot milk?

Ruth. Yes—hot milk.

Walter. Why hot milk?

Ruth. 'Cause after all that liquor you come home with you ought to have some-thing hot in your stomach.

Walter. I don't want no milk.

Ruth. You want some coffee then?

Walter. No, I don't want no coffee. I don't want nothing hot to drink. (*Almost plaintively.*) Why you always trying to give me something to eat?

Ruth (*standing and looking at him helplessly*). What *else* can I give you, Walter Lee Younger?

She stands and looks at him and presently turns to go out again. He lifts his head and watches her going away from him in a new mood which began to emerge when he asked her "Who cares about you?"

Walter. It's been rough, ain't it, baby? (*She hears and stops but does not turn around and he continues to her back.*) I guess between two people there ain't never as much understood as folks generally thinks there is. I mean like between me and you—(*She turns to face him.*) How we gets to the place where we scared to talk softness to each other. (*He waits, thinking hard himself.*) Why you think it got to be like that? (*He is thoughtful, almost as a child would be.*) Ruth, what is it gets into people ought to be close?

Ruth. I don't know, honey. I think about it a lot.

Walter. On account of you and me, you mean? The way things are with us. The way something done come down between us.

Ruth. There ain't so much between us, Walter . . . Not when you come to me and try to talk to me. Try to be with me . . . a little even.

Walter (*total honesty*). Sometimes . . . sometimes . . . I don't even know how to try.

Ruth. Walter—

Walter. Yes?

Ruth (*coming to him, gently and with misgiving, but coming to him*). Honey . . . life don't have to be like this. I mean sometimes people can do things so that things are better . . . You remember how we used to talk when Travis was born . . .

about the way we were going to live . . . the kind of house . . . (*She is stroking his head.*) Well, it's all starting to slip away from us . . .

He turns her to him and they look at each other and kiss, tenderly and hungrily. The door opens and Mama enters—Walter breaks away and jumps up. A beat.

Walter. Mama, where have you been?

Mama. My—them steps is longer than they used to be. Whew! (*She sits down and ignores him.*) How you feeling this evening, Ruth?

Ruth shrugs, disturbed at having been interrupted and watching her husband knowingly.

Walter. Mama, where have you been all day?

Mama (*still ignoring him and leaning on the table and changing to more comfortable shoes*). Where's Travis?

Ruth. I let him go out earlier and he ain't come back yet. Boy, is he going to get it!

Walter. Mama!

Mama (*as if she has heard him for the first time*). Yes, son?

Walter. Where did you go this afternoon?

Mama. I went downtown to tend to some business that I had to tend to.

Walter. What kind of business?

Mama. You know better than to question me like a child, Brother.

Walter (*rising and bending over the table*). Where were you, Mama? (*Bringing his fists down and shouting.*) Mama, you didn't go do something with that insurance money, something crazy?

The front door opens slowly, interrupting him, and Travis peeks his head in, less than hopefully.

Travis (*to his mother*). Mama, I—

Ruth. "Mama I" nothing! You're going to get it, boy! Get on in that bedroom and get yourself ready!

Travis. But I—

Mama. Why don't you all never let the child explain hisself.

Ruth. Keep out of it now, Lena.

Mama clamps her lips together, and Ruth advances toward her son menacingly.

Ruth. A thousand times I have told you not to go off like that—

Mama (*holding out her arms to her grandson*). Well—at least let me tell him something. I want him to be the first one to hear . . . Come here, Travis. (*The boy obeys, gladly.*) Travis—(*She takes him by the shoulder and looks into his face.*)—you know that money we got in the mail this morning?

Travis. Yes'm—

Mama. Well—what you think your grandmama gone and done with that money?

Travis. I don't know, Grandmama.

Mama (*putting her finger on his nose for emphasis*). She went out and she bought you a house! (*The explosion comes from Walter at the end of the revelation and he jumps up and turns away from all of them in a fury. Mama continues, to Travis.*) You glad about the house? It's going to be yours when you get to be a man.

Travis. Yeah—I always wanted to live in a house.

Mama. All right, gimme some sugar then—(*Travis puts his arms around her neck as she watches her son over the boy's shoulder. Then, to Travis, after the embrace.*) Now when you say your prayers tonight, you thank God and your grandfather—'cause it was him who give you the house—in his way.

Ruth (*taking the boy from Mama and pushing him toward the bedroom*). Now you get out of here and get ready for your beating.

Travis. Aw, Mama—

Ruth. Get on in there—(*Closing the door behind him and turning radiantly to her mother-in-law.*) So you went and did it!

Mama (*quietly, looking at her son with pain*). Yes, I did.

Ruth (*raising both arms classically*). PRAISE GOD! (*Looks at Walter a moment, who says nothing. She crosses rapidly to her husband.*) Please, honey—let me be glad . . . you be glad too. (*She has laid her hands on his shoulders, but he shakes himself free of her roughly, without turning to face her.*) Oh, Walter . . . a home . . . a home. (*She comes back to Mama.*) Well—where is it? How big is it? How much it going to cost?

Mama. Well—

Ruth. When we moving?

Mama (*smiling at her*). First of the month.

Ruth (*throwing back her head with jubilance*). Praise God!

Mama (*tentatively, still looking at her son's back turned against her and Ruth*). It's—it's a nice house too . . . (*She cannot help speaking directly to him. An imploring quality in her voice, her manner, makes her almost like a girl now.*) Three bedrooms—nice big one for you and Ruth . . . Me and Beneatha still have to share our room, but Travis have one of his own—and (*With difficulty.*) I figure if the—new baby—is a boy, we could get one of them double-decker outfits . . . And there's a yard with a little patch of dirt where I could maybe get to grow me a few flowers . . . And a nice big basement . . .

Ruth. Walter honey, be glad—

Mama (*still to his back, fingering things on the table*). 'Course I don't want to make it sound fancier than it is . . . It's just a plain little old house—but it's made good and solid—and it will be *ours*. Walter Lee—it makes a difference in a man when he can walk on floors that belong to *him* . . .

Ruth. Where is it?

Mama (*frightened at this telling*). Well—well—it's out there in Clybourne Park—

Ruth's radiance fades abruptly, and Walter finally turns slowly to face his mother with incredulity and hostility.

Ruth. Where?

Mama *(matter-of-factly).* Four o six Clybourne Street, Clybourne Park.

Ruth. Clybourne Park? Mama, there ain't no colored people living in Clybourne Park.

Mama *(almost idiotically).* Well, I guess there's going to be some now.

Walter *(bitterly).* So that's the peace and comfort you went out and bought for us today!

Mama *(raising her eyes to meet his finally).* Son—I just tried to find the nicest place for the least amount of money for my family.

Ruth *(trying to recover from the shock).* Well—well—'course I ain't one never been 'fraid of no crackers, mind you—but—well, wasn't there no other houses nowhere?

Mama. Them houses they put up for colored in them areas way out all seem to cost twice as much as other houses. I did the best I could.

Ruth *(struck senseless with the news, in its various degrees of goodness and trouble, she sits a moment, her fists propping her chin in thought, and then she starts to rise, bringing her fists down with vigor, the radiance spreading from cheek to cheek again).* Well—well—All I can say is—if this is my time in life—MY TIME—to say good-bye—*(And she builds with momentum as she starts to circle the room with an exuberant, almost tearfully happy release.)*—to these Goddamned cracking walls!—*(She pounds the walls.)*—and these marching roaches!—*(She wipes at an imaginary army of marching roaches.)*—and this cramped little closet which ain't now or never was no kitchen! . . . then I say it loud and good, HALLELUJAH! AND GOOD-BYE MISERY . . . I DON'T NEVER WANT TO SEE YOUR UGLY FACE AGAIN! *(She laughs joyously, having practically destroyed the apartment, and flings her arms up and lets them come down happily, slowly, reflectively, over her abdomen, aware for the first time perhaps that the life therein pulses with happiness and not despair.)* Lena?

Mama *(moved, watching her happiness).* Yes, honey?

Ruth *(looking off).* Is there—is there a whole lot of sunlight?

Mama *(understanding).* Yes, child, there's a whole lot of sunlight.

Long pause.

Ruth *(collecting herself and going to the door of the room Travis is in).* Well—I guess I better see 'bout Travis. *(To Mama.)* Lord, I sure don't feel like whipping nobody today!

She exits.

Mama *(the mother and son are left alone now and the mother waits a long time, considering deeply, before she speaks).* Son—you—you understand what I done, don't you? *(Walter is silent and sullen.)* I—I just seen my family falling apart today . . . just falling to pieces in front of my eyes . . . We couldn't of gone on like we was today. We was going backwards 'stead of forwards—talking 'bout killing babies and wishing each other was dead . . . When it gets like that in life—you just got to do something different, push on out and do something bigger . . . *(She waits.)* I wish you say something, son . . . I wish you'd say how deep inside you you think I done the right thing—

Walter. *(crossing slowly to his bedroom door and finally turning there and speaking measuredly).* What you need me to say you done right for? *You* the head of this family. You run our lives like you want to. It was your money and you did what you wanted with it. So what you need for me to say it was all right for? *(Bitterly, to hurt her as deeply as he knows is possible.)* So you butchered up a dream of mine—you—who always talking 'bout your children's dreams . . .

Mama. Walter Lee—

He just closes the door behind him. Mama sits alone, thinking heavily.

Curtain.

Scene 2.

Time: Friday night, a few weeks later.

At rise: Packing crates mark the intention of the family to move. Beneatha and George come in, presumably from an evening out again.

George. O.K. . . . O.K., whatever you say . . . *(They both sit on the couch. He tries to kiss her. She moves away.)* Look, we've had a nice evening; let's not spoil it, huh? . . .

He again turns her head and tries to nuzzle in and she turns away from him, not with distaste but with momentary lack of interest; in a mood to pursue what they were talking about.

Beneatha. I'm *trying* to talk to you.

George. We always talk.

Beneatha. Yes—and I love to talk.

George *(exasperated; rising).* I know it and I don't mind it sometimes . . . I want you to cut it out, see—The moody stuff, I mean. I don't like it. You're a nice-looking girl . . . all over. That's all you need, honey, forget the atmosphere. Guys aren't going to go for the atmosphere—they're going to go for what they see. Be glad for that. Drop the Garbo routine. It doesn't go with you. As for myself, I want a nice—*(Groping.)*—simple *(Thoughtfully.)*—sophisticated girl . . . not a poet—O.K.?

He starts to kiss her, she rebuffs him again and he jumps up.

Beneatha. Why are you angry, George?

George. Because this is stupid! I don't go out with you to discuss the nature of "quiet desperation" or to hear all about your thoughts—because the world will go on thinking what it thinks regardless—

Beneatha. Then why read books? Why go to school?

George (*with artificial patience, counting on his fingers*). It's simple. You read books—to learn facts—to get grades—to pass the course—to get a degree. That's all—it has nothing to do with thoughts.

A long pause.

Beneatha. I see. (*He starts to sit.*) Good night, George.

George looks at her a little oddly, and starts to exit. He meets Mama coming in.

George. Oh—hello, Mrs. Younger.
Mama. Hello, George, how you feeling?
George. Fine—fine, how are you?
Mama. Oh, a little tired. You know them steps can get you after a day's work. You all have a nice time tonight?
George. Yes—a fine time. A fine time.
Mama. Well, good night.
George. Good night. (*He exits. Mama closes the door behind her.*)
Mama. Hello, honey. What you sitting like that for?
Beneatha. I'm just sitting.
Mama. Didn't you have a nice time?
Beneatha. No.
Mama. No? What's the matter?
Beneatha. Mama, George is a fool—honest. (*She rises.*)
Mama (*hustling around unloading the packages she has entered with. She stops*). Is he, baby?
Beneatha. Yes.

Beneatha makes up Travis's bed as she talks.

Mama. You sure?
Beneatha. Yes.
Mama. Well—I guess you better not waste your time with no fools.

Beneatha looks up at her mother, watching her put groceries in the refrigerator. Finally she gathers up her things and starts into the bedroom. At the door she stops and looks back at her mother.

Beneatha. Mama—
Mama. Yes, baby—
Beneatha. Thank you.
Mama. For what?
Beneatha. For understanding me this time.

She exits quickly and the mother stands, smiling a little, looking at the place where Beneatha just stood. Ruth enters.

Ruth. Now don't you fool with any of this stuff, Lena—

Mama. Oh, I just thought I'd sort a few things out. Is Brother here?

Ruth. Yes.

Mama *(with concern).* Is he—

Ruth *(reading her eyes).* Yes.

Mama is silent and someone knocks on the door. Mama and Ruth exchange weary and knowing glances and Ruth opens it to admit the neighbor, Mrs. Johnson,[1] who is a rather squeaky wide-eyed lady of no particular age, with a newspaper under her arm.

Mama *(changing her expression to acute delight and a ringing cheerful greeting).* Oh—hello there, Johnson.

Johnson *(this is a woman who decided long ago to be enthusiastic about EVERY-THING in life and she is inclined to wave her wrist vigorously at the height of her exclamatory comments).* Hello there, yourself! H'you this evening, Ruth?

Ruth *(not much of a deceptive type).* Fine, Mis' Johnson, h'you?

Johnson. Fine. *(Reaching out quickly, playfully, and patting Ruth's stomach.)* Ain't you starting to poke out none yet! *(She mugs with delight at the over familiar remark and her eyes dart around looking at the crates and packing preparation; Mama's face is a cold sheet of endurance.)* Oh, ain't we getting ready round here, though! Yessir! Lookathere! I'm telling you the Youngers is really getting ready to "move on up a little higher!"—Bless God!

Mama *(a little drily, doubting the total sincerity of the Blesser).* Bless God.

Johnson. He's good, ain't He?

Mama. Oh yes, He's good.

Johnson. I mean sometimes He works in mysterious ways . . . but He works, don't He!

Mama *(the same).* Yes, He does.

Johnson. I'm just sooooooo happy for y'all. And this here child—*(About Ruth.)* looks like she could just pop open with happiness, don't she. Where's all the rest of the family?

Mama. Bennie's gone to bed—

Johnson. Ain't no . . . *(The implication is pregnancy.)* sickness done hit you—I hope . . . ?

Mama. No—she just tired. She was out this evening.

Johnson *(all is a coo, an emphatic coo).* Aw—ain't that lovely. She still going out with the little Murchison boy?

Mama *(drily).* Ummmm huh.

Johnson. That's lovely. You sure got lovely children, Younger. Me and Isaiah talks all the time 'bout what fine children you was blessed with. We sure do.

Mama. Ruth, give Mis' Johnson a piece of sweet potato pie and some milk.

---

[1] This character and the scene of her visit were cut from the original production and early editions of the play.

Johnson. Oh honey, I can't stay hardly a minute—I just dropped in to see if there was anything I could do. *(Accepting the food easily.)* I guess y'all seen the news what's all over the colored paper this week . . .

Mama. No—didn't get mine yet this week.

Johnson *(lifting her head and blinking with the spirit of catastrophe).* You mean you ain't read 'bout them colored people that was bombed out their place out there?

Ruth straightens with concern and takes the paper and reads it. Johnson notices her and feeds commentary.

Johnson. Ain't it something how bad these here white folks is getting here in Chicago! Lord, getting so you think you right down in Mississippi! *(With a tremendous and rather insincere sense of melodrama.)* 'Course I thinks it's wonderful how our folk keeps on pushing out. You hear some of these Negroes round here talking 'bout how they don't go where they ain't wanted and all that—but not me, honey! *(This is a lie.)* Wilhemenia Othella Johnson goes anywhere, any time she feels like it! *(With head movement for emphasis.)* Yes I do! Why if we left it up to these here crackers, the poor niggers wouldn't have nothing—*(She clasps her hand over her mouth.)* Oh, I always forgets you don't 'low that word in your house.

Mama *(quietly, looking at her).* No—I don't 'low it.

Johnson *(vigorously again).* Me neither! I was just telling Isaiah yesterday when he come using it in front of me—I said, "Isaiah, it's just like Mis' Younger says all the time—"

Mama. Don't you want some more pie?

Johnson. No—no thank you; this was lovely. I got to get on over home and have my midnight coffee. I hear some people say it don't let them sleep but I finds I can't close my eyes right lessen I done had that laaaast cup of coffee . . . *(She waits. A beat. Undaunted.)* My Goodnight coffee, I calls it!

Mama *(with much eye-rolling and communication between herself and Ruth).* Ruth, why don't you give Mis' Johnson some coffee.

Ruth gives Mama an unpleasant look for her kindness.

Johnson *(accepting the coffee).* Where's Brother tonight?

Mama. He's lying down.

Johnson. Mmmmmmm, he sure gets his beauty rest, don't he? Good-looking man. Sure is a good-looking man! *(Reaching out to pat Ruth's stomach again.)* I guess that's how come we keep on having babies around here. *(She winks at Mama.)* One thing 'bout Brother, he always know how to have a *good* time. And sooooo ambitious! I bet it was his idea y'all moving out to Clybourne Park. Lord—I bet this time next month y'all's names will have been in the papers plenty—*(Holding up her hands to mark off each word of the headline she can see in front of her.)* "NEGROES INVADE CLYBOURNE PARK—BOMBED!"

Mama *(she and Ruth look at the woman in amazement).* We ain't exactly moving out there to get bombed.

Johnson. Oh honey—you know I'm praying to God every day that don't nothing like that happen! But you have to think of life like it is—and these here Chicago peckerwoods is some baaaad peckerwoods.

Mama *(wearily).* We done thought about all that Mis' Johnson.

Beneatha comes out of the bedroom in her robe and passes through to the bathroom. Mrs. Johnson turns.

Johnson. Hello there, Bennie!

Beneatha *(crisply).* Hello, Mrs. Johnson.

Johnson. How is school?

Beneatha *(crisply).* Fine, thank you. *(She goes out.)*

Johnson *(insulted).* Getting so she don't have much to say to nobody.

Mama. The child was on her way to the bathroom.

Johnson. I know—but sometimes she act like ain't got time to pass the time of day with nobody ain't been to college. Oh—I ain't criticizing her none. It's just—you know how some of our young people gets when they get a little education. *(Mama and Ruth say nothing, just look at her.)* Yes—well. Well, I guess I better get on home. *(Unmoving.)* 'Course I can understand how she must be proud and everything—being the only one in the family to make something of herself. I know just being a chauffeur ain't never satisfied Brother none. He shouldn't feel like that, though. Ain't nothing wrong with being a chauffeur.

Mama. There's plenty wrong with it.

Johnson. What?

Mama. Plenty. My husband always said being any kind of a servant wasn't a fit thing for a man to have to be. He always said a man's hands was made to make things, or to turn the earth with—not to drive nobody's car for 'em—or—*(She looks at her own hands.)* carry they slop jars. And my boy is just like him—he wasn't meant to wait on nobody.

Johnson *(rising, somewhat offended).* Mmmmmmmmm. The Youngers is too much for me! *(She looks around.)* You sure one proud-acting bunch of colored folks. Well—I always thinks like Booker T. Washington said that time—"Education has spoiled many a good plow hand"—

Mama. Is that what old Booker T. said?

Johnson. He sure did.

Mama. Well, it sounds just like him. The fool.

Johnson *(indignantly).* Well—he was one of our great men.

Mama. Who said so?

Johnson *(nonplussed).* You know, me and you ain't never agreed about some things, Lena Younger. I guess I better be going—

Ruth *(quickly).* Good night.

Johnson. Good night. Oh—*(Thrusting it at her.)* You can keep the paper! *(With a trill.)* 'Night.

Mama. Good night, Mis' Johnson.

Mrs. Johnson exits.

Ruth. If ignorance was gold . . .
Mama. Shush. Don't talk about folks behind their backs.
Ruth. You do.
Mama. I'm old and corrupted. (*Beneatha enters.*) You was rude to Mis' Johnson, Beneatha, and I don't like it at all.
Beneatha (*at her door*). Mama, if there are two things we, as a people, have got to overcome, one is the Ku Klux Klan—and the other is Mrs. Johnson. (*She exits.*)
Mama. Smart aleck.

The phone rings.

Ruth. I'll get it.
Mama. Lord, ain't this a popular place tonight.
Ruth (*at the phone*). Hello—Just a minute. (*Goes to door.*) Walter, it's Mrs. Arnold. (*Waits. Goes back to the phone. Tense.*) Hello. Yes, this is his wife speaking . . . He's lying down now. Yes . . . well, he'll be in tomorrow. He's been very sick. Yes—I know we should have called, but we were so sure he'd be able to come in today. Yes—yes, I'm very sorry. Yes . . . Thank you very much. (*She hangs up. Walter is standing in the doorway of the bedroom behind her.*) That was Mrs. Arnold.
Walter (*indifferently*). Was it?
Ruth. She said if you don't come in tomorrow that they are getting a new man . . .
Walter. Ain't that sad—ain't that crying sad.
Ruth. She said Mr. Arnold has had to take a cab for three days . . . Walter, you ain't been to work for three days! (*This is a revelation to her.*) Where you been, Walter Lee Younger? (*Walter looks at her and starts to laugh.*) You're going to lose your job.
Walter. That's right . . . (*He turns on the radio.*)
Ruth. Oh, Walter, and with your mother working like a dog every day—

A steamy, deep blues pours into the room.

Walter. That's sad too—Everything is sad.
Mama. What you been doing for these three days, son?
Walter. Mama—you don't know all the things a man what got leisure can find to do in this city . . . What's this—Friday night? Well—Wednesday I borrowed Willy Harris's car and I went for a drive . . . just me and myself and I drove and drove . . . Way out . . . way past South Chicago, and I parked the car and I sat and looked at the steel mills all day long. I just sat in the car and looked at them big black chimneys for hours. Then I drove back and I went to the Green Hat. (*Pause.*) And Thursday—Thursday I borrowed the car again and I got in it and I pointed it the other way and I drove the other way—for hours—way, way up

to Wisconsin, and I looked at the farms. I just drove and looked at the farms. Then I drove back and I went to the Green Hat. *(Pause.)* And today—today I didn't get the car. Today I just walked. All over the Southside. And I looked at the Negroes and they looked at me and finally I just sat down on the curb at Thirty-ninth and South Parkway and I just sat there and watched the Negroes go by. And then I went to the Green Hat. You all sad? You all depressed? And you know where I am going right now—

Ruth goes out quietly.

Mama. Oh, Big Walter, is this the harvest of our days?

Walter. You know what I like about the Green Hat? I like this little cat they got there who blows a sax . . . He blows. He talks to me. He ain't but 'bout five feet tall and he's got a conked head and his eyes is always closed and he's all music—

Mama *(rising and getting some papers out of her handbag).* Walter—

Walter. And there's this other guy who plays the piano . . . and they got a sound. I mean they can work on some music . . . They got the best little combo in the world in the Green Hat . . . You can just sit there and drink and listen to them three men play and you realize that don't nothing matter worth a damn, but just being there—

Mama. I've helped do it to you, haven't I, son? Walter I been wrong.

Walter. Naw—you ain't never been wrong about nothing, Mama.

Mama. Listen to me, now. I say I been wrong, son. That I been doing to you what the rest of the world been doing to you. *(She turns off the radio.)* Walter—*(She stops and he looks up slowly at her and she meets his eyes pleadingly.)* What you ain't never understood is that I ain't got nothing, don't own nothing, ain't never really wanted nothing that wasn't for you. There ain't nothing as precious to me . . . There ain't nothing worth holding on to, money, dreams, nothing else—if it means—if it means it's going to destroy my boy. *(She takes an envelope out of her handbag and puts it in front of him and he watches her without speaking or moving.)* I paid the man thirty-five hundred dollars down on the house. That leaves sixty-five hundred dollars. Monday morning I want you to take this money and take three thousand dollars and put it in a savings account for Beneatha's medical schooling. The rest you put in a checking account—with your name on it. And from now on any penny that come out of it or that go in it is for you to look after. For you to decide. *(She drops her hands a little helplessly.)* It ain't much, but it's all I got in the world and I'm putting it in your hands. I'm telling you to be the head of this family from now on like you supposed to be.

Walter *(stares at the money).* You trust me like that, Mama?

Mama. I ain't never stop trusting you. Like I ain't never stop loving you.

She goes out, and Walter sits looking at the money on the table. Finally, in a decisive gesture, he gets up, and, in mingled joy and desperation, picks up the money. At the same moment, Travis enters for bed.

Travis. What's the matter, Daddy? You drunk?

Walter *(sweetly, more sweetly than we have ever known him).* No, Daddy ain't drunk. Daddy ain't going to never be drunk again . . .

Travis. Well, good night, Daddy.

The father has come from behind the couch and leans over, embracing his son.

Walter. Son, I feel like talking to you tonight.

Travis. About what?

Walter. Oh, about a lot of things. About you and what kind of man you going to be when you grow up . . . Son—son, what do you want to be when you grow up?

Travis. A bus driver.

Walter *(laughing a little).* A what? Man, that ain't nothing to want to be!

Travis. Why not?

Walter. 'Cause, man—it ain't big enough—you know what I mean.

Travis. I don't know then. I can't make up my mind. Sometimes Mama asks me that too. And sometimes when I tell her I just want to be like you—she says she don't want me to be like that and sometimes she says she does. . . .

Walter *(gathering him up in his arms).* You know what, Travis? In seven years you going to be seventeen years old. And things is going to be very different with us in seven years, Travis. . . . One day when you are seventeen I'll come home— home from my office downtown somewhere—

Travis. You don't work in no office, Daddy.

Walter. No—but after tonight. After what your daddy gonna do tonight, there's going to be offices—a whole lot of offices. . . .

Travis. What you gonna do tonight, Daddy?

Walter. You wouldn't understand yet, son, but your daddy's gonna make a transaction . . . a business transaction that's going to change our lives. . . . That's how come one day when you 'bout seventeen years old I'll come home and I'll be pretty tired, you know what I mean, after a day of conferences and secretaries getting things wrong the way they do . . . 'cause an executive's life is hell, man—*(The more he talks the farther away he gets.)* And I'll pull the car up on the driveway . . . just a plain black Chrysler, I think, with white walls—no—black tires. More elegant. Rich people don't have to be flashy . . . though I'll have to get something a little sportier for Ruth—maybe a Cadillac convertible to do her shopping in. . . . And I'll come up the steps to the house and the gardener will be clipping away at the hedges and he'll say, "Good evening, Mr. Younger." And I'll say, "Hello, Jefferson, how are you this evening?" And I'll go inside and Ruth will come downstairs and meet me at the door and we'll kiss each other and she'll take my arm and we'll go up to your room to see you sitting on the floor with the catalogues of all the great schools in America around you. . . . All the great schools in the world! And—and I'll say, all right son—it's your seventeenth birthday, what is it you've decided? . . . Just tell me where you want to go to school and you'll *go.* Just tell me, what it is you want to be—and you'll *be* it. . . .

Whatever you want to be—Yessir! (*He holds his arms open for Travis.*) You just name it, son . . . (*Travis leaps into them.*) and I hand you the world!

Walter's voice has risen in pitch and hysterical promise and on the last line he lifts Travis high.

Blackout.

Scene 3.

Time. Saturday, moving day, one week later.
    Before the curtain rises, Ruth's voice, a strident, dramatic church alto, cuts through the silence.
    It is, in the darkness, a triumphant surge, a penetrating statement of expectation: "Oh, Lord, I don't feel no ways tired! Children, oh, glory hallelujah!"
    As the curtain rises we see that Ruth is alone in the living room, finishing up the family's packing. It is moving day. She is nailing crates and tying cartons. Beneatha enters, carrying a guitar case, and watches her exuberant sister-in-law.

Ruth. Hey!
Beneatha (*putting away the case*). Hi.
Ruth (*pointing at a package*). Honey—look in that package there and see what I found on sale this morning at the South Center. (*Ruth gets up and moves to the package and draws out some curtains.*) Lookahere—hand-turned hems!
Beneatha. How do you know the window size out there?
Ruth (*who hadn't thought of that*). Oh—Well, they bound to fit something in the whole house. Anyhow, they was too good a bargain to pass up. (*Ruth slaps her head, suddenly remembering something.*) Oh, Bennie—I meant to put a special note on that carton over there. That's your mama's good china and she wants 'em to be very careful with it.
Beneatha. I'll do it.

Beneatha finds a piece of paper and starts to draw large letters on it.

Ruth. You know what I'm going to do soon as I get in that new house?
Beneatha. What?
Ruth. Honey—I'm going to run me a tub of water up to here . . . (*With her fingers practically up to her nostrils.*) And I'm going to get in it—and I am going to sit . . . and sit . . . and sit in that hot water and the first person who knocks to tell *me* to hurry up and come out—
Beneatha. Gets shot at sunrise.
Ruth (*laughing happily*). You said it, sister! (*Noticing how large Beneatha is absent-mindedly making the note.*) Honey, they ain't going to read that from no airplane.
Beneatha (*laughing herself*). I guess I always think things have more emphasis if they are big, somehow.

Ruth (*looking up at her and smiling*). You and your brother seem to have that as a philosophy of life. Lord, that man—done changed so 'round here. You know—you know what we did last night? Me and Walter Lee?

Beneatha. What?

Ruth (*smiling to herself*). We went to the movies. (*Looking at Beneatha to see if she understands.*) We went to the movies. You know the last time me and Walter went to the movies together?

Beneatha. No.

Ruth. Me neither. That's how long it been. (*Smiling again.*) But we went last night. The picture wasn't much good, but that didn't seem to matter. We went—and we held hands.

Beneatha. Oh, Lord!

Ruth. We held hands—and you know what?

Beneatha. What?

Ruth. When we come out of the show it was late and dark and all the stores and things was closed up . . . and it was kind of chilly and there wasn't many people on the streets . . . and we was still holding hands, me and Walter.

Beneatha. You're killing me.

Walter enters with a large package. His happiness is deep in him; he cannot keep still with his newfound exuberance. He is singing and wiggling and snapping his fingers. He puts his package in a corner and puts a phonograph record, which he has brought in with him, on the record player. As the music, soulful and sensuous, comes up he dances over to Ruth and tries to get her to dance with him. She gives in at last to his raunchiness and in a fit of giggling allows herself to be drawn into his mood. They dip and she melts into his arms in a classic, body-melting "slow drag."

Beneatha (*regarding them a long time as they dance, then drawing in her breath for a deeply exaggerated comment which she does not particularly mean*). Talk about—olddddddddddd-fashioneddddddd—Negroes!

Walter (*stopping momentarily*). What kind of Negroes?

He says this in fun. He is not angry with her today, nor with anyone. He starts to dance with his wife again.

Beneatha. Old-fashioned.

Walter (*as he dances with Ruth*). You know, when these *New Negroes* have their convention—(*Pointing at his sister.*)—that is going to be the chairman of the Committee on Unending Agitation. (*He goes on dancing, then stops.*) Race, race, race! . . . Girl, I do believe you are the first person in the history of the entire human race to successfully brainwash yourself. (*Beneatha breaks up and he goes on dancing. He stops again, enjoying his tease.*) Damn, even the N double A C P takes a holiday sometimes! (*Beneatha and Ruth laugh. He dances with Ruth some more and starts to laugh and stops and pantomimes someone over an operating table.*) I can just see that chick someday looking down at some poor cat on an operating table and before she starts to slice him, she says . . . *(Pulling his sleeves back maliciously.)* "By the way, what are your views on civil rights down there? . . ."

He laughs at her again and starts to dance happily. The bell sounds.

Beneatha. Sticks and stones may break my bones but . . . words will never hurt me!

Beneatha goes to the door and opens it as Walter and Ruth go on with the clowning. Beneatha is somewhat surprised to see a quiet-looking middle-aged white man in a business suit holding his hat and a briefcase in his hand and consulting a small piece of paper.

Man. Uh—how do you do, miss. I am looking for a Mrs.—*(He looks at the slip of paper.)* Mrs. Lena Younger? *(He stops short, struck dumb at the sight of the oblivious Walter and Ruth.)*

Beneatha *(smoothing her hair with slight embarrassment).* Oh—yes, that's my mother. Excuse me. *(She closes the door and turns to quiet the other two.)* Ruth! Brother! *(Enunciating precisely but soundlessly: "There's a white man at the door!" They stop dancing, Ruth cuts off the phonograph, Beneatha opens the door. The man casts a curious quick glance at all of them.)* Uh—come in please.

Man *(coming in).* Thank you.

Beneatha. My mother isn't here just now. Is it business?

Man. Yes . . . well, of a sort.

Walter *(freely, the Man of the House).* Have a seat. I'm Mrs. Younger's son. I look after most of her business matters.

Ruth and Beneatha exchange amused glances.

Man *(regarding Walter, and sitting).* Well—My name is Karl Lindner . . .

Walter *(stretching out his hand).* Walter Younger. This is my wife—*(Ruth nods politely.)*—and my sister.

Lindner. How do you do.

Walter *(amiably, as he sits himself easily on a chair, leaning forward on his knees with interest and looking expectantly into the newcomer's face).* What can we do for you, Mr. Lindner!

Lindner *(some minor shuffling of the hat and briefcase on his knees).* Well—I am a representative of the Clybourne Park Improvement Association—

Walter *(pointing).* Why don't you sit your things on the floor?

Lindner. Oh—yes. Thank you. *(He slides the briefcase and hat under the chair.)* And as I was saying—I am from the Clybourne Park Improvement Association and we have had it brought to our attention at the last meeting that you people—or at least your mother—has bought a piece of residential property at—*(He digs for the slip of paper again.)*—four o six Clybourne Street . . .

Walter. That's right. Care for something to drink? Ruth, get Mr. Lindner a beer.

Lindner *(upset for some reason).* Oh—no, really. I mean thank you very much, but no thank you.

Ruth *(innocently).* Some coffee?

Lindner. Thank you, nothing at all.

Beneatha is watching the man carefully.

Lindner. Well, I don't know how much you folks know about our organization. *(He is a gentle man; thoughtful and somewhat labored in his manner.)* It is one of these community organizations set up to look after—oh, you know, things like block upkeep and special projects and we also have what we call our New Neighbors Orientation Committee . . .

Beneatha *(drily).* Yes—and what do they do?

Lindner *(turning a little to her and then returning the main force to Walter).* Well— it's what you might call a sort of welcoming committee, I guess. I mean they, we—I'm the chairman of the committee—go around and see the new people who move into the neighborhood and sort of give them the lowdown on the way we do things out in Clybourne Park.

Beneatha *(with appreciation of the two meanings, which escape Ruth and Walter).* Un-huh.

Lindner. And we also have the category of what the association calls—*(He looks elsewhere.)*—uh—special community problems . . .

Beneatha. Yes—and what are some of those?

Walter. Girl, let the man talk.

Lindner *(with understated relief).* Thank you. I would sort of like to explain this thing in my own way. I mean I want to explain to you in a certain way.

Walter. Go ahead.

Lindner. Yes. Well. I'm going to try to get right to the point. I'm sure we'll all appreciate that in the long run.

Beneatha. Yes.

Walter. Be still now!

Lindner. Well—

Ruth *(still innocently).* Would you like another chair—you don't look comfortable.

Lindner *(more frustrated than annoyed).* No, thank you very much. Please. Well— to get right to the point, I—*(A great breath, and he is off at last.)* I am sure you people must be aware of some of the incidents which have happened in various parts of the city when colored people have moved into certain areas—*(Beneatha exhales heavily and starts tossing a piece of fruit up and down in the air.)* Well— because we have what I think is going to be a unique type of organization in American community life—not only do we deplore that kind of thing—but we are trying to do something about it. *(Beneatha stops tossing and turns with a new and quizzical interest to the man.)* We feel—*(gaining confidence in his mission because of the interest in the faces of the people he is talking to.)*—we feel that most of the trouble in this world, when you come right down to it—*(He hits his knee* *for emphasis.)*—most of the trouble exists because people just don't sit down and talk to each other.

Ruth *(nodding as she might in church, pleased with the remark)*. You can say that again, mister.

Lindner *(more encouraged by such affirmation)*. That we don't try hard enough in this world to understand the other fellow's problem. The other guy's point of view.

Ruth. Now that's right.

Beneatha and Walter merely watch and listen with genuine interest.

Lindner. Yes—that's the way we feel out in Clybourne Park. And that's why I was elected to come here this afternoon and talk to you people. Friendly like, you know, the way people should talk to each other and see if we couldn't find some way to work this thing out. As I say, the whole business is a matter of *caring* about the other fellow. Anybody can see that you are a nice family of folks, hard working and honest I'm sure. *(Beneatha frowns slightly, quizzically, her head tilted regarding him.)* Today everybody knows what it means to be on the outside of *something*. And of course, there is always somebody who is out to take advantage of people who don't always understand.

Walter. What do you mean?

Lindner. Well—you see our community is made up of people who've worked hard as the dickens for years to build up that little community. They're not rich and fancy people; just hard-working, honest people who don't really have much but those little homes and a dream of the kind of community they want to raise their children in. Now, I don't say we are perfect and there is a lot wrong in some of the things they want. But you've got to admit that a man, right or wrong, has the right to want to have the neighborhood he lives in a certain kind of way. And at the moment the overwhelming majority of our people out there feel that people get along better, take more of a common interest in the life of the community, when they share a common background. I want you to believe me when I tell you that race prejudice simply doesn't enter into it. It is a matter of the people of Clybourne Park believing, rightly or wrongly, as I say, that for the happiness of all concerned that our Negro families are happier when they live in their *own* communities.

Beneatha *(with a grand and bitter gesture)*. This, friends, is the Welcoming Committee!

Walter *(dumfounded, looking at Lindner)*. Is this what you came marching all the way over here to tell us?

Lindner. Well, now we've been having a fine conversation. I hope you'll hear me all the way through.

Walter *(tightly)*. Go ahead, man.

Lindner. You see—in the face of all the things I have said, we are prepared to make your family a very generous offer . . .

Beneatha. Thirty pieces and not a coin less!

Walter. Yeah?

Lindner (*putting on his glasses drawing a form out of the briefcase*). Our association is prepared, through the collective effort of our people, to buy the house from you at a financial gain to your family.

Ruth. Lord have mercy, ain't this the living gall!

Walter. All right, you through?

Lindner. Well, I want to give you the exact terms of the financial arrangement—

Walter. We don't want to hear no exact terms of no arrangements. I want to know if you got any more to tell us 'bout getting together?

Lindner (*taking off his glasses*). Well—I don't suppose that you feel . . .

Walter. Never mind how I feel—you got any more to say 'bout how people ought to sit down and talk to each other? . . . Get out of my house, man.

He turns his back and walks to the door.

Lindner (*looking around at the hostile faces and reaching and assembling his hat and briefcase*). Well—I don't understand why you people are reacting this way. What do you think you are going to gain by moving into a neighborhood where you just aren't wanted and where some elements—well—people can get awful worked up when they feel that their whole way of life and everything they've ever worked for is threatened.

Walter. Get out.

Lindner (*at the door, holding a small card*). Well—I'm sorry it went like this.

Walter. Get out.

Lindner (*almost sadly regarding Walter*). You just can't force people to change their hearts, son.

He turns and puts his card on a table and exits. Walter pushes the door to with stinging hatred, and stands looking at it. Ruth just sits and Beneatha just stands. They say nothing. Mama and Travis enter.

Mama. Well—this all the packing got done since I left out of here this morning. I testify before God that my children got all the energy of the *dead!* What time the moving men due?

Beneatha. Four o'clock. You had a caller, Mama.

She is smiling, teasingly.

Mama. Sure enough—who?

Beneatha (*her arms folded saucily*). The Welcoming Committee.

Walter and Ruth giggle.

Mama (*innocently*). Who?

Beneatha. The Welcoming Committee. They said they're sure going to be glad to see you when you get there.

Walter (*devilishly*). Yeah, they said they can't hardly wait to see your face.

Laughter.

Mama *(sensing their facetiousness).* What's the matter with you all?

Walter. Ain't nothing the matter with us. We just telling you 'bout the gentleman who came to see you this afternoon. From the Clybourne Park Improvement Association.

Mama. What he want?

Ruth *(in the same mood as Beneatha and Walter).* To welcome you, honey.

Walter. He said they can't hardly wait. He said the one thing they don't have, that they just *dying* to have out there is a fine family of fine colored people! *(To Ruth and Beneatha.)* Ain't that right!

Ruth *(mockingly).* Yeah! He left his card—

Beneatha *(handing card to Mama).* In case.

Mama reads and throws it on the floor—understanding and looking off as she draws her chair up to the table on which she has put her plant and some sticks and some cord.

Mama. Father, give us strength. *(Knowingly—and without fun.)* Did he threaten us?

Beneatha. Oh—Mama—they don't do it like that any more. He talked Brotherhood. He said everybody ought to learn how to sit down and hate each other with good Christian fellowship.

She and Walter shake hands to ridicule the remark.

Mama *(sadly).* Lord, protect us . . .

Ruth. You should hear the money those folks raised to buy the house from us. All we paid and then some.

Beneatha. What they think we going to do—eat 'em?

Ruth. No, honey, marry 'em.

Mama *(shaking her head).* Lord, Lord, Lord . . .

Ruth. Well—that's the way the crackers crumble. *(A beat.)* Joke.

Beneatha *(laughingly noticing what her mother is doing).* Mama, what are you doing?

Mama. Fixing my plant so it won't get hurt none on the way . . .

Beneatha. Mama, you going to take *that* to the new house?

Mama. Un-huh—

Beneatha. That raggedy-looking old thing?

Mama *(stopping and looking at her).* It expresses ME!

Ruth *(with delight, to Beneatha).* So there, Miss Thing!

Walter comes to Mama suddenly and bends down behind her and squeezes her in his arms with all his strength. She is overwhelmed by the suddenness of it and, though delighted, her manner is like that of Ruth and Travis.

Mama. Look out now, boy! You make me mess up my thing here!

Walter *(his face lit, he slips down on his knees beside her, his arms still about her).*
Mama . . . you know what it means to climb up in the chariot?

Mama *(gruffly, very happy).* Get on away from me now . . .

Ruth *(near the gift-wrapped package, trying to catch Walter's eye).* Psst—

Walter. What the old song say, Mama . . .

Ruth. Walter—Now?

She is pointing at the package.

Walter *(speaking the lines, sweetly, playfully, in his mother's face).*

I got wings . . . you got wings . . .
All God's Children got wings . . .

Mama. Boy—get out of my face and do some work . . .

Walter.

When I get to heaven gonna put on my wings,
Gonna fly all over God's heaven . . .

Beneatha *(teasingly, from across the room).* Everybody talking 'bout heaven ain't
going there!

Walter *(to Ruth, who is carrying the box across to them).* I don't know, you think we
ought to give her that . . . Seems to me she ain't been very appreciative around
here.

Mama *(eying the box, which is obviously a gift).* What is that?

Walter *(taking it from Ruth and putting it on the table in front of Mama).* Well—
what you all think? Should we give it to her?

Ruth. Oh—she was pretty good today.

Mama. I'll good you—

She turns her eyes to the box again.

Beneatha. Open it, Mama.

*She stands up, looks at it, turns and looks at all of them, and then presses her hands
together and does not open the package.*

Walter *(sweetly).* Open it, Mama. It's for you. *(Mama looks in his eyes. It is the first
present in her life without its being Christmas. Slowly she opens her package and
lifts out, one by one, a brand-new sparkling set of gardening tools. Walter continues,
prodding.)* Ruth made up the note—read it . . .

Mama *(picking up the card and adjusting her glasses).* "To our own Mrs. Miniver—
Love from Brother, Ruth, and Beneatha." Ain't that lovely . . .

Travis *(tugging at his father's sleeve).* Daddy, can I give her mine now?

Walter. All right, son. *(Travis flies to get his gift.)*

Mama. Now I don't have to use my knives and forks no more . . .

Walter. Travis didn't want to go in with the rest of us, Mama. He got his own. (*Somewhat amused.*) We don't know what it is . . .

Travis (*racing back in the room with a large hatbox and putting it in front of his grandmother*). Here!

Mama. Lord have mercy, baby. You done gone and bought your grandmother a hat?

Travis (*very proud*). Open it!

She does and lifts out an elaborate, but very elaborate, wide gardening hat, and all the adults break up at the sight of it.

Ruth. Travis, honey, what is that?

Travis (*who thinks it is beautiful and appropriate*). It's a gardening hat! Like the ladies always have on in the magazines when they work in their gardens.

Beneatha (*giggling fiercely*). Travis—we were trying to make Mama Mrs. Miniver—not Scarlett O'Hara!

Mama (*indignantly*). What's the matter with you all! This here is a beautiful hat! (*Absurdly.*) I always wanted me one just like it!

She pops it on her head to prove it to her grandson, and the hat is ludicrous and considerably oversized.

Ruth. Hot dog! Go, Mama!

Walter (*doubled over with laughter*). I'm sorry, Mama—but you look like you ready to go out and chop you some cotton sure enough!

They all laugh except Mama, out of deference to Travis's feelings.

Mama (*gathering the boy up to her*). Bless your heart—this is the prettiest hat I ever owned—(*Walter, Ruth, and Beneatha chime in—noisily, festively, and insincerely congratulating Travis on his gift.*) What are we all standing around here for? We ain't finished packin' yet. Bennie, you ain't packed one book.

The bell rings.

Beneatha. That couldn't be the movers . . . it's not hardly two good yet—

Beneatha goes into her room. Mama starts for door.

Walter (*turning, stiffening*). Wait—wait—I'll get it.

He stands and looks at the door.

Mama. You expecting company, son?

Walter (*just looking at the door*). Yeah—yeah . . .

Mama looks at Ruth, and they exchange innocent and unfrightened glances.

Mama *(not understanding).* Well, let them in, son.
Beneatha *(from her room).* We need some more string.
Mama. Travis—you run to the hardware and get me some string cord.

Mama goes out and Walter turns and looks at Ruth. Travis goes to a dish for money.

Ruth. Why don't you answer the door, man?
Walter *(suddenly bounding across the floor to embrace her).* 'Cause sometimes it hard to let the future begin! *(Stooping down in her face.)*

I got wings! You got wings!
All God's children got wings!

He crosses to the door and throws it open. Standing there is a very slight little man in a not-too-prosperous business suit and with haunted frightened eyes and a hat pulled down tightly, brim up, around his forehead. Travis passes between the men and exits. Walter leans deep in the man's face, still in his jubilance.

When I get to heaven gonna put on my wings,
Gonna fly all over God's heaven . . .

The little man just stares at him.

Heaven—

Suddenly he stops and looks past the little man into the empty hallway.

Where's Willy, man?
Bobo. He ain't with me.
Walter *(not disturbed).* Oh—come on in. You know my wife.
Bobo *(dumbly, taking off his hat).* Yes—h'you, Miss Ruth.
Ruth *(quietly, a mood apart from her husband already, seeing Bobo).* Hello, Bobo.
Walter. You right on time today . . . Right on time. That's the way! *(He slaps Bobo on his back.)* Sit down . . . lemme hear.

Ruth stands stiffly and quietly in back of them, as though somehow she senses death, her eyes fixed on her husband.

Bobo *(his frightened eyes on the floor, his hat in his hands).* Could I please get a drink of water, before I tell you about it, Walter Lee?

Walter does not take his eyes off the man. Ruth goes blindly to the tap and gets a glass of water and brings it to Bobo.

Walter. There ain't nothing wrong, is there?

Bobo. Lemme tell you—

Walter. Man—didn't nothing go wrong?

Bobo. Lemme tell you—Walter Lee. *(Looking at Ruth and talking to her more than to Walter.)* You know how it was. I got to tell you how it was. I mean first I got to tell you how it was all the way . . . I mean about the money I put in, Walter Lee . . .

Walter *(with taut agitation now).* What about the money you put in?

Bobo. Well—it wasn't much as we told you—me and Willy—*(He stops.)* I'm sorry, Walter. I got a bad feeling about it. I got a real bad feeling about it . . .

Walter. Man, what you telling me about all this for? . . . Tell me what happened in Springfield . . .

Bobo. Springfield.

Ruth *(like a dead woman).* What was supposed to happen in Springfield?

Bobo *(to her).* This deal that me and Walter went into with Willy—Me and Willy was going to go down to Springfield and spread some money 'round so's we wouldn't have to wait so long for the liquor license . . . That's what we were going to do. Everybody said that was the way you had to do, you understand, Miss Ruth?

Walter. Man—what happened down there?

Bobo *(a pitiful man, near tears).* I'm trying to tell you, Walter.

Walter *(screaming at him suddenly).* THEN TELL ME, GODDAMMIT . . . WHAT'S THE MATTER WITH YOU?

Bobo. Man . . . I didn't go to no Springfield, yesterday.

Walter *(halted, life hanging in the moment).* Why not?

Bobo *(the long way, the hard way to tell).* 'Cause I didn't have no reasons to . . .

Walter. Man, what are you talking about!

Bobo. I'm talking about the fact that when I got to the train station yesterday morning—eight o'clock like we planned . . . Man—*Willy didn't never show up.*

Walter. Why . . . where was he . . . where is he?

Bobo. That's what I'm trying to tell you . . . I don't know . . . I waited six hours . . . I called his house . . . and I waited . . . six hours . . . I waited in that train station six hours . . . *(Breaking into tears.)* That was all the extra money I had in the world . . . *(Looking up at Walter with the tears running down his face.)* Man, *Willy is gone.*

Walter. Gone, what you mean Willy is gone? Gone where? You mean he went by himself. You mean he went off to Springfield by himself—to take care of getting the license—*(Turns and looks anxiously at Ruth.)* You mean maybe he didn't want too many people in on the business down there? *(Looks to Ruth again, as before.)* You know Willy got his own ways. *(Looks back to Bobo.)* Maybe you was late yesterday and he just went on down there without you. Maybe—maybe—he's been callin' you at home tryin' to tell you what happened or something. Maybe—maybe—he just got sick. He's somewhere—he's got to be somewhere. We just got to find him—me and you got to find him. *(Grabs Bobo senselessly by the collar and starts to shake him.)* We got to!

Bobo *(in sudden angry, frightened agony).* What's the matter with you, Walter! When a cat take off with your money he don't leave you no road maps!

Walter (*turning madly, as though he is looking for Willy in the very room*). Willy! . . . Willy . . . don't do it . . . Please don't do it . . . Man, not with that money . . . Man, please, not with that money . . . Oh, God . . . Don't let it be true . . . (*He is wandering around, crying out for Willy and looking for him or perhaps for help from God.*) Man . . . I trusted you . . . Man, I put my life in your hands . . . (*He starts to crumple down on the floor as Ruth just covers her face in horror. Mama opens the door and comes into the room, with Beneatha behind her.*) Man . . . (*He starts to pound the floor with his fists, sobbing wildly.*) THAT MONEY IS MADE OUT OF MY FATHER'S FLESH—

Bobo (*standing over him helplessly*). I'm sorry, Walter . . . (*only Walter's sobs reply. Bobo puts on his hat.*) I had my life staked on this deal, too . . .

He exits.

Mama (*to Walter*). Son—(*She goes to him, bends down to him, talks to his bent head.*) Son . . . Is it gone? Son, I gave you sixty-five hundred dollars. Is it gone? All of it? Beneatha's money too?

Walter (*lifting his head slowly*). Mama . . . I never . . . went to the bank at all . . .

Mama (*not wanting to believe him*). You mean . . . your sister's school money . . . you used that too . . . Walter? . . .

Walter. Yessss! All of it . . . It's all gone . . .

There is total silence. Ruth stands with her face covered with her hands; Beneatha leans forlornly against a wall, fingering a piece of red ribbon from the mother's gift. Mama stops and looks at her son without recognition and then, quite without thinking about it, starts to beat him senselessly in the face. Beneatha goes to them and stops it.

Beneatha. Mama!

Mama stops and looks at both of her children and rises slowly and wanders vaguely, aimlessly away from them.

Mama. I seen . . . him . . . night after night . . . come in . . . and look at that rug . . . and then look at me . . . the red showing in his eyes . . . the veins moving in his head . . . I seen him grow thin and old before he was forty . . . working and working and working like somebody's old horse . . . killing himself . . . and you—you give it all away in a day—(*She raises her arms to strike him again.*)

Beneatha. Mama—

Mama. Oh, God . . . (*She looks up to Him.*) Look down here—and show me the strength.

Beneatha. Mama—

Mama (*folding over*). Strength . . .

Beneatha (*plaintively*). Mama . . .

Mama. Strength!

Curtain.

ACT III

Time: An hour later.

At curtain, there is a sullen light of gloom in the living room, gray light not unlike that which began the first scene of Act I. At left we can see Walter within his room, alone with himself. He is stretched out on the bed, his shirt out and open, his arms under his head. He does not smoke, he does not cry out, he merely lies there, looking up at the ceiling, much as if he were alone in the world.

In the living room Beneatha sits at the table, still surrounded by the now almost ominous packing crates. She sits looking off. We feel that this is a mood struck perhaps an hour before, and it lingers now, full of the empty sound of profound disappointment. We see on a line from her brother's bedroom the sameness of their attitudes. Presently the bell rings and Beneatha rises without ambition or interest in answering. It is Asagai, smiling broadly, striding into the room with energy and happy expectation and conversation.

Asagai. I came over . . . I had some free time. I thought I might help with the packing. Ah, I like the look of packing crates! A household in preparation for a journey! It depresses some people . . . but for me . . . it is another feeling. Something full of the flow of life, do you understand? Movement, progress . . . It makes me think of Africa.

Beneatha. Africa!

Asagai. What kind of a mood is this? Have I told you how deeply you move me?

Beneatha. He gave away the money, Asagai . . .

Asagai. Who gave away what money?

Beneatha. The insurance money. My brother gave it away.

Asagai. Gave it away?

Beneatha. He made an investment! With a man even Travis wouldn't have trusted with his most worn-out marbles.

Asagai. And it's gone?

Beneatha. Gone!

Asagai. I'm very sorry . . . And you, now?

Beneatha. Me? . . . Me? . . . Me, I'm nothing . . . Me. When I was very small . . . we used to take our sleds out in the wintertime and the only hills we had were the ice-covered stone steps of some houses down the street. And we used to fill them in with snow and make them smooth and slide down them all day . . . and it was very dangerous, you know . . . far too steep . . . and sure enough one day a kid named Rufus came down too fast and hit the sidewalk and we saw his face just split open right there in front of us . . . And I remember standing there looking at his bloody open face thinking that was the end of Rufus. But the ambulance came and they took him to the hospital and they fixed the broken bones and they sewed it all up . . . and the next time I saw Rufus he just had a little line down the middle of his face . . . I never got over that . . .

Asagai. What?

Beneatha. That that was what one person could do for another, fix him up—sew up the problem, make him all right again. That was the most marvelous thing in the world . . . I wanted to do that. I always thought it was the one concrete thing in the world that a human being could do. Fix up the sick, you know—and make them whole again. This was truly being God . . .

Asagai. You wanted to be God?

Beneatha. No—I wanted to cure. It used to be so important to me. I wanted to cure. It used to matter. I used to care. I mean about people and how their bodies hurt . . .

Asagai. And you've stopped caring?

Beneatha. Yes—I think so.

Asagai. Why?

Beneatha (bitterly). Because it doesn't seem deep enough, close enough to what ails mankind! It was a child's way of seeing things—or an idealist's.

Asagai. Children see things very well sometimes—and idealists even better.

Beneatha. I know that's what you think. Because you are still where I left off. You with all your talk and dreams about Africa! You still think you can patch up the world. Cure the Great Sore of Colonialism—(Loftily, mocking it.) with the Penicillin of Independence—!

Asagai. Yes!

Beneatha. Independence and then what? What about all the crooks and thieves and just plain idiots who will come into power and steal and plunder the same as before—only now they will be black and do it in the name of the new Independence—WHAT ABOUT THEM?!

Asagai. That will be the problem for another time. First we must get there.

Beneatha. And where does it end?

Asagai. End? Who even spoke of an end? To life? To living?

Beneatha. An end to misery! To stupidity! Don't you see there isn't any real progress, Asagai, there is only one large circle that we march in, around and around, each of us with our own little picture in front of us—our own little mirage that we think is the future.

Asagai. That is the mistake.

Beneatha. What?

Asagai. What you just said—about the circle. It isn't a circle—it is simply a long line—as in geometry, you know, one that reaches into infinity. And because we cannot see the end—we also cannot see how it changes. And it is very odd but those who see the changes—who dream, who will not give up—are called idealists . . . and those who see only the circle—we call them the "realists"!

Beneatha. Asagai, while I was sleeping in that bed in there, people went out and took the future right out of my hands! And nobody asked me, nobody consulted me—they just went out and changed my life!

Asagai. Was it your money?

Beneatha. What?

Asagai. Was it your money he gave away?

Beneatha. It belonged to all of us.

Asagai. But did you earn it? Would you have had it at all if your father had not died?

Beneatha. No.

Asagai. Then isn't there something wrong in a house—in a world—where all dreams, good or bad, must depend on the death of a man? I never thought to see *you* like this, Alaiyo. You! Your brother made a mistake and you are grateful to him so that now you can give up the ailing human race on account of it! You talk about what good is struggle, what good is anything! Where are we all going and why are we bothering!

Beneatha. AND YOU CANNOT ANSWER IT!

Asagai (*shouting over her*). I LIVE THE ANSWER! (*Pause.*) In my village at home it is the exceptional man who can even read a newspaper . . . or who ever sees a book at all. I will go home and much of what I will have to say will seem strange to the people of my village. But I will teach and work and things will happen, slowly and swiftly. At times it will seem that nothing changes at all . . . and then again the sudden dramatic events which make history leap into the future. And then quiet again. Retrogression even. Guns, murder, revolution. And I even will have moments when I wonder if the quiet was not better than all that death and hatred. But I will look about my village at the illiteracy and disease and ignorance and I will not wonder long. And perhaps . . . perhaps I will be a great man . . . I mean perhaps I will hold on to the substance of truth and find my way always with the right course . . . and perhaps for it I will be butchered in my bed some night by the servants of empire . . .

Beneatha. *The martyr!*

Asagai (*he smiles*). . . . or perhaps I shall live to be a very old man, respected and esteemed in my new nation . . . And perhaps I shall hold office and this is what I'm trying to tell you, Alaiyo: perhaps the things I believe now for my country will be wrong and outmoded, and I will not understand and do terrible things to have things my way or merely to keep my power. Don't you see that there will be young men and women—not British soldiers then, but my own black countrymen—to step out of the shadows some evening and slit my then useless throat? Don't you see they have always been there . . . that they always will be. And that such a thing as my own death will be an advance? They who might kill me even . . . actually replenish all that I was.

Beneatha. Oh, Asagai, I know all that.

Asagai. Good! Then stop moaning and groaning and tell me what you plan to do.

Beneatha. Do?

Asagai. I have a bit of a suggestion.

Beneatha. What?

Asagai (*rather quietly for him*). That when it is all over—that you come home with me—

Beneatha (*staring at him and crossing away with exasperation*). Oh—Asagai—at this moment you decide to be romantic!

Asagai (*quickly understanding the misunderstanding*). My dear, young creature of the New World—I do not mean across the city—I mean across the ocean: home—to Africa.

Beneatha (*slowly understanding and turning to him with murmured amazement*). To Africa?

Asagai. Yes! . . . (*smiling and lifting his arms playfully.*) Three hundred years later the African Prince rose up out of the seas and swept the maiden back across the middle passage over which her ancestors had come—

Beneatha (*unable to play*). To—to Nigeria?

Asagai. Nigeria. Home. (*Coming to her with genuine romantic flippancy.*) I will show you our mountains and our stars; and give you cool drinks from gourds and teach you the old songs and the ways of our people—and, in time, we will pretend that—(*Very softly.*)—you have only been away for a day. Say that you'll come—(*He swings her around and takes her full in his arms in a kiss which proceeds to passion.*)

Beneatha (*pulling away suddenly*). You're getting me all mixed up—

Asagai. Why?

Beneatha. Too many things—too many things have happened today. I must sit down and think. I don't know what I feel about anything right this minute.

She promptly sits down and props her chin on her fist.

Asagai (*charmed*). All right, I shall leave you. No—don't get up. (*Touching her, gently, sweetly.*) Just sit awhile and think . . . Never be afraid to sit awhile and think. (*He goes to door and looks at her.*) How often I have looked at you and said, "Ah—so this is what the New World hath finally wrought . . ."

He exits. Beneatha sits on alone. Presently Walter enters from his room and starts to rummage through things, feverishly looking for something. She looks up and turns in her seat.

Beneatha (*hissingly*). Yes—just look at what the New World hath wrought! . . . Just look! (*She gestures with bitter disgust.*) There he is! *Monsieur le petit bourgeois noir*[2]—himself! There he is—Symbol of a Rising Class! Entrepreneur! Titan of the system! (*Walter ignores her completely and continues frantically and destructively looking for something and hurling things to floor and tearing things out of their place in his search. Beneatha ignores the eccentricity of his actions and goes on with the monologue of insult.*) Did you dream of yachts on Lake Michigan, Brother? Did you see yourself on that Great Day sitting down at the Conference Table, surrounded by all the mighty bald-headed men in America? All halted, waiting, breathless, waiting for your pronouncements on industry? Waiting for you—Chairman of the Board! (*Walter finds what he is looking for—a small piece of white paper—and pushes it in his pocket and puts on his coat and rushes out without ever having looked at her. She shouts after him.*) I look at you and I see the final triumph of stupidity in the world!

---

[2] Mr. Black Bourgeoisie.

The door slams and she returns to just sitting again. Ruth comes quickly out of Mama's room.

Ruth. Who was that?

Beneatha. Your husband.

Ruth. Where did he go?

Beneatha. Who knows—maybe he has an appointment at U.S. Steel.

Ruth *(anxiously, with frightened eyes).* You didn't say nothing bad to him, did you?

Beneatha. Bad? Say anything bad to him? No—I told him he was a sweet boy and full of dreams and everything is strictly peachy keen, as the ofay kids say!

Mama enters from her bedroom. She is lost, vague, trying to catch hold, to make some sense of her former command of the world, but it still eludes her. A sense of waste overwhelms her gait; a measure of apology rides on her shoulders. She goes to her plant, which has remained on the table, looks at it, picks it up and takes it to the window sill and sits it outside, and she stands and looks at it a long moment. Then she closes the window, straightens her body with effort and turns around to her children.

Mama. Well—ain't it a mess in here, though? *(A false cheerfulness, a beginning of something.)* I guess we all better stop moping around and get some work done. All this unpacking and everything we got to do. *(Ruth raises her head slowly in response to the sense of the line; and Beneatha in similar manner turns very slowly to look at her mother.)* One of you all better call the moving people and tell 'em not to come.

Ruth. Tell 'em not to come?

Mama. Of course, baby. Ain't no need in 'em coming all the way here and having to go back. They charges for that too. *(She sits down, fingers to her brow, thinking.)* Lord, ever since I was a little girl, I always remembers people saying, "Lena—Lena Eggleston, you aims too high all the time. You needs to slow down and see life a little more like it is. Just slow down some." That's what they always used to say down home—"Lord, that Lena Eggleston is a high-minded thing. She'll get her due one day!"

Ruth. No, Lena . . .

Mama. Me and Big Walter just didn't never learn right.

Ruth. Lena, no! We gotta go. Bennie—tell her . . .

She rises and crosses to Beneatha with her arms outstretched. Beneatha doesn't respond.

Tell her we can still move . . . the notes ain't but a hundred and twenty-five a month. We got four grown people in this house—we can work . . .

Mama *(to herself).* Just aimed too high all the time—

Ruth *(turning and going to Mama fast—the words pouring out with urgency and desperation).* Lena—I'll work . . . I'll work twenty hours a day in all the kitchens in Chicago . . . I'll strap my baby on my back if I have to and scrub all the floors in America and wash all the sheets in America if I have to—but we got to MOVE! We got to get OUT OF HERE!!

Mama reaches out absently and pats Ruth's hand.

Mama. No—I sees things differently now. Been thinking 'bout some of the things we could do to fix this place up some. I seen a second-hand bureau over on Maxwell Street just the other day that could fit right there. *(She points to where the new furniture might go. Ruth wanders away from her.)* Would need some new handles on it and then a little varnish and it look like something brand-new. And—we can put up them new curtains in the kitchen . . . Why this place be looking fine. Cheer us all up so that we forget trouble ever come . . . *(To Ruth.)* And you could get some nice screens to put up in your room round the baby's bassinet . . . *(She looks at both of them pleadingly.)* Sometimes you just got to know when to give up some things . . . and hold on to what you got . . .

Walter enters from the outside, looking spent and leaning against the door, his coat hanging from him.

Mama. Where you been, son?
Walter *(breathing hard).* Made a call.
Mama. To who, son?
Walter. To The Man. *(He heads for his room.)*
Mama. What man, baby?
Walter *(stops in the door).* The Man, Mama. Don't you know who The Man is?
Ruth. Walter Lee?
Walter. The Man. Like the guys in the streets say—The Man. Captain Boss—Mistuh Charley . . . Old Cap'n Please Mr. Bossman . . .
Beneatha *(suddenly).* Lindner!
Walter. That's right! That's good. I told him to come right over.
Beneatha *(fiercely, understanding).* For what? What do you want to see him for!
Walter *(looking at his sister).* We going to do business with him.
Mama. What you talking 'bout, son?
Walter. Talking 'bout life, Mama. You all always telling me to see life like it is. Well—I laid in there on my back today . . . and I figured it out. Life just like it is. Who gets and who don't get. *(He sits down with his coat on and laughs.)* Mama, you know it's all divided up. Life is. Sure enough. Between the takers and the "tooken." *(He laughs.)* I've figured it out finally. *(He looks around at them.)* Yeah. Some of us always getting "tooken." *(He laughs.)* People like Willy Harris, they don't never get "tooken." And you know why the rest of us do? 'Cause we all mixed up. Mixed up bad. We get to looking 'round for the right and the wrong; and we worry about it and cry about it and stay up nights trying to figure out 'bout the wrong and the right of things all the time . . . And all the time, man, them takers is out there operating, just taking and taking. Willy Harris? Shoot—Willy Harris don't even count. He don't even count in the big scheme of things. But I'll say one thing for old Willy Harris . . . he's taught me something. He's taught me to keep my eye on what counts in this world. Yeah—*(Shouting out a little.)* Thanks, Willy!

Ruth. What did you call that man for, Walter Lee?

Walter. Called him to tell him to come on over to the show. Gonna put on a show for the man. Just what he wants to see. You see, Mama, the man came here today and he told us that them people out there where you want us to move—well they so upset they willing to pay us *not* to move! *(He laughs again.)* And—and oh, Mama—you would of been proud of the way me and Ruth and Bennie acted. We told him to get out . . . Lord have mercy! We told the man to get out! Oh, we was some proud folks this afternoon, yeah. *(He lights a cigarette.)* We were still full of that old-time stuff . . .

Ruth *(coming toward him slowly).* You talking 'bout taking them people's money to keep us from moving in that house?

Walter. I ain't just talking 'bout it, baby—I'm telling you that's what's going to happen!

Beneatha. Oh, God! Where is the bottom! Where is the real honest-to-God bottom so he can't go any farther!

Walter. See—that's the old stuff. You and that boy that was here today. You all want everybody to carry a flag and a spear and sing some marching songs, huh? You wanna spend your life looking into things and trying to find the right and the wrong part, huh? Yeah. You know what's going to happen to that boy someday—he'll find himself sitting in a dungeon, locked in forever—and the takers will have the key! Forget it, baby! There ain't no causes—there ain't nothing but taking in this world, and he who takes most is smartest—and it don't make a damn bit of difference *how.*

Mama. You making something inside me cry, son. Some awful pain inside me.

Walter. Don't cry, Mama. Understand. That white man is going to walk in that door able to write checks for more money than we ever had. It's important to him and I'm going to help him . . . I'm going to put on the show, Mama.

Mama. Son—I come from five generations of people who was slaves and share-croppers—but ain't nobody in my family never let nobody pay 'em no money that was a way of telling us we wasn't fit to walk the earth. We ain't never been that poor. *(Raising her eyes and looking at him.)* We ain't never been that—dead inside.

Beneatha. Well—we are dead now. All the talk about dreams and sunlight that goes on in this house. It's all dead now.

Walter. What's the matter with you all! I didn't make this world! It was give to me this way! Hell, yes, I want me some yachts someday! Yes, I want to hang some real pearls 'round my wife's neck. Ain't she supposed to wear no pearls? Somebody tell me—tell me, who decides which women is suppose to wear pearls in this world. I tell you I am a *man*—and I think my wife should wear some pearls in this world!

This last line hangs a good while and Walter begins to move about the room. The word "Man" has penetrated his consciousness; he mumbles it to himself repeatedly between strange agitated pauses as he moves about.

Mama. Baby, how you going to feel on the inside?

Walter. Fine! . . . Going to feel fine . . . a man . . .

Mama. You won't have nothing left then, Walter Lee.

Walter *(coming to her).* I'm going to feel fine, Mama. I'm going to look that son-of-a-bitch in the eyes and say—*(He falters.)*—and say, "All right, Mr. Lindner—*(He falters even more.)*—that's *your* neighborhood out there! You got the right to keep it like you want! You got the right to have it like you want! Just write the check and—the house is yours." And—and I am going to say—*(His voice almost breaks.)* "And you—you people just put the money in my hand and you won't have to live next to this bunch of stinking niggers! . . ." *(He straightens up and moves away from his mother, walking around the room.)* And maybe—maybe I'll just get down on my black knees . . . *(He does so; Ruth and Bennie and Mama watch him in frozen horror.)* "Captain, Mistuh, Bossman—(Groveling and grinning and wringing his hands in profoundly anguished imitation of the slow-witted movie stereotype.)* A-hee-hee-hee! Oh, yassuh boss! Yasssssuh! Great white—*(Voice breaking, he forces himself to go on.)*—Father, just gi' ussen de money, fo' God's sake, and we's—we's ain't gwine come out deh and dirty up yo' white folks neighborhood . . ." *(He breaks down completely.)* And I'll feel fine! Fine! FINE! *(He gets up and goes into the bedroom.)*

Beneatha. That is not a man. That is nothing but a toothless rat.

Mama. Yes—death done come in this here house. *(She is nodding, slowly, reflectively.)* Done come walking in my house on the lips of my children. You what supposed to be my beginning again. You—what supposed to be my harvest. *(To Beneatha.)* You—you mourning your brother?

Beneatha. He's no brother of mine.

Mama. What you say?

Beneatha. I said that that individual in that room is no brother of mine.

Mama. That's what I thought you said. You feeling like you better than he is today? *(Beneatha does not answer.)* Yes? What you tell him a minute ago? That he wasn't a man? Yes? You give him up for me? You done wrote his epitaph too—like the rest of the world? Well, who give you the privilege?

Beneatha. Be on my side for once! You saw what he just did, Mama! You saw him—down on his knees. Wasn't it you who taught me to despise any man who would do that? Do what he's going to do?

Mama. Yes—I taught you that. Me and your daddy. But I thought I taught you something else too . . . I thought I taught you to love him.

Beneatha. Love him? There is nothing left to love.

Mama. There is *always* something left to love. And if you ain't learned that, you ain't learned nothing. *(Looking at her.)* Have you cried for that boy today? I don't mean for yourself and for the family 'cause we lost the money. I mean for him: what he been through and what it done to him. Child, when do you think is the time to love somebody the most? When they done good and made things easy for everybody? Well then, you ain't through learning—because that ain't the time at all. It's when he's at his lowest and can't believe in hisself 'cause the world done whipped him so! When you starts measuring somebody, measure him right, child, measure him right. Make sure you done taken into account what hills and valleys he come through before he got to wherever he is.

Travis bursts into the room at the end of the speech, leaving the door open.

Travis. Grandmama—the moving men are downstairs! The truck just pulled up.
Mama *(turning and looking at him).* Are they, baby? They downstairs?

She sighs and sits. Lindner appears in the doorway. He peers in and knocks lightly, to gain attention, and comes in. All turn to look at him.

Lindner *(hat and briefcase in hand).* Uh—hello . . .

Ruth crosses mechanically to the bedroom door and opens it and lets it swing open freely and slowly as the lights come up on Walter within, still in his coat, sitting at the far corner of the room. He looks up and out through the room to Lindner.

Ruth. He's here.

A long minute passes and Walter slowly gets up.

Lindner *(coming to the table with efficiency, putting his briefcase on the table and starting to unfold papers and unscrew fountain pens).* Well, I certainly was glad to hear from you people. *(Walter has begun the trek out of the room, slowly and awkwardly, rather like a small boy, passing the back of his sleeve across his mouth from time to time.)* Life can really be so much simpler than people let it be most of the time. Well—with whom do I negotiate? You, Mrs. Younger, or your son here? *(Mama sits with her hands folded on her lap and her eyes closed as Walter advances. Travis goes closer to Lindner and looks at the papers curiously.)* Just some official papers, sonny.
Ruth. Travis, you go downstairs—
Mama *(opening her eyes and looking into Walter's).* No. Travis, you stay right here. And you make him understand what you doing, Walter Lee. You teach him good. Like Willy Harris taught you. You show where our five generations done come to. *(Walter looks from her to the boy, who grins at him innocently.)* Go ahead, son—*(She folds her hands and closes her eyes.)* Go ahead.
Walter *(at last crosses to Lindner, who is reviewing the contract).* Well, Mr. Lindner. *(Beneatha turns away.)* We called you—*(There is a profound, simple groping quality in his speech.)*—because, well, me and my family *(He looks around and shifts from one foot to the other.)* Well—we are very plain people . . .
Lindner. Yes—
Walter. I mean—I have worked as a chauffeur most of my life—and my wife here, she does domestic work in people's kitchens. So does my mother. I mean—we are plain people . . .
Lindner. Yes, Mr. Younger—
Walter *(really like a small boy, looking down at his shoes and then up at the man).* And—uh—well, my father, well, he was a laborer most of his life. . . .
Lindner *(absolutely confused).* Uh, yes—yes, I understand. *(He turns back to the contract.)*

Walter *(a beat; staring at him).* And my father—*(With sudden intensity.)* My father almost *beat a man to death* once because this man called him a bad name or something, you know what I mean?

Lindner *(looking up, frozen).* No, no, I'm afraid I don't—

Walter *(a beat. The tension hangs; then Walter steps back from it).* Yeah. Well— what I mean is that we come from people who had a lot of *pride.* I mean—we are very proud people. And that's my sister over there and she's going to be a doctor—and we are very proud—

Lindner. Well—I am sure that is very nice, but—

Walter. What I am telling you is that we called you over here to tell you that we are very proud and that this—*(Signaling to Travis.)* Travis, come here. *(Travis crosses and Walter draws him before him facing the man.)* This is my son, and he makes the sixth generation our family in this country. And we have all thought about your offer—

Lindner. Well, good . . . good—

Walter. And we have decided to move into our house because my father—my father—he earned it for us brick by brick. *(Mama has her eyes closed and is rocking back and forth as though she were in church, with her head nodding the Amen yes.)* We don't want to make no trouble for nobody or fight no causes, and we will try to be good neighbors. And that's *all* we got to say about that. *(He looks the man absolutely in the eyes.)* We don't want your money. *(He turns and walks away.)*

Lindner *(looking around at all of them).* I take it then—that you have decided to occupy . . .

Beneatha. That's what the man said.

Lindner *(to Mama in her reverie).* Then I would like to appeal to you, Mrs. Younger. You are older and wiser and understand things better I am sure . . .

Mama. I am afraid you don't understand. My son said we was going to move and there ain't nothing left for me to say. *(Briskly.)* You know how these young folks is nowadays, mister. Can't do a thing with 'em! *(As he opens his mouth, she rises.)* Good-bye.

Lindner *(folding up his materials).* Well—if you are that final about it . . . there is nothing left for me to say. *(He finishes, almost ignored by the family, who are concentrating on Walter Lee. At the door Lindner halts and looks around.)* I sure hope you people know what you're getting into.

He shakes his head and exits.

Ruth *(looking around and coming to life).* Well, for God's sake—if the moving men are here—LET'S GET THE HELL OUT OF HERE!

Mama *(into action).* Ain't it the truth! Look at all this here mess. Ruth, put Travis's good jacket on him . . . Walter Lee, fix your tie and tuck your shirt in, you look like somebody's hoodlum! Lord have mercy, where is my plant? *(She flies to get it amid the general bustling of the family, who are deliberately trying to ignore the nobility of the past moment.)* You all start on down . . . Travis child, don't go empty-handed . . . Ruth, where did I put that box with my skillets in it?

I want to be in charge of it myself . . . I'm going to make us the biggest dinner we ever ate tonight . . . Beneatha, what's the matter with them stockings? Pull them things up, girl . . .

The family starts to file out as two moving men appear and begin to carry out the heavier pieces of furniture, bumping into the family as they move about.

Beneatha. Mama, Asagai asked me to marry him today and go to Africa—
Mama (*in the middle of her getting-ready activity*). He did? You ain't old enough to marry nobody—(*Seeing the moving men lifting one of her chairs precariously.*) Darling, that ain't no bale of cotton, please handle it so we can sit in it again! I had that chair twenty-five years . . .

The movers sigh with exasperation and go on with their work.

Beneatha (*girlishly and unreasonably trying to pursue the conversation*). To go to Africa, Mama—be a doctor in Africa . . .
Mama (*distracted*). Yes, baby—
Walter. *Africa!* What he want you to go to Africa for?
Beneatha. To practice there . . .
Walter. Girl, if you don't get all them silly ideas out your head! You better marry yourself a man with some loot . . .
Beneatha (*angrily, precisely as in the first scene of the play*). What have you got to do with who I marry!
Walter. Plenty. Now I think George Murchison—
Beneatha. *George Murchison!* I wouldn't marry him if he was Adam and I was Eve!

Walter and Beneatha go out yelling at each other vigorously and the anger is loud and real till their voices diminish. Ruth stands at the door and turns to Mama and smiles knowingly.

Mama (*fixing her hat at last*). Yeah—they something all right, my children . . .
Ruth. Yeah—they're something. Let's go, Lena.
Mama (*stalling, starting to look around at the house*). Yes—I'm coming. Ruth—
Ruth. Yes?
Mama (*quietly, woman to woman*). He finally come into his manhood today, didn't he? Kind of like a rainbow after the rain . . .
Ruth (*biting her lip lest her own pride explode in front of Mama*). Yes, Lena.

Walter's voice calls for them raucously.

Walter (*off stage*). Y'all come on! These people charges by the hour, you know!
Mama (*waving Ruth out vaguely*). All right, honey—go on down. I be down directly.

Ruth hesitates, then exits. Mama stands, at last alone in the living room, her plant on the table before her as the lights start to come down. She looks around at all the walls and ceilings and suddenly, despite herself, while the children call below, a great heaving thing rises in her and she puts her fist to her mouth to stifle it, takes a final desperate look, pulls her coat about her, pats her hat, and goes out. The lights dim down. The door opens and she comes back in, grabs her plant, and goes out for the last time.

Curtain.

FOR ANALYSIS

1. In what ways does the opening **dialogue** between Ruth and Walter establish the major **themes** of the play?

2. Describe the shared values and dreams that give the family its cohesiveness.

3. Describe Walter's view of women. Is his view validated by the actions of the women? Explain.

4. Describe the contrast between Beneatha's two suitors, George Murchison and Joseph Asagai, and explain how it contributes to the theme of the play.

5. What is the significance of Mama's plant?

6. In what ways does the dialogue between Beneatha and Asagai that opens act III advance the theme of the play and prepare us for the ending?

7. Karl Lindner asserts that "the overwhelming majority of our people out there feel that people get along better, take more of a common interest in the life of the community, when they share a common background" (act II, scene 3). Is this a reasonable argument? Or is Lindner a racist? Explain.

8. In what sense is this play a celebration of African American life and culture?

9. Describe the speech patterns of the main **characters**. What function do the differences in **diction** serve? Is there any relationship between a character's diction and his or her moral standing in the play? Explain.

10. Even though he is dead, Big Walter is an important presence in the play. Examine the ways in which his presence is created, and explain what he represents.

WRITING TOPICS

1. Argue for or against the proposition that this play, written in 1959, is dated in its portrayal of black life and race relations.

2. Read Hughes's poem "Harlem" (p. 429), from which the title of the play is taken, and write an essay describing why you think Hansberry found the line appropriate as the title for her play.

3. Describe the significance of money in the play.

4. Write an essay in which you speculate on what happens to the members of the Younger family once they have moved into their new home.

MAKING CONNECTIONS

Compare and contrast the dynamics of family life in this play with those of the family in Walker's "Everyday Use" (p. 586). Which family do you think is more successful in coping with its problems? Explain.

LLOYD W. BROWN (B. 1938)

LORRAINE HANSBERRY AS ICONIST: A REAPPRAISAL OF *A RAISIN IN THE SUN*   1974

Ever since the sixties the reputation and significance of several established Black American writers have become issues in the running ethnopolitical debates on Black American literature. James Baldwin, Ralph Ellison, and LeRoi Jones, for example, have been at the center of confrontations between "militants" and "moderates," Black "extremists" and white "liberals," integrationists and Black nationalists, and so on. And it is increasingly evident that Lorraine Hansberry has joined this list of controversial writers, especially on the basis of her first play, *A Raisin in the Sun* (1959). On the anti-integrationist side, Harold Cruse deplores *Raisin* as "the artistic, aesthetic and class-inspired culmination of the efforts of the Harlem left-wing literary and cultural in-group to achieve integration of the Negro in the arts." In other words, it is a "most cleverly written piece of glorified soap opera," a "second-rate" play about working-class Blacks who "mouth middle class ideology." Moreover, the alleged shortcomings of Lorraine Hansberry's integrationist philosophy are linked, somehow, with her supposed inferiority as a dramatic artist: "*A Raisin in the Sun* demonstrated that the Negro playwright has lost the intellectual and, therefore, technical and creative, ability to deal with his own special ethnic group materials in dramatic form" (Cruse, 1968: 278–281).

On the other side of the debate, both C. W. E. Bigsby (1967: 152) and Richard A. Duprey have praised Hansberry precisely because, in their view, she transcends those "special ethnic group materials." Thus, according to Duprey (1967: 210), *Raisin* is full of human insights that transcend any racial "concerns," and Bigsby praises her compassion and her understanding of the need to "transcend" history. In short, Hansberry's work has been caught up in the continuing conflict between the ethnic criteria of social protesters and the pro-integrationist's ethos of love and reconciliation. And when a critic such as Jordan Miller (1971: 161) is confronted with this kind of debate he responds with the art-for-art's-sake thesis. He refuses to discuss Hansberry's work "on the basis of any form of racial consciousness" or "in any niche of social significance," and insists instead on the critic's "obligation" to judge the dramatist's work as "dramatic literature quite apart from other factors."

These three representative viewpoints need to be emphasized here because, taken together, they demonstrate a continuing problem in the study of Black literature: the tendency, for one reason or another, to isolate questions of structure or technique from those of social, or racial, significance. Harold Cruse's reservations about *Raisin* begin with assumptions based, not so much on a searching analysis of the text, but on a jaundiced view of Hansberry's social background (Black middle class) and ideological activities (left-wing "in-groups"). Consequently, his allegations about her dramatic technique are really a species of non sequitur: Hansberry's play is a bourgeois integrationist work, *therefore* it lacks "technical . . . ability." At the opposite extreme Jordan Miller would have us concentrate on the play as a "dramatic structure"—to the esoteric exclusion of Hansberry's obvious preoccupation with "social signifi-cance" and "racial consciousness." But this erudite escapism does no more jus-tice to Hansberry's art than Harold Cruse's ideological bias, for, once again, the artist's total achievement is being obscured by the critic's determination to treat technique and social content as if these are unrelated or mutually exclusive.

Bigsby does offer some analysis of Hansberry's dramatic techniques, but the attempt is limited by his preconception that *Raisin* is primarily an integra-tionist manifesto. The rhetorical design of Hansberry's title is a case in point. Bigsby assumes that the play as a whole incorporates all the thematic tensions (destruction versus fulfillment, despair versus self-realization) that dominate "Harlem," the Langston Hughes poem from which Hansberry takes her title. And this reading of the play's title justifies the critic's view that the play "clearly represents Lorraine Hansberry's own faith" in the inevitability of change built on courage and compassion (Bigsby, 1967: 161). But the fact is that the phrase, "a raisin in the sun," does not embody all of the thematic tensions in Hughes' poem. On the contrary, it is one of the ominous negatives which counterbal-ance positive possibilities in the conflicts of "Harlem":

> What happens to a dream deferred?
> Does it dry up
> like a raisin in the sun?
> Or fester like a sore—
> And then run?
> Does it stink like rotten meat?
> Or crust and sugar over—
> like a syrupy sweet?

In effect, the connotations of Hansberry's title establish an ironic context 5 which is crucial to an understanding of the play's themes and design. Hughes clusters the ambiguities and tensions of his poem around the experience of a "dream deferred"—a deferred dream may simply end in the drying up of hope (like a raisin in the sun) or, paradoxically, the adversities of frustra-tion may motivate the "syrupy sweet" realization of human potential. Conse-quently, when Hansberry selects the "raisin" phrase she limits the thematic relevance of Hughes' poem to her play: her themes are concerned, not so much with a fulfilled faith in inevitable changes for the better, but with the drying up of dreams. Hence the basic contextual irony of the title, and of the themes which flow from it, is based on an acceptance of the dream ideal—spiritual and material fulfillment in America—and, simultaneously, on a realistic recogni-tion of those (like Walter Younger) whose dreams, or hopes, have dried up. The point is not that Lorraine Hansberry rejects integration or the economic and moral promise of the American dream, but that she remains loyal to this dream ideal while looking, realistically, at its corruption in the United States. Once we recognize this fundamental strategy, then we will begin to accept the ironic nuances of the play as intrinsic qualities of Hansberry's dramatic insights rather than as the "unintentional" irony that Bigsby (1967: 159) attributes to the work. Indeed, there has been a curiously persistent refusal to credit Hansberry with any capacity for irony, and this has led critics to interpret thematic conflicts as mere confusion, contradictions, or as a rather insipid species of eclecticism. On the much-debated Pan-African theme, for example, Harold R. Isaacs (1960: 33) finds it difficult to reconcile Hansberry's Black nationalist sympathies and her long-term ideal of human reconciliation. But the complex grasp of self-esteem and human solidarity as compatibles is no more "contradictory" than W. E. B. DuBois's (1969: 3) famous and well-considered ideal of ethnic self-awareness coexisting with human unity, or Frantz Fanon's (1968: 246–247) deliberate emphasis on an ideal internationalism which accommodates national identities and roles. Consequently, it is not really an exaggeration of her dramatic insights to assume that the romanticization of Africa, in the person of Asagai, goes hand in hand with the emphasis on the Youngers' American commitment. Indeed, Hansberry's ironic grasp of the Black American's duality enables her to portray (rather than merely succumb to) the African nostalgia which has been nurtured by the Youngers' dreams but which remains realistically counterbalanced by the inexorable facts of the Youngers' American identity (complete with the pervasive American dream). In short, we need to break away from the old condescension which assumes, arbitrarily, that perceptual conflicts within the play are merely reflections of Hansberry's personal confusions rather than reflections of her ironic insight into social and psychological ambiguities that already exist. And, in this connection, the need to reevaluate her themes is especially strong with respect to two interwoven themes: (1) the ambiguity of the American dream itself, and (2) integration as the Black American's means of realizing the dream.

The more familiar irony of the Youngers' poverty is obvious enough: their deprivations expose the gap between the American dream and the Black American reality. But, equally important, both the nature of Walter Younger's ambitions and the success of George Murchison emphasize another paradox. Ideally the promise of the American dream is aimed at the total personality of the individual: the dream is defined not only in moral terms—freedom, equality, justice, and self-realization—but also in material and socio-economic terms. However, in practice, the moral ideals of the dream are invariably subordinated to material criteria and ambitions. Hence the socioeconomic advantages of the affluent society have been culturally ennobled as the passport to spiritual fulfillment, in much the same way that the physical freedom of the slave is a prerequisite for the total realization of human dignity.

The dialectical materialism in which the American dream is rooted [is] the very staple of the society's cultural modes—as in the television commercials and billboard advertisements in which toothpaste, automobiles, or deodorants promise emotional and sexual fulfillment, or in which images of novelty justify built-in obsolescence by appealing to the dream ideal of inevitable change as improvement, newness as fulfillment, and modernity as achievement. And in Hansberry's play this intrinsic ambiguity of the American dream is demonstrated by the Murchison family, especially by George, whose bourgeois materialism illustrates the American propensity to confuse material achievement with the total promise of the American dream. Thus, however well intentioned, Bigsby (1965: 157) actually reduces Hansberry's social insights to the level of idealistic naivete when he assumes that she dissociates the socioeconomic issue from "the need for spiritual replenishment which can only come with a return of dignity." And when critics such as Harold Cruse dismiss *Raisin* as bourgeois soap opera, they ignore the dramatist's fundamental ambivalence toward the American dream: having affirmed her faith in the human possibilities of the dream by deploring its deferment in the lives of some Americans (as indicated in her title), Lorraine Hansberry underscores the moral ambiguities that are inherent in the process of actually realizing the dream, in the lives of other Americans (like the Murchisons).

Moreover, when Hansberry dwells on the deferred dreams of the poor, she heightens the ironic paradox of all these ambiguities. For in the cultural psychology of the Youngers' community (and of Langston Hughes's Harlem) the deprived and the disadvantaged are like the affluent bourgeoisie in that they, too, view materialistic achievements as self-justifying, even self-redeeming, goals. The acquisition of material things (either across the counter in legal trade, or in the "revenge" looting of urban riots) is really a means of participating vicariously in the affluent society. This vicarious participation increases in value in direct ratio to the deprived individual's role of "outsider." And Walter Younger is an outsider on two counts: he is both Black and poor. Hence Walter's unabashed obsession with the insurance money as a key to instant affluence fits the materialistic priorities of the outsider's dream. In presenting the moral conflict between the spiritual promises of the dream ideal and the frank materialism of the impoverished dreamer, Hansberry is being faithful to the cultural psychology of American poverty, and to the ironic basis of her thematic design. And, viewed in this context, the importance of the money in the Youngers' eventual choice—the purchase of a house in a white neighborhood—is not the unintentional irony that C. W. E. Bigsby condescendingly attributes to Hansberry. On the contrary, this emphasis on money as the key to moral and spiritual fulfillment is consistent with the playwright's ironic overview of the socioeconomics of the American dream ideal.

The ambiguous implications of the money are also integrated with the ironies which underlie Hansberry's treatment of ideological choices between integration or separation. The crucial factor in the presentation of these choices is the play's strong hints that the choices have already been severely limited by the negative emphasis of the "raisin" title. Given the pervasive connotations of dried up hopes and deferred dreams, then the very notion of choice, with all its attendant implications of free will, has been restricted to a set of ironically balanced alternatives. From the viewpoint of the integrationist ideal, Mama is commendable in her determination to use the insurance check to buy the house. And this choice, such as it is, offers its own advantages over Walter's crassly materialistic scheme to invest the money into a dubious liquor scheme. But if housing integration is praiseworthy on the ideal principles of the American dream, then it is difficult to accept the Younger venture into a determined and hostile neighborhood as a complete fulfillment of the dream ideal. The embittering realities of enforced housing integration in Hansberry's own family life is ample evidence that she was well aware that enforced or legal integration is rather different from the ideal concept of integration as the complete reconciliation of human beings. Once again, Hansberry has ironically juxtaposed the ideal possibilities of the dream with the limitations of the American reality. Mama's (and Walter's) moral triumph over white racists is real enough, and it is undoubtedly significant in the confirmation of Walter's self-respect. But as the humiliations and hardships of the Hansberry family demonstrated in a white Chicago neighborhood, the tactical defeat of individual racists is not, ipso facto, the destruction of racism. At best it is a self-ennobling start without the certainty of a satisfactory conclusion based on genuine reconciliation. Compassion and understanding may very well be the dominant social values espoused by *Raisin*, as Bigsby and Duprey argue. But a realistic, rather than ideologically subjective, reading of the play hardly supports their view that these qualities "transcend" (racist?) history. For it is obvious enough that compassion and understanding can only transcend conflict and division if such ideals are shared equally by all sides. And it should be equally obvious that the Youngers' new white neighbors are neither compassionate nor understanding. In other words, the integration which is eventually realized at the end of the play has been severely, and realistically, limited by Hansberry's awareness of the contradiction between the dream ideals of reconciliation and equality, and the social realities of hatred and unresolved conflict. So without debunking the integrationist ideal, Hansberry confirms the inexorable barriers and the frustrations represented by her dominant raisin symbol.

Conversely, the rebuff to Walter's liquor-store scheme is no more decisive, 10 morally, than the triumph of Mama's integrationism. Admittedly, Walter is no businessman; and his scheme is motivated by a self-serving materialism which, as we have seen, is intrinsic to the moral and psychological ambiguities of the American dream itself. But the fact still remains that the long-term socioeconomic problems of the Younger family have not been solved by the final disposition of the money on behalf of Mama's crusade for integration and for the reclamation of (Walter's) Black manhood. The Youngers now own a house in a better (white) neighborhood, but Walter's prospects for even a moderate socioeconomic self-sufficiency remain bleak; and there have been no changes in the general economic frustrations which have left their mark on both the furnishings and Ruth Younger's features:

the furnishings of this room were actually selected with care and love and even hope—and brought to this apartment and arranged with taste and pride.

That was a long time ago. Now the once loved pattern of the couch upholstery has to fight to show itself from under acres of crocheted doilies and couch covers which have themselves finally come to be more important than the upholstery. And here a table or a chair has been moved to disguise the worn places in the carpet; but the carpet has fought back by showing its weariness, with depressing uniformity, elsewhere on its surface.

Weariness has, in fact, won this room. . . . All pretenses but living itself have long since vanished from the very atmosphere of this room. . . .

Ruth is about thirty . . . it is apparent that life has been little that she expected, and disappointment has already begun to hang in her face. In a few years, before thirty-five even, she will be known among her people as a "settled woman" (Hansberry, 1966: 11–12).

Despite the pride and ebullience with which the play concludes, it is difficult, even then, to escape the grim reminders of these furniture symbols in the opening scene—the more difficult because the concluding scene is dominated by the same pieces of furniture as they are transferred from the old apartment to the new house. The point is that Hansberry offers no easy promise that the old frustrations and "weariness" will be left behind, or that there will be inevitable change in terms of socioeconomic achievement and complete human reconciliation. For after we have duly acknowledged all the bourgeois excesses and the poverty-inspired expectations which encourage exclusively materialistic images of the American dream, among the Murchisons and the Youngers alike, it is still a fact that the American dream ideal seeks to fulfill both the material and spiritual needs of the human personality. And as long as material and attitudinal barriers persist there will be no complete realization of the American dream for the Youngers. What they do achieve at the end of the play is neither the transcendental social triumphs envisioned by Bigsby's integrationist ethic, nor the facile soap-opera resolutions derided by the pro-separatist Cruse. Their main achievement lies in an incipient (rather than full-blown) self-esteem; but within the ironic design of Hansberry's themes, this is still counterbalanced by the forbidding prospects for both material opportunities and social regeneration as a whole. The African student, Asagai, is really an idealistic embodiment of that kind of self-esteem, but he is far from being the mouthpiece of Hansberry's ideology, as Bigsby (1967: 161) argues. For his ringing rhetoric of optimistic self-esteem comes easily in an Africa already being swept by the now famous winds of anticolonial change. But the uncertain future of the Youngers and the persistent "weariness" of that old furniture undercut, or qualify, this optimism in an American context. And this, surely, is the ultimate irony of the play: that moral malaise and spiritual weariness have tarnished the characteristically American optimism in dreams-for-change, change-as-improvement, and improvement-as-humanization; that despite all the hallowed myths of change and the cherished dream of ideals of human fulfillment, American society allows far less room for optimism about real change than do the despised societies of the so-called underdeveloped world.

REFERENCES

Bigsby, C. W. E. (1967) *Confrontation and Commitment: A Study of Contemporary American Drama 1959–1966.* Columbia: Univ. of Missouri Press.

Cruse, H. (1968) *The Crisis of the Negro Intellectual.* New York: Apollo.

DuBois, W. E. B. (1969) *Darkwater: Voices from Within the Veil.* New York: Schocken.

Duprey, R. A. (1967) "Today's dramatists," in *American Theatre.* Volume 10 of Stratford-Upon-Avon Studies. London.

Fanon, F. (1968) *The Wretched of the Earth* (C. Farrington, trans.). New York: Black Cat.

Hansberry, L. (1966) *A Raisin in the Sun.* New York: Signet.

Hughes, L. (1959) "Harlem," p. 268 in *Selected Poems.* New York: Alfred A. Knopf.

Isaacs, H. R. (1960) "Five writers and their African ancestors." *Phylon* 21, 4: 33.

Miller, J. (1971) "Lorraine Hansberry," C. W. E. Bigsby (ed.) *Poetry and Drama,* Volume 2 of *The Black American Writer.* Baltimore: Pelican.

MAKING ARGUMENTS

1. How does Brown characterize the controversies over Hansberry's plays? What does he have to say about the arguments critics have made?

2. What kinds of reading/interpretive mistakes does Brown say these critics make? What does he say they should have done instead?

3. What role does Brown claim irony plays in *A Raisin in the Sun*?

MARGARET B. WILKERSON (B. ?)

A RAISIN IN THE SUN: ANNIVERSARY OF AN AMERICAN CLASSIC 1999

Rarely, if ever, has a play by a Black-American been accorded the status of a classic. Parochialism and polemics, critics have claimed, render works based on Black experience unattractive and of limited or temporary appeal. Yet Lorraine Hansberry's *A Raisin in the Sun*, the first play by a Black woman to be produced on Broadway and to win the New York Drama Critics' Circle Award in 1959, has become an American classic within a quarter of a century. According to Samuel French, Inc., an estimated two hundred productions were mounted during the 1983–84 theatre season alone, including critical successes at the Goodman Theatre in Chicago, Yale Repertory Theatre, and the St. Louis Repertory Theatre. In a 1983 review in the *New York Times*, Mel Gussow called this play about a 1950s Black family in Chicago "an enduring work of contemporary theatre."[1] Lloyd Richards, director of the Yale Repertory and director of the original 1959 production, labeled *A Raisin in the Sun*, "An historic . . . and . . . a timeless piece."[2] Frank Rich, in his 1983 review of the Goodman Theatre revival, claimed that the play was dated only by "its dependence on plot mechanics."[3] The St. Louis Repertory Company's production attracted unprecedented sell-out crowds in 1984, while a 1986 production at the Roundabout Theatre drew the admiration of off-Broadway audiences. What accounts for the extraordinary appeal of *A Raisin in the Sun*? How has it transcended the racial parochialisms of American audiences?

A variety of factors have contributed to its enduring success: the finely crafted text; a brilliant cast in the original production and subsequent casts with talented performers; its historic reception on Broadway in the 1958–59 season and subsequent impact on a new generation of artists; and the events of the past quarter century that confirmed Hansberry's prescience. However, textual additions and revisions since the original production, some as recent as 1984, have sharpened the major issues of the play, revitalizing the work for contemporary audiences. This essay will discuss the various social, historical, and artistic factors that have contributed to the play's contemporary relevance and popularity, with particular focus on recent script revisions published by Samuel French, Inc., in the 1984 Anniversary Edition of the play.

The history of that first production is the stuff of which theatre legend is made. "Housewife's Play Is a Hit," read one local headline,[4] indicating the sheer luck and nerve that allowed *A Raisin in the Sun*—a play written by an unknown Black woman, produced by inexperienced newcomers, and directed by an untried young Black man—to reach the professional New York stage. Although Sidney Poitier brought "star quality" to the show, the other performers (with the exception of Claudia McNeil) had yet to make their mark on the American theatre. Yet the talent of this first cast proved extraordinary and the chemistry perfect for a memorable show. Today the names of playwright Lorraine Hansberry, director Lloyd Richards, producers Phil Rose and David Cogan, actors Sidney Poitier, Claudia McNeil, Lou Gossett, Glynn Turman, Diana Sands, Ivan Dixon, Ruby Dee, Ossie Davis, understudies Douglas Turner Ward, Lonne Elder, Beah Richards, and others are widely known for their contributions to theatre.

Starting from a half empty house in New Haven, *A Raisin in the Sun* attracted larger audiences on its out-of-town trials through Chicago and other cities

---

*All notes are Wilkerson's.

[1] Mel Gussow, "Stage: *A Raisin in the Sun* at Yale," *New York Times*. 9 November 1983, C23.

[2] Samuel G. Freedman, "Yale Marking 25th Anniversary of *Raisin in Sun*," *New York Times*, 1 November 1983, C13.

[3] Frank Rich, "Theater: *Raisin in Sun*, Anniversary in Chicago," *New York Times*, 5 October 1983, C24.

[4] Sidney Fields, "Housewife's Play Is A Hit," *New York Daily Mirror*, 16 March 1959.

until a last minute rush for tickets in Philadelphia earned it a Broadway house. It had taken a year to raise the $100,000 needed for the show—the "smart money" would not take a risk on a serious play about a Black family. The tenuousness of its production life ended, however, with its New York opening. The show ran on Broadway for nineteen months and won the New York Drama Critics' Circle Award against such plays as Tennessee Williams' *Sweet Bird of Youth*, Archibald MacLeish's *J.B.*, and Eugene O'Neill's *A Touch of the Poet*.

The play's phenomenal reception can be attributed, in part, to its timeliness, for this drama reflects that moment in U.S. history when the country was poised on the brink of cataclysmic social and legal upheavals that would forever change its character. In his 1959 review of the show, Walter Kerr observed that Hansberry "reads the precise temperature of a race at that time in its history when it cannot retreat and cannot quite find the way to move forward. The mood is forty-nine parts anger and forty-nine parts control, with a very narrow escape hatch for the steam these abrasive contraries build up. Three generations stand poised, and crowded, on a detonating-cap."[5] 5

The tensions of the times that Kerr sensed in the play had been captured earlier in a short, provacative poem by Langston Hughes, a work that had given Hansberry the title and theme of her drama. "What happens to a dream deferred," asked the poet in his historical collection of poems on Harlem. "Does it dry up like a raisin in the sun . . . or does it explode?"[6] Lorraine Hansberry answered by fashioning a play about the struggles and frustrations of a working-class Black family living in Chicago's South Side ghetto during the 1950s. Crowded into a cramped, roach-infested kitchenette, this family of laborers wages a constant battle to survive and to maintain hope for a better future. When Lena Younger (Mama), the elder of the household, receives a $10,000 widow's benefit, each family member sees the money as fulfillment of a private dream. The conflict is sharpest between the dual protagonists of the play, Mama and her thirty-five-year-old son, Walter Lee, who lives with his sister (Beneatha), his wife (Ruth), and son (Travis) in his mother's home. Walter, frustrated by his dead-end chauffeur's job, wants to invest in a liquor store as a way out of their economic and psychological trap. But Mama, seeking more physical space for the family and the psychological freedom it would bring, puts a down payment on a house that happens to be in Clybourne Park, a white neighborhood. Her decision decimates Walter who views the money as his last chance to gain some economic control over his life. When Mama realizes how deeply her decision has hurt her son, she entrusts him with the remaining money with a portion to be placed in a savings account for his sister's college education and the rest for Walter to do with as he wishes. His good fortune is short-lived, however, because he loses the money in a dubious business deal.

[5] Walter Kerr, "No Clear Path and No Retreat," *New York Herald Tribune*, Lively Arts Section, 22 March 1959, 1–2.

[6] The Langston Hughes poem, "Harlem," is reprinted as introduction to the text of *A Raisin in the Sun* in all editions.

A disillusioned man, Walter faces his mother and family in a highly emotional scene; when presented with the opportunity to recover his losses by selling out to the Clybourne Park Association (which is determined to keep the neighborhood white), he decides to take their offer despite its demeaning implications. However, Walter comes to realize that he cannot live with this denigration of his family's pride and consequently rejects the proposal. The play ends as the family begins to move to the new house.

The spirit and struggles of the Younger family symbolized the social progress and setbacks characteristic of the 1950s, and the Broadway audience of that time could not help but notice. In 1955, three years before the opening of *A Raisin in the Sun*, the Supreme Court had declared racial segregation in public schools illegal, marking a climax to decades of advocacy and legal challenges, but initiating a new level of resistance. The Montgomery bus boycott was staged the same year, marking the beginning of Martin Luther King's visible leadership in the Civil Rights Movement. Boycotts and sit-ins intensified as federal troops were called in to prevent interference with school integration in Little Rock, Arkansas. As the struggle continued in the United States, it was also raging in Africa as Ghana became an independent nation, signaling the imminent demise of European colonialism.

During the play's run and shortly thereafter, Black and white Freedom Riders headed South and were greeted by a wave of terrorism as Southern segregationists retaliated; lunch counters in over 100 Southern cities were integrated; sit-ins and protests accelerated; Martin Luther King was arrested and jailed repeatedly; Black children were murdered, and churches were burned by racists, while the President of the United States shattered precedent by declaring that segregation was morally wrong. The bloody years continued as public figures like Medgar Evers and President John F. Kennedy were assassinated.

"[Hansberry] saw history, whole," wrote Frank Rich in his 1983 review of the play, ". . . the present and the future in the light of the past."[7] The time was ripe for a play that could somehow bridge the gap between Blacks and whites in the U.S. while communicating the urgency and necessity of the civil rights struggle. Black militancy born of anger, frustration, and deferred dreams was captured in the explosive and desperate Walter Lee. Rosa Parks's sudden refusal to move to the back of the bus, which became the catalyst for the historic Montgomery bus boycott, was mirrored in Lena Younger's apolitical decision to live in Clybourne Park, and her unintentional challenge of the restrictive covenants of the day. The rise of independent African nations was reflected in the presence of Asagai, the African student, who brings home the reality of his people's struggle for liberation, while Beneatha's adulation of things Africaine anticipated a new wave of hair and dress styles that Black Americans would soon adopt. In an uncanny way, Hansberry sensed what was to come. Her prescience extended even a decade beyond to the assertion of women's rights and women's equality through the assertive Beneatha who aspires to be a doctor, and the loyal, loving

---

[7] Rich, "Theater: *A Raisin in the Sun*," C24.

Ruth who seriously contemplates an abortion. The play touched the vibrating nerve of a country on the verge of change and a people on the move.

The timeliness of the play was equalled only by the captivating characters with whom white audiences were willing to identify and of whom Black audiences could be proud. Lena Younger was a strong point of identification. She was everybody's Mama—strong, caring, determined—the glue that held the family together. The self-sacrificing love of wife and mother were recognizable in Ruth's quiet strength and giving nature. Although Walter Lee was a new kind of character for white audiences, intended as a "ghetto hero" by Hansberry, the generational conflict with his mother was very familiar. For Blacks, Walter was a welcome affirmation of the urgency and potency of the Black struggle, while his sister, the ebullient Beneatha, represented its intellectual potential. Each character was molded with skill, humor, and the best tools of realistic theatre. The human qualities of Hansberry's characters came through without negating their racial integrity, and the play was loudly acclaimed on that account. 10

Critics praised the play as much for what it did not do as for its achievements. It presented characters who were neither sentimentalized nor stereotyped. There was no special pleading. The play was honest and had integrity. It did not preach political dogma, reviewers claimed. Even the F.B.I. file on Hansberry confirmed that the play was not propagandistic, according to the agents' report. Apparently, it did not pose a danger to the Republic. Because the humanity of this family was so brilliantly exposed, white audiences could see themselves reflected in those Black faces. Because the racial experience was so authentically portrayed, Blacks found a new voice and created a vital, provocative theatre movement in the next decade. However, during the 1960s, Black critic Harold Cruse labeled the play a "glorified soap opera,"[8] reflecting a few reviewers' growing impatience with realistic plot structures and disagreement with what they perceived to be the play's political views. Nevertheless, the vitality and sharp definition of characters, the wit and humor of its sparkling dialogue, and the continued affirmation of the play's "message" by Black and white audiences alike, have far outweighed that criticism, causing audiences to return year after year to relive the now well-known rituals of the Younger family. However, A Raisin in the Sun is also a play of ideas and functions on a deeper, philosophical level, which until recently has been obscured to some extent by the racial prism through which it was originally viewed.

Writing in her scrapbook of reviews, Hansberry agreed with a 1959 passage by Daniel Gottlieb of the Hartford Times: the playwright "manages to weave the threads of the Negro-white conflict, materialism vs. spiritualism, and the individual vs. his conscience into the play."[9] The seductiveness of material values is at issue in the play and the Youngers' struggle for a spiritual and economic future poses fundamental questions about the American dream of success. As

---

[8] Harold Cruse, *The Crisis of the Negro Intellectual* (New York: William Morrow & Company, Inc., 1967), 278.

[9] Daniel W. Gottlieb, "*A Raisin in the Sun* Premieres at Schubert," *Hartford Times*, 24 January 1959.

Gregory Mosher, Director of the Goodman Theatre, asks, "Is Walter Lee right when he says money is all that matters? How important is economic success in securing rights for a minority group? Such goals give you power, but do they also corrupt you?"[10] In order to advance materially, must the Youngers also become materialistic? The contradiction between the profitable, economic values of acquisition, power, and status and the "unprofitable" values of integrity, justice, and freedom runs deep in the American psyche. Walter's desire to "make it" is as American as Mama's determination to retain the family's pride and honor.

Although the original production script contained ample confirmation of this theme, events of the last twenty-five years both offstage and on have helped audiences to perceive these fundamental issues more clearly. The re-insertion of some omitted lines has sharpened and clarified the philosophical content without altering the basic structure of the play. Some scenes were cut in the original production in order to minimize risk; the producers and director chose to keep the playing time as tight as possible without sacrificing the playwright's values. Among the scenes and lines that were eliminated were three portions of dialogue which have since been restored to more recent publications and were included in 1983–84 productions.[11] These sections offer important insights to the character of Walter Lee and Mama, the play's dual protagonists, and greatly strengthen the articulation of the fundamental theme.

The debate over materialism and integrity is framed by Walter Lee and Mama whose conflict drives the play. However, the full implications of Walter's desires must be grasped in order to perceive the deeper levels of the debate. The New American Library edition (1966) and the 25th Anniversary edition published in 1984 restored a scene which is key to this understanding. Inserted at the end of Act II, Scene 2, the scene shows a brief moment between Walter and his young son, Travis. Walter, who has just been entrusted with the remaining $6500 by his mother and who sees his dream of economic success within his grasp, speaks in a tender tone not heard before from him:

> *You wouldn't understand yet, son, but your daddy's gonna make a transaction . . . a business transaction that's going to change our lives. . . . That's how come one day when you 'bout seventeen years old I'll come home and I'll be pretty tired, you know what I mean, after a day of conferences and secretaries getting things wrong the way they do . . . 'cause an executive's life is hell, man—. . . And I'll pull the car up on the driveway . . . just a plain black Chrysler, I think, with white walls—no—black tires. More elegant. Rich people don't have to be flashy . . . though I'll have to get something a little sportier for Ruth—maybe a Cadillac convertible to do her shopping in. . . . And I'll*

---

[10] Tom Valeo, "Issues Raised by *Raisin* Haven't Begun to Dry Up," *Chicago Sunday Herald,* 2 October 1983, sec. 5, 4.

[11] In discussing these scenes, the following sources will be used: the original Samuel French acting edition and the Random House Edition, both published in 1959; the New American Library (N.A.L.) edition published in 1966; the 25th Anniversary Samuel French Acting Edition published in 1984; and the 1961 film version.

come up the steps to the house and the gardener will be clipping away at the hedges and he'll say "Good evening, Mr. Younger." And I'll say, "Hello, Jefferson, how are you this evening?" And I'll go inside and Ruth will come downstairs and meet me at the door and we'll kiss each other and she'll take my arm and we'll go up to your room to see you sitting on the floor with the catalogues of all the great schools in America around you. . . . All the great schools in the World! And—and I'll say, all right son—it's your seventeenth birthday, what is it you've decided? Just tell me where you want to go to school and you'll go. Just tell me, what it is you want to be—and you'll be it. . . . Whatever you want to be—Yessir! You just name it, son . . . and I hand you the world![12]*

The placement of this speech is critical to its import for it catches Walter in a rare, reflective moment. Throughout the play, the audience has seen the restless side of Walter, constantly at odds with his family, desperately trying to convince his strong-willed mother of the importance of his plans. This speech is Walter's only chance in the play to explain his ideas fully, without interruption and criticism. While the speech verifies Walter's desire to shape a better future for his son, it also signals a shift in his value system—one which will make the outrageous offer from the white homeowners' association both attractive and logical. Walter is willing to buy into a system of roles and class stratification in order to realize his dream. His image is typical Americana—the independent male who controls the world and around whom the universe revolves. Wife, secretary, gardener, Cadillac, sports car—all are complements to his material universe. His manhood is at stake, he believes, and the women around him with their traditional values are holding him back.

Walter's speech was also deleted from the 1961 film version of the play. In its place was a brief exchange between Mama and Walter in which Walter equates his investment opportunity with his parents' move North out of the economic and spiritual traps of the Deep South. The money represents his chance to board his generation's train to the North. Without the Walter/Travis scene, however, the text lacks the subtle class and sexist implications of the American dream that Walter seeks.

To sharpen this fundamental debate, Lena Younger/Mama must be rescued from the persistent image of passivity, accommodation, and self-satisfaction associated with the Black Mammy stereotype. She must be revealed for what, in fact, she is, according to Hansberry: "The Black matriarch incarnate: The bulwark of the Negro family since slavery; the embodiment of the Negro will to transcendance. It is she who, in the mind of the Black poet, scrubs the floors of a nation in order to create Black diplomats and university professors. It is she who, while seeming to cling to traditional restraints, drives the young on into the fire hoses and one day simply refuses to move to the back of the bus in Montgomery."[13]

15

---

[12] Lorraine Hansberry, *A Raisin in the Sun/The Sign in Sidney Brustein's Window* (New York: New American Library, 1966), 88–89.

[13] Lorraine Hansberry, "The Origins of Character" (Address to the American Academy of Psychotherapists, New York, 5 October 1963).

The original production script also included a scene in Act II, Scene 2, that clarified this image of Mama. However, the entire scene, along with the character of Mrs. Johnson, was eliminated in order to trim the show's playing time. It has now been published for the first time in the addendum of the 1984 Samuel French edition and has been included in several recent productions. The original producers may have sacrificed too much, underestimating the persistence of the Mammy stereotype in the American psyche. The perception of Lena Younger as a conservative, retarding force has been a difficult one to shed. Although the dialogue in this scene is carried by Mrs. Johnson, a nosy neighbor and somewhat humorous character, Mama's responses clearly place her in the militant forefront. Mrs. Johnson, always the happy bearer of bad news, makes explicit the danger in the family's move and Mama's quiet determination to take the risk.

Johnson. I guess y'all seen the news what's all over the colored paper this week . . .

Mama. No—didn't get mine yet this week.

Johnson. You mean you ain't read 'bout them colored people that was bombed out their place out there? . . . Ain't it something how bad these here white folks is getting here in Chicago! Lord, getting so you think you right down in Mississippi! . . . 'Course I thinks it's wonderful how our folks keeps on pushing out. . . . Lord—I bet this time next month y'all's names will have been in the papers plenty—. . . "NEGROES INVADE CLYBOURNE PARK—BOMBED!"

Mama. We ain't exactly moving out there to get bombed.

Johnson. Oh, honey—you know I'm praying to God every day that don't nothing like that happen! But you have to think of life like it is—and these here Chicago peckerwoods is some baaaad peckerwoods.

Mama. We done thought about all that, Mis' Johnson.[14]

The conversation continues with Mrs. Johnson carrying most of the dialogue, while Mama speaks briefly, but with quiet authority. Then Lena Younger makes a surprising philosophical connection.

Johnson. [S]ometimes . . . [Beneatha] act like she ain't got time to pass the time of day with nobody ain't been to college. Oh—I ain't criticizing her none. It's just—you know how some of our young people gets when they get a little education. . . . 'Course I can understand how she must be proud and everything—being the only one in the family to make something of herself! I know just being a chauffeur ain't never satisfied Brother none. He shouldn't feel like that, though. Ain't nothing wrong with being a chauffeur.

Mama. There's plenty wrong with it.

Johnson. What?

---

14 Lorraine Hansberry, *A Raisin in the Sun*, 25th Anniversary Edition (New York: Samuel French, Inc., 1984), 137–39.

Mama. Plenty. My husband always said being any kind of a servant wasn't
a fit thing for a man to have to be. He always said a man's hands was made
to make things, or to turn the earth with—not to drive nobody's car for
'em—or—. . . carry they slop jars. And my boy is just like him—. . .

Johnson. Mmmmmmmmm. The Youngers is too much for me! . . . You
sure one proud-acting bunch of colored folks. Well—I always thinks like
Booker T. Washington said that time—"Education has spoiled many a
good plow hand"—

Mama. Is that what old Booker T. said?

Johnson. He sure did.

Mama. Well, it sounds just like him. The fool.

Johnson. Well—he was one of our great men.

Mama. Who said so?[15]

The physical image of Mama (large, dark, dominant) suggests the Mammy 20
stereotype of countless American plays and films, but her criticism of Booker
T. Washington's ideas in this passage aligns her with Washington's intellectual
opponent, W. E. B. DuBois. DuBois and other militant advocates for civil rights
founded the National Association for the Advancement for Colored People
(NAACP), the organization that provided much of the legal bases for protesting segregation. The Washington/DuBois debate framed the philosophical and
political issues facing Black-Americans and the fight for human and civil rights
early in this century. The stereotype of the Black Mammy suggests complicity
with Washington's emphasis on accommodation and economic self-sufficiency.
However, in an ironic twist, Hansberry equates Mama's determination with the
militant spirit of DuBois's position and Walter's entrepreneurial interests with
the materialism associated with Washington's philosophy. Lena Younger is not
the accommodating Mammy who chooses the passive, safe path, but rather the
folk figure, the courageous spirit that lends credence and power to the militant
struggle. In her own determined way, she gives birth to revolutionaries and is
herself a progressive force. The explicit reference to Washington in this scene
illuminates the "revolutionary" aspect of Lena and sharply delineates the
philosophical difference between Mama and Walter.

Hansberry's final and most definitive framing of the philosophical issues
occurs at the beginning of Act III in the dialogue between Asagai and Beneatha.
Abridged in early publications of the script, most of this exchange was cut from
the film. As in the earlier Walter/Travis scene, the placement of this scene is
important. It occurs just after the highly emotional moment when Walter and
Mama discover that the money is gone. The audience, affected by the sheer magnitude of the loss, is now invited to reflect on the family's future. At a time when
Mama's faith is being sorely tested and the materialistic underpinnings of Walter's
faith have been destroyed, what values will shape the family's response? Here
Hansberry places a key dialogue—the debate between Asagai and Beneatha.

[15] Ibid., 139–40.

Some critics dismiss this section as a distracting, verbose passage, out of place in this realistic piece of theatre.[16] Yet a closer examination of the unabridged scene reveals its crucial role in the philosophical progression of the theme.

The question here is not whether the family should move or stay, but rather what they will learn from this tragedy. Will they act out of an affirmation of life or be paralyzed by despair? Asagai focuses on Beneatha, but Hansberry focuses her critique on Walter and all those who would base their future on the acquisition of things. As the money goes, so goes Beneatha's and Walter's faith in humankind. "Man is foul!" Beneatha says, "And the human race deserves its misery! . . . From now on, I worship truth—and the truth is that people are puny, small and selfish."[17] The logical extension of this "truth" is to ignore human values and to act, if one does at all, out of selfishness and the needs of the existential moment. This idea enables Walter later in Act III to consider any means to recover the lost money. But Asagai counters:

> Why is it that you despairing ones always think that only you have the truth? I never thought to see you like this, Alaiyo. You! Your brother made a mistake—and you are grateful to him so that now you can give up the ailing human race on account of it! You talk about what good is struggle; what good is anything! Where are we all going and why are we bothering![18]

Beneatha responds:

> *AND YOU CANNOT ANSWER IT!*[19]

Asagai shouts over her: "I LIVE THE ANSWER!"[20] Asagai proposes his being, his life, his very existence—and the meaning that commitment creates—as the embodiment of his answer. Asagai acts out of a belief in the transcendent power of man and woman, a belief that cannot be shaken by the loss of money, material things, or even the devastation of human betrayal. This faith will be his armor when he returns to his troubled homeland to fight against terrible odds—poverty and ignorance, not to mention the British and the French—to achieve the full liberation of his people.

Asagai expresses in philosophical and political terms the affirmation that Lena Younger has lived. At this moment, he is her symbolic son—the long-desired reuniting of Africans and Afro-Americans through shared beliefs, not color alone. The debate anticipates the ambivalence of Walter's emotions as he is torn, up to the very end of the play, between an act of despair and an act of affirmation. Ironically, affirmation carries no assurances. For just as Asagai

---

[16] For example, see Max Lerner, "A Dream Deferred," *New York Post*, 8 April 1959, 2. The "theme of the African heritage and possible future of the Negro is marginal to the main theme of the play."

[17] Lorraine Hansberry, *A Raisin in the Sun/The Sign*, 114.

[18] Ibid.

[19] Ibid., 114–15.

[20] Ibid., 115.

does not know whether he will be revered or murdered for his efforts on behalf of his people, so Walter and the Younger family will face an uncertain future in their new neighborhood. Although Asagai prevails in the debate, Walter must peer into the abyss of despair and lost pride before he can finally acknowledge the progressive, enlightened values of his forebears—the spirit of life which has allowed humankind to transcend its condition.

The play repudiates the kind of materialism that values money and acquisi- 25 tion over human dignity and life. The spirit of humankind, Hansberry insists, must affirm freedom, justice, integrity, caring—at the expense of comfort or even life itself. It is a courageous statement made in the face of the desperate economic needs of the Youngers of the nation. It is offered as a framework for the liberation struggles of the world, in defiance of traditional American notions of success. The uncut scene in Act III gives full expression to the debate and heightens the philosophical questions implicit in the Youngers' struggle. When this scene is cut, as in the film, or abridged, as in the early publications and the original production, the import of Hansberry's philosophical position is diminished and the intellectual dimensions of Beneatha and Asagai are trivialized. The Yale production used the full version of this scene with great success. One critic even claimed that this scene could well be the climax of the play.[21]

Hansberry's sensing of future trends was most evident in another casualty of the original production script: Beneatha adopts a natural hairstyle (long before the "Afro" became popular) and a bourgeois George Murchison is surprisingly appreciative of the look.[22] But the most dramatic change in the play occurred long before the show went into rehearsal. In an earlier version of the script, Hansberry wrote a more somber ending in which the family is shown sitting in the darkened living room of their new house, armed and awaiting an attack by their white neighbors. The accepted and ever popular upbeat ending, which shows a jubilant family moving to their new home, was no less true than the other ending. This more positive view did, however, emphasize the Youngers' evolution and progress rather than the violent, retrogressive attitudes of the racists who awaited them.

Despite the loss of much of the play's philosophical dimension, *A Raisin in the Sun* was a smashing success in 1959 and has continued to attract audiences for a quarter of a century. The productions that recent audiences have applauded are for the most part based on an expanded text that includes portions of the scenes discussed in this essay and that provides greater definition of major characters and theme. The heavy financial risks associated with professional productions resulted in a necessarily conservative handling of the original production and robbed early audiences of the full import of Hansberry's achievement. It may have been asking too much of 1959 audiences to cope with the full vision of the play. Only the very naive would have expected

[21] Markland Taylor, "*Raisin, Jerusalem* a Case of Good vs. Poor Playwriting," *New Haven Register*, 13 November 1983, D9.

[22] The "Afro" was deleted because it was not attractive on actress Diana Sands.

them to accept the intellectual dimension emanating from the experiences of a working-class Black family and the pen of a Black woman writer during the heat and turmoil of those days. The timeliness of the play has not diminished. Its criticism of materialistic values is more poignant amidst the affluence and poverty of American society in the 1980s. At the same time, its depiction of the Black struggle against pernicious, persistent racism remains current as racial intolerance continues to pervade the country's institutions, albeit in more subtle forms. Perhaps because the idea of Black stage characters is not as exotic as it once was, the 1980s audience can perceive the full meaning of the play. Perhaps they are more capable of comprehending the theatre of Black experience, not only as literal portrayal, but as a metaphor for the American experience. Hansberry, however, did not wait for such enlightenment on the part of her audience; she insisted on restoring many of the deleted scenes as soon as possible. It is to her credit that she did so. Her literary executor, Robert Nemiroff, has continued in the same spirit, making other scenes available since the playwright's death. The expanded text has revitalized the play for this generation and has added a new dimension to the exploration of Black experience in the American theatre.

MAKING ARGUMENTS

1. Why does Wilkerson believe audiences found Hansberry's play relevant when it was first staged?

2. Why does she think contemporary audiences still find it relevant?

3. What significance does she assign to the textual restorations made to the original production script in later years? What do they change about the play? How do they strengthen its appeal?

ROBIN BERNSTEIN (B. 1969)

INVENTING A FISHBOWL: WHITE SUPREMACY AND THE CRITICAL RECEPTION OF LORRAINE HANSBERRY'S *A RAISIN IN THE SUN* 1999

When Lorraine Hansberry's *A Raisin in the Sun* opened on Broadway in 1959, the vast majority of white critics praised the play's "universality." One reviewer wrote, "A Negro wrote this show. It is played, with one exception, by Negroes. Half the audiences here are Negroes. Even so, it isn't written for Negroes. . . . It's a show about people, white or colored. . . . I see *A Raisin in the Sun* as part of the general culture of the U.S."[1] The phrase "happens to be" appeared with remarkable frequency among reviews: the play was "about human beings, who happen to be Negroes"[2] (or "a family that happens to be colored"[3]); Sidney Poitier played "the angry young man who happens to be a Negro."[4]

Other white reviewers, however, praised the play not for its universality, but for its particularity. "The play is honest," wrote Brooks Atkinson, critic for the *New York Times*. "[Hansberry] has told the inner as well as the outer truth about a Negro family in the southside of Chicago at the present time."[5] "This Negro play," wrote another reviewer, "celebrates with slow impressiveness a triumph of racial pride."[6]

How can a play be simultaneously specific and universal? This apparent paradox is easily resolved with the assertion that African-Americans are precisely as human—and African-American cultures just as universal or particular—as members of any other group. Hansberry herself pointed out the nonexistence of the paradox:

> Interviewer: *The question, I'm sure, is asked you many times—you must be tired of it—someone comes up to you and says: "This is not really a Negro play; why, this could be about anybody! It's a play about people!" What is your reaction? What do you say?*
>
> Hansberry: *Well[,] I hadn't noticed the contradiction because I'd always been under the impression that Negroes are people. . . . One of the most sound ideas in dramatic writing is that in order to create the universal, you must pay very great attention to the specific.*[7]

Hansberry's solution to the apparent paradox did not go unnoticed or unremarked. Novelist John Oliver Killens and historian and editor Lerone Bennett, Jr., for example, both noted Hansberry's ability to be "universal in her particularity."[8]

The paradox, then, is that a paradox was perceived at all, or that it continued to be perceived after Hansberry (and, later, Killens, Bennett, and

---

*All notes are Bernstein's.

[1] George Murray, "'Raisin in Sun' Terrific Theater," *Chicago American* (27 February 1959), 19.

[2] Sydney J. Harris, "Sydney Harris Reviews: 'A Raisin in the Sun,'" *Chicago Daily News* (11 February 1959), 39.

[3] George Oppenheimer, "On Stage," newspaper unknown (25 March 1959), in file, "*A Raisin in the Sun*. Clippings," Billy Rose Collection, New York Public Library for the Performing Arts.

[4] Claudia Cassidy, "On the Aisle: Warm Heart, Backbone, Funnybone in Blackstone Play and Cast," *Chicago Daily Tribune* (12 February 1959), F1.

[5] Brooks Atkinson, "A Raisin in the Sun," in *On Stage: Selected Theater Reviews from The New York Times, 1920–1970*, ed. Bernard Beckerman and Howard Siegman (New York, 1970), 402.

[6] "A Simple Story: Triumph of Negro Pride," *London Times* (5 August 1959), n.p., in file, "*A Raisin in the Sun*. Clippings," Billy Rose Collection, New York Public Library for the Performing Arts.

[7] Lorraine Hansberry [assembled and edited by Robert Nemiroff]. *To Be Young. Gifted, and Black* (New York, 1970), 128.

[8] Lerone Bennett, Jr., and Margaret G. Burroughs, "A Lorraine Hansberry Rap," *Freedomways: A Quarterly Review of the Freedom Movement*, 19 (1979): 232.

others[9]) had publicly resolved it. Why did critics persistently categorize *Raisin* as either universal *or* specifically black? Why, when critics noted the fact that the play successfully communicated both universal and particular concerns, did they remark on this fact as a paradox or contradiction? In other words, why was the appearance of a paradox created and maintained?

This essay attempts to tease out some of the meanings fueling and produced 5 by the creation and maintenance of the apparent contradiction between universality and particularity. Although the focus, obviously, is on *A Raisin in the Sun*, the same apparent paradox is constructed for many other artistic works from the past and present. This essay, then, (a) lays groundwork to analyze the apparently contradictory claims that a piece (any piece) is both "universal" and "specific" to a minority experience and (b) helps illuminate the reasons for a cultural *need* for the appearance of the paradox.

The claim that the play's characters are universal "people" without specific ties to African-American culture appears simply racist ("This is a well-written play; white people can relate to it; therefore it cannot be a black play"). Conversely, the assertion that the play is *not* universal but exclusively specific to African-Americans— that is, that the characters exist outside the category of "human"—seems equally racist. Upon closer examination, however, it is possible to discern both racist and anti-racist impulses in each claim.

The "particularizing" assertion can be separated into several different strands. In the most racist form, critics in this mode refused to acknowledge any difference between Hansberry's characters and stereotyped images of blacks. A few months after the play opened, Hansberry noted "some of the prior attitudes which were brought into the theatre from the world outside. For in the minds of many, [the character of] Walter remains, despite the play, despite performance, what American racial traditions *wish* him to be: an exotic."[10] If audiences went to the theatre to see "the simple, lovable, and glandular 'Negro,' "[11] they would find him, regardless of what actually occurred on stage. Hansberry wrote,

> *My colleagues and I were reduced to mirth and tears by that gentleman writing his review of our play in a Connecticut paper who remarked of his pleasure at seeing how "our dusky brethren" could "come up with a song and hum their troubles away." It did not disturb the writer in the least that there is no such implication in the entire three acts. He did not need it in the play; he had it in his head.*[12]

---

[9] I have chosen not to attempt to create any chronology of criticism. In other words, I have not traced the ways in which the play's critical reception changed over time, nor have I foregrounded time as an important factor in this study. My purpose in this paper is not to write a history of the play's critical reception, but rather to unpack the ideas that have swirled around the play from 1959 until today. Also because I am not foregrounding any chronology, I use the words "African-American" and "black" interchangeably when I refer to people of a non-specified time; I use "Negro" only when I refer specifically to blacks prior to the early 1960s.

[10] Lorraine Hansberry, "Willie Loman, Walter Younger, and He Who Must Live," *The Village Voice* (12 August 1959), 7, 8 (original emphasis). In this article, the word "racial" was misprinted as "radical"; however, on 19 August, the *Voice* corrected it to "racial." I have corrected the quote for ease in reading.

[11] Ibid., 8.

[12] Ibid.

Similarly, Elliot Norton wrote for the *Boston Record* that Hansberry's characters "have been endowed with the light-hearted humor which seems to be inherent to their race."[13]

Such blatant racism is related to the more subtle "people's culture" approach Eric Lott attacked in *Love and Theft: Blackface Minstrelsy and the American Working Class*. Lott defined the "people's culture" position as one that views minstrelsy as a more-or-less accurate reflection or aspect of "authentic" Negro culture. Lott's attack on this approach's ahistoricity and inaccuracy might seem inapplicable to *Raisin*, which was obviously and deliberately locatable in black culture. However, the "people's culture" stance resembled that of some of the reviewers in that both approaches sought—or demanded access to "authentic" black culture, as evidenced in critics' repeated praising of *Raisin* as "honest drama" with "vigor as well as veracity."[14] In other words, the "people's culture" approach and that of some of *Raisin's* critics shared a common *impulse to access* perceived authentic black culture. And in doing so, of course, these approaches re-asserted whiteness as the norm.

The play's ability to appear to encapsulate "Negro experience" in the readily knowable, digestible, and non-threatening form of theatrical realism arguably satisfied this impulse and thus constituted the primary reason for the play's success among white audiences. In other words, the play's realism satisfied its white viewers in much the same way that minstrelsy satisfied its viewers by providing them with easy access to consumable, perceived "Negro culture." *A Raisin in the Sun*, then, by making black experiences appear understandable to and consumable by white audiences, simultaneously made those experiences *collectable*. The bourgeois white viewer could display his or her new-found knowledge much as one might display a collection of "primitive" art; as James Clifford argues, "cultural description [can be] presented as a form of collecting."[15]

Collecting is a performance of power. To collect is to construct, limit, contain, display, and define. As Clifford observed, collections (even nonmaterial ones such as collected experiences of theatregoing) are necessarily organized taxonomically and hierarchically; thus collectors assert power over their possessions (which serve as metonyms for cultures).[16] The impulse for the white theatregoer to collect knowledge of "authentic" black experiences—through minstrelsy or through *Raisin's* realism—is therefore an impulse to perform (and thus actualize) white power.

Collecting is closely related to conservation, another performance of power to which Clifford devoted some attention: "Collecting—at least in the West, where time is generally thought to be linear and irreversible—implies a rescue

10

---

[13] Elliot Norton, "'A Raisin in the Sun' Bristles with Power," *Boston Record* (13 September 1960), C74.

[14] Frank Ashton and Brooks Atkinson, respectively, quoted in Lorraine Hansberry, *A Raisin in the Sun* (New York, 1966), back cover.

[15] James Clifford, *The Predicament of Culture: Twentieth-Century Ethnography, Literature, and Art* (Cambridge, MA, 1988), 215.

[16] Ibid., 218.

of phenomena from inevitable historical decay or loss."[17] Clifford described the collecting of "primitive" visual art and the anthropological collecting of non-material knowledge as similarly conservative projects: "Both discourses assume a primitive world in need of preservation, redemption, and representation."[18] White audiences' nonmaterial collecting of minority experiences through theatre attendance, then, could involve a similar conservative impulse. And, as Clifford's colleague Donna Haraway noted, conservation is always intertwined with subjugation: "Once domination is complete, conservation is urgent."[19]

Finally, the assertion that *A Raisin in the Sun* was specifically and exclusively black effectively erased from the play Hansberry's class analysis. Many African-American critics and scholars have noticed and commented on this aspect of the play, but almost no white commentators have. Hansberry complained,

Some writers have been astonishingly incapable of discussing [the character of Walter's] purely class aspirations and have persistently confounded them with what they consider to be an exotic being's longing to "wheel and deal" in what they consider to be (and what Walter never can) "the white man's world."[20]

The erasure of Hansberry's class analysis suggests white critics' unwillingness to engage with a black writer's intellect. In other words, white audiences who came to the theatre to see (and collect the experiences of) the "simple, lovable, and glandular 'Negro'"[21] (and who encountered, to their disappointment, non-stereotyped characters[22]) could have preserved their mission by willfully ignoring anything that did not contribute to that project. Even the FBI, which investigated Lorraine Hansberry as a possible "danger to the Republic," labeled the play "not propagandistic."[23] This description, regarded as flattering by the FBI, revealed an unwillingness to engage with—or even recognize—the politics of the play.

---

[17] Ibid., 231.

[18] Ibid., 200.

[19] Donna Haraway, *Primate Visions: Gender, Race, and Nature in the World of Modern Science* (New York, 1989), 34.

[20] Hansberry, "Willie Loman," 8 (original emphasis). See note 10.

[21] Ibid., 8.

[22] The assertion that the characters are not stereotyped is not without controversy. Many critics, both black and white, have noted that the play "abounds with types: Mama is a tyrannical but good-natured matriarch; Walter, a frustrated young man surrounded by too many women; Beneatha, a free-thinking college student; the African Asagai, a poetic revolutionary; and the one white man, a cliché-ridden suburbanite" (Doris E. Abramson, *Negro Playwrights in the American Theatre, 1925–1959* [New York, 1967], 254). In particular, the character of Mama was "charged by critics" with being "a reactionary black 'mammy'" (Adrienne Rich, "The Problem with Lorraine Hansberry," *Freedomways: A Quarterly Review of the Freedom Movement*, 19 [1979], 252)—a characterization vociferously contradicted by black writers such as Amiri Baraka and Margaret B. Wilkerson (Amiri Baraka, "'Raisin in the Sun's' Enduring Passion," *The Washington Post* [16 November 1986], n.p., in file, "'A Raisin in the Sun': Clippings," Billy Rose Collection, New York Public Library for the Performing Arts; Margaret B. Wilkerson, "*A Raisin in the Sun*: Anniversary of an American Classic" in *Performing Feminisms: Feminist Critical Theory and Theatre*, ed. Sue-Ellen Case [Baltimore, 1990], 122, 125, 128). The point is not that the play was necessarily devoid of stereotypes, but rather that any stereotypes it may have contained were certainly far less pronounced and racist than those of minstrelsy.

[23] Wilkerson, "Anniversary" 122. See note 22.

By ignoring Hansberry's politics and recognizing only the play's specificity to black culture, white critics erased Hansberry's authority to speak about anything but herself. This action positioned blacks as if in a fishbowl: they could look at each other, but not at anything beyond their immediate context. This fishbowl could sit comfortably, decoratively, on a shelf in a white household; white people could peer through the glass (which contained and controlled the exotics and simultaneously kept the white spectator safely separated from the creatures) and enjoy their collection. In other words, erasing Hansberry's authority to speak about anything but her (white-defined) culture created a "glass" barrier that separated white audiences from the play's black creators and characters and rendered the subaltern collectable—and thus produced white power.

Furthermore, this "fishbowl" dynamic created a unidirectional gaze; that is 15 to say, it positioned blacks as the object of both blacks' and whites' gazes, and simultaneously positioned whites as the empowered, invisible inspector. This action reified blacks' lives and experiences as collectable and simultaneously precluded the possibility of blacks inverting the dynamic and collecting (and thus disempowering) whites and their experiences. The fish cannot collect the humans outside the bowl.

The interpretation of *Raisin* as specifically black (and distinctly not universal), however, also had non-racist, or even anti-racist, aspects, most of which originated from African-American writers.

Hansberry wrote the play in response to a racist performance:

One night, after seeing a play I won't mention, I suddenly became disgusted with a whole body of material about Negroes. Cardboard characters. Cute dialect bits. Or hip-swinging musicals from exotic sources.[24]

The critic from Connecticut, then, was not entirely wrong when he read racist stereotypes into Hansberry's play: these stereotypes were diegetically present.

Black audiences apparently also read the play in the context of racist stereotypes. According to James Baldwin, the play drew unprecedented numbers of African-Americans to the theatre because "never before in American theater history had so much of the truth of black people's lives been seen on stage."[25] Overlap occurred, then, between the racist impulse to collect black experiences and the anti-racist impulse to see one's own experience reflected on stage (and to see stereotypes extirpated): both impulses hinged on the highly suspect notion of authenticity. The fact that two opposing impulses could exist in the same space contributed to the appearance of a paradox.

[24] Lorraine Hansberry, quoted in Nan Robertson, "Dramatist Against Odds," *New York Times* (8 March 1959), in file, "A Raisin in the Sun," Schomburg Collection, New York Public Library; quoted in Abramson, 240.

[25] Elizabeth Brown-Guillory, *Their Place on the Stage: Black Women Playwrights in America* (Westport, CT, 1988), 34.

The play itself emphasized particularity within particularity through the character of Joseph Asagai, a Nigerian. According to Alex Haley, Hansberry achieved two goals through the character of Asagai. First, she

> helped to dispel the myth of the 'cannibal' with a bone in his hair. Her educated African character . . . was certainly the first time a large audience had seen and heard an African portrayed as carrying himself with dignity and being, moreover, a primary spokesman for sanity and progress. It must also have been the first time a mass audience had ever seen a black woman gracefully don African robes or wear an "afro" hairstyle.[26]

Asagai, then, continued Hansberry's project of creating individual, specifically black characters who testified against stereotypes. Second, as Haley noted, *A Raisin in the Sun* was the first artistic work to popularize (on a large scale) the concept of a relationship between African-Americans and Africans.[27] By teasing out this relationship that specifically separated African-Americans from all other Americans, Hansberry again employed the particularizing approach— but to anti-racist ends.

As several critics—and Hansberry herself—have noted, however, Hansberry's 20 particularism funneled into her universalism. Margaret B. Wilkerson posited that Hansberry's simultaneous particularism and universalism enabled *Raisin* to function as a bridge:

> Hansberry . . . [insists] upon a thorough probing of the individual within the specifics of culture, ethnicity and gender. In the midst of her expansiveness, she refuses to diminish the pain, suffering or truths of any one group in order to benefit another, a factor which makes her plays particularly rich and her characters thoroughly complex. Hence, she can write authentically about a black family in A Raisin in the Sun and yet produce, in the same instance, a play which appeals to both Blacks and whites, bridging for a moment the historical and cultural gaps between them.
>
> Her universalism, which redefines that much abused term, grows out of a deep, complex encounter with the specific terms of human experience as it occurs for Blacks, women, whites and many other groups of people. Her universalism is not facile, nor does it gloss over the things that divide people. She engages those issues, works through them, to find whatever may be, a priori, the human commonality that lies beneath.[28]

Obviously, there was an anti-racist project inherent to the demand that white audiences see themselves (i.e., the "universal") in black characters. And audiences responded to this demand: scholars such as Lerone Bennett, Jr., commented

---

[26] Alex Haley, "The Once and Future Vision of Lorraine Hansberry," *Freedomways: A Quarterly Review of the Freedom Movement*, 19 (1979), 279.

[27] Ibid, 278–79.

[28] Margaret B. Wilkerson, "Lorraine Hansberry: The Complete Feminist," *Freedomways: A Quarterly Review of the Freedom Movement*, 19 (1979), 237.

on the "curious identification some elements of the non-black community felt toward the play."[29] However, within this dynamic—which Hansberry deliberately created from an anti-racist politic—racist interpretations abounded.

The universalist interpretation of the play was used to deny and erase the particularity on which Hansberry insisted. In this way, universalism functioned much like the collecting instinct of the "people's culture" approach: the latter sought black culture in order to acquire and preserve it—and thus assert power over it; the former denied and erased black culture in order to control and assert power over it. Once again, opposing projects overlapped and contributed to the appearance of a paradox.

Furthermore, critics' lauding of *Raisin* for its "universal" appeal must be read in the context of the critics' more typical dismissal of black theatre "as social rather than artistic, as parochial rather than universal."[30] The interpretation of *Raisin* as artistic (i.e., apolitical) and universal, then, in addition to erasing crucial components of the play, denigrated all other black theatre. The elevation of *Raisin* to the status of universal made the play a token.

More subtly, the universalist impulse among white critics functioned to absorb the particular into the white/universal or to reduce the particular other to a reflection of the white self—both of which had the effect of inflating the white/universal.[31] In an essay on an exhibit of "primitive" art at the Museum of Modern Art, Clifford described a "disquieting quality of modernism: its taste for appropriating or redeeming otherness, for constructing non-Western arts in its own image, for discovering universal, ahistorical 'human' capabilities."[32] The point is not that Hansberry's work was modernist or non-Western, but rather that white critics, thinking in the modernist mode, treated *Raisin* as an exotic "other" and therefore sought "universal" qualities within it. Again, nuances of the apparent paradox are revealed: universalism flows into particularism, which in turn flows back into universalism.

What should be clear from this discussion is the fluidity, overlap, and mutual permeability of the categories of "universal" and "particular." Fluidity, overlap, and mutual permeability do not, however, constitute a paradox (which would require the simultaneous existence of two or more mutually exclusive trajectories). The appearance of a paradox depends on the assumption that universality and particularity are static.

---

[29] Bennett and Burroughs, 230. See note 8.

[30] Margaret B. Wilkerson, "Critics, Standards and Black Theatre," in *The Theater of Black Americans: A Collection of Critical Essays*, ed. Errol Hill (New York, 1987), 319.

[31] In an interesting variation, some critics argued that Hansberry's characters were *universal minorities*. For example, the characters "could belong to almost any minority race or sect"; *Raisin* "could be a play by Clifford Odets about Jews in the Bronx" or "could just as easily be about Jews or Communists" (Oppenheimer, 19; Milton Shulman, "I Fear We've Heard this Note Before," *Evening Standard* [5 August 1959], n.p., in file, "*A Raisin in the Sun*: Clippings," Billy Rose Collection, New York Public Library for the Performing Arts; Don Cook, "'Raisin in the Sun vs. London Critics," *New York Herald Tribune* [30 August 1959], n.p., in file, "*A Raisin in the Sun*: Clippings," Billy Rose Collection, New York Public Library for the Performing Arts). The reviewers thus used *Raisin* simultaneously to erase differences among minority cultures, to segregate and marginalize *all* such cultures from the white majority, and thus to center and empower white gentiles.

[32] Clifford, 193. See note 15.

The introduction of the idea of motion not only resolves the apparent para- 25 dox (as Hansberry did in 1959 with her assertion that universality flows out of particularity), but also illuminates the reasons for the illusion of—and the cultural need for—the paradox: to view the "universal" and the "particular" as a dialectic rather than a pair of static opposites frozen in a paradox is to destabilize the "universal," that is, whiteness.

All the white critics' categorizations of the play—as particular, as distinctly not particular but universal, as apolitical, as a tokenized masterpiece—constructed black experiences as collectable. The unidirectionality of collecting (the fish cannot collect the humans outside the bowl) stabilizes whiteness and thus reifies white power. Hansberry's solution to the apparent paradox—that particularity and universality are not static, contradictory opposites—suggested that the fishbowl's glass does not exist (or at least that the glass is an unstable illusion), that blacks are not inherently collectable, that whites are not necessarily immune from being collected. Hansberry's resolution of the paradox, then, was antiracist both in its content ("I'd always been under the impression that Negroes *are* people"[33]) and in its destabilization of the static categories of "universal" and "particular," "collector" and "collected"—categories on whose stability white power depends. White critics, then, maintained the illusion of the paradox—despite the availability of a simple solution—in order to stabilize both whiteness and the segregation of Negroes and whites, and thus to produce and enhance white power.

The level of desperation to maintain the paradox and thus stabilize whiteness is best appreciated through an examination of a misquotation in the *New York Times* that reversed Hansberry's fluid belief in universalism-through-particularity. The progression of the misquotation, as described by Robert Nemiroff, Hansberry's ex-husband and literary executor, is worth quoting at length:

> [Hansberry] is . . . "quoted" as follows: "I told them this wasn't a 'Negro play.' It was a play about honest-to-God, believable, many-sided people who happened to be Negroes."
>
> In her scrapbook, beside a clipping of this interview, Lorraine wrote these words: "Never said NO such thing. Miss Robertson [the interviewer] goofed—letter sent post-haste—Tune in next week. . . ." But she need not have waited. The letter of correction was never printed. A month later, in a second profile ("Her Dream Came True" 4/9/59), presumably by another writer, the alleged statement was repeated. And from there it spread like a prairie fire. In short order, a second "quote" was mysteriously appended to the first to complete the equation: "I'm not a Negro writer—but a writer who happens to be a Negro." And now nothing could stop it, for it seemed to solve the problem for white Americans—how to classify the author of "The Best Play of the Year" while, at the same time, avoid honoring the special qualities that made her what she was. By the time Lorraine died, the phrase had undergone, in the New York Times obituary, a further metamorphosis: "The work was described not as a Negro play but one about people who happen to be Negroes.

[33] Hansberry, *To Be Young*, 128. See note 7.

*And its author, too, insisted throughout her short lifetime that she was not a Negro
playwright, but. . . ." etc.*

*Thus, the words Lorraine never spoke became in effect her credo as an artist, as
if it were the driving passion of her life.*[34]

The persistence and expansion of the misquotation (which can still be found
in many scholarly texts) demonstrates the urgency and effort with which
the paradox was maintained. The misquotation located Hansberry squarely
within the universalist stance—but reacting to the particularist interpretation (in other words, it invoked the particularist interpretation as much as it
did the universalist). The misquotation thus maintained the illusion of two
mutually exclusive interpretations locked in battle with each other. It appeared
to resolve the paradox (by using Hansberry's authority as the writer and as a
"Negro" to "prove" the universalist interpretation and "discredit" the particularist position), but in fact it merely maintained it by erasing the possibility of a
fluid relationship between the universal and the particular.

Fluidity was also frozen (and thus the paradox was maintained and whiteness stabilized) through critics' re-invention of *Raisin* as a "timeless classic."
Upon the play's opening, the question of whether the play was timely or timeless arose as immediately as the question of whether it was universal or specific
to black culture. "We do not know if Miss Hansberry has written a timeless
play," wrote a reviewer for the *Philadelphia Inquirer*, "but she certainly has
written a timely one."[35] George Murray noted in the *Chicago American* that the
play "couldn't be better timed for box office success. Its advent coincides with
a rising wave of general interest in the Negro. The wave began as a ground-
swell after World War II. It is visible in the South's integration fight, in high
court decisions, the National Association for the Advancement of Colored
People's muscle-flexing."[36] With the benefit of twenty years' hindsight, Bennett
observed, "the timing [of the play's opening] was perfect. Remember, this
was 1959, five years after the Supreme Court decision on school desegrega-
tion, four years after Montgomery, the eve of the sit-ins. The time was ripe for
Lorraine Hansberry. She was a kind of herald, a person announcing the coin-
ing of something. It was in the air, I think, and whites felt it as well as Blacks."[37]

Before long, the votes swung overwhelmingly in the direction of dubbing
A Raisin in the Sun "timeless," that is, a masterpiece. Upon the play's revival
in 1983, Lloyd Richards, director of the original production, called the play "a
timeless piece."[38] As Wilkerson observed, *A Raisin in the Sun* is one of the only
black plays ever to have been "accorded the status of a classic."[39]

[34] Robert Nemiroff, "A Lorraine Hansberry Bibliography," *Freedomways: A Quarterly Review of the Freedom Movement*, 19 (1979), 286–87.

[35] Henry T. Murdock, "Poitier in Timely Play on Trials of Negroes," *Philadelphia Inquirer* (27 January 1959), n.p., in file, "*A Raisin in the Sun*: Clippings," Billy Rose Collection, New York Public Library for the Performing Arts.

[36] Murray, 19. See note 1.

[37] Bennett and Burroughs, 229.

[38] Samuel G. Freedman, "Yale Marking 25th Anniversary of *Raisin in Sun*," *New York Times* (1 November 1983), C13, quoted in Wilkerson, "Anniversary," 119.

[39] Wilkerson, "Anniversary," 119.

The process by which classics or masterpieces are so labeled is politically charged, to say the least. When the artistic work slides along the dialectic of universality and particularity (i.e., when the work is labeled "ethnic"), however, the political ramifications become even more acute. As Clifford observed, some collectable "ethnographic specimens" (as the particularists viewed *Raisin*) are recognized as artistic masterpieces because they fit so-called "universal" aesthetics.[40] To label an "ethnically specific" play a "masterpiece," then, is to label it exceptional, to separate it from its ethnic tradition. It was impossible in 1959—and it is arguably still impossible today—to label the work of a minority artist a "masterpiece" without simultaneously asserting its universality. In other words, the process of labeling a "minority" play a masterpiece necessarily invoked and engaged with the apparent paradox of universality versus particularity. The creation and maintenance of the illusion of the paradox enables some "exceptional" works by minorities to be declared masterpieces and simultaneously facilitates the relegation to the back of the bus of artistic works labeled "non-masterpieces." The "paradox," in other words, acts as a gate to separate (or stabilize the separation of) "masterpieces" from "non-masterpieces," white from black, collector from collected, "universal" from "particular," "timeless" from "timely." And as the "paradox" acts as a gate, those with the power to maintain the illusion of the paradox (e.g., white critics) invent themselves as gatekeepers.

Lerone Bennett, Jr., was correct when he called Hansberry "a kind of herald, a person announcing the coming of something," as when he described a nameless something "in the air . . . and whites felt it as well as Blacks."[41] Perhaps that subconsciously anticipated "something"—so feared by the creators and maintainers of the paradox—was a postmodern, globalized culture in which boundaries between universal and particular, white and nonwhite, collector and collected, are unstable. A world in which the subaltern speaks back; in which culture flows not only from the "top-down," but in all chaotic directions; a world, in the words of Arjun Appadurai, in which "the United States [and by extension, whiteness] is no longer the puppeteer of a world system of images, but is only one node of a complex transnational construction of imaginary landscapes."[42] Through the desperate creation and maintenance of the appearance of the paradox—which in turn created and maintained a static boundary between universal and particular, white and black—white people created the illusion that they could collect minority experiences without being collected themselves.

MAKING ARGUMENTS

1. What does Bernstein mean by "the universal" and "the particular"? How does she believe they relate? What part does this relation play in her argument?

2. What is the "'fishbowl' dynamic" (para. 15) to which Bernstein refers? Why is it significant?

3. What is Bernstein's argument about paradox? Do you agree?

[40] Clifford, 206.

[41] Bennett and Burroughs, 229.

[42] Arjun Appadurai, "Disjuncture and Difference in the Global Cultural Economy," in *The Phantom Public Sphere*, ed. Bruce Robbins (Minneapolis, 1993), 273.

MARILYN STASIO (B. 1940)

VARIETY REVIEW OF A RAISIN IN THE SUN[1] 2014

Raisin made its way into the history books for very good reason when it had its Broadway premiere (in the same theater, let it be noted) more than 50 years ago. It was, after all, the first play by an African-American woman to be produced on Broadway. (The importance of that comes through loud and clear in a pre-curtain airing of the scribe's well-known interview with Studs Terkel.) The play went on to win the New York Drama Critics Circle's award for best play. And, as a work of sociologically astute drama, it presented a penetrating look into the lives of working-class black Americans at a time when this silent minority was finding its voice and beginning to ask for the hard-won rights and privileges it had been promised.

But it isn't the historical value of Hansberry's heartfelt family drama that is moving audiences to tears. It's watching and sharing the hopes and dreams and heartaches of a multigenerational family—not unlike your own—struggling to hold itself together as the changing times are challenging all its traditional belief systems and core values.

When people think of *Raisin*, what quickly comes to mind is the dramatic scene in which Karl Lindner (in a precision-tooled perf only to be expected from director-thesp David Cromer), a weaselly emissary from a white neighborhood, appears at the Younger apartment (a rabbit warren of cramped, crowded, airless spaces on Mark Thompson's realistic set) to present the family with a hefty bribe not to move into the house they have just bought. This, in turn, sets up the searing scene at the end of the show, played with great passion by Washington, in which Walter Lee Younger finally mans up to resolve the family crisis.

But *Raisin* is about a lot more than race relations in 1950s Chicago. It's the very model of the modern well-made play, which means that every piece in its jigsaw plot locks into its central theme—the survival of the African-American family. As the title reference to Langston Hughes' powerful poem pointedly tells us, the play is about dreams, the many deeply desired and often conflicting dreams that are flying around in this family, making everybody crazy.

Lena Younger, the formidable matriarch played by the formidable Latanya 5 Richardson Jackson, dreams of moving the family into a real home—a place where her sickly little potted plant can put down roots and grow. Her grown-up child of a son, Walter Lee, desperately dreams of leaving his chauffeur's job and opening a liquor store where he can put up his feet and do as white executives do—talk big and do nothing. Walter's worn-out wife, Ruth (Sophie Okonedo, as utterly mesmerizing here as she was in *Hotel Rawanda*), dreams of seeing her petulant husband so happy that he'll remember she exists.

---

[1] Marilyn Stasio/*Variety* © Variety Media, LLC.

Beneatha Younger, the family brain and Hansberry's obvious stand-in, fares brilliantly in Anika Noni Rose's delicious performance. Her dreams are very much those of her race and generation: a college education, a career in medicine, freedom to travel and choose an exciting husband, and—here's what sets her aside from the rest of the more convention-bound Youngers—to explore her personal identity and African heritage. Although helmer Kenny Leon generally treats the material with respect and keeps it from slipping too obviously into sitcom farce, he lets loose (as does costumer Ann Roth) when Beneatha stuns the family with the African duds and folk dances she picked up from her Nigerian boyfriend.

The family's tragedy is that everyone, even smart-as-a-whip Beneatha, is really, really slow (or, in Walter Lee's case, too selfish) to see how achieving their own individual dreams might cost others theirs. In Playwriting 101 terms, that conflict is dramatized by the $10,000 insurance money that Mama Lena has inherited from her late husband, but everyone else—and especially grabby Walter Lee—has designs on.

The conflicts in the household are about power as much as money. True believer Lena slaps down Beneatha hard when she asserts the atheist creed she picked up at school. Walter Lee asserts his manhood by wringing out Ruth like a dishrag. But it does always get back to money, and the standoff between Lena and Walter Lee over that $10,000 is the elemental generational battle between parents, whose dominance means that everyone has to live by their old-fashioned values, and their impatient children, whose newfangled notions have yet to pass the test of time.

It's an old battle, as old as the family structure itself. But Hansberry presents it with such clear-eyed intelligence and warmhearted affection that you can't help wishing the Youngers all the happiness they can hold.

MAKING ARGUMENTS

1. Does Stasio have a central argument in her review? If so, what is it? If not, why not?

2. What does Stasio claim *A Raisin in the Sun* is about? One thing? More than one thing? One thing more than another?

3. How does she support this claim? Do you think she does so successfully?

MAKING CONNECTIONS

1. What role does the idea of Africa play in both *A Raisin in the Sun* and in its reception, according to Brown and Wilkerson?

2. How does the idea of the American dream surface in these pieces? Do all of the writers raise it? Do they all work with the same definition?

3. Which of these essays discusses the role of politics in drama? What do they have to say about it? Why is it important in work on this play in particular?

4. Which of these pieces treat the relation of class and race in this play and in American society? Do they treat it in the same way?

5. The selections in this casebook include both scholarly criticism and journalistic reviews. Compare the work in the two genres. How do they differ? How do their differences reflect the demands and expectations of the genres?

DAVID HENRY HWANG (B. 1957)

TRYING TO FIND CHINATOWN 1996

CHARACTERS

Benjamin, Caucasian male, early twenties.
Ronnie, Asian American male, mid-twenties.

Time and Place

A street corner on the Lower East Side, New York City. The present.

Note on Music

Obviously, it would be foolish to require that the actor portraying Ronnie perform the specified violin music live. The score of this play can be played on tape over the house speakers, and the actor can feign playing the violin using a bow treated with soap. However, in order to effect a convincing illusion, it is desirable that the actor possess some familiarity with the violin or another stringed instrument.

Darkness. Over the house speakers, sound fades in: Hendrix-like virtuoso rock 'n' roll riffs—heavy feedback, distortion, phase shifting, wah-wah—amplified over a tiny Fender pug-nose.

Lights fade up to reveal that the music's being played over a solid-body electric violin by Ronnie, a Chinese American male in his mid-twenties; he is dressed in retro-'60s clothing and has a few requisite '90s body mutilations. He's playing on a sidewalk for money, his violin case open before him; change and a few stray bills have been left by previous passersby.

Benjamin enters; he's in his early twenties, blond, blue-eyed, a midwestern tourist in the big city. He holds a scrap of paper in his hands, scanning street signs for an address. He pauses before Ronnie, listens for a while. With a truly bravura run, Ronnie concludes the number and falls to his knees, gasping. Benjamin applauds.

Benjamin. Good. That was really great. *(Pause)* I didn't . . . I mean, a fiddle . . . I mean, I'd heard them at square dances, on country stations and all, but I never . . . wow, this must really be New York City!

(Benjamin applauds, starts to walk on. Still on his knees, Ronnie clears his throat loudly.)

Oh, I . . . you're not just doing this for your health, right?

(Benjamin reaches in his pocket, pulls out a couple of coins. Ronnie clears his throat again.)

Look, I'm not a millionaire, I'm just . . .

(Benjamin pulls out his wallet, removes a dollar bill. Ronnie nods his head and gestures toward the violin case as he takes out a pack of cigarettes, lights one.)

Ronnie. And don't call it a "fiddle," OK?

Benjamin. Oh. Well, I didn't mean to—

Ronnie. You sound like a wuss. A hick. A dipshit.

Benjamin. It just slipped out. I didn't really—

Ronnie. If this was a fiddle, I'd be sitting here with a cob pipe, stomping my cowboy boots and kicking up hay. Then I'd go home and fuck my cousin.

Benjamin. Oh! Well, I don't really think—

Ronnie. Do you see a cob pipe? Am I fucking my cousin?

Benjamin. Well, no, not at the moment, but—

Ronnie. All right. Then this is a violin, now you give me your money, and I ignore the insult. Herein endeth the lesson.

(Pause.)

Benjamin. Look, a dollar's more than I've ever given to a . . . to someone asking for money.

Ronnie. Yeah, well, this is New York. Welcome to the cost of living.

Benjamin. What I mean is, maybe in exchange, you could help me—?

Ronnie. Jesus Christ! Do you see a sign around my neck reading "Big Apple Fucking Tourist Bureau"?

Benjamin. I'm just looking for an address, I don't think it's far from here, maybe you could . . . ?

(Benjamin holds out his scrap of paper, Ronnie snatches it away.)

Ronnie. You're lucky I'm such a goddamn softy. *(He looks at the paper)* Oh, fuck you. Just suck my dick, you and the cousin you rode in on.

Benjamin. I don't get it! What are you—?

Ronnie. Eat me. You know exactly what I—

Benjamin. I'm just asking for a little—

Ronnie. "13 Doyers Street"? Like you don't know where that is?

Benjamin. Of course I don't know! That's why I'm asking—

Ronnie. C'mon, you trailer-park refugee. You don't know that's Chinatown?

Benjamin. Sure I know that's Chinatown.

Ronnie. I know you know that's Chinatown.

Benjamin. So? That doesn't mean I know where Chinatown—

Ronnie. So why is it that you picked *me*, of all the street musicians in the city—to point you in the direction of Chinatown? Lemme guess—is it the earring? No, I don't think so. The Hendrix riffs? Guess again, you fucking moron.

Benjamin. Now, wait a minute. I see what you're—

Ronnie. What are you gonna ask me next? Where you can find the best dim sum in the city? Whether I can direct you to a genuine opium den? Or do I happen to know how you can meet Miss Saigon for a night of nookie-nookie followed by a good old-fashioned ritual suicide? Now, get your white ass off my sidewalk. One dollar doesn't even begin to make up for all this aggravation. Why don't you go back home and race bullfrogs, or whatever it is you do for—?

Benjamin. Brother, I can absolutely relate to your anger. Righteous rage, I suppose, would be a more appropriate term. To be marginalized, as we are, by a white racist patriarchy, to the point where the accomplishments of our people are obliterated from the history books, this is cultural genocide of the first order, leading to the fact that you must do battle with all of Euro-America's emasculating and brutal stereotypes of Asians—the opium den, the sexual objectification of the Asian female, the exoticized image of a tourist's Chinatown which ignores the exploitation of workers, the failure to unionize, the high rate of mental illness and tuberculosis—against these, each day, you rage, no, not as a victim, but as a survivor, yes, brother, a glorious warrior survivor!

(Silence.)

Ronnie. Say what?

Benjamin. So, I hope you can see that my request is not—

Ronnie. Wait, wait.

Benjamin. —motivated by the sorts of racist assumptions—

Ronnie. But, but where . . . how did you learn all that?

Benjamin. All what?

Ronnie. All that—you know—oppression stuff—tuberculosis . . .

Benjamin. It's statistically irrefutable. TB occurs in the community at a rate—

Ronnie. Where did *you* learn it?

Benjamin. I took Asian American studies. In college.

Ronnie. Where did you go to college?

Benjamin. University of Wisconsin. Madison.

Ronnie. Madison, Wisconsin?

Benjamin. That's not where the bridges are, by the way.

Ronnie. Huh? Oh, right . . .

Benjamin. You wouldn't believe the number of people who—

Ronnie. They have Asian American studies in Madison, Wisconsin? Since when?

Benjamin. Since the last Third World Unity hunger strike. *(Pause)* Why do you look so surprised? We're down.

Ronnie. I dunno. It just never occurred to me, the idea of Asian students in the Midwest going on a hunger strike.

Benjamin. Well, a lot of them had midterms that week, so they fasted in shifts. *(Pause)* The administration never figured it out. The Asian students put that "They all look alike" stereotype to good use.

Ronnie. OK, so they got Asian American studies. That still doesn't explain—

Benjamin. What?

Ronnie. Well . . . what *you* were doing taking it?

Benjamin. Just like everyone else. I wanted to explore my roots. And, you know, the history of oppression which is my legacy. After a lifetime of assimilation, I wanted to find out who I really am.

(Pause.)

Ronnie. And did you?

Benjamin. Sure. I learned to take pride in my ancestors who built the railroads, my Popo who would make me a hot bowl of jok with thousand-day-old eggs when the white kids chased me home yelling, "Gook! Chink! Slant-eyes!"

Ronnie. OK, OK, that's enough!

Benjamin. Painful to listen to, isn't it?

Ronnie. I don't know what kind of bullshit ethnic studies program they're running over in Wuss-consin, but did they bother to teach you that in order to find your Asian "roots," it's a good idea to first be Asian?

(Pause.)

Benjamin. Are you speaking metaphorically?

Ronnie. No! Literally! Look at your skin!

Benjamin. You know, it's very stereotypical to think that all Asian skin tones conform to a single hue.

Ronnie. You're white! Is this some kind of redneck joke or something? Am I the first person in the world to tell you this?

Benjamin. Oh! Oh! Oh!

Ronnie. I know real Asians are scarce in the Midwest, but . . . Jesus!

Benjamin. No, of course, I . . . I see where your misunderstanding arises.

Ronnie. Yeah. It's called, "You white."

Benjamin. It's just that—in my hometown of Tribune, Kansas, and then at school—see, everyone knows me—so this sort of thing never comes up. *(He offers his hand)* Benjamin Wong. I forget that a society wedded to racial constructs constantly forces me to explain my very existence.

Ronnie. Ronnie Chang. Otherwise known as "The Bow Man."

Benjamin. You see, I was adopted by Chinese American parents at birth. So, clearly, I'm an Asian American—

Ronnie. Even though you're blond and blue-eyed.

Benjamin. Well, you can't judge my race by my genetic heritage alone.

Ronnie. If genes don't determine race, what does?

Benjamin. Perhaps you'd prefer that I continue in denial, masquerading as a white man?

Ronnie. You can't just wake up and say, "Gee, I *feel* black today."

Benjamin. Brother, I'm just trying to find what you've already got.

Ronnie. What do I got?

Benjamin. A home. With your people. Picketing with the laundry workers. Taking refuge from the daily slights against your masculinity in the noble image of Gwan Gung.

Ronnie. Gwan who?

Benjamin. C'mon—the Chinese god of warriors and—what do you take me for? There're altars to him up all over the community.

Ronnie. I dunno what community you're talking about, but it's sure as hell not mine.

(Pause.)

Benjamin. What do you mean?

Ronnie. I mean, if you wanna call Chinatown *your* community, OK, knock yourself out, learn to use chopsticks, big deal. Go ahead, try and find your "roots" in
some dim sum parlor with headless ducks hanging in the window. Those places
don't tell you a thing about who *I* am.

Benjamin. Oh, I get it.

Ronnie. You get what?

Benjamin. You're one of those self-hating, *assimilated* Chinese Americans, aren't
you?

Ronnie. Oh, Jesus.

Benjamin. You probably call yourself "Oriental," huh? Look, maybe I can help you.
I have some books I can—

Ronnie. Hey, I read all those Asian identity books when you were still slather-
ing on industrial-strength sunblock. *(Pause)* Sure, I'm Chinese. But folks like
you act like that means something. Like, all of a sudden, you know who I am.
You think identity's that simple? That you can wrap it all up in a neat package
and say, "I have ethnicity, therefore I am"? All you fucking ethnic fundamentalists. Always settling for easy answers. You say you're looking for identity, but
you can't begin to face the real mysteries of the search. So instead, you go skin-
deep, and call it a day. *(Pause. He turns away from Benjamin and starts to play his
violin—slow and bluesy.)*

Benjamin. So what are you? "Just a human being"? That's like saying you *have*
no identity. If you asked me to describe my dog, I'd say more than, "He's just a
dog."

Ronnie. What—you think if I deny the importance of my race, I'm nobody?
There're worlds out there, worlds you haven't even begun to understand. Open
your eyes. Hear with your ears.

*(Ronnie holds his violin at chest level, but does not attempt to play during the fol-
lowing monologue. As he speaks, rock and jazz violin tracks fade in and out over
the house speakers, bringing to life the styles of music he describes.)*

I concede—it was called a fiddle long ago—but that was even before the birth
of jazz. When the hollering in the fields, the rank injustice of human bondage,
the struggle of God's children against the plagues of the devil's white man, when
all these boiled up into that bittersweet brew, called by later generations, the
blues. That's when fiddlers like Son Sims held their chin rests at their chests,
and sawed away like the hillbillies still do today. And with the coming of ragtime appeared the pioneer Stuff Smith, who sang as he stroked the catgut, with
his raspy, Louis Armstrong–voice—gruff and sweet like the timber of horsehair
riding south below the fingerboard—and who finally sailed for Europe to find
ears that would hear. Europe—where Stephane Grappelli initiated a magical
French violin, to be passed from generation to generation—first he, to Jean-Luc
Ponty, then Ponty to Didier Lockwood. Listening to Grappelli play "A Nightingale Sang in Berkeley Square" is to understand not only the song of birds, but
also how they learn to fly, fall in love on the wing, and finally falter one day, to

wait for darkness beneath a London street lamp. And Ponty—he showed how the modern violin man can accompany the shadow of his own lead lines, which cascade, one over another, into some nether world beyond the range of human hearing. Joe Venuti. Noel Pointer. Sven Asmussen. Even the Kronos Quartet, with their arrangement of "Purple Haze." Now, tell me, could any legacy be more rich, more crowded with mythology and heroes to inspire pride? What can I say if the banging of a gong or the clinking of a pickax on the Transcontinental Railroad fails to move me even as much as one note, played through a violin MIDI controller by Michael Urbaniak? *(He puts his violin to his chin, begins to play a jazz composition of his own invention)* Does it have to sound like Chinese opera before people like you decide I know who I am?

(Benjamin stands for a long moment, listening to Ronnie play. Then, he drops his dollar into the case, turns and exits right. Ronnie continues to play a long moment. Then Benjamin enters downstage left, illuminated in his own spotlight. He sits on the floor of the stage, his feet dangling off the lip. As he speaks, Ronnie continues playing his tune, which becomes underscoring for Benjamin's monologue. As the music continues, does it slowly begin to reflect the influence of Chinese music?)

Benjamin. When I finally found Doyers Street, I scanned the buildings for Number 13. Walking down an alley where the scent of freshly steamed char siu bao lingered in the air, I felt immediately that I had entered a world where all things were finally familiar. *(Pause)* An old woman bumped me with her shopping bag—screaming to her friend in Cantonese, though they walked no more than a few inches apart. Another man—shouting to a vendor in Sze-Yup. A youth, in white undershirt, perhaps a recent newcomer, bargaining with a grocer in Hokkien. I walked through this ocean of dialects, breathing in the richness with deep gulps, exhilarated by the energy this symphony brought to my step. And when I finally saw the number 13, I nearly wept at my good fortune. An old tenement, paint peeling, inside walls no doubt thick with a century of grease and broken dreams—and yet, to me, a temple—the house where my father was born. I suddenly saw it all: Gung Gung, coming home from his sixteen-hour days pressing shirts he could never afford to own, bringing with him candies for my father, each sweet wrapped in the hope of a better life. When my father left the ghetto, he swore he would never return. But he had, this day, in the thoughts and memories of his son, just six months after his death. And as I sat on the stoop, I pulled a hua-moi from my pocket, sucked on it, and felt his spirit returning. To this place where his ghost, and the dutiful hearts of all his descendants, would always call home. *(He listens for a long moment)* And I felt an ache in my heart for all those lost souls, denied this most important of revelations: to know who they truly are.

(Benjamin sucks his salted plum and listens to the sounds around him. Ronnie continues to play. The two remain oblivious of one another. Lights fade slowly to black.)

End of play

FOR ANALYSIS

1. Two things about Benjamin are revealed in his first big speech (p. 814). What are they? What two different sets of stereotypes make them surprising?

2. Why does Benjamin consider himself Chinese? Why does Ronnie disagree?

3. The second-to-last stage direction (not counting "End of play") ends: "As the music continues, does it slowly begin to reflect the influence of Chinese music?" (p. 817). Why might Hwang have written this stage direction? What comment might it be making about the discussion the two **characters** have been having?

MAKING ARGUMENTS

Ronnie and Benjamin disagree about the importance of ethnic heritage to identity. Make an argument for the view you find more persuasive, using the play and anything else you think supports your argument.

WRITING TOPIC

Hwang writes **dialogue** in a very particular way for each character. Describe the **style** of each character's lines, and compare them. What does the way in which each talks say about him as a person? What do the similarities and differences between the ways they talk say about the similarities and differences between them as people?

MAKING CONNECTIONS

1. Compare this play to Chin's poem "How I Got That Name" (p. 672). How does each work relate Chinese identity to mainstream "white" American identity?

2. Compare Ronnie's attitudes about Asian stereotypes to the responses about gender stereotypes by the speakers in "Connecting Poems: Working Mothers" (p. 696). How are these responses—and the issues they concern—similar? How are they different?

NONFICTION

VIRGINIA WOOLF (1882–1941)

WHAT IF SHAKESPEARE HAD HAD A SISTER?[1] 1929

It was disappointing not to have brought back in the evening some important statement, some authentic fact. Women are poorer than men because— this or that. Perhaps now it would be better to give up seeking for the truth, and receiving on one's head an avalanche of opinion hot as lava, discoloured as dish-water. It would be better to draw the curtains; to shut out distractions; to light the lamp; to narrow the enquiry and to ask the historian, who records not opinions but facts, to describe under what conditions women lived, not throughout the ages, but in England, say in the time of Elizabeth.

For it is a perennial puzzle why no woman wrote a word of that extraordinary literature when every other man, it seemed, was capable of song or sonnet. What were the conditions in which women lived, I asked myself; for fiction, imaginative work that is, is not dropped like a pebble upon the ground, as science may be; fiction is like a spider's web, attached ever so lightly perhaps, but still attached to life at all four corners. Often the attachment is scarcely perceptible; Shakespeare's plays, for instance, seem to hang there complete by themselves. But when the web is pulled askew, hooked up at the edge, torn in the middle, one remembers that these webs are not spun in midair by incorporeal creatures, but are the work of suffering human beings, and are attached to grossly material things, like health and money and the houses we live in.

I went, therefore, to the shelf where the histories stand and took down one of the latest, Professor Trevelyan's *History of England*. Once more I looked up

---

[1] *A Room of One's Own*, from which this essay is taken, is based on two lectures Woolf delivered on women and literature at Newnham College and Girton College, Cambridge University. In the opening chapter, Woolf declares that without "money and a room of her own," a woman cannot write fiction. In the following chapter, she recounts her unsuccessful attempt to turn up information at the British Library on the lives of women. This essay is from Chapter 3, from which a few passages are omitted. The essay ends with the concluding paragraph of the book.

Women, found "position of," and turned to the pages indicated. "Wife-beating," I read, "was a recognized right of man, and was practiced without shame by high as well as low. . . . Similarly," the historian goes on, "the daughter who refused to marry the gentleman of her parents' choice was liable to be locked up, beaten and flung about the room, without any shock being inflicted on public opinion. Marriage was not an affair of personal affection, but of family avarice, particularly in the 'chivalrous' upper classes. . . . Betrothal often took place while one or both of the parties was in the cradle, and marriage when they were scarcely out of the nurses' charge." That was about 1470, soon after Chaucer's time. The next reference to the position of women is some two hundred years later, in the time of the Stuarts. "It was still the exception for women of the upper and middle class to choose their own husbands, and when the husband had been assigned, he was lord and master, so far at least as law and custom could make him. Yet even so," Professor Trevelyan concludes, "neither Shakespeare's women nor those of authentic seventeenth-century memoirs, like the Verneys and the Hutchinsons, seem wanting in personality and character." Certainly, if we consider it, Cleopatra must have had a way with her; Lady Macbeth, one would suppose, had a will of her own; Rosalind, one might conclude, was an attractive girl. Professor Trevelyan is speaking no more than the truth when he remarks that Shakespeare's women do not seem wanting in personality and character. Not being a historian, one might go even further and say that women have burnt like beacons in all the works of all the poets from the beginning of time—Clytemnestra, Antigone, Cleopatra, Lady Macbeth, Phèdre, Cressida, Rosalind, Desdemona, the Duchess of Malfi, among the dramatists; then among the prose writers: Millamant, Clarissa, Becky Sharp, Anna Karenina, Emma Bovary, Madame de Guermantes[2]—the names flock to mind, nor do they recall women "lacking in personality and character." Indeed, if woman had no existence save in the fiction written by men, one would imagine her a person of the utmost importance; very various; heroic and mean; splendid and sordid; infinitely beautiful and hideous in the extreme; as great as a man, some think even greater. But this is woman in fiction. In fact, as Professor Trevelyan points out, she was locked up, beaten and flung about the room.

A very queer, composite being thus emerges. Imaginatively she is of the highest importance; practically she is completely insignificant. She pervades poetry from cover to cover; she is all but absent from history. She dominates the lives of kings and conquerors in fiction; in fact she was the slave of any boy whose parents forced a ring upon her finger. Some of the most inspired words, some of the most profound thoughts in literature fell from her lips; in real life she could hardly read, could scarcely spell, and was the property of her husband.

It was certainly an odd monster that one made up by reading the historians 5 first and the poets afterwards—a worm winged like an eagle; the spirit of life and beauty in a kitchen chopping up suet. But these monsters, however amusing to the imagination, have no existence in fact. What one must do to bring her to

---

[2] Female characters from great works of literature.

life was to think poetically and prosaically at one and the same moment, thus keeping in touch with fact—that she is Mrs. Martin, aged thirty-six, dressed in blue, wearing a black hat and brown shoes; but not losing sight of fiction either—that she is a vessel in which all sorts of spirits and forces are coursing and flashing perpetually. The moment, however, that one tries this method with the Elizabethan woman, one branch of illumination fails; one is held up by the scarcity of facts. One knows nothing detailed, nothing perfectly true and substantial about her. History scarcely mentions her. And I turned to Professor Trevelyan again to see what history meant to him. I found by looking at his chapter headings that it meant—

"The Manor Court and the Methods of Open-field Agriculture . . . The Cistercians and Sheep-farming . . . The Crusades . . . The University . . . The House of Commons . . . The Hundred Years' War . . . The Wars of the Roses . . . The Renaissance Scholars . . . The Dissolution of the Monasteries . . . Agrarian and Religious Strife . . . The Origin of English Seapower . . . The Armada . . ." and so on. Occasionally an individual woman is mentioned, an Elizabeth, or a Mary; a queen or a great lady. But by no possible means could middle-class women with nothing but brains and character at their command have taken part in any one of the great movements which, brought together, constitute the historian's view of the past. Nor shall we find her in any collection of anecdotes. Aubrey hardly mentions her.[3] She never writes her own life and scarcely keeps a diary; there are only a handful of her letters in existence. She left no plays or poems by which we can judge her . . . Here am I asking why women did not write poetry in the Elizabethan age, and I am not sure how they were educated; whether they were taught to write; whether they had sitting-rooms to themselves; how many women had children before they were twenty-one; what, in short, they did from eight in the morning till eight at night. They had no money evidently; according to Professor Trevelyan they were married whether they liked it or not before they were out of the nursery, at fifteen or sixteen very likely. It would have been extremely odd, even upon this showing, had one of them suddenly written the plays of Shakespeare, I concluded, and I thought of that old gentleman, who is dead now, but was a bishop, I think, who declared that it was impossible for any woman, past, present, or to come, to have the genius of Shakespeare. He wrote to the papers about it. He also told a lady who applied to him for information that cats do not as a matter of fact go to heaven, though they have, he added, souls of a sort. How much thinking those old gentlemen used to save one! How the borders of ignorance shrank back at their approach! Cats do not go to heaven. Women cannot write the plays of Shakespeare.

Be that as it may, I could not help thinking, as I looked at the works of Shakespeare on the shelf, that the bishop was right at least in this; it would have been impossible, completely and entirely, for any woman to have written the plays of Shakespeare in the age of Shakespeare. Let me imagine, since facts are so hard to come by, what would have happened had Shakespeare had

---

[3] John Aubrey (1626–1697), author of *Brief Lives*, a biographical work.

a wonderfully gifted sister, called Judith, let us say. Shakespeare himself went, very probably—his mother was an heiress—to the grammar school, where he may have learnt Latin—Ovid, Virgil and Horace—and the elements of grammar and logic. He was, it is well known, a wild boy who poached rabbits, perhaps shot a deer, and had, rather sooner than he should have done, to marry a woman in the neighbourhood, who bore him a child rather quicker than was right. That escapade sent him to seek his fortune in London. He had, it seemed, a taste for the theatre; he began by holding horses at the stage door. Very soon he got work in the theatre, became a successful actor, and lived in the hub of the universe, meeting everybody, knowing everybody, practising his art on the boards, exercising his wits in the streets, and even getting access to the palace of the queen. Meanwhile his extraordinarily gifted sister, let us suppose, remained at home. She was as adventurous, as imaginative, as agog to see the world as he was. But she was not sent to school. She had no chance of learning grammar and logic, let alone of reading Horace and Virgil. She picked up a book now and then, one of her brother's perhaps, and read a few pages. But then her parents came in and told her to mend the stockings or mind the stew and not moon about with books and papers. They would have spoken sharply but kindly, for they were substantial people who knew the conditions of life for a woman and loved their daughter—indeed, more likely than not she was the apple of her father's eye. Perhaps she scribbled some pages up in an apple loft on the sly, but was careful to hide them or set fire to them. Soon, however, before she was out of her teens, she was to be betrothed to the son of a neighbouring wool-stapler. She cried out that marriage was hateful to her, and for that she was severely beaten by her father. Then he ceased to scold her. He begged her instead not to hurt him, not to shame him in this matter of her marriage. He would give her a chain of beads or a fine petticoat, he said; and there were tears in his eyes. How could she disobey him? How could she break his heart? The force of her own gift alone drove her to it. She made up a small parcel of her belongings, let herself down by a rope one summer's night and took the road to London. She was not seventeen. The birds that sang in the hedge were not more musical than she was. She had the quickest fancy, a gift like her brother's, for the tune of words. Like him, she had a taste for the theatre. She stood at the stage door; she wanted to act, she said. Men laughed in her face. The manager—a fat, loose-lipped man—guffawed. He bellowed something about poodles dancing and women acting—no woman, he said, could possibly be an actress.[4] He hinted—you can imagine what. She could get no training in her craft. Could she even seek her dinner in a tavern or roam the streets at midnight? Yet her genius was for fiction and lusted to feed abundantly upon the lives of men and women and the study of their ways. At last—for she was very young, oddly like Shakespeare the poet in her face, with the same grey eyes and rounded brows—at last Nick Greene the actor-manager took pity on her; she found herself with

---

[4] In Shakespeare's day, women's roles were played by males.

child by that gentleman and so—who shall measure the heat and violence of the poet's heart when caught and tangled in a woman's body?—killed herself one winter's night and lies buried at some cross-roads where the omnibuses now stop outside the Elephant and Castle.[5]

That, more or less, is how the story would run, I think, if a woman in Shakespeare's day had had Shakespeare's genius. But for my part, I agree with the deceased bishop, if such he was—it is unthinkable that any woman in Shakespeare's day should have had Shakespeare's genius. For genius like Shakespeare's is not born among labouring, uneducated, servile people. It was not born in England among the Saxons and the Britons. It is not born today among the working classes. How, then, could it have been born among women whose work began, according to Professor Trevelyan, almost before they were out of the nursery, who were forced to it by their parents and held to it by all the power of law and custom? Yet genius of a sort must have existed among women as it must have existed among the working classes. Now and again an Emily Brontë or a Robert Burns blazes out and proves its presence.[6] But certainly it never got itself on to paper. When, however, one reads of a witch being ducked, of a woman possessed by devils, of a wise woman selling herbs, or even of a very remarkable man who had a mother, then I think we are on the track of a lost novelist, a suppressed poet, of some mute and inglorious[7] Jane Austen, some Emily Brontë who dashed her brains out on the moor or moped and mowed about the highways crazed with the torture that her gift had put her to. Indeed, I would venture to guess that Anon, who wrote so many poems without signing them, was often a woman. It was a woman Edward Fitzgerald,[8] I think, suggested who made the ballads and the folk-songs, crooning them to her children, beguiling her spinning with them, or the length of the winter's night.

This may be true or it may be false—who can say?—but what is true in it, so it seemed to me, reviewing the story of Shakespeare's sister as I had made it, is that any woman born with a great gift in the sixteenth century would certainly have gone crazed, shot herself, or ended her days in some lonely cottage outside the village, half witch, half wizard, feared and mocked at. For it needs little skill in psychology to be sure that a highly gifted girl who had tried to use her gift for poetry would have been so thwarted and hindered by other people, so tortured and pulled asunder by her own contrary instincts, that she must have lost her health and sanity to a certainty. No girl could have walked to London and stood at a stage door and forced her way into the presence of actor-managers without doing herself a violence and suffering an anguish which may have been irrational—for chastity may be a fetish invented by certain societies for unknown reasons—but were none the less inevitable. Chastity had then, it has even now, a religious importance in a woman's life, and has so

---

[5] A tavern.

[6] Emily Brontë (1818–1848), English novelist, and Robert Burns (1759–1796), Scottish poet.

[7] Thomas Gray's description in "Elegy Written in a Country Churchyard" of a peasant whose underdeveloped poetic genius might be as powerful as the great John Milton's.

[8] Edward FitzGerald (1809–1883), translator and poet.

wrapped itself round with nerves and instincts that to cut it free and bring it to the light of day demands courage of the rarest. To have lived a free life in London in the sixteenth century would have meant for a woman who was poet and playwright a nervous stress and dilemma which might well have killed her. Had she survived, whatever she had written would have been twisted and deformed, issuing from a strained and morbid imagination. And undoubtedly, I thought, looking at the shelf where there are no plays by women, her work would have gone unsigned. That refuge she would have sought certainly. It was the relic of the sense of chastity that dictated anonymity to women even so late as the nineteenth century. Currer Bell, George Eliot, George Sand,[9] all the victims of inner strife as their writings prove, sought ineffectively to veil themselves by using the name of a man. Thus they did homage to the convention, which if not implanted by the other sex was liberally encouraged by them (the chief glory of a woman is not to be talked of, said Pericles,[10] himself a much-talked-of man), that publicity in women is detestable. . . .

That woman, then, who was born with a gift of poetry in the sixteenth cen-   10
tury, was an unhappy woman, a woman at strife against herself. All the conditions of her life, all her own instincts, were hostile to the state of mind which is needed to set free whatever is in the brain. But what is the state of mind that is most propitious to the act of creation, I asked? Can one come by any notion of the state that furthers and makes possible that strange activity? Here I opened the volume containing the Tragedies of Shakespeare. What was Shakespeare's state of mind, for instance, when he wrote *Lear* and *Antony and Cleopatra*? It was certainly the state of mind most favourable to poetry that there has ever existed. But Shakespeare himself said nothing about it. We only know casually and by chance that he "never blotted a line."[11] Nothing indeed was ever said by the artist himself about his state of mind until the eighteenth century perhaps. Rousseau[12] perhaps began it. At any rate, by the nineteenth century self-consciousness had developed so far that it was the habit for men of letters to describe their minds in confessions and autobiographies. Their lives also were written, and their letters were printed after their deaths. Thus, though we do not know what Shakespeare went through when he wrote *Lear*, we do know what Carlyle went through when he wrote the *French Revolution*; what Flaubert went through when he wrote *Madame Bovary*; what Keats was going through when he tried to write poetry against the coming of death and the indifference of the world.

And one gathers from this enormous modern literature of confession and self-analysis that to write a work of genius is almost always a feat of prodigious difficulty. Everything is against the likelihood that it will come from the writer's mind whole and entire. Generally material circumstances are against it. Dogs

---

[9] The pseudonyms of Charlotte Brontë (1816–1855) and Mary Ann Evans (1819–1880), English novelists, and Amandine-Aurore-Lucie Dupin (1804–1876), French novelist.

[10] Pericles (ca. 495–429 BCE), Athenian statesman and general.

[11] According to Ben Jonson, Shakespeare's contemporary.

[12] Jean-Jacques Rousseau (1712–1778), French philosopher, author of *The Confessions of Jean-Jacques Rousseau*.

will bark; people will interrupt; money must be made; health will break down. Further, accentuating all these difficulties and making them harder to bear is the world's notorious indifference. It does not ask people to write poems and novels and histories; it does not need them. It does not care whether Flaubert finds the right word or whether Carlyle scrupulously verifies this or that fact. Naturally, it will not pay for what it does not want. And so the writer, Keats, Flaubert, Carlyle, suffers, especially in the creative years of youth, every form of distraction and discouragement. A curse, a cry of agony, rises from those books of analysis and confession. "Mighty poets in their misery dead"[13]—that is the burden of their song. If anything comes through in spite of this, it is a miracle, and probably no book is born entire and uncrippled as it was conceived.

But for women, I thought, looking at the empty shelves, these difficulties were infinitely more formidable. In the first place, to have a room of her own, let alone a quiet room or a sound-proof room, was out of the question, unless her parents were exceptionally rich or very noble, even up to the beginning of the nineteenth century. Since her pin money, which depended on the good will of her father, was only enough to keep her clothed, she was debarred from such alleviations as came even to Keats or Tennyson or Carlyle, all poor men, from a walking tour, a little journey to France, from the separate lodging which, even if it were miserable enough, sheltered them from the claims and tyrannies of their families. Such material difficulties were formidable; but much worse were the immaterial. The indifference of the world which Keats and Flaubert and other men of genius have found so hard to bear was in her case not indifference but hostility. The world did not say to her as it said to them, Write if you choose; it makes no difference to me. The world said with a guffaw, Write? What's the good of your writing? . . .

I told you in the course of this paper that Shakespeare had a sister; but do not look for her in Sir Sidney Lee's life of the poet. She died young—alas, she never wrote a word. She lies buried where the omnibuses now stop, opposite the Elephant and Castle. Now my belief is that this poet who never wrote a word and was buried at the cross-roads still lives. She lives in you and me, and in many other women who are not here tonight, for they are washing up the dishes and putting the children to bed. But she lives; for great poets do not die; they are continuing presences; they need only the opportunity to walk among us in the flesh. This opportunity, as I think, it is now coming within your power to give her. For my belief is that if we live another century or so—I am talking of the common life which is the real life and not of the little separate lives which we live as individuals—and have five hundred a year each of us and rooms of our own; if we have the habit of freedom and the courage to write exactly what we think; if we escape a little from the common sitting-room and see human beings not always in their relation to each other but in relation to reality; and the sky, too, and the trees or whatever it may be in themselves; if we look past

---

[13] From William Wordsworth's poem "Resolution and Independence."

Milton's bogey, for no human being should shut out the view; if we face the fact, for it is a fact, that there is no arm to cling to, but that we go alone and that our relation is to the world of reality and not only to the world of men and women, then the opportunity will come and the dead poet who was Shakespeare's sister will put on the body which she has so often laid down. Drawing her life from the lives of the unknown who were her forerunners, as her brother did before her, she will be born. As for her coming without that preparation, without that effort on our part, without that determination that when she is born again she shall find it possible to live and write her poetry, that we cannot expect, for that would be impossible. But I maintain that she would come if we worked for her, and that so to work, even in poverty and obscurity, is worth while.

FOR ANALYSIS

1. How does Woolf explain the contrast between the women of fact and women as they have been portrayed in fiction?

2. What answers do historians provide to the "perennial puzzle" Woolf mentions in the first sentence of paragraph 2? What generalizations might we make about the meaning of "history" on the basis of Woolf's research into the status of women?

3. Analyze the effect of Woolf's concluding remarks about the bishop (para. 6): "Cats do not go to heaven. Women cannot write the plays of Shakespeare." Then consider her later comment (para. 8), "I agree with the deceased bishop, if such he was—it is unthinkable that any woman in Shakespeare's day should have had Shakespeare's genius." Does this contradict what she has been saying?

4. Explain the link Woolf makes between chastity and the problem of the gifted woman writer (para. 9).

5. In what ways does the first part of Woolf's essay prepare the reader to accept her imagined life of Shakespeare's sister?

MAKING ARGUMENTS

Do you believe that our culture has changed so significantly in its attitudes toward women that Woolf's arguments have lost their relevance? Write an essay arguing why or why not.

WRITING TOPIC

Speculate on why, while being as economically dependent on men as servants were throughout much of Western history, women were sometimes portrayed in fiction as being "as great as a man, some think even greater" (para. 3).

MAKING CONNECTIONS

1. Among the women who "have burnt like beacons" (para. 3) in the works of great male writers, Woolf cites Desdemona in Shakespeare's *Othello* (p. 984). Do you agree with her assessment? Might Woolf have included Nora in Ibsen's *A Doll's House* (p. 213) and Mama in Hansberry's *A Raisin in the Sun* (p. 710)? Explain.

2. What do you think Woolf would think of Mrs. Peters and Mrs. Hale in Susan Glaspell's *Trifles* (p. 1073) and Calixta in Kate Chopin's "The Storm" (p. 861)?

GEORGE ORWELL (1903–1950)

SHOOTING AN ELEPHANT   1936

In Moulmein, in lower Burma, I was hated by large numbers of people—the only time in my life that I have been important enough for this to happen to me. I was sub-divisional police officer of the town, and in an aimless, petty kind of way anti-European feeling was very bitter. No one had the guts to raise a riot, but if a European woman went through the bazaars alone somebody would probably spit betel juice over her dress. As a police officer I was an obvious target and was baited whenever it seemed safe to do so. When a nimble Burman tripped me up on the football field and the referee (another Burman) looked the other way, the crowd yelled with hideous laughter. This happened more than once. In the end the sneering yellow faces of young men that met me everywhere, the insults hooted after me when I was at a safe distance, got badly on my nerves. The young Buddhist priests were the worst of all. There were several thousands of them in the town and none of them seemed to have anything to do except stand on street corners and jeer at Europeans.

All this was perplexing and upsetting. For at that time I had already made up my mind that imperialism was an evil thing and the sooner I chucked up my job and got out of it the better. Theoretically—and secretly, of course—I was all for the Burmese and all against their oppressors, the British. As for the job I was doing, I hated it more bitterly than I can perhaps make clear. In a job like that you see the dirty work of Empire at close quarters. The wretched prisoners huddling in the stinking cages of the lock-ups, the grey, cowed faces of the long-term convicts, the scarred buttocks of the men who had been flogged with bamboos—all these oppressed me with an intolerable sense of guilt. But I could get nothing into perspective. I was young and ill-educated and I had had to think out my problems in the utter silence that is imposed on every Englishman in the East. I did not even know that the British Empire is dying, still less did I know that it is a great deal better than the younger empires that are going to supplant it. All I knew was that I was stuck between my hatred of the empire I served and my rage against the evil-spirited little beasts who tried to make my job impossible. With one part of my mind I thought of the British[1] as an unbreakable tyranny, as something clamped down, *in saecula saeculorum*,[2] upon the will of prostrate peoples; with another part I thought that the greatest joy in the world would be to drive a bayonet into a Buddhist priest's guts. Feelings like these are the normal by-products of imperialism; ask any Anglo-Indian official, if you can catch him off duty.

[1] The imperial British government of India and Burma.
[2] For eternity.

One day something happened which in a roundabout way was enlightening. It was a tiny incident in itself, but it gave me a better glimpse than I had had before of the real nature of imperialism—the real motive for which despotic governments act. Early one morning the sub-inspector at a police station the other end of the town rang me up on the 'phone and said that an elephant was ravaging the bazaar. Would I please come and do something about it? I did not know what I could do, but I wanted to see what was happening and I got on to a pony and started out. I took my rifle, an old .44 Winchester and much too small to kill an elephant, but I thought the noise might be useful *in terrorem*. Various Burmans stopped me on the way and told me about the elephant's doings. It was not, of course, a wild elephant, but a tame one which had gone "must." It had been chained up, as tame elephants always are when their attack of "must" is due, but on the previous night it had broken its chain and escaped. Its mahout,[3] the only person who could manage it when it was in that state, had set out in pursuit, but had taken the wrong direction and was now twelve hours' journey away, and in the morning the elephant had suddenly reappeared in the town. The Burmese population had no weapons and were quite helpless against it. It had already destroyed somebody's bamboo hut, killed a cow and raided some fruit-stalls and devoured the stock; also it had met the municipal rubbish van and, when the driver jumped out and took to his heels, had turned the van over and inflicted violences upon it.

The Burmese sub-inspector and some Indian constables were waiting for me in the quarter where the elephant had been seen. It was a very poor quarter, a labyrinth of squalid bamboo huts, thatched with palm-leaf, winding all over a steep hillside. I remember that it was a cloudy, stuffy morning at the beginning of the rains. We began questioning the people as to where the elephant had gone and, as usual, failed to get any definite information. That is invariably the case in the East; a story always sounds clear enough at a distance, but the nearer you get to the scene of events the vaguer it becomes. Some of the people said that the elephant had gone in one direction, some said that he had gone in another, some professed not even to have heard of any elephant. I had almost made up my mind that the whole story was a pack of lies, when we heard yells a little distance away. There was a loud, scandalized cry of "Go away, child! Go away this instant!" and an old woman with a switch in her hand came round the corner of a hut, violently shooing away a crowd of naked children. Some more women followed, clicking their tongues and exclaiming; evidently there was something that the children ought not to have seen. I rounded the hut and saw a man's dead body sprawling in the mud. He was an Indian, a black Dravidian coolie, almost naked, and he could not have been dead many minutes. The people said that the elephant had come suddenly upon him round the corner of the hut, caught him with its trunk, put its foot on his back and ground him into the earth. This was the rainy season and the ground was soft, and his face had scored a trench a foot deep and a couple of yards long. He was lying on his

---

[3] The keeper and driver of an elephant.

belly with arms crucified and head sharply twisted to one side. His face was coated with mud, the eyes wide open, the teeth bared and grinning with an expression of unendurable agony. (Never tell me, by the way, that the dead look peaceful. Most of the corpses I have seen look devilish.) The friction of the great beast's foot had stripped the skin from his back as neatly as one skins a rabbit. As soon as I saw the dead man I sent an orderly to a friend's house nearby to borrow an elephant rifle. I had already sent back the pony, not wanting it to go mad with fright and throw me if it smelt the elephant.

The orderly came back in a few minutes with a rifle and five cartridges, and 5 meanwhile some Burmans had arrived and told us that the elephant was in the paddy fields below, only a few hundred yards away. As I started forward practically the whole population of the quarter flocked out of the houses and followed me. They had seen the rifle and were all shouting excitedly that I was going to shoot the elephant. They had not shown much interest in the elephant when he was merely ravaging their homes, but it was different now that he was going to be shot. It was a bit of fun to them, as it would be to an English crowd; besides they wanted the meat. It made me vaguely uneasy. I had no intention of shooting the elephant—I had merely sent for the rifle to defend myself if necessary—and it is always unnerving to have a crowd following you. I marched down the hill, looking and feeling a fool, with the rifle over my shoulders and an ever-growing army of people jostling at my heels. At the bottom, when you got away from the huts, there was a metalled road and beyond that a miry waste of paddy fields a thousand yards across, not yet ploughed but soggy from the first rains and dotted with coarse grass. The elephant was standing eight yards from the road, his left side towards us. He took not the slightest notice of the crowd's approach. He was tearing up branches of grass, beating them against his knees to clean them and stuffing them into his mouth.

I had halted on the road. As soon as I saw the elephant I knew with perfect certainty that I ought not to shoot him. It is a serious matter to shoot a working elephant—it is comparable to destroying a huge and costly piece of machinery—and obviously one ought not to do it if it can possibly be avoided. And at that distance, peacefully eating, the elephant looked no more dangerous than a cow. I thought then and I think now that his attack of "must" was already passing off; in which case he would merely wander harmlessly about until the mahout came back and caught him. Moreover, I did not in the least want to shoot him. I decided that I would watch him for a little while to make sure that he did not turn savage again, and then go home.

But at that moment I glanced round at the crowd that had followed me. It was an immense crowd, two thousand at the least and growing every minute. It blocked the road for a long distance on either side. I looked at the sea of yellow faces above the garish clothes—faces all happy and excited over this bit of fun, all certain that the elephant was going to be shot. They were watching me as they would watch a conjurer about to perform a trick. They did not like me, but with the magical rifle in my hands I was momentarily worth watching. And suddenly I realized that I should have to shoot the elephant after all. The people expected it of me and I had got to do it; I could feel their two thousand wills pressing me forward, irresistibly. And it was at this moment, as I stood there with the rifle in my hands, that I first grasped the hollowness, the futility of the white man's dominion in the East. Here was I, the white man with his gun, standing in front of the unarmed native crowd—seemingly the leading actor of the piece; but in reality I was only an absurd puppet pushed to and fro by the will of those yellow faces behind. I perceived in this moment that when the white man turns tyrant it is his own freedoms that he destroys. He becomes a sort of hollow, posing dummy, the conventionalized figure of a sahib. For it is the condition of his rule that he shall spend his life in trying to impress the "natives," and so in every crisis he has got to do what the "natives" expect of him. He wears a mask, and his face grows to fit it. I had got to shoot the elephant. I had committed myself to doing it when I sent for the rifle. A sahib has got to act like a sahib; he has got to appear resolute, to know his own mind and do definite things. To come all that way, rifle in hand, with two thousand people marching at my heels, and then to trail feebly away, having done nothing—no, that was impossible. The crowd would laugh at me. And my whole life, every white man's life in the East, was one long struggle not to be laughed at.

But I did not want to shoot the elephant. I watched him beating his bunch of grass against his knees, with that preoccupied grandmotherly air that elephants have. It seemed to me that it would be murder to shoot him. At that age I was not squeamish about killing animals, but I had never shot an elephant and never wanted to. (Somehow it always seems worse to kill a *large* animal.) Besides, there was the beast's owner to be considered. Alive, the elephant was worth at least a hundred pounds; dead, he would only be worth the value of his tusks, five pounds, possibly. But I had to act quickly. I turned to some experienced-looking Burmans who had been there when we arrived, and asked them how the elephant had been behaving. They all said the same thing: he took no notice of you if you left him alone, but he might charge if you went too close to him.

It was perfectly clear to me what I ought to do. I ought to walk up to within, say, twenty-five yards of the elephant and test his behavior. If he charged, I could shoot; if he took no notice of me, it would be safe to leave him until the mahout came back. But also I knew that I was going to do no such thing. I was a poor shot with a rifle and the ground was soft mud into which one would sink at every step. If the elephant charged and I missed him, I should have about as much chance as a toad under a steam-roller. But even then I was not thinking particularly of my own skin, only of the watchful yellow faces behind. For at that moment, with the crowd watching me, I was not afraid in the ordinary sense, as I would have been if I had been alone. A white man mustn't be frightened in front of "natives"; and so, in general, he isn't frightened. The sole thought in my mind was that if anything went wrong those two thousand Burmans would see me pursued, caught, trampled on and reduced to a grinning corpse like that Indian up the hill. And if that happened it was quite probable that some of them would laugh. That would never do. There was only one alternative. I shoved the cartridges into the magazine and lay down on the road to get a better aim.

The crowd grew very still, and a deep, low, happy sigh, as of people who see the 10
theatre curtain go up at last, breathed from innumerable throats. They were going
to have their bit of fun after all. The rifle was a beautiful German thing with cross-
hair sights. I did not then know that in shooting an elephant one would shoot to
cut an imaginary bar running from ear-hole to ear-hole. I ought, therefore, as the
elephant was sideways on, to have aimed straight at his ear-hole; actually I aimed
several inches in front of this, thinking the brain would be further forward.

When I pulled the trigger I did not hear the bang or feel the kick—one never
does when a shot goes home—but I heard the devilish roar of glee that went up
from the crowd. In that instant, in too short a time, one would have thought,
even for the bullet to get there, a mysterious, terrible change had come over
the elephant. He neither stirred nor fell, but every line of his body had altered.
He looked suddenly stricken, shrunken, immensely old, as though the frightful
impact of the bullet had paralysed him without knocking him down. At last,
after what seemed a long time—it might have been five seconds, I dare say—
he sagged flabbily to his knees. His mouth slobbered. An enormous senility
seemed to have settled upon him. One could have imagined him thousands of
years old. I fired again into the same spot. At the second shot he did not collapse
but climbed with desperate slowness to his feet and stood weakly upright, with
legs sagging and head drooping. I fired a third time. That was the shot that did
for him. You could see the agony of it jolt his whole body and knock the last
remnant of strength from his legs. But in falling he seemed for a moment to
rise, for as his hind legs collapsed beneath him he seemed to tower upward like
a huge rock toppling, his trunk reaching skywards like a tree. He trumpeted, for
the first and only time. And then down he came, his belly towards me, with a
crash that seemed to shake the ground even where I lay.

I got up. The Burmans were already racing past me across the mud. It was
obvious that the elephant would never rise again, but he was not dead. He was
breathing very rhythmically with long rattling gasps, his great mound of a side
painfully rising and falling. His mouth was wide open—I could see far down
into caverns of pale pink throat. I waited a long time for him to die, but his
breathing did not weaken. Finally I fired my two remaining shots into the spot
where I thought his heart must be. The thick blood welled out of him like red
velvet, but still he did not die. His body did not even jerk when the shots hit
him, the tortured breathing continued without a pause. He was dying, very
slowly and in great agony, but in some world remote from me where not even
a bullet could damage him further. I felt that I had got to put an end to that
dreadful noise. It seemed dreadful to see the great beast lying there, powerless
to move and yet powerless to die, and not even to be able to finish him. I sent
back for my small rifle and poured shot after shot into his heart and down his
throat. They seemed to make no impression. The tortured gasps continued as
steadily as the ticking of a clock.

In the end I could not stand it any longer and went away. I heard later that it
took him half an hour to die. Burmans were bringing dahs[4] and baskets even

[4] Knives.

before I left, and I was told they had stripped his body almost to the bones by the afternoon.

Afterwards, of course, there were endless discussions about the shooting of the elephant. The owner was furious, but he was only an Indian and could do nothing. Besides, legally I had done the right thing, for a mad elephant has to be killed, like a mad dog, if its owner fails to control it. Among the Europeans opinion was divided. The older men said I was right, the younger men said it was a damn shame to shoot an elephant for killing a coolie, because an elephant was worth more than any damn Coringhee coolie. And afterwards I was very glad that the coolie had been killed; it put me legally in the right and it gave me a sufficient pretext for shooting the elephant. I often wondered whether any of the others grasped that I had done it solely to avoid looking a fool.

FOR ANALYSIS

1. Examine carefully paragraphs 11 and 12, in which Orwell describes the death of the elephant. Is the reader meant to take the passage only literally, or can a case be made that the elephant's death is imbued with **symbolic** meaning? Explain.

2. Orwell tells us repeatedly that his sympathies are with the Burmese. Yet he describes them as "evil-spirited little beasts" (para. 2). Explain this ambivalence.

3. What does the experience described in paragraph 7 teach Orwell?

4. What is your reaction to Orwell's final comment: "I was very glad that the coolie had been killed; it put me legally in the right and it gave me a sufficient pretext for shooting the elephant. I often wondered whether any of the others grasped that I had done it solely to avoid looking a fool"?

5. Midway through the essay (para. 7), Orwell discloses the significance the event had for him. Why does he disclose it then rather than save it for the conclusion?

MAKING ARGUMENTS

Do you agree with Orwell's rationalization that under the circumstances he had no choice but "to shoot the elephant" (para. 7)? Build an argument for your answer.

WRITING TOPICS

1. In a brief paragraph, summarize the lesson Orwell learned from his experience.

2. What does Orwell conclude about the position of foreign authorities in a hostile country?

3. Describe a situation in which you were required to behave in an official capacity in a way that contradicted your personal beliefs.

MAKING CONNECTIONS

1. Compare the techniques and arguments used in this essay to attack imperialism with those used in Swift's "A Modest Proposal" (p. 481).

2. While they are dissimilar in subject matter, this story and Bambara's "The Lesson" (p. 98) culminate in climactic events that change the **protagonists**. Compare those events and their effect on the two protagonists.

SABRINA JONES (B. 1960)

LITTLE HOUSE IN THE BIG CITY   2011

FOR ANALYSIS

1. What is Jones's topic here? What is her argument?

2. How does Jones build her argument? What kinds of sources does she use for evidence? Personal? Historical?

3. A second historical development emerges late in Jones's graphic essay. What is it? How does it threaten city life?

MAKING ARGUMENTS

Jones chooses to tell the story of "Little House in the Big City" in the medium of graphic **narrative** that she could have just as easily told in text. Make an argument for or against this choice using as evidence close observation of how the piece works and any ideas you may have about how narrative, both graphic and text-based, is supposed to work.

WRITING TOPIC

Describe the town or city in which you live or are from originally if those are different (and you want to). See if you can turn up some facts on its history, especially the history of its development; if not, speculate on the origin of its features. How did this place get to be the place it is now? Has it turned out the way everyone or anyone wanted it to? Is it still changing?

MAKING CONNECTIONS

Find two or three poems in this book that are interested in the way people live in cities (an example would be Jonathan Swift's "Market Women's Cries" on p. 646). Do they share concerns with this piece by Jones? Do they have different concerns? How do they express them?

EULA BISS (B. 1977)

TIME AND DISTANCE OVERCOME 2008

"Of what use is such an invention?" *The New York World* asked shortly after Alexander Graham Bell first demonstrated his telephone in 1876. The world was not waiting for the telephone.

Bell's financial backers asked him not to work on his new invention anymore because it seemed too dubious an investment. The idea on which the telephone depended—the idea that every home in the country could be connected with a vast network of wires suspended from poles set an average of one hundred feet apart—seemed far more unlikely than the idea that the human voice could be transmitted through a wire.

Even now it is an impossible idea, that we are all connected, all of us.

"At the present time we have a perfect network of gas pipes and water pipes throughout our large cities," Bell wrote to his business partners, in defense of his idea. "We have main pipes laid under the streets communicating by side pipes with the various dwellings. . . . In a similar manner it is conceivable that cables of telephone wires could be laid under ground, or suspended overhead, communicating by branch wires with private dwellings, counting houses, shops, manufactories, etc., uniting them through the main cable. . . ."

Imagine the mind that could imagine this. That could see us all connected 5 through one branching cable. The mind of a man who wanted to invent, more than the telephone, a machine that would allow the deaf to hear.

For a short time, the telephone was little more than a novelty. For twenty-five cents you could see it demonstrated by Bell himself, in a church, along with some singing and recitations by local talent. From a mile away, Bell would receive a call from "the invisible Mr. Watson." Then the telephone became a plaything of the rich. A Boston banker paid for a private line between his office and his home so that he could let his family know exactly when he would be home for dinner.

Mark Twain was among the first to own a telephone, but he wasn't completely taken with it. "The human voice carries entirely too far as it is," he remarked.

By 1889, *The New York Times* was reporting a "War on Telephone Poles." Wherever telephone companies were erecting poles, homeowners and business owners were sawing them down, or defending their sidewalks with rifles.

In Red Bank, New Jersey, property owners threatened to tar and feather the workers putting up telephone poles. One judge granted a group of homeowners an injunction to prevent the telephone company from erecting any new poles. Another judge found that a man who had cut down a pole because it was "obnoxious" was not guilty of malicious mischief.

Telephone poles, newspaper editorials complained, were an urban blight. 10 The poles carried a wire for each telephone—sometimes hundreds of wires.

844

And in some places there were also telegraph wires, power lines, and trolley cables. The sky was filled with wires.

The War on Telephone Poles was fueled, in part, by that terribly American concern for private property and a reluctance to surrender it to a shared utility. And then there was a fierce sense of aesthetics, an obsession with purity, a dislike for the way the poles and wires marred a landscape that those other new inventions, skyscrapers and barbed wire, were just beginning to complicate. And then perhaps there was also a fear that distance, as it had always been known and measured, was collapsing.

The city council in Sioux Falls, South Dakota, ordered policemen to cut down all the telephone poles in town. And the Mayor of Oshkosh, Wisconsin, ordered the police chief and the fire department to chop down the telephone poles there. Only one pole was chopped down before the telephone men climbed all the poles along the line, preventing any more chopping. Soon, Bell Telephone Company began stationing a man at the top of each pole as soon as it had been set, until enough poles had been set to string a wire between them, at which point it became a misdemeanor to interfere with the poles. Even so, a constable cut down two poles holding forty or fifty wires. And a homeowner sawed down a recently wired pole then fled from police. The owner of a cannery ordered his workers to throw dirt back into the hole the telephone company was digging in front of his building. His men threw the dirt back in as fast as the telephone workers could dig it out. Then he sent out a team with a load of stones to dump into the hole. Eventually, the pole was erected on the other side of the street.

Despite the War on Telephone Poles, it would take only four years after Bell's first public demonstration of the telephone for every town of over 10,000 people to be wired, although many towns were wired only to themselves. And by the turn of the century, there were more telephones than bathtubs in America.

"Time and dist. overcome," read an early advertisement for the telephone. Rutherford B. Hayes pronounced the installation of a telephone in the White House "one of the greatest events since creation." The telephone, Thomas Edison declared, "annihilated time and space, and brought the human family in closer touch."

In 1898, in Lake Comorant, Mississippi, a black man was hanged from a telephone pole. And in Weir City, Kansas. And in Brook Haven, Mississippi. And in Tulsa, where the hanged man was riddled with bullets. In Pittsburg, Kansas, a black man's throat was slit and his dead body was strung up on a telephone pole. Two black men were hanged from a telephone pole in Lewisburg, West Virginia. And two in Hempstead, Texas, where one man was dragged out of the courtroom by a mob and another was dragged out of jail.

A black man was hanged from a telephone pole in Belleville, Illinois, where a fire was set at the base of the pole and the man was cut down half-alive, covered in coal oil, and burned. While his body was burning, the mob beat it with clubs and nearly cut it to pieces.

Lynching, the first scholar of the subject determined, is an American invention. Lynching from bridges, from arches, from trees standing alone in fields, from trees in front of the county courthouse, from trees used as public billboards, from trees barely able to support the weight of a man, from telephone poles, from street lamps, and from poles erected for that purpose. From the middle of the nineteenth century to the middle of the twentieth century black men were lynched for crimes real and imagined, for "disputing with a white man," for "unpopularity," for "asking a white woman in marriage," for "peeping in a window."

The children's game of "telephone" depends on the fact that a message passed quietly from one ear to another to another will get distorted at some point along the line.

In Pine Bluff, Arkansas, a black man charged with kicking a white girl was hanged from a telephone pole. In Long View, Texas, a black man accused of attacking a white woman was hanged from a telephone pole. In Greenville, Mississippi, a black man accused of attacking a white telephone operator was hanged from a telephone pole. "The negro only asked time to pray." In Purcell, Oklahoma, a black man accused of attacking a white woman was tied to a telephone pole and burned. "Men and women in automobiles stood up to watch him die."

The poles, of course, were not to blame. It was only coincidence that they 20 became convenient as gallows, because they were tall and straight, with a crossbar, and because they stood in public places. And it was only coincidence that the telephone pole so closely resembled a crucifix.

Early telephone calls were full of noise. "Such a jangle of meaningless noises had never been heard by human ears," Herbert Casson wrote in his 1910 *History of the Telephone.* "There were the rustling of leaves, the croaking of frogs, the hissing of steam, the flapping of birds' wings. . . . There were spluttering and bubbling, jerking and rasping, whistling and screaming."

In Shreveport, a black man charged with attacking a white girl was hanged from a telephone pole. "A knife was left sticking in the body." In Cumming, Georgia, a black man accused of assaulting a white girl was shot repeatedly then hanged from a telephone pole. In Waco, Texas, a black man convicted of killing a white woman was taken from the courtroom by a mob and burned, then his charred body was hung from a telephone pole.

A postcard was made from the photo of a burned man hanging from a telephone pole in Texas, his legs broken off below the knee and his arms curled up and blackened. Postcards of lynchings were sent out as greetings and warnings until 1908, when the Postmaster General declared them unmailable. "This is the barbecue we had last night," reads one.

"If we are to die," W. E. B. Du Bois wrote in 1911, "in God's name let us not perish like bales of hay." And "if we must die," Claude McKay wrote ten years later, "let it not be like hogs. . . ."

In Danville, Illinois, a black man was hanged from a telephone pole, cut 25 down, burned, shot, and stoned with bricks. "At first the negro was defiant,"

The New York Times reported, "but just before he was hanged he begged hard for his life."

In the photographs, the bodies of the men lynched from telephone poles are silhouetted against the sky. Sometimes two men to a pole, hanging above the buildings of a town. Sometimes three. They hung like flags in still air.

In Cumberland, Maryland, a mob used a telephone pole as a battering ram to break into the jail where a black man charged with the murder of a policeman was being held. They kicked him to death then fired twenty shots into his head. They wanted to burn his body, but a minister asked them not to.

The lynchings happened everywhere, all over the United States. From shortly before the invention of the telephone to long after the first trans-Atlantic call. More in the South, and more in rural areas. In the cities and in the North there were race riots.

Riots in Cincinnati, New Orleans, Memphis, New York, Atlanta, Philadelphia, Houston. . . .

During the race riots that destroyed the black section of Springfield, Ohio, a black man was shot and hanged from a telephone pole.

During the race riots that set fire to East St. Louis and forced five hundred black people to flee their homes, a black man was hanged from a telephone pole. The rope broke and his body fell into the gutter. "Negros are lying in the gutters every few feet in some places," read the newspaper account.

In 1921, the year before Bell died, four companies of the National Guard were called out to end a race war in Tulsa that began when a white woman accused a black man of rape. Bell had lived to complete the first call from New York to San Francisco, which required 14,000 miles of copper wire and 130,000 telephone poles.

My grandfather was a lineman. He broke his back when a telephone pole fell. "Smashed him onto the road," my father says.

When I was young, I believed that the arc and swoop of telephone wires along the roadways were beautiful. I believed that the telephone poles, with their glass transformers catching the evening sun, were glorious. I believed my father when he said, "My dad could raise a pole by himself." And I believed that the telephone itself was a miracle.

Now, I tell my sister, these poles, these wires do not look the same to me. Nothing is innocent, my sister reminds me. But nothing, I would like to think, remains unrepentant.

One summer, heavy rains fell in Nebraska and some green telephone poles grew small leafy branches.

A Note on "Time and Distance Overcome"

I began my research for this essay by searching for every instance of the phrase "telephone pole" in the *New York Times* from 1880 to 1920, which resulted in 370 articles. As I read through these articles, starting with the oldest and working forward in time, I was not prepared to discover, in the process, a litany of lynchings. I had not intended to write an essay about lynching, but I found that, given what my research was yielding, I could not avoid it. After reading an article headlined "Colored Scoundrel Lynched," and then another head-lined "Mississippi Negro Lynched," and then another headlined "Texas Negro Lynched," I searched for every instance of the word "lynched" in the *New York Times* from 1880 to 1920, which resulted in 2,354 articles.

I refer, in this essay, to the first scholar of lynching, meaning James E. Cutler, author of the 1905 book *Lynch-Law*, in which he writes, on the first page, "lynching is a criminal practice which is peculiar to the United States." This is debatable, of course, and very possibly not true, but there is good evidence that the Italian Antonio Meucci invented a telephone years before Bell began working on his device, so as long as we are going to lay claim to one invention, we might as well take responsibility for the other.

FOR ANALYSIS

1. When does "Time and Distance Overcome" become about more than the advent and spread of the telephone? Make a list of the additional concerns and historical developments Biss connects to Bell's invention. What unites these things?

2. Track some of the ironies in Biss's essay, for example, ways in which earlier statements about the value of the telephone (or the negative value of the pole, to some) can be seen differently later.

3. What do you make of the essay's final image?

MAKING ARGUMENTS

The formal technique of juxtaposition is crucial to the way this essay works. Make an argument, relying on a firm definition of juxtaposition and the evidence of particular textual observations, for why this is so and for how the technique is successful.

WRITING TOPIC

In her note, Biss writes: "I had not intended to write an essay about lynching, but I found that, given what my research was yielding, I could not avoid it." Try to do some-thing similar by researching the history of something everyday and important like the telephone and seeing what unexpected histories emerge. Keep a log of your attempts: it is unlikely you will succeed on your first try, and a record of your failures may itself be instructive about the ways in which research can lead to planned and unplanned outcomes.

MAKING CONNECTIONS

Read Biss's essay with Carolyn Forché's "The Colonel" (p. 436). What similarities and/or differences do you see in the way that Biss and Forché represent violence in their works?

There are different ways to feel alien to or excluded from a culture. Many people tend to think of immigrants this way: that they often experience a dislocation that is more than geographical, as their cultural environment changes while individual identity lags behind. But there are also ways in which native-born people can feel as if they do not belong. Sometimes this exclusion is felt as a result of racial or ethnic identity in places where the mainstream culture is defined partly by these things, but it can also be the result of differences in social class. All of these "outsider" positions can give writers a unique vantage point. As you read these essays, think about what the experiences of these authors allow them to see. Do they see things in America that native-born people, or people born to the dominant or majority ethnicity or class, may not? Do they see themselves differently, too?

BHARATI MUKHERJEE (B. 1940)

TWO WAYS TO BELONG IN AMERICA 1996

This is a tale of two sisters from Calcutta, Mira and Bharati, who have lived in the United States for some thirty-five years, but who find themselves on different sides in the current debate over the status of immigrants.

I am an American citizen and she is not. I am moved that thousands of long-term residents are finally taking the oath of citizenship. She is not.

Mira arrived in Detroit in 1960 to study child psychology and preschool education. I followed her a year later to study creative writing at the University of Iowa. When we left India, we were almost identical in appearance and attitude. We dressed alike, in saris; we expressed identical views on politics, social issues, love, and marriage in the same Calcutta convent-school accent. We would endure our two years in America, secure our degrees, then return to India to marry the grooms of our father's choosing.

Instead, Mira married an Indian student in 1962 who was getting his business administration degree at Wayne State University. They soon acquired the labor certifications necessary for the green card of hassle-free residence and employment.

Mira still lives in Detroit, works in the Southfield, Michigan, school system, 5 and has become nationally recognized for her contributions in the fields of preschool education and parent-teacher relationships. After thirty-six years as a legal immigrant in this country, she clings passionately to her Indian citizenship and hopes to go home to India when she retires.

In Iowa City in 1963, I married a fellow student, an American of Canadian parentage. Because of the accident of his North Dakota birth, I bypassed labor-certification requirements and the race-related "quota" system that favored the applicant's country of origin over his or her merit. I was prepared for (and even welcomed) the emotional strain that came with marrying outside my ethnic community. In thirty-three years of marriage, we have lived in every part of North America. By choosing a husband who was not my father's selection, I was opting for fluidity, self-invention, blue jeans and T-shirts, and renouncing three thousand years (at least) of caste-observant, "pure culture" marriage in the Mukherjee family. My books have often been read as unapologetic (and in some quarters overenthusiastic) texts for cultural and psychological "mongrelization." It's a word I celebrate.

Mira and I have stayed sisterly close by phone. In our regular Sunday morning conversations, we are unguardedly affectionate. I am her only blood relative on this continent. We expect to see each other through the looming crises of aging and ill health without being asked. Long before Vice President Gore's "Citizenship U.S.A." drive, we'd had our polite arguments over the ethics of retaining an overseas citizenship while expecting the permanent protection and economic benefits that come with living and working in America.

Like well-raised sisters, we never said what was really on our minds, but we probably pitied one another. She, for the lack of structure in my life, the erasure of Indianness, the absence of an unvarying daily core. I, for the narrowness of her perspective, her uninvolvement with the mythic depths or the superficial pop culture of this society. But, now, with the scapegoating of "aliens" (documented or illegal) on the increase, and the targeting of long-term legal immigrants like Mira for new scrutiny and new self-consciousness, she and I find ourselves unable to maintain the same polite discretion. We were always unacknowledged adversaries, and we are now, more than ever, sisters.

"I feel used," Mira raged on the phone the other night. "I feel manipulated and discarded. This is such an unfair way to treat a person who was invited to stay and work here because of her talent. My employer went to the I.N.S. and petitioned for the labor certification. For over thirty years, I've invested my creativity and professional skills into the improvement of this country's preschool system. I've obeyed all the rules, I've paid my taxes, I love my work, I love my students, I love the friends I've made. How dare America now change its rules in midstream? If America wants to make new rules curtailing benefits of legal immigrants, they should apply only to immigrants who arrive after those rules are already in place." To my ears, it sounded like the description of a long-enduring, comfortable yet loveless marriage, without risk or recklessness. Have we the right to demand, and to expect, that we be loved? (That, to me, is the subtext of the arguments by immigration advocates.) My sister is an expatriate, professionally generous and creative, socially courteous and gracious, and that's as far as her Americanization can go. She is here to maintain an identity, not to transform it.

I asked her if she would follow the example of others who have decided to become citizens because of the anti-immigration bills in Congress. And here, 10 she surprised me. "If America wants to play the manipulative game, I'll play it too," she snapped. "I'll become a U.S. citizen for now, then change back to Indian when I'm ready to go home. I feel some kind of irrational attachment to India that I don't to America. Until all this hysteria against legal immigrants, I was totally happy. Having my green card meant I could visit any place in the world I wanted to and then come back to a job that's satisfying and that I do very well."

In one family, from two sisters alike as peas in a pod, there could not be a wider divergence of immigrant experience. America spoke to me—I married it—I embraced the demotion from expatriate aristocrat to immigrant nobody, surrendering those thousands of years of "pure culture," the saris, the delightfully accented English. She retained them all. Which of us is the freak?

Mira's voice, I realize, is the voice not just of the immigrant South Asian community but of an immigrant community of the millions who have stayed rooted in one job, one city, one house, one ancestral culture, one cuisine, for the entirety of their productive years. She speaks for greater numbers than I possibly can. Only the fluency of her English and the anger, rather than fear, born of confidence from her education, differentiate her from the seamstresses, the domestics, the technicians, the shop owners, the millions of hardworking but effectively silenced documented immigrants as well as their less fortunate "illegal" brothers and sisters.

Nearly twenty years ago, when I was living in my husband's ancestral homeland of Canada, I was always well employed but never allowed to feel part of the local Quebec or larger Canadian society. Then, through a Green Paper that invited a national referendum on the unwanted side effects of "nontraditional" immigration, the government officially turned against its immigrant communities, particularly those from South Asia.

I felt then the same sense of betrayal that Mira feels now.

I will never forget the pain of that sudden turning, and the casual racist outbursts the Green Paper elicited. That sense of betrayal had its desired effect and drove me, and thousands like me, from the country.   15

Mira and I differ, however, in the ways in which we hope to interact with the country that we have chosen to live in. She is happier to live in America as expatriate Indian than as an immigrant American. I need to feel like a part of the community I have adopted (as I tried to feel in Canada as well). I need to put roots down, to vote and make the difference that I can. The price that the immigrant willingly pays, and that the exile avoids, is the trauma of self-transformation.

FOR ANALYSIS

1. What does Mukherjee mean by "mongrelization" (para. 6)?

2. What is the "trauma of self-transformation" (para. 16)? Are there traumas felt by those who choose to remain faithful to their original identity?

3. What are Mukherjee's feelings about the culture she left behind? What does she value? To what does she object?

MAKING ARGUMENTS

Immigration is a controversial political issue. Where do you stand on it? Should the United States make it easier or harder for immigrants to enter the country, to gain access to social services, to stay without becoming citizens, or to become citizens?

WRITING TOPIC

Mukherjee's sister describes her attachment to India as "irrational" (para. 10), yet she maintains it. Does Mukherjee agree with her sister? Is she similarly attached to her nation, only her new one rather than her old one? Do you think feeling a deep connection to a nation and culture is irrational?

LACY M. JOHNSON (B. 1978)

WHITE TRASH PRIMER 2009

You live with your mama and daddy, your two sisters, three dogs, two horses and exactly twelve cats on a farm so far from town you barely see the street lights' bright white tossed over the horizon. Your mama grows a garden of fresh green vegetables right outside your back door and you and your sisters pick peas and tomatoes in the afternoon while mama hangs clean white sheets on the clothesline and the hot sun freckles your shoulders with small brown spots. When your daddy comes up to the house all sweating and covered in hayseed you set the table and make sure the silverware's in all the right places or you have to drink water with your dinner instead of tea.

You attend second service every Sunday since the day you are born and Brother Dan or Brother Darrell preach about the glory and grace of Jesus Christ and you accept Him as your Lord and Savior or you burn in hell and this is why you've been baptized twice and saved exactly twenty-seven times. Every week your mama and you and your sisters get real dressed up in the pretty cotton dresses she makes special for wearing to church. Your mama's always made all your clothes special with her own two hands and you are grateful for each hem until the rich kids in your Sunday School don't look at you even when you sit right next to them. Your daddy says vanity's an expensive sin but sometimes your mama drives you and your sisters to Wal-Mart anyway and she buys you underwear and socks and a pair of Lee jeans that are exactly two inches shorter than your legs and she presses her lips real tight together the whole time. One day she stops making pretty cotton dresses but the rich kids still don't look at you. They never look at you.

You and your sisters have always got on real good together. On hot summer days you pack peanut-butter sandwiches in a napkin your sister ties to your belt loop and you spend all day wandering the woods along the farm. Your daddy cuts a path with the brush hog and builds a square fort with sixteen knotty black logs instead of dragging them up to the house for firewood. You stop there every day to eat your lunch and you go skinny dipping in the creek and splash your little sister with the cold cold water and sometimes she tells your daddy and all three of you get spanked. Sometimes at night your sister comes to sleep in your bed and you stay up late talking real soft together with your heads under the covers like two peas in a pod and your daddy has to get on you for staying up past your bedtime. One night after mama and daddy are in bed your sister tells you she's moving to an apartment above the Five and Dime downtown and you pull the covers back to see her face in the dark and she says you can come to her place to see her anytime you like. The next day she takes all of her clothes out of her closet and packs them up in a big black trash bag and carries them over her shoulder out the door. Your mama and daddy holler real loud when they find out your sister is living in sin with a black man and you don't get to see her for some time.

Your daddy lets you drive his pickup truck on the gravel road to your house when he's real tired even if you're not old enough because he says it's something you need to know how to do. When you're driving he turns on the radio and listens to Paul Harvey. Sometimes he disagrees with Paul Harvey and explains to you why he is right instead of resting. Sometimes he listens with his eyes closed and his head leaned back against the window. You know he's worrying over money because when your daddy worries over money his forehead gets to looking like tilled soil, mounded in rows like the creek bottom. He works real hard on the farm but the soybeans aren't selling and neither is the corn and the fence needs repairs and the plow's all busted so you take the truck into town without asking and you apply for a job at the fancy Wal-Mart but they don't call you to come in for an INTERVIEW. You apply six times and when they do call you pack peanut-butter sandwiches every day for lunch and every time you get a paycheck you put it in your daddy's bank and sometimes his eyes get to watering and you think he might be going soft. You save every penny you earn, but disappointment's what you get for dreaming because every penny ain't enough. Your daddy's a proud man and his eyes water the hardest you've ever seen when he signs the papers that sell the farm but this time you don't think it's cause he's soft.

You move into a white house with blue shutters and a yard with exactly ⁵ thirteen trees on a paved street in town and your daddy tears down all the walls and puts up new ones cause black mold spreads where you can't see. He works at the power plant and drops his yellow hard hat by the front door and your mama waits on rich folks at the restaurant and gets real dressed up for work every night and you don't have to set the table anymore cause you and your sister eat peanut-butter sandwiches for dinner and watch cable television before you go to bed. Sometimes you cut the sandwiches into circles with the mouth of a glass and sometimes you add pink and white candy sprinkles mama keeps in the cupboard for cupcakes and you tell your sister you've made her a SURPRISE. You walk to high school every day and you smoke cigarettes and cough down the peach schnapps your mama keeps hidden in the very back of the highest kitchen cabinet and even though it burns your stomach like hell fire you follow the kids to the one-block downtown and drive your truck in circles cause it's the only thing to do. You make friends with a girl your same age and she lets you spend the night at her place sometimes and you sleep real soundly in the AIR CONDITIONING. Sometimes she sneaks her boyfriend in and they have sex in the bed right next to you. One night he brings his friend over and he kisses you and claws your clothes off and you just want to sleep but his breath is stale and sweet like the beer your daddy drinks and when you try to push him off and tell him to stop he puts a pillow over your face and jams himself right up inside you and you can hardly breathe it burns so bad but there is nothing God will do.

You try real hard to get good grades in college cause you know exactly how much it cost but you work forty hours a week at Wal-Mart and sometimes you're so damn tired you can't read the PSYCHOLOGY open in front of you. Sometimes you don't know the words in front of you but you don't have a dictionary and if you fake it your teachers always know that you are faking. Your mama calls and asks how you're doing and you tell her you're doing great, mama, just great and one day she calls to tell you she has CANCER. Your hands sweat and your knees tremble together with sixteen of your cousins and your aunts and uncles and grandparents on both sides and both of your sisters in your mama's hospital room holding hands around her bed while your daddy asks the good Lord for STRENGTH. You don't even breathe until she's waking up from surgery with her mouth pawing open and each time you look she is weaker and smaller and closer to dying and each time your daddy palms his forehead he leaves tracks like the old creek bottom, but now you know it's not just money he worries over, so you tell him you'll drop out of school just till she's better but you don't plan to go back for some time.

You ask your mama how she feels when she picks you up from your apartment to take you to TACO BELL and she pushes you into the bathroom to show you where her breast used to be and hands you the silicon fist she keeps in her bra. You hold it with both hands. You order food. You sit down and when she's half-way through with her second SOFT TACO SUPREME you show her the pink flower tattoo your older sister bought you for your eighteenth birthday. Your mama doesn't say anything but her lips pressed real tight together tell you she is mad. Before she walks out the door and drives away she meets your eyes with hers and you know exactly what she means.

You hide that you are poor. You save up for a pair of LEVI's jeans and put shirts on layaway. You take furniture from your neighbor's dumpster and thank your luck that they are wasteful. You fog your apartment for roaches and clean with bleach so they don't come out when you have company. You wash your car in the driveway with a hose and dishsoap. Your sister comes to visit and colors your hair NICE AND EASY 98 LIGHTEST BLONDE and paints your fingernails and toenails FIRE ENGINE RED. You make friends with a girl at work who is the same size as you and she gives you things she doesn't like anymore: a blue dress from the mall, a pair of black pumps, a pretty barrette with fake red crystals for your hair. She sets you up on dates with men and at dinner you order steaks and alcoholic drinks even if you're not old enough to drink. Sometimes you let them take you back to the fancy places where they live and if you have sex with them they take you shopping or to Springfield for the weekend and you thank your luck that they are gullible.

You act real tough but you've got a weak spot for HARLEY DAVIDSON motorcycles and a tall man in a leather coat with a broad chest and long black hair makes you want to ride. He takes you down a blacktop road clear out into nowhere and the whole time you've got that great big machine growling right under you, you're reeling in the smell of pine trees and wide green fields. So your fingers tighten on his arm. And your blond hair blows from underneath your helmet and all you can think about with the wind keeping your eyes closed tight is going and staying gone. When he stops his bike on the side of the road and turns around to hold your face real gentle between his hands you let him kiss you. And he takes you home without asking you for anything.

Your mama puts your picture in the paper when you go back to school. 10 You take classes with black folks and brown folks and yellow folks and make friends with who you like. Your parents take you out to dinner with your sisters and when your daddy is half-way through with his second beer and his cheeks are glowing with the red blood rushing to his face he lifts his glass and says that he is proud of you. When he finishes his third beer he goes out to sleep in the car and your mama gives you three brand new black pens and a pad of PostIts from her purse. You study real damn hard this time cause you know this is your last earthly chance to make something of yourself and you buy a dictionary at a yard sale and think you might learn every word if you have DETERMINATION and RESOLVE. When Wal-Mart doesn't let you off to study for a test you tell them to kiss your poor white ass and you apply for student loans and when they give out credit cards on campus you accept exactly three. Your English professor says you have POTENTIAL and you hold this real close to your heart when you're walking up to get your diploma and sixteen of your cousins and your aunts and uncles and grandparents on both sides and your two sisters are hooting and hollering from the stands and your mama blows an air horn and your daddy yells your name so loud and true it's like he's calling you to come up from the creek bottom. And you hear him calling for some time.

FOR ANALYSIS

1. What significance does the title have? What does Johnson mean by "white trash"? What is a "primer"?

2. How would you characterize the **style** of the **prose** with which Johnson writes "White Trash Primer"?

3. What **point of view** is this essay written in? What effect does it have on you as you read?

MAKING ARGUMENTS

Reflect on how you relate to the use of the word *you* in "White Trash Primer." How does it make you feel? Do you feel included by it or excluded by it? Why? Argue for or against Johnson's use of the second-person ("you") **point of view**. Cite specific moments when you feel that it is effective or ineffective, and explain why. If you are arguing against it, try to include an argument for an alternative that attempts to explain why it would have been better.

WRITING TOPIC

Johnson's essay closes on an emotional note. Going back through the essay, note the different **tones** she creates, and reflect on how she prepares her readers for the feelings evoked by the end of the essay.

MAKING CONNECTIONS

1. Both of these essays are in part about what Mukherjee calls "the trauma of self-transformation" (para. 16). What is the nature of Johnson's transformation? How does Johnson present it? Is it traumatic?

2. Mukherjee's essay is about immigration, while Johnson's is not. Yet both are about different ways to be in America—different ways to live, different ways to see yourself and be seen by others. Compare the situations the two essays take as their subjects and the ways the two treat those situations.

3. Imagine a conversation between Mukherjee and Johnson on the subject of culture. What might each of them mean by the term? How might their definitions be similar, and how might they be different?

FURTHER QUESTIONS
FOR THINKING AND WRITING

1. Explain how Virginia Woolf's observations in "What If Shakespeare Had Had a Sister?" illuminate Emily's situation in William Faulkner's "A Rose for Emily." **Writing Topic:** In an essay, argue for or against the proposition that women have achieved absolute equality in the United States.

2. Emily Dickinson's "What Soft—Cherubic Creatures—" and e. e. cummings's "the Cambridge ladies who live in furnished souls" both address certain culturally determined behavior patterns among women. Describe the behavior depicted in these poems. How do the authors feel about the behavior? What devices reveal the authors' attitudes? **Writing Topic:** Define the social tradition that produced the women in these poems. Either defend that tradition as crucial to the social order, or offer a cultural variation that would give women a different social role.

3. The speakers in Marilyn Chin's "How I Got That Name" and T. S. Eliot's "The Love Song of J. Alfred Prufrock" exhibit quite different attitudes about their identities. Describe each speaker's attitude toward his identity, and identify which aspects of the poems define those attitudes. In what sense are the speakers' identities culturally determined? **Writing Topic:** In an imaginative essay, describe each speaker's early life, and suggest what cultural forces shaped each of them.

4. Some of the works in this section focus on intergenerational tensions within a culture. Compare such tensions among parents and offspring in Alice Walker's "Everyday Use" and Sherman Alexie's "War Dances."

5. The struggle of women to achieve equality is the subject of many works in this section. **Writing Topic:** Examine some of the feminist works in this section. What, if any, common threads do you find running through them, either in content or in the use of literary devices?

6. Homer in William Faulkner's "A Rose for Emily" and Prufrock in T. S. Eliot's "The Love Song of J. Alfred Prufrock" are both, in some sense, cultural outsiders. **Writing Topic:** Compare their positions in the dominant culture, the resulting conflicts or tensions, and the strategies they employ in dealing with their status.

LOVE AND HATE

Two Lovers, 1630, by Riza 'Abbasi (1565–1635). A.H. 1039/1629–30. Safavid period.
From Iran. Tempera and gold on paper, H. 7⅛ in. × W. 4¹¹⁄₁₆ in. (18.1 × 11.9 cm).
Purchase, Francis M. Weld Gift, 1950 (50.164).

Love and death, it is often noted, are the two great themes of literature. Many of the literary works we have placed in the sections "Innocence and Experience," "Conformity and Rebellion," and "Culture and Identity" speak of love and death as well. But in those works, other thematic interests dominate. In this section, we gather a number of works in which love and hate are thematically central.

The rosy conception of love presented in many popular and sentimental stories does not prepare us for the complicated reality we face. We know that the course of true love never runs smoothly, but in those popular stories the obstacles that hinder the lovers are simple and external. If the young lover can land the high-paying job or convince the beloved's parents that he or she is worthy despite social differences, all will be well. But love in life is rarely that simple. The external obstacles may be insuperable, or the obstacles may lie deep within the personality. The major obstacle may well be an individual's difficult and painful effort to understand that he or she has been deceived by an immature or sentimental conception of love.

In this age of psychological awareness, the claims of the flesh are well recognized. But psychology teaches us, as well, to recognize the aggressive aspect of the human condition. The omnipresent selfishness that civilization attempts to check may be aggressively violent as well as lustful. Thus, on one hand, we have the simple eroticism of Kate Chopin's "The Storm" and, on the other, the more complicated, dangerous attraction of Joyce Carol Oates's "Where Are You Going, Where Have You Been?" And Matthew Arnold in "Dover Beach" finds love the only refuge from a chaotic world in which "ignorant armies clash by night."

The cliché has it that love and hate are closely related, and much evidence supports this proposition. But why should love and hate, seeming opposites, lie so close together in the emotional lives of men and women? We are all egos, separate from each other. And as separate individuals, we develop elaborate behavior mechanisms that defend us from each other. But the erotic love relationship differs from other relationships in that it may be defined as a rejection of separateness. The common metaphor speaks of two lovers as joining, as merging into one. That surrender of the "me" to join in an "us" leaves lovers uniquely vulnerable to psychic injury. In short, the defenses are down, and the self-esteem of each of the lovers depends importantly on the behavior of the other. If the lover is betrayed by the beloved, the emotional consequences are uniquely disastrous—hence the peculiarly close relationship between passionate hatred and erotic love.

Words like *love* and *hate* are so general that poets rarely use them except as one term in a metaphor designed to project sharply some aspect of emotional life. The simple sexuality in poems such as Andrew Marvell's "To His Coy Mistress" and Ben Jonson's "Song, To Celia" may be juxtaposed with the hatred and violence generated in *Othello* by sexual jealousy or with the angry impulses of the spurned speaker in Carolyn Kizer's "Bitch." And Sharon Olds's description of lust in "Sex without Love" notes an aspect of love quite overlooked by Robert Burns in "A Red, Red Rose."

Perhaps more than anything, the works in this section celebrate the elemental impulses of men and women that run counter to those rational formulations by which we govern our lives. We pursue Othello's love for Desdemona and Iago's hate for Othello and arrive at an irreducible mystery, for neither Othello's love nor Iago's hate yields satisfactorily to rational explanation. Reason does not tell us why Othello and Desdemona love one another or why Iago hates rather than honors Othello.

Love is an act of faith springing from our deep-seated need to join with another human being not only in physical nakedness but in emotional and spiritual nakedness as well. While hate is a denial of that faith and therefore a retreat into spiritual isolation, love is an attempt to break out of the isolation.

QUESTIONS FOR THINKING AND WRITING

As you read the selections in this section, consider the following questions. You may want to write out your thoughts informally in a journal or notebook as a way of preparing to respond to the selections, or you may wish to make one of these questions the basis for a formal essay.

1. What is love? What is the source of your definition (literature, personal observation, discussions with those you trust)? Have you ever been in love? How did you know? Do you know someone who is in love? How has it changed that person?

2. Have you ever truly hated someone or something? Describe the circumstances, and characterize your hatred.

3. Do you believe that love and hate are closely related? Have you experienced a change from love to hatred, or do you know someone who has? Explain.

4. There are different kinds of love—love of family, of humankind, of a cause. Describe several different kinds of love, and examine your own motives and behavior in different love relationships. Is it possible that certain kinds of love necessarily generate certain hatreds? Explain.

FICTION

KATE CHOPIN (1851–1904)

THE STORM 1898

I

The leaves were so still that even Bibi thought it was going to rain. Bobinôt, who was accustomed to converse on terms of perfect equality with his little son, called the child's attention to certain sombre clouds that were rolling with sinister intention from the west, accompanied by a sullen, threatening roar. They were at Friedheimer's store and decided to remain there till the storm had passed. They sat within the door on two empty kegs. Bibi was four years old and looked very wise.

"Mama'll be 'fraid, yes," he suggested with blinking eyes.

"She'll shut the house. Maybe she got Sylvie helpin' her this evenin,'" Bobinôt responded reassuringly.

"No; she ent got Sylvie. Sylvie was helpin' her yistiday," piped Bibi.

Bobinôt arose and going across to the counter purchased a can of shrimps, of which Calixta was very fond. Then he returned to his perch on the keg and sat stolidly holding the can of shrimps while the storm burst. It shook the wooden store and seemed to be ripping great furrows in the distant field. Bibi laid his little hand on his father's knee and was not afraid.

II

Calixta, at home, felt no uneasiness for their safety. She sat at a side window sewing furiously on a sewing machine. She was greatly occupied and did not notice the approaching storm. But she felt very warm and often stopped to mop her face on which the perspiration gathered in beads. She unfastened her white sacque at the throat. It began to grow dark, and suddenly realizing the situation she got up hurriedly and went about closing windows and doors.

Out on the small front gallery she had hung Bobinôt's Sunday clothes to air and she hastened out to gather them before the rain fell. As she stepped outside,

Alcée Laballière rode in at the gate. She had not seen him very often since her marriage, and never alone. She stood there with Bobinôt's coat in her hands, and the big rain drops began to fall. Alcée rode his horse under the shelter of a side projection where the chickens had huddled and there were plows and a harrow piled up in the corner.

"May I come and wait on your gallery till the storm is over, Calixta?" he asked.

"Come 'long in, M'sieur Alcée."

His voice and her own startled her as if from a trance, and she seized Bobinôt's 10
vest. Alcée, mounting to the porch, grabbed the trousers and snatched Bibi's braided jacket that was about to be carried away by a sudden gust of wind. He expressed an intention to remain outside, but it was soon apparent that he might as well have been out in the open: the water beat in upon the boards in driving sheets, and he went inside, closing the door after him. It was even necessary to put something beneath the door to keep the water out.

"My! what a rain! It's good two years since it rain' like that," exclaimed Calixta as she rolled up a piece of bagging and Alcée helped her to thrust it beneath the crack.

She was a little fuller of figure than five years before when she married; but she had lost nothing of her vivacity. Her blue eyes still retained their melting quality; and her yellow hair, dishevelled by the wind and rain, kinked more stubbornly than ever about her ears and temples.

The rain beat upon the low, shingled roof with a force and clatter that threatened to break an entrance and deluge them there. They were in the dining room—the sitting room—the general utility room. Adjoining was her bed room, with Bibi's couch along side her own. The door stood open, and the room with its white, monumental bed, its closed shutters, looked dim and mysterious.

Alcée flung himself into a rocker and Calixta nervously began to gather up from the floor the lengths of a cotton sheet which she had been sewing.

"If this keeps up, *Dieu sait*[1] if the levees goin' to stan' it!" she exclaimed. 15

"What have you got to do with the levees?"

"I got enough to do! An' there's Bobinôt with Bibi out in that storm—if he only didn' left Friedheimer's!"

"Let us hope, Calixta, that Bobinôt's got sense enough to come in out of a cyclone."

She went and stood at the window with a greatly disturbed look on her face. She wiped the frame that was clouded with moisture. It was stiflingly hot. Alcée got up and joined her at the window, looking over her shoulder. The rain was coming down in sheets obscuring the view of far-off cabins and enveloping the distant wood in a gray mist. The playing of the lightning was incessant. A bolt struck a tall chinaberry tree at the edge of the field. It filled all visible space with a blinding glare and the crash seemed to invade the very boards they stood upon.

---

[1] God knows.

Calixta put her hands to her eyes, and with a cry, staggered backward. 20
Alcée's arm encircled her, and for an instant he drew her close and spasmodically to him.

"*Bonté!*"[2] she cried, releasing herself from his encircling arm and retreating
from the window, "the house'll go next! If I only knew we're Bibi was!" She
would not compose herself; she would not be seated. Alcée clasped her shoulders and looked into her face. The contact of her warm, palpitating body when
he had unthinkingly drawn her into his arms, had aroused all the old-time
infatuation and desire for her flesh.

"Calixta," he said, "don't be frightened. Nothing can happen. The house is
too low to be struck, with so many tall trees standing about. There! aren't you
going to be quiet? say, aren't you?" He pushed her hair back from her face that
was warm and steaming. Her lips were as red and moist as pomegranate seed.
Her white neck and a glimpse of her full, firm bosom disturbed him powerfully. As she glanced up at him the fear in her liquid blue eyes had given place
to a drowsy gleam that unconsciously betrayed a sensuous desire. He looked
down into her eyes and there was nothing for him to do but to gather her lips
in a kiss. It reminded him of Assumption.[3]

"Do you remember—in Assumption, Calixta?" he asked in a low voice broken by passion. Oh! she remembered; for in Assumption he had kissed her and
kissed and kissed her; until his senses would well nigh fail, and to save her he
would resort to a desperate flight. If she was not an immaculate dove in those
days, she was still inviolate; a passionate creature whose very defenselessness
had made her defense, against which his honor forbade him to prevail. Now—
well, now—her lips seemed in a manner free to be tasted, as well as her round,
white throat and her whiter breasts.

They did not heed the crashing torrents, and the roar of the elements made
her laugh as she lay in his arms. She was a revelation in that dim, mysterious
chamber; as white as the couch she lay upon. Her firm, elastic flesh that was
knowing for the first time its birthright, was like a creamy lily that the sun
invites to contribute its breath and perfume to the undying life of the world.

The generous abundance of her passion, without guile or trickery, was like a 25
white flame which penetrated and found response in depths of his own sensuous nature that had never yet been reached.

When he touched her breasts they gave themselves up in quivering ecstasy,
inviting his lips. Her mouth was a fountain of delight. And when he possessed
her, they seemed to swoon together at the very borderland of life's mystery.

He stayed cushioned upon her, breathless, dazed, enervated, with his heart
beating like a hammer upon her. With one hand she clasped his head, her lips
lightly touching his forehead. The other hand stroked with a soothing rhythm
his muscular shoulders.

[2] An exclamation: Goodness!
[3] A holiday commemorating the ascent of the Virgin Mary to heaven. Assumption is also the name
of a Louisiana parish (county) where Calixta and Alcée had a rendezvous in an earlier story.

The growl of the thunder was distant and passing away. The rain beat softly upon the shingles, inviting them to drowsiness and sleep. But they dared not yield.

The rain was over; and the sun was turning the glistening green world into a palace of gems. Calixta, on the gallery, watched Alcée ride away. He turned and smiled at her with a beaming face; and she lifted her pretty chin in the air and laughed aloud.

III

Bobinôt and Bibi, trudging home, stopped without at the cistern to make 30 themselves presentable.

"My! Bibi, w'at will yo' mama say! You ought to be ashame'. You oughtn' put on those good pants. Look at 'em! An' that mud on yo' collar! How you got that mud on yo' collar, Bibi? I never saw such a boy!" Bibi was the picture of pathetic resignation. Bobinôt was the embodiment of serious solicitude as he strove to remove from his own person and his son's the signs of their tramp over heavy roads and through wet fields. He scraped the mud off Bibi's bare legs and feet with a stick and carefully removed all traces from his heavy brogans. Then, prepared for the worst—the meeting with an over-scrupulous housewife, they entered cautiously at the back door.

Calixta was preparing supper. She had set the table and was dripping coffee at the hearth. She sprang up as they came in.

"Oh, Bobinôt! You back! My! but I was uneasy. W'ere you been during the rain? An' Bibi? he ain't wet? he ain't hurt?" She had clasped Bibi and was kissing him effusively. Bobinôt's explanations and apologies which he had been composing all along the way, died on his lips as Calixta felt him to see if he were dry, and seemed to express nothing but satisfaction at their safe return.

"I brought you some shrimps, Calixta," offered Bobinôt, hauling the can from his ample side pocket and laying it on the table.

"Shrimps! Oh, Bobinôt! you too good fo' anything!" and she gave him a 35 smacking kiss on the cheek that resounded. "*J'vous réponds,*[4] we'll have a feas' to night! umph-umph!"

Bobinôt and Bibi began to relax and enjoy themselves, and when the three seated themselves at table they laughed much and so loud that anyone might have heard them as far away as Laballière's.

IV

Alcée Laballière wrote to his wife, Clarisse, that night. It was a loving letter, full of tender solicitude. He told her not to hurry back, but if she and the babies liked it at Biloxi, to stay a month longer. He was getting on nicely; and though

---

[4] I'm telling you.

he missed them, he was willing to bear the separation a while longer—realizing that their health and pleasure were the first things to be considered.

V

As for Clarisse, she was charmed upon receiving her husband's letter. She and the babies were doing well. The society was agreeable; many of her old friends and acquaintances were at the bay. And the first free breath since her marriage seemed to restore the pleasant liberty of her maiden days. Devoted as she was to her husband, their intimate conjugal life was something which she was more than willing to forego for a while.

So the storm passed and everyone was happy.

FOR ANALYSIS

1. Aside from the child Bibi, there are four **characters** in this story—two married couples. How did you respond to each of these characters? What are the sources for your reactions?

2. How do the characters in the story feel about themselves? About each other? On what evidence in the story do you base your response?

3. Discuss the title of the story.

4. During the second half of the nineteenth century, certain American writers, including Kate Chopin, evoked a sense of region in their work. What region of the United States provides the **setting** for this story? How do you know?

5. What aspects of this story's **style** contribute to its realism?

MAKING ARGUMENTS

Chopin is often thought of as a Naturalist writer—that is, as one of the writers of the period who saw human life as determined by forces beyond their control, such as economics, biology, or the environment. Based on the evidence you find in "The Storm," make the argument that Chopin is or is not a Naturalist.

WRITING TOPICS

1. Write an essay on modern marriage, using this story to support your analysis.

2. Comment on the story's final line. Is "the storm" literal or **symbolic**? If everyone is "happy," do you believe they have the right to be? Or is such a question irrelevant? Explain.

MAKING CONNECTIONS

Read this story against Galway Kinnell's "After Making Love We Hear Footsteps" (p. 951). How do the children function in relation to the sex in each work? What does the boy's presence after the act mean in each selection?

ZORA NEALE HURSTON (1891–1960)

SWEAT 1926

I

It was eleven o'clock of a Spring night in Florida. It was Sunday. Any other night, Delia Jones would have been in bed for two hours by this time. But she was a washwoman, and Monday morning meant a great deal to her. So she collected the soiled clothes on Saturday when she returned the clean things. Sunday night after church, she sorted and put the white things to soak. It saved her almost a half-day's start. A great hamper in the bedroom held the clothes that she brought home. It was so much neater than a number of bundles lying around.

She squatted on the kitchen floor beside the great pile of clothes, sorting them into small heaps according to color, and humming a song in a mournful key, but wondering through it all where Sykes, her husband, had gone with her horse and buckboard.

Just then something long, round, limp, and black fell upon her shoulders and slithered to the floor beside her. A great terror took hold of her. It softened her knees and dried her mouth so that it was a full minute before she could cry out or move. Then she saw that it was the big bull whip her husband liked to carry when he drove.

She lifted her eyes to the door and saw him standing there bent over with laughter at her fright. She screamed at him.

"Sykes, what you throw dat whip on me like dat? You know it would skeer me—looks just like a snake, an' you knows how skeered Ah is of snakes."

"Course Ah knowed it! That's how come Ah done it." He slapped his leg with his hand and almost rolled on the ground in his mirth. "If you such a big fool dat you got to have a fit over a earth worm or a string, Ah don't keer how bad Ah skeer you."

"You ain't got no business doing it. Gawd knows it's a sin. Some day Ah'm gointuh drop dead from some of yo' foolishness. 'Nother thing, where you been wid mah rig? Ah feeds dat pony. He ain't fuh you to be drivin' wid no bull whip."

"You sho' is one aggravatin' nigger woman!" he declared and stepped into the room. She resumed her work and did not answer him at once. "Ah done tole you time and again to keep them white folks' clothes outa dis house."

He picked up the whip and glared at her. Delia went on with her work. She went out into the yard and returned with a galvanized tub and set it on the wash-bench. She saw that Sykes had kicked all of the clothes together again, and now stood in her way truculently, his whole manner hoping, *praying*, for an argument. But she walked calmly around him and commenced to re-sort the things.

"Next time, Ah'm gointer kick 'em outdoors," he threatened as he struck a 10 match along the leg of his corduroy breeches.

Delia never looked up from her work, and her thin, stooped shoulders sagged further.

"Ah ain't for no fuss t'night, Sykes. Ah just come from taking sacrament at the church house."

He snorted scornfully. "Yeah, you just come from de church house on a Sunday night, but heah you is gone to work on them clothes. You ain't nothing but a hypocrite. One of them amen-corner Christians—sing, whoop, and shout, then come home and wash white folks' clothes on the Sabbath."

He stepped roughly upon the whitest pile of things, kicking them helter-skelter as he crossed the room. His wife gave a little scream of dismay, and quickly gathered them together again.

"Sykes, you quit grindin' dirt into these clothes! How can Ah git through by 15 Sat'day if Ah don't start on Sunday?"

"Ah don't keer if you never git through. Anyhow, Ah done promised Gawd and a couple of other men, Ah ain't gointer have it in mah house. Don't gimme no lip neither, else Ah'll throw 'em out and put mah fist up side yo' head to boot."

Delia's habitual meekness seemed to slip from her shoulders like a blown scarf. She was on her feet; her poor little body, her bare knuckly hands bravely defying the strapping hulk before her.

"Looka heah, Sykes, you done gone too fur. Ah been married to you fur fifteen years, and Ah been takin' in washin' fur fifteen years. Sweat, sweat, sweat! Work and sweat, cry and sweat, pray and sweat!"

"What's that got to do with me?" he asked brutally.

"What's it got to do with you, Sykes? Mah tub of suds is filled yo' belly with 20 vittles more times than yo' hands is filled it. Mah sweat is done paid for this house and Ah reckon Ah kin keep on sweatin' in it."

She seized the iron skillet from the stove and struck a defensive pose, which act surprised him greatly, coming from her. It cowed him and he did not strike her as he usually did.

"Naw you won't," she panted, "that ole snaggle-toothed black woman you runnin' with ain't comin' heah to pile up on *mah* sweat and blood. You ain't paid for nothin' on this place, and Ah'm gointer stay right heah till Ah'm toted out foot foremost."

"Well, you better quit gittin' me riled up, else they'll be totin' you out sooner than you expect. Ah'm so tired of you Ah don't know whut to do. Gawd! How Ah hates skinny wimmen!"

A little awed by this new Delia, he sidled out of the door and slammed the back gate after him. He did not say where he had gone, but she knew too well. She knew very well that he would not return until nearly daybreak also. Her work over, she went on to bed but not to sleep at once. Things had come to a pretty pass!

She lay awake, gazing upon the debris that cluttered their matrimonial 25 trail. Not an image left standing along the way. Anything like flowers had long ago been drowned in the salty stream that had been pressed from her heart. Her tears, her sweat, her blood. She had brought love to the union and he had brought a longing after the flesh. Two months after the wedding, he had given her the first brutal beating. She had the memory of his numerous trips to Orlando with all of his wages when he had returned to her penniless, even before the first year had passed. She was young and soft then, but now she thought of her knotty, muscled limbs, her harsh knuckly hands, and drew herself up into an unhappy little ball in the middle of the big feather bed. Too late now to hope for love, even if it were not Bertha it would be someone else. This case differed from the others only in that she was bolder than the others. Too late for everything except her little home. She had built it for her old days, and planted one by one the trees and flowers there. It was lovely to her, lovely.

Somehow, before sleep came, she found herself saying aloud: "Oh well, whatever goes over the Devil's back, is got to come under his belly. Sometime or ruther, Sykes, like everybody else, is gointer reap his sowing." After that she was able to build a spiritual earthworks against her husband. His shells could no longer reach her. AMEN. She went to sleep and slept until he announced his presence in bed by kicking her feet and rudely snatching the covers away.

"Gimme some kivah heah, an' git yo' damn foots over on yo' own side! Ah oughter mash you in yo' mouf fuh drawing dat skillet on me."

Delia went clear to the rail without answering him. A triumphant indifference to all that he was or did.

II

The week was full of work for Delia as all other weeks, and Saturday found her behind her little pony, collecting and delivering clothes.

It was a hot, hot day near the end of July. The village men on Joe Clarke's 30 porch even chewed cane listlessly. They did not hurl the cane-knots as usual. They let them dribble over the edge of the porch. Even conversation had collapsed under the heat.

"Heah come Delia Jones," Jim Merchant said, as the shaggy pony came 'round the bend of the road toward them. The rusty buckboard was heaped with baskets of crisp, clean laundry.

"Yep," Joe Lindsay agreed. "Hot or col', rain or shine, jes'ez reg'lar ez de weeks roll roun' Delia carries 'em an' fetches 'em on Sat'day."

"She better if she wanter eat," said Moss. "Syke Jones ain't wuth de shot an' powder hit would tek tuh kill 'em. Not to *huh* he ain't."

"He sho' ain't," Walter Thomas chimed in. "It's too bad, too, cause she wuz a right pretty li'l trick when he got huh. Ah'd uh mah'ied huh mahself if he hadnter beat me to it."

Delia nodded briefly at the men as she drove past. 35

"Too much knockin' will ruin *any* 'oman. He done beat huh 'nough tuh kill three women, let 'lone change they looks," said Elijah Moseley. "How Syke kin stommuck dat big black greasy Mogul he's layin' roun' wid, gits me. Ah swear dat eight-rock couldn't kiss a sardine can Ah done thowed out de back do' 'way las' yeah."

"Aw, she's fat, thass how come. He's allus been crazy 'bout fat women," put in Merchant. "He'd a' been tied up wid one long time ago if he could a' found one tuh have him. Did Ah tell yuh 'bout him come sidlin' roun' *mah* wife—bringin' her a basket uh peecans outa his yard fuh a present? Yessir, mah wife! She tol' him tuh take 'em right straight back home, 'cause Delia works so hard ovah dat washtub she reckon everything on de place taste lak sweat an' soapsuds. Ah jus' wisht Ah'd a' caught 'im roun' dere! Ah'd a' made his hips ketch on fiah down dat shell road."

"Ah know he done it, too. Ah sees 'im grinnin' at every 'oman dat passes," Walter Thomas said. "But even so, he useter eat some mighty big hunks uh humble pie tuh git dat li'l 'oman he got. She wuz ez pritty ez a speckled pup! Dat wuz fifteen years ago. He useter be so skeered uh losin' huh, she could make him do some parts of a husband's duty. Dey never wuz de same in de mind."

"There oughter be a law about him," said Lindsay. "He ain't fit tuh carry guts tuh a bear."

Clarke spoke for the first time. "Tain't no law on earth dat kin make a man   40 be decent if it ain't in 'im. There's plenty men dat takes a wife lak dey do a joint uh sugar-cane. It's round, juicy, an' sweet when dey gits it. But dey squeeze an' grind, squeeze an' grind an' wring tell dey wring every drop uh pleasure dat's in 'em out. When dey's satisfied dat dey is wrung dry, dey treats 'em jes' lak dey do a cane-chew. Dey thows 'em away. Dey knows whut dey is doin' while dey is at it, an' hates theirselves fuh it but they keeps on hangin' after huh tell she's empty. Den dey hates huh fuh bein' a cane-chew an' in de way."

"We oughter take Syke an' dat stray 'oman uh his'n down in Lake Howell swamp an' lay on de rawhide till they cain't say Lawd a' mussy. He allus wuz uh ovahbearin niggah, but since dat white 'oman from up north done teached 'im how to run a automobile, he done got too beggety to live—an' we oughter kill 'im," Old Man Anderson advised.

A grunt of approval went around the porch. But the heat was melting their civic virtue and Elijah Moseley began to bait Joe Clarke.

"Come on, Joe, git a melon outa dere an' slice it up for yo' customers. We'se all sufferin' wid de heat. De bear's done got *me!*"

"Thass right, Joe, a watermelon is jes' whut Ah needs tuh cure de eppizu-dicks," Walter Thomas joined forces with Moseley. "Come on dere, Joe. We all is steady customers an' you ain't set us up in a long time. Ah chooses dat long, bowlegged Floridy favorite."

"A god, an' be dough. You all gimme twenty cents and slice away," Clarke   45 retorted. "Ah needs a col' slice m'self. Heah, everybody chip in. Ah'll lend y'all mah meat knife."

The money was all quickly subscribed and the huge melon brought forth. At that moment, Sykes and Bertha arrived. A determined silence fell on the porch and the melon was put away again.

Merchant snapped down the blade of his jacknife and moved toward the store door.

"Come on in, Joe, an' gimme a slab uh sow belly an' uh pound uh coffee— almost fuhgot 'twas Sat'day. Got to git on home." Most of the men left also.

Just then Delia drove past on her way home, as Sykes was ordering magnificently for Bertha. It pleased him for Delia to see.

"Git whutsoever yo' heart desires, Honey. Wait a minute, Joe. Give huh two   50
bottles uh strawberry soda-water, uh quart parched ground-peas, an' a block uh chewin' gum."

With all this they left the store, with Sykes reminding Bertha that this was his town and she could have it if she wanted it.

The men returned soon after they left, and held their watermelon feast.

"Where did Syke Jones git da 'oman from nohow?" Lindsay asked.

"Ovah Apopka. Guess dey musta been cleanin' out de town when she lef'. She don't look lak a thing but a hunk uh liver wid hair on it."

"Well, she sho' kin squall," Dave Carter contributed. "When she gits ready   55
tuh laff, she jes' opens huh mouf an' latches it back tuh de las' notch. No ole granpa alligator down in Lake Bell ain't got nothin' on huh."

III

Bertha had been in town three months now. Sykes was still paying her room-rent at Della Lewis'—the only house in town that would have taken her in. Sykes took her frequently to Winter Park to "stomps." He still assured her that he was the swellest man in the state.

"Sho' you kin have dat li'l ole house soon's Ah git dat 'oman outa dere. Everything b'longs tuh me an' you sho' kin have it. Ah sho' 'bominates uh skinny 'oman. Lawdy, you sho' is got one portly shape on you! You kin git *anything* you wants. Dis is *mah* town an' you sho' kin have it."

Delia's work-worn knees crawled over the earth in Gethsemane[1] and up the rocks of Calvary many, many times during these months. She avoided the villagers and meeting places in her efforts to be blind and deaf. But Bertha nullified this to a degree, by coming to Delia's house to call Sykes out to her at the gate.

Delia and Sykes fought all the time now with no peaceful interludes. They slept and ate in silence. Two or three times Delia had attempted a timid friendliness, but she was repulsed each time. It was plain that the breaches must remain agape.

The sun had burned July to August. The heat streamed down like a million   60
hot arrows, smiting all things living upon the earth. Grass withered, leaves

---

[1] Gethsemane is the garden where, according to the Bible, Jesus and his disciples prayed the night before Jesus was crucified on Calvary (which is also known as Golgotha, "the place of the skull").

browned, snakes went blind in shedding, and men and dogs went mad. Dog days!

Delia came home one day and found Sykes there before her. She wondered, but started to go on into the house without speaking, even though he was standing in the kitchen door and she must either stoop under his arm or ask him to move. He made no room for her. She noticed a soap box beside the steps, but paid no particular attention to it, knowing that he must have brought it there. As she was stooping to pass under his outstretched arm, he suddenly pushed her backward, laughingly.

"Look in de box dere Delia, Ah done brung yuh somethin'!"

She nearly fell upon the box in her stumbling, and when she saw what it held, she all but fainted outright.

"Syke! Syke, mah Gawd! You take dat rattlesnake 'way from heah! You *got-tuh*. Oh, Jesus, have mussy!"

"Ah ain't got tuh do nuthin' uh de kin'—fact is Ah ain't got tuh do nothin' 65
but die. Tain't no use uh you puttin' on airs makin' out lak you skeered uh dat snake—he's gointer stay right heah tell he die. He wouldn't bite me cause Ah knows how tuh handle 'im. Nohow he wouldn't risk breakin' out his fangs 'gin *yo* skinny laigs."

"Naw, now Syke, don't keep dat thing 'round tryin' tuh skeer me tuh death. You knows Ah'm even feared uh earth worms. Thass de biggest snake Ah evah did se. Kill 'im Syke, please."

"Doan ast me tuh do nothin' fuh yuh. Goin' 'round tryin' tuh be so damn asterperious. Naw, Ah ain't gonna kill it. Ah think uh damn sight mo' uh him dan you! Dat's a nice snake an' anybody doan lak 'im kin jes' hit de grit."

The village soon heard that Sykes had the snake, and came to see and ask questions.

"How de hen-fire did you ketch dat six-foot rattler, Syke?" Thomas asked.

"He's full uh frogs so he cain't hardly move, thass how Ah eased up on 'im. 70
But Ah'm a snake charmer an' knows how tuh handle 'em. Shux, dat ain't nothin'. Ah could ketch one eve'y day if Ah so wanted tuh."

"Whut he needs is a heavy hick'ry club leaned real heavy on his head. Dat's de bes' way tuh charm a rattlesnake."

"Naw, Walt, y'all jes' don't understand dese diamon' backs lak Ah do," said Sykes in a superior tone of voice.

The village agreed with Walter, but the snake stayed on. His box remained by the kitchen door with its screen wire covering. Two or three days later it had digested its meal of frogs and literally came to life. It rattled at every movement in the kitchen or the yard. One day as Delia came down the kitchen steps she saw his chalky-white fangs curved like scimitars hung in the wire meshes. This time she did not run away with averted eyes as usual. She stood for a long time in the doorway in a red fury that grew bloodier for every second that she regarded the creature that was her torment.

That night she broached the subject as soon as Sykes sat down to the table.

"Syke, Ah wants you tuh take dat snake 'way fum heah. You done starved 75
me an' Ah put up widcher, you done beat me an Ah took dat, but you don kilt
all mah insides bringin' dat varmint heah."

Sykes poured out a saucer full of coffee and drank it deliberately before he
answered her.

"A whole lot Ah keer 'bout how you feels inside uh out. Dat snake ain't goin'
no damn wheah till Ah gits ready fuh 'im tuh go. So fur as beatin' is concerned,
yuh ain't took near all dat you gointer take ef yuh stay 'round *me*."

Delia pushed back her plate and got up from the table. "Ah hates you,
Sykes," she said calmly. "Ah hates you tuh de same degree dat Ah useter
love yuh. Ah done took an' took till mah belly is full up tuh mah neck. Dat's
de reason Ah got mah letter fum de church an' moved mah membership
tuh Woodbridge—so Ah don't haftuh take no sacrament wid yuh. Ah don't
wantuh see yuh 'round me atall. Lay 'round wid dat 'oman all yuh wants
tuh, but gwan 'way from me an' mah house. Ah hates yuh lak uh suck-egg
dog."

Sykes almost let the huge wad of corn bread and collard greens he was chewing fall out of his mouth in amazement. He had a hard time whipping himself
up to the proper fury to try to answer Delia.

"Well, Ah'm glad you does hate me. Ah'm sho' tiahed uh you hangin' ontuh 80
me. Ah don't want yuh. Look at yuh stringey ole neck! Yo' rawbony laigs an'
arms is enough tuh cut uh man tuh death. You looks jes' lak de devvul's doll-
baby tuh *me*. You cain't hate me no worse dan Ah hates you. Ah been hatin'
you fuh years."

"Yo' ole black hide don't look lak nothin' tuh me, but uh passle uh wrinkled
up rubber, wid yo' big ole yeahs flappin' on each side lak uh paih uh buzzard
wings. Don't think Ah'm gointuh be run 'way fum mah house neither. Ah'm
goin' tuh de white folks 'bout *you*, mah young man, de very nex' time you lay
yo' han's on me. Mah cup is done run ovah." Delia said this with no signs of
fear and Sykes departed from the house, threatening her, but made not the
slightest move to carry out any of them.

That night he did not return at all, and the next day being Sunday, Delia was
glad she did not have to quarrel before she hitched up her pony and drove the
four miles to Woodbridge.

She stayed to the night service—"love feast"—which was very warm and full
of spirit. In the emotional winds her domestic trials were borne far and wide so
that she sang as she drove homeward,

Jurden water, black an' col
Chills de body, not de soul
An'Ah wantah cross Jurden in uh calm time.

She came from the barn to the kitchen door and stopped.

"Whut's de mattah, ol' Satan, you ain't kicken' up yo' racket?" She addressed
the snake's box. Complete silence. She went on into the house with a new hope

in its birth struggles. Perhaps her threat to go to the white folks had fright-ened Sykes! Perhaps he was sorry! Fifteen years of misery and suppression had brought Delia to the place where she would hope *anything* that looked towards a way over or through her wall of inhibitions.

She felt in the match-safe behind the stove at once for a match. There was 85 only one there.

"Dat niggah wouldn't fetch nothin' heah tuh save his rotten neck, but he kin run thew whut Ah brings quick enough. Now he done toted off nigh on tuh haff uh box uh matches. He done had dat 'oman heah in mah house, too."

Nobody but a woman could tell how she knew this even before she struck the match. But she did and it put her into a new fury.

Presently she brought in the tubs to put the white things to soak. This time she decided she need not bring the hamper out of the bedroom; she would go in there and do the sorting. She picked up the pot-bellied lamp and went in. The room was small and the hamper stood hard by the foot of the white iron bed. She could sit and reach through the bedposts—resting as she worked.

"Ah wantah cross Jurden in uh calm time." She was singing again. The mood of the "love feast," had returned. She threw back the lid of the basket almost gaily. Then, moved by both horror and terror, she sprang back toward the door. *There lay the snake in the basket!* He moved sluggishly at first, but even as she turned round and round, jumped up and down in an insanity of fear, he began to stir vigorously. She saw him pouring his awful beauty from the basket upon the bed, then she seized the lamp and ran as fast as she could to the kitchen. The wind from the open door blew out the light and the darkness added to her terror. She sped to the darkness of the yard, slamming the door after her before she thought to set down the lamp. She did not feel safe even on the ground, so she climbed up in the hay barn.

There for an hour or more she lay sprawled upon the hay a gibbering wreck. 90

Finally she grew quiet, and after that came coherent thought. With this stalked through her a cold, bloody rage. Hours of this. A period of introspection, a space of retrospection, then a mixture of both. Out of this an awful calm.

"Well, Ah done de bes' Ah could. If things ain't right, Gawd knows tain't mah fault."

She went to sleep—a twitch sleep—and woke up to a faint gray sky. There was a loud hollow sound below. She peered out. Sykes was at the woodpile, demolishing a wire-covered box.

He hurried to the kitchen door, but hung outside there some minutes before he entered, and stood some minutes more inside before he closed it after him.

The gray in the sky was spreading. Delia descended without fear now, and 95 crouched beneath the low bedroom window. The drawn shade shut out the dawn, shut in the night. But the thin walls held back no sound.

"Dat ol' scratch is woke up now!" She mused at the tremendous whirr inside, which every woodsman knows, is one of the sound illusions. The rattler is a ventriloquist. His whirr sounds to the right, to the left, straight ahead, behind, close under foot—everywhere but where it is. Woe to him who guesses wrong unless he is prepared to hold up his end of the argument! Sometimes he strikes without rattling at all.

Inside, Sykes heard nothing until he knocked a pot lid off the stove while trying to reach the match-safe in the dark. He had emptied his pockets at Bertha's.

The snake seemed to wake up under the stove and Sykes made a quick leap into the bedroom. In spite of the gin he had had, his head was clearing now.

"Mah Gawd!" he chattered, "ef Ah could on'y strack uh light!"

The rattling ceased for a moment as he stood paralyzed. He waited. It seemed that the snake waited also.   100

"Oh, fuh de light! Ah thought he'd be too sick"—Sykes was muttering to himself when the whirr began again, closer, right underfoot this time. Long before this, Sykes' ability to think had been flattened down to primitive instinct and he leaped—onto the bed.

Outside Delia heard a cry that might have come from a maddened chimpanzee, a stricken gorilla. All the terror, all the horror, all the rage that man possibly could express, without a recognizable human sound.

A tremendous stir inside there, another series of animal screams, the intermittent whirr of the reptile. The shade torn violently down from the window, letting in the red dawn, a huge brown hand seizing the window stick, great dull blows upon the wooden floor punctuating the gibberish of sound long after the rattle of the snake had abruptly subsided. All this Delia could see and hear from her place beneath the window, and it made her ill. She crept over to the four o'clocks and stretched herself on the cool earth to recover.

She lay there. "Delia, Delia!" She could hear Sykes calling in a most despairing tone as one who expected no answer. The sun crept on up, and he called. Delia could not move—her legs had gone flabby. She never moved, he called, and the sun kept rising.

"Mah Gawd!" She heard him moan, "Mah Gawd fum Heben!" She heard   105
him stumbling about and got up from her flower-bed. The sun was growing warm. As she approached the door she heard him call out hopefully, "Delia, is dat you Ah heah?"

She saw him on his hands and knees as soon as she reached the door. He crept an inch or two toward her—all that he was able, and she saw his horribly swollen neck and his one open eye shining with hope. A surge of pity too strong to support bore her away from that eye that must, could not, fail to see the tubs. He would see the lamp. Orlando with its doctors was too far. She could scarcely reach the chinaberry tree, where she waited in the growing heat while inside she knew the cold river was creeping up and up to extinguish that eye which must know by now that she knew.

FOR ANALYSIS

1. What purpose do the men on the porch serve in the story? How are we supposed to take their opinions on Delia and Sykes?

2. While this story is about an unfortunate situation, the **tone** is not uniformly grave. How does Hurston manipulate tone? What are the effects of her choice to mix it up?

3. How do you feel about Delia's actions at the end of the story? Do you blame her? Has her love turned to hate, or does she still hope for love?

MAKING ARGUMENTS

One of the men on the porch says, "Tain't no law on earth dat kin make a man be decent if it ain't in 'im" (para. 40). Reflect on the nature of decentness, with special attention to its source. Do you think people are or are not inherently decent? Or do you think the circumstances of their lives play a part in shaping their characters? Make an argument one way or the other.

WRITING TOPIC

Stories are seldom written using dialect anymore. Why do you think that is? What do you think of Hurston's use of dialect?

MAKING CONNECTIONS

Think about this story in connection to a very different story, O'Connor's "A Good Man Is Hard to Find" (p. 141). Both stories feature religious belief prominently, though in very different ways. How does belief inform each story? How do the characters relate to it?

RAYMOND CARVER (1938–1988)

WHAT WE TALK ABOUT
WHEN WE TALK ABOUT LOVE 1981

My friend Mel McGinnis was talking. Mel McGinnis is a cardiologist, and sometimes that gives him the right.

The four of us were sitting around his kitchen table drinking gin. Sunlight filled the kitchen from the big window behind the sink. There were Mel and me and his second wife, Teresa—Terri, we called her—and my wife, Laura. We lived in Albuquerque then. But we were all from somewhere else.

There was an ice bucket on the table. The gin and the tonic water kept going around, and we somehow got on the subject of love. Mel thought real love was nothing less than spiritual love. He said he'd spent five years in a seminary before quitting to go to medical school. He said he still looked back on those years in the seminary as the most important years in his life.

Terri said the man she lived with before she lived with Mel loved her so much he tried to kill her. Then Terri said, "He beat me up one night. He dragged me around the living room by my ankles. He kept saying, 'I love you, I love you, you bitch.' He went on dragging me around the living room. My head kept knocking on things." Terri looked around the table. "What do you do with love like that?"

She was a bone-thin woman with a pretty face, dark eyes, and brown hair 5 that hung down her back. She liked necklaces made of turquoise, and long pendant earrings.

"My God, don't be silly. That's not love, and you know it," Mel said. "I don't know what you'd call it, but I sure know you wouldn't call it love."

"Say what you want to, but I know it was," Terri said. "It may sound crazy to you, but it's true just the same. People are different, Mel. Sure, sometimes he may have acted crazy. Okay. But he loved me. In his own way maybe, but he loved me. There was love there, Mel. Don't say there wasn't."

Mel let out his breath. He held his glass and turned to Laura and me. "The man threatened to kill me," Mel said. He finished his drink and reached for the gin bottle. "Terri's a romantic. Terri's of the kick-me-so-I'll-know-you-love-me school. Terri, hon, don't look that way." Mel reached across the table and touched Terri's cheek with his fingers. He grinned at her.

"Now he wants to make up," Terri said.

"Make up what?" Mel said. "What is there to make up? I know what I know. 10 That's all."

"How'd we get started on this subject, anyway?" Terri said. She raised her glass and drank from it. "Mel always has love on his mind," she said. "Don't you, honey?" She smiled, and I thought that was the last of it.

"I just wouldn't call Ed's behavior love. That's all I'm saying, honey," Mel said. "What about you guys?" Mel said to Laura and me. "Does that sound like love to you?"

"I'm the wrong person to ask," I said. "I didn't even know the man. I've only heard his name mentioned in passing. I wouldn't know. You'd have to know the particulars. But I think what you're saying is that love is an absolute."

Mel said, "The kind of love I'm talking about is. The kind of love I'm talking about, you don't try to kill people."

Laura said, "I don't know anything about Ed, or anything about the situa- 15 tion. But who can judge anyone else's situation?"

I touched the back of Laura's hand. She gave me a quick smile. I picked up Laura's hand. It was warm, the nails polished, perfectly manicured. I encircled the broad wrist with my fingers, and I held her.

"When I left, he drank rat poison," Terri said. She clasped her arms with her hands. "They took him to the hospital in Sante Fe. That's where we lived then, about ten miles out. They saved his life. But his gums went crazy from it. I mean they pulled away from his teeth. After that, his teeth stood out like fangs. My God," Terri said. She waited a minute, then let go of her arms and picked up her glass.

"What people won't do!" Laura said.

"He's out of the action now," Mel said. "He's dead."

Mel handed me the saucer of limes. I took a section, squeezed it over my 20 drink, and stirred the ice cubes with my finger.

"It gets worse," Terri said. "He shot himself in the mouth. But he bungled that too. Poor Ed," she said. Terri shook her head.

"Poor Ed nothing," Mel said. "He was dangerous."

Mel was forty-five years old. He was tall and rangy with curly soft hair. His face and arms were brown from the tennis he played. When he was sober, his gestures, all his movements, were precise, very careful.

"He did love me though, Mel. Grant me that," Terri said. "That's all I'm asking. He didn't love me the way you love me. I'm not saying that. But he loved me. You can grant me that, can't you?"

"What do you mean, he bungled it?" I said. 25

Laura leaned forward with her glass. She put her elbows on the table and held her glass in both hands. She glanced from Mel to Terri and waited with a look of bewilderment on her open face, as if amazed that such things happened to people you were friendly with.

"How'd he bungle it when he killed himself?" I said.

"I'll tell you what happened," Mel said. "He took this twenty-two pistol he'd bought to threaten Terri and me with. Oh, I'm serious, the man was always threatening. You should have seen the way we lived in those days. Like fugitives. I even bought a gun myself. Can you believe it? A guy like me? But I did. I bought one for self-defense and carried it in the glove compartment. Some- times I'd have to leave the apartment in the middle of the night. To go to the hospital, you know? Terri and I weren't married then, and my first wife had the house and kids, the dog, everything, and Terri and I were living in this apartment here. Sometimes, as I say, I'd get a call in the middle of the night and have to go in to the hospital at two or three in the morning. It'd be dark out there in the parking lot, and I'd break into a sweat before I could even get to my car. I never knew if he was going to come up out of the shrubbery or from behind a car and start shooting. I mean, the man was crazy. He was capable of wiring a bomb, anything. He used to call my service at all hours and say he needed to talk to the doctor, and when I'd return the call, he'd say, 'Son of a bitch, your days are numbered.' Little things like that. It was scary, I'm telling you."

"I still feel sorry for him," Terri said.

"It sounds like a nightmare," Laura said. "But what exactly happened after he shot himself?"

Laura is a legal secretary. We'd met in a professional capacity. Before we knew it, it was a courtship. She's thirty-five, three years younger than I am. In addition to being in love, we like each other and enjoy one another's company. She's easy to be with.

"What happened?" Laura said.

Mel said, "He shot himself in the mouth in his room. Someone heard the shot and told the manager. They came in with a passkey, saw what had happened, and called an ambulance. I happened to be there when they brought him in, alive but past recall. The man lived for three days. His head swelled up to twice the size of a normal head. I'd never seen anything like it, and I hope I never do again. Terri wanted to go in and sit with him when she found out about it. We had a fight over it. I didn't think she should see him like that. I didn't think she should see him, and I still don't."

"Who won the fight?" Laura said.

"I was in the room with him when he died," Terri said. "He never came up out of it. But I sat with him. He didn't have anyone else."

"He was dangerous," Mel said. "If you call that love, you can have it."

"It was love," Terri said. "Sure, it's abnormal in most people's eyes. But he was willing to die for it. He did die for it."

"I sure as hell wouldn't call it love," Mel said. "I mean, no one knows what he did it for. I've seen a lot of suicides, and I couldn't say anyone ever knew what they did it for."

Mel put his hands behind his neck and tilted his chair back. "I'm not interested in that kind of love," he said. "If that's love, you can have it."

Terri said, "We were afraid. Mel even made a will out and wrote to his brother in California who used to be a Green Beret. Mel told him who to look for if something happened to him."

Terri drank from her glass. She said, "But Mel's right—we lived like fugitives. We were afraid. Mel was, weren't you, honey? I even called the police at one point, but they were no help. They said they couldn't do anything until Ed actually did something. Isn't that a laugh?" Terri said.

She poured the last of the gin into her glass and waggled the bottle. Mel got up from the table and went to the cupboard. He took down another bottle.

"Well, Nick and I know what love is," Laura said. "For us, I mean," Laura said. She bumped my knee with her knee. "You're supposed to say something now," Laura said, and turned her smile on me.

For an answer, I took Laura's hand and raised it to my lips. I made a big production out of kissing her hand. Everyone was amused.

"We're lucky," I said.

"You guys," Terri said. "Stop that now. You're making me sick. You're still on the honeymoon, for God's sake. You're still gaga, for crying out loud. Just wait. How long have you been together now? How long has it been? A year? Longer than a year?"

"Going on a year and a half," Laura said, flushed and smiling.

"Oh, now," Terri said. "Wait a while."

She held her drink and gazed at Laura.

"I'm only kidding," Terri said.

Mel opened the gin and went around the table with the bottle.

"Here, you guys," he said. "Let's have a toast. I want to propose a toast. A toast to love. To true love," Mel said.

We touched glasses.

"To love," we said.

Outside in the backyard, one of the dogs began to bark. The leaves of the aspen that leaned past the window ticked against the glass. The afternoon sun was like a presence in this room, the spacious light of ease and generosity. We could have been anywhere, somewhere enchanted. We raised our glasses again and grinned at each other like children who had agreed on something forbidden.

"I'll tell you what real love is," Mel said. "I mean, I'll give you a good example. And then you can draw your own conclusions." He poured more gin into his glass. He added an ice cube and a sliver of lime. We waited and sipped our drinks. Laura and I touched knees again. I put a hand on her warm thigh and left it there.

"What do any of us really know about love?" Mel said. "It seems to me we're just beginners at love. We say we love each other and we do, I don't doubt it. I love Terri and Terri loves me, and you guys love each other too. You know the kind of love I'm talking about now. Physical love, that impulse that drives you to someone special, as well as love of the other person's being, his or her essence, as it were. Carnal love and, well, call it sentimental love, the day-to-day caring about the other person. But sometimes I have a hard time accounting for the fact that I must have loved my first wife too. But I did, I know I did. So I suppose I am like Terri in that regard. Terri and Ed." He thought about it and then he went on. "There was a time when I thought I loved my first wife more than life itself. But now I hate her guts. I do. How do you explain that? What happened to that love? What happened to it, is what I'd like to know. I wish someone could tell me. Then there's Ed. Okay, we're back to Ed. He loves Terri so much he tries to kill her and he winds up killing himself." Mel stopped talking and swallowed from his glass. "You guys have been together eighteen months and you love each other. It shows all over you. You glow with it. But you both loved other people before you met each other. You've both been married before, just like us. And you probably loved other people before that too, even. Terri and I have been together five years, been married for four. And the terrible thing, the terrible thing is, but the good thing too, the saving grace, you might say, is that if something happened to one of us—excuse me for saying this—but if something happened to one of us tomorrow I think the other one, the other person, would grieve for a while, you know, but then the surviving party would go out and love again, have someone else soon enough. All this, all of this love we're talking about, it would just be a memory. Maybe not even a memory. Am I wrong? Am I way off base? Because I want you to set me straight if you think I'm wrong. I want to know. I mean, I don't know anything, and I'm the first one to admit it."

"Mel, for God's sake," Terri said. She reached out and took hold of his wrist. "Are you getting drunk? Honey? Are you drunk?"

"Honey, I'm just talking," Mel said. "All right? I don't have to be drunk to say what I think. I mean, we're all just talking, right?" Mel said. He fixed his eyes on her.

"Sweetie, I'm not criticizing," Terri said.   60

She picked up her glass.

"I'm not on call today," Mel said. "Let me remind you of that. I am not on call," he said.

"Mel, we love you," Laura said.

Mel looked at Laura. He looked at her as if he could not place her, as if she was not the woman she was.

"Love you too, Laura," Mel said. "And you, Nick, love you too. You know   65 something?" Mel said. "You guys are our pals," Mel said.

He picked up his glass.

Mel said, "I was going to tell you about something. I mean, I was going to prove a point. You see, this happened a few months ago, but it's still going on right now, and it ought to make us feel ashamed when we talk like we know what we're talking about when we talk above love."

"Come on now," Terri said. "Don't talk like you're drunk if you're not drunk."

"Just shut up for once in your life," Mel said very quietly. "Will you do me a favor and do that for a minute? So as I was saying, there's this old couple who had this car wreck out on the interstate. A kid hit them and they were all torn to shit and nobody was giving them much chance to pull through."

Terri looked at us and then back at Mel. She seemed anxious, or maybe that's 70
too strong a word.

Mel was handing the bottle around the table.

"I was on call that night," Mel said. "It was May or maybe it was June. Terri
and I had just sat down to dinner when the hospital called. There'd been this
thing out on the interstate. Drunk kid, teenager, plowed his dad's pickup into
this camper with this old couple in it. They were up in their mid-seventies, that
couple. The kid—eighteen, nineteen, something—he was DOA. Taken the steering wheel through his sternum. The old couple, they were alive, you understand.
I mean, just barely. But they had everything. Multiple fractures, internal injuries,
hemorrhaging, contusions, lacerations, the works, and they each of them had
themselves concussions. They were in a bad way, believe me. And, of course, their
age was two strikes against them. I'd say she was worse off than he was. Ruptured
spleen along with everything else. Both kneecaps broken. But they'd been wearing their seatbelts and, God knows, that's what saved them for the time being."

"Folks, this is an advertisement for the National Safety Council," Terri said.
"This is your spokesman, Dr. Melvin R. McGinnis, talking." Terri laughed.
"Mel," she said, "sometimes you're just too much. But I love you, hon," she said.

"Honey, I love you," Mel said.

He leaned across the table. Terri met him halfway. They kissed. 75

"Terri's right," Mel said as he settled himself again. "Get those seatbelts on.
But seriously, they were in some shape, those oldsters. By the time I got down
there, the kid was dead, as I said. He was off in a corner, laid out on a gurney. I
took one look at the old couple and told the ER nurse to get me a neurologist
and an orthopedic man and a couple of surgeons down there right away."

He drank from his glass. "I'll try to keep this short," he said. "So we took the
two of them up to the OR and worked like fuck on them most of the night.
They had these incredible reserves, those two. You see that once in a while. So
we did everything that could be done, and toward morning we're giving them
a fifty-fifty chance, maybe less than that for her. So here they are, still alive the
next morning. So, okay, we move them into the ICU, which is where they both
kept plugging away at it for two weeks, hitting it better and better on all the
scopes. So we transfer them out to their own room."

Mel stopped talking. "Here," he said, "let's drink this cheapo gin the hell up.
Then we're going to dinner, right? Terri and I know a new place. That's where
we'll go, to this new place we know about. But we're not going until we finish
up this cut-rate, lousy gin."

Terri said, "We haven't actually eaten there yet. But it looks good. From the
outside, you know."

"I like food," Mel said. "If I had it to do all over again, I'd be a chef, you 80
know? Right, Terri?" Mel said.

He laughed. He fingered the ice in his glass.

"Terri knows," he said. "Terri can tell you. But let me say this. If I could come
back again in a different life, a different time and all, you know what? I'd like to

come back as a knight. You were pretty safe wearing all that armor. It was all right being a knight until gunpowder and muskets and pistols came along."

"Mel would like to ride a horse and carry a lance," Terri said.

"Carry a woman's scarf with you everywhere," Laura said.

"Or just a woman," Mel said.   85

"Shame on you," Laura said.

Terri said, "Suppose you came back as a serf. The serfs didn't have it so good in those days," Terri said.

"The serfs never had it good," Mel said. "But I guess even the knights were vessels to someone. Isn't that the way it worked? But then everyone is always a vessel to someone. Isn't that right? Terri? But what I liked about knights, besides their ladies, was that they had that suit of armor, you know, and they couldn't get hurt very easy. No cars in those days, you know? No drunk teenagers to tear into your ass."

"Vassals," Terri said.

"What?" Mel said.   90

"Vassals," Terri said. "They were called vassals, not vessels."

"Vassals, vessels," Mel said, "what the fuck's the difference? You knew what I meant anyway. All right," Mel said. "So I'm not educated. I learned my stuff. I'm a heart surgeon, sure, but I'm just a mechanic. I go in and I fuck around and I fix things. Shit," Mel said.

"Modesty doesn't become you," Terri said.

"He's just a humble sawbones," I said. "But sometimes they suffocated in all that armor, Mel. They'd even have heart attacks if it got too hot and they were too tired and worn out. I read somewhere that they'd fall off their horses and not be able to get up because they were too tired to stand with all that armor on them. They got trampled by their own horses sometimes."

"That's terrible," Mel said. "That's a terrible thing, Nicky. I guess they'd just   95 lay there and wait until somebody came along and made a shish kebab out of them."

"Some other vessel," Terri said.

"That's right," Mel said. "Some vassal would come along and spear the bastard in the name of love. Or whatever the fuck it was they fought over in those days."

"Same things we fight over these days," Terri said.

Laura said, "Nothing's changed."

The color was still high in Laura's cheeks. Her eyes were bright. She brought   100 her glass to her lips.

Mel poured himself another drink. He looked at the label closely as if studying a long row of numbers. Then he slowly put the bottle down on the table and slowly reached for the tonic water.

"What about the old couple?" Laura said. "You didn't finish that story you started."

Laura was having a hard time lighting her cigarette. Her matches kept going out.

The sunshine inside the room was different now, changing, getting thinner. But the leaves outside the window were still shimmering, and I stared at the pattern they made on the panes and on the Formica counter. They weren't the same patterns, of course.

"What about the old couple?" I said. 105

"Older but wiser," Terri said.

Mel stared at her.

Terri said, "Go on with your story, hon. I was only kidding. Then what happened?"

"Terri, sometimes," Mel said.

"Please, Mel," Terri said. "Don't always be so serious, sweetie. Can't you 110 take a joke?"

"Where's the joke?" Mel said.

He held his glass and gazed steadily at his wife.

"What happened?" Laura said.

Mel fastened his eyes on Laura. He said, "Laura, if I didn't have Terri and if I didn't love her so much, and if Nick wasn't my best friend, I'd fall in love with you, I'd carry you off, honey," he said.

"Tell your story," Terri said. "Then we'll go to that new place, okay?" 115

"Okay," Mel said. "Where was I?" he said. He stared at the table and then he began again.

"I dropped in to see each of them every day, sometimes twice a day if I was up doing other calls anyway. Casts and bandages, head to foot, the both of them. You know, you've seen it in the movies. That's just the way they looked, just like in the movies. Little eye-holes and nose-holes and mouth-holes. And she had to have her legs slung up on top of it. Well, the husband was very depressed for the longest while. Even after he found out that his wife was going to pull through, he was still very depressed. Not about the accident, though. I mean, the accident was one thing, but it wasn't everything. I'd get up to his mouth-hole, you know, and he'd say no, it wasn't the accident exactly but it was because he couldn't see her through his eye-holes. He said that was what was making him feel so bad. Can you imagine? I'm telling you, the man's heart was breaking because he couldn't turn his goddamn head and *see* his goddamn wife."

Mel looked around the table and shook his head at what he was going to say.

"I mean, it was killing the old fart just because he couldn't *look* at the fucking woman."

We all looked at Mel.

"Do you see what I'm saying?" he said. 120

Maybe we were a little drunk by then. I know it was hard keeping things in focus. The light was draining out of the room, going back through the window where it had come from. Yet nobody made a move to get up from the table to turn on the overhead light.

"Listen," Mel said. "Let's finish this fucking gin. There's about enough left here for one shooter all around. Then let's go eat. Let's go to the new place."

"He's depressed," Terri said. "Mel, why don't you take a pill?"

Mel shook his head. "I've taken everything there is."

"We all need a pill now and then," I said.

"Some people are born needing them," Terri said.

She was using her finger to rub at something on the table. Then she stopped rubbing.

"I think I want to call my kids," Mel said. "Is that all right with everybody? I'll call my kids," he said.

Terri said, "What if Marjorie answers the phone? You guys, you've heard us on the subject of Marjorie? Honey, you know you don't want to talk to Marjorie. It'll make you feel even worse."

"I don't want to talk to Marjorie," Mel said. "But I want to talk to my kids."

"There isn't a day goes by that Mel doesn't say he wishes she'd get married again. Or else die," Terri said. "For one thing," Terri said, "she's bankrupting us. Mel says it's just to spite him that she won't get married again. She has a boyfriend who lives with her and the kids, so Mel is supporting the boyfriend too."

"She's allergic to bees," Mel said. "If I'm not praying she'll get married again, I'm praying she'll get herself stung to death by a swarm of fucking bees."

"Shame on you," Laura said.

"Bzzzzzzz," Mel said, turning his fingers into bees and buzzing them at Terri's throat. Then he let his hands drop all the way to his sides.

"She's vicious," Mel said. "Sometimes I think I'll go up there dressed like a beekeeper. You know, that hat that's like a helmet with the plate that comes down over your face, the big gloves, and the padded coat? I'll knock on the door and let loose a hive of bees in the house. But first I'd make sure the kids were out, of course."

He crossed one leg over the other. It seemed to take him a lot of time to do it. Then he put both feet on the floor and leaned forward, elbows on the table, his chin cupped in his hands.

"Maybe I won't call the kids, after all. Maybe it isn't such a hot idea. Maybe we'll just go eat. How does that sound?"

"Sounds fine to me," I said. "Eat or not eat. Or keep drinking. I could head right on out into the sunset."

"What does that mean, honey?" Laura said.

"It just means what I said," I said. "It means I could just keep going. That's all it means."

"I could eat something myself," Laura said. "I don't think I've ever been so hungry in my life. Is there something to nibble on?"

"I'll put out some cheese and crackers," Terri said.

But Terri just sat there. She did not get up to get anything.

Mel turned his glass over. He spilled it out on the table.

"Gin's gone," Mel said.

Terri said, "Now what?"

I could hear my heart beating. I could hear everyone's heart. I could hear the human noise we sat there making, not one of us moving, not even when the room went dark.

FOR ANALYSIS

1. What is your reaction to Mel? Is he likable? What does his profession—a scientist and a cardiologist—represent?

2. What is the significance of Mel's account of the old couple injured in the car accident?

3. Do Mel's feelings about his ex-wife parallel Ed's feelings about Terri? Explain.

MAKING ARGUMENTS

Raymond Carver is known for his **style**, sometimes called minimalism, characterized by spare language, attention to description, and an inclination to let elements of a story speak for themselves. As became clear later in his career and after his death, much of that style was the product of the interventions of his editor, Gordon Lish; in fact, many of Carver's early stories were originally much longer and much more expansive. Based on this story but drawing especially on your ideas about how fiction should work and what it should do, argue either that Lish did Carver a favor or that Carver would have been better off without him.

WRITING TOPIC

In an essay, examine the various relationships in the story: Nick and Laura, Mel and Terri, Terri and Ed, Mel and his ex-wife Marjorie, and the injured old couple. How are they similar, and how are they different? Do they all have anything in common? Conclude your essay with a comment on "what we talk about when we talk about love."

MAKING CONNECTIONS

Compare the marriages in this story, past and present, to the relationship between Sykes and Delia in Hurston's "Sweat" (p. 866). Think in terms of not only love and hate but also any other terms you can imagine. Are there some that are better or worse? What do "better" and "worse" mean to you, in this context?

JOYCE CAROL OATES   (B. 1938)

WHERE ARE YOU GOING,
WHERE HAVE YOU BEEN?   1970

FOR BOB DYLAN[1]

Her name was Connie. She was fifteen and she had a quick nervous giggling habit of craning her neck to glance into mirrors, or checking other people's faces to make sure her own was all right. Her mother, who noticed everything and knew everything and who hadn't much reason any longer to look at her own face, always scolded Connie about it. "Stop gawking at yourself, who are you? You think you're so pretty?" she would say. Connie would raise her eyebrows at these familiar complaints and look right through her mother, into a shadowy vision of herself as she was right at that moment: she knew she was pretty and that was everything. Her mother had been pretty once too, if you could believe those old snapshots in the album, but now her looks were gone and that was why she was always after Connie.

"Why don't you keep your room clean like your sister? How've you got your hair fixed—what the hell stinks? Hair spray? You don't see your sister using that junk."

Her sister June was twenty-four and still lived at home. She was a secretary in the high school Connie attended, and if that wasn't bad enough—with her in the same building—she was so plain and chunky and steady that Connie had to hear her praised all the time by her mother and her mother's sisters. June did this, June did that, she saved money and helped clean the house and cooked and Connie couldn't do a thing, her mind was all filled with trashy daydreams. Their father was away at work most of the time and when he came home he wanted supper and he read the newspaper at supper and after supper he went to bed. He didn't bother talking much to them, but around his bent head Connie's mother kept picking at her until Connie wished her mother was dead and she herself was dead and it was all over. "She makes me want to throw up sometimes," she complained to her friends. She had a high, breathless, amused voice which made everything she said sound a little forced, whether it was sincere or not.

There was one good thing: June went places with girl friends of hers, girls who were just as plain and steady as she, and so when Connie wanted to do that her mother had no objections. The father of Connie's best girl friend drove the girls the three miles to town and left them off at a shopping plaza, so

---

[1] Bob Dylan (b. 1941) is an influential folk-rock musician and songwriter. Oates has commented that she had in mind Dylan's song "It's All Over Now, Baby Blue" when she wrote this story.

that they could walk through the stores or go to a movie, and when he came to pick them up again at eleven he never bothered to ask what they had done.

They must have been familiar sights, walking around that shopping plaza 5 in their shorts and flat ballerina slippers that always scuffed the sidewalk, with charm bracelets jingling on their thin wrists; they would lean together to whisper and laugh secretly if someone passed by who amused or interested them. Connie had long dark blond hair that drew anyone's eye to it, and she wore part of it pulled up on her head and puffed out and the rest of it she let fall down her back. She wore a pull-over jersey blouse that looked one way when she was at home and another way when she was away from home. Everything about her had two sides to it, one for home and one for anywhere that was not home: her walk that could be childlike and bobbing, or languid enough to make anyone think she was hearing music in her head, her mouth which was pale and smirking most of the time, but bright and pink on these evenings out, her laugh which was cynical and drawling at home—"Ha, ha, very funny"—but high-pitched and nervous anywhere else, like the jingling of the charms on her bracelet.

Sometimes they did go shopping or to a movie, but sometimes they went across the highway, ducking fast across the busy road, to a drive-in restaurant where older kids hung out. The restaurant was shaped like a big bottle, though squatter than a real bottle, and on its cap was a revolving figure of a grinning boy who held a hamburger aloft. One night in mid-summer they ran across, breathless with daring, and right away someone leaned out a car window and invited them over, but it was just a boy from high school they didn't like. It made them feel good to be able to ignore him. They went up through the maze of parked and cruising cars to the bright-lit, fly-infested restaurant, their faces pleased and expectant as if they were entering a sacred building that loomed out of the night to give them what haven and what blessing they yearned for. They sat at the counter and crossed their legs at the ankles, their thin shoulders rigid with excitement, and listened to the music that made everything so good: the music was always in the background like music at a church service, it was something to depend upon.

A boy named Eddie came in to talk with them. He sat backwards on his stool, turning himself jerkily around in semi-circles and then stopping and turning again, and after a while he asked Connie if she would like something to eat. She said she did and so she tapped her friend's arm on her way out—her friend pulled her face up into a brave droll look—and Connie said she would meet her at eleven, across the way. "I just hate to leave her like that," Connie said earnestly, but the boy said that she wouldn't be alone for long. So they went out to his car and on the way Connie couldn't help but let her eyes wander over the windshields and faces all around her, her face gleaming with a joy that had nothing to do with Eddie or even this place; it might have been the music. She drew her shoulders up and sucked in her breath with the pure pleasure of being alive, and just at that moment she happened to glance at a face just a few feet from hers. It was a boy with shaggy black hair, in a convertible jalopy painted gold. He stared at her and then his lips widened into a grin. Connie slit her eyes at him and turned away, but she couldn't help glancing back and there he was still watching her. He wagged a finger and laughed and said, "Gonna get you, baby," and Connie turned away without Eddie noticing anything.

She spent three hours with him, at the restaurant where they ate hamburgers and drank Cokes in wax cups that were always sweating, and then down an alley a mile or so away, and when he left her off at five to eleven only the movie house was still open at the plaza. Her girl friend was there, talking with a boy. When Connie came up the two girls smiled at each other and Connie said, "How was the movie?" and the girl said, "*You* should know." They rode off with the girl's father, sleepy and pleased, and Connie couldn't help but look at the darkened shopping plaza with its big empty parking lot and its signs that were faded and ghostly now, and over at the drive-in restaurant where cars were still circling tirelessly. She couldn't hear the music at this distance.

Next morning June asked her how the movie was and Connie said, "So-so."

She and that girl and occasionally another girl went several times a week 10 that way, and the rest of the time Connie spent around the house—it was summer vacation—getting in her mother's way and thinking, dreaming, about the boys she met. But all the boys fell back and dissolved into a single face that was not even a face, but an idea, a feeling, mixed up with the urgent insistent pounding of the music and the humid night air of July. Connie's mother kept dragging her back to the daylight by finding things for her to do or saying, suddenly, "What's this about the Pettinger girl?"

And Connie would say nervously, "Oh, her. That dope." She always drew thick clear lines between herself and such girls, and her mother was simple and kindly enough to believe her. Her mother was so simple, Connie thought, that it was maybe cruel to fool her so much. Her mother went scuffling around the house in old bedroom slippers and complained over the telephone to one sister about the other, then the other called up and the two of them complained about the third one. If June's name was mentioned her mother's tone was approving, and if Connie's name was mentioned it was disapproving. This did not really mean she disliked Connie and actually Connie thought that her mother preferred her to June because she was prettier, but the two of them kept up a pretense of exasperation, a sense that they were tugging and struggling over something of little value to either of them. Sometimes, over coffee, they were almost friends, but something would come up—some vexation that was like a fly buzzing suddenly around their heads—and their faces went hard with contempt.

One Sunday Connie got up at eleven—none of them bothered with church—and washed her hair so that it could dry all day long, in the sun. Her parents and sister were going to a barbecue at an aunt's house and Connie said no, she wasn't interested, rolling her eyes to let her mother know just what she thought of it. "Stay home alone then," her mother said sharply. Connie sat out back in a lawn chair and watched them drive away, her father quiet and bald, hunched around so that he could back the car out, her mother with a look that was still angry and not at all softened through the windshield, and in the back seat poor old June all dressed up as if she didn't know what a barbecue was, with all the running yelling kids and the flies. Connie sat with her eyes closed in the sun, dreaming and dazed with the warmth about her as if this were a kind of love, the caresses of love, and her mind slipped over onto thoughts of the boy she had been with the night before and how nice he had been, how sweet it always was, not the way someone like June would suppose but sweet, gentle, the way it was in movies and promised in songs; and when she opened her eyes she hardly knew where she was, the back yard ran off into weeds and a fence-line of trees and behind it the sky was perfectly blue and still. The asbestos "ranch house" that was now three years old still startled her—it looked small. She shook her head as if to get awake.

It was too hot. She went inside the house and turned on the radio to drown out the quiet. She sat on the edge of her bed, barefoot, and listened for an hour and a half to a program called XYZ Sunday Jamboree, record after record of hard, fast, shrieking songs she sang along with, interspersed by exclamations from "Bobby King": "An' look here you girls at Napoleon's—Son and Charley want you to pay real close attention to this song coming up!"

And Connie paid close attention herself, bathed in a glow of slow-pulsed joy that seemed to rise mysteriously out of the music itself and lay languidly about the airless little room, breathed in and breathed out with each gentle rise and fall of her chest.

After a while she heard a car coming up the drive. She sat up at once,   15 startled, because it couldn't be her father so soon. The gravel kept crunching all the way in from the road—the driveway was long—and Connie ran to the window. It was a car she didn't know. It was an open jalopy, painted a bright gold that caught the sunlight opaquely. Her heart began to pound and her fingers snatched at her hair, checking it, and she whispered "Christ. Christ," wondering how bad she looked. The car came to a stop at the side door and the horn sounded four short taps as if this were a signal Connie knew.

She went into the kitchen and approached the door slowly, then hung out the screen door, her bare toes curling down off the step. There were two boys in the car and now she recognized the driver: he had shaggy, shabby black hair that looked crazy as a wig and he was grinning at her.

"I ain't late, am I?" he said.

"Who the hell do you think you are?" Connie said.

"Toldja I'd be out, didn't I?"

"I don't even know who you are."   20

She spoke sullenly, careful to show no interest or pleasure, and he spoke in a fast bright monotone. Connie looked past him to the other boy, taking her time. He had fair brown hair, with a lock that fell onto his forehead. His sideburns gave him a fierce, embarrassed look, but so far he hadn't even bothered to glance at her. Both boys wore sunglasses. The driver's glasses were metallic and mirrored everything in miniature.

"You wanta come for a ride?" he said.

Connie smirked and let her hair fall loose over one shoulder.

"Don'tcha like my car? New paint job," he said. "Hey."

"What?" 25

"You're cute."

She pretended to fidget, chasing flies away from the door.

"Don'tcha believe me, or what?" he said.

"Look, I don't even know who you are," Connie said in disgust.

"Hey, Ellie's got a radio, see. Mine's broke down." He lifted his friend's arm 30 and showed her the little transistor the boy was holding, and now Connie began to hear the music. It was the same program that was playing inside the house.

"Bobby King?" she said.

"I listen to him all the time. I think he's great."

"He's kind of great," Connie said reluctantly.

"Listen, that guy's *great*. He knows where the action is."

Connie blushed a little, because the glasses made it impossible for her to see 35 just what this boy was looking at. She couldn't decide if she liked him or if he was just a jerk, and so she dawdled in the doorway and wouldn't come down or go back inside. She said, "What's all that stuff painted on your car?"

"Can'tcha read it?" He opened the door very carefully, as if he was afraid it might fall off. He slid out just as carefully, planting his feet firmly on the ground, the tiny metallic world in his glasses slowing down like gelatine hardening and in the midst of it Connie's bright green blouse. "This here is my name, to begin with," he said. ARNOLD FRIEND was written in tarlike black letters on the side, with a drawing of a round grinning face that reminded Connie of a pumpkin, except it wore sunglasses. "I wanta introduce myself, I'm Arnold Friend and that's my real name and I'm gonna be your friend, honey, and inside the car's Ellie Oscar, he's kinda shy." Ellie brought his transistor radio up to his shoulder and balanced it there. "Now these numbers are a secret code, honey," Arnold Friend explained. He read off the numbers 33, 19, 17 and raised his eyebrows at her to see what she thought of that, but she didn't think much of it. The left rear fender had been smashed and around it was written on the gleaming gold background: DONE BY CRAZY WOMAN DRIVER. Connie had to laugh at that. Arnold Friend was pleased at her laughter and looked up at her. "Around the other side's a lot more—you wanta come and see them?"

"No."

"Why not?"

"Why should I?"

"Don'tcha wanta see what's on the car? Don'tcha wanta go for a ride?" 40

"I don't know."

"Why not?"

"I got things to do."

"Like what?"

"Things." 45

He laughed as if she had said something funny. He slapped his thighs. He was standing in a strange way, leaning back against the car as if he were balancing himself. He wasn't tall, only an inch or so taller than she would be if she came down to him. Connie liked the way he was dressed, which was the way all of them dressed: tight faded jeans stuffed into black, scuffed boots, a belt that pulled his waist in and showed how lean he was, and a white pull-over shirt that was a little soiled and showed the hard small muscles of his arms and shoulders. He looked as if he possibly did hard work, lifting and carrying things. Even his neck looked muscular. And his face was a familiar face, some-how: the jaw and chin and cheeks slightly darkened, because he hadn't shaved for a day or two, and the nose long and hawk-like, sniffing as if she were a treat he was going to gobble up and it was all a joke.

"Connie, you ain't telling the truth. This is your day set aside for a ride with me and you know it," he said, still laughing. The way he straightened and recovered from his fit of laughing showed that it had been all fake.

"How do you know what my name is?" she said suspiciously.

"It's Connie."

"Maybe and maybe not."   50

"I know my Connie," he said, wagging his finger. Now she remembered him even better, back at the restaurant, and her cheeks warmed at the thought of how she sucked in her breath just at the moment she passed him—how she must have looked to him. And he had remembered her. "Ellie and I came out here especially for you," he said. "Ellie can sit in back. How about it?"

"Where?"

"Where what?"

"Where're we going?"

He looked at her. He took off the sunglasses and she saw how pale the skin   55
around his eyes was, like holes that were not in shadow but instead in light. His eyes were chips of broken glass that catch the light in an amiable way. He smiled. It was as if the idea of going for a ride somewhere, to some place, was a new idea to him.

"Just for a ride, Connie sweetheart."

"I never said my name was Connie," she said.

"But I know what it is. I know your name and all about you, lots of things," Arnold Friend said. He had not moved yet but stood still leaning back against the side of his jalopy. "I took a special interest in you, such a pretty girl, and found out all about you like I know your parents and sister are gone somewheres and I know where and how long they're going to be gone, and I know who you were with last night, and your best girl friend's name is Betty. Right?"

He spoke in a simple lilting voice, exactly as if he were reciting the words to a song. His smile assured her that everything was fine. In the car, Ellie turned up the volume on his radio and did not bother to look around at them.

"Ellie can sit in the back seat," Arnold Friend said. He indicated his friend   60
with a casual jerk of his chin, as if Ellie did not count and she should not bother with him.

"How'd you find out all that stuff?" Connie said.

"Listen: Betty Schultz and Tony Fitch and Jimmy Pettinger and Nancy Pettinger," he said, in a chant. "Raymond Stanley and Bob Hutter—"

"Do you know all those kids?"

"I know everybody."

"Look, you're kidding. You're not from around here." 65

"Sure."

"But—how come we never saw you before?"

"Sure you saw me before," he said. He looked down at his boots, as if he were a little offended. "You just don't remember."

"I guess I'd remember you," Connie said.

"Yeah?" He looked up at this, beaming. He was pleased. He began to mark 70 time with the music from Ellie's radio, tapping his fists lightly together. Connie looked away from his smile to the car, which was painted so bright it almost hurt her eyes to look at it. She looked at that name, ARNOLD FRIEND. And up at the front fender was an expression that was familiar—MAN THE FLYING SAUCERS. It was an expression kids had used the year before, but didn't use this year. She looked at it for a while as if the words meant something to her that she did not yet know.

"What're you thinking about? Huh?" Arnold Friend demanded. "Not worried about your hair blowing around in the car, are you?"

"No."

"Think I maybe can't drive good?"

"How do I know?"

"You're a hard girl to handle. How come?" he said. "Don't you know I'm your 75 friend? Didn't you see me put my sign in the air when you walked by?"

"What sign?"

"My sign." And he drew an X in the air, leaning out toward her. They were maybe ten feet apart. After his hand fell back to his side, the X was still in the air, almost visible. Connie let the screen door close and stood perfectly still inside it, listening to the music from her radio and the boy's blend together. She stared at Arnold Friend. He stood there so stiffly relaxed, pretending to be relaxed, with one hand idly on the door handle as if he were keeping himself up that way and had no intention of ever moving again. She recognized most things about him, the tight jeans that showed his thighs and buttocks and the greasy leather boots and the tight shirt, and even that slippery friendly smile of his, that sleepy dreamy smile that all the boys used to get across ideas they didn't want to put into words. She recognized all this and also the singsong way he talked, slightly mocking, kidding, but serious and a little melancholy, and she recognized the way he tapped one fist against the other in homage to the perpetual music behind him. But all these things did not come together.

She said suddenly, "Hey, how old are you?"

His smile faded. She could see then that he wasn't a kid, he was much older— thirty, maybe more. At this knowledge her heart began to pound faster.

"That's a crazy thing to ask. Can'tcha see I'm your own age?" 80

"Like hell you are."

"Or maybe a couple years older, I'm eighteen."

"Eighteen?" she said doubtfully.

He grinned to reassure her and lines appeared at the corners of his mouth. His teeth were big and white. He grinned so broadly his eyes became slits and she saw how thick the lashes were, thick and black as if painted with a black tarlike material. Then he seemed to become embarrassed, abruptly, and looked over his shoulder at Ellie. "*Him*, he's crazy," he said. "Ain't he a riot, he's a nut, a real character." Ellie was still listening to the music. His sunglasses told nothing about what he was thinking. He wore a bright orange shirt unbuttoned halfway to show his chest, which was a pale, bluish chest and not muscular like Arnold Friend's. His shirt collar was turned up all around and the very tips of the collar pointed out past his chin as if they were protecting him. He was pressing the transistor radio up against his ear and sat there in a kind of daze, right in the sun.

"He's kinda strange," Connie said.   85

"Hey, she says you're kinda strange! Kinda strange!" Arnold Friend cried. He pounded on the car to get Ellie's attention. Ellie turned for the first time and Connie saw with shock that he wasn't a kid either—he had a fair, hairless face, cheeks reddened slightly as if the veins grew too close to the surface of his skin, the face of a forty-year-old baby. Connie felt a wave of dizziness rise in her at this sight and she stared at him as if waiting for something to change the shock of the moment, make it all right again. Ellie's lips kept shaping words, mumbling along, with the words blasting in his ear.

"Maybe you two better go away," Connie said faintly.

"What? How come?" Arnold Friend cried. "We come out here to take you for a ride. It's Sunday." He had the voice of the man on the radio now. It was the same voice, Connie thought. "Don'tcha know it's Sunday all day and honey, no matter who you were with last night today you're with Arnold Friend and don't you forget it!—Maybe you better step out here," he said, and this last was in a different voice. It was a little flatter, as if the heat was finally getting to him.

"No. I got things to do."

"Hey."   90

"You two better leave."

"We ain't leaving until you come with us."

"Like hell I am—"

"Connie, don't fool around with me. I mean, I mean, don't fool *around*," he said, shaking his head. He laughed incredulously. He placed his sunglasses on top of his head, carefully, as if he were indeed wearing a wig, and brought the stems down behind his ears. Connie stared at him, another wave of dizziness and fear rising in her so that for a moment he wasn't even in focus but was just a blur, standing there against his gold car, and she had the idea that he had driven up the driveway all right but had come from nowhere before that and belonged nowhere and that everything about him and even about the music that was so familiar to her was only half real.

"If my father comes and sees you—"   95

"He ain't coming. He's at the barbecue."

"How do you know that?"

"Aunt Tillie's. Right now they're—uh—they're drinking. Sitting around," he said vaguely, squinting as if he were staring all the way to town and over to Aunt Tillie's backyard. Then the vision seemed to get clear and he nodded energetically. "Yeah. Sitting around. There's your sister in a blue dress, huh? And high heels, the poor sad bitch—nothing like you, sweetheart! And your mother's helping some fat woman with the corn, they're cleaning the corn—husking the corn—"

"What fat woman?" Connie cried.

"How do I know what fat woman. I don't know every goddam fat woman in   100 the world!" Arnold Friend laughed.

"Oh, that's Mrs. Hornby. . . . Who invited her?" Connie said. She felt a little light-headed. Her breath was coming quickly.

"She's too fat. I don't like them fat. I like them the way you are, honey," he said, smiling sleepily at her. They stared at each other for awhile, through the screen door. He said softly, "Now what you're going to do is this: you're going to come out that door. You're going to sit up front with me and Ellie's going to sit in the back, the hell with Ellie, right? This isn't Ellie's date. You're my date. I'm your lover, honey."

"What? You're crazy—"

"Yes, I'm your lover. You don't know what that is but you will," he said. "I know that too. I know all about you. But look: it's real nice and you couldn't ask for nobody better than me, or more polite. I always keep my word. I'll tell you how it is, I'm always nice at first, the first time. I'll hold you so tight you won't think you have to try to get away or pretend anything because you'll know you can't. And I'll come inside you where it's all secret and you'll give in to me and you'll love me—"

"Shut up! You're crazy!" Connie said. She backed away from the door. She   105 put her hands against her ears as if she'd heard something terrible, something not meant for her. "People don't talk like that, you're crazy," she muttered. Her heart was almost too big now for her chest and its pumping made sweat break out all over her. She looked out to see Arnold Friend pause and then take a step toward the porch lurching. He almost fell. But, like a clever drunken man, he managed to catch his balance. He wobbled in high boots and grabbed hold of one of the porch posts.

"Honey?" he said. "You still listening?"

"Get the hell out of here!"

"Be nice, honey. Listen."

"I'm going to call the police—"

He wobbled again and out of the side of his mouth came a fast spat curse,   110 an aside not meant for her to hear. But even this "Christ!" sounded forced. Then he began to smile again. She watched this smile come, awkward as if he were smiling from inside a mask. His whole face was a mask, she thought wildly, tanned down onto his throat but then running out as if he had plastered make-up on his face but had forgotten about his throat.

"Honey—? Listen, here's how it is. I always tell the truth and I promise you this: I ain't coming in the house after you."

"You better not! I'm going to call the police if you—if you don't—"

"Honey," he said, talking right through her voice, "honey, I'm not coming in there but you are coming out here. You know why?"

She was panting. The kitchen looked like a place she had never seen before, some room she had run inside but which wasn't good enough, wasn't going to help her. The kitchen window had never had a curtain, after three years, and there were dishes in the sink for her to do—probably—and if you ran your hand across the table you'd probably feel something sticky there.

"You listening, honey? Hey?" 115

"— going to call the police—"

"Soon as you touch the phone I don't need to keep my promise and can come inside. You won't want that."

She rushed forward and tried to lock the door. Her fingers were shaking. "But why lock it," Arnold Friend said gently, talking right into her face. "It's just a screen door. It's just nothing." One of his boots was at a strange angle, as if his foot wasn't in it. It pointed out to the left, bent at the ankle. "I mean, anybody can break through a screen door and glass and wood and iron or anything else he needs to, anybody at all and specially Arnold Friend. If the place got lit up with a fire honey you'd come running out into my arms, right into my arms and safe at home—like you knew I was your lover and'd stopped fooling around. I don't mind a nice shy girl but I don't like no fooling around." Part of those words were spoken with a slight rhythmic lilt, and Connie somehow recognized them—the echo of a song from last year, about a girl rushing into her boy friend's arms and coming home again—

Connie stood barefoot on the linoleum floor, staring at him. "What do you want?" she whispered.

"I want you," he said. 120

"What?"

"Seen you that night and thought, that's the one, yes sir. I never needed to look any more."

"But my father's coming back. He's coming to get me. I had to wash my hair first—" She spoke in a dry, rapid voice, hardly raising it for him to hear.

"No, your daddy is not coming and yes, you had to wash your hair and you washed it for me. It's nice and shining and all for me, I thank you, sweetheart," he said, with a mock bow, but again he almost lost his balance. He had to bend and adjust his boots. Evidently his feet did not go all the way down; the boots must have been stuffed with something so that he would seem taller. Connie stared out at him and behind him Ellie in the car, who seemed to be looking off toward Connie's right, into nothing. This Ellie said, pulling the words out of the air one after another as if he were just discovering them, "You want me to pull out the phone?"

"Shut your mouth and keep it shut," Arnold Friend said, his face red from 125 bending over or maybe from embarrassment because Connie had seen his boots. "This ain't none of your business."

"What—what are you doing? What do you want?" Connie said. "If I call the police they'll get you, they'll arrest you—"

"Promise was not to come in unless you touch that phone, and I'll keep that promise," he said. He resumed his erect position and tried to force his shoulders back. He sounded like a hero in a movie, declaring something important. He spoke too loudly and it was as if he were speaking to someone behind Connie. "I ain't made plans for coming in that house where I don't belong but just for you to come out to me, the way you should. Don't you know who I am?"

"You're crazy," she whispered. She backed away from the door but did not want to go into another part of the house, as if this would give him permission to come through the door. "What do you . . . You're crazy, you . . ."

"Huh? What're you saying, honey?"

Her eyes darted everywhere in the kitchen. She could not remember what it 130 was, this room.

"This is how it is, honey: you come out and we'll drive away, have a nice ride. But if you don't come out we're gonna wait till your people come home and then they're all going to get it."

"You want that telephone pulled out?" Ellie said. He held the radio away from his ear and grimaced, as if without the radio the air was too much for him.

"I toldja shut up, Ellie," Arnold Friend said, "you're deaf, get a hearing aid, right? Fix yourself up. This little girl's no trouble and's gonna be nice to me, so Ellie keep to yourself, this ain't your date—right? Don't hem in on me. Don't hog. Don't crush. Don't bird dog. Don't trail me," he said in a rapid meaningless voice, as if he were running through all the expressions he'd learned but was no longer sure which one of them was in style, then rushing on to new ones, making them up with his eyes closed, "Don't crawl under my fence, don't squeeze in my chipmunk hole, don't sniff my glue, suck my popsicle, keep your own greasy fingers on yourself!" He shaded his eyes and peered in at Connie, who was backed against the kitchen table. "Don't mind him honey he's just a creep. He's a dope. Right? I'm the boy for you and like I said you come out here nice like a lady and give me your hand, and nobody else gets hurt, I mean, your nice old bald-headed daddy and your mummy and your sister in her high heels. Because listen: why bring them in this?"

"Leave me alone," Connie whispered.

"Hey, you know that old woman down the road, the one with the chickens 135 and stuff—you know her?"

"She's dead!"

"Dead? What? You know her?" Arnold Friend said.

"She's dead—"

"Don't you like her?"

"She's dead—she's—she isn't here any more—" 140

"But don't you like her, I mean, you got something against her? Some grudge or something?" Then his voice dipped as if he were conscious of a rudeness. He touched the sunglasses perched on top of his head as if to make sure they were still there. "Now you be a good girl."

"What are you going to do?"

"Just two things, or maybe three," Arnold Friend said. "But I promise it won't last long and you'll like me that way you get to like people you're close to. You will. It's all over for you here, so come on out. You don't want your people in any trouble, do you?"

She turned and bumped against a chair or something, hurting her leg, but she ran into the back room and picked up the telephone. Something roared in her ear, a tiny roaring, and she was so sick with fear that she could do nothing but listen to it—the telephone was clammy and very heavy and her fingers groped down to the dial but were too weak to touch it. She began to scream into the phone, into the roaring. She cried out, she cried for her mother, she felt her breath start jerking back and forth in her lungs as if it were something Arnold Friend were stabbing her with again and again with no tenderness. A noisy sorrowful wailing rose all about her and she was locked inside it the way she was locked inside that house.

After a while she could hear again. She was sitting on the floor with her wet back against the wall. 145

Arnold Friend was saying from the door, "That's a good girl. Put the phone back."

She kicked the phone away from her.

"No, honey. Pick it up. Put it back right."

She picked it up and put it back. The dial tone stopped.

"That's a good girl. Now come outside." 150

She was hollow with what had been fear, but what was now just an emptiness. All that screaming had blasted it out of her. She sat, one leg cramped under her, and deep inside her brain was something like a pinpoint of light that kept going and would not let her relax. She thought, I'm not going to see my mother again. She thought, I'm not going to sleep in my bed again. Her bright green blouse was all wet.

Arnold Friend said, in a gentle-loud voice that was like a stage voice, "The place where you came from ain't there any more, and where you had in mind to go is cancelled out. This place you are now—inside your daddy's house—is nothing but a cardboard box I can knock down any time. You know that and always did know it. You hear me?"

She thought, I have got to think. I have to know what to do.

"We'll go out to a nice field, out in the country here where it smells so nice and it's sunny," Arnold Friend said. "I'll have my arms around you so you won't need to try to get away and I'll show you what love is like, what it does. The hell with this house! It looks solid all right," he said. He ran a fingernail down the screen and the noise did not make Connie shiver, as it would have the day before. "Now put your hand on your heart, honey. Feel that? That feels solid too but we know better, be nice to me, be sweet like you can because

what else is there for a girl like you but to be sweet and pretty and give in?—
and get away before her people come back?"

She felt her pounding heart. Her hand seemed to enclose it. She thought   155
for the first time in her life that it was nothing that was hers, that belonged to
her, but just a pounding, living thing inside this body that wasn't really hers
either.

"You don't want them to get hurt," Arnold Friend went on. "Now get up,
honey. Get up all by yourself."

She stood up.

"Now turn this way. That's right. Come over here to me—Ellie, put that
away, didn't I tell you? You dope. You miserable creepy dope," Arnold said.
His words were not angry but only part of an incantation. The incantation was
kindly. "Now come out through the kitchen to me honey and let's see a smile,
try it, you're a brave sweet little girl and now they're eating corn and hotdogs
cooked to bursting over an outdoor fire, and they don't know one thing about
you and never did and honey, you're better than them because not a one of
them would have done this for you."

Connie felt the linoleum under her feet; it was cool. She brushed her hair
back out of her eyes. Arnold Friend let go of the post tentatively and opened
his arms for her, his elbows pointing in toward each other and his wrists limp,
to show that this was an embarrassed embrace and a little mocking, he didn't
want to make her self-conscious.

She put out her hand against the screen. She watched herself push the door   160
slowly open as if she were safe back somewhere in the other doorway, watching this body and this head of long hair moving out into the sunlight where
Arnold Friend waited.

"My sweet little blue-eyed girl," he said, in a half-sung sigh that had nothing to do with her brown eyes but was taken up just the same by the vast sunlit
reaches of the land behind him and on all sides of him, so much land that Connie had never seen before and did not recognize except to know that she was
going to it.

For Analysis

1. Describe Connie in your own words. What are the sources of her values? What
sort of love experience does she imagine?

2. When she agrees to go with Eddie, what do you suppose they did in the "alley a
mile or so away" (para. 8)?

3. How does Arnold Friend differ from Eddie?

4. Why is attention paid in the story to Arnold's boots?

5. How does Ellie's repeated proposal that Arnold pull out the phone affect your
understanding of Arnold and Ellie's motives?

6. Does Connie go to Arnold simply to protect her family from his threats? Explain.

7. What is going to happen to Connie? Why?

8. The story is told by a **third-person narrator**—yet it is limited, essentially, to Connie's viewpoint. Would multiple viewpoints—her mother's, June's, Eddie's, her friend's, Arnold's—enhance or impair the story's impact?

MAKING ARGUMENTS

Do you believe that Connie knows what is likely to happen to her when she steps outside her house? Is she simply too naïve to see it? Is one of these alternatives somehow worse than the other? Using evidence from the story, argue that Arnold Friend is an incarnation of the devil or some fairy-tale villain.

WRITING TOPIC

In your experience, do some women find dangerous and unstable men more attractive than gentle and kind men? Support your arguments with **allusions** to Oates's story and other stories you have read.

MAKING CONNECTIONS

Compare the situation in this story to that in Galchen's "Wild Berry Blue" (p. 130). Both situations are in some ways dangerous; both are in some ways about innocence. How are they similar in these regards? How are they different?

LYDIA MILLET (B. 1968)

LOVE IN INFANT MONKEYS 2009

Harry Harlow had a general hypothesis: Mothers are useful, in scientific terms. They have an intrinsic value, even beyond their breast milk. Call it their company.

In this hypothesis he was bucking a trend in American psychology. For decades experts on parenting had been advising mothers to show their children as little affection as possible. Too much affection was coddling, and coddling weakened a child. "When you are tempted to pet your child," said a president of the American Psychological Association in a speech, "remember that mother love is a dangerous instrument." This school of thought ran counter to what was believed by those not indebted for their child-rearing strategies to a rigorously monitored testing process. But it was dominant in the scholarship. To refute it, Harlow decided, the value of love would have to be demonstrated in a controlled experimental setting.

He worked long hours, seldom leaving his laboratory. With his experiments he made a name for himself, appearing on television programs and traveling the country on speaking engagements. He was seen as a rebel and an iconoclast. He spoke boldly of mother love, calling it "contact comfort." He stressed its value to emotional health.

But he spoke harshly of his test subjects. "The only thing I care about is whether a monkey will turn out a property I can publish," he said. "I don't have any love for them. I never have. How could you love a monkey?"

To know how love works, a scientist must study its absence. This is simple 5 scientific method; Harry admitted it. The suffering of lesser beings is often the price of knowledge. As he put it, "If my work will save only one million human children, I can't get overly concerned about ten monkeys."

Others were doing bold animal experiments at the same time, in the fifties, when Harry started, and after. Rats were dropped in boiling water, cats pinned down for months until their legs withered, dogs irradiated until their skin crisped, monkeys shot in the heads and stomachs or immobilized to have their spinal cords severed. When it came to the treatment of research animals, Harry was squarely in the mainstream. Only his willingness to speak bluntly was avant-garde.

He gathered disciples around him, young women and men who would continue his work, and decades later he would still be revered by psychology. While acknowledging the problem of what some might call animal cruelty, later scholars would view his collateral damage as a necessary unpleasantness. His chief biographer, a woman journalist, described him as a rose in a cornfield.

900

He was a high-functioning alcoholic, and there were long periods in his life when he was rarely sober. He had wives—first one, then another, then the first one again. He had two sets of children he never saw.

Harry Frederick Harlow had been born Harry Frederick Israel. Around the time of his doctoral dissertation he had changed his last name, not because he was Jewish—for he was not, in fact, Jewish—but because the name Israel sounded Jewish, and this made it hard to secure a good job. He did not dislike Jews; indeed, he admired them for their intelligence and their education. But others in academia had certain prejudices. A famous professor who was also his first mentor did not wish him to continue to be mistaken for a Jew, so Harry deferred to him.

It was a minor accommodation. 10

One way to prove the hypothesis was to take a newborn monkey away from its mother and never give it back. Put it in a bare box, observe it. Anxiety first, shown in trembling and shaking; then come the screams. Watch it huddle, small limbs clutching. Make careful notations. Next, construct a wire mannequin that holds a milk bottle. See if the baby thinks the mannequin is its mother. When it does not think so, give it a mannequin draped with terry cloth, but no milk. See it cling to this milkless cloth mannequin.

Repeat experiment with numerous infants. Make notations.

Second, place infant monkeys in isolation, with neither monkeys nor human contact save the sight of the researchers' hands entering the box to change bedding or food. Leave them there for thirty days. Make careful notations. When the infants are removed, watch two among them starve themselves till they expire. Notations. Repeat with longer isolation periods. First six months, then a year. If necessary, force-feed upon removal from box. Observe: If left in boxes for twelve months, infants will no longer move. Only life signs: pulse and respiration. Upon removal from box, such damaged infants may have to be reisolated for the duration of their short lives. Notations.

Third, attempt to breed the isolate monkeys to produce needed new experimental subjects. When the monkeys show no inclination to mate, inseminate the females. Observe the birth of infants. Observe that the longest-isolated mothers kill infants by chewing off fingers and toes or crushing heads with their teeth. Notations.

Fourth, create bad-mother surrogates: mothers with spikes, mothers that 15 blast cold wind. Put baby monkeys on them. Observe: Time after time, baby monkeys return. Bad mother is better than none.

Only 8:00 pm, and he was already slurring. He would swing by that party. What the hell. Suomi had said he'd be there.

But first, check the experiments.

Walking along the row of vertical chambers, he gave cursory glances inside—one, two, three subjects in a row had given up trying to climb out of their wells of isolation. The pits were designed, of course, to make it impossible to escape.

One subject scrambled and fell back, a weak young female. She looked up with her great round black eyes. Blink blink. She was afraid, but still plucky. Still game to try to get out, change her situation. The others were abject at the bottom of their separate holes, knew by now they could never climb the sides of the wells. As far as they knew, they were in there for good. Plucky got you nowhere if you were a lab monkey.

Then the boxes where Bill had dosed the subjects with reserpine. These mon- 20 keys, too, huddled unmoving. Serotonin had been suppressed; this seemed to equate almost uniformly with complete listlessness, complete passivity. Might be other factors, but still: very interesting.

Back past the so-called pits of despair, where the young female—what had they named her? Minestrone?—was still trying to climb the walls and falling repeatedly. She squeaked at him. Well, not at him, technically. She did not know he was there; she could not see him. She could see no one. She was alone.

Harlow got in the car. Drove. Wasn't far. Hated faculty parties, hardly ever went to them: frivolous. Took him away from his work.

He said this to a new female grad student who met him on the walkway, exclaiming at his presence. She had long curly hair and wore no brassiere.

"Dr. Harlow! I can't believe you actually made it!"

"Work allatime," he said, nodding and shrugging at once. Not as easy as he'd 25 thought it would be. Pulled it together, though. "Lucky. Always have smart wives to help me with it."

She shot him a look of pity: Everyone knew the second smart wife was on her cancer deathbed.

"Some of the faculty," he went on, "these guys don't even work on Sundays. Not serious."

She was looking at him like he was a baby bird fallen from its nest. The free-love ones were maternal. Always acting like everyone's little mommy.

Save it up for the kiddies, he thought. Wasted on me.

These days, Peggy dying like this, maybe he should take a break more 30 often—the depression, for one thing. Felt like the top of his head was weighing him down. Headaches constantly. Chest squashed and nervous stomach. Nothing compared to the chemo, but still. Hair and skin greasy. Plus he was tired, face ached with it. Didn't know if he could have kept his head up if he'd stayed at his desk. Fell asleep with a cigarette in his mouth last night, woke up with a stack of papers smoldering. Something smelled wrong. Burned his eyebrow half off, it turned out.

He patted his pocket for his cigarettes. Full pack. His students were going to be here. Chance to talk to Steve again about the chambers. Steve had said not to call them *dungeons*. Bad for public opinion.

Bullshit, but Steve was good at that side of it. Spade a spade, goddammit.

Saw a garden hose sticking out of a spigot against the side of the house. Turned it on, with some difficulty. Wrestled with the hose till cool water sputtered into his mouth. Cleared his head. Tongue felt less mealy. He wiggled the tongue around in his mouth. Testing it.

"Harry!—I can't believe this—Harry!"

Fat woman from the department, what did she do? Personnel? Payroll? 35 Lumbering.

"Ha, ha," he said, dropping the hose, stepping up onto the stoop and lurching into the doorjamb.

"So you're finally out of your cave! Look who's here! It's *Harry*! Can you guys believe this? Come on in!"

There was the good-looking girl from East Germany who was interested in the nuclear-family experiments, smoking in the corner with Jim. Poor Jim, that plagiarism thing with Peggy. Unfair. But nothing he could do about it. Couldn't get in the middle. He shrugged, itchy.

The jacket: How long had he been wearing it? Felt oily. Maybe it was the shirt. Was it supposed to be white? He could not remember. Gray, beige or white? What color was the shirt to begin with?

"Get you a highball, Harry?" 40

It was a hard-to-breathe night. Humid, filmy. He squinted. Barely see the kids in the corner, but all of them seemed to be looking at him.

The fat payroll said something about gin. He nodded. Headache getting worse. Bands of light spanning his field of vision.

"Harry," said a guy from the right. "Harry Harlow, right? Hey, I read 'Love in Infant Monkeys.' Great paper."

"Huh," grunted Harry, "Seen Suomi?"

"Steve's not here yet," said the guy, either frowning or leering. No idea who it 45 was. Might be the chancellor, for all he knew. Wished he would disappear.

"Huh," Harry muttered. Guy was already veering toward something out the side door, where a fountain was playing. A twinkle of water? Mermaids?

"Lie down a little," he told the payroll woman, hovering with a heavy tumbler. He accepted it gratefully, drank it down and gave it right back. Good to be prompt. Aftertaste was hinky. "Spare daybed, maybe? Dark room? Cot thing?"

"Certainly," said the woman. "There, there. You poor dear." She leaned close and whispered with obscene intimacy: "How's she *doing*?"

Wasn't a baby bird, for Chrissake. No broken wing. Piece of his mind; tell her straight she resembled a water buffalo. Should be roaming the Serengeti with her quadruped friends. "Holding up, holding up," he mumbled. "Brave girl, Peggy." Hadn't seen her for more than five minutes since what, Tuesday? Busy. She knew; she understood perfectly.

He persevered to the room at the back. Secluded. The water buffalo showed 50 him in. Closed the door in her face. "No buffalos," he said, quietly but firmly.

He fell down on the bed and felt a brief satisfaction.

When he woke, the party was over. Brimming ashtrays everywhere. Skinny kid fast asleep on the couch, legs straight, sneakers splayed on the sofa arm. He stood over the kitchen sink, full of squeezed-out lemon halves and olives.

He splashed water on his face and gargled out of a used glass. Didn't see a clean one. Who cared. His mouth was pure alcohol, would neutralize the germs. Made his way out of the bungalow, thirsty as hell. Needed something real to drink.

White light; he blinked on the stoop. It was early morning. Sunday? Legs felt heavy, but he would go to the lab. Still had a faint headache, but bearable now.

Lab was empty. Students must be sitting on their asses this weekend. Pure mediocrity.

Walking the gauntlet of the pits of despair he glanced into Minestrone's 55 setup. Saw the top of her head. She was just sitting there. He kept watching; she did not move. Not a spark animated the creature. Finally given up. Now broken. Her spindly arms hung loose from the sockets, doing nothing. Hunched little figure, staring. Nothing there. It had gone.

Had a flask in a special file cabinet. Headed for it. Deep swig.

In the nightmare, which he'd had in other forms before, he stood beside his beautiful boxes, the boxes of his own design, the boxes that B. F. Skinner himself had admired. He mistook each infant monkey for a beloved soul. In that way the nightmare was confusing. He saw each infant in the heart of its mother, precious, unique, held so close because the mother was willing to die for it. The mother, in the dream, knew what he was doing as he took the infant from her. She was fully aware of what was happening to her and her baby. It was as though she were being forced to watch the infant waste away, left alone in the box—not for the length of its life, perhaps, but for the length of its self, until the self flew out and was forever gone.

In the nightmare it was always the mother monkey he faced, not the infants. The mother, with her wild, desperate eyes. He felt what he could think of only as her passion, like a heat emanating. The mother was crazy with love, mad with a singular devotion. All she wanted was the safety of her infant. She would chew off her feet for it. She would do anything.

But she was trapped, simply trapped. He had put her in a cage, and the cage was too strong for her. When he took the baby from her arms, her panic rose so high it could rise no higher; if she knew how to beg she would beg till the end of the world, scream until her throat split. *Give me my baby back.*

He knew the feeling of loss that would last till she died. He knew it the way 60 he knew a distant country. They had their own customs there.

FOR ANALYSIS

1. What is the nature of the **paradox** concerning the topic of Harry Harlow's research and his feeling about his test subjects?

2. Why are the details about Harlow's personal past life important: his drinking, his name change, his relationship with his children? Why do you think Millet includes them?

3. What do Harlow's experiments prove?

4. What is the significance of Harlow's dream?

MAKING ARGUMENTS

1. What is the deep connection between Harlow's personal life and his experiments? Make an argument to answer this question, using your observations about the text as support.

2. Animal experimentation has led to many scientific breakthroughs. At the same time, many see it as cruel and unnecessary. Do some research on the topic and construct an argument against or in defense of the practice.

WRITING TOPICS

1. "Love in Infant Monkeys" is not **didactic** fiction—that is, it does not attempt to teach us the right way to think about something. Can you detect a position nonetheless? What is it? How does the story convey it without being direct?

2. Millet makes excellent use of free indirect discourse, or the representation of a **character's** thoughts not between quotation marks or after "He thought that" but in the **narrator's** statements, which slide in and out of observations and verbal formulations that originate with the character. List a few places where she does this, and reflect on the effects of her use of the device. How does it work? What does it do to and for readers?

MAKING CONNECTIONS

1. Read this story alongside the "Making Change" case study in the "Conformity and Rebellion" chapter (p. 506). Is there anything in that cluster about effecting social change that connects to "Love in Infant Monkeys"?

2. Compare Millet's story and Egan's story "Safari" (p. 393). How do the **characters** think about nonhuman animal life? Do they value it? Do the stories critique and/or champion their ways of thinking about nonhuman animals?

Junot Díaz   (B. 1968)

Drown   1996

M y mother tells me Beto's home, waits for me to say something, but I
keep watching the TV. Only when she's in bed do I put on my jacket
and swing through the neighborhood to see. He's a pato now but two years ago
we were friends and he would walk into the apartment without knocking, his
heavy voice rousing my mother from the Spanish of her room and drawing me
up from the basement, a voice that crackled and made you think of uncles or
grandfathers.

We were raging then, crazy the way we stole, broke windows, the way we
pissed on people's steps and then challenged them to come out and stop us.
Beto was leaving for college at the end of the summer and was delirious from
the thought of it—he hated everything about the neighborhood, the break-
apart buildings, the little strips of grass, the piles of garbage around the cans,
and the dump, especially the dump.

I don't know how you can do it, he said to me. I would just find me a job
anywhere and go.

Yeah, I said. I wasn't like him. I had another year to go in high school, no
promises elsewhere.

Days we spent in the mall or out in the parking lot playing stickball, but   5
nights were what we waited for. The heat in the apartments was like something
heavy that had come inside to die. Families arranged on their porches, the
glow from their TVs washing blue against the brick. From my family apartment you could smell the pear trees that had been planted years ago, four to
a court, probably to save us all from asphyxiation. Nothing moved fast, even
the daylight was slow to fade, but as soon as night settled Beto and I headed
down to the community center and sprang the fence into the pool. We were
never alone, every kid with legs was there. We lunged from the boards and
swam out of the deep end, wrestling and farting around. At around midnight
abuelas, with their night hair swirled around spiky rollers, shouted at us from
their apartment windows. ¡Sinvergüenzas! Go home!

I pass his apartment but the windows are dark; I put my ear to the busted-up
door and hear only the familiar hum of the air conditioner. I haven't decided yet
if I'll talk to him. I can go back to my dinner and two years will become three.

Even from four blocks off I can hear the racket from the pool—radios
too—and wonder if we were ever that loud. Little has changed, not the stink
of chlorine, not the bottles exploding against the lifeguard station. I hook my
fingers through the plastic-coated hurricane fence. Something tells me that he
will be here; I hop the fence, feeling stupid when I sprawl on the dandelions
and the grass.

Nice one, somebody calls out.

Fuck me, I say. I'm not the oldest motherfucker in the place, but it's close. I take off my shirt and my shoes and then knife in. Many of the kids here are younger brothers of the people I used to go to school with. Two of them swim past, black and Latino, and they pause when they see me, recognizing the guy who sells them their shitty dope. The crackheads have their own man, Lucero, and some other guy who drives in from Paterson, the only full-time commuter in the area.

The water feels good. Starting at the deep end I glide over the slick-tiled 10 bottom without kicking up a spume or making a splash. Sometimes another swimmer churns past me, more a disturbance of water than a body. I can still go far without coming up. While everything above is loud and bright, everything below is whispers. And always the risk of coming up to find the cops stabbing their searchlights out across the water. And then everyone running, wet feet slapping against the concrete, yelling, Fuck you, officers, you puto sucios, fuck you.

When I'm tired I wade through to the shallow end, past some kid who's kissing his girlfriend, watching me as though I'm going to try to cut in, and I sit near the sign that runs the pool during the day. *No Horseplay, No Running, No Defecating, No Urinating, No Expectorating*. At the bottom someone has scrawled in *No Whites, No Fat Chiks* and someone else has provided the missing *c*. I laugh. Beto hadn't known what expectorating meant though he was the one leaving for college. I told him, spitting a greener by the side of the pool.

Shit, he said. Where did you learn that?

I shrugged.

Tell me. He hated when I knew something he didn't. He put his hands on my shoulders and pushed me under. He was wearing a cross and cutoff jeans. He was stronger than me and held me down until water flooded my nose and throat. Even then I didn't tell him; he thought I didn't read, not even dictionaries.

We live alone. My mother has enough for the rent and groceries and I cover 15 the phone bill, sometimes the cable. She's so quiet that most of the time I'm startled to find her in the apartment. I'll enter a room and she'll stir, detaching herself from the cracking plaster walls, from the stained cabinets, and fright will pass through me like a wire. She has discovered the secret to silence: pouring café without a splash, walking between rooms as if gliding on a cushion of felt, crying without a sound. You have traveled to the East and learned many secret things, I've told her. You're like a shadow warrior.

And you're like a crazy, she says. Like a big crazy.

When I come in she's still awake, her hands picking clots of lint from her skirt. I put a towel down on the sofa and we watch television together. We settle on the Spanish-language news: drama for her, violence for me. Today a child has survived a seven-story fall, busting nothing but his diaper. The hysterical babysitter, about three hundred pounds of her, is head-butting the microphone.

It's a goddamn miraclevilla, she cries.

My mother asks me if I found Beto. I tell her that I didn't look.

That's too bad. He was telling me that he might be starting at a school for 20 business.

So what?

She's never understood why we don't speak anymore. I've tried to explain, all wise-like, that everything changes, but she thinks that sort of saying is only around so you can prove it wrong.

He asked me what you were doing.

What did you say?

I told him you were fine. 25

You should have told him I moved.

And what if he ran into you?

I'm not allowed to visit my mother?

She notices the tightening of my arms. You should be more like me and your father.

Can't you see I'm watching television? 30

I was angry at him, wasn't I? But now we can talk to each other.

Am I watching television here or what?

Saturdays she asks me to take her to the mall. As a son I feel I owe her that much, even though neither of us has a car and we have to walk two miles through redneck territory to catch the M15.

Before we head out she drags us through the apartment to make sure the windows are locked. She can't reach the latches so she has me test them. With the air conditioner on we never open windows but I go through the routine anyway. Putting my hand on the latch is not enough—she wants to hear it rattle. This place just isn't safe, she tells me. Lorena got lazy and look what they did to her. They punched her and kept her locked up in her place. Those morenos ate all her food and even made phone calls. Phone calls!

That's why we don't have long-distance, I tell her but she shakes her head. 35 That's not funny, she says.

She doesn't go out much, so when she does it's a big deal. She dresses up, even puts on makeup. Which is why I don't give her lip about taking her to the mall even though I usually make a fortune on Saturdays, selling to those kids going down to Belmar or out to Spruce Run.

I recognize like half the kids on the bus. I keep my head buried in my cap, praying that nobody tries to score. She watches the traffic, her hands somewhere inside her purse, doesn't say a word.

When we arrive at the mall I give her fifty dollars. Buy something, I say, hating the image I have of her, picking through the sale bins, wrinkling everything. Back in the day, my father would give her a hundred dollars at the end of each summer for my new clothes and she would take nearly a week to spend it, even though it never amounted to more than a couple of t-shirts and two pairs of jeans. She folds the bills into a square. I'll see you at three, she says.

I wander through the stores, staying in sight of the cashiers so they won't have reason to follow me. The circuit I make has not changed since my looting days. Bookstore, record store, comic-book shop, Macy's. Me and Beto used to steal like mad from these places, two, three hundred dollars of shit in an outing. Our system was simple—we walked into a store with a shopping bag and came out loaded. Back then security wasn't tight. The only trick was in the exit. We stopped right at the entrance of the store and checked out some worthless piece of junk to stop people from getting suspicious. What do you think? we asked each other. Would she like it? Both of us had seen bad shoplifters at work. All grab and run, nothing smooth about them. Not us. We idled out of the stores slow, like a fat seventies car. At this, Beto was the best. He even talked to mall security, asked them for directions, his bag all loaded up, and me, standing ten feet away, shitting my pants. When he finished he smiled, swinging his shopping bag up to hit me.

You got to stop that messing around, I told him. I'm not going to jail for 40 bullshit like that.

You don't go to jail for shoplifting. They just turn you over to your old man.

I don't know about you, but my pops hits like a motherfucker.

He laughed. You know my dad. He flexed his hands. The nigger's got arthritis.

My mother never suspected, even when my clothes couldn't all fit in my closet, but my father wasn't that easy. He knew what things cost and knew that I didn't have a regular job.

You're going to get caught, he told me one day. Just you wait. When you do 45 I'll show them everything you've taken and then they'll throw your stupid ass away like a bad piece of meat.

He was a charmer, my pop, a real asshole, but he was right. Nobody can stay smooth forever, especially kids like us. One day at the bookstore, we didn't even hide the drops. Four issues of the same *Playboy* for kicks, enough audio books to start our own library. No last minute juke either. The lady who stepped in front of us didn't look old, even with her white hair. Her silk shirt was half unbuttoned and a silver horn necklace sat on the freckled top of her chest. I'm sorry fellows, but I have to check your bag, she said. I kept moving, and looked back all annoyed, like she was asking us for a quarter or something. Beto got polite and stopped. No problem, he said, slamming the heavy bag into her face. She hit the cold tile with a squawk, her palms slapping the ground. There you go, Beto said.

Security found us across from the bus stop, under a Jeep Cherokee. A bus had come and gone, both of us too scared to take it, imagining a plainclothes waiting to clap the cuffs on. I remember that when the rent-a-cop tapped his nightstick against the fender and said, You little shits better come out here real slow, I started to cry. Beto didn't say a word, his face stretched out and gray, his hand squeezing mine, the bones in our fingers pressing together.

Nights I drink with Alex and Danny. The Malibou Bar is no good, just washouts and the sucias we can con into joining us. We drink too much, roar at each other and make the skinny bartender move closer to the phone. On the wall hangs a cork dartboard and a Brunswick Gold Crown blocks the bathroom, its bumpers squashed, the felt pulled like old skin.

When the bar begins to shake back and forth like a rumba, I call it a night and go home, through the fields that surround the apartments. In the distance you can see the Raritan, as shiny as an earthworm, the same river my homeboy goes to school on. The dump has long since shut down, and grass has spread over it like a sickly fuzz, and from where I stand, my right hand directing a colorless stream of piss downward, the landfill might be the top of a blond head, square and old.

In the mornings I run. My mother is already up, dressing for her house-cleaning job. She says nothing to me, would rather point to the mangú she has prepared than speak.

I run three miles easily, could have pushed a fourth if I were in the mood. I keep an eye out for the recruiter who prowls around our neighborhood in his dark K-car. We've spoken before. He was out of uniform and called me over, jovial, and I thought I was helping some white dude with directions. Would you mind if I asked you a question?

No.

Do you have a job?

Not right now.

Would you like one? A real career, more than you'll get around here?

I remember stepping back. Depends on what it is, I said.

Son, I know somebody who's hiring. It's the United States government.

Well. Sorry, but I ain't Army material.

That's exactly what I used to think, he said, his ten piggy fingers buried in his carpeted steering wheel. But now I have a house, a car, a gun and a wife. Discipline. Loyalty. Can you say that you have those things? Even one?

He's a southerner, red-haired, his drawl so out of place that the people around here laugh just hearing him. I take to the bushes when I see his car on the road. These days my guts feel loose and cold and I want to be away from here. He won't have to show me his Desert Eagle or flash the photos of the skinny Filipino girls sucking dick. He'll only have to smile and name the places and I'll listen.

When I reach the apartment, I lean against my door, waiting for my heart to slow, for the pain to lose its edge. I hear my mother's voice, a whisper from the kitchen. She sounds hurt or nervous, maybe both. At first I'm terrified that Beto's inside with her but then I look and see the phone cord, swinging lazily. She's talking to my father, something she knows I disapprove of. He's in Florida now, a sad guy who calls her and begs for money. He swears that if she moves down there he'll leave the woman he's living with. These are lies, I've told her, but she still calls him. His words coil inside of her, wrecking her sleep for days. She opens the refrigerator door slightly so that the whir of the compressor masks their conversation. I walk in on her and hang up the phone. That's enough, I say.

She's startled, her hand squeezing the loose folds of her neck. That was him, she says quietly.

On school days Beto and I chilled at the stop together but as soon as that bus came over the Parkwood hill I got to thinking about how I was failing gym and screwing up math and how I hated every single living teacher on the planet. I'll see *you* in the p.m., I said.

He was already standing on line. I just stood back and grinned, my hands 65
in my pockets. With our bus drivers you didn't have to hide. Two of them didn't give a rat fuck and the third one, the Brazilian preacher, was too busy talking Bible to notice anything but the traffic in front of him.

Being truant without a car was no easy job but I managed. I watched a lot of TV and when it got boring I trooped down to the mall or the Sayreville library, where you could watch old documentaries for free. I always came back to the neighborhood late, so the bus wouldn't pass me on Ernston and nobody could yell Asshole! out the windows. Beto would usually be home or down by the swings, but other times he wouldn't be around at all. Out visiting other neighborhoods. He knew a lot of folks I didn't—a messed-up black kid from Madison Park, two brothers who were into that N.Y. club scene, who spent money on platform shoes and leather backpacks. I'd leave a message with his parents and then watch some more TV. The next day he'd be out at the bus stop, too busy smoking a cigarette to say much about the day before.

You need to learn how to walk the world, he told me. There's a lot out there.

Some nights me and the boys drive to New Brunswick. A nice city, the Raritan so low and silty that you don't have to be Jesus to walk over it. We hit the Melody and the Roxy, stare at the college girls. We drink a lot and then spin out onto the dance floor. None of the chicas ever dance with us, but a glance or a touch can keep us talking shit for hours.

Once the clubs close we go to the Franklin Diner, gorge ourselves on pancakes, and then, after we've smoked our pack, head home. Danny passes out in the back seat and Alex cranks the window down to keep the wind in his eyes. He's fallen asleep in the past, wrecked two cars before this one. The streets have been picked clean of students and townies and we blow through every light, red or green. At the Old Bridge Turnpike we pass the fag bar, which never seems to close. Patos are all over the parking lot, drinking and talking.

Sometimes Alex will stop by the side of the road and say, Excuse me. When 70
somebody comes over from the bar he'll point his plastic pistol at them, just to see if they'll run or shit their pants. Tonight he just puts his head out the window. Fuck you! he shouts and then settles back in his seat, laughing.

That's original, I say.

He puts his head out the window again. Eat me, then!

Yeah, Danny mumbles from the back. Eat me.

Twice. That's it.

The first time was at the end of that summer. We had just come back from the pool and were watching a porn video at his parents' apartment. His father was a nut for these tapes, ordering them from wholesalers in California and Grand Rapids. Beto used to tell me how his pop would watch them in the middle of the day, not caring a lick about his moms, who spent the time in the kitchen, taking hours to cook a pot of rice and gandules. Beto would sit down with his pop and neither of them would say a word, except to laugh when somebody caught it in the eye or the face.

We were an hour into the new movie, some vaina that looked like it had been filmed in the apartment next door, when he reached into my shorts. What the fuck are you doing? I asked, but he didn't stop. His hand was dry. I kept my eyes on the television, too scared to watch. I came right away, smearing the plastic sofa covers. My legs started shaking and suddenly I wanted out. He didn't say anything to me as I left, just sat there watching the screen.

The next day he called and when I heard his voice I was cool but I wouldn't go to the mall or anywhere else. My mother sensed that something was wrong and pestered me about it, but I told her to leave me the fuck alone, and my pops, who was home on a visit, stirred himself from the couch to slap me down. Mostly I stayed in the basement, terrified that I would end up abnormal, a fucking pato, but he was my best friend and back then that mattered to me more than anything. This alone got me out of the apartment and over to the pool that night. He was already there, his body pale and flabby under the water. Hey, he said. I was beginning to worry about you.

Nothing to worry about, I said.

We swam and didn't talk much and later we watched a Skytop crew pull a bikini top from a girl stupid enough to hang out alone. Give it, she said, covering herself, but these kids howled, holding it up over her head, the shiny laces flopping just out of reach. When they began to pluck at her arms, she walked away, leaving them to try the top on over their flat pecs.

He put his hand on my shoulder, my pulse a code under his palm. Let's go, he said. Unless of course you're not feeling good.

I'm feeling fine, I said.

Since his parents worked nights we pretty much owned the place until six the next morning. We sat in front of his television, in our towels, his hands bracing against my abdomen and thighs. I'll stop if you want, he said and I didn't respond. After I was done, he laid his head in my lap. I wasn't asleep or awake, but caught somewhere in between, rocked slowly back and forth the way surf holds junk against the shore, rolling it over and over. In three weeks he was leaving. Nobody can touch me, he kept saying. We'd visited the school and I'd seen how beautiful the campus was, with all the students drifting from dorm to class. I thought of how in high school our teachers loved to crowd us into their lounge every time a space shuttle took off from Florida. One teacher, whose family had two grammar schools named after it, compared us to the shuttles. A few of you are going to make it. Those are the orbiters. But the majority of you are just going to burn out. Going nowhere. He dropped his hand onto his desk. I could already see myself losing altitude, fading, the earth spread out beneath me, hard and bright.

I had my eyes closed and the television was on and when the hallway door crashed open, he jumped up and I nearly cut my dick off struggling with my shorts. It's just the neighbor, he said, laughing. He was laughing, but I was saying, Fuck this, and getting my clothes on.

I believe I see him in his father's bottomed-out Cadillac, heading towards the turnpike, but I can't be sure. He's probably back in school already. I deal close to home, trooping up and down the same dead-end street where the kids drink and smoke. These punks joke with me, pat me down for taps, sometimes too hard. Now that strip malls line Route 9, a lot of folks have part-time jobs; the kids stand around smoking in their aprons, name tags dangling heavily from pockets.

When I get home, my sneakers are filthy so I take an old toothbrush to their 85 soles, scraping the crap into the tub. My mother has thrown open the windows and propped open the door. It's cool enough, she explains. She has prepared dinner— rice and beans, fried cheese, tostones. Look what I bought, she says, showing me two blue t-shirts. They were two for one so I bought you one. Try it on.

It fits tight but I don't mind. She cranks up the television. A movie dubbed into Spanish, a classic, one that everyone knows. The actors throw themselves around, passionate, but their words are plain and deliberate. It's hard to imagine anybody going through life this way. I pull out the plug of bills from my pockets. She takes it from me, her fingers soothing the creases. A man who treats his plata like this doesn't deserve to spend it, she says.

We watch the movie and the two hours together makes us friendly. She puts her hand on mine. Near the end of the film, just as our heroes are about to fall apart under a hail of bullets, she takes off her glasses and kneads her temples, the light of the television flickering across her face. She watches another minute and then her chin lists to her chest. Almost immediately her eyelashes begin to tremble, a quiet semaphore. She is dreaming, dreaming of Boca Raton, of strolling under the jacarandas with my father. You can't be anywhere forever, was what Beto used to say, what he said to me the day I went to see him off. He handed me a gift, a book, and after he was gone I threw it away, didn't even bother to open it and read what he'd written.

I let her sleep until the end of the movie and when I wake her she shakes her head, grimacing. You better check those windows, she says. I promise her I will.

FOR ANALYSIS

1. Díaz peppers "Drown" with Spanish words and phrases. What is the effect of his doing so? Do you think the effect depends on the individual reader? Why do you think he does it? Why do you think he doesn't offer translations?

2. The **narrator** describes one drug dealer as "the only full-time commuter in the area" (para. 9). What is the significance of this comment? What does it reveal about how the narrator thinks of his neighborhood?

3. Why is the narrator steering clear of Beto?

4. Why do you think the narrator's academic career has gone the way it has? How do you think he feels about it?

MAKING ARGUMENTS

1. Borrowing the teacher's shuttle **metaphor** (para. 82), is the **narrator** going to be an orbiter or will he just burn out? Make an argument for what you think the future holds for him based on the evidence in the text.

2. The narrator's drug dealing is dealt with pretty matter-of-factly in the story. Depending on the state, the drug being sold and the quantity possessed, if a drug dealer is arrested in the United States he or she could end up in prison for a very long time. Read up on drug laws, "the war on drugs," and contemporary statistics about incarceration, think about the narrator's life, and, using this evidence, make an argument about the way we deal with drug use and the drug trade in the United States today.

WRITING TOPICS

1. Write or outline a sequel to "Drown." Beto says, "You can't be anywhere forever" (para. 87). Does the **narrator** stay or does he leave and change his life?

2. Is this story more about love or hate? Think about all of the opportunities for **characters** in "Drown" to love or to hate—each other, the place they live and the way they live there, themselves—and think about whether they love, or hate, or both. What do your answers tell you about the author's vision of life?

MAKING CONNECTIONS

1. Compare how the **narrator** in "Drown" talks about his parents with the way Dagoberto Gilb talks about his in "I Knew She Was Beautiful" (p. 1111). How does each author/narrator understand his parents in the context of their environment?

2. Reread Soto's "Behind Grandma's House" (p. 203) and compare it to "Drown." How does each describe the relationship between a young person and a parental figure? Is it possible to imagine Díaz's narrator having a grandmother like Soto's?

CHIMAMANDA NGOZI ADICHIE (B. 1977)

MY AMERICAN JON 2007

There is something forlorn about Baltimore; I thought of this every Thursday when my taxi sped down Charles Street on my way to the train station to visit Jon in New York City. The buildings were connected to one another in faded slumping rows, but what really held my attention was the people: hunched in puffy jackets, waiting for buses, slouching in corners, making me wonder again and again why the dankest, drabbest parts of all the American cities I knew were full of black people. My taxi drivers were mostly Punjabi or Ethiopian. It was an Ethiopian who asked where my accent was from and then said, "You don't look African at all," when I told him Nigeria.

"Why don't I look African?" I asked.

"Because your blouse is too tight."

"It is not too tight," I said.

"I thought you were from Jamaica or one of those places," he said, looking in 5 the rear-view with both disapproval and concern. "You have to be very careful or America will corrupt you."

Later, I told Jon about this conversation and how the driver's sincerity had infuriated me and how I had gone to the station bathroom to see if my pink blouse was too tight. Jon laughed. But I was sure he understood; this was during the early months, the good months of our relationship.

We met at a poetry reading. I had come up to New York to hear the new Nigerian poet Chioma Ekemma read from her *Love Economies*. During the Q&A, the questions were not about why she chose to write poems without active verbs, or which poets she admired, but what could be done about poverty in Nigeria and would women ever achieve equality there and wasn't she lucky that she could come to America and find her voice? She was gracious— too gracious, I thought. Then Jon raised his hand from two rows ahead of me and said tourism was the easiest way to fix the Nigerian economy and it was a shame Nigeria was not tourist friendly. No hostels. No good roads. No back packers. He spoke with absolute authority. Chioma Ekemma nodded enthusiastically. I raised my hand and said one could fix an economy in other ways that did not involve richer people going to gawk at the lives of poorer people who could never gawk back. There was some scattered clapping; I noticed the most vigorous came from the black people. Chioma Ekemma said something conciliatory and moved on to the next question. She was clearly thinking of keeping the peace so that as many people as possible would buy her book.

Jon was staring at me; a white man wearing a metal wristband who thought he could pontificate about my country irritated me. I stared back. I imagined him taking in my afro-shaped twists, my severe black frames, with distaste.

But there was something else between us, between the chairs and people separating us: a sparkle, a star, a spark. His face was solemn when he came over after the reading and said I had really felt strongly back there and did I want to get coffee and have a little bit more of a debate. It amused me, the way he said "debate." But we did debate, about devaluation and deregulation and debt, and later, when we kissed at Penn station in a sudden press of our bodies before I got on the train, it was as if the debate was continuing, the way our tongues darted around inside our mouths without meeting.

He had never been with a black woman; he told me this the following weekend with a self-mocking toss of his head, as if this were something he should have done long ago but had somehow neglected. I laughed and he laughed and in the morning sunlight that streamed in through the windows of his apartment, his skin took on a bright and foreign translucence. After we broke up two years later, I would tell people that race was the reason, that he was too white and I was too black and the midway too skewed in his favor. In truth, we broke up after I cheated. The cheating was very good, me on top gliding and moaning and grasping the hair on the chest of the other man. But I told Jon that it had meant nothing. I told him that I had hated myself although I was filled with well-being, with a sublime sense not just of satisfaction but of accomplishment.

At first, Jon was disbelieving. "No, you didn't have a one-night stand. You're 10 such a liar."

I did lie to him sometimes, playful little lies like calling to say I could not come that weekend when I was just outside his door. But I did not lie about the big things.

"It's true," I said.

He got up and turned down the volume of the stereo and paced and looked through the tall windows at the cars and people below. "Unknown Soldier" was playing. Jon loved Fela Kuti; it was the reason he'd visited Nigeria and attended Nigerian events, perhaps the reason he thought he knew how to save Nigeria.

"Why?" he asked finally.

I should not have been pleased by the prospect of telling Jon why I had 15 cheated. I sat down on the sofa and said, "It was desire."

It was desire. It felt as though gentle peppers had been squirted at the bottom of my stomach, a surge of pure aching desire that I was grateful for feeling and was determined not to waste.

"Desire?" Jon was watching me. Maybe he was thinking that it had always been good between us. So I got up and held him close and said that even though it had been a physical desire, the act itself had meant nothing because my self-loathing made pleasure impossible. Jon did not push me away. He said, "The sin is not the sex, Amaka, the sin is the betrayal. So it doesn't matter whether or not you enjoyed it."

That all-knowing tone of Jon's had always made me stiffen. If the circumstances were different, I would have asked him, "Did the people at Yale teach you how to talk with such authority about things you know nothing about? I had often asked him this in the past. Such as when, two or so months into our relationship, I arrived at his apartment and he kissed me and gestured to the table and said, "Surprise. Tickets to Paris for three days. We leave tonight. You'll be back in time to teach Tuesday."

"Jon, I just cannot jet off to Paris. I have a Nigerian passport and I have to apply for a visa."

"Come on, you're an American resident. You don't need a visa to go to Paris."   20

"I do."

"No you don't."

After I showed him on the Internet that Nigerian citizens who were resident in America did in fact need a visa to get into Europe—a process that required bank statements, health insurance, all sorts of proof that you would not stay back and become a burden to Europe—Jon muttered "Ridiculous," as though it was the French embassy and not he who had been wrong. We did go to Paris, though. Jon changed the ticket dates. We went together to the French embassy but I went alone to the window where a woman wearing silver eyeshadow glanced at me, at my passport, back at me, and said she would not approve the visa because Nigerian passport-holders were high-risk and it seemed suspicious to her that I was going to Paris for just three days.

"But . . ." I started to say and she made an impatient gesture and pushed my documents across under the glass. Jon got up then, tall and sinewy and angry, and told her I was going to Paris as his guest and my documents included his bank statements and my employment letter and insurance and everything else, if only she'd look at them. "We're together," he added, as if it was necessary to make it clear. The woman smirked. She said I should have explained myself better. She made a show of looking through the documents and said the visa would be ready for pick-up in two days.

It filled me with a dizzying pride, how Jon would often stand up for me, speak   25 for me, protect me, make me omelets, give me pedicures in the bubbling foot bath, slip his hand into mine as we walked, speak in the first-person plural. "*O na-eji gi ka akwa*: he holds you like an egg," Aunty Adanna said admiringly when she finally accepted that I was serious with a white man and asked me to bring him to lunch. Aunty Adanna was one of those Nigerian immigrants who, when they spoke to white people, adopted a risible American accent. I took Jon to her seven-room home in Columbia, outside Baltimore, and suddenly she was calling her son "Mek," my bewildered teenage cousin whom we had always called Nnaemeka, and talking about how good he was at golf. She spoke of *fufu* and soup, which Jon had eaten many times before in New York, as if Nigerian food could not be worthy unless it was like something American. This is like your mashed potatoes, she told him, this is just like your clam chowder. She spoke of her swimming pool needing to be drained. She told anecdotes about the patients at her medical practice.

Jon asked when last she had been back in Nigeria and she said it had been six years; she could not bear the dirt and chaos and she did not know what the matter was with all of those corrupt people in government. "Matter" came out sounding like "marah." Even though Jon had not asked, she proudly told him she had lived in America for eighteen years, that she had sponsored my trip here eight years ago after my Nigerian university kept going on strike after strike. I stabbed the chicken in my soup and said nothing. I was ashamed. I was ashamed that she did not have books in her house and that when Jon brought up Zimbabwe, she had no idea what was going on there and so to cover my shame I muttered "Philistine" as we drove away.

"Nigerian doctors and engineers and lawyers don't read anything unless it has the possibility of leading them to bigger paychecks," I said. Jon laughed and said it had nothing to do with Nigeria, it was the same for the American bourgeoisie and, leaning over to kiss me, said that Aunty Adanna had been sweet, the way she was so keen to make him comfortable. It wasn't sweet, it was pathetic, but I liked that Jon said that and I liked that he wanted to be liked by my family.

I had never felt that love I read about in books, that inexorable thing that made characters take all sorts of unlikely decisions. By the time I met Jon, I had convinced myself that the feeling was like an orgasm; a certain percentage of women would never have one after all. At first, each long weekend with Jon in New York was a pleasant break to look forward to after teaching three days a week at the Shipley school. Soon, each weekend became something I longed for, and then something I needed. I realized that what I felt for Jon was becoming an inexorable thing when I saw the flyer advertising a teaching position in a New York City private academy on a board outside the general office and immediately went in to ask the secretary, Nakeya, if she knew more. She shook her head and said it wasn't a good idea.

"They like you here and you'll rise quickly if you stay, Amaka," she said. I persisted. She said the academy was a good place although the pay at Shipley was better, the student body there was richer, though, and the class size smaller. She added in a lower voice that they were a little conservative and it was best if I took my twists out for the interview. "You know how our hair can make them feel threatened?" Nakeya asked with a smile.

I knew. Why adults would feel threatened by hair has never ceased to amaze me but, after I called the academy and was asked to come in for an interview, I removed my twists and straightened my hair with a hot comb that burned my scalp. I was even willing to buy blonde dye. I wanted the job. I wanted to be in New York City with Jon. I had been rashly honest at my Shipley school interview, telling them that I had just graduated from Johns Hopkins graduate creative writing program, had published only a few poems in journals, was struggling to complete a collection and was unsure how to make a living. For the academy interview, I decided I would be more circumspect. I told the two white men and one Hispanic woman that teaching was my first love and poetry my second.

They were attentive, they nodded often as if to show approval. I didn't tell Jon about it because I wanted to surprise him but after I got the e-mail only three days later, thanking me and telling me they had selected a better-qualified applicant, I told Jon. He smiled, his big generous smile. He asked me to resign from the Shipley school, to move in with him and take some time off and focus on my poetry and, if I was worried about not paying rent, I could do so in kind. We laughed. We laughed so often during the early months. I put up an advertisement for subletting my Baltimore apartment, put my furniture in storage, and moved in with Jon.

Later, almost two years later, on the day I told Jon that I had cheated, I wondered whether my moving in had contributed in some way; perhaps things would have been different if I had stayed in Baltimore, visiting for long weekends. That day, it took hours of sidestepping each other, of drinking tea, of Jon lying face up on the couch, before he asked, "Who is he?"

I told him the man's name: Ifeanyi. We had met years ago at the wedding of a friend of Aunty Adanna's. He had called me a few times and then, recently, he moved from Atlanta to Harlem and we met for coffee and the desire happened and we took the train to his place.

Jon said, "You gave him what he wanted."

It was an odd thing for Jon to say, the sort of thing Aunty Adanna, who per- 35
sisted in speaking about sex as if it were something a woman gave a man at a loss to herself, would say. I corrected Jon gently. "I took what I wanted. If I gave him anything, then it was incidental."

"Listen to yourself, just fucking listen to yourself!" Jon's voice thickened and he got up and shook me and then stopped, but did not apologize. "Amaka, I would never have cheated on you. I didn't even think about it in the past two years, I didn't think about it," he said and I realized that he was already looking at us through the lens of the past tense. It puzzled me, the ability of romantic love to mutate so completely. Where did it go? Was the real thing somehow connected to blood since love for children and parents did not change or die in the way love for romantic partners did?

"You won't forgive me," I said.

"I don't think we should be talking about forgiveness right now."

Jon was the kind of man for whom fidelity came easily, the kind who did not turn to glance at pretty women on the street simply because it did not occur to him. He sat down on the couch and I felt a terrible loss because I had become used to knowing that he was undisputedly there, to the cultured ease in the life he gave me, to his upper-class tickets and his boat and house in Connecticut and the smiling uniformed doorman in his apartment building. Even though I had shrugged, non-committal, the two times he brought up marriage, I often thought of it. The first time I told him I was not sure I wanted to get married. The second time I said I was uncomfortable about bringing mixed-race children into the world. He laughed. How could I buy into the tragic mulatto cliché? It was so much bullshit. He recited the names of our—his, really—biracial friends who seemed perfectly fine with being as they were. His tone was arch, superior, and perhaps he was right and it was bullshit but this was truly how I felt and it did not help that Jon approached my misgivings about race with an intellectual wave of his hand.

And who says that race did not play a role in our break-up? Who says we 40
were not lying all those times we clung to the comforting idea of complexity? It wasn't about race, we would say, it was complex—Jon speaking first and me promptly agreeing. What if the reasons for most things didn't require blurred lines? What about the day we walked into a Maine restaurant with white-linen-covered tables, and the waiter looked at us and asked Jon, "Table for one?" Or when the new Indian girlfriend of Jon's golf partner Ashish said she had

enjoyed her graduate experience at Yale but had disliked how close the ghetto was and then her hand flew to her mouth after "ghetto" and she turned to me and said, "Oh, I'm so sorry," and Jon nodded as if to accept the apology on my behalf.

What about when he, Jon, said he hated the predatory way a black man had looked at me in Central Park and I realized I had never heard him use the word predatory before? Or the long weekend in Montreal when the strawberry-haired owner of the bed and breakfast refused to acknowledge me and spoke and smiled at Jon and I was not sure whether she disliked black people or simply liked Jon and later in the room, for the first time I did not agree that it was complex, at least not in the way I had agreed all the other times. I shouted at Jon, "The worst thing is never being sure when it is race and not race and you'll never have this baggage!" And he held me and said I was overreacting and tired.

What about the evening we attended a reading at the Mercantile Library and afterwards Jon's friend Evan, who wrote travel books, told me he was sure it had to feel like shit when ignorant people suggested I had been published in the *Best American Poetry* because I was black and Jon merely shook his head when I told him that the ignorant people had to be Evan himself because nobody else had suggested this. And what about the first time I met Jon's mother? She talked about her Kenyan safari in the seventies, about Mandela's majestic grace, about her adoration for Harry Belafonte, and I worried that she would lapse into Ebonics or Swahili. As we left her rambling house in Vermont where she had an organic garden in her backyard, Jon said it was not really about race, it was more complex than that, it was that she was too hyperaware of difference and consequently too eager to bridge it.

"And she does that with me, too. She likes to talk about only the things she thinks I'm interested in," he said. This he did often: a constant equalizing of our experiences, a refusal to see that what I experienced was different from his.

And what about Jon's wife? Jon was divorced from a woman who he described as brilliant and needy. She lived in Cambridge but was on sabbatical in Europe and so did not feature in our lives during the first months, the good months. Then she came back and began to call often. She was unhappy, she wasn't sure what she wanted to do, she wasn't tenure-track, she had given up on her book. Jon often put her on speaker and said soothing things to her about hanging in there and ended the conversation by mentioning me. "I have to go, Amaka and I are late already." "I have to go, I'm cooking Amaka dinner."

On the evening we were to go and see *Thom Pain* off-Broadway, she called 45 and hung up after only a minute or so and he said she was awfully drunk and had called to confess that she still loved him and felt bad that he was with someone else and worse that the someone else was black. He was laughing. I wanted to cry. I am tough, believe me, but that day, as I stared at the high-heeled sandals I was about to slip on, I wanted to cry. All I said was, "I can't go to the theater." This woman whom I did not know had brought out in Jon something I loathed with a visceral lurch in my chest: an inability to show necessary outrage. For this new power of hers, I resented her. When, finally, we met, her unremarkably small breasts delighted me, the lines around her eyes and the saggy skin of her neck delighted me. It was at Ashish's garden party. She wore a pretty jersey dress and a limp string of green beads around her neck and smiled too brightly as we were introduced.

"Jon has told me so much about you," she said.

"You sound different," I said.

"What?"

"When you call Jon puts you on speaker so I can follow the conversation and you sound nothing like you do on the phone," I said, smiling.

She looked away and then back at me before she excused herself to go find a 50 drink. When I went to the bathroom, I was not surprised that she had followed me. She was standing by the door when I came out.

"It's not real," she said.

"What's not real?" I asked. I was bored with her. I was a little disappointed that Jon had not been with a less predictable woman.

"What you're doing isn't real. If it was, he wouldn't be trying so hard."

I turned and walked back outside to the party, hoping she thought I was taking the high road when the truth was that I had no idea what to say in response. On the day that I told Jon I had cheated, about eight months after that garden party, I repeated her words to Jon and said I had never told him about it because a part of me had always suspected that it was true.

"That what was true?" Jon asked. 55

"You were trying too hard to prove that my being black didn't matter and it was as if it wasn't a good thing and so we had to pretend it wasn't there and sometimes I wanted it to matter because it does matter but we never really talked, truly talked, about any of this."

Jon started to laugh. "This is rich," he said. "Now you blame it on race? What are you talking about? We've always talked about everything. And you told me you didn't even remember I was white!"

I had indeed said that and it was true, but only when we were alone, when we were silent, when we sat side by side and watched a film, or lay side by side and passed *New York Times* sections to each other. And yes, we did talk about race, either in the slippery way that admitted nothing and engaged nothing and ended with that word "complexity"; or as jokes that left me with a small and numb discomfort; or as intellectual nuggets to be examined and then put aside because it was not about us (such as when he read somewhere that mainstream women's magazine sales fall with a light-skinned black on the cover and plummet with a dark-skinned black).

Jon was still laughing, his bitter laughter.

"I should leave," I said. "I'll go and stay with Aunty Adanna for a while." 60

"No, wait." Jon got up. "Will you see him again?"

I shook my head.

"Does he mean anything to you?"

Again, I shook my head.

"We can talk. Maybe we can work through this." 65

I nodded. He placed his hand on my chin and gently tilted my head up and looked into my eyes. "You don't want to, do you? You want to make this look like my decision but it's really yours. You don't want to be forgiven. You don't want to work through this," he said, with that all-knowing authority of his and I stood there and said nothing.

A week later, I was back in Baltimore, a little drunk and a little happy and a little lonely, speeding down Charles Street in a taxi with a Punjabi driver who was proudly telling me that his children did better than American children at school.

FOR ANALYSIS

1. What is the first moment of foreshadowing you notice in "My American Jon"?

2. How does the **narrator** discuss the topic of romantic love? Is it something she understands? Does she approach it from the outside, as if it were alien to her?

3. How would you characterize the narrator? Do you think she is a good person? Does she? How would you characterize Jon? How would the narrator? Is there any way to form an opinion of Jon outside of the narrator's?

MAKING ARGUMENTS

1. The **narrator** wonders if her moving in contributed to her cheating on Jon. Make the argument that it was a major factor or, alternatively, make the argument that their breakup was predetermined by other factors.

2. The narrator, a Nigerian immigrant, is African American in a different way than American-born people of distant African descent. Make an argument for the centrality of this fact to "My American Jon."

WRITING TOPICS

1. Jon describes the **narrator's** aunt as no different from "American bourgeoisie" (para. 27). What does he mean by this? Why is the narrator ashamed of her aunt? Reflect on the intersections of social class and the difficulties of assimilation.

2. There is a moment in the story when the narrator describes Jon as suddenly looking at their relationship "through the lens of the past tense" (para. 36). Adichie's entire story is told in the past tense, which is the default for contemporary fiction, but it also signals that the events are related in retrospect—that is, from the start the narrator is looking back. How does this retrospective orientation inform the story? What does it imply? What does it make possible—and impossible?

MAKING CONNECTIONS

1. Read this story alongside "Sex without Love" (p. 958) by Sharon Olds. What relationship between physical love and romantic love does each presume?

2. Compare "My American Jon" to the poems in the "America through Immigrants' Eyes" cluster in "Culture and Identity" (p. 701). What does the **narrator's** representation of her experience share with those poems? How is it different?

**CONNECTING STORIES:
HAVING IT ALL**

The two stories in this cluster deal with a difficult subject (one that we want you to discover as you read). While it has become a difficult political subject over the years, it is treated in these stories as a difficult personal subject, one that touches the root of romantic and sexual relationships, and tests them. As you read these two stories, think about this subject's ramifications for the individuals involved and for the way they understand their own values and priorities.

ERNEST HEMINGWAY (1899–1961)

HILLS LIKE WHITE ELEPHANTS 1927

The hills across the valley of the Ebro were long and white. On this side there was no shade and no trees and the station was between two lines of rails in the sun. Close against the side of the station there was the warm shadow of the building and a curtain, made of strings of bamboo beads, hung across the open door into the bar, to keep out flies. The American and the girl with him sat at a table in the shade, outside the building. It was very hot and the express from Barcelona would come in forty minutes. It stopped at this junction for two minutes and went on to Madrid.

"What should we drink?" the girl asked. She had taken off her hat and put it on the table.

"It's pretty hot," the man said.

"Let's drink beer."

"*Dos cervezas*," the man said into the curtain.   5

"Big ones?" a woman asked from the doorway.

"Yes. Two big ones."

The woman brought two glasses of beer and two felt pads. She put the felt pads and the beer glasses on the table and looked at the man and the girl. The girl was looking off at the line of hills. They were white in the sun and the country was brown and dry.

"They look like white elephants," she said.

"I've never seen one," the man drank his beer.   10

"No, you wouldn't have."

"I might have," the man said. "Just because you say I wouldn't have doesn't prove anything."

The girl looked at the bead curtain. "They've painted something on it," she said. "What does it say?"

"Anis del Toro. It's a drink."

"Could we try it?"   15

The man called "Listen" through the curtain. The woman came out from the bar.

"Four reales."

"We want two Anis del Toro."

"With water?"

"Do you want it with water?"   20

"I don't know," the girl said. "Is it good with water?"

"It's all right."

"You want them with water?" asked the woman.

"Yes, with water."

"It tastes like licorice," the girl said and put the glass down.   25

"That's the way with everything."

"Yes," said the girl. "Everything tastes of licorice. Especially all the things you've waited so long for, like absinthe."

"Oh, cut it out."

"You started it," the girl said. "I was being amused. I was having a fine time."

"Well, let's try and have a fine time."   30

"All right. I was trying. I said the mountains looked like white elephants. Wasn't that bright?"

"That was bright."

"I wanted to try this new drink: that's all we do, isn't it—look at things and try new drinks?"

"I guess so."

The girl looked across at the hills.   35

"They're lovely hills," she said. "They don't really look like white elephants. I just meant the coloring of their skin through the trees."

"Should we have another drink?"

"All right."

The warm wind blew the bead curtain against the table.

"The beer's nice and cool," the man said.   40

"It's lovely," the girl said.

"It's really an awfully simple operation, Jig," the man said. "It's not really an operation at all."

The girl looked at the ground the table legs rested on.

"I know you wouldn't mind it, Jig. It's really not anything. It's just to let the air in."

The girl did not say anything.   45

"I'll go with you and I'll stay with you all the time. They just let the air in and then it's all perfectly natural."

"Then what will we do afterward?"

"We'll be fine afterward. Just like we were before."

"What makes you think so?"

"That's the only thing that bothers us. It's the only thing that's made us 50
unhappy."

The girl looked at the bead curtain, put her hand out, and took hold of two of the strings of beads.

"And you think then we'll be all right and be happy."

"I know we will. You don't have to be afraid. I've known lots of people that have done it."

"So have I," said the girl. "And afterward they were all so happy."

"Well," the man said, "if you don't want to you don't have to. I wouldn't 55 have you do it if you didn't want to. But I know it's perfectly simple."

"And you really want to?"

"I think it's the best thing to do. But I don't want you to do it if you don't really want to."

"And if I do it you'll be happy and things will be like they were and you'll love me?"

"I love you now. You know I love you."

"I know. But if I do it, then it will be nice again if I say things are like white 60 elephants, and you'll like it?"

"I'll love it. I love it now but I just can't think about it. You know how I get when I worry."

"If I do it you won't ever worry?"

"I won't worry about that because it's perfectly simple."

"Then I'll do it. Because I don't care about me."

"What do you mean?" 65

"I don't care about me."

"Well, I care about you."

"Oh, yes. But I don't care about me. And I'll do it and then everything will be fine."

"I don't want you to do it if you feel that way."

The girl stood up and walked to the end of the station. Across, on the other 70 side, were fields of grain and trees along the banks of the Ebro. Far away, beyond the river, were mountains. The shadow of a cloud moved across the field of grain and she saw the river through the trees.

"And we could have all this," she said. "And we could have everything and every day we make it more impossible."

"What did you say?"

"I said we could have everything."

"We can have everything."

"No, we can't."

"We can have the whole world." 75

"No, we can't."

"We can go everywhere."

"No, we can't. It isn't ours any more."

"It's ours."

"No, it isn't. And once they take it away, you never get it back." 80

"But they haven't taken it away."

"We'll wait and see."

"Come on back in the shade," he said. "You mustn't feel that way."

"I don't feel any way," the girl said. "I just know things." 85

"I don't want you to do anything that you don't want to do——"

"Nor that isn't good for me," she said. "I know. Could we have another beer?"

"All right. But you've got to realize——"

"I realize," the girl said. "Can't we maybe stop talking?"

They sat down at the table and the girl looked across at the hills on the dry 90
side of the valley and the man looked at her and at the table.

"You've got to realize," he said, "that I don't want you to do it if you don't want
to. I'm perfectly willing to go through with it if it means anything to you."

"Doesn't it mean anything to you? We could get along."

"Of course it does. But I don't want anybody but you. I don't want any one
else. And I know it's perfectly simple."

"Yes, you know it's perfectly simple."

"It's all right for you to say that, but I do know it." 95

"Would you do something for me now?"

"I'd do anything for you."

"Would you please please please please please please please stop talking?"

He did not say anything but looked at the bags against the wall of the station.
There were labels on them from all the hotels where they had spent nights.

"But I don't want you to," he said, "I don't care anything about it." 100

"I'll scream," the girl said.

The woman came out through the curtains with two glasses of beer and
put them down on the damp felt pads. "The train comes in five minutes," she
said.

"What did she say?" asked the girl.

"That the train is coming in five minutes."

The girl smiled brightly at the woman, to thank her. 105

"I'd better take the bags over to the other side of the station," the man said.
She smiled at him.

"All right. Then come back and we'll finish the beer."

He picked up the two heavy bags and carried them around the station to
the other tracks. He looked up the tracks but could not see the train. Coming
back, he walked through the barroom, where people waiting for the train were
drinking. He drank an Anis at the bar and looked at the people. They were all
waiting reasonably for the train. He went out through the bead curtain. She
was sitting at the table and smiled at him.

"Do you feel better?" he asked.

"I feel fine," she said. "There's nothing wrong with me. I feel fine." 110

FOR ANALYSIS

1. What is a "white elephant"?

2. What do you think the couple is arguing about? Is it more than one thing?

MAKING ARGUMENTS

How do you think the story will turn out? Is there a happy ending in store for this couple? Make your argument with the support of textual evidence.

WRITING TOPICS

1. How would you characterize Hemingway's **style**? Focus on what he includes and what he leaves out. What are the effects of his stylistic choices?

2. Much attention is paid in the story to **setting**—to where the main **characters** are sitting in relation to the things around them. Write an analysis of setting in this story. What might the relations of the characters to their surroundings mean? How might it reinforce certain ideas about their situation?

DAVID FOSTER WALLACE (1962–2008)

GOOD PEOPLE 2007

They were up on a picnic table at that park by the lake, by the edge of the lake, with part of a downed tree in the shallows half hidden by the bank. Lane A. Dean, Jr., and his girlfriend, both in bluejeans and button-up shirts. They sat up on the table's top portion and had their shoes on the bench part that people sat on to picnic or fellowship together in carefree times. They'd gone to different high schools but the same junior college, where they had met in campus ministries. It was springtime, and the park's grass was very green and the air suffused with honeysuckle and lilacs both, which was almost too much. There were bees, and the angle of the sun made the water of the shallows look dark. There had been more storms that week, with some downed trees and the sound of chainsaws all up and down his parents' street. Their postures on the picnic table were both the same forward kind with their shoulders rounded and elbows on their knees. In this position the girl rocked slightly and once put her face in her hands, but she was not crying. Lane was very still and immobile and looking past the bank at the downed tree in the shallows and its ball of exposed roots going all directions and the tree's cloud of branches all half in the water. The only other individual nearby was a dozen spaced tables away, by himself, standing upright. Looking at the torn-up hole in the ground there where the tree had gone over. It was still early yet and all the shadows wheeling right and shortening. The girl wore a thin old checked cotton shirt with pearl-colored snaps with the long sleeves down and always smelled very good and clean, like someone you could trust and care about even if you weren't in love. Lane Dean had liked the smell of her right away. His mother called her *down to earth* and liked her, thought she was good people, you could tell—she made this evident in little ways. The shallows lapped from different directions at the tree as if almost teething on it. Sometimes when alone and thinking or struggling to turn a matter over to Jesus Christ in prayer, he would find himself putting his fist in his palm and turning it slightly as if still playing and pounding his glove to stay sharp and alert in center. He did not do this now; it would be cruel and indecent to do this now. The older individual stood beside his picnic table—he was at it but not sitting—and looked also out of place in a suit coat or jacket and the kind of men's hat Lane's grandfather wore in photos as a young insurance man. He appeared to be looking across the lake. If he moved, Lane didn't see it. He looked more like a picture than a man. There were not any ducks in view.

One thing Lane Dean did was reassure her again that he'd go with her and be there with her. It was one of the few safe or decent things he could really say. The second time he said it again now she shook her head and laughed in an unhappy way that was more just air out her nose. Her real laugh was different. Where he'd be was the waiting room, she said. That he'd be thinking about her and feeling bad for her, she knew, but he couldn't be in there with her. This was so obviously true that he felt like a ninny that he'd kept on about it and now knew what she had thought every time he went and said it—it hadn't brought her comfort or eased the burden at all. The worse he felt, the stiller he sat. The whole thing felt balanced on a knife or wire; if he moved to put his arm up or touch her the whole thing could tip over. He hated himself for sitting so frozen. He could almost visualize himself tiptoeing past something explosive. A big stupid-looking tiptoe, like in a cartoon. The whole last black week had been this way and it was wrong. He knew it was wrong, knew something was required of him that was not this terrible frozen care and caution, but he pretended to himself he did not know what it was that was required. He pretended it had no name. He pretended that not saying aloud what he knew to be right and true was for her sake, was for the sake of her needs and feelings. He also worked dock and routing at UPS, on top of school, but had traded to get the day off after they'd decided together. Two days before, he had awakened very early and tried to pray but could not. He was freezing more and more solid, he felt like, but he had not thought of his father or the blank frozenness of his father, even in church, which had once filled him with such pity. This was the truth. Lane Dean, Jr., felt sun on one arm as he pictured in his mind an image of himself on a train, waving mechanically to something that got smaller and smaller as the train pulled away. His father and his mother's father had the same birthday, a Cancer. Sheri's hair was colored an almost corn blond, very clean, the skin through her central part pink in the sunlight. They'd sat here long enough that only their right side was shaded now. He could look at her head, but not at her. Different parts of him felt unconnected to each other. She was smarter than him and they both knew it. It wasn't just school—Lane Dean was in accounting and business and did all right; he was hanging in there. She was a year older, twenty, but it was also more—she had always seemed to Lane to be on good terms with her life in a way that age could not account for. His mother had put it that she *knew what it is she wanted*, which was nursing and not an easy program at

Peoria Junior College, and plus she worked hostessing at the Embers and had bought her own car. She was serious in a way Lane liked. She had a cousin that died when she was thirteen, fourteen, that she'd loved and been close with. She only talked about it that once. He liked her smell and her downy arms and the way she exclaimed when something made her laugh. He had liked just being with her and talking to her. She was serious in her faith and values in a way that Lane had liked and now, sitting here with her on the table, found himself afraid of. This was an awful thing. He was starting to believe that he might not be serious in his faith. He might be somewhat of a hypocrite, like the Assyrians in Isaiah, which would be a far graver sin than the appointment—he had decided he believed this. He was desperate to be good people, to still be able to feel he was good. He rarely before now had thought of damnation and Hell—that part of it didn't speak to his spirit—and in worship services he more just tuned himself out and tolerated Hell when it came up, the same way you tolerate the job you've got to have to save up for what it is you want. Her tennis shoes had little things doodled on them from sitting in her class lectures. She stayed looking down like that. Little notes or reading assignments in Bic in her neat round hand on the rubber elements around the sneaker's rim. Lane A. Dean, looking now at her inclined head's side's barrettes in the shape of blue ladybugs. The appointment was for afternoon, but when the doorbell had rung so early and his mother'd called to him up the stairs, he had known, and a terrible kind of blankness had commenced falling through him.

He told her that he did not know what to do. That he knew if he was the salesman of it and forced it upon her that was awful and wrong. But he was trying to understand—they'd prayed on it and talked it through from every different angle. Lane said how sorry she knew he was, and that if he was wrong in believing they'd truly decided together when they decided to make the appointment she should please tell him, because he thought he knew how she must have felt as it got closer and closer and how she must be so scared, but that what he couldn't tell was if it was more than that. He was totally still except for moving his mouth, it felt like. She did not reply. That if they needed to pray on it more and talk it through, then he was here, he was ready, he said. The appointment could get moved back; if she just said the word they could call and push it back to take more time to be sure in the decision. It was still so early in it—they both knew that, he said. This was true, that he felt this way, and yet he also knew he was also trying to say things that would get her to open up and say enough back that he could see her and read her heart and know what to say to get her to go through with it. He knew this without admitting to himself that this was what he wanted, for it would make him a hypocrite and liar. He knew, in some locked-up little part of him, why it was that he'd gone to no one to open up and seek their life counsel, not Pastor Steve or the prayer partners at campus ministries, not his UPS friends or the spiritual counselling available through his parents' old church. But he did not know why Sheri herself had not gone to Pastor Steve—he could not read her heart. She was blank and hidden. He so fervently wished it never happened. He felt like he knew now why it was a true sin and not just a leftover rule from past society. He felt like he had been brought low by it and humbled and now did believe that the rules were there for a reason. That the rules were concerned with him personally, as an individual. He promised God he had learned his lesson. But what if that, too, was a hollow promise, from a hypocrite who repented only after, who promised submission but really only wanted a reprieve? He might not even know his own heart or be able to read and know himself. He kept thinking also of 1 Timothy and the hypocrite therein who *disputeth over words*. He felt a terrible inner resistance but could not feel what it was that it resisted. This was the truth. All the different angles and ways they had come at the decision together did not ever include it—the word—for had he once said it, avowed that he did love her, loved Sheri Fisher, then it all would have been transformed. It would not be a different stance or angle, but a difference in the very thing they were praying and deciding on together. Sometimes they had prayed together over the phone, in a kind of half code in case anybody accidentally picked up the extension. She continued to sit as if thinking, in the pose of thinking, like that one statue. They were right up next to each other on the table. He was looking over past her at the tree in the water. But he could not say he did: it was not true.

But neither did he ever open up and tell her straight out he did not love her. This might be his *lie by omission*. This might be the frozen resistance—were he to look right at her and tell her he didn't, she would keep the appointment and go. He knew this. Something in him, though, some terrible weakness or lack of values, could not tell her. It felt like a muscle he did not have. He didn't know why; he just could not do it, or even pray to do it. She believed he was good, serious in his values. Part of him seemed willing to more or less just about lie to someone with that kind of faith and trust, and what did that make him? How could such a type of individual even pray? What it really felt like was a taste of the reality of what might be meant by Hell. Lane Dean had never believed in Hell as a lake of fire or a loving God consigning folks to a burning lake of fire—he knew in his heart this was not true. What he believed in was a living God of compassion and love and the possibility of a personal relationship with Jesus Christ through whom this love was enacted in human time. But sitting here beside this girl as unknown to him now as outer space, waiting for whatever she might say to unfreeze him, now he felt like he could see the edge or outline of what a real vision of Hell might be. It was of two great and terrible armies within himself, opposed and facing each other, silent. There would be battle but no victor. Or never a battle—the armies would stay like that, motionless, looking across at each other, and seeing therein something so different and alien from themselves that they could not understand, could not hear each other's speech as even words or read anything from what their face looked like, frozen like that, opposed and uncomprehending, for all human time. Two-hearted, a hypocrite to yourself either way.

When he moved his head, a part of the lake further out flashed with sun— 5 the water up close wasn't black now, and you could see into the shallows and see that all the water was moving but gently, this way and that—and in this same way he besought to return to himself as Sheri moved her leg and started to turn beside him. He could see the man in the suit and gray hat standing motionless now at the lake's rim, holding something under one arm and looking across at the opposite side where a row of little forms on camp chairs sat in a way that meant they had lines in the water for crappie—which mostly only your blacks from the East Side ever did—and the little white shape at the row's end a Styrofoam creel. In his moment or time at the lake now just to come, Lane Dean first felt he could take this all in whole: everything seemed distinctly lit, for the circle of the pin oak's shade had rotated off all the way, and they sat now in sun with their shadow a two-headed thing in the grass before them. He was looking or gazing again at where the downed tree's branches seemed to all bend so sharply just under the shallows' surface when he was given to know that through all this frozen silence he'd despised he had, in truth, been praying, or some little part of his heart he could not hear had, for he was answered now with a type of vision, what he would later call within his own mind a vision or *moment of grace*. He was not a hypocrite, just broken and split off like all men. Later on, he believed that what happened was he'd had a moment of almost seeing them both as Jesus saw them—as blind but groping, wanting to please God despite their inborn fallen nature. For in that same given moment he saw, quick as light, into Sheri's heart, and was made to know what would occur here as she finished turning to him and the man in the hat watched the fishing and the downed elm shed cells into the water. This down-to-earth girl that smelled good and wanted to be a nurse would take and hold one of his hands in both of hers to unfreeze him and make him look at her, and she would say that she cannot do it. That she is sorry she did not know this sooner, that she hadn't meant to lie—she agreed because she'd wanted to believe that she could, but she cannot. That she will carry this and have it; she has to. With her gaze clear and steady. That all night last night she prayed and searched inside herself and decided this is what love commands of her. That Lane should please please sweetie let her finish. That listen—this is her own decision and obliges him to nothing. That she knows he does not love her, not that way, has known it all this time, and that it's all right. That it is as it is and it's all right. She will carry this, and have it, and love it and make no claim on Lane except his good wishes and respecting what she has to do. That she releases him, all claim, and hopes he finishes up at P.J.C. and does so good in his life and has all joy and good things. Her voice will be clear and steady, and she will be lying, for Lane has been given to read her heart. To see through her. One of the opposite side's blacks raises his arm in what may be greeting, or waving off a bee. There is a mower cutting grass someplace off behind them. It will be a terrible, last-ditch gamble born out of the desperation in Sheri Fisher's soul, the knowledge that she can neither do this thing today nor carry a child alone and shame her family. Her values blocked the way either way, Lane could see, and she has no other options or choice—this lie is not a sin. Galatians 4:16, *Have I then become your enemy?* She is gambling that he is good. There on the table, neither frozen nor yet moving, Lane Dean, Jr., sees all this, and is moved with pity, and also with something more, something without any name he knows, that is given to him in the form of a question that never once in all the long week's thinking and division had even so much as occurred—why is he so sure he doesn't love her? Why is one kind of love any different? What if he has no earthly idea what love is? What would even Jesus do? For it was just now he felt her two small strong soft hands on his, to turn him. What if he was just afraid, if the truth was no more than this, and if what to pray for was not even love but simple courage, to meet both her eyes as she says it and trust his heart?

FOR ANALYSIS

1. What truths does Lane feel unable to confront?

2. There are many biblical references in "Good People," and Lane often frames his thoughts in religious terms. How does the story present his faith, and faith in general?

3. How would you describe the **style** in which this story is written? How does the style serve the story's treatment of its subject and characters?

4. The **protagonist** is said to think that "He was desperate to be good people, to still be able to feel he was good" (para. 2). How does what happens at the end of the story affect this desire?

MAKING ARGUMENTS

David Foster Wallace's work is known for its self-awareness, complicated **irony**, and flashy, erudite-crossed-with-slang language. "Good People" is of course much different. Supposing for the moment that Wallace chose to use a different **style** to write a story from the point of this particular character, what do you think of the choice? Should writers always write in language their **characters** might use, or should they write they way they write, regardless? Is to do otherwise—to write simply for people the writer perceives as themselves simple—condescending or simply realistic? Make an argument based both on the text and on other fiction you have read.

WRITING TOPICS

1. List appearances of **images** of division, doubleness, halfness, and dichotomy in the story. Reflect on your list: Why do you think there are so many of these instances? Is the story ultimately about division, or is it about its opposite—wholeness or union? How so?

2. What kind of note do you think the story ends on? Does it imply a happy future for the two characters, or do more difficulties lie ahead? What happens next? Write the next part of their story.

MAKING CONNECTIONS

1. Is it possible to read "Good People" as being consciously written in the shadow of "Hills Like White Elephants"? In what ways could it be seen to echo the earlier story? In what ways could it be seen to diverge? Do you think Wallace might even be offering a commentary on Hemingway's story?

2. In what way are both of these stories about characters wanting to have it all? What does "having it all" entail in each story? Is it possible in either?

3. Compare the two stories' treatment of abortion. How does each bring it up? How does each talk about it—directly or indirectly? How do the characters feel about it? How, as far as you can tell, do the authors themselves feel about it?

POETRY

SAPPHO   (CA. 610–CA. 580 BCE)

WITH HIS VENOM[1]

With his venom

Irresistible
and bittersweet

that loosener
of limbs, Love

reptile-like
strikes me down

CATULLUS   (CA. 84–CA. 54 BCE)

85

I hate and love. Why I do so, perhaps you ask.
I know not, but I feel it, and I am in torment.

FOR ANALYSIS

1. In the original Latin, the first sentence of the poem is *Odi et amo*, "I hate and I love." It illustrates something general about the poem, which is the absence of adjectives and, for the most part, nouns. What is the effect of this choice on the reader?

2. This poem is one of twenty-six that Catullus wrote about a woman with whom he was in love. Many are not entirely happy poems, taking as their subjects infidelity, quarrels, and other topics not usually thought of as the stuff of love poetry. Is this a love poem?

With His Venom
    [1] Translated by Mary Barnard.

Write a love/hate poem, and afterward reflect on your poetic choices. What kinds of **imagery** and **figurative language** did you choose? Do you think they are generally good choices for this kind of poem? If so, what makes them so? If not, why not?

WILLIAM SHAKESPEARE (1564–1616)

SONNETS 1609

18

Shall I compare thee to a summer's day?
Thou art more lovely and more temperate:
Rough winds do shake the darling buds of May,
And summer's lease hath all too short a date:
Sometime too hot the eye of heaven shines,
And often is his gold complexion dimmed;
And every fair from fair sometimes declines,
By chance or nature's changing course untrimmed;
But thy eternal summer shall not fade,
Nor lose possession of that fair thou ow'st,°   owns 10
Nor shall death brag thou wander'st in his shade,
When in eternal lines to time thou grow'st:
    So long as men can breathe, or eyes can see,
    So long lives this, and this gives life to thee.

FOR ANALYSIS

1. Why does the speaker in the poem argue that "a summer's day" is an inappropriate **metaphor** for his beloved?

2. What is "this" in line 14?

MAKING ARGUMENTS

Line 10's "ow'st" has been read as either "ownest" or "owest" and so as meaning either "owns" or "owes." Argue for one or the other reading. Why do you think one works better than the other? What do you take each to mean?

29

When, in disgrace with fortune and men's eyes,
I all alone beweep my outcast state

And trouble deaf heaven with my bootless cries
And look upon myself and curse my fate,
Wishing me like to one more rich in hope,
Featured like him, like him with friends possessed,
Desiring this man's art and that man's scope,
With what I most enjoy contented least;
Yet in these thoughts myself almost despising,
Haply I think on thee, and then my state,   10
Like to the lark at break of day arising
From sullen earth, sings hymns at heaven's gate;
     For thy sweet love remembered such wealth brings
     That then I scorn to change my state with kings.

64

When I have seen by Time's fell hand defac'd
The rich-proud cost of outworn buried age;
When sometime lofty towers I see down-raz'd,
And brass eternal slave to mortal rage;
When I have seen the hungry ocean gain
Advantage on the kingdom of the shore,
And the firm soil win of the watery main,
Increasing store with loss, and loss with store;
When I have seen such interchange of state,
Or state itself confounded to decay;   10
Ruin hath taught me thus to ruminate—
That Time will come and take my love away.
     This thought is as a death, which cannot choose
     But weep to have that which it fears to lose.

FOR ANALYSIS

1. Why does the **narrator** "weep" in the final line? Does he or she mourn the actual death of a loved one? If not death, then what causes the weeping?

2. This poem could have been included in this book's final chapter, "Life and Death." Why do you think it was included in this chapter? Is it simply a poem about death? If not, what does it have to say about love beyond the fear of a loved one's death?

MAKING ARGUMENTS

This poem is usually read as a recognition of the inevitability of death and the pain it causes. Make the argument that the ruminations at the end of the poem offer something positive from this recognition. Is there some alternative offered to the weeping of line 14?

116

Let me not to the marriage of true minds
Admit impediments. Love is not love
Which alters when it alteration finds,
Or bends with the remover to remove:
Oh, no! it is an ever-fixèd mark,
That looks on tempests and is never shaken;
It is the star to every wandering bark,
Whose worth's unknown, although his height be taken.
Love's not Time's fool, though rosy lips and cheeks
Within his bending sickle's compass come;   10
Love alters not with his brief hours and weeks,
But bears it out even to the edge of doom.
    If this be error and upon me proved,
    I never writ, nor no man ever loved.

130

My mistress' eyes are nothing like the sun;
Coral is far more red than her lips' red;
If snow be white, why then her breasts are dun;
If hairs be wires, black wires grow on her head.
I have seen roses damasked,° red and white,   variegated
But no such roses see I in her cheeks;
And in some perfumes is there more delight
Than in the breath that from my mistress reeks.
I love to hear her speak, yet well I know
That music hath a far more pleasing sound;   10
I grant I never saw a goddess go;
My mistress, when she walks, treads on the ground.
    And yet, by heaven, I think my love as rare
    As any she belied with false compare.[1]

FOR ANALYSIS

1. It seems at first like the speaker might be insulting his "mistress." Is he? What evidence supports your answer?

2. Annotate the poem so that the **sonnet's rhyme** scheme is clear. Where does the scheme change—that is, where does the pattern of alternating pairs of lines whose last words rhyme (for example, in lines 1–4 "sun," "red," "dun," "head," or ABAB) shift to a different pattern? How does the poem take advantage of this shift to make meaning?

3. How do the last two lines echo the first line?

[1] I.e., as any woman misrepresented with false comparisons.

MAKING ARGUMENTS

Make an argument connecting the attitude Shakespeare **satirizes** in Sonnet 130 to a present-day phenomenon. Do attitudes exist today like those Shakespeare observed in his time?

WRITING TOPIC

This poem plays off the tradition of **Petrarchan** love poetry, whose conventions include the worshipful idealization of the woman who is the subject of the poem. How does Shakespeare's poem **satirize** this kind of love poetry?

JOHN DONNE (1572–1631)

THE FLEA   1633

Mark but this flea, and mark in this,
How little that which thou deniest me is;
It sucked me first, and now sucks thee,
And in this flea our two bloods mingled be;
Thou know'st that this cannot be said
A sin, nor shame, nor loss of maidenhead,
    Yet this enjoys before it woo,
    And pampered swells with one blood made of two,
    And this, alas, is more than we would do.

Oh stay, three lives in one flea spare,   10
Where we almost, yea more than married, are.
This flea is you and I, and this
Our marriage bed and marriage temple is;
Though parents grudge, and you, we are met,
And cloistered in these living walls of jet,
    Though use° make you apt to kill me   custom
    Let not to that, self-murder added be,
    And sacrilege, three sins in killing three.

Cruel and sudden, hast thou since
Purpled thy nail, in blood of innocence?   20
Wherein could this flea guilty be,
Except in that drop which it sucked from thee?
Yet thou triumph'st, and say'st that thou
Find'st not thy self nor me the weaker now;
    'Tis true, then learn how false fears be;
    Just so much honor, when thou yield'st to me,
    Will waste, as this flea's death took life from thee.

FOR ANALYSIS

1. What does the woman addressed in this poem deny the poet (l. 2)?

2. What is the woman about to do at the beginning of the second **stanza**? What argument does the poet use to save the flea?

3. How does the poet turn the flea's life and death to his own purposes?

MAKING ARGUMENTS

While in the poem itself the speaker uses the flea to try to persuade someone to sleep with him, Donne himself is not using the poem in the same way. Make an argument for what you think he *is* doing, using the poem itself and research on Donne's work as support.

WRITING TOPIC

In a paragraph, discuss your response to Donne's use of a flea to animate a seduction poem.

A VALEDICTION: FORBIDDING MOURNING   1633

As virtuous men pass mildly away,
    And whisper to their souls to go,
Whilst some of their sad friends do say
    The breath goes now, and some say, No;

So let us melt, and make no noise,
    No tear-floods, nor sigh-tempests move,
'Twere profanation of our joys
    To tell the laity our love.

Moving of th' earth° brings harms and fears,   earthquake
    Men reckon what it did and meant;   10
But trepidation of the spheres,
    Though greater far, is innocent.[1]

Dull sublunary° lovers' love   under the moon
    (Whose soul is sense) cannot admit
Absence, because it doth remove
    Those things which elemented it.

---

[1] The movement of the heavenly spheres is harmless.

But we by a love so much refined
  That our selves know not what it is,
Inter-assuréd of the mind,
  Care less, eyes, lips, and hands to miss.   20

Our two souls therefore, which are one,
  Though I must go, endure not yet
A breach, but an expansion,
  Like gold to airy thinness beat.

If they be two, they are two so
  As stiff twin compasses are two;
Thy soul, the fixed foot, makes no show
  To move, but doth, if th' other do.

And though it in the center sit,
  Yet when the other far doth roam,   30
It leans and harkens after it,
  And grows erect, as that comes home.

Such wilt thou be to me, who must
  Like th' other foot, obliquely run;
Thy firmness makes my circle just,
  And makes me end where I begun.

FOR ANALYSIS

1. Two kinds of love are described in this poem: spiritual and physical. How does the **simile** drawn in the first two **stanzas** help define the differences between them?

2. How does the contrast between earthquakes and the movement of the spheres in stanza 3 further develop the contrast between the two types of love?

3. Explain the comparison between a drawing compass and the lovers in the last three stanzas.

MAKING ARGUMENTS

Do some research on **metaphor** so that you understand the difference between two ways of seeing metaphor—as a poetic device or as a fundamental tool of cognition, a way in which we use language to understand the world. Using this research and Donne's poem, make an argument about these ways of thinking about metaphor. Is one more important? Is one more fundamental? Are they not as different as they seem?

BEN JONSON   (1572–1637)

SONG, TO CELIA[1]   1616

Drink to me only with thine eyes,
   And I will pledge with mine;
Or leave a kiss but in the cup,
   And I'll not look for wine.
The thirst that from the soul doth rise
   Doth ask a drink divine;
But might I of Jove's nectar sup,
   I would not change for thine.
I sent thee late a rosy wreath,
   Not so much honoring thee   10
As giving it a hope, that there
   It could not withered be.
But thou thereon didst only breathe,
   And sent'st it back to me;
Since when it grows, and smells, I swear,
   Not of itself but thee.

ROBERT HERRICK   (1591–1674)

TO THE VIRGINS, TO MAKE MUCH OF TIME   1648

Gather ye rosebuds while ye may,
   Old Time is still a-flying;
And this same flower that smiles today,
   Tomorrow will be dying.

The glorious lamp of heaven, the sun,
   The higher he's a-getting,
The sooner will his race be run,
   And nearer he's to setting.

That age is best which is the first,
   When youth and blood are warmer;
But being spent, the worse, and worst   10
   Times still succeed the former.

Song, To Celia
[1] A widely recorded song.

940

Then be not coy, but use your time;
　And while ye may, go marry:
For having lost but once your prime,
　You may for ever tarry.

ANNE BRADSTREET   (CA. 1612–1672)

TO MY DEAR AND LOVING HUSBAND   1678

If ever two were one, then surely we.
If ever man were loved by wife, then thee;
If ever wife was happy in a man,
Compare with me ye women if you can.
I prize thy love more than whole mines of gold
Or all the riches that the East doth hold.
My love is such that rivers cannot quench,
Nor ought but love from thee give recompense.
Thy love is such I can no way repay;
The heavens reward thee manifold, I pray.   10
Then while we live, in love let's so persever,
That when we live no more we may live ever.

WILLIAM BLAKE   (1757–1827)

A POISON TREE   1794

I was angry with my friend:
I told my wrath, my wrath did end.
I was angry with my foe:
I told it not, my wrath did grow.

And I watered it in fears,
Night & morning with my tears;
And I sunnéd it with smiles,
And with soft deceitful wiles.

And it grew both day and night,
Till it bore an apple bright.
And my foe beheld its shine,
And he knew that it was mine,   10

And into my garden stole,
When the night had veil'd the pole;
In the morning glad I see
My foe outstretched beneath the tree.

FOR ANALYSIS

1. Is anything gained from the parallel readers might draw between this tree and the tree in the Garden of Eden? Explain.

2. Explain what the "poison" is.

3. Does your own experience verify the first **stanza** of the poem?

MAKING ARGUMENTS

Given the workings of identification, what is the reader's reaction to the event discovered in the poem's last line? What do you think it is supposed to be? What would it mean for us to be happy about it, or unhappy? Make an argument for how the poem wants us to react at the poem's end, using evidence from the text and any sense you have from reading other poems by Blake of what he might have wanted.

ROBERT BURNS   (1759–1796)

A RED, RED ROSE   1796

O My Luve's like a red, red rose,
   That's newly sprung in June;
O My Luve's like a melodie
   That's sweetly played in tune.

As fair art thou, my bonnie lass,
   So deep in luve am I;
And I will luve thee still, my dear,
   Til a' the seas gang dry.

Till a' the seas gang dry, my dear,
   And the rocks melt wi' the sun:
O I will love thee still, my dear,
   While the sands o' life shall run.

And fare thee weel, my only luve,
   And fare thee weel awhile!
And I will come again, my luve,
   Though it were ten thousand mile.

MATTHEW ARNOLD (1822–1888)

DOVER BEACH 1867

The sea is calm tonight.
The tide is full, the moon lies fair
Upon the straits; on the French coast the light
Gleams and is gone; the cliffs of England stand,
Glimmering and vast, out in the tranquil bay.
Come to the window, sweet is the night-air!
Only, from the long line of spray
Where the sea meets the moon-blanched land,
Listen! you hear the grating roar
Of pebbles which the waves draw back, and fling,   10
At their return, up the high strand,
Begin, and cease, and then again begin,
With tremulous cadence slow, and bring
The eternal note of sadness in.

Sophocles long ago
Heard it on the Aegean, and it brought
Into his mind the turbid ebb and flow
Of human misery; we
Find also in the sound a thought,
Hearing it by this distant northern sea.   20

The Sea of Faith
Was once, too, at the full, and round earth's shore
Lay like the folds of a bright girdle furled.
But now I only hear
Its melancholy, long, withdrawing roar,
Retreating, to the breath
Of the night-wind, down the vast edges drear
And naked shingles° of the world.   pebble beaches

Ah, love, let us be true
To one another! for the world, which seems   30
To lie before us like a land of dreams,
So various, so beautiful, so new,
Hath really neither joy, nor love, nor light,
Nor certitude, nor peace, nor help for pain;
And we are here as on a darkling plain
Swept with confused alarms of struggle and flight,
Where ignorant armies clash by night.

ROBERT FROST   (1874–1963)

FIRE AND ICE   1923

Some say the world will end in fire,
Some say in ice,
From what I've tasted of desire
I hold with those who favor fire.
But if it had to perish twice,
I think I know enough of hate
To say that for destruction ice
Is also great
And would suffice.

DOROTHY PARKER   (1893–1967)

ONE PERFECT ROSE   1926

A single flow'r he sent me, since we met.
    All tenderly his messenger he chose;
Deep-hearted, pure, with scented dew still wet—
    One perfect rose.

I knew the language of the floweret;
    "My fragile leaves," it said, "his heart enclose."
Love long has taken for his amulet
    One perfect rose.

Why is it no one ever sent me yet
    One perfect limousine, do you suppose?
Ah no, it's always just my luck to get
    One perfect rose.

THEODORE ROETHKE   (1908–1963)

I KNEW A WOMAN   1958

I knew a woman, lovely in her bones,
When small birds sighed, she would sigh back at them;
Ah, when she moved, she moved more ways than one:

The shapes a bright container can contain!
Of her choice virtues only gods should speak,
Or English poets who grew up on Greek
(I'd have them sing in chorus, cheek to cheek).

How well her wishes went! She stroked my chin,
She taught me Turn, and Counter-turn, and Stand;
She taught me Touch, that undulant white skin;   10
I nibbled meekly from her proffered hand;
She was the sickle; I, poor I, the rake,
Coming behind her for her pretty sake
(But what prodigious mowing we did make).

Love likes a gander, and adores a goose:
Her full lips pursed, the errant note to seize;
She played it quick, she played it light and loose;
My eyes, they dazzled at her flowing knees;
Her several parts could keep a pure repose,
Or one hip quiver with a mobile nose   20
(She moved in circles, and those circles moved).

Let seed be grass, and grass turn into hay:
I'm martyr to a motion not my own;
What's freedom for? To know eternity.
I swear she cast a shadow white as stone.
But who would count eternity in days?
These old bones live to learn her wanton ways:
(I measure time by how a body sways).

For Analysis

1. What is the **rhyme** scheme of this poem?
2. What does line 3 mean?
3. Describe the two principal **images** in the second **stanza**.

Making Arguments

Roethke was known in his earlier poems for painstaking attention to the self; with his love poems, he turns to others, the love-objects of the poem. Make an argument about this turn: are these poems still about the self also? When we think about love, talk about it, write about, are *in* it, how much is the self still important? Use as evidence the poem and anything else that might support your notions about love.

Writing Topic

In an essay, describe the role of motion in this celebration of a woman's beauty.

ELIZABETH BISHOP   (1911–1979)

ONE ART   1976

The art of losing isn't hard to master;
so many things seem filled with the intent
to be lost that their loss is no disaster.

Lose something every day. Accept the fluster
of lost door keys, the hour badly spent.
The art of losing isn't hard to master.

Then practice losing farther, losing faster:
places, and names, and where it was you meant
to travel. None of these will bring disaster.

I lost my mother's watch. And look! my last, or   10
next-to-last, of three loved houses went.
The art of losing isn't hard to master.

I lost two cities, lovely ones. And, vaster,
some realms I owned, two rivers, a continent.
I miss them, but it wasn't a disaster.

—Even losing you (the joking voice, a gesture
I love) I shan't have lied. It's evident
the art of losing's not too hard to master
though it may look like (*Write* it!) like disaster.

JOHN FREDERICK NIMS   (1913–1999)

LOVE POEM   1947

My clumsiest dear, whose hands shipwreck vases,
At whose quick touch all glasses chip and ring,
Whose palms are bulls in china, burrs in linen,
And have no cunning with any soft thing

Except all ill at ease fidgeting people:
The refugee uncertain at the door
You make at home; deftly you steady
The drunk clambering on his undulant floor.

Unpredictable dear, the taxi drivers' terror,
Shrinking from far headlights pale as a dime   10

Yet leaping before red apoplectic streetcars—
Misfit in any space. And never on time.

A wrench in clocks and the solar system. Only
With words and people and love you move at ease.
In traffic of wit expertly maneuver
And keep us, all devotion, at your knees.

Forgetting your coffee spreading on our flannel,
Your lipstick grinning on our coat,
So gayly in love's unbreakable heaven
Our souls on glory of spilt bourbon float.   20

Be with me darling early and late. Smash glasses—
I will study wry music for your sake.
For should your hands drop white and empty
All the toys of the world would break.

LISEL MUELLER (B. 1924)

HAPPY AND UNHAPPY FAMILIES I 1996

If all happy families are alike,[1]
then so are the unhappy families,
whose lives we celebrate
because they are motion and heat,
because they are what we think of as *life.*
Someone is lying and someone else
is being lied to. Someone is beaten
and someone else is doing the beating.
Someone is praying, or weeps
because she does not know how to pray.   10
Someone drinks all night;
someone cowers in corners;
someone threatens and someone pleads.
Bitter words at the table,
bitter sobs in the bedroom;
reprisal breathed on the bathroom mirror.
The house crackles with secrets;
everyone draws up a plan of escape.
Somebody shatters without a sound.
Sometimes one of them leaves the house   20

Happy and Unhappy Families I
[1] An allusion to the celebrated opening line of Leo Tolstoy's novel *Anna Karenina* (1873–1876).

on a stretcher, in terrible silence.
How much energy suffering takes!
It is like a fire that burns and burns
but cannot burn down to extinction.
Unhappy families are never idle;
they are where the action is,
unlike the others, the happy ones,
who never raise their voices
and spit no blood, who do nothing
to deserve their happiness.   30

FOR ANALYSIS

1. How does the speaker describe unhappy families? What do you think are the characteristics of happy families?

2. Describe the **images** used to identify the sources of unhappiness.

3. Describe the conditions that generate happy families (ll. 27–30). Do you agree with the speaker? Explain.

MAKING ARGUMENTS

In line 22, the speaker laments, "How much energy suffering takes!" Do you agree? How much energy does happiness take? Make an argument about the relative energy required to suffer versus to be happy based both on the words of the poem and other works of literature you have read.

WRITING TOPIC

Argue for or against the proposition that all happy (or unhappy) families are alike. On what assumptions do you base your argument?

CAROLYN KIZER   (1925–2014)

BITCH   1984

Now, when he and I meet, after all these years,
I say to the bitch inside me, don't start growling.
He isn't a trespasser anymore,
Just an old acquaintance tipping his hat.
My voice says, "Nice to see you,"
As the bitch starts to bark hysterically.
He isn't an enemy now,
Where are your manners, I say, as I say,
"How are the children? They must be growing up."
At a kind word from him, a look like the old days,   10
The bitch changes her tone: she begins to whimper.

She wants to snuggle up to him, to cringe.
Down, girl! Keep your distance
Or I'll give you a taste of the choke-chain.
"Fine, I'm just fine," I tell him.
She slobbers and grovels.
After all, I am her mistress. She is basically loyal.
It's just that she remembers how she came running
Each evening, when she heard his step;
How she lay at his feet and looked up adoringly   20
Though he was absorbed in his paper;
Or, bored with her devotion, ordered her to the kitchen
Until he was ready to play.
But the small careless kindnesses
When he'd had a good day, or a couple of drinks,
Come back to her now, seem more important
Than the casual cruelties, the ultimate dismissal.
"It's nice to know you are doing so well," I say.
He couldn't have taken you with him;
You were too demonstrative, too clumsy,   30
Not like the well-groomed pets of his new friends.
"Give my regards to your wife," I say. You gag
As I drag you off by the scruff,
Saying, "Goodbye! Goodbye! Nice to have seen you again."

FOR ANALYSIS

1. Who is being addressed in lines 13 and 14?

2. In what ways does the title suit the poem? In answering this question, consider the **tone** of "Bitch," as well as the many **connotations** of the word.

3. What is "the ultimate dismissal" referred to in line 27?

4. How would you describe the speaker's present feelings about her former relationship?

AFTERNOON HAPPINESS   2002

FOR JOHN

At a party I spy a handsome psychiatrist,
And wish, as we all do, to get her advice for free.
Doctor, I'll say, I'm supposed to be a poet.
All life's awfulness has been grist to me.
We learn that happiness is a Chinese meal,
While sorrow is a nourishment forever.
My new environment is California Dreamer.

I'm fearful I'm forgetting how to brood.
And, Doctor, another thing has got me worried:
I'm not drinking as much as I should . . .   10

At home, I want to write a happy poem
On love, or a love poem of happiness.
But they won't do, the tensions of every day,
The rub, the minor abrasions of any two
Who share one space. All, there's no substitute for tragedy!
But in this chapter, tragedy belongs
To that other life, the old life before *us*.
Here is my aphorism of the day:
Happy people are monogamous.
Even in California. So how does the poem play   20

Without the paraphernalia of betrayal and loss?
I don't have a jealous eye or fear
And neither do you. In truth, I'm fond
Of your ex-mate, whom I name "my wife-in-law."
My former husband, that old disaster, is now just funny,
So laugh we do, in what Cyril Connolly
Has called the endless, nocturnal conversation
Of marriage. Which may be the best part.
Darling, must I love you in light verse
Without the tribute of profoundest art?   30

Of course it won't last. You will break my heart
Or I yours, by dying. I could weep over that.
But now it seems forced, here in these heaven hills,
The mourning doves mourning, the squirrels mating,
My old cat warm in my lap, here on our terrace
As from below comes a musical cursing
As you mend my favorite plate. Later of course
I could pick a fight; there is always material in that.
But we don't come from fighting people, those
Who scream out red-hot iambs in their hate.   40

No, love, the heavy poem will have to come
From *temps perdu*, fertile with pain, or perhaps
Detonated by terrors far beyond this place
Where the world rends itself, and its tainted waters
Rise in the east to erode our safety here.
Much as I want to gather a lifetime thrift
And craft, my cunning skills tied in a knot for you,
There is only this useless happiness as gift.

FOR ANALYSIS

1. Explain the comparison in lines 5 and 6.
2. Why does the speaker seem to think that happiness is a problem for poets?
3. How is this poem about more than poets? What other concerns surface?

MAKING ARGUMENTS

Would you say this is a happy poem? A sad poem? Something in between? Make an argument for whichever of these options you believe is the case.

GALWAY KINNELL   (1927–2014)

AFTER MAKING LOVE WE HEAR FOOTSTEPS   1980

For I can snore like a bullhorn
or play loud music
or sit up talking with any reasonably sober Irishman
and Fergus will only sink deeper
into his dreamless sleep, which goes by all in one flash,
but let there be that heavy breathing
or a stifled come-cry anywhere in the house
and he will wrench himself awake
and make for it on the run—as now, we lie together,
after making love, quiet, touching along the length of our bodies,   10
familiar touch of the long-married,
and he appears—in his baseball pajamas, it happens,
the neck opening so small
he has to screw them on, which one day may make him wonder
about the mental capacity of baseball players—
and says, "Are you loving and snuggling? May I join?"
He flops down between us and hugs us and snuggles himself to sleep,
his face gleaming with satisfaction at being this very child.

In the half darkness we look at each other
and smile   20
and touch arms across his little, startlingly muscled body—
this one whom habit of memory propels to the ground of his making,
sleeper only the mortal sounds can sing awake,
this blessing love gives again into our arms.

FOR ANALYSIS

1. What two things appear in this poem that rarely appear together in poems? What is it like to read about them together? Why?

2. What expectation is set up by the event related in lines 6–9? Is it met? Does the speaker have the reaction to this event that we expect?

3. What function might lines 12–15 serve? How do they stand apart from the rest of the poem, and how do they fit in?

MAKING ARGUMENTS

There is an important thread running through much of Western culture concerning how we think about our bodies and sex—that the mind or soul is separate from the body, that sex is for procreation only, that we should be ashamed of our bodies and of sex. (See Blake for an alternate thread.) Make the argument that Kinnell's poem can be read as arguing against this set of ideas. How does it do it? Directly? Indirectly?

WRITING TOPICS

1. Do you believe the explanation in line 22? Do you have to for the poem to work?

2. Though it is not explicitly expressed, what might the speaker be said to be discovering in this poem?

ADRIENNE RICH   (1929–2012)

LIVING IN SIN   1955

She had thought the studio would keep itself;
no dust upon the furniture of love.
Half heresy, to wish the taps less vocal,
the panes relieved of grime. A plate of pears,
a piano with a Persian shawl, a cat
stalking the picturesque amusing mouse
had risen at his urging.
Not that at five each separate stair would writhe
under the milkman's tramp; that morning light
so coldly would delineate the scraps   10
of last night's cheese and three sepulchral bottles;
that on the kitchen shelf among the saucers
a pair of beetle-eyes would fix her own—
Envoy from some village in the moldings . . .
Meanwhile, he, with a yawn,
sounded a dozen notes upon the keyboard,
declared it out of tune, shrugged at the mirror,
rubbed at his beard, went out for cigarettes;
while she, jeered by the minor demons,
pulled back the sheets and made the bed and found   20
a towel to dust the table-top,
and let the coffee-pot boil over on the stove.
By evening she was back in love again,

though not so wholly but throughout the night
she woke sometimes to feel the daylight coming
like a relentless milkman up the stairs.

Sylvia Plath (1932–1963)

Daddy 1965

You do not do, you do not do
Any more, black shoe
In which I have lived like a foot
For thirty years, poor and white,
Barely daring to breathe or Achoo.

Daddy, I have had to kill you,
You died before I had time—
Marble-heavy, a bag full of God,
Ghastly statue with one gray toe
Big as a Frisco seal   10

And a head in the freakish Atlantic
Where it pours bean green over blue
In the waters off beautiful Nauset.
I used to pray to recover you.
Ach, du.[1]

In the German tongue, in the Polish town
Scraped flat by the roller
Of wars, wars, wars.
But the name of the town is common.
My Polack friend   20

Says there are a dozen or two.
So I never could tell where you
Put your foot, your root,
I never could talk to you.
The tongue stuck in my jaw.

It stuck in a barb wire snare.
Ich, ich, ich, ich,[2]
I could hardly speak.

Daddy
  [1] German for "Oh, you."
  [2] German for "I, I, I, I."

I thought every German was you.
And the language obscene   30

An engine, an engine
Chuffing me off like a Jew.
A Jew to Dachau, Auschwitz, Belsen.
I began to talk like a Jew.
I think I may well be a Jew.

The snows of the Tyrol, the clear beer of Vienna
Are not very pure or true.
With my gypsy ancestress and my weird luck
And my Taroc pack and my Taroc pack
I may be a bit of a Jew.   40

I have always been scared of *you*,
With your Luftwaffe,[3] your gobbledygoo.
And your neat mustache
And your Aryan eye, bright blue.
Panzer-man,[4] panzer-man, O You—

Not God but a swastika
So black no sky could squeak through.
Every woman adores a Fascist,
The boot in the face, the brute
Brute heart of a brute like you.   50

You stand at the blackboard, daddy,
In the picture I have of you,
A cleft in your chin instead of your foot
But no less a devil for that, no not
Any less the black man who

Bit my pretty red heart in two.
I was ten when they buried you.
At twenty I tried to die
And get back, back, back to you.
I thought even the bones would do   60

But they pulled me out of the sack,
And they stuck me together with glue.
And then I knew what to do.

---

[3] Name of the German air force during World War II.
[4] *Panzer* refers to German armored divisions during World War II.

I made a model of you,
A man in black with a Meinkampf⁵ look

And a love of the rack and the screw.
And I said I do, I do.
So daddy, I'm finally through.
The black telephone's off at the root,
The voices just can't worm through.   70

If I've killed one man, I've killed two—
The vampire who said he was you
And drank my blood for a year,
Seven years, if you want to know.
Daddy, you can lie back now.

There's a stake in your fat black heart
And the villagers never liked you.
They are dancing and stamping on you.
They always *knew* it was you.
Daddy, daddy, you bastard, I'm through.   80

FOR ANALYSIS

1. How do the **allusions** to Nazism function in the poem?

2. Does the poem exhibit the speaker's love for her father or her hatred of him? Explain.

3. What type of man does the speaker marry (see ll. 61–70)?

4. How does the speaker **characterize** her husband and her father in the last two **stanzas**? Might the "Daddy" of the last line of the poem refer to something more than the speaker's father? Explain.

MAKING ARGUMENTS

One could imagine someone taking offense at lines 31–35, in which the speaker **alludes** to Nazi camps and identifies with the Jewish people. Argue for or against this position. Why is it offensive? Alternatively, why is it not? Use as support for your argument the evidence of the poem and your knowledge (research can help) of the history of World War II and the Jews of Europe.

WRITING TOPICS

1. What is the effect of the peculiar structure, idiosyncratic **rhyme**, unusual words (such as *achoo, gobbledygoo*), and repetitions in the poem?

2. What emotional associations does the title "Daddy" possess? Are those associations reinforced or contradicted by the poem?

⁵ *My Struggle*, the title of Adolf Hitler's autobiography.

LUCILLE CLIFTON (B. 1936–2010)

THERE IS A GIRL INSIDE 1977

there is a girl inside.
she is randy as a wolf.
she will not walk away
and leave these bones
to an old woman.

she is a green tree
in a forest of kindling.
she is a green girl
in a used poet.

she has waited
patient as a nun   10
for the second coming,
when she can break through gray hairs
into blossom

and her lovers will harvest
honey and thyme
and the woods will be wild
with the damn wonder of it.

FOR ANALYSIS

1. Who is the "girl" of this poem? What is she "inside" of?

2. What are the "bones" of the first **stanza**? What does the speaker's statement that
she will not defer to an old woman tell us about her?

3. Describe the prevailing **metaphor** of the poem.

MAKING ARGUMENTS

The connection of the ideas of vitality and sexuality runs deep—just think about the
fertility rituals and **symbols** that have accompanied spring festivals for centuries.
Make an argument about the importance of that connection to "There Is a Girl Inside,"
using as support the poem and anything relevant you find about the way people think
about youth and liveliness and sex.

WRITING TOPIC

In an essay, discuss the appropriateness of the **images** Clifton uses to make her point.

SEAMUS HEANEY (B. 1939–2013)

VALEDICTION 1966

Lady with the frilled blouse
And simple tartan skirt,
Since you have left the house
Its emptiness has hurt
All thought. In your presence
Time rode easy, anchored
On a smile; but absence
Rocked love's balance, unmoored
The days. They buck and bound
Across the calendar   10
Pitched from the quiet sound
Of your flower-tender
Voice. Need breaks on my strand;
You've gone, I am at sea.
Until you resume command
Self is in mutiny.

FOR ANALYSIS

1. What is the central figure of speech (beginning in the middle of line 5) that animates this poem?

2. How are *time*, *love's balance*, and *the days* affected by the "lady's" behavior?

3. What sort of voice would a "flower-tender / Voice" (ll. 12–13) be?

MAKING ARGUMENTS

"All you need is love," John Lennon sang, but is it enough? In "Valediction," the speaker seems to say good-bye not only to his lover but also to himself. Make an argument about love and the need to maintain one's own identity. Is it okay to be at sea when left alone, or is it evidence of having lost oneself? Use the poem, other literature or songs, and/or your own experience to support your argument.

WRITING TOPIC

Write an essay or a poem, serious or humorous, in which you use an extended **metaphor** to describe a fundamental emotion or experience—for example, how falling in love is like racing a car, or how the anguish of separation is like a visit to a dentist, or how attending classes is like a long hike through a desert.

BILLY COLLINS (B. 1941)

SONNET 1999

All we need is fourteen lines, well, thirteen now,
and after this one just a dozen
to launch a little ship on love's storm-tossed seas,
then only ten more left like rows of beans.
How easily it goes unless you get Elizabethan[1]
and insist the iambic bongos must be played
and rhymes positioned at the ends of lines,
one for every station of the cross.
But hang on here while we make the turn
into the final six where all will be resolved,   10
where longing and heartache will find an end,
where Laura will tell Petrarch[2] to put down his pen,
take off those crazy medieval tights,
blow out the lights, and come at last to bed.

SHARON OLDS (B. 1942)

SEX WITHOUT LOVE 1984

How do they do it, the ones who make love
without love? Beautiful as dancers,
gliding over each other like ice skaters
over the ice, fingers hooked
inside each other's bodies, faces
red as steak, wine, wet as the
children at birth whose mothers are going to
give them away. How do they come to the
come to the   come to the   God   come to the
still waters, and not love   10
the one who came there with them, light
rising slowly as steam off their joined
skin? These are the true religious,
the purists, the pros, the ones who will not
accept a false Messiah, love the

Sonnet
[1] The entry for *sonnet* in the "Glossary of Literary Terms" (p. 1418) distinguishes between the English and the Italian, or *Petrarchan*, sonnet.
[2] Francesco Petrarca (1304–1374), who employed the sonnet form named for him. Laura was the idealized woman he celebrated in his sonnets.

priest instead of the God. They do not
mistake the lover for their own pleasure,
they are like great runners: they know they are alone
with the road surface, the cold, the wind,
the fit of their shoes, their over-all cardio-   20
vascular health—just factors, like the partner
in the bed, and not the truth, which is the
single body alone in the universe
against its own best time.

FOR ANALYSIS

1. Describe the speaker's attitude toward "the ones who make love / without love"
(ll. 1–2).

2. Who are the "These" of line 13?

3. What is the effect of the repetitions in lines 8 and 9?

4. What does "factors" of line 21 refer to?

5. Put into your own words the "truth" referred to in the final three lines. Does the
speaker use the word straightforwardly or **ironically**? Explain.

MAKING ARGUMENTS

Is sex without love a bad thing? If so, why? If not, why not? Make an argument on one
side or the other, making detailed reference to the counterargument and refuting it
using support from whatever seems relevant—history, religion, philosophy, or anything else that you can use to bolster your argument.

WYATT PRUNTY   (B. 1947)

LEARNING THE BICYCLE   2000

FOR HEATHER

The older children pedal past
Stable as little gyros, spinning hard
To supper, bath, and bed, until at last
We also quit, silent and tired
Beside the darkening yard where trees
Now shadow up instead of down.
Their predictable lengths can only tease
Her as, head lowered, she walks her bike alone
Somewhere between her wanting to ride
And her certainty she will always fall.   10

Tomorrow, though I will run behind,
Arms out to catch her, she'll tilt then balance wide
Of my reach, till distance makes her small,
Smaller, beyond the place I stop and know
That to teach her I had to follow
And when she learned to let her go.

FOR ANALYSIS

1. Describe the form and **rhyme** scheme of this poem. How does it differ from a **sonnet**?

2. What does the speaker learn from the experience of teaching his daughter to ride a bicycle?

WRITING TOPIC

Write an analysis of the poem's formal structure, noting how the poem shifts somewhat at lines 5, 9, and 11. How does the poem's organization and **rhyme** scheme mimic a typical **sonnet**?

ADRIAN BLEVINS (B. 1964)

CASE AGAINST APRIL 2003

For a long time I was absolutely idiotic,
by which I mean I lashed and pulsed
like the cosmos of tissue at present on fire
inside the bodies of my students—
it being springtime, it being the season
of being naked under the cherry trees.
I'm not saying dig a hole and fall in it;

I'm not saying buy a cabin and a nanny goat
and walk around re-naming the forget-me-nots
after the lovers who said they'd slay you   10
and, well, *did*—for who ever heard
of a plant named Greg? Nevertheless,
sex is laughable; it's ultimately ridiculous;
it's what God invented since he couldn't have

Comedy Central. And still the young people
who aren't pushing their tongues
against the tongues of others
are weeping like babies
being prodded with thermometers
for the lack of good tongues   20
to lean their own tongues against.

I hear them complaining
about their would-be boyfriends and girlfriends,
and it's like they are all about to die,
like their hearts have spontaneously combusted
and little cell splinters are poking their lungs
and they're losing their balance,
falling like hail

or like meteors with pretty faces,
which is why when I say *up*, they look down.   30
And though I'm all for biology,
for the divine plan of multiplication
that calls for the pink of bodies
being bodies with other bodies
in beds and in bushes,
I'm sorry for all the time I wasted
being dramatic over the boys and their mustaches.
Maybe the heart, it gets colder.
But maybe the heart,
it learns a little self-preservation   40
and pulls the shades down
one window at a time. And it's not dark
in here. Really, there's a kind of light
between the marrow and the bone,
and sweet patches of grass to lie down on,
and muskrats and pied pipers
if that's the way you like to see the world,
if to get your kicks you choose to be delirious.
I mean, if you happen to be romantic

and don't mind splitting apart with longing   50
like a child in a toy store
with everywhere these primary colors
seeming to want to open what could be mouths
and seeming to want to sing what could be songs
if only you could catch your breath—
if only your heart would just stop seizing.

FOR ANALYSIS

1. What does April stand for here? Against what is the speaker making her case?

2. Where does the speaker come down on the issues of romance and love and sex?
Is this poem's stance as simple as the title makes it seem?

MAKING ARGUMENTS

Argue for or against the "self-preservation" the speaker claims to have learned (l. 40).
Is romantic love feverish and foolish? Is it necessary and wonderful? Is it some

combination of both? Refer to the poem and to anything else—other poems (or stories, plays, or essays) about love, ideas from other fields such as biology or sociology—or just life in making your argument.

WRITING TOPIC

The title's mention of April **alludes** to a long history of references to that month in poetry. Spend a few minutes of research on other famous poetic Aprils. While they all refer to the same month, do they all do so in exactly the same way? What are the variations? How does this new knowledge affect your reading of the poem?

DAISY FRIED (B. 1967)

ECONO MOTEL, OCEAN CITY 2010

Korean monster movie on the SyFy channel,
lurid *Dora the Explorer* blanket draped tentlike
over Baby's portacrib to shield us from unearned
innocence. The monster slings its carapace
in reverse swan dive up the embankment, triple-jointed bug legs
clattering, bathroom door ajar, exhaust roaring,
both of us naked, monster chomps
fast food stands, all that quilted aluminum, eats through streams
of running people, the promiscuously cheerful guilty American
scientist dies horribly. Grease-dusted ceiling fan   10
paddles erratically, two spars missing. Sheets whirled
to the polluted rug. I reach under the bed, fish out
somebody else's crunched beer can, my forearm comes out
dirty. Monster brachiates from bridge girders like a gibbon
looping round and around uneven bars, those are your fingers
in my tangles or my fingers, my head hangs
half off the king-size, monster takes tiny child actor
to its bone stash. Pillow's wet. The warped ceiling mirror
makes us look like fat porno dwarfs
in centripetal silver nitrate ripples. My glasses on the side table   20
tipped onto scratchproof lenses, earpieces sticking up
like arms out of disaster rubble. Your feet hooked over my feet. What miasma
lays gold dander down on forms of temporary
survivors wandering the promenade? You pull Dora
back over us—Baby's dead to the world—intrude
your propagandistic intimacy jokes,
unforgiving. "What, in a motel room?" I say.

Purple clouds roll back to reveal Armageddon
a dream in bad digital unreality. Explosions repeat patterns like
fake flames dance on fake fireplace logs. Sad Armageddon ⁣ 30
of marriage: how pretty much nice
we meant to be, and couldn't make a difference.

CONNECTING POEMS:
LOOKING BACK ON LOVE

The four poems in this cluster tap into two of the most widely represented
aspects of poetry: the act of looking back and the subject of love. Recol-
lecting, recreating, and reflecting on the past is one of the things writers do
most; loving others is one of the things people do most. As you read these
poems, think about how each of these writers confronts these fundamental
acts and how the most basic parts of each of these phenomena relate—how
looking back so often entails remembering love, and how loving is so much
about loss.

SIR THOMAS WYATT   (1503–1542)

THEY FLEE FROM ME   1557

They flee from me that sometime did me seek
With naked foot, stalking in my chamber.
I have seen them gentle, tame, and meek,
That now are wild and do not remember
That sometime they put themself in danger
To take bread at my hand; and now they range,
Busily seeking with a continual change.

Thanked be fortune it hath been otherwise
Twenty times better; but once in special,
In thin array after a pleasant guise,   10
When her loose gown from her shoulders did fall,
And she me caught in her arms long and small;
Therewithall sweetly did me kiss
And softly said, "Dear heart, how like you this?"

It was no dream: I lay broad waking.
But all is turned thorough my gentleness
Into a strange fashion of forsaking;

And I have leave to go of her goodness,
And she also, to use newfangleness.
But since that I so kindly am served   20
I would fain know what she hath deserved.

FOR ANALYSIS

1. What picture of himself does the speaker paint in the first **stanza**? How does he relate to women? How does that change by the third stanza?

2. What is this poem's **conceit**? If unsure, consider the pun in line 14 ("heart" for "hart"). How does Wyatt use this conceit?

3. Do you think lines 18 and 20 are intended to be read straight or **ironically**? What's the difference for your understanding of the poem?

MAKING ARGUMENTS

Look up Wyatt online and do some reading. What do you notice about his life that might inform this poem? Can you read the poem the same way after learning the long, convoluted tale of his personal life? Regardless of whether your answer is yes or no, make the argument that you can't read it the same, using evidence from your research and the poem.

WRITING TOPIC

Newfangleness is a word Wyatt borrowed from fourteenth-century poet Geoffrey Chaucer. Look it up. What is its significance to the poem? What other words are key in the poem?

LADY MARY WROTH   (CA. 1587–CA. 1651)

"COME DARKEST NIGHT, BECOMING SORROW BEST"   1621

Come darkest night, becoming sorrow best;
   Light; leave thy light; fitt for a lightsome soule;
   Darknes doth truly sure with mee oprest
   Whom absence power doth from mirthe controle:

The very trees with hanging heads condole
   Sweet sommers parting, and of leaves distrest
   In dying coulers make a griefe-full role;
   Soe much (alas) to sorrow are they prest,

Thus of dead leaves her farewell carpett's made:
   Theyr fall, theyr branches, all theyr mournings prove;   10
   With leavles, naked bodies, whose huese vade
   From hopefull greene, to wither in theyr love,

If trees, and leaves for absence, mourners bee
Noe mervaile that I grieve, who like want see.

FOR ANALYSIS

1. What is this poem's **mood**? How does Wroth achieve it?

2. How does the speaker feel about her feelings? Does she try to fight them off?
Does she accept them? Does she welcome them?

MAKING ARGUMENTS

Grief is a complicated thing, an emotional response to loss. There are entire branches
of the psychological and social sciences devoted to understanding what it is, what
forms it takes, and how different personalities and different cultures conceive of it and
deal with it. Make an argument about the workings of grief in this poem concerning
the speaker as griever. How does the speaker grieve? Is the speaker going through
something or stuck in something? Is grief something to be worked through?

WRITING TOPIC

The sentimental or pathetic fallacy is the name given by critics to the practice of
assigning humanlike feelings and actions to inanimate objects, often natural ones.
"Pathetic" here is not negative (nor is "fallacy"); instead, it has to do with *pathos*, or
feeling. List Wroth's use of the pathetic fallacy in this poem. Do you think there is anything fallacious or false about it?

SHARON OLDS (B. 1942)

MY FATHER'S DIARY 1998

I get into bed with it, and spring
the scarab legs of its locks. Inside,
the stacked, shy wealth of his print—
he could not write in script, so the pages
are sturdy with the beamwork of printedness,
WENT TO LOOK AT A CAR, DAD
IN A GOOD MOOD AT DINNER, WENT
TO TRY OUT SOME NEW TENNIS RACQUETS,
LUNCH WITH MOM, life of ease—
except when he spun his father's DeSoto on the   10
ice, and a young tree whirled up to the
hood, throwing up her arms—until
LOIS. PLAYED TENNIS, WITH LOIS,
LUNCH WITH MOM AND LOIS, LOIS
LIKED THE CAR, DRIVING WITH LOIS,
LONG DRIVE WITH LOIS. And then,
LOIS! I CAN'T BELIEVE IT! SHE IS SO

GOOD, SO SWEET, SO GENEROUS, I HAVE
NEVER, WHAT HAVE I EVER DONE
TO DESERVE SUCH A GIRL? Between the dark   20
legs of the capitals, moonlight, soft
tines of the printed letter gentled
apart, nectar drawn from serif, the
self of the grown boy pouring
out, the heart's charge, the fresh
man kneeling in pine-needle weave,
worshipping her. It was my father
good, it was my father grateful,
it was my father dead, who had left me
these small structures of his young brain—   30
he wanted me to know him, he wanted
someone to know him.

FOR ANALYSIS

1. This poem is about the speaker's father as a boy, so retrospect—literally, looking
back—is built into the situation. How does Olds set the stage for this situation in the
poem's opening?

2. What does the speaker discover about her father? How does she feel about what
she discovers?

MAKING ARGUMENTS

The presence of handwriting in "My Father's Diary" looms larger than one might
expect. Paying close attention to the language and **imagery** of the poem, argue that
the handwriting is more significant to it than if it were a stray observation about the
physical appearance of the diary's pages. How does Olds use it? Where and how does
she refer to it? Why does it take on importance?

WRITING TOPIC

There seems to be a lot left out of this poem, a great deal left unsaid about the father
and the daughter's relationship with or her feelings about him. Drawing on the textual
evidence in this poem and on your own imagination, write a short **prose** description
of the man and his relationship with his daughter.

DEAN YOUNG   (B. 1955)

WINGED PURPOSES   2009

Fly from me does all I would have stay,
the blossoms did not stay, stayed not the frost
in the yellow grass. Every leash snapped,
every contract void, and flying in the crows

lingers but a moment in the graveyard oaks
yet inside me it never stops so I can't tell
who is chasing, who chased, I can sleep
into afternoon and still wake soaring.
So out come the bats, down spiral swifts
into the chimneys, Hey, I'm real, say the dream-   10
figments then are gone like breath-prints
on a window, handwriting in snow. Whatever
I hold however flies apart, the children skip
into the park come out middle-aged
with children of their own. Your laugh
over the phone, will it ever answer me again?
Too much flying, photons perforating us,
voices hurtling into outer space, Whitman
out past Neptune, Dickinson retreating
yet getting brighter. Remember running   20
barefoot across hot sand into the sea's
hovering, remember my hand as we darted
against the holiday Broadway throng,
catching your train just as it was leaving?
Hey, it's real, your face like a comet,
horses coming from the field for morning
oats, insects hitting a screen, the message
nearly impossible to read, obscured by light
because carried by Mercury: I love you,
I'm coming. Sure, what fluttered is now gone,   30
maybe a smudge left, maybe a delicate under-
feather only then that too, yes, rained away.
And when the flying is flown and the heart's
a useless sliver in a glacier and the gown
hangs still as meat in a locker and eyesight
is dashed-down glass and the mouth rust-
stoppered, will some twinge still pass between us,
still some fledgling pledge?

FOR ANALYSIS

1. What does the speaker wish would stay that does not? How does he feel about these things?

2. While this poem is about memory and loss, would you say the **tone** is uniformly dark? Why or why not?

MAKING ARGUMENTS

Emily Dickinson and Walt Whitman make cameos in "Winged Purposes." Make an argument for why you think casting director Dean Young hired them. Possible avenues to consider: literary history (When were they alive and writing? When is

Young?); the nature(s) of their poetry; the importance of memory not only in poetry but in life; and other such topics.

WRITING TOPIC

Write a short description of Young's **style**. Is the language spare or flowery, intimate or oratorical? Is the **imagery** focused or encyclopedic? Why do the choices you think Young made in writing this poem fit the ideas and feelings he's trying to express?

MAKING CONNECTIONS

1. All of these poems are in some way about looking back on love. How does each look back? In anger? Wistfully? How does the nature of their looking back help to shape the poems?

2. Compare Wyatt's "They Flee From Me" (p. 963) to Young's "Winged Purposes." While both are about things going away from the speaker, they take very different approaches to the topic. Wyatt pursues a single **conceit** throughout the poem; comparing Young's poem to Wyatt's, would you say he follows the same path? If not, what does he do differently? What is the effect of his choice?

3. Love and its loss is surely one of the oldest **themes** in literature. Compare the two twentieth-century poems in this cluster to those from the sixteenth and seventeenth centuries. What are the differences? Are they superficial or more profound?

CONNECTING POEMS: REMEMBERING FATHERS

No relationship is more primary to the human experience than that between parent and child. The relationship of mother or father to baby is one of complete responsibility and complete dependence, but this changes as both grow older and the emotional terrain becomes more tricky and harder to read. The poems in this unit express just a few of the very different kinds of emotions fathers and their children feel for each other, in the context of some of the many difficulties people encounter in life. As you read, take note of how the poems address the ways in which parents' and children's expectations of each other are or are not met and the ways in which feelings are or are not expressed.

THEODORE ROETHKE   (1908–1963)

MY PAPA'S WALTZ   1948

The whiskey on your breath
Could make a small boy dizzy;
But I hung on like death:
Such waltzing was not easy.

We romped until the pans
Slid from the kitchen shelf;
My mother's countenance
Could not unfrown itself.

The hand that held my wrist
Was battered on one knuckle;
At every step you missed
My right ear scraped a buckle.   10

You beat time on my head
With a palm caked hard by dirt,
Then waltzed me off to bed
Still clinging to your shirt.

FOR ANALYSIS

1. Why is **iambic trimeter** an appropriate **meter** for this poem?
2. What details reveal the kind of person the father is?
3. How would you describe the boy's feelings about his father? The father's about the boy?

MAKING ARGUMENTS

Some read this poem as more funny than not, while some read the humor as dark
and consider the darkness of the poem to be the overriding **tone**. Make an argument
concerning this critical disagreement, paying close attention to individual words and
phrases and larger effects of the lines, **stanzas**, and the poem as a whole.

WRITING TOPIC

Describe this poem's tone. What in the way it describes the events, from the title to the
conceit, expresses this tone?

ROBERT HAYDEN   (1913–1980)

THOSE WINTER SUNDAYS   1975

Sundays too my father got up early
and put his clothes on in the blueblack cold,
then with cracked hands that ached
from labor in the weekday weather made
banked fires blaze. No one ever thanked him.

I'd wake and hear the cold splintering, breaking.
When the rooms were warm, he'd call,
and slowly I would rise and dress,
fearing the chronic angers of that house,

Speaking indifferently to him,
who had driven out the cold
and polished my good shoes as well.
What did I know, what did I know
of love's austere and lonely offices?

10

FOR ANALYSIS

1. Why Sundays "too" (l. 1)?

2. What does *offices* mean (l. 14) in this poem? Why do you think Hayden chooses this word?

3. From when in his life does the speaker describe those winter Sundays? How does his relation to the event color his description?

MAKING ARGUMENTS

Arguably, the final **couplet** of "Winter Sundays" is (as is often case) the most powerful moment in the poem. Make the unwinnable (because unprovable, not because demonstrably wrong) argument that the sentiment expressed there—of regret for what past ignorance led one to do or not do—is as powerful as any other you know of.

WRITING TOPICS

1. In the last line of the second **stanza**, the speaker refers to "the chronic angers of that house." How does the anger the speaker fears relate to the "love" of the poem's last line?

2. Has there been a time in your life when you neglected to thank someone you should have or to appreciate something you should have? How does the recollection make you feel?

LI-YOUNG LEE   (B. 1957)

EATING ALONE   1986

I've pulled the last of the year's young onions.
The garden is bare now. The ground is cold,
brown and old. What is left of the day flames
in the maples at the corner of my
eye. I turn, a cardinal vanishes.
By the cellar door, I wash the onions,
then drink from the icy metal spigot.

Once, years back, I walked beside my father
among the windfall pears. I can't recall
our words. We may have strolled in silence. But
I still see him bend that way—left hand braced

10

on knee, creaky—to lift and hold to my
eye a rotten pear. In it, a hornet
spun crazily, glazed in slow, glistening juice.

It was my father I saw this morning
waving to me from the trees. I almost
called to him, until I came close enough
to see the shovel, leaning where I had
left it, in the flickering, deep green shade.

White rice steaming, almost done. Sweet green peas   20
fried in onions. Shrimp braised in sesame
oil and garlic. And my own loneliness.
What more could I, a young man, want.

FOR ANALYSIS

1. Why is the speaker eating alone?

2. How do the repeated references to youth and age, things being finished or almost done, function in the poem?

3. Why do you think the poet might have chosen to include the **image** of the hornet?

MAKING ARGUMENTS

The importance of food to this poem cannot be overstated. The same could be true of its importance to culture. Read up as much as time will allow on the cultural uses and meanings of food (that is, beyond keeping people alive) and, using the evidence of any of the works in this book, make an argument concerning the importance of food in literature specifically (as opposed to in culture, or the way we live, more broadly). If at a loss, consider the usefulness to your argument of the idea that literature is how we think about culture.

WRITING TOPICS

1. Read the last **stanza** closely. What is the effect of the **imagery**? What kind of question is asked in the last line? What do you think Lee was trying to do at the end of his poem?

2. Why do you think the poet chooses to write about a son remembering his father through the preparation of a meal? What is the significance of eating?

MAKING CONNECTIONS

1. Violence—actual or possible—is a presence in many of these poems. How do these poems express violence, explicitly and implicitly? Why is it such a presence?

2. In these poems, love is expressed in funny ways or goes unexpressed even when it is felt. What are some of the different ways in which these poems represent or hint at love?

3. In "Winter Sundays," Hayden alludes to the work parents do outside the home with the phrase "labor in the weekday weather" (1.4). What role does the work providers do outside the home play in these poems? What is its significance?

CONNECTING POEMS: LOVE STINKS

None of the poems in this cluster professes a romantic view of romantic love—that is, none of these poems assumes the possibility of uncomplicated, cupids-and-angels kind of love in real life. As you read these poems in which love is shown to stink, observe the ways in which it does not. That love sometimes or even often brings pain and misery matters only because it sometimes does not.

CATULLUS   (CA. 84–CA. 54 BCE)

70

My woman says that she prefers to be married to no one
than to me, not even if Jupiter himself should seek her.
She says: but what a woman says to her passionate lover,
she ought to write on the wind and swift-flowing water.

FOR ANALYSIS

1. What does it mean to write something on the wind or on water?

2. What significance does the reference to Jupiter carry?

MAKING ARGUMENTS

Make an argument about this short poem: Is the **tone** humorous, dark, or both?

WRITING TOPIC

When have you promised something you had no intention of doing? When have you promised something you might have meant, sort of, but didn't stick to keeping the promise? Reflect on that moment, on your motivations, and on how you feel about it looking back.

APHRA BEHN   (1640–1689)

LOVE IN FANTASTIQUE TRIUMPH SATT   1684

Love in Fantastique Triumph satt
Whilst Bleeding Hearts a round him flow'd,
For whom fresh paines he did Create,
And strange Tyranick power he show'd;

From thy Bright Eyes he took his fire,
Which round about, in sport he hurl'd;
But 'twas from mine he took desire,
Enough to undo the Amorous World.

From me he took his sighs and tears,
From thee his Pride and Crueltie;
From me his Languishments and Feares,
And every Killing Dart from thee;
Thus thou and I, the God have arm'd,
And sett him up a Deity;
But my poor heart alone is harm'd,
Whilst thine the Victor is, and free.

10

FOR ANALYSIS

1. Who is the speaker? To whom does she speak?

2. What is the background of this poem—that is, what is the relationship between the speaker and the immediate audience, and what has happened between them?

3. How has love triumphed in this poem?

MAKING ARGUMENTS

As Michael Jackson says to Paul McCartney in the song "The Girl Is Mine," "I'm a lover, not a fighter." The opposition of love and war, love and violence, loving and fighting, is an old one. An alternate title under which this poem is often published is "Love Armed," which makes even more plain that Love, **personified** in this poem, *is* a fighter. Using any evidence you wish, from your own life to literature to what you may take as universal human truths, make an argument for the ways in which, to quote a song coincidentally also released in 1982 (one month later), "love is a battlefield."

WRITING TOPIC

Imagine a response to this poem in which speaker and spoken-to are switched.

EDNA ST. VINCENT MILLAY   (1892-1950)

I KNOW I AM BUT SUMMER TO YOUR HEART (SONNET XXVII)

I know I am but summer to your heart,
And not the full four seasons of the year;
And you must welcome from another part
Such noble moods as are not mine, my dear.
No gracious weight of golden fruits to sell
Have I, nor any wise and wintry thing;

And I have loved you all too long and well
To carry still the high sweet breast of Spring.
Wherefore I say: O love, as summer goes,
I must be gone, steal forth with silent drums,   10
That you may hail anew the bird and rose
When I come back to you, as summer comes.
Else will you seek, at some not distant time,
Even your summer in another clime.

FOR ANALYSIS

1. What is the speaker *not*, to the person to whom he or she speaks? How are these things/qualities described?

2. What *is* the speaker to the person to whom he or she speaks? How are these things/qualities described?

3. Describe the **tone** of this poem. Is it angry? Wistful? Accepting? Ultimately, is it despairing or hopeful?

MAKING ARGUMENTS

The first six lines of the poem contain a number of negative words, variations of *no* and *not*, and the entire poem is filled with negation—with what is not true, not the case, not possessed. Make an argument for why Millay might have chosen to write the poem in this way. What is the effect? How does it fit well with the poem's subject?

WRITING TOPIC

Imagine a version of this poem in which Millay had done something differently. Maybe she argues that she should be everything to her lover, or that her lover should just leave her, or maybe she frames the poem not in negatives but in positives. Write the poem, if you want, or simply describe it.

FAIZ AHMED FAIZ (1911–1984)

BE NEAR ME 1987

Be near me now,
My tormenter, my love, be near me—
At this hour when night comes down,
When, having drunk from the gash of sunset, darkness comes
With the balm of musk in its hands, its diamond lancets,
When it comes with cries of lamentation,
                              with laughter with songs;
Its blue-gray anklets of pain clinking with every step.
At this hour when hearts, deep in their hiding places,

Have begun to hope once more, when they start their vigil   10
For hands still enfolded in sleeves;
When wine being poured makes the sound
                 of inconsolable children
           who, though you try with all your heart,
                 cannot be soothed.
When whatever you want to do cannot be done,
When nothing is of any use;
—At this hour when night comes down,
When night comes, dragging its long face,
                 dressed in mourning,   20

Be with me,
My tormenter, my love, be near me.

FOR ANALYSIS

1. Why does the speaker call his or her lover "my tormenter" (ll. 2 and 22)?
2. At this hour when night comes down,
2. What is the significance of night in "Be Near Me"?

MAKING ARGUMENTS

Make an argument about this poem's **tone**. Is it uniform or changing? If the former, what is it, and how is it created? If the latter, what are the different tones and how are each created?

WRITING TOPIC

Read through the poem again and list all of the ways in which things are described in ways that emphasize pain and violence, from **diction** to **imagery** even to sound. Create an alternate list of ways the poem could have been written to describe a love that brings not pain but pleasure, or calm, or something other than that which is Faiz's subject here.

ANDREA HOLLANDER   (B. 1947)

BETRAYAL   2009

They decide finally not to speak
of it, the one blemish in their otherwise
blameless marriage. It happened

as these things do, before the permanence
was set, before the children grew
complicated, before the quench

of loving one another became all
each of them wanted from this life.
Years later the bite

of not knowing (and not wanting   10
to know) still pierces the doer
as much as the one to whom it was done:

the threadbare lying, the insufferable longing,
the inimitable lack of touching, the undoing
undone.

FOR ANALYSIS

1. What is the "one blemish" (l. 2)?

2. Where in time, relative to the event that is the poem's subject, is this poem situated? Why is this significant?

MAKING ARGUMENTS

Hollander chooses not to provide any details of the betrayal in "Betrayal," yet it is so important that it is the title of the poem. Make an argument for why she made this choice, taking into account the poem's subject and form and considering alternative ways she might have written the poem as counterarguments.

WRITING TOPIC

Reflect on a time when you betrayed someone, in one way or another (it doesn't have to be romantic); or, if you have lived a blameless life, reflect on a time when you were betrayed. How does the event compare to Hollander's account of a betrayal, even one that may not have happened?

CASE STUDY IN ARGUMENT
SEDUCTIVE REASONING

Andrew Marvell's poem "To His Coy Mistress" is one of the best-known poems in English. In the poems by A. D. Hope, Peter DeVries, and Annie Finch in this cluster, Marvell's poem is held up as an example of social attitudes and poetic tropes. Reading these poems alongside Marvell's, note the complicated and varied ways in which they not only make arguments about what's wrong with "To His Coy Mistress" but also press their own claims about seduction, romance, and what comes after.

ANDREW MARVELL (1621–1678)

TO HIS COY MISTRESS 1681

Had we but world enough, and time,
This coyness, lady, were no crime.
We would sit down, and think which way
To walk, and pass our long love's day.
Thou by the Indian Ganges' side
Shouldst rubies find; I by the tide
Of Humber would complain. I would
Love you ten years before the flood,
And you should, if you please, refuse
Til the conversion of the Jews.   10
My vegetable love should grow
Vaster than empires and more slow;
An hundred years should go to praise
Thine eyes, and on thy forehead gaze;
Two hundred to adore each breast,
But thirty thousand to the rest;
An age at least to every part,
And the last age should show your heart.
For, lady, you deserve this state,
Nor would I love at lower rate.   20
    But at my back I always hear
Time's wingéd chariot hurrying near;
And yonder all before us lie
Deserts of vast eternity.
Thy beauty shall no more be found,
Nor, in thy marble vault, shall sound

My echoing song; then worms shall try
That long-preserved virginity,
And your quaint honor turn to dust,
And into ashes all my lust: 30
The grave's a fine and private place,
But none, I think, do there embrace.
   Now therefore, while the youthful hue
Sits on thy skin like morning dew,
And while thy willing soul transpires
At every pore with instant fires,
Now let us sport us while we may,
And now, like amorous birds of prey,
Rather at once our time devour
Than languish in his slow-chapped° power.   slow-jawed 40
Let us roll our strength and all
Our sweetness up into one ball,
And tear our pleasures with rough strife
Thorough° the iron gates of life: through
Thus, though we cannot make our sun
Stand still, yet we will make him run.

FOR ANALYSIS

1. State the argument of the poem (see ll. 1–2, 21–22, 33–34).

2. Compare the figures of speech in lines 1–20 with those in lines 33–46. How do they differ?

3. Describe the attitude toward life recommended by the poet.

MAKING ARGUMENTS

Analyze "To His Coy Mistress" as an argument. How does the speaker press his case? How does he support his claim?

A. D. HOPE (1907–2000)

HIS COY MISTRESS TO MR. MARVELL   1978

Since you have world enough and time
Sir, to admonish me in rhyme,
Pray Mr. Marvell, can it be
You think to have persuaded me?
Then let me say: you want the art
To woo, much less to win my heart.

The verse was splendid, all admit,
And, sir, you have a pretty wit.
All that indeed your poem lacked
Was logic, modesty, and tact,   10
Slight faults and ones to which I own,
Your sex is generally prone;
But though you lose your labour, I
Shall not refuse you a reply:

First, for the language you employ:
A term I deprecate is "coy";
The ill-bred miss, the bird-brained Jill,
May simper and be coy at will;
A lady, sir, as you will find,
Keeps counsel, or she speaks her mind,   20
Means what she says and scorns to fence
And palter with feigned innocence.

The ambiguous "mistress" next you set
Beside this graceless epithet.
"Coy mistress," sir? Who gave you leave
To wear my heart upon your sleeve?
Or to imply, as sure you do,
I had no other choice than you
And must remain upon the shelf
Unless I should bestir myself?   30
Shall I be moved to love you, pray,
By hints that I must soon decay?
No woman's won by being told
How quickly she is growing old;
Nor will such ploys, when all is said,
Serve to stampede us into bed.

When from pure blackmail, next you move
To bribe or lure me into love,
No less inept, my rhyming friend,
Snared by the means, you miss your end.   40
"Times winged chariot," and the rest
As poetry may pass the test;
Readers will quote those lines, I trust,
Till you and I and they are dust;
But I, your destined prey, must look
Less at the bait than at the hook,
Nor, when I do, can fail to see
Just what it is you offer me:

Love on the run, a rough embrace
Snatched in the fury of the chase, 50
The grave before us and the wheels
Of Time's grim chariot at our heels,
While we, like "am'rous birds of prey,"
Tear at each other by the way.

To say the least, the scene you paint
Is, what you call my honour, quaint!
And on this point what prompted you
So crudely, and in public too,
To canvass and, indeed, make free
With my entire anatomy? 60
Poets have licence, I confess,
To speak of ladies in undress;
Thighs, hearts, brows, breasts are well enough,
In verses this is common stuff;
But—well I ask: to draw attention
To worms in—what I blush to mention,
And prate of dust upon it too!
Sir, was this any way to woo?

Now therefore, while male self-regard
Sits on your cheek, my hopeful bard, 70
May I suggest, before we part,
The best way to a woman's heart
Is to be modest, candid, true;
Tell her you love and show you do;
Neither cajole nor condescend
And base the lover on the friend;
Don't bustle her or fuss or snatch:
A suitor looking at his watch
Is not a posture that persuades
Willing, much less reluctant maids. 80

Remember that she will be stirred
More by the spirit than the word;
For truth and tenderness do more
Than coruscating metaphor.
Had you addressed me in such terms
And prattled less of graves and worms,
I might, who knows, have warmed to you;
But, as things stand, must bid adieu
(Though I am grateful for the rhyme)
And wish you better luck next time. 90

FOR ANALYSIS

1. What is the speaker's attitude toward Mr. Marvell?
2. How would you describe the speaker's **tone**? How does it serve the poem?

MAKING ARGUMENTS

Analyze "His Coy Mistress to Mr. Marvell" as an argument. How does the speaker press her case? How does she support her claim?

WRITING TOPIC

Pick a poem from this book or elsewhere and write (or outline) a similar response to it.

PETER DeVRIES (1910-1993)

TO HIS IMPORTUNATE MISTRESS (ANDREW MARVELL UPDATED) 1986

Had we but world enough, and time,
My coyness, lady, were a crime,
But at my back I always hear
Time's winged chariot, striking fear
The hour is nigh when creditors
Will prove to be my predators.
As wages of our picaresque,
Bag lunches bolted at my desk
Must stand as fealty to you
For each expensive rendezvous.   10
Obeisance at your marble feet
Deserves the best-appointed suite,
And would have, lacked I not the pelf
To pleasure also thus myself;
But amply sumptuous amorous scenes
Rule out the rake of modest means.

Since mistress presupposes wife,
It means a doubly costly life;
For fools by second passion fired
A second income is required,   20
The earning which consumes the hours
They'd hoped to spend in rented bowers.
To hostelries the worst of fates
That weekly raise their daily rates!

I gather, lady, from your scoffing
A bloke more solvent in the offing.
So revels thus to rivals go
For want of monetary flow.
How vexing that inconsistent cash
The constant suitor must abash,   30
Who with excuses vainly pled
Must rue the undishevelled bed,
And that for paltry reasons given
His conscience may remain unriven.

FOR ANALYSIS

1. How would you describe the relation of this poem, line by line (including the title), to Marvell's?

2. Rather than focusing on romantic and sexual love, what does this poem emphasize most?

MAKING ARGUMENTS

Analyze "To His Importunate Mistress" as an argument. How does the speaker frame his argument? How does he support it?

WRITING TOPIC

The history of literature in English is marked by the waxing and waning of attention to the economic. From a history of tales and poems about courtly love, royal intrigue, and religious feeling emerges, here and there and more so the later you get, the daily business of financial solvency and even survival. Reflect on this tension in literary history. Should literature be above these concerns or should it focus on how people make do in the world?

ANNIE FINCH   (B. 1956)

COY MISTRESS   1997

(IN ANSWER TO THE POEM BY ANDREW MARVELL)

Sir, I am not a bird of prey:
a Lady does not seize the day.
I trust that brief Time will unfold
our youth, before he makes us old.
How could we two write lines of rhyme
were we not fond of numbered Time
and grateful to the vast and sweet
trials his days will make us meet:

The Grave's not just the body's curse;
no skeleton can pen a verse!
So while this numbered World we see,
let's sweeten Time with poetry,
and Time, in turn, may sweeten Love
and give us time our love to prove.
You've praised my eyes, forehead, breast:
you've all our lives to praise the rest.

10

FOR ANALYSIS

1. What word appears more than any other in this poem? Why?
2. What is the poem's **tone**? How is it created?
3. What is the thing most valued in this poem?

MAKING ARGUMENTS

Make the argument that Finch's shifting of the focus from Marvell's (seduction) to her poem's focus, poetry, is more than a diversion or an expression of professional colleagueship but a feminist statement. Use the two poems as evidence and read up on feminist thought if you need to.

WRITING TOPIC

Finch's poem is a direct response to Marvell's "To His Coy Mistress" (p. 977). Imagine a different response to Marvell's poem. What else could be said in reply? Who else could say it?

MAKING CONNECTIONS

1. Argument is often thought of as more the province of essays than poems, but as these poems make plain, poetry has its own resources. Compare the ways the different works in this cluster use poetic form to make their arguments.
2. What is the significance of time in these poems? To which poems is it most important? How is it important in each?
3. Compare Finch's and Hope's responses to Marvell. How are they similar? How do they differ?

DRAMA

WILLIAM SHAKESPEARE (1564–1616)

OTHELLO   CA. 1604

CHARACTERS

Duke of Venice
Brabantio, a Senator
Senators
Gratiano, Brother to Brabantio
Lodovico, Kinsman to Brabantio
Othello, a noble Moor; in the
    service of the Venetian State
Cassio, his Lieutenant
Iago, his Ancient
Roderigo, a Venetian Gentleman

Montano, Othello's predecessor
    in the Government of Cyprus
Clown, Servant to Othello
Desdemona, Daughter to
    Brabantio, and Wife to Othello
Emilia, Wife to Iago
Bianca, Mistress to Cassio
Sailor, Officers, Gentlemen,
Messengers, Musicians,
Heralds, Attendants

Scene
For the first Act, in Venice; during the rest of the Play, at a Sea-port in Cyprus

ACT I

Scene 1.   Venice. A Street.

(Enter Roderigo and Iago.)

Roderigo.   Tush! Never tell me; I take it much unkindly
    That thou, Iago, who has had my purse
    As if the strings were thine, shouldst know of this.[1]

---

[1] I.e., Othello's successful courtship of Desdemona.

Iago. 'Sblood,[2] but you will not hear me:
    If ever I did dream of such a matter,
    Abhor me.
Roderigo. Thou told'st me thou didst hold him[3] in thy hate.
Iago. Despise me if I do not. Three great ones of the city,
    In personal suit to make me his lieutenant,
    Off-capp'd[4] to him; and, by the faith of man,   10
    I know my price, I am worth no worse a place;
    But he, as loving his own pride and purposes,
    Evades them, with a bombast circumstance[5]
    Horribly stuff'd with epithets of war;
    And, in conclusion,
    Nonsuits[6] my mediators;[7] for, 'Certes,'[8] says he,
    'I have already chosen my officer.'
    And what was he?
    Forsooth, a great arithmetician,
    One Michael Cassio, a Florentine,   20
    A fellow almost damn'd in a fair wife;[9]
    That never set a squadron in the field,
    Nor the division of a battle knows
    More than a spinster; unless[10] the bookish theoric,[11]
    Wherein the togèd consuls can propose
    As masterly as he: mere prattle, without practice,
    Is all his soldiership. But he, sir, had the election;
    And I—of whom his eyes had seen the proof
    At Rhodes, at Cyprus, and on other grounds
    Christian and heathen—must be be-lee'd[12] and calm'd   30
    By debitor and creditor; this counter-caster,[13]
    He, in good time, must his lieutenant be,
    And I—God bless the mark!—his Moorship's ancient.[14]
Roderigo. By heaven, I rather would have been his hangman.
Iago. Why, there's no remedy: 'tis the curse of service,
    Preferment goes by letter and affection,
    Not by the old gradation,[15] where each second
    Stood heir to the first. Now, sir, be judge yourself,
    Whe'r[16] I in any just term am affin'd[17]
    To love the Moor.

---

[2] By God's blood.   [3] I.e., Othello.   [4] Took off their caps.   [5] Pompous wordiness, circumlocution.
[6] Turns down.   [7] Spokesmen.   [8] In truth.   [9] A much debated phrase. In the Italian source the
Captain (i.e., Cassio) was married, and it may be that Shakespeare originally intended Bianca to be Cassio's
wife but later changed his mind and failed to alter the phrase here accordingly. Or perhaps Iago simply
sneers at Cassio as a notorious ladies' man.   [10] Except.   [11] Theory.   [12] Left without wind for my sails.
[13] Bookkeeper (cf. "arithmetician" above).   [14] Ensign (but Iago's position in the play seems to be that of
Othello's aide-de-camp).   [15] Seniority.   [16] Whether.   [17] Obliged.

Roderigo.   I would not follow him then. 40

Iago. O! sir, content you;

I follow him to serve my turn upon him;
We cannot all be masters, nor all masters
Cannot be truly follow'd. You shall mark
Many a duteous and knee-crooking knave,
That, doting on his own obsequious bondage,
Wears out his time, much like his master's ass,
For nought but provender, and when he's old, cashier'd;
Whip me such honest knaves. Others there are
Who, trimm'd in forms and visages of duty, 50
Keep yet their hearts attending on themselves,
And, throwing but shows of service on their lords,
Do well thrive by them, and when they have lin'd their coats
Do themselves homage: these fellows have some soul;
And such a one do I profess myself. For, sir,
It is as sure as you are Roderigo,
Were I the Moor, I would not be Iago:
In following him, I follow but myself;
Heaven is my judge, not I for love and duty,
But seeming so, for my peculiar end: 60
For when my outward action doth demonstrate
The native act and figure of my heart
In compliment extern,[18] 'tis not long after
But I will wear my heart upon my sleeve
For daws to peck at: I am not what I am.

Roderigo. What a full fortune does the thick-lips owe,[19]

If he can carry 't thus!

Iago.   Call up her father;

Rouse him, make after him, poison his delight,
Proclaim him in the streets, incense her kinsmen,
And, though he in a fertile climate dwell,[20] 70
Plague him with flies; though that his joy be joy,
Yet throw such changes of vexation on 't
As it may lose some colour.

Roderigo. Here is her father's house; I'll call aloud.

Iago. Do; with like timorous[21] accent and dire yell

As when, by night and negligence, the fire
Is spied in populous cities.

Roderigo. What, ho! Brabantio: Signior Brabantio, ho!

Iago. Awake! what, ho! Brabantio! thieves! thieves! thieves!

---

[18] External show.   [19] Own.   [20] I.e., is fortunate.   [21] Frightening.

Look to your house, your daughter, and your bags!   80
Thieves! thieves!

(Enter Brabantio, above, at a window.)

Brabantio. What is the reason of this terrible summons?
   What is the matter there?
Roderigo. Signior, is all your family within?
Iago. Are your doors lock'd?
Brabantio.   Why? wherefore ask you this?
Iago. 'Zounds!²² sir, you're robb'd; for shame, put on your gown;
   Your heart is burst, you have lost half your soul;
   Even now, now, very now, an old black ram
   Is tupping²³ your white ewe. Arise, arise!
   Awake the snorting²⁴ citizens with the bell,   90
   Or else the devil will make a grandsire of you.
   Arise, I say.
Brabantio. What! have you lost your wits?
Roderigo. Most reverend signior, do you know my voice?
Brabantio. Not I, what are you?
Roderigo. My name is Roderigo.
Brabantio.   The worser welcome:
   I have charg'd thee not to haunt about my doors:
   In honest plainness thou hast heard me say
   My daughter is not for thee; and now, in madness,
   Being full of supper and distempering draughts,   100
   Upon malicious knavery dost thou come
   To start my quiet.
Roderigo. Sir, sir, sir!
Brabantio.   But thou must needs be sure
   My spirit and my place²⁵ have in them power
   To make this bitter to thee.
Roderigo.   Patience, good sir.
Brabantio. What tell'st thou me of robbing? this is Venice;
   My house is not a grange.²⁶
Roderigo.   Most grave Brabantio,
   In simple and pure soul I come to you.
Iago. 'Zounds! sir, you are one of those that will not serve God if the devil bid
   you. Because we come to do you service and you think we are ruffians, you'll
   have your daughter covered with a Barbary horse; you'll have your nephews
   neigh to you; you'll have coursers for cousins and gennets²⁷ for germans.²⁸   112
Brabantio. What profane wretch art thou?

---

²² By God's wounds.   ²³ Copulating.   ²⁴ Snoring.   ²⁵ Position.   ²⁶ Isolated farmhouse.
²⁷ Spanish horses.   ²⁸ Blood relations.

Iago. I am one, sir, that comes to tell you, your daughter and the Moor are now
  making the beast with two backs.

Brabantio. Thou art a villain.

Iago.   You are—a senator.

Brabantio. This thou shalt answer; I know thee, Roderigo.

Roderigo. Sir, I will answer any thing. But, I beseech you,
  If 't be your pleasure and most wise consent,—
  As partly, I find, it is,—that your fair daughter,   120
  At this odd-even[29] and dull watch o' the night,
  Transported with no worse nor better guard
  But with a knave of common hire, a gondolier,
  To the gross clasps of a lascivious Moor,—
  If this be known to you, and your allowance,[30]
  We then have done you bold and saucy wrongs;
  But if you know not this, my manners tell me
  We have your wrong rebuke. Do not believe
  That, from[31] the sense of all civility,
  I thus would play and trifle with your reverence: 130
  Your daughter, if you have not given her leave,
  I say again, hath made a gross revolt;
  Tying her duty, beauty, wit and fortunes
  In[32] an extravagant[33] and wheeling stranger
  Of here and every where. Straight satisfy yourself:
  If she be in her chamber or your house,
  Let loose on me the justice of the state
  For thus deluding you.

Brabantio.   Strike on the tinder, ho!
  Give me a taper! call up all my people!
  This accident[34] is not unlike my dream;
  Belief of it oppresses me already.   140
  Light, I say! light!   *(Exit, from above.)*

Iago.   Farewell, for I must leave you:
  It seems not meet nor wholesome to my place
  To be produc'd,[35] as, if I stay, I shall,
  Against the Moor; for I do know the state,
  However this may gall him with some check,[36]
  Cannot with safety cast him; for he's embark'd
  With such loud reason to the Cyprus wars,—
  Which even now stand in act,—that, for their souls,
  Another of his fathom[37] they have none,   150
  To lead their business; in which regard,
  Though I do hate him as I do hell-pains,

---

[29] Between night and morning.   [30] By your approval.   [31] Away from.   [32] To.   [33] Expatriate.
[34] Happening.   [35] I.e., as a witness.   [36] Restraining adversity.   [37] Caliber, ability.

Yet, for necessity of present life,
I must show out a flag and sign of love,
Which is indeed but sign. That you shall surely find him,
Lead to the Sagittary[38] the raised search;
And there will I be with him. So, farewell.   *(Exit.)*

(Enter below, Brabantio, and servants with torches.)

Brabantio. It is too true an evil: gone she is,
And what's to come of my despised time
Is nought but bitterness. Now, Roderigo,   160
Where didst thou see her? O, unhappy girl!
With the Moor, sayst thou? Who would be a father!
How didst thou know 'twas she? O, she deceives me
Past thought. What said she to you? Get more tapers!
Raise all my kindred! Are they married, think you?
Roderigo. Truly, I think they are.
Brabantio. O heaven! How got she out? O treason of the blood:
Fathers, from hence trust not your daughters' minds
By what you see them act. Are there not charms
By which the property of youth and maidhood   170
May be abus'd? Have you not read, Roderigo,
Of some such thing?
Roderigo.   Yes, sir, I have indeed.
Brabantio. Call up my brother. O! that you had had her.
Some one way, some another! Do you know
Where we may apprehend her and the Moor?
Roderigo. I think I can discover him, if you please
To get good guard and go along with me.
Brabantio. Pray you, lead on. At every house I'll call;
I may command at most. Get weapons, ho!
And raise some special officers of night.   180
On, good Roderigo; I'll deserve[39] your pains.   *(Exeunt.)*

Scene 2.   Another Street.

(Enter Othello, Iago, and Attendants, with torches.)

Iago. Though in the trade of war I have slain men,
Yet do I hold it very stuff o' the conscience
To do no contriv'd murder: I lack iniquity
Sometimes to do me service. Nine or ten times
I had thought to have yerk'd[40] him here under the ribs.

---

[38] The name of an inn (?).   [39] I.e., reward.   [40] Stabbed.

Othello. 'Tis better as it is.

Iago.   Nay, but he prated,
And spoke such scurvy and provoking terms
Against your honour
That, with the little godliness I have,
I did full hard forbear him. But, I pray, sir,   10
Are you fast married? Be assur'd of this,
That the magnifico⁴¹ is much belov'd,
And hath in his effect a voice potential
As double⁴² as the duke's; he will divorce you,
Or put upon you what restraint and grievance
The law—with all his might to enforce it on—
Will give him cable.⁴³

Othello.   Let him do his spite:
My services which I have done the signiory⁴⁴
Shall out-tongue his complaints. 'Tis yet to know,⁴⁵
Which when I know that boasting is an honour   20
I shall promulgate, I fetch my life and being
From men of royal siege, and my demerits⁴⁶
May speak unbonneted⁴⁷ to as proud a fortune
As this⁴⁸ that I have reach'd; for know, Iago,
But that I love the gentle Desdemona,
I would not my unhoused⁴⁹ free condition
Put into circumscription and confine
For the sea's worth. But, look! what lights come yond?

Iago. Those are the raised⁵⁰ father and his friends:
You were best⁵¹ go in.

Othello.   Not I; I must be found: 30
My parts, my title, and my perfect⁵² soul
Shall manifest me rightly. Is it they?

Iago. By Janus,⁵³ I think no.

(Enter Cassio and certain Officers, with torches.)

Othello. The servants of the duke, and my lieutenant.
The goodness of the night upon you, friends!
What is the news?

Cassio.   The duke does greet you, general,
And he requires your haste-post-haste appearance,
Even on the instant.

Othello.   What is the matter, think you?

---

⁴¹ One of the grandees, or rulers, of Venice; here, Brabantio.   ⁴² Iago means that Brabantio's influence equals that of the Doge's with his double vote.   ⁴³ I.e., scope.   ⁴⁴ The Venetian government.
⁴⁵ I.e., the signiory does not as yet know.   ⁴⁶ Merits.   ⁴⁷ I.e., as equals.   ⁴⁸ I.e., that of Desdemona's family.   ⁴⁹ Unconfined.   ⁵⁰ Aroused.   ⁵¹ Had better.   ⁵² Untroubled by a bad conscience.
⁵³ The two-faced Roman god of portals and doors and (hence) of beginnings and ends.

Cassio. Something from Cyprus, as I may divine.
It is a business of some heat;[54] the galleys   40
Have sent a dozen sequent[55] messengers
This very night at one another's heels,
And many of the consuls,[56] rais'd and met,
Are at the duke's already. You have been hotly call'd for;
When, being not at your lodging to be found,
The senate hath sent about three several[57] quests
To search you out.
Othello.   'Tis well I am found by you.
I will but spend a word here in the house,
And go with you.   *(Exit.)*
Cassio.   Ancient, what makes he here?
Iago. Faith, he to-night hath boarded a land carrack;[58]   50
If it prove lawful prize, he's made for ever.
Cassio. I do not understand.
Iago.   He's married.
Cassio.   To who?

(Re-enter Othello.)

Iago. Marry,[59] to—Come, captain, will you go?
Othello.   Have with you.
Cassio. Here comes another troop to seek for you.
Iago. It is Brabantio. General, be advis'd;
He comes to bad intent.

(Enter Brabantio, Roderigo, and Officers, with torches and weapons.)

Othello.   Holla! stand there!
Roderigo. Signior, it is the Moor.
Brabantio.   Down with him, thief!

(They draw on both sides.)

Iago. You, Roderigo! Come, sir, I am for you.[60]
Othello. Keep up your bright swords, for the dew will rust them.
Good signior, you shall more command with years   60
Than with your weapons.
Brabantio. O thou foul thief! where hast thou stow'd my daughter?
Damn'd as thou art, thou hast enchanted her;
For I'll refer me to all things of sense,
If she in chains of magic were not bound,
Whether a maid so tender, fair, and happy,

---

[54] Urgency.   [55] Following one another.   [56] I.e., senators.   [57] Separate.   [58] Treasure ship.   [59] By the
Virgin Mary.   [60] Let you and me fight.

So opposite to marriage that she shunn'd
The wealthy curled darlings of our nation,
Would ever have, to incur a general mock,
Run from her guardage to the sooty bosom   70
Of such a thing as thou; to fear, not to delight.
Judge me the world, if 'tis not gross in sense[61]
That thou hast practis'd on her with foul charms,
Abus'd her delicate youth with drugs or minerals
That weaken motion:[62] I'll have 't disputed on;
'Tis probable, and palpable to thinking.
I therefore apprehend and do attach[63] thee
For an abuser of the world, a practiser
Of arts inhibited and out of warrant.[64]
Lay hold upon him: if he do resist,   80
Subdue him at his peril.

Othello.   Hold your hands,
Both you of my inclining,[65] and the rest:
Were it my cue to fight, I should have known it
Without a prompter. Where will you that I go
To answer this your charge?

Brabantio.   To prison; till fit time
Of law and course of direct session[66]
Call thee to answer.

Othello.   What if I do obey?
How may the duke be therewith satisfied,
Whose messengers are here about my side,
Upon some present[67] business of the state   90
To bring me to him?

Officer.   'Tis true, most worthy signior;
The duke's in council, and your noble self,
I am sure, is sent for.

Brabantio.   How! the duke in council!
In this time of the night! Bring him away.
Mine's not an idle cause: the duke himself,
Or any of my brothers of the state,[68]
Cannot but feel this wrong as 'twere their own;
For if such actions may have passage free,
Bond-slaves and pagans shall our statesmen be.   *(Exeunt.)*

Scene 3. A Council Chamber.

(The Duke and Senators sitting at a table. Officers attending.)

Duke. There is no composition[69] in these news
That gives them credit.

---

[61] Obvious.   [62] Normal reactions.   [63] Arrest.   [64] Prohibited and illegal.   [65] Party.   [66] Normal process of law.   [67] Immediate, pressing.   [68] Fellow senators.   [69] Consistency, agreement.

First Senator.   Indeed, they are disproportion'd;
    My letters say a hundred and seven galleys.
Duke. And mine, a hundred and forty.
Second Senator.   And mine, two hundred:
    But though they jump[70] not on a just[71] account,—
    As in these cases, where the aim[72] reports,
    'Tis oft with difference,—yet do they all confirm
    A Turkish fleet, and bearing up to Cyprus.
Duke. Nay, it is possible enough to judgment:
    I do not so secure me in[73] the error,   10
    But the main article[74] I do approve[75]
    In fearful sense.
Sailor (within).   What, ho! what, ho! what, ho!
Officer. A messenger from the galleys.

(Enter a Sailor.)

Duke.   Now, what's the business?
Sailor. The Turkish preparation makes for Rhodes;
    So was I bid report here to the state
    By Signior Angelo.
Duke. How say you by this change?
First Senator.   This cannot be
    By no[76] assay[77] of reason; 'tis a pageant[78]
    To keep us in false gaze.[79] When we consider
    The importancy of Cyprus to the Turk,   20
    And let ourselves again but understand,
    That as it more concerns the Turk than Rhodes,
    So may he with more facile question bear[80] it,
    For that it stands not in such warlike brace,[81]
    But altogether lacks the abilities
    That Rhodes is dress'd in: if we make thought of this,
    We must not think the Turk is so unskilful
    To leave that latest which concerns him first,
    Neglecting an attempt of ease and gain,
    To wake and wage a danger profitless.   30
Duke. Nay, in all confidence, he's not for Rhodes.
Officer. Here is more news.

(Enter a Messenger.)

Messenger. The Ottomites,[82] reverend and gracious,
    Steering with due course toward the isle of Rhodes,
    Have there injointed[83] them with an after fleet.[84]

---

[70] Coincide.   [71] Exact.   [72] Conjecture.   [73] Draw comfort from.   [74] Substance.   [75] Believe.
[76] Any.   [77] Test.   [78] (Deceptive) show.   [79] Looking in the wrong direction.   [80] More easily capture.
[81] State of defense.   [82] Turks.   [83] Joined.   [84] Fleet that followed after.

First Senator. Ay, so I thought. How many, as you guess?

Messenger. Of thirty sail; and now they do re-stem[85]
    Their backward course, bearing with frank appearance
    Their purposes toward Cyprus. Signior Montano,
    Your trusty and most valiant servitor,   40
    With his free duty[86] recommends[87] you thus,
    And prays you to believe him.

Duke. 'Tis certain then, for Cyprus.
    Marcus Luccicos, is not he in town?

First Senator. He's now in Florence.

Duke. Write from us to him; post-post-haste dispatch.

First Senator. Here comes Brabantio and the valiant Moor.

(Enter Brabantio, Othello, Iago, Roderigo, and Officers.)

Duke. Valiant Othello, we must straight employ you
    Against the general enemy Ottoman.
    (To Brabantio.) I did not see you; welcome, gentle signior;   50
    We lack'd your counsel and your help to-night.

Brabantio. So did I yours. Good your Grace, pardon me;
    Neither my place nor aught I heard of business
    Hath rais'd me from my bed, nor doth the general care
    Take hold of me, for my particular grief
    Is of so flood-gate[88] and o'erbearing nature
    That it engluts and swallows other sorrows
    And it is still itself.

Duke.   Why, what's the matter?

Brabantio. My daughter! O! my daughter.

Duke.   ⎫
Senators. ⎭   Dead?

Brabantio.   Ay, to me;
    She is abus'd, stol'n from me, and corrupted   60
    By spells and medicines bought of mountebanks;
    For nature so preposterously to err,
    Being not deficient, blind, or lame of sense,
    Sans[89] witchcraft could not.

Duke. Whoe'er he be that in this foul proceeding
    Hath thus beguil'd your daughter of herself
    And you of her, the bloody book of law
    You shall yourself read in the bitter letter
    After your own sense; yea, though our proper[90] son
    Stood[91] in your action.[92]

Brabantio.   Humbly I thank your Grace.   70
    Here is the man, this Moor; whom now, it seems,

---

[85] Steer again.   [86] Unqualified expressions of respect.   [87] Informs.   [88] Torrential.   [89] Without.
[90] Own.   [91] Were accused.   [92] Suit.

Your special mandate for the state affairs
Hath hither brought.

Duke.
Senators. } We are very sorry for it.

Duke *(to Othello).* What, in your own part, can you say to this?

Brabantio. Nothing, but this is so.

Othello. Most potent, grave, and reverend signiors,
My very noble and approv'd[93] good masters,
That I have ta'en away this old man's daughter,
It is most true; true, I have married her:
The very head and front of my offending   80
Hath this extent, no more. Rude am I in my speech,
And little bless'd with the soft phrase of peace;
For since these arms of mine had seven years' pith,[94]
Till now some nine moons wasted,[95] they have us'd
Their dearest action in the tented field;
And little of this great world can I speak,
More than pertains to feats of broil and battle;
And therefore little shall I grace my cause
In speaking for myself. Yet, by your gracious patience,
I will a round[96] unvarnish'd tale deliver   90
Of my whole course of love; what drugs, what charms,
What conjuration, and what mighty magic,
For such proceeding I am charg'd withal,
I won his daughter.

Brabantio.   A maiden never bold;
Of spirit so still and quiet, that her motion
Blush'd at herself;[97] and she, in spite of nature,
Of years, of country, credit, every thing,
To fall in love with what she fear'd to look on!
It is a judgment maim'd and most imperfect
That will confess[98] perfection so could err   100
Against all rules of nature, and must be driven
To find out practices of cunning hell,
Why this should be. I therefore vouch again
That with some mixtures powerful o'er the blood,
Or with some dram conjur'd to this effect,
He wrought upon her.

Duke.   To vouch this, is no proof,
Without more certain and more overt test
Than these thin habits[99] and poor likelihoods
Of modern[100] seeming do prefer against him.

---

[93] Tested (by past experience).   [94] Strength.   [95] Past.   [96] Blunt.   [97] I.e. (her modesty was such that) she blushed at her own emotions; or: she could not move without blushing.   [98] Assert.   [99] Weak appearances.   [100] Commonplace.

First Senator. But, Othello, speak: 110
    Did you by indirect and forced courses
    Subdue and poison this young maid's affections;
    Or came it by request and such fair question[101]
    As soul to soul affordeth?
Othello.   I do beseech you;
    Send for the lady to the Sagittary,
    And let her speak of me before her father:
    If you do find me foul in her report,
    The trust, the office I do hold of you,
    Not only take away, but let your sentence
    Even fall upon my life.
Duke.   Fetch Desdemona hither. 120
Othello. Ancient, conduct them; you best know the place.

                              (Exeunt Iago and Attendants.)

    And, till she come, as truly as to heaven
    I do confess the vices of my blood,
    So justly to your grave ears I'll present
    How I did thrive in this fair lady's love,
    And she in mine.
Duke. Say it, Othello.
Othello. Her father lov'd me; oft invited me;
    Still[102] question'd me the story of my life
    From year to year, the battles, sieges, fortunes 130
    That I have pass'd.
    I ran it through, even from my boyish days
    To the very moment that he bade me tell it;
    Wherein I spake of most disastrous chances,
    Of moving accidents by flood and field,
    Of hair-breadth 'scapes i' the imminent deadly breach,
    Of being taken by the insolent foe
    And sold to slavery, of my redemption thence
    And portance[103] in my travel's history;
    Wherein of antres[104] vast and deserts idle,[105] 140
    Rough quarries, rocks, and hills whose heads touch heaven,
    It was my hint[106] to speak, such was the process;
    And of the Cannibals that each other eat,
    The Anthropophagi,[107] and men whose heads
    Do grow beneath their shoulders. This to hear
    Would Desdemona seriously incline;
    But still the house-affairs would draw her thence;
    Which ever as she could with haste dispatch,

---

[101] Conversation.   [102] Always, regularly.   [103] Behavior.   [104] Caves.   [105] Empty, sterile.
[106] Opportunity.   [107] Man-eaters.

She'd come again, and with a greedy ear
Devour up my discourse. Which I observing,   150
Took once a pliant[108] hour, and found good means
To draw from her a prayer of earnest heart
That I would all my pilgrimage dilate,[109]
Whereof by parcels[110] she had something heard,
But not intentively:[111] I did consent;
And often did beguile her of her tears,
When I did speak of some distressful stroke
That my youth suffer'd. My story being done,
She gave me for my pains a world of sighs:
She swore, in faith, 'twas strange, 'twas passing[112] strange;   160
'Twas pitiful, 'twas wondrous pitiful:
She wish'd she had not heard it, yet she wish'd
That heaven had made her[113] such a man; she thank'd me,
And bade me, if I had a friend that lov'd her,
I should but teach him how to tell my story,
And that would woo her. Upon this hint I spake.
She lov'd me for the dangers I had pass'd,
And I lov'd her that she did pity them.
This only is the witchcraft I have us'd:
Here comes the lady; let her witness it.   170

(Enter Desdemona, Iago, and Attendants.)

Duke. I think this tale would win my daughter too.
  Good Brabantio,
  Take up this mangled matter at the best;
  Men do their broken weapons rather use
  Than their bare hands.

Brabantio.   I pray you, hear her speak:
  If she confess that she was half the wooer,
  Destruction on my head, if my bad blame
  Light on the man! Come hither, gentle mistress:
  Do you perceive in all this noble company
  Where most you owe obedience?

Desdemona.   My noble father,   180
  I do perceive here a divided duty:
  To you I am bound for life and education;
  My life and education both do learn[114] me
  How to respect you; you are the lord of duty,
  I am hitherto your daughter: but here's my husband;
  And so much duty as my mother show'd
  To you, preferring you before her father,

---

[108] Suitable.   [109] Relate in full.   [110] Piecemeal.   [111] In sequence.   [112] Surpassing.   [113] Direct object; not "for her."   [114] Teach.

So much I challenge[115] that I may profess
Due to the Moor my lord.

Brabantio.   God be with you! I have done.
Please it your Grace, on to the state affairs;   190
I had rather to adopt a child than get it.
Come hither, Moor:
I here give thee that with all my heart
Which, but thou hast[116] already, with all my heart
I would keep from thee. For your sake,[117] jewel,
I am glad at soul I have no other child;
For thy escape would teach me tyranny,
To hang clogs on them. I have done, my lord.

Duke. Let me speak like yourself and lay a sentence,[118]
Which as a grize[119] or step, may help these lovers   200
Into your favour.
When remedies are past, the griefs are ended
By seeing the worst, which[120] late on hopes depended.
To mourn a mischief that is past and gone
Is the next way to draw new mischief on.
What cannot be preserv'd when Fortune takes,
Patience her injury a mockery makes.[121]
The robb'd that smiles steals something from the thief;
He robs himself that spends a bootless grief.

Brabantio. So let the Turk of Cyprus us beguile;   210
We lose it not so long as we can smile.
He bears the sentence[122] well that nothing bears
But the free comfort which from thence he hears;
But he bears both the sentence and the sorrow
That, to pay grief, must of poor patience borrow.
These sentences, to sugar, or to gall,
Being strong on both sides, are equivocal:[123]
But words are words: I never yet did hear
That the bruis'd heart was pierced[124] through the ear.
I humbly beseech you, proceed to the affairs of state.   220

Duke. The Turk with a most mighty preparation makes for Cyprus. Othello, the
fortitude[125] of the place is best known to you; and though we have there a substitute of most allowed sufficiency,[126] yet opinion, a sovereign mistress of effects,
throws a more safer voice on you:[127] you must therefore be content to slubber[128]
the gloss of your new fortunes with this more stubborn[129] and boisterous
expedition.

---

[115] Claim as right.   [116] Didn't you have it.   [117] Because of you.   [118] Provide a maxim.   [119] Step.
[120] The antecedent is "griefs."   [121] To suffer an irreparable loss patiently is to make light of injury (i.e.,
to triumph over adversity).   [122] (1) Verdict, (2) Maxim.   [123] Sententious comfort (like the Duke's
trite maxims) can hurt as well as soothe.   [124] (1) Lanced (i.e., cured), (2) Wounded.   [125] Strength.
[126] Admitted competence.   [127] General opinion, which mainly determines action, thinks Cyprus
safer with you in command.   [128] Besmear.   [129] Rough.

Othello. The tyrant custom, most grave senators,
Hath made the flinty and steel couch of war
My thrice-driven[130] bed of down: I do agnize[131]
A natural and prompt alacrity   230
I find in hardness, and do undertake
These present wars against the Ottomites.
Most humbly therefore bending to your state,[132]
I crave fit disposition[133] for my wife,
Due reference of place and exhibition,[134]
With such accommodation and besort[135]
As levels with[136] her breeding.

Duke.   If you please,
Be 't at her father's.

Brabantio.   I'll not have it so.

Othello. Nor I.

Desdemona. Nor I; I would not there reside,   240
To put my father in impatient thoughts
By being in his eye. Most gracious duke,
To my unfolding[137] lend your gracious ear;
And let me find a charter[138] in your voice
To assist my simpleness.

Duke. What would you, Desdemona?

Desdemona. That I did love the Moor to live with him,
My downright violence and storm of fortunes
May trumpet to the world; my heart's subdu'd
Even to the very quality of my lord;[139]   250
I saw Othello's visage in his mind,
And to his honours and his valiant parts
Did I my soul and fortunes consecrate.
So that, dear lords, if I be left behind,
A moth of peace, and he go to the war,
The rites[140] for which I love him are bereft me,
And I a heavy interim shall support[141]
By his dear[142] absence. Let me go with him.

Othello. Let her have your voices.
Vouch with me, heaven, I therefore beg it not   260
To please the palate of my appetite,
Nor to comply with heat,—the young affects[143]
In me defunct,—and proper satisfaction,
But to be free and bounteous to her mind;

---

[130] Made as soft as possible.   [131] Recognize.   [132] Submitting to your authority.   [133] Disposal.   [134] Provision.   [135] Fitness.   [136] Is proper to.   [137] Explanation.   [138] Permission.
[139] I.e., I have become a soldier, like Othello.   [140] I.e., of marriage, or of war, or of both.   [141] Endure.
[142] Closely concerning (i.e., Desdemona).   [143] The passions of youth (hence, here, *immoderate* sexual passion).

And heaven defend[144] your good souls that you think
I will your serious and great business scant
For[145] she is with me. No, when light-wing'd toys
Of feather'd Cupid seel[146] with wanton dulness
My speculative and offic'd instruments,[147]
That[148] my disports corrupt and taint my business,   270
Let housewives make a skillet of my helm,
And all indign[149] and base adversities
Make head against my estimation![150]

Duke. Be it as you shall privately determine,
Either for her stay or going. The affair cries haste,
And speed must answer it.

First Senator. You must away to-night.

Othello.   With all my heart.

Duke. At nine i' the morning here we'll meet again.
Othello, leave some officer behind,
And he shall our commission bring to you;   280
With such things else of quality and respect
As doth import you.[151]

Othello.   So please your Grace, my ancient;
A man he is of honesty and trust:
To his conveyance I assign my wife,
With what else needful your good grace shall think
To be sent after me.

Duke.   Let it be so.
Good-night to every one. *(To Brabantio.)* And, noble signior,
If virtue no delighted[152] beauty lack,
Your son-in-law is far more fair than black.

First Senator. Adieu, brave Moor! use Desdemona well.   290

Brabantio. Look to her, Moor, if thou hast eyes to see:
She has deceiv'd her father, and may thee.

(Exeunt Duke, Senators, Officers, &c.)

Othello. My life upon her faith! Honest Iago,
My Desdemona must I leave to thee:
I prithee, let thy wife attend on her;
And bring them after in the best advantage.[153]
Come, Desdemona; I have but an hour
Of love, of worldly matters and direction,
To spend with thee: we must obey the time.

(Exeunt Othello and Desdemona.)

---

[144] Forbid.   [145] Because.   [146] Blind (v.) by sewing up the eyelids (a term from falconry).   [147] Reflective and executive faculties and organs.   [148] So that.   [149] Shameful.   [150] Reputation.   [151] Concern. [152] Delightful.   [153] Opportunity.

Roderigo. Iago!　300

Iago. What sayst thou, noble heart?

Roderigo. What will I do, think'st thou?

Iago. Why, go to bed, and sleep.

Roderigo. I will incontinently[154] drown myself.

Iago. Well, if thou dost, I shall never love thee after. Why, thou silly gentleman!

Roderigo. It is silliness to live when to live is torment; and then have we a prescription to die when death is our physician.

Iago. O! villainous; I have looked upon the world for four times seven years, and since I could distinguish betwixt a benefit and an injury, I never found man that knew how to love himself. Ere I would say, I would drown myself for the love of a guinea-hen, I would change my humanity with a baboon.　312

Roderigo. What should I do? I confess it is my shame to be so fond;[155] but it is not in my virtue[156] to amend it.

Iago. Virtue! a fig! 'tis in ourselves that we are thus, or thus. Our bodies are our gardens, to the which our wills are gardeners; so that if we will plant nettles or sow lettuce, set hyssop and weed up thyme, supply it with one gender[157] of herbs or distract it with many, either to have it sterile with idleness or manured with industry, why, the power and corrigible[158] authority of this lies in our wills. If the balance of our lives had not one scale of reason to poise another of sensuality, the blood and baseness of our natures would conduct us to most preposterous conclusions; but we have reason to cool our raging motions, our carnal stings, our unbitted[159] lusts, whereof I take this that you call love to be a sect or scion.[160]　324

Roderigo. It cannot be.

Iago. It is merely a lust of the blood and a permission of the will. Come, be a man. Drown thyself! drown cats and blind puppies. I have professed me thy friend, and I confess me knit to thy deserving with cables of perdurable toughness; I could never better stead thee than now. Put money in thy purse; follow these wars; defeat thy favour[161] with a usurped[162] beard; I say, put money in thy purse. It cannot be that Desdemona should long continue her love to the Moor,—put money in thy purse,—nor he his to her. It was a violent commencement in her, and thou shalt see an answerable sequestration;[163] put but money in thy purse. These Moors are changeable in their wills;—fill thy purse with money:—the food that to him now is as luscious as locusts,[164] shall be to him shortly as bitter as coloquintida.[165] She must change for youth: when she is sated with his body, she will find the error of her choice. She must have change, she must: therefore put money in thy purse. If thou wilt needs damn thyself, do it a more delicate way than drowning. Make all the money thou canst. If

---

[154] Forthwith.　[155] Infatuated.　[156] Strength.　[157] Kind.　[158] Corrective.　[159] I.e., uncontrolled.　[160] Offshoot.　[161] Change thy appearance (for the worse?).　[162] Assumed.　[163] Estrangement.　[164] Sweet-tasting fruits (perhaps the carob, the edible seedpod of an evergreen tree in the Mediterranean area).　[165] Purgative derived from a bitter apple.

sanctimony and a frail vow betwixt an erring[166] barbarian and a supersubtle[167] Venetian be not too hard for my wits and all the tribe of hell, thou shalt enjoy her; therefore make money. A pox of drowning thyself! it is clean out of the way: seek thou rather to be hanged in compassing thy joy than to be drowned and go without her. 344

Roderigo. Wilt thou be fast to my hopes, if I depend on the issue?[168]

Iago. Thou art sure of me: go, make money. I have told thee often, and I retell thee again and again, I hate the Moor; my cause is hearted; thine hath no less reason. Let us be conjunctive[169] in our revenge against him; if thou canst cuckold him, thou dost thyself a pleasure, me a sport. There are many events in the womb of time which will be delivered. Traverse;[170] go: provide thy money. We will have more of this to-morrow. Adieu. 351

Roderigo. Where shall we meet i' the morning?

Iago. At my lodging.

Roderigo. I'll be with thee betimes.

Iago. Go to: farewell. Do you hear, Roderigo?

Roderigo. What say you?

Iago. No more of drowning, do you hear?

Roderigo. I am changed. I'll sell all my land.

Iago. Go to; farewell! put money enough in your purse.   (*Exit Roderigo.*)

Thus do I ever make my fool my purse; 360
For I mine own gain'd knowledge should profane,
If I would time expend with such a snipe[171]
But for my sport and profit. I hate the Moor,
And it is thought abroad[172] that 'twixt my sheets
He has done my office: I know not if 't be true,
But I, for mere suspicion in that kind,
Will do as if for surety.[173] He holds me well;[174]
The better shall my purpose work on him.
Cassio's a proper[175] man; let me see now:
To get his place; and to plume up[176] my will 370
In double knavery; how, how? Let's see:
After some time to abuse Othello's ear
That he[177] is too familiar with his wife:
He hath a person and a smooth dispose[178]
To be suspected; framed[179] to make women false,
The Moor is of a free and open nature,
That thinks men honest that but seem to be so,
And will as tenderly be led by the nose
As asses are.
I have 't; it is engender'd: hell and night 380
Must bring this monstrous birth to the world's light.   (*Exit.*)

---

[166] Vagabond.   [167] Exceedingly refined.   [168] Rely on the outcome.   [169] Allied.   [170] March.
[171] Dupe.   [172] People think.   [173] As if it were certain.   [174] In high regard.   [175] Handsome.
[176] Make ready.   [177] I.e., Cassio.   [178] Bearing.   [179] Designed, apt.

ACT II

Scene 1. A Sea-port Town in Cyprus. An open place near the Quay.

(Enter Montano and two Gentlemen.)

Montano. What from the cape can you discern at sea?
First Gentleman. Nothing at all: it is a high-wrought flood;
    I cannot 'twixt the heaven and the main[180]
    Descry a sail.
Montano. Methinks the wind hath spoke aloud at land;
    A fuller blast ne'er shook our battlements;
    If it hath ruffian'd so upon the sea,
    What ribs of oak, when mountains melt on them,
    Can hold the mortise?[181] What shall we hear of this?
Second Gentleman. A segregation[182] of the Turkish fleet;   10
    For do but stand upon the foaming shore,
    The chidden billow seems to pelt the clouds;
    The wind-shak'd surge, with high and monstrous mane,
    Seems to cast water on the burning bear[183]
    And quench the guards of the ever-fixed pole:[184]
    I never did like[185] molestation view
    On the enchafed[186] flood.
Montano.   If that[187] the Turkish fleet
    Be not enshelter'd and embay'd, they are drown'd;
    It is impossible they bear it out.

(Enter a Third Gentleman.)

Third Gentleman. News, lad! our wars are done.   20
    The desperate tempest hath so bang'd the Turks
    That their designment halts;[188] a noble ship of Venice
    Hath seen a grievous wrack and suffrance[189]
    On most part of their fleet.
Montano. How! is this true?
Third Gentleman.   The ship is here put in,
    A Veronesa;[190] Michael Cassio,
    Lieutenant to the warlike Moor Othello,
    Is come on shore: the Moor himself's at sea,
    And is in full commission here for Cyprus.
Montano. I am glad on 't; 'tis a worthy governor.   30
Third Gentleman. But this same Cassio, though he speak of comfort
    Touching the Turkish loss, yet he looks sadly

---

[180] Ocean. [181] Hold the joints together. [182] Scattering. [183] Ursa Minor (the Little Dipper).
[184] Polaris, the North Star, almost directly above the Earth's axis, is part of the constellation of the Little
Bear, or Dipper. [185] Similar. [186] Agitated. [187] If. [188] Plan is stopped. [189] Damage. [190] Probably
a *type* of ship, rather than a ship from Verona—not only because Verona is an inland city but also because
of "a noble ship of Venice" above.

And prays the Moor be safe; for they were parted
With foul and violent tempest.
Montano.   Pray heaven he be;
For I have serv'd him, and the man commands
Like a full soldier. Let's to the sea-side, ho!
As well to see the vessel that's come in
As to throw out our eyes for brave Othello,
Even till we make the main and the aerial blue
An indistinct regard.[191]   40
Third Gentleman. Come, let's do so;
For every minute is expectancy
Of more arrivance.

(Enter Cassio.)

Cassio. Thanks, you the valiant of this warlike isle,
That so approve the Moor. O! let the heavens
Give him defence against the elements,
For I have lost him on a dangerous sea.
Montano. Is he well shipp'd?
Cassio. His bark is stoutly timber'd, and his pilot
Of very expert and approv'd allowance;[192]   50
Therefore my hopes, not surfeited to death,[193]
Stand in bold cure.[194]

(Within, 'A sail!—a sail!—a sail!' Enter a Messenger.)

Cassio. What noise?
Messenger. The town is empty; on the brow o' the sea
Stand ranks of people, and they cry 'A sail!'
Cassio. My hopes do shape him for the governor.

(Guns heard.)

Second Gentleman. They do discharge their shot of courtesy;
Our friends at least.
Cassio.   I pray you, sir, go forth.
And give us truth who 'tis that is arriv'd.
Second Gentleman. I shall.   *(Exit.)* 60
Montano. But, good lieutenant, is your general wiv'd?
Cassio. Most fortunately: he hath achiev'd a maid
That paragons[195] description and wild fame;
One that excels the quirks[196] of blazoning pens,

---

[191] Till our (straining) eyes can no longer distinguish sea and sky.   [192] Admitted and proven
to be expert.   [193] Overindulged.   [194] With good chance of being fulfilled.   [195] Exceeds, surpasses.
[196] Ingenuities.

And in th' essential vesture of creation[197]
Does tire the ingener.[198]

(Re-enter Second Gentleman.)

How now! who has put in?
Second Gentleman. 'Tis one Iago, ancient to the general.
Cassio. He has had most favourable and happy speed:
  Tempests themselves, high seas, and howling winds,
  The gutter'd[199] rocks, and congregated sands,   70
  Traitors ensteep'd[200] to clog the guiltless keel,
  As having sense of beauty, do omit
  Their mortal[201] natures, letting go safely by
  The divine Desdemona.
Montano.   What is she?
Cassio. She that I spake of, our great captain's captain,
  Left in the conduct of the bold Iago,
  Whose footing[202] here anticipates our thoughts
  A se'nnight's[203] speed. Great Jove, Othello guard,
  And swell his sail with thine own powerful breath,
  That he may bless this bay with his tall[204] ship,   80
  Make love's quick pants in Desdemona's arms,
  Give renew'd fire to our extincted spirits,
  And bring all Cyprus comfort!

(Enter Desdemona, Emilia, Iago, Roderigo, and Attendants.)

O! behold,
  The riches of the ship is come on shore.
  Ye men of Cyprus, let her have your knees.
  Hail to thee, lady! and the grace of heaven,
  Before, behind thee, and on every hand,
  Enwheel thee round!
Desdemona.   I thank you, valiant Cassio.
  What tidings can you tell me of my lord?
Cassio. He is not yet arriv'd; nor know I aught   90
  But that he's well, and will be shortly here.
Desdemona. O! but I fear—How lost you company?
Cassio. The great contention of the sea and skies
  Parted our fellowship. But hark! a sail.

(Cry within, 'A sail—a sail!' Guns heard.)

Second Gentleman. They give their greeting to the citadel:
  This likewise is a friend.

---

[197] I.e., just as God made her; or: (even in) the (mere) essence of human nature.   [198] Inventor (i.e., of her praises?).   [199] Jagged; or: submerged.   [200] Submerged.   [201] Deadly.   [202] Landing.   [203] Week's.
[204] Brave.

Cassio.　　　　　　　　See for the news!　　　　　　*(Exit Gentleman.)*

　　Good ancient, you are welcome:—*(To Emilia.)* welcome, mistress.

　　Let it not gall your patience, good Iago,

　　That I extend my manners; 'tis my breeding

　　That gives me this bold show of courtesy.　　　　*(Kissing her.)*　100

Iago.　Sir, would she give you so much of her lips

　　As of her tongue she oft bestows on me,

　　You'd have enough.

Desdemona.　　　　　Alas! she has no speech.

Iago.　In faith, too much;

　　I find it still when I have list[205] to sleep:

　　Marry, before your ladyship, I grant,

　　She puts her tongue a little in her heart,

　　And chides with thinking.[206]

Emilia.　You have little cause to say so.

Iago.　Come on, come on; you are pictures[207] out of doors,　110

　　Bells[208] in your parlours, wild cats in your kitchens,

　　Saints in your injuries, devils being offended,

　　Players[209] in your housewifery,[210] and housewives[211] in your beds.

Desdemona.　O! fie upon thee, slanderer.

Iago.　Nay, it is true, or else I am a Turk:

　　You rise to play and go to bed to work.

Emilia.　You shall not write my praise.

Iago.　　　　　　　　No, let me not.

Desdemona.　What wouldst thou write of me, if thou shouldst praise me?

Iago.　O gentle lady, do not put me to 't,

　　For I am nothing if not critical.　　　　　　　　　120

Desdemona.　Come on; assay. There's one gone to the harbour?

Iago.　Ay, madam.

Desdemona *(aside).*　I am not merry, but I do beguile

　　The thing I am by seeming otherwise.

　　(To Iago.) Come, how wouldst thou praise me?

Iago.　I am about it; but indeed my invention

　　Comes from my pate[212] as birdlime does from frize;[213]

　　It plucks out brains and all: but my muse labours

　　And thus she is deliver'd.

　　If she be fair and wise, fairness and wit,　　　　　130

　　The one's for use, the other useth it.

Desdemona.　Well prais'd! How if she be black and witty?

Iago.　If she be black,[214] and thereto have a wit,

　　She'll find a white that shall her blackness fit.

Desdemona.　Worse and worse.

---

[205] Wish.　[206] I.e., without words.　[207] I.e., made up, "painted."　[208] I.e., jangly.　[209] Triflers, wastrels.
[210] Housekeeping.　[211] (1) Hussies, (2) (unduly) frugal with their sexual favors, (3) businesslike, serious.
[212] Head.　[213] Coarse cloth.　[214] Brunette, dark haired.

Emilia. How if fair and foolish?

Iago. She never yet was foolish that was fair,
For even her folly[215] help'd to an heir.

Desdemona. These are old fond[216] paradoxes to make fools laugh i' the alehouse.
What miserable praise has thou for her that's foul and foolish? 140

Iago. There's none so foul and foolish thereunto,
But does foul pranks which fair and wise ones do.

Desdemona. O heavy ignorance! thou praisest the worst best. But what praise
couldst thou bestow on a deserving woman indeed, one that, in the authority of
her merit, did justly put on the vouch[217] of very malice itself?

Iago. She that was ever fair and never proud,
Had tongue at will and yet was never loud,
Never lack'd gold and yet went never gay,
Fled from her wish and yet said 'Now I may,'
She that being anger'd, her revenge being nigh, 150
Bade her wrong stay and her displeasure fly,
She that in wisdom never was so frail
To change the cod's head for the salmon's tail,[218]
She that could think and ne'er disclose her mind,
See suitors following and not look behind,
She was a wight, if ever such wight were,—

Desdemona. To do what?

Iago. To suckle fools and chronicle small beer.[219]

Desdemona. O most lame and impotent conclusion! Do not learn of him, Emilia,
though he be thy husband. How say you, Cassio? Is he not a most profane and
liberal[220] counsellor? 161

Cassio. He speaks home,[221] madam; you may relish him more in the soldier than
in[222] the scholar.

Iago (aside). He takes her by the palm: ay, well said, whisper; with as little a web
as this will I ensnare as great a fly as Cassio. Ay, smile upon her, do; I will gyve[223]
thee in thine own courtship. You say true, 'tis so, indeed. If such tricks as these
strip you out of your lieutenantry, it had been better you had not kissed your
three fingers so oft, which now again you are most apt to play the sir[224] in. Very
good; well kissed! an excellent courtesy! 'tis so, indeed. Yet again your fingers to
your lips? would they were clyster-pipes[225] for your sake! (A trumpet heard.) The
Moor! I know his trumpet.[226] 171

Cassio. 'Tis truly so.

Desdemona. Let's meet him and receive him.

Cassio. Lo! where he comes.

(Enter Othello and Attendants.)

---

[215] Here also, wantonness. [216] Foolish. [217] Compel the approval. [218] To make a foolish
exchange (a bawdy secondary meaning is probable). [219] I.e., keep petty household accounts.
[220] Free-spoken, licentious. [221] To the mark, aptly. [222] As . . . as. [223] Entangle. [224] Gentleman.
[225] Syringes, enema pipes. [226] I.e., Othello's distinctive trumpet call.

Othello. O my fair warrior!

Desdemona.   My dear Othello!

Othello. It gives me wonder great as my content
    To see you here before me. O my soul's joy!
    If after every tempest come such calms,
    May the winds blow till they have waken'd death!
    And let the labouring bark climb hills of seas   180
    Olympus-high, and duck again as low
    As hell's from heaven! If it were now to die,
    'Twere now to be most happy, for I fear
    My soul hath her content so absolute
    That not another comfort like to this
    Succeeds in unknown fate.

Desdemona.   The heavens forbid
    But that our loves and comforts should increase
    Even as our days do grow!

Othello. Amen to that, sweet powers!
    I cannot speak enough of this content;   190
    It stops me here; it is too much of joy:
    And this, and this, the greatest discords be   *(Kissing her.)*
    That e'er our hearts shall make!

Iago *(aside).*   O! you are well tun'd now,
    But I'll set down[227] the pegs that make this music,
    As honest as I am.

Othello.   Come, let us to the castle.
    News, friends; our wars are done, the Turks are drown'd.
    How does my old acquaintance of this isle?
    Honey, you shall be well desir'd[228] in Cyprus;
    I have found great love amongst them. O my sweet,
    I prattle out of fashion, and I dote   200
    In mine own comforts. I prithee, good Iago,
    Go to the bay and disembark my coffers.
    Bring thou the master to the citadel;
    He is a good one, and his worthiness
    Does challenge much respect. Come, Desdemona,
    Once more well met at Cyprus.

                              (Exeunt all except Iago and Roderigo.)

Iago. Do thou meet me presently at the harbour. Come hither. If thou be'st valiant,
as they say base men being in love have then a nobility in their natures more
than is native to them, list[229] me. The lieutenant to-night watches on the court of
guard:[230] first, I must tell thee this, Desdemona is directly in love with him.   210

Roderigo. With him! Why, 'tis not possible.

---

[227] Loosen.   [228] Welcomed.   [229] Listen to.   [230] Guardhouse.

Iago. Lay thy finger thus, and let thy soul be instructed. Mark me with what violence she first loved the Moor but for bragging and telling her fantastical lies; and will she love him still for prating? let not thy discreet heart think it. Her eye must be fed; and what delight shall she have to look on the devil? When the blood is made dull with the act of sport, there should be, again to inflame it, and to give satiety a fresh appetite, loveliness in favour, sympathy in years, manners, and beauties; all which the Moor is defective in. Now, for want of these required conveniences, her delicate tenderness will find itself abused, begin to heave the gorge,[231] disrelish and abhor the Moor; very nature will instruct her in it, and compel her to some second choice. Now, sir, this granted, as it is a most pregnant[232] and unforced position, who stands so eminently in the degree of this fortune as Cassio does? a knave very voluble, no further conscionable[233] than in putting on the mere form of civil and humane seeming, for the better compassing of his salt[234] and most hidden loose affection? why, none; why, none: a slipper[235] and subtle knave, a finder-out of occasions, that has an eye can stamp and counterfeit advantages, though true advantage never present itself; a devilish knave! Besides, the knave is handsome, young, and hath all those requisites in him that folly and green minds look after; a pestilent complete knave! and the woman hath found him already.

Roderigo. I cannot believe that in her; she is full of most blessed condition.

Iago. Blessed fig's end! the wine she drinks is made of grapes;[236] if she had been blessed she would never have loved the Moor; blessed pudding! Didst thou not see her paddle with the palm of his hand? didst not mark that?

Roderigo. Yes, that I did; but that was but courtesy.

Iago. Lechery, by this hand! an index[237] and obscure prologue to the history of lust and foul thoughts. They met so near with their lips, that their breaths embraced together. Villainous thoughts, Roderigo! when these mutualities so marshal the way, hard at hand comes the master and main exercise, the incorporate[238] conclusion. Pish![239] But, sir, be you ruled by me: I have brought you from Venice. Watch you to-night; for the command, I'll lay 't upon you: Cassio knows you not. I'll not be far from you: do you find some occasion to anger Cassio, either by speaking too loud, or tainting[240] his discipline; or from what other course you please, which the time shall more favourably minister.

Roderigo. Well.

Iago. Sir, he is rash and very sudden in choler, and haply may strike at you: provoke him, that he may; for even out of that will I cause these of Cyprus to mutiny, whose qualification[241] shall come into no true taste again but by the displanting of Cassio. So shall you have a shorter journey to your desires by the means I shall then have to prefer[242] them; and the impediment most profitably removed, without the which there were no expectation of our prosperity.

Roderigo. I will do this, if I can bring it to any opportunity.

---

[231] Vomit. [232] Obvious. [233] Conscientious. [234] Lecherous. [235] Slippery. [236] I.e., she is only flesh and blood. [237] Pointer. [238] Carnal. [239] Exclamation of disgust. [240] Disparaging. [241] Appeasement. [242] Advance.

Iago. I warrant thee. Meet me by and by at the citadel: I must fetch his necessaries ashore. Farewell.

Roderigo. Adieu. *(Exit.)*

Iago. That Cassio loves her, I do well believe it;
That she loves him, 'tis apt,[243] and of great credit:[244]
The Moor, howbeit that I endure him not,   260
Is of a constant, loving, noble nature;
And I dare think he'll prove to Desdemona
A most dear[245] husband. Now, I do love her too;
Not out of absolute lust,—though peradventure[246]
I stand accountant[247] for as great a sin,—
But partly led to diet my revenge,
For that I do suspect the lusty Moor
Hath leap'd into my seat; the thought whereof
Doth like a poisonous mineral gnaw my inwards;
And nothing can or shall content my soul   270
Till I am even'd with him, wife for wife;
Or failing so, yet that I put the Moor
At least into a jealousy so strong
That judgment cannot cure. Which thing to do,
If this poor trash[248] of Venice, whom I trash[249]
For his quick hunting, stand the putting-on,[250]
I'll have our Michael Cassio on the hip;
Abuse him to the Moor in the rank garb,[251]
For I fear Cassio with my night-cap too,
Make the Moor thank me, love me, and reward me   280
For making him egregiously an ass
And practising upon his peace and quiet
Even to madness. 'Tis here, but yet confus'd:
Knavery's plain face is never seen till us'd. *(Exit.)*

Scene 2.   A Street.

(Enter a Herald with a proclamation; people following.)

Herald.   It is Othello's pleasure, our noble and valiant general, that, upon certain tidings now arrived, importing the mere[252] perdition of the Turkish fleet, every man put himself into triumph; some to dance, some to make bonfires, each man to what sport and revels his addiction leads him; for, besides these beneficial news, it is the celebration of his nuptial. So much was his pleasure should be proclaimed. All offices[253] are open, and there is full liberty of feasting from this present hour of five till the bell have told eleven. Heaven bless the isle of Cyprus and our noble general Othello! *(Exeunt.)*

---

[243] Natural, probable.   [244] Easily believable.   [245] A pun on the word in the sense of expensive.   [246] Perchance, perhaps.   [247] Accountable.   [248] I.e., Roderigo.   [249] Check, control.   [250] Inciting.   [251] Gross manner.   [252] Utter.   [253] Kitchens and storehouses.

Scene 3. A Hall in the Castle.

(Enter Othello, Desdemona, Cassio, and Attendants.)

Othello. Good Michael, look you to the guard to-night:
  Let's teach ourselves that honourable stop,[254]
  Not to outsport discretion.
Cassio. Iago hath direction what to do:
  But, notwithstanding, with my personal[255] eye
  Will I look to 't.
Othello.   Iago is most honest.
  Michael, good-night; to-morrow with your earliest
  Let me have speech with you. *(To Desdemona.)* Come, my dear love,
  The purchase made, the fruits are to ensue;
  That profit's yet to come 'twixt me and you.   10
  Good-night.

(Exeunt Othello, Desdemona, and Attendants.)

(Enter Iago.)

Cassio. Welcome, Iago; we must to the watch.
Iago. Not this hour, lieutenant; 'tis not yet ten o' the clock. Our general casts us
  thus early for the love of his Desdemona, who let us not therefore blame; he hath
  not yet made wanton the night with her, and she is sport for Jove.
Cassio. She's a most exquisite lady.
Iago. And, I'll warrant her, full of game.
Cassio. Indeed, she is a most fresh and delicate creature.
Iago. What an eye she has! methinks it sounds a parley[256] of provocation.
Cassio. An inviting eye: and yet methinks right modest.   20
Iago. And when she speaks, is it not an alarum[257] to love?
Cassio. She is indeed perfection.
Iago. Well, happiness to their sheets! Come, lieutenant, I have a stoup of wine,
  and here without are a brace[258] of Cyprus gallants that would fain have a mea-
  sure to the health of black Othello.
Cassio. Not to-night, good Iago: I have very poor and unhappy brains for
  drinking: I could well wish courtesy would invent some other custom of
  entertainment.
Iago. O! they are our friends; but one cup: I'll drink for you.   29
Cassio. I have drunk but one cup to-night, and that was craftily qualified[259] too,
  and, behold, what innovation[260] it makes here: I am unfortunate in the infirmity, and dare not task my weakness with any more.
Iago. What, man! 'tis a night of revels; the gallants desire it.

---

[254] Discipline.   [255] Own.   [256] Conference.   [257] Call-to-arms.   [258] Pair.   [259] Diluted.   [260] Change, revolution.

Cassio. Where are they?

Iago. Here at the door; I pray you, call them in.

Cassio. I'll do 't; but it dislikes me.   *(Exit.)*

Iago. If I can fasten but one cup upon him,
    With that which he hath drunk to-night already,
    He'll be as full of quarrel and offence
    As my young mistress' dog. Now, my sick fool Roderigo,   40
    Whom love has turn'd almost the wrong side out,
    To Desdemona hath to-night carous'd
    Potations pottle-deep;[261] and he's to watch.
    Three lads of Cyprus, noble swelling spirits,
    That hold their honours in a wary distance,[262]
    The very elements[263] of this warlike isle,
    Have I to-night fluster'd with flowing cups,
    And they watch too. Now, 'mongst this flock of drunkards,
    Am I to put our Cassio in some action
    That may offend the isle. But here they come.   50
    If consequence[264] do but approve my dream,
    My boat sails freely, both with wind and stream.

(Re-enter Cassio, with him Montano, and Gentlemen. Servant following with wine.)

Cassio. 'Fore God, they have given me a rouse[265] already.

Montano. Good faith, a little one; not past a pint, as I am a soldier.

Iago. Some wine, ho!
    (Sings.)   And let me the canakin[266] clink, clink;
            And let me the canakin clink:
            A soldier's a man;
            A life's but a span;
            Why then let a soldier drink.   60
    Some wine, boys!

Cassio. 'Fore God, an excellent song.

Iago. I learned it in England, where indeed they are most potent in potting; your Dane, your German, and your swag-bellied[267] Hollander,—drink ho!—are nothing to your English.

Cassio. Is your Englishman so expert in his drinking?

Iago. Why, he drinks you[268] with facility your Dane dead drunk; he sweats not to overthrow your Almain;[269] he gives your Hollander a vomit ere the next pottle can be filled.

Cassio. To the health of our general!   70

Montano. I am for it, lieutenant; and I'll do you justice.

---

[261] Bottoms-up.   [262] Take offense easily.   [263] Types.   [264] Succeeding events.   [265] Drink.   [266] Small cup.   [267] With a pendulous belly.   [268] The "ethical" dative, i.e., you'll see that he drinks.   [269] German.

Iago. O sweet England!

> (*Sings.*) King Stephen was a worthy peer,
>> His breeches cost him but a crown;
> He held them sixpence all too dear,
>> With that he call'd the tailor lown.[270]
> He was a wight of high renown,
>> And thou art but of low degree:
> 'Tis pride that pulls the country down,
>> Then take thine auld cloak about thee.   80

Some wine, ho!

Cassio. Why, this is a more exquisite song than the other.

Iago. Will you hear 't again?

Cassio. No; for I hold him to be unworthy of his place that does those things. Well, God's above all; and there be souls must be saved, and there be souls must not be saved.

Iago. It's true, good lieutenant.

Cassio. For mine own part,—no offence to the general, nor any man of quality,— I hope to be saved.

Iago. And so do I too, lieutenant.   90

Cassio. Ay; but, by your leave, not before me; the lieutenant is to be saved before the ancient. Let's have no more of this; let's to our affairs. God forgive us our sins! Gentlemen, let's look to our business. Do not think, gentlemen, I am drunk: this is my ancient; this is my right hand, and this is my left hand. I am not drunk now; I can stand well enough, and speak well enough.

All. Excellent well.

Cassio. Why, very well, then; you must not think then that I am drunk.

> (*Exit.*)

Montano. To the platform, masters; come, let's set the watch.

Iago. You see this fellow that is gone before;
> He is a soldier fit to stand by Caesar   100
> And give direction; and do but see his vice;
> 'Tis to his virtue a just equinox,[271]
> The one as long as the other; 'tis pity of him.
> I fear the trust Othello puts him in,
> On some odd time of his infirmity,
> Will shake this island.

Montano.   But is he often thus?

Iago. 'Tis evermore the prologue to his sleep;
> He'll watch the horologe a double set,[272]
> If drink rock not his cradle.

Montano.   It were well
> The general were put in mind of it.   110
> Perhaps he sees it not; or his good nature

---

[270] Lout, rascal.   [271] Equivalent.   [272] Stand watch twice twelve hours.

Prizes the virtue that appears in Cassio,
And looks not on his evils. Is not this true?

(Enter Roderigo.)

Iago *(aside to him).* How now, Roderigo!
I pray you, after the lieutenant; go.   *(Exit Roderigo.)*
Montano. And 'tis great pity that the noble Moor
Should hazard such a place as his own second
With one of an ingraft[273] infirmity;
It were an honest action to say
So to the Moor.
Iago.   Not I, for this fair island: 120
I do love Cassio well, and would do much
To cure him of this evil. But hark! what noise?

(Cry within, 'Help! Help!' Re-enter Cassio, driving in Roderigo.)

Cassio. You rogue! you rascal!
Montano.   What's the matter, lieutenant?
Cassio. A knave teach me my duty!
I'll beat the knave into a twiggen[274] bottle.
Roderigo. Beat me!
Cassio.   Dost thou prate, rogue?

(Striking Roderigo.)

Montano *(staying him).* Nay, good lieutenant;
I pray you, sir, hold your hand.
Cassio.   Let me go, sir,
Or I'll knock you o'er the mazzard.[275]
Montano.   Come, come; you're drunk.
Cassio. Drunk!   130

(They fight.)

Iago *(aside to Roderigo).* Away, I say! go out, and cry a mutiny.

(Exit Roderigo.)

Nay, good lieutenant! God's will, gentlemen!
Help, ho! Lieutenant! sir! Montano! sir!
Help, masters! Here's a goodly watch indeed!

(Bell rings.)

Who's that that rings the bell? Diablo, ho!

---

[273] Ingrained.   [274] Wicker.   [275] Head.

The town will rise: God's will! lieutenant, hold!
You will be sham'd for ever.

(Re-enter Othello and Attendants.)

Othello.   What is the matter here?
Montano. 'Zounds! I bleed still; I am hurt to the death.

(He faints.)

Othello. Hold, for your lives!   140
Iago. Hold, ho, lieutenant! Sir! Montano! gentlemen!
  Have you forgot all sense of place and duty?
  Hold! the general speaks to you; hold for shame!
Othello. Why, how now, ho! from whence ariseth this?
  Are we turn'd Turks, and to ourselves do that
  Which heaven hath forbid the Ottomites?
  For Christian shame put by this barbarous brawl;
  He that stirs next to carve for his own rage
  Holds his soul light; he dies upon his motion.
  Silence that dreadful bell! it frights the isle   150
  From her propriety. What is the matter, masters?
  Honest Iago, that look'st dead with grieving,
  Speak, who began this? On thy love, I charge thee.
Iago. I do not know; friends all but now, even now,
  In quarter²⁷⁶ and in terms like bride and groom
  Devesting²⁷⁷ them for bed; and then, but now,—
  As if some planet had unwitted men,—
  Swords out, and tilting one at other's breast,
  In opposition bloody. I cannot speak
  Any beginning to this peevish odds,²⁷⁸   160
  And would in action glorious I had lost
  Those legs that brought me to a part of it!
Othello. How comes it, Michael, you are thus forgot?
Cassio. I pray you, pardon me; I cannot speak.
Othello. Worthy Montano, you were wont be civil;
  The gravity and stillness of your youth
  The world hath noted, and your name is great
  In mouths of wisest censure:²⁷⁹ what's the matter,
  That you unlace²⁸⁰ your reputation thus
  And spend your rich opinion²⁸¹ for the name   170
  Of a night-brawler? give me answer to it.
Montano. Worthy Othello, I am hurt to danger;
  Your officer, Iago, can inform you,

---

²⁷⁶ On duty.   ²⁷⁷ Undressing.   ²⁷⁸ Silly quarrel.   ²⁷⁹ Judgment.   ²⁸⁰ Undo.   ²⁸¹ High reputation.

While I spare speech, which something now offends[282] me,
Of all that I do know; nor know I aught
By me that 's said or done amiss this night,
Unless self-charity be sometimes a vice,
And to defend ourselves it be a sin
When violence assails us.

Othello.   Now, by heaven,
My blood begins my safer guides to rule,   180
And passion, having my best judgment collied,[283]
Assays to lead the way. If I once stir,
Or do but lift this arm, the best of you
Shall sink in my rebuke. Give me to know
How this foul rout began, who set it on;
And he that is approv'd[284] in this offence,
Though he had twinn'd with me—both at a birth—
Shall lose me. What! in a town of war,
Yet wild, the people's hearts brimful of fear,
To manage private and domestic quarrel,   190
In night, and on the court and guard of safety!
'Tis monstrous. Iago, who began 't?

Montano. If partially affin'd,[285] or leagu'd in office,
Thou dost deliver more or less than truth,
Thou art not soldier.

Iago.   Touch me not so near;
I had rather[286] have this tongue cut from my mouth
Than it should do offence to Michael Cassio;
Yet, I persuade myself, to speak the truth
Shall nothing wrong him. Thus it is, general.
Montano and myself being in speech,   200
There comes a fellow crying out for help,
And Cassio following with determin'd sword
To execute upon him. Sir, this gentleman
Steps in to Cassio, and entreats his pause;
Myself the crying fellow did pursue,
Lest by his clamour, as it so fell out,
The town might fall in fright; he, swift of foot,
Outran my purpose, and I return'd the rather
For that I heard the clink and fall of swords,
And Cassio high in oath, which till to-night   210
I ne'er might say before. When I came back,—
For this was brief,—I found them close together,
At blow and thrust, even as again they were
When you yourself did part them.

---

[282] Pains, harms.   [283] Clouded.   [284] Proved (i.e., guilty).   [285] Favorably biased (by ties of friendship, or as Cassio's fellow officer).   [286] More quickly.

More of this matter can I not report:
But men are men; the best sometimes forget:
Though Cassio did some little wrong to him,
As men in rage strike those that wish them best,
Yet, surely Cassio, I believe, receiv'd
From him that fled some strange indignity,   220
Which patience could not pass.
Othello.   I know, Iago.
Thy honesty and love doth mince[287] this matter,
Making it light to Cassio. Cassio, I love thee;
But never more be officer of mine.

(Enter Desdemona, attended.)

Look! if my gentle love be not rais'd up;
(To Cassio.) I'll make thee an example.
Desdemona.   What's the matter?
Othello. All's well now, sweeting; come away to bed.
Sir, for your hurts, myself will be your surgeon.
Lead him off.   *(Montano is led off.)*
Iago, look with care about the town,   230
And silence those whom this vile brawl distracted.
Come, Desdemona; 'tis the soldier's life,
To have their balmy slumbers wak'd with strife.

                                    (Exeunt all but Iago and Cassio.)

Iago. What! are you hurt, lieutenant?
Cassio. Ay; past all surgery.
Iago. Marry, heaven forbid!
Cassio. Reputation, reputation, reputation! O! I have lost my reputation. I have
lost the immortal part of myself, and what remains is bestial. My reputation,
Iago, my reputation!
Iago. As I am an honest man, I thought you had received some bodily wound;
there is more offence in that than in reputation. Reputation is an idle and most
false imposition;[288] oft got without merit, and lost without deserving: you
have lost no reputation at all, unless you repute yourself such a loser. What!
man; there are ways to recover the general again; you are but now cast in his
mood,[289] a punishment more in policy[290] than in malice; even so as one would
beat his offenceless dog to affright an imperious lion. Sue to him again, and he
is yours.
Cassio. I will rather sue to be despised than to deceive so good a commander with
so slight, so drunken and so indiscreet an officer. Drunk! and speak parrot![291]

---

[287] Tone down.   [288] Something external.   [289] Dismissed because he is angry.   [290] I.e., more for
the sake of the example or to show his fairness.   [291] I.e., without thinking.

and squabble, swagger, swear, and discourse fustian[292] with one's own shadow! O thou invisible spirit of wine! if thou hast no name to be known by, let us call thee devil!

Iago. What was he that you followed with your sword? What hath he done to you?

Cassio. I know not.

Iago. Is 't possible?

Cassio. I remember a mass of things, but nothing distinctly; a quarrel, but nothing wherefore. O God! that men should put an enemy in their mouths to steal away their brains; that we should, with joy, pleasance,[293] revel, and applause, transform ourselves into beasts.   260

Iago. Why, but you are now well enough; how came you thus recovered?

Cassio. It hath pleased the devil drunkenness to give place to the devil wrath; one unperfectness shows me another, to make me frankly despise myself.

Iago. Come, you are too severe a moraler. As the time, the place, and the condition of this country stands, I could heartily wish this had not befallen, but since it is as it is, mend it for your own good.

Cassio. I will ask him for my place again; he shall tell me I am a drunkard! Had I as many mouths as Hydra,[294] such an answer would stop them all. To be now a sensible man, by and by a fool, and presently a beast! O strange! Every inordinate cup is unblessed and the ingredient[295] is a devil.   270

Iago. Come, come; good wine is a good familiar creature if it be well used; exclaim no more against it. And, good lieutenant, I think you think I love you.

Cassio. I have well approved it, sir. I drunk!

Iago. You or any man living may be drunk at some time, man. I'll tell you what you shall do. Our general's wife is now the general; I may say so in this respect, for that he hath devoted and given up himself to the contemplation, mark, and denotement of her parts and graces: confess yourself freely to her; importune her; she'll help to put you in your place again. She is of so free, so kind, so apt, so blessed a disposition, that she holds it a vice in her goodness not to do more than she is requested. This broken joint between you and her husband entreat her to splinter;[296] and, my fortunes against any lay[297] worth naming, this crack of your love shall grow stronger than it was before.   282

Cassio. You advise me well.

Iago. I protest, in the sincerity of love and honest kindness.

Cassio. I think it freely; and betimes in the morning I will beseech the virtuous Desdemona to undertake for me. I am desperate of my fortunes if they check me here.

Iago. You are in the right. Good-night, lieutenant; I must to the watch.

Cassio. Good-night, honest Iago!   *(Exit.)*

Iago. And what's he then that says I play the villain?   290
When this advice is free I give and honest,
Probal[298] to thinking and indeed the course

---

[292] I.e., nonsense.   [293] Pleasure.   [294] Many-headed snake in Greek mythology.   [295] Contents.
[296] Bind up with splints.   [297] Wager.   [298] Provable.

To win the Moor again? For 'tis most easy
The inclining Desdemona to subdue
In any honest suit; she's fram'd as fruitful[299]
As the free elements. And then for her
To win the Moor, were 't to renounce his baptism,
All seals and symbols of redeemed sin,
His soul is so enfetter'd to her love,
That she may make, unmake, do what she list,   300
Even as her appetite shall play the god
With his weak function.[300] How am I then a villain
To counsel Cassio to this parallel[301] course,
Directly to his good? Divinity of hell!
When devils will the blackest sins put on,
They do suggest at first with heavenly shows,
As I do now; for while this honest fool
Plies Desdemona to repair his fortunes,
And she for him pleads strongly to the Moor,
I'll pour this pestilence into his ear   310
That she repeals[302] him for her body's lust;
And, by how much she strives to do him good,
She shall undo her credit with the Moor.
So will I turn her virtue into pitch,
And out of her own goodness make the net
That shall enmesh them all.

(Re-enter Roderigo.)

Iago. How now, Roderigo!

Roderigo. I do follow here in the chase, not like a hound that hunts, but one that fills up the cry.[303] My money is almost spent; I have been to-night exceedingly well cudgelled; and I think the issue will be, I shall have so much experience for my pains; and so, with no money at all and a little more wit, return again to Venice.

Iago. How poor are they that have not patience!
What wound did ever heal but by degrees?
Thou know'st we work by wit and not by witchcraft,
And wit depends on dilatory time.
Does 't not go well? Cassio hath beaten thee,
And thou by that small hurt hast cashiered Cassio.
Though other things grow fair against the sun,
Yet fruits that blossom first will first be ripe:
Content thyself awhile. By the mass, 'tis morning;   330
Pleasure and action make the hours seem short.

---

[299] Generous.   [300] Faculties.   [301] Purposeful.   [302] I.e., seeks to recall.   [303] Pack (hunting term).

Retire thee; go where thou art billeted:
Away, I say; thou shalt know more hereafter:
Nay, get thee gone. *(Exit Roderigo.)* Two things are to be done,
My wife must move for Cassio to her mistress;
I'll set her on;
Myself the while to draw the Moor apart,
And bring him jump[304] when he may Cassio find
Soliciting his wife: ay, that's the way:
Dull not device by coldness and delay.   *(Exit.)*

ACT III

Scene 1.   Cyprus. Before the Castle.

(Enter Cassio, and some Musicians.)

Cassio. Masters, play here, I will content your pains;[305]
Something that's brief; and bid 'Good-morrow, general.'   *(Music.)*

(Enter Clown.)

Clown. Why, masters, have your instruments been in Naples, that they speak i'
the nose[306] thus?
First Musician. How, sir, how?
Clown. Are these, I pray you, wind-instruments?
First Musician. Ay, marry, are they, sir.
Clown. O! thereby hangs a tale.
First Musician. Whereby hangs a tale, sir?
Clown. Marry, sir, by many a wind-instrument that I know. But, masters, here's
money for you; and the general so likes your music, that he desires you, for love's
sake, to make no more noise with it.   12
First Musician. Well, sir, we will not.
Clown. If you have any music that may not be heard, to 't again; but, as they say, to
hear music the general does not greatly care.
First Musician. We have none such, sir.
Clown. Then put up your pipes in your bag, for I'll away.
Go; vanish into air; away!   *(Exeunt Musicians.)*
Cassio. Dost thou hear, mine honest friend?
Clown. No, I hear not your honest friend; I hear you.   20
Cassio. Prithee, keep up thy quillets.[307] There's a poor piece of gold for thee. If the
gentlewoman that attends the general's wife be stirring, tell her there's one Cas-
sio entreats her a little favour of speech: wilt thou do this?

---

[304] At the exact moment.   [305] Reward your efforts.   [306] Naples was notorious for venereal disease, and syphilis was believed to affect the nose.   [307] Quibbles.

Clown. She is stirring, sir: if she will stir hither, I shall seem to notify unto her.

Cassio. Do, good my friend. *(Exit Clown.)*

(Enter Iago.)

In happy time, Iago.

Iago. You have not been a-bed, then?

Cassio. Why, no; the day had broke
Before we parted. I have made bold, Iago,
To send in to your wife; my suit to her
Is, that she will to virtuous Desdemona   30
Procure me some access.

Iago.   I'll send her to you presently;
And I'll devise a mean to draw the Moor
Out of the way, that your converse and business
May be more free.

Cassio. I humbly thank you for 't. *(Exit Iago.)*
                I never knew
A Florentine more kind and honest.[308]

(Enter Emilia.)

Emilia. Good-morrow, good lieutenant: I am sorry
For your displeasure,[309] but all will soon be well.
The general and his wife are talking of it,
And she speaks for you stoutly: the Moor replies   40
That he you hurt is of great fame in Cyprus
And great affinity,[310] and that in wholesome wisdom
He might not but refuse you; but he protests he loves you,
And needs no other suitor but his likings
To take the safest occasion by the front[311]
To bring you in again.[312]

Cassio.   Yet, I beseech you,
If you think fit, or that it may be done,
Give me advantage of some brief discourse
With Desdemona alone.

Emilia.   Pray you, come in:
I will bestow you where you shall have time   50
To speak your bosom[313] freely.

Cassio.   I am much bound to you. *(Exeunt.)*

Scene 2. A Room in the Castle.

(Enter Othello, Iago, and Gentlemen.)

---

[308] Cassio means that not even a fellow Florentine could behave to him in a friendlier fashion than
does Iago.   [309] Disgrace.   [310] Family connection.   [311] Forelock.   [312] Restore you (to Othello's
favor).   [313] Heart, inmost thoughts.

Othello. These letters give, Iago, to the pilot,
  And by him do my duties to the senate;
  That done, I will be walking on the works;
  Repair there to me.
Iago.   Well, my good lord, I'll do 't.
Othello. This fortification, gentlemen, shall we see 't?
Gentlemen. We'll wait upon your lordship.   *(Exeunt.)*

Scene 3.   Before the Castle.

(Enter Desdemona, Cassio, and Emilia.)

Desdemona. Be thou assur'd, good Cassio, I will do
  All my abilities in thy behalf.
Emilia. Good madam, do: I warrant it grieves my husband,
  As if the case were his.
Desdemona. O! that's an honest fellow. Do not doubt, Cassio,
  But I will have my lord and you again
  As friendly as you were.
Cassio.   Bounteous madam,
  Whatever shall become of Michael Cassio,
  He's never any thing but your true servant.
Desdemona. I know 't; I thank you. You do love my lord;   10
  You have known him long; and be you well assur'd
  He shall in strangeness[314] stand no further off
  Than in a politic[315] distance.
Cassio.   Ay, but, lady,
  That policy may either last so long,
  Or feed upon such nice[316] and waterish diet,
  Or breed itself so out of circumstance,
  That, I being absent and my place supplied,
  My general will forget my love and service.
Desdemona. Do not doubt[317] that; before Emilia here
  I give thee warrant of thy place. Assure thee,   20
  If I do vow a friendship, I'll perform it
  To the last article; my lord shall never rest;
  I'll watch him tame,[318] and talk him out of patience;
  His bed shall seem a school, his board a shrift;[319]
  I'll intermingle every thing he does
  With Cassio's suit. Therefore be merry, Cassio;
  For thy solicitor shall rather die
  Than give thy cause away.[320]

(Enter Othello and Iago, at a distance.)

---

[314] Aloofness.   [315] I.e., dictated by policy.   [316] Slight, trivial.   [317] Fear.   [318] Outwatch him (i.e., keep him awake) till he submits.   [319] Confessional.   [320] Abandon your cause.

Emilia. Madam, here comes my lord.

Cassio. Madam, I'll take my leave.   30

Desdemona. Why, stay, and hear me speak.

Cassio. Madam, not now; I am very ill at ease,
  Unfit for mine own purposes.

Desdemona. Well, do your discretion.   *(Exit Cassio.)*

Iago. Ha! I like not that.

Othello.   What dost thou say?

Iago. Nothing, my lord: or if—I know not what.

Othello. Was not that Cassio parted from my wife?

Iago. Cassio, my lord? No, sure, I cannot think it,
  That he would steal away so guilty-like,
  Seeing you coming.

Othello.   I do believe 'twas he.   40

Desdemona. How now, my lord!
  I have been talking with a suitor here,
  A man that languishes in your displeasure.

Othello. Who is 't you mean?

Desdemona. Why, your lieutenant, Cassio. Good my lord,
  If I have any grace or power to move you,
  His present[321] reconciliation take;
  For if he be not one that truly loves you,
  That errs in ignorance and not in cunning,
  I have no judgment in an honest face.   50
  I prithee[322] call him back.

Othello.   Went he hence now?

Desdemona. Ay, sooth; so humbled,
  That he hath left part of his grief with me,
  To suffer with him. Good love, call him back.

Othello. Not now, sweet Desdemona; some other time.

Desdemona. But shall 't be shortly?

Othello.   The sooner, sweet, for you.

Desdemona. Shall 't be to-night at supper?

Othello.   No, not to-night.

Desdemona. To-morrow dinner, then?

Othello.   I shall not dine at home;
  I meet the captains at the citadel.

Desdemona. Why, then, to-morrow night; or Tuesday morn;   60
  Or Tuesday noon, or night; or Wednesday morn:
  I prithee name the time, but let it not
  Exceed three days: in faith, he's penitent;
  And yet his trespass, in our common reason,—
  Save that they say, the wars must make examples
  Out of their best,—is not almost[323] a fault

---

[321] Immediate.   [322] Pray thee.   [323] Hardly.

To incur a private check.[324] When shall he come?
Tell me, Othello: I wonder in my soul,
What you could ask me, that I should deny,
Or stand so mammering[325] on. What! Michael Cassio,   70
That came a wooing with you, and so many a time,
When I have spoke of you dispraisingly,
Hath ta'en your part; to have so much to do
To bring him in! Trust me, I could do much,—

Othello. Prithee, no more; let him come when he will;
I deny thee nothing.

Desdemona.   Why, this is not a boon;
'Tis as I should entreat you wear your gloves,
Or feed on nourishing dishes, or keep you warm,
Or sue to you to do a peculiar profit
To your own person: nay, when I have a suit   80
Wherein I mean to touch your love indeed,
It shall be full of poise[326] and difficult weight,
And fearful to be granted.

Othello.   I will deny thee nothing:
Whereon, I do beseech thee, grant me this,
To leave me but a little to myself.

Desdemona. Shall I deny you? no: farewell, my lord.

Othello. Farewell, my Desdemona: I'll come to thee straight.

Desdemona. Emilia, come. Be as your fancies teach you;
Whate'er you be, I am obedient.   *(Exit, with Emilia.)*

Othello. Excellent wretch![327] Perdition catch my soul,   90
But I do love thee! and when I love thee not,
Chaos is[328] come again.

Iago. My noble lord,—

Othello.   What dost thou say, Iago?

Iago. Did Michael Cassio, when you woo'd my lady,
Know of your love?

Othello. He did, from first to last: why dost thou ask?

Iago. But for a satisfaction of my thought;
No further harm.

Othello.   Why of thy thought, Iago?

Iago. I did not think he had been acquainted with her.

Othello. O! yes; and went between us very oft.   100

Iago. Indeed!

Othello. Indeed! ay, indeed; discern'st thou aught in that?
Is he not honest?

Iago.   Honest, my lord?

Othello.   Honest! ay, honest.

---

[324] (Even) a private reprimand. [325] Shilly-shallying. [326] Weight. [327] Here, a term of endearment.
[328] Will have.

Iago. My lord, for aught I know.

Othello. What dost thou think?

Iago.   Think, my lord!

Othello.   Think, my lord!

By heaven, he echoes me,
As if there were some monster in his thought
Too hideous to be shown. Thou dost mean something:
I heard thee say but now, thou lik'dst not that,
When Cassio left my wife; what didst not like? 110
And when I told thee he was of my counsel
In my whole course of wooing, thou criedst, 'Indeed!'
And didst contract and purse thy brow together,
As if thou then hadst shut up in thy brain
Some horrible conceit.³²⁹ If thou dost love me,
Show me thy thought.

Iago. My lord, you know I love you.

Othello.   I think thou dost;
And, for³³⁰ I know thou art full of love and honesty,
And weigh'st thy words before thou givest them breath,
Therefore these stops³³¹ of thine fright me the more; 120
For such things in a false disloyal knave
Are tricks of custom, but in a man that's just
They are close dilations,³³² working from the heart
That passion cannot rule.

Iago.   For Michael Cassio,
I dare be sworn I think that he is honest.

Othello. I think so too.

Iago.   Men should be what they seem;
Or those that be not, would they might seem none!

Othello. Certain men should be what they seem.

Iago. Why then, I think Cassio's an honest man.

Othello. Nay, yet there's more in this. 130
I pray thee, speak to me as to thy thinkings,
As thou dost ruminate, and give thy worst of thoughts
The worst of words.

Iago.   Good my lord, pardon me;
Though I am bound to every act of duty,
I am not bound to³³³ that all slaves are free to.
Utter my thoughts? Why, say they are vile and false;
As where's that palace whereinto foul things
Sometimes intrude not? who has a breast so pure
But some uncleanly apprehensions³³⁴
Keep leets and law-days,³³⁵ and in session sit 140
With meditations lawful?

---

³²⁹ Fancy.   ³³⁰ Because.   ³³¹ Interruptions, hesitations.   ³³² Secret (i.e., involuntary, unconscious)
revelations.   ³³³ Bound with regard to.   ³³⁴ Conceptions.   ³³⁵ Sittings of the local courts.

Othello. Thou dost conspire against thy friend, Iago,
    If thou but think'st him wrong'd, and mak'st his ear
    A stranger to thy thoughts.

Iago.   I do beseech you,
    Though I perchance am vicious in my guess,—
    As, I confess, it is my nature's plague
    To spy into abuses, and oft my jealousy[336]
    Shapes faults that are not,—that your wisdom yet,
    From one that so imperfectly conceits,
    Would take no notice, nor build yourself a trouble   150
    Out of his scattering and unsure observance.
    It were not for your quiet nor your good,
    Nor for my manhood, honesty, or wisdom,
    To let you know my thoughts.

Othello.   What dost thou mean?

Iago. Good name in man and woman, dear my lord,
    Is the immediate jewel of[337] their souls:
    Who steals my purse steals trash; 'tis something, nothing;
    'Twas mine, 'tis his, and has been slave to thousands;
    But he that filches from me my good name
    Robs me of that which not enriches him,   160
    And makes me poor indeed.

Othello. By heaven, I'll know thy thoughts.

Iago. You cannot, if my heart were in your hand;
    Nor shall not, whilst 'tis in my custody.

Othello. Ha!

Iago.   O! beware, my lord, of jealousy;
    It is the green-ey'd monster which doth mock
    The meat it feeds on: that cuckold[338] lives in bliss
    Who, certain of his fate, loves not his wronger;
    But, O! what damned minutes tells[339] he o'er
    Who dotes, yet doubts; suspects, yet soundly loves!   170

Othello. O misery!

Iago. Poor and content is rich, and rich enough,
    But riches fineless[340] is as poor as winter
    To him that ever fears he shall be poor.
    Good heaven, the souls of all my tribe defend
    From jealousy!

Othello.   Why, why is this?
    Think'st thou I'd make a life of jealousy,
    To follow still the changes of the moon
    With fresh suspicions? No; to be once in doubt
    Is once to be resolved. Exchange me for a goat   180

---

[336] Suspicion.   [337] Jewel closest to.   [338] Husband of an adulterous woman.   [339] Counts.
[340] Boundless.

When I shall turn the business of my soul
To such exsufflicate[341] and blown[342] surmises,
Matching thy inference. 'Tis not to make me jealous
To say my wife is fair, feeds well, loves company,
Is free of speech, sings, plays, and dances well;
Where virtue is, these are more virtuous:
Nor from mine own weak merits will I draw
The smallest fear, or doubt of her revolt;
For she had eyes, and chose me. No, Iago;
I'll see before I doubt; when I doubt, prove;   190
And, on the proof, there is no more but this,
Away at once with love or jealousy!

Iago. I am glad of it; for now I shall have reason
To show the love and duty that I bear you
With franker spirit; therefore, as I am bound,
Receive it from me; I speak not yet of proof.
Look to your wife; observe her well with Cassio;
Wear your eye thus, not jealous nor secure:
I would not have your free and noble nature
Out of self-bounty[343] be abus'd; look to 't: 200
I know our country disposition[344] well;
In Venice they do let heaven see the pranks
They dare not show their husbands; their best conscience
Is not to leave 't undone, but keep 't unknown.

Othello. Dost thou say so?

Iago. She did deceive her father, marrying you;
And when she seem'd to shake and fear your looks,
She lov'd them most.

Othello.   And so she did.

Iago.   Why, go to,[345] then;
She that so young could give out such a seeming,
To seel her father's eyes up close as oak,   210
He thought 'twas witchcraft; but I am much to blame;
I humbly do beseech you of your pardon
For too much loving you.

Othello.   I am bound to thee for ever.

Iago. I see, this hath a little dash'd your spirits.

Othello. Not a jot, not a jot.

Iago.   I' faith, I fear it has.
I hope you will consider what is spoke
Comes from my love. But I do see you're mov'd;
I am to pray you not to strain my speech
To grosser issues nor to larger reach
Than to suspicion.   220

---

[341] Spat out (?).   [342] Fly-blown.   [343] Innate generosity.   [344] I.e., that of Venice.   [345] Colloquialism;
here, something like "all right."

Othello. I will not.

Iago.   Should you do so, my lord,
My speech should fall into such vile success
As my thoughts aim not at. Cassio's my worthy friend—
My lord, I see you're mov'd.

Othello.   No, not much mov'd:
I do not think but Desdemona's honest.[346]

Iago. Long live she so! and long live you to think so!

Othello. And yet, how nature erring from itself,—

Iago. Ay, there's the point: as, to be bold with you,
Not to affect many proposed matches
Of her own clime,[347] complexion, and degree,[348]   230
Whereto, we see, in all things nature tends;
Foh! one may smell in such, a will most rank,
Foul disproportion, thoughts unnatural.
But pardon me; I do not in position[349]
Distinctly[350] speak of her, though I may fear
Her will, recoiling[351] to her better judgment,
May fall to match you with her country forms
And happily[352] repent.

Othello.   Farewell, farewell:
If more thou dost perceive, let me know more;
Set on thy wife to observe. Leave me, Iago.   240

Iago. My lord, I take my leave.   *(Going.)*

Othello. Why did I marry? This honest creature, doubtless,
Sees and knows more, much more, than he unfolds.

Iago *(returning).* My lord, I would I might entreat your honour
To scan this thing no further; leave it to time.
Although 'tis fit that Cassio have his place,
For, sure he fills it up with great ability,
Yet, if you please to hold him off awhile,
You shall by that perceive him and his means:
Note if your lady strain his entertainment[353]   250
With any strong or vehement importunity;
Much will be seen in that. In the mean time,
Let me be thought too busy[354] in my fears,
As worthy cause I have to fear I am,
And hold her free, I do beseech your honour.

Othello. Fear not my government.

Iago. I once more take my leave.   *(Exit.)*

Othello. This fellow's of exceeding honesty,
And knows all qualities, with a learned spirit,
Of human dealings; if I do prove her haggard,[355]   260

---

[346] Chaste.   [347] Country.   [348] Social rank.   [349] In definite assertion.   [350] Specifically.   [351] Reverting.
[352] Perhaps.   [353] Urge his re-welcome (i.e., to Othello's trust and favor).   [354] Meddlesome.   [355] Wild hawk.

Though that her jesses[356] were my dear heart-strings,
I'd whistle her off and let her down the wind,[357]
To prey at fortune. Haply, for I am black,
And have not those soft parts of conversation
That chamberers[358] have, or, for I am declin'd
Into the vale of years—yet that's not much—
She's gone, I am abus'd;[359] and my relief
Must be to loathe her. O curse of marriage!
That we can call these delicate creatures ours,
And not their appetites. I had rather be a toad, 270
And live upon the vapour of a dungeon,
Than keep a corner in the thing I love
For others' uses. Yet, 'tis the plague of great ones;
Prerogativ'd[360] are they less than the base;
'Tis destiny unshunnable, like death:
Even then this forked plague[361] is fated to us
When we do quicken.[362]
                    Look! where she comes.
If she be false, O! then heaven mocks itself.
I'll not believe it.

(Re-enter Desdemona and Emilia.)

Desdemona.   How now, my dear Othello!
Your dinner and the generous[363] islanders 280
By you invited, do attend your presence.
Othello. I am to blame.
Desdemona.   Why do you speak so faintly?
Are you not well?
Othello. I have a pain upon my forehead here.[364]
Desdemona. Faith, that's with watching; 'twill away again:
Let me but bind it hard, within this hour
It will be well.
Othello.   Your napkin[365] is too little:

(She drops her handkerchief.)

Let it alone. Come, I'll go in with you.
Desdemona. I am very sorry that you are not well.

                    (Exeunt Othello and Desdemona.)

---

[356] Leather thongs by which the hawk's legs were strapped to the trainer's wrist.   [357] I'd let her
go and take care of herself.   [358] Courtiers; or (more specifically) gallants, frequenters of bed
chambers.   [359] Deceived.   [360] Privileged.   [361] I.e., the cuckold's proverbial horns.   [362] Are conceived, come alive.   [363] Noble.   [364] Othello again refers to his cuckoldom.   [365] Handkerchief.

Emilia. I am glad I have found this napkin;   290
  This was her first remembrance from the Moor;
  My wayward husband hath a hundred times
  Woo'd me to steal it, but she so loves the token,
  For he conjur'd her she should ever keep it,
  That she reserves it evermore about her
  To kiss and talk to. I'll have the work ta'en out,[366]
  And giv 't Iago:
  What he will do with it heaven knows, not I;
  I nothing but[367] to please his fantasy.[368]

(Enter Iago.)

Iago. How now! what do you here alone?   300
Emilia. Do not you chide; I have a thing for you.
Iago. A thing for me? It is a common thing—
Emilia. Ha!
Iago. To have a foolish wife.
Emilia. O! is that all? What will you give me now
  For that same handkerchief?
Iago.   What handkerchief?
Emilia. What handkerchief!
  Why, that the Moor first gave to Desdemona:
  That which so often you did bid me steal.
Iago. Hath stol'n it from her?   310
Emilia. No, faith; she let it drop by negligence,
  And, to the advantage, I, being there, took 't up.
  Look, here it is.
Iago.   A good wench; give it me.
Emilia. What will you do with 't, that you have been so earnest
  To have me filch it?
Iago.   Why, what's that to you?   *(Snatches it.)*
Emilia. If it be not for some purpose of import
  Give 't me again; poor lady! she'll run mad
  When she shall lack it.
Iago. Be not acknown on 't;[369] I have use for it.
  Go, leave me.   *(Exit Emilia.)*
  I will in Cassio's lodging lose this napkin,
  And let him find it; trifles light as air
  Are to the jealous confirmations strong
  As proofs of holy writ; this may do something.
  The Moor already changes with my poison:
  Dangerous conceits are in their natures poisons,

---

[366] Pattern copied.   [367] I.e., only want.   [368] Whim.   [369] You know nothing about it.

Which at the first are scarce found to distaste,[370]
But with a little act upon the blood,
Burn like the mines of sulphur. I did say so:
Look! where he comes!

(Enter Othello.)

                    Not poppy,[371] nor mandragora,[372]   330
Nor all the drowsy syrups[373] of the world,
Shall ever medicine thee to that sweet sleep
Which thou ow'dst yesterday.
Othello.   Ha! ha! false to me?
Iago. Why, how now, general! no more of that.
Othello. Avaunt! be gone! thou hast set me on the rack;
  I swear 'tis better to be much abus'd
  Than but to know 't a little.
Iago.   How now, my lord!
Othello. What sense had I of her stol'n hours of lust?
  I saw 't not, thought it not, it harm'd not me;
  I slept the next night well, was free and merry;   340
  I found not Cassio's kisses on her lips;
  He that is robb'd, not wanting what is stol'n,
  Let him not know 't, and he's not robb'd at all.
Iago. I am sorry to hear this.
Othello. I had been happy, if the general camp,[374]
  Pioners[375] and all, had tasted her sweet body,
  So[376] I had nothing known. O! now, for ever
  Farewell the tranquil mind; farewell content!
  Farewell the plumed troop and the big wars
  That make ambition virtue! O, farewell!   350
  Farewell the neighing steed, and the shrill trump,
  The spirit-stirring drum, the ear-piercing fife,
  The royal banner, and all quality,
  Pride, pomp, and circumstance[377] of glorious war!
  And, O you mortal engines,[378] whose rude throats
  The immortal Jove's dread clamours counterfeit,
  Farewell! Othello's occupation's gone!
Iago. Is it possible, my lord?
Othello. Villain, be sure thou prove my love a whore,
  Be sure of it; give me the ocular proof;   360
  Or, by the worth of mine eternal soul,
  Thou hadst been better have been born a dog
  Than answer my wak'd wrath.

---

[370] Scarce can be tasted.   [371] Opium.   [372] A soporific.   [373] I.e., soporifics.   [374] Whole army.
[375] Lowest rank of manual laborers in the army.   [376] As long as.   [377] Pageantry.   [378] Deadly artillery.

Iago.   Is 't come to this?

Othello. Make me to see 't; or, at the least, so prove it,
That the probation[379] bear no hinge nor loop
To hang a doubt on; or woe upon thy life!

Iago. My noble lord—

Othello. If thou dost slander her and torture me,
Never pray more; abandon all remorse;
On horror's head horrors accumulate;   370
Do deeds to make heaven weep, all earth amaz'd;
For nothing canst thou to damnation add
Greater than that.

Iago.   O grace! O heaven forgive me!
Are you a man! have you a soul or sense?
God be wi' you; take mine office. O wretched fool!
That liv'st to make thine honesty a vice.
O monstrous world! Take note, take note, O world!
To be direct and honest is not safe.
I thank you for this profit,[380] and, from hence
I'll love no friend, sith[381] love breeds such offence.   380

Othello. Nay, stay; thou shouldst be honest.

Iago. I should be wise; for honesty's a fool,
And loses that it works for.

Othello.   By the world,
I think my wife be honest and think she is not;
I think that thou art just and think thou art not.
I'll have some proof. Her name, that was as fresh
As Dian's[382] visage, is now begrim'd and black
As mine own face. If there be cords or knives,
Poison or fire or suffocating streams,
I'll not endure it. Would I were satisfied!   390

Iago. I see, sir, you are eaten up with passion.
I do repent me that I put it to you.
You would be satisfied?

Othello.   Would! nay, I will.

Iago. And may; but how? how satisfied, my lord?
Would you, the supervisor,[383] grossly gape on;
Behold her tupp'd?

Othello.   Death and damnation! O!

Iago. It were a tedious[384] difficulty, I think,
To bring them to that prospect; damn them then,
If ever mortal eyes do see them bolster[385]
More[386] than their own! What then? how then?   400
What shall I say? Where's satisfaction?

---

[379] Proof.   [380] Lesson.   [381] Since.   [382] Diana's, the goddess of the moon.   [383] Observer.   [384] Laborious.
[385] Lie together.   [386] Other.

It is impossible you should see this,
Were they as prime[387] as goats, as hot as monkeys,
As salt as wolves in pride,[388] and fools as gross
As ignorance made drunk; but yet, I say,
If imputation, and strong circumstances,
Which lead directly to the door of truth,
Will give you satisfaction, you may have it.

Othello. Give me a living reason she's disloyal.

Iago. I d not like the office;   410
But, ch I am enter'd in this cause so far,
Prick'd to 't by foolish honesty and love,
I will go on. I lay with Cassio lately;
And, being troubled with a raging tooth,
I could not sleep.
There are a kind of men so loose of soul
That in their sleeps will mutter their affairs;
One of this kind is Cassio.
In sleep I heard him say, 'Sweet Desdemona,
Let us be wary, let us hide our loves!'   420
And then, sir, would he gripe[389] and wring my hand,
Cry, 'O, sweet creature!' and then kiss me hard,
As if he pluck'd up kisses by the roots,
That grew upon my lips; then laid his leg
Over my thigh, and sigh'd, and kiss'd; and then
Cried, 'Cursed fate, that gave thee to the Moor!'

Othello. O monstrous! monstrous!

Iago.   Nay, this was but his dream.

Othello. But this denoted a foregone conclusion:[390]
'Tis a shrewd doubt,[391] though it be but a dream.

Iago. And this may help to thicken other proofs   430
That do demonstrate thinly.

Othello.   I'll tear her all to pieces.

Iago. Nay, but be wise; yet we see nothing done;
She may be honest yet. Tell me but this:
Have you not sometimes seen a handkerchief
Spotted with strawberries in your wife's hand?

Othello. I gave her such a one; 'twas my first gift.

Iago. I know not that; but such a handkerchief—
I am sure it was your wife's—did I to-day
See Cassio wipe his beard with.

Othello.   If it be that,—

Iago. If it be that, or any that was hers,   440
It speaks against her with the other proofs.

---

[387] Lustful.   [388] Heat.   [389] Seize.   [390] Previous consummation.   [391] (1) Cursed, (2) Acute, suspicion.

Othello. O! that the slave had forty thousand lives;
 One is too poor, too weak for my revenge.
 Now do I see 'tis true. Look here, Iago;
 All my fond love thus do I blow to heaven:
 'Tis gone.
 Arise, black vengeance, from the hollow hell!
 Yield up, O love! thy crown and hearted throne
 To tyrannous hate. Swell, bosom, with thy fraught,[392]
 For 'tis of aspics'[393] tongues!
Iago.   Yet be content.[394]   450
Othello. O! blood, blood, blood!
Iago. Patience, I say; your mind, perhaps, may change.
Othello. Never, Iago. Like to the Pontic sea,[395]
 Whose icy current and compulsive course
 Ne'er feels retiring ebb, but keeps due on
 To the Propontic and the Hellespont,[396]
 Even so my bloody thoughts, with violent pace,
 Shall ne'er look back, ne'er ebb to humble love,
 Till that a capable[397] and wide revenge
 Swallow them up.   (Kneels.)
       Now, by yond marble heaven,   460
 In the due reverence of a sacred vow
 I here engage my words.
Iago.   Do not rise yet.   (Kneels.)
 Witness, you ever-burning lights above!
 You elements that clip[398] us round about!
 Witness, that here Iago doth give up
 The execution of his wit, hands, heart,
 To wrong'd Othello's service! Let him command,
 And to obey shall be in me remorse,[399]
 What bloody business ever.[400]   (They rise.)
Othello.   I greet thy love,
 Not with vain thanks, but with acceptance bounteous,   470
 And will upon the instant put thee to 't:
 Within these three days let me hear thee say
 That Cassio 's not alive.
Iago. My friend is dead; 'tis done at your request:
 But let her live.
Othello.   Damn her, lewd minx! O, damn her!
 Come, go with me apart; I will withdraw.
 To furnish me with some swift means of death
 For the fair devil. Now art thou my lieutenant.
Iago. I am your own for ever.   (Exeunt.)

---

[392] Burden.   [393] Poisonous snakes.   [394] Patient.   [395] The Black Sea.   [396] The Sea of Marmara, the Dardanelles.   [397] Comprehensive.   [398] Encompass.   [399] Probably a corrupt line; the meaning appears to be: "to obey shall be my solemn obligation."   [400] Soever.

Scene 4. Before the Castle.

(Enter Desdemona, Emilia, and Clown.)

Desdemona. Do you know, sirrah,[401] where Lieutenant Cassio lies?[402]
Clown. I dare not say he lies any where.
Desdemona. Why, man?
Clown. He is a soldier; and for one to say a soldier lies, is stabbing.[403]
Desdemona. Go to;[404] where lodges he?
Clown. To tell you where he lodges is to tell you where I lie.
Desdemona. Can anything be made of this?
Clown. I know not where he lodges, and for me to devise[405] a lodging, and say he lies here or he lies there, were to lie in mine own throat.
Desdemona. Can you inquire him out, and be edified by report? 10
Clown. I will catechize the world for him; that is, make questions, and by them answer.
Desdemona. Seek him, bid him come hither; tell him I have moved my lord in his behalf, and hope all will be well.
Clown. To do this is within the compass of man's wit, and therefore I will attempt the doing it. *(Exit.)*
Desdemona. Where should I lose that handkerchief, Emilia?
Emilia. I know not, madam.
Desdemona. Believe me, I had rather have lost my purse
Full of cruzadoes;[406] and, but my noble Moor 20
Is true of mind, and made of no such baseness
As jealous creatures are, it were enough
To put him to ill thinking.
Emilia. Is he not jealous?
Desdemona. Who! he? I think the sun where he was born
Drew all such humours from him.
Emilia. Look! where he comes.
Desdemona. I will not leave him now till Cassio
Be call'd to him.

(Enter Othello.)

Desdemona. How is 't with you, my lord?
Othello. Well, my good lady. *(Aside.)* O! hardness to dissemble.
How do you, Desdemona?
Desdemona. Well, my good lord.
Othello. Give me your hand. This hand is moist,[407] my lady. 30
Desdemona. It yet has felt no age nor known no sorrow.
Othello. This argues fruitfulness and liberal[408] heart;
Hot, hot, and moist; this hand of yours requires

[401] Common form of address to inferiors. [402] Lives. [403] I.e., is cause for stabbing. [404] Here apparently: "Come on!" [405] Invent. [406] Portuguese gold coins. [407] A supposed symptom of a lustful nature. [408] With overtones of: too free, loose.

A sequester[409] from liberty, fasting and prayer,
Much castigation, exercise devout;
For here 's a young and sweating devil here,
That commonly rebels. 'Tis a good hand,
A frank one.

Desdemona. You may, indeed, say so;
For 'twas that hand that gave away my heart. 40

Othello. A liberal hand; the hearts of old gave hands,
But our new heraldry[410] is hands not hearts.

Desdemona. I cannot speak of this. Come now, your promise.

Othello. What promise, chuck?[411]

Desdemona. I have sent to bid Cassio come speak with you.

Othello. I have a salt and sorry rheum offends me.
Lend me thy handkerchief.

Desdemona.   Here, my lord.

Othello. That which I gave you.

Desdemona.   I have it not about me.

Othello. Not?

Desdemona. No, indeed, my lord.

Othello.   That is a fault.
That handkerchief 50
Did an Egyptian[412] to my mother give;
She was a charmer,[413] and could almost read
The thoughts of people; she told her, while she kept it,
'Twould make her amiable[414] and subdue my father
Entirely to her love, but if she lost it
Or made a gift of it, my father's eye
Should hold her loathed, and his spirits should hunt
After new fancies.[415] She dying gave it me;
And bid me, when my fate would have me wive,
To give it her. I did so; and take heed on 't; 60
Make it a darling like your precious eye;
To lose 't or give 't away, were such perdition
As nothing else could match.

Desdemona.   Is 't possible?

Othello. 'Tis true; there 's magic in the web of it;
A sibyl,[416] that had number'd in the world
The sun to course two hundred compasses,
In her prophetic fury sew'd the work;
The worms were hallow'd that did breed the silk,
And it was dy'd in mummy[417] which the skilful
Conserv'd of maidens' hearts.

---

[409] Separation.   [410] I.e., new heraldic symbolism (Othello means that the new way is not to give the heart together with the hand).   [411] Common term of endearment.   [412] Gypsy.   [413] Sorceress.   [414] Lovable, desirable.   [415] Loves.   [416] Prophetess.   [417] Drug (medicinal or magic) derived from embalmed bodies.

Desdemona.　　　　　　　Indeed! is 't true?　　　　　70
Othello. Most veritable; therefore look to 't well.
Desdemona. Then would to heaven that I had never seen it!
Othello. Ha! wherefore?
Desdemona. Why do you speak so startingly and rash?
Othello. Is 't lost? is 't gone? speak, is it out o' the way?
Desdemona. Heaven bless us!
Othello. Say you?
Desdemona. It is not lost; but what an if[418] it were?
Othello. How!
Desdemona. I say, it is not lost.
Othello.　　　　　　　Fetch 't, let me see 't!　　　　80
Desdemona. Why, so I can, sir, but I will not now.
　This is a trick to put me from my suit:
　Pray you let Cassio be receiv'd again.
Othello. Fetch me the handkerchief; my mind misgives.
Desdemona. Come, come;
　You'll never meet a more sufficient[419] man.
Othello. The handkerchief!
Desdemona.　　　　　　I pray, talk[420] me of Cassio.
Othello. The handkerchief!
Desdemona.　　　　　A man that all his time
　Hath founded his good fortunes on your love,
　Shar'd dangers with you,—　　　　　　90
Othello. The handkerchief!
Desdemona. In sooth, you are to blame.
Othello. Away!　　　　　　　　　　　(*Exit.*)
Emilia. Is not this man jealous?
Desdemona. I ne'er saw this before.
　Sure, there's some wonder in this handkerchief;
　I am most unhappy in the loss of it.
Emilia. 'Tis not a year or two shows us a man;
　They are all but stomachs, and we all but[421] food;
　They eat us hungerly, and when they are full　　100
　They belch us. Look you! Cassio and my husband.

(*Enter Iago and Cassio.*)

Iago. There is no other way; 'tis she must do 't:
　And, lo! the happiness;[422] go and importune her.
Desdemona. How now, good Cassio! what 's the news with you?
Cassio. Madam, my former suit: I do beseech you
　That by your virtuous means I may again
　Exist, and be a member of his love

---

[418] If.　[419] Adequate.　[420] Talk to.　[421] Only . . . only.　[422] "What luck!"

Whom I with all the office[423] of my heart
Entirely honour; I would not be delay'd.
If my offence be of such mortal kind   110
That nor my service past, nor present sorrows,
Nor purpos'd merit in futurity,
Can ransom me into his love again,
But to know so must be my benefit;
So shall I clothe me in a forc'd content,
And shut myself up in some other course
To fortune's alms.

Desdemona.   Alas! thrice-gentle Cassio!
My advocation is not now in tune;
My lord is not my lord, nor should I know him,
Were he in favour[424] as in humour alter'd.   120
So help me every spirit sanctified,
As I have spoken for you all my best
And stood within the blank of[425] his displeasure
For my free speech. You must awhile be patient;
What I can do I will, and more I will
Than for myself I dare: let that suffice you.

Iago. Is my lord angry?

Emilia.   He went hence but now,
And certainly in strange unquietness.

Iago. Can he be angry? I have seen the cannon,
When it hath blown his ranks[426] into the air,   130
And, like the devil, from his very arm
Puff'd his own brother; and can he be angry?
Something of moment[427] then; I will go meet him;
There's matter in 't indeed, if he be angry.

Desdemona. I prithee, do so. *(Exit Iago.)* Something, sure, of state,[428]
Either from Venice, or some unhatch'd[429] practice
Made demonstrable here in Cyprus to him,
Hath puddled[430] his clear spirit; and, in such cases
Men's natures wrangle with inferior things,
Though great ones are their object. 'Tis even so;   140
For let our finger ache, and it indues[431]
Our other healthful members even to that sense
Of pain. Nay, we must think men are not gods,
Nor of them look for such observancy[432]
As fits the bridal.[433] Beshrew me much, Emilia,
I was—unhandsome warrior as I am—
Arraigning his unkindness with[434] my soul;

---

[423] Duty.   [424] Appearance.   [425] As the target for.   [426] I.e., his soldiers.   [427] Important.   [428] Public affairs.
[429] Abortive or budding plot.   [430] Muddied.   [431] Brings, leads.   [432] Attention.   [433] Wedding.   [434] To.

But now I find I had suborn'd the witness,[435]
And he 's indicted falsely.

Emilia. Pray heaven it be state matters, as you think,   150
And no conception,[436] nor no jealous toy[437]
Concerning you.

Desdemona. Alas the day! I never gave him cause.

Emilia. But jealous souls will not be answer'd so;
They are not ever jealous for the cause,
But jealous for they are jealous; 'tis a monster
Begot upon itself, born on itself.

Desdemona. Heaven keep that monster from Othello's mind!

Emilia. Lady, amen.

Desdemona. I will go seek him. Cassio, walk hereabout;   160
If I do find him fit, I'll move your suit
And seek to effect it to my uttermost.

Cassio. I humbly thank your ladyship.

                                    (Exeunt Desdemona and Emilia.)

(Enter Bianca.)

Bianca. Save you, friend Cassio!

Cassio.   What make you from home?
How is it with you, my most fair Bianca?
I' faith, sweet love, I was coming to your house.

Bianca. And I was going to your lodging, Cassio.
What! keep a week away? seven days and nights?
Eight score eight hours? and lovers' absent hours,
More tedious than the dial eight score times?   170
O weary reckoning!

Cassio.   Pardon me, Bianca,
I have this while with leaden thoughts been press'd;
But I shall, in a more continuate[438] time,
Strike off[439] this score of absence. Sweet Bianca,

(Giving her Desdemona's handkerchief.)

Take me this work out.

Bianca.   O Cassio! whence came this?
This is some token from a newer friend;
To the felt absence now I feel a cause;
Is 't come to this? Well, well.

Cassio.   Go to, woman!
Throw your vile guesses in the devil's teeth,

---

[435] I.e., caused my soul to bring in wrong charges.   [436] Fancy, supposition.   [437] Fancy.   [438] Uninterrupted.
[439] Cancel (i.e., make up for).

From whence you have them. You are jealous now   180
That this is from some mistress, some remembrance:
No, in good troth, Bianca.

Bianca.   Why, whose is it?

Cassio. I know not, sweet; I found it in my chamber.
I like the work well; ere it be demanded,—[440]
As like enough it will,—I'd have it copied;
Take it and do 't; and leave me for this time.

Bianca. Leave you! wherefore?

Cassio. I do attend here on[441] the general,
And think it no addition,[442] nor my wish,
To have him see me woman'd.

Bianca.   Why, I pray you?   190

Cassio. Not that I love you not.

Bianca.   But that you do not love me.
I pray you, bring me on the way a little
And say if I shall see you soon at night.

Cassio. 'Tis but a little way that I can bring you,
For I attend here; but I'll see you soon.

Bianca. 'Tis very good; I must be circumstanc'd.[443]

                                                        (*Exeunt.*)

ACT IV

Scene 1. Cyprus. Before the Castle.

(*Enter Othello and Iago.*)

Iago. Will you think so?

Othello.   Think so, Iago!

Iago.   What!
To kiss in private?

Othello.   An unauthoriz'd kiss.

Iago. Or to be naked with her friend a-bed
An hour or more, not meaning any harm?

Othello. Naked a-bed, Iago, and not mean harm?
It is hypocrisy against the devil:[444]
They that mean virtuously, and yet do so,
The devil their virtue tempts, and they tempt heaven.

Iago. If they do nothing, 'tis a venial slip;
But if I give my wife a handkerchief,—   10

Othello. What then?

---

[440] Asked for.   [441] Wait for.   [442] Advantage, credit.   [443] Governed by circumstances.   [444] I.e., by not committing the sin which the situation invites.

Iago. Why, then, 'tis hers, my lord; and, being hers,
   She may, I think, bestow 't on any man.

Othello. She is protectress of her honour too;
   May she give that?

Iago. Her honour is an essence that 's not seen;
   They have it very oft that have it not:[445]
   But for the handkerchief,—

Othello. By heaven, I would most gladly have forgot it:—
   Thou said'st,—O! it comes o'er my memory,   20
   As doth the raven[446] o'er the infected house,
   Boding to all,—he had my handkerchief.

Iago. Ay, what of that?

Othello.   That's not so good now.

Iago.   What,
   If I had said I had seen him do you wrong?
   Or heard him say, as knaves be such abroad,[447]
   Who having, by their own importunate suit,
   Or voluntary dotage[448] of some mistress,
   Convinced or supplied them,[449] cannot choose
   But they must blab.

Othello.   Hath he said any thing?

Iago. He hath, my lord; but be you well assur'd,   30
   No more than he'll unswear.

Othello.   What hath he said?

Iago. Faith, that he did— I know not what he did.

Othello. What? what?

Iago. Lie—

Othello. With her?

Iago.   With her, on her; what you will.

Othello. Lie with her; lie on her! We say, lie on her, when they belie her. Lie with her! that's fulsome. Handkerchief,—confessions,—handkerchief! To confess, and be hanged for his labour. First, to be hanged, and then to confess: I tremble at it. Nature would not invest herself in such shadowing passion without some instruction.[450] It is not words that shake me thus. Pish! Noses, ears, and lips. Is it possible?—Confess!—Handkerchief!—O devil!   41

(Falls in a trance.)

Iago. Work on,
   My medicine, work! Thus credulous fools are caught;
   And many worthy and chaste dames even thus,

---

[445] I.e., some unchaste women are thought chaste.   [446] (1) A bad omen, (2) A carrier of the plague.   [447] As there are some such in the world.   [448] Foolish affection.   [449] Overcome (their reluctance) or satisfied (their desires).   [450] I would not fall into such passion unless there were some real grounds for it.

All guiltless, meet reproach. What, ho! my lord!
My lord, I say! Othello!

(Enter Cassio.)

How now, Cassio!
Cassio. What's the matter?
Iago. My lord is fallen into an epilepsy;[451]
   This is his second fit; he had one yesterday.
Cassio. Rub him about the temples.
Iago.   No, forbear;   50
   The lethargy[452] must have his quiet course,
   If not, he foams at mouth, and by and by
   Breaks out to savage madness. Look! he stirs;
   Do you withdraw yourself a little while,
   He will recover straight; when he is gone,
   I would on great occasion[453] speak with you.   *(Exit Cassio.)*
   How is it, general? have you not hurt your head?
Othello. Dost thou mock me?[454]
Iago.   I mock you! no, by heaven.
   Would you would bear your fortune like a man!
Othello. A horned man's a monster and a beast.
Iago. There's many a beast then, in a populous city,   60
   And many a civil[455] monster.
Othello. Did he confess it?
Iago.   Good sir, be a man;
   Think every bearded fellow that's but yok'd
   May draw[456] with you; there's millions now alive
   That nightly lie in those unproper[457] beds
   Which they dare swear peculiar;[458] your case is better.
   O! 'tis the spite of hell, the fiend's arch-mock,
   To lip[459] a wanton in a secure[460] couch,
   And to suppose her chaste. No, let me know;   70
   And knowing what I am, I know what she shall be.
Othello. O! thou art wise; 'tis certain.
Iago.   Stand you awhile apart;
   Confine yourself but in a patient list.[461]
   Whilst you were here o'erwhelmed with your grief,—
   A passion most unsuiting such a man,—
   Cassio came hither; I shifted him away,
   And laid good 'scuse upon your ecstasy;[462]
   Bade him anon return and here speak with me;

---

[451] Seizure, fit.   [452] Coma.   [453] Important matter.   [454] Another allusion to the cuckold's horns. [455] Citizen.   [456] I.e., pull the burden of cuckoldom.   [457] Not exclusively their own.   [458] Exclusively their own.   [459] Kiss.   [460] I.e., without suspicion of having a rival.   [461] Bounds of patience. [462] Derangement, trance.

The which he promis'd. Do but encave yourself,
And mark the fleers, the gibes, and notable scorns,   80
That dwell in every region of his face;
For I will make him tell the tale anew,
Where, how, how oft, how long ago, and when
He hath, and is again to cope[463] your wife:
I say, but mark his gesture. Marry, patience;
Or I shall say you are all in all in spleen,[464]
And nothing of a man.

Othello.   Dost thou hear, Iago?
I will be found most cunning in my patience;
But—dost thou hear?—most bloody.

Iago.   That's not amiss:
But yet keep time[465] in all. Will you withdraw?   *(Othello goes apart.)*
Now will I question Cassio of Bianca,
A housewife[466] that by selling her desires
Buys herself bread and clothes; it is a creature
That dotes on Cassio; as 'tis the strumpet's plague
To beguile many and be beguil'd by one.
He, when he hears of her, cannot refrain
From the excess of laughter. Here he comes:

(Re-enter Cassio.)

As he shall smile, Othello shall go mad;
And his unbookish[467] jealousy must construe
Poor Cassio's smiles, gestures, and light behaviour   100
Quite in the wrong. How do you now, lieutenant?

Cassio. The worser that you give me the addition[468]
Whose want[469] even kills me.

Iago. Ply Desdemona well, and you are sure on 't.
(Speaking lower.) Now, if this suit lay in Bianca's power,
How quickly should you speed!

Cassio.   Alas! poor caitiff![470]

Othello. Look! how he laughs already!

Iago. I never knew woman love man so.

Cassio. Alas! poor rogue, I think i' faith, she loves me.

Othello. Now he denies it faintly, and laughs it out.   110

Iago. Do you hear, Cassio?

Othello.   Now he importunes him
To tell it o'er: go to; well said, well said.

Iago. She gives it out that you shall marry her;
Do you intend it?

Cassio. Ha, ha, ha!

---

[463] Close with.   [464] Completely overcome by passion.   [465] Maintain control.   [466] Hussy.
[467] Unpracticed, naive.   [468] Title.   [469] The want of which.   [470] Wretch.

Othello. Do you triumph, Roman?[471] do you triumph?

Cassio. I marry her! what? a customer?[472] I prithee, bear some charity to my wit;[473] do not think it so unwholesome. Ha, ha, ha!

Othello. So, so, so, so. They laugh that win.[474]

Iago. Faith, the cry goes that you shall marry her. 120

Cassio. Prithee, say true.

Iago. I am a very villain else.

Othello. Have you scored me?[475] Well.

Cassio. This is the monkey's own giving out: she is persuaded I will marry her, out of her own love and flattery, not out of my promise.

Othello. Iago beckons me;[476] now he begins the story.

Cassio. She was here even now; she haunts me in every place. I was the other day talking on the sea-bank with certain Venetians, and thither comes this bauble,[477] and, by this hand, she falls me thus about my neck;—

Othello. Crying, 'O dear Cassio!' as it were; his gesture imports it. 130

Cassio. So hangs and lolls and weeps upon me; so hales[478] and pulls me; ha, ha, ha!

Othello. Now he tells how she plucked him to my chamber. O! I see that nose of yours, but not the dog I shall throw it to.

Cassio. Well, I must leave her company.

Iago. Before me![479] look, where she comes.

Cassio. 'Tis such another fitchew![480] marry, a perfumed one.

(Enter Bianca.)

What do you mean by this haunting of me? 138

Bianca. Let the devil and his dam haunt you! What did you mean by that same handkerchief you gave me even now? I was a fine fool to take it. I must take out the work! A likely piece of work, that you should find it in your chamber, and not know who left it there! This is some minx's token, and I must take out the work! There, give it your hobby-horse;[481] wheresoever you had it I'll take out no work on 't.

Cassio. How now, my sweet Bianca! how now, how now!

Othello. By heaven, that should be[482] my handkerchief!

Bianca. An you'll come to supper to-night, you may; an you will not, come when you are next prepared[483] for. *(Exit.)*

Iago. After her, after her.

Cassio. Faith, I must; she'll rail in the street else.

Iago. Will you sup there? 150

Cassio. Faith, I intend so.

Iago. Well, I may chance to see you, for I would very fain[484] speak with you.

---

[471] I.e., one who triumphs (?).   [472] Courtesan, prostitute.   [473] Give me credit for some sense.   [474] "He who laughs last laughs longest" (?).   [475] Wounded, defaced (?); or: settled my account (?).   [476] Signals.   [477] Plaything.   [478] Hauls.   [479] An exclamation of surprise.   [480] Polecat, noted both for its strong smell and for its lechery.   [481] Harlot.   [482] I.e., I think that is.   [483] Expected (Bianca means that if he does not come that night, she will never want to see him again).   [484] Gladly.

Cassio. Prithee come; will you?

Iago. Go to; say no more.   *(Exit Cassio.)*

Othello *(advancing).* How shall I murder him, Iago?

Iago. Did you perceive how he laughed at his vice?

Othello. O! Iago!

Iago. And did you see the handkerchief?

Othello. Was that mine?   160

Iago. Yours, by this hand; and to see how he prizes the foolish woman your wife!
She gave it him, and he hath given it his whore.

Othello. I would have him nine years a-killing. A fine woman! a fair woman! a
sweet woman!

Iago. Nay, you must forget that.

Othello. Ay, let her rot, and perish, and be damned to-night; for she shall not live.
No, my heart is turned to stone; I strike it, and it hurts my hand. O! the world
hath not a sweeter creature; she might lie by an emperor's side and command
him tasks.

Iago. Nay, that's not your way.[485]   170

Othello. Hang her! I do but say what she is. So delicate with her needle! An
admirable musician! O, she will sing the savageness out of a bear. Of so high
and plenteous wit and invention!

Iago. She's the worse for all this.

Othello. O! a thousand, a thousand times. And then, of so gentle a condition![486]

Iago. Ay, too gentle.[487]

Othello. Nay, that's certain;—but yet the pity of it, Iago!
O! Iago, the pity of it, Iago!

Iago. If you are so fond over her iniquity, give her patent to offend; for, if it touch
not you, it comes near nobody.

Othello. I will chop her into messes.[488] Cuckold me!

Iago. O! 'tis foul in her.

Othello. With mine officer!

Iago. That's fouler.

Othello. Get me some poison, Iago; this night: I'll not expostulate with her, lest
her body and beauty unprovide my mind again.[489] This night, Iago.

Iago. Do it not with poison, strangle her in her bed, even the bed she hath
contaminated.

Othello. Good, good; the justice of it pleases; very good.   190

Iago. And for Cassio, let me be his undertaker;[490] you shall hear more by
midnight.

Othello. Excellent good. *(A trumpet within.)* What trumpet is that same?

Iago. Something from Venice, sure. 'Tis Lodovico,
Come from the duke; and see, your wife is with him.

(Enter Lodovico, Desdemona, and Attendants.)

---

[485] Proper course.   [486] So much the high-born lady.   [487] I.e., yielding.   [488] Bits.   [489] Unsettle my
intention.   [490] Dispatcher.

Lodovico. God save you, worthy general!
Othello. With all my heart, sir.
Lodovico. The duke and senators of Venice greet you.

(Gives him a packet.)

Othello. I kiss the instrument of their pleasures.

(Opens the packet, and reads.)

Desdemona. And what's the news, good cousin Lodovico?
Iago. I am very glad to see you, signior;   200
  Welcome to Cyprus.
Lodovico. I thank you. How does Lieutenant Cassio?
Iago. Lives, sir.
Desdemona. Cousin, there's fall'n between him and my lord
  An unkind[491] breach; but you shall make all well.
Othello. Are you sure of that?
Desdemona. My lord?
Othello *(reads).* 'This fail you not to do, as you will'—
Lodovico. He did not call; he's busy in the paper.
  Is there division[492] twixt my lord and Cassio?   210
Desdemona. A most unhappy one; I would do much
  To atone[493] them, for the love I bear to Cassio.
Othello. Fire and brimstone!
Desdemona. My lord?
Othello. Are you wise?
Desdemona. What! is he angry?
Lodovico. May be the letter mov'd him;
  For, as I think, they do command him home,
  Deputing Cassio in his government.
Desdemona. Trust me, I am glad on 't.
Othello. Indeed!
Desdemona. My lord?
Othello. I am glad to see you mad.
Desdemona. Why, sweet Othello?
Othello. Devil!   *(Strikes her.)*
Desdemona. I have not deserved this.   220
Lodovico. My lord, this would not be believ'd in Venice,
  Though I should swear I saw 't; 'tis very much;
  Make her amends, she weeps.
Othello. O devil, devil!
  If that the earth could teem with woman's tears,
  Each drop she falls[494] would prove a crocodile.[495]

---

[491] Unnatural.   [492] Estrangement.   [493] Reconcile.   [494] Lets fall.   [495] The crocodile's tears were supposed to be hypocritical.

Out of my sight!

Desdemona. I will not stay to offend you. *(Going.)*

Lodovico. Truly, an obedient lady;

I do beseech your lordship, call her back.

Othello. Mistress!

Desdemona. My lord?

Othello. What would you with her, sir? 230

Lodovico. Why, I, my lord?

Othello. Ay; you did wish that I would make her turn:

Sir, she can turn, and turn, and yet go on,

And turn again; and she can weep, sir, weep;

And she's obedient, as you say, obedient,

Very obedient. Proceed you in your tears.

Concerning this, sir—O well-painted passion!—

I am commanded home. Get you away;

I'll send for you anon. Sir, I obey the mandate,

And will return to Venice. Hence! avaunt![496]   *(Exit Desdemona.)*

Cassio shall have my place. And, sir, to-night,

I do entreat that we may sup together;

You are welcome, sir, to Cyprus. Goats and monkeys!   *(Exit.)*

Lodovico. Is this the noble Moor whom our full senate

Call all-in-all sufficient? is this the noble nature

Whom passion could not shake? whose solid virtue

The shot of accident nor dart of chance

Could neither graze nor pierce?

Iago. He is much chang'd.

Lodovico. Are his wits safe? is he not light of brain?

Iago. He's that he is; I may not breathe my censure. 250

What he might be, if, what he might, he is not,

I would to heaven he were![497]

Lodovico. What! strike his wife!

Iago. Faith, that was not so well; yet would I knew

That stroke would prove the worst!

Lodovico. Is it his use?

Or did the letters work upon his blood,

And new-create this fault?

Iago. Alas, alas!

It is not honesty in me to speak

What I have seen and known. You shall observe him,

And his own courses[498] will denote him so

That I may save my speech. Do but go after 260

And mark how he continues.

Lodovico. I am sorry that I am deceiv'd in him.   *(Exeunt.)*

---

[496] Begone!   [497] Another of Iago's gnomic speeches; perhaps approximately: "If now he is not himself, I wish he would be what he could be!"   [498] Actions.

Scene 2. A Room in the Castle.

(Enter Othello and Emilia.)

Othello. You have seen nothing, then?
Emilia. Nor ever heard, nor ever did suspect.
Othello. Yes, you have seen Cassio and her together.
Emilia. But then I saw no harm, and then I heard
    Each syllable that breath made up between them.
Othello. What! did they never whisper?
Emilia.   Never, my lord.
Othello. Nor send you out o' the way?
Emilia. Never.
Othello. To fetch her fan, her gloves, her mask, nor nothing?[499]
Emilia. Never, my lord.
Othello. That's strange.
Emilia. I durst, my lord, to wager she is honest,
    Lay down my soul at stake: if you think other,
    Remove your thought; it doth abuse your bosom.
    If any wretch have put this in your head,
    Let heaven requite it with the serpent's curse!
    For, if she be not honest, chaste, and true,
    There's no man happy; the purest of their wives
    Is foul as slander.
Othello.   Bid her come hither; go.   *(Exit Emilia.)*
    She says enough; yet she 's a simple[500] bawd
    That cannot say as much. This is a subtle whore,
    A closet lock and key of villainous secrets;
    And yet she 'll kneel and pray; I have seen her do 't.

(Re-enter Emilia with Desdemona.)

Desdemona. My lord, what is your will?
Othello.   Pray, chuck, come hither.
Desdemona. What is your pleasure?
Othello.   Let me see your eyes;
    Look in my face.
Desdemona.   What horrible fancy 's this?
Othello *(to Emilia).* Some of your function,[501] mistress;
    Leave procreants alone and shut the door;
    Cough or cry 'hem' if any body come;
    Your mystery,[502] your mystery; nay, dispatch.   *(Exit Emilia.)*
Desdemona. Upon my knees, what doth your speech import?
    I understand a fury in your words.
    But not the words.

---

[499] Anything.   [500] Simpleminded.   [501] To your duty, business.   [502] Trade.

Othello. Why, what art thou?

Desdemona. Your wife, my lord; your true
And loyal wife.

Othello. Come, swear it, damn thyself;
Lest, being like one of heaven, the devils themselves
Should fear to seize thee; therefore be double-damn'd;
Swear thou art honest.

Desdemona. Heaven doth truly know it.

Othello. Heaven truly knows that thou art false as hell.

Desdemona. To whom, my lord? with whom? how am I false? 40

Othello. Ah! Desdemona; away, away, away!

Desdemona. Alas, the heavy day!—Why do you weep?
Am I the motive of these tears, my lord?
If haply you my father do suspect
An instrument of this your calling back,
Lay not your blame on me; if you have lost him,
Why, I have lost him too.

Othello. Had it pleas'd heaven
To try me with affliction, had he rain'd
All kinds of sores and shames on my bare head,
Steep'd me in poverty to the very lips, 50
Given to captivity me and my utmost hopes,
I should have found in some part of my soul
A drop of patience; but, alas! to make me
The fixed figure for the time of scorn[503]
To point his slow and moving finger at;
Yet could I bear that too; well, very well:
But there, where I have garner'd[504] up my heart,
Where either I must live or bear no life,
The fountain from the which my current runs
Or else dries up; to be discarded thence! 60
Or keep it as a cistern for foul toads
To knot and gender in![505] Turn thy complexion there,[506]
Patience, thou young and rose-lipp'd cherubin;
Ay, there, look grim as hell!

Desdemona. I hope my noble lord esteems me honest.

Othello. O! ay; as summer flies are in the shambles,[507]
That quicken even with blowing. O thou weed!
Who art so lovely fair and smell'st so sweet
That the sense aches at thee, would thou hadst ne'er been born.

Desdemona. Alas! what ignorant sin have I committed? 70

Othello. Was this fair paper, this most goodly book,
Made to write 'whore' upon? What committed!
Committed! O thou public commoner![508]

---

[503] I.e., the scornful world. [504] Stored. [505] Bunch up and procreate. [506] I.e., change your color
to suit the "cistern for foul toads." [507] Slaughterhouse. [508] Harlot.

I should make very forges of my cheeks,
That would to cinders burn up modesty,
Did I but speak thy deeds. What committed!
Heaven stops the nose at it and the moon winks,[509]
The bawdy wind that kisses all it meets
Is hush'd within the hollow mine of earth,
And will not hear it. What committed!   80
Impudent strumpet!

Desdemona.   By heaven, you do me wrong.

Othello. Are not you a strumpet?

Desdemona.   No, as I am a Christian.
If to preserve this vessel for my lord
From any other foul unlawful touch
Be not to be a strumpet, I am none.

Othello. What! not a whore?

Desdemona.   No, as I shall be sav'd.

Othello. Is it possible?

Desdemona. O! heaven forgive us.

Othello.   I cry you mercy,[510] then;
I took you for that cunning whore of Venice
That married with Othello. You, mistress,   90
That have the office opposite to Saint Peter,
And keep the gate of hell!

(Re-enter Emilia.)

                    You, you, ay, you!
We have done our course; there's money for your pains.
I pray you, turn the key and keep our counsel.   *(Exit.)*

Emilia. Alas! what does this gentleman conceive?[511]
How do you, madam? how do you, my good lady?

Desdemona. Faith, half asleep.

Emilia. Good madam, what 's the matter with my lord?

Desdemona. With who?

Emilia. Why, with my lord, madam.   100

Desdemona. Who is thy lord?

Emilia.   He that is yours, sweet lady.

Desdemona. I have none; do not talk to me, Emilia;
I cannot weep, nor answer have I none,
But what should go by water.[512] Prithee, to-night
Lay on my bed my wedding sheets: remember:
And call thy husband hither.

Emilia.   Here is a change indeed!   *(Exit.)*

---

[509] Closes her eyes.   [510] Beg your pardon.   [511] Imagine.   [512] Be conveyed by means of tears.

Desdemona. 'Tis meet I should be us'd so, very meet.
How have I been behav'd, that he might stick
The small'st opinion on my least misuse?[513]

(Re-enter Emilia, with Iago.)

Iago. What is your pleasure, madam? How is it with you?   110
Desdemona. I cannot tell. Those that do teach young babes
Do it with gentle means and easy tasks;
He might have chid me so; for, in good faith,
I am a child to chiding.
Iago.   What 's the matter, lady?
Emilia. Alas, Iago, my lord hath so bewhor'd her,
Thrown such despite[514] and heavy terms upon her,
As true hearts cannot bear.
Desdemona. Am I that name, Iago?
Iago.   What name, fair lady?
Desdemona. Such as she says my lord did say I was.
Emilia. He call'd her whore; a beggar in his drink   120
Could not have laid such terms upon his callat.[515]
Iago. Why did he so?
Desdemona. I do not know; I am sure I am none such.
Iago. Do not weep, do not weep. Alas the day!
Emilia. Has she forsook so many noble matches,
Her father and her country and her friends,
To be call'd whore? would it not make one weep?
Desdemona. It is my wretched fortune.
Iago.   Beshrew[516] him for it!
How comes this trick upon him?
Desdemona.   Nay, heaven doth know.
Emilia. I will be hang'd, if some eternal villain,   130
Some busy and insinuating rogue,
Some cogging[517] cozening slave, to get some office,
Have not devis'd this slander; I'll be hang'd else.
Iago. Fie! there is no such man; it is impossible.
Desdemona. If any such there be, heaven pardon him!
Emilia. A halter pardon him, and hell gnaw his bones!
Why should he call her whore? who keeps her company?
What place? what time? what form? what likelihood?
The Moor 's abus'd by some most villainous knave,
Some base notorious knave, some scurvy fellow.   140
O heaven! that such companions[518] thou'dst unfold,

---

[513] The least suspicion on my slightest misconduct.   [514] Abuse.   [515] Slut.   [516] Curse.   [517] Cheating.
[518] Fellows (derogatory).

And put in every honest hand a whip
To lash the rascals naked through the world,
Even from the east to west!

Iago.   Speak within door.

Emilia. O! fie upon them. Some such squire he was
That turn'd your wit the seamy side without,[519]
And made you to suspect me with the Moor.

Iago. You are a fool; go to.

Desdemona.   O good Iago,
What shall I do to win my lord again?
Good friend, go to him; for, by this light of heaven,   150
I know not how I lost him. Here I kneel:
If e'er my will did trespass 'gainst his love,
Either in discourse of thought or actual deed,
Or that mine eyes, mine ears, or any sense,
Delighted them[520] in any other form;
Or that I do not yet,[521] and ever did,
And ever will, though he do shake me off
To beggarly divorcement, love him dearly,
Comfort forswear me! Unkindness may do much;
And his unkindness may defeat[522] my life,   160
But never taint my love. I cannot say 'whore':
It does abhor me now I speak the word;
To do the act that might the addition earn
Not the world's mass of vanity could make me.

Iago. I pray you be content, 'tis but his humour;
The business of the state does him offence,
And he does chide with you.

Desdemona.   If 'twere no other,—

Iago. 'Tis but so, I warrant.   *(Trumpets.)*
Hark! how these instruments summon to supper;
The messengers of Venice stay the meat: 170
Go in, and weep not; all things shall be well.

                                    (Exeunt Desdemona and Emilia.)

(Enter Roderigo.)

How now, Roderigo!

Roderigo. I do not find that thou dealest justly with me.

Iago. What in the contrary?[523]

Roderigo. Every day thou daffest me[524] with some device, Iago; and rather, as
it seems to me now, keepest from me all conveniency,[525] than suppliest me
with the least advantage of hope. I will indeed no longer endure it, nor am I yet
persuaded to put up[526] in peace what already I have foolishly suffered.

---

[519] Outward.   [520] Found delight.   [521] Still.   [522] Destroy.   [523] I.e., what reason do you have for
saying that?   [524] You put me off.   [525] Favorable circumstances.   [526] Put up with.

Iago. Will you hear me, Roderigo?

Roderigo. Faith, I have heard too much, for your words and performances are no kin together. 181

Iago. You charge me most unjustly.

Roderigo. With nought but truth. I have wasted myself out of my means. The jewels you have had from me to deliver to Desdemona would half have corrupted a votarist;[527] you have told me she has received them, and returned me expectations and comforts of sudden respect[528] and acquaintance, but I find none.

Iago. Well; go to; very well.

Roderigo. Very well! go to! I cannot go to, man; nor 'tis not very well: by this hand, I say, it is very scurvy, and begin to find myself fobbed[529] in it. 190

Iago. Very well.

Roderigo. I tell you 'tis not very well. I will make myself known to Desdemona; if she will return me my jewels, I will give over my suit and repent my unlawful solicitation; if not, assure yourself I will seek satisfaction of you.

Iago. You have said now.[530]

Roderigo. Ay, and said nothing, but what I protest intendment of doing.

Iago. Why, now I see there's mettle in thee, and even from this instant do build on thee a better opinion than ever before. Give me thy hand, Roderigo; thou hast taken against me a most just exception; but yet, I protest, I have dealt most directly in thy affair. 200

Roderigo. It hath not appeared.

Iago. I grant indeed it hath not appeared, and your suspicion is not without wit and judgment. But, Roderigo, if thou hast that in thee indeed, which I have greater reason to believe now than ever, I mean purpose, courage, and valour, this night show it: if thou the next night following enjoy not Desdemona, take me from this world with treachery and devise engines for[531] my life.

Roderigo. Well, what is it? is it within reason and compass?

Iago. Sir, there is especial commission come from Venice to depute Cassio in Othello's place. 210

Roderigo. Is that true? why, then Othello and Desdemona return again to Venice.

Iago. O, no! he goes into Mauritania, and takes away with him the fair Desdemona, unless his abode be lingered here by some accident; wherein none can be so determinate[532] as the removing of Cassio.

Roderigo. How do you mean, removing of him?

Iago. Why, by making him uncapable of Othello's place; knocking out his brains.

Roderigo. And that you would have me do? 219

Iago. Ay; if you dare do yourself a profit and a right. He sups to-night with a harlotry,[533] and thither will I go to him; he knows not yet of his honourable fortune. If you will watch his going thence,—which I will fashion to fall out between

---

[527] Nun.   [528] Immediate consideration.   [529] Cheated.   [530] I.e., "I suppose you're through?" (?); or: "Now you're talking"(?).   [531] Devices against.   [532] Effective.   [533] Harlot.

twelve and one,—you may take him at your pleasure; I will be near to second your attempt, and he shall fall between us. Come, stand not amazed at it, but go along with me; I will show you such a necessity in his death that you shall think yourself bound to put it on him. It is now high supper-time, and the night grows to waste; about it.

Roderigo. I will hear further reason for this.

Iago. And you shall be satisfied. *(Exeunt.)*

Scene 3. Another Room in the Castle.

(Enter Othello, Lodovico, Desdemona, Emilia, and Attendants.)

Lodovico. I do beseech you, sir, trouble yourself no further.

Othello. O! pardon me; 'twill do me good to walk.

Lodovico. Madam, good-night; I humbly thank your ladyship.

Desdemona. Your honour is most welcome.

Othello. Will you walk, sir?

O! Desdemona,—

Desdemona. My lord?

Othello. Get you to bed on the instant; I will be returned forthwith; dismiss your attendant there; look it be done.

Desdemona. I will, my lord. *(Exeunt Othello, Lodovico, and Attendants.)*

Emilia. How goes it now? He looks gentler than he did. 10

Desdemona. He says he will return incontinent;[534]

He hath commanded me to go to bed,

And bade me to dismiss you.

Emilia. Dismiss me!

Desdemona. It was his bidding; therefore, good Emilia,

Give me my nightly wearing, and adieu:

We must not now displease him.

Emilia. I would you had never seen him.

Desdemona. So would not I; my love doth so approve him,

That even his stubbornness,[535] his checks[536] and frowns,—

Prithee, unpin me,—have grace and favour in them. 20

Emilia. I have laid those sheets you bade me on the bed.

Desdemona. All's one.[537] Good faith! how foolish are our minds!

If I do die before thee, prithee, shroud me

In one of those same sheets.

Emilia. Come, come, you talk.

Desdemona. My mother had a maid call'd Barbara;

She was in love, and he she lov'd prov'd mad[538]

And did forsake her; she had a song of 'willow';

---

[534] At once. [535] Roughness. [536] Rebukes. [537] I.e., it doesn't matter. [538] Wild.

An old thing 'twas, but it express'd her fortune,
And she died singing it; that song to-night
Will not go from my mind; I have much to do   30
But to go hang my head all at one side,
And sing it like poor Barbara. Prithee, dispatch.

Emilia. Shall I go fetch your night-gown?

Desdemona.   No, unpin me here.
This Lodovico is a proper man.

Emilia. A very handsome man.

Desdemona. He speaks well.

Emilia. I know a lady in Venice would have walked barefoot to Palestine for a
touch of his nether lip.

Desdemona (*sings*).

> The poor soul sat sighing by a sycamore tree,
>   Sing all a green willow;
> Her hand on her bosom, her head on her knee,   40
>   Sing willow, willow, willow:
> The fresh streams ran by her, and murmur'd her moans;
>   Sing willow, willow, willow:
> Her salt tears fell from her and soften'd the stones;—

Lay by these:—
>   Sing willow, willow, willow:

Prithee, hie thee;[539] he 'll come anon.—

>   Sing all a green willow must be my garland.
>   Let nobody blame him, his scorn I approve,—   50

Nay, that's not next. Hark! who is it that knocks?

Emilia. It is the wind.

Desdemona.

> I call'd my love false love; but what said he then?
>   Sing willow, willow, willow:
> If I court moe[540] women, you 'll couch with moe men.

So, get thee gone; good-night. Mine eyes do itch;
Doth that bode weeping?

Emilia.   'Tis neither here nor there.

Desdemona. I have heard it said so. O! these men, these men!
Dost thou in conscience think, tell me, Emilia,
That there be women do abuse their husbands   60
In such gross kind?

---

[539] Hurry.   [540] More.

Emilia.   There be some such, no question.

Desdemona. Wouldst thou do such a deed for all the world?

Emilia. Why, would not you?

Desdemona.   No, by this heavenly light!

Emilia. Nor I neither by this heavenly light;
I might do 't as well i' the dark.

Desdemona. Wouldst thou do such a deed for all the world?

Emilia. The world is a huge thing; 'tis a great price
For a small vice.

Desdemona.   In troth, I think thou wouldst not.

Emilia. In troth, I think I should, and undo 't when I had done. Marry, I would
not do such a thing for a joint-ring,[541] nor measures of lawn,[542] nor for gowns,
petticoats, nor caps, nor any petty exhibition;[543] but for the whole world, who
would not make her husband a cuckold to make him a monarch? I should
venture purgatory for 't.

Desdemona. Beshrew me, if I would do such a wrong
For the whole world.

Emilia. Why, the wrong is but a wrong i' the world; and having the world for
your labour, 'tis a wrong in your own world, and you might quickly make it
right.

Desdemona. I do not think there is any such woman.

Emilia. Yes, a dozen; and as many to the vantage,[544] as   80
Would store[545] the world they played for.
But I do think it is their husbands' faults
If wives do fall. Say that they slack their duties,
And pour our treasures into foreign laps,
Or else break out in peevish jealousies,
Throwing restraint upon us; or say they strike us,
Or scant[546] our former having[547] in despite;
Why, we have galls;[548] and though we have some grace,
Yet have we some revenge. Let husbands know
Their wives have sense like them; they see and smell,   90
And have their palates both for sweet and sour,
As husbands have. What is it that they do
When they change us for others? Is it sport?[549]
I think it is; and doth affection breed it?
I think it doth; is 't frailty that thus errs?
It is so too; and have not we affections,
Desires for sport, and frailty, as men have?
Then, let them use us well; else let them know,
The ills we do, their ills instruct us so.

Desdemona. Good-night, good night; heaven me such usage[550] send,   100
Not to pick bad from bad, but by bad mend!   (*Exeunt.*)

---

[541] Ring made in separable halves.   [542] Fine linen.   [543] Offer, gift.   [544] Over and above.
[545] Populate.   [546] Reduce.   [547] Allowance.   [548] Spirits, temper.   [549] Lust, sexual enjoyment.
[550] Habits (?), treatment (?).

ACT V

Scene 1.   Cyprus. A Street.

(Enter Iago and Roderigo.)

Iago. Here, stand behind this bulk,[551] straight will he come:
Wear thy good rapier bare, and put it home.
Quick, quick; fear nothing; I 'll be at thy elbow.
It makes us, or it mars us; think on that,
And fix most firm thy resolution.
Roderigo. Be near at hand; I may miscarry in 't.
Iago. Here, at thy hand: be bold, and take thy stand.   *(Retires.)*
Roderigo. I have no great devotion to the deed;
And yet he has given me satisfying reasons:
'Tis but a man gone: forth, my sword; he dies.   10
Iago. I have rubb'd this young quat[552] almost to the sense,[553]
And he grows angry. Now, whether he kill Cassio,
Or Cassio him, or each do kill the other,
Every way makes my gain: live Roderigo,
He calls me to a restitution large
Of gold and jewels that I bobb'd[554] from him,
As gifts to Desdemona;
It must not be: if Cassio do remain,
He hath a daily beauty in his life
That makes me ugly: and, besides, the Moor   20
May unfold me to him; there stand I in much peril.
No, he must die. But so;[555] I hear him coming.

(Enter Cassio.)

Roderigo. I know his gait; 'tis he. Villain, thou diest!

(Makes a pass at Cassio.)

Cassio. That thrust had been mine enemy indeed
But that my coat is better than thou know'st;
I will make proof of thine.

(Draws, and wounds Roderigo.)

Roderigo.   O! I am slain.

(Iago from behind wounds Cassio in the leg, and exit.)

---

[551] Jutting part of a wall.   [552] Pimple.   [553] To the quick.   [554] Swindled.   [555] I.e., that's the only way.

Cassio. I am maim'd for ever. Help, ho! murder! murder!   (*Falls.*)

(*Enter Othello, at a distance.*)

Othello. The voice of Cassio: Iago keeps his word.
Roderigo. O! villain that I am!
Othello.   It is e'en so.
Cassio. O, help, ho! light! a surgeon!   30
Othello. 'Tis he: O brave Iago, honest and just!
    That hast such noble sense of thy friend's wrong;
    Thou teachest me. Minion,[556] your dear lies dead,
    And your unblest fate hies; strumpet, I come!
    Forth of my heart those charms, thine eyes, are blotted;
    Thy bed lust-stain'd shall with lust's blood be spotted.   (*Exit.*)

(*Enter Lodovico and Gratiano, at a distance.*)

Cassio. What ho! no watch? no passage?[557] murder! murder!
Gratiano. 'Tis some mischance; the cry is very direful.
Cassio. O, help!
Lodovico. Hark!   40
Roderigo. O wretched villain!
Lodovico. Two or three groans: it is a heavy[558] night;
    These may be counterfeits; let 's think 't unsafe
    To come in to the cry[559] without more help.
Roderigo. Nobody come? then shall I bleed to death.
Lodovico. Hark!

(*Re-enter Iago, with a light.*)

Gratiano. Here 's one comes in his shirt, with light and weapons.
Iago. Who 's there? whose noise is this that cries on murder?
Lodovico. We do not know.
Iago.   Did not you hear a cry?
Cassio. Here, here! for heaven's sake, help me.
Iago.   What's the matter?   50
Gratiano. This is Othello's ancient, as I take it.
Lodovico. The same indeed; a very valiant fellow.
Iago. What are you here that cry so grievously?
Cassio. Iago? O! I am spoil'd, undone by villains!
    Give me some help.
Iago. O me, lieutenant! what villains have done this?
Cassio. I think that one of them is hereabout,
    And cannot make away.

---

[556] (Cassio's) darling, i.e., Desdemona.   [557] Passer-by.   [558] Dark.   [559] Where the cry comes from.

Iago. O treacherous villains!

(To Lodovico and Gratiano.) What are you there? come in, and
give some help. 60

Roderigo. O! help me here.

Cassio. That's one of them.

Iago. O murderous slave! O villain!

(Stabs Roderigo.)

Roderigo. O damn'd Iago! O inhuman dog!

Iago. Kill men i' the dark! Where be these bloody thieves?
How silent is this town! Ho! murder! murder!
What may you be? are you of good or evil?

Lodovico. As you shall prove us, praise us.

Iago. Signior Lodovico?

Lodovico. He, sir.

Iago. I cry you mercy. Here 's Cassio hurt by villains. 70

Gratiano. Cassio!

Iago. How is it, brother?

Cassio. My leg is cut in two.

Iago. Marry, heaven forbid.
Light, gentlemen; I 'll bind it with my shirt.

(Enter Bianca.)

Bianca. What is the matter, ho? who is 't that cried?

Iago. Who is 't that cried!

Bianca. O my dear Cassio! my sweet Cassio!
O Cassio, Cassio, Cassio!

Iago. O notable strumpet! Cassio, may you suspect
Who they should be that have thus mangled you? 80

Cassio. No.

Gratiano. I am sorry to find you thus; I have been to seek you.

Iago. Lend me a garter. So. O! for a chair,
To bear him easily hence!

Bianca. Alas; he faints! O Cassio, Cassio, Cassio!

Iago. Gentlemen all, I do suspect this trash[560]
To be a party in this injury.
Patience awhile, good Cassio. Come, come.
Lend me a light. Know we this face, or no?
Alas! my friend and my dear countryman, 90
Roderigo? no: yes, sure, O heaven! Roderigo.

Gratiano. What! of Venice?

Iago. Even he, sir, did you know him?

---

[560] I.e., Bianca.

Gratiano.   Know him! ay.

Iago. Signior Gratiano? I cry you gentle pardon;
  These bloody accidents must excuse my manners,
  That so neglected you.

Gratiano.   I am glad to see you.

Iago. How do you, Cassio? O! a chair, a chair!

Gratiano. Roderigo!

(A chair brought in.)

Iago. He, he, 'tis he,—O! that 's well said; the chair:
  Some good men bear him carefully from hence;
  I 'll fetch the general's surgeon. *(To Bianca.)* For you, mistress,   100
  Save you your labour. He that lies slain here, Cassio,
  Was my dear friend. What malice was between you?

Cassio. None in the world; nor do I know that man.

Iago *(to Bianca).* What! look you pale? O! bear him out o' the air—

(Cassio and Roderigo are borne off.)

  Stay you, good gentlemen. Look you pale, mistress?—
  Do you perceive the gastness[561] of her eye?
  Nay, if you stare, we shall hear more anon.
  Behold her well; I pray you, look upon her.
  Do you see, gentlemen? nay, guiltiness will speak   110
  Though tongues were out of use.

(Enter Emilia.)

Emilia. 'Las! what 's the matter? what 's the matter, husband?

Iago. Cassio hath here been set on in the dark
  By Roderigo and fellows that are 'scaped:
  He 's almost slain, and Roderigo dead.

Emilia. Alas! good gentleman; alas! good Cassio!

Iago. This is the fruit of whoring. Prithee, Emilia,
  Go know of Cassio where he supp'd to-night.
  (To Bianca.) What! do you shake at that?

Bianca. He supp'd at my house; but I therefore shake not.   120

Iago. O! did he so? I charge you, go with me.

Emilia. Fie, fie, upon thee, strumpet!

Bianca. I am no strumpet, but of life as honest
  As you that thus abuse me.

Emilia.   As I! foh! fie upon thee!

Iago. Kind gentlemen, let 's go see poor Cassio dress'd.[562]

---

[561] Terror.   [562] Bandaged.

Come, mistress, you must tell 's another tale.
Emilia, run you to the citadel,
And tell my lord and lady what hath happ'd.
Will you go on afore? *(Aside.)* This is the night
That either makes me or fordoes[563] me quite.   *(Exeunt.)*

Scene 2.   A Bedchamber in the Castle. Desdemona in bed asleep. A light
burning.

(Enter Othello.)

Othello. It is the cause,[564] it is the cause, my soul;
Let me not name it to you, you chaste stars!
It is the cause. Yet I 'll not shed her blood,
Nor scar that whiter skin of hers than snow,
And smooth as monumental alabaster.
Yet she must die, else she 'll betray more men.
Put out the light, and then put out the light:
If I quench thee, thou flaming minister,[565]
I can again thy former light restore,
Should I repent me; but once put out thy light,   10
Thou cunning'st[566] pattern of excelling nature,
I know not where is that Promethean[567] heat
That can thy light relume.[568] When I have pluck'd the rose,
I cannot give it vital growth again,
It needs must wither: I 'll smell it on the tree. *(Kisses her.)*
O balmy breath, that dost almost persuade
Justice to break her sword! One more, one more.
Be thus when thou art dead, and I will kill thee,
And love thee after. One more, and this the last:
So sweet was ne'er so fatal. I must weep,   20
But they are cruel tears; this sorrow 's heavenly,
It strikes where it doth love. She wakes.
Desdemona. Who 's there? Othello?
Othello.   Ay, Desdemona.
Desdemona. Will you come to bed, my lord?
Othello. Have you pray'd to-night, Desdemona?
Desdemona.   Ay, my lord.
Othello. If you bethink yourself of any crime
   Unreconcil'd as yet to heaven and grace,
   Solicit for it straight.
Desdemona. Alas! my lord, what may you mean by that?

---

[563] Ruins.   [564] I.e., Desdemona's unchastity (Othello means that the severity of the punishment is
required by the nature of her sin).   [565] I.e., the candle.   [566] Most intricately wrought.   [567] In Greek
mythology the demigod Prometheus stole fire from the gods and gave it to man.   [568] Relight.

Othello. Well, do it, and be brief; I will walk by:[569]   30
    I would not kill thy unprepared spirit;
    No; heaven forfend![570] I would not kill thy soul.

Desdemona. Talk you of killing?

Othello.   Ay, I do.

Desdemona.   Then heaven
    Have mercy on me!

Othello.   Amen! with all my heart.

Desdemona. If you say so, I hope you will not kill me.

Othello. Hum!

Desdemona. And yet I fear you; for you are fatal then
    When your eyes roll so. Why I should fear I know not,
    Since guiltiness I know not; but yet I feel I fear.

Othello. Think on thy sins.

Desdemona.   They are loves I bear to you.   40

Othello. Ay, and for that thou diest.

Desdemona. That death's unnatural that kills for loving.
    Alas! why gnaw you so your nether lip?
    Some bloody passion shakes your very frame;
    These are portents,[571] but yet, I hope, I hope
    They do not point on me.

Othello.   Peace, and be still!

Desdemona. I will so. What's the matter?

Othello. That handkerchief which I so lov'd and gave thee
    Thou gav'st to Cassio.

Desdemona.   No, by my life and soul!
    Send for the man and ask him.

Othello.   Sweet soul, take heed,   50
    Take heed of perjury; thou 'rt on thy death-bed.

Desdemona. Ay, but not yet to die.

Othello.   Yes, presently;[572]
    Therefore confess thee freely of thy sin;
    For to deny each article with oath
    Cannot remove nor choke the strong conception[573]
    That I do groan withal. Thou art to die.

Desdemona. Then Lord have mercy on me!

Othello.   I say, amen.

Desdemona. And have you mercy too! I never did
    Offend you in my life; never lov'd Cassio
    But with such general warranty[574] of heaven   60
    As I might love; I never gave him token.

Othello. By heaven, I saw my handkerchief in 's hand.
    O perjur'd woman! thou dost stone[575] my heart,
    And mak'st me call what I intend to do

---

[569] Nearby.   [570] Forbid.   [571] Omens.   [572] At once.   [573] Belief.   [574] Permission.   [575] Turn to stone.

A murder, which I thought a sacrifice:
I saw the handkerchief.
Desdemona.   He found it then;
I never gave it him. Send for him hither;
Let him confess a truth.
Othello.   He had confessed.
Desdemona. What, my lord?
Othello. That he hath us'd thee.
Desdemona.   How? Unlawfully?
Othello.   Ay.   70
Desdemona. He will not say so.
Othello.   No; his mouth is stopp'd:
Honest Iago hath ta'en order for 't.[576]
Desdemona. O! my fear interprets. What! is he dead?
Othello. Had all his hairs been lives, my great revenge
Had stomach[577] for them all.
Desdemona. Alas! he is betray'd and I undone.
Othello. Out, strumpet! Weep'st thou for him to my face?
Desdemona. O! banish me, my lord, but kill me not!
Othello. Down, strumpet!
Desdemona. Kill me to-morrow; let me live to-night!   80
Othello. Nay, if you strive,—
Desdemona. But half an hour!
Othello.   Being done, there is no pause.
Desdemona. But while I say one prayer!
Othello.   It is too late.   (*He smothers her.*)
Emilia (*within*). My lord, my lord! what, ho! my lord, my lord!
Othello. What noise is this? Not dead? Not yet quite dead?
I that am cruel am yet merciful;
I would not have thee linger in thy pain.
So, so.
Emilia (*within*). What, ho! my lord, my lord!
Othello.   Who's there?
Emilia (*within*). O! good my lord, I would speak a word with you!   90
Othello. Yes; 'tis Emilia: by and by.[578] She's dead.
'Tis like[579] she comes to speak of Cassio's death;
The noise was high. Ha! no more moving?
Still as the grave. Shall she come in? were 't good?[580]
I think she stirs again: no. What 's best to do?
If she come in she'll sure speak to my wife:
My wife! my wife! what wife? I have no wife;
O, insupportable! O heavy hour!
Methinks it should be now a huge eclipse
Of sun and moon, and that the affrighted globe   100

---

[576] Taken steps.   [577] Appetite.   [578] I.e., "just a moment."   [579] Likely.   [580] Would that be wise.

Should yawn[581] at alteration.

Emilia (*within*).   I do beseech you

That I may speak with you, O! good my lord.

Othello. I had forgot thee: O! come in, Emilia:

Soft, by and by: let me the curtains draw.

Where art thou?   (*Unlocks the door.*)

(*Enter Emilia.*)

     What's the matter with thee now?

Emilia. O! my good lord, yonder's foul murder done.

Othello. What! now?

Emilia. But now, my lord.

Othello. It is the very error[582] of the moon;

She comes more near the earth than she was wont,   110

And makes men mad.

Emilia. Cassio, my lord, has kill'd a young Venetian

Call'd Roderigo.

Othello.   Roderigo kill'd!

And Cassio kill'd?

Emilia.   No, Cassio is not kill'd.

Othello. Not Cassio kill'd! then murder's out of tune,

And sweet revenge grows harsh.

Desdemona. O! falsely, falsely murder'd.

Emilia.   Alas! what cry is that?

Othello. That! what?

Emilia. Out, and alas! that was my lady's voice:

Help! Help, ho! help! O lady, speak again!   120

Sweet Desdemona! O! sweet mistress, speak.

Desdemona. A guiltless death I die.

Emilia. O! who hath done this deed?

Desdemona. Nobody; I myself; farewell:

Commend me to my kind lord. O! farewell!   (*Dies.*)

Othello. Why, how should she be murder'd?

Emilia.   Alas! who knows?

Othello. You heard her say herself it was not I.

Emilia. She said so; I must needs report the truth.

Othello. She's like a liar gone to burning hell;

'Twas I that kill'd her.

Emilia.   O! the more angel she,   130

And you the blacker devil.

Othello. She turn'd to folly, and she was a whore.

Emilia. Thou dost belie her, and thou art a devil.

Othello. She was false as water.

---

[581] Open up (as in an earthquake).   [582] Straying.

Emilia.   Thou art rash as fire to say
   That she was false! O! she was heavenly true.
Othello. Cassio did tup her; ask thy husband else.
   O! I were damn'd beneath all depth in hell
   But that I did proceed[583] upon just grounds
   To this extremity. Thy husband knew it all.
Emilia. My husband!   140
Othello. Thy husband.
Emilia. That she was false to wedlock?
Othello. Ay, with Cassio. Nay, had she been true,
   If heaven would make me such another world
   Of one entire and perfect chrysolite,[584]
   I'd not have sold her for it.
Emilia. My husband!
Othello.   Ay, 'twas he that told me first:
   An honest man he is, and hates the slime
   That sticks on filthy deeds.
Emilia.   My husband!
Othello. What needs this iterance,[585] woman? I say thy husband.   150
Emilia. O mistress! villany hath made mocks with love.
   My husband say that she was false!
Othello.   He, woman;
   I say, thy husband: dost understand the word?
   My friend, thy husband, honest, honest Iago.
Emilia. If he say so, may his pernicious soul
   Rot half a grain a day! he lies to the heart:
   She was too fond of her most filthy bargain.[586]
Othello. Ha!
Emilia. Do thy worst:
   This deed of thine is no more worthy heaven   160
   Than thou wast worthy her.
Othello.   Peace! you were best.[587]
Emilia. Thou hast not half the power to do me harm
   As I have to be hurt. O gull! O dolt!
   As ignorant as dirt! thou hast done a deed,—
   I care not for thy sword; I'll make thee known,
   Though I lost twenty lives. Help! help, ho! help!
   The Moor has kill'd my mistress! murder! murder!

(Enter Montano, Gratiano, Iago, and others.)

Montano. What is the matter? How now, general!
Emilia. O! are you come, Iago? you have done well,
   That men must lay their murders on your neck.   170

---

[583] Had I not proceeded.   [584] Topaz.   [585] Repetition.   [586] I.e., Othello.   [587] You'd better be quiet.

Gratiano. What is the matter?

Emilia. Disprove this villain if thou be'st a man:
He says thou told'st him that his wife was false.
I know thou didst not, thou 'rt not such a villain.
Speak, for my heart is full.

Iago. I told him what I thought, and told no more
Than what he found himself was apt and true.

Emilia. But did you ever tell him she was false?

Iago. I did.

Emilia. You told a lie, an odious damned lie; 180
Upon my soul, a lie, a wicked lie;
She false with Cassio! Did you say with Cassio?

Iago. With Cassio, mistress. Go to, charm[588] your tongue.

Emilia. I will not charm my tongue; I am bound to speak.
My mistress here lies murder'd in her bed.

All. O heavens forfend!

Emilia. And your reports have set the murder on.

Othello. Nay, stare not, masters; it is true, indeed.

Gratiano. 'Tis a strange truth.

Montano. O monstrous act!

Emilia.   Villany! villany! villany! 190
I think upon 't, I think, I smell 't; O villany!
I thought so then;[589] I'll kill myself for grief.
O! villany, villany!

Iago. What! are you mad? I charge you, get you home.

Emilia. Good gentlemen, let me have leave to speak:
'Tis proper I obey him, but not now.
Perchance, Iago, I will ne'er go home.

Othello. O! O! O!   *(Falls on the bed.)*

Emilia.   Nay, lay thee down and roar,
For thou hast kill'd the sweetest innocent
That e'er did lift up eye.

Othello.   O! she was foul.   *(Rises.)*
I scarce did know you, uncle. There lies your niece,
Whose breath, indeed, these hands have newly stopp'd:
I know this act shows terrible and grim.

Gratiano. Poor Desdemona! I am glad thy father's dead.
Thy match was mortal to him, and pure grief
Shore[590] his old thread in twain: did he live now,
This sight would make him do a desperate turn,
Yea, curse his better angel from his side,
And fall to reprobation.[591]

---

[588] I.e., into silence. [589] Cf. "I will be hang'd, if some eternal villain, / Some busy and insinuating rogue, / Some cogging cozening slave, to get some office, / Have not devis'd this slander; . . ." (IV, 2, 130 ff.). Emilia means not that she guessed Iago's guilt but that she rightly guessed the slanderer's motive. [590] Cut. [591] Damnation.

Othello. 'Tis pitiful; but yet Iago knows   210
    That she with Cassio hath the act of shame
    A thousand times committed; Cassio confess'd it:
    And she did gratify[592] his amorous works
    With that recognizance and pledge of love
    Which I first gave her. I saw it in his hand:
    It was a handkerchief, an antique token
    My father gave my mother.
Emilia. O heaven! O heavenly powers!
Iago.   Come, hold your peace.
Emilia. 'Twill out, 'twill out; I hold my peace, sir? no;
    No, I will speak as liberal as the north;[593]   220
    Let heaven and men and devils, let them all,
    All, all, cry shame against me, yet I'll speak.
Iago. Be wise, and get you home.
Emilia.   I will not.

(Iago threatens to stab Emilia.)

Gratiano.   Fie!
    Your sword upon a woman!
Emilia. O thou dull Moor! that handkerchief thou speak'st of
    I found by fortune and did give my husband;
    For often, with a solemn earnestness,
    More than, indeed, belong'd to such a trifle,
    He begg'd of me to steal it.
Iago.   Villainous whore!
Emilia. She give it Cassio! no, alas! I found it,   230
    And I did give 't my husband.
Iago.   Filth, thou liest!
Emilia. By heaven, I do not, I do not, gentlemen.
    O murderous coxcomb![594] what should such a fool
    Do with so good a wife?
Othello.   Are there no stones[595] in heaven
    But what serve for the thunder? Precious villain!

(He runs at Iago. Iago stabs Emilia.)

Gratiano. The woman falls; sure, he has kill'd his wife.   *(Exit Iago.)*
Emilia. Ay, ay; O! lay me by my mistress' side.
Gratiano. He 's gone; but his wife 's kill'd.
Montano. 'Tis a notorious[596] villain. Take you this weapon,
    Which I have here recover'd from the Moor.   240

---

[592] Reward.   [593] I.e., the north wind (?), the supposedly free-spoken people of north England (?).
[594] Idiot.   [595] I.e., thunderbolts (to strike Iago down).   [596] Notable.

Come, guard the door without; let him not pass,
But kill him rather. I'll after that same villain,
For 'tis a damned slave.   (*Exeunt Montano and Gratiano.*)

Othello.   I am not valiant neither,
But every puny whipster[597] gets my sword.
But why should honour outlive honesty?
Let it go all.

Emilia.   What did thy song bode, lady?
Hark, canst thou hear me? I will play the swan,
And die in music:—
(*Sings.*)   Willow, willow, willow.
Moor, she was chaste; she lov'd thee, cruel Moor;
So come my soul to bliss as I speak true;   250
So speaking as I think, I die, I die.   (*Dies.*)

Othello. I have another weapon in this chamber;
It is a sword of Spain, the ice-brook's temper.[598]
O! here it is. Uncle, I must come forth.

Gratiano (*within*). If thou attempt it, it will cost thee dear:
Thou hast no weapon, and perforce must suffer.

Othello. Look in upon me then, and speak with me,
Or, naked[599] as I am, I will assault thee.

(*Re-enter Gratiano.*)

Gratiano. What is the matter?

Othello.   Behold! I have a weapon;
A better never did itself sustain   260
Upon a soldier's thigh: I have seen the day,
That with this little arm, and this good sword,
I have made my way through more impediments
Than twenty times your stop: but, O vain boast!
Who can control his fate? 'tis not so now.
Be not afraid, though you do see me weapon'd;
Here is my journey's end, here is my butt,[600]
And very sea-mark of my utmost sail.[601]
Do you go back dismay'd? 'tis a lost fear;
Man but a rush[602] against Othello's breast,   270
And he retires. Where should Othello go?
Now how dost thou look now? O ill-starr'd wench!
Pale as thy smock! when we shall meet at compt,[603]
This look of thine will hurl my soul from heaven,
And fiends will snatch at it. Cold, cold, my girl!

---

[597] I.e., a small boy whipping a top.   [598] Tempered in icy water (or the reference may
be to Innsbruck, famed for the quality of its steel, but this hardly fits "a sword of Spain").
[599] Unarmed.   [600] Goal, end, limit.   [601] Destination of my farthest journey.   [602] Wield but a reed.
[603] On the day of judgment.

Even like thy chastity.
O! cursed, cursed slave. Whip me, ye devils,
From the possession of this heavenly sight!
Blow me about in winds! roast me in sulphur!
Wash me in steep-down gulfs of liquid fire! 280
O Desdemona! Desdemona! dead!
Oh! Oh! Oh!

(Enter Lodovico, Montano, Cassio carried in a chair, and Officers with Iago, prisoner.)

Lodovico. Where is this rash and most unfortunate man?
Othello. That's he that was Othello; here I am.
Lodovico. Where is that viper? bring the villain forth.
Othello. I look down towards his feet;[604] but that 's a fable.
  If that thou be'st a devil, I cannot kill thee. *(Wounds Iago.)*
Lodovico. Wrench his sword from him. *(Othello is disarmed.)*
Iago.   I bleed, sir; but not kill'd.
Othello. I am not sorry neither; I'd have thee live;
  For, in my sense,[605] 'tis happiness to die. 290
Lodovico. O thou Othello! that wert once so good,
  Fall'n in the practice[606] of a damned slave,[607]
  What shall be said to thee?
Othello.   Why, any thing:
  An honourable murderer, if you will;
  For nought did I in hate, but all in honour.
Lodovico. This wretch hath part confess'd his villany:
  Did you and he consent in Cassio's death?
Othello. Ay.
Cassio. Dear general, I never gave you cause.
Othello. I do believe it, and I ask your pardon. 300
  Will you, I pray, demand that demi-devil
  Why he hath thus ensnar'd my soul and body?
Iago. Demand me nothing: what you know, you know:
  From this time forth I never will speak word.
Lodovico. What! not to pray?
Gratiano.   Torments will ope[608] your lips.
Othello. Well, thou dost best.
Lodovico. Sir, you shall understand what hath befall'n,
  Which, as I think, you know not. Here is a letter
  Found in the pocket of the slain Roderigo,
  And here another; the one of them imports 310
  The death of Cassio to be undertook
  By Roderigo.

---

[604] I.e., for the Devil's cloven hoof.   [605] The way I feel.   [606] Plot, machination.   [607] I.e., Iago.   [608] Open.

Othello. O villain!

Cassio.   Most heathenish and most gross!

Lodovico. Now here's another discontented paper,
    Found in his pocket too; and this, it seems,
    Roderigo meant to have sent this damned villain,
    But that, belike,[609] Iago in the interim[610]
    Came in and satisfied him.

Othello.   O the pernicious caitiff!
    How came you, Cassio, by that handkerchief
    That was my wife's?

Cassio.   I found it in my chamber;   320
    And he himself confess'd but even now
    That there he dropp'd it for a special purpose
    Which wrought to his desire.

Othello.   O fool! fool! fool!

Cassio. There is besides in Roderigo's letter
    How he upbraids Iago that he made him
    Brave me upon the watch; whereon it came
    That I was cast:[611] and even but now he spake,
    After long seeming dead, Iago hurt him,
    Iago set him on.

Lodovico. You must forsake this room and go with us;   330
    Your power and your command is taken off,
    And Cassio rules in Cyprus. For this slave,
    If there be any cunning cruelty
    That can torment him much and hold him long,
    It shall be his. You shall close prisoner rest,
    Till that the nature of your fault be known
    To the Venetian state. Come, bring him away.

Othello. Soft you; a word or two before you go.
    I have done the state some service, and they know 't;
    No more of that. I pray you, in your letters,   340
    When you shall these unlucky deeds relate,
    Speak of me as I am; nothing extenuate,
    Nor set down aught[612] in malice: then, must you speak
    Of one that lov'd not wisely but too well;
    Of one not easily jealous, but, being wrought,
    Perplex'd[613] in the extreme; of one whose hand
    Like the base Indian,[614] threw a pearl away
    Richer than all his tribe; of one whose subdu'd[615] eyes
    Albeit unused to the melting mood,

---

[609] Most likely.   [610] In the meantime.   [611] Dismissed.   [612] Anything.   [613] Distracted.   [614] The Folio reads "Iudean." Both readings denote the foolish infidel who fails to appreciate the treasure he possesses.   [615] Overcome (by grief).

Drop tears as fast as the Arabian trees   350
Their med'cinable gum. Set you down this;
And say besides, that in Aleppo once,
Where a malignant and a turban'd Turk
Beat a Venetian and traduc'd the state,
I took by the throat the circumcised dog,
And smote him, thus.   *(Stabs himself.)*
Lodovico. O bloody period![616]
Gratiano.   All that's spoke is marr'd.
Othello. I kiss'd thee ere I killed thee; no way but this.
                                         (Falling upon Desdemona.)
     Killing myself to die upon a kiss.   *(Dies.)*
Cassio. This did I fear, but thought he had no weapon;   360
     For he was great of heart.
Lodovico *(to Iago).*   O Spartan dog!
     More fell[617] than anguish, hunger, or the sea.
     Look on the tragic loading of this bed;
     This is thy work; the object poisons sight;
     Let it be hid. Gratiano, keep the house,
     And seize upon the fortunes of the Moor,
     For they succeed on you. To you, lord governor,
     Remains the censure of this hellish villain,
     The time, the place, the torture; O! enforce it.
     Myself will straight aboard, and to the state   370
     This heavy act with heavy heart relate.   *(Exeunt.)*

FOR ANALYSIS

1. In what sense might it be said that Othello is responsible for his own downfall?

2. Discuss the functions of the minor **characters**, such as Roderigo, Bianca, and Emilia.

3. Is the rapidity of Othello's emotional collapse (act III, scene 3) plausible? Does his race contribute to his emotional turmoil? Explain.

4. The first part of act IV, scene 2 (until Othello exits), is sometimes called the "brothel" scene. What features of Othello's language and behavior justify this designation?

5. Why does Iago kill Roderigo?

6. What are the benefits of moving the main characters to Cyprus rather than setting the drama in Venice?

7. Compare the speeches of Cassio and Iago in act II, scene 1. What do the differences in language and **style** reveal about their characters?

8. Carefully review the play to determine how much time elapses between the arrival in Cyprus and the end of the action. Can you find narrated events that could not possibly have occurred within that time frame? What effect do the chronological inconsistencies have on you? Explain.

[616] Ending.   [617] Grim, cruel.

MAKING ARGUMENTS

In a note that Romantic poet Samuel Taylor Coleridge wrote in his copy of Shakespeare's play, Iago is described in a now-famous phrase as possessing a "motiveless malignity," that is, a desire to do evil for evil's sake, and for no other reason. Do you find the reasons that Iago gives for his actions consistent and convincing, or do you agree with Coleridge? Why?

WRITING TOPICS

1. Write an analysis of the **figurative language** in Iago's soliloquies at the end of act I and at the end of act II, scene 1.

2. Choose a minor **character**, such as Roderigo, Emilia, or Bianca, and in a carefully reasoned essay, explain how the character contributes to the design of the play.

3. Discuss the relationship between love and hate in this **tragedy**.

MAKING CONNECTIONS

1. Place yourself in Othello's position. How would you respond to Iago's machinations? If you were in Desdemona's position, how would you deal with Othello's apparently bizarre behavior?

2. Compare Desdemona's hope that her virtue will win out to the hope (or cynicism) of the wife Terri in Carver's "What We Talk About When We Talk About Love" (p. 876). Why do you think Desdemona remains submissive?

SUSAN GLASPELL   (1882–1948)

TRIFLES   1916

CHARACTERS

George Henderson, county
   attorney
Henry Peters, sheriff

Lewis Hale, a neighboring farmer
Mrs. Peters
Mrs. Hale

Scene

*The kitchen in the now abandoned farmhouse of John Wright, a gloomy kitchen, and
left without having been put in order—the walls covered with a faded wall paper.
Down right is a door leading to the parlor. On the right wall above this door is a built-
in kitchen cupboard with shelves in the upper portion and drawers below. In the rear
wall at right, up two steps is a door opening onto stairs leading to the second floor. In
the rear wall at left is a door to the shed and from there to the outside. Between these
two doors is an old-fashioned black iron stove. Running along the left wall from the
shed door is an old iron sink and sink shelf, in which is set a hand pump. Downstage
of the sink is an uncurtained window. Near the window is an old wooden rocker.
Center stage is an unpainted wooden kitchen table with straight chairs on either side.
There is a small chair down right. Unwashed pans under the sink, a loaf of bread
outside the breadbox, a dish towel on the table—other signs of incompleted work. At
the rear the shed door opens and the Sheriff comes in followed by the County Attorney and Hale. The Sheriff and Hale are men in middle life, the County Attorney is a
young man; all are much bundled up and go at once to the stove. They are followed
by the two women—the Sheriff's wife, Mrs. Peters, first; she is a slightly wiry woman,
with a thin nervous face. Mrs. Hale is larger and would ordinarily be called more
comfortable looking, but she is disturbed now and looks fearfully about as she enters.
The women have come in slowly, and stand close together near the door.*

County Attorney *(at stove rubbing his hands)*. This feels good. Come up to the
   fire, ladies.
Mrs. Peters *(after taking a step forward)*. I'm not—cold.
Sheriff *(unbuttoning his overcoat and stepping away from the stove to right of table
   as if to mark the beginning of official business)*. Now, Mr. Hale, before we move
   things about, you explain to Mr. Henderson just what you saw when you came
   here yesterday morning.
County Attorney *(crossing down to left of the table)*. By the way, has anything been
   moved? Are things just as you left them yesterday?
Sheriff *(looking about)*. It's just about the same. When it dropped below zero last
   night I thought I'd better send Frank out this morning to make a fire for us—

(sits right of center table) no use getting pneumonia with a big case on, but I told him not to touch anything except the stove—and you know Frank.

County Attorney. Somebody should have been left here yesterday.

Sheriff. Oh—yesterday. When I had to send Frank to Morris Center for that man who went crazy—I want you to know I had my hands full yesterday. I knew you could get back from Omaha by today and as long as I went over everything here myself—

County Attorney. Well, Mr. Hale, tell just what happened when you came here yesterday morning.

Hale *(crossing down to above table).* Harry and I started to town with a load of potatoes. We came along the road from my place and as I got here I said, "I'm going to see if I can't get John Wright to go in with me on a party telephone." I spoke to Wright about it once before and he put me off, saying folks talked too much anyway, and all he asked was peace and quiet—I guess you know about how much he talked himself; but I thought maybe if I went to the house and talked about it before his wife, though I said to Harry that I didn't know as what his wife wanted made much difference to John————

County Attorney. Let's talk about that later, Mr. Hale. I do want to talk about that, but tell now just what happened when you got to the house.

Hale. I didn't hear or see anything; I knocked at the door, and still it was all quiet inside. I knew they must be up, it was past eight o'clock. So I knocked again, and I thought I heard somebody say, "Come in." I wasn't sure. I'm not sure yet, but I opened the door—this door *(indicating the door by which the two women are still standing)* and there in that rocker—*(pointing at it)* sat Mrs. Wright. *(They all look at the rocker down left.)*

County Attorney. What—was she doing?

Hale. She was rockin' back and forth. She had her apron in her hand and was kind of—pleating it.

County Attorney. And how did she—look?

Hale. Well, she looked queer.

County Attorney. How do you mean—queer?

Hale. Well, as if she didn't know what she was going to do next. And kind of done up.

County Attorney *(takes out notebook and pencil and sits left of center table).* How did she seem to feel about your coming?

Hale. Why, I don't think she minded—one way or another. She didn't pay much attention. I said, "How do, Mrs. Wright, it's cold, ain't it?" And she said, "Is it?"—and went on kind of pleating at her apron. Well, I was surprised; she didn't ask me to come up to the stove, or to set down, but just sat there, not even looking at me, so I said, "I want to see John." And then she—laughed. I guess you would call it a laugh. I thought of Harry and the team outside, so I said a little sharp: "Can't I see John?" "No," she says, kind o' dull like. "Ain't he home?" says I. "Yes," says she, "he's home." "Then why can't I see him?" I asked her, out of patience. " 'Cause he's dead," says she. "*Dead?*" says I. She just nodded her head, not getting a bit excited, but rockin' back and forth. "Why—where is he?" says I, not knowing what to say. She just pointed upstairs—like that. *(Himself pointing to the room above.)* I started for the stairs, with the idea of going up there. I walked from there to here—then I says, "Why, what did he die of?" "He died of a rope round his neck," says she, and just went on, pleatin' at her apron. Well, I went out and called Harry. I thought I might—need help. We went upstairs and there he was lyin'————

County Attorney. I think I'd rather have you go into that upstairs, where you can point it all out. Just go on now with the rest of the story.

Hale. Well, my first thought was to get that rope off. It looked . . . *(stops; his face twitches)* . . . but Harry, he went up to him, and he said, "No, he's dead all right, and we'd better not touch anything." So we went back downstairs. She was still sitting that same way. "Has anybody been notified?" I asked. "No," says she, unconcerned. "Who did this, Mrs. Wright?" said Harry. He said it business-like—and she stopped pleatin' of her apron. "I don't know," she says. "You don't *know*?" says Harry. "No," says she. "Weren't you sleepin' in the bed with him?" says Harry. "Yes," says she, "but I was on the inside." "Somebody slipped a rope round his neck and strangled him and you didn't wake up?" says Harry. "I didn't wake up," she said after him. We must 'a' looked as if we didn't see how that could be, for after a minute she said, "I sleep sound." Harry was going to ask her more questions but I said maybe we ought to let her tell her story first to the coroner, or the sheriff, so Harry went fast as he could to Rivers' place, where there's a telephone.

County Attorney. And what did Mrs. Wright do when she knew that you had gone for the coroner?

Hale. She moved from the rocker to that chair over there *(pointing to a small chair in the down right corner)* and just sat there with her hands held together and looking down. I got a feeling that I ought to make some conversation, so I said I had come in to see if John wanted to put in a telephone, and at that she started to laugh, and then she stopped and looked at me—scared. *(The County Attorney, who has had his notebook out, makes a note.)* I dunno, maybe it wasn't scared. I wouldn't like to say it was. Soon Harry got back, and then Dr. Lloyd came and you, Mr. Peters, and so I guess that's all I know that you don't.

County Attorney *(rising and looking around).* I guess we'll go upstairs first—and then out to the barn and around there. *(To the Sheriff.)* You're convinced that there was nothing important here—nothing that would point to any motive?

Sheriff. Nothing here but kitchen things.

(The County Attorney, after again looking around the kitchen, opens the door of a cupboard closet in right wall. He brings a small chair from right—gets on it and looks on a shelf. Pulls his hand away, sticky.)

County Attorney. Here's a nice mess. *(The women draw nearer up center.)*

Mrs. Peters *(to the other woman).* Oh, her fruit; it did freeze. *(To the Lawyer.)* She worried about that when it turned so cold. She said the fire'd go out and her jars would break.

Sheriff *(rises).* Well, can you beat the woman! Held for murder and worryin' about her preserves.

County Attorney *(getting down from chair).* I guess before we're through she may have something more serious than preserves to worry about. *(Crosses down right center.)*

Hale. Well, women are used to worrying over trifles. *(The two women move a little closer together.)*

County Attorney *(with the gallantry of a young politician).* And yet, for all their worries, what would we do without the ladies? *(The women do not unbend. He goes below the center table to the sink, takes a dipperful of water from the pail, and pouring it into a basin, washes his hands. While he is doing this the Sheriff and Hale cross to cupboard, which they inspect. The County Attorney starts to wipe his hands on the roller towel, turns it for a cleaner place.)* Dirty towels! *(Kicks his foot against the pans under the sink.)* Not much of a housekeeper, would you say, ladies?

Mrs. Hale *(stiffly).* There's a great deal of work to be done on a farm.

County Attorney. To be sure. And yet *(with a little bow to her)* I know there are some Dickson County farmhouses which do not have such roller towels.

(He gives it a pull to expose its full length again.)

Mrs. Hale. Those towels get dirty awful quick. Men's hands aren't always as clean as they might be.

County Attorney. Ah, loyal to your sex, I see. But you and Mrs. Wright were neighbors. I suppose you were friends, too.

Mrs. Hale *(shaking her head).* I've not seen much of her of late years. I've not been in this house—it's more than a year.

County Attorney *(crossing to women up center).* And why was that? You didn't like her?

Mrs. Hale. I liked her all well enough. Farmers' wives have their hands full, Mr. Henderson. And then————

County Attorney. Yes————?

Mrs. Hale *(looking about).* It never seemed a very cheerful place.

County Attorney. No—it's not cheerful. I shouldn't say she had the homemaking instinct.

Mrs. Hale. Well, I don't know as Wright had, either.

County Attorney. You mean that they didn't get on very well?

Mrs. Hale. No, I don't mean anything. But I don't think a place'd be any cheerfuller for John Wright's being in it.

County Attorney. I'd like to talk more of that a little later. I want to get the lay of things upstairs now.

(He goes past the women to up right where steps lead to a stair door.)

Sheriff. I suppose anything Mrs. Peters does'll be all right. She was to take in some clothes for her, you know, and a few little things. We left in such a hurry, yesterday.

County Attorney. Yes, but I would like to see what you take, Mrs. Peters, and keep an eye out for anything that might be of use to us.

Mrs. Peters. Yes, Mr. Henderson.

(The men leave by up right door to stairs. The women listen to the men's steps on the stairs, then look about the kitchen.)

Mrs. Hale *(crossing left to sink).* I'd hate to have men coming into my kitchen, snooping around and criticizing.

(She arranges the pans under sink which the Lawyer had shoved out of place.)

Mrs. Peters. Of course it's no more than their duty.

(Crosses to cupboard up right.)

Mrs. Hale. Duty's all right, but I guess that deputy sheriff that came out to make the fire might have got a little of this on. *(Gives the roller towel a pull.)* Wish I'd thought of that sooner. Seems mean to talk about her for not having things slicked up when she had to come away in such a hurry.

(Crosses right to Mrs. Peters at cupboard.)

Mrs. Peters *(who has been looking through cupboard, lifts one end of towel that covers a pan).* She had bread set.

(Stands still.)

Mrs. Hale *(eyes fixed on a loaf of bread beside the breadbox, which is on a low shelf of the cupboard).* She was going to put this in there. *(Picks up a loaf, abruptly drops it. In a manner of returning to familiar things.)* It's a shame about her fruit. I wonder if it's all gone. *(Gets up on the chair and looks.)* I think there's some here that's all right, Mrs. Peters. Yes—here; *(holding it toward the window)* this is cherries, too. *(Looking again.)* I declare I believe that's the only one. *(Gets down, jar in her hand. Goes to the sink and wipes it off on the outside.)* She'll feel awful bad after all her hard work in the hot weather. I remember the afternoon I put up my cherries last summer.

(She puts the jar on the big kitchen table, center of the room. With a sigh, is about to sit down in the rocking chair. Before she is seated realizes what chair it is; with a

slow look at it, steps back. The chair which she has touched rocks back and forth. Mrs. Peters moves to center table and they both watch the chair rock for a moment or two.)

Mrs. Peters *(shaking off the mood which the empty rocking chair has evoked. Now in a businesslike manner she speaks).* Well I must get those things from the front room closet. *(She goes to the door at the right but, after looking into the other room, steps back.)* You coming with me, Mrs. Hale? You could help me carry them. *(They go in the other room; reappear, Mrs. Peters carrying a dress, petticoat, and skirt, Mrs. Hale following with a pair of shoes.)* My, it's cold in there.

(She puts the clothes on the big table and hurries to the stove.)

Mrs. Hale *(right of center table examining the skirt).* Wright was close. I think maybe that's why she kept so much to herself. She didn't even belong to the Ladies' Aid. I suppose she felt she couldn't do her part, and then you don't enjoy things when you feel shabby. I heard she used to wear pretty clothes and be lively, when she was Minnie Foster, one of the town girls singing in the choir. But that—oh, that was thirty years ago. This all you want to take in?

Mrs. Peters. She said she wanted an apron. Funny thing to want, for there isn't much to get you dirty in jail, goodness knows. But I suppose just to make her feel more natural. *(Crosses to cupboard.)* She said they was in the top drawer in this cupboard. Yes, here. And then her little shawl that always hung behind the door. *(Opens stair door and looks.)* Yes, here it is.

(Quickly shuts door leading upstairs.)

Mrs. Hale *(abruptly moving toward her).* Mrs. Peters?
Mrs. Peters. Yes, Mrs. Hale?

(At up right door.)

Mrs. Hale. Do you think she did it?
Mrs. Peters *(in a frightened voice).* Oh, I don't know.
Mrs. Hale. Well, I don't think she did. Asking for an apron and her little shawl. Worrying about her fruit.
Mrs. Peters *(starts to speak, glances up, where footsteps are heard in the room above. In a low voice).* Mr. Peters says it looks bad for her. Mr. Henderson is awful sarcastic in a speech and he'll make fun of her sayin' she didn't wake up.
Mrs. Hale. Well, I guess John Wright didn't wake when they was slipping that rope under his neck.
Mrs. Peters *(crossing slowly to table and placing shawl and apron on table with other clothing).* No, it's strange. It must have been done awful crafty and still. They say it was such a—funny way to kill a man, rigging it all up like that.

Mrs. Hale (*crossing to left of Mrs. Peters at table*). That's just what Mr. Hale said. There was a gun in the house. He says that's what he can't understand.

Mrs. Peters. Mr. Henderson said coming out that what was needed for the case was a motive; something to show anger, or—sudden feeling.

Mrs. Hale (*who is standing by the table*). Well, I don't see any signs of anger around here. (*She puts her hand on the dish towel, which lies on the table, stands looking down at table, one-half of which is clean, the other half messy.*) It's wiped to here. (*Makes a move as if to finish work, then turns and looks at loaf of bread outside the breadbox. Drops towel. In that voice of coming back to familiar things.*) Wonder how they are finding things upstairs. (*Crossing below table to down right.*) I hope she had it a little more red-up[1] up there. You know, it seems kind of *sneaking*. Locking her up in town and then coming out here and trying to get her own house to turn against her!

Mrs. Peters. But, Mrs. Hale, the law is the law.

Mrs. Hale. I s'pose 'tis. (*Unbuttoning her coat.*) Better loosen up your things, Mrs. Peters. You won't feel them when you go out.

(*Mrs. Peters takes off her fur tippet, goes to hang it on chair back left of table, stands looking at the work basket on floor near down left window.*)

Mrs. Peters. She was piecing a quilt.

(*She brings the large sewing basket to the center table and they look at the bright pieces, Mrs. Hale above the table and Mrs. Peters left of it.*)

Mrs. Hale. It's a log cabin pattern. Pretty, isn't it? I wonder if she was goin' to quilt it or just knot it?

(*Footsteps have been heard coming down the stairs. The Sheriff enters followed by Hale and the County Attorney.*)

Sheriff. They wonder if she was going to quilt it or just knot it!

(*The men laugh, the women look abashed.*)

County Attorney (*rubbing his hands over the stove*). Frank's fire didn't do much up there, did it? Well, let's go out to the barn and get that cleared up.

(*The men go outside by up left door.*)

Mrs. Hale (*resentfully*). I don't know as there's anything so strange, our takin' up our time with little things while we're waiting for them to get the evidence.

[1] A slang expression for "make attractive."

(She sits in chair right of table smoothing out a block with decision.) I don't see as it's anything to laugh about.

Mrs. Peters *(apologetically).* Of course they've got awful important things on their minds.

(Pulls up a chair and joins Mrs. Hale at the left of the table.)

Mrs. Hale *(examining another block).* Mrs. Peters, look at this one. Here, this is the one she was working on, and look at the sewing! All the rest of it has been so nice and even. And look at this! It's all over the place! Why, it looks as if she didn't know what she was about!

(After she has said this they look at each other, then start to glance back at the door. After an instant Mrs. Hale has pulled at a knot and ripped the sewing.)

Mrs. Peters. Oh, what are you doing, Mrs. Hale?

Mrs. Hale *(mildly).* Just pulling out a stitch or two that's not sewed very good. *(Threading a needle.)* Bad sewing always made me fidgety.

Mrs. Peters *(with a glance at door, nervously).* I don't think we ought to touch things.

Mrs. Hale. I'll just finish up this end. *(Suddenly stopping and leaning forward.)* Mrs. Peters?

Mrs. Peters. Yes, Mrs. Hale?

Mrs. Hale. What do you suppose she was so nervous about?

Mrs. Peters. Oh—I don't know. I don't know as she was nervous. I sometimes sew awful queer when I'm just tired. *(Mrs. Hale starts to say something, looks at Mrs. Peters, then goes on sewing.)* Well, I must get these things wrapped up. They may be through sooner than we think. *(Putting apron and other things together.)* I wonder where I can find a piece of paper, and string.

(Rises.)

Mrs. Hale. In that cupboard, maybe.

Mrs. Peters *(crosses right looking in cupboard).* Why, here's a bird-cage. *(Holds it up.)* Did she have a bird, Mrs. Hale?

Mrs. Hale. Why, I don't know whether she did or not—I've not been here for so long. There was a man around last year selling canaries cheap, but I don't know as she took one; maybe she did. She used to sing real pretty herself.

Mrs. Peters *(glancing around).* Seems funny to think of a bird here. But she must have had one, or why would she have a cage? I wonder what happened to it?

Mrs. Hale. I s'pose maybe the cat got it.

Mrs. Peters. No, she didn't have a cat. She's got that feeling some people have about cats—being afraid of them. My cat got in her room and she was real upset and asked me to take it out.

Mrs. Hale. My sister Bessie was like that. Queer, ain't it?

Mrs. Peters *(examining the cage).* Why, look at this door. It's broke. One hinge is pulled apart.

(Takes a step down to Mrs. Hale's right.)

Mrs. Hale *(looking too).* Looks as if someone must have been rough with it.

Mrs. Peters. Why, yes.

(She brings the cage forward and puts it on the table.)

Mrs. Hale *(glancing toward up left door).* I wish if they're going to find any evidence they'd be about it. I don't like this place.

Mrs. Peters. But I'm awful glad you came with me, Mrs. Hale. It would be lonesome for me sitting here alone.

Mrs. Hale. It would, wouldn't it? *(Dropping her sewing.)* But I tell you what I do wish, Mrs. Peters. I wish I had come over sometimes when *she* was here. I—*(looking around the room)*—wish I had.

Mrs. Peters. But of course you were awful busy, Mrs. Hale—your house and your children.

Mrs. Hale *(rises and crosses left).* I could've come. I stayed away because it weren't cheerful—and that's why I ought to have come. I—*(looking out left window)*—I've never liked this place. Maybe because it's down in a hollow and you don't see the road. I dunno what it is, but it's a lonesome place and always was. I wish I had come over to see Minnie Foster sometimes. I can see now—

(Shakes her head.)

Mrs. Peters *(left of table and above it).* Well, you mustn't reproach yourself, Mrs. Hale. Somehow we just don't see how it is with other folks until—something turns up.

Mrs. Hale. Not having children makes less work—but it makes a quiet house, and Wright out to work all day, and no company when he did come in. *(Turning from window.)* Did you know John Wright, Mrs. Peters?

Mrs. Peters. Not to know him; I've seen him in town. They say he was a good man.

Mrs. Hale. Yes—good; he didn't drink, and kept his word as well as most, I guess, and paid his debts. But he was a hard man, Mrs. Peters. Just to pass the time of day with him—*(Shivers.)* Like a raw wind that gets to the bone. *(Pauses, her eye falling on the cage.)* I should think she would 'a' wanted a bird. But what do you suppose went with it?

Mrs. Peters. I don't know, unless it got sick and died.

(She reaches over and swings the broken door, swings it again, both women watch it.)

Mrs. Hale. You weren't raised round here, were you? (*Mrs. Peters shakes her head.*) You didn't know—her?

Mrs. Peters. Not till they brought her yesterday.

Mrs. Hale. She—come to think of it, she was kind of like a bird herself—real sweet and pretty, but kind of timid and—fluttery. How—she—did—change. (*Silence: then as if struck by a happy thought and relieved to get back to everyday things. Crosses right above Mrs. Peters to cupboard, replaces small chair used to stand on to its original place down right.*) Tell you what, Mrs. Peters, why don't you take the quilt in with you? It might take up her mind.

Mrs. Peters. Why, I think that's a real nice idea, Mrs. Hale. There couldn't possibly be any objection to it could there? Now, just what would I take? I wonder if her patches are in here—and her things.

(*They look in the sewing basket.*)

Mrs. Hale (*crosses to right of table*). Here's some red. I expect this has got sewing things in it. (*Brings out a fancy box.*) What a pretty box. Looks like something somebody would give you. Maybe her scissors are in here. (*Opens box. Suddenly puts her hand to her nose.*) Why———(*Mrs. Peters bends nearer, then turns her face away.*) There's something wrapped up in this piece of silk.

Mrs. Peters. Why, this isn't her scissors.

Mrs. Hale (*lifting the silk*). Oh, Mrs. Peters—it's———

(*Mrs. Peters bends closer.*)

Mrs. Peters. It's the bird.

Mrs. Hale. But, Mrs. Peters—look at it! Its neck! Look at its neck! It's all—other side *to*.

Mrs. Peters. Somebody—wrung—its—neck.

(*Their eyes meet. A look of growing comprehension, of horror. Steps are heard outside. Mrs. Hale slips box under quilt pieces, and sinks into her chair. Enter Sheriff and County Attorney. Mrs. Peters steps down left and stands looking out of window.*)

County Attorney (*as one turning from serious things to little pleasantries*). Well, ladies, have you decided whether she was going to quilt it or knot it?

(*Crosses to center above table.*)

Mrs. Peters. We think she was going to—knot it.

(*Sheriff crosses to right of stove, lifts stove lid, and glances at fire, then stands warming hands at stove.*)

County Attorney. Well, that's interesting, I'm sure. (*Seeing the bird-cage.*) Has the bird flown?

Mrs. Hale (*putting more quilt pieces over the box*). We think the—cat got it.

County Attorney (*preoccupied*). Is there a cat?

(*Mrs. Hale glances in a quick covert way at Mrs. Peters.*)

Mrs. Peters (*turning from window takes a step in*). Well, not *now*. They're superstitious, you know. They leave.

County Attorney (*to Sheriff Peters, continuing an interrupted conversation*). No sign at all of anyone having come from the outside. Their own rope. Now let's go up again and go over it piece by piece. (*They start upstairs.*) It would have to have been someone who knew just the———

(*Mrs. Peters sits down left of table. The two women sit there not looking at one another, but as if peering into something and at the same time holding back. When they talk now it is in the manner of feeling their way over strange ground, as if afraid of what they are saying, but as if they cannot help saying it.*)

Mrs. Hale (*hesitatively and in hushed voice*). She liked the bird. She was going to bury it in that pretty box.

Mrs. Peters (*in a whisper*). When I was a girl—my kitten—there was a boy took a hatchet, and before my eyes—and before I could get there———(*Covers her face an instant.*) If they hadn't held me back I would have—(*catches herself, looks upstairs where steps are heard, falters weakly*)—hurt him.

Mrs. Hale (*with a slow look around her*). I wonder how it would seem never to have had any children around. (*Pause.*) No, Wright wouldn't like the bird—a thing that sang. She used to sing. He killed that, too.

Mrs. Peters (*moving uneasily*). We don't know who killed the bird.

Mrs. Hale. I knew John Wright.

Mrs. Peters. It was an awful thing was done in this house that night, Mrs. Hale. Killing a man while he slept, slipping a rope around his neck that choked the life out of him.

Mrs. Hale. His neck. Choked the life out of him.

(*Her hand goes out and rests on the bird-cage.*)

Mrs. Peters (*with rising voice*). We don't know who killed him. We don't know.

Mrs. Hale (*her own feeling not interrupted*). If there'd been years and years of nothing, then a bird to sing to you, it would be awful—still, after the bird was still.

Mrs. Peters (*something within her speaking*). I know what stillness is. When we homesteaded in Dakota, and my first baby died—after he was two years old, and me with no other then———

Mrs. Hale (*moving*). How soon do you suppose they'll be through looking for the evidence?

Mrs. Peters. I know what stillness is. *(Pulling herself back.)* The law has got to punish crime, Mrs. Hale.

Mrs. Hale *(not as if answering that).* I wish you'd seen Minnie Foster when she wore a white dress with blue ribbons and stood up there in the choir and sang. *(A look around the room.)* Oh, I wish I'd come over here once in a while! That was a crime! That was a crime! Who's going to punish that?

Mrs. Peters *(looking upstairs).* We mustn't—take on.

Mrs. Hale. I might have known she needed help! I know how things can be—for women. I tell you, it's queer, Mrs. Peters. We live close together and we live far apart. We all go through the same things—it's all just a different kind of the same thing. *(Brushes her eyes, noticing the jar of fruit, reaches out for it.)* If I was you I wouldn't tell her her fruit was gone. Tell her it ain't. Tell her it's all right. Take this in to prove it to her. She—she may never know whether it was broke or not.

Mrs. Peters *(takes the jar, looks about for something to wrap it in; takes petticoat from the clothes brought from the other room, very nervously begins winding this around the jar. In a false voice).* My, it's a good thing the men couldn't hear us. Wouldn't they just laugh! Getting all stirred up over a little thing like a— dead canary. As if that could have anything to do with—with—wouldn't they laugh!

(The men are heard coming downstairs.)

Mrs. Hale *(under her breath).* Maybe they would—maybe they wouldn't.

County Attorney. No, Peters, it's all perfectly clear except a reason for doing it. But you know juries when it comes to women. If there was some definite thing. *(Crosses slowly to above table. Sheriff crosses down right. Mrs. Hale and Mrs. Peters remain seated at either side of table.)* Something to show—something to make a story about—a thing that would connect up with this strange way of doing it———

(The women's eyes meet for an instant. Enter Hale from outer door.)

Hale *(remaining by door).* Well, I've got the team around. Pretty cold out there.

County Attorney. I'm going to stay awhile by myself. *(To the Sheriff.)* You can send Frank out for me, can't you? I want to go over everything. I'm not satisfied that we can't do better.

Sheriff. Do you want to see what Mrs. Peters is going to take in?

(The Lawyer picks up the apron, laughs.)

County Attorney. Oh, I guess they're not very dangerous things the ladies have picked out. *(Moves a few things about, disturbing the quilt pieces which cover the box. Steps back.)* No, Mrs. Peters doesn't need supervising. For that matter a sheriff's wife is married to the law. Ever think of it that way, Mrs. Peters?

Mrs. Peters. Not—just that way.

Sheriff (*chuckling*). Married to the law. (*Moves to down right door to the other room.*) I just want you to come in here a minute, George. We ought to take a look at these windows.

County Attorney (*scoffingly*). Oh, windows!

Sheriff. We'll be right out, Mr. Hale.

(*Hale goes outside. The Sheriff follows the County Attorney into the room. Then Mrs. Hale rises, hands tight together, looking intensely at Mrs. Peters, whose eyes make a slow turn, finally meeting Mrs. Hale's. A moment Mrs. Hale holds her, then her own eyes point the way to where the box is concealed. Suddenly Mrs. Peters throws back quilt pieces and tries to put the box in the bag she is carrying. It is too big. She opens box, starts to take bird out, cannot touch it, goes to pieces, stands there helpless. Sound of a knob turning in the other room. Mrs. Hale snatches the box and puts it in the pocket of her big coat. Enter County Attorney and Sheriff, who remain down right.*)

County Attorney (*crosses to up left door facetiously*). Well, Henry, at least we found out that she was not going to quilt it. She was going to—what is it you call it, ladies?

Mrs. Hale (*standing center below table facing front, her hand against her pocket*). We call it—knot it, Mr. Henderson.

Curtain.

FOR ANALYSIS

1. What is the meaning of the title? Glaspell titled a short-story version of the play "A Jury of Her Peers." Is that a better title than *Trifles*? Explain.

2. What are the major differences between Mrs. Hale and Mrs. Peters?

3. At one point, Mrs. Peters tells Mrs. Hale a childhood story about a boy who killed her kitten. Why is she reminded of this event? What does it tell us about her reaction to the Wrights' marriage?

4. Which of the two women undergoes the most noticeable character development? Explain.

5. In what ways do the relationships between the two couples—Mrs. Hale and Mrs. Peters, and Henry Peters and Lewis Hale—change by the end of the play?

6. Do Henry Peters and Lewis Hale change in the course of the play?

7. Why are the men unable to see the clues that become obvious to the women?

8. Can you suggest why Mrs. Wright is the only one identified by her birth name?

MAKING ARGUMENTS

Argue for or against the proposition that Mrs. Hale and Mrs. Peters are morally obligated to tell the county attorney what they know about the murder.

WRITING TOPIC

Show how the discussion of Mrs. Wright's quilt embodies the major **themes** of *Trifles*.

MAKING CONNECTIONS

1. What similarities in attitudes toward women do you find in this play and in Ibsen's *A Doll's House* (p. 213)?

2. Do you think it is fair to say that Mrs. Wright in this play and the **narrator** in Gilman's "The Yellow Wallpaper" (p. 548) are people whose lives have been blighted by a patriarchal society that confines women to narrow, stereotypical roles? Explain.

LYNN NOTTAGE (B. 1964)

POOF! 1993

CHARACTERS

Samuel, Loureen's husband
Loureen, a demure housewife, early thirties
Florence, Loureen's best friend, early thirties

Time: *The present*

Place: *Kitchen*

A Note: *Nearly half the women on death row in the United States were convicted of killing abusive husbands. Spontaneous combustion is not recognized as a capital crime.*

Darkness.

Samuel *(In the darkness).* WHEN I COUNT TO TEN I DON' WANT TO SEE YA! I DON' WANT TO HEAR YA! ONE, TWO, THREE, FOUR—
Loureen *(In the darkness).* DAMN YOU TO HELL, SAMUEL!

A bright flash.
    Lights rise. A huge pile of smoking ashes rests in the middle of the kitchen. Loureen, a demure housewife in her early thirties, stares down at the ashes incredulously. She bends and lifts a pair of spectacles from the remains. She ever so slowly backs away.

Samuel? Uh! *(Places the spectacles on the kitchen table)* Uh! . . . Samuel? *(Looks around)* Don't fool with me now. I'm not in the mood. *(Whispers)* Samuel? I didn't mean it really. I'll be good if you come back . . . Come on now, dinner's waiting. *(Chuckles, then stops abruptly)* Now stop your foolishness . . . And let's sit down. *(Examines the spectacles)* Uh! *(Softly)* Don't be cross with me. Sure I forgot to pick up your shirt for tomorrow. I can wash another, I'll do it right now. Right now! Sam? . . . *(Cautiously)* You hear me! *(Awaits a response)* Maybe I didn't ever intend to wash your shirt. *(Pulls back as though about to receive a blow; a moment)* Uh! *(Sits down and dials the telephone)* Florence, honey, could you come on down for a moment. There's been a . . . little . . . accident . . . Quickly please. Uh!

Loureen hangs up the phone. She gets a broom and a dust pan. She hesitantly approaches the pile of ashes. She gets down on her hands and knees and takes a closer look. A fatuous grin spreads across her face. She is startled by a sudden knock on the

1087

door. She slowly walks across the room like a possessed child. Loureen lets in Florence, her best friend and upstairs neighbor. Florence, also a housewife in her early thirties, wears a floral housecoat and a pair of oversized slippers. Without acknowledgment Loureen proceeds to saunter back across the room.

Florence. HEY!

Loureen *(Pointing at the ashes)*. Uh! . . . *(She struggles to formulate words, which press at the inside of her mouth, not quite realized)* Uh! . . .

Florence. You all right? What happened? *(Sniffs the air)* Smells like you burned something? *(Stares at the huge pile of ashes)* What the devil is that?

Loureen *(Hushed)*. Samuel . . . It's Samuel, I think.

Florence. What's he done now?

Loureen. It's him. It's him. *(Nods her head repeatedly)*

Florence. Chile, what's wrong with you? Did he finally drive you out your mind? I knew something was going to happen sooner or later.

Loureen. Dial 911, Florence!

Florence. Why? You're scaring me!

Loureen. Dial 911!

Florence picks up the telephone and quickly dials.

I think I killed him.

Florence hangs up the telephone.

Florence. What?

Loureen *(Whimpers)*. I killed him! I killed Samuel!

Florence. Come again? . . . He's dead dead?

Loureen wrings her hands and nods her head twice, mouthing "dead dead." Florence backs away.

No, stop it, I don't have time for this. I'm going back upstairs. You know how Samuel hates to find me here when he gets home. You're not going to get me this time. *(Louder)* Y'all can have your little joke, I'm not part of it! *(A moment. She takes a hard look into Loureen's eyes; she squints)* Did you really do it this time?

Loureen *(Hushed)*. I don't know how or why it happened, it just did.

Florence. Why are you whispering?

Loureen. I don't want to talk too loud—something else is liable to disappear.

Florence. Where's his body?

Loureen *(Points to the pile of ashes)*. There! . . .

Florence. You burned him?

Loureen. I DON'T KNOW! *(Covers her mouth as if to muffle her words; hushed)* I think so.

Florence. Either you did or you didn't, what you mean you don't know? We're talking murder, Loureen, not oven settings.

Loureen. You think I'm playing?

Florence. How many times have I heard you talk about being rid of him. How many times have we sat at this very table and laughed about the many ways we could do it and how many times have you done it? None.

Loureen (*Lifting the spectacles*). A pair of cheap spectacles, that's all that's left. And you know how much I hate these. You ever seen him without them, no! . . . He counted to four and disappeared. I swear to God!

Florence. Don't bring the Lord into this just yet! Sit down now . . . What you got to sip on?

Loureen. I don't know whether to have a stiff shot of scotch or a glass of champagne.

Florence takes a bottle of sherry out of the cupboard and pours them each a glass. Loureen downs hers, then holds out her glass for more.

He was . . .

Florence. Take your time.

Loureen. Standing there.

Florence. And?

Loureen. He exploded.

Florence. Did that muthafucka hit you again?

Loureen. No . . . he exploded. Boom! Right in front of me. He was shouting like he does, being all colored, then he raised up that big crusty hand to hit me, and poof, he was gone . . . I barely got words out and I'm looking down at a pile of ash.

Florence belts back her sherry. She wipes her forehead and pours them both another.

Florence. Chile, I'll give you this, in terms of color you've matched my husband Edgar, the story king. He came in at six Sunday morning, talking about he'd hit someone with his car, and had spent all night trying to outrun the police. I felt sorry for him. It turns out he was playing poker with his paycheck no less. You don't want to know how I found out . . . But I did.

Loureen. You think I'm lying?

Florence. I certainly hope so, Loureen. For your sake and my heart's.

Loureen. Samuel always said if I raised my voice something horrible would happen. And it did. I'm a witch . . . the devil spawn!

Florence. You've been watching too much television.

Loureen. Never seen anything like this on television. Wish I had, then I'd know what to do . . . There's no question, I'm a witch. (*Looks at her hands with disgust*)

Florence. Chile, don't tell me you've been messing with them mojo women again? What did I tell ya.

Loureen, agitated, stands and sits back down.

Loureen. He's not coming back. Oh no, how could he? It would be a miracle! Two in one day . . . I could be canonized. Worse yet, he could be . . . All that needs to happen now is for my palms to bleed and I'll be eternally remembered as Saint Loureen, the patron of battered wives. Women from across the country will make pilgrimages to me, laying pies and pot roast at my feet and asking the good saint to make their husbands turn to dust. How often does a man like Samuel get damned to hell, and go?

She breaks down. Florence moves to console her friend, then realizes that Loureen is actually laughing hysterically.

Florence. You smoking crack?
Loureen. Do I look like I am?
Florence. Hell, I've seen old biddies creeping out of crack houses, talking about they were doing church work.
Loureen. Florence, please be helpful, I'm very close to the edge! . . . I don't know what to do next! Do I sweep him up? Do I call the police? Do I . . .

The phone rings.

Oh God.
Florence. You gonna let it ring?

Loureen reaches for the telephone slowly.

Loureen. NO! (*Holds the receiver without picking it up, paralyzed*) What if it's his mother? . . . She knows!

The phone continues to ring. They sit until it stops. They both breathe a sigh of relief.

I should be mourning, I should be praying, I should be thinking of the burial, but all that keeps popping into my mind is what will I wear on television when I share my horrible and wonderful story with a studio audience . . . (*Whimpers*) He's made me a killer, Florence, and you remember what a gentle child I was. (*Whispers*) I'm a killer, I'm a killer, I'm a killer.
Florence. I wouldn't throw that word about too lightly even in jest. Talk like that gets around.
Loureen. You think they'll lock me up? A few misplaced words and I'll probably get the death penalty, isn't that what they do with women like me, murderesses?
Florence. Folks have done time for less.
Loureen. Thank you, just what I needed to hear!
Florence. What did you expect, that I was going to throw up my arms and congratulate you? Why'd you have to go and lose your mind at this time of day, while I got a pot of rice on the stove and Edgar's about to walk in the door and

wonder where his goddamn food is. (*Losing her cool*) And he's going to start in on me about all the nothing I've been doing during the day and why I can't work and then he'll mention how clean you keep your home. And I don't know how I'm going to look him in the eye without . . .

Loureen. I'm sorry, Florence. Really. It's out of my hands now.

She takes Florence's hand and squeezes it.

Florence (*Regaining her composure*). You swear on your right tit?

Loureen (*Clutching both breasts*). I swear on both of them!

Florence. Both your breasts, Loureen! You know what will happen if you're lying. (*Loureen nods; hushed*) Both your breasts Loureen?

Loureen. Yeah!

Florence (*Examines the pile of ashes, then shakes her head*). Oh sweet, sweet Jesus. He must have done something truly terrible.

Loureen. No more than usual. I just couldn't take being hit one more time.

Florence. You've taken a thousand blows from that man, couldn't you've turned the cheek and waited? I'd have helped you pack. Like we talked about.

A moment.

Loureen. Uh! . . . I could blow on him and he'd disappear across the linoleum. (*Snaps her fingers*) Just like that. Should I be feeling remorse or regret or some other "R" word? I'm strangely jubilant, like on prom night when Samuel and I first made love. That's the feeling! (*The women lock eyes*) Uh!

Florence. Is it . . .

Loureen. Like a ton of bricks been lifted from my shoulders, yeah.

Florence. Really?

Loureen. Yeah!

Florence walks to the other side of the room.

Florence. You bitch!

Loureen. What?

Florence. We made a pact.

Loureen. I know.

Florence. You've broken it . . . We agreed that when things got real bad for both of us we'd . . . you know . . . together . . . Do I have to go back upstairs to that? . . . What next?

Loureen. I thought you'd tell me! . . . I don't know!

Florence. I don't know!

Loureen. I don't know!

Florence begins to walk around the room, nervously touching objects. Loureen sits, wringing her hands and mumbling softly to herself.

Florence. Now you got me, Loureen, I'm truly at a loss for words.

Loureen. Everybody always told me, "Keep your place, Loureen." My place, the silent spot on the couch with a wine cooler in my hand and a pleasant smile that warmed the heart. All this time I didn't know why he was so afraid for me to say anything, to speak up. Poof! . . . I've never been by myself, except for them two weeks when he won the office pool and went to Reno with his cousin Mitchell. He wouldn't tell me where he was going until I got that postcard with the cowboy smoking a hundred cigarettes . . . Didn't Sonny Larkin look good last week at Caroline's? He looked good, didn't he . . .

Florence nods. She nervously picks up Samuel's jacket, which is hanging on the back of the chair. She clutches it unconsciously.

NO! No! Don't wrinkle that, that's his favorite jacket. He'll kill me. Put it back!

Florence returns the jacket to its perch. Loureen begins to quiver.

I'm sorry. (*She grabs the jacket and wrinkles it up*) There! (*She then digs into the coat pockets and pulls out his wallet and a movie stub*) Look at that, he said he didn't go to the movies last night. Working late. (*Frantically thumbs through his wallet*) Picture of his motorcycle, Social Security card, driver's license, and look at that from our wedding. (*Smiling*) I looked good, didn't I? (*She puts the pictures back in the wallet and holds the jacket up to her face*) There were some good things. (*She then sweeps her hand over the jacket to remove the wrinkles, and folds it ever so carefully, and finally throws it in the garbage*) And out of my mouth those words made him disappear. All these years and just words, Florence. That's all they were.

Florence. I'm afraid I won't ever get those words out. I'll start resenting you, honey. I'm afraid won't anything change for me.

Loureen. I been to that place.

Florence. Yeah? But now I wish I could relax these old lines (*Touches her forehead*) for a minute maybe. Edgar has never done me the way Samuel did you, but he sure did take the better part of my life.

Loureen. Not yet, Florence.

Florence (*Nods*). I have the children to think of . . . right?

Loureen. You can think up a hundred things before . . .

Florence. Then come upstairs with me . . . we'll wait together for Edgar and then you can spit out your words and . . .

Loureen. I can't do that.

Florence. Yes you can. Come on now.

Loureen shakes her head no.

Well, I guess my mornings are not going to be any different.

Loureen. If you can say for certain, then I guess they won't be. I couldn't say that.

Florence. But you got a broom and a dust pan, you don't need anything more than that . . . He was a bastard and nobody will care that he's gone.

Loureen. Phone's gonna start ringing soon, people are gonna start asking soon, and they'll care.

Florence. What's your crime? Speaking your mind?

Loureen. Maybe I should mail him to his mother. I owe her that. I feel bad for her, she didn't understand how it was. I can't just throw him away and pretend like it didn't happen. Can I?

Florence. I didn't see anything but a pile of ash. As far as I know you got a little careless and burned a chicken.

Loureen. He was always threatening not to come back.

Florence. I heard him.

Loureen. It would've been me eventually.

Florence. Yes.

Loureen. I should call the police, or someone.

Florence. Why? What are you gonna tell them? About all those times they refused to help, about all those nights you slept in my bed 'cause you were afraid to stay down here? About the time he nearly took out your eye 'cause you flipped the television channel?

Loureen. No.

Florence. You've got it, girl!

Loureen. Good-bye to the fatty meats and the salty food. Good-bye to the bourbon and the bologna sandwiches. Good-bye to the smell of his feet, his breath and his bowel movements . . . (*A moment. She closes her eyes and, reliving a horrible memory, she shudders*) Good-bye. (*Walks over to the pile of ashes*) Samuel? . . . Just checking.

Florence. Good-bye Samuel.

They both smile.

Loureen. I'll let the police know that he's missing tomorrow . . .

Florence. Why not the next day?

Loureen. Chicken's warming in the oven, you're welcome ɔ stay.

Florence. Chile, I got a pot of rice on the stove, kids are probably acting out . . . and Edgar, well . . . Listen, I'll stop in tomorrow.

Loureen. For dinner?

Florence. Edgar wouldn't stand for that. Cards maybe.

Loureen. Cards.

The women hug for a long moment. Florence exits. Loureen stands over the ashes for a few moments contemplating what to do. She finally decides to sweep them under the carpet, and then proceeds to set the table and sit down to eat her dinner.

End of Play

FOR ANALYSIS

1. What does the interplay between Loureen and her friend Florence add to the play?

2. Nottage's play is about a serious subject but is not itself always serious. How would you characterize *Poof!*'s **tone**? How do the play's attitudes and **moods** work with and/or against its subjects?

3. Would you describe *Poof!* as a realistic play? Is its subject "real"? Its **plot**? What does it mean to say a work of imaginative literature is realistic?

MAKING ARGUMENTS

Poof! is noteworthy for (among other things) its combination of realism and the fantastic. Make an argument about this aspect of the play and its effectiveness as a piece of drama. Would it have been more effective if it dramatized the experience of women living in abusive relationships? Is its present effectiveness the result of its use of the fantastic?

WRITING TOPIC

Reimagine *Poof!* as told or seen from Samuel's **point of view**. Would you still have the play begin at the end of Samuel's life? Where would you set it? Would Samuel be alone? If not, with whom would you have him talk? Reflect on your choices: could you explore the same situations and **themes** that Nottage does in her version of the play, or would you be led in different directions?

MAKING CONNECTIONS

1. Compare Nottage's depiction of violence to Roethke's in "My Papa's Waltz" (p. 968). Taking into account differences in genre, how do Roethke's and Nottage's choices compare? What are the effects of each?

2. Read *Poof!* against Hurston's "Sweat" (p. 866). How does each work treat its main character? How does each work treat the husband? What does each have to say about his death, and about his wife's part in that death?

NONFICTION

PAUL (D. CA. 64 CE)

1 CORINTHIANS 13   CA. 56

If I speak in the tongues of men° and of angels, but have not love, I am a noisy gong or a clanging cymbal. [2] And if I have prophetic powers, and understand all mysteries and all knowledge, and if I have all faith, so as to remove mountains, but have not love, I am nothing. [3] If I give away all I have, and if I deliver my body to be burned, but have not love, I gain nothing.

[4] Love is patient and kind; love is not jealous or boastful; [5] it is not arrogant or rude. Love does not insist on its own way; it is not irritable or resentful; [6] it does not rejoice at wrong, but rejoices in the right. [7] Love bears all things, believes all things, hopes all things, endures all things.

[8] Love never ends; as for prophesies, they will pass away; as for tongues, they will cease; as for knowledge, it will pass away. [9] For our knowledge is imperfect and our prophecy is imperfect; [10] but when the perfect comes, the imperfect will pass away. [11] When I was a child, I spoke like a child, I thought like a child, I reasoned like a child; when I became a man, I gave up childish ways. [12] For now we see in a mirror dimly, but then face to face. Now I know in part; then I shall understand fully, even as I have been fully understood. [13] So faith, hope, love abide, these three; but the greatest of these is love.

FOR ANALYSIS

1. How does Paul emphasize the significance of love in verses 1–3?

2. What does Paul mean by "now" and "then" in verse 12?

3. In verse 13, Paul mentions "faith, hope, love" as abiding values. What do you understand by "faith" and "hope"? What do you think "love" means to Paul? Why does he rank it above the others?

°Glossolalia, the ecstatic uttering of unintelligible sounds that some interpret as a deeply religious experience.

MAKING ARGUMENTS

This passage is often chosen as a reading at weddings. Just to be contrary, and regardless of your opinion, make the argument that it offers bad advice about love.

WRITING TOPICS

1. Read Paul's First Epistle to the Corinthians (preferably in a well-annotated study Bible), and analyze the relationship of chapter 13 to the rest of the epistle.

2. This text, translated from the original Greek, is taken from the Revised Standard Version of the Bible. Read the same passage in two or three other versions (for example, the King James Version, the Douay Version, the New American Bible), and compare the translations in terms of **style** and effectiveness.

MAKING CONNECTIONS

How do you think the **characters** in Carver's "What We Talk About When We Talk About Love" (p. 876) would respond to Paul's definition of *love* or the absence of love?

NO NAME WOMAN 1970

Y ou must not tell anyone," my mother said, "what I am about to tell you. In China your father had a sister who killed herself. She jumped into the family well. We say that your father has all brothers because it is as if she had never been born.

"In 1924 just a few days after our village celebrated seventeen hurry-up weddings—to make sure that every young man who went 'out on the road' would responsibly come home—your father and his brothers and your grandfather and his brothers and your aunt's new husband sailed for America, the Gold Mountain. It was your grandfather's last trip. Those lucky enough to get contracts waved good-bye from the decks. They fed and guarded the stowaways and helped them off in Cuba, New York, Bali, Hawaii. 'We'll meet in California next year,' they said. All of them sent money home.

"I remember looking at your aunt one day when she and I were dressing; I had not noticed before that she had such a protruding melon of a stomach. But I did not think, 'She's pregnant,' until she began to look like other pregnant women, her shirt pulling and the white tops of her black pants showing. She could not have been pregnant, you see, because her husband had been gone for years. No one said anything. We did not discuss it. In early summer she was ready to have the child, long after the time when it could have been possible.

"The village had also been counting. On the night the baby was to be born the villagers raided our house. Some were crying. Like a great saw, teeth strung with lights, files of people walked zigzag across our land, tearing the rice. Their lanterns doubled in the disturbed black water, which drained away through the broken bunds. As the villagers closed in, we could see that some of them, probably men and women we knew well, wore white masks. The people with long hair hung it over their faces. Women with short hair made it stand up on end. Some had tied white bands around their foreheads, arms, and legs.

"At first they threw mud and rocks at the house. Then they threw eggs 5 and began slaughtering our stock. We could hear the animals scream their deaths—the roosters, the pigs, a last great roar from the ox. Familiar wild heads flared in our night windows; the villagers encircled us. Some of the faces stopped to peer at us, their eyes rushing like searchlights. The hands flattened against the panes, framed heads, and left red prints.

"The villagers broke in the front and the back doors at the same time, even though we had not locked the doors against them. Their knives dripped with the blood of our animals. They smeared blood on the doors and walls. One woman swung a chicken, whose throat she had slit, splattering blood in red arcs about her. We stood together in the middle of our house, in the family hall with the pictures and tables of the ancestors around us, and looked straight ahead.

"At that time the house had only two wings. When the men came back, we would build two more to enclose our courtyard and a third one to begin a second courtyard. The villagers pushed through both wings, even your grandparents' rooms, to find your aunt's, which was also mine until the men returned. From this room a new wing for one of the younger families would grow. They ripped up her clothes and shoes and broke her combs, grinding them underfoot. They tore her work from the loom. They scattered the cooking fire and rolled the new weaving in it. We could hear them in the kitchen breaking our bowls and banging the pots. They overturned the great waist-high earthenware jugs; duck eggs, pickled fruits, vegetables burst out and mixed in acrid torrents. The old woman from the next field swept a broom through the air and loosed the spirits-of-the-broom over our heads. 'Pig.' 'Ghost.' 'Pig,' they sobbed and scolded while they ruined our house.

"When they left, they took sugar and oranges to bless themselves. They cut pieces from the dead animals. Some of them took bowls that were not broken and clothes that were not torn. Afterward we swept up the rice and sewed it back up into sacks. But the smells from the spilled preserves lasted. Your aunt gave birth in the pigsty that night. The next morning when I went for the water, I found her and the baby plugging up the family well.

"Don't let your father know that I told you. He denies her. Now that you have started to menstruate, what happened to her could happen to you. Don't humiliate us. You wouldn't like to be forgotten as if you had never been born. The villagers are watchful."

Whenever she had to warn us about life, my mother told stories that ran 10 like this one, a story to grow up on. She tested our strength to establish realities. Those in the emigrant generations who could not reassert brute survival died young and far from home. Those of us in the first American generations have had to figure out how the invisible world the emigrants built around our childhoods fit in solid America.

The emigrants confused the gods by diverting their curses, misleading them with crooked streets and false names. They must try to confuse their offspring as well, who, I suppose, threaten them in similar ways—always trying to get things straight, always trying to name the unspeakable. The Chinese I know hide their names; sojourners take new names when their lives change and guard their real names with silence.

Chinese Americans, when you try to understand what things in you are Chinese, how do you separate what is peculiar to childhood, to poverty, insanities, one family, your mother who marked your growing with stories, from what is Chinese? What is Chinese tradition and what is the movies?

If I want to learn what clothes my aunt wore, whether flashy or ordinary, I would have to begin, "Remember Father's drowned-in-the-well sister?"

I cannot ask that. My mother has told me once and for all the useful parts. She will add nothing unless powered by Necessity, a riverbank that guides her life. She plants vegetable gardens rather than lawns; she carries the odd-shaped tomatoes home from the fields and eats food left for the gods.

Whenever we did frivolous things, we used up energy; we flew high kites. We children came up off the ground over the melting cones our parents brought home from work and the American movie on New Year's Day—*Oh, You Beautiful Doll* with Betty Grable one year, and *She Wore a Yellow Ribbon* with John Wayne another year. After the one carnival ride each, we paid in guilt; our tired father counted his change on the dark walk home.

Adultery is extravagance. Could people who hatch their own chicks and eat the embryos and the heads for delicacies and boil the feet in vinegar for party food, leaving only the gravel, eating even the gizzard lining—could such people engender a prodigal aunt? To be a woman, to have a daughter in starvation time was a waste enough. My aunt could not have been the lone romantic who gave up everything for sex. Women in the old China did not choose. Some man had commanded her to lie with him and be his secret evil. I wonder whether he masked himself when he joined the raid on her family. 15

Perhaps she had encountered him in the fields or on the mountain where the daughters-in-law collected fuel. Or perhaps he first noticed her in the marketplace. He was not a stranger because the village housed no strangers. She had to have dealings with him other than sex. Perhaps he worked an adjoining field, or he sold her the cloth for the dress she sewed and wore. His demand must have surprised, then terrified her. She obeyed him; she always did as she was told.

When the family found a young man in the next village to be her husband, she had stood tractably beside the best rooster, his proxy, and promised before they met that she would be his forever. She was lucky that he was her age and she would be the first wife, an advantage secure now. The night she first saw him, he had sex with her. Then he left for America. She had almost forgotten what he looked like. When she tried to envision him, she only saw the black and white face in the group photograph the men had had taken before leaving.

The other man was not, after all, much different from her husband. They both gave orders: she followed. "If you tell your family, I'll beat you. I'll kill you. Be here again next week." No one talked sex, ever. And she might have separated the rapes from the rest of living if only she did not have to buy her oil from him or gather wood in the same forest. I want her fear to have lasted just as long as rape lasted so that the fear could have been contained. No drawn-out fear. But women at sex hazarded birth and hence lifetimes. The fear did not stop but permeated everywhere. She told the man, "I think I'm pregnant." He organized the raid against her.

On nights when my mother and father talked about their life back home, sometimes they mentioned an "outcast table" whose business they still seemed to be settling, their voices tight. In a commensal tradition, where food is precious, the powerful older people made wrongdoers eat alone. Instead of letting them start separate new lives like the Japanese, who could become samurais and geishas, the Chinese family, faces averted but eyes glowering sideways, hung on to the offenders and fed them leftovers. My aunt must have lived in the same house as my parents and eaten at an outcast table. My mother spoke about the raid as if she had seen it, when she and my aunt, a daughter-in-law to a different household, should not have been living together at all. Daughters-in-law lived with their husbands' parents, not their own; a synonym for marriage in Chinese is "taking a daughter-in-law." Her husband's parents could have sold her, mortgaged her, stoned her. But they had sent her back to her own mother and father, a mysterious act hinting at disgraces not told me. Perhaps they had thrown her out to deflect the avengers.

She was the only daughter; her four brothers went with her father, husband, and uncles "out on the road" and for some years became Western men. When the goods were divided among the family, three of the brothers took land, and the youngest, my father, chose an education. After my grandparents gave their daughter away to her husband's family, they had dispensed all the adventure and all the property. They expected her alone to keep the traditional ways, which her brothers, now among the barbarians, could fumble without detection. The heavy, deep-rooted women were to maintain the past against the flood, safe for returning. But the rare urge west had fixed upon our family, and so my aunt crossed boundaries not delineated in space. 20

The work of preservation demands that the feelings playing about in one's guts not be turned into action. Just watch their passing like cherry blossoms. But perhaps my aunt, my forerunner, caught in a slow life, let dreams grow and fade and after some months or years went toward what persisted. Fear at the enormities of the forbidden kept her desires delicate, wire and bone. She looked at a man because she liked the way the hair was tucked behind his ears, or she liked the question-mark line of a long torso curving at the shoulder and straight at the hip. For warm eyes or a soft voice or a slow walk—that's all—a few hairs, a line, a brightness, a sound, a pace, she gave up family. She offered us up for a charm that vanished with tiredness, a pigtail that didn't toss when the wind died. Why, the wrong lighting could erase the dearest thing about him.

It could very well have been, however, that my aunt did not take subtle enjoyment of her friend, but, a wild woman, kept rollicking company. Imagining her free with sex doesn't fit, though. I don't know any women like that, or men either. Unless I see her life branching into mine, she gives me no ancestral help.

To sustain her being in love, she often worked at herself in the mirror, guessing at the colors and shapes that would interest him, changing them frequently in order to hit on the right combination. She wanted him to look back.

On a farm near the sea, a woman who tended her appearance reaped a reputation for eccentricity. All the married women blunt-cut their hair in flaps about their ears or pulled it back in tight buns. No nonsense. Neither style blew easily into heart-catching tangles. And at their weddings they displayed themselves in their long hair for the last time. "It brushed the backs of my knees," my mother tells me. "It was braided, and even so, it brushed the backs of my knees."

At the mirror my aunt combined individuality into her bob. A bun could 25 have been contrived to escape into black streamers blowing in the wind or in quiet wisps about her face, but only the older women in our picture album wear buns. She brushed her hair back from her forehead, tucking the flaps behind her ears. She looped a piece of thread, knotted into a circle between her index fingers and thumbs, and ran the double strand across her forehead. When she closed her fingers as if she were making a pair of shadow geese bite, the string twisted together catching the little hairs. Then she pulled the thread away from her skin, ripping the hairs out neatly, her eyes watering from the needles of pain. Opening her fingers, she cleaned the thread, then rolled it along her hairline and the tops of her eyebrows. My mother did the same to me and my sisters and herself. I used to believe that the expression "caught by the short hairs" meant a captive held with a depilatory string. It especially hurt at the temples, but my mother said we were lucky we didn't have to have our feet bound when we were seven. Sisters used to sit on their beds and cry together, she said, as their mothers or their slave removed the bandages for a few minutes each night and let the blood gush back into their veins. I hope that the man my aunt loved appreciated a smooth brow, that he wasn't just a tits-and-ass man.

Once my aunt found a freckle on her chin, at a spot that the almanac said predestined her for unhappiness. She dug it out with a hot needle and washed the wound with peroxide.

More attention to her looks than these pullings of hairs and pickings at spots would have caused gossip among the villagers. They owned work clothes and good clothes, and they wore good clothes for feasting the new seasons. But since a woman combing her hair hexes beginnings, my aunt rarely found an occasion to look her best. Women looked like great sea snails—the corded wood, babies, and laundry they carried were the whorls on their backs. The Chinese did not admire a bent back; goddesses and warriors stood straight. Still there must have been a marvelous freeing of beauty when a worker laid down her burden and stretched and arched.

Such commonplace loveliness, however, was not enough for my aunt. She dreamed of a lover for the fifteen days of New Year's, the time for families to exchange visits, money, and food. She plied her secret comb. And sure enough she cursed the year, the family, the village, and herself.

Even as her hair lured her imminent lover, many other men looked at her. Uncles, cousins, nephews, brothers would have looked, too, had they been home between journeys. Perhaps they had already been restraining their curiosity, and they left, fearful that their glances, like a field of nesting birds, might be startled and caught. Poverty hurt, and that was their first reason for leaving. But another, final reason for leaving the crowded house was the never-said.

She may have been unusually beloved, the precious only daughter, spoiled 30 and mirror-gazing because of the affection the family lavished on her. When her husband left, they welcomed the chance to take her back from the in-laws; she could live like the little daughter for just a while longer. There are stories that my grandfather was different from other people, "crazy ever since the little Jap bayoneted him in the head." He used to put his naked penis on the dinner table, laughing. And one day he brought home a baby girl, wrapped up inside his brown Western-style greatcoat. He had traded one of his sons, probably my father, the youngest, for her. My grandmother made him trade back. When he finally got a daughter of his own, he doted on her. They must have all loved her, except perhaps my father, the only brother who never went back to China, having once been traded for a girl.

Brothers and sisters, newly men and women, had to efface their sexual color and present plain miens. Disturbing hair and eyes, a smile like no other, threatened the ideal of five generations living under one roof. To focus blurs, people shouted face to face and yelled from room to room. The immigrants I know have loud voices, unmodulated to American tones even after years away from the village where they called their friendships out across the fields. I have not been able to stop my mother's screams in public libraries or over telephones. Walking erect (knees straight, toes pointed forward, not pigeon-toed, which is Chinese-feminine) and speaking in an inaudible voice, I have tried to turn myself American-feminine. Chinese communication was loud, public. Only sick people had to whisper. But at the dinner table, where the family members came nearest one another, no one could talk, not the outcasts nor any eaters. Every word that falls from the mouth is a coin lost. Silently they gave and accepted food with both hands. A preoccupied child who took his bowl with one hand got a sideways glare. A complete moment of total attention is due everyone alike. Children and lovers have no singularity here, but my aunt used a secret voice, a separate attentiveness.

She kept the man's name to herself throughout her labor and dying; she did not accuse him that he be punished with her. To save her inseminator's name she gave silent birth.

He may have been somebody in her own household, but intercourse with a man outside the family would have been no less abhorrent. All the village were kinsmen, and the titles shouted in loud country voices never let kinship be forgotten. Any man within visiting distance would have been neutralized as a lover—"brother," "younger brother," "older brother"—115 relationship titles. Parents researched birth charts probably not so much to assure good fortune as to circumvent incest in a population that has but one hundred surnames. Everybody has eight million relatives. How useless then sexual mannerisms, how dangerous.

As if it came from an atavism deeper than fear, I used to add "brother" silently to boys' names. It hexed the boys, who would or would not ask me to dance, and made them less scary and as familiar and deserving of benevolence as girls.

But, of course, I hexed myself also—no dates. I should have stood up, both 35 arms waving, and shouted out across libraries, "Hey, you! Love me back." I had no idea, though, how to make attraction selective, how to control its direction and magnitude. If I made myself American-pretty so that the five or six Chinese boys in the class fell in love with me, everyone else—the Caucasian, Negro, and Japanese boys—would too. Sisterliness, dignified and honorable, made much more sense.

Attraction eludes control so stubbornly that whole societies designed to organize relationships among people cannot keep order, not even when they bind people to one another from childhood and raise them together. Among the very poor and the wealthy, brothers married their adopted sisters, like doves. Our family allowed some romance, paying adult brides' prices and providing dowries so that their sons and daughters could marry strangers. Marriage promises to turn strangers into friendly relatives—a nation of siblings.

In the village structure, spirits shimmered among the live creatures, balanced and held in equilibrium by time and land. But one human being flaring up into violence could open up a black hole, a maelstrom that pulled in the sky. The frightened villagers, who depended on one another to maintain the real, went to my aunt to show her a personal, physical representation of the break she had made in the "roundness." Misallying couples snapped off the future, which was to be embodied in true offspring. The villagers punished her for acting as if she could have a private life, secret and apart from them.

If my aunt had betrayed the family at a time of large grain yields and peace, when many boys were born, and wings were being built on many houses, perhaps she might have escaped such severe punishment. But the men—hungry, greedy, tired of planting in dry soil, cuckolded—had been forced to leave the village in order to send food-money home. There were ghost plagues, bandit plagues, wars with the Japanese, floods. My Chinese brother and sister had died of an unknown sickness. Adultery, perhaps only a mistake during good times, became a crime when the village needed food.

The round moon cakes and round doorways, the round tables of graduated size that fit one roundness inside another, round windows and rice bowls— these talismans had lost their power to warn this family of the law: a family must be whole, faithfully keeping the descent line by having sons to feed the old and the dead, who in turn look after the family. The villagers came to show my aunt and her lover-in-hiding a broken house. The villagers were speeding up the circling of events because she was too shortsighted to see that her infidelity had already harmed the village, that waves of consequences would return unpredictably, sometimes in disguise, as now, to hurt her. This roundness had to be made coin-sized so that she would see its circumference: punish her at the birth of her baby. Awaken her to the inexorable. People who refused fatalism because they could invent small resources insisted on culpability. Deny accidents and wrest fault from the stars.

After the villagers left, their lanterns now scattering in various directions 40 toward home, the family broke their silence and cursed her. "Aiaa, we're going to die. Death is coming. Death is coming. Look what you've done. You've killed us. Ghost! Dead ghost! Ghost! You've never been born." She ran out into the fields, far enough from the house so that she could no longer hear their voices, and pressed herself against the earth, her own land no more. When she felt the birth coming, she thought that she had been hurt. Her body seized together. "They've hurt me too much," she thought. "This is gall, and it will kill me." With forehead and knees against the earth, her body convulsed and then relaxed. She turned on her back, lay on the ground. The black well of sky and stars went out and out and out forever; her body and her complexity seemed to disappear. She was one of the stars, a bright dot in blackness, without home, without a companion, in eternal cold and silence. An agoraphobia rose in her, speeding higher and higher, bigger and bigger; she would not be able to contain it; there would be no end to fear.

Flayed, unprotected against space, she felt pain return, focusing her body. This pain chilled her—a cold, steady kind of surface pain. Inside, spasmodically, the other pain, the pain of the child, heated her. For hours she lay on the ground, alternately body and space. Sometimes a vision of normal comfort obliterated reality: she saw the family in the evening gambling at the dinner table, the young people massaging their elders' backs. She saw them congratulating one another, high joy on the mornings the rice shoots came up. When these pictures burst, the stars drew yet further apart. Black space opened.

She got to her feet to fight better and remembered that old-fashioned women gave birth in their pigsties to fool the jealous, pain-dealing gods, who do not snatch piglets. Before the next spasms could stop her, she ran to the pigsty, each step a rushing out into emptiness. She climbed over the fence and knelt in the dirt. It was good to have a fence enclosing her, a tribal person alone.

Laboring, this woman who had carried her child as a foreign growth that sickened her every day, expelled it at last. She reached down to touch the hot, wet, moving mass, surely smaller than anything human, and could feel that it was human after all—fingers, toes, nails, nose. She pulled it up on to her belly, and it lay curled there, butt in the air, feet precisely tucked one under the other. She opened her loose shirt and buttoned the child inside. After resting, it squirmed and thrashed and she pushed it up to her breast. It turned its head this way and that until it found her nipple. There, it made little snuffling noises. She clenched her teeth at its preciousness, lovely as a young calf, a piglet, a little dog.

She may have gone to the pigsty as a last act of responsibility: she would protect this child as she had protected its father. It would look after her soul, leaving supplies on her grave. But how would this tiny child without family find her grave when there would be no marker for her anywhere, neither in the earth nor the family hall? No one would give her a family hall name. She had taken the child with her into the wastes. At its birth the two of them had felt the same raw pain of separation, a wound that only the family pressing tight could close. A child with no descent line would not soften her life but only trail after her, ghostlike, begging her to give it purpose. At dawn the villagers on their way to the fields would stand around the fence and look.

Full of milk, the little ghost slept. When it awoke, she hardened her breasts 45 against the milk that crying loosens. Toward morning she picked up the baby and walked to the well.

Carrying the baby to the well shows loving. Otherwise abandon it. Turn its face into the mud. Mothers who love their children take them along. It was probably a girl; there is some hope of forgiveness for boys.

"Don't tell anyone you had an aunt. Your father does not want to hear her name. She has never been born." I have believed that sex was unspeakable and words so strong and fathers so frail that "aunt" would do my father mysterious harm. I have thought that my family, having settled among immigrants who had also been their neighbors in the ancestral land, needed to clean their name, and a wrong word would incite the kinspeople even here. But there is more to this silence: they want me to participate in her punishment. And I have.

In the twenty years since I heard this story I have not asked for details nor said my aunt's name; I do not know it. People who can comfort the dead can also chase after them to hurt them further—a reverse ancestor worship. The real punishment was not the raid swiftly inflicted by the villagers, but the family's deliberately forgetting her. Her betrayal so maddened them, they saw to it that she would suffer forever, even after death. Always hungry, always needing, she would have to beg food from other ghosts, snatch and steal it from those whose living descendants give them gifts. She would have to fight the ghosts massed at crossroads for the buns a few thoughtful citizens leave to decoy her away from village and home so that the ancestral spirits could feast unharassed. At peace, they could act like gods, not ghosts, their descent lines providing them with paper suits and dresses, spirit money, paper houses, paper automobiles, chicken, meat, and rice into eternity—essences delivered up in smoke and flames, steam and incense rising from each rice bowl. In an attempt to make the Chinese care for people outside the family, Chairman Mao encourages us now to give our paper replicas to the spirits of outstanding soldiers and workers, no matter whose ancestors they may be. My aunt remains forever hungry. Goods are not distributed evenly among the dead.

My aunt haunts me—her ghost drawn to me because now, after fifty years of neglect, I alone devote pages of paper to her, though not origamied into houses and clothes. I do not think she always means me well. I am telling on her, and she was a spite suicide, drowning herself in the drinking water. The Chinese are always very frightened of the drowned one, whose weeping ghost, wet hair hanging and skin bloated, waits silently by the water to pull down a substitute.

FOR ANALYSIS

1. In what sense did the **narrator** participate in her aunt's punishment?

2. Given the Chinese belief system, what is the No Name Woman's most significant punishment?

3. What evidence in the essay supports the view that the Chinese villagers favored males over females?

4. Why does the woman enter the pigsty to give birth?

5. What factors intensify the ferocity of the villagers' attack on the house?

6. Discuss the significance of the assertion in paragraph 49: "I alone devote pages of paper to her, though not origamied into houses and clothes."

7. Reread the essay, noting scenes the speaker seems to invent. What reasons might Kingston have for imagining the events that she could not have known?

MAKING ARGUMENTS

The final sentence of this essay is haunting, both literally and **figuratively**. Make an argument about the significance of its final image—the threat of the ghost of the drowned pulling down a substitute—to the essay as a whole.

WRITING TOPIC

Describe the No Name Woman's sin. Was it a sin against the absent husband of her hastily arranged marriage, against her extended family, against the village, against the gods?

MAKING CONNECTIONS

Some authors, such as Chopin in "The Storm" (p. 861), seem to treat sexual infidelity casually; others, such as Shakespeare in *Othello* (p. 984), treat it murderously. Give reasons to support each view.

GRACE TALUSAN (B. 1972)

MY FATHER'S NOOSE   2007

When my father was a boy, his mother hung him.

 Enter Tondo, a Manila slum, and stand in the kitchen of his childhood home. Look up. The crusty knot is still there, tied around the light fixture.

I imagine my father, Totoy, at ten. He hasn't graduated yet to long pants and shoes; his shorts and T-shirt are faded and soft from the wear of three older brothers.

Totoy has done something to make his mother angrier than she's ever been. And now, Totoy balances on a stack of vegetable crates, his neck connected to the ceiling. He's wearing one rubber slipper, and after slapping him on the ears, his mother has tucked the other slipper under the bowtie of her apron. If Totoy becomes dizzy and loses balance, or if Inang kicks the crates away, he might save himself by curling his fingers around the rope and pulling against the noose as if it were the mouth on a drawstring bag.

But his mother plants his palms to his hips and she looks up at him. She 5 doesn't say a word, but Totoy hears, "Don't try to save yourself. Don't you dare."

He moves only his eyes and from this height, he notices his mother is balding. Her gray hair is loosely bunned and there are triangles of white flesh between the comb tracks. Her body is thick and intimidating, fleshy roll layered onto fat, souvenirs from eleven pregnancies. Totoy is number seven.

When she's angry, she makes noise and breaks things and stares until you look away. One by one, Totoy's siblings return from school and work, take a step into the kitchen, and right back out without a word.

With a pestle, she pounds garlic in the mortar bowl. She raises the butcher knife to her shoulder and chops heads from fish. She'll fry the bodies for dinner and save the heads and tails for soup the next day.

What does Totoy think as he stands there watching his mother prepare dinner? Does he believe he will taste that dinner? Perhaps his mother will remove the crates and watch him suffocate and kick until the knot is as tight as it will go; allow his siblings to play tetherball with his body; or keep him tied there, hanging from the kitchen.

His siblings are hiding, staying far away from the kitchen. Even if his father 10 could be found—perhaps he is playing pool in a neighborhood bar or perhaps he is earning money by taking a passenger from the market to their home on the sidecar of his tricycle—Totoy's father wouldn't save him. Mother knows best, and she tells him, "I'm doing this because you're my son. You need to learn right from wrong."

Totoy doesn't know this yet: he will survive. Fifteen years later, he will have me, a daughter. But he will never forgive his mother, and half a century later, he won't attend her funeral. Totoy will try his best not to abuse his children. But he's his mother's son. He will.

FOR ANALYSIS

1. What circumstances of Totoy's mother's life help to explain (if not justify) her actions? Do you judge her less harshly because of what you know about her life?

2. Why does Totoy's mother say she does this to him? Does it work? If so, how? If not, why not?

3. Part of the power of this brief essay comes from the way it ends. How does the ending extend the meaning of the event described?

MAKING ARGUMENTS

How would Totoy's mother justify her actions? Do you think she could put together a convincing argument for the necessity of her actions? What might she include in such an argument? Construct an argument for the notion that people (of all ages) manifest this combination of desire for and fear of physical intimacy. Use as evidence anything from literature, film, music, or life (yours or others').

WRITING TOPIC

Write a brief arresting essay (or story) in which you use some of Talusan's techniques (such as a shocking opening or an ending with a twist).

MAKING CONNECTIONS

1. Compare "My Father's Noose" to one or more of the poems in "Connecting Poems: Remembering Fathers" in Love and Hate (p. 968). How do the two (or more) works address the ways in which love expresses itself? How do they show how love can look similar to hate?

2. Though about quite different situations, Talusan's essay and Hayden's poem "Those Winter Sundays" (p. 969) both recognize the hard work parents do to care for their children, the love that motivates that work, and the toll that work sometimes takes on those who do it. How do the selections differ? What do the children in each poem learn from their experiences?

SONYA CHUNG (B. 1973)

GETTING IT RIGHT 1999

My mother called today from the other coast asking if I got the package she sent. I said no, and then the buzzer buzzed, and the UPS man knocked on the door with the package. "Call me back after you've opened it," my mother said.

Inside the big brown box, I find another flat, rectangular box, covered with a lime-green rice paper—very thin, textured, fibrous. In the center of the box top, some kind of Asian graphic: purple lines forming what looks to me like a stick figure sitting cross-legged, but is probably a Chinese character. I open the box. Underneath pink tissue paper, a hand mirror. Octagonal, technically, but wider at the top, narrowing towards the bottom. A beautiful dark wood, mahogany perhaps, but lighter. Koa? A large tassle of bright colors—red, neon pink, lime green, royal blue, electric yellow—trailing down from the handle. A Korean giveaway. The backside of the mirror proper: embroidered flowers, pale pink, and small leaves in all shades of green, red veins accenting. Another Chinese character in the left-hand corner. Buried in the tissue paper, the note says: *from Jagunummah, youngest aunt. In Korea, mother gives to daughter on wedding day. I think it means "happiness" but not sure. Be sure to send thank you note.*

Back to the big brown box, I find 50 lavender packages of birth control pills, floating in foam peanuts. The note reads: *thought you running low.* I notice the expiration date on all of them: 10/93. Next, a mouse pad bearing the snow-capped mountains of Yosemite National Park—*from our trip last year. I keep forget to send to you.* Finally, an envelope: photos from Christmas day, my family minus my husband and me. My father smiling wide, wearing the wool zipper-front vest we sent him, my mother's corduroy floral backside to the camera as she bends over to pick up crumpled wrapping paper, my sisters both with eyes blinking shut (who took the photo? I wonder). Double prints.

Last night, in the silence after the ugly argument, I lay in bed thinking, in a Jimmy Stewart-esque way, what would happen if I were to disappear. If I simply ceased to exist.

I call my mother back and thank her for everything. I ask what's new, and she says she wants to buy a computer, she's been researching. "What about all those megahertz of memory?" she asks, mixing up computer terms. "Do I need all that? I want one of those big screens and big sound systems; you know, for music and for old people." I tell her to go with mail order, so she can get the 800-number help desk. "You think?" she says. "What about zip drive? You have a zip drive?" 5

My mother used to rummage through piles of papers around the house, asking, "Where is that L.L. Crew J. catalogue?"

Today, we talk about the rain, my father's business, his secretary who is suicidal *again*. All the while, I'm carefully laying out the contents of the package on my bedroom floor: the mirror from my aunt that my mother forgot to give me when I got married, the expired pills, the mouse pad for my mouseless ergonomic keyboard, the terribly shot photos. And as my mother tells me about the latest deal between Microsoft and Sony, about how despite Sony's reputation for unreliability Microsoft is forging some kind of partnership based on mutual interest, I find myself covering the mouthpiece on the telephone, blubbering uncontrollably, dripping tears onto lime-green rice paper. I am remembering what it is to feel the largeness of love, the relief of simple gifts, given in earnest. I am thinking of my first week of college, of the package of crumbled cookies my mother sent me, the note enclosed boldly saying: *Hope your first day is as smooth as a sail.*

FOR ANALYSIS

1. What is the significance to the essay of the event recounted in the fourth paragraph?

2. Why does the author cry as she talks to her mother on the phone?

3. To what does the title refer?

MAKING ARGUMENTS

The photographs mentioned in Chung's essay capture the **narrator's** complicated feelings of love, embarrassment, and separation—geographic and emotional—from her birth family. Are these the most important objects described in this essay? Make an argument that they are, or that some other object is more important, explaining its significance.

WRITING TOPIC

While Chung makes fun of her mother's errors in idiomatic English and other things she sees as shortcomings, she does so with fondness. Do you have similar things you could note about a parent or caregiver? If you are a parent or caregiver yourself, how would a child of yours answer this question?

MAKING CONNECTIONS

1. Select a poem in this book that considers immigrant experience in America and compare it to this essay. How does the author's treatment of assimilation compare to Chung's?

2. Read this essay alongside Lee's "Eating Alone" (p. 970) and compare the ways in which the two treat the combinations of traditional and adopted cultures to immigrant experience. How is filial love expressed at the point where the two cross?

Connecting Nonfiction: Looking for Love in All the Wrong Places

It is hard to imagine two more different pieces of nonfiction. As you will see, these two authors approach the subject of love from different angles and with different strategies. That both arrive at compelling and similar places is testament to the literary version of the truism that there's more than one way to skin a cat. As you read, think about the way these two writers approach their subjects, and how both are able to tell affecting, complicated stories about the ways we look for love.

DAGOBERTO GILB   (B. 1950)

I Knew She Was Beautiful   2000

I was holding her hand at a train depot. I can still feel my arm in the air, limp and soft with trust. It must have been Union Station, Los Angeles, and I don't know where we were going or why. I was thrilled. I was small, probably just walking, and looking up at her I swear I knew then that she was beautiful. She was wearing a hat, one of those brimless hats women wore in the fifties that matched the rest of the outfit. There was a red rose in the hat, I'm sure. It wasn't a real rose but a lacy decorative one. Almost all my other early images of her are from the department stores we used to go to together. She's trying clothes on, everybody paying attention to her, or standing at a cosmetics counter, my mommy and the women around talking fast and unashamed, giggling, playing with the silver and gold and glass tubes, the jars and sprays, the smallest brushes, the colored powders. The train depot on that trip was the black-and-white of a dream, and the indoors had the faraway feel of the outdoors, its expanse as dusty as a memory.

I think it was La Cienega. It was a Spanish name, and the other stores where she modelled—downtown or on Wilshire Boulevard, department stores like the Broadway and Robinson's—didn't have Spanish names. The store didn't seem large. Just elegant. Racks of women's clothes with beads and jewels, collars and sleeves, strings and straps and bows, low in the front, low in the back. I went into the dressing room, where all the models were changing from one thing into another for the show that day. I watched them, breathing the cool mist of perfume, as they hurried through the step-throughs and pull-offs of dress and undress—the zippers and snaps, the gritty static or smooth wisp of on and off. Skin that was legs and arms, and round hips that cut into small waists; bras, even a breast, and panties that showed that darkened mystery hair. The piccolo of women's voices. I was a good boy, they said. I would be such a handsome man. I remember the warmth of their touch, like that of my favorite blanket. I used to scissor my fingers onto its nylon end seam to go to sleep, my thumb in my mouth, sucking. Even then I knew it was women, their attraction and allure, that I loved, *mi* mommy and her friends, her best friend, the woman from Puerto Rico who she could whisper to in Spanish. But it was this day I remember because on the other side of the store there was an old man in a uniform tinting a display window that faced the street. There were mannequins behind him and he let me go through a half door to sit between him and them. He brushed on the tint, the glass becoming a yellow brown, that biting, tart odor, and I looked out at the people and cars passing by on the other side of the window. I would run from him back to the dressing room, from one scent to the other, back and forth, the fumes subliminal and intoxicating as I ran from the old man with the paintbrush and can in the room no one got to sit in to the beautiful women in their underwear.

She loved to go to Hollywood Park, and we went to the last race because admission was free. I loved to go, too, and not just because of the horses, the earth shuddering under me as they left the gate and pounded across the finish line. I liked to collect the bet stubs like baseball cards, the losers thrown down, a trail of litter that began in the parking lot until it carpeted the grandstands. I collected fives and tens, win, place, or show. Win stubs were the hardest to find. Wandering the track was like walking on a beach looking for unbroken shells. We'd go down to the general-admission area, at track level, or we'd walk right over to a nicer area, where there were chairs and tables and drinks, and sometimes we were invited to sit in a private glass-enclosed clubhouse. A man would offer to buy us drinks, and I'd get a Roy Rogers—grenadine and Coke. She gave me the green olives on toothpicks from her drink to eat. The man who bought the drinks might say something at a distance first, and then approach. Usually, she just told a waiter, or the man himself, thank you so much, polite, generously happy about the drinks, but that would be it, and there we'd be, her and me at the races. I was her date. I was her man. Those men, in their suits and their blazers, snugged or loosened ties, stinking in their colognes, snapping bills off silver money clips, they were obvious, stupid, easy even for me to figure out. She might light a cigarette. She didn't smoke, though, for the taste. It was a look she wanted. I'd complain that I couldn't find betting stubs. She'd tell me to look around where we were sitting, and I'd search the tops of the starched tablecloths, the ashtrays, hunting the big losers. One time, I found four hundred-dollar tickets to win, creased the long way.

She was seeing this one man. Years later, I learned that she'd been seeing him for some time, even before she and my father divorced, which was soon after I was born. His voice was loud by design, the way a horn is loud. She used to ask me, Do you like him? He took us to baseball games. The Tigers and Angels and Yankees, the Dodgers and Giants and Pirates. The year Roger Maris hit sixty-one home runs I caught one of his B.P. homers. The loud man let me hang around after the games and get autographs. He was a big man, a fireman, and sometimes we visited him at his station. I was too scared to slide down the pole. It was too fat, too thick. I played handball alone in a white room beside the red trucks. He wasn't a bad man, but I didn't like him very much. I couldn't explain why, except that he was loud when he talked, and even though he bought me ice cream anytime I wanted it, he was no fun. And so I would answer her. No, I would say.

We were in the kitchen. I was sitting in one of those heavy metal chairs with 5 glossy vinyl covering—we had two of them—and my mom got mad at me. I was used to this. She had a job now in a dental office, and things like this happened because she was tired when she came home. But this time he was there. They were always going out, and I was left at home alone with our knobless television and a TV dinner, sometimes two, because I was getting taller, flexing muscles I could see in my arms. He only came inside our house once in a while, and she must have told me to go away, to get out of the kitchen. In that loud voice he told me to do what she said. I sat there. Then he was louder, really yelling. I sat there. And so he grabbed me and I held onto the metal rails under the chair and he picked it up along with me. I'm not leaving! I told him. You don't tell me! He was furious, and my mom was yelling now, too, and she told him to leave me alone, and he stopped, dropping the chair and me in it. I went into the bedroom and I was crying, waiting for her to come. She hit me sometimes, and when she got there that's what I was expecting. Instead she held me and she was smiling. She was proud of me. She said, You're such a man already.

At school the kids said things. I knew it. I was bigger than they were and more athletic, and angry all the time, and it wasn't like they were going to say anything much to my face. My mom was a Mexican and my mom was divorced, and one time a girl told me her mom didn't like mine and she didn't like me, either. I didn't hang out with too many kids. There was this one boy— he had his own bedroom, with toys everywhere. He had a basketball, and a hoop on the garage. I would want to play, but he was soft, blubbery, and I'd shoot alone for as long as his mom would let me. She was always smoking and drinking coffee in a stained white mug and talking on the phone, and once I came over and she took me into their clean bathroom and got a washcloth and washed my neck and behind my ears, scrubbed so hard it hurt. She was supposed to be a friend of my mom's, but I knew she wasn't, not really, because whenever my mom came to collect me only my mom talked.

Sometimes my mom would take me to the Food Giant and buy me a chili dog with finely grated cheese on the top that would melt in a minute. When she went out, which was a lot, she left me some money and I'd ride a bike down to the Thrifty and buy a half-gallon square of chocolate ice cream. She didn't cook, except on my birthday, when she made *chile verde* that stewed for hours. She'd buy tamales from a bakery on Whittier Boulevard. In the morning, before she went to work and I went to school, we had breakfast at a coffee shop, and she'd give me her hash-brown potatoes. Even then, at that hour, men looked at her. Even then, men would come up to our table, squat so that they could talk to her. Introduce themselves. I was starting junior high, I had touched a girl, looked at nudie magazines, and I knew what these men wanted. I was such a good-looking boy, they would tell her. When they guessed at my age, they missed by years, and then the talk would be about her beauty—how could such a young woman have a son so old? She was too polite to them, and one time I remember this man's eyes looking at my mom. I wanted us to be alone. I didn't want her to be polite. I was so mad at her. I was so mad then that I think I never got over it.

She'd stopped modelling, but when she and her Puerto Rican friend got together they talked about the other models' getting fat butts and saggy *chiches*, girdles and falsies. Her Puerto Rican friend was marrying a man who owned the biggest sailboat ever and they were going around the world in it. He was so rich he didn't have to work. My mom had to work. It made her tired. She was going out on more dates, too, so she was always busy. She talked wistfully about Pancho Gonzalez, the tennis star. Another friend of hers was supposed to be his cousin. She was a woman who talked too fast and too much, and she drank, and she laughed wrong. She and my mom both bleached their hair platinum, but this friend's was ugly and cheap looking. She was a *fea*, short and plump and pimply, but she thought she was as pretty as my mom. She was bad news, I knew, because by then I was smarter than my mom seemed to be. This "cousin" did not help my mom win Pancho Gonzalez, but they got drunk a lot together. My mom's Puerto Rican friend stopped coming around. Maybe she was sailing on the Pacific Ocean, maybe not yet, but she was married, and she was rich, and we weren't.

Though the modelling jobs weren't around anymore, the pretty clothes were. Bills came in the mail daily. I answered the phone and a bill collector would ask for her and I'd say she wasn't home even if she was. She was working for a dentist who was a Mormon, and she was dating him, too, and two old biddies started coming to our door lecturing my mom, and I listened to them with her. I answered their questions because she didn't know the answers. She wanted to become a Mormon, she didn't care how. We went to the dentist's house for Thanksgiving, my first Thanksgiving dinner. His mother had a bun of white and gray hair and a frilly apron just like one of those grandmothers on a TV show. We had to sit at a long dinner table, crowded with people. It was a feast of full bowls and platters, and I ate so much turkey and mashed potatoes that I got sick, but I didn't think it was because I overate. It was because they didn't like my mom. Well, I didn't like these people from the start. My mom and I spoke to each other, and they looked at us as if we were being secretive, as if we were talking in Spanish, not in English. After dinner we were taking a walk around the neighborhood with the dentist—it was green with overgrown trees and grass, and there weren't always sidewalks, and the idea was that he should get to know me a little—when my mom said that something was wrong, she was bleeding. She assured me it wasn't that kind of bleeding, teased me for not understanding immediately, but he didn't laugh. He didn't like this, didn't want to have to find an open store, couldn't believe she wouldn't be prepared. She sloughed that off, wanting to be cheerful. She wanted to make him happy. But he didn't laugh. This was the man I'd been lying about to new junior-high friends. Before I met him, my mom had told me that she was going to marry him. My dad, I'd tell these guys, snooty, was a dentist. I wanted us to be richer than them. After that day I don't remember ever hearing her talk about him again, and I never asked.

Two or three times my mom took me to an old lady's house. It was an old 10 house, with old things, and I had to have good manners and eat boring food. The woman thought I was a bright boy and liked it when I visited, my mom told me, and I might be getting an inheritance from her. When the old lady died, I went to the funeral parlor with my mom to pay last respects. There were no other people there, and still I felt as though we were being watched like thieves. The casket was open, but I didn't look close. It was like a church, with wooden pews and crosses and Jesuses, though no Virgins. My mom's knees went onto the padded kneel board, and as they did she made a loud *pedo*. I don't think I'd ever heard that from her before. She looked at me and I looked at her and we both tried to hold back from laughing. The more we did, the worse it hurt, and the stronger was the desire to laugh. She kept kneeling there, her hands folded and her head down as though she were praying, but really she was giggling and then we both started laughing too hard. There was no inheritance for either of us.

One night I was watching TV when a man who my mom worked for, someone I think she'd also gone out with, came to the door screaming about her. She was out on a date. He was wailing about money, what had she done with his money. He was drunk and howling and cussing. I knew about drunk because sometimes there were bottles in the house, broken glasses, laughter. I knew who this man was because he'd shot someone. Mom had told me about him, and I'd heard her tell her friends. He kept beating on the door, and it finally blew open right in front of me just as a cop neighbor I'd called came running up. A week later she married a man raised near Lancaster. I'd never heard of him, I'd never met him before. He was the cousin of a woman she'd worked with. He had the stupidest grin, as stupid as his hick name. He asked me if there was one thing he could do for me. I said I wanted him to take me to see Washington, D.C., and he grinned that dumb grin and said he would. I actually believed him. He and my mom went to Arizona for a week for their honeymoon, and after that we moved in. He wore a different clean green uniform every day for his job, and most of the rest of the time, too. There were deer heads and birds and fish on the walls. Maple furniture, a family table with matching chairs. He had a son who was a taxidermist, and he was proud of him. My mom's new husband was an electrician and a couple of times I worked for him and that's when I heard him tell his working friends he just felt so lucky to be married to such a pretty Mexican gal. A few weeks later she went on the TV show "Let's Make a Deal" and she was chosen. When Monty Hall asked her name, she told him her new name without a flinch. But she didn't win anything big—twenty or forty bucks, that was all—and she didn't get to pick a door.

Not too long afterward, she asked me to go to lunch with her. We hadn't gone out together, the two of us, for some time because she was so busy with her new husband. They were beginning to have arguments about bills and money, and they raced to get the mail first. The lunch wasn't only with my mom. It was with the loud man, the fireman, she'd dated before. He took us to a restaurant. I don't remember the food, only that when he pulled into the driveway of the apartment building where we lived, she jumped out of the car and rushed to the front door, and I was stuck in the back seat and this old boyfriend leaned over to talk to me. He told me he loved my mom and he was sorry and he wished something or other, I don't know. It was a speech, and it seemed as if he might cry or already was crying, but I told him I had to go. Maybe this was why I didn't like him. Big as he was, he was too loud, and yet he would cry. I think the car was a Thunderbird coupe, and I didn't even enjoy that. Things weren't good between my mom and her husband, and I knew she wasn't happy—I figured that she'd been sneaking out for these lunches with the fireman for a while—but I started avoiding my mom and her husband as much as possible. I never liked the deer meat or the maple furniture or the Hank Snow music, and I ate with my new neighborhood friends, stayed as late as I could. Then my mom and her husband separated, and we moved to an apartment complex on the south side of town. She would just lie on the couch, half awake, half asleep, depressed. We didn't talk too much. I had a job, and even though I was getting in fights at school and she was getting calls from the vice-principal about suspensions and swats and the rest, she didn't really care, and I didn't think it was such a big deal, either.

She married the loud fireman, who was almost ten years younger than she was—though nobody ever thought so—and who loved her after all this time. He bought her a brand-new house and everything that went in it, and it was as if we were rich, though I didn't feel as though anything was mine. It was all theirs. His and hers. He wasn't there very much. He worked hard at two jobs—he drove a Brink's truck, too—and she had all the money she'd ever dreamed of because he gave her his paychecks as if she were a financial wizard. When we were alone, or when she was joking in front of the women who would visit, she would say that he could be boring and dull, and that if he wasn't gone most of the time, if she didn't keep him working two jobs . . . Then she'd laugh, and everyone laughed with her. She always had food, and always a drink. There were jugs of wine and there was beer and liquor. There was a new blender, the best. He loved to drink with her, too. He loved everything she did, everything she bought, and she bought everything. She was the best thing that he could ever imagine happening to him, his life was full of sunlight and colors he'd never seen. I wasn't around much, going back to my old friends in my old high school, going to a new job to have my own money, partying myself now, playing with drugs and liquor and girlfriends, but I was happy that she wasn't worried anymore. Since she didn't have to do anything but please him, she pleased him. He didn't like "spicy" food, so she learned to cook potatoes and roasts. She babied him when he got home, made him feel like he ran the world. They drank together. They talked to each other and had fun when they drank. When she was around him, she became like him. When he thought he should be serious, he droned philosophically about black people and illegal aliens. My mom was an illegal alien, born out of wedlock in Mexico City and baptized at the Basilica Santa María de Guadalupe. She often tried to stop him when he went off on a long editorial, but it wasn't always worth it to her.

My mother was becoming a person I wouldn't want to know, and sometimes, especially when I was reminding her of a past that she didn't want to remember, she'd get mad. Once I told a neighbor that her husband wasn't my real father. I didn't know that I wasn't supposed to say this. I was sorry I embarrassed her. I didn't even care about my real father much, I only saw him a couple of days a year, but the only times my mother's husbands were fathers were when others made that assumption. They were just men to me, part of her life, not mine. Another time, after a year of living in this new house, with this new husband, I made her so angry by something I'd said or done, she told me she didn't know where I'd come from. She meant it, too, looking at me like I was an utter stranger, a lousy tenant.

On a Tuesday morning, just before dawn, I jerked myself out of a dream. It was so vivid I turned on a light and wrote it down. In the dream, a voice was talking to me, asking me if I wanted to talk to my mother. Why wouldn't I? Because we never did anymore, hadn't really talked in decades. When we did, there was nothing but awkwardness and mutual disapproval between us, and for several years there was nothing at all. I'd moved far away, to El Paso. The voice in the dream was asking me questions from my mother, and I started responding to the dream, to the voice, and straight to my mom. I answered the voice, yes, I always loved her. She had to know that I didn't care about whatever it was that had come between us, that I would remember only how much I loved her. I was always proud of her. I thought she was the best mommy, the most beautiful woman. I said I understood everything she'd gone through. Of course I didn't think only about the past, our troubles. Of course I forgave her, and I told her I wanted her to forgive me, too. And then I was overcome by a sob that wasn't in my dream but in my body and my mouth and my eyes.

Two days later, her husband called me. He was calm and positive. My mom, he said, had been taken to the hospital Tuesday. She was found unconscious. There was a problem with her liver. She was in intensive care, but he was convinced she'd be home soon. He just thought I should know. I thought this sounded much more serious, and I called the hospital. A nurse there said I was right, usually it was only a matter of time, it could be at any moment, though it could also take days or even a few weeks. I asked about the liver, whether it was the usual reason a liver goes. She asked, Well, was she always the life of the party? I got a plane ticket. I remembered a previous visit, and finding an empty vodka bottle—plastic, the cheapest brand you could buy—in the corner of the bedroom where I was sleeping, and where she kept a mountain of purses and shoes and wallets. I found another, most of it gone, behind a closet door.

I rented a car at the airport and went to the hospital. She was bloated, her hair a tousle—a woman who never missed a hairdresser's appointment—an unappealing white gown tied around her. Tubes needled into her hand and arm, a clear mask was over her mouth and nose. When she heard me, her eyes opened. She had no voice. I talked. Years had passed, she knew little about my life. She knew that I did construction work, thought it was all I did, ever, didn't know anything about the other life I led, the one as a writer. I never told her. I was afraid that she would only be his wife, not my mom, and she wouldn't care in the appropriate way. Or that she would be too relieved, and that all those other years I'd been struggling, when she disapproved of me, even thought I deserved whatever misery befell me, would be forgotten. I didn't want to give that up so easily. These were the reasons I had told her nothing. But I knew my mom would be proud. I knew she would be happy for me. I told her that I was a writer, and that I'd had a book published, another one just out. I had been going to New York City and Washington, D.C. I'd gone there more than once, and I never paid. Her eyes smiled so big. I knew she would like this the most. She always wanted to travel the world. Can you believe they even give me money? I asked her. She was proud of me, and she was as surprised as I was about it. And then I told her why I had to come. I told her about the dream I'd had two nights before, on the first night she spent in the hospital. My mom's eyes stopped moving. I said, I talked to you, you were talking to me, we were talking. She nodded—her whole weakened body squirmed while she was nodding. I knew it, and yet I wouldn't believe this story if I'd heard it. It was such a *telenovela* deathbed scene, mother and son, both weeping about a psychic conversation routed hundreds of miles through the smog and traffic and over the mountains and across three deserts, from one dream to another, so that we wouldn't miss telling each other for the last time before she died. She was as stunned as I was, as happy. You know? She kept nodding, looking at me, crying. Oh, Mom, I said.

FOR ANALYSIS

1. What else does Gilb know about his mother, other than that she was beautiful?

2. How does Gilb relate to the men in his mother's life? What do they have in common with each other? How does he see them?

3. What does Gilb's mother value? How does that contrast with what Gilb thinks is important? How do you read the final scene in relation to this difference?

MAKING ARGUMENTS

1. Some readers of this essay will object to the story of the dream. If you are one of them, how would you argue that such a thing could not happen? If you are not, how would you argue that it could?

2. Do you think the difficulty of Gilb's mother's life—her trouble with men, with responsibility, with alcohol—are of her own making or the result of circumstance? Make an argument in response to this question using the essay and any ideas and facts about individual psychology, social forces, or anything else you find relevant as evidence.

WRITING TOPIC

Do you think Gilb's mother was a good parent? A bad parent? Reflect on Gilb's portrayal of her—what does he think of her parenting? Does he judge her? Should we?

PABLO PIÑERO STILLMANN   (B. 1982)

LIFE, LOVE, HAPPINESS: A FOUND ESSAY FROM THE TWITTERVERSE[1]   2013

#Pisces often wonder what the meaning of #Life truly is. The meaning of life is to give life meaning. #WorkHard. For an example: Me: "Mom you look skinnier." Mom: "Thanks, now what do you want?" About to take my son up on the mountain and show him the meaning of life by having him kill a bear. YOLO. We tell our kids it's not about winning, it's about having fun. But all they see on TV are the biggest games: politics and war. What about love!??? I value a good friendship. I'm craving spontaneity, change, and maybe just something different to look forward to. Because that's what life is all about! We live in a World where losing your phone is more dramatic than losing your virginity. We live in a world full of people who are pretending to be something they're not. We live in a world where entertainers make way more money than people who save lives. We live in a really messed up world so appreciate the little bit of good you do see in people. If you think faking an orgasm is bad, wait until you meet someone who fakes a relationship. If you meet someone off OKC and the next day they delete their profile, that's good right? Or maybe you sucked so bad they gave up. Hmm. I want someone who'll save my texts just to look at them when they missed me . . . Ugh, I just want someone I can bake and cook for all the time. THE ONLY THING I WANT IN LIFE IS A FOLLOW FROM THE BOYS OK. IS THAT TOO MUCH TO ASK FOR, GOD? WHY DO YOU HATE ME ☹ I'm sorry that I am not good enough. I'm sorry that I am annoying. I'm sorry that I am lame. I'm sorry that I am not pretty enough. I have so much fun being single in the daylight or when I'm with friends, but when I'm all by myself I instantly become bored & depressed. Slowly dying with boredom and loneliness. WOO YEAH! I'm so unhappy with my life. No one understands. When will you realize? Baby, I'm not like the rest . . . Bitch, I'm special! I'm not odd, just different. You may not understand me 'cause maybe

[1] Contributors, in order of appearance: @PiscesAreUs, @Swiperboy, @YoDaddyAsia, @LeeBLVD, @patrickptomey, @PablodaJunkie, ©AsianPersuashin, @Narioo, ©mirzsunshine, @WeKnowComedy, @NiceTweets_, @Ask_Ricky, @Beauty_OMG, @sierranickellxo, @saraelizabethW, @MrEpicMind, @RaqNavaXO, @YumOneDirection, @RuzanaLah, @Khvlen, @wohlaa, @NCs_Finesttt, @caioschelege, @ohyescokyes, @iCanBUrDestiny_, @GirlDictionary, @gloriacharper, @bayorwheezy, @c0ndoms, @Thebieberjunkie, @OliviaDresher.

I don't want you to. I'm not to be like everyone else. I'm unique. If you ignore me, I will ignore you. If you don't start the conversation, we won't talk. If you don't put in the effort, why should I? I just bought a whole bunch of new cute clothes. I deserve to be taken out on a date. I just wanna hold you and never let go! If I could kill myself without affecting anyone else's life, I'd be gone tonight. Suicide is stupid? You wanna know what is stupid? Hurting someone so much emotionally, that they think suicide is the only answer. That feeling of waves crashing over me, the waves as helpless as myself.

FOR ANALYSIS

1. What kind of essay is this? Who wrote these words? What's with the hashtags?

2. How would you characterize the **tone** of this essay? Is it uniform or does it shift, and if the latter, where and how?

3. Many of these found sentences are clichés, but not all of them. How would you characterize the kinds of statements the author has collected here? Do you think they comment on the ideas of cliché and common wisdom?

MAKING ARGUMENTS

Some people think that different forms of social media make people write in different ways, that the sentences on one social medium are different from the sentences on another, for various reasons. Do you believe this? Construct an argument on this topic, in support of or refuting this idea or changing the terms of the discussion entirely.

WRITING TOPICS

1. The author, in a blog post on the origins of this essay, wrote that it came out of his anxieties about the waning of interest in literature and a resulting determination to confront its biggest competition—what he calls "the screen"—rather than running from it, and the form this confrontation took was a series of found essays composed of others' tweets. Reflect on this strategy. What is the result of this confrontation? What does it tell us about all the screens that distract us from books? Are they only a distraction or are there points of commonality?

2. Compose your own found essay from tweets or Facebook posts or any other social media. Be careful to respect the privacy of others while doing so.

MAKING CONNECTIONS

1. How are the people in Gilb's essay—perhaps including Gilb himself—looking for love in all the wrong places? How are those in Stillmann's essay doing the same thing? What commonalities do you find in the way they do this?

2. Gilb sees his mother as focused on love—of a lover, a husband, sexual or romantic— at the expense of other things, including perhaps care of her son. Compare the way Gilb reveals this side of his mother to the way Stillmann chooses and arranges his tweets. When does love and the search for love become the essays' subjects—from the start? Sometime later? How does it happen?

FURTHER QUESTIONS
FOR THINKING AND WRITING

1. How do the works in this section support the contention that love and hate are closely related emotions? **Writing Topic:** Discuss the relationship between love and hate in Raymond Carver's "What We Talk About When We Talk About Love" and William Shakespeare's *Othello.*

2. What images are characteristically associated with love in the prose and poetry of this section? What images are associated with hate? **Writing Topic:** Compare the image patterns in William Shakespeare's Sonnets 18 and 130 or the image patterns in John Donne's "A Valediction: Forbidding Mourning" and Robert Burns's "A Red, Red Rose."

3. The Greeks have three words that can be translated by the English word *love: eros, agape,* and *philia.* Describe the differences among these three types of love. **Writing Topic:** Find a story or poem that is representative of each type of love. In analyzing each work, discuss the extent to which the primary notion of love being addressed or celebrated is tempered by the other two types.

4. William Blake's "A Poison Tree," Carolyn Kizer's "Bitch," and Sylvia Plath's "Daddy" all seem to describe aspects of hate. Distinguish among the different varieties of hatred expressed in each poem. **Writing Topic:** Compare and contrast the source of the speaker's hatred in two of these poems.

5. Which works in this section treat love and/or hate in a way that corresponds most closely with your own experience or conception of those emotional states? Which contradict your experience? **Writing Topic:** For each case, isolate the elements in the work that provoke your response, and discuss them in terms of their "truth" or "falsity."

LIFE AND DEATH

Death and Life, Gustav Klimt. Before 1911, finished 1915. Oil on canvas, 178 × 198 cm.

The inevitability of death is not implied in the biblical story of creation; it required an act of disobedience before an angry God passed a sentence of hard labor and mortality on humankind: "In the sweat of your face you shall eat bread till you return to the ground, for out of it you were taken; you are dust and to dust you shall return." These words, written down some 2,800 years ago, preserve one ancient explanation for a persistently enigmatic condition of life and a persistent awareness of the implications of our actions. From earliest times men and women have attempted to characterize death, to cultivate beliefs about it, and to let it inform how they spend their time among the living. The mystery and certainty of death, in every age, make it an important theme for literary art.

Beliefs about the nature of death vary widely. The ancient Jews of the Pentateuch reveal no conception of immortality. Ancient Buddhist writings describe death as a mere translation from one painful life to another in an ongoing process of atonement that only the purest can avoid. The Christians conceive of a soul, separate from the body, which at the body's death is freed for a disembodied eternal life. The speaker in Robert Frost's "Stopping by Woods on a Snowy Evening" gazes into the dark woods filling up with snow, momentarily drawn toward the peace it represents; but Frost's is a secular poem, and the speaker turns back to life. In much religious poetry—John Donne's sonnet "Death, Be Not Proud" is an outstanding example—death is celebrated as a release from a burdensome existence into the eternal happiness of the afterlife. More recently, attitudes about death have reflected the great intellectual revolutions that affected all thought. For example, the Darwinian revolution replaced humans, the greatest glory of God's creation, with upright primates whose days are likely to be numbered by the flux between the fire and ice of geological history; and the Freudian revolution robbed men and women of their proudest certainty—the conviction that they possessed a dependable and controlling rational mind. In the context of Western tradition, these ideas serve to diminish us, to mock our self-importance. And, inevitably, these shifts lead us to alter our conception of death.

Death often inspires evaluation, or re-evaluation. Another's death affords us the opportunity to look back on a life and judge its worth; it also impels us to look again at our own lives. Simple awareness of the fact of death is sometimes enough to make us worry about what we are doing with our lives—a theme explored by poets in the "Seizing the Day" cluster in this chapter—and reactions to such a realization can range from Rainer Maria Rilke's cautionary encouragement "You must change your life" to James Wright's resigned declaration "I have wasted my life."

The view that establishes death as the great leveler, bringing citizens and emperors to the selfsame dust, is apparent in such poems as Percy Bysshe Shelley's "Ozymandias" and A. E. Housman's "To an Athlete Dying Young." This leveling view of death leads easily to the tradition wherein life itself is made absurd by the fact of death. Shakespeare's Macbeth finally declares that life is "a tale / Told by an idiot, full of sound and fury, / Signifying nothing." And the contemplation of suicide, which the pain and absurdity of life would seem to commend, provokes responses such as Edwin Arlington Robinson's ironic "Richard Cory." Some rage against death, as Dylan Thomas does in "Do Not Go Gentle into That Good Night"; others caution a quiet resignation, like Frost in "After Apple-Picking." Much fine poetry on death is elegiac—it speaks the melancholy response of the living to the fact of death. And reminders of this fact do not arise only from the death of a solitary person or within a grieving community: we are faced with it when we recognize the lives and deaths of the animals with whom we share the planet, as we see in the "Animal Fates" cluster. These writers urge us to see that the animal world is an inextricable part of the human experience; it isn't there simply to help us think about our own deaths and lives, but exists in its own right as a world worthy of attention, one whose own cycle of life and death can be shaped, sometimes quite harmfully, by human actions.

In short, literary treatments of death and how it shapes life display immense diversity. In Leo Tolstoy's "The Death of Iván Ilých," dying leads to a redemptive awareness. Leslie Marmon Silko's "The Man to Send Rain Clouds" explores sacrificial death as a means to control nature. In Victor Hernández Cruz's "Problems with Hurricanes" the comic lightens the weight of death. The inevitability of death and the way one confronts it paradoxically give life its meaning and its value.

QUESTIONS FOR THINKING AND WRITING

As you read the selections in this section, consider the following questions. You may want to write out your thoughts informally in a journal as a way of preparing to respond to the selections, or you may wish to make one of these questions the basis for a formal essay.

1. Has a close relative or friend of yours died? Was the person young or old, vigorous or in poor health? How did you feel? How might the circumstances of death alter one's feelings toward death or toward the person who died?

2. Do you believe that some essential part of you will survive the death of your body? On what do you base the belief? How does this belief alter your feelings about the death of people close to you? How does it alter your own behavior?

3. Are there any circumstances that justify suicide? Explain. If you believe that some suicides are justifiable, would it also be justifiable to help someone end his or her life? Explain.

4. Are there any circumstances that justify killing someone? Explain.

5. Imagine as best you can the circumstances of your own death. Describe them.

6. Write your own obituary. How would you like to be remembered? If you want, instead of the reserved, respectful tone characteristic of the genre, write something funny or satirical, but still take the exercise seriously. What are the important things you want people to remember about you, that you did or said? What kind of person were you really?

FICTION

EDGAR ALLAN POE   (1809–1849)

THE CASK OF AMONTILLADO   1846

The thousand injuries of Fortunato I had borne as I best could, but when he ventured upon insult, I vowed revenge. You, who so well know the nature of my soul, will not suppose, however, that I gave utterance to a threat. At *length* I would be avenged; this was a point definitely settled—but the very definitiveness with which it was resolved precluded the idea of risk. I must not only punish, but punish with impunity. A wrong is unredressed when retribution overtakes its redresser. It is equally unredressed when the avenger fails to make himself felt as such to him who has done the wrong.

It must be understood that neither by word nor deed had I given Fortunato cause to doubt my good will. I continued, as was my wont, to smile in his face, and he did not perceive that my smile *now* was at the thought of his immolation.

He had a weak point—this Fortunato—although in other regards he was a man to be respected and even feared. He prided himself on his connoisseurship in wine. Few Italians have the true virtuoso spirit. For the most part their enthusiasm is adopted to suit the time and opportunity to practise imposture upon the British and Austrian *millionnaires*. In painting and gemmary Fortunato, like his countrymen, was a quack, but in the matter of old wines he was sincere. In this respect I did not differ from him materially;—I was skillful in the Italian vintages myself, and bought largely whenever I could.

It was about dusk, one evening during the supreme madness of the carnival season, that I encountered my friend. He accosted me with excessive warmth, for he had been drinking much. The man wore motley. He had on a tight-fitting parti-striped dress, and his head was surmounted by the conical cap and bells. I was so pleased to see him, that I thought I should never have done wringing his hand.

I said to him—"My dear Fortunato, you are luckily met. How remarkably 5 well you are looking to-day! But I have received a pipe[1] of what passes for Amontillado, and I have my doubts."

[1] Large wine cask.

"How?" said he, "Amontillado? A pipe? Impossible! And in the middle of the carnival!"

"I have my doubts," I replied; "and I was silly enough to pay the full Amontillado price without consulting you in the matter. You were not to be found, and I was fearful of losing a bargain."

"Amontillado!"

"I have my doubts."

"Amontillado!"

"And I must satisfy them."   10

"Amontillado!"

"As you are engaged, I am on my way to Luchesi. If any one has a critical turn, it is he. He will tell me—"

"Luchesi cannot tell Amontillado from Sherry."

"And yet some fools will have it that his taste is a match for your own."   15

"Come, let us go."

"Whither?"

"To your vaults."

"My friend, no; I will not impose upon your good nature. I perceive you have an engagement. Luchesi—"

"I have no engagement;—come."   20

"My friend, no. It is not the engagement, but the severe cold with which I perceive you are afflicted. The vaults are insufferably damp. They are encrusted with nitre."

"Let us go, nevertheless. The cold is merely nothing. Amontillado! You have been imposed upon; and as for Luchesi, he cannot distinguish Sherry from Amontillado."

Thus speaking, Fortunato possessed himself of my arm. Putting on a mask of black silk, and drawing a *roquelaure*[2] closely about my person, I suffered him to hurry me to my palazzo.

There were no attendants at home; they had absconded to make merry in honor of the time. I had told them that I should not return until the morning, and had given them explicit orders not to stir from the house. These orders were sufficient, I well knew, to insure their immediate disappearance, one and all, as soon as my back was turned.

I took from their sconces two flambeaux, and giving one to Fortunato, 25 bowed him through several suites of rooms to the archway that led into the vaults. I passed down a long and winding staircase, requesting him to be cautious as he followed. We came at length to the foot of the descent, and stood together on the damp ground of the catacombs of the Montresors.

The gait of my friend was unsteady, and the bells upon his cap jingled as he strode.

"The pipe," said he.

"It is farther on," said I; "but observe the white web-work which gleams from these cavern walls."

[2] Short cloak.

He turned towards me, and looked into my eyes with two filmy orbs that distilled the rheum of intoxication.

"Nitre?" he asked, at length.

"Nitre," I replied. "How long have you had that cough?"

"Ugh! ugh! ugh!—ugh! ugh! ugh!—ugh! ugh! ugh!—ugh! ugh! ugh!—ugh! ugh! ugh!"

My poor friend found it impossible to reply for many minutes.

"It is nothing," he said, at last.

"Come," I said, with decision, "we will go back; your health is precious. You are rich, respected, admired, beloved; you are happy, as once I was. You are a man to be missed. For me it is no matter. We will go back; you will be ill, and I cannot be responsible. Besides, there is Luchesi—"

"Enough," he said; "the cough is a mere nothing: it will not kill me. I shall not die of a cough."

"True—true," I replied; "and, indeed, I had no intention of alarming you unnecessarily—but you should use all proper caution. A draught of this Medoc will defend us from the damps."

Here I knocked off the neck of a bottle which I drew from a long row of its fellows that lay upon the mould.

"Drink," I said, presenting him the wine.

He raised it to his lips with a leer. He paused and nodded to me familiarly, while his bells jingled.

"I drink," he said, "to the buried that repose around us."

"And I to your long life."

He again took my arm, and we proceeded.

"These vaults," he said, "are extensive."

"The Montresors," I replied, "were a great and numerous family."

"I forget your arms."

"A huge human foot d'or, in a field azure; the foot crushes a serpent rampant whose fangs are imbedded in the heel."

"And the motto?"

"*Nemo me impune lacessit.*"[3]

"Good!" he said.

The wine sparkled in his eyes and the bells jingled. My own fancy grew warm with the Medoc. We had passed through walls of piled bones, with casks and puncheons intermingling, into the inmost recesses of the catacombs. I paused again, and this time I made bold to seize Fortunato by an arm above the elbow.

"The nitre!" I said; "see, it increases. It hangs like moss upon the vaults. We are below the river's bed. The drops of moisture trickle among the bones. Come, we will go back ere it is too late. Your cough—"

"It is nothing," he said; "let us go on. But first, another draught of the Medoc."

---

[3] No one provokes me with impunity (the motto of Scotland).

I broke and reached him a flagon of De Grâve. He emptied it at a breath. His eyes flashed with a fierce light. He laughed and threw the bottle upwards with a gesticulation I did not understand.

I looked at him in surprise. He repeated the movement—a grotesque one.   55

"You do not comprehend?" he said.

"Not I," I replied.

"Then you are not of the brotherhood."

"How?"

"You are not of the masons."[4]   60

"Yes, yes," I said; "yes, yes."

"You? Impossible! A mason?"

"A mason," I replied.

"A sign," he said.

"It is this," I answered, producing a trowel from beneath the folds of my   65
roquelaure.

"You jest," he exclaimed, recoiling a few paces. "But let us proceed to the Amontillado."

"Be it so," I said, replacing the tool beneath the cloak, and again offering him my arm. He leaned upon it heavily. We continued our route in search of the Amontillado. We passed through a range of low arches, descended, passed on, and descending again, arrived at a deep crypt, in which the foulness of the air caused our flambeaux rather to glow than flame.

At the most remote end of the crypt there appeared another less spacious. Its walls had been lined with human remains piled to the vault overhead, in the fashion of the great catacombs of Paris. Three sides of this interior crypt were still ornamented in this manner. From the fourth the bones had been thrown down, and lay promiscuously upon the earth, forming at one point a mound of some size. Within the wall thus exposed by the displacing of the bones, we perceived a still interior recess, in depth about four feet, in width three, in height six or seven. It seemed to have been constructed for no especial use within itself, but formed merely the interval between two of the colossal supports of the roof of the catacombs, and was backed by one of their circumscribing walls of solid granite.

It was in vain that Fortunato, uplifting his dull torch, endeavored to pry into the depths of the recess. Its termination the feeble light did not enable us to see.

"Proceed," I said; "herein is the Amontillado. As for Luchesi—"   70

"He is an ignoramus," interrupted my friend, as he stepped unsteadily forward, while I followed immediately at his heels. In an instant he had reached the extremity of the niche, and finding his progress arrested by the rock, stood stupidly bewildered. A moment more and I had fettered him to the granite. In its surface were two iron staples, distant from each other about two feet, horizontally. From one of these depended a short chain, from the other a

---

[4] A member of the Freemasons, an international secretive mutual aid society.

padlock. Throwing the links about his waist, it was but the work of a few seconds to secure it. He was too much astounded to resist. Withdrawing the key I stepped back from the recess.

"Pass your hand," I said, "over the wall; you cannot help feeling the nitre. Indeed it is *very* damp. Once more let me *implore* you to return. No? Then I must positively leave you. But I must first render you all the little attentions in my power."

"The Amontillado!" ejaculated my friend, not yet recovered from his astonishment.

"True," I replied; "the Amontillado."

As I said these words I busied myself among the pile of bones of which I have 75 before spoken. Throwing them aside, I soon uncovered a quantity of building-stone and mortar. With these materials and with the aid of my trowel, I began vigorously to wall up the entrance of the niche.

I had scarcely laid the first tier of the masonry when I discovered that the intoxication of Fortunato had in a great measure worn off. The earliest indication I had of this was a low moaning cry from the depth of the recess. It was *not* the cry of a drunken man. There was then a long and obstinate silence. I laid the second tier, and the third, and the fourth; and then I heard the furious vibrations of the chain. The noise lasted for several minutes, during which, that I might hearken to it with the more satisfaction, I ceased my labors and sat down upon the bones. When at last the clanking subsided, I resumed the trowel, and finished without interruption the fifth, the sixth, and the seventh tier. The wall was now nearly upon a level with my breast. I again paused, and holding the flambeaux over the masonwork, threw a few feeble rays upon the figure within.

A succession of loud and shrill screams, bursting suddenly from the throat of the chained form, seemed to thrust me violently back. For a brief moment I hesitated—I trembled. Unsheathing my rapier, I began to grope with it about the recess; but the thought of an instant reassured me. I placed my hand upon the solid fabric of the catacombs, and felt satisfied. I reapproached the wall. I replied to the yells of him who clamored. I re-echoed—I aided—I surpassed them in volume and in strength. I did this, and the clamorer grew still.

It was now midnight, and my task was drawing to a close. I had completed the eighth, the ninth, and the tenth tier. I had finished a portion of the last and the eleventh; there remained but a single stone to be fitted and plastered in. I struggled with its weight; I placed it partially in its destined position. But now there came from out the niche a low laugh that erected the hairs upon my head. It was succeeded by a sad voice, which I had difficulty in recognizing as that of the noble Fortunato. The voice said—

"Ha! ha! ha!—he! he! he!—a very good joke indeed—an excellent jest. We will have many a rich laugh about it at the palazzo—he! he! he!—over our wine—he! he! he!"

"The Amontillado!" I said.

"He! he! he!—he! he! he!—yes, the Amontillado. But is it not getting late? Will not they be awaiting us at the palazzo, the Lady Fortunato and the rest? Let us be gone."

"Yes," I said, "let us be gone."

"For the love of God, Montresor!"

"Yes," I said, "for the love of God!"

But to these words I hearkened in vain for a reply. I grew impatient. I called aloud; 85

"Fortunato!"

No answer. I called again;

"Fortunato!"

No answer still, I thrust a torch through the remaining aperture and let it fall within. There came forth in return only a jingling of the bells. My heart grew sick—on account of the dampness of the catacombs. I hastened to make an end of my labor. I forced the last stone into its position; I plastered it up. Against the new masonry I reerected the old rampart of bones. For the half of a century no mortal has disturbed them. *In pace requiescat!*[5]

FOR ANALYSIS

1. We are not told how Fortunato insulted Montresor. Would the story be more effective if we knew? Explain.

2. Are there any clues that suggest when and to whom Montresor tells his tale? Explain.

3. How is Montresor able to lure Fortunato into the catacombs?

4. Describe the qualities that Montresor insists on as the characteristics of a successful vengeance.

5. Describe the **style** of this story, particularly the speech of the characters. What effect does the archaic flavor contribute to the tale?

MAKING ARGUMENTS

Choose a short section of the story—say, three or four paragraphs—and carefully analyze the language line by line (particularly as it differs from ordinary colloquial English). Make an argument for or against this change, using as evidence your story of how this story works or doesn't work and of how stories work generally.

WRITING TOPIC

In an essay, imagine and describe the circumstances and the nature of Fortunato's insult.

MAKING CONNECTIONS

Compare this story with Jackson's "The Lottery" (p. 367), which also ends with an unexpected and horrible murder. What similarities do you find? What differences?

---

[5] May he rest in peace.

LEO TOLSTOY (1828–1910)

THE DEATH OF IVÁN ILÝCH[1]   1886

CHAPTER I

During an interval in the Melvínski trial in the large building of the Law Courts the members and public prosecutor met in Iván Egóro-vich Shébek's private room, where the conversation turned on the celebrated Krasóvski case. Fëdor Vasílievich warmly maintained that it was not subject to their jurisdiction, Iván Egórovich maintained the contrary, while Peter Iván-ovich, not having entered into the discussion at the start, took no part in it but looked through the *Gazette* which had just been handed in.

"Gentlemen," he said, "Iván Ilých has died!"

"You don't say so!"

"Here, read it yourself," replied Peter Ivánovich, handing Fëdor Vasílievich the paper still damp from the press. Surrounded by a black border were the words: "Praskóvya Fëdorovna Goloviná, with profound sorrow, informs rela-tives and friends of the demise of her beloved husband Iván Ilých Golovín, Member of the Court of Justice, which occurred on February the 4th of this year 1882. The funeral will take place on Friday at one o'clock in the afternoon."

Iván Ilých had been a colleague of the gentlemen present and was liked by 5 them all. He had been ill for some weeks with an illness said to be incurable. His post had been kept open for him, but there had been conjectures that in case of his death Alexéev might receive his appointment, and that either Vín-nikov or Shtábel would succeed Alexéev. So on receiving the news of Iván Ilých's death the first thought of each of the gentlemen in that private room was of the changes and promotions it might occasion among themselves or their acquaintances.

"I shall be sure to get Shtábel's place or Vínnikov's," thought Fëdor Vasílievich. "I was promised that long ago, and the promotion means an extra eight hundred rubles a year for me besides the allowance."

"Now I must apply for my brother-in-law's transfer from Kalúga," thought Peter Ivánovich. "My wife will be very glad, and then she won't be able to say that I never do anything for her relations."

"I thought he would never leave his bed again," said Peter Ivánovich aloud. "It's very sad."

"But what really was the matter with him?"

"The doctors couldn't say—at least they could, but each of them said some- 10 thing different. When last I saw him I thought he was getting better."

---

[1] Translated by Aylmer Maude.

"And I haven't been to see him since the holidays. I always meant to go."

"Had he any property?"

"I think his wife had a little—but something quite trifling."

"We shall have to go to see her, but they live so terribly far away."

"Far away from you, you mean. Everything's far away from your place."   15

"You see, he never can forgive my living on the other side of the river," said Peter Ivánovich, smiling at Shébek. Then, still talking of the distances between different parts of the city, they returned to the Court.

Besides considerations as to the possible transfers and promotions likely to result from Iván Ilých's death, the mere fact of the death of a near acquaintance aroused, as usual, in all who heard of it the complacent feeling that, "it is he who is dead and not I."

Each one thought or felt, "Well, he's dead but I'm alive!" But the more intimate of Iván Ilých's acquaintances, his so-called friends, could not help thinking also that they would now have to fulfill the very tiresome demands of propriety by attending the funeral service and paying a visit of condolence to the widow.

Fëdor Vasílievich and Peter Ivánovich had been his nearest acquaintances. Peter Ivánovich had studied law with Iván Ilých and had considered himself to be under obligations to him.

Having told his wife at dinner-time of Iván Ilých's death, and of his conjec-   20
ture that it might be possible to get her brother transferred to their circuit, Peter Ivánovich sacrificed his usual nap, put on his evening clothes, and drove to Iván Ilých's house.

At the entrance stood a carriage and two cabs. Leaning against the wall in the hall downstairs near the cloak-stand was a coffin-lid covered with cloth of gold, ornamented with gold cord and tassels, that had been polished up with metal powder. Two ladies in black were taking off their fur cloaks. Peter Ivánovich recognized one of them as Iván Ilých's sister, but the other was a stranger to him. His colleague Schwartz was just coming downstairs, but on seeing Peter Ivánovich enter he stopped and winked at him, as if to say: "Iván Ilých has made a mess of things—not like you and me."

Schwartz's face with his Piccadilly whiskers, and his slim figure in evening dress, had as usual an air of elegant solemnity which contrasted with the playfulness of his character and had a special piquancy here, or so it seemed to Peter Ivánovich.

Peter Ivánovich allowed the ladies to precede him and slowly followed them upstairs. Schwartz did not come down but remained where he was, and Peter Ivánovich understood that he wanted to arrange where they should play bridge that evening. The ladies went upstairs to the widow's room, and Schwartz with seriously compressed lips but a playful look in his eyes, indicated by a twist of his eyebrows the room to the right where the body lay.

Peter Ivánovich, like everyone else on such occasions, entered feeling uncertain what he would have to do. All he knew was that at such times it is always safe to cross oneself. But he was not quite sure whether one should make obeisances while doing so. He therefore adopted a middle course. On entering the room he began crossing himself and made a slight movement resembling a bow. At the same time, as far as the motion of his head and arm allowed, he surveyed the room. Two young men—apparently nephews, one of whom was a high-school pupil—were leaving the room, crossing themselves as they did so. An old woman was standing motionless, and a lady with strangely arched eyebrows was saying something to her in a whisper. A vigorous, resolute Church Reader, in a frock-coat, was reading something in a loud voice with an expression that precluded any contradiction. The butler's assistant, Gerásim, stepping lightly in front of Peter Ivánovich, was strewing something on the floor. Noticing this, Peter Ivánovich was immediately aware of a faint odour of a decomposing body.

The last time he had called on Iván Ilých, Peter Ivánovich had seen Gerásim 25 in the study. Iván Ilých had been particularly fond of him and he was performing the duty of a sick nurse.

Peter Ivánovich continued to make the sign of the cross slightly inclining his head in an intermediate direction between the coffin, the Reader, and the icons on the table in a corner of the room. Afterwards, when it seemed to him that this movement of his arm in crossing himself had gone on too long, he stopped and began to look at the corpse.

The dead man lay, as dead men always lie, in a specially heavy way, his rigid limbs sunk in the soft cushions of the coffin, with the head forever bowed on the pillow. His yellow waxen brow with bald patches over his sunken temples was thrust up in the way peculiar to the dead, the protruding nose seeming to press on the upper lip. He was much changed and had grown even thinner since Peter Ivánovich had last seen him, but, as is always the case with the dead, his face was handsomer and above all more dignified than when he was alive. The expression on the face said that what was necessary had been accomplished, and accomplished rightly. Besides this there was in that expression a reproach and a warning to the living. This warning seemed to Peter Ivánovich out of place, or at least not applicable to him. He felt a certain discomfort and so he hurriedly crossed himself once more and turned and went out of the door—too hurriedly and too regardless of propriety, as he himself was aware.

Schwartz was waiting for him in the adjoining room with legs spread wide apart and both hands toying with his top-hat behind his back. The mere sight of that playful, well-groomed, and elegant figure refreshed Peter Ivánovich. He felt that Schwartz was above all these happenings and would not surrender to any depressing influences. His very look said that this incident of a church service for Iván Ilých could not be a sufficient reason for infringing the order of the session—in other words, that it would certainly not prevent his unwrapping a new pack of cards and shuffling them that evening while a footman placed four fresh candles on the table: in fact, there was no reason for supposing that this incident would hinder their spending the evening agreeably. Indeed he said this in a whisper as Peter Ivánovich passed him, proposing that they should meet for a game at Fëdor Vasílievich's. But apparently Peter Ivánovich was not destined to play bridge that evening. Praskóvya Fëdorovna (a short, fat woman who despite all efforts to the contrary had continued to broaden steadily from her shoulders downwards and who had the same extraordinarily arched eyebrows as the lady who had been standing by the coffin), dressed all in black, her head covered with lace, came out of her own room with some other ladies, conducted them to the room where the dead body lay, and said: "The service will begin immediately. Please go in."

Schwartz, making an indefinite bow, stood still, evidently neither accepting nor declining this invitation. Praskóvya Fëdorovna recognizing Peter Ivánovich, sighed, went close up to him, took his hand, and said: "I know you were a true friend to Iván Ilých . . ." and looked at him awaiting some suitable response. And Peter Ivánovich knew that, just as it had been the right thing to cross himself in that room, so what he had to do here was to press her hand, sigh, and say, "Believe me . . ." So he did all this and as he did it felt that the desired result had been achieved: that both he and she were touched.

"Come with me. I want to speak to you before it begins," said the widow.   30 "Give me your arm."

Peter Ivánovich gave her his arm and they went to the inner rooms, passing Schwartz who winked at Peter Ivánovich compassionately.

"That does for our bridge! Don't object if we find another player. Perhaps you can cut in when you do escape," said his playful look.

Peter Ivánovich sighed still more deeply and despondently, and Praskóvya Fëdorovna pressed his arm gratefully. When they reached the drawing-room, upholstered in pink cretonne and lighted by a dim lamp, they sat down at the table—she on a sofa and Peter Ivánovich on a low pouffe, the springs of which yielded spasmodically under his weight. Praskóvya Fëdorovna had been on the point of warning him to take another seat, but felt that such a warning was out of keeping with her present condition and so changed her mind. As he sat down on the pouffe Peter Ivánovich recalled how Iván Ilých had arranged this room and had consulted him regarding this pink cretonne with green leaves. The whole room was full of furniture and knick-knacks, and on her way to the sofa the lace of the widow's black shawl caught on the carved edge of the table. Peter Ivánovich rose to detach it, and the springs of the pouffe, relieved of his weight, rose also and gave him a push. The widow began detaching her shawl herself, and Peter Ivánovich again sat down, suppressing the rebellious springs of the pouffe under him. But the widow had not quite freed herself and Peter Ivánovich got up again, and again the pouffe rebelled and even creaked. When this was all over she took out a clean cambric handkerchief and began to weep. The episode with the shawl and the struggle with the pouffe had cooled Peter Ivánovich's emotions and he sat there with a sullen look on his face. This awkward situation was interrupted by Sokolóv, Iván Ilých's butler, who came to report that the plot in the cemetery that Praskóvya Fëdorovna had chosen would cost two hundred rubles. She stopped weeping and, looking at Peter Ivánovich with the air of a victim, remarked in French that it was very hard for her. Peter Ivánovich made a silent gesture signifying his full conviction that it must indeed be so.

"Please smoke," she said in a magnanimous yet crushed voice, and turned to discuss with Sokolóv the price of the plot for the grave.

Peter Ivánovich while lighting his cigarette heard her inquiring very circum- 35 stantially into the price of different plots in the cemetery and finally decide which she would take. When that was done she gave instructions about engaging the choir. Sokolóv then left the room.

"I look after everything myself," she told Peter Ivánovich, shifting the albums that lay on the table; and noticing that the table was endangered by his cigarette-ash, she immediately passed him an ashtray, saying as she did so: "I consider it an affectation to say that my grief prevents my attending to practical affairs. On the contrary, if anything can—I won't say console me, but—distract me, it is seeing to everything concerning him." She again took out her handkerchief as if preparing to cry, but suddenly, as if mastering her feeling, she shook herself and began to speak calmly. "But there is something I want to talk to you about."

Peter Ivánovich bowed, keeping control of the springs of the pouffe, which immediately began quivering under him.

"He suffered terribly the last few days."

"Did he?" said Peter Ivánovich.

"Oh, terribly! He screamed unceasingly, not for minutes but for hours. For the 40 last three days he screamed incessantly. It was unendurable. I cannot understand how I bore it; you could hear him three rooms off. Oh, what I have suffered!"

"Is it possible that he was conscious all that time?" asked Peter Ivánovich.

"Yes," she whispered. "To the last moment. He took leave of us a quarter of an hour before he died, and asked us to take Volódya away."

The thought of the sufferings of this man he had known so intimately, first as a merry little boy, then as a school-mate, and later as a grown-up colleague, suddenly struck Peter Ivánovich with horror, despite an unpleasant consciousness of his own and this woman's dissimulation. He again saw that brow, and that nose pressing down on the lip, and felt afraid for himself.

"Three days of frightful suffering and then death! Why, that might suddenly, at any time, happen to me," he thought, and for a moment felt terrified. But—he did not himself know how—the customary reflection at once occurred to him that this had happened to Iván Ilých and not to him, and that it should not and could not happen to him, and that to think that it could would be yielding to depression which he ought not to do, as Schwartz's expression plainly showed. After which reflection Peter Ivánovich felt reassured, and began to ask with interest about the details of Iván Ilých's death, as though death was an accident natural to Iván Ilých but certainly not to himself.

After many details of the really dreadful physical sufferings Iván Ilých 45 had endured (which details he learnt only from the effect those sufferings had produced on Praskóvya Fëdorovna's nerves) the widow apparently found it necessary to get to business.

"Oh, Peter Ivánovich, how hard it is! How terribly, terribly hard!" and she again began to weep.

Peter Ivánovich sighed and waited for her to finish blowing her nose. When she had done so he said, "Believe me . . ." and she again began talking and brought out what was evidently her chief concern with him—namely, to question him as to how she could obtain a grant of money from the government on the occasion of her husband's death. She made it appear that she was asking Peter Ivánovich's advice about her pension, but he soon saw that she already knew about that to the minutest detail, more even than he did himself. She knew how much could be got out of the government in consequence of her husband's death, but wanted to find out whether she could not possibly extract something more. Peter Ivánovich tried to think of some means of doing so, but after reflecting for a while and, out of propriety, condemning the government for its niggardliness, he said he thought that nothing more could be got. Then she sighed and evidently began to devise means of getting rid of her visitor. Noticing this, he put out his cigarette, rose, pressed her hand, and went out into the anteroom.

In the dining-room where the clock stood that Iván Ilých had liked so much and had bought at an antique shop, Peter Ivánovich met a priest and a few acquaintances who had come to attend the service, and he recognized Iván Ilých's daughter, a handsome young woman. She was in black and her slim figure appeared slimmer than ever. She had a gloomy, determined, almost angry expression, and bowed to Peter Ivánovich as though he were in some way to blame. Behind her, with the same offended look, stood a wealthy young man, an examining magistrate, whom Peter Ivánovich also knew and who was her fiancé, as he had heard. He bowed mournfully to them and was about to pass into the death-chamber, when from under the stairs appeared the figure of Iván Ilých's schoolboy son, who was extremely like his father. He seemed a little Iván Ilých, such as Peter Ivánovich remembered when they studied law together. His tear-stained eyes had in them the look that is seen in the eyes of boys of thirteen or fourteen who are not pure-minded. When he saw Peter Ivánovich he scowled morosely and shamefacedly. Peter Ivánovich nodded to him and entered the death-chamber. The service began: candles, groans, incense, tears, and sobs. Peter Ivánovich stood looking gloomily down at his feet. He did not look once at the dead man, did not yield to any depressing influence, and was one of the first to leave the room. There was no one in the anteroom, but Gerásim darted out of the dead man's room, rummaged with his strong hands among the fur coats to find Peter Ivánovich's and helped him on with it.

"Well, friend Gerásim," said Peter Ivánovich, so as to say something. "It's a sad affair, isn't it?"

"It's God's will. We shall all come to it some day," said Gerásim, displaying 50 his teeth—the even, white teeth of a healthy peasant—and, like a man in the thick of urgent work, he briskly opened the front door, called the coachman, helped Peter Ivánovich into the sledge, and sprang back to the porch as if in readiness for what he had to do next.

Peter Ivánovich found the fresh air particularly pleasant after the smell of incense, the dead body, and carbolic acid.

"Where to, sir?" asked the coachman.

"It's not too late even now. . . . I'll call round on Fëdor Vasílievich."

He accordingly drove there and found them just finishing the first rubber, so that it was quite convenient for him to cut in.

CHAPTER II

Iván Ilých's life had been most simple and most ordinary and therefore most terrible. 55

He had been a member of the Court of Justice, and died at the age of forty-five. His father had been an official who after serving in various ministries and departments in Petersburg had made the sort of career which brings men to positions from which by reason of their long service they cannot be dismissed, though they are obviously unfit to hold any responsible position, and for whom therefore posts are specially created, which though fictitious carry salaries of from six to ten thousand rubles that are not fictitious, and in receipt of which they live on to a great age.

Such was the Privy Councillor and superfluous member of various superfluous institutions, Ilyá Epímovich Golovín.

He had three sons, of whom Iván Ilých was the second. The eldest son was following in his father's footsteps only in another department, and was already approaching that stage in the service at which a similar sinecure would be reached. The third son was a failure. He had ruined his prospects in a number of positions and was now serving in the railway department. His father and brothers, and still more their wives, not merely disliked meeting him, but avoided remembering his existence unless compelled to do so. His sister had married Baron Greff, a Petersburg official of her father's type. Iván Ilých was *le phénix de la famille*[2] as people said. He was neither as cold and formal as his elder brother nor as wild as the younger, but was a happy mean between them—an intelligent, polished, lively and agreeable man. He had studied with his younger brother at the School of Law, but the latter had failed to complete the course and was expelled when he was in the fifth class. Iván Ilých finished the course well. Even when he was at the School of Law he was just what he remained for the rest of his life: a capable, cheerful, good-natured, and sociable man, though strict in the fulfilment of what he considered to be his duty: and he considered his duty to be what was so considered by those in authority. Neither as a boy nor as a man was he a toady, but from early youth was by nature attracted to people of high station as a fly is drawn to the light, assimilating their ways and views of life and establishing friendly relations with them. All the enthusiasms of childhood and youth passed without leaving much trace on him; he succumbed to sensuality, to vanity, and latterly among the highest classes to liberalism, but always within limits which his instinct unfailingly indicated to him as correct.

---

[2] The phoenix of the family, here meaning "rare bird" or "prodigy."

At school he had done things which had formerly seemed to him very horrid and made him feel disgusted with himself when he did them; but when later on he saw that such actions were done by people of good position and that they did not regard them as wrong, he was able not exactly to regard them as right, but to forget about them entirely or not be at all troubled at remembering them.

Having graduated from the School of Law and qualified for the tenth rank 60 of the civil service, and having received money from his father for his equipment, Iván Ilých ordered himself clothes at Scharmer's, the fashionable tailor, hung a medallion inscribed *respice finem*[3] on his watch-chain, took leave of his professor and the prince who was patron of the school, had a farewell dinner with his comrades at Donon's first-class restaurant, and with his new and fashionable portmanteau, linen, clothes, shaving and other toilet appliances, and a travelling rug, all purchased at the best shops, he set off for one of the provinces where, through his father's influence, he had been attached to the Governor as an official for special service.

In the province Iván Ilých soon arranged as easy and agreeable a position for himself as he had had at the School of Law. He performed his official tasks, made his career, and at the same time amused himself pleasantly and decorously. Occasionally he paid official visits to country districts, where he behaved with dignity both to his superiors and inferiors, and performed the duties entrusted to him, which related chiefly to the sectarians,[4] with an exactness and incorruptible honesty of which he could not but feel proud.

In official matters, despite his youth and taste for frivolous gaiety, he was exceedingly reserved, punctilious, and even severe; but in society he was often amusing and witty, and always good-natured, correct in his manner, and *bon enfant*, as the governor and his wife—with whom he was like one of the family—used to say of him.

In the provinces he had an affair with a lady who made advances to the elegant young lawyer, and there was also a milliner; and there were carousals with aides-de-camp who visited the district, and after-supper visits to a certain outlying street of doubtful reputation; and there was too some obsequiousness to his chief and even to his chief's wife, but all this was done with such a tone of good breeding that no hard names could be applied to it. It all came under the heading of the French saying: "Il faut que jeunesse se passe."[5] It was all done with clean hands, in clean linen, with French phrases, and above all among people of the best society and consequently with the approval of people of rank.

So Iván Ilých served for five years and then came a change in his official life. The new and reformed judicial institutions were introduced, and new men were needed. Iván Ilých became such a new man. He was offered the post

---

[3] Regard the end.
[4] A large sect, whose members were placed under many legal restrictions, which broke away from the Orthodox Church in the seventeenth century.
[5] Youth must have its fling.

of Examining Magistrate, and he accepted it though the post was in another province and obliged him to give up the connections he had formed and to make new ones. His friends met to give him a send-off; they had a group-photograph taken and presented him with a silver cigarette-case, and he set off to his new post.

As examining magistrate Iván Ilých was just as *comme il faut*[6] and deco- 65 rous a man, inspiring general respect and capable of separating his official duties from his private life, as he had been when acting as an official on special service. His duties now as examining magistrate were far more interesting and attractive than before. In his former position it had been pleasant to wear an undress uniform made by Scharmer, and to pass through the crowd of petitioners and officials who were timorously awaiting an audience with the governor, and who envied him as with free and easy gait he went straight into his chief's private room to have a cup of tea and a cigarette with him. But not many people had then been directly dependent on him—only police officials and the sectarians when he went on special missions—and he liked to treat them politely, almost as comrades, as if he were letting them feel that he who had the power to crush them was treating them in this simple, friendly way. There were then but few such people. But now, as an examining magistrate, Iván Ilých felt that everyone without exception, even the most important and self-satisfied, was in his power, and that he need only write a few words on a sheet of paper with a certain heading, and this or that important, self-satisfied person would be brought before him in the role of an accused person or a witness, and if he did not choose to allow him to sit down, would have to stand before him and answer his questions. Iván Ilých never abused his power; he tried on the contrary to soften its expression, but the consciousness of it and of the possibility of softening its effect, supplied the chief interest and attraction of his office. In his work itself, especially in his examinations, he very soon acquired a method of eliminating all considerations irrelevant to the legal aspect of the case, and reducing even the most complicated case to a form in which it would be presented on paper only in its externals, completely excluding his personal opinion of the matter, while above all observing every prescribed formality. The work was new and Iván Ilých was one of the first men to apply the new Code of 1864.[7]

On taking up the post of examining magistrate in a new town, he made new acquaintances and connections, placed himself on a new footing, and assumed a somewhat different tone. He took up an attitude of rather dignified aloofness towards the provincial authorities, but picked out the best circle of legal gentlemen and wealthy gentry living in the town and assumed a tone of slight dissatisfaction with the government, of moderate liberalism, and of enlightened citizenship. At the same time, without at all altering the elegance of his toilet, he ceased shaving his chin and allowed his beard to grow as it pleased.

[6] Proper.
[7] Judicial procedures were reformed after the emancipation of the serfs in 1861.

Iván Ilých settled down very pleasantly in this new town. The society there, which inclined towards opposition to the Governor, was friendly, his salary was larger, and he began to play *vint*,[8] which he found added not a little to the pleasure of life, for he had a capacity for cards, played good-humouredly, and calculated rapidly and astutely, so that he usually won.

After living there for two years he met his future wife, Praskóvya Fëdorovna Míkhel, who was the most attractive, clever, and brilliant girl of the set in which he moved, and among other amusements and relaxations from his labours as examining magistrate, Iván Ilých established light and playful relations with her.

While he had been an official on special service he had been accustomed to dance, but now as an examining magistrate it was exceptional for him to do so. If he danced now, he did it as if to show that though he served under the reformed order of things, and had reached the fifth official rank, yet when it came to dancing he could do it better than most people. So at the end of an evening he sometimes danced with Praskóvya Fëdorovna, and it was chiefly during these dances that he captivated her. She fell in love with him. Iván Ilých had at first no definite intention of marrying, but when the girl fell in love with him he said to himself: "Really, why shouldn't I marry?"

Praskóvya Fëdorovna came of a good family, was not bad looking and had some little property. Iván Ilých might have aspired to a more brilliant match, but even this was good. He had his salary, and she, he hoped, would have an equal income. She was well connected, and was a sweet, pretty, and thoroughly correct young woman. To say that Iván Ilých married because he fell in love with Praskóvya Fëdorovna and found that she sympathized with his views of life would be as incorrect as to say that he married because his social circle approved of the match. He was swayed by both these considerations: the marriage gave him personal satisfaction, and at the same time it was considered the right thing by the most highly placed of his associates.

So Iván Ilých got married.

The preparations for marriage and the beginning of married life, with its conjugal caresses, the new furniture, new crockery, and new linen, were very pleasant until his wife became pregnant—so that Iván Ilých had begun to think that marriage would not impair the easy, agreeable, gay and always decorous character of his life, approved of by society and regarded by himself as natural, but would even improve it. But from the first months of his wife's pregnancy, something new, unpleasant, depressing, and unseemly, and from which there was no way of escape, unexpectedly showed itself.

His wife, without any reason—*de gaieté de coeur*[9] as Iván Ilých expressed it to himself—began to disturb the pleasure and propriety of their life. She began to be jealous without any cause, expected him to devote his whole attention to her, found fault with everything, and made coarse and ill-mannered scenes.

---

[8] A card game similar to bridge.
[9] Of a joyous heart. Iván uses the expression ironically.

At first Iván Ilých hoped to escape from the unpleasantness of this state of affairs by the same easy and decorous relation to life that had served him heretofore: he tried to ignore his wife's disagreeable moods, continued to live in his usual easy and pleasant way, invited friends to his house for a game of cards, and also tried going out to his club or spending his evenings with friends. But one day his wife began upbraiding him so vigorously, using such coarse words, and continued to abuse him every time he did not fulfil her demands, so resolutely and with such evident determination not to give way till he submitted—that is, till he stayed at home and was bored just as she was—that he became alarmed. He now realized that matrimony—at any rate with Praskóvya Fëdorovna—was not always conducive to the pleasures and amenities of life but on the contrary often infringed both comfort and propriety, and that he must therefore entrench himself against such infringement. And Iván Ilých began to seek for means of doing so. His official duties were the one thing that imposed upon Praskóvya Fëdorovna, and by means of his official work and the duties attached to it he began struggling with his wife to secure his own independence.

With the birth of their child, the attempts to feed it and the various failures 75 in doing so, and with the real and imaginary illnesses of mother and child, in which Iván Ilých's sympathy was demanded but about which he understood nothing, the need of securing for himself an existence outside his family life became still more imperative.

As his wife grew more irritable and exacting and Iván Ilých transferred the centre of gravity of his life more and more to his official work, so did he grow to like his work better and became more ambitious than before.

Very soon, within a year of his wedding, Iván Ilých had realized that marriage, though it may add some comforts to life, is in fact a very intricate and difficult affair towards which in order to perform one's duty, that is, to lead a decorous life approved of by society, one must adopt a definite attitude just as towards one's official duties.

And Iván Ilých evolved such an attitude towards married life. He only required of it those conveniences—dinner at home, housewife, and bed—which it could give him, and above all that propriety of external forms required by public opinion. For the rest he looked for lighthearted pleasure and propriety, and was very thankful when he found them, but if he met with antagonism and querulousness he at once retired into his separate fenced-off world of official duties, where he found satisfaction.

Iván Ilých was esteemed a good official, and after three years was made Assistant Public Prosecutor. His new duties, their importance, the possibility of indicting and imprisoning anyone he chose, the publicity his speeches received, and the success he had in all these things, made his work still more attractive.

More children came. His wife became more and more querulous and 80 ill-tempered, but the attitude Iván Ilých had adopted towards his home life rendered him almost impervious to her grumbling.

After seven years' service in that town he was transferred to another province as Public Prosecutor. They moved, but were short of money and his wife did not like the place they moved to. Though the salary was higher the cost of living was greater, besides which two of their children died and family life became still more unpleasant for him.

Praskóvya Fëdorovna blamed her husband for every inconvenience they encountered in their new home. Most of the conversations between husband and wife, especially as to the children's education, led to topics which recalled former disputes, and those disputes were apt to flare up again at any moment. There remained only those rare periods of amorousness which still came to them at times but did not last long. These were islets at which they anchored for a while and then again set out upon that ocean of veiled hostility which showed itself in their aloofness from one another. This aloofness might have grieved Iván Ilých had he considered that it ought not to exist, but he now regarded the position as normal, and even made it the goal at which he aimed in family life. His aim was to free himself more and more from those unpleasantnesses and to give them a semblance of harmlessness and propriety. He attained this by spending less and less time with his family, and when obliged to be at home he tried to safeguard his position by the presence of outsiders. The chief thing however was that he had his official duties. The whole interest of his life now centered in the official world and that interest absorbed him. The consciousness of his power, being able to ruin anybody he wished to ruin, the importance, even the external dignity of his entry into court, or meetings with his subordinates, his success with superiors and inferiors, and above all his masterly handling of cases, of which he was conscious—all this gave him pleasure and filled his life, together with chats with his colleagues, dinners, and bridge. So that on the whole Iván Ilých's life continued to flow as he considered it should do—pleasantly and properly.

So things continued for another seven years. His eldest daughter was already sixteen, another child had died, and only one son was left, a schoolboy and a subject of dissension. Iván Ilých wanted to put him in the School of Law, but to spite him Praskóvya Fëdorovna entered him at the High School. The daughter had been educated at home and had turned out well: the boy did not learn badly either.

CHAPTER III

So Iván Ilých lived for seventeen years after his marriage. He was already a Public Prosecutor of long standing, and had declined several proposed transfers while awaiting a more desirable post, when an unanticipated and unpleasant occurrence quite upset the peaceful course of his life. He was expecting to be offered the post of presiding judge in a University town, but Happe somehow came to the front and obtained the appointment instead. Iván Ilých became irritable, reproached Happe, and quarreled both with him and with his immediate superiors—who became colder to him and again passed him over when other appointments were made.

This was in 1880, the hardest year of Iván Ilých's life. It was then that it 85 became evident on the one hand that his salary was insufficient for them to live on, and on the other that he had been forgotten, and not only this, but that what was for him the greatest and most cruel injustice appeared to others a quite ordinary occurrence. Even his father did not consider it his duty to help him. Iván Ilých felt himself abandoned by everyone, and that they regarded his position with a salary of 3,500 rubles as quite normal and even fortunate. He alone knew that with the consciousness of the injustices done him, with his wife's incessant nagging, and with the debts he had contracted by living beyond his means, his position was far from normal.

In order to save money that summer he obtained leave of absence and went with his wife to live in the country at her brother's place.

In the country, without his work, he experienced *ennui* for the first time in his life, and not only *ennui* but intolerable depression, and he decided that it was impossible to go on living like that, and that it was necessary to take energetic measures.

Having passed a sleepless night pacing up and down the veranda, he decided to go to Petersburg and bestir himself, in order to punish those who had failed to appreciate him and to get transferred to another ministry.

Next day, despite many protests from his wife and her brother, he started for Petersburg with the sole object of obtaining a post with a salary of five thousand rubles a year. He was no longer bent on any particular department, or tendency, or kind of activity. All he now wanted was an appointment to another post with a salary of five thousand rubles, either in the administration, in the banks, with the railways, in one of the Empress Márya's Institutions,[10] or even in the customs—but it had to carry with it a salary of five thousand rubles and be in a ministry other than that in which they had failed to appreciate him.

And this quest of Iván Ilých's was crowned with remarkable and unexpected 90 success. At Kursk an acquaintance of his, F. I. Ilyín, got into the first-class carriage, sat down beside Iván Ilých, and told him of a telegram just received by the Governor of Kursk announcing that a change was about to take place in the ministry: Peter Ivánovich was to be superseded by Iván Semënovich.

The proposed change, apart from its significance for Russia, had a special significance for Iván Ilých, because by bringing forward a new man, Peter Petróvich, and consequently his friend Zachár Ivánovich, it was highly favourable for Iván Ilých, since Zachár Ivánovich was a friend and colleague of his.

In Moscow this news was confirmed, and on reaching Petersburg Iván Ilých found Zachár Ivánovich and received a definite promise of an appointment in his former Department of Justice.

A week later he telegraphed to his wife: "Zachár in Miller's place. I shall receive appointment on presentation of report."

Thanks to this change of personnel, Iván Ilých had unexpectedly obtained an appointment in his former ministry which placed him two stages above

---

[10] A charitable organization founded in the late eighteenth century by the empress Márya.

his former colleagues besides giving him five thousand rubles salary and three thousand five hundred rubles for expenses connected with his removal. All his ill humour towards his former enemies and the whole department vanished, and Iván Ilých was completely happy.

He returned to the country more cheerful and contented than he had 95 been for a long time. Praskóvya Fëdorovna also cheered up and a truce was arranged between them. Iván Ilých told of how he had been fêted by everybody in Petersburg, how all those who had been his enemies were put to shame and now fawned on him, how envious they were of his appointment, and how much everybody in Petersburg had liked him.

Praskóvya Fëdorovna listened to all this and appeared to believe it. She did not contradict anything, but only made plans for their life in the town to which they were going. Iván Ilých saw with delight that these plans were his plans, that he and his wife agreed, and that, after a stumble, his life was regaining its due and natural character of pleasant lightheartedness and decorum.

Iván Ilých had come back for a short time only, for he had to take up his new duties on the 10th of September. Moreover, he needed time to settle into the new place, to move all his belongings from the province, and to buy and order many additional things: in a word, to make such arrangements as he had resolved on, which were almost exactly what Praskóvya Fëdorovna too had decided on.

Now that everything had happened so fortunately, and that he and his wife were at one in their aims and moreover saw so little of one another, they got on together better than they had done since the first years of marriage. Iván Ilých had thought of taking his family away with him at once, but the insistence of his wife's brother and her sister-in-law, who had suddenly become particularly amiable and friendly to him and his family, induced him to depart alone.

So he departed, and the cheerful state of mind induced by his success and by the harmony between his wife and himself, the one intensifying the other, did not leave him. He found a delightful house, just the thing both he and his wife had dreamt of. Spacious, lofty reception rooms in the old style, a convenient and dignified study, rooms for his wife and daughter, a study for his son—it might have been specially built for them. Iván Ilých himself superintended the arrangements, chose the wallpapers, supplemented the furniture (preferably with antiques which he considered particularly *comme il faut*), and supervised the upholstering. Everything progressed and progressed and approached the ideal he had set himself: even when things were only half completed they exceeded his expectations. He saw what a refined and elegant character, free from vulgarity, it would all have when it was ready. On falling asleep he pictured to himself how the reception-room would look. Looking at the yet unfinished drawing-room he could see the fireplace, the screen, the what-not, the little chairs dotted here and there, the dishes and plates on the walls, and the bronzes, as they would be when everything was in place. He was pleased by the thought of how his wife and daughter, who shared his taste in this matter, would be impressed by it. They were certainly not expecting as much.

He had been particularly successful in finding, and buying cheaply, antiques which gave a particularly aristocratic character to the whole place. But in his letters he intentionally understated everything in order to be able to surprise them. All this so absorbed him that his new duties—though he liked his official work—interested him less than he had expected. Sometimes he even had moments of absent-mindedness during the Court Sessions, and would consider whether he should have straight or curved cornices for his curtains. He was so interested in it all that he often did things himself, rearranging the furniture, or rehanging the curtains. Once when mounting a step-ladder to show the upholsterer, who did not understand, how he wanted the hangings draped, he made a false step and slipped, but being a strong and agile man he clung on and only knocked his side against the knob of the window frame. The bruised place was painful but the pain soon passed, and he felt particularly bright and well just then. He wrote: "I feel fifteen years younger." He thought he would have everything ready by September, but it dragged on till mid-October. But the result was charming not only in his eyes but to everyone who saw it.

In reality it was just what is usually seen in the houses of people of moder- 100 ate means who want to appear rich, and therefore succeed only in resembling others like themselves: there were damasks, dark wood, plants, rugs, and dull and polished bronzes—all the things people of a certain class have in order to resemble other people of that class. His house was so like the others that it would never have been noticed, but to him it all seemed to be quite exceptional. He was very happy when he met his family at the station and brought them to the newly furnished house all lit up, where a footman in a white tie opened the door into the hall decorated with plants, and when they went on into the drawing room and the study uttering exclamations of delight. He conducted them everywhere, drank in their praises eagerly, and beamed with pleasure. At tea that evening, when Praskóvya Fëdorovna among other things asked him about his fall, he laughed and showed them how he had gone flying and had frightened the upholsterer.

"It's a good thing I'm a bit of an athlete. Another man might have been killed, but I merely knocked myself, just here; it hurts when it's touched, but it's passing off already—it's only a bruise."

So they began living in their new home—in which, as always happens, when they got thoroughly settled in they found they were just one room short—and with the increased income, which as always was just a little (some five hundred rubles) too little, but it was all very nice.

Things went particularly well at first, before everything was finally arranged and while something had still to be done: this thing bought, that thing ordered, another thing moved, and something else adjusted. Though there were some disputes between husband and wife, they were both so well satisfied and had so much to do that it all passed off without any serious quarrels. When nothing was left to arrange it became rather dull and something seemed to be lacking, but they were then making acquaintances, forming habits, and life was growing fuller.

Iván Ilých spent his mornings at the law court and came home to dinner, and at first he was generally in a good humour, though he occasionally
became irritable just on account of his house. (Every spot on the tablecloth or
the upholstery, and every broken window-blind string, irritated him. He had
devoted so much trouble to arranging it all that every disturbance of it distressed him.) But on the whole his life ran its course as he believed life should
do: easily, pleasantly, and decorously.

He got up at nine, drank his coffee, read the paper, and then put on his   105
undress uniform and went to the law courts. There the harness in which he
worked had already been stretched to fit him and he donned it without a hitch:
petitioners, inquiries at the chancery, the chancery itself, and the sittings public and administrative. In all this the thing was to exclude everything fresh
and vital, which always disturbs the regular course of official business, and to
admit only official relations with people, and then only on official grounds.
A man would come, for instance, wanting some information. Iván Ilých, as
one in whose sphere the matter did not lie, would have nothing to do with
him: but if the man had some business with him in his official capacity, something that could be expressed on officially stamped paper, he would do everything, positively everything he could within the limits of such relations, and
in doing so would maintain the semblance of friendly human relations, that
is, would observe the courtesies of life. As soon as the official relations ended,
so did everything else. Iván Ilých possessed this capacity to separate his real
life from the official side of affairs and not mix the two, in the highest degree,
and by long practice and natural aptitude had brought it to such a pitch that
sometimes, in the manner of a virtuoso, he would even allow himself to let the
human and official relations mingle. He let himself do this just because he felt
that he could at any time he chose resume the strictly official attitude again
and drop the human relation. And he did it all easily, pleasantly, correctly, and
even artistically. In the intervals between the sessions he smoked, drank tea,
chatted a little about politics, a little about general topics, a little about cards,
but most of all about official appointments. Tired, but with the feelings of a
virtuoso—one of the first violins who has played his part in an orchestra with
precision—he would return home to find that his wife and daughter had been
out paying calls, or had a visitor, and that his son had been to school, had done
his homework with his tutor, and was duly learning what is taught at High
Schools. Everything was as it should be. After dinner, if they had no visitors,
Iván Ilých sometimes read a book that was being much discussed at the time,
and in the evening settled down to work, that is, read official papers, compared the depositions of witnesses, and noted paragraphs of the Code applying
to them. This was neither dull nor amusing. It was dull when he might have
been playing bridge, but if no bridge was available it was at any rate better than
doing nothing or sitting with his wife. Iván Ilých's chief pleasure was giving
little dinners to which he invited men and women of good social position, and
just as his drawing-room resembled all other drawing-rooms so did his enjoyable little parties resemble all other such parties.

Once they even gave a dance. Iván Ilých enjoyed it and everything went off well, except that it led to a violent quarrel with his wife about the cakes and sweets. Praskóvya Fëdorovna had made her own plans, but Iván Ilých insisted on getting everything from an expensive confectioner and ordered too many cakes, and the quarrel occurred because some of those cakes were left over and the confectioner's bill came to forty-five rubles. It was a great and disagreeable quarrel. Praskóvya Fëdorovna called him "a fool and an imbecile," and he clutched at his head and made angry allusions to divorce.

But the dance itself had been enjoyable. The best people were there, and Iván Ilých had danced with Princess Trúfonova, a sister of the distinguished founder of the Society "Bear My Burden."

The pleasures connected with his work were pleasures of ambition; his social pleasures were those of vanity; but Iván Ilých's greatest pleasure was playing bridge. He acknowledged that whatever disagreeable incident happened in his life, the pleasure that beamed like a ray of light above everything else was to sit down to bridge with good players, not noisy partners, and of course to four-handed bridge (with five players it was annoying to have to stand out, though one pretended not to mind), to play a clever and serious game (when the cards allowed it) and then to have supper and drink a glass of wine. After a game of bridge, especially if he had won a little (to win a large sum was unpleasant), Iván Ilých went to bed in specially good humour.

So they lived. They formed a circle of acquaintances among the best people and were visited by people of importance and by young folk. In their views as to their acquaintances, husband, wife and daughter were entirely agreed, and tacitly and unanimously kept at arm's length and shook off the various shabby friends and relations who, with much show of affection, gushed into the drawing-room with its Japanese plates on the walls. Soon these shabby friends ceased to obtrude themselves and only the best people remained in the Golovíns' set.

Young men made up to Lisa, and Petríshchev, an examining magistrate and 110 Dmítri Ivanovich Petríshchev's son and sole heir, began to be so attentive to her that Iván Ilých had already spoken to Praskóvya Fëdorovna about it, and considered whether they should not arrange a party for them or get up some private theatricals.

So they lived, and all went well, without change, and life flowed pleasantly.

CHAPTER IV

They were all in good health. It could not be called ill health if Iván Ilých sometimes said that he had a queer taste in his mouth and felt some discomfort in his left side.

But this discomfort increased and, though not exactly painful, grew into a sense of pressure in his side accompanied by ill humour. And his irritability became worse and worse and began to mar the agreeable, easy, and correct life that had established itself in the Golovín family. Quarrels between husband

and wife became more and more frequent, and soon the ease and amenity disappeared and even the decorum was barely maintained. Scenes again became frequent, and very few of those islets remained on which husband and wife could meet without explosion. Praskóvya Fëdorovna now had good reason to say that her husband's temper was trying. With characteristic exaggeration she said he had always had a dreadful temper, and that it had needed all her good nature to put up with it for twenty years. It was true that now the quarrels were started by him. His bursts of temper always came just before dinner, often just as he began to eat his soup. Sometimes he noticed that a plate or dish was chipped, or the food was not right, or his son put his elbow on the table, or his daughter's hair was not done as he liked it, and for all this he blamed Praskóvya Fëdorovna. At first she retorted and said disagreeable things to him, but once or twice he fell into such a rage at the beginning of dinner that she realized it was due to some physical derangement brought on by taking food, and so she restrained herself and did not answer, but only hurried to get the dinner over. She regarded this self-restraint as highly praiseworthy. Having come to the conclusion that her husband had a dreadful temper and made her life miserable, she began to feel sorry for herself, and the more she pitied herself the more she hated her husband. She began to wish he would die; yet she did not want him to die because then his salary would cease. And this irritated her against him still more. She considered herself dreadfully unhappy just because not even his death could save her, and though she concealed her exasperation, that hidden exasperation of hers increased his irritation also.

After one scene in which Iván Ilých had been particularly unfair and after which he had said in explanation that he certainly was irritable but that it was due to his not being well, she said that if he was ill it should be attended to, and insisted on his going to see a celebrated doctor.

He went. Everything took place as he had expected and as it always does. 115 There was the usual waiting and the important air assumed by the doctor, with which he was so familiar (resembling that which he himself assumed in court), and the sounding and listening, and the questions which called for answers that were foregone conclusions and were evidently unnecessary, and the look of importance which implied that "if only you put yourself in our hands we will arrange everything—we know indubitably how it has to be done, always in the same way for everybody alike." It was all just as it was in the law courts. The doctor put on just the same air towards him as he himself put on towards an accused person.

The doctor said that so-and-so indicated that there was so-and-so inside the patient, but if the investigation of so-and-so did not confirm this, then he must assume that and that. If he assumed that and that, then . . . and so on. To Iván Ilých only one question was important: was his case serious or not? But the doctor ignored that inappropriate question. From his point of view it was not the one under consideration, the real question was to decide between a floating kidney, chronic catarrh, or appendicitis. It was not a question of Iván Ilých's life or death, but one between a floating kidney and appendicitis. And that question the doctor solved brilliantly, as it seemed to Iván Ilých, in favour of the appendix, with the reservation that should an examination of the urine give fresh indications the matter would be reconsidered. All this was just what Iván Ilých had himself brilliantly accomplished a thousand times in dealing with men on trial. The doctor summed up just as brilliantly, looking over his spectacles triumphantly and even gaily at the accused. From the doctor's summing up Iván Ilých concluded that things were bad, but that for the doctor, and perhaps for everybody else, it was a matter of indifference, though for him it was bad. And this conclusion struck him painfully, arousing in him a great feeling of pity for himself and of bitterness towards the doctor's indifference to a matter of such importance.

He said nothing of this, but rose, placed the doctor's fee on the table, and remarked with a sigh: "We sick people probably often put inappropriate questions. But tell me, in general, is this complaint dangerous, or not? . . ."

The doctor looked at him sternly over his spectacles with one eye, as if to say: "Prisoner, if you will not keep to the questions put to you, I shall be obliged to have you removed from the court."

"I have already told you what I consider necessary and proper. The analysis may show something more." And the doctor bowed.

Iván Ilých went out slowly, seated himself disconsolately in his sledge, and drove home. All the way home he was going over what the doctor had said, trying to translate those complicated, obscure, scientific phrases into plain language and find in them an answer to the question: "Is my condition bad? Is it very bad? Or is there as yet nothing much wrong?" And it seemed to him that the meaning of what the doctor had said was that it was very bad. Everything in the streets seemed depressing. The cabmen, the houses, the passersby, and the shops, were dismal. His ache, this dull gnawing ache that never ceased for a moment, seemed to have acquired a new and more serious significance from the doctor's dubious remarks. Iván Ilých now watched it with a new and oppressive feeling. 120

He reached home and began to tell his wife about it. She listened, but in the middle of his account his daughter came in with her hat on, ready to go out with her mother. She sat down reluctantly to listen to this tedious story, but could not stand it long, and her mother too did not hear him to the end.

"Well, I am very glad," she said. "Mind now to take your medicine regularly. Give me the prescription and I'll send Gerásim to the chemist's." And she went to get ready to go out.

While she was in the room Iván Ilých had hardly taken time to breathe, but he sighed deeply when she left it.

"Well," he thought, "perhaps it isn't so bad after all."

He began taking his medicine and following the doctor's directions, which had been altered after the examination of the urine. But then it happened that there was a contradiction between the indications drawn from the examination of the urine and the symptoms that showed themselves. It turned out that what was happening differed from what the doctor had told him, and that he 125 had either forgotten, or blundered, or hidden something from him. He could not, however, be blamed for that, and Iván Ilých still obeyed his orders implicitly and at first derived some comfort from doing so.

From the time of his visit to the doctor, Iván Ilých's chief occupation was the exact fulfilment of the doctor's instructions regarding hygiene and the taking of medicine, and the observation of his pain and his excretions. His chief interests came to be people's ailments and people's health. When sickness, deaths, or recoveries were mentioned in his presence, especially when the illness resembled his own, he listened with agitation which he tried to hide, asked questions, and applied what he heard to his own case.

The pain did not grow less, but Iván Ilých made efforts to force himself to think that he was better. And he could do this so long as nothing agitated him. But as soon as he had any unpleasantness with his wife, any lack of success in his official work, or held bad cards at bridge, he was at once acutely sensible of his disease. He had formerly borne such mischances, hoping soon to adjust what was wrong, to master it and attain success, or make a grand slam. But now every mischance upset him and plunged him into despair. He would say to himself: "There now, just as I was beginning to get better and the medicine had begun to take effect, comes this accursed misfortune, or unpleasantness. . . ." And he was furious with the mishap, or with the people who were causing the unpleasantness and killing him, for he felt that this fury was killing him but could not restrain it. One would have thought that it should have been clear to him that this exasperation with circumstances and people aggravated his illness, and that he ought therefore to ignore unpleasant occurrences. But he drew the very opposite conclusion: he said that he needed peace, and he watched for everything that might disturb it and became irritable at the slightest infringement of it. His condition was rendered worse by the fact that he read medical books and consulted doctors. The progress of his disease was so gradual that he could deceive himself when comparing one day with another—the difference was so slight. But when he consulted the doctors it seemed to him that he was getting worse, and even very rapidly. Yet despite this he was continually consulting them.

That month he went to see another celebrity, who told him almost the same as the first had done but put his questions rather differently, and the interview with this celebrity only increased Iván Ilých's doubts and fears. A friend of a friend of his, a very good doctor, diagnosed his illness again quite differently from the others, and though he predicted recovery, his questions and suppositions bewildered Iván Ilých still more and increased his doubts. A homeopathist diagnosed the disease in yet another way, and prescribed medicine which Iván Ilých took secretly for a week. But after a week, not feeling any improvement and having lost confidence both in the former doctor's treatment and in this one's, he became still more despondent. One day a lady acquaintance mentioned a cure effected by a wonder-working icon. Iván Ilých caught himself listening attentively and beginning to believe that it had occurred. This incident alarmed him. "Has my mind really weakened to such an extent?" he asked himself. "Nonsense! It's all rubbish. I mustn't give way to nervous fears but having chosen a doctor must keep strictly to his treatment. That is what I will do. Now it's all settled. I won't think about it, but will follow the treatment seriously till summer, and then we shall see. From now there must be no more of this wavering!" This was easy to say but impossible to carry out. The pain in his side oppressed him and seemed to grow worse and more incessant, while the taste in his mouth grew stranger and stranger. It seemed to him that his breath had a disgusting smell, and he was conscious of a loss of appetite and strength. There was no deceiving himself: something terrible, new, and more important than anything before in his life, was taking place within him of which he alone was aware. Those about him did not understand or would not understand it, but thought everything in the world was going on as usual. That tormented Iván Ilých more than anything. He saw that his household, especially his wife and daughter who were in a perfect whirl of visiting, did not understand anything of it and were annoyed that he was so depressed and so exacting, as if he were to blame for it. Though they tried to disguise it he saw that he was an obstacle in their path, and that his wife had adopted a definite line in regard to his illness and kept to it regardless of anything he said or did. Her attitude was this: "You know," she would say to her friends, "Iván Ilých can't do as other people do, and keep to the treatment prescribed for him. One day he'll take his drops and keep strictly to his diet and go to bed in good time, but the next day unless I watch him he'll suddenly forget his medicine, eat sturgeon—which is forbidden—and sit up playing cards till one o'clock in the morning."

"Oh, come, when was that?" Iván Ilých would ask in vexation. "Only once at Peter Ivánovich's."

"And yesterday with Shébek."   130

"Well, even if I hadn't stayed up, this pain would have kept me awake."

"Be that as it may you'll never get well like that, but will always make us wretched."

Praskóvya Fëdorovna's attitude to Iván Ilých's illness, as she expressed it both to others and to him, was that it was his own fault and was another of the annoyances he caused her. Iván Ilých felt that this opinion escaped her involuntarily—but that did not make it easier for him.

At the law courts too, Iván Ilých noticed, or thought he noticed, a strange attitude towards himself. It sometimes seemed to him that people were watching him inquisitively as a man whose place might soon be vacant. Then again, his friends would suddenly begin to chaff him in a friendly way about his low spirits, as if the awful, horrible, and unheard-of thing that was going on within him, incessantly gnawing at him and irresistibly drawing him away, was a very agreeable subject for jests. Schwartz in particular irritated him by his jocularity, vivacity, and *savoir-faire*, which reminded him of what he himself had been ten years ago.

Friends came to make up a set and they sat down to cards. They dealt, bend-   135
ing the new cards to soften them, and he sorted the diamonds in his hand and

found he had seven. His partner said "No trumps" and supported him with two diamonds. What more could be wished for? It ought to be jolly and lively. They would make a grand slam. But suddenly Iván Ilých was conscious of that gnawing pain, that taste in his mouth, and it seemed ridiculous that in such circumstances he should be pleased to make a grand slam.

He looked at his partner Mikháil Mikháylovich, who rapped the table with his strong hand and instead of snatching up the tricks pushed the cards courteously and indulgently towards Iván Ilých that he might have the pleasure of gathering them up without the trouble of stretching out his hand for them. "Does he think I am too weak to stretch out my arm?" thought Iván Ilých, and forgetting what he was doing he over-trumped his partner, missing the grand slam by three tricks. And what was most awful of all was that he saw how upset Mikháil Mikháylovich was about it but did not himself care. And it was dreadful to realize why he did not care.

They all saw that he was suffering and said: "We can stop if you are tired. Take a rest." Lie down? No, he was not at all tired, and he finished the rubber. All were gloomy and silent. Iván Ilých felt that he had diffused this gloom over them and could not dispel it. They had supper and went away, and Iván Ilých was left alone with the consciousness that his life was poisoned and was poisoning the lives of others, and that this poison did not weaken but penetrated more and more deeply into his whole being.

With this consciousness, and with physical pain besides the terror, he must go to bed, often to lie awake the greater part of the night. Next morning he had to get up again, dress, go to the law courts, speak, and write; or if he did not go out, spend at home those twenty-four hours a day each of which was a torture. And he had to live thus all alone on the brink of an abyss, with no one who understood or pitied him.

CHAPTER V

So one month passed and then another. Just before the New Year his brother-in-law came to town and stayed at their house. Iván Ilých was at the law courts and Praskóvya Fëdorovna had gone shopping. When Iván Ilých came home and entered his study he found his brother-in-law there—a healthy, florid man—unpacking his portmanteau himself. He raised his head on hearing Iván Ilých's footsteps and looked up at him for a moment without a word. That stare told Iván Ilých everything. His brother-in-law opened his mouth to utter an exclamation of surprise but checked himself, and that action confirmed it all.

"I have changed, eh?"

"Yes, there is a change."

And after that, try as he would to get his brother-in-law to return to the subject of his looks, the latter would say nothing about it. Praskóvya Fëdorovna came home and her brother went out to her. Iván Ilých locked the door and began to examine himself in the glass, first full face, then in profile. He took up a portrait of himself taken with his wife, and compared it with what he saw in the glass. The change in him was immense. Then he bared his arms to the elbow, looked at them, drew the sleeves down again, sat down on an ottoman, and grew blacker than night.

"No, no, this won't do!" he said to himself, and jumped up, went to the table, took up some law papers and began to read them, but could not continue. He unlocked the door and went into the reception-room. The door leading to the drawing room was shut. He approached it on tiptoe and listened.

"No, you are exaggerating!" Praskóvya Fëdorovna was saying.

"Exaggerating! Don't you see it? Why, he's a dead man! Look at his eyes— there's no light in them. But what is it that is wrong with him?" 145

"No one knows. Nikoláevich (that was another doctor) said something, but I don't know what. And Leshchetítsky (this was the celebrated specialist) said quite the contrary . . ."

Iván Ilých walked away, went to his own room, lay down, and began musing: "The kidney, a floating kidney." He recalled all the doctors had told him of how it detached itself and swayed about. And by an effort of imagination he tried to catch that kidney and arrest it and support it. So little was needed for this, it seemed to him. "No, I'll go to see Peter Ivánovich again." (That was the friend whose friend was a doctor.) He rang, ordered the carriage, and got ready to go.

"Where are you going, Jean?" asked his wife, with a specially sad and exceptionally kind look.

This exceptionally kind look irritated him. He looked morosely at her.

"I must go to see Peter Ivánovich." 150

He went to see Peter Ivánovich, and together they went to see his friend, the doctor. He was in, and Iván Ilých had a long talk with him.

Reviewing the anatomical and physiological details of what in the doctor's opinion was going on inside him, he understood it all.

There was something, a small thing, in the vermiform appendix. It might all come right. Only stimulate the energy of one organ and check the activity of another, then absorption would take place and everything would come right. He got home rather late for dinner, ate his dinner, and conversed cheerfully, but could not for a long time bring himself to go back to work in his room. At last, however, he went to his study and did what was necessary, but the consciousness that he had put something aside—an important, intimate matter which he would revert to when his work was done—never left him. When he had finished his work he remembered that this intimate matter was the thought of his vermiform appendix. But he did not give himself up to it, and went to the drawing-room for tea. There were callers there, including the examining magistrate who was a desirable match for his daughter, and they were conversing, playing the piano and singing. Iván Ilých, as Praskóvya Fëdorovna remarked, spent that evening more cheerfully than usual, but he never for a moment forgot that he had postponed the important matter of the appendix. At eleven o'clock he said good-night and went to his bedroom. Since his illness he had slept alone in a small room next to his study.

He undressed and took up a novel by Zola, but instead of reading it he fell into thought, and in his imagination that desired improvement in the vermiform appendix occurred. There was the absorption and evacuation and the reestablishment of normal activity. "Yes, that's it!" he said to himself. "One need only assist nature, that's all." He remembered his medicine, rose, took it, and lay down on his back watching for the beneficent action of the medicine and for it to lessen the pain. "I need only take it regularly and avoid all injurious influences. I am already feeling better, much better." He began touching his side: it was not painful to the touch. "There, I really don't feel it. It's much better already." He put out the light and turned on his side . . . "The appendix is getting better, absorption is occurring." Suddenly he felt the old, familiar, dull, gnawing pain, stubborn and serious. There was the same familiar loathsome taste in his mouth. His heart sank and he felt dazed. "My God! My God!" he muttered. "Again, again! and it will never cease." And suddenly the matter presented itself in a quite different aspect. "Vermiform appendix! Kidney!" he said to himself. "It's not a question of appendix or kidney, but of life and . . . death. Yes, life was there and now it is going, going and I cannot stop it. Yes. Why deceive myself? Isn't it obvious to everyone but me that I'm dying, and that it's only a question of weeks, days . . . it may happen this moment. There was light and now there is darkness. I was here and now I'm going there! Where?" A chill came over him, his breathing ceased, and he felt only the throbbing of his heart.

"When I am not, what will there be? There will be nothing. Then where shall I be when I am no more? Can this be dying? No, I don't want to!" He jumped up and tried to light the candle, felt for it with trembling hands, dropped candle and candlestick on the floor, and fell back on his pillow.

"What's the use? It makes no difference," he said to himself, staring with wide-open eyes into the darkness. "Death. Yes, death. And none of them know or wish to know it, and they have no pity for me. Now they are playing." (He heard through the door the distant sound of a song and its accompaniment.) "It's all the same to them, but they will die too! Fools! I first, and they later, but it will be the same for them. And now they are merry . . . the beasts!"

Anger choked him and he was agonizingly, unbearably miserable. "It is impossible that all men have been doomed to suffer this awful horror!" He raised himself.

"Something must be wrong. I must calm myself—must think it all over from the beginning." And he again began thinking. "Yes, the beginning of my illness: I knocked my side, but I was still quite well that day and the next. It hurt a little, then rather more. I saw the doctors, then followed despondency and anguish, more doctors, and I drew nearer to the abyss. My strength grew less and I kept coming nearer and nearer, and now I have wasted away and there is no light in my eyes. I think of the appendix—but this is death! I think of mending the appendix, and all the while here is death! Can it really be death?" Again terror seized him and he gasped for breath. He leant down and began feeling for the matches, pressing with his elbow on the stand beside the bed.

It was in his way and hurt him, he grew furious with it, pressed on it still harder, and upset it. Breathless and in despair he fell on his back, expecting death to come immediately.

Meanwhile the visitors were leaving. Praskóvya Fëdorovna was seeing them off. She heard something fall and came in.

"What has happened?"

"Nothing. I knocked it over accidentally."   160

She went out and returned with a candle. He lay there panting heavily, like a man who has run a thousand yards, and stared upwards at her with a fixed look.

"What is it, Jean?"

"No . . . o . . . thing. I upset it." ("Why speak of it? She won't understand," he thought.)

And in truth she did not understand. She picked up the stand, lit his candle, and hurried away to see another visitor off. When she came back he still lay on his back, looking upwards.

"What is it? Do you feel worse?"   165

"Yes."

She shook her head and sat down.

"Do you know, Jean, I think we must ask Leshchetítsky to come and see you here."

This meant calling in the famous specialist, regardless of expense. He smiled malignantly and said "No." She remained a little longer and then went up to him and kissed his forehead.

While she was kissing him he hated her from the bottom of his soul and   170
with difficulty refrained from pushing her away.

"Good-night. Please God you'll sleep."

"Yes."

CHAPTER VI

Iván Ilých saw that he was dying, and he was in continual despair.

In the depth of his heart he knew he was dying, but not only was he not accustomed to the thought, he simply did not and could not grasp it.

The syllogism he had learnt from Kiezewetter's Logic:[11] "Caius is a man,   175
men are mortal, therefore Caius is mortal," had always seemed to him correct as applied to Caius, but certainly not as applied to himself. That Caius—man in the abstract—was mortal, was perfectly correct, but he was not Caius, not an abstract man, but a creature quite, quite separate from all others. He had been little Ványa, with a mamma and a papa; with Mitya and Volódya, and the toys, a coachman and a nurse, afterwards with Kátenka and with all the joys, griefs, and delights of childhood, boyhood, and youth. What did Caius know

[11] Karl Kiezewetter (1766–1819), author of an outline of logic widely used in Russian schools at the time.

of the smell of that striped leather ball Ványa had been so fond of? Had Caius kissed his mother's hand like that, and did the silk of her dress rustle so for Caius? Had he rioted like that at school when the pastry was bad? Had Caius been in love like that? Could Caius preside at a session as he did? "Caius really was mortal, and it was right for him to die; but for me, little Ványa, Iván Ilých, with all my thoughts and emotions, it's altogether a different matter. It cannot be that I ought to die. That would be too terrible."

Such was his feeling.

"If I had to die like Caius I should have known it was so. An inner voice would have told me so, but there was nothing of the sort in me and I and all my friends felt that our case was quite different from that of Caius. And now here it is!" he said to himself. "It can't be. It's impossible! But here it is. How is this? How is one to understand it?"

He could not understand it, and tried to drive this false, incorrect, morbid thought away and to replace it by other proper and healthy thoughts. But that thought, and not the thought only but the reality itself, seemed to come and confront him.

And to replace that thought he called up a succession of others, hoping to find in them some support. He tried to get back into the former current of thoughts that had once screened the thought of death from him. But strange to say, all that had formerly shut off, hidden, and destroyed, his consciousness of death, no longer had that effect. Iván Ilých now spent most of his time in attempting to re-establish that old current. He would say to himself: "I will take up my duties again—after all I used to live by them." And banishing all doubts he would go to the law courts, enter into conversation with his colleagues, and sit carelessly as was his wont, scanning the crowd with a thoughtful look and leaning both his emaciated arms on the arms of his oak chair; bending over as usual to a colleague and drawing his papers nearer he would interchange whispers with him, and then suddenly raising his eyes and sitting erect would pronounce certain words and open the proceedings. But suddenly in the midst of those proceedings the pain in his side, regardless of the stage the proceedings had reached, would begin its own gnawing work. Iván Ilých would turn his attention to it and try to drive the thought of it away, but without success. *It* would come and stand before him and look at him, and he would be petrified and the light would die out of his eyes, and he would again begin asking himself whether *It* alone was true. And his colleagues and subordinates would see with surprise and distress that he, the brilliant and subtle judge, was becoming confused and making mistakes. He would shake himself, try to pull himself together, manage somehow to bring the sitting to a close, and return home with the sorrowful consciousness that his judicial labours could not as formerly hide from him what he wanted them to hide, and could not deliver him from *It*. And what was worst of all was that *It* drew his attention to itself not in order to make him take some action but only that he should look at *It*, look it straight in the face: look at it and without doing anything, suffer inexpressibly.

And to save himself from this condition Iván Ilých looked for consolations— 180 new screens—and new screens were found and for a while seemed to save him, but then they immediately fell to pieces or rather became transparent, as if *It* penetrated them and nothing could veil *It*.

In these latter days he would go into the drawing-room he had arranged— that drawing-room where he had fallen and for the sake of which (how bitterly ridiculous it seemed) he had sacrificed his life—for he knew that his illness originated with that knock. He would enter and see that something had scratched the polished table. He would look for the cause of this and find that it was the bronze ornamentation of an album, that had got bent. He would take up the expensive album which he had lovingly arranged, and feel vexed with his daughter and her friends for their untidiness—for the album was torn here and there and some of the photographs turned upside down. He would put it carefully in order and bend the ornamentation back into position. Then it would occur to him to place all those things in another corner of the room, near the plants. He could call the footman, but his daughter or wife would come to help him. They would not agree, and his wife would contradict him, and he would dispute and grow angry. But that was all right, for then he did not think about *It*. *It* was invisible.

But then, when he was moving something himself, his wife would say: "Let the servants do it. You will hurt yourself again." And suddenly *It* would flash through the screen and he would see it. It was just a flash, and he hoped it would disappear, but he would involuntarily pay attention to his side. "It sits there as before, gnawing just the same!" And he could no longer forget *It*, but could distinctly see it looking at him from behind the flowers. "What is it all for?"

"It really is so! I lost my life over that curtain as I might have done when storming a fort. Is that possible? How terrible and how stupid. It can't be true! It can't, but it is."

He would go to his study, lie down, and again be alone with *It*: face to face with *It*. And nothing could be done with *It* except to look at it and shudder.

CHAPTER VII

How it happened it is impossible to say because it came about step by step, 185 unnoticed, but in the third month of Iván Ilých's illness, his wife, his daughter, his son, his acquaintances, the doctors, the servants, and above all he himself, were aware that the whole interest he had for other people was whether he would soon vacate his place, and at last release the living from the discomfort caused by his presence and be himself released from his sufferings.

He slept less and less. He was given opium and hypodermic injections of morphine, but this did not relieve him. The dull depression he experienced in a somnolent condition at first gave him a little relief, but only as something new, afterwards it became as distressing as the pain itself or even more so.

Special foods were prepared for him by the doctors' orders, but all those foods became increasingly distasteful and disgusting to him.

For his excretions also special arrangements had to be made, and this was a torment to him every time—a torment from the uncleanliness, the unseemliness, and the smell, and from knowing that another person had to take part in it.

But just through this most unpleasant matter Iván Ilých obtained comfort. Gerásim, the butler's young assistant, always came in to carry the things out. Gerásim was a clean, fresh peasant lad, grown stout on town food and always cheerful and bright. At first the sight of him, in his clean Russian peasant costume, engaged on that disgusting task embarrassed Iván Ilých.

Once when he got up from the commode too weak to draw up his trousers, 190 he dropped into a soft armchair and looked with horror at his bare, enfeebled thighs with the muscles so sharply marked on them.

Gerásim with a firm light tread, his heavy boots emitting a pleasant smell of tar and fresh winter air, came in wearing a clean Hessian apron, the sleeves of his print shirt tucked up over his strong bare young arms; and refraining from looking at his sick master out of consideration for his feelings, and restraining the joy of life that beamed from his face, he went up to the commode.

"Gerásim!" said Iván Ilých in a weak voice.

Gerásim started, evidently afraid he might have committed some blunder, and with a rapid movement turned his fresh, kind, simple young face which just showed the first downy signs of a beard.

"Yes, sir?"

"That must be very unpleasant for you. You must forgive me. I am helpless." 195

"Oh, why, sir," and Gerásim's eyes beamed and he showed his glistening white teeth, "what's a little trouble? It's a case of illness with you, sir."

And his deft strong hands did their accustomed task, and he went out of the room stepping lightly. Five minutes later he as lightly returned.

Iván Ilých was still sitting in the same position in the armchair.

"Gerásim," he said when the latter had replaced the freshly-washed utensil. "Please come here and help me." Gerásim went up to him. "Lift me up. It is hard for me to get up, and I have sent Dmítri away."

Gerásim went up to him, grasped his master with his strong arms deftly but 200 gently, in the same way that he stepped—lifted him, supported him with one hand, and with the other drew up his trousers and would have set him down again, but Iván Ilých asked to be led to the sofa. Gerásim, without an effort and without apparent pressure, led him, almost lifting him, to the sofa and placed him on it.

"Thank you. How easily and well you do it all!"

Gerásim smiled again and turned to leave the room. But Iván Ilých felt his presence such a comfort that he did not want to let him go.

"One thing more, please move up that chair. No, the other one—under my feet. It is easier for me when my feet are raised."

Gerásim brought the chair, set it down gently in place, and raised Iván Ilých's legs on to it. It seemed to Iván Ilých that he felt better while Gerásim was holding up his legs.

"It's better when my legs are higher," he said. "Place that cushion under 205 them."

Gerásim did so. He again lifted the legs and placed them, and again Iván Ilých felt better while Gerásim held his legs. When he set them down Iván Ilých fancied he felt worse.

"Gerásim," he said. "Are you busy now?"

"Not at all, sir," said Gerásim, who had learnt from the townsfolk how to speak to gentlefolk.

"What have you still to do?"

"What have I to do? I've done everything except chopping the logs for 210 tomorrow."

"Then hold my legs up a bit higher, can you?"

"Of course I can. Why not?" And Gerásim raised his master's legs higher and Iván Ilých thought that in that position he did not feel any pain at all.

"And how about the logs?"

"Don't trouble about that, sir. There's plenty of time."

Iván Ilých told Gerásim to sit down and hold his legs, and began to talk to 215 him. And strange to say it seemed to him that he felt better while Gerásim held his legs up.

After that Iván Ilých would sometimes call Gerásim and get him to hold his legs on his shoulders, and he liked talking to him. Gerásim did it all easily, willingly, simply, and with a good nature that touched Iván Ilých. Health, strength, and vitality in other people were offensive to him, but Gerásim's strength and vitality did not mortify but soothed him.

What tormented Iván Ilých most was the deception, the lie, which for some reason they all accepted, that he was not dying but was simply ill, and that he only need keep quiet and undergo a treatment and then something very good would result. He however knew that do what they would nothing would come of it, only still more agonizing suffering and death. This deception tortured him—their not wishing to admit what they all knew and what he knew, but wanting to lie to him concerning his terrible condition, and wishing and forcing him to participate in that lie. Those lies—lies enacted over him on the eve of his death and destined to degrade this awful, solemn act to the level of their visitings, their curtains, their sturgeon for dinner—were a terrible agony for Iván Ilých. And strangely enough, many times when they were going through their antics over him he had been within a hairbreadth of calling out to them: "Stop lying! You know and I know that I am dying. Then at least stop lying about it!" But he had never had the spirit to do it. The awful, terrible act of his dying was, he could see, reduced by those about him to the level of a casual, unpleasant, and almost indecorous incident (as if someone entered a drawing-room diffusing an unpleasant odour) and this was done by that very decorum which he had served all his life long. He saw that no one felt for him, because no one even wished to grasp his position. Only Gerásim recognized it and pitied him. And so Iván Ilých felt at ease only with him. He felt comforted when Gerásim supported his legs (sometimes all night long) and refused to go to bed, saying, "Don't you worry, Iván Ilých. I'll get sleep enough later on," or when he suddenly became familiar and exclaimed: "If you weren't sick it would be another matter, but as it is, why should I grudge a little trouble?" Gerásim alone did not lie; everything showed that he alone understood the facts of the case and did not consider it necessary to disguise them, but simply felt sorry for his emaciated and enfeebled master. Once when Iván Ilých was sending him away he even said straight out: "We shall all of us die, so why should I grudge a little trouble?"—expressing the fact that he did not think his work burdensome, because he was doing it for a dying man and hoped someone would do the same for him when his time came.

Apart from this lying, or because of it, what most tormented Iván Ilých was that no one pitied him as he wished to be pitied. At certain moments after prolonged suffering he wished most of all (though he would have been ashamed to confess it) for someone to pity him as a sick child is pitied. He longed to be petted and comforted. He knew he was an important functionary, that he had a beard turning grey, and that therefore what he longed for was impossible, but still he longed for it. And in Gerásim's attitude towards him there was something akin to what he wished for, and so that attitude comforted him. Iván Ilých wanted to weep, wanted to be petted and cried over, and then his colleague Shébek would come, and instead of weeping and being petted, Iván Ilých would assume a serious, severe, and profound air, and by force of habit would express his opinion on a decision of the Court of Cassation and would stubbornly insist on that view. This falsity around him and within him did more than anything else to poison his last days.

CHAPTER VIII

It was morning. He knew it was morning because Gerásim had gone, and Peter the footman had come and put out the candles, drawn back one of the curtains, and begun quietly to tidy up. Whether it was morning or evening, Friday or Sunday, made no difference, it was all just the same: the gnawing, unmitigated, agonizing pain, never ceasing for an instant, the consciousness of life inexorably waning but not yet extinguished, that approach of that ever dreaded and hateful Death which was the only reality, and always the same falsity. What were days, weeks, hours, in such a case?

"Will you have some tea, sir?"   220

"He wants things to be regular, and wishes the gentlefolk to drink tea in the morning," thought Iván Ilých, and only said "No."

"Wouldn't you like to move onto the sofa, sir?"

"He wants to tidy up the room, and I'm in the way. I am uncleanliness and disorder," he thought, and said only:

"No, leave me alone."

The man went on bustling about. Iván Ilých stretched out his hand. Peter 225 came up, ready to help.

"What is it, sir?"

"My watch."

Peter took the watch which was close at hand and gave it to his master.

"Half-past eight. Are they up?"

"No, sir, except Vladímir Ivánich" (the son) "who has gone to school. Pra- 230
skóvya Fëdorovna ordered me to wake her if you asked for her. Shall I do so?"

"No, there's no need to." "Perhaps I'd better have some tea," he thought,
and added aloud: "Yes, bring me some tea."

Peter went to the door but Iván Ilých dreaded being left alone. "How can I
keep him here? Oh yes, my medicine." "Peter, give me my medicine." "Why
not? Perhaps it may still do me some good." He took a spoonful and swallowed it. "No, it won't help. It's all tomfoolery, all deception," he decided as
soon as he became aware of the familiar, sickly, hopeless taste. "No, I can't
believe in it any longer. But the pain, why this pain? If it would only cease just
for a moment!" And he moaned. Peter turned towards him. "It's all right. Go
and fetch me some tea."

Peter went out. Left alone Iván Ilých groaned not so much with pain, terrible
though that was, as from mental anguish. Always and for ever the same, always
these endless days and nights. If only it would come quicker! If only *what* would
come quicker? Death, darkness? . . . No, no! Anything rather than death!

When Peter returned with the tea on a tray, Iván Ilých stared at him for a
time in perplexity, not realizing who and what he was. Peter was disconcerted
by that look and his embarrassment brought Iván Ilých to himself.

"Oh, tea! All right, put it down. Only help me to wash and put on a clean shirt." 235

And Iván Ilých began to wash. With pauses for rest, he washed his hands
and then his face, cleaned his teeth, brushed his hair, and looked in the glass.
He was terrified by what he saw, especially by the limp way in which his hair
clung to his pallid forehead.

While his shirt was being changed he knew that he would be still more
frightened at the sight of his body, so he avoided looking at it. Finally he was
ready. He drew on a dressing-gown, wrapped himself in a plaid, and sat down
in the armchair to take his tea. For a moment he felt refreshed, but as soon as
he began to drink the tea he was again aware of the same taste, and the pain
also returned. He finished it with an effort, and then lay down stretching out
his legs, and dismissed Peter.

Always the same. Now a spark of hope flashes up, then a sea of despair rages,
and always pain; always pain, always despair, and always the same. When alone
he had a dreadful and distressing desire to call someone, but he knew beforehand
that with others present it would be still worse. "Another dose of morphine—to
lose consciousness. I will tell him, the doctor, that he must think of something
else. It's impossible, impossible, to go on like this."

An hour and another pass like that. But now there is a ring at the door bell.
Perhaps it's the doctor? It is. He comes in fresh, hearty, plump, and cheerful, with that look on his face that seems to say: "There now, you're in a panic
about something, but we'll arrange it all for you directly!" The doctor knows
this expression is out of place here, but he has put it on once for all and can't

take it off—like a man who has put on a frock-coat in the morning to pay a round of calls.

The doctor rubs his hands vigorously and reassuringly. 240

"Brr! How cold it is! There's such a sharp frost; just let me warm myself!" he says, as if it were only a matter of waiting till he was warm, and then he would put everything right.

"Well now, how are you?"

Iván Ilých feels that the doctor would like to say: "Well, how are our affairs?" but that even he feels that this would not do, and says instead: "What sort of a night have you had?"

Iván Ilých looks at him as much as to say: "Are you really never ashamed of lying?" But the doctor does not wish to understand this question, and Iván Ilých says: "Just as terrible as ever. The pain never leaves me and never subsides. If only something . . ."

"Yes, you sick people are always like that. . . . There, now I think I am warm 245 enough. Even Praskóvya Fёdorovna, who is so particular, could find no fault with my temperature. Well, now I can say good-morning," and the doctor presses his patient's hand.

Then, dropping his former playfulness, he begins with a most serious face to examine the patient, feeling his pulse and taking his temperature, and then begins the sounding and auscultation.

Iván Ilých knows quite well and definitely that all this is nonsense and pure deception, but when the doctor, getting down on his knee, leans over him, putting his ear first higher then lower, and performs various gymnastic movements over him with a significant expression on his face, Iván Ilých submits to it all as he used to submit to the speeches of the lawyers, though he knew very well that they were all lying and why they were lying.

The doctor, kneeling on the sofa, is still sounding him when Praskóvya Fёdorovna's silk dress rustles at the door and she is heard scolding Peter for not having let her know of the doctor's arrival.

She comes in, kisses her husband, and at once proceeds to prove that she has been up a long time already, and only owing to a misunderstanding failed to be there when the doctor arrived.

Iván Ilých looks at her, scans her all over, sets against her the whiteness and 250 plumpness and cleanness of her hands and neck, the gloss of her hair, and the sparkle of her vivacious eyes. He hates her with his whole soul. And the thrill of hatred he feels for her makes him suffer from her touch.

Her attitude towards him and his disease is still the same. Just as the doctor had adopted a certain relation to his patient which he could not abandon, so had she formed one towards him—that he was not doing something he ought to do and was himself to blame, and that she reproached him lovingly for this—and she could not now change that attitude.

"You see he doesn't listen to me and doesn't take his medicine at the proper time. And above all he lies in a position that is no doubt bad for him—with his legs up."

She described how he made Gerásim hold his legs up.

The doctor smiled with a contemptuous affability that said: "What's to be done? These sick people do have foolish fancies of that kind, but we must forgive them."

When the examination was over the doctor looked at his watch, and then Praskóvya Fëdorovna announced to Iván Ilých that it was of course as he pleased, but she had sent to-day for a celebrated specialist who would examine him and have a consultation with Michael Danílovich (their regular doctor).

"Please don't raise any objections. I am doing this for my own sake," she said ironically, letting it be felt that she was doing it all for his sake and only said this to leave him no right to refuse. He remained silent, knitting his brows. He felt that he was so surrounded and involved in a mesh of falsity that it was hard to unravel anything.

Everything she did for him was entirely for her own sake, and she told him she was doing for herself what she actually was doing for herself, as if that was so incredible that he must understand the opposite.

At half-past eleven the celebrated specialist arrived. Again the sounding began and the significant conversations in his presence and in another room, about the kidneys and the appendix, and the questions and answers, with such an air of importance that again, instead of the real question of life and death which now alone confronted him, the question arose of the kidney and appendix which were not behaving as they ought to and would now be attacked by Michael Danílovich and the specialist and forced to amend their ways.

The celebrated specialist took leave of him with a serious though not hopeless look, and in reply to the timid question Iván Ilých, with eyes glistening with fear and hope, put to him as to whether there was a chance of recovery, said that he could not vouch for it but there was a possibility. The look of hope with which Iván Ilých watched the doctor out was so pathetic that Praskóvya Fëdorovna, seeing it, even wept as she left the room to hand the doctor his fee.

The gleam of hope kindled by the doctor's encouragement did not last long. The same room, the same pictures, curtains, wall-paper, medicine bottles, were all there, and the same aching suffering body, and Iván Ilých began to moan. They gave him a subcutaneous injection and he sank into oblivion.

It was twilight when he came to. They brought him his dinner and he swallowed some beef tea with difficulty, and then everything was the same again and night was coming on.

After dinner, at seven o'clock, Praskóvya Fëdorovna came into the room in evening dress, her full bosom pushed up by her corset, and with traces of powder on her face. She had reminded him in the morning that they were going to the theater. Sarah Bernhardt was visiting the town and they had a box, which he had insisted on their taking. Now he had forgotten about it and her toilet offended him, but he concealed his vexation when he remembered that he had himself insisted on their securing a box and going because it would be an instructive and aesthetic pleasure for the children.

Praskóvya Fëdorovna came in, self-satisfied but yet with a rather guilty air. She sat down and asked how he was, but, as he saw, only for the sake of asking and not in order to learn about it, knowing that there was nothing to learn—and then went on to what she really wanted to say: that she would not on any account have gone but that the box had been taken and Helen and their daughter were going, as well as Petríshchev (the examining magistrate, their daughter's fiancé) and that it was out of the question to let them go alone; but that she would have much preferred to sit with him for a while; and he must be sure to follow the doctor's orders while she was away.

"Oh, and Fëdor Petróvich" (the fiancé) "would like to come in. May he? And Lisa?"

"All right." 265

Their daughter came in in full evening dress, her fresh young flesh exposed (making a show of that very flesh which in his own case caused so much suffering), strong, healthy, evidently in love, and impatient with illness, suffering, and death, because they interfered with her happiness.

Fëdor Petróvich came in too, in evening dress, his hair curled á la Capoul, a tight stiff collar round his long sinewy neck, an enormous white shirt-front and narrow black trousers tightly stretched over his strong thighs. He had one white glove tightly drawn on, and was holding his opera hat in his hand.

Following him the schoolboy crept in unnoticed, in a new uniform, poor little fellow, and wearing gloves. Terribly dark shadows showed under his eyes, the meaning of which Iván Ilých knew well.

His son had always seemed pathetic to him, and now it was dreadful to see the boy's frightened look of pity. It seemed to Iván Ilých that Vásya was the only one besides Gerásim who understood and pitied him.

They all sat down and again asked how he was. A silence followed. Lisa asked 270 her mother about the opera-glasses, and there was an altercation between mother and daughter as to who had taken them and where they had been put. This occasioned some unpleasantness.

Fëdor Petróvich inquired of Iván Ilých whether he had ever seen Sarah Bernhardt. Iván Ilých did not at first catch the question, but then replied: "No, have you seen her before?"

"Yes, in *Adrienne Lecouvreur*."[12]

Praskóvya Fëdorovna mentioned some roles in which Sarah Bernhardt was particularly good. Her daughter disagreed. Conversation sprang up as to the elegance and realism of her acting—the sort of conversation that is always repeated and is always the same.

In the midst of the conversation Fëdor Petróvich glanced at Iván Ilých and became silent. The others also looked at him and grew silent. Iván Ilých was staring with glittering eyes straight before him, evidently indignant with them. This had to be rectified, but it was impossible to do so. The silence had to be

---

[12] A play by the French dramatist Eugène Scribe (1791–1861).

broken, but for a time no one dared to break it and they all became afraid that the conventional deception would suddenly become obvious and the truth become plain to all. Lisa was the first to pluck up courage and break that silence, but by trying to hide what everybody was feeling, she betrayed it.

"Well, if we are going it's time to start," she said, looking at her watch, 275 a present from her father, and with a faint and significant smile at Fëdor Petróvich relating to something known only to them. She got up with a rustle of her dress.

They all rose, said good-night, and went away.

When they had gone it seemed to Iván Ilých that he felt better; the falsity had gone with them. But the pain remained—that same pain and that same fear that made everything monotonously alike, nothing harder and nothing easier. Everything was worse.

Again minute followed minute and hour followed hour. Everything remained the same and there was no cessation. And the inevitable end of it all became more and more terrible.

"Yes, send Gerásim here," he replied to a question Peter asked.

CHAPTER IX

His wife returned late at night. She came in on tiptoe, but he heard her, opened 280 his eyes, and made haste to close them again. She wished to send Gerásim away and to sit with him herself, but he opened his eyes and said: "No, go away."

"Are you in great pain?"

"Always the same."

"Take some opium."

He agreed and took some. She went away.

Till about three in the morning he was in a state of stupefied misery. It seemed 285 to him that he and his pain were being thrust into a narrow, deep black sack, but though they were pushed further and further in they could not be pushed to the bottom. And this, terrible enough in itself, was accompanied by suffering. He was frightened yet wanted to fall through the sack, he struggled but yet co-operated. And suddenly he broke through, fell, and regained consciousness. Gerásim was sitting at the foot of the bed dozing quietly and patiently, while he himself lay with his emaciated stockinged legs resting on Gerásim's shoulders; the same shaded candle was there and the same unceasing pain.

"Go away, Gerásim," he whispered.

"It's all right, sir. I'll stay a while."

"No. Go away."

He removed his legs from Gerásim's shoulders, turned sideways onto his arm, and felt sorry for himself. He only waited till Gerásim had gone into the next room and then restrained himself no longer but wept like a child. He wept on account of his helplessness, his terrible loneliness, the cruelty of man, the cruelty of God, and the absence of God.

"Why hast Thou done all this? Why hast Thou brought me here? Why, why 290
dost Thou torment me so terribly?"

He did not expect an answer and yet wept because there was no answer and
could be none. The pain again grew more acute, but he did not stir and did not
call. He said to himself: "Go on! Strike me! But what is it for? What have I done
to Thee? What is it for?"

Then he grew quiet and not only ceased weeping but even held his breath
and became all attention. It was as though he were listening not to an audible
voice but to the voice of his soul, to the current of thoughts arising within him.

"What is it you want?" was the first clear conception capable of expression
in words, that he heard.

"What do you want? What do you want?" he repeated to himself.

"What do I want? To live and not to suffer," he answered. 295

And again he listened with such concentrated attention that even his pain
did not distract him.

"To live? How?" asked his inner voice.

"Why, to live as I used to—well and pleasantly."

"As you lived before, well and pleasantly?" the voice repeated.

And in imagination he began to recall the best moments of his pleasant life. 300
But strange to say none of those best moments of his pleasant life now seemed
at all what they had then seemed—none of them except the first recollections
of childhood. There, in childhood, there had been something really pleasant
with which it would be possible to live if it could return. But the child who
had experienced that happiness existed no longer, it was like a reminiscence of
somebody else.

As soon as the period began which had produced the present Iván Ilých, all
that had then seemed joys now melted before his sight and turned into something trivial and often nasty.

And the further he departed from childhood and the nearer he came to
the present the more worthless and doubtful were the joys. This began with
the School of Law. A little that was really good was still found there—there
was lightheartedness, friendship, and hope. But in the upper classes there
had already been fewer of such good moments. Then during the first years of
his official career, when he was in the service of the Governor, some pleasant
moments again occurred: they were the memories of love for a woman. Then
all became confused and there was still less of what was good; later on again
there was still less that was good, and the further he went the less there was. His
marriage, a mere accident, then the disenchantment that followed it, his wife's
bad breath and the sensuality and hypocrisy: then that deadly official life and
those preoccupations about money, a year of it, and two, and ten, and twenty,
and always the same thing. And the longer it lasted the more deadly it became.
"It is as if I had been going downhill while I imagined I was going up. And that
is really what it was. I was going up in public opinion, but to the same extent life
was ebbing away from me. And now it is all done and there is only death."

"Then what does it mean? Why? It can't be that life is so senseless and hor-rible. But if it really has been so horrible and senseless, why must I die and die in agony? There is something wrong!"

"Maybe I did not live as I ought to have done," it suddenly occurred to him. "But how could that be, when I did everything properly?" he replied, and immediately dismissed from his mind this, the sole solution of all the riddles of life and death, as something quite impossible.

"Then what do you want now? To live? Live how? Live as you lived in the law courts when the usher proclaimed 'The judge is coming!' " "The judge is coming, the judge!" he repeated to himself. "Here he is, the judge. But I am not guilty!" he exclaimed angrily. "What is it for?" And he ceased crying, but turning his face to the wall continued to ponder on the same question: Why, and for what purpose, is there all this horror? But however much he pon-dered he found no answer. And whenever the thought occurred to him, as it often did, that it all resulted from his not having lived as he ought to have done, he at once recalled the correctness of his whole life and dismissed so strange an idea. 305

CHAPTER X

Another fortnight passed. Iván Ilých now no longer left his sofa. He would not lie in bed but lay on the sofa, facing the wall nearly all the time. He suffered ever the same unceasing agonies and in his loneliness pondered always on the same insoluble question: "What is this? Can it be that it is Death?" And the inner voice answered: "Yes, it is Death."

"Why these sufferings?" And the voice answered, "For no reason—they just are so." Beyond and besides this there was nothing.

From the very beginning of his illness, ever since he had first been to see the doctor, Iván Ilých's life had been divided between two contrary and alternat-ing moods: now it was despair and the expectation of this uncomprehended and terrible death, and now hope and an intently interested observation of the functioning of his organs. Now before his eyes there was only a kidney or an intestine that temporarily evaded its duty, and now only that incomprehen-sible and dreadful death from which it was impossible to escape.

These two states of mind had alternated from the very beginning of his ill-ness, but the further it progressed the more doubtful and fantastic became the conception of the kidney, and the more real the sense of impending death.

He had but to call to mind what he had been three months before and what he was now, to call to mind with what regularity he had been going downhill, for every possibility of hope to be shattered. 310

Latterly during that loneliness in which he found himself as he lay facing the back of the sofa, a loneliness in the midst of a populous town and sur-rounded by numerous acquaintances and relations but that yet could not have been more complete anywhere—either at the bottom of the sea or under the earth—during that terrible loneliness Iván Ilých had lived only in memories of the past. Pictures of his past rose before him one after another. They always began with what was nearest in time and then went back to what was most remote—to his childhood—and rested there. If he thought of the stewed prunes that had been offered him that day, his mind went back to the raw shrivelled French plums of his childhood, their peculiar flavor and the flow of saliva when he sucked their stones, and along with the memory of that taste came a whole series of memories of those days: his nurse, his brother, and their toys. "No, I mustn't think of that. . . . It is too painful," Iván Ilých said to himself, and brought himself back to the present—to the button on the back of the sofa and the creases in its morocco. "Morocco is expensive, but it does not wear well: there had been a quarrel about it. It was a different kind of quarrel and a different kind of morocco that time when we tore father's portfolio and were punished, and mamma brought us some tarts. . . ." And again his thoughts dwelt on his childhood, and again it was painful and he tried to banish them and fix his mind on something else.

Then again together with that chain of memories another series passed through his mind—of how his illness had progressed and grown worse. There also the further back he looked the more life there had been. There had been more of what was good in life and more of life itself. The two merged together. "Just as the pain went on getting worse and worse so my life grew worse and worse," he thought. "There is one bright spot there at the back, at the beginning of life, and afterwards all becomes blacker and blacker and proceeds more and more rapidly—in inverse ratio to the square of the distance from death," thought Iván Ilých. And the example of a stone falling downwards with increasing velocity entered his mind. Life, a series of increasing sufferings, flies, further and further towards its end—the most terrible suffering. "I am flying. . . ." He shuddered, shifted himself, and tried to resist, but was already aware that resistance was impossible, and again with eyes weary of gazing but unable to cease seeing what was before them, he stared at the back of the sofa and waited—awaiting that dreadful fall and shock and destruction.

"Resistance is impossible!" he said to himself. "If I could only understand what it is all for! But that too is impossible. An explanation would be possible if it could be said that I have not lived as I ought to. But it is impossible to say that," and he remembered all the legality, correctitude, and propriety of his life. "That at any rate can certainly not be admitted," he thought, and his lips smiled ironically as if someone could see that smile and be taken in by it. "There is no explanation! Agony, death. . . . What for?"

CHAPTER XI

Another two weeks went by in this way and during that fortnight an event occurred that Iván Ilých and his wife had desired. Petríshchev formally proposed. It happened in the evening. The next day Praskóvya Fëdorovna came into her husband's room considering how best to inform him of it, but that very night there had been a fresh change for the worse in his condition. She found him still lying on the sofa but in a different position. He lay on his back, groaning and staring fixedly straight in front of him.

She began to remind him of his medicines, but he turned his eyes towards 315 her with such a look that she did not finish what she was saying; so great an animosity, to her in particular, did that look express.

"For Christ's sake, let me die in peace!" he said.

She would have gone away, but just then their daughter came in and went up to say good morning. He looked at her as he had done at his wife, and in reply to her inquiry about his health said dryly that he would soon free them all of himself. They were both silent and after sitting with him for a while went away.

"Is it our fault?" Lisa said to her mother. "It's as if we were to blame! I am sorry for papa, but why should we be tortured?"

The doctor came at his usual time. Iván Ilých answered "Yes" and "No," never taking his angry eyes from him, and at last said: "You know you can do nothing for me, so leave me alone."

"We can ease your sufferings." 320

"You can't even do that. Let me be."

The doctor went into the drawing-room and told Praskóvya Fëdorovna that the case was very serious and that the only resource left was opium to allay her husband's sufferings, which must be terrible.

It was true, as the doctor said, that Iván Ilých's physical sufferings were terrible, but worse than the physical sufferings were his mental sufferings which were his chief torture.

His mental sufferings were due to the fact that that night, as he looked at Gerásim's sleepy, good-natured face with its prominent cheek-bones, the question suddenly occurred to him: "What if my whole life has really been wrong?"

It occurred to him that what had appeared perfectly impossible before, 325 namely that he had not spent his life as he should have done, might after all be true. It occurred to him that his scarcely perceptible attempts to struggle against what was considered good by the most highly placed people, those scarcely noticeable impulses which he had immediately suppressed, might have been the real thing, and all the rest false. And his professional duties and the whole arrangement of his life and of his family, and all his social and official interests, might all have been false. He tried to defend all those things to himself and suddenly felt the weakness of what he was defending. There was nothing to defend.

"But if that is so," he said to himself, "and I am leaving this life with the consciousness that I have lost all that was given me and it is impossible to rectify it—what then?"

He lay on his back and began to pass his life in review in quite a new way. In the morning when he saw first his footman, then his wife, then his daughter, and then the doctor, their every word and movement confirmed to him the awful truth that had been revealed to him during the night. In them he saw himself—all that for which he had lived—and saw clearly that it was not real at all, but a terrible and huge deception which had hidden both life and death.

This consciousness intensified his physical suffering tenfold. He groaned and tossed about, and pulled at his clothing which choked and stifled him. And he hated them on that account.

He was given a large dose of opium and became unconscious, but at noon his sufferings began again. He drove everybody away and tossed from side to side.

His wife came to him and said:

"Jean, my dear, do this for me. It can't do any harm and often helps. Healthy people often do it." 330

He opened his eyes wide.

"What? Take communion? Why? It's unnecessary! However. . . ."

She began to cry.

"Yes, do, my dear. I'll send for our priest. He is such a nice man."

"All right. Very well," he muttered. 335

When the priest came and heard his confession, Iván Ilých was softened and seemed to feel a relief from his doubts and consequently from his sufferings, and for a moment there came a ray of hope. He again began to think of the vermiform appendix and the possibility of correcting it. He received the sacrament with tears in his eyes.

When they laid him down again afterwards he felt a moment's ease, and the hope that he might live awoke in him again. He began to think of the operation that had been suggested to him. "To live! I want to live!" he said to himself.

His wife came in to congratulate him after his communion, and when uttering the usual conventional words she added:

"You feel better, don't you?"

Without looking at her he said "Yes." 340

Her dress, her figure, the expression of her face, the tone of her voice, all revealed the same thing. "This is wrong, it is not as it should be. All you have lived for and still live for is falsehood and deception, hiding life and death from you." And as soon as he admitted that thought, his hatred and his agonizing physical suffering again sprang up, and with that suffering a consciousness of the unavoidable, approaching end. And to this was added a new sensation of grinding shooting pain and a feeling of suffocation.

The expression of his face when he uttered that "yes" was dreadful. Having uttered it, he looked her straight in the eyes, turned on his face with a rapidity extraordinary in his weak state and shouted:

"Go away! Go away and leave me alone!"

CHAPTER XII

From that moment the screaming began that continued for three days, and was so terrible that one could not hear it through two closed doors without horror. At the moment he answered his wife he realized that he was lost, that there was no return, that the end had come, the very end, and his doubts were still unsolved and remained doubts.

"Oh! Oh! Oh!" he cried in various intonations. He had begun by screaming 345
"I won't!" and continued screaming on the letter "o."

For three whole days, during which time did not exist for him, he struggled
in that black sack into which he was being thrust by an invisible, resistless
force. He struggled as a man condemned to death struggles in the hands of
the executioner, knowing that he cannot save himself. And every moment he
felt that despite all his efforts he was drawing nearer and nearer to what terrified him. He felt that his agony was due to his being thrust into that black hole
and still more to his not being able to get right into it. He was hindered from
getting into it by his conviction that his life had been a good one. That very
justification of his life held him fast and prevented his moving forward, and it
caused him most torment of all.

Suddenly some force struck him in the chest and side, making it still harder
to breathe, and he fell through the hole and there at the bottom was a light.
What had happened to him was like the sensation one sometimes experiences
in a railway carriage when one thinks one is going backwards while one is
really going forwards and suddenly becomes aware of the real direction.

"Yes, it was all not the right thing," he said to himself, "but that's no matter.
It can be done. But what *is* the right thing?" he asked himself, and suddenly
grew quiet.

This occurred at the end of the third day, two hours before his death. Just
then his schoolboy son had crept softly in and gone up to the bedside. The
dying man was still screaming desperately and waving his arms. His hand fell
on the boy's head, and the boy caught it, pressed it to his lips, and began to cry.

At that very moment Iván Ilých fell through and caught sight of the light, 350
and it was revealed to him that though his life had not been what it should
have been, this could still be rectified. He asked himself, "What *is* the right
thing?" and grew still, listening. Then he felt that someone was kissing his
hand. He opened his eyes, looked at his son, and felt sorry for him. His wife
came up to him and he glanced at her. She was gazing at him open-mouthed,
with undried tears on her nose and cheek and a despairing look on her face.
He felt sorry for her too.

"Yes, I am making them wretched," he thought. "They are sorry, but it will be
better for them when I die." He wished to say this but had not the strength to
utter it. "Besides, why speak? I must act," he thought. With a look at his wife he
indicated his son and said: "Take him away . . . sorry for him . . . sorry for you
too. . . ." He tried to add, "forgive me," but said "forego" and waved his hand,
knowing that He whose understanding mattered would understand.

And suddenly it grew clear to him that what had been oppressing him
and would not leave him was all dropping away at once from two sides, from
ten sides, and from all sides. He was sorry for them, he must act so as not to
hurt them: release them and free himself from these sufferings. "How good
and how simple!" he thought. "And the pain?" he asked himself. "What has
become of it? Where are you, pain?"

He turned his attention to it.

"Yes, here it is. Well, what of it? Let the pain be."

"And death . . . where is it?"   355

He sought his former accustomed fear of death and did not find it. "Where is it? What death?" There was no fear because there was no death.

In place of death there was light.

"So that's what it is!" he suddenly exclaimed aloud. "What joy!"

To him all this happened in a single instant, and the meaning of that instant did not change. For those present his agony continued for another two hours. Something rattled in his throat, his emaciated body twitched, then the gasping and rattle became less and less frequent.

"It is finished!" said someone near him.   360

He heard these words and repeated them in his soul.

"Death is finished," he said to himself. "It is no more!"

He drew in a breath, stopped in the midst of a sigh, stretched out, and died.

FOR ANALYSIS

1. Discuss the evidence that Ilých's death is a moral judgment—that is, a punishment for his life.

2. Discuss "The Death of Iván Ilých" from Paul's perspective revealed in 1 Corinthians 13 (p. 1095). What accounts for the change in Ilých's attitude toward his approaching death?

3. Discuss the fact that Gerásim, Ilých's peasant servant, is more sympathetic to his condition than Ilých's family is.

4. Suggest a reason for Tolstoy's decision to begin the story immediately after Ilých's death and then move back to recount the significant episodes of his life.

MAKING ARGUMENTS

Ilých's life is described as "most simple and most ordinary and therefore most terrible" (para. 55). What is it exactly about his life that makes it so terrible? Would any life that was simple and ordinary be terrible? Make an argument for your answer to this question, with close reference to the text as support.

WRITING TOPICS

1. At the conclusion of the story, Ilých achieves peace and understanding, and the questions that have been torturing him are resolved. He realizes that "though his life had not been what it should have been, this could still be rectified" (para. 350). What does this mean?

2. In an essay, compare and contrast the attitudes of various **characters** to Ilých's mortal illness. How do his colleagues respond? His wife? His children? His servant Gerásim?

MAKING CONNECTIONS

Compare the significance of death to the **characters** in this story with the significance of death to the characters in one or both of the following works: Katherine Anne Porter's "The Jilting of Granny Weatherall" (p. 1227) and Leslie Marmon Silko's "The Man to Send Rain Clouds" (p. 1209).

KATE CHOPIN (1850–1904)

THE STORY OF AN HOUR 1894

Knowing that Mrs. Mallard was afflicted with a heart trouble, great care was taken to break to her as gently as possible the news of her husband's death.

It was her sister Josephine who told her, in broken sentences; veiled hints that revealed in half concealing. Her husband's friend Richards was there, too, near her. It was he who had been in the newspaper office when intelligence of the railroad disaster was received, with Brently Mallard's name leading the list of "killed." He had only taken the time to assure himself of its truth by a second telegram, and had hastened to forestall any less careful, less tender friend in bearing the sad message.

She did not hear the story as many women have heard the same, with a paralyzed inability to accept its significance. She wept at once, with sudden, wild abandonment, in her sister's arms. When the storm of grief had spent itself she went away to her room alone. She would have no one follow her.

There stood, facing the open window, a comfortable, roomy armchair. Into this she sank, pressed down by a physical exhaustion that haunted her body and seemed to reach into her soul.

She could see in the open square before her house the tops of trees that were 5 all aquiver with the new spring life. The delicious breath of rain was in the air. In the street below a peddler was crying his wares. The notes of a distant song which some one was singing reached her faintly, and countless sparrows were twittering in the eaves.

There were patches of blue sky showing here and there through the clouds that had met and piled one above the other in the west facing her window.

She sat with her head thrown back upon the cushion of the chair, quite motionless, except when a sob came up into her throat and shook her, as a child who had cried itself to sleep continues to sob in its dreams.

She was young, with a fair, calm face, whose lines bespoke repression and even a certain strength. But now there was a dull stare in her eyes, whose gaze was fixed away off yonder on one of those patches of blue sky. It was not a glance of reflection, but rather indicated a suspension of intelligent thought.

There was something coming to her and she was waiting for it, fearfully. What was it? She did not know; it was too subtle and elusive to name. But she felt it, creeping out of the sky, reaching toward her through the sounds, the scents, and the color that filled the air.

Now her bosom rose and fell tumultuously. She was beginning to recognize 10 this thing that was approaching to possess her, and she was striving to beat it back with her will—as powerless as her two white slender hands would have been.

When she abandoned herself a little whispered word escaped her slightly parted lips. She said it over and over under her breath: "free, free, free!" The vacant stare and the look of terror that had followed it went from her eyes. They stayed keen and bright. Her pulses beat fast, and the coursing blood warmed and relaxed every inch of her body.

She did not stop to ask if it were or were not a monstrous joy that held her. A clear and exalted perception enabled her to dismiss the suggestion as trivial.

She knew that she would weep again when she saw the kind, tender hands folded in death; the face that had never looked save with love upon her, fixed and gray and dead. But she saw beyond that bitter moment a long procession of years to come that would belong to her absolutely. And she opened and spread her arms out to them in welcome.

There would be no one to live for her during those coming years: she would live for herself. There would be no powerful will bending hers in that blind persistence with which men and women believe they have a right to impose a private will upon a fellow-creature. A kind intention or a cruel intention made the act seem no less a crime as she looked upon it in that brief moment of illumination.

And yet she had loved him—sometimes. Often she had not. What did it mat- 15
ter! What could love, the unsolved mystery, count for in face of this possession of self-assertion which she suddenly recognized as the strongest impulse of her being!

"Free! Body and soul free!" she kept whispering.

Josephine was kneeling before the closed door with her lips to the keyhole, imploring for admission. "Louise, open the door! I beg; open the door—you will make yourself ill. What are you doing, Louise? For heaven's sake open the door."

"Go away. I am not making myself ill." No; she was drinking in a very elixir of life through that open window.

Her fancy was running riot along those days ahead of her. Spring days, and summer days, and all sorts of days that would be her own. She breathed a quick prayer that life might be long. It was only yesterday she had thought with a shudder that life might be long.

She arose at length and opened the door to her sister's importunities. There 20
was a feverish triumph in her eyes, and she carried herself unwittingly like a goddess of Victory. She clasped her sister's waist, and together they descended the stairs. Richards stood waiting for them at the bottom.

Some one was opening the front door with a latchkey. It was Brently Mallard who entered, a little travel-stained, composedly carrying his gripsack and umbrella. He had been far from the scene of accident, and did not even know there had been one. He stood amazed at Josephine's piercing cry; at Richards' quick motion to screen him from the view of his wife.

But Richards was too late.

When the doctors came they said she had died of heart disease—of joy that kills.

FOR ANALYSIS

1. How does Chopin's story begin? Are we introduced to **character**, **setting**, and **plot** first, or do we find things out gradually? Does all the important action happen in the story's present, or has some already happened? What are the effects of beginning the story this way?

2. How did you feel as you read of Mrs. Mallard's reactions to the news? Did your feelings change as hers did? How did all of this make you feel about her as a person?

3. How would you describe **point of view** in this story? From what perspective is the story told? How do we know what we know? What are the effects of this use of point of view?

MAKING ARGUMENTS

Argue for or against the proposition that "The Story of an Hour" is informed by feminism. What makes Mrs. Mallard unexpectedly joyful at the initial bad news? What is it that seems to kill her? Use as evidence your observations about the text and your knowledge/research about feminist thought.

WRITING TOPIC

Write about a time in your own life when your reaction to an event was not what others might have expected it to be. What did this situation feel like? How did you deal with the fact that you were not meeting expectations? Were these expectations fair?

MAKING CONNECTIONS

What do Mrs. Mallard and the main character in Gilman's "The Yellow Wallpaper" (p. 548) have in common? How are the two **characters** different in terms of their situations and their reactions to them?

TIM O'BRIEN (B. 1946)

THE THINGS THEY CARRIED 1986

First Lieutenant Jimmy Cross carried letters from a girl named Martha, a junior at Mount Sebastian College in New Jersey. They were not love letters, but Lieutenant Cross was hoping, so he kept them folded in plastic at the bottom of his rucksack. In the late afternoon, after a day's march, he would dig his foxhole, wash his hands under a canteen, unwrap the letters, hold them with the tips of his fingers, and spend the last hour of light pretending. He would imagine romantic camping trips into the White Mountains in New Hampshire. He would sometimes taste the envelope flaps, knowing her tongue had been there. More than anything, he wanted Martha to love him as he loved her, but the letters were mostly chatty, elusive on the matter of love. She was a virgin, he was almost sure. She was an English major at Mount Sebastian, and she wrote beautifully about her professors and roommates and midterm exams, about her respect for Chaucer and her great affection for Virginia Woolf. She often quoted lines of poetry; she never mentioned the war, except to say, Jimmy, take care of yourself. The letters weighed ten ounces. They were signed "Love, Martha," but Lieutenant Cross understood that "Love" was only a way of signing and did not mean what he sometimes pretended it meant. At dusk, he would carefully return the letters to his rucksack. Slowly, a bit distracted, he would get up and move among his men, checking the perimeter, then at full dark he would return to his hole and watch the night and wonder if Martha was a virgin.

The things they carried were largely determined by necessity. Among the necessities or near necessities were P-38 can openers, pocket knives, heat tabs, wrist watches, dog tags, mosquito repellent, chewing gum, candy, cigarettes, salt tablets, packets of Kool-Aid, lighters, matches, sewing kits, Military Payment Certificates, C rations, and two or three canteens of water. Together, these items weighed between fifteen and twenty pounds, depending upon a man's habits or rate of metabolism. Henry Dobbins, who was a big man, carried extra rations; he was especially fond of canned peaches in heavy syrup over pound cake. Dave Jensen, who practiced field hygiene, carried a toothbrush, dental floss, and several hotel-size bars of soap he'd stolen on R&R[1] in Sydney, Australia. Ted Lavender, who was scared, carried tranquilizers until he was shot in the head outside the village of Than Khe in mid-April. By necessity, and because it was SOP,[2] they all carried steel helmets that weighed five pounds including the liner and camouflage cover. They carried the standard

[1] Rest and recreation.
[2] Standard operating procedure.

fatigue jackets and trousers. Very few carried underwear. On their feet they carried jungle boots—2.1 pounds—and Dave Jensen carried three pairs of socks and a can of Dr. Scholl's foot powder as a precaution against trench foot. Until he was shot, Ted Lavender carried six or seven ounces of premium dope, which for him was a necessity. Mitchell Sanders, the RTO, carried condoms. Norman Bowker carried a diary. Rat Kiley carried comic books. Kiowa, a devout Baptist, carried an illustrated New Testament that had been presented to him by his father, who taught Sunday school in Oklahoma City, Oklahoma. As a hedge against bad times, however, Kiowa also carried his grandmother's distrust of the white man, his grandfather's old hunting hatchet. Necessity dictated. Because the land was mined and booby-trapped, it was SOP for each man to carry a steel-centered, nylon-covered flak jacket, which weighed 6.7 pounds, but which on hot days seemed much heavier. Because you could die so quickly, each man carried at least one large compress bandage, usually in the helmet band for easy access. Because the nights were cold, and because the monsoons were wet, each carried a green plastic poncho that could be used as a raincoat or ground sheet or makeshift tent. With its quilted liner, the poncho weighed almost two pounds, but it was worth every ounce. In April, for instance, when Ted Lavender was shot, they used his poncho to wrap him up, then to carry him across the paddy, then to lift him into the chopper that took him away.

They were called legs or grunts.

To carry something was to "hump" it, as when Lieutenant Jimmy Cross humped his love for Martha up the hills and through the swamps. In its intransitive form, "to hump" meant "to walk," or "to march," but it implied burdens far beyond the intransitive.

Almost everyone humped photographs. In his wallet, Lieutenant Cross carried two photographs of Martha. The first was a Kodachrome snapshot signed "Love," though he knew better. She stood against a brick wall. Her eyes were gray and neutral, her lips slightly open as she stared straight-on at the camera. At night, sometimes, Lieutenant Cross wondered who had taken the picture, because he knew she had boyfriends, because he loved her so much, and because he could see the shadow of the picture taker spreading out against the brick wall. The second photograph had been clipped from the 1968 Mount Sebastian yearbook. It was an action shot—women's volleyball—and Martha was bent horizontal to the floor, reaching, the palms of her hands in sharp focus, the tongue taut, the expression frank and competitive. There was no visible sweat. She wore white gym shorts. Her legs, he thought, were almost certainly the legs of a virgin, dry and without hair, the left knee cocked and carrying her entire weight, which was just over one hundred pounds. Lieutenant Cross remembered touching that left knee. A dark theater, he remembered, and the movie was *Bonnie and Clyde*, and Martha wore a tweed skirt, and during the final scene, when he touched her knee, she turned and looked at him in a sad, sober way that made him pull his hand back, but he would always remember the feel of the tweed skirt and the knee beneath it and the sound of the gunfire that killed Bonnie and Clyde, how embarrassing it was, how slow and oppressive. He remembered kissing her good night at the dorm door. Right then, he thought, he should've done something brave. He should've carried her up the stairs to her room and tied her to the bed and touched that left knee all night long. He should've risked it. Whenever he looked at the photographs, he thought of new things he should've done.

What they carried was partly a function of rank, partly of field specialty.

As a first lieutenant and platoon leader, Jimmy Cross carried a compass, maps, code books, binoculars, and a .45-caliber pistol that weighed 2.9 pounds fully loaded. He carried a strobe light and the responsibility for the lives of his men.

As an RTO, Mitchell Sanders carried the PRC-25 radio, a killer, twenty-six pounds with its battery.

As a medic, Rat Kiley carried a canvas satchel filled with morphine and plasma and malaria tablets and surgical tape and comic books and all the things a medic must carry, including M&M's for especially bad wounds, for a total weight of nearly twenty pounds.

As a big man, therefore a machine gunner, Henry Dobbins carried the 10 M-60, which weighed twenty-three pounds unloaded, but which was almost always loaded. In addition, Dobbins carried between ten and fifteen pounds of ammunition draped in belts across his chest and shoulders.

As PFCs or Spec 4s, most of them were common grunts and carried the standard M-16 gas-operated assault rifle. The weapon weighed 7.5 pounds unloaded, 8.2 pounds with its full twenty-round magazine. Depending on numerous factors, such as topography and psychology, the riflemen carried anywhere from twelve to twenty magazines, usually in cloth bandoliers, adding on another 8.4 pounds at minimum, fourteen pounds at maximum. When it was available, they also carried M-16 maintenance gear—rods and steel brushes and swabs and tubes of LSA oil—all of which weighed about a pound. Among the grunts, some carried the M-79 grenade launcher, 5.9 pounds unloaded, a reasonably light weapon except for the ammunition, which was heavy. A single round weighed ten ounces. The typical load was twenty-five rounds. But Ted Lavender, who was scared, carried thirty-four rounds when he was shot and killed outside Than Khe, and he went down under an exceptional burden, more than twenty pounds of ammunition, plus the flak jacket and helmet and rations and water and toilet paper and tranquilizers and all the rest, plus the unweighed fear. He was dead weight. There was no twitching or flopping. Kiowa, who saw it happen, said it was like watching a rock fall, or a big sandbag or something—just boom, then down—not like the movies where the dead guy rolls around and does fancy spins and goes ass over teakettle—not like that, Kiowa said, the poor bastard just flat-fuck fell. Boom. Down. Nothing else. It was a bright morning in mid-April. Lieutenant Cross felt the pain. He blamed himself. They stripped off Lavender's canteens and ammo, all the heavy things, and Rat Kiley said the obvious, the guy's dead, and Mitchell Sanders used his radio to report one U.S. KIA and to request a chopper. Then they wrapped Lavender in his poncho. They carried him out to a dry paddy, established security, and sat smoking the dead man's dope until the chopper came. Lieutenant Cross kept to himself. He pictured Martha's smooth young face, thinking he loved her more than anything, more than his men, and now Ted Lavender was dead because he loved her so much and could not stop thinking about her. When the dust-off arrived, they carried Lavender aboard. Afterward they burned Than Khe. They marched until dusk, then dug their holes, and that night Kiowa kept explaining how you had to be there, how fast it was, how the poor guy just dropped like so much concrete. Boom-down, he said. Like cement.

In addition to the three standard weapons—the M-60, M-16, and M-79—they carried whatever presented itself, or whatever seemed appropriate as a means of killing or staying alive. They carried catch-as-catch-can. At various times, in various situations, they carried M-14s and CAR-15s and Swedish Ks and grease guns and captured AK-47s and Chi-Coms and RPGs and Simonov carbines and black-market Uzis and .38-caliber Smith & Wesson handguns and 66 mm LAWs and shotguns and silencers and blackjacks and bayonets and C-4 plastic explosives. Lee Strunk carried a slingshot; a weapon of last resort, he called it. Mitchell Sanders carried brass knuckles. Kiowa carried his grandfather's feathered hatchet. Every third or fourth man carried a Claymore antipersonnel mine—3.5 pounds with its firing device. They all carried fragmentation grenades—fourteen ounces each. They all carried at least one M-18 colored smoke grenade—twenty-four ounces. Some carried CS or tear-gas grenades. Some carried white-phosphorus grenades. They carried all they could bear, and then some, including a silent awe for the terrible power of the things they carried.

In the first week of April, before Lavender died, Lieutenant Jimmy Cross received a good-luck charm from Martha. It was a simple pebble, an ounce at most. Smooth to the touch, it was a milky-white color with flecks of orange and violet, oval-shaped, like a miniature egg. In the accompanying letter, Martha wrote that she had found the pebble on the Jersey shoreline, precisely where the land touched water at high tide, where things came together but also separated. It was this separate-but-together quality, she wrote, that had inspired her to pick up the pebble and to carry it in her breast pocket for several days, where it seemed weightless, and then to send it through the mail, by air, as a token of her truest feelings for him. Lieutenant Cross found this romantic. But he wondered what her truest feelings were, exactly, and what she meant by separate-but-together. He wondered how the tides and waves had come into play on that afternoon along the Jersey shoreline when Martha saw the pebble and bent down to rescue it from geology. He imagined bare feet. Martha was a poet, with the poet's sensibilities, and her feet would be brown and bare, the toenails unpainted, the eyes chilly and somber like the ocean in March, and though it was painful, he wondered who had been with her that afternoon. He imagined a pair of shadows moving along the strip of sand where things came together but also separated. It was phantom jealousy, he knew, but he couldn't help himself. He loved her so much. On the march, through the hot days of early April, he carried the pebble in his mouth, turning it with his tongue, tasting sea salts and moisture. His mind wandered. He had difficulty keeping his attention on the war. On occasion he would yell at his men to spread out the column, to keep their eyes open, but then he would slip away into daydreams, just pretending, walking barefoot along the Jersey shore, with Martha, carrying nothing. He would feel himself rising. Sun and waves and gentle winds, all love and lightness.

What they carried varied by mission.

When a mission took them to the mountains, they carried mosquito net- 15 ting, machetes, canvas tarps, and extra bug juice.

If a mission seemed especially hazardous, or if it involved a place they knew to be bad, they carried everything they could. In certain heavily mined AOs, where the land was dense with Toe Poppers and Bouncing Betties, they took turns humping a twenty-eight-pound mine detector. With its headphones and big sensing plate, the equipment was a stress on the lower back and shoulders, awkward to handle, often useless because of the shrapnel in the earth, but they carried it anyway, partly for safety, partly for the illusion of safety.

On ambush, or other night missions, they carried peculiar little odds and ends. Kiowa always took along his New Testament and a pair of moccasins for silence. Dave Jensen carried night-sight vitamins high in carotin. Lee Strunk carried his slingshot; ammo, he claimed, would never be a problem. Rat Kiley carried brandy and M&M's. Until he was shot, Ted Lavender carried the starlight scope, which weighed 6.3 pounds with its aluminum carrying case. Henry Dobbins carried his girlfriend's pantyhose wrapped around his neck as a comforter. They all carried ghosts. When dark came, they would move out single file across the meadows and paddies to their ambush coordinates, where they would quietly set up the Claymores and lie down and spend the night waiting.

Other missions were more complicated and required special equipment. In mid-April, it was their mission to search out and destroy the elaborate tunnel complexes in the Than Khe area south of Chu Lai. To blow the tunnels, they carried one-pound blocks of pentrite high explosives, four blocks to a man, sixty-eight pounds in all. They carried wiring, detonators, and battery-powered clackers. Dave Jensen carried earplugs. Most often, before blowing the tunnels, they were ordered by higher command to search them, which was considered bad news, but by and large they just shrugged and carried out orders. Because he was a big man, Henry Dobbins was excused from tunnel duty. The others would draw numbers. Before Lavender died there were seventeen men in the platoon, and whoever drew the number seventeen would strip off his gear and crawl in head first with a flashlight and Lieutenant Cross's

.45-caliber pistol. The rest of them would fan out as security. They would sit down or kneel, not facing the hole, listening to the ground beneath them, imagining cobwebs and ghosts, whatever was down there—the tunnel walls squeezing in—how the flashlight seemed impossibly heavy in the hand and how it was tunnel vision in the very strictest sense, compression in all ways, even time, and how you had to wiggle in—ass and elbows—a swallowed-up feeling—and how you found yourself worrying about odd things—will your flashlight go dead? Do rats carry rabies? If you screamed, how far would the sound carry? Would your buddies hear it? Would they have the courage to drag you out? In some respects, though not many, the waiting was worse than the tunnel itself. Imagination was a killer.

On April 16, when Lee Strunk drew the number seventeen, he laughed and muttered something and went down quickly. The morning was hot and very still. Not good, Kiowa said. He looked at the tunnel opening, then out across a dry paddy toward the village of Than Khe. Nothing moved. No clouds or birds or people. As they waited, the men smoked and drank Kool-Aid, not talking much, feeling sympathy for Lee Strunk but also feeling the luck of the draw. You win some, you lose some, said Mitchell Sanders, and sometimes you settle for a rain check. It was a tired line and no one laughed.

Henry Dobbins ate a tropical chocolate bar. Ted Lavender popped a tran- 20 quilizer and went off to pee.

After five minutes, Lieutenant Jimmy Cross moved to the tunnel, leaned down, and examined the darkness. Trouble, he thought—a cave-in maybe. And then suddenly, without willing it, he was thinking about Martha. The stresses and fractures, the quick collapse, the two of them buried alive under all that weight. Dense, crushing love. Kneeling, watching the hole, he tried to concentrate on Lee Strunk and the war, all the dangers, but his love was too much for him, he felt paralyzed, he wanted to sleep inside her lungs and breathe her blood and be smothered. He wanted her to be a virgin and not a virgin, all at once. He wanted to know her. Intimate secrets—why poetry? Why so sad? Why the grayness in her eyes? Why so alone? Not lonely, just alone—riding her bike across campus or sitting off by herself in the cafeteria. Even dancing, she danced alone—and it was the aloneness that filled him with love. He remembered telling her that one evening. How she nodded and looked away. And how, later, when he kissed her, she received the kiss without returning it, her eyes wide open, not afraid, not a virgin's eyes, just flat and uninvolved.

Lieutenant Cross gazed at the tunnel. But he was not there. He was buried with Martha under the white sand at the Jersey shore. They were pressed together, and the pebble in his mouth was her tongue. He was smiling. Vaguely, he was aware of how quiet the day was, the sullen paddies, yet he could not bring himself to worry about matters of security. He was beyond that. He was just a kid at war, in love. He was twenty-two years old. He couldn't help it.

A few moments later Lee Strunk crawled out of the tunnel. He came up grinning, filthy but alive. Lieutenant Cross nodded and closed his eyes while the others clapped Strunk on the back and made jokes about rising from the dead.

Worms, Rat Kiley said. Right out of the grave. Fuckin' zombie.

The men laughed. They all felt great relief. 25

Spook City, said Mitchell Sanders.

Lee Strunk made a funny ghost sound, a kind of moaning, yet very happy, and right then, when Strunk made that high happy moaning sound, when he went *Ahhooooo*, right then Ted Lavender was shot in the head on his way back from peeing. He lay with his mouth open. The teeth were broken. There was a swollen black bruise under his left eye. The cheekbone was gone. Oh shit, Rat Kiley said, the guy's dead. The guy's dead, he kept saying, which seemed profound—the guy's dead. I mean really.

The things they carried were determined to some extent by superstition. Lieutenant Cross carried his good-luck pebble. Dave Jensen carried a rabbit's foot. Norman Bowker, otherwise a very gentle person, carried a thumb that had been presented to him as a gift by Mitchell Sanders. The thumb was dark brown, rubbery to the touch, and weighed four ounces at most. It had been cut from a VC[3] corpse, a boy of fifteen or sixteen. They'd found him at the bottom of an irrigation ditch, badly burned, flies in his mouth and eyes. The boy wore black shorts and sandals. At the time of his death he had been carrying a pouch of rice, a rifle, and three magazines of ammunition.

You want my opinion, Mitchell Sanders said, there's a definite moral here.

He put his hand on the dead boy's wrist. He was quiet for a time, as if count- 30 ing a pulse, then he patted the stomach, almost affectionately, and used Kiowa's hunting hatchet to remove the thumb.

Henry Dobbins asked what the moral was.

Moral?

You know. *Moral.*

Sanders wrapped the thumb in toilet paper and handed it across to Norman Bowker. There was no blood. Smiling, he kicked the boy's head, watched the flies scatter, and said, It's like with that old TV show—Paladin. Have gun, will travel.

Henry Dobbins thought about it. 35

Yeah, well, he finally said. I don't see no moral.

There it *is*, man.

Fuck off.

They carried USO stationery and pencils and pens. They carried Sterno, safety pins, trip flares, signal flares, spools of wire, razor blades, chewing tobacco, liberated joss sticks and statuettes of the smiling Buddha, candles, grease pencils, *The Stars and Stripes,*[4] fingernail clippers, Psy Ops leaflets, bush hats, bolos, and much more. Twice a week, when the resupply choppers came in, they carried hot chow in green Mermite cans and large canvas

---

[3] Vietcong.
[4] The military's officially sanctioned overseas newspaper.

bags filled with iced beer and soda pop. They carried plastic water containers, each with a two-gallon capacity. Mitchell Sanders carried a set of starched
tiger fatigues for special occasions. Henry Dobbins carried Black Flag insecticide. Dave Jensen carried empty sandbags that could be filled at night for
added protection. Lee Strunk carried tanning lotion. Some things they carried in common. Taking turns, they carried the big PRC-77 scrambler radio,
which weighed thirty pounds with its battery. They shared the weight of
memory. They took up what others could no longer bear. Often, they carried
each other, the wounded or weak. They carried infections. They carried chess
sets, basketballs, Vietnamese-English dictionaries, insignia of rank, Bronze
Stars and Purple Hearts, plastic cards imprinted with the Code of Conduct.
They carried diseases, among them malaria and dysentery. They carried lice
and ringworm and leeches and paddy algae and various rots and molds. They
carried the land itself—Vietnam, the place, the soil—a powdery orange-red
dust that covered their boots and fatigues and faces. They carried the sky. The
whole atmosphere, they carried it, the humidity, the monsoons, the stink of
fungus and decay, all of it, they carried gravity. They moved like mules. By
daylight they took sniper fire, at night they were mortared, but it was not battle, it was just the endless march, village to village, without purpose, nothing
won or lost. They marched for the sake of the march. They plodded along
slowly, dumbly, leaning forward against the heat, unthinking, all blood and
bone, simple grunts, soldiering with their legs, toiling up the hills and down
into the paddies and across the rivers and up again and down, just humping,
one step and then the next and then another, but no volition, no will, because
it was automatic, it was anatomy, and the war was entirely a matter of posture
and carriage, the hump was everything, a kind of inertia, a kind of emptiness,
a dullness of desire and intellect and conscience and hope and human sensibility. Their principles were in their feet. Their calculations were biological. They
had no sense of strategy or mission. They searched the villages without knowing what to look for, not caring, kicking over jars of rice, frisking children and
old men, blowing tunnels, sometimes setting fires and sometimes not, then
forming up and moving on to the next village, then other villages, where it
would always be the same. They carried their own lives. The pressures were
enormous. In the heat of early afternoon, they would remove their helmets
and flak jackets, walking bare, which was dangerous but which helped ease the
strain. They would often discard things along the route of march. Purely for
comfort, they would throw away rations, blow their Claymores and grenades,
no matter, because by nightfall the resupply choppers would arrive with more
of the same, then a day or two later still more, fresh watermelons and crates of
ammunition and sunglasses and woolen sweaters—the resources were stunning—sparklers for the Fourth of July, colored eggs for Easter. It was the great
American war chest—the fruits of science, the smokestacks, the canneries, the
arsenals at Hartford, the Minnesota forests, the machine shops, the vast fields
of corn and wheat—they carried like freight trains; they carried it on their
backs and shoulders—and for all the ambiguities of Vietnam, all the mysteries

and unknowns, there was at least the single abiding certainty that they would never be at a loss for things to carry.

After the chopper took Lavender away, Lieutenant Jimmy Cross led his men 40 into the village of Than Khe. They burned everything. They shot chickens and dogs, they trashed the village well, they called in artillery and watched the wreckage, then they marched for several hours through the hot afternoon, and then at dusk, while Kiowa explained how Lavender died, Lieutenant Cross found himself trembling.

He tried not to cry. With his entrenching tool, which weighed five pounds, he began digging a hole in the earth.

He felt shame. He hated himself. He had loved Martha more than his men, and as a consequence Lavender was now dead, and this was something he would have to carry like a stone in his stomach for the rest of the war.

All he could do was dig. He used his entrenching tool like an ax, slashing, feeling both love and hate, and then later, when it was full dark, he sat at the bottom of his foxhole and wept. It went on for a long while. In part, he was grieving for Ted Lavender, but mostly it was for Martha, and for himself, because she belonged to another world, which was not quite real, and because she was a junior at Mount Sebastian College in New Jersey, a poet and a virgin and uninvolved, and because he realized she did not love him and never would.

Like cement, Kiowa whispered in the dark. I swear to God—boom-down. Not a word.

I've heard this, said Norman Bowker.   45

A pisser, you know? Still zipping himself up. Zapped while zipping.

All right, fine. That's enough.

Yeah, but you had to see it, the guy just—

I *heard*, man. Cement. So why not shut the fuck *up*?

Kiowa shook his head sadly and glanced over at the hole where Lieutenant 50 Jimmy Cross sat watching the night. The air was thick and wet. A warm, dense fog had settled over the paddies and there was the stillness that precedes rain.

After a time Kiowa sighed.

One thing for sure, he said. The Lieutenant's in some deep hurt. I mean that crying jag—the way he was carrying on—it wasn't fake or anything, it was real heavy-duty hurt. The man cares.

Sure, Norman Bowker said.

Say what you want, the man does care.

We all got problems.   55

Not Lavender.

No, I guess not, Bowker said. Do me a favor, though.

Shut up?

That's a smart Indian. Shut up.

Shrugging, Kiowa pulled off his boots. He wanted to say more, just to 60 lighten up his sleep, but instead he opened his New Testament and arranged it beneath his head as a pillow. The fog made things seem hollow and unattached. He tried not to think about Ted Lavender, but then he was thinking how fast it was, no drama, down and dead, and how it was hard to feel anything except surprise. It seemed un-Christian. He wished he could find some great sadness, or even anger, but the emotion wasn't there and he couldn't make it happen. Mostly he felt pleased to be alive. He liked the smell of the New Testament under his cheek, the leather and ink and paper and glue, whatever the chemicals were.He liked hearing the sounds of night. Even his fatigue, it felt fine, the stiff muscles and the prickly awareness of his own body, a floating feeling. He enjoyed not being dead. Lying there, Kiowa admired Lieutenant Jimmy Cross's capacity for grief. He wanted to share the man's pain, he wanted to care as Jimmy Cross cared. And yet when he closed his eyes, all he could think was Boom-down, and all he could feel was the pleasure of having his boots off and the fog curling in around him and the damp soil and the Bible smells and the plush comfort of night.

After a moment Norman Bowker sat up in the dark.

What the hell, he said. You want to talk, *talk*. Tell it to me.

Forget it.

No, man, go on. One thing I hate, it's a silent Indian.

For the most part they carried themselves with poise, a kind of dignity. 65 Now and then, however, there were times of panic, when they squealed or wanted to squeal but couldn't, when they twitched and made moaning sounds and covered their heads and said Dear Jesus and flopped around on the earth and fired their weapons blindly and cringed and sobbed and begged for the noise to stop and went wild and made stupid promises to themselves and to God and to their mothers and fathers, hoping not to die. In different ways, it happened to all of them. Afterward, when the firing ended, they would blink and peek up. They would touch their bodies, feeling shame, then quickly hiding it. They would force themselves to stand. As if in slow motion, frame by frame, the world would take on the old logic—absolute silence, then the wind, then sunlight, then voices. It was the burden of being alive. Awkwardly, the men would reassemble themselves, first in private, then in groups, becoming soldiers again. They would repair the leaks in their eyes. They would check for casualties, call in dust-offs, light cigarettes, try to smile, clear their throats and spit and begin cleaning their weapons. After a time someone would shake his head and say, No lie, I almost shit my pants, and someone else would laugh, which meant it was bad, yes, but the guy had obviously not shit his pants, it wasn't that bad, and in any case nobody would ever do such a thing and then go ahead and talk about it. They would squint into the dense, oppressive sunlight. For a few moments, perhaps, they would fall silent, lighting a joint and tracking its passage from man to man, inhaling, holding in the humiliation. Scary stuff, one of them might say. But then someone else would grin or flick his eyebrows and say, Roger-dodger, almost cut me a new asshole, *almost*.

There were numerous such poses. Some carried themselves with a sort of wistful resignation, others with pride or stiff soldierly discipline or good humor or macho zeal. They were afraid of dying but they were even more afraid to show it.

They found jokes to tell.

They used a hard vocabulary to contain the terrible softness. *Greased*, they'd say. *Offed, lit up, zapped while zipping*. It wasn't cruelty, just stage presence. They were actors and the war came at them in 3-D. When someone died, it wasn't quite dying, because in a curious way it seemed scripted, and because they had their lines mostly memorized, irony mixed with tragedy, and because they called it by other names, as if to encyst and destroy the reality of death itself. They kicked corpses. They cut off thumbs. They talked grunt lingo. They told stories about Ted Lavender's supply of tranquilizers, how the poor guy didn't feel a thing, how incredibly tranquil he was.

There's a moral here, said Mitchell Sanders.

They were waiting for Lavender's chopper, smoking the dead man's dope. 70

The moral's pretty obvious, Sanders said, and winked. Stay away from drugs. No joke, they'll ruin your day every time.

Cute, said Henry Dobbins.

Mind-blower, get it? Talk about wiggy—nothing left, just blood and brains.

They made themselves laugh.

There it is, they'd say, over and over, as if the repetition itself were an act 75 of poise, a balance between crazy and almost crazy, knowing without going. There it is, which meant be cool, let it ride, because oh yeah, man, you can't change what can't be changed, there it is, there it absolutely and positively and fucking well *is*.

They were tough.

They carried all the emotional baggage of men who might die. Grief, terror, love, longing—these were intangibles, but the intangibles had their own mass and specific gravity, they had tangible weight. They carried shameful memories. They carried the common secret of cowardice barely restrained, the instinct to run or freeze or hide, and in many respects this was the heaviest burden of all, for it could never be put down, it required perfect balance and perfect posture. They carried their reputations. They carried the soldier's greatest fear, which was the fear of blushing. Men killed, and died, because they were embarrassed not to. It was what had brought them to the war in the first place, nothing positive, no dreams of glory or honor, just to avoid the blush of dishonor. They died so as not to die of embarrassment. They crawled into tunnels and walked point and advanced under fire. Each morning, despite the unknowns, they made their legs move. They endured. They kept humping. They did not submit to the obvious alternative, which was simply to close the eyes and fall. So easy, really. Go limp and tumble to the ground and let the muscles unwind and not speak and not budge until your buddies picked you up and lifted you into the chopper that would roar and dip its nose and carry you off to the world. A mere matter of falling, yet no one ever fell. It was not courage, exactly; the object was not valor. Rather, they were too frightened to be cowards.

By and large they carried these things inside, maintaining the masks of composure. They sneered at sick call. They spoke bitterly about guys who had found release by shooting off their own toes or fingers. Pussies, they'd say. Candyasses. It was fierce, mocking talk, with only a trace of envy or awe, but even so, the image played itself out behind their eyes.

They imagined the muzzle against flesh. They imagined the quick, sweet pain, then the evacuation to Japan, then a hospital with warm beds and cute geisha nurses.

They dreamed of freedom birds.   80

At night, on guard, staring into the dark, they were carried away by jumbo jets. They felt the rush of takeoff. *Gone!* they yelled. And then velocity, wings and engines, a smiling stewardess—but it was more than a plane, it was a real bird, a big sleek silver bird with feathers and talons and high screeching. They were flying. The weights fell off, there was nothing to bear. They laughed and held on tight, feeling the cold slap of wind and altitude, soaring, think-ing *It's over, I'm gone!*—they were naked, they were light and free—it was all lightness, bright and fast and buoyant, light as light, a helium buzz in the brain, a giddy bubbling in the lungs as they were taken up over the clouds and the war, beyond duty, beyond gravity and mortification and global entangle-ments—*Sin loi!* they yelled, *I'm sorry, motherfuckers, but I'm out of it, I'm goofed, I'm on a space cruise, I'm gone!*—and it was a restful, disencumbered sensation, just riding the light waves, sailing that big silver freedom bird over the mountains and oceans, over America, over the farms and great sleeping cities and cemeteries and highways and the golden arches of McDonald's. It was flight, a kind of fleeing, a kind of falling, falling higher and higher, spin-ning off the edge of the earth and beyond the sun and through the vast, silent vacuum where there were no burdens and where everything weighed exactly nothing. *Gone!* they screamed, *I'm sorry but I'm gone!* And so at night, not quite dreaming, they gave themselves over to lightness, they were carried, they were purely borne.

On the morning after Ted Lavender died, First Lieutenant Jimmy Cross crouched at the bottom of his foxhole and burned Martha's letters. Then he burned the two photographs. There was a steady rain falling, which made it difficult, but he used heat tabs and Sterno to build a small fire, screening it with his body, holding the photographs over the tight blue flame with the tips of his fingers.

He realized it was only a gesture. Stupid, he thought. Sentimental, too, but mostly just stupid.

Lavender was dead. You couldn't burn the blame.

Besides, the letters were in his head. And even now, without photographs,   85
Lieutenant Cross could see Martha playing volleyball in her white gym shorts and yellow T-shirt. He could see her moving in the rain.

When the fire died out, Lieutenant Cross pulled his poncho over his shoulders and ate breakfast from a can.

There was no great mystery, he decided.

In those burned letters Martha had never mentioned the war, except to say, Jimmy, take care of yourself. She wasn't involved. She signed the letters "Love," but it wasn't love, and all the fine lines and technicalities did not matter.

The morning came up wet and blurry. Everything seemed part of everything else, the fog and Martha and the deepening rain.

It was a war, after all. 90

Half smiling, Lieutenant Jimmy Cross took out his maps. He shook his head hard, as if to clear it, then bent forward and began planning the day's march. In ten minutes, or maybe twenty, he would rouse the men and they would pack up and head west, where the maps showed the country to be green and inviting. They would do what they had always done. The rain might add some weight, but otherwise it would be one more day layered upon all the other days.

He was realistic about it. There was that new hardness in his stomach.

No more fantasies, he told himself.

Henceforth, when he thought about Martha, it would be only to think that she belonged elsewhere. He would shut down the daydreams. This was not Mount Sebastian, it was another world, where there were no pretty poems or midterm exams, a place where men died because of carelessness and gross stupidity. Kiowa was right. Boom-down, and you were dead, never partly dead.

Briefly, in the rain, Lieutenant Cross saw Martha's gray eyes gazing back 95 at him.

He understood.

It was very sad, he thought. The things men carried inside. The things men did or felt they had to do.

He almost nodded at her, but didn't.

Instead he went back to his maps. He was now determined to perform his duties firmly and without negligence. It wouldn't help Lavender, he knew that, but from this point on he would comport himself as a soldier. He would dispose of his good-luck pebble. Swallow it, maybe, or use Lee Strunk's slingshot, or just drop it along the trail. On the march he would impose strict field discipline. He would be careful to send out flank security, to prevent straggling or bunching up, to keep his troops moving at the proper pace and at the proper interval. He would insist on clean weapons. He would confiscate the remainder of Lavender's dope. Later in the day, perhaps, he would call the men together and speak to them plainly. He would accept the blame for what had happened to Ted Lavender. He would be a man about it. He would look them in the eyes, keeping his chin level, and he would issue the new SOPs in a calm, impersonal tone of voice, an officer's voice, leaving no room for argument or discussion. Commencing immediately, he'd tell them, they would no longer abandon equipment along the route of march. They would police up their acts. They would get their shit together, and keep it together, and maintain it neatly and in good working order.

He would not tolerate laxity. He would show strength, distancing himself. 100

Among the men there would be grumbling, of course, and maybe worse, because their days would seem longer and their loads heavier, but Lieutenant Cross reminded himself that his obligation was not to be loved but to lead. He would dispense with love; it was not now a factor. And if anyone quarreled or complained, he would simply tighten his lips and arrange his shoulders in the correct command posture. He might give a curt little nod. Or he might not. He might just shrug and say Carry on, then they would saddle up and form into a column and move out toward the villages of Than Khe.

FOR ANALYSIS

1. What are the various meanings of "Things" in the title?

2. What is the **narrator's** attitude toward war? Does his attitude differ from the attitudes of the soldiers he is describing? Explain.

3. How do Lieutenant Cross's thoughts about Martha fit into the overall **thematic** pattern of the story?

4. What is the attitude of the men toward the enemy?

5. How effective do you find the cataloging of things as a way to tell this story? Explain.

MAKING ARGUMENTS

Another story in *The Things They Carried*, the book this story comes from, is entitled "How to Tell a True War Story." In it, the implicit argument is that there are different kinds of truth, and that reporting factual truth isn't always as instructive—doesn't always impart what an event or situation was like—as fiction can be. Does it matter to you if the wealth of detail in this story is accurate? Construct an argument about truth and fiction, making reference to both the story and larger ideas about these issues.

WRITING TOPIC

Discuss the meaning of heroism in this story.

MAKING CONNECTIONS

Compare and contrast O'Brien's perspective on war with Owen's in "Dulce et Decorum Est" (p. 445). Which do you find to be a more effective antiwar statement? Explain.

HELENA MARÍA VIRAMONTES (B. 1954)

THE MOTHS 1985

I was fourteen years old when Abuelita requested my help. And it seemed only fair. Abuelita had pulled me through the rages of scarlet fever by placing, removing, and replacing potato slices on the temples of my forehead; she had seen me through several whippings, an arm broken by a dare jump off Tío Enrique's toolshed, puberty, and my first lie. Really, I told Amá, it was only fair.

Not that I was her favorite granddaughter or anything special. I wasn't even pretty or nice like my older sisters and I just couldn't do the girl things they could do. My hands were too big to handle the fineries of crocheting or embroidery and I always pricked my fingers or knotted my colored threads time and time again while my sisters laughed and called me bull hands with their cute waterlike voices. So I began keeping a piece of jagged brick in my sock to bash my sisters or anyone who called me bull hands. Once, while we all sat in the bedroom, I hit Teresa on the forehead, right above her eyebrow and she ran to Amá with her mouth open, her hand over her eye while blood seeped between her fingers. I was used to the whippings by then.

I wasn't respectful either. I even went so far as to doubt the power of Abuelita's slices, the slices she said absorbed my fever. "You're still alive, aren't you?" Abuelita snapped back, her pasty gray eye beaming at me and burning holes in my suspicions. Regretful that I had let secret questions drop out of my mouth, I couldn't look into her eyes. My hands began to fan out, grow like a liar's nose until they hung by my side like low weights. Abuelita made a balm out of dried moth wings and Vicks and rubbed my hands, shaped them back to size and it was the strangest feeling. Like bones melting. Like sun shining through the darkness of your eyelids. I didn't mind helping Abuelita after that, so Amá would always send me over to her.

In the early afternoon Amá would push her hair back, hand me my sweater and shoes, and tell me to go to Mama Luna's. This was to avoid another fight and another whipping, I knew. I would deliver one last direct shot on Marisela's arm and jump out of our house, the slam of the screen door burying her cries of anger, and I'd gladly go help Abuelita plant her wild lilies or jasmine or heliotrope or cilantro or hierbabuena in red Hills Brothers coffee cans. Abuelita would wait for me at the top step of her porch holding a hammer and nail and empty coffee cans. And although we hardly spoke, hardly looked at each other as we worked over root transplants, I always felt her gray eye on me. It made me feel, in a strange sort of way, safe and guarded and not alone. Like God was supposed to make you feel.

On Abuelita's porch, I would puncture holes in the bottom of the coffee 5
cans with a nail and a precise hit of a hammer. This completed, my job was
to fill them with red clay mud from beneath her rose bushes, packing it softly,
then making a perfect hole, four fingers round, to nest a sprouting avocado
pit, or the spidery sweet potatoes that Abuelita rooted in mayonnaise jars
with toothpicks and daily water, or prickly chayotes that produced vines that
twisted and wound all over her porch pillars, crawling to the roof, up and over
the roof, and down the other side, making her small brick house look like it
was cradled within the vines that grew pear-shaped squashes ready for the
pick, ready to be steamed with onions and cheese and butter. The roots would
burst out of the rusted coffee cans and search for a place to connect. I would
then feed the seedlings with water.

But this was a different kind of help, Amá said, because Abuelita was dying.
Looking into her gray eye, then into her brown one, the doctor said it was just
a matter of days. And so it seemed only fair that these hands she had melted
and formed found use in rubbing her caving body with alcohol and mari-
huana, rubbing her arms and legs, turning her face to the window so that she
could watch the Bird of Paradise blooming or smell the scent of clove in the air.
I toweled her face frequently and held her hand for hours. Her gray wiry hair
hung over the mattress. Since I could remember, she'd kept her long hair in
braids. Her mouth was vacant and when she slept, her eyelids never closed all
the way. Up close, you could see her gray eye beaming out the window, staring
hard as if to remember everything. I never kissed her. I left the window open
when I went to the market.

Across the street from Jay's Market there was a chapel. I never knew its
denomination, but I went in just the same to search for candles. I sat down
on one of the pews because there were none. After I cleaned my fingernails,
I looked up at the high ceiling. I had forgotten the vastness of these places,
the coolness of the marble pillars and the frozen statues with blank eyes. I was
alone. I knew why I had never returned.

That was one of Apá's biggest complaints. He would pound his hands on
the table, rocking the sugar dish or spilling a cup of coffee and scream that
if I didn't go to mass every Sunday to save my goddamn sinning soul, then
I had no reason to go out of the house, period. Punto final. He would grab my
arm and dig his nails into me to make sure I understood the importance of
catechism. Did he make himself clear? Then he strategically directed his anger
at Amá for her lousy ways of bringing up daughters, being disrespectful and
unbelieving, and my older sisters would pull me aside and tell me if I didn't
get to mass right this minute, they were all going to kick the holy shit out of
me. Why am I so selfish? Can't you see what it's doing to Amá, you idiot? So
I would wash my feet and stuff them in my black Easter shoes that shone with
Vaseline, grab a missal and veil, and wave good-bye to Amá.

I would walk slowly down Lorena to First to Evergreen, counting the cracks
on the cement. On Evergreen I would turn left and walk to Abuelita's. I liked

her porch because it was shielded by the vines of the chayotes and I could get a good look at the people and car traffic on Evergreen without them knowing. I would jump up the porch steps, knock on the screen door as I wiped my feet and call Abuelita? mi Abuelita? As I opened the door and stuck my head in, I would catch the gagging scent of toasting chile on the placa. When I entered the sala, she would greet me from the kitchen, wringing her hands in her apron. I'd sit at the corner of the table to keep from being in her way. The chiles made my eyes water. Am I crying? No, Mama Luna, I'm sure not crying. I don't like going to mass, but my eyes watered anyway, the tears dropping on the tablecloth like candle wax. Abuelita lifted the burnt chiles from the fire and sprinkled water on them until the skins began to separate. Placing them in front of me, she turned to check the menudo. I peeled the skins off and put the flimsy, limp looking green and yellow chiles in the molcajete and began to crush and crush and twist and crush the heart out of the tomato, the clove of garlic, the stupid chiles that made me cry, crushed them until they turned into liquid under my bull hand. With a wooden spoon, I scraped hard to destroy the guilt, and my tears were gone. I put the bowl of chile next to a vase filled with freshly cut roses. Abuelita touched my hand and pointed to the bowl of menudo that steamed in front of me. I spooned some chile into the menudo and rolled a corn tortilla thin with the palms of my hands. As I ate, a fine Sunday breeze entered the kitchen and a rose petal calmly feathered down to the table.

I left the chapel without blessing myself and walked to Jay's. Most of the time Jay didn't have much of anything. The tomatoes were always soft and the cans of Campbell soups had rusted spots on them. There was dust on the tops of cereal boxes. I picked up what I needed: rubbing alcohol, five cans of chicken broth, a big bottle of Pine Sol. At first Jay got mad because I thought I had forgotten the money. But it was there all the time, in my back pocket.

When I returned from the market, I heard Amá crying in Abuelita's kitchen. She looked up at me with puffy eyes. I placed the bags of groceries on the table and began putting the cans of soup away. Amá sobbed quietly. I never kissed her. After a while, I patted her on the back for comfort. Finally: "¿Y mi Amá?" she asked in a whisper, then choked again and cried into her apron.

Abuelita fell off the bed twice yesterday, I said, knowing that I shouldn't have said it and wondering why I wanted to say it because it only made Amá cry harder. I guess I became angry and just so tired of the quarrels and beatings and unanswered prayers and my hands just there hanging helplessly by my side. Amá looked at me again, confused, angry, and her eyes were filled with sorrow. I went outside and sat on the porch swing and watched the people pass. I sat there until she left. I dozed off repeating the words to myself like rosary prayers: when do you stop giving when do you start giving when do you. . . . and when my hands fell from my lap, I awoke to catch them. The sun was setting, an orange glow, and I knew Abuelita was hungry.

There comes a time when the sun is defiant. Just about the time when moods change, inevitable seasons of a day, transitions from one color to another, that hour or minute or second when the sun is finally defeated, finally sinks into the realization that it cannot with all its power to heal or burn, exist forever, there comes an illumination where the sun and earth meet, a final burst of burning red orange fury reminding us that although endings are inevitable, they are necessary for rebirths, and when that time came, just when I switched on the light in the kitchen to open Abuelita's can of soup, it was probably then that she died.

The room smelled of Pine Sol and vomit and Abuelita had defecated the remains of her cancerous stomach. She had turned to the window and tried to speak, but her mouth remained open and speechless. I heard you, Abuelita, I said, stroking her cheek, I heard you. I opened the windows of the house and let the soup simmer and overboil on the stove. I turned the stove off and poured the soup down the sink. From the cabinet I got a tin basin, filled it with lukewarm water and carried it carefully to the room. I went to the linen closet and took out some modest bleached white towels. With the sacredness of a priest preparing his vestments, I unfolded the towels one by one on my shoulders. I removed the sheets and blankets from her bed and peeled off her thick flannel nightgown. I toweled her puzzled face, stretching out the wrinkles, removing the coils of her neck, toweled her shoulders and breasts. Then I changed the water. I returned to towel the creases of her stretch-marked stomach, her sporadic vaginal hairs, and her sagging thighs. I removed the lint from between her toes and noticed a mapped birthmark on the fold of her buttock. The scars on her back which were as thin as the life lines on the palms of her hands made me realize how little I really knew of Abuelita. I covered her with a thin blanket and went into the bathroom. I washed my hands, and turned on the tub faucets and watched the water pour into the tub with vitality and steam. When it was full, I turned off the water and undressed. Then, I went to get Abuelita.

She was not as heavy as I thought and when I carried her in my arms, her body fell into a V, and yet my legs were tired, shaky, and I felt as if the distance between the bedroom and bathroom was miles and years away. Amá, where are you?

I stepped into the bathtub one leg first, then the other. I bent my knees slowly to descend into the water slowly so I wouldn't scald her skin. There, there, Abuelita, I said, cradling her, smoothing her as we descended, I heard you. Her hair fell back and spread across the water like eagle's wings. The water in the tub overflowed and poured onto the tile of the floor. Then the moths came. Small, gray ones that came from her soul and out through her mouth fluttering to light, circling the single dull light bulb of the bathroom. Dying is lonely and I wanted to go to where the moths were, stay with her and plant chayotes whose vines would crawl up her fingers and into the clouds; I wanted to rest my head on her chest with her stroking my hair, telling me about the moths that lay within the soul and slowly eat the spirit up; I wanted to return to the waters of the womb with her so that we would never be alone again. I wanted. I wanted my Amá. I removed a few strands of hair from Abuelita's face and held her small light head within the hollow of my neck. The bathroom was filled with moths, and for the first time in a long time I cried, rocking us, crying for her, for me, for Amá, the sobs emerging from the depths of anguish, the misery of feeling half born, sobbing until finally the sobs rippled into circles and circles of sadness and relief. There, there, I said to Abuelita, rocking us gently, there, there.

FOR ANALYSIS

1. Why do you think the observation that the **narrator** does not kiss people is repeated?

2. Why is it important that the old person with whom the narrator connects is a woman and not a man?

3. In what ways is the grandmother's death important to the narrator? Why, when the narrator holds her body at the end of the story, does she say that she rocks "us"?

MAKING ARGUMENTS

Does the story read significantly differently if you do or don't believe that the moths at the end actually exist? How so? Make an argument one way or the other. What do you choose to believe?

WRITING TOPIC

Reread "The Moths" and keep a reading log, tracking your emotions as you go. Then reflect on what elements of the story made you feel these ways.

MAKING CONNECTIONS

1. Compare the relationships between the two elderly women and their caregivers in "The Moths" and Katherine Anne Porter's "The Jilting of Granny Weatherall" (p. 1227). How are they similar? How are they different?

2. How does telling the story of an older woman's death from her **point of view** differ from telling it from the younger woman's point of view? What effects does each have? Why do you think the authors chose to tell their stories the way they did?

THE NATURALS   2014

C aperton's stepmother, Stell, called.

"Your father," Stell said.

"Larry?" Caperton said.

"He's dying. You can say Dad."

"He's done deathbed before."

"It's different," Stell said. "The doctors agree now. And your father, well, no grand speeches about not going gentle, for one thing. For another, he looks out of it, pushed down. He shops online. He watches TV. I think you should be here."

"Command performance?"

"Don't be a crumbum."

Caperton took the short flight from O'Hare to Newark on one of the new boutique lines. Shortbread, cappuccinos, and sea-salted nuts in great jars sated travellers, gratis, at the gate. The in-flight magazine resembled an avant-garde culture journal Caperton once read with fervor. The cover depicted the airline's female pilots as cockpit kittens with tapered blazers and tilted caps. It was blunted wit, but startling for a commercial carrier. Caperton took note. Among other things, he consulted for a living. That morning, he'd been in meetings about a redo for a small chunk of lakefront. They'd discussed the placement of a Dutch-designed information kiosk; one of the city-council guys kept calling it "the koisk."

"The koisk should be closer to the embankment," the guy, a boy, bony in his dark suit, said.

"We can work on that," a rival consultant Caperton had not known would be present said. "The main thing is we're trying to tell a story here. A lakefront narrative."

Were they supposed to make bids in the room together?

"My opinions are vaguely aligned with that," Caperton said.

"But what color will the koisk be?"

Caperton felt the surge of a strange desire to shelter this apprentice politician from future displays of idiocy, as you might a defective son, though Caperton had no children. He liked kids, just not what they represented. He wasn't exactly sure what that meant, but it sounded significant, even if Daphne had finally left him over it, had a baby by herself with some Princeton-rower sperm.

Aloft in coach, Caperton found himself squeezed up against the trunk of a human sequoia. The man's white T-shirt stretched to near-transparency over his twitch-prone pecs. His hair shone aerosol gold. His cheek pulsed with each chew of a gum wad he occasionally spat into his palm and sculpted. He winked at Caperton, pressed the pink bolus flat, and slit a crude face in it with his thumbnail.

"I'm doing voodoo on the pilot."

"A good time for it," Caperton said.

"Don't be scared. The plane flies itself. I'll cure him before we land."

"I'd appreciate that."

"What brings you up into the sky today?"

"A personal matter."

"Fuck, I should hope so. Can you imagine wasting a minute of your life on something that wasn't personal? Something that didn't mean anything to you? And, I mean, especially if you're helping other people. Like a mission of mercy. That should always be personal. Otherwise you're just doing it for the likes. What's your line of work?"

"It's tricky," Caperton said. "It's kind of conceptual marketing, kind of design. I'm a free-range cultural consultant. But my passion is public space."

"Wow. Do you have all that bullshit on one business card?"

The man's enormous biceps jumped.

"Sorry," he said. "That comment was a little aggro of me. The juice does that sometimes."

"The juice?"

"I don't hide it. In my field, I don't have to. We're entertainers."

"What's your field?" Caperton asked.

"Dude, I'm a pro wrestler. What the fuck else would I be?"

"A bodybuilder?"

"Jesus, no! Those guys are pathetic narcissists. They were all abused by their fathers. Every one of them. Don't you know me? I'm the Rough Beast of Bethlehem. I wrestle on the Internet. You don't watch, I take it?"

"No," Caperton said.

"You think it's stupid."

"Not at all."

"You think that, now that we're post-kayfabe, it's ultra-moronic, right?"

"Post-kayfabe?"

"Kayfabe was the code we followed. Don't break character. Pretend it's not staged. Now we wink at the audience and they wink back."

"Oh, when did that go into effect?" Caperton said.

The Rough Beast snorted. "You don't get it at all, buddy. It's not about wrestling. It's about stories. We're storytellers."

Caperton studied him. "Somebody at my job just said that."

"It's true! You have to be able to tell the story to get people on board for anything. A soft drink, a suck sesh, elective surgery, gardening, even your thing—public space? I prefer private space, but that's cool. Anyway, nobody cares about anything if there isn't a story attached. Ask the team that wrote the Bible. Ask Vincent Allan Poe."

"But doesn't it seem kind of creepy?" Caperton said. "All of us just going around calling ourselves storytellers?"

The Rough Beast shrugged. "Well, you can be negative. That's the easy way 45 out."

Caperton thought it might be the hard way out. The Beast slipped his gum into his mouth.

"Gardening?" Caperton said, after a moment, but by then the Beast had his earbuds in.

Stell met Caperton in front of his childhood house, in Nearmont. She leaned against the doorway the way his mother once did. They were not quite the same type, but ballpark, as his father would say. Larry preferred tall, semi-controlling women with light, wavy hair. Stell preferred to smoke pot, laugh, cook, yell at Larry, read good novels, and watch her shows. She'd proved a perfect stepmother, and she and Caperton flourished in their family roles, except for the deal with the refrigerator—or, rather, Stell's deal with Caperton rummaging freely in the refrigerator. "Deal" was weak wording for it. "Nearly unassuageable rage" seemed more accurate. Stell just thought it would be better if Caperton waited outside the kitchen area. She'd be more than happy to get him whatever he wanted. It would just be better, it really would, if he waited over there at the edge or even beyond the edge of the kitchen area.

Caperton harbored a secret ancestral claim to what his forebears had known as the icebox. There had been only so much depredation and madness an American child could endure in the past century. That's why the government had invented the after-school snack. But he supposed he'd evolved. This was Stell's house now, and, whatever her idiosyncrasies about the accessibility of chilled provisions, she'd kept his father's energy up for years, saved him from a fatal spiral when Caperton's mother died, even, or especially, if she'd been his mistress at the time.

For his part, Caperton's father called Stell the Bossman. Whenever she left 50 the room he would twinkle his snow-blue eyes at Caperton and, his throat choked with affection, say, "What a goddam cunt, huh?"

Larry had been married three times, cancered twice. Now the liver, as he put it, was negotiating a severance package. Larry had spent decades on the road, and Caperton used to picture a bawdy shadow life for his father, whiskey sours at a sleek, cushioned bar, a woman with his tie in her teeth. These were bitter visions, but he knew, guiltily, that the anger wasn't really for his mother's sake. He just didn't understand why the man seemed so antsy at home, as though he couldn't enjoy even a few moments of family life, drinking hot cocoa and over-praising young Caperton's tediously improvised puppet shows or the lumpy space soldiers he pinched without talent from bright clay. Why were there so few trips to the toy store, or the zoo, or the toy store at the zoo, or, better yet, the snack stand beside the toy store at the zoo?

"First World problems," Daphne once told him.

"That's why they're so painful."

Caperton had wanted to be, with his father, a team. But Larry had a team, his work buddies, gruff chums whose cruel whinnies carried through the house those Sundays they came to watch football or smoke cigars on the patio. Like Larry, these hard cases were not gangsters but grade-school-textbook salesmen. Larry worked his regions year-round, his returns heralded by the appearance of the exquisite red-and-gold Jade Dragon takeout cartons. Every business trip ended with egg rolls and spareribs and enough monosodium glutamate to goon them all into an animate diorama of menu item No. 14: Happy Family.

His father would debrief them, long, duck-sauced fingers curled around a 55 frosted stein. He'd sing of the specialty foods of the nation—the Cincinnati chilies, avocado-and-sprout sandwiches, and spice-rubbed hams of the culinary mosaic—or describe the historic hotels he'd slept in, name the ones with the tastiest pillow mints, the fluffiest towels, the most impressive water pressure. Caperton had found receipts in his father's overcoat, though, and they all said Howard Johnson. Larry hardly mentioned the people he'd seen or what he and the other salesmen had done, unless they'd scored big on a sale. Many schools, he explained, still taught from textbooks that conjectured a moon shot. Once, he said, he told a school board in Delaware that he'd be delighted to inform Commander Neil Armstrong himself what passed for scientific knowledge in their district. Caperton and his mother whooped, and Larry grinned into his stein. A triumph for Enlightenment values, plus commission.

After Caperton's mother died, his father retired and built birdhouses for a while. He meant well, but to a grown Caperton these designs were rather Cabrini-Green-ish, huge and institutional, as though Larry meant to warehouse the local jays and sparrows in balsa-wood towers of utter marginalization. It troubled Caperton to the point that he considered talking to his father about it, but then construction halted. Crises of the body beckoned. Lung inflammations, nano-strokes, mystery cysts, myeloma scares. Caperton raced home for it all. But Larry couldn't deliver, until, apparently, now.

Caperton kissed Stell and followed her into the house, past the foyer bench and ancient wall hooks. He saw the mauve sofa where he and his father watched movies while his mother died upstairs—Westerns and sports sagas, mostly. Larry loved the one about the ancient, pretty baseball player who steps out of some Hooverville limbo to lead his club in a pennant race. Bad fuckers bribe him to tank the big game, but the hero jacks one, as Larry liked to say, into the stadium lights. Sparks shower down. The republic is renewed.

"In the book, he strikes out," Caperton once told his father.

"I know. That's why it's a stupid book. Why go through all that trouble to make a great story and then give it an ending like that? That takes real bitterness."

Caperton had said nothing, but thought there might be something brave 60 about the bitterness.

"Your father's sleeping now," Stell said. "Would you like some coffee? Maybe a sandwich?"

He noticed a new strain in Stell's face. Her hands nipped at each other like little animals. Could he stop himself even if he wanted to?

"I can make one later," Caperton said.

"I don't think that'll work. I can make one now."

"I can make it. I'll just look around in the fridge." 65

"I don't . . . that can't . . ."

"It's no problem," Caperton said.

"Just let me make you a sandwich now. No big deal."

"Exactly. I can make it, no biggie."

"But you don't know what's there." 70

"I can look."

"No, honey, please don't do this. It's hard to see what's in the fridge. The bulb is out. But I know what's there. Tell me what you want."

"I want a turkey-pastrami sandwich with capers and spicy pickles and sharp English mustard on a fresh-baked croissant."

"What?"

"Stell, just let me look in the fridge. I have a right. I was looking in that fridge 75 when you were just an old hippie in Jersey City."

Stell stared at the carpet. She looked widowed already. Caperton agreed to let her make him a turkey on wheat, which she would store until he was ready.

"I just hope there's room in the fridge," Stell said.

"Hope is what we have," Caperton said, because he was a crumbum.

Caperton stood in his old bedroom, now Stell's study. Photographs of her family—nieces, cousins, a stern, tanned uncle—covered the bookshelves. Her people were much comelier than the dough-nosed Capertons. He recognized a few of his old textbooks behind the photographs, but most of the library was Stell's, an odd mix of self-help and hard science. He pulled out one on the human genome and flipped through it, pulled out another called "Narrative Medicine: How Stories Save Lives." Stell had a master's in this discipline. She counselled doctors not to be arrogant jerks, to listen to their patients, or clients, or consumers, or whatever doctors called the people they often helped and occasionally killed. She taught patients how to craft their personal tales. It seemed both noble and, perhaps, a lot of bullshit on one card.

Now a pain sliced along his upper torso. He'd felt it before, like being cinched 80 in a hot metal belt. Sometimes the pangs brought him to his knees, left him breathless, but they always faded. Caperton wheezed and clung to a bookshelf for a moment. He was stressed, the doctor had said, because he was anxious. Or maybe the other way around.

A lakefront, he wished he'd said at the meeting, was a place where you could stroll and enjoy the sunshine and the lake. Wasn't that enough? Why bring history into it? History was slaughter and slaves. Stories were devices for deluding ourselves and others, like Larry's pillow mints.

Was this pretentious? Caperton had worried about being pretentious since college, when somebody told him he was pretentious. He knew he was just naïve. Why did he continue to struggle for perspective when others had moved on? A secret dunce gene? A genome? Maybe the scary belt that squeezed him was a warning: stop thinking your shallow thoughts.

Stay in the story, moron.

He pulled a faded red sneaker box from under the bed. Here resided all the junk, the objets d'crap of his years in this room: buttons, paper clips, lozenge tins, cassette tapes, rolling papers, a tiny airport brandy bottle, the watchband from his uncle's Seiko, guitar picks and toothpicks and a photograph of his mother leaning on the birch tree in the yard. Probably a box in Daphne's parents' house brimmed with similar detritus. A rabbit's-foot key chain, the fur dyed electric blue. A comic-book version of "The Waves." Desiccated lip balm and a plastic ruby ring.

They'd met at an office party not that many years before, traded a few catch- 85 phrases from the sitcoms of their youth. That and the sex seemed enough. But then came the dumb baby question. People thought they could work on you. Wear you down. They assumed you didn't really mean what you said.

Caperton found a condom in the shoebox, the wrapper worn and crinkled, the expiration date three or four Presidents ago, a Herbert Walker rubber, a forgotten land mine that required defusing before some innocents got maimed, or had a baby too early, led stunted lives with little chance for either of them or their issue to someday stand in a room and listen to an elected official say "koisk."

Caperton unbent a paper clip and pricked at the wrapper. He noticed something gunked on the tip of the paper clip, like tar or bong resin. How could that shit stay gooey for so long? The universe was an unanswered question. Had Caperton read that? Heard it on public radio? He couldn't track what spoke through him anymore. He moaned and held the condom up to the window. Daylight poured through the constellation of holes.

Stell stuck her head in.

"He's up," she said.

Larry sat in bed with a tablet in his lap. Caperton noticed the device first, 90 then his father's freckled stick arms and ashy cheeks.

"I'm ordering tons of garbage. Stuff for the house. Gadgets. Why not? I should get some congressional shopping medal."

"I'll make it my life's work that you get one," Caperton said.

"What *is* your life's work, anyway?"

"Stell says it's serious this time."

Larry looked down at the tablet, swiped the screen with a long, chapped finger. 95

"It's always been serious," he said. "Since you get born it's serious. I mean, I have a greater understanding now. Dying is natural. We're built to do it. We discuss this in my six-months-and-under group."

"Your what?"

"It's online. No pity parties. Death is just a part of the story."

"I thought it was the end of the story."

"Mr. Doom-and-Gloom."   100

"Jesus, Dad, you're the one in bed. What do the doctors say?"

"Have you met my doctors? They have pimples. Peach fuzz. They're all virgins."

"How do you know?"

"My tumors know."

"O.K.," Caperton said. 105

"The way you kids say O.K.," Larry said. "Sounds like it's not O.K."

"It's nice to be called a kid."

"I'm indulging you," Larry said. "Sit down."

Caperton took the rocker near the window.

"How long can you be here?" Larry said. 110

"I'll be back and forth. I'll be here."

"I realize I was the boy who cried death. I'm sorry to put you out. But I think I need you. Or Stell will need you."

"I'll be around," Caperton said. "I'll be there and back again."

"Guess you've seen all of this before."

"In this very room," Caperton said. 115

"I know," Larry said. "In this very bed."

The painting above the headboard was new, and Caperton couldn't quite tell what it depicted, with its fat swirls of white and gray. It was some kind of ship, or the spume of a whale, or a spiral-whipped wave in a storm.

Maybe it had been on the wall for a long time, but certainly not when his mother died. Or had it? He'd once been proud of the precision with which he recalled his mother's final weeks: the order of familial arrivals, their withered utterances, the last four things his mother ate (mashed potatoes, applesauce, cinnamon oatmeal, cherry ice cream, in that order), the exact position of the water pitcher on the walnut table. But now he couldn't remember if that painting had been there.

"You know," Larry said, "I had this English professor who used to talk about the death of the individual. 'The death of the individual,' he'd say. I had no idea if he was for it or against it. But at least now I know what he was talking about."

"I don't think he was talking about this."

"The hell you say," Larry said. 120

Back in his room, Caperton checked up on the lakefront. There were no new developments, just as after all these meetings there would be no new development. It was all a joke. Most of his working hours he spent tracking down his paychecks.

He composed a text to Daphne, which he still did sometimes, though she never responded, even when he lied and said that Gates Mandela McAdoo was a wonderful name for her child. Now he wrote, "Here with Larry and Stell. Not good." He erased "Not good" and replaced it with "More soon." The moment he sent it an e-mail zipped in from the airline, a survey about his flight. He was about to answer the questions when he remembered the purpose of his trip. Still, he'd rather not be rude. "Flight was great," he replied, "but I'm dealing with some difficult personal matters." Probably only robots would read the message, but sometimes it was crucial to clear the emotional desk.

He lay down on his old bed, a narrow, thin-mattressed cheapo he'd once cherished as a snuggle palace. He closed his eyes and had one of those mini-dreams he sometimes had before falling asleep. His teasers. This one featured the Rough Beast. They trudged through the rubble of a ruined city. Before them rose a bangled tower, a high, corroded structure made of pig iron, tiles, beach glass, and bottle caps. The Rough Beast paused after each step.

"Public or private?" he whispered. "Public or private?"   125

Caperton flew at the Beast, bashed him to the ground.

"That's it, baby!" the Beast cried. "Hurt my shit!"

Now there were different voices, and Caperton woke. A man who looked familiar but unplaceable stood just outside the open door.

"Hello," he said. "This must seem strange. But don't be alarmed. Stell told me to rouse you."

Stell brought out tea and joined the man on the sofa in the living room.   130
Caperton sat down on an ottoman. The man had stiff white hair, a velvet black unibrow. He jiggled Stell's hand in his lap.

"It's such a joy for me to see you again. I wish it were under better circumstances. Do you remember me?"

"You're Burt," Caperton said. "You used to come over with the other guys."

"That's right. Last time I saw you, you were yay high." Burt lifted his boot off the carpet.

"Really? That's very tiny. I must have been a barely viable fetus then."

Burt chuckled, nudged Stell.   135

"Larry said he was a tough cookie. Your father loves you, you know."

"I know."

"Do you?" Burt said.

"Maybe you know better."

"Your father's from a different generation, that's all. We weren't allowed to   140
show our emotions."

"I've met men your age who overcame that."

"Outliers," Burt said. "Or possibly fags. I always liked you, you know. Even when you were a little kid and I could tell you were judging us."

"Us?"

"The gang."

Burt pulled Stell's knuckles to his lips.   145

"Hey, pal, my father's not dead yet."

"Cool it, Omelet," Burt said. "Stell and I go back. I introduced your father to her. We're like family. Anyway, I hear you're a consultant."

"Yes."

"It's a very worthy path. I retired from the sales department about ten years after your father. Since then, I've taken up a new calling."

"What's that?"   150

"Burt's a storyteller," Stell said.

"No shit."

"I must admit it's true," Burt said. "Every Saturday I go down to the library and tell stories to the children. I'm sure I bore the pants off them, but I get a thrill."

"Tell me a story."

"Well, I don't know if this is really a good time for—"   155

"Just tell me a story."

Burt told Caperton a story. It had a boy in it, an eagle feather, a shiny blue turtle. There was an ogre in a cave. Rivers were crossed on flimsy ropes, wise witches sought for counsel, bandits hunted and rehabilitated. The blue turtle led the boy to a princess. The princess fought the ogre and saved the boy. Caperton soaked up every word and couldn't take his eyes off Burt's brow, which lifted at the close of the tale.

"Bravo," Stell said.

"Pulled that one out of my butt," Burt said.

"That's why you're a genius," Stell said. "Am I right?"   160

Caperton shrugged. "I don't know. Seemed a little cheesy to me."

"Helps if you're five," Burt said. "Not some snide turd turning forty."

Caperton stood.

"You're right, Burt. What can I say? I'm feeling peckish."

Stell shrieked. "Please, don't go in there! What do you want? I'll get your   165
sandwich! Or do you want something else? Just tell me what you want! Let me make it for you!"

Caperton opened the fridge and in the darkness saw what he wanted. What he could make. He scooped up a bag of bread, a tomato, a hard-boiled egg. Stell charged him, crumpled against his hip, wrapped up his knees. The egg flew away. Caperton slit the bread bag open with his thumbnail, balled up a soft slice of seven-grain and shoved it in his mouth. He bit into the tomato and seeds ran down his wrists, pulp splotched the wall.

"Stop!" Stell said. "What are you doing?"

"I'm having an after-school snack," Caperton snarled, and fisted up another bread ball, licked the tomato's bright wound.

"You're sick!" Stell said, and from her knees tried to shove him clear of the kitchen.

Caperton bent over her, whispered, "Thanks for the medical narrative."   170

He ripped open his shirt and crushed the mutilated tomato against his chest. Juice glistened in dark burls of hair. He thought that maybe he was about to make a serious declaration, or even try to laugh the whole thing off, when he felt a twinge, a test cinch for another spell of nervous woe. The Belt of Intermittent Sorrow, which he somehow now named the moment it went tight, squeezed him to the kitchen floor.

That night he texted Daphne: *Can't sleep in this bed. It's crazy here. Creepy. Like a bad play. Or a bad production of a good play. How is little Gates? I'm sure you're a wonderful mother. Maybe if mine hadn't died I would have felt differently. Who knows? You know I'll always love you. More later. Talk soon.*

Minutes later Caperton heard his text tone: shod hooves on cobblestones.

Let me introduce myself. My name is Miles and I'm the nanny. I was a Division II nose tackle not very long ago. If you keep texting Daphne I'll come to your house and feed you your phone. Daphne does not wish to receive messages from you, now or in the future. Good day.

Good day?

Caperton shivered in his shoddy childhood cot. *Let the sobbing begin,* he texted to himself, and sank into hard slumber beneath his dank duvet.

The next morning Caperton stood beside a taxi in the driveway. Stell gathered him in for a hug.

"I'm sorry," Caperton said, fingering the pierced condom in his pocket.

"Stop saying that. Just go see a doctor. And a therapist."

"I will. I'll be back for the weekend. I'll be back and forth."

"I know," Stell said.

Burt stood on the lawn in cop shades.

Was he protecting Stell from her hair-trigger stepson? Standing vigil for his dying amigo?

Just before coming outside, Caperton had checked on his father. Larry had maybe taken a little bit of a bad turn. He looked pretty damn sick.

"Work beckons, huh?" Larry nodded at Caperton's coat.

"Afraid so. Be here Saturday."

Caperton took his father's hand.

"Listen," Caperton said. "I realize I've been an idiot, Dad. All my pointless rage. I've wasted so much time trying to get a certain feeling back. But it's a child's feeling, and I can't have it anymore. But I love you. I really do. Know that. And let's not hold back. With the time we have, let's say everything to each other. That's all I want."

Something like a ship's light, far away, began to glow, stately and forlorn, in Larry's eyes. He gripped his son's hand harder.

"I know you're strapped for time," Larry said, his voice raspier in just the past day. "But there's this new show on cable, you really should watch it. It's amazing."

"A show?"

"No, really," Larry said, strained upward, and coughed in Caperton's ear the name of the showrunner, and how this fellow had also created another hit series.

"The character arcs are groundbreaking," Larry said. "It's a golden age of cable television."

"Sounds great."

"I'd wait to watch it with you," Larry said. "But, well, you know . . ."

"I'll be back," Caperton said.

"And forth." Larry said. "I'm glad. I need you, son."

Caperton was not surprised to see the Rough Beast in the terminal. The Internet wrestler sipped from a demitasse at a granite countertop near the gate. Caperton thought to approach him, but the quest for symmetry seemed a mistake. Besides, the Beast wouldn't remember a snide turd like him.

Caperton had two seats to himself on the plane. He wished he could relish the boon, but it made him anxious. A free seat meant that anybody could take it at any time, lumber up from the back rows looking for relief—a fatty, a talker, the ghost of his mother, Death itself, Burt.

Caperton took the aisle seat, the better to defend the window and, about twenty minutes into the flight, heard a loud grunt, felt a hard pinch on his earlobe.

"How are you, man?" the Beast said. "What's the story?"

A pill from Stell had introduced Caperton to a new flippancy.

"The story, Mr. Beast? It's ongoing. Arcing hard. It's an arcing savage, an astonishment machine."

"Booyah! And how's your personal matter?"

"Everything's going to be O.K., my man, within the context of nothing ever being O.K."

"Brother has been on a philosophical fact-finding mission, come back with the news." The Beast proffered five, belly-high.

"Please," a flight attendant said, approaching from business. "No congregating."

"Nobody's congregating," the Beast said.

"We can't allow congregating for security reasons."

"Just shooting the breeze here, sweetness. No box cutters."

"Sir."

"Maybe you're too young for that reference."

"Please sit down."

"O.K., fine," the Beast said, and walked back to his row.

When the plane landed, Caperton lifted his half-unzipped bag from under the seat and noticed a sandwich tucked under some socks. Pastrami and capers. On a croissant. Caperton chewed and waited for the plane to reach the gate. It would be an odd time now. Larry, the Fates willing, might hold on for a while. They would have a chance to grow close again. Caperton knew he would not run from this. Even if his father doubted him, he knew he would be there when it counted.

He checked his phone and saw the messages stack up in comforting fashion. Life might be looking down, but at least coms were up. It took just the briefest skim of his messages for all comfort to vanish. Now he could only ponder how strange it was that you could move at these outrageous speeds through the air and know everything known and still control nothing. For example, during this one quick flight his father had died, and the bony young councilman, the Prince of Koisks, had kicked him off the project. Also, there was an e-mail from the airline he'd just flown explaining how much they respected his time and offering consolation for his current difficulties. Worse than robots, really.

Caperton called the only person he could call. Daphne answered and told him to hold on. Another voice came on the line.

"This is Miles."

"Jesus, I thought she made you up."

"No, I'm very much an entity of your dimension. Somebody who could find you and stomp on your urethra in what we foolishly call real time. Did you not receive the text message?"

"I did," Caperton said.

"But you thought calling was O.K.?"

"Did you say you were the nanny?"

"Goodbye, Mr.—"

"No, Miles, please don't hang up. Just stay on the line for a minute. For sixty   225
seconds. That's all. I'm having a bad moment. I don't need Daphne. You'll do
fine. My father just died. Please just . . . I just . . ."

"Why don't you emulate your old man," Miles said, hung up.

Caperton groaned, shook, curled up in his seats, and watched people stand
and grope at the overhead bins. He heard the Beast barrel through the throng
behind him. Here he loomed again.

"Caught the end of your call."

"Yeah," Caperton said.

"We'll be here awhile, waiting for all these people. Shove over."   230

Caperton slid toward the window and the Rough Beast sat down. He patted
Caperton's knee.

"Terrible about your pops. Mine went easy. Keeled over on his city snow-
plow up in Rochester. But that doesn't make it any better for you."

"No."

"It's O.K. You're with me now. Everything will be O.K. Cry for your father.
What man doesn't cry for his father? Let it out."

Caperton cooled his forehead on the window. The Beast stroked his back.   235

"They say it's a cycle, but there is no cycle. You get jerked in and reamed out.
That's all."

Caperton could not cry again. Also, he thought he might be onto a new
phase. Lumped nullity. Drool drooped from his lip. He looked up and saw that
the plane was empty.

"I'm sorry," one of the flight attendants said. "But it's time to leave."

"We'll leave soon," the Beast said. "When it's time."

"But it's time now."   240

"No, it's not!" the Rough Beast shouted, cocked his hand for a karate chop.
"This man's in the middle of a fucking hinge moment! I'll waste you all!"

One of the flight attendants called security on her walkie-talkie. The others
dashed for the door.

Caperton, who now felt a wider and more fiery belt of perhaps increasingly
frequent sorrow begin to singe him, slid to his knees and crushed his face into
the seat back. The underside of the locked and upright tray, cool and vaguely
pebbled, was heaven on his skin.

FOR ANALYSIS

1. What is Caperton's line of work? What does it tell us about him?

2. How are we supposed to feel about Caperton's neighbor on the plane? Is there any
larger significance to the story in his professional name?

3. What deaths is this story about? Just Larry's, or others, actual and **metaphorical**? If
others, how do they relate?

4. Caperton notices a book in his stepmother's home office titled "Narrative Medicine: How Stories Save Lives" (para. 79). How are stories important in "The Naturals"? Do they save lives? What or what else can they do (and/or not do)?

MAKING ARGUMENTS

Caperton's father likes the movie version of *The Natural* better than the original Bernard Malamud novel because the book doesn't have the movie's happy ending. Make an argument about endings, happy and otherwise, in narratives. Why are they important? What do they mean? Is it better to have one or the other?

WRITING TOPICS

1. "The Naturals" is characteristic of Lipsyte's work in its combination of the serious and the comic. Reread the story and track where the **tone** shifts. Reflect on your observations and try to describe his **style** generally, in this regard, and how it is at work in this story.

2. Reflect on the title of this story. Why do you think Lipsyte chose it, beyond the obvious reference? To what or whom else might it refer, and how?

MAKING CONNECTIONS

Consider this story next to Alexie's "War Dances" (p. 594). There are similarities in the situation and the **plot**; how do what Caperton's father calls the "character arcs" (para. 193) of the two **protagonists** compare?

CONNECTING STORIES: MOURNING RITUALS

It is hard (though not impossible) to imagine two more different stories about the same thing, but Leslie Marmon Silko's and Allegra Goodman's stories manage to cover a lot of the same terrain while walking quite divergent paths. As you read these stories, consider how the characters in them think about death and mourning, how the rest of their lives are inextricably tied to their thoughts, and how the significance of death trumps both everything and nothing at the same time.

LESLIE MARMON SILKO (B. 1948)

THE MAN TO SEND RAIN CLOUDS   1981

They found him under a big cottonwood tree. His Levi jacket and pants were faded light blue so that he had been easy to find. The big cottonwood tree stood apart from a small grove of winterbare cottonwoods which grew in the wide, sandy arroyo. He had been dead for a day or more, and the sheep had wandered and scattered up and down the arroyo. Leon and his brother-in-law, Ken, gathered the sheep and left them in the pen at the sheep camp before they returned to the cottonwood tree. Leon waited under the tree while Ken drove the truck through the deep sand to the edge of the arroyo. He squinted up at the sun and unzipped his jacket—it sure was hot for this time of year. But high and northwest the blue mountains were still in snow. Ken came sliding down the low, crumbling bank about fifty yards down, and he was bringing the red blanket.

Before they wrapped the old man, Leon took a piece of string out of his pocket and tied a small gray feather in the old man's long white hair. Ken gave him the paint. Across the brown wrinkled forehead he drew a streak of white and along the high cheekbones he drew a strip of blue paint. He paused and watched Ken throw pinches of corn meal and pollen into the wind that fluttered the small gray feather. Then Leon painted with yellow under the old man's broad nose, and finally, when he had painted green across the chin, he smiled.

"Send us rain clouds, Grandfather." They laid the bundle in the back of the pickup and covered it with a heavy tarp before they started back to the pueblo.

They turned off the highway onto the sandy pueblo road. Not long after they passed the store and post office they saw Father Paul's car coming toward them. When he recognized their faces he slowed his car and waved them to stop. The young priest rolled down the car window.

"Did you find old Teofilo?" he asked loudly.   5

Leon stopped the truck. "Good morning, Father. We were just out to the sheep camp. Everything is O.K. now."

"Thank God for that. Teofilo is a very old man. You really shouldn't allow him to stay at the sheep camp alone."

"No, he won't do that any more now."

"Well, I'm glad you understand. I hope I'll be seeing you at Mass this week—we missed you last Sunday. See if you can get old Teofilo to come with you." The priest smiled and waved at them as they drove away.

Louise and Teresa were waiting. The table was set for lunch, and the coffee 10 was boiling on the black iron stove. Leon looked at Louise and then at Teresa.

"We found him under a cottonwood tree in the big arroyo near sheep camp. I guess he sat down to rest in the shade and never got up again." Leon walked toward the old man's bed. The red plaid shawl had been shaken and spread carefully over the bed, and a new brown flannel shirt and pair of stiff new Levi's were arranged neatly beside the pillow. Louise held the screen door open while Leon and Ken carried in the red blanket. He looked small and shriveled, and after they dressed him in the new shirt and pants he seemed more shrunken.

It was noontime now because the church bells rang the Angelus. They ate the beans with hot bread, and nobody said anything until after Teresa poured the coffee.

Ken stood up and put on his jacket. "I'll see about the gravediggers. Only the top layer of soil is frozen. I think it can be ready before dark."

Leon nodded his head and finished his coffee. After Ken had been gone for a while, the neighbors and clanspeople came quietly to embrace Teofilo's family and to leave food on the table because the gravediggers would come to eat when they were finished.

The sky in the west was full of pale yellow light. Louise stood outside with 15 her hands in the pockets of Leon's green army jacket that was too big for her. The funeral was over, and the old men had taken their candles and medicine bags and were gone. She waited until the body was laid into the pickup before she said anything to Leon. She touched his arm, and he noticed that her hands were still dusty from the corn meal that she had sprinkled around the old man. When she spoke, Leon could not hear her.

"What did you say? I didn't hear you."

"I said that I had been thinking about something."

"About what?"

"About the priest sprinkling holy water for Grandpa. So he won't be thirsty."

Leon stared at the new moccasins that Teofilo had made for the ceremo- 20 nial dances in the summer. They were nearly hidden by the red blanket. It was getting colder, and the wind pushed gray dust down the narrow pueblo road. The sun was approaching the long mesa where it disappeared during the winter. Louise stood there shivering and watching his face. Then he zipped up his jacket and opened the truck door. "I'll see if he's there."

Ken stopped the pickup at the church, and Leon got out; and then Ken drove down the hill to the graveyard where people were waiting. Leon knocked at the old carved door with its symbols of the Lamb. While he waited he looked up at the twin bells from the king of Spain with the last sunlight pouring around them in their tower.

The priest opened the door and smiled when he saw who it was. "Come in! What brings you here this evening?"

The priest walked toward the kitchen, and Leon stood with his cap in his hand, playing with the earflaps and examining the living room—the brown sofa, the green armchair, and the brass lamp that hung down from the ceiling by links of chain. The priest dragged a chair out of the kitchen and offered it to Leon.

"No thank you, Father. I only came to ask you if you would bring your holy water to the graveyard."

The priest turned away from Leon and looked out the window at the patio full of shadows and the dining-room windows of the nuns' cloister across the patio. The curtains were heavy, and the light from within faintly penetrated; it was impossible to see the nuns inside eating supper. "Why didn't you tell me he was dead? I could have brought the Last Rites anyway."

Leon smiled. "It wasn't necessary, Father."

The priest stared down at his scuffed brown loafers and the worn hem of his cassock. "For a Christian burial it was necessary."

His voice was distant, and Leon thought that his blue eyes looked tired.

"It's O.K. Father, we just want him to have plenty of water."

The priest sank down into the green chair and picked up a glossy missionary magazine. He turned the colored pages full of lepers and pagans without looking at them.

"You know I can't do that, Leon. There should have been the Last Rites and a funeral Mass at the very least."

Leon put on his green cap and pulled the flaps down over his ears. "It's getting late, Father. I've got to go."

When Leon opened the door Father Paul stood up and said, "Wait." He left the room and came back wearing a long brown overcoat. He followed Leon out the door and across the dim churchyard to the adobe steps in front of the church. They both stooped to fit through the low adobe entrance. And when they started down the hill to the graveyard only half of the sun was visible above the mesa.

The priest approached the grave slowly, wondering how they had managed to dig into the frozen ground, and then he remembered that this was New Mexico, and saw the pile of cold loose sand beside the hole. The people stood close to each other with little clouds of steam puffing from their faces. The priest looked at them and saw a pile of jackets, gloves, and scarves in the yellow, dry tumbleweeds that grew in the graveyard. He looked at the red blanket, not sure that Teofilo was so small, wondering if it wasn't some perverse Indian trick—something they did in March to ensure a good harvest—wondering if maybe old Teofilo was actually at sheep camp corraling the sheep for the night. But there he was, facing into a cold dry wind and squinting at the last sunlight, ready to bury a red wool blanket while the faces of his parishioners were in shadow with the last warmth of the sun on their backs.

His fingers were stiff, and it took him a long time to twist the lid off the holy 35 water. Drops of water fell on the red blanket and soaked into dark icy spots. He sprinkled the grave and the water disappeared almost before it touched the dim, cold sand; it reminded him of something—he tried to remember what it was, because he thought if he could remember he might understand this. He sprinkled more water; he shook the container until it was empty, and the water fell through the light from sundown like August rain that fell while the sun was still shining, almost disappearing before it touched the wilted squash flowers.

The wind pulled at the priest's brown Franciscan robe and swirled away the corn meal and pollen that had been sprinkled on the blanket. They lowered the bundle into the ground, and they didn't bother to untie the stiff pieces of new rope that were tied around the ends of the blanket. The sun was gone, and over on the highway the eastbound lane was full of headlights. The priest walked away slowly. Leon watched him climb the hill, and when he had disappeared within the tall, thick walls, Leon turned to look up at the high blue mountains in the deep snow that reflected a faint red light from the west. He felt good because it was finished, and he was happy about the sprinkling of the holy water; now the old man could send them big thunderclouds for sure.

FOR ANALYSIS

1. Why do Leon and Ken not tell Father Paul that Teofilo is dead? Why do they later ask Father Paul to bring holy water to the funeral?

2. Two rituals associated with death—the Native American and the Roman Catholic— seem to conflict. Why does Teofilo's family seek the priest's help? Why does Father Paul agree to help them?

3. Although the story is mostly told from the **point of view** of an omniscient narrator, at one point we share two characters' thoughts. What effect does this shift generate?

4. Why do you think Silko included the detail (in the last paragraph) about the automobile lights on the highway?

5. Why does Leon feel good at the end of the story?

MAKING ARGUMENTS

Why do so many if not all cultures have elaborate, codified rituals for handling death? Make an argument based on research, the story, and your own thoughts on what death means to people and to communities and on how rituals and processes plug into those meanings.

WRITING TOPIC

"The Man to Send Rain Clouds" remains silent about the characters' spirituality: there is no **narrator** commenting on whether their rituals and beliefs are effective or true. How did you respond to the different **points of view** on death and the natural world presented in the story? How might the characters respond to your points of view about the world? Where did you get them?

ALLEGRA GOODMAN (B. 1967)

APPLE CAKE 2014

Her sisters flinched because she was the youngest, but she looked so old. Jeanne was just seventy-four, and no one had ever thought . . . They didn't speak of it. They would not allow themselves, but Helen was eighty, Sylvia seventy-eight. They'd married first, been mothers first. They were older. They should have been frailer. How could Jeanne be first to go?

Their baby sister lay propped up on pillows. Jeanne, who had celebrated her first birthday in eyelet lace, a slice of cake on the tray of her high chair, and her sisters on either side. Their living doll, with her blond curls and round blue eyes. They'd pulled her in their wagon over grass bumpy with apples from the apple tree. It was dreadful to approach her now—her hair just wisps, her voice nearly gone, her cough breaking every sentence. Horror, pity, shame. They felt all that at once, to see her now and to remember her as she had been. They were sorry and they were glad to feel so alive, their steps firm in their low-heeled shoes. Their own bodies sound, rejoicing with each breath. What a terrible thing to say! They would never have admitted it. Their own strength, their own good fortune and their guilt—they could never put it into words. No one should!

"How are you, darling?" Helen asked.

Jeanne didn't answer.

"Did you see the orchid Richard sent?" Sylvia turned a tall white orchid   5
toward Jeanne's chair.

Jeanne glanced at her nephew's gift. There were so many. Blossoms filled the first-floor music studio where Jeanne had to live because she couldn't take the stairs. The orchid from Richard, the sunflowers from her daughter-in-law, Melanie, the roses from the Auerbachs next door. Wherever she looked, she saw arrangements from neighbors, nieces, grandchildren. The piano tuner had sent a basket of mums, which were losing petals, shedding everywhere. The cards said, "All our love," and "Thinking of you," and even "Healing light." This from her niece Wendy, the music therapist.

"Look how beautiful they are," Sylvia said. She meant, Do you see how much everybody loves you?

Jeanne made a face. The flowers depressed her, especially those that were already wilting. When she looked at the mums, she felt she wasn't dying fast enough.

Her sisters sat chattering about the heat, the traffic, and the rain. They were afraid to leave her alone—she had lived by herself for fifteen years, a widow. She lived alone because she liked it. Her late husband had been difficult, to say the least.

According to Jeanne's sons, her Tudor home was much too big. According to   10
Phoebe, her twenty-year-old granddaughter, Jeanne's house wasted energy. For years, everybody had been telling Jeanne to move. Now nobody mentioned it.

These were the privileges of hospice. You didn't have to blow insulation into your walls. No one suggested assisted living or criticized your carbon footprint, which would disappear entirely in weeks, or even days. On the other hand, everyone came to see you and confide in you. Jeanne didn't believe in God or any kind of afterlife, but lung cancer made believers of her family, so that she, who despised superstition, became a touchstone and talisman to the rest of them. Her sisters were always pressing her cold hands.

Helen told Jeanne, "Pam and Wendy are coming up this weekend."

Jeanne nodded.

"Richard's coming, too," Sylvia said. Her only child was having a terrible time, switching jobs, divorcing, and she felt he deserved credit for dropping everything to see his aunt. Pam was coming up from Providence, and Wendy lived in Brooklyn, but Richard had to drive all the way from Philly.

Jeanne closed her eyes and listened to her sisters say, She's tired. She's 15
exhausted. She heard them echo and repeat each other. She has to rest. Yes, she has to rest. She was looking at the sun, red through her closed eyelids.

The autumn sun felt good, but darkness was better, because everybody left except Shawn, the night nurse. Then Jeanne lay awake in her rented hospital bed and listened to symphonies and choral rhapsodies, quartets, and concertos on WGBH, Boston's classical radio. When she heard a solo violin, her fingers curled reflexively; her left hand knew.

Her sons had pushed away her music stands and moved the piano to make room for Shawn, now dozing in his straight-backed chair. Jeanne assumed he had another job during the day, and she saw that he was trying to study as well. He was always reading a textbook, but he never got very far. Just before dawn, the book slipped off his lap onto the floor.

Shawn started up and saw Jeanne staring at him from her bed. "I'm sorry. I'm sorry. Ma'am." He bent down for the book.

She said, "You rest."

"No, I'm here if you need something." 20

"Sleep."

His eyes widened. There was no way he was going back to sleep. He'd lose his job.

"I'll let you know if anything happens," Jeanne said.

Her sons and their wives came to see her every afternoon. First, Steve and Andrea would sit by her side. Andrea showed videos on her phone of their huge boys, born just eighteen months apart, lion cubs who played high-school soccer. They were coming to see Jeanne right after regionals. Andrea was going to drive them straight from the field, cleats and all.

Next came Dan and Melanie. They had just the one daughter, Phoebe. Melanie 25
had gained fifty pounds when she was pregnant. She never had another child, and she never lost the weight. "Phoebe sends her love," Melanie said.

Dan explained, "She wants to be here, but she won't fly."

Jeanne tried to picture her ecological granddaughter biking from Ann Arbor. She imagined Phoebe's long blond hair streaming out from under her helmet. "Her schoolwork is more important."

"Actually, she's taking the semester off," Melanie said.

"What was that?"

Dan frowned, upset with Melanie for mentioning this. "She says she wants 30
to work with her hands."

"Preferably in the dirt," Melanie said. "She wants to be a farmer and write
poetry."

Jeanne couldn't help laughing. Her breath came short and quick. For a few
moments, she couldn't breathe at all, and then she couldn't see. With help from
her day nurse, Lorraine, Jeanne sat up, and wiped the tears from her eyes.

"I don't think dropping out is funny," Dan said.

"She isn't dropping out," Melanie said. "She just needs a little time."

Jeanne croaked, "Let her do what she wants."   35

Dan and Melanie looked crushed, and Jeanne felt sorry for them—but why
did everyone expect her to be so concerned?

Illness did not bring out the angel in her. At first, she'd appreciated visitors,
but as she lingered on they didn't leave. Her sisters kept bringing in their
middle-aged children—for what? Good-byes? Advice? Some final blessing?
Sylvia begged, "Tell Richard to stop smoking!"

Oh, really, Jeanne thought. That's what I am. Exhibit A. She studied her
ruddy nephew. His wife had just won custody of the children, and the dog. "I
enjoyed smoking," Jeanne said. "Your mother did, too."

Sylvia shrank back as though Jeanne had struck her, but she said nothing. It
was too late, apparently, to retaliate.

Jeanne's sons appeared, and they looked terrible, both of them. Dan wore 40
wire-rimmed glasses. He was thick in the middle and he had hardly any hair.
It amused and saddened Jeanne to see him look so much like his late father.
As for Steve, he had a bad back, so he had to walk around the room. He made
Jeanne dizzy, pacing up and down.

Her daughters-in-law got emotional—especially Melanie, herself a doctor.
Please, Jeanne thought. I lost my parents when I was half your age. We're all
over fifty here.

She pretended to sleep, and then she really did drop off. When she woke, her
sisters were hovering over her. Some of us have overstayed our welcome, Jeanne
thought. And then, with sudden shock, No: I'm the one. That would be me.

Sardonic as she was, husk that she was, she shuddered at the thought of
disappearing, of losing consciousness and irony, her music, her unrenovated
house, her sun. Cancer had consumed her body, drugs clouded her mind. Even
so, Jeanne held on. Barely eating, scarcely speaking, she endured. Her nieces
and her nephew sat with her. Wendy sang and strummed her battered guitar.
Jeanne's soccer-playing grandsons arrived. Zach cracked his knuckles. Nate
jiggled his right leg. The boys were like a pair of jackrabbits, all ears and feet.

The hospice nurses said that Jeanne would drift away in a day or two, but
four days passed, and then a fifth. It was awkward, because her sons had to
take off work, and her grandchildren could miss only so many days of school.
Should they stay or should they go? Did it make sense to return home and then
come right back for the funeral?

Helen said, "We need a plan." Oldest and bossiest, she told Jeanne, "We need 45
to know your wishes."

"To get up," Jeanne said immediately.

Later, in the hall, Sylvia turned on Helen. "How can you speak to her like that?"

Helen was amazed at the question. "Well, we can't ask her when she's gone!"

Sylvia began to cry.

"Don't get hysterical," Helen snapped. 50

"I'm not hysterical. I have feelings. Be considerate."

"I am considerate," Helen said. "I'm doing for Jeanne what I hope someone
would do for me. If I didn't have a living will."

Weeping, Sylvia retreated to the dining room to criticize her husband, Lew.

That afternoon, at Jeanne's bedside, Helen appealed to her daughter Pam, a
tax attorney. "She left no instructions."

At the word "instructions," Jeanne opened her eyes. It was disconcerting the 55
way she did that. Just as Helen slipped into the past tense, Jeanne roused herself.
Then everyone hurried to her side again.

Sons and daughters-in-law watched Jeanne's face.

"Melanie," Jeanne whispered.

"What is it?" Melanie asked. Already the tears. Always the tears.

"Half a bagel," Jeanne said.

That sent them off again, scrambling to Rosenfeld's. The two couples took 60
Dan's Volvo to Newton Centre, even as they told each other there was no way.
Melanie, the doctor, said, "She'll never eat a whole half a bagel."

"Does that matter?" Dan demanded, as he drove.

"No," Melanie said. "Of course not."

"If my mother wants half a bagel, she's getting half a bagel."

Melanie said, "No poppy. She could aspirate the seeds."

"Get her an egg bagel," Steve suggested from the back seat. 65

Andrea corrected him. "She doesn't like egg. She likes plain."

By the time they returned with a dozen bagels, two large containers of whipped
cream cheese, a side of lox, and a chocolate babka, Jeanne was sleeping again.

The nurses stopped predicting when she would drift away. Now they said
that only Jeanne would know when it was time. Lorraine suggested that everybody share a moment. Was there unfinished business in the family? Sometimes people had to forgive each other before they could let go.

Tremulous, angelic, Sylvia told Helen, "I forgive you."

"Oh, for God's sake," Helen said. There was nothing to forgive. There was 70
simply the great divide between them: Helen told the truth, while Sylvia tried
to paper over everything.

"She never listens to me," Sylvia told the family assembled at Jeanne's bedside.
"I'm invisible to her."

Amazed at this mixed metaphor, Helen said, "Obviously I see you."

At this point, Dan spoke up. "I think we need to focus on the time we have
together."

"Amen," Lorraine said, and everyone was jealous, because she liked Dan best.

Look at you, Jeanne thought. All vying for attention! Even so, she forgave 75
everybody. Good night, she told them silently. Farewell. She wished that she
could send a blanket dispensation. After which she could stay and they would
leave.

In fact, she looked a little better. She drank some juice and tried a bite of
toast. She asked for her violin. She couldn't play it. She couldn't even open the
case, but she kept it near her on the window ledge next to her bed. She wanted
her instrument where she could see it.

Like a cat, Jeanne slept most of the day, but, waking, she seemed a heightened, sharper version of herself. When Pam drove up from Providence for the
second time, Jeanne asked why she'd never married. When Melanie sniffled,
Jeanne said, "Stop feeling sorry for yourself."

Obviously, Melanie was sad because she was afraid of her own death. Jeanne
could see it in her eyes. Jeanne's sisters were even worse. They looked at her
and thought only of their mortality.

But this was cruel! Not just unkind. Untrue. Jeanne's sisters thought nothing
of themselves. Sylvia berated Lew all the way home to Weston. Helen stayed
up late in Brookline, baking. Lemon squares, and brownies, pecan bars, apple
cake, sandy almond cookies. Alone in her kitchen, she wrapped these offerings
in waxed paper and froze them in tight-lipped containers.

Her husband, Charles, ventured, "You should get some rest." 80

What a thing to say! How could anybody rest? Helen had not pursued a
career like Jeanne, the music teacher, or three successive husbands, like Sylvia.
No, Helen had always been a homemaker. Now her family needed sustenance,
so she doubled every recipe and froze half. After all, there would be a memorial service, and shivah afterward. Helen could already picture Jeanne's students descending with their parents. Sylvia hadn't baked in years, because Lew
was diabetic. As for Melanie and Andrea—what would they throw together?
A box of doughnut holes? No. Helen was the baker of the family. What she felt
could not be purchased. She grieved from scratch.

And yet Jeanne kept on living. Her sisters held vigil; her sons came up on
weekends. In the kitchen, her family nibbled Helen's lemon squares. Melanie
urged brownies on the nurses. "Take these," she told Lorraine. "We can't eat
them all, but Helen won't stop baking."

"Sweetheart," Lorraine said, "everybody mourns in her own way."

Helen mourned her sister deeply. She arrived each day with shopping bags.
Her cake was tender with sliced apples, but her almond cookies crumbled at
the touch. Her pecan bars were awful, sticky-sweet and hard enough to break
your teeth. They remained untouched in the dining room, because Helen
never threw good food away.

Sometimes Jeanne asked in a confused voice why everyone had come. And 85
then there were moments when she remembered and took charge. She ordered
Melanie to take all the plants and flowers to Newton-Wellesley Hospital. She

told Wendy to put her guitar away. After this, she asked to speak to her sons alone. She lay in bed and watched Dan and Steve approach. This is it, the two of them were thinking. "We'll see," Jeanne said.

Guilty, nervous, Steve asked, "What did you say?"

"These are my wishes," Jeanne said.

Dan pulled up a chair, but Steve paced up and down.

"Stop that."

"What are your wishes? "Dan asked.   90

"First of all"—Jeanne looked at Steve—"don't pace. Second of all . . ."

They waited.

"No funeral."

"A private burial?" Dan ventured.

"No burial."   95

Astonished, Steve said, "You have the plot." He might as well have added, And it's paid for.

"I don't want it."

Steve protested, "But it's next to Dad."

"Yes, I am aware of that."

Dan's glasses were fogging up. He took them off and wiped them on the bottom   100
of his sweater. "You shared your life with Dad for thirty-eight years."

"Exactly."

If Jeanne had another plan, she did not reveal it to her sons. If she had a good word to say about their father, she did not say it. Fiercely, she insisted that there would be no burial. No memorial. Privately, she decided not to die.

Jeanne's voice grew stronger as she kept living. Outside, the leaves were turning. AAA Sparkling Windows and Gutters called to schedule a cleaning. Still, she endured.

Uneasily, the family dispersed. Jeanne's grandsons returned to school. Jeanne's sons and their wives went back to work. Even Melanie stopped crying. Her mother-in-law was a medical miracle. She was going to outlast them all. Only the nurses kept the faith. Lorraine said that sometimes older people held on for an occasion. They willed themselves to stay alive for one final milestone. A wedding. A grandchild's graduation.

No one could think of a milestone, apart from Richard's divorce. Nobody   105
was marrying or graduating. The next family birthday was in May. Everyone had shared a moment. Nieces and nephew and grandchildren had . . . Wait! They'd forgotten Phoebe, writing poetry in Michigan, working with her hands, refusing to fly.

Melanie and Dan spoke to Phoebe on the phone. They called her from Jeanne's house, and then Melanie called again from the car as Dan drove home. She talked to Phoebe about respect and compassion—thinking about others, not just about the earth.

Meanwhile, Helen and Sylvia kept coming every day, baleful, fearful, sorry for their lot. Helen wanted to bring her rabbi to the house.

"No rabbis," Jeanne said. "No members of the clergy."

"Well, what would you suggest?" Helen demanded.

Sylvia cried, "How dare you scream at her?"   110

"Only one of us is screaming," Helen said.

Sylvia left the room, and then she left the house. Maybe she raised her voice at times. Maybe she felt overwhelmed. The situation was overwhelming. Jeanne's death unimaginable, and now—even worse—postponed. There was nothing to be done, and yet Helen managed to do it. As usual, she took over everything. Sylvia was up all night, she was so upset. "It's all about Helen," Sylvia told Lew. "Her plan, her rabbi, her stale old pecan bars."

Columbus Day, when the family gathered at the house, Sylvia arrived with fresh-baked apple cake, warm from her oven, fragrant in its pan.

Heads up, suddenly alert, Jeanne's huge grandsons sniffed the cake. Can I have a piece? Can I have some?

In the kitchen, Sylvia turned the cake out on a plate and sliced big wedges   115
for the boys. Then Dan and Melanie had pieces, as did Steve and Andrea. In the dining room, Helen's defrosted brownies, pecan bars, and almond cookies sat undisturbed. Charles did take a brownie out of loyalty, but he slipped into the kitchen for Sylvia's cake.

"I smell baked apples," Jeanne whispered in the studio. The bed seemed to swallow her up, and yet she spoke.

"It's my recipe," Helen said. "I gave that recipe to Sylvia twenty years ago."

"Yes, I remember," Jeanne said. "She bakes a very good apple cake."

"I bake the same one! I brought you apple cake last week!"

"I know, but I like hers better," Jeanne said.   120

Helen marched into the kitchen and gazed at the last crumbs of Sylvia's cake. Zach and Nate were eating standing up. Melanie and Dan, Steve and Andrea, were eating at the table. Then Helen caught her own husband throwing away a paper plate.

"*Et tu*, Charles," Lew said.

"You used my recipe," Helen told Sylvia.

"Yes, I did," Sylvia replied, with such an air that even Zach and Nate knew she meant, What's it to you?

The next day, Sylvia brought her homemade jelly rolls, soft sponges rolled   125
with tangy apricot, dusted on top with coconut flakes. She had not baked jelly rolls in fifteen years, and the whole family fell upon them. Even Lew, so careful with his diet, took a tiny piece. Only Helen and Jeanne abstained. Helen would not, and Jeanne could not partake.

She was sick of visitors, but she made an effort to say a few words to each one. She advised her younger son, Dan, to look into hair-replacement therapy. She told Melanie to try antidepressants. Maybe they would help her lose some weight. As for Steve and Andrea, they were neglecting music. Neither of their boys played an instrument. Jeanne told Andrea to look into marching band, since the boys loved sports so much. Or, if they refused to practice, there were youth choirs. With some ear training, they might learn to sing.

Andrea was speechless for a moment. Then she said slowly, "I realize that music is important to you."

"My life," Jeanne whispered.

"Would you like to see your students?" Steve asked.

Jeanne thought of her young violinists—George, with his sweet tone and his 130 tendency to rush. Sophie, who forgot to count. Wyatt had a good ear but didn't work at all. Emma would not relax her tight goat-trill vibrato.

Andrea said, "Would you like some of them to come and play for you?"

"God, no," Jeanne said.

Sisters, sons, daughters-in-law were always begging to know what they could do. Jeanne gazed out the window at her sugar maple, and she told them what she wanted, since they asked.

They carried her into the garden, where she could see the trees. Tethered to her wheelchair and to her oxygen, she turned her face up to the fiery maples, the gold oaks, the breezy sky. How good the world smelled, the fresh damp grass.

She leaned back and she smiled, and her family thought she was at peace. 135 They were wrong. She was not at peace; quite the opposite. She was happy. Full of plans.

She told Helen she would see the rabbi. She would have a conversation with him. "Thank you," Helen said.

Rabbi Lieberman, when he arrived the next day, looked about twelve. He could have come for lessons. He wore a suit, but he seemed to Jeanne not much bigger than a child.

"Jeanne wanted to have a conversation with you," Helen said.

Jeanne told the rabbi, "You should know that I'm an atheist."

The rabbi nodded. "Yes, I understand." 140

Jeanne added, "I don't have time for organized religion."

"You're in good company," the rabbi said.

Jeanne frowned to find him so accommodating. Didn't rabbis believe anything anymore? "But you believe in God," she said.

"I do."

Jeanne looked at Helen. "That's a relief," she said. 145

"You see?" Helen told her sister, and she meant, You see, it's a relief, a comfort to think of the Creator. "You see?"

"Belief is very personal," the rabbi said.

"I agree," Jeanne said. "That's why we should keep it to ourselves."

The rabbi smiled.

"My family would like to bury me." 150

Helen broke in. "You know that's not true."

"They want to bury me next to my late husband," Jeanne said. "I would like to go somewhere else."

"Where would you like to go?"

"I'd like to be scattered," Jeanne said.

"Cremated?" Rabbi Lieberman asked delicately. 155

"That's not Jewish," Helen declared.

Jeanne looked at the rabbi, who seemed reluctant to speak.

"It's not our tradition," the rabbi said at last.

"Good."

"And how will we visit you?" Helen demanded.   160

Jeanne said, "Why do you assume that I want visitors?"

Helen's tears startled Jeanne. Not you, she thought. Helen never cried.

"I would visit," Helen said.

"Oh, fine," Jeanne said. "Go ahead and bury me. I won't mind."

"Thank you," Helen whispered.   165

After all, Jeanne reasoned, she would never feel it. She wouldn't even know.
"Do what you want," she told her sister. "Cover me with rocks."

They wore her down. They came in shifts. Jeanne closed her eyes and listened to the house. Doors closing. Water running. The crackle of crumbs
flying up the vacuum cleaner. Raised voices. Furious words. Helen baked
mandelbrot from their mother Esther's recipe. Sylvia countered with Esther's
honey cake.

Jeanne tasted none of it, but she remained the cause, the crux of the matter, the still fixed point of the entire family. How long had she been sleeping?
When would she wake? She was as surprised as anyone to find herself alive
each morning. She opened her eyes and everyone turned to her as to an oracle.
She did her best to keep them busy. "Take a day off," she told Helen. "Serve on
a committee." She turned to Sylvia. "Bring me another apple cake."

"You're angry at me," Helen told Jeanne later when they were alone.

Jeanne shook her head.   170

"You're angry because I have beliefs."

Jeanne said, "I don't hold any of your beliefs against you." She said this, but
she added silently, I do think less of you.

"Sylvia covers her apples with brown sugar," Helen said. "She sugars everything."

"Of course she does," Jeanne said. After all, people liked sweet things. Anything sweet and easy. The bitter, dark, and complicated could not compete.
This had always pained her before, but she enjoyed the injustice of it now. Joy
mixed with fear as she looked out the window and saw scarlet trees. How dazzling the world was. How strange.

She heard voices at her door and saw a beautiful girl, dressed all in rags. At   175
last, her granddaughter, Phoebe, had arrived with her gold hair trailing down
her back. She'd come on the bus from Michigan, and she'd brought a young
man, a huntsman in a rough leather shirt.

Jeanne clasped her granddaughter's hand, but Phoebe started back, shocked
by Jeanne's ghastly face.

Oh, you're afraid of me, Jeanne thought. Grandmother, what big eyes you
have, what withered cheeks.

"Sharp nails," Phoebe murmured, looking down at Jeanne's claws.

The wolf inside Jeanne whispered, The better to eat you with, my dear. But
Jeanne said, "Introduce me."

Phoebe didn't understand.   180

Jeanne turned to Phoebe's deerslayer. "What's your name?"

"I'm Christian."

Jeanne had no breath, but laughter racked her body anyway. She held on to Phoebe, and she began to shake.

Dan and Melanie did not find Phoebe's boyfriend funny, nor did they laugh about his name. He was twenty-eight years old, without a full-time job. He said he wanted to raise blueberries. They did not appreciate meeting him like this. They did not appreciate meeting him at all. He sat on the couch with his arms wrapped around Phoebe, as though she belonged to him. They couldn't even have a conversation with their daughter. And yet Christian withstood every hint and every disapproving look. He nuzzled their only child, and he ate. Unblinking, he finished off Helen's pecan bars. He devoured Sylvia's apple cake.

Now that Phoebe had arrived, Jeanne was supposed to let go, but she stayed 185
alive to gaze at Phoebe's lovely face. "Where's your violin?" she asked.

Phoebe looked down at her hiking boots.

"You sold it, didn't you?"

Phoebe began to cry.

"It doesn't matter. In the grand scheme of things . . ."

Phoebe waited for Jeanne. Then she said, "What is it?"   190

Oh, who can remember, Jeanne thought. Maybe she was sleeping. It was hard to tell. She could have been dreaming, or talking in her sleep. "You played well, but other people play much better."

"Thanks, Grandma," Phoebe said, and suddenly Jeanne saw her as a little child, golden-haired, sitting on the beach. She could see Phoebe sand-dusted in her bathing suit. The rippling tide around her, deep-blue waves, white foam.

Jeanne lost consciousness the next day. Dan and Steve kissed their mother's forehead. Once more, everybody said goodbye, but another day passed, and then a third. Finally, at night, when she was all alone except for Shawn, Jeanne cried out.

"Mrs. Rubinstein!" He tried to make her comfortable, but she fought him. She didn't want help. She wanted to open her eyes, to rise up from her bed. She wanted music and she wanted apples. She wanted to touch the sandy beach, to feel summer's heat. She wanted all this, but she couldn't have it. She died because she couldn't breathe.

In the morning, Jeanne's sons tried to make arrangements. Everybody sat in 195
the dining room, and Helen insisted that her rabbi lead prayers.

Sylvia turned on her. "She said no memorial service. You know she hated organized religion!"

"Stop shrieking at me," Helen said.

"We are honoring Jeanne's life, not yours."

Dan intervened. "A simple burial."

"No service," Steve added.   200

"But she didn't want a burial," Sylvia reminded them.

Helen drew herself up. "She said fine."

"Because you pressured her!"

"I would never pressure anyone," Helen said.

"Oh, really!"   205

"She told me fine."

"Nobody else heard her."

"The rabbi heard."

"Because the two of you were pressuring her into it."

"For the last time, she wasn't pressured. She said yes. Bury me."   210

"Because she was dying! That's why she agreed."

Even as they argued in the dining room, the rental company came to collect Jeanne's cannisters of oxygen. Someone was on the phone about the hospital bed, now stripped bare.

"She wanted to be scattered," Sylvia declared.

"She said, Bury me. She told the rabbi."

"She didn't believe in rabbis!"   215

"Does that mean he never existed?" Helen shot back. "Does that mean the conversation never happened?"

"Stop," Dan begged them, but they would not stop.

"As far as you're concerned," Sylvia said, "the only conversations that happen are the ones happening to you."

Now Helen lost her temper entirely. "I asked her to make plans, and you accused me of having no feelings! I talked about instructions, because I knew this was going to happen!"

"She stated her wishes a thousand times." Sylvia spoke with resolve. "She said 220 she wanted to be scattered."

"That is what she said," Dan admitted.

"She never wavered," Sylvia told Helen.

"She changed her mind!" Helen cried out, but no one believed her. Once, Helen had been the sane one. Now they treated her as though she were delusional. Sylvia had begun the insurrection. She'd waged this war for weeks. Helen's voice broke, even as she appealed to them all. "Jeanne talked to the rabbi and she said, Bury me, and that's the truth!"

Sylvia fixed her eyes on Helen. "Don't get hysterical."

But of course it wasn't up to them. Dan and Steve made all the plans. They 225 interpreted their mother's wishes. There would be no burial, just a celebration of Jeanne's life.

Privately, their wives spoke to Sylvia and Helen. They said that the reception after the service would be catered, and for the sake of the family they requested no homemade desserts. They asked Jeanne's sisters to promise. No cookies, no pecan bars. Absolutely no cake.

"I will do whatever you decide," Helen said with dignity.

"And so will I," Sylvia said.

Helen added, "I would never use an occasion like this to call attention to myself."

No rabbi spoke at the celebration of Jeanne's life. Jeanne's student Emma 230 Kantor played Bach, and Dan spoke about how Jeanne's music had filled the house. Steve talked about what he had learned from his mother: "Don't quit. Don't feel sorry for yourself. Don't just stand there, do something." These were the lessons he remembered, although Jeanne's actual words had been "Don't pace."

In the front row of the funeral chapel, Sylvia sat wearing tinted glasses. She didn't think that she could speak. However, when the time came she walked up to the lectern and the words began to come. She'd written them all down on college-ruled paper.

"All my friends were jealous when she was born," Sylvia said. "But I didn't even let them touch her. She was a perfect baby and an angel. From the time she was born, she was my special charge. I used to dress her and play with her. I was her teacher when we played school on the porch. And this is why . . . this is why it's so difficult . . . impossible to . . ."

Sylvia broke down, and her son rushed to the lectern to comfort her, which made her cry even more. How could he keep smoking after all this? How could his wife, his college sweetheart, leave him?

Lew was standing. He helped her take her seat, and she sat between the two of them, her husband and her son, and the tears kept coming—until Helen began to speak.

"It is perhaps appropriate that I speak last, because I am the oldest," Helen   235
said. "And yet I have no monopoly on my sister. Like every human, she belonged to many people, not just one. She had parents." Helen stared straight at Sylvia. "She had two older sisters. She was a beloved member of our family. Daughter, sister, mother, cousin, friend. She was a musician. She was a teacher who spent countless hours instructing children. She was not sentimental, but she was giving."

Now Sylvia took off her glasses. Now she wiped the last tears from her eyes.

"She did not love tradition," Helen said, "but in her final days she spoke of God."

"Not true!" Sylvia whispered to Lew.

"She talked about belief."

Louder, Sylvia whispered to her husband, "That's just not true!"   240

As Helen spoke, Sylvia rattled her notes, her own words left unsaid. She wanted to stand up and finish her eulogy. She wanted to deliver her bright version of Jeanne's life, the true picture, unvarnished with religion, but it was too late. Already Helen was speaking about eternity. Already she was reciting Kaddish.

Sylvia wanted to cry out and stop the prayer. She whispered loud enough for those around her to hear, "This is not what Jeanne wanted!" Apart from that, she suffered in silence. She would not ruin the memorial. She would never make a scene.

To close the service Jeanne's twelve-year-old student, George Leong, played the Meditation on a Theme from "Thaïs." He didn't rush until the last cascading phrases at the end. Horse knows the way, Jeanne would have said.

After the celebration, the family convened at Jeanne's house to sit shivah for one day. No one could take off another week. Silent, staring, Helen watched the caterers serve quiche and crudités and sweet noodle kugel in a silver chafing dish.

Fresh-fruit platters stood in for dessert, along with factory-made cookies and weak coffee.

In the living room, Melanie and Andrea tried to comfort friends and neigh- 245 bors who were shaken by Jeanne's passing. Several confided that Jeanne's sudden death had prompted them to enjoy life while they could. The Auerbachs next door had decided to tour the Galápagos Islands. After that, they hoped to see the northern lights. They had a list.

In Jeanne's studio, Dan and Steve and their cousins, Pam, Wendy, and Richard, talked about how they used to play Wiffle ball together in the back yard. Someone asked Helen to look for the photo albums, but she sat in a daze. As for Sylvia, she was nowhere to be seen.

Late in the day, just as the guests began to leave, Sylvia slipped into the house. Sober, Lew followed, carrying a tube pan.

"Lew?" Andrea said in a warning voice. "What is that?"

Lew kept moving. He knew that this was the nuclear option, and he felt culpable, but he loved his wife.

In the dining room, Sylvia sliced her fresh-baked apple cake. The caterers 250 were still packing up. Their chafing dishes were hardly cold when the house filled with the cake's fragrance. Jeanne's grandsons ran straight to the table. Christian appeared with Phoebe right behind him.

The scent of apples woke Helen from her trance. She marched into the dining room and saw the family eating; she saw what Sylvia had done, and her eyes brightened; her whole body tensed with indignation.

That was the end.

Melanie tried. Everybody tried. Nobody could reconcile Jeanne's sisters. This was all a misunderstanding, their children said. Don't be stubborn, their children pleaded. Andrea said that they only had each other now, but they refused to listen. Dan said life was short. They didn't care. In fact, they knew it wasn't true. Their lives were long.

Lorraine was right. Everybody mourned in his or her own way. Phoebe wrote a poem, and Melanie did in fact start taking antidepressants. Richard began dating a woman he'd met at a bar. Pam adopted a shelter dog. As for Jeanne's sisters, they would not forgive each other for Jeanne's death. They would not reconcile, not even when the whole family gathered at Singing Beach in the spring to scatter Jeanne's ashes in the ocean. Wendy stood on the sand and asked the sisters, in Jeanne's memory, to open their hearts and to embrace each other so that they might begin to heal, but no, not even then.

FOR ANALYSIS

1. How would you characterize **point of view** in this story? Whose point of view do we see from for most of the story? What other points of view are we granted access to? What is the effect of this splitting?

2. What is your reaction to this sentence: "When she looked at the mums, she felt she wasn't dying fast enough" (para. 8)? Does it strike you as the kind of thing you tend to hear in narratives about death? What is its significance in the story?

3. Why do Melanie and Dan call Phoebe?

MAKING ARGUMENTS

Make an argument about Helen and Sylvia. How are we supposed to feel about them? How are we to judge their actions and reactions? What purpose do these **characters** serve in the story?

WRITING TOPICS

Irony is an important device in this story. Reread the story and note instances of irony, and how they work in themselves and in the larger story. What do you think the larger function of irony is in "Apple Cake"?

MAKING CONNECTIONS

Although there are three stories in this book about elderly women, they are not as a rule a staple of fiction. Think about this story alongside Faulkner's "A Rose for Emily" (p. 623) and Katherine Anne Porter's "The Jilting of Granny Weatherall" (p. 1227). What do these stories have in common, and where do they part ways? On the evidence of this small sample, what can you say about fiction about older women?

CONNECTING STORIES:
BETWEEN LIFE AND DEATH

The two stories in this unit share their subject—the moment of death—but regardless of the amount of action on the level of plot, their real focus is not on the event but on the minds of their main characters. As you read these unusual and emotionally affecting stories, consider the difficulties entailed in writing about something you and your readers can never have experienced— death itself—and also the possibilities such an absence of experience opens up.

KATHERINE ANNE PORTER   (1890–1980)

THE JILTING OF
GRANNY WEATHERALL   1930

She flicked her wrist neatly out of Doctor Harry's pudgy careful fingers and pulled the sheet up to her chin. The brat ought to be in knee breeches. Doctoring around the country with spectacles on his nose! "Get along now, take your schoolbooks and go. There's nothing wrong with me."

Doctor Harry spread a warm paw like a cushion on her forehead where the forked green vein danced and made her eyelids twitch. "Now, now, be a good girl, and we'll have you up in no time."

"That's no way to speak to a woman nearly eighty years old just because she's down. I'd have you respect your elders, young man."

"Well, Missy, excuse me." Doctor Harry patted her cheek. "But I've got to warn you, haven't I? You're a marvel, but you must be careful or you're going to be good and sorry."

"Don't tell me what I'm going to be. I'm on my feet now, morally speaking. 5 It's Cornelia. I had to go to bed to get rid of her."

Her bones felt loose, and floated around in her skin, and Doctor Harry floated like a balloon around the foot of the bed. He floated and pulled down his waistcoat and swung his glasses on a cord. "Well, stay where you are, it certainly can't hurt you."

"Get along and doctor your sick," said Granny Weatherall. "Leave a well woman alone. I'll call for you when I want you. . . . Where were you forty years ago when I pulled through milk-leg and double pneumonia? You weren't even born. Don't let Cornelia lead you on," she shouted, because Doctor Harry appeared to float up to the ceiling and out. "I pay my own bills, and I don't throw my money away on nonsense!"

She meant to wave good-by, but it was too much trouble. Her eyes closed of themselves, it was like a dark curtain drawn around the bed. The pillow rose and floated under her, pleasant as a hammock in a light wind. She listened to the leaves rustling outside the window. No, somebody was swishing newspapers: no, Cornelia and Doctor Harry were whispering together. She leaped broad awake, thinking they whispered in her ear.

"She was never like this, *never* like this!" "Well, what can we expect?" "Yes, eighty years old. . . ."

Well, and what if she was? She still had ears. It was like Cornelia to whis- 10
per around doors. She always kept things secret in such a public way. She was always being tactful and kind. Cornelia was dutiful; that was the trouble with her. Dutiful and good: "So good and dutiful," said Granny, "that I'd like to spank her." She saw herself spanking Cornelia and making a fine job of it.

"What'd you say, Mother?"

Granny felt her face tying up in hard knots.

"Can't a body think, I'd like to know?"

"I thought you might want something."

"I do. I want a lot of things. First off, go away and don't whisper." 15

She lay and drowsed, hoping in her sleep that the children would keep out and let her rest a minute. It had been a long day. Not that she was tired. It was always pleasant to snatch a minute now and then. There was always so much to be done, let me see: tomorrow.

Tomorrow was far away and there was nothing to trouble about. Things were finished somehow when the time came; thank God there was always a little margin over for peace: then a person could spread out the plan of life and tuck in the edges orderly. It was good to have everything clean and folded away, with the hair brushes and tonic bottles sitting straight on the white embroidered linen: the day started without fuss and the pantry shelves laid out with rows of jelly glasses and brown jugs and white stone-china jars with blue whirligigs and words painted on them: coffee, tea, sugar, ginger, cinnamon, allspice: and the bronze clock with the lion on top nicely dusted off. The dust that lion could collect in twenty-four hours! The box in the attic with all those letters tied up, well she'd have to go through that tomorrow. All those letters— George's letters and John's letters and her letters to them both—lying around for the children to find afterwards made her uneasy. Yes, that would be tomorrow's business. No use to let them know how silly she had been once.

While she was rummaging around she found death in her mind and it felt clammy and unfamiliar. She had spent so much time preparing for death there was no need for bringing it up again. Let it take care of itself now. When she was sixty she had felt very old, finished, and went around making farewell trips to see her children and grandchildren, with a secret in her mind: this is the very last of your mother, children! Then she made her will and came down with a long fever. That was all just a notion like a lot of other things, but it was lucky too, for she had once and for all got over the idea of dying for a long time. Now she couldn't be worried. She hoped she had better sense now. Her father had lived to be one hundred and two years old and had drunk a noggin of strong hot toddy on his last birthday. He told the reporters it was his daily habit, and he owed his long life to that. He had made quite a scandal and was very pleased about it. She believed she'd just plague Cornelia a little.

"Cornelia! Cornelia!" No footsteps, but a sudden hand on her cheek. "Bless you, where have you been?"

"Here, mother."

"Well, Cornelia, I want a noggin of hot toddy."

"Are you cold, darling?"

"I'm chilly, Cornelia. Lying in bed stops the circulation. I must have told you that a thousand times."

Well, she could just hear Cornelia telling her husband that Mother was getting childish and they'd have to humor her. The thing that most annoyed her was that Cornelia thought she was deaf, dumb, and blind. Little hasty glances and tiny gestures tossed around her and over her head saying, "Don't cross her, let her have her way, she's eighty years old," and she sitting there as if she lived in a thin glass cage. Sometimes Granny almost made up her mind to pack up and move back to her own house where nobody could remind her every minute that she was old. Wait, wait, Cornelia, till your own children whisper behind your back!

In her day she had kept a better house and had got more work done. She wasn't too old yet for Lydia to be driving eighty miles for advice when one of the children jumped the track, and Jimmy still dropped in and talked things over: "Now, Mammy, you've a good business head, I want to know what you think of this? . . ." Old Cornelia couldn't change the furniture around without asking. Little things, little things! They had been so sweet when they were little. Granny wished the old days were back again with the children young and everything to be done over. It had been a hard pull, but not too much for her. When she thought of all the food she had cooked, and all the clothes she had cut and sewed, and all the gardens she had made—well, the children showed it. There they were, made out of her, and they couldn't get away from that. Sometimes she wanted to see John again and point to them and say, Well, I didn't do so badly, did I? But that would have to wait. That was for tomorrow. She used to think of him as a man, but now all the children were older than their father, and he would be a child beside her if she saw him now. It seemed strange and there was something wrong in the idea. Why, he couldn't possibly recognize her. She had fenced in a hundred acres once, digging the post holes herself and clamping the wires with just a negro boy to help. That changed a woman. John would be looking for a young woman with the peaked Spanish comb in her hair and the painted fan. Digging post holes changed a woman. Riding country roads in the winter when women had their babies was another thing: sitting up nights with sick horses and sick negroes and sick children and hardly ever losing one. John, I hardly ever lost one of them! John would see that in a minute, that would be something he could understand, she wouldn't have to explain anything!

It made her feel like rolling up her sleeves and putting the whole place to rights again. No matter if Cornelia was determined to be everywhere at once, there were a great many things left undone in this place. She would start tomorrow and do them. It was good to be strong enough for everything, even if all you made melted and changed and slipped under your hands, so that by the time you finished you almost forgot what you were working for. What was it I set out to do? she asked herself intently, but she could not remember. A fog rose over the valley, she saw it marching across the creek swallowing the trees and moving up the hill like an army of ghosts. Soon it would be at the near edge of the orchard, and then it was time to go in and light the lamps. Come in, children, don't stay out in the night air.

Lighting the lamps had been beautiful. The children huddled up to her and breathed like little calves waiting at the bars in the twilight. Their eyes followed the match and watched the flame rise and settle in a blue curve, then they moved away from her. The lamp was lit, they didn't have to be scared and hang on to mother any more. Never, never, never more. God, for all my life I thank Thee. Without Thee, my God, I could never have done it. Hail, Mary, full of grace.

I want you to pick all the fruit this year and see that nothing is wasted. There's always someone who can use it. Don't let good things rot for want of using. You waste life when you waste good food. Don't let things get lost. It's bitter to lose things. Now, don't let me get to thinking, not when I am tired and taking a little nap before supper. . . .

The pillow rose about her shoulders and pressed against her heart and the memory was being squeezed out of it: oh, push down the pillow, somebody: it would smother her if she tried to hold it. Such a fresh breeze blowing and such a green day with no threats in it. But he had not come, just the same. What does a woman do when she has put on the white veil and set out the white cake for a man and he doesn't come? She tried to remember. No, I swear he never harmed me but in that. He never harmed me but in that . . . and what if he did? There was the day, the day, but a whirl of dark smoke rose and covered it, crept up and over into the bright field where everything was planted so carefully in orderly rows. That was hell, she knew hell when she saw it. For sixty years she had prayed against remembering him and against losing her soul in the deep pit of hell, and now the two things were mingled in one and the thought of him was a smoky cloud from hell that moved and crept in her head when she had just got rid of Doctor Harry and was trying to rest a minute. Wounded vanity, Ellen, said a sharp voice in the top of her mind. Don't let your wounded vanity get the upper hand of you. Plenty of girls get jilted. You were jilted, weren't you? Then stand up to it. Her eyelids wavered and let in streamers of blue-gray light like tissue paper over her eyes. She must get up and pull the shades down or she'd never sleep. She was in bed again and the shades were not down. How could that happen? Better turn over, hide from the light, sleeping in the light gave you nightmares. "Mother, how do you feel now?" and a stinging wetness on her forehead. But I don't like having my face washed in cold water!

Hapsy? George? Lydia? Jimmy? No, Cornelia, and her features were swollen 30 and full of little puddles. "They're coming, darling, they'll all be here soon." Go wash your face, child, you look funny.

Instead of obeying, Cornelia knelt down and put her head on the pillow. She seemed to be talking but there was no sound. "Well, are you tongue-tied? Whose birthday is it? Are you going to give a party?"

Cornelia's mouth moved urgently in strange shapes. "Don't do that, you bother me, daughter."

"Oh, no, Mother, Oh, no. . . ."

Nonsense. It was strange about children. They disputed your every word. "No what, Cornelia?"

"Here's Doctor Harry."

"I won't see that boy again. He just left five minutes ago."

"That was this morning, Mother. It's night now. Here's the nurse."

"This is Doctor Harry, Mrs. Weatherall. I never saw you look so young and happy!"

"Ah, I'll never be young again—but I'd be happy if they'd let me lie in peace and get rested."

She thought she spoke up loudly, but no one answered. A warm weight on her forehead, a warm bracelet on her wrist, and a breeze went on whispering, trying to tell her something. A shuffle of leaves in the everlasting hand of God. He blew on them and they danced and rattled. "Mother, don't mind, we're going to give you a little hypodermic." "Look here, daughter, how do ants get in this bed? I saw sugar ants yesterday." Did you send for Hapsy too?

It was Hapsy she really wanted. She had to go a long way back through a great many rooms to find Hapsy standing with a baby on her arm. She seemed to herself to be Hapsy also, and the baby on Hapsy's arm was Hapsy and himself and herself, all at once, and there was no surprise in the meeting. Then Hapsy melted from within and turned flimsy as gray gauze and the baby was a gauzy shadow, and Hapsy came up close and said, "I thought you'd never come," and looked at her very searchingly and said, "You haven't changed a bit!" They leaned forward to kiss, when Cornelia began whispering from a long way off, "Oh, is there anything you want to tell me? Is there anything I can do for you?"

Yes, she had changed her mind after sixty years and she would like to see George. I want you to find George. Find him and be sure to tell him I forgot him. I want him to know I had my husband just the same and my children and my house like any other woman. A good house too and a good husband that I loved and fine children out of him. Better than I hoped for even. Tell him I was given back everything he took away and more. Oh, no, oh, God, no, there was something else besides the house and the man and the children. Oh, surely they were not all? What was it? Something not given back. . . . Her breath crowded down under her ribs and grew into a monstrous frightening shape with cutting edges; it bored up into her head, and the agony was unbelievable. Yes, John, get the doctor now, no more talk, my time has come.

When this one was born it should be the last. The last. It should have been born first, for it was the one she had truly wanted. Everything came in good time. Nothing left out, left over. She was strong. In three days she would be as well as ever. Better. A woman needed milk in her to have her full health.

"Mother, do you hear me?"

"I've been telling you—"

"Mother, Father Connolly's here."

"I went to Holy Communion only last week. Tell him I'm not so sinful as all that."

"Father just wants to speak to you."

He could speak as much as he pleased. It was like him to drop in and inquire about her soul as if it were a teething baby, and then stay on for a cup of tea and a round of cards and gossip. He always had a funny story of some sort, usually about an Irishman who made his little mistakes and confessed them, and the point lay in some absurd thing he would blurt out in the confessional showing his struggles between naive piety and original sin. Granny felt easy about her soul. Cornelia, where are your manners? Give Father Connolly a chair. She had her secret comfortable understanding with a few favorite saints who cleared a straight road to God for her. All as surely signed and sealed as the papers for the new Forty Acres. Forever . . . heirs and assigns forever. Since the day the wedding cake was not cut, but thrown out and wasted. The whole bottom dropped out of the world, and there she was blind and sweating with nothing under her feet and the walls falling away. His hand had caught her under the breast, she had not fallen, there was the freshly polished floor with the green rug on it, just as before. He had cursed like a sailor's parrot and said, "I'll kill him for you." Don't lay a hand on him, for my sake leave something to God. "Now, Ellen, you must believe what I tell you. . . ."

So there was nothing, nothing to worry about any more, except sometimes 50
in the night one of the children screamed in a nightmare, and they both hustled out shaking and hunting for the matches and calling, "There, wait a minute, here we are!" John, get the doctor now, Hapsy's time has come. But there was Hapsy standing by the bed in a white cap. "Cornelia, tell Hapsy to take off her cap, I can't see her plain."

Her eyes opened very wide and the room stood out like a picture she had seen somewhere. Dark colors with the shadows rising towards the ceiling in long angles. The tall black dresser gleamed with nothing on it but John's picture, enlarged from a little one, with John's eyes very black when they should have been blue. You never saw him, so how do you know how he looked? But the man insisted the copy was perfect, it was very rich and handsome. For a picture, yes, but it's not my husband. The table by the bed had a linen cover and a candle and a crucifix. The light was blue from Cornelia's silk lampshades. No sort of light at all, just frippery. You had to live forty years with kerosene lamps to appreciate honest electricity. She felt very strong and she saw Doctor Harry with a rosy nimbus around him.

"You look like a saint, Doctor Harry, and I vow that's as near as you'll ever come to it."

"She's saying something."

"I heard you, Cornelia. What's all this carrying on?"

"Father Connolly's saying—" 55

Cornelia's voice staggered and bumped like a cart in a bad road. It rounded corners and turned back again and arrived nowhere. Granny stepped up in the cart very lightly and reached for the reins, but a man sat beside her and she knew him by his hands, driving the cart. She did not look in his face, for she knew without seeing, but looked instead down the road where the trees leaned over and bowed to each other and a thousand birds were singing a Mass. She felt like singing too, but she put her hand in the bosom of her dress and pulled out a rosary, and Father Connolly murmured Latin in a very solemn voice and tickled her feet. My God, will you stop that nonsense? I'm a married woman. What if he did run away and leave me to face the priest by myself? I found another a whole world better. I wouldn't have exchanged my husband for anybody except St. Michael himself, and you may tell him that for me with a thank you in the bargain.

Light flashed on her closed eyelids, and a deep roaring shook her. Cornelia, is that lightning? I hear thunder. There's going to be a storm. Close all the windows. Call the children in. . . . "Mother, here we are, all of us." "Is that you, Hapsy?" "Oh, no, I'm Lydia. We drove as fast as we could." Their faces drifted above her, drifted away. The rosary fell out of her hands and Lydia put it back. Jimmy tried to help, their hands fumbled together, and Granny closed two fingers around Jimmy's thumb. Beads wouldn't do, it must be something alive. She was so amazed her thoughts ran round and round. So, my dear Lord, this is my death and I wasn't even thinking about it. My children have come to see me die. But I can't, it's not time. Oh, I always hated surprises. I wanted to give Cornelia the amethyst set—Cornelia, you're to have the amethyst set, but Hapsy's to wear it when she wants, and, Doctor Harry, do shut up. Nobody sent for you. Oh, my dear Lord, do wait a minute. I meant to do something about the Forty Acres, Jimmy doesn't need it and Lydia will later on, with that worthless husband of hers. I meant to finish the altar cloth and send six bottles of wine to Sister Borgia for her dyspepsia. I want to send six bottles of wine to Sister Borgia, Father Connolly, now don't let me forget.

Cornelia's voice made short turns and tilted over and crashed. "Oh, Mother, oh, Mother, oh, Mother. . . ."

"I'm not going, Cornelia. I'm taken by surprise. I can't go."

You'll see Hapsy again. What about her? "I thought you'd never come." 60 Granny made a long journey outward, looking for Hapsy. What if I don't find her? What then? Her heart sank down and down, there was no bottom to death, she couldn't come to the end of it. The blue light from Cornelia's lampshade drew into a tiny point in the center of her brain, it flickered and winked like an eye, quietly it fluttered and dwindled. Granny lay curled down within herself, amazed and watchful, staring at the point of light that was herself; her body was now only a deeper mass of shadow in an endless darkness and this darkness would curl around the light and swallow it up. God, give a sign!

For the second time there was no sign. Again no bridegroom and the priest in the house. She could not remember any other sorrow because this grief wiped them all away. Oh, no, there's nothing more cruel than this—I'll never forgive it. She stretched herself with a deep breath and blew out the light.

FOR ANALYSIS

1. Characterize Granny Weatherall. What facts about her life does the story provide?

2. Why, after sixty years, does the jilting by George loom so large in Granny's mind? Should we accept her own strong statements that the pain of the jilting was more

than compensated for by the happiness she ultimately found with her husband, her children, and her grandchildren? Defend your response.

3. Who is Hapsy? Why do you think she is not present?

4. Why doesn't the author present Granny's final thoughts in an orderly and sequential way?

5. Granny is revealed to us not only through her direct thoughts but also through the many images that float through her mind—a "fog" (para. 26), a "breeze blowing" (para. 29), a "whirl of dark smoke" (para. 29), and others. What do these images reveal about Granny?

MAKING ARGUMENTS

The majority of literature is about people younger than the eponymous **character** of Porter's story. Indeed, it is fair to say that only a small minority of stories and novels and poems are about the elderly. While this is not something decided by committee or fiat, it is a fact; is it a lamentable one? Does it reflect well, poorly, or not at all on how we think about and treat the older members of our societies? Make an argument about age in literature using this story, other works of literature, and any knowledge or research about age in society that you find relevant.

WRITING TOPIC

The final paragraph echoes Christ's parable of the bridegroom (Matthew 25:1–3). If you are not familiar with this parable, find a copy of the New Testament in print or online and read it. Why does Granny connect this final, deep religious grief with the grief she felt when George jilted her? What does this biblical **allusion** add to the story?

TOBIAS WOLFF (B. 1945)

BULLET IN THE BRAIN   1995

The line was endless. Anders couldn't get to the bank until just before it closed and now he was stuck behind two women whose loud, stupid conversation put him in a murderous temper. He was never in the best of tempers anyway, Anders—a book critic known for the weary, elegant savagery with which he dispatched almost everything he reviewed.

With the line still doubled around the rope, one of the tellers stuck a Position Closed sign in her window and walked to the back of the bank, where she leaned against a desk and began to pass the time with a man shuffling papers. The women in front of Anders broke off their conversation and watched the teller with hatred. "Oh, that's nice," one of them said. She turned to Anders and added, confident of his accord, "One of those little human touches that keep us coming back."

Anders had conceived his own towering hatred of the teller, but he immediately turned it on the presumptuous crybaby in front of him. "Damned unfair," he said. "Tragic, really. If they're not chopping off the wrong leg, or bombing your ancestral village, they're closing their positions."

She stood her ground. "I didn't say it was tragic," she said. "I just think it's a pretty lousy way to treat your customers."

"Unforgivable," Anders said. "Heaven will take note." 5

She sucked in her cheeks but stared past him and said nothing. Anders saw that the other woman, her friend, was looking in the same direction. And then the tellers stopped what they were doing, and the customers slowly turned, and silence came over the bank. Two men wearing black ski masks and blue business suits were standing to the side of the door. One of them had a pistol pressed against the guard's neck. The guard's eyes were closed, and his lips were moving. The other man had a sawed-off shotgun. "Keep your big mouth shut!" the man with the pistol said, though no one had spoken a word. "One of you tellers hits the alarm, you're all dead meat. Got it?"

The tellers nodded.

"Oh, bravo," Anders said. "Dead meat." He turned to the woman in front of him. "Great script, eh? The stern, brass-knuckled poetry of the dangerous classes."

She looked at him with drowning eyes.

The man with the shotgun pushed the guard to his knees. He handed the 10 shotgun to his partner and yanked the guard's wrists up behind his back and locked them together with a pair of handcuffs. He then toppled him onto the floor with a kick between the shoulder blades. He took his shotgun back and went over to the security gate at the end of the counter. He was short and heavy and moved with peculiar slowness, even torpor. "Buzz him in," his partner said. The man with the shotgun sauntered along the line of tellers, handing each of them a Hefty bag. When he came to the empty position he looked over at the man with the pistol, who said, "Whose slot is that?"

Anders watched the teller. She put her hand to her throat and turned to the man she'd been talking to. He nodded. "Mine," she said.

"Then get your ugly ass in gear and fill that bag."

"There you go," Anders said to the woman in front of him. "Justice is done."

"Hey! Bright boy! Did I tell you to talk?"

"No," Anders said. 15

"Then shut your trap."

"Did you hear that?" Anders said. "'Bright boy.' Right out of 'The Killers.'"

"Please be quiet," the woman said.

"Hey, you deaf or what?" The man with the pistol walked over to Anders. He poked the weapon into Anders' gut. "You think I'm playing games?"

"No," Anders said, but the barrel tickled like a stiff finger and he had to 20 fight back the titters. He did this by making himself stare into the man's eyes, which were clearly visible behind the holes in the mask: pale-blue and rawly red-rimmed. The man's left eyelid kept twitching. He breathed out a piercing, ammoniac smell that shocked Anders more than anything that had happened, and he was beginning to develop a sense of unease when the man prodded him again with the pistol.

"You like me, bright boy?" he said. "You want to suck my dick?"

"No," Anders said.

"Then stop looking at me."

Anders fixed his gaze on the man's shiny wing-tip shoes.

"Not down there. Up there." He stuck the pistol under Anders' chin and 25 pushed it upward until Anders was looking at the ceiling.

Anders had never paid much attention to that part of the bank, a pompous old building with marble floors and counters and pillars and gilt scrollwork over the tellers' cages. The domed ceiling had been decorated with mythological figures whose fleshy, toga-draped ugliness Anders had taken in at a glance many years earlier and afterward declined to notice. Now he had no choice but to scrutinize the painter's work. It was worse than he remembered, and all of it executed with the utmost gravity. The artist had a few tricks up his sleeve and used them again and again—a certain rosy blush on the underside of the clouds, a coy backward glance on the faces of the cupids and fauns. The ceiling was crowded with various dramas, but the one that caught Anders' eye was Zeus and Europa—portrayed, in this rendition, as a bull ogling a cow from behind a haystack. To make the cow sexy, the painter had canted her hips suggestively and given her long, droopy eyelashes, through which she gazed back at the bull with sultry welcome. The bull wore a smirk and his eyebrows were arched. If there'd been a bubble coming out of his mouth, it would have said, "Hubba hubba."

"What's so funny, bright boy?"

"Nothing."

"You think I'm comical? You think I'm some kind of clown?"

"No." 30

"You think you can fuck with me?"

"No."

"Fuck with me again, you're history. *Capeesh?*"

Anders burst out laughing. He covered his mouth with both hands and said, "I'm sorry, I'm sorry," then snorted helplessly through his fingers and said, "*Capeesh*, oh, God, *capeesh*," and at that the man with the pistol raised the pistol and shot Anders right in the head.

The bullet smashed Anders' skull and plowed through his brain and exited 35 behind his right ear, scattering shards of bone into the cerebral cortex, the corpus callosum, back toward the basal ganglia, and down into the thalamus. But before all this occurred, the first appearance of the bullet in the cerebrum set off a crackling chain of ion transports and neurotransmissions. Because of their peculiar origin, these traced a peculiar pattern, flukishly calling to life a summer afternoon some forty years past, and long since lost to memory. After striking the cranium, the bullet was moving at nine hundred feet per second, a pathetically sluggish, glacial pace compared with the synaptic lightning that flashed around it. Once in the brain, that is, the bullet came under the mediation of brain time, which gave Anders plenty of leisure to contemplate the scene that, in a phrase he would have abhorred, "passed before his eyes."

It is worth noting what Anders did not remember, given what he did remember. He did not remember his first lover, Sherry, or what he had most madly loved about her, before it came to irritate him—her unembarrassed carnality, and especially the cordial way she had with his unit, which she called Mr. Mole, as in "Uh-oh, looks like Mr. Mole wants to play," and "Let's hide Mr. Mole!" Anders did not remember his wife, whom he had also loved, before she exhausted him with her predictability, or his daughter, now a sullen professor of economics at Dartmouth. He did not remember standing just outside his daughter's door as she lectured her bear about his naughtiness and described the truly appalling punishments Paws would receive unless he changed his ways. He did not remember a single line of the hundreds of poems he had committed to memory in his youth so that he could give himself the shivers at will—not "Silent, upon a peak in Darien," or "My God, I heard this day," or "All my pretty ones? Did you say all? O hell-kite! All?" None of these did he remember, not one. Anders did not remember his dying mother saying of his father, "I should have stabbed him in his sleep."

He did not remember Professor Josephs telling his class how the Spartans had released Athenian prisoners from their mines if they could recite Aeschylus, and then reciting Aeschylus himself, right there, in the Greek. Anders did not remember how his eyes had burned at those sounds. He did not remember the surprise of seeing a college classmate's name on the jacket of a novel not long after they graduated, or the respect he had felt after reading the book. He did not remember the pleasure of giving respect.

Nor did Anders remember seeing a woman leap to her death from the building opposite his own, just days after his daughter was born. He did not remember shouting, "Lord have mercy!" He did not remember deliberately crashing his father's car into a tree, or having his ribs kicked in by three policemen at an antiwar rally, or waking himself up with laughter. He did not remember when he began to regard the heap of books on his desk with boredom and dread, or when he grew angry at writers for writing them. He did not remember when everything began to remind him of something else.

This is what he remembered. Heat. A baseball field. Yellow grass, the whirr of insects, himself leaning against a tree as the boys of the neighborhood gather for a pickup game. The captains, precociously large boys named Burns and Darsch, argue the relative genius of Mantle and Mays. They have been worrying this subject all summer, and it has become tedious to Anders; an oppression, like the heat.

Then the last two boys arrive, Coyle and a cousin of his from Mississippi. 40 Anders has never met Coyle's cousin before and will never see him again. He says hi with the rest but takes no further notice of him until they've chosen sides and Darsch asks the cousin what position he wants to play. "Shortstop," the boy says. "Short's the best position they is." Anders turns and looks at him. He wants to hear Coyle's cousin repeat what he's just said, but he knows better than to ask. The others will think he's being a jerk, ragging the kid for his grammar. But that isn't it, not at all—it's that Anders is strangely roused, elated, by those final two words, their pure unexpectedness and their music. He takes the field in a trance, repeating them to himself.

The bullet is already in the brain; it won't be outrun forever, or charmed to a halt. In the end, it will do its work and leave the troubled skull behind, dragging its comet's tail of memory and hope and talent and love into the marble hall of commerce. That can't be helped. But for now Anders can still make time. Time for the shadows to lengthen on the grass, time for the tethered dog to bark at the flying ball, time for the boy in right field to smack his sweat-blackened mitt and softly chant, *They is, they is, they is.*

FOR ANALYSIS

1. How do you feel about the main **character** at the beginning of the story? How does Wolff establish our initial sense of him so quickly?

2. What does the main character do for a living? How does he feel about it? How does the rest of the story, even though it never explicitly mentions this profession again, depend on our being able to trace how he came to the profession and how he feels about it?

3. The "life flashing before the eyes" idea is an old standby in stories. How does Wolff use it? Does he follow the expectations we might have when we see this **plot** device used?

4. How do you feel about the main character by the story's end? Has your sense of him changed? If so, how?

MAKING ARGUMENTS

Think about "Bullet in the Brain" in conjunction with Wallace's "Commencement Speech: Kenyon College" (p. 309). Despite the difference in genre (and many other differences), what subject do they share? Which do you find more effective in treating this shared idea?

WRITING TOPIC

One of the things that makes this story powerful is the way in which it gets inside the head—literally—of its main **character**, particularly because it does so at such an unusual moment. Imagine your own kind of story like this, where you as the writer get inside the head of a character at an unlikely moment. Describe this story, or write it if you want. How do you capitalize on an opportunity to present what's inside someone's mind at such a moment? What can you do to make it seem real? What can you do to make it emotionally affecting?

MAKING CONNECTIONS

1. "The Jilting of Granny Weatherall" and "Bullet in the Brain" are both deeply affecting stories. What is the importance of our identification with the main **character** to the emotional impact each story has? How much depends on our liking them? How much depends on the way they bring us inside their minds?

2. Each of these stories takes the moment of death as an opportunity to look back on the main character's life. How does each do this? What does each focus on? Why?

3. Compare the representations of the moment of death in these two stories. How are they similar? How are they different? Do you find one more effective? If so, why?

POETRY

ANONYMOUS

EDWARD

1

"Why does your brand° sae° drap wi' bluid,   sword/so
    Edward, Edward,
Why does your brand sae drap wi' bluid,
    And why sae sad gang° ye, O?"   go
"O I ha'e killed my hawk sae guid,
    Mither, mither,
O I ha'e killed my hawk sae guid,
    And I had nae mair but he, O."

2

"Your hawke's bluid was never sae reid,°   red
    Edward, Edward,   10
Your hawke's bluid was never sae reid,
    My dear son I tell thee, O."
"O I ha'e killed my reid-roan steed,
    Mither, mither,
O I ha'e killed my reid-roan steed,
    That erst was sae fair and free, O."

3

"Your steed was auld, and ye ha'e gat mair,
    Edward, Edward,
Your steed was auld, and ye ha'e gat mair,
    Some other dule° ye drie,° O."   grief/suffer   20
"O I ha'e killed my fader dear,
    Mither, mither,

1239

O I ha'e killed my fader dear,
    Alas, and wae° is me, O!"   woe

4

"And whatten penance wul ye drie for that,
        Edward, Edward?
And whatten penance wul ye drie for that,
    My dear son, now tell me, O?"
"I'll set my feet in yonder boat,
        Mither, mither,   30
I'll set my feet in yonder boat,
    And I'll fare over the sea, O."

5

"And what wul ye do wi' your towers and your ha',
        Edward, Edward?
And what wul ye do wi' your towers and your ha',
    That were sae fair to see, O?"
"I'll let them stand tul they down fa',
        Mither, mither,
I'll let them stand tul they down fa',
    For here never mair maun° I be, O."   must 40

6

"And what wul ye leave to your bairns° and your wife,   children
        Edward, Edward?
And what wul ye leave to your bairns and your wife,
    Whan ye gang over the sea, O?"
"The warlde's° room, let them beg thrae° life,   world's/through
        Mither, mither,
The warlde's room, let them beg thrae life,
    For them never mair wul I see, O."

7

"And what wul ye leave to your ain mither dear,
        Edward, Edward?   50
And what wul ye leave to your ain mither dear,
    My dear son, now tell me, O?"

"The curse of hell frae° me sall° ye bear,   *from/shall*
    Mither, mither,
The curse of hell frae me sall ye bear,
  Sic° counsels ye gave to me, O."   *such*

FOR ANALYSIS

1. Why does the mother reject Edward's answers to her first two questions?

2. Does the poem provide any clues to the murderer's motive?

3. Edward has murdered his father and then bitterly turns away from his mother, wife, and children. What basis is there in the poem for nevertheless sympathizing with Edward?

MAKING ARGUMENTS

Do a little research on murder **ballads**, and make an argument based on that evidence and on your reading of "Edward" for why murder ballads exist. Why do people write them? Why do people like to hear them? What need(s) do they meet? What purpose do they serve?

WRITING TOPIC

What effects are achieved through the question-and-answer technique and the repetition of lines?

WILLIAM SHAKESPEARE   (1564–1616)

SONNET   1609

73

That time of year thou mayst in me behold
When yellow leaves, or none, or few, do hang
Upon those boughs which shake against the cold,
Bare ruined choirs, where late the sweet birds sang.
In me thou see'st the twilight of such day
As after sunset fadeth in the west;
Which by and by black night doth take away,
Death's second self, that seals up all in rest.
In me thou see'st the glowing of such fire,
That on the ashes of his youth doth lie,   10

As the deathbed whereon it must expire,
Consumed with that which it was nourished by.
This thou perceiv'st, which makes thy love more strong,
To love that well which thou must leave ere long.

FEAR NO MORE
THE HEAT O' THE SUN   1623

Fear no more the heat o' the sun,[1]
   Nor the furious winter's rages;
Thou thy worldly task hast done,
   Home art gone, and ta'en thy wages:
Golden lads and girls all must,
As chimney-sweepers, come to dust.

Fear no more the frown o' the great;
   Thou art past the tyrant's stroke;
Care no more to clothe and eat;
   To thee the reed is as the oak:
The scepter, learning, physic,° must[2]   medicine   10
All follow this, and come to dust.

Fear no more the lightning flash,
   Nor the all-dreaded thunder stone;[3]
Fear not slander, censure rash;
   Thou hast finished joy and moan:
All lovers young, all lovers must
Consign to° thee, and come to dust.   agree with

No exorciser harm thee!
Nor no witchcraft charm thee!   20
Ghost unlaid forbear thee!
Nothing ill come near thee!
Quiet consummation have;
And renownéd be thy grave!

Fear No More the Heat o' the Sun
  [1] From Cymbeline, act IV, scene 2.
  [2] I.e., kings, scholars, and physicians.
  [3] It was believed that thunder was caused by falling meteorites.

JOHN DONNE (1572–1631)

DEATH, BE NOT PROUD 1633

Death be not proud, though some have calléd thee
Mighty and dreadful, for thou art not so;
For those whom thou think'st thou dost overthrow
Die not, poor Death, nor yet canst thou kill me.
From rest and sleep, which but thy pictures be,
Much pleasure; then from thee much more must flow,
And soonest our best men with thee do go,
Rest of their bones, and soul's delivery.
Thou art slave to fate, chance, kings, and desperate men,
And dost with poison, war, and sickness dwell,   10
And poppy or charms can make us sleep as well
And better than thy stroke; why swell'st thou then?
One short sleep past, we wake eternally
And death shall be no more; Death, thou shalt die.

JONATHAN SWIFT (1667–1745)

A SATIRICAL ELEGY ON THE DEATH
OF A LATE FAMOUS GENERAL 1722

His Grace! impossible! what dead!
Of old age too, and in his bed!
And could that mighty warrior fall?
And so inglorious, after all!
Well, since he's gone, no matter how,
The last loud trump must wake him now:
And, trust me, as the noise grows stronger,
He'd wish to sleep a little longer.
And could he be indeed so old
As by the newspapers we're told?   10
Threescore, I think, is pretty high;
'Twas time in conscience he should die
This world he cumbered long enough;
He burnt his candle to the snuff;
And that's the reason, some folks think,
He left behind so great a stink.
Behold his funeral appears,
Nor widow's sighs, nor orphan's tears,

Wont at such times each heart to pierce,
Attend the progress of his hearse.   20
But what of that, his friends may say,
He had those honours in his day.
True to his profit and his pride,
He made them weep before he died.

    Come hither, all ye empty things,
Ye bubbles raised by breath of kings;
Who float upon the tide of state,
Come hither, and behold your fate.
Let pride be taught by this rebuke,
How very mean a thing's a Duke;   30
From all his ill-got honours flung,
Turned to that dirt from whence he sprung.

FOR ANALYSIS

1. How would you describe the **tone** of this poem? Give examples.

2. How does the speaker feel about the general? How does he feel about the general's death?

3. What about the poem changes in its second **stanza**?

4. To where is the speaker asking "ye empty things" (l. 25) to come in the second stanza? Why?

MAKING ARGUMENTS

Swift wrote this poem about a contemporary of his, John Churchill, Duke of Marlborough, whom Swift believed was a war profiteer. Do a little reading on this subject and make an argument about whether knowing this information makes you read the poem differently, or if it has no effect. As you construct your argument, think about methods of literary criticism, about whether historical context is crucial or extraneous to interpretation.

WRITING TOPIC

Write a **satirical elegy** for a deceased public figure. Don't get personal or ad hominem, but criticize him or her on the basis of important public acts you find worthy of criticism (that is, think about why you don't like what this person did in his or her career). Make sure to have your facts as straight as you can get them, with outside help, and try to be creative; don't copy Swift, but be inspired by him to find your own way to say good-bye.

MAKING CONNECTIONS

Read Swift's poem alongside the poems in the "Connecting Poems: Soldiers' Protests" cluster in Conformity and Rebellion (p. 444). Is this a protest poem? Is Swift antiwar? What is the target of his **satire**?

PERCY BYSSHE SHELLEY (1792–1822)

OZYMANDIAS[1]   1818

I met a traveller from an antique land
Who said: Two vast and trunkless legs of stone
Stand in the desert . . . Near them, on the sand,
Half sunk, a shattered visage lies, whose frown,
And wrinkled lip, and sneer of cold command,
Tell that its sculptor well those passions read
Which yet survive, stamped on these lifeless things,
The hand that mocked them, and the heart that fed:
And on the pedestal these words appear:
"My name is Ozymandias, king of kings: 10
Look on my works, ye Mighty, and despair!"
Nothing beside remains. Round the decay
Of that colossal wreck, boundless and bare
The lone and level sands stretch far away.

JOHN KEATS (1795–1821)

ODE ON A GRECIAN URN   1820

I

Thou still unravished bride of quietness,
   Thou foster child of silence and slow time,
Sylvan historian, who canst thus express
   A flowery tale more sweetly than our rhyme:
What leaf-fringed legend haunts about thy shape
   Of deities or mortals, or of both,
      In Tempe or the dales of Arcady?[1]
   What men or gods are these? What maidens loath?
What mad pursuit? What struggle to escape?
      What pipes and timbrels? What wild ecstasy?   10

II

Heard melodies are sweet, but those unheard
   Are sweeter; therefore, ye soft pipes, play on;
Not to the sensual ear, but, more endeared,

Ozymandias
   [1] Egyptian monarch of the thirteenth century B.C., said to have erected a huge statue of himself.
Ode on a Grecian Urn
   [1] Tempe and Arcady are valleys in Greece famous for their beauty. In ancient times, Tempe was regarded as sacred to Apollo.

Pipe to the spirit ditties of no tone:
Fair youth, beneath the trees, thou canst not leave
   Thy song, nor ever can those trees be bare;
     Bold Lover, never, never canst thou kiss,
Though winning near the goal—yet, do not grieve;
     She cannot fade, though thou hast not thy bliss,
Forever wilt thou love, and she be fair!   20

III

Ah, happy, happy boughs! that cannot shed
   Your leaves, nor ever bid the Spring adieu;
And, happy melodist, unweariéd,
   Forever piping songs forever new;
More happy love! more happy, happy love!
   Forever warm and still to be enjoyed,
     Forever panting, and forever young;
All breathing human passion far above,[2]
     That leaves a heart high-sorrowful and cloyed,
      A burning forehead, and a parching tongue.   30

IV

Who are these coming to the sacrifice?
   To what green altar, O mysterious priest,
Lead'st thou that heifer lowing at the skies,
   And all her silken flanks with garlands dressed?
What little town by river or sea shore,
   Or mountain-built with peaceful citadel,
     Is emptied of this folk, this pious morn?
And, little town, thy streets forevermore
   Will silent be; and not a soul to tell
     Why thou art desolate, can e'er return.   40

V

O Attic[3] shape! Fair attitude! with brede
   Of marble men and maidens overwrought,
With forest branches and the trodden weed;
   Thou, silent form, dost tease us out of thought
As doth eternity: Cold Pastoral!
   When old age shall this generation waste,

---

[2] I.e., far above all breathing human passion.
[3] Athenian, thus simple and graceful.

Thou shalt remain, in midst of other woe
Than ours, a friend to man, to whom thou say'st,
"Beauty is truth, truth beauty,—that is all
Ye know on earth, and all ye need to know."   50

FOR ANALYSIS

1. Describe the scene the poet sees depicted on the urn. Describe the scene the poet imagines as a consequence of the scene on the urn.

2. Why are the boughs, the piper, and the lovers happy in **stanza** III?

3. Explain the assertion of stanza II: "Heard melodies are sweet, but those unheard / Are sweeter."

4. Does the poem support the assertion of the last two lines? What do they mean?

MAKING ARGUMENTS

Perhaps the most famous lines of this poem—which is filled with well-known lines—come at the poem's close, ending with "Beauty is truth," and so on (l. 49). They are also the source of the greatest critical disagreements, as some readers find these lines define the poem, while others feel they nearly ruin it. Make an argument concerning these lines; if it helps, do a bit of reading on what the critics have said (for example, I. A. Richards, T. S. Eliot), and think about who voices these lines, whether they are endorsed or the speech of a "**character**," and whether they are critiqued or championed.

WRITING TOPIC

Discuss Keats's view of the connection between art and life. With this in mind, consider the meaning of the phrase "Cold Pastoral!" (l. 45).

EMILY DICKINSON   (1830–1886)

AFTER GREAT PAIN, A FORMAL FEELING COMES   CA. 1863

After great pain, a formal feeling comes—
The Nerves sit ceremonious, like Tombs—
The stiff Heart questions was it He, that bore,
And Yesterday, or Centuries before?

The Feet, mechanical, go round—
Of Ground, or Air, or Ought—
A Wooden way
Regardless grown,
A Quartz contentment, like a stone—

This is the Hour of Lead—   10
Remembered, if outlived,

As Freezing persons, recollect the Snow—
First—Chill—then Stupor—then the letting go—

FOR ANALYSIS

Is this poem about physical or psychic pain? Explain.

WRITING TOPIC

What is the meaning of "stiff Heart" (l. 3) and "Quartz contentment" (l. 9)? What part
do they play in the larger pattern of **images** in this poem?

I HEARD A FLY BUZZ—
WHEN I DIED   CA. 1862

I heard a Fly buzz—when I died—
The Stillness in the Room
Was like the Stillness in the Air—
Between the Heaves of Storm—

The Eyes around—had wrung them dry—
And Breaths were gathering firm
For that last Onset—when the King
Be witnessed—in the Room—

I willed my Keepsakes—Signed away
What portion of me be   10
Assignable—and then it was
There interposed a Fly—

With Blue—uncertain stumbling Buzz—
Between the light—and me—
And then the Windows failed—and then
I could not see to see—

APPARENTLY WITH NO SURPRISE   CA. 1884

Apparently with no surprise
To any happy Flower,
The Frost beheads it at its play
In accidental power.
The blond Assassin passes on,
The Sun proceeds unmoved
To measure off another Day
For an Approving God.

CASE STUDY IN WORDS AND IMAGES

POEMS ABOUT PAINTINGS

The works in this section offer a unique opportunity to reflect on the ways meaning can be conveyed through different media. Most of the poems here are linked with the paintings that inspired them; others appear with paintings thematically similar in their treatment of death. While all these groupings offer an opportunity for rich examination, the ones featuring poems inspired by a particular painting open up even more complex areas for analysis: not only can the painting and the poem be considered independently of each other, but the poem can also be analyzed as a reading of the painting—an interpretation in words of a visual object.

As you enter into a dialogue between the works of art and the poems, jot down your reactions to each painting in some detail before reading the accompanying poem. After you have read a poem, compare your reactions to the poet's. Did reading the poem clarify or in any other way alter your response to the painting? Are the poems successful or even comprehensible without reference to the paintings? How are the works alike or different? With paired works, why does the poet choose to emphasize certain details of a painting and ignore others? What accounts for the order in which the poet deals with the details of the painting? Is the poet attempting an accurate and neutral description of the painting or making some judgment about it?

If you wish to look beyond the individual work, you might consider researching one of the poets and investigating why he or she was so moved by the painting as to write about it. Or you might examine the historical context of both the poem and the painting for any illuminating connections.

W. H. AUDEN (1907–1973)

MUSÉE DES BEAUX ARTS 1940

About suffering they were never wrong,
The Old Masters: how well they understood
Its human position; how it takes place
While someone else is eating or opening a window or just walking dully along;
How, when the aged are reverently, passionately waiting
For the miraculous birth, there always must be
Children who did not specially want it to happen, skating
On a pond at the edge of the wood:
They never forgot
That even the dreadful martyrdom must run its course   10

Anyhow in a corner, some untidy spot
Where the dogs go on with their doggy life and the torturer's horse
Scratches its innocent behind on a tree.

In Brueghel's *Icarus*,[1] for instance: how everything turns away
Quite leisurely from the disaster; the plowman may
Have heard the splash, the forsaken cry,
But for him it was not an important failure; the sun shone
As it had to on the white legs disappearing into the green
Water; and the expensive delicate ship that must have seen
Something amazing, a boy falling out of the sky,   20
Had somewhere to get to and sailed calmly on.

Landscape with the Fall of Icarus, ca. 1560, by Pieter Brueghel the Elder.

Musée d'Art Ancien. Scala/Art Resource, NY.

[1] This poem describes and comments on Pieter Brueghel's painting *Landscape with the Fall of Icarus* (reproduced above). According to myth, Daedalus and his son Icarus made wings, whose feathers they attached with wax, to escape Crete. Icarus flew so near the sun that the wax melted and he fell into the sea.

FOR ANALYSIS

1. Look up the story of Icarus. What aspects of the human condition or human nature does the story embody? How does Brueghel interpret the story? What other interpretations are possible? Compare Sexton's interpretation of the legend in her poem "To a Friend Whose Work Has Come to Triumph," which can be found in her volume *All My Pretty Ones* (1962).

2. Does the poem offer an accurate interpretation of the painting? Explain.

3. Which details of the painting does the poem describe? Does the poet omit details you found important?

LAWRENCE FERLINGHETTI   (B. 1919)
IN GOYA'S GREATEST SCENES   1958

In Goya's greatest scenes[1] we seem to see
                                        the people of the world
    exactly at the moment when
            they first attained the title of
                        'suffering humanity'
        They writhe upon the page
                        in a veritable rage
                            of adversity
        Heaped up
                groaning with babies and bayonets   10
                        under cement skies
        in an abstract landscape of blasted trees
            bent statues bats wings and beaks
                    slippery gibbets
            cadavers and carnivorous cocks
    and all the final hollering monsters
            of the
                'imagination of disaster'
        they are so bloody real
                    it is as if they really still existed   20

    And they do

---

[1] Francisco José de Goya (1746–1828), famous Spanish artist, celebrated for his representations of "suffering humanity."

Only the landscape is changed
They still are ranged along the roads
plagued by legionaires
false windmills and demented roosters

They are the same people
only further from home
on freeways fifty lanes wide
on a concrete continent
spaced with bland billboards   30
illustrating imbecile illusions of happiness
The scene shows fewer tumbrils[2]
but more maimed citizens
in painted cars
and they have strange license plates
and engines
that devour America

The Third of May, 1808, Madrid, 1814, by Francisco de Goya. Oil on canvas, 266 × 345 cm. Museo del Prado.

[2] Carts in which prisoners were conducted to the place of execution.

FOR ANALYSIS

1. While *The Third of May, 1808, Madrid* commemorates the uprising of the Spanish people against the invading forces of Napoleon, it has come to be seen as a powerful and universal statement against the brutalities of war. Goya also created a series of eighty-five etchings entitled *The Disasters of War* (1810–1820), which shows how individuals are transformed into "suffering humanity" when they are savaged by war. Compare the painting and some of the etchings as views of the disasters of war. Does the use of color in the painting and of black and white in the etchings cause different responses in the viewer? Explain.

2. Goya represents suffering and death in their most elemental, physical sense. Do you find Ferlinghetti's transformation of suffering and death from the literal to the **metaphoric** in the second half of his poem successful? Explain.

ANNE SEXTON (1928-1974)

THE STARRY NIGHT 1961

That does not keep me from having a terrible need of—shall I say the word—religion. Then I go out at night to paint the stars.
—Vincent van Gogh in a letter to his brother

The town does not exist
except where one black-haired tree slips
up like a drowned woman into the hot sky.
The town is silent. The night boils with eleven stars
Oh starry starry night! This is how
I want to die

It moves. They are all alive.
Even the moon bulges in its orange irons
to push children, like a god from its eye.
The old unseen serpent swallows up the stars.   10
Oh starry starry night! This is how
I want to die:

into that rushing beast of the night,
sucked up by that great dragon, to split
from my life with no flag,
no belly,
no cry.

The Starry Night, 1889, by Vincent van Gogh (1853–1890). Oil on canvas, 29″ × 36¼″. Acquired through the Lillie P. Bliss Bequest. (472.1941). The Museum of Modern Art, New York, NY, USA. Reproduced by permission.

FOR ANALYSIS

1. In what ways does your reaction to the painting agree with Sexton's? In what ways does it differ? Does her poem open your eyes to elements of the painting you had not initially seen? Explain.

2. The first two **stanzas** of the poem end with the refrain "This is how / I want to die." What does "This" refer to? In what sense might *The Starry Night* be described as a painting about death?

3. Around the time of this painting, van Gogh was much preoccupied with cypress trees. He wrote his brother, "The tree is as beautiful of line and proportion as an Egyptian obelisk. And the green has such a quality of distinction. It is a splash of black in a sunny landscape, but it is one of the most interesting black notes, and the most difficult to hit off exactly that I can imagine." How is Sexton's reference to the cypress tree in the opening lines of her poem related to her overall reading of the painting?

4. Describe the difference in brushstrokes van Gogh uses for the sky and those he uses for the village. How is this difference related to the painting's **theme**?

5. *The Starry Night* was painted in the town of Saint-Rémy. Later in the same year, van Gogh did another painting, this one in the town of Arles, to which he gave the same title. Look up this later painting, and compare the differences in the painter's handling of light, both natural and artificial.

6. Some of van Gogh's paintings have been described as mystical. Which of his two *Starry Night* paintings does the term best fit? Explain. What similarities and differences do you find between the depiction of the village and the sky in the two works?

DONALD FINKEL (1929–2008)

THE GREAT WAVE: HOKUSAI   1959

But we will take the problem in its most obscure manifestation, and suppose that our spectator is an average Englishman. A trained observer, carefully hidden behind a screen, might notice a dilation in his eyes, even an intake of his breath, perhaps a grunt.
—Herbert Read, The Meaning of Art

It is because the sea is blue,
Because Fuji is blue, because the bent blue
Men have white faces, like the snow
On Fuji, like the crest of the wave in the sky the color of their
Boats. It is because the air
Is full of writing, because the wave is still: that nothing
Will harm these frail strangers,
That high over Fuji in an earthcolored sky the fingers
Will not fall; and the blue men
Lean on the sea like snow, and the wave like a mountain leans   10
Against the sky.

              In the painter's sea
All fishermen are safe. All anger bends under his unity.
But the innocent bystander, he merely
'Walks round a corner, thinking of nothing': hidden
Behind a screen we hear his cry.
He stands half in and half out of the world; he is the men,
But he cannot see below Fuji
The shore the color of sky; he is the wave, he stretches
His claws against strangers. He is   20
Not safe, not even from himself. His world is flat.
He fishes a sea full of serpents, he rides his boat
Blindly from wave to wave toward Ararat.

The Great Wave Off Kanagawa, 1831–1833, by Katsushika Hokusai. Polychrome woodblock print; ink and color on paper. 10⅛ʺ × 14¹⁵⁄₁₆ʺ (25.7 × 37.9 cm). The Metropolitan Museum of Art, H. O. Havemeyer Collection, Bequest of Mrs. H. O. Havemeyer, 1929 (JP1847).

Image copyright © The Metropolitan Museum of Art. Image source: Art Resource, NY.

FOR ANALYSIS

1. The "average Englishman" or indeed any other eyewitness to the actual scene depicted in this print would reasonably assume that the men in the boats are in imminent danger of being drowned by the enormous, menacing wave about to crash down upon them. Yet that is not how the poet interprets the scene. On what basis does he declare "that nothing / Will harm these frail strangers" (ll. 6–7) and that "In the painter's sea / All fishermen are safe" (ll. 12–13)?

2. What does Finkel mean when he says, "In the painter's sea / All fishermen are safe. All anger bends under his unity" (ll. 12–13)? How has the artist's representation of nature changed its reality—that is, eliminated the danger and imposed unity?

3. What does the "innocent bystander" not understand that the poet does? Why is the bystander not safe from himself? In contrast to the world represented by the artist, what kind of world does the bystander inhabit? Why is his sea "full of serpents" (l. 22), and why is his boat headed for Ararat (l. 23)?

4. Finkel's epigraph is taken from a passage in section 1, paragraph 17, of Herbert Read's *The Meaning of Art* (1968). Read the passage, which defines "the problem," and explain why Finkel uses it to introduce his poem.

5. Compare Finkel's poem with Keats's "Ode on a Grecian Urn" (p. 1245), and discuss the similarities and differences in the way they interpret the visual work that has inspired them to poetry.

BECAUSE I COULD NOT STOP FOR DEATH   CA. 1863

Because I could not stop for Death—
He kindly stopped for me—
The Carriage held but just Ourselves—
And Immortality.

We slowly drove—He knew no haste
And I had put away
My labor and my leisure too,
For his Civility—

We passed the School, where Children strove
At Recess—in the Ring—   10
We passed the Fields of Gazing Grain—
We passed the Setting Sun—

Or rather—He passed Us—
The Dews drew quivering and chill—
For only Gossamer, my Gown—
My Tippet—only Tulle—

We paused before a House that seemed
A Swelling of the Ground—
The Roof was scarcely visible—
The Cornice—in the Ground—   20

Since then—'tis Centuries—and yet
Feels shorter than the Day
I first surmised the Horses' Heads
Were toward Eternity—

GERARD MANLEY HOPKINS   (1844–1889)

GOD'S GRANDEUR   1918

The world is charged with the grandeur of God.
    It will flame out, like shining from shook foil°   metal foil
    It gathers to a greatness, like the ooze of oil
Crushed. Why do men then now not reck° his rod?   heed
Generations have trod, have trod, have trod;

1257

And all is seared with trade; bleared, smeared with toil;
   And wears man's smudge and shares man's smell: the soil
Is bare now, nor can foot feel, being shod.

And for all this, nature is never spent;
   There lives the dearest freshness deep down things;   10
And though the last lights off the black West went
   Oh, morning, at the brown brink eastward, springs—
Because the Holy Ghost over the bent
   World broods with warm breast and with ah! bright wings.

A. E. HOUSMAN   (1859–1936)

TO AN ATHLETE DYING YOUNG   1896

The time you won your town the race
We chaired you through the market place;
Man and boy stood cheering by,
And home we brought you shoulder-high.

Today, the road all runners come,
Shoulder-high we bring you home,
And set you at your threshold down,
Townsman of a stiller town.

Smart lad, to slip betimes away
From fields where glory does not stay,
And early though the laurel grows   10
It withers quicker than the rose.

Eyes the shady night has shut
Cannot see the record cut,
And silence sounds no worse than cheers
After earth has stopped the ears:

Now you will not swell the rout
Of lads that wore their honors out,
Runners whom renown outran
And the name died before the man.   20

So set, before its echoes fade,
The fleet foot on the sill of shade,

And hold to the low lintel up
The still-defended challenge cup.

And round that early-laureled head
Will flock to gaze the strengthless dead
And find unwithered on its curls
The garland briefer than a girl's.

WILLIAM BUTLER YEATS   (1865–1939)

SAILING TO BYZANTIUM[1]   1927

1

That is no country for old men. The young
In one another's arms, birds in the trees
—Those dying generations—at their song,
The salmon-falls, the mackerel-crowded seas,
Fish, flesh, or fowl, commend all summer long
Whatever is begotten, born, and dies.
Caught in that sensual music all neglect
Monuments of unaging intellect.

2

An aged man is but a paltry thing,
A tattered coat upon a stick, unless
Soul clap its hands and sing, and louder sing   10
For every tatter in its mortal dress,
Nor is there singing school but studying
Monuments of its own magnificence;
And therefore I have sailed the seas and come
To the holy city of Byzantium.

Sailing to Byzantium
    [1] Capital of the ancient Eastern Roman Empire, Byzantium (modern Istanbul) is celebrated for
its great art, including mosaics (in ll. 17–18, Yeats addresses the figures in one of these mosaics). In
A Vision, Yeats cites Byzantium as possibly the only civilization that had achieved what he called "Unity
of Being"—a state where "religious, aesthetic, and practical life were one."

3

O sages standing in God's holy fire
As in the gold mosaic of a wall,
Come from the holy fire, perne in a gyre,[2]
And be the singing-masters of my soul.
Consume my heart away; sick with desire   20
And fastened to a dying animal
It knows not what it is; and gather me
Into the artifice of eternity.

4

Once out of nature I shall never take
My bodily form from any natural thing,
But such a form as Grecian goldsmiths make
Of hammered gold and gold enameling
To keep a drowsy Emperor awake;[3]
Or set upon a golden bough to sing   30
To lords and ladies of Byzantium
Of what is past, or passing, or to come.

FOR ANALYSIS

1. This poem incorporates a series of contrasts, among them "that" country and Byzantium, and the real birds of the first **stanza** and the artificial bird of the final stanza. What others do you find?

2. What are the meanings of "generations" (l. 3)?

3. For what is the poet "sick with desire" (l. 21)?

4. In what sense is eternity an "artifice" (l. 24)?

MAKING ARGUMENTS

Do some reading on Yeats, in particular on his idiosyncratic view of human history but also on his other poems, for example "The Second Coming" (p. 424). Make an argument concerning the final line of "Sailing to Byzantium." What is past? What is passing? Most importantly, what would you argue Yeats sees coming, and how does he feel about it?

WRITING TOPIC

In what ways are the **images** of bird and song used throughout this poem?

---

[2] I.e., whirl in a spiral motion. Yeats associated this motion with the cycles of history and the fate of the individual. Here he entreats the sages represented in the mosaic to take him out of the natural world described in the first stanza and into the eternal world of art.

[3] "I have read somewhere," Yeats wrote, "that in the Emperor's palace at Byzantium was a tree made of gold and silver, and artificial birds that sang." The poet wishes to become an artificial bird (a work of art) in contrast to the real birds of the first stanza.

EDWIN ARLINGTON ROBINSON   (1869–1935)

RICHARD CORY   1897

Whenever Richard Cory went down town,
We people on the pavement looked at him:
He was a gentleman from sole to crown,
Clean favored, and imperially slim.

And he was always quietly arrayed,
And he was always human when he talked;
But still he fluttered pulses when he said,
"Good-morning," and he glittered when he walked.

And he was rich—yes, richer than a king—
And admirably schooled in every grace: 10
In fine, we thought that he was everything
To make us wish that we were in his place.

So on we worked, and waited for the light,
And went without the meat, and cursed the bread;
And Richard Cory, one calm summer night,
Went home and put a bullet through his head.

ROBERT FROST   (1874–1963)

AFTER APPLE-PICKING   1914

My long two-pointed ladder's sticking through a tree
Toward heaven still,
And there's a barrel that I didn't fill
Beside it, and there may be two or three
Apples I didn't pick upon some bough.
But I am done with apple-picking now.
Essence of winter sleep is on the night,
The scent of apples: I am drowsing off.
I cannot rub the strangeness from my sight
I got from looking through a pane of glass   10
I skimmed this morning from the drinking trough
And held against the world of hoary grass.
It melted, and I let it fall and break.
But I was well
Upon my way to sleep before it fell,
And I could tell
What form my dreaming was about to take.

Magnified apples appear and disappear,
Stem end and blossom end,
And every fleck of russet showing clear. 20
My instep arch not only keeps the ache,
It keeps the pressure of a ladder-round.
I feel the ladder sway as the boughs bend.
And I keep hearing from the cellar bin
The rumbling sound
Of load on load of apples coming in.
For I have had too much
Of apple-picking: I am overtired
Of the great harvest I myself desired.
There were ten thousand thousand fruit to touch, 30
Cherish in hand, lift down, and not let fall.
For all
That struck the earth,
No matter if not bruised or spiked with stubble,
Went surely to the cider-apple heap
As of no worth.
One can see what will trouble
This sleep of mine, whatever sleep it is.
Were he not gone,
The woodchuck could say whether it's like his 40
Long sleep, as I describe its coming on,
Or just some human sleep.

FOR ANALYSIS

1. What does apple-picking **symbolize**?

2. At the end of the poem, why is the speaker uncertain about what kind of sleep is coming on him?

MAKING ARGUMENTS

Do you think the speaker's "sleep" will be troubled? What does the poem seem to think the future holds for him, after life? Make an argument in response to these questions, supporting your claim with specific textual observations.

'OUT, OUT—'[1]   1916

The buzz-saw snarled and rattled in the yard
And made dust and dropped stove-length sticks of wood,
Sweet-scented stuff when the breeze drew across it.

[1] The title is taken from the famous speech of Macbeth upon hearing that his wife has died (*Macbeth,* act v, scene 5).

And from there those that lifted eyes could count
Five mountain ranges one behind the other
Under the sunset far into Vermont.
And the saw snarled and rattled, snarled and rattled,
As it ran light, or had to bear a load.
And nothing happened: day was all but done.
Call it a day, I wish they might have said
To please the boy by giving him the half hour
That a boy counts so much when saved from work.
His sister stood beside them in her apron
To tell them 'Supper.' At the word, the saw,
As if to prove saws knew what supper meant,
Leaped out at the boy's hand, or seemed to leap—
He must have given the hand. However it was,
Neither refused the meeting. But the hand!
The boy's first outcry was a rueful laugh,
As he swung toward them holding up the hand
Half in appeal, but half as if to keep
The life from spilling. Then the boy saw all—
Since he was old enough to know, big boy
Doing a man's work, though a child at heart—
He saw all spoiled. 'Don't let him cut my hand off—
The doctor, when he comes. Don't let him, sister!'
So. But the hand was gone already.
The doctor put him in the dark of ether.
He lay and puffed his lips out with his breath.
And then—the watcher at his pulse took fright.
No one believed. They listened at his heart.
Little—less—nothing!—and that ended it.
No more to build on there. And they, since they
Were not the one dead, turned to their affairs.

NOTHING GOLD CAN STAY 1923

Nature's first green is gold,
Her hardest hue to hold.
Her early leaf's a flower;
But only so an hour.
Then leaf subsides to leaf.
So Eden sank to grief,
So dawn goes down to day.
Nothing gold can stay.

FOR ANALYSIS

1. Does this poem protest or accept the transitoriness of things?

2. Why does Frost use the word *subsides* in line 5 rather than a word like *expands* or *grows*?

3. How are "Nature's first green" (l. 1), "Eden" (l. 6), and "dawn" (l. 7) linked together?

STOPPING BY WOODS ON A SNOWY EVENING 1923

Whose woods these are I think I know.
His house is in the village though;
He will not see me stopping here
To watch his woods fill up with snow.

My little horse must think it queer
To stop without a farmhouse near
Between the woods and frozen lake
The darkest evening of the year.

He gives his harness bells a shake
To ask if there is some mistake.
The only other sound's the sweep
Of easy wind and downy flake.

The woods are lovely, dark and deep,
But I have promises to keep,
And miles to go before I sleep,
And miles to go before I sleep.

FOR ANALYSIS

1. What does the description of the horse tell us about the speaker?

2. What function does the repetition in the last two lines of the poem serve?

3. Why does the speaker refer to the owner of the woods in the opening **stanza**?

MAKING ARGUMENTS

Like many of Frost's poems, this one seems simple. Argue for the idea that, behind its simple, even lovely surface, this poem is (to continue borrowing from l. 13) "dark and deep." Build your argument from observations of the poem's specifics, both to demonstrate the simplicity and argue that it possesses dark depths.

DESIGN   1936

I found a dimpled spider, fat and white,
On a white heal-all, holding up a moth
Like a white piece of rigid satin cloth—
Assorted characters of death and blight
Mixed ready to begin the morning right,
Like the ingredients of a witches' broth—
A snow-drop spider, a flower like a froth,
And dead wings carried like a paper kite.

What had that flower to do with being white,
The wayside blue and innocent heal-all?   10
What brought the kindred spider to that height,
Then steered the white moth thither in the night?
What but design of darkness to appall?—
If design govern in a thing so small.

WRITING TOPIC

Compare this poem with Dickinson's "Apparently with no surprise" (p. 1248).

PABLO NERUDA   (1904–1973)

THE DEAD WOMAN   1972

If suddenly you do not exist,
if suddenly you are not living,
I shall go on living.

I do not dare,
I do not dare to write it,
if you die.

I shall go on living.

Because where a man has no voice,
there, my voice.

Where blacks are beaten,
I can not be dead.   10
When my brothers go to jail
I shall go with them.

When victory,
not my victory
but the great victory
arrives,
even though I am mute I must speak:
I shall see it come even though I am blind.

No, forgive me.   20
If you are not living,
if you, beloved, my love,
if you
have died,
all the leaves will fall on my breast,
it will rain upon my soul night and day,
the snow will burn my heart,
I shall walk with cold and fire and death and snow,
my feet will want to march toward where you sleep,
but   30
I shall go on living,
because you wanted me to be, above all things,
untamable,
and, love, because you know that I am not just one man
but all men.

CZESŁAW MIŁOSZ   (1911–2004)

A SONG ON THE END OF THE WORLD[1]   1944

On the day the world ends
A bee circles a clover,
A fisherman mends a glimmering net.
Happy porpoises jump in the sea,
By the rainspout young sparrows are playing
And the snake is gold-skinned as it should always be.

On the day the world ends
Women walk through the fields under their umbrellas,
A drunkard grows sleepy at the edge of a lawn,
Vegetable peddlers shout in the street   10
And a yellow-sailed boat comes nearer the island,
The voice of a violin lasts in the air
And leads into a starry night.

[1] Translated by Anthony Milosz.

And those who expected lightning and thunder
Are disappointed.
And those who expected signs and archangels' trumps
Do not believe it is happening now.
As long as the sun and the moon are above,
As long as the bumblebee visits a rose,
As long as rosy infants are born   20
No one believes it is happening now.

Only a white-haired old man, who would be a prophet
Yet is not a prophet, for he's much too busy,
Repeats while he binds his tomatoes:
There will be no other end of the world,
There will be no other end of the world.

FOR ANALYSIS

1. How would you describe the **tone** of this poem? Is it sad? Foreboding? Does it feel more positive than negative?

2. Think again about the title of the poem. How is this a song about the end of the world? How is it not? What else is it about? How do these two things relate?

MAKING ARGUMENTS

The poem was written in 1944 in Warsaw. Based on a bit of research, make an argument for the importance of the place and time of its creation to the poem.

DYLAN THOMAS   (1914–1953)

DO NOT GO GENTLE INTO
THAT GOOD NIGHT   1952

Do not go gentle into that good night,
Old age should burn and rave at close of day;
Rage, rage against the dying of the light.

Though wise men at their end know dark is right,
Because their words had forked no lightning they
Do not go gentle into that good night.

Good men, the last wave by, crying how bright
Their frail deeds might have danced in a green bay,
Rage, rage against the dying of the light.

Wild men who caught and sang the sun in flight,   10
And learn, too late, they grieved it on its way,
Do not go gentle into that good night.

Grave men, near death, who see with blinding sight
Blind eyes could blaze like meteors and be gay,
Rage, rage against the dying of the light.

And you, my father, there on the sad height,
Curse, bless, me now with your fierce tears, I pray.
Do not go gentle into that good night.
Rage, rage against the dying of the light.

FOR ANALYSIS

1. What do wise, good, wild, and grave men have in common?

2. Why does the poet use the adjective *gentle* rather than the adverb *gently* in the title?

3. What is the "sad height" (l. 16)?

MAKING ARGUMENTS

"Do Not Go Gentle into That Good Night" is filled with paradoxes, even before it starts, in its title (which is really just its first line). How would you construct an argument for the importance of **paradox** not formally but thematically? Build your argument from observations about how Thomas uses paradox and from claims for paradox as a way to think about his subject.

WRITING TOPIC

This poem is a **villanelle**, which means that it contains only two rhymes and that the first and third lines alternate as the third lines in each **stanza** following and form a final **couplet**. Why do you think Thomas chose this form for his poem? How does it relate to the poem's subject and its treatment of that subject?

DONALD HALL   (B. 1928)

AFFIRMATION   2002

To grow old is to lose everything.
Aging, everybody knows it.
Even when we are young,
we glimpse it sometimes, and nod our heads
when a grandfather dies.
Then we row for years on the midsummer
pond, ignorant and content. But a marriage,
that began without harm, scatters
into debris on the shore,
and a friend from school drops   10

cold on a rocky strand.
If a new love carries us
past middle age, our wife will die
at her strongest and most beautiful.
New women come and go. All go.
The pretty lover who announces
that she is temporary
is temporary. The bold woman,
middle-aged against our old age,
sinks under an anxiety she cannot withstand. 20
Another friend of decades estranges himself
in words that pollute thirty years.
Let us stifle under mud at the pond's edge
and affirm that it is fitting
and delicious to lose everything.

FOR ANALYSIS

1. What exactly does this poem affirm?

2. The first and last lines of the poem end with "to lose everything." If the poem begins and ends the same way, does anything change in the middle? If so, what?

MAKING ARGUMENTS

"Affirmation" is not what you would call a cheery poem. Rather than heeding the contemporary encouragement to think positively, look on the bright side, and see the glass as half full, this poem affirms what some would call the biggest fact of life, certainly its final fact. Positive psychology, for example, would not approve. Argue for or against this choice to face the dark side of life. Do you think it is a good choice? Is it healthy? Base your argument on the workings of the poem and also on your own ideas (and others that you turn up in your reading) about life and how we think about it.

WRITING TOPIC

Did you identify with the "we" in lines 3 through 5? Or lines 6 and 7? How aware are you of the fact that, as Hall puts it, "all go" (l. 15)? Reflect on the ways in which you do and don't think about the inevitable fact of death.

MAKING CONNECTIONS

The last sentence of the poem seems to allude to Owen's "Dulce et Decorum Est" (p. 445). Why do you think Hall might have made this **allusion**?

MARVIN KLOTZ (1930-2014)

REQUIEM 2007

FOR S.S.

Inside the skin's where it happens.
Amazing what that space contains—
Interstices, the roads, all mapped
By what we've done—our lives' refrain,

A song within the skin. Childhood
Anxieties, first love, the rough
And tumble scars, ecstatic good—
All melt, and cool—become one tough

Amalgam: our unburnished selves.
There reside affections, taste, pain,   10
And politics. And there we delve
Among the crystal cracks, to gain
That sense of who we are, to find,
Among inchoate parts, a center.

Sometimes, inside the skin, the mind
Demurs, sweeps out all debris—vents,
And leaves that arid space within
Where plain grief abides, untarnished
By our lives' complex and foolish
Stuff—just empty, inside the skin.   20

MARY OLIVER (B. 1935)

WHEN DEATH COMES 1992

When death comes
like the hungry bear in autumn;
when death comes and takes all the bright coins from his purse

to buy me, and snaps the purse shut;
when death comes
like the measle-pox;

when death comes
like an iceberg between the shoulder blades,

1270

I want to step through the door full of curiosity, wondering:
what is it going to be like, that cottage of darkness?   10

And therefore I look upon everything
as a brotherhood and a sisterhood,
and I look upon time as no more than an idea,
and I consider eternity as another possibility,

and I think of each life as a flower, as common
as a field daisy, and as singular,

and each name a comfortable music in the mouth,
tending, as all music does, toward silence,

and each body a lion of courage, and something
precious to the earth.   20

When it's over, I want to say: all my life
I was a bride married to amazement.
I was the bridegroom, taking the world into my arms.

When it's over, I don't want to wonder
if I have made of my life something particular, and real.
I don't want to find myself sighing and frightened,
or full of argument.

I don't want to end up simply having visited this world.

FOR ANALYSIS

1. This poem turns on a series of **images**. Describe each image associated with approaching death, evaluating its effectiveness and appropriateness.

2. What is the "cottage of darkness" (l. 10)?

3. What images are associated with life and experience? Are they effective? Explain.

4. What is wrong with "simply having visited this world" (l. 28)?

MAKING ARGUMENTS

Much of Oliver's imagery here is drawn from nature; in fact, she is known as a nature poet. How would you argue that this sustained attention to the natural world informs this poem's approach to thinking about death?

WRITING TOPIC

Lines 24–27 express the poet's attitude toward life as its end approaches. In an essay, explain how a life that is "particular, and real" leads naturally to a death that does not generate either sighing and fear, or argument.

ALICIA OSTRIKER (B. 1937)

DAFFODILS 2005

FOR DAVID LEHMAN

> Ten thousand saw I at a glance
> Tossing their heads in sprightly dance.
> —WILLIAM WORDSWORTH

> Going to hell so many times tears it
> Which explains poetry.
> —JACK SPICER

The day the war against Iraq begins
I'm photographing the yellow daffodils
With their outstretched arms and ruffled cups
Blowing in the wind of Jesus Green

Edging the lush grassy moving river
Along with the swans and ducks
Under a soft March Cambridge sky
Embellishing the earth like a hand

Starting to illustrate a children's book
Where people in light clothes come out   10
To play, to frisk and run about
With their lovers, friends, animals, and children

As down every stony back road of history
They've always done in the peaceful springs
—Which in a sense is also hell because
The daffodils do look as if they dance

And make some of us in the park want to dance
And breathe deeply and I know that
Being able to eat and incorporate beauty like this
I am privileged and by that token can   20

Taste pain, roll it on my tongue, it's good
The cruel wars are good the stupidity is good,
The primates hiding in their caves are very good,
They do their best, which explains poetry.

What explains poetry is that life is hard
But better than the alternatives,

The no and the nothing. Look at this light
And color, a splash of brilliant yellow

Punctuating an emerald text, white swans
And mottled brown ducks floating quietly along   30
Whole and alive, like an untorn language
That lacks nothing, that excludes

Nothing. Period. Don't you think
It is our business to defend it
Even the day our masters start a war?
To defend the day we see the daffodils?

FOR ANALYSIS

1. How does the physical **setting** of the poem and the way it is described contrast with the day on which it is set?

2. What is the effect of ending the poem with questions? What kind of questions are they?

3. By the end of the poem, it is clear what the speaker thinks "explains poetry." What is it? How does it explain poetry?

MAKING ARGUMENTS

Arguments over whether literature should be political are as old as literature and politics themselves. Critic Lionel Trilling described their intersection as "the dark and bloody crossroads where literature and politics meet," "bloody" in the sense that they are argued over violently. Using this poem as evidence, but also relying on your thoughts about this issue and anything you can learn from others' statements on the matter, make your own argument about politics in poetry.

WRITING TOPIC

As the first **epigraph** makes plain, this poem alludes to William Wordsworth's 1807 poem "I Wandered Lonely as a Cloud" (often referred to as "Daffodils"). Find a copy of Wordsworth's poem and write a short essay explaining Ostriker's **allusion**. Why does she point to that poem in particular? What about the subject and spirit of her poem is illuminated by bringing to mind Wordsworth's?

SEAMUS HEANEY   (B. 1939–2013)

MID-TERM BREAK   1966

I sat all morning in the college sick bay
Counting bells knelling classes to a close.
At two o'clock our neighbors drove me home.

In the porch I met my father crying—
He had always taken funerals in his stride—
And Big Jim Evans saying it was a hard blow.

The baby cooed and laughed and rocked the pram
When I came in, and I was embarrassed
By old men standing up to shake my hand

And tell me they were "sorry for my trouble," 10
Whispers informed strangers I was the eldest,
Away at school, as my mother held my hand

In hers and coughed out angry tearless sighs.
At ten o'clock the ambulance arrived
With the corpse, stanched and bandaged by the nurses.

Next morning I went up into the room. Snowdrops
And candles soothed the bedside; I saw him
For the first time in six weeks. Paler now,

Wearing a poppy bruise on his left temple,
He lay in the four foot box as in his cot. 20
No gaudy scars, the bumper knocked him clear.

A four foot box, a foot for every year.

FOR ANALYSIS

1. Although it contains little **rhyme**, this poem is remarkably musical. Identify the **assonance** and **alliteration** that permeate the poem.

2. What event does the poem describe?

3. How is the poem's title relevant?

MAKING ARGUMENTS

Different poems depend on different effects. "Mid-term Break" depends in large measure on the timing of the disclosure of information. Make an argument about the use of this surprise ending—do you find it powerful? Will its power persist through multiple readings? Do you find it gimmicky, like the twist at the end of an O. Henry story?

WRITING TOPIC

Describe the family and the society revealed in this short poem.

JANE KENYON   (1947–1995)

LET EVENING COME   1996

Let the light of late afternoon
shine through chinks in the barn, moving
up the bales as the sun moves down.

Let the cricket take up chafing
as a woman takes up her needles
and her yarn. Let evening come.

Let dew collect on the hoe abandoned
in long grass. Let the stars appear
and the moon disclose her silver horn.

Let the fox go back to its sandy den.   10
Let the wind die down. Let the shed
go black inside. Let evening come.

To the bottle in the ditch, to the scoop
in the oats, to air in the lung
let evening come.

Let it come, as it will, and don't
be afraid. God does not leave us
comfortless, so let evening come.

FOR ANALYSIS

1. What does evening signify in this poem?

2. Why do you think Kenyon includes "air in the lung" (l. 14) as one of the things that
evening should be allowed to come to?

3. How would you characterize the sounds and **rhythms** of this poem? How do they
serve the subject?

MAKING ARGUMENTS

"Let Evening Come" was published shortly after the death of its author. Reflect on how
knowing this might change your reading experience or interpretation of the poem.
Does it change your sense of what the poem is about? Does it change its emotional
tone? Should it? Should knowing something about the life of a writer change how you
read that writer's work?

WRITING TOPIC

Do you have an opinion on the poem's assertion that "God does not leave us /
comfortless" (ll. 17–18)? What does it mean? Does your agreement or disagreement with that assertion change how you feel about the poem?

YUSEF KOMUNYAKAA   (B. 1947)

FACING IT   1988

My black face fades,
hiding inside the black granite.
I said I wouldn't,
dammit: No tears.
I'm stone. I'm flesh.
My clouded reflection eyes me
like a bird of prey, the profile of night
slanted against morning. I turn
this way—the stone lets me go.
I turn that way—I'm inside   10
the Vietnam Veterans Memorial
again, depending on the light
to make a difference.
I go down the 58,022 names,
half-expecting to find
my own in letters like smoke.
I touch the name Andrew Johnson;
I see the booby trap's white flash.
Names shimmer on a woman's blouse
but when she walks away   20
the names stay on the wall.
Brushstrokes flash, a red bird's
wings cutting across my stare.
The sky. A plane in the sky.
A white vet's image floats
closer to me, then his pale eyes
look through mine. I'm a window.
He's lost his right arm
inside the stone. In the black mirror
a woman's trying to erase names: 30
No, she's brushing a boy's hair.

FOR ANALYSIS

1. What is the speaker in "Facing It" facing? Is it one thing? More than one thing? If
more than one, does "facing" mean the same thing for each "it"?

2. In what ways does the poem refer to the war itself? Does it include direct representation of the violence or the participants? Indirect representation? Why do you think
Komunyakaa chose to refer to it in these ways?

MAKING ARGUMENTS

With the support of research into other memorials—restricting yourself to those in
Washington, DC, would make sense—make an argument about the Vietnam Veterans

1276

Memorial. Is it appropriate? Inappropriate? Does it or does it not comport with your sense of what these kinds of memorials should be and do?

WRITING TOPIC

The Vietnam Veterans Memorial was controversial when it first opened. (If you are not familiar with the memorial, refer to a picture of it.) How does "Facing It" engage how the memorial is experienced by people? What might it have to say to those who criticize the memorial as unpatriotic or disrespectful?

VICTOR HERNÁNDEZ CRUZ   (B. 1949)

PROBLEMS WITH HURRICANES   1991

A campesino looked at the air
And told me:
With hurricanes it's not the wind
or the noise or the water.
I'll tell you he said:
it's the mangoes, avocados
Green plantains and bananas
flying into town like projectiles.

How would your family
feel if they had to tell   10
The generations that you
got killed by a flying
Banana.

Death by drowning has honor
If the wind picked you up
and slammed you
Against a mountain boulder
This would not carry shame
But
to suffer a mango smashing   20
Your skull
or a plantain hitting your
Temple at 70 miles per hour
is the ultimate disgrace.

The campesino takes off his hat—
As a sign of respect

towards the fury of the wind
and says:
Don't worry about the noise
Don't worry about the water   30
Don't worry about the wind—
If you are going out
beware of mangoes
And all such beautiful
sweet things.

MARK HALLIDAY (B. 1949)

CHICKEN SALAD 2007

Three hours before he died,
my father felt he should have an answer
when I asked what he might like to eat.
He remembered a kind of chicken salad he liked
weeks ago when living was more possible
and he said, "Maybe that chicken salad"
but because of the blood in his mouth
and because of his shortness of breath
he had to say it several times before I understood.
So I went out and bought a container of chicken salad,   10
grateful for the illusion of helping,
but when I brought it back to the apartment
my father studied it for thirty seconds
and set it aside on the bed. I wasn't ready
to know what the eyes of the nurse at the hospice
had tried to tell me before dawn, so I said,
"Don't you want your chicken salad, Daddy?"
He glanced at it from a distance of many miles—
little tub of chicken salad down on the planet of
slaughtered birds and mastication, digestion, excretion—   20
and murmured. "Maybe later." He was in
the final austerity
which I was too frazzled to quite recognize
but ever since his death I see with stony clarity
the solitary dignity of
the totality of his knowing
how far beyond the pleasure of chicken salad
he had gone already and would go.

MARIE HOWE (B. 1950)

WHAT THE LIVING DO 1998

Johnny, the kitchen sink has been clogged for days, some utensil
    probably fell down there.
And the Drano won't work but smells dangerous, and the crusty
    dishes have piled up

waiting for the plumber I still haven't called. This is the everyday
    we spoke of.
It's winter again: the sky's a deep, headstrong blue, and the sunlight
    pours through

the open living-room windows because the heat's on too high in
    here and I can't turn it off.
For weeks now, driving, or dropping a bag of groceries in the
    street, the bag breaking,

I've been thinking: This is what the living do. And yesterday,
    hurrying along those
wobbly bricks in the Cambridge sidewalk, spilling my coffee
    down my wrist and sleeve,

I thought it again, and again later, when buying a hairbrush:
    This is it.
Parking. Slamming the car door shut in the cold. What you
    called that yearning.   10

What you finally gave up. We want the spring to come and the
    winter to pass. We want
whoever to call or not call, a letter, a kiss—we want
    more and more and then more of it.

But there are moments, walking, when I catch a glimpse of myself
    in the window glass,
say, the window of the corner video store, and I'm gripped by a
    cherishing so deep

for my own blowing hair, chapped face, and unbuttoned coat
    that I'm speechless:
I am living. I remember you.

FOR ANALYSIS

1. Who do you think Johnny might be?
2. What is it that Johnny "finally gave up" (l. 11)?

3. What kinds of things make the speaker stop and think about Johnny? How does she characterize these thoughts?

MAKING ARGUMENTS

The situation of "What the Living Do," its subject, is not unfamiliar to us. What makes this poem is not the idea—that one shape grief can take is this one—but the way in which that shape is realized in the shape of the poem. Make an argument for this claim, using the poem's structure and **rhythm** as evidence.

WRITING TOPIC

Often we think of the dead in terms of loss—of who they were, of what they meant to us, of how they are gone. The speaker in "What the Living Do" thinks of them in terms of what the title names—what those of us still here do in our everyday lives. Write an essay in which you describe the ways in which you think of those who are no longer with us.

MARK TURPIN   (B. 1953)

THE MAN WHO BUILT THIS HOUSE   2003

First realize he didn't build it for himself,
and that changes a man, and the way he thinks
about building a house. There is joy but
it's a colder type—he'd as easily joy in
tearing it down, as we have done, down
to the bare frame, loaded boxes of lath
and plaster, stirring a dust unstirred since
well, we know the date: Thursday, June 19, 1930.
Date on the newspaper stuffed between
the doorbell battery and the box it lodged in.   10
Not so long ago, seventy years, historical
only to a Californian. The headline: "Admiral Byrd
Given Welcome In N.Y." "Rear Admiral
Richard E. Byrd, conqueror of the South Pole."
Safe to say, the man who built this house
is gone or nearly gone by now—and we think
of the houses we have built, and the strangers
who will certainly, eventually come to change
or tear them down—that further event that
needs to happen. And there is a foulness   20
to this dust, dust locked in walls till
we arrived to release it to the world again.
So, maybe, all is as it should be. Still, the man

himself haunts me. I noticed it—especially
after my apprentice saw fit to criticize his work,
this neat but spindly frame of rough 2 × 4's—
2 × 4's for the walls, the rafters, even for the ceiling joists
(that he tied to the ridge to keep the ceiling from sagging)
that functioned adequately all these years
till we knocked it loose. And so, for reasons   30
my apprentice wouldn't understand, I admit
a liking, yes, for him and for this sketch
of a house, the lightness of his eye, as if
there might be something else to think about:
a sister taken sick, or maybe just a book or
a newspaper with a coffee and a smoke, as if
to say to the world: This is all you take from me.
Of course, having lived here a month already,
I know better—accustomed now to the
hieroglyphs of his keel marks, his red crayon   40
with an arrow denoting the sole plate of a wall,
imaginary, invisible lines that he
unknowing, passes on to me, numbers and lines
radiating from the corners and the eaves
—where the bird nests hide inside the vents—
all lining up, falling plumb, coming square and true
for me, and all his offhand easiness just a guise
for a mind too quick ever to be satisfied
—just moving quickly through the motions.
And, now, what he has to show for it, hauled away   50
in boxes and bags, and me about to alter
what's left—not like Byrd's Pole, fixed
forever. The pure radiating lines forever
flowing and unalterable—lines of mind only,
without a house attached. And yet, even a South Pole
doesn't seem much of an accomplishment to us—
to have merely found another place on Earth.
There is a special pity that we reserve
for the dead, trapped in their newspapers'
images of time, wearing what they wore,   60
doing what they did. I feel as much for this man here,
and for the force it took to pull a chalked string
off the floor, let it snap, and, make a wall.
Something apart from something else,
not forever but for a little while.
He must have felt it too, a man like him,
else why leave the newspaper for us?

DILRUBA AHMED (B. 1973)

SNAKE OIL, SNAKE BITE 2013

They staunched the wound with a stone.
They drew blue venom from his blood
    until there was none.
When his veins ran true his face remained
lifeless and all the mothers of the village
wept and pounded their chests until the sky
    had little choice
but to grant their supplications. God made
    the boy breathe again.

God breathes life into us, it is said,
only once. But this case was an exception.
God drew back in a giant gust and blew life into the boy
and like a stranded fish, he shuddered, oceanless.   10

It was true: the boy lived.
He lived for a very long time. The toxins
were an oil slick: contaminated, cleaned.
But just as soon as the women
kissed redness back into his cheeks
the boy began to die again.
He continued to die for the rest of his life.
The dying took place slowly, sweetly.
The dying took a very long time.

FOR ANALYSIS

1. Who saves the boy's life?
2. What is the **tone** at the poem's end?

MAKING ARGUMENTS

Make an argument about the presence of the divine in this poem. Is this a religious
poem? Does the speaker endorse the mothers' opinion that God saves the boy? If so,
does the poem endorse the speaker?

WRITING TOPIC

Reread the poem and annotate it by speaker. That is, note who is responsible for each
line of the poem (beyond the poet herself, who of course is ultimately responsible for
all of it). Reflect on your observations. Is this poem more complicated than it at first
seems? Does recognizing possible shifts in **point of view** complicate your understanding of the poem? How?

CONNECTING POEMS: ANIMAL FATES

The poems in this unit focus on the ways in which our own reflections on mortality can involve the animal world beyond the human. They consider the decisions people must make when faced with the death of animals, the way such deaths can make us think about our own lives, and the thoughts about the mysteries of life itself that as innocent a gesture as playing with a cat can prompt.

ELIZABETH BISHOP (1911–1979)

THE FISH 1946

I caught a tremendous fish
and held him beside the boat
half out of water, with my hook
fast in a corner of his mouth.
He didn't fight.
He hadn't fought at all.
He hung a grunting weight,
battered and venerable
and homely. Here and there
his brown skin hung in strips   10
like ancient wallpaper,
and its pattern of darker brown
was like wallpaper:
shapes like full-blown roses
stained and lost through age.
He was speckled with barnacles,
fine rosettes of lime,
and infested
with tiny white sea-lice,
and underneath two or three   20
rags of green weed hung down.
While his gills were breathing in
the terrible oxygen
—the frightening gills,
fresh and crisp with blood,
that can cut so badly—
I thought of the coarse white flesh

packed in like feathers,
the big bones and the little bones,
the dramatic reds and blacks   30
of his shiny entrails,
and the pink swim-bladder
like a big peony.
I looked into his eyes
which were far larger than mine
but shallower, and yellowed,
the irises backed and packed
with tarnished tinfoil
seen through the lenses
of old scratched isinglass.   40
They shifted a little, but not
to return my stare.
—It was more like the tipping
of an object toward the light.
I admired his sullen face,
the mechanism of his jaw,
and then I saw
that from his lower lip
—if you could call it a lip—
grim, wet, and weaponlike,   50
hung five old pieces of fish-line,
or four and a wire leader
with the swivel still attached,
with all their five big hooks
grown firmly in his mouth.
A green line, frayed at the end
where he broke it, two heavier lines,
and a fine black thread
still crimped from the strain and snap
when it broke and he got away.   60
Like medals with their ribbons
frayed and wavering,
a five-haired beard of wisdom
trailing from his aching jaw.
I stared and stared
and victory filled up
the little rented boat,
from the pool of bilge
where oil had spread a rainbow
around the rusted engine   70
to the bailer rusted orange,
the sun-cracked thwarts,
the oarlocks on their strings,

the gunnels—until everything
was rainbow, rainbow, rainbow!
And I let the fish go.

FOR ANALYSIS

1. What is the nature of the speaker's "victory" (l. 66)?

2. Where does the poem turn—that is, where does the poem shift its attention to
something that changes what it is about and what it means?

MAKING ARGUMENTS

Bishop's poem hinges on the decision to let the fish go. While this is not really the
poem's subject, it could be taken as a commentary on sportfishing and hunting, a pastime enjoyed by millions but also criticized by many. Make an argument defending
or attacking this pastime based on whatever evidence and support you think will help
you make your case.

WRITING TOPIC

"The Fish" is packed with details. List the details Bishop includes, breaking them
down into the groups in which they appear (e.g., those describing the fish's skin, those
describing the boat). Then reflect on how the poem uses these details. How do they
create pictures, set moods, imply thoughts and feelings?

WILLIAM STAFFORD   (1914–1995)

TRAVELING THROUGH THE DARK   1962

Traveling through the dark I found a deer
dead on the edge of the Wilson River road.
It is usually best to roll them into the canyon:
that road is narrow; to swerve might make more dead.

By glow of the tail-light I stumbled back of the car
and stood by the heap, a doe, a recent killing;
she had stiffened already, almost cold.
I dragged her off; she was large in the belly.

My fingers touching her side brought me the reason—
her side was warm; her fawn lay there waiting,   10
alive, still, never to be born.
Beside that mountain road I hesitated.

The car aimed ahead its lowered parking lights;
under the hood purred the steady engine.

I stood in the glare of the warm exhaust turning red;
around our group I could hear the wilderness listen.

I thought hard for us all—my only swerving—,
then pushed her over the edge into the river.

FOR ANALYSIS

1. Why is it best to clear the dead deer off the road? Why does the speaker hesitate?

2. How is the speaker's car described? Why do you think Stafford describes it this way?

3. Stafford uses versions of the word *swerve* twice. Why do you think he uses them?

MAKING ARGUMENTS

There are estimates that 350,000 deer are killed by cars each year. For some, this is a tragedy for the animals; for others, it is more concerning because of the danger to drivers and passengers. Where do you stand on this situation? Could it be avoided? Is it a necessary evil given the modern world's car-based way of life?

WRITING TOPIC

Stafford chose not to explain how the deer came to be dead, perhaps in part because it is obvious that cars kill deer on this road often. Why else might he not have mentioned it? What could this poem be saying about this unnamed cause?

JOHN UPDIKE (1932-2009)

DOG'S DEATH 1993

She must have been kicked unseen or brushed by a car.
Too young to know much, she was beginning to learn
To use the newspapers spread on the kitchen floor
And to win, wetting there, the words, "Good dog! Good dog!"

We thought her shy malaise was a shot reaction.
The autopsy disclosed a rupture in her liver.
As we teased her with play, blood was filling her skin
And her heart was learning to lie down forever.

· · ·

Monday morning, as the children were noisily fed
And sent to school, she crawled beneath the youngest's bed.   10
We found her twisted and limp but still alive.
In the car to the vet's, on my lap, she tried

To bite my hand and died. I stroked her warm fur
And my wife called in a voice imperious with tears.

Though surrounded by love that would have upheld her,
Nevertheless she sank and, stiffening, disappeared.

Back home, we found that in the night her frame,
Drawing near to dissolution, had endured the shame
Of diarrhea and had dragged across the floor
To a newspaper carelessly left there. *Good dog.*   20

FOR ANALYSIS

1. Why is the dog's dying described the way it is in line 8?

2. Are the speaker and his family to blame for the dog's death? Do they feel they are?

3. Why do you think Updike ends the poem the way he does—in particular, why with that sentence?

MAKING ARGUMENTS

There is a difference between sentiment and sentimentality. Argue that Updike's poem is characterized by the former or the latter.

WRITING TOPIC

Many of us are very attached to our pets and think of them as members of the family. There are some people who find this very odd, even indulgent and irrational. What do you think about the way people feel about their pets? Write a reflection on this question, using as material not only your own feelings and experiences but your observations and knowledge of relevant issues.

WILLIAM GREENWAY   (B. 1947)

PIT PONY   1987

There are only a few left, he says,
kept by old Welsh miners, souvenirs, like
gallstones or gold teeth, torn
from this "pit," so cold and wet my
breath comes out a soul up
into my helmet's lantern
beam, anthracite walls running,
gleaming, and the floors iron-rutted
with tram tracks, the almost pure
rust that grows and waves like   10
orange moss in the gutters of water
that used to rise and drown.
He makes us turn all lights off, almost
a mile down. While children scream
I try to see anything, my hand touching
my nose, my wife beside me—darkness palpable,

a velvet sack over our heads, even the glow
of watches left behind. This is where
they were born, into this nothing, felt
first with their cold noses for the shaggy   20
side and warm bag of black
milk, pulled their trams for twenty
years through pitch, past birds
that didn't sing, through doors
opened by five-year-olds who sat
in the cheap, complete blackness listening
for steps, a knock. And they
died down here, generation after
generation. The last one, when it
dies in the hills, not quite blind, the mines   30
closed forever, will it die strangely? Will it
wonder dimly why it was exiled from the rest
of its race, from the dark flanks of the soft
mother, what these timbers are that hold up
nothing but blue? If this is the beginning
of death, this wind, these stars?

For Analysis

1. What are there only a few of left in the poem's first line?

2. While down in the mine, the speaker imagines life for the ponies that worked
there. How might the speaker's act of imagination be affected by the fact that he is
touring the mine with his family?

3. What is the **tone** of the poem's description of the pony's lives in the pits? How
about the tone of the description of life aboveground? Is it what you might expect?
Why or why not?

Making Arguments

We anthropomorphize animals. But that doesn't mean that they don't have consciousness—emotions, attachments, self-awareness—according to many people.
Others think they are far more different from us and that we shouldn't pretend to
know what could be going on in their heads, if anything. Make an argument about
"Pit Pony" in this context. Can a poet attempt to empathize with a nonhuman
subject? Does our having sympathy for them depend on what we imagine their
feelings are?

Writing Topic

Write (or describe) a poem written in whole or in part from the **point of view** of an
animal, and reflect on what you've written. How is the animal's life like and unlike
human life? Can our imagination of an animal's interior life ever approach what it's
actually like?

MAKING CONNECTIONS

1. How do these poems create moments in which the speakers think of animals as individual beings? How do they create personal (or emotional) connections with animals?

2. Some of these poems confront humans with a dilemma about killing animals. How does each resolve its dilemma? How does each poem present the decision that is made? Do any of them judge the decision?

3. What do humans do for animals in these poems? What do animals do for humans? Reflect on what these poems as a group say about the relationship between humans and nonhuman animals.

CONNECTING POEMS: SEIZING THE DAY

This section contains a range of poems, some quite similar, some very different; all could be said to fall in the line of poems that confront the idea that at some point in our lives, we feel as if we must seize the day, or that we have failed to do so. As you read, listen for the way in which these poets reflect on life's way of reminding us that we're not here forever.

RAINER MARIA RILKE   (1875–1926)

ARCHAIC TORSO OF APOLLO[1]   1908

We cannot know his legendary head
with eyes like ripening fruit. And yet his torso
is still suffused with brilliance from inside,
like a lamp, in which his gaze, now turned to low,

gleams in all its power. Otherwise
the curved breast could not dazzle you so, nor could
a smile run through the placid hips and thighs
to that dark center where procreation flared.

Otherwise this stone would seem defaced
beneath the translucent cascade of the shoulders   10
and would not glisten like a wild beast's fur:

would not, from all the borders of itself,
burst like a star: for here there is no place
that does not see you. You must change your life.

---

[1] Translated by Stephen Mitchell

FOR ANALYSIS

1. Who was Apollo? Why can we not know his legendary head?

2. How would you describe the poem's **tone**? What is the experience it expresses?

3. Who utters the poem's last sentence? Who is "you"?

4. What motivates the poem's final statement? Were you expecting it?

MAKING ARGUMENTS

Look at the final sentence in this poem: is it a gimmick? Criticize or defend this famous last sentence, arguing on the evidence of how the poem works, what the last line is trying to do, and whether or not it is effective.

WRITING TOPIC

Rilke worked for sculptor Auguste Rodin for a time, studying his sculptures and sculpture in general because he wanted his poetry to be less **abstract** and more **concrete**. Write or describe an alternative poem to this in which the ideas are explored and the sentiments are expressed with less concrete **imagery**. How might you do it? How would it compare to Rilke's?

JAMES WRIGHT (1927–1980)

LYING IN A HAMMOCK AT WILLIAM DUFFY'S FARM IN PINE ISLAND, MINNESOTA 1990

Over my head, I see the bronze butterfly,
Asleep on the black trunk,
Blowing like a leaf in green shadow.
Down the ravine behind the empty house,
The cowbells follow one another
Into the distances of the afternoon.
To my right,
In a field of sunlight between two pines,
The droppings of last year's horses
Blaze up into golden stones.   10
I lean back, as the evening darkens and comes on.
A chicken hawk floats over, looking for home.
I have wasted my life.

FOR ANALYSIS

1. What is the speaker doing as he sees the things he describes in this poem?

2. What unites the different things the speaker sees? Is there anything more than the fact that he can see them from where he lies?

3. What might the last line mean? Does what the speaker has been doing constitute the wasting of his life, or has he wasted his life not doing more of it? Defend your answer.

4. Do you think there might be any special significance to the fact that the day is ending at the end of the poem? What might it be?

MAKING ARGUMENTS

Argue either that the speaker's realization is one of regret at having spent too much time in hammocks, or that the speaker's realization is one of regret at not having spent enough time in hammocks. If a hammock is available, spend some time in it considering this question first.

WRITING TOPIC

Poets sit around a lot, thinking and looking at things. Write an essay in which you honestly consider the writing of poetry as an activity, calling, or profession. Is it a noble profession? A necessary one? Is it a nice thing to have people doing? Is it a waste of time? Explain your answer(s).

BILLY COLLINS   (B. 1941)

THE SANDHILL CRANES
OF NEBRASKA   2011

Too bad you weren't here six months ago,
was a lament I heard on my visit to Nebraska.
You could have seen the astonishing spectacle
of the sandhill cranes, thousands of them
feeding and even dancing on the shores of the Platte River.

There was no point in pointing out
the impossibility of my being there then
because I happened to be somewhere else,
so I nodded and put on a look of mild disappointment
if only to be part of the commiseration.   10

It was the same look I remember wearing
about six months ago in Georgia
when I was told that I had just missed
the spectacular annual outburst of azaleas,
brilliant against the green backdrop of spring

and the same in Vermont six months before that
when I arrived shortly after
the magnificent foliage had gloriously peaked,
Mother Nature, as she is called,
having touched the hills with her many-colored brush,   20

a phenomenon that occurs, like the others,
around the same time every year when I am apparently off
in another state, stuck in a motel lobby
with the local paper and a styrofoam cup of coffee,
busily missing God knows what.

FOR ANALYSIS

1. Why does the speaker miss the various events he mentions?
2. What do these events have in common?
3. How does the speaker feel about missing these things? How do you know?
4. What is important about the details Collins provides in the final **stanza**?

MAKING ARGUMENTS

How would you make an argument for line 22's "apparently" as the most important
line in the poem? Why is it more than something thrown in for **rhythm** or **tone**? Is the
speaker really missing things for the reason he states here?

WRITING TOPIC

"Mother nature, as she is called," in Collins's words (l. 19), is the source of much attention in poetry, from the **pastoral** poems of ancient Greece to the poems of the British
Romantics. Often the poems take nature as a topic in order to reflect on human life or
grand metaphysical questions about existence or religion. Write about "The Sandhill
Cranes of Nebraska" as a nature poem. How does Collins represent nature in this
poem? Why does he take nature as a subject here?

BARBARA RAS (B. 1949)

YOU CAN'T HAVE IT ALL 1997

But you can have the fig tree and its fat leaves like clown hands
gloved with green. You can have the touch of a single eleven-year-old finger
on your cheek, waking you at one a.m. to say the hamster is back.
You can have the purr of the cat and the soulful look
of the black dog, the look that says, If I could I would bite
every sorrow until it fled, and when it is August,
you can have it August and abundantly so. You can have love,
though often it will be mysterious, like the white foam
that bubbles up at the top of the bean pot over the red kidneys
until you realize foam's twin is blood.   10
You can have the skin at the center between a man's legs,
so solid, so doll-like. You can have the life of the mind,
glowing occasionally in priestly vestments, never admitting pettiness,

never stooping to bribe the sullen guard who'll tell you
all roads narrow at the border.
You can speak a foreign language, sometimes,
and it can mean something. You can visit the marker on the grave
where your father wept openly. You can't bring back the dead,
but you can have the words *forgive* and *forget* hold hands
as if they meant to spend a lifetime together. And you can be grateful   20
for makeup, the way it kisses your face, half spice, half amnesia, grateful
for Mozart, his many notes racing one another towards joy, for towels
sucking up the drops on your clean skin, and for deeper thirsts,
for passion fruit, for saliva. You can have the dream,
the dream of Egypt, the horses of Egypt and you riding in the hot sand.
You can have your grandfather sitting on the side of your bed,
at least for a while, you can have clouds and letters, the leaping
of distances, and Indian food with yellow sauce like sunrise.
You can't count on grace to pick you out of a crowd
but here is your friend to teach you how to high jump,   30
how to throw yourself over the bar, backwards,
until you learn about love, about sweet surrender,
and here are periwinkles, buses that kneel, farms in the mind
as real as Africa. And when adulthood fails you,
you can still summon the memory of the black swan on the pond
of your childhood, the rye bread with peanut butter and bananas
your grandmother gave you while the rest of the family slept.
There is the voice you can still summon at will, like your mother's,
it will always whisper, you can't have it all,
but there is this.   40

FOR ANALYSIS

1. Why is the first word of the poem "But"?

2. Who is "you"?

3. Do you ever have a sense of what "it all" means? Find the moments where the speaker says you can't have something. What connects those things?

MAKING ARGUMENTS

"At least for a while" (l. 27)—what is the significance of this phrase? Make an argument for its meaning and importance to the poem. How does it relate to the larger **themes** of the poem? How does it relate to the title? How does it also relate to the theme of this cluster?

WRITING TOPIC

Reread "You Can't Have It All" and record your reflections on these questions: What connects the different items in this poem? Where are their clear transitions or associations between two items, or phrases, or **images**? Where are there jumps without

connection, logical or otherwise? Afterward, review your reflections and try to describe
the method behind Ras's choices.

TONY HOAGLAND (B. 1953)

I HAVE NEWS FOR YOU   2010

There are people who do not see a broken playground swing
as a symbol of ruined childhood

and there are people who don't interpret the behavior
of a fly in a motel room as a mocking representation of their thought process.

There are people who don't walk past an empty swimming pool
and think about past pleasures unrecoverable

and then stand there blocking the sidewalk for other pedestrians.
I have read about a town somewhere in California where human beings

do not send their sinuous feeder roots
deep into the potting soil of others' emotional lives   10

as if they were greedy six-year-olds
sucking the last half-inch of milkshake up through a noisy straw;

and other persons in the Midwest who can kiss without
debating the imperialist baggage of heterosexuality.

Do you see that creamy, lemon-yellow moon?
There are some people, unlike me and you,

who do not yearn after fame or love or quantities of money as
            unattainable as that moon;
thus, they do not later
                  have to waste more time
defaming the object of their former ardor.   20

Or consequently run and crucify themselves
in some solitary midnight Starbucks Golgotha.

I have news for you—
there are people who get up in the morning and cross a room

and open a window to let the sweet breeze in
and let it touch them all over their faces and bodies.

FOR ANALYSIS

1. What kind of person is the speaker describing who does all these things he says others do not do?

2. What does the poem get out of describing the phenomenon on which it focuses in negative terms? That is, why does it talk about some people who don't do these things rather than people who do them?

3. Do you find this poem humorous? If so, what is the source of the humor? How does Hoagland convey it?

4. Does the poem say one kind of person is better than the other? Is it that simple? What do you think the poem might be saying about this question? Does it matter that the speaker is not one of those who can walk by one of these opportunities to muse without musing?

MAKING ARGUMENTS

Make an argument about the poem that answers these questions: Is the speaker one of these people? Is he not? If he is, how does he feel about it? If not, how does he feel about that?

WRITING TOPIC

Which kind of person are you? Or are you some combination? Do you have friends or family who seem to be one or the other? Write a short portrait of a person or people in light of Hoagland's distinction. How do you see this person (even if it's you)? How do others see him or her?

MAKING CONNECTIONS

1. The poems in this section are all in one way or another about opportunities taken or not taken, lives well spent or wasted, things noticed or ignored. Are there any poems that could be seen to have very different takes on these phenomena? Pick two and make the argument.

2. There is a long tradition of *carpe diem* poetry. The phrase originates with the Roman poet Horace. Find the original quote. What does the second half, after *carpe diem*, say about the source of the urgency to seize opportunities rather than let them pass by?

3. In these poems about how people choose to live their lives, there are a fair number of references to death. Find a few across the poems. What does each mean in the context of the poem?

DRAMA

EDWARD ALBEE   (B. 1928)

THE SANDBOX   1959

CHARACTERS

The Young Man, Twenty-five. A good-looking, well-built boy in a bathing suit.
Mommy, Fifty-five. A well-dressed, imposing woman.
Daddy, Sixty. A small man; gray, thin.

Grandma, Eighty-six. A tiny, wizened woman with bright eyes.
The Musician, No particular age, but young would be nice.

Note: When, in the course of the play, Mommy and Daddy call each other by these names, there should be no suggestion of regionalism. These names are of empty affection and point up the pre-senility and vacuity of their characters.

Scene
A bare stage, with only the following: Near the footlights, far stage-right, two simple chairs set side by side, facing the audience; near the footlights, far stage-left, a chair facing stage-right with a music stand before it; farther back, and stage-center, slightly elevated and raked, a large child's sandbox with a toy pail and shovel; the background is the sky, which alters from brightest day to deepest night.

At the beginning, it is brightest day; the Young Man is alone on stage, to the rear of the sandbox, and to one side. He is doing calisthenics; he does calisthenics until quite at the very end of the play. These calisthenics, employing the arms only, should suggest the beating and fluttering of wings. The Young Man is, after all, the Angel of Death.

(*Mommy and Daddy enter from stage-left, Mommy first.*)

Mommy (*Motioning to Daddy*). Well, here we are; this is the beach.
Daddy (*Whining*). I'm cold.
Mommy (*Dismissing him with a little laugh*). Don't be silly; it's as warm as toast. Look at that nice young man over there: *he* doesn't think it's cold. (*Waves to the Young Man*) Hello.

Young Man *(With an endearing smile).* Hi!

Mommy *(Looking about).* This will do perfectly . . . don't you think so, Daddy? There's sand there . . . and the water beyond. What do you think, Daddy?

Daddy *(Vaguely).* Whatever you say, Mommy.

Mommy *(With the same little laugh).* Well, of course . . . whatever I say. Then, it's settled, is it?

Daddy *(Shrugs).* She's *your* mother, not mine.

Mommy. *I* know she's my mother. What do you take me for? *(A pause)* All right, now; let's get on with it. *(She shouts into the wings, stage-left)* You! Out there! You can come in now.

(The Musician enters, seats himself in the chair, stage-left, places music on the music stand, is ready to play. Mommy nods approvingly)

Mommy. Very nice; very nice. Are you ready, Daddy? Let's go get Grandma.

Daddy. Whatever you say, Mommy.

Mommy *(Leading the way out, stage-left).* Of course, whatever I say. *(To the Musician)* You can begin now.

(The Musician begins playing; Mommy and Daddy exit; the Musician, all the while playing, nods to the Young Man)

Young Man *(With the same endearing smile).* Hi!

(After a moment, Mommy and Daddy re-enter, carrying Grandma. She is borne in by their hands under her armpits; she is quite rigid; her legs are drawn up; her feet do not touch the ground; the expression on her ancient face is that of puzzlement and fear)

Daddy. Where do we put her?

Mommy *(The same little laugh).* Wherever I say, of course. Let me see . . . well . . . all right, over there . . . in the sandbox. *(Pause)* Well, what are you waiting for, Daddy? . . . The sandbox!

(Together they carry Grandma over to the sandbox and more or less dump her in)

Grandma *(Righting herself to a sitting position; her voice a cross between a baby's laugh and cry).* Ahhhhhh! Graaaaa!

Daddy *(Dusting himself).* What do we do now?

Mommy *(To the Musician).* You can stop now.

(The Musician stops)

(Back to Daddy) What do you mean, what do we do now? We go over there and sit down, of course. *(To the Young Man)* Hello there.

Young Man *(Again smiling).* Hi!

(Mommy and Daddy move to the chairs, stage-right, and sit down. A pause)

Grandma *(Same as before).* Ahhhhhh! Ah-haaaaaa! Graaaaaa!
Daddy. Do you think . . . do you think she's . . . comfortable?
Mommy *(Impatiently).* How would I know?
Daddy *(Pause).* What do we do now?
Mommy *(As if remembering).* We . . . wait. We . . . sit here . . . and we wait . . . that's what we do.
Daddy *(After a pause).* Shall we talk to each other?
Mommy *(With that little laugh; picking something off her dress).* Well, *you* can talk, if you want to . . . if you can think of anything to *say* . . . if you can think of anything *new*.
Daddy *(Thinks).* No . . . I suppose not.
Mommy *(With a triumphant laugh).* Of course not!
Grandma *(Banging the toy shovel against the pail).* Haaaaaa! Ahhaaaaaa!
Mommy *(Out over the audience).* Be quiet, Grandma . . . just be quiet, and wait.

(Grandma throws a shovelful of sand at Mommy)

Mommy *(Still out over the audience).* She's throwing sand at me! You stop that, Grandma; you stop throwing sand at Mommy! *(To Daddy)* She's throwing sand at me.

(Daddy looks around at Grandma, who screams at him)

Grandma. GRAAAAAA!
Mommy. Don't look at her. Just . . . sit here . . . be very still . . . and wait. *(To the Musician)* You . . . uh . . . you go ahead and do whatever it is you do.

(The Musician plays)

(Mommy and Daddy are fixed, staring out beyond the audience. Grandma looks at them, looks at the Musician, looks at the sandbox, throws down the shovel)

Grandma. Ah-haaaaaa! Graaaaaa! *(Looks for reaction; gets none. Now . . . directly to the audience)* Honestly! What a way to treat an old woman! Drag her out of the house . . . stick her in a car . . . bring her out here from the city . . . dump her in a pile of sand . . . and leave her here to set. I'm eighty-six years old! I was married when I was seventeen. To a farmer. He died when I was thirty. *(To the Musician)* Will you stop that, please?

(The Musician stops playing).

I'm a feeble old woman . . . how do you expect anybody to hear me over that peep! peep! peep! *(To herself)* There's no respect around here. *(To the Young Man)* There's no respect around here!

Young Man *(Same smile).* Hi!

Grandma *(After a pause, a mild double-take, continues, to the audience).* My husband died when I was thirty *(indicates Mommy),* and I had to raise that big cow over there all by my lonesome. You can imagine what *that* was like. Lordy! *(To the Young Man)* Where'd they get *you*?

Young Man. Oh . . . I've been around for a while.

Grandma. I'll bet you have! Heh, heh, heh. Will you look at you!

Young Man *(Flexing his muscles).* Isn't that something? *(Continues his calisthenics)*

Grandma. Boy, oh boy; I'll say. Pretty good.

Young Man *(Sweetly).* I'll say.

Grandma. Where ya from?

Young Man. Southern California.

Grandma *(Nodding).* Figgers, figgers. What's your name, honey?

Young Man. I don't know. . . .

Grandma *(To the audience).* Bright, too!

Young Man. I mean . . . I mean, they haven't given me one yet . . . the studio . . .

Grandma *(Giving him the once-over).* You don't say . . . you don't say. Well . . . uh, I've got to talk some more . . . don't you go 'way.

Young Man. Oh, no.

Grandma *(Turning her attention back to the audience).* Fine; fine. *(Then, once more, back to the Young Man)* You're . . . you're an actor, hunh?

Young Man *(Beaming).* Yes. I am.

Grandma. *(To the audience again; shrugs).* I'm smart that way. *Anyhow,* I had to raise . . . *that* over there all by my lonesome; and what's next to her there . . . that's what she married. Rich? I tell you . . . money, money, money. They took me off the *farm* . . . which was real decent of them . . . and they moved me into the big town house with *them* . . . fixed a nice place for me under the stove . . . gave me an army blanket . . . and my own dish . . . my very own dish! So, what have I got to complain about? Nothing, of course. I'm not complaining. *(She looks up at the sky, shouts to someone offstage)* Shouldn't it be getting dark now, dear?

(The lights dim; night comes on. The Musician begins to play; it becomes deepest night. There are spots on all the players, including the Young Man, who is, of course, continuing his calisthenics)

Daddy *(Stirring).* It's nighttime.

Mommy. Shhhh. Be still . . . wait.

Daddy *(Whining).* It's so hot.

Mommy. Shhhhhh. Be still . . . wait.

Grandma *(To herself).* That's better. Night. *(To the Musician)* Honey, do you play all through this part?

(The Musician nods)

Well, keep it nice and soft; that's a good boy.

(The Musician nods again; plays softly)

That's nice.

(There is an off-stage rumble)

Daddy *(Starting).* What was that?

Mommy *(Beginning to weep).* It was nothing.

Daddy. It was . . . it was . . . thunder . . . or a wave breaking . . . or something.

Mommy *(Whispering, through her tears).* It was an off-stage rumble and you know what *that* means. . . .

Daddy. I forget. . . .

Mommy *(Barely able to talk).* It means the time has come for poor Grandma . . . and I can't bear it!

Daddy *(Vacantly).* I . . . I suppose you've got to be brave.

Grandma *(Mocking).* That's right, kid; be brave. You'll bear up; you'll get over it.

(Another off-stage rumble . . . louder)

Mommy. Ohhhhhhhhhh . . . poor Grandma . . . poor Grandma. . . .

Grandma *(To Mommy).* I'm fine! I'm all right! It hasn't happened yet!

(A violent off-stage rumble. All the lights go out, save the spot on the Young Man; the Musician stops playing)

Mommy. Ohhhhhhhhhh . . . Ohhhhhhhhhh. . . .

(Silence)

Grandma. Don't put the lights up yet . . . I'm not ready; I'm not quite ready. *(Silence)* All right, dear . . . I'm about done.

(The lights come up again, to brightest day; the Musician begins to play. Grandma is discovered, still in the sandbox, lying on her side, propped up on an elbow, half covered, busily shoveling sand over herself)

Grandma *(Muttering).* I don't know how I'm supposed to do anything with this goddamn toy shovel. . . .

Daddy. Mommy! It's daylight!

Mommy *(Brightly).* So it is! Well! Our long night is over. We must put away our tears, take off our mourning . . . and face the future. It's our duty.

Grandma *(Still shoveling; mimicking)* . . . take off our mourning . . . face the future. . . . Lordy!

(Mommy and Daddy rise, stretch. Mommy waves to the Young Man)

Young Man *(With that smile).* Hi!

(Grandma plays dead. (!) Mommy and Daddy go over to look at her; she is a little more than half buried in the sand; the toy shovel is in her hands, which are crossed on her breast)

Mommy *(Before the sandbox; shaking her head).* Lovely! It's . . . it's hard to be sad . . . she looks . . . so happy. *(With pride and conviction)* It pays to do things well. *(To the Musician)* All right, you can stop now, if you want to. I mean, stay around for a swim, or something; it's all right with us. *(She sighs heavily)* Well, Daddy . . . off we go.

Daddy. Brave Mommy!

Mommy. Brave Daddy!

(They exit, stage-left)

Grandma. *(After they leave; lying quite still).* It pays to do things well . . . Boy, oh boy! *(She tries to sit up)* . . . well, kids . . . *(but she finds she can't)* . . . I . . . I can't get up. I . . . I can't move. . . .

(The Young Man stops his calisthenics, nods to the Musician, walks over to Grandma, kneels down by the sandbox)

Grandma. I . . . can't move. . . .

Young Man. Shhhhh . . . be very still. . . .

Grandma. I . . . I can't move. . . .

Young Man. Uh . . . ma'am; I . . . I have a line here.

Grandma. Oh, I'm sorry, sweetie; you go right ahead.

Young Man. I am . . . uh . . . I am . . .

Grandma. Take your time, dear.

Young Man *(Prepares; delivers the line like a real amateur).* I am the Angel of Death. I am . . . uh . . . I am come for you.

Grandma. What . . . wha . . . *(Then, with resignation)* . . . ohhhh . . . ohhhh . . . I see.

(The Young Man bends over, kisses Grandma gently on the forehead)

Grandma *(Her eyes closed, her hands folded on her breast again, the shovel between her hands, a sweet smile on her face).* Well . . . that was very nice, dear . . .

Young Man *(Still kneeling).* Shhhhhh . . . be still. . . .

Grandma. What I meant was . . . you did that very well, dear. . . .

Young Man *(Blushing).* . . . oh . . .

Grandma. No; I mean it. You've got that . . . you've got a quality.

Young Man *(With his endearing smile).* Oh . . . thank you; thank you very much . . . ma'am.

Grandma *(Slowly; softly—as the Young Man puts his hands on top of Grandma's).* You're . . . you're welcome . . . dear.

(Tableau. The Musician continues to play as the curtain slowly comes down)

Curtain

FOR ANALYSIS

1. How would you characterize the relationship between Mommy and Daddy on the one hand and Grandma on the other? How do they treat her? What can you tell about them and their feelings?

2. What are Mommy and Daddy waiting for?

3. Is this a realistic play? How so, and/or how not?

4. As odd as this play is, do you still feel emotion by its end? If so, what causes it?

MAKING ARGUMENTS

While Albee is a giant of American theater and this is one of his better-known works, not every critic loved this play when it first appeared. Make an argument in defense of the play against these critics. What do you imagine their criticisms might have been? How would you counter them?

WRITING TOPIC

Think about the absurdism of this play. Describe how it is absurdist (defining what that means—research is fine here) and reflect on what it means to write about this subject in this way.

MAKING CONNECTIONS

1. Compare *The Sandbox* to Nottage's *Poof!* (p. 1087). How are their methods similar? How do they differ? How are their subjects related? Can you identify a shared connection between their methods and their subjects?

2. Revisit Goodman's "Apple Cake" (p. 1213) and think about it in the light of this (very different) play. Do they share observations about the relationship between adult children and their parents and the nature of the moment when elderly parents die?

NONFICTION

JOHN DONNE (1572–1631)

MEDITATION XVII, FROM DEVOTIONS UPON EMERGENT OCCASIONS 1623

Nunc lento sonitu dicunt morieris.
Now this bell tolling softly for another says to me, Thou must die.

Perchance he for whom this bell tolls may be so ill as that he knows not it tolls for him; and perchance I may think myself so much better than I am, as that they who are about me and see my state may have caused it to toll for me, and I know not that. The church is catholic, universal, so are all her actions; all that she does belongs to all. When she baptizes a child, that action 5 concerns me; for that child is thereby connected to that head which is my head too, and ingrafted into that body whereof I am a member. And when she buries a man, that action concerns me: all mankind is of one author and is one volume; when one man dies, one chapter is not torn out of the book, but translated into a better language; and every chapter must be so translated. God employs sev- 10 eral translators; some pieces are translated by age, some by sickness, some by war, some by justice; but God's hand is in every translation, and his hand shall bind up all our scattered leaves again for that library where every book shall lie open to one another. As therefore the bell that rings to a sermon calls not upon the preacher only, but upon the congregation to come, so this bell calls us all; 15 but how much more me, who am brought so near the door by this sickness. There was a contention as far as a suit[1] (in which piety and dignity, religion and estimation, were mingled) which of the religious orders should ring to prayers first in the morning; and it was determined that they should ring first that rose earliest. If we understand aright the dignity of this bell that tolls for our evening 20 prayer, we would be glad to make it ours by rising early, in that application, that it might be ours as well as his whose indeed it is. The bell doth toll for him that

[1] An argument settled by a lawsuit.

thinks it doth, and though it intermit again, yet from that minute that that occasion wrought upon him, he is united to God. Who casts not up his eye to the sun when it rises? but who takes off his eye from a comet when that breaks out? 25 Who bends not his ear to any bell which upon any occasion rings? but who can remove it from that bell which is passing a piece of himself out of this world? No man is an island, entire of itself; every man is a piece of the continent, a part of the main. If a clod be washed away by the sea, Europe is the less, as well as if a promontory were, as well as if a manor of thy friend's or of thine own were. Any 30 man's death diminishes me, because I am involved in mankind; and therefore never send to know for whom the bell tolls; it tolls for thee. Neither can we call this a begging of misery or a borrowing of misery, as though we were not miserable enough of ourselves but must fetch in more from the next house, in taking upon us the misery of our neighbors. Truly it were an excusable covetousness 35 if we did; for affliction is a treasure, and scarce any man hath enough of it. No man hath affliction enough that is not matured and ripened by it, and made fit for God by that affliction. If a man carry treasure in bullion, or in a wedge of gold, and have none coined into current moneys, his treasure will not defray him as he travels. Tribulation is treasure in the nature of it, but it is not current 40 money in the use of it, except we get nearer and nearer our home, heaven, by it. Another man may be sick too, and sick to death, and this affliction may lie in his bowels as gold in a mine and be of no use to him; but this bell that tells me of his affliction digs out and applies that gold to me, if by this consideration of another's danger I take mine own into contemplation and so secure myself by 45 making my recourse to my God, who is our only security.

FOR ANALYSIS

1. What does Donne mean when he says that the death bell "tolls for thee" (l. 32)?

2. Toward the end of his meditation, Donne states that "tribulation is treasure" (l. 40). What does he mean? What will that treasure purchase?

3. Donne is justly admired for his use of **figurative language**. What extended **metaphors** does he use to characterize humankind and death?

MAKING ARGUMENTS

Look up the larger work from which this meditation is drawn. Make an argument concerning the relation to the biographical and theological in this work. How does one relate to the other? How does this relation manifest in the work?

WRITING TOPICS

1. What does Donne mean by "affliction is a treasure" (l. 36)? Do you agree? Explain.

2. Identify and analyze the **figurative language** Donne uses to illuminate the human condition and his attitude toward death.

MAKING CONNECTIONS

Read this meditation with Donne's "Death, Be Not Proud" (p. 1243). What attitude does each have toward death? How does each offer alternatives to fear of death and sadness about death?

E. B. WHITE (1899–1985)

ONCE MORE TO THE LAKE 1941

One summer, along about 1904, my father rented a camp on a lake in Maine and took us all there for the month of August. We all got ring-worm from some kittens and had to rub Pond's Extract on our arms and legs night and morning, and my father rolled over in a canoe with all his clothes on; but outside of that the vacation was a success and from then on none of us ever thought there was any place in the world like that lake in Maine. We returned summer after summer—always on August 1st for one month. I have since become a salt-water man, but sometimes in summer there are days when the restlessness of the tides and the fearful cold of the sea water and the incessant wind which blows across the afternoon and into the evening make me wish for the placidity of a lake in the woods. A few weeks ago this feeling got so strong I bought myself a couple of bass hooks and a spinner and returned to the lake where we used to go, for a week's fishing and to revisit old haunts.

I took along my son, who had never had any fresh water up his nose and who had seen lily pads only from train windows. On the journey over to the lake I began to wonder what it would be like. I wondered how time would have marred this unique, this holy spot—the coves and streams, the hills that the sun set behind, the camps and the paths behind the camps. I was sure that the tarred road would have found it out and I wondered in what other ways it would be desolated. It is strange how much you can remember about places like that once you allow your mind to return into the grooves which lead back. You remember one thing, and that suddenly reminds you of another thing. I guess I remembered clearest of all the early mornings, when the lake was cool and motionless, remembered how the bedroom smelled of the lumber it was made of and of the wet woods whose scent entered through the screen. The partitions in the camp were thin and did not extend clear to the top of the rooms, and as I was always the first up I would dress softly so as not to wake the others, and sneak out into the sweet outdoors and start out in the canoe, keeping close along the shore in the long shadows of the pines. I remembered being very careful never to rub my paddle against the gunwale for fear of disturbing the stillness of the cathedral.

The lake had never been what you would call a wild lake. There were cottages sprinkled around the shores, and it was in farming country although the shores of the lake were quite heavily wooded. Some of the cottages were owned by nearby farmers, and you would live at the shore and eat your meals at the farm-house. That's what our family did. But although it wasn't wild, it was a fairly large and undisturbed lake and there were places in it which, to a child at least, seemed infinitely remote and primeval.

I was right about the tar: it led to within half a mile of the shore. But when I got back there, with my boy, and we settled into a camp near a farmhouse and into the kind of summertime I had known, I could tell that it was going to be pretty much the same as it had been before—I knew it, lying in bed the first morning, smelling the bedroom, and hearing the boy sneak quietly out and go off along the shore in a boat. I began to sustain the illusion that he was I, and therefore, by simple transposition, that I was my father. This sensation persisted, kept cropping up all the time we were there. It was not an entirely new feeling, but in this setting it grew much stronger. I seemed to be living a dual existence. I would be in the middle of some simple act, I would be picking up a bait box or laying down a table fork, or I would be saying something, and suddenly it would be not I but my father who was saying the words or making the gesture. It gave me a creepy sensation.

We went fishing the first morning. I felt the same damp moss covering the worms in the bait can, and saw the dragonfly alight on the tip of my rod as it hovered a few inches from the surface of the water. It was the arrival of this fly that convinced me beyond any doubt that everything was as it always had been, that the years were a mirage and there had been no years. The small waves were the same, chucking the rowboat under the chin as we shed at anchor, and the boat was the same boat, the same color green and the ribs broken in the same places, and under the floor-boards the same freshwater leavings and débris—the dead helgramite, the wisps of moss, the rusty discarded fishhook, the dried blood from yesterday's catch. We stared silently at the tips of our rods, at the dragonflies that came and went. I lowered the tip of mine into the water, tentatively, pensively dislodging the fly, which darted two feet away, poised, darted two feet back, and came to rest again a little farther up the rod. There had been no years between the ducking of this dragonfly and the other one—the one that was part of memory. I looked at the boy, who was silently watching his fly, and it was my hands that held his rod, my eyes watching. I felt dizzy and didn't know which rod I was at the end of.

We caught two bass, hauling them in briskly as though they were mackerel, pulling them over the side of the boat in a businesslike manner without any landing net, and stunning them with a blow on the back of the head. When we got back for a swim before lunch, the lake was exactly where we had left it, the same number of inches from the dock, and there was only the merest suggestion of a breeze. This seemed an utterly enchanted sea, this lake you could leave to its own devices for a few hours and come back to, and find that it had not stirred, this constant and trustworthy body of water. In the shallows, the dark, water-soaked sticks and twigs, smooth and old, were undulating in clusters on the bottom against the clean ribbed sand, and the track of the mussel was plain. A school of minnows swam by, each minnow with its small, individual shadow, doubling the attendance, so clear and sharp in the sunlight. Some of the other campers were in swimming, along the shore, one of them with a cake of soap, and the water felt thin and clear and insubstantial. Over the years there had been this person with the cake of soap, this cultist, and here he was. There had been no years.

Up to the farmhouse to dinner through the teeming, dusty field, the road under our sneakers was only a two-track road. The middle track was missing, the one with the marks of the hooves and the splotches of dried, flaky manure. There had always been three tracks to choose from in choosing which track to walk in; now the choice was narrowed down to two. For a moment I missed terribly the middle alternative. But the way led past the tennis court, and something about the way it lay there in the sun reassured me; the tape had loosened along the backline, the alleys were green with plantains and other weeds, and the net (installed in June and removed in September) sagged in the dry noon, and the whole place steamed with midday heat and hunger and emptiness. There was a choice of pie for dessert, and one was blueberry and one was apple, and the waitresses were the same country girls, there having been no passage of time, only the illusion of it as in a dropped curtain—the waitresses were still fifteen; their hair had been washed, that was the only difference—they had been to the movies and seen the pretty girls with the clean hair.

Summertime, oh summertime, pattern of life indelible, the fade proof lake, the woods unshatterable, the pasture with the sweetfern and the juniper forever and ever, summer without end; this was the background, and the life along the shore was the design, the cottages with their innocent and tranquil design, their tiny docks with the flagpole and the American flag floating against the white clouds in the blue sky, the little paths over the roots of the trees leading from camp to camp and the paths leading back to the outhouses and the can of lime for sprinkling, and at the souvenir counters at the store the miniature birch-bark canoes and the post cards that showed things looking a little better than they looked. This was the American family at play, escaping the city heat, wondering whether the newcomers at the camp at the head of the cove were "common" or "nice," wondering whether it was true that the people who drove up for Sunday dinner at the farmhouse were turned away because there wasn't enough chicken.

It seemed to me, as I kept remembering all this, that those times and those summers had been infinitely precious and worth saving. There had been jollity and peace and goodness. The arriving (at the beginning of August) had been so big a business in itself, at the railway station the farm wagon drawn up, the first smell of the pineladen air, the first glimpse of the smiling farmer, and the great importance of the trunks and your father's enormous authority in such matters, and the feel of the wagon under you for the long ten-mile haul, and at the top of the last long hill catching the first view of the lake after eleven months of not seeing this cherished body of water. The shouts and cries of the other campers when they saw you, and the trunks to be unpacked, to give up their rich burden. (Arriving was less exciting nowadays, when you sneaked up in your car and parked it under a tree near the camp and took out the bags and in five minutes it was all over, no fuss, no loud wonderful fuss about trunks.)

Peace and goodness and jollity. The only thing that was wrong now, really, 10 was the sound of the place, an unfamiliar nervous sound of the outboard motors. This was the note that jarred, the one thing that would sometimes break the illusion and set the years moving. In those other summertimes, all motors were inboard; and when they were at a little distance, the noise they made was a sedative, an ingredient of summer sleep. They were one-cylinder and two-cylinder engines, and some were make-and-break and some were jump-spark, but they all made a sleepy sound across the lake. The one-lungers throbbed and muttered, and the twin-cylinder ones purred and purred, and that was a quiet sound too. But now the campers all had outboards. In the day-time, in the hot mornings, these motors made a petulant, irritable sound; at night, in the still evening when the afterglow lit the water, they whined about one's ears like mosquitoes. My boy loved our rented outboard, and his great desire was to achieve singlehanded mastery over it, and authority, and he soon learned the trick of choking it a little (but not too much), and the adjustment of the needle valve. Watching him I would remember the things you could do with the old one-cylinder engine with the heavy flywheel, how you could have it eating out of your hand if you got really close to it spiritually. Motor boats in those days didn't have clutches, and you would make a landing by shutting off the motor at the proper time and coasting in with a dead rudder. But there was a way of reversing them, if you learned the trick, by cutting the switch and putting it on again exactly on the final dying revolution of the flywheel, so that it would kick back against compression and begin reversing. Approaching a dock in a strong following breeze, it was difficult to slow up sufficiently by the ordinary coasting method, and if a boy felt he had complete mastery over his motor, he was tempted to keep it running beyond its time and then reverse it a few feet from the dock. It took a cool nerve, because if you threw the switch a twentieth of a second too soon you could catch the flywheel when it still had speed enough to go up past center, and the boat would leap ahead, charging bull-fashion at the dock.

We had a good week at the camp. The bass were biting well and the sun shone endlessly, day after day. We would be tired at night and lie down in the accu-mulated heat of the little bedrooms after the long hot day and the breeze would stir almost imperceptibly outside and the smell of the swamp drift in through the rusty screens. Sleep would come easily and in the morning the red squir-rel would be on the roof, tapping out his gay routine. I kept remembering ev-erything, lying in bed in the mornings—the small steamboat that had a long rounded stern like the lip of a Ubangi, and how quietly she ran on the moonlight sails, when the older boys played their mandolins and the girls sang and we ate doughnuts dipped in sugar, and how sweet the music was on the water in the shining night, and what it had felt like to think about girls then. After breakfast we would go up to the store and the things were in the same place—the minnows in a bottle, the plugs and spinners disarranged and pawed over by the youngsters from the boys' camp, the fig newtons and the Beeman's gum. Outside, the road was tarred and cars stood in front of the store. Inside, all was just as it had always been, except there was more Coca-Cola and not so much Moxie and root beer and birch beer and sarsaparilla. We would walk out with a bottle of pop apiece and sometimes the pop would backfire up our noses and hurt. We explored the streams, quietly, where the turtles slid off the sunny logs and dug their way into the soft bottom; and we lay on the town wharf and fed worms to the tame bass. Everywhere we went I had trouble making out which was I, the one walking at my side, the one walking in my pants.

One afternoon while we were there at that lake a thunderstorm came up. It was like the revival of an old melodrama that I had seen long ago with childish awe. The second-act climax of the drama of the electrical disturbance over a lake in America had not changed in any important respect. This was the big scene, still the big scene. The whole thing was so familiar, the first feeling of oppression and heat and a general air around camp of not wanting to go very far away. In mid-afternoon (it was all the same) a curious darkening of the sky, and a lull in everything that had made life tick; and then the way the boats suddenly swung the other way at their moorings with the coming of a breeze out of the new quarter, and the premonitory rumble. Then the kettle drum, then the snare, then the bass drum and cymbals, then crackling light against the dark, and the gods grinning and licking their chops in the hills. Afterward the calm, the rain steadily rustling in the calm lake, the return of light and hope and spirits, and the campers running out in joy and relief to go swimming in the rain, their bright cries perpetuating the deathless joke about how they were getting simply drenched, and the children screaming with delight at the new sensation of bathing in the rain, and the joke about getting drenched linking the generations in a strong indestructible chain. And the comedian who waded in carrying an umbrella.

When the others went swimming my son said he was going in too. He pulled his dripping trunks from the line where they had hung all through the shower, and wrung them out. Languidly, and with no thought of going in, I watched him, his hard little body, skinny and bare, saw him wince slightly as he pulled up around his vitals the small, soggy, icy garment. As he buckled the swollen belt suddenly my groin felt the chill of death.

For Analysis

1. How is the lake the same as it was in the past? How has it changed?

2. Why is it important that White brings his son along on this trip?

3. What does the trip remind White of? What does that reminiscence make him aware of?

Making Arguments

Nostalgia is a powerful force, personally and culturally. Make an argument that the nostalgia in White's essay concerns not only his own life but also the history of some larger group he belongs to.

Writing Topics

1. Note the kinds of details White selects in painting his portrait of the lake. Reflect on his choices: Why is the lake "fade proof," the woods "unshatterable" (para. 8)?

2. Write a short narrative of a trip you took or a visit you made that brought you back to when you were younger. Try to include as much descriptive detail as you can, and try to make that detail work to express the feelings you had.

MAKING CONNECTIONS

There are a number of works of literature in this book that look at parents from children's perspective. Compare those in the "Connecting Poems: Remembering Fathers" cluster in Love and Hate (p. 968) to "Once More to the Lake." How are the concerns raised in these works different? How does fatherhood look from a father's point of view as opposed to a child's?

JILL CHRISTMAN (B. 1969)

THE SLOTH 2002

There is a nothingness of temperature, a point on the body's mercury where our blood feels neither hot nor cold. I remember a morning swim on the black sand eastern coast of Costa Rica four months after my twenty-two-year-old fiancé was killed in a car accident. Walking into the water, disembodied by grief, I felt no barriers between my skin, the air, and the water.

Later, standing under a trickle of water in the wooden outdoor shower, I heard a rustle, almost soundless, and looking up, expecting something small, I saw my first three-toed sloth. Mottled and filthy, he hung by his meat-hook claws not five feet above my head in the cecropia tree. He peered down at me, his flattened head turned backwards on his neck. Here is a fact: a sloth cannot regulate the temperature of his blood. He must live near the equator.

I thought I knew slow, but this guy, this guy was *slow*. The sound I heard was his wiry-haired blond elbow, brushed green with living algae, stirring a leaf as he reached for the next branch. Pressing my wet palms onto the rough wooden walls, I watched the sloth move in the shadows of the canopy. Still reaching. And then still reaching.

What else is this slow? Those famous creatures of slow—the snail, the tortoise—they move faster. Much. This slow seemed impossible, not real, like a trick of my sad head. Dripping and naked in the jungle, I thought, *That sloth is as slow as grief.* We were numb to the speed of the world. We were one temperature.

FOR ANALYSIS

1. What emotion other than grief is present in this essay?

2. How does the author approach the subject of her grief? What are the effects of writing about it in this way? Would representing it and discussing it more directly have been more or less effective for you?

MAKING ARGUMENTS

Make an argument concerning anthropomorphization. Is Christman guilty of it in this essay? Use as evidence your understanding of the term and your reading of the essay.

WRITING TOPIC

Write about a time when you felt something strongly. Is there an animal you could have compared yourself to? How?

MAKING CONNECTIONS

Read "The Sloth" with any or all of the selections in "Connecting Poems: Animal Fates" (p. 1293). How does Christman's use of the sloth compare to the way these other writers use animals in their work?

FEET IN SMOKE   2011

On the morning of April 21, 1995, my elder brother, Worth (short for Elsworth), put his mouth to a microphone in a garage in Lexington, Kentucky, and in the strict sense of having been "shocked to death," was electrocuted. He and his band, the Moviegoers, had stopped for a day to rehearse on their way from Chicago to a concert in Tennessee, where I was in school. Just a couple of days earlier, he had called to ask if there were any songs I wanted to hear at the show. I asked for something new, a song he'd written and played for me the last time I'd seen him, on Christmas Day. Our holidays always end the same way, with the two of us up late drinking and trying out our "tunes" on each other. There's something biologically satisfying about harmonizing with a sibling. We've gotten to where we communicate through music, using guitars the way fathers and sons use baseball, as a kind of emotional code. Worth is seven years older than I am, an age difference that can make brothers strangers. I'm fairly sure the first time he ever felt we had anything to talk about was the day he caught me in his basement bedroom at our old house in Indiana, trying to teach myself how to play "Radio Free Europe" on a black Telecaster he'd forbidden me to touch.

The song I had asked for, "Is It All Over," was not a typical Moviegoers song. It was simpler and more earnest than the infectious pop-rock they made their specialty. The changes were still unfamiliar to the rest of the band, and Worth had been about to lead them through the first verse, had just leaned forward to sing the opening lines—"Is it all over? I'm scanning the paper / For someone to replace her"—when a surge of electricity arced through his body, magnetizing the mike to his chest like a tiny but obstinate missile, searing the first string and fret into his palm, and stopping his heart. He fell backward and crashed, already dying.

Possibly you know most of this already. I got many of my details from a common source, an episode of *Rescue 911* (the reality show hosted by William Shatner) that aired about six months after the accident. My brother played himself in the dramatization, which was amusing for him, since he has no memory whatsoever of the real event. For the rest of us, his family and friends, the segment is hard to watch.

The story Shatner tells, which ends at the moment we learned that my brother would live, is different from the story I know. But his version offers a useful reminder of the danger, where medical emergencies are involved, of talking too much about "miracles." Not to knock the word—the staff at Humana Hospital in Lexington called my brother's case "miraculous," and they've seen any number of horrifying accidents and inexplicable recoveries—but it tends to obscure the human skill and coolheadedness that go into saving somebody's life. I think of Liam, my brother's best friend and bandmate, who managed not to fall apart while he cradled Worth in his arms until help arrived, and who'd warned him when the band first started practicing to put on his Chuck Taylors, the rubber soles of which were the only thing that kept him from being zapped into a more permanent fate than the one he did endure. I think of Captain Clarence Jones, the fireman and paramedic who brought Worth back to life, strangely with two hundred joules of pure electric shock (and who later responded to my grandmother's effusive thanks by giving all the credit to the Lord). Without people like these and doubtless others whom I never met and Shatner didn't mention, there would have been no miracle.

It was afternoon when I heard about the accident from my father, who called 5 and told me flatly that my brother had been "hurt." I asked if Worth would live, and there was a nauseating pause before his "I don't know." I got in the car and drove from Tennessee to Lexington, making the five-hour trip in about three and a half hours. In the hospital parking lot I was met by two of my uncles on my mother's side, fraternal twins, both of them Lexington businessmen. They escorted me up to the ICU and, in the elevator, filled me in on Worth's condition, explaining that he'd flatlined five times in the ambulance on the way to the hospital, his heart locked in something that Captain Jones, in his interview for *Rescue 911*, diagnosed as "asystole," which Jones described as "just another death-producing rhythm." As I took him to mean, my brother's pulse had been almost one continuous beat, like a drumroll, but feeble, not actually sending the blood anywhere. By the time I showed up, his heart was at least beating on its own power, but a machine was doing all his breathing for him. The worst news had to do with his brain, which we were told displayed 1 percent activity, vegetable status.

In the waiting room, a heavyset nurse who looked to be in her sixties came up and introduced herself as Nancy. She took me by the hand and led me through two silent, automatic glass doors into Intensive Care. My brother was a nightmare of tubes and wires, dark machines silently measuring every internal event, a pump filling and emptying his useless lungs. The stench of dried spit was everywhere in the room. His eyes were closed, his every muscle slack. It seemed that only the machines were still alive, possessed of some perverse will that wouldn't let them give up on this body.

I stood frozen, staring at him. The nurse spoke to me from the corner of the room in an unexpected tone of admonishment, which stung me at the time and even in retrospect seems hard to account for. "It ain't like big brother's gonna wake up tomorrow and be all better," she said. I looked at her stupidly. Had I not seemed shocked enough?

"Yes, I realize that," I said, and asked to be alone. When the door closed behind me, I went up to the side of the bed. Worth and I have different fathers, making us half brothers, technically, though he was already living with my dad when I was born, which means that I've never known life without him. Nonetheless we look nothing alike. He has thick dark hair and olive skin and was probably the only member of our family in the hospital that night with green as opposed to blue eyes. I leaned over into his face. The normal flush of his cheeks had gone white, and his lips were parted to admit the breathing tube. There was no sign of anything, of life or struggle or crisis, only the gruesomely robotic sounds of the oxygen machine pumping air into his chest and drawing it out again. I heard my uncles, their voices composed with strain, telling me about the 1 percent brain activity. I leaned closer, putting my mouth next to my brother's right ear. "Worth," I said, "it's John."

Without warning, all six feet and four inches of his body came to life, writhing against the restraints and what looked like a thousand invasions of his orifices and skin. His head reared back, and his eyes swung open on me. The pupils were almost nonexistent. They stayed open only for the briefest instant, focusing loosely on mine before falling shut. But what an instant! As a volunteer fireman in college, I had once helped to pull a dead man out of an overturned truck, and I remember the look of his open eyes as I handed him to the next person in line—I'd been expecting pathos, some shadow of whatever had been the last thought to cross his mind, but his eyes were just marbles, mere things. My brother's eyes had been nothing like that. They were, if anything, the terrified eyes of a man who was trying to climb out of a well: the second he moves, he slips back to the bottom. Worth's head fell back onto the pillow motionless, his body exhausted from that brief effort at reentering the world. I put down his hand, which I'd taken without knowing it, and stepped back into the hallway.

Worth spent that night, and the second day and night, in a coma. There were no outward signs of change, but the machines began to pick up indications of increased brain function. The neurosurgeon, an Irishman, explained to us (in what must have been, for him, child's language) that the brain is itself an electrical machine, and that the volts that had flowed from my brother's vintage Gibson amplifier and traumatized his body were in some sense still racing around in his skull. There was a decent chance, the doctor said, that he would emerge from the coma, but no one could say what would be left; no one could say who would emerge. The period of waiting comes back to me as a collage of awful food, nurses' cautious encouragement, and the disquieting presence of my brother supine in his bed, an oracle who could answer all our questions but refused to speak. We rotated in and out of his room like tourists circulating through a museum.

"On the third day" (I would never have said it myself, but Shatner does it for me on the show), Worth woke up. The nurses led us into his room, their faces almost proud, and we found him sitting up—gingerly resting on his elbows, with heavy-lidded eyes, as if at any moment he might decide he liked the coma better and slip back into it. His face lit up like a simpleton's whenever one of us entered the room, and he greeted each of us by our names in a barely audible rasp. He seemed to know us, but hadn't the slightest idea what we were all doing there, or where "there" might be—though he did come up with theories on the last point over the next two weeks, chief among them a wedding reception, a high school poker game, and at one point some kind of holding cell.

I've tried many times over the years to describe for people the person who woke up from that electrified near-death, the one who remained with us for about a month before he went back to being the person we'd known and know now. It would save one a lot of trouble to be able to say "it was like he was on acid," but that wouldn't be quite true. Instead, he seemed to be living one of those imaginary acid trips we used to pretend to be on in junior high, before we tried the real thing and found out it was slightly less magical—"Hey, man, your nose is like a star or something, man." He had gone there. My father and I kept notes, neither of us aware that the other was doing it, trying to get down all of Worth's little disclosures before they faded. I have my own list here in front of me. There's no best place to begin. I'll just transcribe a few things:

Squeezed my hand late on the night of the 23rd. Whispered, "That's the human experience."

While eating lunch on the 24th, suddenly became convinced that I was impersonating his brother. Demanded to see my ID. Asked me, "Why would you want to impersonate John?" When I protested, "But, Worth, don't I look like John?" he replied, "You look exactly like him. No wonder you can get away with it."

On the day of the 25th, stood up from his lunch, despite my attempts to restrain him, spilling the contents of his tray everywhere. Glanced at my hands, tight around his shoulders, and said, "I am not . . . repulsed . . . by man-to-man love. But I'm not into it."

Evening of the 25th. Gazing at own toes at end of bed, remarked, "That'd make a nice picture: Feet in Smoke."

Day of the 26th. Referred to heart monitor as "a solid, congealed bag of nutrients."

Night of the 26th. Tried to punch me with all his strength while I worked with Dad and Uncle John to restrain him in his bed, swinging and missing me by less than an inch. The IV tubes were tearing loose from his arms. His eyes were terrified, helpless. I think he took us for fascist goons.

Evening of the 27th. Unexpectedly jumped up from his chair, a perplexed expression on his face, and ran to the wall. Rubbed palms along a small area of the wall, like a blind man. Turned. Asked, "Where's the piñata?" Shuffled into hallway. Noticed a large nurse walking away from us down the hall. Muttered, "If she's got our piñata, I'm gonna be pissed."

The experience went from tragedy to tragicomedy to outright farce on a sliding continuum, so it's hard to pinpoint just when one let onto another. He was the most delightful drunk you'd ever met—I had to follow him around the hospital like a sidekick to make sure he didn't fall, because he couldn't stop moving, couldn't concentrate on anything for longer than a second. He became a holy fool. He looked down into his palm, where the fret and string had burned a deep, red cross into his skin, and said, "Hey, it'd be stigmata if there weren't all those ants crawling in it." He introduced my mother and father to each other as if they'd never met, saying, "Mom, meet Dad; Dad, meet Dixie Jean." Asked by the neurosurgeon if he knew how to spell his own name, he said, "Well, doctor, if you were Spenser, you might spell it w-o-r-t-h-E."

Another of the nurses, when I asked her if he'd ever be normal again, said, "Maybe, but wouldn't it be wonderful just to have him like this?" She was right; she humbled me. I can't imagine anything more hopeful or hilarious than having a seat at the spectacle of my brother's brain while it reconstructed reality. Like a lot of people, I'd always assumed, in a sort of cut-rate Hobbesian way, that the center of the brain, if you could ever find it, would inevitably be a pretty dark place, that whatever is good or beautiful about being human is a result of our struggles against everything innate, against physical nature. My brother changed my mind about all that. Here was a consciousness reduced to its matter, to a ball of crackling synapses—words that he knew how to use but couldn't connect to the right things; strange new objects for which he had to invent names; unfamiliar people who approached and receded like energy fields—and it was a good place to be, you might even say a poetic place. He had touched death, or death had touched him, but he seemed to find life no less interesting for having done so.

There is this one other remark: 15

Late afternoon of April 25. The window slats casting bars of shadow all over his room in the ICU. I had asked my mom and dad if they'd mind giving me a moment alone with him, since I still wasn't sure he knew quite who I was. I did know he wasn't aware of being inside a hospital; his most recent idea was that we were all back at my grandparents' house having a party, and at one point he slipped loose and went to the nurses' station to find out whether his tux was ready. Now we were sitting there in his room. Neither of us was speaking. Worth was jabbing a fork into his Jell-O, and I was just watching, waiting to see what would come out. Earlier that morning, he'd been scared by the presence of so many "strangers," and I didn't want to upset him any more. Things went on in silence like this for maybe five minutes.

Very quietly, he began to weep, his shoulders heaving with the force of emotion. I didn't touch him. A minute went by. I asked, "Worth, why are you crying?"

"I was thinking of the vision I had when I knew I was dead."

Certain that I'd heard him right, I asked him again anyway. He repeated it in the same flat tone: "I was thinking of the vision I had when I knew I was dead."

How could he know he'd been dead, when he didn't even know we were in a   20 hospital, or that anything unusual had happened to him? Had a sudden clarity overtaken him?

"What was it? What was your vision?"

He looked up. The tears were gone. He seemed calm and serious. "I was on the banks of the River Styx," he said. "The boat came to row me across, but . . . instead of Charon, it was Huck and Jim. Only, when Huck pulled back his hood, he was an old man . . . like, ninety years old or something."

My brother put his face in his hands and cried a little more. Then he seemed to forget all about it. According to my notes, the next words out of his mouth were, "Check this out—I've got the Andrews Sisters in my milkshake."

We've never spoken of it since. It's hard to talk to my brother about anything related to his accident. He has a monthlong tape erasure in his memory that starts the second he put his lips to that microphone. He doesn't remember the shock, the ambulance, having died, coming back to life. Even when it was time for him to leave the hospital, he had managed only to piece together that he was late for a concert somewhere, and my last memory of him from that period is his leisurely wave when I told him I had to go back to school. "See you at the show," he called across the parking lot. When our family gets together, the subject of his accident naturally bobs up, but he just looks at us with a kind of suspicion. It's a story about someone else, a story he thinks we might be fudging just a bit.

When I can't sleep I still sometimes will try to decipher that vision. My 25 brother was never much of a churchgoer (he proclaimed himself a deist at age fifteen) but had been an excellent student of Latin in high school. His teacher, a sweet and brilliant old bun-wearing woman named Rank, drilled her classes in classical mythology. Maybe when it came time for my brother to have his near-death experience, to reach down into his psyche and pull up whatever set of myths would help him make sense of the fear, he reached for the ones he'd found most compelling as a young man. For most people, that involves the whole tunnel-of-light business; for my brother, the underworld.

The question of where he got Huck and Jim defeats me. My father was a great Mark Twain fanatic—he got fired from the only teaching job he ever held for keeping the first graders in at recess, to make them listen to records of an actor reading the master's works—and he came up with the only clue: the accident had occurred on the eighty-fifth anniversary of Twain's death, in 1910.

I'm just glad they decided to leave my brother on this side of the river.

FOR ANALYSIS

1. Why should you wear rubber-bottomed shoes when playing electric instruments?

2. What is a "holy fool" (para. 13)? Why does Sullivan describe his brother as one?

3. What does Sullivan learn from his brother's accident and recovery about the essence of human nature that he didn't know before?

MAKING ARGUMENTS

Even though it is about a serious incident, there is a lot of humor in "Feet in Smoke." Make an argument about the appropriateness of this combination.

WRITING TOPICS

The first of the notes from his brother's "little disclosures" Sullivan shares tells of Worth squeezing his hand and whispering, "That's the human experience" (para. 12). How might the rest of this list represent the human experience? What kinds of things does Worth say, and what do they tell us about life?

MAKING CONNECTIONS

Compare this essay to White's "Once More to the Lake" (p. 1305). While both consider the intrusion of death into everyday life, they do it in very different manners. Describe the way each of these essays brings up and treats the fact of our mortality.

These two fantastic new essays are among the saddest in this book, and among the most interesting. They are about the same subject, generally, but approach that subject in very different ways and with very different goals in mind. As you read, notice how both manage to be intensely personal, yet do so in different ways.

JONATHAN LETHEM   (B. 1964)

13, 1977, 21   2006

1. In the summer of 1977 I saw *Star Wars*—the original, which is all I want to discuss here—twenty-one times. Better to blurt this at the start so I'm less tempted to retreat from what still seems to me a sort of raw, howling confession, one I've long hidden in shame. Again, to pin myself like a Nabokovian butterfly (no high-lit reference is going to bail me out here, I know) to my page in geek history: I watched *Star Wars* twenty-one times in the space of four months. I was that kid alone in the ticket line, slipping past ushers who'd begun to recognize me, muttering in impatience at a urinal before finding my favorite seat. That was me, occult as a porn customer, yes, though I've sometimes denied it. Now, a quarter-century later, I'm ready for my close-up. Sort of.

2. That year I was thirteen, and likely as ideal an audience member as any mogul could have drooled for. Say every kid in the United States with even the passingest fondness for comic books or adventure fiction, *any kid with a television, even*, had bought a ticket for the same film in a single summer: blah, blah, right, that's what happened. So figure that for every hundred kids who traveled an ordinary path (*Cool movie, wouldn't mind seeing it again with my friends*) there might be one who'd make himself ill returning to the cookie jar five or six times (*It's really still good the fourth time, I swear!*) before copping to a tummy ache. Next figure that for each *five* hundred, one or two would slip into some brain-warped identificatory obsession (*I am Star Wars, Star Wars am me, goo goo ga joob*) and return to the primal site often enough to push into the realm of trance and memorization. That's me, with my gaudy *twenty-one*, like DiMaggio's *fifty-six*. But what actually occurred within the secret brackets of that experience? What emotions lurk within that ludicrous temple of hours? *What the fuck was I thinking?*

3. Every one of those twenty-one viewings took place at the Loew's Astor Plaza on Forty-fourth Street, just off Times Square. I'd never seen a movie there before (and unless you count *The Empire Strikes Back*, I didn't again until

1999—*The Matrix*). And I've still never seen *Star Wars* anywhere else. The Astor Plaza was a low, deep-stretched hall with a massive screen and state-of-the-art sound, and newly enough renovated to be free of too much soda-rotted carpet, a plague among New York theaters those days. Though architecturally undistinguished, it was a superior place to see anything, I suppose. But for me it was a shrine meant for just one purpose—I took it as weirdly significant that "Astor" could be rearranged into "astro"—and in a very *New Yorker*–coverish way I believed it to be the only real and right place to see *Star Wars*, the very ground zero of the phenomenon. I felt a definite but not at all urgent pity for any benighted fools stuck watching it elsewhere. I think I associated the Astor Plaza with the Death Star, in a way. Getting in always felt like an accomplishment, both elevating and slightly dangerous.

4. Along those lines I should say it was vaguely unnerving to be a white kid in spectacles routinely visiting Times Square by subway in the middle of the 1970s. Nobody ever said anything clearly about what was wrong or fascinating about that part of the city we lived in—the information was absorbed in hints and mutterings from a polyphony of sources. In fact, though I was conscious of a certain seamy energy in those acres of sex shows and drug dealers and their furtive sidewalk customers, I was never once hassled (and this was a time when my home neighborhood, in Brooklyn, was a minefield for me personally). But the zone's reputation ensured I'd always plan my visits to fall wholly within summer's long daylight hours.

5. Problem: it doesn't seem at all likely that I went to the movie alone the first time, but I can't remember who I was with. I've polled a few of my likeliest friends from that period, but they're unable to help. In truth I can't recall a "first time" in any real sense, though I do retain a flash memory of the moment the prologue first began to crawl in tilted perspective up the screen, an Alice-in-Wonderland doorway to dream. I'd been so primed, so attuned and ready to love it (I remember mocking my friend Evan for his thinking that the title meant it was going to be some kind of all-star cavalcade of a comedy, like *It's a Mad Mad Mad Mad World* or *Smokey and the Bandit*) that my first time was gulped impatiently, then covered quickly in the memory of return visits. From the first I was "seeing it again." I think this memory glitch is significant. I associate it with my practice of bluffing familiarity with various drug experiences, later (not much later). My refusal to recall or admit to a first time was an assertion of maturity: I was *always already* a *Star Wars* fanatic.

6. I didn't buy twenty-one tickets. My count was amassed by seeing the movie twice in a day over and over again. And one famous day (famous to myself) I sat through it three times. That practice of seeing a film twice through originated earlier. Somebody—my mother?—had floated the idea that it wasn't important to be on time for a movie, or even to check the screening times before going. Instead, moviegoing in Brooklyn Heights or on Fulton Street with my brother or with friends, we'd pop in at any point in the story, watch to

the end, then sit through the break and watch the beginning. Which led naturally, if the film was any good, to staying past the original point of entry to see the end twice. Which itself led to routinely twice-watching a movie we liked, even if we hadn't been late. This was encouraged, partly according to a general *Steal This Book*–ish anticapitalist imperative for taking freebies in my parents' circle in the seventies. Of course somebody—my mother?—had also figured out a convenient way to get the kids out of the house for long stretches.

7. I hate arriving late for movies now and would never watch one in this broken fashion. (It seems to me, though, that I probably learned something about the construction of narratives from the practice.) The lifelong moviegoing habit which does originate for me with *Star Wars* is that of sitting in movie theaters alone. I probably only had company in the Loew's Astor Plaza four or five times. The rest of my visits were solitary, which is certainly central to any guesses I'd make about the emotional meaning of the ritual viewings.

8. I still go to the movies alone, all the time. In the absenting of self which results—so different from the quality of solitude at my writing desk—this seems to me as near as I come in my life to any reverent or worshipful or meditational practice. That's not to say it isn't also indulgent, with a frisson of guilt, of stolen privilege, every time. I'm acutely conscious of this joyous guilt in the fact that when as a solitary moviegoer I take a break to go to the bathroom *I can return to another part of the theater and watch from a different seat.* I first discovered this thrill during my *Star Wars* summer, and it's one which never diminishes. The rupture of the spectator's contract with perspective feels as transgressive as wife-swapping.

9. The function or dysfunction of my *Star Wars* obsession was paradoxical. I was using the movie as a place to hide, sure. That's obvious. At the same time, this activity of hiding inside the Loew's Astor Plaza, and inside my private, *deeper-than-yours, deeper-than-anyone's* communion with the film itself, was something I boasted widely about. By building my lamebrain World Record for screenings (fat chance, I learned later) I was teaching myself to package my own craving for solitude, and my own obsessive tendencies, as something to be admired. *You can't join me inside this box where I hide,* I was saying, *but you sure can praise the box. You're permitted to marvel at me for going inside.*

10. What I was hiding from is easy, though. My parents had separated a couple of years earlier. Then my mother had begun having seizures, been diagnosed with a brain tumor, and had had the first of two surgeries. The summer of *Star Wars* she was five or six months from the second, unsuccessful surgery, and a year from dying.

11. I took my brother, and he stayed through it twice. We may have done that together more than once—neither of us clearly remembers. I took a girl, on a quasi-date: Alissa, the sister of my best friend, Joel. I took my mother. I tried to take my grandmother.

12. That same summer I once followed Alissa to a ballet class at Carnegie Hall and hung around the studio, expressing a polite curiosity which was cover for another, less polite curiosity. The instructor was misled or chose to misunderstand—a thirteen-year-old boy willing to set foot inside a ballet studio was a commodity, a raw material. I was offered free classes, and the teacher called my house and strong-armed my parents. I remember vividly my mother's pleasure in refusing on my behalf—I was too much of a coward—and how strongly she fastened on the fact that my visit had had nothing to do with any interest in ballet. For years this seemed to me an inexplicable cruelty in my mother toward the ballet teacher. Later I understood that in those first years of adolescence I was giving off a lot of signals to my parents that I might be gay. I was a delicate, obedient, and bookish kid, a constant teacher's pet. Earlier that year my father had questioned me regarding a series of distended cartoon noses I'd drawn in ballpoint on my loose-leaf binder—they had come out looking a lot like penises. And my proclaimed favorite *Star Wars* character was the tweaking English robot, C-3P0.

13. I did and do find C-3P0 sexy. It's as if a strand of DNA from Fritz Lang's fetishized girl robot in *Metropolis* has carried forward to the bland world of *Star Wars*. Also, whereas Carrie Fisher's robes went to her ankles, C-3P0 is obviously naked, and ashamed of it.

14. Alissa thought the movie was okay (my overstated claims generally cued a compensating shrug in others) and that was our last date, if it was a date. We're friends now.

15. I don't know how much of an effort it was for my mother to travel by subway to a movie theater in Manhattan by the summer of '77, but I do know it was unusual, and that she was certainly doing it to oblige me. It might have been one of our last ventures out together, before it was impossible for her. I remember fussing over rituals inside the theater, showing her my favorite seat, and straining not to watch her watch it throughout, not to hang on her every reaction. Afterward she too found the movie just okay. It wasn't her kind of thing, but she could understand why I liked it so much. Those were pretty close to her exact words. Maybe with her characteristic Queens hard-boiled tone: *I see why you like it, kiddo.* Then, in a turn I find painful to relate, she left me there to watch it a second time, and took the subway home alone. What a heartbreaking rehearsal! I was saying, in effect: *Come and see my future, post-mom self. Enact with me your parting from it. Here's the world of cinema and stories and obsessive identification I'm using to survive your going—now go.* How generous of her to play in this masquerade, if she knew.

16. I spent a certain amount of time that year trying hopelessly to distract my grandmother from the coming loss of her only child—it would mostly wreck her—by pushing my new enthusiasms at her. For instance she and I had a recurrent argument about rock and roll, one which it now strikes me was probably a faint echo, for her, of struggles over my mother's dropping out of Queens

College in favor of a Greenwich Village beatnik-folk lifestyle. I worked to find a hit song she couldn't quibble with, and thought I'd found one in Wings' "Mull of Kintyre," which is really just a strummy faux-Irish folk song. I played it for her at top volume and she grimaced, her displeasure not at the music but at the apparent trump card I'd played. Then, on the fade, Paul McCartney gave out a kind *of whoop-whoop* holler and my grandmother seized on this, with relish: "You hear that? He had to go and scream. It wasn't good enough just to sing, he had to scream like an animal!" Her will was too much for me. So when she resisted being dragged to *Star Wars* I probably didn't mind, being uninterested in having her trample on my secret sand castle. She and I were ultimately in a kind of argument about whether or not our family was a site of tragedy, and I probably sensed I was on the losing end of that one.

17. My father lived in a commune for part of that summer, though my mother's illness sometimes drew him back into the house. There was a man in the commune—call him George Lucas—whose married life, which included two young children, was coming apart. George Lucas was the person I knew who'd seen *Star Wars* the most times, apart from me, and we had a ritualized bond over it. He'd ask me how many times I'd seen the film and I'd report, like an emissary with good news from the front. George Lucas had a copy of the soundtrack and we'd sit in the commune's living room and play it on the stereo, which I seem to remember being somewhat unpopular with the commune's larger membership. George Lucas, who played piano and had some classical training, would always proclaim that the score was *really pretty good symphonic composition*—he'd also play me Gustav Holst's *Planets Suite* as a kind of primer, and to show me how the Death Star theme came from Holst's Jupiter—and I would dutifully parrot this for my friends, with great severity: John Williams's score was *really pretty good symphonic composition*.

18. The movie itself, right: of course, I must have enjoyed it immensely the first few times. That's what I least recall. Instead I recall now how as I memorized scenes I fought my impatience, and yet fought not to know I was fighting impatience—all that mattered were the winnowed satisfactions of crucial moments occurring once again, like stations of the cross: "Help me, Obi-Wan Kenobi, you're my only hope," "These aren't the droids you're looking for," "If you strike me down, I'll become more powerful than you can possibly imagine," and the dunk shot of Luke's missiles entering the Death Star's duct. I hated, absolutely, the scene in the Death Star's sewers. I hated Han Solo and Princess Leia's flirtation, after a while, feeling I was being manipulated, that it was too mannered and rote: of course they're grumbling now, that's how it *always* goes. I hated the triumphalist ceremony at the end, though the spiffing-up of the robots was a consolation, a necessary relief. I think I came to hate a lot of the film, but I couldn't permit myself to know it. I even came, within a year or so, to hate the fact that I'd seen the movie twenty-one times.

19. Why that number? Probably I thought it was safely ridiculous and extreme to get my record into the twenties, yet stopping at only twenty seemed too

mechanically round. Adding one more felt plausibly arbitrary, more *realistic*. That was likely all I could stand. Perhaps at twenty-one I'd also attained the symbolic number of adulthood, of maturity. By bringing together *thirteen* and *twenty-one* I'd made *Star Wars* my Bar Mitzvah, a ritual I didn't have and probably could have used that year. Now I was a man.

20. By the time I was fifteen, not only had I long since quit boasting about my love of *Star Wars* but it had become privately crucial to have another favorite movie inscribed in its place. I decided Kubrick's *2001: A Space Odyssey* was a suitably noble and alienated choice, but that in order to make it official I'd have to see it more times than *Star Wars*. An exhausting proposition, but I went right at it. One day at the Thalia on West Ninety-fifth Street I sat alone through *2001* three times in a row in a nearly empty theater, a commitment of some nine hours. That day I brought along a tape recorder in order to whisper notes on this immersion experience to my friend Eliot—I also taped *Also sprach Zarathustra* all six times. If *Star Wars* was my Bar Mitzvah then *2001* was getting laid, an experience requiring a more persuasive maturity, and one which I more honestly enjoyed, especially fifteen or twenty showings in. Oddly enough, though, I never did completely overwrite *Star Wars* with *2001*. Instead I stuck at precisely twenty-one viewings of the second movie as well, leaving the two in a dead heat. Even that number was only attained years later, at the University Theater in Berkeley, California, two days after the 1989 Loma Prieta earthquake. There was a mild aftershock which rumbled the old theater during the Star Gate sequence, a nice touch.

21. I'll never see another film so many times, though I still count. I've seen *The Searchers* twelve times—a cheat, since it was partly research. Otherwise, I usually peak out at six or seven viewings, as with *Bringing Up Baby* and *Three Women* and *Love Streams* and *Vertigo*, all films I believe I love more than either *Star Wars* or *2001*. But that kid who still can't decide which of the two futuristic epics to let win the struggle for his mortal soul, the kid who left the question hanging, the kid who partly invented himself in the vacuum collision of *Star Wars* and real loss—that kid is me.

For Analysis

1. Explain the title. Why is it an unusual title? Why do you think the author might have decided to use it?

2. Number 18 begins, "The movie itself, right." Is this essay about *Star Wars* at all? If so, how? If not, what is it really about?

3. Although she is mentioned in number 6, Lethem's mother's illness isn't brought up until number 10. Why do you think he waits so long?

Making Arguments

Culture criticism—reviews of specific works of literature, film, music, and theater, and longer pieces about these fields—is an important and ever-changing branch of writing.

Where such work is available changes, and how it is written changes. Argue that Lethem's brand of personal criticism as shown here is better, worse, or just different from more traditional, objective criticism.

WRITING TOPIC

Reread the essay and keep a reading log. At multiple points, reflect on what you thought the essay was about then and where you thought it was going. When you are done, write a reflection on the essay's structure. Consider difficulty, linearity or the lack thereof, and anything else that jumps out at you.

RUTH MARGALIT   (B. 1983)

THE UNMOTHERED   2014

When I was growing up in Israel, there was a short-lived show on television called "*Hahaverim Shel Yael*" ("Yael's Friends"), which featured a peppy girl who introduced short clips acted out by puppets. The actress who played Yael was probably in her twenties, but she was dressed up to look like a child, in flowery dresses and pigtails. I loved that program, in which the puppets occassionally crossed into real life and made a mess of Yael's studio. Right before the opening music came on, Yael would look into the camera and fake-whisper to the viewers, "Tell your mother to turn up the volume!" Once, as my twin sister and I were settling down on the sofa to watch, my mother overheard this opening bit. "And what about those who don't have a mother?" she asked.

I must have been seven or eight at the time. I was irritated with her for asking that question, forever ruining the show for me. But I shouldn't have been surprised. It summed up, I now realize, her parenting philosophy. The way she didn't baby us, but treated us like thoughtful people, capable of empathy. The way she was always fully there—registering, questioning. But mostly, I think, it showed her unyielding belief in fairness, which, years later, I would hear her define as justice played out in the private sphere. (She was a philosophy professor, preoccupied with definitions.) It was a particular kind of fairness, one that centered on a child's sensibility. Once, when I asked her whom she loved more, my sister or me, she answered, simply, "You." Incredulous, my sister posed the same question. "Who do you love more, *Ima*? Ruth or me?" "You," my mother said. We tried again. Each time, my mother invariably told whoever asked that she loved her more. "This doesn't make any sense," we finally said. She smiled and told us, "Sure it does. Don't you see? I love *you* more and I love *you* more." This was her sense of fairness: no kid wants to hear that they are loved the *same* as their sister.

This Mother's Day, three and a half years after she died, I find myself turning over her question in my mind. *And what about those who don't have a mother?*

"CALL MOM" said a sign the other day, and something inside me clenched. In my inbox, at work, an email waited from the New York *Times*: a limited offer to "treat Mom" to a free gift. It's nothing, I tell myself. A day for advertisers. So I shrug off the sales and the offers, the cards and the flowers. I press delete. Still, I now mark Mother's Day on my private calendar of grief. Anyone who has experienced a loss must have one of those. There's August 29th, my mother's birthday—forever stopped at sixty-four. September 17th, my parents' anniversary—a day on which I now make a point of calling my father, and we both make a point of talking about anything but. There's June 6th, the day she was diagnosed—when a cough that she had told us was "annoying" her and a leg that she had been dragging, thinking she must have pulled a muscle, turned out to be symptoms of Stage IV lung cancer. And then there's October 16th: the day she died, four months and ten days after the diagnosis. The year becomes a landscape filled with little mines.

Trust me, I'm too aware of the fact that my mother is gone to wish her here 5 in any serious way on Mother's Day. But does the holiday have to be in May, when the lilacs are in full bloom? When a gentle breeze stirs—the kind of breeze that reminds me of days when she would recline on a deck chair on our Jerusalem porch, head tilted back, urging me to "sit a while"?

Meghan O'Rourke has a wonderful word for the club of those without mothers. She calls us not motherless but unmothered. It feels right—an ontological word rather than a descriptive one. I had a mother, and now I don't. This is not a characteristic one can affix, like being paperless, or odorless. The emphasis should be on absence.

I remember driving back to my apartment in Tel Aviv for the first time after those first agitated days in the hospital. A man was out on the street walking his dog. I stared at him, waiting for some sign of acknowledgment that the fundamentals of life had changed. He kept on strolling, of course. How stupid of me, to think that everyone knew.

They say time heals. It's true that the pain wears off, slightly, around the edge, like a knife in need of whetting. But here's what they're missing: It gets harder to explain to myself why I haven't seen her. A month can make sense. (*I took a trip; she was busy with work.*) Even six months is excusable. (*I moved; she's on sabbatical.*) But how to make sense of more than three years worth of distance? How to comprehend that time will only drive my mother and me farther and farther apart?

I've learned that some mourners experience anticipatory grief, mourning their loved ones before they have died, while others experience delayed grief—a postponed reaction to the loss. It might sound strange, but I used to think that I experienced both.

I fully grieved the day we were given the diagnosis. My mother was told that 10 she would be admitted overnight to the cardiology department, because there were no available beds yet to take her in oncology. I heard that phrase—no beds "yet" in oncology—and knew that we were entering a new universe, with its own set of rules. That night, when I finally had a moment to myself, I stood in the hospital's darkened hallway, stared out a sullied window, and wailed in a way I never have before or since. A passing nurse, seeing me keen, brought me a tiny cup of water and made me sit down. I never told my parents or my siblings about this. I simply wiped my eyes and dutifully returned to my mother's bedside. Every now and then, I try to recall what went through my mind as I was standing in that hallway, crying my heart out. (And if you think that the cliché can't be real—well, then, you're lucky.) The truth is, I was thinking, selfishly, about myself. That my mother would never see me marry. That she would not know my children. That the following summer I would turn twenty-eight—her lucky number—and she might not be there.

But there was also what I experienced as a delayed state of grief. I had begun graduate school at Columbia that August—my mother was by then on a targeted drug treatment called Tarceva that had somewhat stabilized her tumor, and she insisted that I go—when I got a call from my sister telling me that things were deteriorating rapidly, and that I should get on a plane back. I had been lying on a lawn in Central Park, reading, when she called. I hung up and couldn't feel anything.

When I returned to New York in late October, only two days after the Shiva, I threw myself right back into school as though nothing had happened. The trees were undressing for winter, and I walked down the chilly streets of Morningside Heights squinting against a nonexistent sun. What I kept hearing from friends during that time was that I looked "good" and "strong." That I seemed "fine." I didn't *feel* fine, but I also had no idea what to do except carry on. "I don't know how you manage," an old friend told me. "If it had been *my* mother, I wouldn't be able to get out of bed in the morning." She thought she was paying me a compliment, not realizing that that's about the worst thing you can say to someone in mourning—as though by merely starting my days I was betraying my mother. *Am I?* I started to panic. But then I came across Roland Barthes's "Mourning Diary," which he kept immediately following the death of his mother. In it, he writes, "No sooner has she departed than the world deafens me with its *continuance*." I remember reading this and experiencing a physical spasm of recognition. He adds, "I seem to have a kind of ease of control that makes other people think I'm suffering less than they would have imagined. But it comes over me when our love for each other is torn apart once again. The most painful moment at the most abstract moment."

Yes, I remember thinking. Yes, yes, yes. This wasn't delayed grief, after all. It was simply this: grief keeps odd hours, *the most painful moment at the most abstract moment.* Strangely, I began to think of Barthes (whose relationship with his mother famously bordered on the Oedipal) as my grief buddy. Largely preferring books to people around that time, I discovered that he wasn't the only one.

In my journal from that period, instead of writing how I felt, I sought out and copied everything that seemed to express what to me was inexpressible. From Proust, I took: "For henceforth you will always keep something broken about you." From C. S. Lewis: "No one ever told me that grief felt so like fear. I am not afraid but the sensation is like being afraid. The same fluttering in the stomach, the same restlessness, the yawning. I keep on swallowing." From Joan Didion: "A single person is missing for you, and the whole world is empty." From O'Rourke: "Am I really she who has woken up again without a mother? Yes, I am." From a short story by Alice Munro: "What he carried with him, all he carried with him, was a lack, something like a lack of air, of proper behavior in his lungs, a difficulty that he supposed would go on forever." From one by David Long: "Eventually, a truck would come rattling down . . . a car door would chuff, and the world would go on—not where it had left off but on the other side of this nothing time. And when it did, though she couldn't quite see it yet, [she] would begin the never-ending task of not forgetting her mother."

Or this, from my mother's favorite Hebrew poem, in which the poet, Natan 15 Alterman, describes his beloved as "sudden forever." Those two words, as well as the poem's title—"A Meeting for Eternity"—are oxymorons that spell out the contradictions inherent in loss. What is the death of a loved one if not an oxymoron? My mother isn't here, and yet I see her everywhere. I kept on looking for hints of her on the page, as though by retracing her beloved books and poems I would get to reclaim a part of her that was already slipping away.

Two days before she died, my father walked into the hospital room and told me to time a minute. I looked at my watch. When the minute was up, I told him. He said, "Twenty-three. Very good." He had been counting her breaths, I realized. Willing her to stay. And she did—she waited until we were all there, flanking her bed—before letting go.

We buried her just outside of Jerusalem, on a kibbutz, facing the mountains of her youth. She adored her hometown, and ached over what it had become. The growing zealotry, the flickering lights of peace. The news coming out of Israel today—another botched round of negotiations—would have depressed her terribly. Instead, I like to think of what is immutable. The warm wind whistling past those hills. The pine needles crackling underfoot. And on the other side of the mountains, down by the coastal plain—hidden—the sea. Another memory floats by without warning: my mother and me, after a dip in the water. My teeth are chattering. My fingers are raisins. I want to rush toward my towel. But my mother tells me softly, "We don't run to our towels; we walk." That moment distills her essence for me: a hint of old-fashioned formality—a proper woman should know how to carry herself—combined with an implicit imperative. *Hold your head high*, was what she was really telling me. *Take your time. Soon it won't be this cold.*

About two weeks after her death, I wrote in my diary: "The finality of it. When she was sick, at least things kept changing. She felt better, or worse. It was a good time to talk, or it wasn't. *Things happened.* Now nothing is happening. This is it."

A year later, my diary reads: "Hardest thing: overhearing colleagues tell their mothers 'Love you' on the phone. So *casually*."

If, in the first months after losing my mother, I searched for books that 20 made my grief echo and reverberate—that rendered it as shocking as I felt it to be—after a while I found my reading diet largely unsustainable. Part of moving on, I realized, was learning to let my grief buddies go, or at least putting them back on the shelf. That is, until I read Cheryl Strayed's "Wild." No, read isn't quite right. More like ravaged. For some time after the book came out, I purposely avoided it. Something in its subhead—"From Lost to Found"— put me off, as did a few of the reviews praising the book for being "uplifting" and "spiritual." I knew it was about the author's hike through the Pacific Crest Trail, on which she had embarked a few years after the death of her mother, but I expected it to be an Oprahfied memoir—hopelessly positive, sentimental, diluted. I didn't expect to gulp it down in one reading. Nor did I expect that Strayed's experience—of watching her healthy, dominant mother beset by advanced lung cancer—would so closely mirror my own.

Strayed serves her material raw. Of receiving her mother's diagnosis, she writes: "We went to the women's restroom. Each of us locked in separate stalls, weeping. We didn't exchange a word. Not because we felt so alone in our grief, but because we were so together in it, as if we were one body instead of two." Strayed's writing is so piercing and precise that I found myself nodding along as I was reading, as though it were a hymn. (Maybe "spiritual" wasn't far-fetched, after all.) Her mother's death, she writes, "had cut me short at the very height of my youthful arrogance. It had forced me to instantly grow up and forgive her every motherly fault at the same time that it kept me forever a child, my life both ended and begun in that premature place where we'd left off." Nothing I've read has managed to describe that exact point in time, that "place where we'd left off," as accurately as those few lines have. I always thought that literature's draw lay in making me identify with people and situations that were as different from my lived experience as possible. But my mother's death changed that. It made me seek out my own kind—the left-behind and the heartbroken. The unmothered.

There's a word in Hebrew—*malkosh*—that means "last rain." It's a word that only means something in places like Israel, where there's a clear distinction between winter and the long, dry stretch of summer. It's a word, too, that can only be applied in retrospect. When it's raining, you have no way of knowing that the falling drops would be the last ones of the year. But then time goes by, the clouds clear, and you realize that *that* rain shower was the one. Having a mother—being mothered—is similar, in a way. It's a term that I only fully grasp now, with the thirst of hindsight: who she was, who I was for her, what she has equipped me with.

Like a last rain, my mother left behind an earthy scent that lingered long after she was gone. Like a last rain, for a fleeting moment, everything she touched seemed to glow.

FOR ANALYSIS

1. What is the occasion for the author's writing of this essay?

2. What is an **oxymoron**? What is the oxymoron Margalit identifies in her essay?

3. What does the author say literature does for her? Has its usefulness or importance to her changed?

MAKING ARGUMENTS

Make an argument about the much-discussed topic of sensitivity in speech and writing, using as a jumping-off point Margalit's observations about what she sees as unthinking references to mothers. How much should people think about who they might offend or sadden when they make an utterance, spoken or written? How much is the offense people take or the sadness they feel their own responsibility?

WRITING TOPICS

Reflect on your own state of motheredness or unmotheredness (and/or your state with regard to a father or guardian) and on Margalit's use of her reading of literature to deal with her feelings. How does your reading of her essay compare to her reading of Barthes and Proust and Strayed? Do you recognize yourself, or learn about different kinds of experiences, or both?

MAKING CONNECTIONS

1. How do Lethem's use of movies and Margalit's of literature compare? How do they use them? When? What do they get out of them?

2. While neither Lethem nor Margalit hide their feelings about the mother's deaths in these essays, they do deal with explicit statements about grief and mourning differently. How would you characterize that difference? Do they seem appropriate to the circumstances they write about, or to the kind of thing they are writing? Do you find one more congenial?

3. Both of these essays focus much more on self-examination than **character** portrait—that is, they are more about the authors' dealing with their mothers' deaths than about the mothers themselves. Yet the mothers still emerge as figures. How does each author make this happen? What do the outlines of the figures that emerge tell you about each of the authors, as writers and as people?

FURTHER QUESTIONS
FOR THINKING AND WRITING

1. Although A. E. Housman's "To an Athlete Dying Young" and Pablo Neruda's "The Dead Woman" employ different poetic forms, they both embody a poetic mode called **elegy**. Define *elegy* in terms of the characteristic **tone** of these poems. Compare the elegiac tone of these poems. **Writing Topic:** Compare the elegiac tone of one of these poems with the tone of Wilfred Owen's "Dulce et Decorum Est" or Dylan Thomas's "Do Not Go Gentle into That Good Night."

2. What **figurative language** in the prose and poetry of this section is commonly associated with death? With dying? Contrast the characteristic **imagery** of this section with the characteristic imagery of love poetry. **Writing Topic:** Compare the imagery in Shakespeare's Sonnet 18 with the imagery in Sonnet 73.

3. In Leo Tolstoy's "The Death of Iván Ilých" and John Donne's **sonnet** "Death, Be Not Proud," death and dying are considered from a religious viewpoint. **Writing Topic:** Discuss whether these works develop a similar attitude toward death or whether the attitudes they develop differ.

4. Helena María Viramontes, a Mexican American, and Leslie Marmon Silko, an American Indian, both treat death as a ritualistic event. How are their stories similar? How do they differ? **Writing Topic:** Contrast the ritualistic elements in these stories with the religious elements in Tolstoy's "The Death of Iván Ilých."

5. Which works in this section treat death and dying in a way that corresponds most closely to your own attitude toward mortality? Which contradict your attitude? **Writing Topic:** Choose two works, each of which affects you differently, and discuss the elements responsible for your response.

Appendixes

INTRODUCTION

This glossary attempts to define, briefly and in general terms, some major critical approaches to literature. Because literary criticism has to do with the value of literature—not with its history—judgments tend to be subjective, and disagreements frequent and even acrimonious. The truth of a work of art is very different from the truth of a mathematical formula. Certainly one's attitudes toward war, religion, sex, and politics are irrelevant to the truth of a formula but quite relevant to one's judgment of a literary work.

Most critical approaches can, in a general sense, be placed into one of three categories:

1. those that focus exclusively on the work itself, including the internal connections between its various parts and elements,

2. those that approach a work with certain preconceived assumptions against which the work is evaluated, and

3. those that reject any "pure" approach and instead encourage an eclecticism that draws from whatever sources seem best suited to the work and the predilections of the critic.

Most of us are likely to find the third approach most congenial.

Yet any examination of the broad range of literary criticism reveals that groups of critics (and all readers are ultimately critics) share certain assumptions about literature. These assumptions govern the way critics approach a work, the elements they tend to look for and emphasize, the details they find significant or insignificant, and finally, the overall value they place on the work.

We do not suggest that one approach is more valid than another or that the lines dividing the various approaches are always clear and distinct. Readers will perhaps discover one approach more congenial to their temperament, more "true" to their sense of the world, than another. More likely, they will find themselves using more than one approach in dealing with a single work. Many of the diverse approaches described here actually overlap, and even those critics who champion a single abstract theory often draw on a variety of useful approaches when they write about a particular work.

Formalist critics assume that a literary text remains independent of the writer who created it. The function of the critic, then, is to discover how the author has deployed language to create (or perhaps failed to create) a formal and aesthetically satisfying structure. The influential American formalists of the 1940s and 1950s (the New Critics) were fond of describing literary texts as "autonomous," meaning that political, historical, biographical, and other considerations were always secondary if not irrelevant to any discussion of their merits.

Furthermore, formalist critics argue that the various elements of a "great" work interweave to create a seamless whole that embodies "universal" values. Unsurprisingly, the "universal" values formalist critics praise, on close analysis, tend to parallel the moral, political, and cultural ideals of the critics' social class. This tendency becomes even more problematic and complex in dealing with the literature of formerly colonized people.

But the formalist point of view, cherishing the artwork's structure, spawned its own antithesis—a group of theorists called *deconstructionists*. These writers argued that language itself was too shifty to support the expectations of formalist criticism. One reader might read a sentence literally, while another might read it ironically. Hence, their "understanding" of the text would be diametrically opposed.

The deconstructionists believe that intelligent readers cannot be expected to ignore those responses that interfere with some "correct" or "desirable" reading of the piece. Given what they see as the notoriously ambiguous and unstable nature of language, deconstructionist critics argue that a literary text can never have a fixed meaning.

While the formalists and deconstructionists wrestle over the philosophy of language and its implications for the nature of literary texts, other critics pursue quite different primary interests. The term *ethical criticism* describes a variety of approaches, all of which argue that literature, like any other human activity, connects to the real world and, consequently, influences real people. If that is so, our appraisal of a work must take into account the ethical and moral values it embodies. Though it sounds simple enough, in reality the task is difficult and often quite controversial. Ethical criticism is the very opposite of the "art for art's sake" approach, best represented by formalist criticism. The formalist critic tries to isolate the work in a timeless world of universal aesthetic considerations; the ethical critic insists on making judgments about whether a work serves values that are "good" or encourages values that are "bad."

Other critical approaches analyze literary works from still other perspectives. *Reader-response* critics assert that a work of art is created as much by its audience as by the artist. For these critics, art has no significant abstract existence: a reader's experience of the work gives birth to it and contributes crucially to its power and value. Further, since each reader embodies a unique set of experiences and values, each reader's response to the work will in some respects be uniquely personal. *Psychoanalytic* criticism, similar to reader-response, is nevertheless distinctive in its application of psychoanalytic principles to works of art. Those principles, originally derived from the work of Sigmund Freud (1856–1939), now often reflect the views of more recent theorists such as Jacques Lacan (1901–1981). There is, finally, the recently emergent approach called *new historical* criticism, which brings historical knowledge to bear on the analysis of literary works in new and sophisticated ways. The result is a sometimes dizzying proliferation of analyses that argue for the relationship between literature and life.

The glossary that follows reveals the widely diverse and often contradictory views expressed by professional theorists and critics.

Deconstruction   This approach grew out of the work of certain twentieth-century European philosophers, notably Jacques Derrida (1930–2004), whose study of language led to the conclusion that since we can know only through the medium of language, and language is unstable and ambiguous, it is impossible to talk about truth and knowledge and meaning in any absolute sense. Verbal structures, these critics maintained, inevitably contained within themselves oppositions. Derrida asserted that in the Western world, language leads us to think in terms of opposites (for example, soul/body, man/woman, master/slave) that imply what he called "a violent hierarchy," with one of the terms (the first) always being superior to the other (the second). The aim of deconstruction is to show that this hierarchy of values cannot be permanent and absolute.

Readers therefore cannot be expected to ignore the oppositions and contradictions in a text just because they do not contribute to some "correct" or "desirable" reading of the piece that might uphold a particular political, social, or cultural view.

Formalism assures us that the successful artist is the master of language and that he or she consciously deploys all its resources to achieve a rich and unified work. Sensitive readers can aspire to a complete understanding of a work undistorted by their own idiosyncrasies, subjective states, or ideological biases.

Rejecting the formalist assumption about authorial control and conscious design, deconstruction attempts to show that by its very nature, language is constantly "saying" more than the writer can control or even know. Thus, a close study of any text (literary or otherwise) will reveal contradictory and irreconcilable elements.

Deconstructionist critics do not necessarily reject the validity of feminist, Marxist, formalist, and other critical approaches. In fact, they often draw on the insights furnished by them. But the deconstructionist critic says that any discourse or critical approach that fails to recognize the inherently shifting and unstable nature of language is bound to produce only a partial if not misleading interpretation. For example, in his study *America the Scrivener: Deconstruction and the Subject of Literary Studies* (1990), Gregory S. Jay finds Emily Grierson, the protagonist of William Faulkner's story "A Rose for Emily" (p. 623), a "puzzle" and warns against simplistic interpretations:

> As feminist subject, her story speaks of a revolutionary subversion of patriarchy; as herself, a figure of racial and class power, Emily also enacts the love affair of patriarchy with its own past, despite all the signs of decline and degradation. She is a split subject, crossed by rival discourses. What the text forces us to think, then, is the complex and ironic alliances between modes of possession and subjection, desire and ownership, identity and position.

Like Marxism and feminism, deconstruction defines itself both as a critical theory of literature and as a philosophy of human values. Hence, it is applicable not only to literature but also to an understanding of the power relations among humans and the societies they create. In insisting that we recognize the way language embodies and supports class, gender, and other biases, deconstruction challenges both the ethnocentrism of political structures and the idea of "universal values" in literary works.

Ethical Criticism Ethical criticism may range from a casual appraisal of a work's moral content to the more rigorous and systematic analysis driven by a coherent set of stated beliefs and assumptions. A *religious* critic (committed to certain moral positions) might attack a work (regardless of its artfulness or brilliance) because it does not condemn adultery. A *feminist* critic might focus on the way literary works devalue women; a *black* critic, on the way they stereotype blacks; a *Marxist* critic, on the way they support class divisions; and a *new historicist* critic, on the way a dominant class interprets history to protect its own interests. But all of them agree that literary works invite ethical judgments. Most of them also agree that literary works must be judged as another means by which a society both defines and perpetuates its political institutions and cultural values. The feminist critic, the black critic, and the Marxist critic would also agree that the political institutions and cultural values of most Western societies have been carefully designed to serve the interests of a dominant class: white, male, and wealthy.

Ethical criticism takes us out of the comparatively calm, academic world of aesthetic values into the larger world of moral judgments. If a literary work's capacity to promote good or bad behavior becomes the criterion for judging its value, then surely some people will try to suppress works they perceive as morally threatening. It is here that ethical criticism encounters its most vexing and dangerous problem: censorship. The literary critic Wayne Booth, who advocates ethical criticism in his book *The Company We Keep: An Ethics of Fiction* (1988), concedes the danger but notes that teaching itself is a form of censorship in that "we impose our ethical choices on our students when we choose our reading lists."

Feminist Criticism Feminist critics hold that literature is merely one of many expressions of a patriarchal society with a vested interest in keeping women subordinate to men. Thus literature, in the way it portrays gender roles, helps to condition women to accept as normal a society that directs them to become nurses rather than doctors, secretaries rather than attorneys or corporate executives, sex symbols rather than thinkers, elementary school teachers rather than university professors. Beyond this general critique of patriarchy, feminists differ in their detailed analyses. Some have re-examined history to show that a literary canon created by males has slighted and ignored female authors. Others, studying canonical works from a feminist perspective, have come up with fresh readings that challenge conventional interpretations, focusing on how women are empowered in literary texts or through writing literary texts. Some, believing that language itself allows men to impose their power, use literary analyses to expose the gender bias of language. Why, they ask, is the English language so rich in words to describe a quarrelsome, abusive woman (*shrew, harridan, termagant*) but so lacking in comparable terms for men? Some feminists believe that the male bias of language, far deeper than mere words, is actually structural. The constellation of qualities connoted by *masculine* and *feminine*, they say, reveals how deeply the positive (male) and negative (female) values are embedded in the language.

While a psychoanalytic critic might use Freud's Oedipal theories to explain Emily's relationship to Homer Barron in William Faulkner's "A Rose for Emily" (p. 623), the feminist critic Judith Fetterley maintains that the explanation is to be found in the fact that a patriarchal culture instills in us the notion "that men and women are made for each other" and that " 'masculinity' and 'femininity' are the natural reflection of that divinely ordained complement." In a society where there is "a massive differentiation of everything according to sex, one sees that in reality a sexist culture is one in which men and women are not simply incompatible but murderously so. . . . Emily murders Homer Barron because she must at any cost get a man" (*The Resisting Reader: A Feminist Approach to American Fiction*, 1978).

Formalist Criticism Like deconstruction, formalism focuses on the ambiguous and multilayered nature of language but does so to achieve the precisely opposite effect. Formalism assures us that the successful artist is the master of language and consciously deploys all its resources to achieve a rich and unified work. Careful readers can aspire to a complete understanding of a work undistorted by their own idiosyncrasies or subjective states or ideological biases. The formalist rejects the central tenet of the reader-response critic—that a work comes into existence, so to speak, through the interaction of the reader with the work. For the formalist, the work exists independent of any particular reader. The work is a structured and formal aesthetic object comprising such elements as symbol, image, and sound patterns. Political, biographical, or historical considerations not embodied in the work itself are irrelevant.

The formalist sees literature as a sort of Platonic ideal form—immutable and objective. Works close to that ideal are praised for their aesthetic energy and their universality (a characteristic of the greatest literature). Works that do not exhibit this prized formal coherence are dispraised and often dismissed as neither universal nor important. Because formalism focuses on the internal structure of literature above all else, it rejects didactic works—those intended to teach or convey moral observations. During the 1940s and 1950s, when the New Critics (as the formalists were called) dominated academic literary criticism, social protest writing was generally dismissed as subliterary because it lacked the "universality" of great literature. What was important in a work of art was not that it might change people's behavior but that its parts coalesced into a beautiful whole. Consider the following comment by two formalist critics (Caroline Gordon and Allen Tate, *The House of Fiction*, 1950) on Nathaniel Hawthorne's "Young Goodman Brown" (p. 77):

> *The dramatic impact would have been stronger if Hawthorne had let the incidents tell their own story: Goodman Brown's behavior to his neighbors and finally to his wife show us that he is a changed man. Since fiction is a kind of shorthand of human behavior and one moment may represent years in a man's life, we would have concluded that the change was to last his entire life. But Hawthorne's weakness for moralizing and his insufficient technical equipment betray him into the anticlimax of the last paragraph.*

African American writers and critics, for example, complained that the criterion of universality was merely a way of protecting white, conservative social and political dominance. The New Critics dismissed African American literature that sought to deal with racism and the struggle for equality as mere didacticism or agitprop, not to be compared with the great white literary productions that achieved universal import. In a major work of New Criticism published in 1952, the influential critic R. P. Blackmur dismissed *Native Son*, a powerful and now classic novel about white racism, as "one of those books in which everything is undertaken with seriousness except the writing."

Marxist Criticism The Marxist critic sees literature as one activity among many to be studied and judged in terms of a larger and all-encompassing ideology derived from the economic and political doctrines of Karl Marx (1818–1883). Marxism offers a comprehensive theory about the nature of humans and the way in which a few of them manage to seize control of the means of production and thereby exploit the masses of working people. But Marxism is about more than analysis. As Karl Marx himself said, "It is not enough to analyze society; we must also change it."

The Marxist critic analyzes literary works to show how, wittingly or unwittingly, they support the dominant social class or how they, in some way, contribute to the struggle against oppression and exploitation. And since the Marxist critic views literature as just one among the variety of human activities that reflect power relations and class divisions, he or she is likely to be more interested in what a work says than in its formal structure.

The Marxist argues that one cannot properly understand a literary work unless one understands how it reflects the relationship between economic production and social class. Further, this relationship cannot be explored adequately without examining a range of questions that other critical approaches, notably formalism, deem irrelevant. How does the work relate to the profit-driven enterprise of publishing? What does the author's biography reveal about his or her class biases? Does the work accurately portray the class divisions of society? Does the work expose the economic bases of oppression and advance the cause of liberation?

And since Marxist critics see their duty—indeed, the duty of all responsible and humane people—as not merely to describe the world but to change it, they judge literature by the contribution it makes to bringing about revolution or in some way enlightening its readers about oppression and the necessity for class struggle.

For example, a Marxist critic's analysis of Matthew Arnold's poem "Dover Beach" (p. 943) might see it not as a brilliantly structured pattern of images and sounds but as the predictable end product of a dehumanizing capitalist economy in which a small class of oligarchs is willing, at whatever cost, to protect its wealth and power. The Marxist critic, as a materialist who believes that humans make their own history, would find Arnold's reference to the "eternal note of sadness" (l. 14) a mystic evasion of the real sources of his alienation and pain: Arnold's misery can be clearly and unmystically explained by his fearful responses to the socioeconomic conditions of his time.

Arnold's refusal to face this fact leads him to the conclusion typical of a bourgeois artist-intellectual who cannot discern the truth. But the cure for Arnold's pain, the Marxist would argue, cannot be found in a love relationship because relations between people are determined crucially by socioeconomic conditions. The cure for the pain he describes so well will be found in the world of action, in the struggle to create a society that is just and humane. "Dover Beach," the Marxist critic would conclude, is both a brilliant evocation of the alienation and misery caused by a capitalist economy and a testimony to the inability of a bourgeois intellectual to understand what is responsible for his feelings.

New Historical Criticism   There is nothing "new" about historians drawing on literary works as significant documents to support and illuminate historical analysis; nor is there anything "new" about literary critics drawing on history to illuminate literary works. For the historian, Sophocles' *Antigonê* (p. 450) tells us much about the conflict between the old-time religion and the new secularism in fifth-century BCE Athens. The literary critic of *Othello* (p. 984) goes to the historian to understand the way in which Shakespeare and his contemporaries viewed black Africans. But until recently, the provinces of the historian and of the literary critics were pretty much mutually exclusive.

The new historians (influenced by modern theories of language and literature) began to question the very idea of history as it had been practiced. The historians of the past tended, for the most part, to think of history in terms of overarching themes and theses, and attempted to understand it in terms of some perceived Zeitgeist, or "spirit of the times." This kind of history was often linked to nationalism. Hence (for one example), nineteenth-century Americans created the idea of manifest destiny and then used it to explain and justify eastern settlers' movement west and their attendant atrocities against the Native Americans who resided there. When the Nazis came to power in Germany, they developed the idea that true Germans were descended from a superior Aryan race and then used that idea to deprive "inferior races" of civil rights, of property, and finally, of life.

More abstractly, the purpose of writing history was to articulate and reinforce the values and beliefs that gave a culture unity. By that means, some new historians note, history became the story (and the ideas and beliefs and culture) of the rich, the powerful, the privileged, the victorious. The new historians see history not as the search for some grand, unifying thesis but as the articulation of the various kinds of discourse that compete with, contradict, overlap, and modify one another in the constant struggle for dominance. Indeed, the new historians, influenced by deconstructionist views of language, came to question the very idea of historical truth.

The new historians also reject the traditional division between history and other disciplines, appropriating to historical studies many kinds of texts—including literary texts—that traditional historians left to others. These critics assert that without an understanding of the historical context that produced it, no work of literature can really be understood; therefore, in their eyes, literature belongs as much to the historian as to the literary critic. Such critics aim at what they call a "thick" description of a literary work, one that applies to a text as much information as can be gathered about every aspect of the author, his work, and his times. While its practitioners generally share the fundamental ideas outlined here, they can differ widely in the tools and methodologies they use to analyze a literary text. That is to say, a new historian may also be a Marxist, feminist, or deconstructionist.

Postcolonial Criticism Postcolonial criticism belongs to the larger field of postcolonial studies, which evolved in the wake of the liberation of many nations from the domination of the European powers of the nineteenth century. It is distinguished not so much by any singular approach as by its subject: the examination of postcolonial writings that explore the way in which the colonizers imposed their culture and values on native peoples and thus distorted or suppressed their past.

One prominent purpose of postcolonial criticism is to explain and expose the mechanisms the colonizer used—from brute force to subtle psychological techniques—to gain and maintain control. It becomes, in effect, a new lens through which the literature of the colonizing culture can be examined in order to expose its biased judgments about the society it has dominated, its distortions of native culture as compared with the colonizing culture. This kind of analysis will lead the critic away from narrowly defined literary concerns to examine the colonized culture's past, including its precolonial past. Thus postcolonial critics (and historians), by uncovering the past, may give their newly liberated compatriots the means of re-creating an identity and may give its imaginative writers the material for a national literature.

Because postcolonial criticism is a relatively new field, it is still developing its distinctive areas of interest and techniques of analysis. By its nature it is eclectic, drawing on any other literary approach (as well as academic discipline) that seems relevant to a critic's purpose.

Psychoanalytic Criticism Psychoanalytic criticism always proceeds from a set of principles that describes the inner life of men and women. Though differing psychological theorists argue for diverse views, all analysts and all psychoanalytic critics assume that the development of the psyche is analogous to the development of the body. Doctors can provide charts indicating physical growth stages; analysts can supply similar charts indicating stages in the growth of the psyche. Sigmund Freud, for all practical purposes, invented psychoanalysis by creating a theoretical model for the (mostly male) human psyche.

The Oedipus complex is a significant element in that model. Freud contends that everyone moves through a childhood stage of erotic attachment to the parent of the opposite sex and an accompanying hostility and aggression against the parent of the same sex, who is seen as a rival. Such feelings, part of the natural biography of the psyche, pass or are effectively controlled in most cases. But sometimes the child grown to adulthood is still strongly gripped by the Oedipal mode, which then may result in neurotic or even psychotic behavior. Freud did not invent the Oedipus complex—he simply described it. It was always there, especially noticeable in the work of great literary artists who, in every era, demonstrate a special insight into the human condition.

Along with Oedipal feelings, the psyche inevitably embodies aggressive feelings—the urge to attack those who exercise authority, who deny us our primal desires. For the young, the authority figure is frequently a parent. Adults must deal with police, government officials, the boss. As far back as the Hebrew Bible story of the tower of Babel and the old Greek myths in which the giant Titans, led by Cronus, overthrow their father, and Zeus and the Olympians subsequently overthrow Cronus, there is evidence of the rebellion against the parent-authority figure. Freud views that aggressive hostility as another component of the developing psyche. But, in the interest of civilization, society has developed ways to control that aggressiveness.

Freud saw us as divided selves. An unconscious *id* struggles to gratify aggressive and erotic primal urges, while a *superego* (roughly what society calls *conscience*), by producing guilt feelings, struggles to control the id. The *ego* (the self) is defined by the struggle. Thus the Freudian psychoanalytic critic is constantly aware that authors and their characters suffer and resuffer a primal tension that results from the conflict between psychic aggressions and social obligations.

Freud has been succeeded by a number of psychological theorists who present quite different models of the psyche, and recent literary theory has responded to these post-Freudian views. Among the most important are Carl Gustav Jung (1875–1961), who argued that there exists a collective (as well as a racial and individual) unconscious. Residing there are archetypes—original patterns—that emerge into our consciousness in the form of shadowy images that persistently appear and reappear in such literary themes as the search for the father, death and resurrection, the quest, and the double.

The psychoanalytic critic understands literature in terms of the psychic models that Freud and others defined. Originally, such critics tended to analyze literature in an attempt to identify the author's neuroses. More recently, psychoanalytic critics have argued that the patterns they discover in works allow us to tap into and, perhaps, resolve our own neuroses.

Reader-Response Criticism Reader-response criticism (also called *transactional theory*) emerged in the 1970s as one of the many challenges to formalist principles. Reader-response critics focus on the interaction between the work and the reader, holding that, in a sense, a work exists only when it is experienced by the reader. If the work exists only in the mind of the reader, the reader becomes an active participant in the creative process rather than a passive receptacle for an autonomous work. The creation of a work thus becomes a dynamic enterprise between the reader and the text, each acting on the other. The study of the affective power of a work becomes not a fallacy, as formalism holds, but the central focus of criticism. The task of the critic is to investigate this dynamic relationship between reader and text in order to discover how it works.

We know that various readers respond differently to the same text. In fact, the same reader might respond to the text quite differently at a different time. The reader-response critic wants to know why. In what ways do such conditions as age, gender, upbringing, and race account for differing responses? Does the reader's mood at the time of reading make a difference? If you accept the principles of reader-response criticism, the inevitable conclusion—*reductio ad absurdum*, its critics would say—is that there is no limit to the possible readings of any text. Consequently, many reader-response critics qualify the intense subjectivity of their approach by admitting that an "informed" or "educated" reader is likely to produce a more "valid" reading than an "uninformed" or "uneducated" one.

Gaps or blanks in literary texts provide particular opportunities to readers. Every narrative work omits, for example, periods of time that the reader must fill in. In Nathaniel Hawthorne's "Young Goodman Brown" (p. 77), the author omits all the years of Brown's life between his emergence from the forest and his death. The reader is free to imagine that history. The filling in of these blanks enables readers to participate in "creating" a text and reinforces the arguments of reader-response theorists.

BIOGRAPHICAL NOTES ON THE AUTHORS

CHRIS ABANI (b. 1966) Born in Nigeria to an Igbo father and an English mother, Abani wrote his first novel at age sixteen. A political thriller about a foiled government take-over, the book landed Abani in prison for insurrection when a real-life coup was attempted shortly after his novel's publication. Abani has since written three novels: *GraceLand* (2004), which won the PEN/Hemingway Book Prize, *The Virgin of Flames* (2007), and *The Secret History of Las Vegas* (2014). He has also received recognition for his shorter works of fiction *Becoming Abigail* (2006) and *Song for Night* (2007) and for his poetry, including *Dog Woman* (2004) and *Sanctificum* (2010). A graduate of Imo State University, Nigeria, Abani received his MA from the University of London and his PhD from the University of Southern California. Currently a professor of English at Northwestern University, Abani's varied research interests include the living architecture of cities, West African music, and Yoruba and Igbo philosophy and religion. His critical and personal essays on humanitarianism, art, ethics, and our shared political responsibility have appeared in numerous sources, including the *New York Times* and *O* magazine. On being named a United States Artists Ford Fellow in 2014, Abani remarked on the importance of imagination: "The world as we know it is a product of human imagination. Without imagination there is no invention, there are no tools, there is nothing but a more instinctual place of being."

CHIMAMANDA NGOZI ADICHIE (b. 1977) Adichie was born in Enugu, Nigeria, and raised in the town of Nsukka. Her parents were very accomplished: her father was the University of Nigeria's first professor of statistics and later served as deputy vice-chancellor of the university, and her mother was the first female registrar there. Adichie completed her secondary education at the university's school and later studied medicine and pharmacy at the university. At the age of nineteen, she moved to the United States and attended Drexel University on a scholarship to study communication. She then went on to pursue a degree in communication and political science at Eastern Connecticut State University, from which she graduated summa cum laude. She later earned her MA in creative writing at Johns Hopkins University. Her first novel, *Purple Hibiscus* (2003), won the Commonwealth Writers' Prize and the Hurston/Wright Legacy Award. Her second novel, *Half of a Yellow Sun* (2006), was awarded the 2007 Orange Prize for Fiction. Her short fiction has appeared in such publications as the *New Yorker*, *Virginia Quarterly Review*, *Fiction*, *Granta*, *Prospect*, and the *Iowa Review*. In 2008 Adichie was awarded a MacArthur Fellowship and was described as "a writer of great promise, [whose] powerful rendering of the Nigerian experience is enlightening audiences both in her homeland and around the world." Her latest novel, *Americanah* (2013), won the National Book Critics Circle Award. Of her fiction, fellow Nigerian author Chinua Achebe has said that "Adichie knows what is at stake and what to do about it."

DILRUBA AHMED (b. 1973) Ahmed won the Bread Loaf Writers' Conference Bakeless Prize for her book *Dhaka Dust* (2011), and her poetry has appeared in several literary reviews as well as *Indivisible: An Anthology of Contemporary South Asian Poetry* (2010). A writer, editor, and educator with roots in Pennsylvania, Ohio, and Bangladesh, Ahmed received her undergraduate and master's degrees from the University of Pittsburgh and her MFA from Warren Wilson College. Reflecting on why she became a poet, Ahmed credits her literature-loving Bangladeshi parents and her status as an outsider who moved a lot as a child. Poet and critic Vijay Seshadri said of Ahmed's poems, "On the surface, . . . they'd probably seem as exotic to a citizen of Dhaka as they would to a citizen of Duluth. In their depths, though, they seem anything but exotic; they seem to be our own impossible, loving, intimate, bereaved thoughts restored to us transformed and ennobled."

EDWARD ALBEE (b. 1928) Award-winning playwright Edward Albee was born in Washington, DC, and adopted by a wealthy couple with ties to powerful New York theater companies. Albee later rebelled against the snobbery and prejudice he detected amid his affluent upbringing. After being kicked out of Trinity College for skipping classes and compulsory chapel attendance, Albee broke from his parents and moved to New York City in the 1940s. There, he mingled with the avant-garde Greenwich Village circle of artists, musicians, and intellectuals, and his long-term romantic partner and mentor, William Flanagan. Although he was determined to be a writer, Albee's many works of fiction, poetry, and drama were mostly rejected by publishers and producers until he wrote *The Zoo Story* (1958) just before his thirtieth birthday. This critical and commercial success launched Albee's playwriting career. He went on to write several notable plays, including *The American Dream* (1960), before the enormously successful *Who's Afraid of Virginia Woolf?* (1961–62), which won five Tony Awards including best play. Albee continued to produce plays in the decades that followed, often to great critical acclaim. Some of his most successful plays since *Who's Afraid of Virginia Woolf?* include the Pulitzer Prize-winning *Three Tall Women* (1991) and *The Goat, or Who Is Sylvia* (2000, 2002), which won the Tony Award for best new play and was well-received at the box office despite its controversial plot, which features a man who falls in love with a goat. Known for pushing the limits with their experimental use of absurd elements and raw dialogue, Albee's plays unsympathetically examine modern conventions. Albee received the Tony Lifetime Achievement Award in 2005.

SHERMAN ALEXIE (b. 1966) A Spokane/Coeur d'Alene Indian, Sherman Alexie was born on the Spokane Indian Reservation in Wellpinit, Washington. In 1981 he left the reservation school and enrolled in a predominantly white high school, where, according to Alexie, he "kept [his] mouth shut and became a good white Indian." He enrolled at Gonzaga University in Spokane and began to discover his love for literature and his talent for writing. After two years at Gonzaga, he transferred to Washington State University in Pullman, where he began to write seriously. A year after he received his degree, he published two collections of poetry, *The Business of Fancydancing* (1992) and *I Would Steal Horses* (1992), followed the next year by another poetry collection, *First Indian on the Moon* (1993). Alexie then turned to prose, publishing a volume of loosely related stories dealing with life on the reservation, *The Lone Ranger and Tonto Fistfight in Heaven* (1993). One of the stories in this collection, "This Is What It Means to Say Phoenix, Arizona," provided the basis for the film *Smoke Signals* (1998), which Alexie produced and for which he wrote the screenplay. He went on to write two more films: *The Business of Fancydancing* (2002), which he also directed, and *49?* (2003). He has published two other collections of short stories, *The Toughest Indian in the World* (2000) and *Ten Little Indians* (2003), along with a number of collections of poetry, including *Dangerous Astronomy* (2005). Alexie has also penned several novels, among them *Reservation Blues* (1995), *Indian Killer* (1996), and *Flight* (2007). His novel for young adults, *The Absolutely True Diary of a Part-Time Indian* (2007), won the National Book Award for Young People's Literature. Alexie received the PEN/Faulkner

Award for his book *War Dances* (2009), a collection of stories, poems, and question-and-answer sequences that explore generational and artistic complexities. About the criticism he has received from members of his reservation, who find his portrayals of Native Americans and reservation life demeaning, Alexie replied, "I write what I know, and I don't try to mythologize myself, which is what some seem to want, and which some Indian women and men writers are doing, this Earth Mother and Shaman Man thing, trying to create these 'authentic, traditional' Indians. We don't live our lives that way."

JULIA ALVAREZ (b. 1950)   Alvarez was born in New York City to Dominican parents. Her family moved to the Dominican Republic when she was three months old and remained there until she was ten, when her father's involvement in a political uprising forced them to flee to the United States. Her struggle to assimilate into American culture and forge an identity informs much of her work. She published a volume of poetry, *Homecoming* (1984), before writing three novels that brought her great acclaim: *How the García Girls Lost Their Accents* (1991), *In the Time of the Butterflies* (1994), and *¡Yo!* (1997). Her nonfiction book, *Once upon a Quinceañera: Coming of Age in the USA* (2007), was a finalist for the National Book Critics Circle Award. She went on to publish additional works of fiction, nonfiction, and poetry, as well as several children's books. Some of her most recent publications include *Return to Sender* (2009), a novel for children about migrant workers, and the nonfiction book *A Wedding in Haiti: The Story of a Friendship* (2012). Among the places Alvarez has taught are the University of Vermont, George Washington College, and the University of Illinois, Urbana; she is now a writer-in-residence at Middlebury College. Alvarez has said, "When I'm asked what made me into a writer, I point to the watershed experience of coming to this country. Not understanding the language, I had to pay close attention to each word. . . . I also discovered the welcoming world of the imagination and books. There, I sunk my new roots."

MAGGIE ANDERSON (b. 1948)   Anderson was born in New York and has dedicated her life to creating and promoting poetry. In 1971 she cofounded the poetry journal *Trellis* and served as its editor until 1981. In 1989 Anderson took a position teaching creative writing at Kent State University, where she became coordinator of the Wick Poetry Program in 1992. She was also part of the founding committee of the Northeast Ohio Master of Fine Arts in Creative Writing and served as Kent's campus coordinator from 2003 to 2006 and as director of the Northeast Ohio MFA Consortium from 2006 to 2009. When she retired from Kent State in 2009, the university created the Maggie Anderson Endowment Fund to honor her contributions to the college. Anderson's poetry collections include *The Great Horned Owl* (1979), *Years That Answer* (1980), *Cold Comfort* (1986), *A Space Filled with Moving* (1992), and *Windfall: New and Selected Poems* (2000). Her poems have been published in the *Alaska Quarterly*, *Georgia Review*, and *American Poetry Review*. She has received a National Endowment for the Arts Fellowship in Poetry, a West Virginia Commission on the Arts Fellowship in Poetry, an Ohio Arts Council Fellowship, a Pennsylvania Council on the Arts Fellowship, and a MacDowell Colony Fellowship.

MATTHEW ARNOLD (1822–1888)   Born in Middlesex, England, Arnold attended Rugby School, where his father was headmaster, and studied classics at Oxford University. Following his graduation in 1844, he became a fellow at Oxford and a master at Rugby. In 1851 he was appointed inspector of schools in England and was sent by the government to observe educational systems in Europe. He remained in that post for some thirty-five years. As a poet, Arnold took inspiration from Greek tragedies, Keats, and Wordsworth. His collections include *Empedocles on Etna and Other Poems* (1852). An eminent social and literary critic in his later years, Arnold lectured in the United States in 1883 and 1886. His essay "The Function of Criticism" sheds light on his transition from poet to critic. Much of his work is collected in *Complete Prose Works* (eleven volumes, 1960–1977).

HANAN MIKHA'IL 'ASHRAWI (b. 1946)   'Ashrawi was born to a wealthy Christian Palestinian family just two years before Israel became a country—an event the Palestinians call *al-nakba* ("the disaster"). She grew up in Ramallah, a West Bank town outside Jerusalem. She was a student of literature at the American University in Beirut, Lebanon, when the 1967 Six-Day War broke out. When the fighting ended, her hometown, along with significant additional territory west of the river Jordan, was occupied by Israel, and for six years the occupying forces refused to allow Palestinians who had been absent during the war to return to the West Bank. During that period, 'Ashrawi traveled and continued her studies, earning a PhD from the University of Virginia in medieval and comparative literature. She returned to Palestine in 1973, where she established and chaired the department of English at Birzeit University in the West Bank, rose to the position of dean of the Faculty of Arts, and remained a faculty member through 1995. She produced several works on literary theory and on contemporary Palestinian literature. She served on numerous commissions on education and politics in the region and is recognized as an eloquent spokesperson for Palestinian civil, economic, and political rights. Her publications include *Intifada to Independence* (1989) and her autobiography, *This Side of Peace: A Personal Account* (1995).

W. H. AUDEN (1907–1973)   A poet, playwright, translator, librettist, critic, and editor, Wystan Hugh Auden was born in York, England, the son of a medical officer and a nurse. He attended Oxford University from 1925 to 1928, then taught, traveled, and moved from faculty to faculty of several universities in the United States, becoming a naturalized citizen in 1946. He won the Pulitzer Prize in 1948 for his collection *The Age of Anxiety*, an expression he coined to describe the 1930s. While his early writing exhibited Marxist sympathies and reflected the excitement of new Freudian psychoanalytic thought, he later embraced Christianity and produced sharply honed verse in the rhyme and meter of traditional forms.

KOFI AWOONOR (1935–2013)   Born to Ewe parents in Ghana, Awoonor was a writer, a diplomat, and a professor of comparative literature at numerous universities, including State University of New York at Stony Brook, where he received his PhD. Author of literary criticism, political essays, novels, and plays, Awoonor is best-known for his works of poetry, including *Rediscovery and Other Poems* (1964), *Night of My Blood* (1971), *Ride Me, Memory* (1973), *The House by the Sea* (1978), and *The Latin American and Caribbean Notebook* (1992). Awoonor's early poems are notable for drawing on the Ewe oral tradition of his ancestors. While serving as head of the English Department at the University of Cape Coast in Ghana in the mid-1970s, Awoonor was imprisoned without trial for his alleged role in an attempt to overthrow the government. He wrote his book *The House by the Sea* about the time he spent in jail. Kwame Dawes, Awoonor's nephew and editor of the literary journal *Prairie Schooner*, categorized his uncle as one of those "artists and writers . . . who felt themselves deeply engaged in the political realities of the world." In September 2013, while visiting Nairobi, Kenya, Awoonor was killed in the Westgate shopping mall attack by the militant group al-Shabaab. He had been in Nairobi for a literary festival to celebrate and promote his forthcoming book, *The Promise of Hope: New and Selected Poems, 1964–2013* (2014), which was published posthumously.

JAMES BALDWIN (1924–1987)   Born in New York City, the son of a Harlem minister, Baldwin began preaching as a young teenager. Some years later, he experienced a religious crisis, left the church, and moved to New York City's bohemian Greenwich Village, where he began his career as a writer, supporting himself with menial jobs and publishing occasional articles in journals such as the *Nation* and *Commentary*. By the end of the 1940s, Baldwin's anger over the treatment of African Americans led him into exile in France. There, Baldwin completed his acclaimed first novel, *Go Tell It on the Mountain* (1953), a work focusing on a minister's son for which he drew heavily on his own childhood. His next work, *Notes of a Native Son* (1955), a collection of personal, literary, and social essays, secured Baldwin's reputation as a major American writer. Two later collections of essays, *Nobody Knows My Name* (1961) and *The Fire Next Time* (1963), established Baldwin as one of the most powerful voices of the turbulent civil rights movement of the 1960s. But as riots, bombings, and other violence grew more frequent, Baldwin grew increasingly pessimistic over the prospect that white America could ever overcome its racism. That pessimism was deepened by two traumatic events: the 1963 bombing of the Sixteenth Street Baptist Church in Birmingham, Alabama, that killed four young girls attending a Sunday school class, and the assassination of the Reverend Martin Luther King Jr. in 1968. Baldwin began making periodic trips to France, settling there permanently in 1974.

TONI CADE BAMBARA (1939–1995)   Born in New York City, Bambara was educated there as well as in Italy and Paris. Early in her career she worked as an investigator for the New York State Department of Social Welfare, but she later devoted herself to teaching and writing. One of the best representatives of a group of African American writers who emerged in the 1960s, Bambara was a consistent civil rights activist, involved both politically and culturally in African American life. Much of her writing focuses on African American women, particularly as they confront experiences that force them to new awareness. She authored several collections of short stories, including *Gorilla, My Love* (1972) and *The Sea Birds Are Still Alive: Collected Stories* (1977), and two novels, *The Salt Eaters* (1980) and *If Blessing Comes* (1987). She also edited a groundbreaking collection of African American women's writing, *The Black Woman: An Anthology* (1970). Two works, *Deep Sightings and Rescue Missions: Fiction, Essays, and Conversations* (1996) and the novel *These Bones Are Not My Child* (1999), were published posthumously.

APHRA BEHN (ca. 1640–1689)   Little is known for certain about the early life of Aphra Behn, but it is generally believed that she sailed with her parents and brother from England to Surinam in 1663. Behn's best-known work, the short novel *Oroonoko* (1688), grew out of her experience in the South American colony, particularly her friendship with an enslaved African prince. Most likely married to a Dutch man sometime after 1664, Behn was forced to make her own living after her husband died in 1665. Hired to spy on the Dutch for the British Crown, Behn traveled to Antwerp but was left broke and in debt when the king would not reimburse her for her work and expenses. She was sent to debtor's prison in 1668 and later began writing plays, vowing never again to rely on others for money. Although her writing was viewed as too masculine and was criticized as indecent by some contemporaries, "Mrs. Behn" went on to become one of the first professional English writers. In *A Room of One's Own*, Virginia Woolf wrote, "All women together ought to let flowers fall upon the tomb of Aphra Behn, . . . for it was she who earned them the right to speak their minds." Behn's prose continues to be highly regarded for its wit and satirical commentary; her poetry is admired for its distinctive voice. Behn's published works of poetry include *Poems upon Several Occasions: With A Voyage to the Island of Love* (1684) and *Lycidus: Or The Lover in Fashion* (1688).

ROBIN BERNSTEIN (b. 1969)   Cultural historian Robin Bernstein specializes in U.S. performance and theater from the nineteenth century to the present. She holds a PhD in American studies from Yale University and is currently professor of African and African American studies and of studies of women, gender, and sexuality at Harvard University. Her book *Racial Innocence: Performing American Childhood from Slavery to Civil Rights* (2011) won five awards, including the Outstanding Book Award from the Association for Theatre in Higher Education. She is currently working on two books, each focused on an area of her specialty. One examines multiracial lesbian performances over the past century; the other looks at how childhood innocence became racially distributed in the United States. In the latter, Bernstein argues that the history of white children serving as symbols of innocence and black children being perceived as threats helps to explain why children of color are disproportionately incarcerated and why white killings of unarmed black youth are widely viewed as justifiable.

ELIZABETH BISHOP (1911–1979)   Bishop was born in Worcester, Massachusetts. Her father died before she was a year old; four years later, when her mother suffered a mental breakdown, Bishop was taken to live with her grandmother in Nova Scotia. Although her mother lived until 1934, Bishop saw her for the last time in 1916, a visit recalled in one of her rare autobiographical stories, "In the Village." Bishop planned to enter Cornell Medical School after graduating from Vassar, but was persuaded by poet Marianne Moore to become a writer. For the next fifteen years, she was a virtual nomad, traveling in Canada, Europe, and North and South America. In 1951 she finally settled in Rio de Janeiro, where she lived for almost twenty years. During the final decade of her life, Bishop continued to travel, but she resumed living in the United States and taught frequently at Harvard University. She was an austere writer, publishing only four slim volumes of poetry: *North and South* (1946); *A Cold Spring* (1955), which won the Pulitzer Prize; *Questions of Travel* (1965); and *Geography III* (1976), which won the National Book Critics Circle Award. *The Complete Poems, 1927–1979* (1984) was published after her death, as was a collection of her prose. Despite her modest output, she has earned an enduring place of respect among twentieth-century poets.

EULA BISS (b. 1977)   Nonfiction writer Eula Biss received her BA from Hampshire College and her MFA from the University of Iowa. A senior lecturer at Northwestern University, she has written three books, and her essays have appeared in numerous publications. In an interview, Biss said, "One essential element of the personal essay tradition is self-scrutiny." Her book of essays on race and identity, *Notes from No Man's Land: American Essays* (2009), won the National Book Critics Circle Award for criticism. Her most recent book, *On Immunity: An Inoculation* (2014), a National Book Critics Circle Award finalist, examines the history, motivations, politics, and fears surrounding the modern vaccination debate.

WILLIAM BLAKE (1757–1827)   Born in London to an obscure family, Blake was educated at home until he was ten and then enrolled in a drawing school, advancing ultimately to a formal apprenticeship as an engraver. At an early age, Blake exhibited talent as both an artist and a poet. Throughout his life, he read widely among modern philosophers and poets and experienced mystical visions that provided him with the inspiration for many of his poems. Blake devised a process he called illuminated printing, which involved the preparation of drawings and decorative frames to complement his poems. He published *Songs of Innocence* (1789) and *Songs of Experience* (1794) in this fashion. These books, as well as the many subsequent works he wrote and illustrated, earned him a reputation as one of the most important artists of his day. Many of Blake's works assert his conviction that the established church and state hinder rather than nurture human freedom and the sense of divine love.

RICHARD BLANCO (b. 1968) Born in Madrid to Cuban exiles, Blanco immigrated to the United States as an infant and was raised and educated in Miami. He received his BS in civil engineering from Florida International University, where he returned several years later to earn his MFA in creative writing. A critically acclaimed poet, in 2013 Blanco was chosen to serve as the fifth inaugural poet of the United States; this appointment made him the first Latino, immigrant, and openly gay writer to be honored in this role. Currently practicing both engineering and writing, his recent works include *Looking for the Gulf Motel* (2012), *Boston Strong* (2013), and *For All of Us, One Today: An Inaugural Poet's Journey* (2013). An avid traveler, Blanco says his writing explores universal questions that we all ask ourselves on our own journeys: Where am I from? Where do I belong? Who am I in this world?

ADRIAN BLEVINS (b. 1964) Adrian Blevins received her BA in English from Virginia Intermont College, her MA in fiction from Hollins University, and her MFA in poetry from Warren Wilson College in 2002. She then taught at Roanoke College and Hollins University, and she is currently an associate professor of creative writing at Colby College in Waterville, Maine. Her first full-length collection of poetry, *The Brass Girl Brouhaha* (2003), won the 2004 Kate Tufts Discovery Award. Blevins has also received the Rona Jaffe Writers Foundation Award for Poetry, the Lamar York Prize for Nonfiction, and a 1996 Bright Hill Press award for her first chapbook, *The Man Who Went Out for Cigarettes* (1997). Her most recent collections include *Live from the Homesick Jamboree* (2009) and *Bloodline* (2012). Her poems have also appeared in the *American Poetry Review, Poetry, Southern Review, Ploughshares, North American Review*, and *Georgia Review*, among other renowned literary journals.

ANNE BRADSTREET (1612–1672) The first notable poet in American literature, Bradstreet was born in England, where her father, a Puritan, managed the business affairs of the estate of the Earl of Lincoln. Unlike most women of her time, Bradstreet received a good deal of formal education. At age sixteen she married Simon Bradstreet, a graduate of Cambridge University, who, like her father, was a Puritan. Two years later, Bradstreet, her husband, and her parents set sail for the Massachusetts Bay Colony, where her father and husband became governors. Anne and Simon Bradstreet settled on a farm near Andover, on the Merrimac River, where the primitive conditions of life left her unhappy and unsatisfied for a period. Ultimately, she reconciled to this new life and her role as a wife, giving birth to eight children. But despite the demands of domestic life in a frontier village, she read a great deal and wrote poetry, which she circulated among family and friends. One of her relatives, who preserved copies of her poems without her knowledge, took them to England, where they were published in 1650 under the title *The Tenth Muse Lately Sprung Up in America . . . By a Gentlewoman of Those Parts*. The first volume of poetry by an English colonist, it was to be the only volume of Bradstreet's poetry published during her lifetime. She continued to write new poems and to revise her older ones; these later poems were included in the second edition of *The Tenth Muse*, published posthumously in 1678.

GWENDOLYN BROOKS (1917–2000) Brooks, who was born in Topeka, Kansas, attended public schools in Chicago and graduated from Wilson Junior College in 1936. She received early recognition for her talent when she attended a poetry workshop at

Chicago's Southside Community Art Center. Shortly after, she published her first book of poems, *A Street in Bronzeville* (1945). She quickly established her reputation as a major poet with *Annie Allen* (1949), which received the Pulitzer Prize for Poetry, making Brooks the first African American to receive this distinction. Her many honors include her designation as poet laureate of Illinois (1968) and as poetry consultant to Congress (1985–86). Although her poetry always focused on the hardships and joys of being poor and black, she steadily moved away from the apolitical integrationist views of her early years. By the 1960s, she had become a passionate advocate of African American consciousness and activism. In addition to reworking traditional forms such as the ballad and sonnet, Brooks achieved greater power in many poems by juxtaposing formal speech with black vernacular. Her other collections of poems include *The Bean Eaters* (1960), *In the Mecca* (1968), *To Disembark* (1981), and *Children Coming Home* (1992). She also published a novel, *Maude Martha* (1953), and an autobiography, *Report from Part One* (1972). Her final volume of poetry, *Montgomery and Other Poems*, was published posthumously in 2003. Its title is taken from the Alabama city that one critic describes as "one of those iconic sites of the Civil Rights Movement, in large part because of the yearlong bus boycotts from 1955 to 1956."

ALLIE BROSH (b. 1985)   An award-winning blogger known primarily for her autobiographical comics, Brosh was named one of the fifty most influential creative figures in the world by *Advertising Age* in 2013. In her blog, *Hyperbole and a Half*, Brosh creates stories that recount episodes from her childhood, illustrate adventures with her dogs, and delve into the depths of her recent depression. In 2013 her popular blog became the basis for a *New York Times* number-one best-selling book, *Hyperbole and a Half: Unfortunate Situations, Flawed Coping Mechanisms, Mayhem, and Other Things That Happened*. On becoming a published author for the first time, Brosh says she feels "only slightly high and mighty. I'm mostly just relieved to have a less confusing answer when people ask me what my job is."

LLOYD W. BROWN (b. 1938)   Born in Jamaica and a graduate of the University of the West Indies, Lloyd W. Brown continued his studies in Canada and later the United States, where he became professor of comparative literature at the University of Southern California. His published works of literary criticism include *Bits of Ivory: Narrative Techniques in Jane Austen's Fiction* (1973), *West Indian Poetry* (1978, 1984), *Women Writers in Black Africa* (1981), and numerous articles for European, North American, and Caribbean journals. Brown also served as editor for the essay collection *The Black Writer in Africa and the Americas* (1973). Brown's own collection of poetry, *Duppies* (1996), grew out of the persistence of his childhood memories in rural Jamaica.

ROBERT BROWNING (1812–1889)   Born in London, Browning attended a private school and was later tutored at home. After one year as a student of Greek at the University of London, he moved with his family to Hatcham, where he studied, wrote poetry, and practiced writing for the theater. In 1845 he began exchanging poems and letters with the already famous poet Elizabeth Barrett; they eloped in 1846. They moved to Italy, where Browning completed most of his work. When Elizabeth died in 1861, he returned to England and began to establish his own reputation. He is noted especially for his fine dramatic monologues in which a wide range of characters reveal the complexity of human belief and passion. His many volumes include *Dramatis Personae* (1864) and *The Ring and the Book* (1868–1869).

HALLMAN B. BRYANT (b. 1936)   Bryant's literary criticism has appeared in *Literature/ Film Quarterly* and *Studies in Short Fiction* as well as many edited collections. His article "Reading the Map in 'A Good Man Is Hard to Find'" is among the most famous essays on Flannery O'Connor's renowned short story.

ROBERT BURNS (1759–1796)   Born in Scotland to a family of poor tenant farmers, Burns was working in the fields with his father by age twelve. During these early years, the family moved often, in fruitless attempts to improve their lot. Although Burns received formal education only intermittently, he read widely on his own. After the death of his father, Burns and his brother worked vainly to make their farm pay, an effort Burns was able to abandon when his first volume of poetry, *Poems, Chiefly in the Scottish Dialect* (1786) brought him overnight fame. One result of this fame was his appointment as an excise officer, a position that gave him some financial security while he continued to write poetry. Burns's humble origins instilled in him a lifelong sympathy for the poor and downtrodden, the rebels and iconoclasts, as well as a disdain for religion, particularly Calvinism and what he considered the hypocrisy of its "devout" ministers.

RAYMOND CARVER (1938–1988)   Carver was born in Clatskanie, Oregon, the son of a sawmill worker and a mother who did odd jobs. He graduated from high school at age eighteen, and was married and the father of two children before he was twenty. The following years were difficult as he struggled to develop a writing career while supporting a family. While at Chico State College (now California State University at Chico), Carver took a creative writing course that profoundly affected him. He went on to earn a BA (1963) from Humboldt State College in Eureka and spent the following year studying writing at the University of Iowa. As he became known, he began to lecture on English and creative writing at various universities, including the University of Iowa's Writers' Workshop. He taught at Goddard College in Vermont and was professor of English at Syracuse University from 1980 to 1983. In 1983 he received the Mildred and Harold Strauss Living Award, which allowed him to devote the next five years to writing. His first collection of short stories, *Will You Please Be Quiet, Please?* (1976), was nominated for the National Book Award. Other short-story collections include *What We Talk About When We Talk About Love* (1981) and *Cathedral* (1984). He also published five volumes of poems, among them *Near Klamath* (1968), *Ultramarine* (1986), and *A New Path to the Waterfall* (1989); *No Heroics, Please* (1992) was published posthumously. During the last ten years of his life, Carver lived with the poet and short-story writer Tess Gallagher, whom he married shortly before his death.

SANDRA M. CASTILLO (b. 1962)   Castillo was born in Havana, Cuba, and moved to Miami, Florida, with her family in 1970. Her poetry draws heavily from her early experience of emigrating to the United States as well as from her family's relationships, frequently looking back on the life her family left behind when they fled Cuba. Castillo received both her BA and MA in creative writing from Florida State University. Her first published collection was the chapbook *Red Letters* (1991), and her first full-length collection was *My Father Sings to My Embarrassment* (2002), which Cornelius Eady selected for the White Pine Press Poetry Prize. Her poems have been published in *Cimarron Review, Midway Journal, Borderlands: Texas Poetry Review, PALABRA: A Magazine of Chicano & Latino Literary Art*, and the anthology *Cool Salsa: Bilingual Poems on Growing Up Latino in the United States* (1994). In 2012 she received a grant from the National Endowment for the Humanities. She currently teaches at Miami Dade College in Florida.

CATULLUS (ca. 84–ca. 54 BCE) Relatively little is known about the Latin poet Gaius Valerius Catullus. He is believed to have been born into an influential family in Verona, and his father was said to be a friend to Julius Caesar. The Roman philosopher Cicero described Catullus as a "neoteric" poet who rejected the epic poems characteristic of his time, opting instead to compose poems in plain language mainly about personal experiences. All knowledge of Catullus's poetry has been gleaned from a single extant manuscript of 116 poems, or *carmina*, and the majority of what is known about Catullus's short life has been gathered from the experiences and observations presented in these poems.

MARILYN CHIN (b. 1955) Chin emigrated with her family from Hong Kong, grew up in Portland, Oregon, and earned degrees from the University of Massachusetts and the University of Iowa. She is the author of four volumes of poetry—*Dwarf Bamboo* (1987), *The Phoenix Gone, the Terrace Empty* (1994), *Rhapsody in Plain Yellow* (2002), and *Hard Love Province* (2014)—as well as a novel, *Revenge of the Mooncake Vixen* (2009). She has received two grants from the National Endowment for the Arts as well as a Stegner Fellowship, the PEN/Josephine Miles Award, four Pushcart Prizes, and a Fulbright scholarship. She is codirector of the MFA program at San Diego State University. About her work, Chin says, "My poetry both laments and celebrates my 'hyphenated' identity. . . . I am an American poet, a hyphenated American poet, to be precise; and what is American about my poetry is my muse's indomitable conviction to hammer the rich virtues and contradictions of my adopted country into a fusionist's delight."

KATE CHOPIN (1851–1904) Born Kate O'Flaherty in St. Louis, Missouri, Chopin was raised by her mother, grandmother, and great-grandmother, all widows, after her father's death when she was four. In 1870, following her graduation from Sacred Heart Convent, she married Oscar Chopin and moved to New Orleans, where she became a housewife and eventually had six children. After her husband's death in 1882, she returned to her mother's home in St. Louis and began her career as a writer. Her first novel, *At Fault* (1890), and her stories, collected in *Bayou Folk* (1894) and *A Night in Acadie* (1897), gained her a reputation as a vivid chronicler of the lives of Creoles and Acadians (Cajuns) in Louisiana. Many of these stories explore a female protagonist's attempts to achieve self-fulfillment. Her novel *The Awakening* (1899) is probably her most ambitious exploration of this theme. It is the story of a woman whose awakening to her passion and inner self leads her to adultery and suicide. The storm of controversy with which this work was met virtually ended Chopin's literary career.

JILL CHRISTMAN (b. 1969) Christman earned her MFA at the University of Alabama and is currently a professor at Ball State University, where she teaches courses in creative nonfiction. Her memoir, *Darkroom: A Family Exposure* (2002), which chronicles her difficult childhood and a string of family tragedies, won the Associated Writers and Writing Programs (AWP) Award for Creative Nonfiction. More recently, Christman's essays have appeared in journals such as *Brevity*, *Harpur Palate*, and *Mississippi Review*. In 2013 Christman was elected to the board of directors of the AWP and is currently serving as its Midwest representative. She lives with her husband and daughter in Muncie, Indiana.

SONYA CHUNG (b. 1973) Korean American writer Sonya Chung received her BA from Columbia University and her MFA from the University of Washington. She currently teaches fiction writing at Skidmore College. Her stories, reviews, and essays have appeared in periodicals such as the *Threepenny Review* and the *Huffington Post* as well as in books such as *The Late American Novel: Writers on the Future of Books*. She has also published a novel, *Long for This World* (2010), about a family divided between America and a small town in South Korea. Paraphrasing Anne Tyler, Chung says, "I write fiction so I can live many lives." She is a staff writer for the online literature and culture magazine *The Millions*, and the founding editor of *Bloom*, a literary site focused on authors whose first major work was published when they were age forty or older.

SANDRA CISNEROS (b. 1954) Cisneros, the daughter of a Mexican father and a Mexican American mother, grew up in poor neighborhoods of Chicago, where she attended public schools. The only daughter among seven children, Cisneros recalled that because her brothers attempted to control her and expected her to assume a traditional female role, she grew up feeling as if she had "seven fathers." The family's frequent moves, many of them between the United States and Mexico to visit a grandmother, left Cisneros feeling alone and displaced. She found refuge both in reading and in writing poems and stories. In the late 1970s, Cisneros's writing talent earned her admission to the University of Iowa's Writers' Workshop. There, Cisneros observed, "Everyone seemed to have some communal knowledge which I did not have. . . . My classmates were from the best schools in the country. They had been bred as fine hothouse flowers. I was a yellow weed among the city's cracks." This realization led Cisneros to focus her writing on the conflicts and yearnings of her own life and culture. Her writings include four volumes of poetry—*Bad Boys* (1980), *The Rodrigo Poems* (1985), *My Wicked, Wicked Ways* (1987), and *Loose Woman* (1994)—and three volumes of fiction—*The House on Mango Street* (1983), *Woman Hollering Creek and Other Stories* (1991), and *Caramelo* (2002). She is also the author of a bilingual children's book, *Hairs = Pelitos* (1994). She received a prestigious MacArthur Fellowship in 1995. Her most recent works include the children's book *Bravo Bruno!* (2011) and the adult fable *Have You Seen Marie?* (2012).

MICHAEL CLARK (1946–1999) After earning his PhD in American literature from the University of Wisconsin–Madison in 1981, Michael Clark taught creative writing, composition, and American literature at Widener University in Pennsylvania. He published short stories, poems, and essays in numerous magazines. His articles on major American authors such as Herman Melville and James Baldwin appeared in a variety of scholarly journals.

LUCILLE CLIFTON (b. 1936–2010) Born in Depew, New York, Clifton attended Howard University (1953–55) and Fredonia State Teachers College. She worked as a claims clerk in the New York State Division of Employment in Buffalo (1958–60), and as literature assistant in the Office of Education in Washington, DC (1960–71). In 1969 she received the YM-YWHA Poetry Center Discovery Award, and her first collection, *Good Times*, was selected as one of the ten best books of 1969 by the *New York Times*. From 1971 to 1974 she was poet-in-residence at Coppin State College in Baltimore, and in 1979 she was named poet laureate of the state of Maryland. She wrote many collections for children and a free-verse chronicle of five generations of her family, *Generations: A Memoir* (1976). Her final publication was *Voices* (2008). In 2007 Clifton was awarded the Ruth Lilly Poetry Prize, a prestigious honor given to living U.S. poets "whose lifetime accomplishments warrant extraordinary recognition." Noted for celebrating ordinary people and everyday things, Clifton was quoted as saying, "I am a black woman poet, and I sound like one."

JOSHUA CLOVER (b. 1962)   Clover was born in Berkeley, California; he grew up there and just outside of Boston. He graduated from Boston University and the University of Iowa's Writers' Workshop and is currently a professor at the University of California, Davis. Clover has been a regular contributor to the *New York Times Sunday Book Review*, the *Village Voice*, the *Nation*, and *Spin* magazine. He has won two Pushcart Prizes and received a grant from the National Endowment for the Arts. His two volumes of poetry are *Madonna anno domini* (1997), which won the Academy of American Poets' Walt Whitman Award, and *The Totality for Kids* (2006). His more recent books include *1989: Bob Dylan Didn't Have This to Sing About* (2010) and *Of Riot* (2016).

JUDITH ORTIZ COFER (b. 1952)   Cofer was born in Hormigueros, Puerto Rico. She earned a BA (1974) from Augusta College and an MA (1977) from Florida Atlantic University and briefly attended Oxford University. She began her teaching career as a bilingual instructor in Florida public schools and taught at a number of schools, including the University of Miami and the University of Georgia. Her first volume of poems, *Latin Women Pray*, appeared in 1981, and she has since published poetry collections, essays, and a novel. Her recent work includes several collections of stories, poems, and essays about coming of age in the barrio, including *The Year of Our Revolution: New and Selected Stories and Poems* (1998), *Woman in Front of the Sun: On Becoming a Writer* (2000), and *A Love Story Beginning in Spanish* (2005). She has also published two young adult novels—*Call Me María* (2004) and *If I Could Fly* (2011)—as well as several children's books. Cofer points out that her family is an important source for her writing: "The place of birth itself becomes a metaphor for the things we must all leave behind; the assimilation of a new culture is the coming into maturity by accepting the terms necessary for survival."

BILLY COLLINS (b. 1941)   Collins was born in New York City and earned a BA (1963) from the College of the Holy Cross and a PhD (1971) from the University of California, Riverside. He has been teaching at the City University of New York since 1971. *Pokerface*, the first of his several books of poetry, was published in 1977. Collins's later work attracted so much attention that his early poetry books became economically valuable. Consequently, the University of Pittsburgh Press, publisher of *The Art of Drowning* (1995) and *Picnic, Lightning* (1998), at first withheld permission from Random House to reprint earlier poems in Collins's *Sailing around the Room: New and Selected Poems* (2000). The matter was settled, and Random House published his next collection of poems, *Nine Horses* (2002). The struggle between Random House and the University of Pittsburgh Press over the rights to Collins's work made him sufficiently notorious. He has since published *The Trouble with Poetry and Other Poems* (2005), *Ballistics: Poems* (2008), *Horoscopes for the Dead: Poems* (2012), and *Aimless Love* (2013). He has won several poetry prizes as well as fellowships from the New York Foundation for the Arts, the National Endowment for the Arts, and the Guggenheim Foundation. Collins was the poet laureate of the United States from 2001 to 2003 and the poet laureate for New York State from 2004 to 2006. In 2005 he was the first recipient of the Mark Twain Prize for Humor in Poetry. He commented to one journalist: "I think my work has to do with a sense that we are attempting, all the time, to create a logical, rational path through the day. To the left and right there are an amazing set of distractions that we usually can't afford to follow. But the poet is willing to stop anywhere."

RICHARD CRASHAW (1612–1649)   Crashaw was the only son of William Crashaw, a fervently anti-Catholic preacher. Crashaw did not share his father's religious views, however; he was a Catholic sympathizer. He attended Pembroke College, Cambridge, where he earned his BA in 1634. He went to Peterhouse in 1636 and became a fellow of the college in 1637, earning his MA there in 1638. However, in 1644 he was ejected from the college for his religious leanings, after which he fled to France and became a Catholic sometime around 1645. His friend Abraham Cowley later found him destitute in Paris and helped him regain his footing, introducing Crashaw to Charles I's queen, Henrietta Maria, who sent Crashaw to Rome with a recommendation to the pope. Crashaw died in 1649 while serving in the Cathedral of Santa Casa in Loreto. He wrote throughout his life, and his poetry came to be known for its brilliant use of extravagant baroque imagery. His works were first collected by an anonymous friend and published as *Steps to the Temple* in 1646.

VICTOR HERNÁNDEZ CRUZ (b. 1949) Cruz was born in Aguas Buenas, Puerto Rico, and immigrated with his family to New York City in 1954. He recalls, "My family life was full of music, guitars and conga drums, maracas and songs.... Even when it was five below zero in New York [my mother] sang warm tropical ballads." By 1966, he had already completed a collection of verse, *Papa Got His Gun, and Other Poems*, and in 1969 he published *Snaps*. He has edited *Umbra* magazine in New York, lectured at the University of California, Berkeley, and taught at San Francisco State University. Cruz says he writes in three languages: Spanish, English, and bilingual. "From the mixture a totally new language emerges, an intense collision, not just of words, but of attitudes." His other works include *Mainland* (1973), *Tropicalizations* (1976), *Red Beans: Poems* (1991), *Panoramas* (1997), *Maraca: New and Selected Poems, 1965–2000* (2001), *The Mountain in the Sea* (2006), and, most recently, *In the Shadow of Al-Andalus* (2011). Cruz is also coeditor of the poetry anthology *Paper Dance: 55 Latino Poets* (2008).

COUNTEE CULLEN (1903–1946) Born Countee L. Porter in New York City, Cullen was adopted by the Reverend and Mrs. Cullen in 1918 and raised in Harlem. He was extraordinarily precocious, and by 1920 his poems had been published in *Poetry*, the *Nation*, and *Harper's*. He published his famous poem "Heritage" in 1925, the year he graduated from New York University. After earning an MA in English from Harvard in 1926, he taught French in a junior high school and was assistant editor of the National Urban League's *Opportunity: Journal of Negro Life*. Cullen, along with Langston Hughes and Jean Toomer, was a central figure in the Harlem Renaissance of the 1920s. He received a Guggenheim Fellowship in 1929. In addition to five volumes of poetry, he published a novel, *One Way to Heaven* (1932), which deals with the interaction between upper- and lower-class African Americans in Harlem in the 1920s.

E. E. CUMMINGS (1894–1962) Born in Cambridge, Massachusetts, Edward Estlin Cummings attended Harvard University (BA, 1915; MA, 1916), served as a volunteer ambulance driver in France during World War I, was imprisoned for three months in a French detention camp, served in the U.S. Army (1918–19), and then studied art and painting in Paris (1920–24). His prose narrative *The Enormous Room* (1922), a recollection of his imprisonment, brought instant acclaim. Several volumes of poetry followed. His experiments with punctuation, line division, and capitalization make his work immediately recognizable. In a letter to young poets published in a high school newspaper, Cummings said, "[N]othing is quite so easy as using words like somebody else. We all of us do exactly this nearly all the time—and whenever we do it, we're not poets."

EDWIDGE DANTICAT (b. 1969) Danticat's parents immigrated to New York when she was a young child, leaving her and her brother in Haiti to be raised by an uncle. Growing up, Danticat was inspired by the storytelling of her older relatives, who, she says, "were not necessarily powerful people in society, but they were powerful with their word." At age twelve, Danticat moved to New York to be with her parents. She received an undergraduate degree from Barnard College and earned an MFA from Brown University. Her first novel, *Breath, Eyes, Memory* (1994), became a commercial success in 1998 when it was named an Oprah's Book Club selection. Other works by Danticat include the short story collection *Krik? Krak!* (1996), the memoir *Brother, I'm Dying* (2007), which won the National Book Critics Circle Award, and *Claire of the Sea Light* (2013). In 2009 she received the prestigious MacArthur Fellowship. A potent voice for Haitian Americans, Danticat has also worked on documentary films, essays, and anthologies that expose her country's traumatic history. Speaking at Brooklyn College's commencement on the day of Maya Angelou's death in 2014, Danticat invoked Angelou's message about the importance of bravery, saying to the graduating class, "Be brave in spirit; be brave in mind. Because only those with imagination and courage are able to reach beyond the ordinary and take us to the next frontier."

DONALD DAVIE (1922–1995)   Davie was an esteemed poet renowned not only for his poems, but also for his criticism on poetry. Born in Barnsley, Yorkshire, he received his early education at Barnsley Holgate Grammar School. He went on to attend St. Catharine's College in Cambridge, though his studies there were interrupted when he joined the navy in 1941. After spending time in northern Russia, Davie returned to Cambridge in 1944 and completed his studies, earning his BA, MA, and PhD. He then went on to teach English at the University of Essex, at Stanford University, and at Vanderbilt University. Throughout his life, Davie displayed a keen interest in poetic technique as well as the ethical implications of poetic subject matter, which he felt many contemporary poets had lost sight of; his *Purity of Diction in English Verse* (1952) is among the best-known volumes of poetic criticism. Along with poets like Philip Larkin, D. J. Enright, and John Wain, Davie was part of a group known as The Movement, who considered "amoral" poetry unworthy of attention. He published many collections of poetry, the best known of which include *Essex Poems* (1969), *In the Stopping Train* (1977), and *To Scorch or Freeze* (1988). He also penned eighteen volumes of criticism across literary, social, religious, and political subjects. Davie considered himself first and foremost a poet, but he claimed to write criticism "in order to explain to myself the sort of thing I've been doing." He became an active editor, editing the newly launched *PN Review* in 1972 and such collections as *The Late Augustans: Longer Poems of the Eighteenth Century* (1958), *Russian Literature and Modern English Fiction* (1965), and *The New Oxford Book of Christian Verse* (1981), among other titles. He also coedited and supplied the verse translations for *Pasternak: Modern Judgements* (1969), and wrote introductions to Elizabeth Daryush's *Collected Poems* (1976) and the *Collected Poems of Yvor Winters* (1978). When Davie passed away in 1995 at the age of seventy-three, Karl Miller, the former editor of the *London Review of Books,* said of the late poet, "He will be remembered as a man who stood up for poetry at a time when it needed defending."

CARL DENNIS (b. 1939)   Dennis was born in St. Louis, Missouri. He received his BA from the University of Minnesota and his PhD in English literature from the University of California, Berkeley. In 1966 he became assistant professor of English at the University at Buffalo and has since spent the majority of his career there; he became one of the school's artists in residence in 2002. He has published numerous volumes of poetry, including *House of My Own* (1974), *The Outskirts of Troy* (1988), *Meetings with Time* (1992), and *Practical Gods* (2001), for which he won the Pulitzer Prize. His most recent collections are *Unknown Friends* (2007) and *Callings* (2010). He has also published a volume of criticism, *Poetry as*

Persuasion (2001), and contributed to many literary journals and magazines, such as the *Atlantic Monthly, American Poetry Review, Ironwood, Kenyon Review,* the *New Yorker, New Republic, Paris Review, Poetry,* and *Salmagundi.* Dennis has been awarded a fellowship at the Rockefeller Study Center, a National Endowment for the Arts Fellowship in Poetry, a Guggenheim Fellowship, and the Ruth Lilly Poetry Prize, given to living U.S. poets "whose lifetime accomplishments warrant extraordinary recognition."

PETER DEVRIES (1910–1993) The son of Dutch immigrants, DeVries was born and raised in a Calvinist home in Chicago. He attended Calvin College in Michigan and graduated in 1931, in the midst of the Great Depression. He took on several odd jobs in the 1930s before becoming editor of *Poetry* magazine in 1938. During World War II, he served in the U.S. Marines as well as the Office of Strategic Services—the predecessor to the CIA. He joined the *New Yorker* as a staff writer in 1944 and worked there for over four decades. Known primarily as a satirist and a comic writer, DeVries wrote more than twenty novels in addition to short fiction, poetry, essays, and criticism. He once noted that "comedy deals with that portion of our suffering that is exempt from tragedy." Although he received much critical acclaim during his lifetime, all of DeVries's books were out of print by the time he died. *The Blood of the Lamb* (1961) and *Slouching Towards Kalamazoo* (1983) were republished in 2005.

JUNOT DÍAZ (b. 1968) Dominican-born Díaz was raised in New Jersey. His father left when Díaz was a child, leaving his mother to raise four sons on her own. He grew up in a poor, working-class area, but reading the works of authors ranging from Stephen King to Toni Morrison inspired Díaz to become a fiction writer. After receiving his undergraduate degree from Rutgers, he got his MFA from Columbia in 1995; soon thereafter he published his first collection of short stories, *Drown* (1996). He taught for several years at Syracuse University before moving to the Massachusetts Institute of Technology, where he is currently a professor of writing and fiction editor at the *Boston Review*, a political and literary forum. In 2008 Díaz won the Pulitzer Prize and the National Book Critics Circle Award for his book *The Brief Wondrous Life of Oscar Wao* (2007). He is also the recipient of a MacArthur Fellowship, PEN/Malamud Award, Dayton Literary Peace Prize, Guggenheim Fellowship, and PEN/O. Henry Award. His most recent collection of short stories, *This Is How You Lose Her* (2012), was a *New York Times* best seller and a finalist for the National Book Award.

EMILY DICKINSON (1830–1886) Dickinson, one of three children, was born in Amherst, Massachusetts. Her father was a prominent lawyer. Except for one year away at a nearby college and a trip with her sister to Washington, DC, to visit her father when he was serving in Congress, she lived out her life, unmarried, in her parents' home. During her trip to Washington, she met the Reverend Charles Wadsworth, a married man, whom she came to characterize as her "dearest earthly friend." Little is known of this relationship except that Dickinson's feelings for Wadsworth were strong. In 1862 Wadsworth moved to San Francisco, an event that coincided with a period of Dickinson's intense poetic creativity. Also in that year, she initiated a literary correspondence with the critic T. W. Higginson, to whom she sent some of her poems for his opinion. Higginson, although he recognized her talent, was puzzled by her startling originality and urged her to write more conventionally, advice she was unable to follow. Only seven of her poems were published while she was alive, none of them with her consent. After her death, the extraordinary richness of her imaginative life came to light with the discovery of her more than 1,000 poems.

GREGORY DJANIKIAN (b. 1949)   Born in Egypt of Armenian parentage, Djanikian came to the United States at age eight. He is a graduate of the Syracuse University writing program and is director of creative writing at the University of Pennsylvania, where he received his undergraduate degree. Djanikian is the author of several collections of poetry that explore, among other things, family, history, culture, and language. His books include *The Man in the Middle* (1984), *Falling Deeply into America* (1989), *Years Later* (2000), *So I Will Till the Ground* (2007), and, most recently, *Dear Gravity* (2014). His poems have appeared in numerous periodicals, including the *American Scholar*, the *Iowa Review*, *Poetry*, and the *Nation*. His work has also appeared in several anthologies, including *Best American Poetry* (2000) and *Becoming Americans: Four Centuries of Immigrant Writing* (2009).

E. L. DOCTOROW (b. 1931–2015)   Doctorow was born and raised in New York City, where he attended the Bronx High School of Science. After earning an AB degree with honors at Kenyon College, Ohio, he returned to New York for a year of graduate studies and then served in the U.S. Army. On his return to New York, he worked as senior editor for New American Library from 1959 to 1964. During this period, he also worked as a script reader for Columbia Pictures, a job which he said required him "to suffer one lousy Western after another, and it occurred to me that I could lie about the West in a much more interesting way than any of these people were lying." The result was his first novel, *Welcome to Hard Times* (1961), a dark, symbolic novel about the West. Among his subsequent novels are *The Book of Daniel* (1971), a fictionalized account of the lives of Julius and Ethel Rosenberg, executed for conspiracy to commit treason during the Cold War (adapted in 1983 into the film *Daniel*, directed by Sidney Lumet). This novel was followed by *Ragtime* (1975), a sprawling historical novel about early twentieth-century America (adapted in 1981 into the film *Ragtime*, directed by Milos Forman). *Ragtime* was named by the editorial board of the Modern Library as one of the 100 best English-language novels of the twentieth century. Doctorow's novel *The March* (2005) won the PEN/Faulkner Award and the National Book Critics Circle Award, and he then published *Creationists: Selected Essays, 1993–2006*. His final novels were *Homer & Langley* (2009) and *Andrew's Brain* (2014). He received numerous awards and prizes, among them the National Book Award, the National Humanities Medal, the PEN/Saul Bellow Award for Achievement in American Literature, and the American Academy of Arts and Letters Gold Medal for Fiction. From 1982 until shortly before his death in 2015, Doctorow taught at New York University, where he held the Lewis and Loretta Brennan Glucksman Chair of English and American Letters.

JOHN DONNE (1572–1631)   Born in London into a prosperous Roman Catholic family of tradespeople at a time when England was staunchly anti-Catholic, Donne was forced to leave Oxford University without a degree because of his religion. He studied law and at the same time read widely in theology in an attempt to decide whether the Roman or the Anglican Church was the true Catholic Church, a decision he was not able to make for many years. In the meantime, he became known as a witty man of the world and the author of original, often dense, erotic poems. Donne left his law studies, participated in two naval expeditions, and then became secretary to a powerful noble, a job he lost when he was briefly sent to prison for secretly marrying his patron's niece. In 1615, at the age of forty-two, Donne accepted ordination in the Anglican Church. He quickly earned a reputation as one of the greatest preachers of his time. He was dean of St. Paul's from 1621 until his death. In his later years, Donne repudiated the poetry of his youth.

TISHANI DOSHI (b. 1975)   Born in India to a Welsh mother and a Gujarati father, Doshi has published five books of fiction, nonfiction, and poetry. She is also a dancer. When asked about the connection between writing and dance in a 2013 interview for *Port* magazine, Doshi said, "There's the sense that if you're working with words, whether it's fiction or poetry, you're working with the body." Her essays, poems, and short stories have been widely anthologized. She is the recipient of an Eric Gregory Award for Poetry, winner of the All-India Poetry Competition, and her first book of poems, *Countries of the Body* (2006), won the prestigious Forward Prize for Best First Collection. Doshi's debut novel, *The Pleasure Seekers* (2010), was shortlisted for the Hindu Literary Prize. Her most recent works include the poetry collection *Everything Begins Elsewhere* (2013) and *Fountainville* (2013), a retelling of a Welsh legend.

RITA DOVE (b. 1952)   Dove was born in Akron, Ohio, the daughter of an African American research chemist who broke the color barrier in the tire industry. She began writing and staging plays at an early age. In 1970 she was named a Presidential Scholar, an annual award given to the top 100 high school graduates in the country. She attended Miami University in Ohio on a National Merit Scholarship, graduating Phi Beta Kappa in 1973. After completing a Fulbright fellowship at the University of Tübingen, Germany, she returned to the United States and earned an MFA at the University of Iowa's Writers' Workshop. Her earliest poems appeared in two chapbooks, followed by her first volume of poems, *The Yellow House on the Corner* (1980). Since then, she has published more than a half dozen volumes of poetry, including the Pulitzer Prize–winning *Thomas and Beulah* (1987). In recognition of her poetic achievement, she was appointed poet laureate of the United States in 1993. *On the Bus with Rosa Parks* (1999), inspired by a bus trip the author shared with the celebrated heroine of the civil rights movement, was nominated for a National Book Critics Circle Award. Her most recent volumes are *American Smooth* (2004) and *Sonata Mulattica* (2009), and she edited *The Penguin Anthology of Twentieth-Century American Poetry* (2011). Dove is also the author of a collection of short stories, *Fifth Sunday* (1990); a novel, *Through the Ivory Gate* (1992); and a play, *The Darker Face of the Earth* (1997). Among her many other honors, she has received the National Association for the Advancement of Colored People's Great American Artist Award (2003) and the Duke Ellington Lifetime Achievement Award (2001). Most recently, President Barack Obama presented her with the 2011 National Medal of Arts. She is Commonwealth Professor of Creative Writing at the University of Virginia.

BOB DOWELL (b. 1932)   Born and raised in East Texas, Dowell earned his PhD in 1962, at which point he embarked on a teaching career. He taught college English and did stints as academic dean for more than thirty years. In 1999 Dowell retired from college teaching in order to write about the Bible, a subject he knew well from years of teaching a Bible as literature course. He also created a church Bible study forum for understanding Christian doctrine through the use of prose (for the head) and poetry (for the heart). The success of that program led to the publication of *Understanding the Bible: Head and Heart* in three parts: *The Old Testament* (2010), *Matthew through Acts* (2011), and *Romans through Revelations* (2012). In addition to writing, Dowell continues to raise cattle on the family farm where he was born.

BRIAN DOYLE (b. 1956)   Doyle, the son of a journalist and a teacher, was born in New York City and graduated from the University of Notre Dame. He was an editor at *U.S. Catholic* magazine and a writer at *Boston College Magazine* before becoming the editor of *Portland Magazine* at the University of Portland. He is the author of several books, among them *Credo: Essays on Grace, Altar Boys, Bees, Kneeling, Saints, the Mass, Priests, Strong Women,*

Epiphanies, a Wake, and the Haunting Thin Energetic Dusty Figure of Jesus the Christ (1999); *The Wet Engine: Exploring the Mad Wild Miracle of the Heart* (2005); *Epiphanies and Elegies: Very Short Stories* (2006); *Mink River* (2010); and *The Plover* (2014). His work has also appeared in anthologies, such as *The Best Spiritual Writing* and *The Best American Essays*, and a number of periodicals, among them *Atlantic Monthly*, *American Scholar*, *Harper's*, *Gourmet*, and the *London Times*. Doyle served as editor of the Best Catholic Writing series from Loyola Press from 2004 to 2006. He lives with his wife and three children.

PAUL LAURENCE DUNBAR (1872–1906)   The son of former slaves, Dunbar was born in Dayton, Ohio, where he graduated from Dayton High School (1891) and worked for two years as an elevator operator. In 1893 he worked in Chicago at the World's Columbian Exhibition. His first verse collection, *Oak and Ivy*, was published in 1893. William Dean Howells—an eminent editor, author, and critic—encouraged him to write and had him join a lecture bureau in 1896. While Dunbar maintained that African American poetry was not much different from white poetry—and wrote many poems in standard English— he often wrote poems in black dialect that seemed to cater to the racial stereotypes of his white audience. He died of tuberculosis in 1906. His complete works appear in *The Dunbar Reader* (1975).

JENNIFER EGAN (b. 1962)   Egan was born in Chicago and raised in San Francisco. She is the author of several novels including *The Invisible Circus* (1995), which became a feature film; *Look at Me* (2001), a finalist for the National Book Award for fiction; and the best-selling *The Keep* (2006). Her novel *A Visit from the Goon Squad* (2010) won the Pulitzer Prize, the National Book Critics Circle Award for Fiction, and the Los Angeles Times Book Prize. Speaking to *Bomb* magazine about the unconventional nature of *A Visit from the Goon Squad*, Egan said, "I don't experience time as linear. I experience it in layers that seem to coexist. . . . One thing that facilitates that kind of time travel is music, which is why I think music ended up being such an important part of the book." Her short stories have appeared in the *New Yorker*, *Harpers*, *Granta*, *McSweeney's*, and other magazines, as well as in her collection *Emerald City and Other Stories* (1993). She is a recipient of a Guggenheim Fellowship and a National Endowment for the Arts Fellowship in Fiction. Her nonfiction articles appear frequently in the *New York Times Magazine*.

T. S. ELIOT (1888–1965)   Thomas Stearns Eliot was born in St. Louis, Missouri. His father was president of the Hydraulic Press Brick Company, and his mother was a teacher, social worker, and writer. Educated at private academies, Eliot earned two philosophy degrees at Harvard University (BA, 1909; MA, 1910). After graduate study in Paris and England, he worked for eight years as a clerk in Lloyd's Bank in London and became a naturalized British citizen in 1927. He was editor, then director, of Faber & Gwyer Publishers (later Faber & Faber) from 1925 to 1965 and spent time in the United States as a visiting lecturer and scholar. Admirers and detractors alike agree that Eliot was the most imposing and influential poet writing between the world wars. His poems "The Love Song of J. Alfred Prufrock" (1917) and *The Waste Land* (1922) are among his earliest and most famous. Acknowledging his dependence on a preexisting cultural tradition, Eliot explained: "The existing order is complete before the new work arrives; for order to persist after the supervention of novelty, the whole existing order must be altered." Eliot also wrote plays, including *Murder in the Cathedral* (1935) and *The Cocktail Party* (1950). The long-running Broadway musical *Cats* is based on his 1939 verse collection, *Old Possum's Book of Practical Cats*. He won the Nobel Prize in Literature in 1948.

HARLAN ELLISON® (b. 1934)   Born in Cleveland, Ohio, Ellison published his first story when he was thirteen. He left Ohio State University after two years and worked at a variety of odd jobs while establishing himself as a writer. In a career spanning over sixty years, he has written or edited a hundred books and more than 1,700 stories, essays, reviews, articles, motion picture scripts, and teleplays. He has won the Hugo Award ten and a half times; the Nebula Award five times, as well as a Grandmaster Nebula Award (basically a lifetime achievement award); the Edgar Allan Poe Award of the Mystery Writers of America twice; the Bram Stoker Award from the Horror Writers Association six times, including the Lifetime Achievement Award in 1996; the Georges Méliès fantasy film award twice; the World Fantasy Award twice, the second time for lifetime achievement; two Audie Awards (for the best in audio recordings); the British Fantasy Award; and the Silver Pen for journalism from PEN. He was presented with the first Living Legend award by the International Horror Critics at the 1995 World Horror Convention, and in March 1998, the National Women's Committee of Brandeis University honored him with their Words, Wit, Wisdom Award. He is the only scenarist in Hollywood ever to have won the Writers Guild of America award for Most Outstanding Teleplay four times for solo work. His latest books are *Bugf#ck: The Useless Wit & Wisdom of Harlan Ellison* (2011) and a new series with the Publishing 180 program. These books are a mixture of classic stories and essays and original never-before-available teleplays: *Brain Movies: The Original Teleplays of Harlan Ellison* (Volumes One and Two), *Harlan 101: Encountering Ellison*, and *Harlan 101: The Sound of a Scythe Plus Three Classic Novellas*. For the first time, Ellison's collections of essays on television, *The Glass Teat* and *The Other Glass Teat*, have been published in one volume as the complete *Omnibus*. He has also written numerous short stories for various magazines, most recently "How Interesting: A Tiny Man," which garnered Ellison his fourth Nebula Award. In celebration of Ellison's seventy-fifth birthday, documentarian Erik Nelson produced a feature-length film that looks at Ellison's life and work. The documentary, *Dreams with Sharp Teeth*, was released on DVD in May 2009. Ellison currently lives with his wife, Susan, in the Los Angeles area.

RALPH ELLISON (1914–1994)   Ellison was born in Oklahoma City, Oklahoma. He studied music, specifically trumpet and piano, and sculpture before embarking on a writing career. In New York City, encouraged by his friend and fellow writer Richard Wright, Ellison began writing book reviews, essays, and short stories. He also earned money as a freelance photographer. His first novel, *Invisible Man* (1952), for which he is best known, won the National Book Award in 1953. He published two collections of essays, *Shadow and Act* (1964) and *Going to the Territory* (1986). He taught at Bard College, Rutgers University, the University of Chicago, and New York University before dying of pancreatic cancer in 1994. His short stories were collected and published posthumously in *Flying Home and Other Stories* (1996). Ellison wrote more than 2,000 pages for a second novel, *Juneteenth*, over the span of forty years; it was edited down to 368 pages and published in 1999, five years after his death.

LOUISE ERDRICH (b. 1954)   Erdrich was born in Little Falls, Minnesota, and grew up in North Dakota. Her father was German American and her mother was French and Anishinaabe; Erdrich is a member of the Native American Anishinaabe Nation. She earned degrees from Dartmouth College and Johns Hopkins University. Before fully embarking on her writing career, she worked as a lifeguard, waitress, prison poetry teacher, construction flagger, and newspaper editor. She began by publishing poems and short fiction and won the Nelson Algren Prize for her short story "The World's Greatest Fisherman" in 1982. Her first novel, *Love Medicine* (1984), won the National Book Critics Circle Award. She went on to write more than ten other novels, notably *The Beet Queen* (1986), *Tracks* (1988), *The Antelope Wife* (1998), and *The Painted Drum* (2005). In addition to having written five novels for adolescents and three works of nonfiction, Erdrich has published three books of poetry: *Jacklight* (1984), *Baptism of Desire* (1989), and *Original Fire: Selected and New Poems* (2003). Her most recent works include the novels *The Plague of Doves* (2008), *Shadow Tag* (2010), and *The Round House* (2012), which won the National Book Award. She has won several other awards including an O. Henry Award, a Pushcart Prize, the Dayton Literary Peace Prize, and the PEN/Saul Bellow Award for Achievement in American Fiction. Erdrich owns a bookstore in Minneapolis, Minnesota, and hosts annual writing workshops on the Turtle Mountain Indian Reservation in North Dakota.

FAIZ AHMED FAIZ (1911–1984) Often referred to as Pakistan's greatest poet, Faiz was also known for his political ideology. Born to wealthy and educated Muslim parents, Faiz was brought up in a secular tradition of Islam. After his college and postcollege studies, he taught literature and economics courses at universities in India. He served in the British Army during World War II, earning the rank of Lieutenant-Colonel in 1944. He resigned from the military in 1947, the same year he cofounded the Communist Party of Pakistan and became editor of the socialist newspaper the *Pakistan Times*. In 1951 he was arrested for his alleged role in plotting a coup against the right-wing government, and he spent four years in prison. In the 1960s he returned to teaching, held prominent positions in the Pakistan Arts Council, and took on several advisory roles in the culture and education departments of the Pakistani government, which had by that time shifted to the left. A humanist and internationalist committed to global peace, Faiz was awarded the Lenin Peace Prize (the Soviet equivalent of the Nobel Peace Prize) in 1962. His major works include *Naqsh-e-Faryadi* (1943) and *Dast-e-Tah-e-Sung* (1965). Many of his poems have been translated into English and published in collections such as *The Rebel's Silhouette: Selected Poems* (1995) and *The True Subject: Selected Poems of Faiz Ahmed Faiz* (2012).

WILLIAM FAULKNER (1897–1962) Faulkner was born in New Albany, Mississippi, and lived most of his life in Oxford, the seat of the University of Mississippi. Although he did not graduate from high school, he attended the university as a special student from 1919 to 1921. During this period, he also worked as a janitor, a bank clerk, and a postmaster. His southern forebears had held slaves, served during the Civil War, endured the deprivations of Reconstruction, fought duels, and even wrote the occasional romance of the old South. Faulkner mined these generous layers of history in his work. He created the mythical Yoknapatawpha County in northern Mississippi and traced the destinies of its inhabitants from the colonial era to the middle of the twentieth century in such novels as *The Sound and the Fury* (1929), *Light in August* (1932), and *Absalom, Absalom!* (1936). Further, Faulkner described the decline of the pre–Civil War aristocratic families and the rise of mean-spirited money-grubbers in a trilogy: *The Hamlet* (1940), *The Town* (1957), and *The Mansion* (1959). Recognition came late, and Faulkner fought a constant battle to keep afloat financially. During the 1940s, he wrote screenplays in Hollywood, but his achievements brought him the Nobel Prize in 1950.

ALAN FELDMAN (b. 1945) Feldman's poetry has appeared in many top literary publications throughout his career, including the *Atlantic*, the *New Yorker*, *Nation*, *Poetry*, *Kenyon Review*, *Southern Review*, *Ploughshares*, *Iowa Review*, *Threepenny Review*, *Virginia*

Quarterly Review, and others. His work has also been included in many anthologies, including *To Woo and To Wed: Poets on Love and Marriage* (1992), *The Best American Erotic Poems 1800–Present*, and *The Best American Poetry 2001 and 2011*, and Feldman has also been honored with poetry fellowships from the National Endowment for the Arts and the Massachusetts Artists Foundation. In 1979 his collection *The Happy Genius* (1978) won the Elliston Book Award, and his full-length collection *A Sail to Great Island* (2004) won the 2004 Felix Pollak Prize in Poetry. His most recent collection, *Immortality* (2015), was awarded the Four Lakes Prize. Feldman lives in Framingham, Massachusetts, and is married to Nan Hass Feldman, an artist.

LAWRENCE FERLINGHETTI (b. 1919) Born Lawrence Ferling, this irreverent writer assumed his original family name in 1954. He earned a BA in journalism from the University of North Carolina in 1941, served as lieutenant commander in the U.S. Naval Reserve during World War II, and then received graduate degrees from Columbia University and the University of Paris. He worked briefly as a translator of French before rising to prominence in the San Francisco–based Beat literary movement of the 1950s, composed of a group of writers who felt strongly that art should be accessible to all, not just to a small group of intellectuals. Ferlinghetti received great praise from many readers and some critics for his attempts to incorporate American vernacular speech and the rhythms of modern jazz into his writings, while he was roundly attacked by defenders of the status quo. Ferlinghetti has been a prolific writer in all genres. In addition, he cofounded the San Francisco bookstore City Lights and two publishing enterprises, City Lights Books and the Pocket Book Series. In 1998 Ferlinghetti was named San Francisco's first poet laureate. He won the Poetry Society of America's Robert Frost Medal and the Authors Guild Lifetime Achievement Award, and was elected to the American Academy of Arts and Letters in 2003. In 2005 he received the National Book Foundation's first Literarian Award for outstanding service to the American literary community. He has published two novels, many plays, and over two dozen volumes of poetry including *Americus, Book I* (2004) and *Poetry as Insurgent Art* (2007). His early work *A Coney Island of the Mind* (1958) remains his most popular and best-selling poetry collection.

ANNIE FINCH (b. 1956) Finch was born in New Rochelle, New York, and earned degrees from Yale University, the University of Houston, and Stanford University. She taught at the University of Northern Iowa and Miami University of Ohio before assuming her role as director of the MFA program at the University of Southern Maine, which she held for nine years. Among her several books of poetry are *The Encyclopedia of Scotland* (1982), *Eve* (1997), *Calendars* (2003), and *Annie Finch's Greatest Hits* (2007). Her most recent collection of poetry is *Spells: New and Selected Poems* (2012). She has also published several books about poetry including *A Formal Feeling Comes* (1993), *The Ghost of Meter* (1994), *An Exaltation of Forms* (2003), *The Body of Poetry* (2004), *Villanelles* (2010), and *A Poet's Craft: A Comprehensive Guide to Making and Sharing Your Poetry* (2012). She has also written two opera librettos, translated the poems of French Renaissance poet Louise Labé, edited several anthologies of poetry and essays, and created an intertwined feminist poem and opera libretto called *Among the Goddesses: An Epic Libretto in Seven Dreams* (2010). About the influence of other poets on her own work, Finch has said, "I love the way bits of poems I've read, maybe years ago, will find their way subtly, secretly, into the poems I write and surprise me when I find them there. And I love to consciously invoke or copy the form or some other aspect of poems I've read in my own work; it's a wonderful way to pay tribute."

DONALD FINKEL (1929–2008) Donald Finkel was born in New York City, the son of an attorney. He earned a BS (1952) and an MA (1953) from Columbia University. In 1956 he married the writer Constance Urdang. Shortly thereafter, Finkel began a university teaching career at the University of Iowa and in 1960 moved to Washington University in St. Louis where he became poet-in-residence. His interest in Antarctica and exploration produced *Endurance: An Antarctic Idyll* and *Going Under* (1978). The first describes the shipwreck and rescue of Ernest Shackleton's 1914 expedition. The second examines two men who explored Kentucky's Mammoth Cave. His many books, including *Selected Shorter Poems* (1987), *A Splintered Mirror: Chinese Poetry from the Democracy Movement* (1991), and *A Question of Seeing: Poems* (1998), have earned him abundant awards and honors, among them a Guggenheim Fellowship (1967), nomination for a National Book Award (1970), and two nominations for the National Book Critics Circle Award (1975, 1981). His final volume was *Not So the Chairs: Selected and New Poems* (2003).

CAROLYN FORCHÉ (b. 1950) Born in Detroit, Forché earned a BA in international relations and creative writing at Michigan State University in 1972. After graduate study at Bowling Green State University in 1975, she taught at a number of schools, including the University of Arkansas, Vassar College, Columbia University, and George Mason University. She won the Yale Series of Younger Poets Award in 1976 for her first collection, *Gathering the Tribes*. Other honors include a Guggenheim Fellowship and the Lamont Award (1981). Forché was a journalist for Amnesty International in El Salvador in 1983 and Beirut correspondent for the National Public Radio program *All Things Considered*. Her works include the collections of poetry *The Country between Us* (1981) and *The Angel of History* (1994), both embodying her passionate preoccupation with the dehumanizing effects of political repression. Among her most recent publications are a memoir, *The Horse on Our Balcony* (2009), and the poetry collections *Blue Hour* (2003) and *In the Lateness of the World* (2015). In 2013 Forché received the Academy of American Poets Fellowship, given for distinguished poetic achievement. She currently is director of the Lannan Center for Poetics and Social Practice at Georgetown University.

DAISY FRIED (b. 1967) Fried has taught creative writing at Villanova University, Haverford College, the University of Pennsylvania, in Warren Wilson College's low-residency MFA program, and as the Grace Hazard Conkling Writer-in-Residence at Smith College. She has been the recipient of Guggenheim, Hodder, and Pew Fellowships, a Pushcart Prize, and the Cohen Award from *Ploughshares*. Her poetry has been featured in such publications as the *Nation, Poetry, New Republic, American Poetry Review, Antioch Review, Threepenny Review, Ploughshares*, and elsewhere. She has published three books of poetry: *She Didn't Mean to Do It* (2000), which won the Agnes Lynch Starrett Prize, *My Brother Is Getting Arrested Again* (2006), a finalist for the National Book Critics Circle Award, and *Women's Poetry: Poems and Advice* (2013), which was named one of the five best poetry books of the year by *Library Journal*. In 2009 she was awarded *Poetry*'s Editors Prize for Feature Article for her essay "Sing, God-Awful Muse," which discusses *Paradise Lost* and breastfeeding. She lives in Philadelphia with her husband and daughter.

ROBERT FROST (1874–1963) Frost was born in San Francisco but from the age of ten lived in New England. He attended Dartmouth College briefly and then became a teacher, but soon decided to resume his formal training and enrolled at Harvard University. He left Harvard after two years without a degree and for several years supported himself and his growing family by tending a farm his grandfather bought for him. When he was not farming, he read and wrote intensively, though he received little recognition. Discouraged by his lack of success, he sold the farm and moved his family to England, where he published his first volumes of poetry, *A Boy's Will* (1913) and *North of Boston* (1914). After three years in England, Frost returned to the United States a recognized poet. Later volumes, notably *Mountain Interval* (1916), *New Hampshire* (1923), *West-Running Brook* (1928), and *A Further Range* (1936), won Frost wide popularity and numerous awards, including two Pulitzer Prizes. By the time he delivered his poem "The Gift Outright" at the inauguration of President John F. Kennedy in 1961, Frost had achieved the status of unofficial poet laureate of the United States, widely revered and beloved for his folksy manner and seemingly artless, accessible poems.

RIVKA GALCHEN (b. 1976)   Galchen was born in Toronto, though she moved with her parents to the United States when she was just a baby. She entered Princeton University in 1994 to study English, but during her sophomore year she applied to an early admissions program at the Mount Sinai School of Medicine. She received her MD from Mount Sinai in 2003 and went on to earn an MFA from Columbia University. Her work has appeared in the *New Yorker*, *Harper's*, the *New York Times*, the *Believer*, and elsewhere. She has received many literary honors, including the 2006 Rona Jaffe Foundation Writers' Award, and she was included in the *New Yorker's* 2010 "20 Under 40" list. She was also the 2011 Mary Ellen von der Heyden Fiction Fellow at the American Academy in Berlin. Her first novel, *Atmospheric·Disturbances* (2008), has been translated into over twenty languages and won the William J. Saroyan International Prize for Fiction. Her collection of short stories, *American Innovations* was published in 2014. Galchen currently teaches writing at Columbia University and is a contributing editor for *Harper's Magazine*.

TESS GALLAGHER (b. 1943)   Gallagher was born in Port Angeles, Washington, the eldest of five children of a logger and longshoreman. She earned degrees from the University of Washington in Seattle and the University of Iowa. She has been married three times, most recently to writer Raymond Carver. She has taught at a number of institutions, among them St. Lawrence University; the University of Montana, Missoula; the University of Arizona, Tucson; Syracuse University; and Willamette University. Her many awards include an Elliston Award, multiple grants from the National Endowment for the Arts, and a Guggenheim Fellowship. Gallagher has written two collections of short stories, *The Lover of Horses* (1986) and *At the Owl Woman Saloon* (1996), as well as two collections of essays, *A Concert of Tenses* (1983) and *Soul Barnacles* (2003). She has penned more than ten volumes of poetry, including *Instructions to the Double* (1976), *Moon Crossing Bridge* (1992), *I Stop Writing the Poem* (1992), *Dear Ghosts* (2006), and, most recently, *Midnight Lantern: New and Selected Poems* (2011).

DEBORAH GARRISON (b. 1965)   Garrison was born in Ann Arbor, Michigan, and earned degrees from Brown University and New York University. She worked for the *New Yorker*, as part of the editorial staff and as the senior nonfiction editor, for over fifteen years before taking on her current roles as poetry editor at Alfred A. Knopf and senior editor at Pantheon Books. Her poems have appeared in a number of periodicals, among them *Elle*, the *New Yorker*, the *New York Times*, and *Slate*. Her first book of poetry, *A Working Girl Can't Win, and Other Poems* (1998), is considered a poetry best seller. Her second volume of poetry is *The Second Child* (2007). Garrison lives with her husband and three children in Montclair, New Jersey. About her work, both as a poetry editor and a writer, she has said, "There's a real yearning for authenticity. It's just such a pure thing. Poetry isn't being optioned to the movies for $3 million. Poetry is immune to all that stuff. It's a haven."

DAGOBERTO GILB (b. 1950)   Gilb was raised by his mother in Los Angeles. He graduated from the University of California, Santa Barbara, in 1974 with a double major in philosophy and religious studies, and went on to earn his MA in religious studies in 1976. His work has appeared in many magazines, most recently *Harper's*, the *New Yorker*, and *Callaloo*, and has been widely anthologized and translated. Gilb also received a Guggenheim Fellowship and has been a finalist for the National Book Critics Circle Award. Some of his publications include *The Magic of Blood* (1993), which won the PEN/Hemingway Award and was a finalist for the PEN/Faulkner Award; *The Last Known Residence of Mickey Acuña* (1994), a New York Times Notable Book; *Woodcuts of Women* (2001); *Gritos* (2003), a finalist for the 2004 National Book Critics Circle Award; and *The Flowers* (2008). His most recent work is *Before the End, After the Beginning* (2011), a collection of stories that Gilb wrote while recovering from a stroke in 2009. He is currently writer-in-residence and executive director of Centro Victoria: Center for Mexican American Literature and Culture at University of Houston–Victoria.

CHARLOTTE PERKINS GILMAN (1860–1935)   Gilman was born in Hartford, Connecticut. Shortly after her birth, her father deserted the family. Left with two children to support and scant help from their father, her mother was unable to provide her children with a secure and stable childhood. Gilman attended the Rhode Island School of Design for a time and went on to work as a commercial artist and teacher. In 1884 she married Charles Stetson, an artist. Following the birth of her only child the next year, Gilman was immobilized by a deep depression. At the urging of her husband, she became the patient of S. Weir Mitchell, a physician celebrated for his treatment of female nervous disorders. Gilman found the treatment intolerable and finally abandoned it. In 1888, convinced that her marriage threatened her sanity, she moved with her daughter to California and began her productive career as writer and feminist. In 1900, after her divorce, she married her first cousin George Houghton Gilman, enjoying a happy relationship that lasted until his sudden death thirty-four years later. Among Gilman's many works are *Women and Economics* (1899), *The Home: Its Work and Influence* (1903), and *The Man-Made World* (1911), whose thesis is that war and injustice will be eliminated only when women assume a larger role in national and international affairs. Gilman's fiction includes the novels *Moving the Mountain* (1911), *Herland* (1915), and *With Her in Ourland* (1916). Her autobiography, *The Living of Charlotte Perkins Gilman*, was published posthumously in 1935, the year she committed suicide to avoid suffering the final stages of breast cancer.

ALLEN GINSBERG (1926–1997)   Born in Newark, New Jersey, Ginsberg was among the foremost members of the Beat Generation. He matriculated to Columbia University in 1943, where he met Lucien Carr—the man who introduced him to William S. Burroughs, Neal Cassady, John Clellon Holmes, and Jack Kerouac, who would all eventually become renowned Beat poets: writers whose poetry conveyed a sense of spiritual exhaustion and rebellion against the hypocrisy and unprecedented materialism that overtook America in the wake of World War II. In his journal, Ginsberg described the "new vision" to which the Beats led him: "Since art is merely and ultimately self-expressive, we conclude that the fullest art, the most individual, uninfluenced, unrepressed, uninhibited expression of art is true expression and the true art." In 1954 Ginsberg moved to San Francisco where his mentor, William Carlos Williams, introduced him to Kenneth Rexroth, a prominent figure in the San Francisco Renaissance. Rexroth helped to establish Ginsberg as part of the San Francisco poetry scene, a task that came to a head when Ginsberg organized a reading for the Six Gallery on October 7, 1955. This was the first public reading of Ginsberg's "Howl"—a poem that attracted worldwide attention for the poet and his colleagues—and came to be known as the birth of the Beat Generation. Ginsberg labored tirelessly thereafter to promote his work and that of his peers, traveling throughout America and Europe to give readings. Ginsberg's first full-length poetry collection, *Howl and Other Poems* (1956), was widely banned for obscenity when it was first published, but over time "Howl" became one of the most read poems of the century. Ginsberg published nearly two dozen other poetry collections, including *Kaddish and Other Poems* (1961), *Planet News* (1968), *Iron Horse* (1972), and *The Fall of America: Poems of These States* (1973), which won the National Book Award. Ginsberg was also involved in many political activities throughout the 1960s and 1970s, including Vietnam War protests and speaking out in defense of the North American Man/Boy Love Association (NAMBLA). In 1973 he cofounded and directed the Jack Kerouac School of Disembodied Poetics at the Naropa Institute in Colorado. In his later years, Ginsberg became a distinguished professor at Brooklyn College, and in 1993 he was named a *Chevalier des Arts et des Lettres* (Knight of the Order of Arts and Letters) by the French Minister of Culture. He continued to travel throughout his life despite developing both diabetes and Reynaud's disease and suffering two minor strokes in the 1970s. He died in New York in 1997 after a battle with liver cancer.

NIKKI GIOVANNI (b. 1943)   Born Yolande Cornelia Giovanni Jr. in Knoxville, Tennessee, daughter of a probation officer and a social worker, Giovanni graduated with honors from Fisk University in 1967. She attended the University of Pennsylvania School of Social Work and Columbia School of the Arts, was assistant professor of black studies at Queens College (1968), and associate professor of English at Rutgers University (1968–70). She is currently Distinguished Professor of English at Virginia Tech. Giovanni's early work reflects her social activism as an African American college student in the 1960s, while her later works focus on the individual struggle for fulfillment rather than the collective struggle for black empowerment. Her books include *Black Feeling, Black Talk, Black Judgment* (1970), *My House* (1972), and *The Women and the Men* (1975). Among her most recent publications are *Acolytes* (2007), *Hip Hop Speaks to Children* (2008), *Bicycles: Love Poems* (2009), and *Chasing Utopia: A Hybrid* (2013). She was nominated for a Grammy in 2004 for her spoken-word album, *The Nikki Giovanni Poetry Collection*, and in 2009 she was commissioned by National Public Radio's *All Things Considered* to create an inaugural poem for President Barack Obama.

MALCOLM GLADWELL (b. 1963)   Journalist Malcolm Gladwell was born in England and grew up in rural Ontario. In 1984 he received his undergraduate degree in history from the University of Ontario. He was a reporter covering business and science at the *Washington Post* from 1987 until 1996, when he began working as a staff writer at the *New Yorker*. Most of Gladwell's works center around sociological and psychological phenomena that he finds interesting or unexpected, such as the underlying causes of crime rates and the evolution of racism and sexism. He has written five books, all of them on the *New York Times* best-seller list: *The Tipping Point: How Little Things Can Make a Big Difference* (2000), *Blink: The Power of Thinking Without Thinking* (2005), *Outliers: The Story of Success* (2008), *What the Dog Saw: And Other Adventures* (2009), and *David and Goliath: Underdogs, Misfits, and the Art of Battling Giants* (2013). In *Outliers*, Gladwell contends that the key to success in any field lies mostly in practicing a given task for 10,000 hours. In his own experience at the *Washington Post*, he spent 10,000 hours—over the course of ten years—developing his expertise as a journalist.

SUSAN GLASPELL (1882–1948)   Born and raised in Davenport, Iowa, Glaspell began her career as a novelist and author of sentimental short stories for popular magazines. By 1915, she had turned her energies to the theater, becoming one of the founders of the Provincetown Players, a group devoted to experimental drama. In 1916 Glaspell moved with the company, now called the Playwright's Theatre, to Greenwich Village in New York, where for two seasons—as writer, director, and actor—she played an important role in a group that came to have a major influence on the development of American drama. *Trifles* was written to be performed with a group of one-act plays by Eugene O'Neill at the company's summer playhouse on Cape Cod. Among her longer plays that embody a feminist perspective are *The Verge* (1921) and *Allison's House* (1931), a Pulitzer Prize–winning drama based on the life of Emily Dickinson. Among more than forty short stories, some twenty plays, and ten novels, Glaspell's best works deal with the theme of the new woman, presenting a protagonist who embodies the American pioneer spirit of independence and freedom.

LOUISE GLÜCK (b. 1943)   Glück was born in New York City and raised on Long Island. She attended Sarah Lawrence College and Columbia University and has taught at over a dozen institutions, among them the University of Iowa, Columbia University, the University of California, Berkeley, and Harvard University; she currently teaches at Yale University and lives in Cambridge, Massachusetts. Her numerous awards include an Academy of American Poets Prize, a National Book Critics Circle Award, a Pulitzer Prize, and a Wallace Stevens Award. She is also the recipient of fellowships from the Guggenheim Foundation, the Rockefeller Foundation, and the National Endowment for the Arts. Glück was poet laureate of the United States from 2003 to 2004. She is the author of one nonfiction book, *Proofs and Theories: Essays on Poetry* (1994), and a dozen volumes of poetry, including *Firstborn* (1968), *The Triumph of Achilles* (1985), *Ararat* (1990), *The Wild Iris* (1992), *Vita Nova* (1999), *Averno* (2006), and *A Village Life: Poems* (2009). Her most recent works include *Poems 1962–2012* (2012), which won the Los Angeles Times Book Prize, and *Faithful and Virtuous Night* (2014), which won the National Book Award.

ALLEGRA GOODMAN (b. 1967)   Born in Brooklyn, New York, Goodman grew up in Honolulu, where both her parents taught at the University of Hawaii. She began writing fiction at a young age, and her first short story was published in the literary journal *Commentary* during her first semester of college. Her first collection of short stories, *Total Immersion* (1989), was published the day she received her undergraduate degree from Harvard University. She did postgraduate work at Stanford, where she earned a PhD in English literature. Goodman has published five novels: *Kaaterskill Falls* (1998), *Paradise Park* (2001), *Intuition* (2006), *The Other Side of the Island* (2008), and *The Cookbook Collector* (2010). She has taught a writing workshop that focused mainly on revision at Boston University's graduate program in creative writing. On being a writer, Goodman says, "I love my job. Each book teaches me something new about character and plot and structure. I am dedicating my life to learning how to tell a story."

WILLIAM GREENWAY (b. 1947)   Greenway was born and raised in Atlanta, Georgia, and earned his BA from Georgia State University in 1970. After being drafted by the U.S. Navy as an electronics technician in New Orleans, he went on to earn his PhD in modern literature and poetry from Tulane University. Greenway has taught English at Youngstown State University since 1986, where he has been awarded three distinguished professorships in both teaching and scholarship. Greenway has also been honored with the Larry Levis Editors' Prize from *Missouri Review*, the Open Voice Poetry Award from the *Writer's Voice*, the Helen and Laura Krout Memorial Poetry Award, an Academy of American Poets Prize, and an Ohio Arts Council Grant, and he was named the 1994 Georgia Author of the Year. In addition to having published over 600 poems in various top literary journals, Greenway has written nine full-length poetry collections, including *Ascending Order* (2003), winner of the 2004 Ohioana Poetry Book of the Year Award; *Fishing at the End of the World* (2005); and *Everywhere at Once* (2008), which was nominated for the 2008 Ohioana Poetry Book of the Year Award. In a 2010 interview with the YSU Student Literary Arts Association, Greenway said that though his poems "are often set in a real and particular place, the place is changed, almost surrealistically, as in a dream, to a place which, though still recognizable as a particular place, is now universal, an Everywhere which I hope is accessible to everyone."

DONALD HALL (b. 1928)   Hall grew up in Hamden, Connecticut, and attended Phillips Exeter Academy in New Hampshire. He went on to earn his BA from Harvard in 1951, a BLitt from Oxford, and an honorary PhD in literature from Bates College. In 1957 he took a position as an assistant professor of English at the University of Michigan, which is where he met his future wife, the poet Jane Kenyon. After they married, the couple moved to Eagle Pond Farm in rural New Hampshire and led a quiet, harmonious life that both poets recounted in many of their poems. But that quiet life was interrupted in 1989 when Hall was diagnosed with colon cancer. Despite unfavorable odds, he eventually went into remission. In 1994, however, Kenyon was diagnosed with leukemia and died fifteen months later. Her death struck Hall hard, and he attempted to work through his grief in writing. In 1998, on the third anniversary of his wife's death, Hall published *Without: Poems* (1998), a volume *Publishers Weekly* called "a heartbreaking portrait of a marriage that has not quite ended." Hall also wrote a memoir about his and Kenyon's twenty-three-year marriage called *The Best Day the Worst Day: Life with Jane Kenyon* (2005). In addition to these works, some of Hall's most notable collections are *Exiles and Marriages* (1955), which was the Academy of American Poets' Lamont Poetry Selection for 1956; *The Happy Man* (1986), winner of the Lenore Marshall Poetry Prize; and *The One Day* (1988), which won the National Book Critics Circle Award and the *Los Angeles Times* Book Prize and was nominated for a Pulitzer Prize. His more recent books include *The Painted Bed* (2002), *White Apples and the Taste of Stone: Selected Poems 1946–2006* (2006), *The Back Chamber* (2011), and *Essays after Eighty* (2014). Among Hall's many literary honors are two Guggenheim Fellowships, the Poetry Society of America's Robert Frost Medal, a Lifetime Achievement award from the New Hampshire Writers and Publishers Project, and the Ruth Lilly Poetry Prize. Hall also served as poet laureate of New Hampshire from 1984 to 1989 and was appointed the Library of Congress's fourteenth Poet Laureate Consultant in Poetry in 2006. In 2010 he was awarded the National Medal of Arts. He still resides in New Hampshire.

MARK HALLIDAY (b. 1949)   Halliday earned bachelor's and master's degrees from Brown University before earning a doctorate in English literature from Brandeis University. He taught at Wellesley College, the University of Pennsylvania, Western Michigan University, and Indiana University before joining the faculty at Ohio University. He is the author of six volumes of poems: *Little Star* (1987), *Tasker Street* (1992), *Selfwolf* (1999), *Jab* (2002), *Keep This Forever* (2008), and *Thresherphobe* (2013). He was awarded the Rome Prize of the American Academy of Arts and Letters in 2001 and a fellowship from the Guggenheim Foundation in 2006. About the colloquial style of his poetry, Halliday has said, "I love the analogy between a poem and a speech that you might actually hear in real life. . . . People do, over a few beers, let's say, if they're having trouble in their marriage or they're trying to change their lives, they do go from anecdote to meditation to comic speculation and then back to the beer, back to a joke—the movement of thought has those different levels. I love poems that show a speaker living through those moves."

LORRAINE HANSBERRY (1930–1965) Lorraine Hansberry was born into a prosperous, middle-class African American family on the South Side of Chicago. When she was seven, her family went to court over an attempt to deny them the right to buy a home in a restricted white neighborhood. Their lawsuit challenging the restrictive covenant was finally decided in their favor by the U.S. Supreme Court. Hansberry later recalled, "Both of my parents were strong-minded, civic-minded, exceptionally race-minded people who made enormous sacrifices on behalf of the struggle for civil rights throughout their lifetimes." After graduating from the segregated public school system of Chicago, she attended the University of Wisconsin and studied at the Art Institute of Chicago and abroad. She soon gave up her artistic plans and moved to New York City to pursue a writing career. She also became politically active in liberal causes. During a protest demonstration at New York University, she met Robert Nemiroff, a white writer and political activist. They married in 1953. Encouraged by her husband, Hansberry finally completed *A Raisin in the Sun*, a play she had been working on for some time. It opened in 1959, becoming the first play written by a black woman to be produced on Broadway. An immediate success, the play won the New York Drama Critics' Circle Award. A film version, for which she wrote the screenplay, was released in 1961. Her next play, *The Sign in Sidney Brustein's Window* (1964), met with less success. She was working on another play, *Les Blancs*, when she died of cancer (the play was produced in 1970). Although Nemiroff and Hansberry divorced in 1964, he was appointed her literary executor and assembled, from his former wife's writings and words, a dramatic autobiography titled *To Be Young, Gifted, and Black* (1969).

THOMAS HARDY (1840–1928) Hardy was born near Dorchester in southeastern England, on which he based the Wessex of many of his novels and poems. Hardy worked for the ecclesiastical architect John Hicks from 1856 to 1861. He then moved to London to practice architecture and took evening classes at King's College for six years. In 1867 he gave up architecture to become a full-time writer, and after writing short stories and poems, he found success as a novelist. *The Mayor of Casterbridge* (1886) and *Tess of the d'Urbervilles* (1891) reveal Hardy's concern for victims of circumstance and his appeal to humanitarian sympathy in readers. After his novel *Jude the Obscure* (1896) was strongly criticized, Hardy set aside prose fiction and returned to poetry—a genre in which he was most prolific and successful after he reached the age of seventy.

NATHANIEL HAWTHORNE (1804–1864) The son of a merchant sea captain who died in a distant port when Nathaniel was four, Hawthorne grew up in genteel poverty in Massachusetts and Maine. His earliest American ancestor, the magistrate William Hathorne, ordered the whipping of a Quaker woman in Salem. William's son John was one of the three judges at the Salem witch trials of 1692. Aware of his family's role in colonial America, Hawthorne returned to Salem after graduating from Bowdoin College (where future president Franklin Pierce was a friend and classmate), determined to be a writer. He recalled and destroyed copies of his first novel, the mediocre *Fanshawe* (1828). His short stories, often set in Puritan America, revealed a moral complexity that had not troubled his righteous ancestors William and John. His success as an author allowed him to marry Sophia Peabody in 1842, after a four-year engagement. Though his stories were critically praised, they did not earn much money, and in 1846 he used his political connections with the Democratic Party to obtain a job at the U.S. Custom House in Salem. His dismissal in

1849 (when the Democrats lost) produced both anger and resolve. The result was a great American novel, *The Scarlet Letter* (1850), which made him famous and improved his fortune. Although he was friendly with Emerson and his circle of optimistic transcendentalists, some of whom established the utopian socialist community at Brook Farm, Hawthorne's vision of the human condition was considerably darker. Herman Melville dedicated *Moby-Dick* to Hawthorne and characterized him as a man who could say "No! in thunder."

ROBERT HAYDEN (1913–1980) Born in Detroit, Hayden studied at Wayne State University and the University of Michigan (MA, 1944). In 1946 he joined the faculty of Fisk University. He left Fisk in 1968 for a professorship at the University of Michigan, where he remained until his death. He produced some ten volumes of poetry but did not receive the acclaim many thought he deserved until late in life, with the publication of *Words in the Mourning Time: Poems* (1971). In the 1960s, he aroused some hostility from African Americans who wanted him to express more militancy. But Hayden did not want to be part of what he called a "kind of literary ghetto." He considered his own work "a form of prayer—a prayer for illumination, perfection."

TERRANCE HAYES (b. 1971) Hayes was born in Columbia, South Carolina. He studied at Coker College and later earned his MFA from the University of Pittsburgh. He has received many literary honors including a Whiting Award, three *Best American Poetry* selections, a Pushcart Prize, and fellowships from the National Endowment for the Arts, the Guggenheim Foundation, and the MacArthur Foundation. His collections of poetry include *Muscular Music* (1999), winner of the Kate Tufts Discovery Award; *Hip Logic* (2002), which won the 2001 National Poetry Series and was a finalist for the Los Angeles Times Book Award; *Wind in a Box* (2006); *Lighthead* (2010), which won the National Book Award for Poetry; and *How to Be Drawn* (2015). In praise of Hayes's work, Cornelius Eady has said, "First you'll marvel at his skill, his near-perfect pitch, his disarming humor, his brilliant turns of phrase. Then you'll notice the grace, the tenderness, the unblinking truth-telling just beneath his lines, the open and generous way he takes in our world." Hayes is a professor of creative writing at the University of Pittsburgh and lives in Pittsburgh with his wife, the poet Yona Harvey, and their children.

SEAMUS HEANEY (1939–2013) Heaney, the eldest of nine children, was born on his family's farm near Belfast in County Derry, Northern Ireland. He attended local schools, earned a degree in English with first-class honors from Queen's University, Belfast, and received a teacher's certificate in English from St. Joseph's College in Belfast. He published his first writings while a student at St. Joseph's and began a career as a teacher. His first volume of poetry, *Death of a Naturalist* (1966), won several prizes and launched Heaney's distinguished career as a poet. He produced several volumes of essays, including *Finders Keepers: Selected Prose 1971–2001* (2002). Among his numerous volumes of poetry are *The Spirit Level* (1996), *Opened Ground: Poems 1966–1996* (1998), *The Riverbank Field* (2007), and *Articulations* (2008). His 2006 volume, *District and Circle*, won the T. S. Eliot Prize, and his final volume, *Human Chain* (2010), won the Forward Poetry Prize Best Collection 2010 award and the Irish Times Poetry Now Award for 2011. Other publications include *Beowulf: A New Verse Translation* (2002) and *The Burial at Thebes: A Version of Sophocles' Antigone* (2004). He taught at Oxford University, the University of California, Berkeley, and Harvard University. In 1995 Heaney was awarded the Nobel Prize in Literature, and several modern critics have characterized him as "the most important Irish poet since Yeats." An immensely popular poet, he enjoyed the support of a host of "Heaneyboppers" who attended his readings. On the day after he died in 2013, over 80,000 people attending an Irish football match in Dublin cheered for Heaney for three minutes.

ERNEST HEMINGWAY (1899–1961) Born in Oak Park, Illinois, Hemingway became a cub reporter after high school. After World War I—during which he was seriously wounded while serving as an ambulance driver—he lived in Paris, a member of a lively and productive expatriate community characterized by Gertrude Stein as "a lost generation." He lived an active life, not only as a writer but also as a war correspondent, big-game hunter, and fisherman. In such novels as *The Sun Also Rises* (1926), *A Farewell to Arms* (1929), and *For Whom the Bell Tolls* (1940), his fictional characters exhibit a passion for courage and integrity, for grace under pressure. Hemingway's spare, unembellished style reinforced his central theme that one must confront danger and live honorably. He won the Nobel Prize in Literature in 1954. In 1961, unable to write because treatment for mental instability affected his memory, he killed himself with the shotgun he had so often used when hunting.

JUAN FELIPE HERRERA (b. 1948) Herrera was born in Fowler, California, to Mexican migrant farmworkers. He earned a bachelor's degree in social anthropology at the University of California, Los Angeles, a master's degree in social anthropology from Stanford University, and an MFA from the University of Iowa. He taught at California State University at Fresno before assuming his current role as the Tomás Rivera Endowed Chair in the Creative Writing Department at the University of California, Riverside. Herrera describes himself as an educator, poet, writer, artist, performer, and musician. In addition to writing children's books, novels for young adults, prose, and short stories, he is the author of more than a dozen volumes of poetry. Among his most recent publications are *Cinnamon Girl: Letters Found Inside a Cereal Box* (2005), *Downtown Boy* (2005), *187 Reasons Mexicanos Can't Cross the Border: Undocuments 1971–2007* (2007), and *Half of the World in Light: New and Selected Poems* (2008), which won the National Book Critics Circle Award. In 2009 he won the PEN/Beyond Margins Award, and in 2010 he received a Guggenheim Fellowship. Herrera served as California's poet laureate from 2012 to 2014.

ROBERT HERRICK (1591–1674) Born in London, Herrick was apprenticed to his uncle, a goldsmith, for ten years until at age twenty-two he was sent to Cambridge University in recognition of his academic talents. Little is known of the decade following his graduation from Cambridge, although it seems certain that he associated with a circle of literary artists. In 1629, he was appointed vicar at Dean Prior, Devonshire, a rural parish that the sophisticated and cosmopolitan Herrick viewed as a kind of exile. Yet, he was fascinated by the pagan elements of local songs and dances, and often drew upon pre-Christian writers for inspiration. His chief work, *Hesperides* (1648), is a collection of some 1,200 poems—mostly written in Devonshire—about local scenery, customs, and people.

TONY HOAGLAND (b. 1953) Hoagland was born in Fort Bragg, North Carolina, and educated at the University of Iowa and the University of Arizona. He has taught at many institutions, including Kalamazoo College, University of Michigan, Warren Wilson College, and Colby College. He now teaches in the creative writing program at the University of Houston. His poems and critical writings have appeared in such publications as *Ploughshares*, *American Poetry Review*, and the *Pushcart Prize Anthology* (1991). Hoagland's first three collections of poems were chapbooks: *A Change in Plans* (1985), *Talking to Stay Warm* (1986), and *History of Desire* (1990). His first full-length volume of poetry, *Sweet Ruin*

(1992), won the Brittingham Prize in poetry as well as the Zacharas Award from Emerson College. His most recent collections of poetry are *What Narcissism Means to Me* (2003), *Hard Rain* (2005), *Unincorporated Persons in the Late Honda Dynasty: Poems* (2010), and the chapbook *Don't Tell Anyone* (2014). Hoagland has also published two essay collections: *Real Sofistikashun: Essays on Poetry and Craft* (2006) and *Twenty Poems That Could Save America and Other Essays* (2014). In 2005 he won the Poetry Foundation's Mark Twain Award and the Folger Shakespeare Library's O. B. Hardison Jr. Poetry Prize, which honors excellence in teaching as well as in writing. He is also the recipient of fellowships from the National Endowment for the Arts and the Guggenheim Foundation.

ANDREA HOLLANDER (b. 1947)　Born to American parents in Berlin, Germany, and raised in the United States, Hollander is the author of several full-length poetry collections: *House Without a Dreamer* (1995), *The Other Life* (2001), and *Woman in the Painting* (2006). Her most recent work, *Landscape with Female Figure: New & Selected Poems, 1982–2012* (2014) was a finalist for the Oregon Book Award in Poetry. Other honors include a Pushcart Prize for prose memoir, the Runes Poetry Prize, and two poetry fellowships from the National Endowment for the Arts. In 2008 she received the Subiaco Award for Literary Excellence in the Writing and Teaching of Poetry. Her poems and essays have appeared in numerous anthologies including *Writing Poems, The Poets' Grimm*, and *The Autumn House Anthology of Contemporary American Poetry*. Her work also appears regularly in such literary journals as *Poetry, Georgia Review*, and *Gettysburg Review*. For more than twenty-two years, Hollander served as writer-in-residence at Lyon College, which awarded her the Lamar Williamson Prize for Excellence in Teaching. In 2011 she moved to Portland, Oregon, where she teaches writing workshops in poetry and the personal essay.

A. D. HOPE (1907–2000)　Australian poet and essayist Alec Derwent Hope studied at Oxford, where his teachers included novelists J. R. R. Tolkien and C. S. Lewis. Although he didn't excel academically, Hope went on to become a teacher and eventually professor of English at the Australian National University. In the 1930s, Hope began publishing poems in various periodicals, which earned him an international reputation as a poet. Although some found the overt sexuality in his writing to be offensive, Hope's first collection of poetry, *The Wandering Islands* (1955), received critical acclaim, and he continued to win awards in Great Britain and the United States for his work. A prolific writer, Hope published eleven poetry collections, seven critical essay collections, and two plays. Especially in his early writings, Hope was known for his biting satire and critique of contemporary values. He was also an award-winning and fierce critic, feared by many writers for his unapologetic reviews, which one writer nonetheless attributed to "sharply rais[ing] the standard of literary discussion in Australia."

GERARD MANLEY HOPKINS (1844–1889)　Raised in London, Hopkins won a scholarship to Balliol College, Oxford University, where he studied classical literature. He converted to Roman Catholicism in 1866 and two years later entered the Jesuit novitiate. In 1877 he was ordained a Jesuit priest and served in missions in London, Liverpool, Oxford, and Glasgow until 1882. From 1884 to his death in 1889, he was professor of Greek at University College, Dublin. A technically innovative poet, Hopkins saw only three of his poems published during his lifetime. He gained posthumous recognition in 1918 when a friend, the poet laureate Robert Bridges, published Hopkins's complete works. His early poems celebrate the beauty of God's world, but later works reflect his poor health and depression.

A. E. HOUSMAN (1859–1936)   Born in Fockbury, England, and an outstanding student, Alfred Edward Housman nonetheless failed his final examinations at Oxford University in 1881, possibly due to emotional chaos caused by his love for a male classmate. Working as a clerk in the patent office in London, he pursued classical studies on his own, earned an MA, and was appointed chair of Latin at University College, London. In 1910 he became professor of Latin at Cambridge, where he remained until his death in 1936. As a poet, Housman was concerned primarily with the fleetingness of love and the decay of youth. After his first collection, *A Shropshire Lad*, was rejected by several publishers, Housman published it at his own expense in 1896. It gained popularity during World War I, and his 1922 collection, *Last Poems*, was well received. In his lecture "The Name and Nature of Poetry" (1933), Housman argued that poetry should appeal to emotions rather than intellect. *More Poems* (1936) was published posthumously.

MARIE HOWE (b. 1950)   Howe was born in Rochester, New York, and received her MFA from Columbia University in 1983. Her first poetry collection, *The Good Thief* (1988), was selected by Margaret Atwood for the National Poetry Series, and that same year, Stanley Kunitz also selected Howe for a Lavan Younger Poets Award from the Academy of American Poets. Kunitz called Howe's poetry "luminous, intense, and eloquent, rooted in an abundant inner life." Howe's second collection of poetry was *What the Living Do* (1998), which she wrote as something of an elegy for her brother John, who died of AIDS in 1989. Howe was coeditor of the anthology *In the Company of My Solitude: American Writing from the AIDS Pandemic* (1995). Her most recent poetry collection, *The Kingdom of Ordinary Time: Poems* (2008), was a finalist for the Los Angeles Times Book Prize. Among Howe's other honors are grants from the Guggenheim Foundation, the Bunting Institute, and the National Endowment for the Arts. She served as poet laureate for the state of New York from 2012 to 2014. Howe currently lives in New York City and teaches at Sarah Lawrence College, New York University, and Columbia University.

LANGSTON HUGHES (1902–1967)   Hughes was born in Joplin, Missouri. His father was a businessman and lawyer; his mother, a teacher. Hughes attended Columbia University, graduated from Lincoln University in 1929, traveled throughout the world, and held many odd jobs as a young man. While Hughes had a long and prolific career as a writer in all genres, he is still remembered as the central figure of the Harlem Renaissance of the 1920s, a movement that committed itself to the examination and celebration of black life in America and its African heritage. He was the Madrid correspondent for the Baltimore *Afro-American* (1937) and a columnist for the Chicago *Defender* (1943–67) and the New York *Post* (1962–67). His poems of racial affirmation and protest are often infused with the rhythms of blues and jazz music. He wrote over two dozen plays (many musicalized) and founded the Suitcase Theater (Harlem, 1938), the New Negro Theater (Los Angeles, 1939), and the Skyloft Players (Chicago, 1941). His works include *The Weary Blues* (1926), *Montage of a Dream Deferred* (1951), and *The Panther and the Lash: Poems of Our Times* (1969).

ZORA NEALE HURSTON (1891–1960)   Born in Eatonville, Florida, an African American town, Hurston enjoyed a happy early childhood in a town that spared her from racism and with a mother who instilled a strong sense of self-worth in her. With the death of her mother, she was sent off to boarding school but was forced to give up her formal education when her father remarried and refused to give her further financial help. She supported herself with odd jobs, managing to earn a high school diploma and enter Howard University in Washington, DC. Unable to support herself as a full-time student, Hurston quit college after five years, having earned only a year and a half of college credits. She moved to Harlem, determined to pursue a writing career. In New York, she was hired as a personal secretary by the novelist Fannie Hurst, who arranged a scholarship for her at Barnard College. There, she studied with the famous anthropologist Franz Boas and became interested in black folk traditions. She earned her degree from Barnard in 1927 and received a fellowship to study the oral traditions of her hometown. She wrote her first novel, *Jonah's Gourd Vine* (1934), while doing fieldwork in Eatonville. *Mules and Men* (1935), based on the material her fieldwork had produced, was attacked by African American intellectuals and writers for its refusal to acknowledge and confront racism. Nevertheless, Hurston was awarded a Guggenheim Fellowship to study voodoo in the Caribbean, which gave her the material for her second and most celebrated novel, *Their Eyes Were Watching God* (1937). During the last two decades of her life, she continued to write novels, plays, and an autobiography, *Dust Tracks on the Road* (1942), but drew increasing criticism from the African American press for her refusal to publicly condemn segregation. In 1950 she was the subject of a *Miami Herald* news story that carried the headline: "Famous Negro Author Working as a Maid Here 'Just to Live a Little.'" She claimed that she needed a break from writing and that she was busy making plans for writing projects and for a national magazine devoted to domestics. Her last years were troubled by poor health, emotional fatigue, and lack of money. She died of a stroke, penniless, in a welfare home in Fort Pierce, Florida.

DAVID HENRY HWANG (b. 1957)   Hwang was born in Los Angeles, earned a degree from Stanford University, and attended the Yale University School of Drama for one year. His first play, *F.O.B.* (for "fresh off the boat") won an OBIE for best New American Off-Broadway Play of 1980. Hwang has written a number of plays, musicals, operas, and screenplays but is best known for *M. Butterfly*, for which he won a Tony Award in 1988 and received a Pulitzer Prize nomination in 1989. His other awards include fellowships from the Guggenheim Foundation and the National Endowment for the Arts; an OBIE for best playwriting in 1997 and a Tony Award nomination for best Broadway play in 1998 for *Golden Child*; and a Tony Award nomination for his adaptation of the musical *Flower Drum Song* in 2003. Although Hwang once called his Chinese American heritage "a minor detail, like having red hair," cultural conflict and Asian themes are hallmarks of his most acclaimed works. In 2014 he received the Doris Duke Artist Award and became the director of Columbia University's Playwrighting Concentration.

HENRIK IBSEN (1828–1906)   Ibsen was born in the seaport of Skien, Norway, the son of a wealthy merchant. When Ibsen was eight, his father's business failed, and at fifteen he was apprenticed to an apothecary in the tiny town of Grimstad. He hated this profession. To solace himself, he read poetry and theology and began to write. When he was twenty-two, he became a student in Christiania (now Oslo) and published his first play. In 1851 his diligent though unremarkable writing earned him an appointment as theater-poet at a new theater in Bergen, where he remained until 1857, learning both the business and the art of drama. He wrote several plays based on Scandinavian folklore, held positions at two theaters in Christiania, and married. When he was thirty-six, he applied to the government for a poet's pension—a stipend that would have permitted him to devote himself to writing. The stipend was refused. Enraged, he left Norway and, though he was granted the stipend two years later, spent the next twenty-seven years in Italy and Germany, where he wrote the realistic social dramas that established his reputation as the founder of modern theater. Such plays as *Ghosts* (1881), *An Enemy of the People* (1882), and *A Doll's House* (1878) inevitably generated controversy as Ibsen explored venereal disease, the stupidity and greed of the "compact majority," and the position of women in society. In 1891 he returned to live in Christiania, where he was recognized and honored as one of Norway's (and Europe's) finest writers.

SHIRLEY JACKSON (1919–1965) Born in San Francisco, Jackson moved with her family to Rochester, New York, in her teens. An episode of severe depression (a recurrent problem during her life) forced her out of the University of Rochester, but she later graduated from Syracuse University. She married the eminent critic Stanley Edgar Hyman, had four children, and kept to a rigid writing schedule. Although her major work tends toward the ominous, she contributed humorous pieces to popular magazines on the problems of housekeeping and raising children. These were collected in *Life among the Savages* (1953) and *Raising Demons* (1957). She wrote four novels, and her short stories are collected in three volumes: *The Lottery* (1949), *The Magic of Shirley Jackson* (1966), and *Come Along with Me* (1968).

HA JIN (b. 1956) Jin is the pen name of Jin Xuěféi. Born in Liaoning, China, he grew up under the communist regime and was enlisted in the People's Liberation Army for six years. He earned two degrees in China before completing his doctorate at Brandeis University near Boston. Jin taught at Emory University and currently teaches at Boston University, where he is a professor in the English department. He has written three books of poetry: *Between Silences* (1990), *Facing Shadows* (1996), and *Wreckage* (2001). He is also the author of three books of short stories and five novels, most recently *A Free Life* (2007), *A Good Fall* (2009), and *Nanjing Requiem* (2011). He is the recipient of numerous awards, including the Flannery O'Connor Prize for Short Fiction, a PEN/Hemingway Award, two PEN/Faulkner Awards, a National Book Award, and fellowships from the Guggenheim Foundation and the American Academy of Arts and Sciences. His latest work is *A Map of Betrayal* (2014). Jin, who writes entirely in English about thorny Chinese-related themes, has said, "When a writer adopts another language there are a lot of motivations: necessity, ambition, estrangement. Estrangement is a big part of it. . . . It creates a kind of distance. In a way, it enables me to write more objectively."

GEORGIA DOUGLAS JOHNSON (1880–1966) Johnson was born in Atlanta, Georgia, to parents of African American, Native American, and English descent. She graduated from Atlanta University's Normal School in 1896, eventually going on to study music at the Oberlin Conservatory and the Cleveland College of Music. On September 28, 1903, Johnson married Henry Lincoln Johnson, an Atlanta-based lawyer and a prominent supporter of the Republican Party. When her husband accepted an appointment as the recorder of deeds from President William Howard Taft in 1910, the Johnsons moved to Washington, DC. It was during this time that Johnson began to write. She published her first poems in 1916 in the NAACP's magazine *Crisis*, and her first volume of poetry, *The Heart of a Woman*, two years later. She also wrote a weekly column called "Homely Philosophy" from 1926 to 1932. She traveled widely during the 1920s to give poetry readings and published three additional collections during her lifetime: *Bronze* (1922), *An Autumn Love Cycle* (1928), and *Share My World* (1962). She also wrote numerous plays, including *A Sunday Morning in the South* (1925), *Blue Blood* (1926), and *Plumes* (1927). Her house at 1461 S Street Northwest—known as site of the S Street Salon—was a principal meeting place for Harlem Renaissance writers in Washington, DC, and she often held open houses and readings there. Johnson received an honorary doctorate in literature from Atlanta University in 1965, one year before she passed away. She was also inducted posthumously into the Georgia Writers Hall of Fame in 2010.

JAMES WELDON JOHNSON (1871–1938) Johnson was born in Jacksonville, Florida, where from a young age he was encouraged by his parents to study English literature and the European musical tradition—an exception for most African Americans at the time. He later attended Atlanta University, during which time he taught for two summers in the poor, rural town of Hampton, Georgia. This experience exposed him to hardships from which he had been previously sheltered and ignited what became an enduring desire to help the black community. In 1901 Johnson and his brother Rosamond—a talented composer—moved to New York City to pursue a life writing songs for the musical theater. The brothers collaborated on the song "Lift Ev'ry Voice and Sing," which swiftly gained popularity and was adopted by the NAACP as the "Negro National Anthem." Johnson also studied creative literature at Columbia University for three years and became an active member of the Republican Party. He served as treasurer of New York's Colored Republican Club and helped compose songs for Republican candidate Theodore Roosevelt's presidential campaign. In 1906 Johnson was appointed to a job as U.S. consul to Venezuela, where he had poems published in the *Century Magazine* and the *Independent*. In 1912 he pseudonymously published *The Autobiography of an Ex-Colored Man*, the story of a biracial musician who rejects his African American heritage in favor of living a life of leisure among whites. In 1916 Johnson became the national organizer for the NAACP and served as its executive secretary for ten years starting in 1920. He also remained an active literary figure, editing *The Book of American Negro Poetry* (1922), which is to this day a landmark text in African American literature; *The Book of American Negro Spirituals* (1925); and *The Second Book of American Negro Spirituals* (1926). He also published *God's Trombones* (1927), a book of poetry that was greatly influenced by his time spent in Hampton, and *Black Manhattan* (1930), a survey of African American contributions to the artistic scene in New York. In 1934 he published *Negro Americans, What Now?*, an extended political argument in favor of racial integration. Of the adversities that he and other African Americans had faced, he declared, "I will not allow one prejudiced person or one million or one hundred million to blight my life. I will not let prejudice or any of its attendant humiliations and injustices bear me down to spiritual defeat. My inner life is mine, and I shall defend and maintain its integrity against all the powers of hell."

LACY M. JOHNSON (b. 1978) Johnson earned her PhD from the University of Houston's Creative Writing Program. Her work has appeared in *Sentence, Nimrod, Memoir (and), Gulf Coast, Pebble Lake Review*, and *Irish Studies Review*. Her first book, *Trespasses: A Memoir* (2012), explores identity as it is associated with region, and region as it is experienced through memory, history, and theory. Author and critic Nick Flynn said of *Trespasses*: "Utterly hip, while at the same time a voice from another era, *Trespasses* is about 'growing up in a poor farming town in the Great Plains,' an examination of the term 'white trash' through interviews, research, and memory, and an evocation of a place many of us will never see. Yet, at its heart, it is a lyric evocation of self. Plainspoken, tattooed, and brilliant, Lacy Johnson pushes the boundaries of what memoir—and, perhaps more importantly, what any of us—can be." Her most recent book is *The Other Side* (2014), a National Book Critics Circle Award finalist that chronicles her kidnapping and rape by an abusive ex-boyfriend. On writing about this painful event, she says, "When I set out to write this book, it wasn't to 'fix' myself, or to make myself 'whole' again, but to change that story I told myself about who I am, who I was, and who I could still be." Johnson teaches interdisciplinary art at University of Houston.

SABRINA JONES (b. 1960)   Born and raised in Philadelphia, Jones moved to New York City to attend the Pratt Institute, where she earned her BFA in painting. In the 1980s, Jones joined the New York–based editorial collective *WW3 Illustrated*, using the comic book as her medium of choice to convey her personal and political messages. In addition to contributing to most issues of the radical comics magazine *World War 3*, Jones coedited *Girltalk* (1995), an anthology of women's autobiographical comics, and she self-published educational comics with alternative views on the war on drugs and military recruitment. After receiving her MFA in illustration from the School of Visual Arts in 2003, she contributed to *Wobblies! A Graphic History of the Industrial Workers of the World* (2005), wrote *Isadora Duncan, a Graphic Biography* (2008), and illustrated *FDR and the New Deal for Beginners* (2010), by Paul Buhle. Her most recent work is *Race to Incarcerate: A Graphic Retelling* (2013), an adaptation of Marc Mauer's book on America's exploding imprisonment rate. Regarding her decision to focus on comics, she says, "People aren't intimidated by it because it isn't Art—or is it? Either way, I get to do a lot of drawing." Jones also continues to paint, most notably for set designs; she regularly works as a scenic artist for the weekly television show *Saturday Night Live*.

BEN JONSON (1572–1637)   Jonson was born in Westminster, England, and after leaving school, began earning his living as a bricklayer, the trade of his stepfather. Though he never attended college, he taught himself enough to be considered learned. He soon abandoned construction work and earned his reputation as one of the preeminent playwrights of his period. A contemporary of Shakespeare, he also wrote poetry and translations of classical Roman authors for his English Renaissance audience. Among other works, Jonson is the author of the satirical plays *Volpone*, *The Alchemist*, and *Bartholemew Fair*; his best known poems include "On My First Sonne," "To Celia," and "To Penshurst."

CAMDEN JOY (b. 1964)   Writer and musician Tom Adelman adopted the pen name Camden Joy around 1994 when he finished writing his first novel, in which the narrator bears the same name as the pseudonymous author. "My writing felt curiously liberated under a pseudonym," he says, and as Joy, he attempted to blur the lines between music criticism, memoir, and fiction in various underground "guerilla" formats such as street posters and pamphlets. He gained some notoriety as an impassioned writer who focused mainly on the indie rock scene of the early 1990s, and his writing was featured in the *Village Voice*, *Boston Phoenix*, and other alternative weeklies. After Joy's first novel, *The Last Rock Star Book, or, Liz Phair: a Rant*, came out in 1998, he went on to publish other works including the novel *Boy Island* (2000), the novella *Palm Tree 13* (2001), and *Lost Joy* (2002), a collection of his writing from the 1990s. Using his legal name, Tom Adelman, he has also written two nonfiction books on baseball: the best-selling *Long Ball: The Summer of '75—Spaceman, Catfish, Charlie Hustle, and the Greatest World Series Ever Played* (2003) and *Black and Blue: The Golden Arm, the Robinson Boys, and the World Series That Stunned America* (2006). Joy currently produces a podcast about alternative music, "Real Good Music with Camden Joy." In 2015, all books published under the name Camden Joy will be reissued by Verse Chorus Press.

JAMES JOYCE (1882–1941)   Though educated in Jesuit schools, Joyce came to reject Catholicism; and though an expatriate living in Paris, Trieste, and Zurich for most of his adult life, he wrote almost exclusively about his native Dublin. Joyce's rebelliousness, which surfaced during his university career, generated a revolution in modern literature. His novels *Ulysses* (1922) and *Finnegan's Wake* (1939) introduced radically new narrative techniques. "Araby"—from his first collection of short stories, *Dubliners* (1914)—is one of a series of sharply realized vignettes based on Joyce's experiences in Ireland, the homeland he later characterized as "a sow that eats its own farrow." Joyce lived precariously on earnings as a language teacher and also modest contributions from wealthy patrons, support that he justified by becoming one of the most influential novelists of the twentieth century. Because *Ulysses* dealt frankly with sexuality and used coarse language, the U.S. Post Office charged that the novel was obscene and forbade its importation. A celebrated 1933 court decision lifted the ban.

FRANZ KAFKA (1883–1924)   Born into a middle-class, German-speaking Jewish family in Prague, Kafka earned a law degree in 1906 and worked as a claims investigator for an insurance company for most of his adult life. He remained in constant conflict with his domineering father, who belittled his literary aims. He became engaged to a woman in 1912 but broke with her after five years. In 1917 he contracted the tuberculosis that was to kill him at age forty-one. Despite the deadening monotony of his job and his personal anguish, he created a remarkable and original body of work during his short life, including the masterful novels *The Trial* (1925) and *The Castle* (1926). His starkly realistic stories and novels take place in nightmarish dreamworlds where stifling bureaucracy chokes his protagonists and diminishes their dignity and their lives. A fierce perfectionist, Kafka published little during his life and left written instructions to his friend and executor, Max Brod, to destroy his unpublished manuscripts. Fortunately, Brod could not bring himself to comply.

JOHN KEATS (1795–1821)   Keats was born in London, the eldest son of a stable keeper who died in an accident in 1804. His mother died of tuberculosis shortly after remarrying, and the grandmother who raised Keats and his siblings died in 1814. At eighteen, Keats wrote his first poem, "Imitation of Spenser," inspired by Edmund Spenser's long narrative poem *The Faerie Queene*. The thirty-three poems he wrote while training to be a surgeon were published in a collection in 1817, and Keats then gave up medicine for writing. After more traumatic losses in 1818, including the departure of one brother for the United States and the death of his other brother of tuberculosis, Keats wrote his second collection, *Lamia, Isabella, The Eve of St. Agnes, and Other Poems* (1820). Ill with tuberculosis himself, Keats was sent to Rome to recover. He died at twenty-six, but despite his short career he is a major figure of the romantic period.

JANE KENYON (1947–1995)   Kenyon was born in Ann Arbor, Michigan, and attended the University of Michigan, where she received a BA (1970) and MA (1972). While at Michigan she studied under Donald Hall, the eminent poet and teacher, whom she married in the year she received her master's. The couple moved to Eagle Pond Farm in rural New Hampshire, living a quiet life that Kenyon celebrated in many of her early poems. They became well known not only through her poems but also through the books Hall wrote about life on their farm. In her last poems, Kenyon wrote about her struggle with leukemia, which claimed her life at age forty-seven. At the time of her death, she was New Hampshire's poet laureate. During her lifetime, she published four collections of poems, *From Room to Room* (1978), *The Boat of Quiet Hours* (1986), *Let Evening Come* (1990), and *Constance* (1993). Since her death, two additional volumes have been published, *Otherwise: New and Selected Poems* (1996) and *A Hundred White Daffodils: Essays, Interviews, the Akhmatova Translations, Newspaper Columns, and One Poem* (1999). In 1998, on the third anniversary of Kenyon's death, Donald Hall published *Without: Poems*, a volume *Publishers Weekly* called "a heartbreaking portrait of a marriage that has not quite ended."

JAMAICA KINCAID (b. 1949)   Kincaid was born Elaine Potter Richardson in St. Johns, Antigua, in the West Indies, then a British colony. At age seventeen, she left home to become an au pair in New York. Determined to make something of her life, Kincaid took night classes and ultimately earned a high school diploma. She went on to take classes at the New School for Social Research in New York, and attended college in New Hampshire on a scholarship. When she returned to New York, she changed her name to Jamaica Kincaid and began writing. Of her life up to this point, Kincaid told a reporter: "Everyone thought I had a way with words, but it came out as a sharp tongue. No one expected anything from me at all. Had I just sunk in the cracks it would not have been noted. I would have been lucky to be a secretary somewhere." Her first publication, a collection of short stories titled *At the Bottom of the River* (1983), earned her wide critical praise and recognition as a new voice in American fiction. That was followed by three novels, including *The Autobiography of My Mother* (1995). *My Brother* (1997) deals with the death of her brother from AIDS. Her most recent novel is *See Now Then* (2013) and her most recent nonfiction work is *Among Flowers: A Walk in the Himalaya* (2005). The recipient of many literary honors, Kincaid served as a staff writer for the *New Yorker* (1976–95) and visiting professor at Harvard University. She is currently a professor of literature at Claremont McKenna College in California.

MAXINE HONG KINGSTON (b. 1940)   Kingston was born in Stockton, California. She earned a bachelor's degree from the University of California, Berkeley (1962), and a teaching certificate (1965). After teaching English and mathematics at a California high school, she moved to Hawaii and taught language arts and English as a second language at a number of schools. She became a visiting associate professor of English at the University of Hawaii after winning the National Book Critics Circle Award for *The Woman Warrior: Memoirs of a Girlhood among Ghosts* (1976). In that volume, she fashioned a new sort of genre—essays with substantial fictive elements. Her next book, *China Men* (1980), further developed that form and received the National Book Award for Nonfiction. Her most recent works include *To Be the Poet* (2002), *The Fifth Book of Peace* (2003), and *I Love a Broad Margin to My Life* (2011), a free-verse memoir informed by the wide page margins in the Chinese editions of her work. An early critic characterized Kingston's work as the blending of "myth, legend, history, and autobiography into a genre of her own invention." Another argued that though Kingston's works are classified as nonfiction, "in a deeper sense, they are fiction at its best— novels, fairy tales, epic poems." In 1993 Kingston founded the Veteran's Writing Group; she compiled and edited a collection of the group's writings in *Veterans of War, Veterans of Peace* (2006). In 2013 Kingston was awarded the National Medal of Arts.

GALWAY KINNELL (1927–2014)   Born in Providence, Rhode Island, Kinnell graduated summa cum laude from Princeton University, served in the navy during World War II, and returned to earn a master's degree from the University of Rochester. He traveled extensively and lectured in France and Iran before returning to the United States. In 1963 he was a fieldworker for the Congress of Racial Equality (CORE) and his involvement in the American civil rights movement informed what is perhaps his most famous collection of poetry, *Body Rags* (1968). Another of his prominent works, *The Book of Nightmares* (1971), is a book-length poem about the Vietnam War. He was the author of more than twenty additional volumes of poetry, the last one being *Strong Is Your Hold* (2006). Kinnell taught at a large number of institutions and earned numerous awards and honors including a MacArthur Fellowship and a Wallace Stevens Award. He served as chancellor of the Academy of American Poets from 2001 to 2007 before retiring to his home in Vermont, where he died at age eighty-seven.

CAROLYN KIZER (1925–2014) Kizer was born in Spokane, Washington. Her father was a lawyer, her mother a biologist and professor. After graduating from Sarah Lawrence College in 1945, Kizer pursued graduate study at Columbia University and the University of Washington. From 1959 to 1965, she was editor of *Poetry Northwest* (which she founded in 1959 in Seattle) and spent 1964 and 1965 as a State Department specialist in Pakistan, where she taught at a women's college and translated poems from Urdu into English. She chose to leave early, after the U.S. decision to bomb North Vietnam in 1965. Later, she joined archaeological tours in Afghanistan and Iran. She worked as director of literary programs for the National Endowment for the Arts in Washington, DC; taught at several universities; and was poet-in-residence at the University of North Carolina and Ohio University. Her volumes of poetry include *Yin* (1984), which won a Pulitzer Prize the following year; *Mermaids in the Basement: Poems for Women* (1984); *The Nearness of You* (1986); *Harping On: Poems 1985–1995* (1996); *Pro Femina: A Poem* (2000); and *Cool, Calm & Collected: Poems 1960–2000* (2001). She also published two collections of essays—*Proses: On Poems and Poets* (1993) and *Picking and Choosing: Essays on Prose* (1995)—and edited *100 Great Poems by Women: A Golden Ecco Anthology* (1995). Kizer's many awards and honors include the Frost Medal, the Theodore Roethke Memorial Poetry Award, three Pushcart Prizes, and an American Academy of Arts and Letters Award.

MARVIN KLOTZ (1930–2014) Born in New York City, Klotz earned a PhD from New York University and, in 1959, joined the faculty at what later became California State University, Northridge, where he taught for thirty-three years and won Northridge's distinguished teaching award in 1983. He also won two Fulbright professorships (in Vietnam and Iran) and was a National Endowment for the Arts Summer Fellow twice. Klotz was one of the original authors of this textbook. After retiring in 1992, he began writing verse about fractured neighborhoods and a bipolar world.

ETHERIDGE KNIGHT (1931–1991) Knight was born in Corinth, Mississippi, attended two years of public high school in Kentucky, and served in the U.S. Army from 1948 to 1951. After being convicted on a robbery charge and sentenced in 1960 to twenty years in Indiana State Prison, he discovered poetry; his first collection is entitled *Poems from Prison* (1968). Knight was paroled after eight years. From 1968 to 1971 he was poet-in-residence at several universities. An important African American voice in the 1960s and 1970s, Knight rejected the American and European aesthetic tradition, arguing that "the red of this esthetic rose got its color from the blood of black slaves, exterminated Indians, napalmed Vietnamese children." His collection *Belly Song and Other Poems* was nominated for the National Book Award and the Pulitzer Prize in 1973. His awards include National Endowment for the Arts and Guggenheim grants and the 1987 American Book Award for *The Essential Etheridge Knight* (1986).

YUSEF KOMUNYAKAA (b. 1947) Born and raised in Bogalusa, Louisiana, James Willie Brown Jr. later took the surname of his great grandparents who had come from Trinidad on a slave ship. His work often explores themes related to his life in the American South, the civil rights movement in America, and his tour of duty as a soldier during the Vietnam War. He began composing poetry even before he earned degrees from the University of Colorado, Colorado State University, and the University of California, Irvine. He taught at the University of New Orleans, Indiana University at Bloomington, and Princeton University before assuming his current role as a professor in the Creative Writing Program at New York University. He is the author of over a dozen books of poetry but gained attention for *Copacetic* (1984), *I Apologize for the Eyes in My Head* (1986), and *Dien Cai Dau* (1988). His most recent collection is *The Chameleon Couch: Poems* (2012), which was shortlisted for the 2012 International Griffin Poetry Prize. He is best known for *Neon Vernacular: New and Selected Poems* (1993), for which he won the Kingsley Tufts Poetry Award and a Pulitzer Prize. He also received the 2001 Ruth Lilly Poetry Prize, a prestigious honor given to living U.S. poets "whose lifetime accomplishments warrant extraordinary recognition." From 1999 to 2005, Komunyakaa served as chancellor of the American Academy of Poets.

PHILIP LARKIN (1922–1985)   Born in Coventry, Larkin attended St. John's College, Oxford University (BA, 1943; MA, 1947). He was appointed librarian at the University of Hull in 1955, wrote jazz feature articles for the London *Daily Telegraph* from 1961 to 1971, and won numerous poetry awards, including the Queens Gold Medal (1965) and the Benson Medal (1975). His first collection, *The North Ship* (1945), was not well received, but he gained recognition after publication of *The Less Deceived* (1960). Larkin once said, "Form holds little interest for me. Content is everything."

EVELYN LAU (b. 1971)   Lau was born in Vancouver, Canada, to Chinese Canadian parents. Driven by an unhappy family life, she ran away from home and wound up living on the streets of Vancouver working as a prostitute to support her drug addiction. During these turbulent early years, Lau kept a diary, and she published poems in Canadian and American journals even before she ran away. Throughout the years of living on the edge, during which she made a number of suicide attempts and was confined in a psychiatric ward, Lau continued to write. With the help of a sympathetic psychiatrist and her commitment to writing, she managed to pull herself out of the chaos and turn herself into a very successful professional writer. Her first published work was an autobiographical account of her early years, *Runaway: Diary of a Street Kid* (1989). An immediate success, it was filmed as *The Diary of Evelyn Lau* and aired on the Canadian Broadcasting Corporation in 1994. *Runaway* was followed by three volumes of poems, *You Are Not Who You Claim* (1990); *Oedipal Dreams*, nominated for the prestigious Governor General's Award for poetry (1993); and *In the House of Slaves* (1993). Lau is also the author of a novel, *Other Women* (1995), two collections of short stories, and a second memoir, *Inside Out: Reflections on a Life So Far* (2001). Her most recent poetry collections are *Treble* (2005), *Living Under Plastic* (2010), and *A Grain of Rice* (2012). Asked by an interviewer if she had acquired her "beautiful, clear" writing style in school, Lau replied, "Nope. All self-taught. In my teens I took some one-day writers' workshops and things like that. But I've never gone properly back to school."

EMMA LAZARUS (1849–1887)   American poet Emma Lazarus was born in New York City and is best known for her sonnet "The New Colossus" (1883), which appears on a plaque at the base of the Statue of Liberty and features the familiar lines "Give me your tired, your poor, / Your huddled masses yearning to breathe free." One of seven children in a well-established family, she was educated by private tutors and became part of the literary elite in late-nineteenth-century New York, capturing the attention of Ralph Waldo Emerson with her writing. One of the first successful Jewish American authors, she wrote poetry, plays, and a novel, and she edited German poems, including some by Johann Wolfgang von Goethe and Heinrich Heine. In the early 1880s, when anti-Semitic violence swept through Russia, thousands of Jews immigrated to New York. In response, Lazarus became an important activist on the refugees' behalf. She penned articles and a book on Jewish issues, organized relief efforts for the poor, and helped establish a vocational training institute for newcomers. An early advocate for the creation of a Jewish homeland, Lazarus died shortly after her second trip to Europe at the age of thirty-eight.

LI-YOUNG LEE (b. 1957)   Lee was born in Jakarta, Indonesia, to Chinese parents. While there, his father was imprisoned for his religious beliefs, and further anti-Chinese sentiment caused the entire family to flee the country. They traveled in exile for six years before finally settling in the United States. Lee earned a degree from the University of Pittsburgh and attended the University of Arizona and the State University of New York College at Brockport for brief periods. He began writing in earnest in college and is the author of four books of poetry: *Rose* (1986), *The City in Which I Love You* (1990), *Book of My Nights* (2001), and *Behind My Eyes* (2008). He also penned a memoir, *The Winged Seed: A Remembrance* (1995), in which he recounts his family's troubled history and his turbulent youth. Lee has received awards from the Lannan and Whiting Foundations, as well as fellowships from the Guggenheim Foundation and the National Endowment for the Arts.

JONATHAN LETHEM (b. 1964)   Born in Brooklyn, New York, Lethem attended Bennington College in Vermont, dropped out during sophomore year, hitchhiked across the country, and landed in California, where he worked as a clerk in a bookstore for over a decade. He published his first short story in 1989. A prolific writer of novels, short stories, and essays, Lethem's work straddles genres. A profile about Lethem in *Publishers Weekly* noted that his writing "exists somewhere in the previously uncharted interstices between science fiction, western, and coming-of-age novels." His notable novels include his first book, *Gun, with Occasional Music*, published in 1994; *Motherless Brooklyn* (1999), which won a National Book Critics Circle Award; and *The Fortress of Solitude* (2003), which was a *New York Times* best seller. His most recent publications include the collections *The Ecstasy of Influence: Nonfictions, Etc.* (2011) and *Wastelands: Stories of the Apocalypse* (2015), and the novel *Dissident Gardens* (2013). His work has appeared in numerous periodicals, among them *Entertainment Weekly*, *Esquire*, *GQ*, *Harper's*, the *New York Times*, the *New Yorker*, *Rolling Stone*, *Salon*, and the *Village Voice*. In 2010 he was named Disney Professor of Writing at Pomona College in Claremont, California.

PHILIP LEVINE (1928–2015)   The son of Russian Jewish immigrants, Levine was born in Detroit, Michigan, into a household where debates and discussions about radical politics instilled in him a political sensibility and an abiding sympathy for the poor and the powerless. After receiving his BA from Wayne State University (1950), he returned to Detroit and worked at various industrial jobs in the auto industry before enrolling in the University of Iowa in 1955, where he received his MFA (1957). He earned his living teaching poetry, primarily at California State University, Fresno, and Tufts University in Massachusetts. After his first collection of poems, *On the Edge* (1961), Levine published more than twenty volumes of poetry, many of them exhibiting his radical political consciousness. Among them are *Ashes* (1979) and *What Work Is* (1991), both of which received the National Book Award, and *The Simple Truth* (1995), for which he received the Pulitzer Prize. His most recent volumes of poetry are *Breath* (2004) and *News of the World* (2009). In 1997 Levine was elected to the American Academy of Arts and Letters. He summed up his aspirations as an artist by saying, "My hope is to write poetry for people for whom there are no poems." He served as 2011–12 poet laureate of the United States, and in 2013 he was awarded the Wallace Stevens Award from the Academy of American Poets.

SHIRLEY GEOK-LIN LIM (b. 1944)   Lim was born in Malacca, Malaysia, and received her PhD from Brandeis University in 1973. Lim's first collection of poems, *Crossing the Peninsula* (1980), won the Commonwealth Poetry Prize, a first both for an Asian author and a female author. She has written four other books of poetry; three books of short stories; a novel, *Joss and Gold* (2001); and two books of criticism: *Nationalism and Literature* (1993) and *Writing South/East Asia in English: Against the Grain* (1994). Her memoir *Among the White Moon Faces: An Asian-American Memoir of Homelands* (1996) received the 1997 American Book Award. She has edited and coedited several scholarly collections, including *The Forbidden Stitch: An Asian American Women's Anthology* (1989), *Power, Race, and Gender in Academe: Strangers in the Tower?* (1999), and *The Columbia Companion to the Twentieth-Century American Short Story* (2001). She has taught abroad at the National University of Singapore, NIE of Nanyang Technological University, and the University of Hong Kong, and she currently teaches English at the University of California, Santa Barbara.

SAM LIPSYTE (b. 1968)   Fiction writer Sam Lipsyte grew up in New Jersey and attended Brown University, where he received his BA in English. His most recent novel is *The Fun Parts* (2012). He is also the author of *The Ask* (2010) and *Home Land* (2004), both of which were named New York Times Notable Books. His first book, *Venus Drive* (2000), a collection of short stories, was named one of the Twenty-Five Best Books of the year by the *Village Voice Literary Supplement*. Known for his black humor and self-deprecating narrators, his fiction has appeared in the *New Yorker, Paris Review, Harper's*, and *McSweeney's*, among other publications. His essays and reviews have appeared in the *New York Times Book Review, Esquire, GQ*, and the *Washington Post Book World*. A 2008 Guggenheim Fellow, Lipsyte currently teaches at Columbia University's School of the Arts, where he also directs the undergraduate fiction program.

AUDRE LORDE (1934–1992)   Born to middle-class West Indian immigrant parents in New York City, Lorde grew up in Harlem and attended the National University of Mexico (1954), Hunter College (BA, 1959), and Columbia University (MLS, 1961). Her marriage in 1962, which produced two children, ended in divorce in 1970. During these early years, she worked as a librarian, but in 1968 her growing reputation as a writer led to her appointment as lecturer in creative writing at City College of New York. The following year, she was named lecturer in the education department at Herbert H. Lehman College. In 1970 she joined the English department at John Jay College of Criminal Justice, and in 1980 returned to Hunter College as professor of English. Besides teaching, Lorde raised a son and a daughter in an interracial lesbian relationship and was involved in political organizing of other black feminists and lesbians. In the early 1980s, Lorde helped to start Kitchen Table: Women of Color Press, and in 1991 she was named New York State Poet. Lorde is probably best known for her prose writings, among them two collections of essays, *Sister Outsider* (1984) and *Burst of Light* (1988), and the autobiographical *Zami: The Cancer Journals* (1980), a chronicle of her struggle with the breast cancer that ultimately claimed her life. Her poetry publications include *The First Cities* (1968), *The Black Unicorn* (1978), and *Undersong: Chosen Poems Old and New* (1993). Near the end of her life, Lorde made her home on St. Croix, U.S. Virgin Islands, and adopted the African name Gamba Adisa (Warrior—She Who Makes Her Meaning Known).

NAGUIB MAHFOUZ (1911–2006)   Egyptian writer Mahfouz was born and raised in Cairo in a devout Muslim family. Watching from his window as a child, he witnessed British soldiers firing on demonstrators during the Egyptian Revolution of 1919, an event he says had a profound effect on him. He received a BA (1934) in philosophy from what is now Cairo University, and he immediately began working as a civil servant. Although he began writing at a young age, he maintained various positions in the Egyptian civil service until he retired in 1971. His first novel, *Khufu's Wisdom* (1939), began his long and prolific writing career, in which he produced more than thirty-five novels, hundreds of short stories (collected in fifteen volumes), dozens of movie scripts, and five plays. He also produced a weekly newspaper column for over three decades and wrote *Echoes of an Autobiography* in 1994. In 1988 he became the only Arab writer to win the Nobel Prize in Literature, bringing him international fame and introducing his many works to the Western world. Mahfouz's earliest books were mainly historical fiction set in ancient Egypt, but after World War II, he began focusing more on the impact of society on the lives of individuals. One of his most famous works from this period, *The Cairo Trilogy* (1956, 1957), centers around the lives of three generations of fictional families in Cairo from World War I until the overthrow of King Farouk in 1952. His fiction tackles a broad range of topics, some of which were banned in Egypt, such as socialism, homosexuality, and religion. His works and political views also rattled some Islamic fundamentalists, who called for Mahfouz's death. In a 1994 assassination attempt, Mahfouz was stabbed in the neck by an Islamic militant, an event that caused nerve damage to his right arm, greatly hindering his ability to write for the remainder of his life. Widely praised around the world for his contributions to literature, Mahfouz was elected to the American Academy of Arts and Sciences in 2002.

RUTH MARGALIT (b. 1983)   Margalit is an Israeli writer living in New York. Her writing has appeared in the *New Yorker, Slate, Tablet, Bookforum*, and *Haaretz*, where she was a staff writer, among other publications. Her fiction was included in the anthology *Tel Aviv Short Stories*, and her poetry in *Maayan Magazine* (in Hebrew). A graduate of the Columbia Journalism School and of Tel Aviv University, Margalit works on the editorial staff of the *New Yorker*.

ANDREW MARVELL (1621–1678)   Born in Yorkshire and educated at Cambridge University, Marvell received an inheritance on his father's death that allowed him to spend four years traveling the Continent. Though not a Puritan himself, Marvell supported the Puritans' cause during the English Civil War and held a number of posts during the Puritan regime, including that of assistant to the blind John Milton, Oliver Cromwell's Latin secretary. In 1659, a year before the Restoration, Marvell was elected to Parliament, where he served until his death. Soon after the Restoration, Marvell expressed strong disagreements with the government in a series of outspoken and anonymously printed satires. It was for these satires, rather than for his many love poems, that he was primarily known in his own day.

CLAUDE McKAY (1890–1948)   Born in Sunny Ville, Jamaica, McKay had already completed two volumes of poetry before coming to the United States in 1912 at the age of twenty-three (the two volumes earned him awards, which paid his way). The racism he encountered as a black immigrant brought a militant tone to his writing. His popular poem "If We Must Die" (1919) helped to initiate the Harlem Renaissance of the 1920s. Between 1922 and 1934 he lived in Great Britain, Russia, Germany, France, Spain, and Morocco. His writings include four volumes of poems, many essays, the autobiography *A Long Way from Home* (1937), the novel *Home to Harlem* (1928), and a sociological study of Harlem. His conversion to Roman Catholicism in the 1940s struck his audience as an ideological retreat. McKay wrote in a letter to a friend: "[T]o have a religion is very much like falling in love with a woman. You love her for her . . . beauty, which cannot be defined."

BILL McKIBBEN (b. 1960)   Born and raised in the Boston suburb of Lexington, Massachusetts, McKibben attended Harvard University and served as editor of its student newspaper. After graduating from college, he worked as a staff writer for the *New Yorker* for five years before becoming a freelance writer. His debut publication, *The End of Nature* (1989), is regarded as the first book for a general audience about climate change, and has appeared in twenty-four languages. He has since written more than ten books about environmental issues, most recently *Deep Economy: The Wealth of Communities and the Durable Future* (2007), *Eaarth: Making a Life on a Tough New Planet* (2010), and *Oil and Honey: The Education of an Unlikely Activist* (2013). The Schumann Distinguished Scholar in Environmental Studies at Middlebury College and a fellow of the American Academy of Arts and Sciences, he has received numerous awards and honors, including a Guggenheim Fellowship and a Gandhi Peace Award. Called "probably America's most important environmentalist" by the *Boston Globe* and one of the world's 100 most important global thinkers by *Foreign Policy*, he was arrested and jailed in Washington, DC, in 2011 for protesting the proposed Keystone XL pipeline project. He writes frequently for a wide variety of publications around the world, including the *New York Review of Books*, *National Geographic*, and *Rolling Stone*.

PETER MEINKE (b. 1932) Born in Brooklyn, New York, the son of a salesman, Meinke served in the U.S. Army from 1955 to 1957, attended Hamilton College (BA, 1955) and the University of Michigan (MA, 1961), and earned his PhD at the University of Minnesota (1965). He taught English at a New Jersey high school, Hamline University, Presbyterian College (now Eckerd College), and Old Dominion University, where he held the Darden Chair in Creative Writing. His reviews, poems, and stories have appeared in periodicals such as the *Atlantic*, the *New Yorker*, and the *New Republic*. The latest of his published books include *Zinc Fingers: Poems A to Z* (2000), *The Contracted World: New & More Selected Poems* (2006), *Unheard Music: Stories* (2007), and the poetry collection *Lucky Bones* (2014). His collection of stories, *The Piano Tuner*, won the 1986 Flannery O'Connor Award. He has also been the recipient of a National Endowment for the Arts Fellowship in poetry.

HERMAN MELVILLE (1819–1891) The death of his merchant father when Melville was twelve shattered the economic security of his family. The financial panic of 1837 reduced the Melvilles to the edge of poverty, and at age nineteen, Melville went to sea. Economic conditions on his return were still grim, and after a frustrating stint as a country schoolteacher, he again went to sea—this time on a four-year whaling voyage. He deserted the whaler in the South Pacific, lived for some time with cannibals, made his way to Tahiti and Hawaii, and finally joined the navy for a return voyage. He mined his experiences for two successful South Sea adventure books, *Typee* (1846) and *Omoo* (1847). On the strength of these successes he married, but his next novel, *Mardi* (1849), was too heavy-handed an allegory to succeed. Driven by the obligation to support his growing family, Melville returned to sea-adventure stories, with moderate success. But neither his masterpiece, *Moby-Dick* (1851), nor his subsequent short stories and novels found much of an audience, and in 1886 he accepted an appointment as customs inspector in Manhattan, a job he held until retirement. He continued to write, mostly poetry, and lived to see himself forgotten as an author. *Billy Budd*, found among his papers after his death and published in 1924, led to a revival of interest in Melville, now recognized as one of America's greatest writers.

W. S. MERWIN (b. 1927) Merwin was born in New York City and raised in Union City, New Jersey, and Scranton, Pennsylvania. His parents' lives had a profound impact on Merwin's writing: His mother was an orphan who lost her brother and her first child, and his father—a Presbyterian minister—had grown up in a home plagued by domestic violence. Anger, inherited violence, and the poverty that can be bred by such conditions became prominent themes in Merwin's poetry. He attended Princeton University on a scholarship and, after graduating in 1948, spent an additional year there studying Romance language—the origin of his later work as a prolific translator of Spanish, Latin, and French poetry. After college, Merwin married his first wife, Dorothy Jeanne Ferry, and moved to Majorca to tutor the children of wealthy families. There he met Dido Milroy and collaborated with her on a play; they eventually married and moved to London. The couple moved to Boston in 1956 so Merwin could serve as playwright-in-residence at the Poet's Theatre in Cambridge, Massachusetts, but soon returned to Europe. They met and became close friends with Sylvia Plath and Ted Hughes, witnessing the brutal collapse of the couple's marriage and Plath's eventual suicide. In 1968 Merwin moved to New York City and separated from Milroy, who stayed at their home in France. In the late 1970s, Merwin moved to Hawaii and eventually divorced Milroy, marrying Paula Schwartz in 1983. Throughout his lengthy career, Merwin has published over twenty books of poetry, most notably *The Carrier of Ladders* (1971), which won the 1971 Pulitzer Prize for Poetry; *Travels* (1993), which received the Lenore Marshall Poetry Prize; *The River Sound* (1999), a New York Times Notable Book of the Year; *Migration: New & Selected Poems* (2005), which won the 2005 National Book Award; and *The Shadow of Sirius* (2008), which won the Pulitzer Prize for Poetry in 2009. Among Merwin's copious literary awards and honors are fellowships from the Academy of American Poets, the Guggenheim Foundation, the National Endowment for the Arts, and the Rockefeller Foundation. In 2010 the Library of Congress named Merwin the seventeenth U.S. poet laureate. His *Selected Translations* (2013) won the 2014 Harold Morton Landon Translation Award from the Academy of American Poets. His most recent collection of poetry is *The Moon Before Morning* (2014). Merwin currently lives on a former pineapple plantation built atop a dormant volcano in Maui, Hawaii.

ROBERT MEZEY (b. 1935)   Born in Philadelphia, Mezey attended Kenyon College and served a troubled hitch in the U.S. Army before earning his BA from the University of Iowa in 1959. He worked as a probation officer, advertising copywriter, and social worker; did graduate study at Stanford University; and began teaching English at Case Western Reserve University in 1963. After a year as poet-in-residence at Franklin and Marshall College, he joined the English department of California State University, Fresno, spent three years at the University of Utah, and settled in 1976 at Pomona College in Claremont, California. Mezey won the Lamont Award for *The Lovemaker* in 1960 and has published many other poetry collections. In addition, he coedited *Naked Poetry* (1969) and was one of several translators for *Poems from the Hebrew* (1973). His recent work includes *Collected Poems: 1952–1999* (2000), for which he was awarded the 2002 Poet's Prize.

EDNA ST. VINCENT MILLAY (1892–1950)   Born in Rockland, Maine, in 1892, Edna St. Vincent Millay was raised by her divorced mother who imbued a strong cultural and literary sensibility in her children. At age nineteen, Millay won a literary contest for her poem "Renascence," which attracted the attention of a wealthy benefactor who paid for her education at Vassar College. Following her 1917 graduation, Millay emerged as a major figure in the cultural life of Greenwich Village, which at the time served as an incubator of important American literary, artistic, and political movements. As part of this milieu, Millay's work and life came to represent the modern, liberated woman of the Jazz Age. Although she was married for over twenty-five years, Millay was openly bisexual, and both she and her husband carried on extramarital affairs. Her first published work, *Renascence, and Other Poems* (1917), was followed by *A Few Figs from Thistles: Poems and Sonnets* (1920), which was considered controversial for its feminist themes and its exploration of female sexuality. In 1921 she published two dramatic works: *The Lamp and the Bell,* about love between women, and the pacifist play *Aria da Capo*. Her 1922 book, *The Harp-Weaver, and Other Poems*, won the Pulitzer Prize. Subsequent publications by Millay include *The Buck in the Snow, and Other Poems* (1928), *Fatal Interview* (1931), *Wine from These Grapes* (1934), *There Are No Islands, Any More: Lines Written in Passion and in Deep Concern for England, France, and My Own Country* (1940), *Make Bright the Arrows: 1940 Notebook* (1940), and *The Murder of Lidice* (1942). In 1943 Millay was awarded the Frost Medal for her lifetime contribution to American poetry.

LYDIA MILLET (b. 1969)   Millet was born in Boston, Massachusetts, and raised in Toronto. She received her BA in creative writing from the University of North Carolina at Chapel Hill and her MA in environmental policy from Duke University. Her short story collection *Love in Infant Monkeys* (2009) was a finalist for the Pulitzer Prize. She has also written nine novels: *Omnivores* (1996); *George Bush: Dark Prince of Love* (2000); *My Happy Life* (2002), the 2003 winner of the PEN/USA Award for Fiction; *Everyone's Pretty* (2005); *Oh Pure and Radiant Heart* (2005); the trilogy *How the Dead Dream* (2008), *Ghost Lights* (2011), and *Magnificence* (2012), which was a finalist for the National Book Critics Circle Award and the Los Angeles Times Book Prize; and her most recent novel, *Mermaids in Paradise* (2014). Millet has also written several young adult novels including the Dissenters series books *The Fires Beneath the Sea* (2011) and *The Shimmers in the Night* (2012), as well as *Pills and Starships* (2014). She received a Guggenheim Fellowship in 2012 and currently works as a staff writer at the Center for Biological Diversity in Tucson.

CZESŁAW MIŁOSZ (1911–2004)   Born in a Lithuanian-Polish province in pre-revolutionary Russia, Milosz began writing poetry and became active in leftist politics while studying law at the University of Vilnius. He began producing poetry in the 1930s, although much of it would be banned from publication in his home country for half a century. During World War II, he worked as a writer and translator for the Polish resistance, and he helped support Jews seeking to evade Nazi persecution. After the war he became a diplomat for Poland's new communist government, but he soon found the repressiveness of Stalin's Soviet regime to be too restrictive for his writing. He defected to the West in 1951, moving to the United States in 1960. His best-known work of nonfiction, *The Captive Mind* (1953), grew out of his experience of living under totalitarianism and explains why he defected. It begins with the sentence, "Like many of my generation, I could have wished that my life had been a more simple affair." In 1961 Milosz became a professor of Slavic languages and literature at the University of California, Berkeley, where he taught until 1998. In 1980 he received the Nobel Prize in Literature, earning him some fame in his home country where his work had been banned, and many had never heard of him. Some of the most notable collections among his many volumes of poetry and prose include *The World* (1953, trans. 1989), a sequence of twenty "naïve" poems composed in an intentionally rudimentary style during World War II, and *Legends of Modernity: Essays and Letters from Occupied Poland 1942–1943* (1996, trans. 2005). Milosz was awarded the U.S. National Medal of Arts in 1989.

LISEL MUELLER (b. 1924)   Born in Hamburg, Germany, to parents who were both teachers, Mueller moved to the United States in 1939 and became a citizen in 1945. Shortly before earning a BA from the University of Evansville (1944), she married. Later, she bore two children, pursued graduate studies at Indiana University, and held a number of positions, among them receptionist, caseworker, and library assistant. She served as an instructor in poetry writing at Elmhurst College (1969–72) and later as an instructor in the MFA

Writing Program at Goddard College, Vermont. She has received numerous awards, including the Robert M. Ferguson Memorial Award for her first book of poems, *Dependencies* (1965), the Pulitzer Prize for Poetry (1997) for *Alive Together: New and Selected Poems*, and a National Book Award for *The Need to Hold Still* (1980). Commenting on the nature of her verse in *The Private Life* (1976), one critic noted that "she goes after our secrets, this poet; often she finds them." In 2002 Mueller was awarded the Ruth Lilly Poetry Prize, a prestigious honor given to living U.S. poets "whose lifetime accomplishments warrant extraordinary recognition."

BHARATI MUKHERJEE (b. 1940) Born in Calcutta, India, Mukherjee attended the University of Calcutta (BA, 1959), the University of Baroda (MA, 1961), and the University of Iowa, where she earned an MFA (1963) and a PhD (1969). In 1963 she married Clark Blaise, a Canadian writer and professor, and joined the faculty at McGill University in Montreal. In 1973 Mukherjee and her husband visited India and kept separate diaries of the trip, published as *Days and Nights in Calcutta* (1977). The diaries reveal marked differences in their responses: Mukherjee found her home environs, especially the status of women, worse than she remembered, while Blaise, after an initial revulsion at the squalor and poverty, found India a fascinating and attractive culture compared to the West. Mukherjee "left Canada after fifteen years due to the persistent effects of racial prejudice against people of my national origin." Her fiction frequently explores the tensions inevitable in intercultural relationships. Her first novel, *The Tiger's Daughter* (1972), deals with the disappointment of an expatriate's return to India. In her second novel, *Wife* (1975), a psychologically abused woman finally kills her husband. *The Middleman and Other Stories* (1988) won the National Book Critics Circle Award. *Desirable Daughters* (2003) and *The Tree Bride* (2004) are the first two novels in a projected trilogy dealing with Indian expatriates in America. Mukherjee currently teaches at the University of California, Berkeley.

TASLIMA NASRIN (b. 1962) Born and educated in Mymensingh, Bangladesh, Nasrin began writing poetry in her childhood, her earliest works appearing in a literary journal edited by her eldest brother. Following in the footsteps of her father, a doctor, she earned a degree in medicine from Mymensingh Medical College and for a few years practiced as a government doctor. Her study of modern science, Nasrin has written, "made me a rationalist." While practicing medicine, she continued her writing, publishing poems and novels. These works, along with the essays she penned as a syndicated columnist in Bangladesh, earned her a number of important literary prizes in 1992 and 1993. However, her rationalism and her feminism, as well as her 1993 novel *Shame*, enraged Islamic fundamentalists. Forced into hiding by death threats, Nasrin fled to Europe in 1994; she returned to India in 2007 only to flee again after facing further threats and physical violence. She entered India once again in 2008 and lives in hiding under tight security. Nasrin has won several humanitarian awards, among them the UNESCO-Madanjeet Singh Prize in 2004 for the promotion of tolerance and nonviolence and the Simone de Beauvoir feminist award in 2008 in recognition of her writing on women's rights. In an essay titled "Women's Rights," Nasrin writes, "My poetry, my prose, my entire output expresses the deprivation of women who have been exploited for centuries." She has written a multivolume autobiography which includes *Meyebela, My Bengali Girlhood: A Memoir of Growing Up Female in a Muslim World* (2002); *Ka* (*Speak Up*, 2003), which was banned in Bangladesh; *Nei, Kichu Nei* (*Nothing Is There*, 2010); and *Nirbasan* (*Exile*, 2012). Among her other publications are an essay collection, *Narir Kono Desh Nei* (*A Woman Has No Country*, 2007), and several volumes of poetry, most recently *Bondini* (*Prisoner*, 2008).

MAGGIE NELSON (b. 1973)   Nelson has taught in the CalArts MFA writing program since 2005. Before then, she lived in New York City where she received her PhD from the Graduate Center of the City University of New York and taught literature and writing at the Pratt Institute of Art and the New School Graduate Writing Program, among other places. Her essays and reviews have appeared in many publications, including the *New York Times Book Review, Artforum, Bookforum,* and *Cabinet.* She has written several books of poetry, including *Shiner* (2001), *The Latest Winter* (2003), *Jane: A Murder* (2005), and *Something Bright, Then Holes* (2007). She has also published several books of nonfiction including *The Red Parts: A Memoir* (2007), an "autobiographical book about sexual violence and media spectacle"; *Women, the New York School, and Other True Abstractions* (2007), a critical study of poetry and painting that won the Susanne M. Glasscock Award for Interdisciplinary Scholarship; *Bluets* (2009), a reflection on the color blue; and *The Art of Cruelty: A Reckoning* (2011). Her latest book is *The Argonauts* (2015), "a work of 'autotheory' about gender, sexuality, sodomitical maternity, queer family, and the limitations and possibilities of language." Most recently, Nelson has been awarded a 2010 Guggenheim Fellowship in Nonfiction, a 2011 National Endowment for the Arts Grant in Poetry, and a 2013 Innovative Literature grant from Creative Capital.

HOWARD NEMEROV (1920–1991)   Born to well-off Russian Jewish immigrants in New York City, Nemerov was raised in a culturally sophisticated atmosphere and was drawn to the arts at a young age. He received his bachelor's degree from Harvard University (1941), served as a pilot in World War II, and published his first book, the poetry collection *The Image of the Law,* in 1947. He taught at several small colleges in the Northeast before becoming professor of English and Distinguished Poet in Residence at Washington University in St. Louis in 1969. Nemerov published numerous additional collections of poetry, including *The Salt Garden* (1955), *Mirrors and Windows* (1958), and *The Winter Lightning: Selected Poems* (1968). His 1977 publication, *The Collected Poems of Howard Nemerov,* won the Pulitzer Prize, the National Book Award, and the Bollingen Prize. *Trying Conclusions: New and Selected Poems, 1961–1991* (1991) was published the year he died. His well-received novels include *The Melodramatists* (1949), *Federigo: Or the Power of Love* (1954), and *The Homecoming Game* (1957). Of Nemerov, author Joyce Carol Oates wrote, "Romantic, realist, comedian, satirist, relentless and indefatigable brooder upon the most ancient mysteries—Nemerov is not to be classified." His many awards and honors include fellowships from the Academy of American Poets and the Guggenheim Foundation, a National Endowment for the Arts grant, and the National Medal of Arts. He served as poet laureate of the United States from 1988 to 1990, and as chancellor of the American Academy of Poets from 1976 to 1991.

PABLO NERUDA (1904–1973)   Neruda was born in Parral, Chile, the son of a railroad worker. Shortly after leaving college, he joined the Chilean foreign service to begin a distinguished career as consul and ambassador at a variety of posts around the world, including Burma, Ceylon, Indonesia, Siam, Cambodia, Spain, France, and Mexico. He was elected to the Chilean senate as a communist. But when he published letters attacking the policies of Gabriel González Videla, the president of Chile, he was forced into exile. He returned to Chile after the victory of anti-Videla forces and rejoined the foreign service. His vast literary output won many prizes and honors. And, although American readers found it difficult to separate his poetry from his politics, he was, at his prime, generally considered to be the greatest poet writing in Spanish. One critic pointed out that Neruda "never bothered his head about the state of poetry. He has just gone on exuding it as he draws breath." In an essay on impure poetry, Neruda wrote: "Let [this] be the poetry we search for: worn with the hand's obligations, as by acids, steeped in sweat and in smoke, smelling of lilies and urine, spattered diversely by the trades that we love by, inside the law or beyond it. A poetry impure as the clothing we wear, or our bodies, soup-stained, soiled with our shameful behavior, our wrinkles and vigils and dreams, observations and prophecies, declarations of loathing and love, idylls and beasts, the shocks of encounter, political loyalties, denials and doubts, affirmation and taxes." *Five Decades, a Selection: Poems, 1925–1970* appeared in 1974. He was awarded the Nobel Prize in Literature in 1971.

JOHN FREDERICK NIMS (1913–1999)   Nims was born in Muskegon, Michigan, and earned degrees from De Paul University, the University of Notre Dame, and the University of Chicago. He taught at a number of institutions, including the University of Toronto, the University of Illinois, Urbana, Harvard University, and Williams College. He wrote two works of nonfiction, *Western Wind: An Introduction to Poetry* (1974) and *A Local Habitation: Essays on Poetry* (1985). In addition to serving as the editor of *Poetry* magazine from 1978 to 1984, Nims was a talented poet in his own right. He was the author of more than eight collections of poems, including *The Iron Pastoral* (1947), *Of Flesh and Bone* (1967), *The Kiss: A Jambalaya* (1982), and *The Six-Cornered Snowflake* (1990). He was also known as an astute translator, publishing translations of the poetry of Sappho and St. John of the Cross, as well as *Andromache*, a Greek tragedy. His work appeared in a number of periodicals, such as *American Scholar, Atlantic, Harper's, Kenyon Review, Mademoiselle*, and *New Republic*. Among Nims's many awards were fellowships from the Academy of American Poets, the Guggenheim Foundation, and the University of Illinois Institute of the Humanities, as well as grants from the American Academy of Arts and Letters and the National Foundation for the Arts and Humanities.

JEAN NORDHAUS (b. 1939)   Nordhaus earned her BA in philosophy from Barnard College and her PhD in German literature from Yale University. Her work includes a poetry chapbook, *A Language of Hands* (1982), as well as the full-length collections *A Bracelet of Lies* (1987), *My Life in Hiding* (1991), and *The Porcelain Apes of Moses Mendelssohn* (2002), and her latest work, *Innocence* (2006). Nordhaus's poetry has appeared in *The American Poetry Review, Hudson Review, Poetry, Prairie Schooner, Washington Review*, and *West Branch*, and was included in *The Best American Poetry* for 2000. She has served as coordinator for the Folger Shakespeare Library's poetry programs and as president of Washington Writers' Publishing House. She has also taught at the Writer's Center in Bethesda, Maryland. She lives in Washington, DC.

LYNN NOTTAGE (b. 1964)   Nottage was born in Brooklyn, New York. She attended New York's High School of Music and Art and went on to graduate from Brown University and the Yale School of Drama. The MacArthur Foundation, which honored Nottage with a fellowship in 2007, called her "an original voice in American theater, a playwright whose entertaining and thought-provoking works address contemporary issues with empathy and humor." Nottage's plays include *Poof!* (1993), which won the Heideman Award; *Por'Knockers* (1994); *Crumbs from the Table of Joy* (1995); *Mud, River, Stone* (1998), a Blackburn Prize finalist; *Las Meninas* (2002); *Intimate Apparel* (2003), which won New York Drama Critics Circle awards, the 2004 Francesca Primus Prize, and the American Steinberg Theatre Critics New Play Award; *Fabulation, or the Re-Education of Undine* (2004); and *Ruined* (2008), which won the Pulitzer Prize for Drama in 2009. Other honors include a 2005 Guggenheim Fellowship, an OBIE Award for playwriting, two AUDELCO awards, and the 2010 Steinberg Distinguished Playwright Award. Her most recent plays are *By the Way, Meet Vera Stark* (2011) and *Sweat* (2015). Her plays have been produced throughout the United States and Europe at such venues as the Second Stage Theatre in New York, the Tricycle Theatre in London, and the Steppenwolf Theatre in Chicago, among many others. Nottage is currently a visiting lecturer at the Yale School of Drama.

JOYCE CAROL OATES (b. 1938)   Born in Lockport, New York, Oates majored in English at Syracuse University (BA, 1960) as a scholarship student and earned an MA in English (1961) from the University of Wisconsin. While still an undergraduate, she won the *Mademoiselle* college fiction award (1959), beginning an enormously prolific career as a writer and editor. She publishes an average of two books a year, to date well over fifty volumes including novels, short story collections, poetry, drama, and critical essays. Her numerous awards and honors include the 1970 fiction National Book Award for her novel *Them* (1969). She has also won two O. Henry Awards, the National Humanities Medal, a Norman Mailer Prize for Lifetime Achievement, and multiple Pulitzer Prize nominations. She taught at the universities of Detroit and Windsor (Canada) before joining the faculty at Princeton University. Among her many recent publications are the short story collection *Lovely, Dark, Deep* (2014), the memoir *A Widow's Story* (2012), and the novels *The Accursed* (2013), *Carthage* (2014), and *The Sacrifice* (2015). Oates retired from full-time teaching in 2015.

TIM O'BRIEN (b. 1946)   O'Brien was born in Austin, Minnesota, attended public schools, and received a BA summa cum laude from Macalester College. Immediately following graduation, he was drafted into the U.S. Army (1968–70), earning a Purple Heart. On his return to civilian life, he pursued graduate work at Harvard University and worked as a national affairs reporter for the *Washington Post*. His first novel, *If I Die in a Combat Zone, Box Me Up and Ship Me Home* (1973), is a semi-fictionalized account of his own Vietnam experiences. Many of O'Brien's novels either are set in Vietnam or focus on characters haunted by the war: *Northern Lights* (1975); *Going After Cacciato* (1978), which won a National Book Award; *The Nuclear Age* (1985); *The Things They Carried* (1990); and *In the Lake of the Woods* (1994). In an interview, O'Brien explained that his preoccupation with the Vietnam War was part of his need to write with "passion." Writing "good" stories, he went on to say, "requires a sense of passion, and my passion as a human being and as a writer intersect in Vietnam, not in the physical stuff but in the issues of Vietnam—of courage, rectitude, enlightenment, holiness, trying to do the right thing in the world." O'Brien wrote a comic novel, *Tomcat in Love* (1998), about a womanizing professor's midlife crisis, before returning to his earlier themes in his most recent book, *July, July* (2002). He has received several literary awards and fellowships from institutions including the American Academy of Arts and Letters, the Guggenheim Foundation, the National Endowment for the Arts, and the Dayton Literary Peace Prize Foundation. O'Brien is currently professor of creative writing at Texas State University in Austin.

FLANNERY O'CONNOR (1925–1964)   O'Connor, afflicted with lupus erythematosus, spent most of her short life in Milledgeville, Georgia. She began writing while a student at Georgia State College for Women in her hometown, and in 1947 earned an MFA from the University of Iowa. Back in Milledgeville, she lived on a farm with her mother, raised peacocks, and endured constant treatment for her progressive and incurable disease. She traveled and lectured when she could. She wrote two novels, *Wise Blood* (1952) and *The Violent*

Bear It Away (1960), and two collections of stories, *A Good Man Is Hard to Find* (1955) and *Everything That Rises Must Converge* (1965).

FRANK O'HARA (1926–1966)   Born in Baltimore, Maryland, O'Hara was raised in Massachusetts and from 1941 to 1944 studied piano at the New England Conservatory in Boston. Shortly after graduating from high school, O'Hara enlisted in the U.S. Navy and served as a sonarman on the USS *Nicholas*. After receiving an honorable discharge in 1946 he enrolled at Harvard University, where he met fellow poet John Ashbery. O'Hara soon began publishing poems in the *Harvard Advocate* and earned his BA in English in 1950. Thanks to a recommendation from his teacher John Ciardi, O'Hara received a graduate fellowship in comparative literature at the University of Michigan. He earned his MA there in 1951 and published his first collection of poems, *A City in Winter*, the following year. O'Hara then went with Ashbery to New York and became a renowned member of the New York School of poets, which included such authors as Ashbery, James Schuyler, Kenneth Koch, and Barbara Guest. O'Hara's poetry was widely praised for its refreshing originality and playful informality. His poems often recounted everyday activities—frequently from around his beloved New York—in conversational tones (O'Hara referred to these as "I do this, I do that" poems). He sought to capture the immediacy and joy of life in the city in the same way that other poets sought to capture the beauty of nature. In his poem "Meditations in an Emergency," O'Hara wrote, "One need never leave the confines of New York to get all the greenery one wishes—I can't even enjoy a blade of grass unless I know there's a subway handy, or a record store or some other sign that people do not totally *regret* life." He published several volumes of poetry, including *Meditations in an Emergency* (1956), *Lunch Poems* (1964), and *Love Poems (Tentative Title)* (1965). In 1966 his life was cut short in a sand buggy accident on Fire Island. Further volumes of O'Hara's poems were published after his death, most notably *The Collected Poems of Frank O'Hara* (1971), *The Selected Poems of Frank O'Hara* (1974), and *Poems Retrieved: 1950–1966* (1977).

SHARON OLDS (b. 1942)   Born in San Francisco, Olds attended Stanford University (BA, 1964) and Columbia University (PhD, 1972). She joined the faculty of Theodor Herzl Institute in 1976 and has given readings at many colleges. She currently teaches at the Graduate Creative Writing Program at New York University. She won the Madeline Sadin Award from the *New York Quarterly* in 1978 for "The Death of Marilyn Monroe." Often compared to confessional poets Sylvia Plath and Anne Sexton, Olds published her first collection, *Satan Says*, in 1980, and won both the National Book Critics' Circle Award and the Lamont Award for *The Dead and the Living* in 1983. She was poet laureate of New York State from 1998 to 2000 and has received numerous awards including Guggenheim and National Endowment for the Arts Fellowships. Her recent volumes of poetry include *The Unswept Room* (2002), *Strike Sparks: Selected Poems, 1980–2002* (2004), and *One Secret Thing* (2008). For her most recent work, *Stag's Leap* (2012), which explores the details of her divorce after thirty-two years of marriage, Olds won the Pulitzer Prize and became the first American woman to win Britain's T. S. Eliot Prize.

MARY OLIVER (b. 1935)   Mary Oliver was born in Cleveland, Ohio. She spent one year at Ohio State University and a second year at Vassar. Her distinctive poetic talent led to an appointment as the chair of the writing department of the Fine Arts Workshop in Provincetown, Massachusetts (1972–73). Though she never graduated from college, she was awarded the Mather Visiting Professorship at Case Western Reserve University for 1980 and 1982, and among her many awards and honors, she received a National Endowment for the

Arts Fellowship (1972–73) and a Guggenheim Fellowship (1980–81). The first of her several volumes of poems, *No Voyage and Other Poems*, appeared in 1963. Other books include *New and Selected Poems* (1992), *A Poetry Handbook* (1995), and *Blue Pastures* (1995), a collection of prose nature writing. Her most recent volumes are the *New York Times* best-selling collection *Dog Songs* (2013), *A Thousand Mornings* (2013), and *Blue Horses* (2014).

DANIEL OROZCO (b. 1942) Orozco earned his BA from Stanford University and his MFA from the University of Washington. His work has appeared in *Harper's Magazine*, *McSweeney's*, *Zoetrope: All Story*, and other literary magazines, and has been anthologized in *Best American Essays*, *Best American Mystery Stories*, and *Best American Short Stories*. He was also awarded a Pushcart Prize for his story "The Bridge," wherein a rookie bridge painter is awakened from the monotony of his everyday routine by a face-to-face encounter with a woman who has just jumped. "The Bridge" is included in Orozco's collection *Orientation and Other Stories* (2011), which was named a Best of 2011 Short Story Collection by *Kirkus Reviews*. Fellow author Yiyun Lee has said that Orozco "has both the relentlessness and the compassion of a truly great writer." Orozco currently teaches in the Creative Writing Program at the University of Idaho. He was a recipient of the Whiting Award in 2011.

GEORGE ORWELL (1903–1950) Born Eric Blair in India, the son of a minor British colonial officer, Orwell was raised in England. His education at good grammar schools, culminating with a stay at Eton College, introduced him to what he later called the snobbish world of England's middle and upper classes. Denied a university scholarship, he joined the Indian Imperial Police in 1922 and served in Burma until he resigned in 1927, disgusted with the injustice of British imperialism in India and Burma. He was determined to be a writer and, living at the edge of poverty, deliberately mingled with social outcasts and impoverished laborers. These experiences produced *Down and Out in Paris and London* (1933). Although he was a socialist, his experiences while fighting alongside the leftists during the Spanish Civil War disillusioned him, and he embodied his distaste for any totalitarian system in *Animal Farm* (1945)—a satirical attack on the leadership of the Soviet Union. In his pessimistic novel *1984* (1949), he imagined a social order shaped by a propagandistic perversion of language, in which the government, an extension of "Big Brother," uses two-way television to control the citizenry. Orwell succumbed to tuberculosis at the age of forty-seven, but not before he produced six novels, three documentary works, over 700 newspaper articles and reviews, and a volume of essays.

ALICIA OSTRIKER (b. 1937) Ostriker is a professor emerita of Rutgers University and a faculty member of the New England College Low-Residency Poetry MFA Program. A major American poet and critic for decades, her poems have appeared in the *New Yorker*, *Paris Review*, *Antaeus*, *Nation*, *Poetry*, *American Poetry Review*, *Kenyon Review*, *Atlantic*, *MS*, *Tikkun*, and many other literary journals, and have been translated into French, German, Italian, Chinese, Japanese, Hebrew, and Arabic. She has lectured and given performances of her work throughout the United States as well as in Europe, Australia, Israel, Japan, and China. In recognition of her tremendous contribution to the world of poetry, Ostriker has received awards from the National Endowment for the Arts, the Poetry Society of America, the San Francisco State Poetry Center, the Judah Magnes Museum, the New Jersey Arts Council, the Rockefeller Foundation, and the Guggenheim Foundation. She has written twelve volumes of poetry, most recently *The Book of Seventy* (2009), which won the Jewish Book Award for Poetry, and *At the Revelation Restaurant and Other Poems* (2010). She has also authored two seminal critical volumes on women's poetry: *Writing Like* *a Woman* (1983) and *Stealing the Language: The Emergence of Women's Poetry in America* (1987). Her most recent book of criticism is *Dancing at the Devil's Party: Essays on Poetry, Politics, and the Erotic* (2000). She lives in Princeton, New Jersey, with her husband.

WILFRED OWEN (1893–1918)   Born in the Shropshire countryside of England, Owen began writing verse before he matriculated at London University, where he was known as a quiet and contemplative student. After some years of teaching English in France, Owen returned to England and joined the army. Wounded in 1917, he was killed in action leading an attack a few days before the armistice was declared in 1918. Owen's poems, published only after his death, along with his letters from the front to his mother, are perhaps the most powerful and vivid accounts of the horror of war to emerge from World War I.

DOROTHY PARKER (1893–1967)   Parker was born in West End, New Jersey, to a Scottish Presbyterian mother and a Jewish father as "a late unexpected arrival in a loveless family." She was educated in private schools and moved in 1911 to New York, where she lived in a boardinghouse and earned her living by playing piano at a dancing school. In 1915 one of the verses she sent around was accepted by *Vogue* magazine, and the editor later hired her to write captions for fashion illustrations. Her native wit captivated the editor, and he persuaded her to join *Vanity Fair* as drama critic, although she was fired when she wrote unfavorable reviews of several plays. She became the first woman among the regulars of the Algonquin Round Table—a group of writers who met regularly at the Algonquin Hotel in New York City that included Alexander Woollcott, George S. Kaufman, Robert Benchley, and Edna Ferber, among others. A master of irony and scathing wit, Parker, despite a troubled personal life that led to suicide attempts, flourished as a humorist, poet, short-story writer, playwright, and screenwriter.

SUZAN-LORI PARKS (b. 1963)   Parks was born in Fort Knox, Kentucky. The daughter of an army colonel, she moved frequently and attended school in Germany. After earning a degree from Mount Holyoke College, where she began writing plays, and studying at the Yale University School of Drama, she moved to London to study acting. Her first play, *Betting on the Dust Commander*, was produced in New York City in 1987. Her second play, *Imperceptible Metabolites in the Third Kingdom*, won an OBIE as one of the best new American Off-Broadway plays of 1989. Among her other plays are *Venus* (1996); *In the Blood* (1999); *Topdog/Underdog* (2001), winner of a Pulitzer Prize; and *The Book of Grace* (2010). Her most recent work is *Father Comes Home from the Wars* (2014). Parks is also the author of three plays for radio; a novel, *Getting Mother's Body* (2003); and three screenplays, *Girl 6* (1996), *Their Eyes Were Watching God* (2005), and *The Great Debaters* (2007). Her numerous awards include a Whiting Award, a Guggenheim Fellowship, and grants from the Rockefeller Foundation, the National Endowment for the Arts, and the MacArthur Foundation. Parks has taught at Yale University, the University of Michigan, and the Pratt Institute for the Arts. In November 2008, she became the first recipient of the Master Writer Chair at the Public Theater. Parks also serves as a visiting arts professor in dramatic writing at New York University's Tisch School of the Arts.

PAUL (d. ca. 64 CE)   Paul was born Saul in Tarsus of Cilicia (located near the Mediterranean Sea in south-central Turkey, near Syria). He was an important Jerusalem Pharisee who, according to the Acts of the Apostles (Chapter 9), vigorously attacked both intellectually and physically those who proclaimed the deity of Jesus. The same source provides an account of Saul's conversion. Traveling to Damascus to arrest followers of Jesus, he experienced an intense light that blinded him and heard a voice that declared, "I am Jesus, whom you are persecuting." In Tarsus, his blindness was cured by Ananias, a follower of Jesus, and Paul became, arguably, the most important disciple of Jesus in the early church: his letters, and those attributed to him, constitute a quarter of the New Testament. His attempts to preach the new Way in the synagogues of the region were rebuffed, sometimes violently, and Paul was frequently jailed. He became the apostle to the Gentiles, traveling throughout the Mediterranean region to establish churches. His epistles to those young and fragile congregations helped formulate the political, legal, and spiritual institutions of the early church. His final arrest brought him to Rome to answer charges, and after two years of imprisonment, he died about 64 CE.

OMAR PÉREZ (b. 1964)   Pérez was born and raised in Havana, earning a degree in English from the University of Havana and a degree in Italian from the Universitá per Straniere di Siena. At the age of 25, Pérez discovered that his father was the Marxist revolutionary Ernesto "Che" Guevara; Pérez has remained largely mum on the subject since discovering his lineage, preferring to let his own work speak for itself. Pérez has worked as an editor for the magazines *La naranja dulce* and *Mantis*, as a journalist for *El Caimán Barbudo*, and as a translator, boasting notable translations of the Italian-Cuban novelist Alba de Céspedes's *Nadie vuelve atrás* (2003) and William Shakespeare's *As You Like It* (as *Como Les Guste*, 2000). Pérez is also a poet and an ordained Zen Buddhist monk. His poetry collections include *Lingua Franca* (2010), *Oíste hablar del gato de pelea?* (1999, translated as *Did You Hear about the Fighting Cat?* by Kristin Dykstra, 2010), and *Algo de lo Sagrado* (1996, translated as *Something of the Sacred* by Kristin Dykstra and Robert Tejada, 2007). Pérez's poetry explores the intersections of human experience, often intertwining his Zen beliefs with political and cultural messages. In an interview with *Jacket* magazine in 2008, Pérez said that "Poetry is a natural function, like god, or DNA, or rain. The fact that we can give notice of it does not mean that we make it."

CARL PHILLIPS (b. 1959)   Phillips is a professor of English and of African and Afro-American Studies at Washington University in St. Louis, where he also teaches in the creative writing program. He has published many volumes of acclaimed poetry, including *In the Blood* (1992), winner of the Samuel French Morse Poetry Prize; *Cortège* (1995), a finalist for the National Book Critics Circle Award; *From the Devotions* (1998), a finalist for the National Book Award; *Pastoral* (2000), winner of the Lambda Literary Award; *The Tether* (2001), winner of the Kingsley Tufts Poetry Award; and *The Rest of Love* (2004), winner of the Theodore Roethke Memorial Foundation Poetry Prize and the Thom Gunn Award for Gay Male Poetry, and a finalist for the National Book Award. Among his most recent publications are *Double Shadow* (2011), winner of the Los Angeles Times Book Prize for poetry; *Silverchest* (2013), a finalist for the Griffin Poetry Prize; and *The Art of Daring: Risk, Restlessness, Imagination* (2014). Phillips also received the 2006 Academy of American Poets Fellowship, an Award in Literature from the American Academy of Arts and Letters, a Pushcart Prize, the Academy of American Poets Prize, and fellowships from the Guggenheim Foundation and the Library of Congress. He was chancellor of the Academy of American Poets from 2006 to 2012.

MARGE PIERCY (b. 1936)   Born in Detroit, Piercy was the first of her family to attend college. In 1957 she graduated from the University of Michigan (where she won prizes for poetry and fiction) and earned an MA from Northwestern University (1958). She was active in social and political causes and fought for equal treatment of women and minorities while opposing the Vietnam War. She supported herself with odd jobs in Chicago as she pursued a writing career, but her first novel was not published until after her 1969 move to Wellfleet,

Massachusetts, where she still lives. She is an extraordinarily prolific writer. Among her more than a dozen novels are *He, She and It* (1991), *The Longings of Women* (1994), and *City of Darkness, City of Lights* (1996). Her many volumes of poetry include *My Mother's Body* (1985), *Available Light* (1988), *The Earth Shines Secretly: A Book of Days* (1990), and *Mars and Her Children* (1992). She has also written plays and several volumes of nonfiction and has edited the anthology *Early Ripening: American Women's Poetry Now* (1987). In the introduction to a volume of selected poems, *Circles on the Water* (1982), Piercy asserted that she wanted her poems to be "useful," saying, "What I mean by useful is simply that readers will find poems that speak to and for them, will take those poems into their lives and say them to each other and put them up on the bathroom wall and remember bits and pieces of them in stressful or quiet moments. . . . To find ourselves spoken for in art gives dignity to our pain, our anger, our lust, our losses." Most recently, she has published two novels, *The Third Child* (2003) and *Sex Wars: A Novel of Gilded Age in New York* (2005); three collections of poetry, *Colors Passing through Us* (2003), *The Crooked Inheritance* (2006), and *The Hunger Moon: New and Selected Poems, 1980–2010* (2011); and a collection of short stories, *The Cost of Lunch, Etc.* (2014).

SYLVIA PLATH (1932–1963)   Plath was born in Boston, Massachusetts, where her parents taught at Boston University. She graduated summa cum laude in English from Smith College (1955); earned an MA as a Fulbright Scholar at Newnham College, Cambridge (1955–57); and married British poet Ted Hughes (1956). Plath's poetry reveals the anger and anxiety that would eventually lead to her suicide. Her view that all relationships were in some way destructive and predatory surely darkened her life. Yet in 1963, during the month between the publication of her only novel, *The Bell Jar* (about a suicidal college student), and her death, Plath was extraordinarily productive; she produced finished poems every day. Her *Collected Poems* was published in 1981.

EDGAR ALLAN POE (1809–1849)   Poe, the son of traveling actors, was born in Boston. Within a year, his alcoholic father deserted his mother and their three infant children. When his mother died of tuberculosis in Richmond, Virginia, three-year-old Edgar was adopted by John Allan and his wife. Allan, a prosperous businessman, spent time in England, where Poe began his education at private schools. Back in the United States, Allan forced Poe to leave the University of Virginia in 1826, when Poe incurred gambling debts he could not pay. Poe served in the U.S. Army from 1827 to 1829, eventually attaining the rank of sergeant major, and then attended West Point, hoping for further military advancement. Shortly thereafter, Mrs. Allan died of tuberculosis. Poe angrily confronted his foster father about his extramarital affairs, and for this candor he was disowned. Believing that Allan would never reinstate him as heir, Poe deliberately violated rules to provoke his dismissal from the academy. In 1835 Poe began his career as editor, columnist, and reviewer, earning a living he could not make as a writer of stories and poems. He married his thirteen-year-old cousin, Virginia Clemm, in 1836, and lived with her and her mother during a period marked by illness and poverty. Virginia died of tuberculosis in 1847. Poe died, delirious and under mysterious circumstances, in 1849. He perfected the gothic horror story ("Fall of the House of Usher") and originated the modern detective story ("The Gold Bug," "The Murders in the Rue Morgue"). Poe's work fascinated the French poet Baudelaire, who translated it into French.

KATHERINE ANNE PORTER (1890–1980)   Born in Texas and educated mostly at small convent schools, Porter traveled widely in her early years, living for some time in Mexico and, more briefly, in Germany. She gained a reputation primarily as a writer of finely crafted stories, gathered in *The Collected Stories of Katherine Anne Porter* (1965). She published one novel, *Ship of Fools*, in 1962. Porter's output of fiction was small, and she earned her livelihood mostly as a reporter, lecturer, scriptwriter, speaker, and writer-in-residence. Her achievement in fiction was recognized by a National Book Award and Pulitzer Prize for Fiction, both in 1966. Her final work, *The Never-Ending Wrong* (1977), is a memoir about her involvement in the celebrated Sacco-Vanzetti case.

KEVIN POWERS (b. 1980) Born and raised in Richmond, Virginia, Powers served in the Iraq War before receiving his BA from Virginia Commonwealth University and his MFA from the University of Texas at Austin, where he was a Michener Fellow in Poetry. His first novel, *The Yellow Birds* (2012), which drew on his military experiences, has been compared to Tim O'Brien's *The Things They Carried* and won several awards, including the Guardian First Book Award and the PEN/Hemingway Award. It was also a finalist for the National Book Award in Fiction. His debut volume of poetry, *Letter Composed During a Lull in the Fighting* (2014), was shortlisted for the T. S. Eliot Prize. Powers's poems have appeared in the *New Orleans Review*, *Poetry*, and the *New York Quarterly*. According to his 2010 biography in the *Sun Magazine*, "When not thinking about poetry or Italy (where he hopes to live someday)," Powers can be found "riding his Royal Enfield motorcycle through the Texas hill country."

WYATT PRUNTY (b. 1947) Prunty was born in Humboldt, Tennessee. After earning a BA from the University of the South in Sewanee, he went on to earn an MA from Johns Hopkins University and a PhD (1979) from Louisiana State University. His poetry chapbook, *Domestic of the Outer Banks*, was published in 1980. Several volumes followed, among them *Since the Noon Mail Stopped* (1997) and *Unarmed and Dangerous* (2000). His poetry has been anthologized in *Anthology of Magazine Verse and Yearbook of American Poetry* for both 1979 and 1980. He was awarded a poetry prize by *Sewanee Review* (1969) and has been a fellow at the Bread Loaf Writers' Conference. He has taught in the graduate program of the Johns Hopkins Writing Seminars, where he was Elliott Coleman Professor of Poetry. Currently, he serves as Carlton Professor of English at the University of the South, where he teaches poetry, and where he founded and now directs the Sewanee Writers' Conference. His most recent work is a collection of poetry and fiction, *The Lover's Guide to Trapping* (2009).

DUDLEY RANDALL (1914–2000) Born in Washington, DC, Randall worked during the Depression in the Ford Motor Company foundry in Dearborn, Michigan, and then as a carrier and clerk for the U.S. Post Office in Detroit. He served in the U.S. Army Signal Corps (1942–46) and graduated from Wayne State University (BA, 1949) and the University of Michigan (MALS, 1951). He was a librarian at several universities and founded the Broadside Press in 1965 "so black people could speak to and for their people." Randall told *Negro Digest*, "Precision and accuracy are necessary for both white and black writers. . . . 'A black aesthetic' should not be an excuse for sloppy writing." He urged African American writers to reject what was false in white poetry but not to forsake universal concerns in favor of a racial agenda. His works include *On Getting a Natural* (1969) and *A Litany of Friends: New and Selected Poems* (1981). He edited *For Malcolm: Poems on the Life and Death of Malcolm X* (1969) and *The Black Poets* (1971), an extensive anthology of poetry, from slave songs to the present.

BARBARA RAS (b. 1949) Ras was born in New Bedford, Massachusetts, and has traveled extensively, living in Costa Rica, Colombia, and Athens, Georgia. Her work has appeared in many literary journals and magazines, including the *New Yorker*, *Boulevard*, *Massachusetts Review*, *Prairie Schooner*, *American Scholar*, and *Spoon River Poetry Review*. Her debut poetry collection *Bite Every Sorrow* (1998) was selected by C. K. Williams for the Walt Whitman Award in 1997. Her most recent collections are *One Hidden Stuff* (2006) and *The Last Skin* (2010). Ras has been honored with numerous literary awards, including the Kate Tufts Discovery Award, a Guggenheim Fellowship, and the Georgia Author of the Year Award for poetry. She has taught and worked across the country, including at the Warren Wilson MFA Program for Writers and the University of Georgia Press. Currently, she serves as director of Trinity University Press in San Antonio, Texas.

SPENCER REECE (b. 1963) Reece was born in Hartford, Connecticut. He attended Wesleyan University and received an MA from the University of York and an MTS from the Harvard Divinity School. At Wesleyan, the Pulitzer Prize–winning writer Annie Dillard was one of Reece's poetry teachers: Reece describes her as "an early encourager" along with James Merrill, another poet with whom he corresponded. Reece's poetry collection *The Clerk's Tale* (2004), the title poem of which describes an ordinary day at a store in the Mall of America and was inspired by Reece's own experience working as a sales associate at Brooks Brothers, won the Bread Loaf Writers' Conference Bakeless Prize. Reece has also won the 2005 Whiting Award for poetry, a 2009 Pushcart Prize, a Guggenheim Fellowship, and a fellowship from the National Endowment for the Arts. His work has appeared in *Boulevard*, the *New Yorker*, and *American Poetry Review*. Reece was ordained as a minister in 2011 and served as chaplain to Bishop Carlos Lopez-Lozano of the Reformed Episcopal Church in Spain. After receiving a Fulbright grant, he worked on a collaborative writing project with children at a Honduran orphanage from 2012 to 2013. The title poem of his latest poetry collection, *The Road to Emmaus* (2014), appeared in *The Best American Poetry 2012*.

ADRIENNE RICH (1929–2012) Born to a middle-class family, Rich was educated by her parents until she entered public school in the fourth grade. She graduated Phi Beta Kappa from Radcliffe College in 1951, the same year her first book of poems, *A Change of World*, appeared. That volume, chosen by W. H. Auden for the Yale Series of Younger Poets Award, and her next, *The Diamond Cutters and Other Poems* (1955), earned her a reputation as an elegant, controlled stylist. In the 1960s, however, Rich began a dramatic shift away from her earlier mode as she took up political and feminist themes and stylistic experimentation in such works as *Snapshots of a Daughter-in-Law* (1963), *The Necessities of Life* (1966), *Leaflets* (1969), and *The Will to Change* (1971). In *Diving into the Wreck* (1973) and *The Dream of a Common Language* (1978), she continued to experiment with form and to deal with the experiences and aspirations of women from a feminist perspective. In addition to her poetry, Rich published many essays on poetry, feminism, motherhood, and lesbianism. She also won numerous awards, most recently the National Book Foundation's Medal for Distinguished Contribution to American Letters in 2006 and the Lifetime Recognition Award from the Griffin Poetry Prize in 2010. Her recent collections include *Telephone Ringing in the Labyrinth: Poems: 2004–2006* (2007), *A Human Eye: Essays on Art in Society, 1997–2008* (2009), and, her final publication, *Tonight No Poetry Will Serve: Poems 2007–2010* (2011).

RAINER MARIA RILKE (1875–1926) Rilke is widely considered one of the most masterful and lyrically intense German-language poets. Born into an unhappy family in Prague, his parents shipped him away to military school when he was a child. He released his first collection of poetry, *Leben und Lieder* (1894), while enrolled at Charles-Ferdinand University, with two additional collections—*Larenopfer* (*Sacrifice to the Lares*, 1895) and

Traumgekrönt (*Dream-Crowned*, 1896)—following soon after. During his lifetime Rilke authored hundreds of poems that garnered him an ardent following in European literary circles, and over time his poetry has been translated into many other languages. His best-known works among English-language readers are the collection *Duino Elegies* (1923) and his loosely autobiographical novel *The Notebooks of Malte Laurids Brigge* (1910). Rilke also became known for *Letters to a Young Poet*, a series of correspondence between Rilke and Franz Kappus, a nineteen-year-old cadet at the Vienna Military Academy who was discouraged by the prospect of army life. Kappus assembled and published the letters in 1929, three years after Rilke's death.

EDWIN ARLINGTON ROBINSON (1869–1935) Robinson grew up in Gardiner, Maine; attended Harvard University; returned to Gardiner as a freelance writer; and then settled in New York City in 1896. His various odd jobs included a one-year stint as subway-construction inspector. President Theodore Roosevelt, a fan of his poetry, had him appointed to the U.S. Custom House in New York, where he worked from 1905 to 1909. Robinson wrote about people rather than nature, particularly New England characters remembered from his early years. Describing his first volume of poems, *The Torrent and the Night Before* (1896), he told a friend there was not "a single red-breasted robin in the whole collection." Popular throughout his career, Robinson won three Pulitzer Prizes (1921, 1924, and 1927).

THEODORE ROETHKE (1908–1963) Born in Saginaw, Michigan, Roethke was the son of a greenhouse owner, and greenhouses figure prominently in the imagery of his poems. He graduated magna cum laude from the University of Michigan in 1929, where he also earned an MA in 1936 after graduate study at Harvard University. He taught at several universities, coached two varsity tennis teams, and settled at the University of Washington in 1947. Intensely introspective and demanding of himself, Roethke was renowned as a great teacher, though he was sometimes incapacitated by bipolar disorder. His collection *The Waking: Poems 1933–1953* won the Pulitzer Prize in 1954. Other awards include Guggenheim Fellowships in 1945 and 1950, and a National Book Award and the Bollingen Prize in 1959 for *Words for the Wind* (1958).

SALMAN RUSHDIE (b. 1947) Rushdie was born in Bombay into a family of Indian Muslims just two months before Indian independence and four months before South Asia was partitioned into a principally Muslim Pakistan and Hindu India. That process resulted in the murder of hundreds of thousands of people in the fighting that accompanied the vast migration of Hindus to the south and Muslims to the north. Some years later, Rushdie's upper-middle-class family sent him first to a British-style private school in Bombay and then to the elite Rugby School in England. There, Rushdie told an interviewer, he was miserable: "I was suddenly an Indian . . . and at the schoolboy level that was no fun." His Islamic family finally moved from Bombay to Karachi, Pakistan, while Rushdie completed an MA with honors in history at Cambridge University (1968). But shortly after his return to Pakistan, the government prohibited the performance of a television play he had produced and the publication of an article he had written about Pakistan. This numbing experience of official censorship convinced him to return to Britain in late 1968. There he supported himself as an actor and freelance advertising copywriter until he began his successful career as a writer. His second novel, *Midnight's Children* (1981), won three awards, including the prestigious Booker Prize, and was honored as the best Booker Prize novel in the prize's forty-year history. But his eminence seriously affected the conduct of his life when his novel

The Satanic Verses (1988) profoundly offended Muslim sensibilities in some quarters and resulted in a fatwa issued by the Iranian ayatollah Khomeini, who offered a million dollars to the person who would execute Rushdie for blasphemy. Rushdie's most recent book, *Joseph Anton: A Memoir* (2012), recounts his life in exile following the call for his death. Though Iran renounced the fatwa in 1998, in some Islamic quarters Rushdie remains a marked man. In 2007 Rushdie was knighted by Queen Elizabeth II of England, causing another outcry among Muslims; Al Qaeda called the knighthood "an insult to Islam" and threatened to retaliate. Rushdie has been elected to many prestigious positions in the world of letters, including the Royal Society of Literature, and he has served as president of the PEN American Center. His most recent novels are *Shalimar the Clown* (2005) and *The Enchantress of Florence* (2008). Bharati Mukherjee once characterized Rushdie as "up there with Joyce and Solzhenitsyn, an educated, implacable, remorseless dissenter from deep inside the family." And Rushdie characterized himself as one who has "spent my entire life as a writer in opposition, and had indeed conceived the writer's role as including the function as antagonist to the state."

KAY RYAN (b. 1945)   Ryan was born in San Jose and grew up in central and southern California. She attended Antelope Valley College in Lancaster, California, before earning two degrees from University of California, Los Angeles. For over thirty-five years, she was a part-time instructor of English at the College of Marin. Ryan is the author of eight volumes of poetry: *Dragon Acts to Dragon Ends* (1983), *Strangely Marked Metal* (1985), *Flamingo Watching* (1994), *Elephant Rocks* (1997), *Say Uncle* (2000), *The Niagara River* (2005), *The Jam Jar Lifeboat and Other Novelties Exposed* (2008), and *The Best of It: New and Selected Poems* (2010), for which she won the Pulitzer Prize. Her poems have also appeared in a number of periodicals, including *American Scholar*, *Atlantic*, the *New Yorker*, *Paris Review*, and *Poetry* magazine. Among her many awards are fellowships from the Guggenheim Foundation and the National Endowment for the Arts, and the 2004 Ruth Lilly Poetry Prize, a prestigious honor given to living U.S. poets "whose lifetime accomplishments warrant extraordinary recognition." Ryan served two terms as poet laureate of the United States, from 2008 through 2010. In 2011 she was named a MacArthur Fellow, and in 2012 she received the National Humanities Medal.

CARL SANDBURG (1878–1967)   H. L. Mencken once described Carl Sandburg as "indubitably an American in every pulse-beat." Sandburg came from humble beginnings in Galesburg, Illinois. His parents had emigrated to America from northern Sweden and were very poor. Sandburg spent much of his youth working odd jobs to earn money, from driving a milk truck to bricklaying. In 1898 he voluntarily joined the military, serving eight months in Puerto Rico during the Spanish-American War. After leaving the military, he returned to his hometown and enrolled in Lombard College, though he dropped out in 1903 before receiving his degree. He then moved to Milwaukee, and joined the Socialist Party of America, where he met his future wife, Lilian Steichen. The couple moved around frequently in their early years together, eventually settling in Elmhurst in 1919. During that time, Sandburg became an editor for the *Chicago Daily News* and came to be known as a part of the Chicago literary renaissance. In 1919 he won the Pulitzer Prize for Poetry for his collection *Cornhuskers* (1918), which celebrated the ordinary working people of the Midwest. The celebration of America became a trademark of Sandburg's poetry and was reflected in his subsequent poetry collections, some of which include *Smoke and Steel* (1920), *Slabs of the Sunburnt West* (1922), *Good Morning, America* (1928), *The People, Yes* (1936), *Harvest Poems* (1950), *Sandburg's Complete Poems* (1951, which also won a Pulitzer

Prize), and *Honey and Salt* (1963). The 1920s also saw Sandburg tap into American folklore. He made brief yearly tours across America with a banjo or guitar, singing folk songs and reciting poems, and thereafter put those uniquely American experiences into songbooks: *The American Songbag* (1927) and *The New American Songbag* (1950). He also wrote a series of children's books called *Rootabaga Stories* (1922), *Rootabaga Pigeons* (1923), and *Potato Face* (1930), which grew out of his desire to have "American fairy tales" match actual American childhood. Sandburg spent years researching and writing a definitive, two-volume biography of Abraham Lincoln, the second volume of which—*Abraham Lincoln: The War Years* (1939)—also earned Sandburg a Pulitzer Prize. He recorded excerpts from the biography for Caedmon Records in New York City in 1957 and made a recording of Aaron Copland's *Lincoln Portrait* with the New York Philharmonic, for which he won a 1959 Grammy Award. In 1945 Sandburg and his wife moved to an estate in Flat Rock, North Carolina, where they lived until Sandburg's death in 1967.

SAPPHO (ca. 610–ca. 580 BCE)   Almost nothing certain is known of the finest woman lyric poet of the ancient world. Sappho was born to an aristocratic family and had three brothers, one of whom was a court cupbearer, a position limited to the sons of good families. She is associated with the island of Lesbos, set in the Aegean Sea. She married and had a daughter. For over 2,000 years, her reputation depended on fragments of her work quoted by other ancient authors. However, in the late nineteenth century a cache of papyrus and vellum codices, dating from the second to the sixth centuries CE and containing authentic transcriptions of a few of her lyrical poems, was discovered in Egypt. Unlike other ancient Greek poets, she wrote in ordinary Greek rather than in an exalted literary dialect; her lyrics, despite their simple language, conveyed women's concerns with intense emotion.

GEORGE SAUNDERS (b. 1958)   Born in Amarillo, Texas, Saunders grew up in the Chicago suburb of Oak Forest. He received a BS in geophysical engineering from Colorado School of Mines in 1981, and an MA in creative writing from Syracuse University in 1988. His writing, which has been compared to that of Kurt Vonnegut, has appeared in the *New Yorker*, *Harper's*, the *Guardian*, *McSweeney's*, and *GQ*, as well as *Best American* anthologies for short stories, travel writing, and science fiction. Saunders, who has won the National Magazine Award for fiction four times, was a finalist for the PEN/Hemingway Award for his first story collection, *CivilWarLand in Bad Decline* (1996). In 2006 Saunders received a MacArthur Fellowship as well as a Guggenheim Fellowship, and he won the World Fantasy Award for his short story "CommComm." His collection *In Persuasion Nation* (2006) was a finalist for the Story Prize, an award he won for his later collection *Tenth of December* (2013), which was also a finalist for the National Book Award. Among his many other honors, he received an award from the American Academy of Arts and Letters in 2009, and the PEN/Malamud Award in 2013. Saunders has taught at the Syracuse MFA program since 1996.

DAVID SEDARIS (b. 1956)   Sedaris was born in Binghamton, New York, and raised in Raleigh, North Carolina. He attended Kent State University before working odd jobs and eventually earning a degree from the School of the Art Institute of Chicago. Sedaris garnered fame when he began reading essays based on his diary on National Public Radio, first on *Morning Edition* and then, at the behest of host Ira Glass, as a regular contributor to *This American Life*. His first book of humorous stories and autobiographical essays, *Barrel Fever*, was published in 1994. All of his other collections—*Naked* (1997), *Holidays on Ice* (1997), *Me Talk Pretty One Day* (2000), *Dress Your Family in Corduroy and Denim* (2004), *When*

You Are Engulfed in Flames (2008), *Squirrel Seeks Chipmunk: A Modest Bestiary* (2010), *Let's Explore Diabetes with Owls* (2013)—have appeared on the *New York Times* best-seller list. He has also contributed regularly to the *New Yorker* and *Esquire* magazines; coauthored several plays with his sister Amy Sedaris; and been nominated for two Grammys for audio recordings of his own work.

LÉOPOLD SÉDAR SENGHOR (1906–2001) Regarded by many as one of the most important African intellectuals of the twentieth century, Senghor was born to a prosperous family and raised in the French colony of Senegal. He was drawn to French literature from a young age, and after receiving his bachelor's degree in Senegal, he continued his studies in France and began a teaching career there. He served in the French army during World War II and spent two years in German prison camps, where he devoted much of his time to writing poetry. Upon his release from prison in 1942, he returned to his teaching career and worked for the French resistance during the Nazi occupation. After the war, Senghor became active in politics and was elected to represent his colonial homeland in the French National Assembly. An early proponent of the Négritude movement, Senghor used his political influence to advocate for a revival of African pride and to argue against colonial rule. In 1960 he became the first democratically elected president of the newly independent Senegal, a position he held until voluntarily resigning in 1980. Throughout his political career, Senghor maintained his cultural and literary activities, helping to found the journal *Presence Africaine* in 1947, and publishing several works of his own including the English translations *Selected Poems* (1964), *On African Socialism* (1964), *Nocturnes* (1971), *Prose and Poetry* (1976), and *The Collected Poetry* (1991). Senghor won numerous international awards both as a writer and political thinker, and in 1984 he was inducted into the French Academy, becoming the first African member in that body's history.

ANNE SEXTON (1928–1974) Born in Newton, Massachusetts, Sexton attended Garland Junior College and Boston University, where she studied under Robert Lowell. She worked for a year as a fashion model in Boston and later wrote her first poetry collection, *To Bedlam and Part Way Back* (1960), while recovering from a nervous breakdown. Writing a poem almost every day was successful therapy for her. From 1961 to 1963, Sexton was a scholar at the Radcliffe Institute for Independent Study. A confessional poet, Sexton acknowledged her debt to W. D. Snodgrass, whose collection of poetry *Heart's Needle* (1959) influenced her profoundly. Her second collection, *All My Pretty Ones* (1962), includes a quote from a letter by Franz Kafka that expresses her own literary philosophy: "A book should serve as the axe for the frozen sea within us." *Live or Die* (1967), her third collection of poems, won a Pulitzer Prize. She committed suicide in 1974.

WILLIAM SHAKESPEARE (1564–1616) Shakespeare was born at Stratford-on-Avon in April 1564. His father became an important public figure, rising to the position of high bailiff (equivalent to mayor) of Stratford. Although we know practically nothing of Shakespeare's personal life, we may assume that he received a decent grammar school education in literature, logic, and Latin (though not in mathematics or natural science). When he was eighteen he married Anne Hathaway, eight years his senior; six months later their son was born. Two years later, Anne bore twins. We do not know how the young Shakespeare supported his family, and we do not hear of him again until 1592, when a rival London playwright sarcastically refers to him as an "upstart crow." Shakespeare seems to have prospered in the London theater world. He probably began as an actor and earned enough as author and part owner of his company's theaters to acquire property. His sonnets, which were written during the 1590s, reveal rich and varied interests. Some are addressed to an attractive young man (whom the poet urges to marry); others to the mysterious dark lady; still others suggest a love triangle of two men and a woman. His dramas include historical plays based on English dynastic struggles; comedies, both festive and dark; romances such as *Pericles* (1608) and *Cymbeline* (1611) that cover decades in the lives of their characters; and the great tragedies *Hamlet* (1602), *Othello* (1604), *King Lear* (1605), and *Macbeth* (1606). About 1611, at age forty-seven, he retired to the second largest house in Stratford. He died in 1616, leaving behind a body of work that still stands as a pinnacle in world literature.

PERCY BYSSHE SHELLEY (1792–1822)   Born near Horsham, England, Shelley was the son of a wealthy landowner who sat in Parliament. At University College, Oxford University, he befriended Thomas Jefferson Hogg. Both became interested in radical philosophy and quickly became inseparable. After one year at Oxford they were both expelled for writing and circulating a pamphlet entitled "The Necessity of Atheism." Shelley married Harriet Westbrook soon after leaving Oxford. Though they had two children, the marriage was unsuccessful, and in 1814, Shelley left Harriet for Mary Wollstonecraft Godwin, the author of *Frankenstein*. After Harriet's apparent suicide, Shelley and Godwin were married. Escaping legal problems in England, he settled in Pisa, Italy, in 1820, and died in a sailing accident before his thirtieth birthday. A playwright and essayist as well as a romantic poet, Shelley is admired for his dramatic poem "Prometheus Unbound" (1820).

CLAY SHIRKY (b. 1964)   A graduate of Yale University, Shirky holds a joint appointment at New York University as associate professor of journalism and associate arts professor at the Interactive Telecommunications Program. He studies the effects of the Internet on society and has written extensively on the subject since 1996. His columns and writings have appeared in *Business 2.0*, the *New York Times*, the *Wall Street Journal*, the *Harvard Business Review*, and *Wired*, and he is the author of two recent books on social media, *Cognitive Surplus: Creativity and Generosity in a Connected Age* (2010) and *Here Comes Everybody: The Power of Organizing Without Organizations* (2008). Shirky is a fellow at the Berkman Center for Internet and Society, and he was named one of Foreign Policy's "Top 100 Global Thinkers" in 2010.

LESLIE MARMON SILKO (b. 1948)   Born in Albuquerque, New Mexico, Silko grew up on the Laguna Pueblo Reservation. She was educated in Bureau of Indian Affairs schools and at the University of New Mexico, where she graduated with highest honors. After three semesters in the American Indian Law program, Silko decided to devote her talents to writing about Native Americans. Her short stories quickly earned her a reputation; in 1974 she published a volume of poems, *Laguna Woman*. Her novel *Ceremony* (1977) was widely acclaimed and revived interest in her earlier short stories. *Storyteller* (1981) is a semiautobiographical collection of stories and poems. In 1991 the novel *Almanac of the Dead* appeared, and a collection of essays on contemporary Native American life, *Yellow Woman and a Beauty of the Spirit*, followed in 1996. Silko has taught at the University of Arizona and the University of New Mexico, but with a large award from the prestigious MacArthur Foundation, she has been, in her words, "a little less beholden to the everyday world." Her other work includes the novel *Gardens in the Dunes* (1999) and *The Turquoise Ledge* (2010), a memoir that was the first book Silko had published in ten years.

STEVIE SMITH (1902–1971)   Born Florence Margaret Smith in Hull, England, Stevie Smith was a secretary at Newnes Publishing Company in London from 1923 to 1953 and occasionally worked as a writer and broadcaster for the BBC. Though in the 1930s she began publishing verse, which she often illustrated herself, Smith did not reach a wide audience until 1962, with the publication of *Selected Poems* and her appearance in the Penguin Modern Poets series. She is noted for her eccentricity and mischievous humor, often involving an acerbic twist on nursery rhymes, common songs, or hymns. Force-fed with what she considered lifeless language in the New English Bible, she often aimed satirical barbs at religion. Smith won the Queen's Gold Medal for poetry in 1969, two years before her death. She published three novels in addition to her eight volumes of poetry.

REBECCA SOLNIT (b. 1961)   A product of the California public education system from kindergarten through graduate school, writer, historian, and activist Rebecca Solnit is the author of more than a dozen books about environment, landscape, community, art, and politics. Her most recent work, *Men Explain Things to Me* (2014), is a collection of essays focused on the presumption that men know (or think they know) more than women, which "keeps women from speaking up and from being heard when they dare," she writes. "It trains us in self-doubt and self-limitation just as it exercises men's unsupported overconfidence." Solnit's other recent works include the New York Times Notable Books *The Faraway Nearby* (2013) and *A Paradise Built in Hell: The Extraordinary Communities That Arise in Disaster* (2009); *A Field Guide to Getting Lost* (2005); *Hope in the Dark: Untold Histories, Wild Possibilities* (2004); and *Wanderlust: A History of Walking* (1999). She received the National Book Critics Circle Award in criticism for *River of Shadows, Eadweard Muybridge and the Technological Wild West* (2003). A recipient of fellowships from the National Endowment for the Arts and the Guggenheim Foundation, Solnit is a contributing editor to *Harper's* and regular contributor to the political site Tomdispatch.com. When asked in an interview how to change people's minds about an issue without alienating them, Solnit advises, "Know what motivates you. Love does a lot more, and keeps you going in a much better way, than hate. It connects you to people."

SOPHOCLES (496?–406 BCE)   Born into a wealthy family at Colonus, a village just outside Athens, Sophocles distinguished himself early in life as a performer, musician, and athlete. Our knowledge of him is based on a very few ancient laudatory notices, but he certainly had a brilliant career as one of the three great Greek classical tragedians (the other two are Aeschylus, an older contemporary, and Euripides, a younger contemporary). He won the drama competition associated with the Dionysian festival (entries consisted of a tragic trilogy and a farce) at least twenty times, far more often than his two principal rivals. However, *Oedipus Rex*, his most famous tragedy, and the three other plays it was grouped with, took second place (ca. 429 BCE). He lived during the golden age of Athens, when architecture, philosophy, and the arts flourished under Pericles. In 440 BCE Sophocles was elected as one of the ten *strategoi* (military commanders), an indication of his stature in Athens. But his long life ended in sadder times, when the Peloponnesian War (431–404 BCE), between the Athenian empire and an alliance led by Sparta, darkened the region. Though Sophocles wrote some 123 plays, only seven have survived; nonetheless, these few works establish him as the greatest of the ancient Western tragedians.

GARY SOTO (b. 1952)   Soto was born in Fresno, California, to working-class Mexican American parents. He grew up in the San Joaquin Valley and worked as a migrant laborer in California's rich agricultural regions. Uncertain of his abilities, he began his academic career at Fresno City College, moving on to California State University at Fresno and the University of California, Irvine, where he earned an MFA (1976). In 1975 he married Carolyn Oda, a woman of Japanese ancestry. Although his work earned him recognition as early as 1975 (an Academy of American Poets Prize), his first book of poems—*The Elements of San Joaquin*, portraying grim pictures of Mexican American life in California's central valley—didn't appear until 1977. In 1985 he joined the faculty at the University of California, Berkeley, where he taught in both the English and Chicano studies departments. He gave up teaching in 1993 to become a full-time writer but returned to teaching in 2003, at the University of California, Riverside. His prolific output of poetry, memoirs, essays, and fiction continues unabated and has earned him numerous prizes, including an American Book Award from the Before Columbus Foundation for *Living up the Street* (1985). Soto's novel *Buried Onions* (1999) deals with the struggle and discomfort of a teenage boy's life in Fresno, California. *Nickel and Dime* (2000) is a fictional exploration of the interlocking lives of three Mexican American men in California. His latest publications are a novel for teenagers, *Accidental Love* (2006); a collection of stories for adolescents, *Facts of Life: Stories* (2008); two collections of poems, *Partly Cloudy: Poems of Love and Longing* (2009) and *Human Nature* (2010); and a memoir, *What Poets Are Like: Up and Down with the Writing Life* (2013). One critic points out that Soto has transcended the social commentary of his early work and shifted to "a more personal, less politically motivated poetry." Another argues that "Gary Soto has become not an important Chicano poet but an important American poet."

WILLIAM STAFFORD (1914–1993) Born in Hutchinson, Kansas, Stafford earned his bachelor's and master's degrees from the University of Kansas and his doctorate from the University of Iowa. Drafted during World War II, he declared himself a pacifist and conscientious objector and spent several years doing forestry and soil-conservation work instead. He taught at a small number of institutions around the country before settling on Lewis & Clark College and the Pacific Northwest. Stafford did not publish a collection of poetry until he was forty-eight years old; his first volume, *Traveling through the Dark* (1962), won the National Book Award in 1963. An astonishingly prolific writer, he kept a journal for fifty years and composed almost 22,000 poems, 3,000 of which were published in nearly 60 volumes of poetry. Among his many titles are *The Rescued Year* (1966), *Stories That Could Be True: New and Collected Poems* (1977), *Writing the Australian Crawl: Views on the Writer's Vocation* (1978), and *An Oregon Message* (1987). Stafford also contributed to numerous periodicals; authored a memoir, essays, reviews, and a children's book; and edited and translated the works of others. His many awards include a Guggenheim Fellowship, a grant from the National Endowment for the Arts, a Shelley Memorial Award, and a Western States Lifetime Achievement Award in Poetry.

MARILYN STASIO (b. 1940) Writer and literary critic Marilyn Stasio has served as *Variety*'s theater critic since 1999. She has been reviewing crime fiction for the *New York Times Book Review* for over twenty years, and her writing has also appeared in the *New York Post* and *New York* magazine, among other publications.

WALLACE STEVENS (1879–1955) Born in Reading, Pennsylvania, Stevens graduated from Harvard University in 1900, worked for a year as a reporter for the New York *Herald Tribune*, graduated from New York University Law School in 1903, and practiced law in New York for twelve years. From 1916 to 1955, Stevens worked for the Hartford Accident and Indemnity Company, where he was appointed vice president in 1934. He was in his forties when he published his first book of poetry, *Harmonium, Ideas of Order* (1923). Stevens argued that poetry is a "supreme fiction" that shapes chaos and provides order to both nature and human relationships. He illuminates his philosophy in *Ideas of Order* (1935) and *Notes toward a Supreme Fiction* (1942). His *Collected Poems* (1954) won the Pulitzer Prize and established him as a major American poet.

PABLO PIÑERO STILLMANN (b. 1982)   Stillmann moved from Mexico City to the Midwest in 2009 to attend graduate school. He has received fellowships from the Foundation for Mexican Literature and Indiana University. His work has appeared or is forthcoming in the *Normal School, Rumpus, Cream City Review, Brevity, Bodega*, and other journals. He lives and writes in Indianapolis.

JOHN JEREMIAH SULLIVAN (b. 1974)   Born in Louisville, Kentucky, Sullivan attended the University of the South in Tennessee, graduating in 1997. He has written two books, *Blood Horses: Notes of a Sportswriter's Son* (2004) and *Pulphead: Essays* (2011). He is a contributing writer to the *New York Times Magazine*, a contributing editor of *Harper's Magazine*, and southern editor of the *Paris Review*. His essays on sports, politics, music, travel, literature, art, and popular culture can also be found in *GQ*, the *New Yorker*, the *Oxford American*, and *New York* magazine. In 2014 he served as guest editor for the annual collection *Best American Essays*. Sullivan has won numerous awards, including a National Magazine Award, a Pushcart Prize, and a Whiting Award. He lives in Wilmington, North Carolina.

JONATHAN SWIFT (1667–1745)   Born in Dublin, Ireland, of English parents, Swift moved to England following his graduation from Trinity College, Dublin. In 1695 he was ordained minister of the Anglican Church of Ireland and five years later became a parish priest in Laracor, Ireland. The conduct of church business took Swift to England frequently, where his wit and skill in defense of Tory politics made him many influential friends. He was rewarded for his efforts in 1713, when Queen Anne appointed him dean of St. Patrick's Cathedral in Dublin. The accession of George I to the throne in the following year, followed by the Tory's loss of the government to Whig control, ended the political power of Swift and his friends. He spent the rest of his life as dean of St. Patrick's, writing during this period his most celebrated satirical narrative, *Gulliver's Travels* (1726), and his most savage essay, "A Modest Proposal" (1729). Among his many other works are *A Tale of a Tub* and *The Battle of the Books* (both 1704), and many poems.

GRACE TALUSAN (b. 1972)   At age three, Talusan emigrated with her family from the Philippines to the United States. She was raised near Boston and earned degrees from Tufts University and the University of California, Irvine. Talusan taught at the University of Oregon and now teaches at Tufts and the creative writing center GrubStreet. Her work has appeared in *Best American Medical Writing 2009* as well as a number of periodicals, including *Asiaweek, Brevity*, the *Boston Globe, Boston Magazine, Creative Nonfiction*, the *Del Sol Review, Rumpus*, and the *San Diego Reader*.

AMY TAN (b. 1952)   Tan's parents emigrated from China to Oakland, California, before she was born, and she grew up in a rather traditional Chinese household. She earned a BA (1973) and an MA (1974) from San Jose State University and spent an additional two years in postgraduate study at the University of California at Berkeley. Her shift from a premed program to English and linguistics caused a serious break with her mother, and they didn't speak for two years. She was a writer from the outset and earned her living for several years as a medical and freelance technical writer. But her interest in fiction led her to the Squaw Valley Community of Writers, and shortly after returning from a trip to China, she published her first novel, *The Joy Luck Club* (1989), consisting of sixteen interwoven stories that reveal the struggles of four Chinese mothers with their sometimes rebellious daughters. Four more novels followed: *The Kitchen God's Wife* (1991), *The Hundred Secret Senses* (1995), *The Year of No Flood* (1995), and *The Bonesetter's Daughter* (2001). Her most recent publications are the collection of essays *The Opposite of Fate* (2003), as well as the novels *Saving Fish from Drowning* (2005), *Rules for Virgins* (2012), and *The Valley of Amazement* (2013).

SHEILA ORTIZ TAYLOR (b. 1939)   Taylor was born into a Mexican American family in the Silver Lake area of Los Angeles; she grew up between there and Toonerville. Taylor has said, "In every Mexican-American family there is an inscriber of stories, the keeper of the family fictions," a role that she filled within her own family. Taylor earned her BA from California State University, Northridge, and her MA and PhD from the University of California, Los Angeles. In 1973 she began teaching literature and creative writing at Florida State University, which is where she taught until retiring in 2006. She has been honored with a Fulbright scholarship, a State of Florida Individual Artist Fellowship, a National Endowment for the Arts creative writing fellowship, and the Alice B. Reader's Appreciation Medal, and holds memberships in the Modern Language Association, the Authors' Guild, and the Lambda Literary Foundation. She has written six novels, a memoir, and a volume of poetry. Her most recent work is a novel, *Homestead* (2011).

ALEXANDRA TEAGUE (b. 1974)   Teague was born in Fort Worth, Texas, and has since lived many places across the United States, including Arkansas, Missouri, Montana, Florida, Hawaii, California, and Idaho. She earned an MFA from the University of Florida in 1998 and was a 2006–2008 Stegner Fellow at Stanford University. She has also taught at the University of Miami and at City College of San Francisco, and she served as a visiting professor of poetry at the University of Arkansas in the fall of 2010. Teague is currently an assistant professor of poetry at the University of Idaho and was the recipient of a 2011 National Endowment for the Arts Fellowship. Her poetry has appeared in *Best New Poets* 2008 and *Best American Poetry* 2009 as well as such literary journals as the *Missouri Review*, *Iowa Review*, *Southern Poetry Review*, *New England Review*, and others. Her first book of poetry, *Mortal Geography* (2010), won the 2009 Lexi Rudnitsky Prize and the 2010 California Book Award.

ALFRED, LORD TENNYSON (1809–1892)   Tennyson was born in Lincolnshire and attended Trinity College, Cambridge (1828–31), where he won the Chancellor's Medal for poetry in 1829. His 1842 collection, *Poems*, was not well received, but he gained prominence and Queen Victoria's favor with the 1850 publication of *In Memoriam*, an elegy written over seventeen years and inspired by the untimely death of his friend Arthur Hallam in 1833. That same year he married Emily Sellwood, after what had been a fourteen-year engagement. In 1850 he was named poet laureate of England after Wordsworth's death. His works include *Maud and Other Poems* (1855) and *Idylls of the King* (1859), based on the legendary exploits of King Arthur and the knights of the Round Table.

DYLAN THOMAS (1914–1953)   Born in Swansea, Wales, Thomas decided to pursue a writing career directly after grammar school. At age twenty he published his first collection,

Eighteen Poems (1934), but his lack of a university degree deprived him of most opportunities to earn a living as a writer in England. Consequently, his early life (as well as the lives of his wife and children) was darkened by a poverty compounded by his free spending and heavy drinking. A self-proclaimed romanticist, Thomas called his poetry a "record of [his] struggle from darkness towards some measure of light." *The Map of Love* appeared in 1939 and *Deaths and Entrances* in 1946. Later, as a radio playwright and screenwriter, Thomas delighted in the sounds of words, sometimes at the expense of sense. *Under Milk Wood* (produced in 1953) is filled with his private, onomatopoetic language. He suffered from alcoholism and lung ailments and died in a New York hospital in 1953. Earlier that year, he noted in his *Collected Poems*: "These poems, with all their crudities, doubts and confusions are written for the love of man and in Praise of God, and I'd be a damn fool if they weren't."

JAMES THURBER (1894–1961)   American humorist and cartoonist James Thurber, born and raised in Columbus, Ohio, worked as a newspaper writer in Paris and New York before joining the staff of the *New Yorker* in 1927. His contributions to that magazine, both as a writer and an artist, were instrumental in changing the character of American humor. Thurber left the magazine in 1935 but continued to contribute to it for the next two decades. In 1940, failing eyesight—the result of a boyhood accident—forced him to curtail his drawing; by 1952, he had to give it up altogether. He continued to write until his death in 1961. Thurber's humor speaks not only for an era, but also for the confused human condition in general. His stories, fables, plays, drawings, and cartoons have been collected in over thirty volumes. Thurber's work has also been adapted for the stage, television, and movies, and he was honored with a special Tony Award for *A Thurber Carnival* (1961) and an Emmy (Best Comedy) for the Thurber-based *My World and Welcome to It* (1970). On the centennial celebration of his birthday, the U.S. Postal Service imprinted his self-portrait on the postage stamp. Additionally, Thurber House (www.ThurberHouse.org), listed on the National Register of Historic places, was one of Thurber's boyhood homes and now serves as a literary center and Thurber museum. Thurber House continues the legacy of James Thurber and has awarded the Thurber Prize for American humor to such writers as Ian Frazier, Jon Stewart, and Calvin Trillin.

LEO TOLSTOY (1828–1910)   Born in Russia into a family of aristocratic landowners, Tolstoy cut short his university education and joined the army, serving among the primitive Cossacks, who became the subject of his first novel, *The Cossacks* (1863). Tolstoy left the army and traveled abroad, but was disappointed by Western materialism and returned home. After a brief period in St. Petersburg, he became bored with the life of literary celebrity and returned to his family estate. There he wrote his two greatest novels, *War and Peace* (1869) and *Anna Karenina* (1877). Around 1876, Tolstoy experienced a spiritual crisis that ultimately led him to reject his former beliefs, way of life, and literary works. He adopted the simple life of the Russian peasants, rejecting orthodoxy in favor of a rational Christianity that disavowed private property, class divisions, secular and institutional religious authority, as well as all art (including his own) that failed to teach the simple principles he espoused.

NATASHA TRETHEWEY (b. 1966)   Trethewey was born in Gulfport, Mississippi. She earned a BA in English from the University of Georgia, an MA in English and creative writing from Hollins University, and an MFA in poetry from the University of Massachusetts. She has published four collections of poetry: *Domestic Work* (2000), *Bellocq's Ophelia* (2002), *Native Guard* (2006), for which she won the 2007 Pulitzer Prize for Poetry, and

Thrall (2012). Trethewey has also written a book of creative nonfiction, *Beyond Katrina: A Meditation on the Mississippi Gulf Coast* (2010). In addition to several fellowships from the Guggenheim Foundation, the Rockefeller Foundation, and elsewhere, she was awarded the 2008 Mississippi Governor's Award for Excellence in the Arts and named the 2008 Georgia Woman of the Year. She was inducted into the Fellowship of Southern Writers in 2009 and into the Georgia Writers Hall of Fame in 2011. In 2012 she was named poet laureate both for Mississippi and the United States. She is currently the director of the creative writing program at Emory University.

MARK TURPIN (b. 1953) Turpin, the son of a Presbyterian minister, spent twenty-five years working construction before graduating from Boston University with an MA in poetry at the age of forty-seven. His poems have appeared in the *Threepenny Review*, *Paris Review*, *Slate*, *Boston Review*, and *Ploughshares*, among other publications. In 1997 he received the prestigious Whiting Award for a book of poems in the new poets series, *Take Three*. He also won the 2004 Ploughshares John C. Zacharis First Book Award for his collection *Hammer* (2003). He teaches poetry and works as a carpenter in the San Francisco Bay area.

JOHN UPDIKE (1932–2009) Updike was born in Shillington, Pennsylvania, and graduated from Harvard University before attending the Ruskin School of Drawing and Fine Arts in Oxford. In England, he made the acquaintance of E. B. White, who offered Updike a job at the *New Yorker*. After two years at the magazine, he left to pursue his writing. His first book of poetry, *The Carpentered Hen and Other Tame Creatures*, was published in 1958. Updike was a prolific short-story writer, poet, novelist, and critic, having written over sixty books, among them *A & P* (short stories, 1961), *Self-Consciousness: Memoirs* (1989), *Collected Poems 1953–1993* (1993), *Still Looking: Essays on American Art* (2005), and the novels *The Poorhouse Fair* (1959), *Rabbit, Run* (1960), *The Centaur* (1963), *The Witches of Eastwick* (1984), and *In the Beauty of the Lilies* (1996). His recent works include *Terrorist* (2006), *Due Considerations: Essays and Criticism* (2007), and *The Widows of Eastwick* (2008). Until he lost his battle with cancer in 2009, he was a regular contributor to the *New Yorker* and the *New York Review of Books*. His countless awards include a Guggenheim Fellowship, a National Book Award, an O. Henry Prize, a Fulbright Fellowship, a Pulitzer Prize, a National Book Critics Circle Award, a PEN/Faulkner Award, a National Medal of Arts, and a Caldecott Medal. Updike said that it was his aim to "give the mundane its beautiful due."

HELENA MARÍA VIRAMONTES (b. 1954) Viramontes was one of nine children born to a construction worker and a homemaker in East Los Angeles, California. She earned degrees from Immaculate Heart College and the University of California, Irvine, and currently teaches at Cornell University. Her work has appeared in a number of anthologies; in addition, she coedited *Chicana Creativity and Criticism: Charting New Frontiers in American Literature* (1988) and *Chicana (w)rites: On Word and Film* (1995). She received a first prize for fiction from *Statement Magazine* and a fellowship from the National Endowment for the Arts. Viramontes, who writes about Chicano culture and women, is the author of three books: *The Moths and Other Stories* (1985), *Under the Feet of Jesus* (1995), and *Their Dogs Came with Them* (2007), which took her seventeen years to complete.

ALICE WALKER (b. 1944) Born in Eatonton, Georgia, the eighth child of sharecroppers, Walker was educated at Spelman College and Sarah Lawrence College. She has been deeply involved in the civil rights movement, working to register voters in Georgia and on behalf of welfare rights and Head Start in Mississippi. She also worked for the Welfare Department of New York City. She has taught at Wellesley College and Yale University and been an editor of *Ms.* Her nonfiction works include a biography for children, *Langston Hughes: American Poet* (1973); numerous contributions to anthologies about African American writers; and a collection of essays, *In Search of Our Mothers' Gardens: Womanist Prose* (1983). Her novels, all dealing with the African American experience, include *The Third Life of Grange Copeland* (1973); *Meridian* (1976); *The Color Purple* (1982), which won both the Pulitzer Prize and the National Book Award; *The Temple of My Familiar* (1989); and *Possessing the Secret of Joy* (1992). Her short stories are collected in three volumes, *In Love and Trouble: Stories of Black Women* (1973), *You Can't Keep a Good Woman Down* (1981), and *The Way Forward Is with a Broken Heart* (2000). Her recent publications include the memoir *The Chicken Chronicles: Sitting with the Angels Who Have Returned with My Memories: Glorious, Rufus, Gertrude Stein, Splendor, Hortensia, Agnes of God, The Gladyses, & Babe* (2011), the poetry collection *The World Will Follow Joy: Turning Madness into Flowers* (2013), and *The Cushion in the Road: Meditation and Wandering as the Whole World Awakens to Being in Harm's Way* (2013).

DAVID FOSTER WALLACE (1962–2008) Wallace, the son of college professors, was born in Ithaca, New York, and grew up in the cities of Champaign and Urbana in Illinois. He attended Amherst College in Massachusetts where he majored in English and philosophy, with a focus on modal logic and mathematics. He earned his MFA from the University of Arizona; he then went on to teach at Illinois State University and Pomona College in Claremont, California. His first novel, *The Broom of the System*, was published in 1987. His second novel, *Infinite Jest* (1996), earned him praise from both critics and readers. Among his short fiction collections are *Girl with Curious Hair* (1989), *Brief Interviews with Hideous Men* (1999), and *Oblivion: Stories* (2004). His nonfiction work includes *A Supposedly Fun Thing I'll Never Do Again* (1997), *Everything and More: A Compact History of Infinity* (2003), *Consider the Lobster* (2005), and *Both Flesh and Not: Essays* (2012). His work also appeared in a great number of periodicals, including the *Boston Globe*, *Los Angeles Times*, *Nation*, the *New Yorker*, *New York Times*, and *Time* magazine. Among his numerous honors were a writer's award from the Whiting Foundation, a fellowship from the National Endowment for the Arts, and a grant from the MacArthur Foundation. Wallace, who was widely considered one of the best young writers in the United States, battled depression for many years before committing suicide in 2008. His last, unfinished novel, *The Pale King* (2011), was nominated for a Pulitzer Prize.

JAMES WELCH (1940–2003) Welch was born in Browning, Montana. His father was a member of the Blackfeet tribe and his mother a member of the Gros Ventre tribe; growing up, Welch attended schools on the Blackfoot and Fort Belknap reservations. He earned his BA from the University of Montana, which is where he launched his writing career under the tutelage of Richard Hugo. Welch later taught at the University of Washington and at Cornell University and also served on the Parole Board of the Montana Prisons Systems and on the board of directors of the Newberry Library D'Arcy McNickle Center. Welch's first book was a collection of poetry entitled *Riding the Earthboy 40* (1971), which centered on the Native American experience. His first novel, *Winter in the Blood* (1974), also explored this theme. While teaching at Cornell, Welch wrote *The Death of Jim Loney* (1979) and *Fools Crow* (1986), which won the American Book Award, the Pacific Northwest Book Award, and the Los Angeles Times Book Prize. In 1997 Welch received a Lifetime Achievement

Award from the Native Writers Circle, and in 2000 he was named a *Chevalier des Arts et des Lettres* (Knight of the Order of Arts and Letters) by the French Minister of Culture. His novel *The Heartsong of Charging Elk* (2000) garnered another Pacific Northwest Book Award in 2001. Welch and Paul Stekler cowrote the documentary *Last Stand at Little Bighorn* (1992), which aired on PBS and won an Emmy Award. They also coauthored *Killing Custer: The Battle of Little Bighorn and the Fate of the Plains Indians* (1994).Welch died of a heart attack in Missoula, Montana, in 2003.

PHILLIS WHEATLEY (1753–1784) Wheatley was abducted from her home in Africa by slave traders and brought to Boston. There, according to an advertisement on August 3, 1761, in the *Boston Evening Post*, "A parcel of likely Negroes, imported from Africa" was offered "cheap for cash." One of them, a seven- or eight-year-old child, was bought as a house servant for Susannah Wheatley, the wife of a prosperous Boston tailor. The Wheatley family, impressed by the young African's quickness of intellect, taught her English and Christianity as well as Latin, ancient history, and classical literature. As Phillis's formidable talents developed, the family allowed her time to study and to write. Her early poems, the first of them published when she was a young teenager, appeared in local broadside sheets sold on the streets of Boston. In 1773, her fame as a poet growing, she was taken by the Wheatleys' son to London, where thirty-nine of her poems were published as *Poems on Various Subjects Religious and Moral*. The book was an instant success, and Phillis was widely honored and lionized. The "Sable Muse," as the English dubbed her, received a visit from Benjamin Franklin, America's colonial agent in Britain; the Lord Mayor of London honored her with a gift; and even Voltaire praised her poems. As arrangements were being made to present her to George III, she was recalled to America to tend to her ailing mistress. In the following years, upon the deaths of the Wheatleys, she gained her freedom; married another freed slave, John Peters; and bore three children, all of whom died in childhood. During her final years, which were marked by failing health and the burdens of menial work, she did not publish any poems. Her attempt to revive her fortunes by advertising a 300-page volume titled "Poems & Letters on various subjects dedicated to the Right Hon. Benjamin Franklin, Esq." failed to attract enough subscribers. She died, obscure and destitute, when she was about thirty.

E. B. WHITE (1899–1985) Elwyn Brooks White was born in Mount Vernon, New York, a suburb of Manhattan. He served in the U.S. Army before earning a degree from Cornell University and then worked as a journalist at the *Seattle Times* and *Seattle Post-Intelligencer* and in advertising, jobs he loathed. In 1925 White submitted his first article to the *New Yorker*; he joined the staff two years later and contributed to the magazine for nearly sixty years. He was also a columnist for *Harper's* magazine from 1938 to 1943. Although White wrote poetry and published letters, he is perhaps best known for his essays, which varied widely in subject matter but always incorporated his amiable wit. He also took to writing children's literature for a beloved niece, and his books—*Stuart Little* (1945), *Charlotte's Web* (1952), and *Trumpet of the Swan* (1970)—became unqualified classics. Among White's countless awards are a Newbery Honor, a gold medal from the National Institute of Arts and Letters, a Laura Ingalls Wilder Award for "a lasting contribution to children's literature," a National Medal for Literature, and a Pulitzer Prize special citation for the body of his work. He spent most of his life at his home in Maine, where he died at age eighty-six.

WALT WHITMAN (1819–1892) One of nine children, Whitman was born in Huntington, Long Island, in New York, and grew up in Brooklyn, where his father worked as a carpenter. At age eleven, after five years of public school, Whitman took a job as a printer's assistant. He learned the printing trade and, before his twentieth birthday, became editor of the *Long Islander*, a Huntington newspaper. He edited several newspapers in the New York area and one in New Orleans before leaving the newspaper business in 1848. He then lived with his parents, worked as a part-time carpenter, and began writing *Leaves of Grass*, which he first published at his own expense in 1855. After the Civil War (during which he was a devoted volunteer, ministering to the wounded), Whitman was fired from his job in the Department of the Interior by Secretary James Harlan, who considered *Leaves of Grass* obscene. Soon, however, he was rehired in the attorney general's office, where he remained until 1874. In 1881, after many editions, *Leaves of Grass* finally found a publisher willing to print it uncensored. Translations were enthusiastically received in Europe, but Whitman remained relatively unappreciated in the United States; not until after his death would a large audience come to admire his original and innovative expression of American individualism.

MARGARET WILKERSON (b. ?)   Wilkerson received her BA in history (1959) from the University of Redlands, and her MA (1967) and PhD (1972) in dramatic art from the University of California, Berkeley, where she taught and held various chairs for nearly three decades. In the 1970s and 1980s, she was director of the school's Center for the Study, Education, and Advancement of Women. She then served as chair of the Department of African American Studies from 1988 to 1994, and as chair of the Department of Theater, Dance, and Performance Studies from 1995 to 1998, where she founded the UC Berkeley Black Theater Workshop. Wilkerson has been honored for exemplary academic leadership by the Deans' Institute of the Council of Independent Colleges, and she was the first recipient of the Black Theatre Network's Winona Lee Fletcher Award for outstanding scholarship. She has received grants and fellowships from both the Rockefeller and Ford Foundations. Wilkerson is currently the director of media, arts, and culture for the Ford Foundation.

TOBIAS WOLFF (b. 1945)   Wolff was born in Birmingham, Alabama. He holds a First Class Honors degree in English from Hertford College, Oxford, and an MA from Stanford University. He contributes regularly to the *New Yorker, Atlantic, Harper's*, and other literary publications, and his work has been recognized with such honors as the PEN/Malamud Award, the Rea Award, the Los Angeles Times Book Prize, and the PEN/Faulkner Award. He has written two novels, *The Barracks Thief* (1984) and *Old School* (2003), the memoirs *This Boy's Life* (1989) and *In Pharaoh's Army* (1994), and the short-story collections *In the Garden of the North American Martyrs* (1981), *Back in the World* (1985), *The Night in Question* (1997), and *Our Story Begins* (2008), which won the Story Prize. Wolff taught at Syracuse University from 1980 to 1997 and currently teaches English at his alma mater, Stanford University.

VIRGINIA WOOLF (1882–1941)   Woolf was born in London, where she spent most of her life. Because of her frail health and her father's Victorian attitudes about the proper role of women, she received little formal education. Nevertheless, the advantages of an upper-class family (her father, Sir Leslie Stephen, was a distinguished scholar and man of letters who hired tutors for her) and an extraordinarily powerful and inquiring mind allowed Woolf to educate herself. She began keeping a regular diary in her early teens. After moderate success with her first novels, the publication of *To the Lighthouse* (1927) and *Orlando* (1929) established her as a major novelist. While Woolf's reputation rests primarily on her novels, which helped revolutionize fictional technique, she was also a distinguished literary and social critic. A strong supporter of women's rights, she expressed her views on the subject in a series of lectures published as *A Room of One's Own* (1929) and in a collection of essays, *Three Guineas* (1938). Her reputation grew with the publication of her letters and diaries following her suicide by drowning.

WILLIAM WORDSWORTH (1770–1850)   Born in Cockermouth in the Lake District of England, Wordsworth was educated at Cambridge University. During a summer tour in France in 1790, Wordsworth had an affair with Annette Vallon that resulted in the birth of a daughter. The tour also made Wordsworth an ardent defender of the French Revolution of 1789 and kindled his sympathies for the plight of the common person. Wordsworth's acquaintance with Samuel Taylor Coleridge in 1795 began a close friendship that led to the collaborative publication of *Lyrical Ballads* in 1798. Wordsworth supplied a celebrated preface to the second edition in 1800, in which he announced himself a nature poet of pantheistic leanings, committed to democratic equality and the language of common people. He finished *The Prelude* in 1805, but it was not published until after his death. As he grew older, Wordsworth grew increasingly conservative, and though he continued to write prolifically, little that he wrote during the last decades of his life attained the heights of his earlier work. In 1843 he was appointed poet laureate.

JAMES WRIGHT (1927–1980)   Wright was born in Martins Ferry, Ohio, into a family afflicted by poverty and misfortune. His parents had never attended school beyond the eighth grade, and Wright himself graduated from high school a year late due to a nervous breakdown that forced him to take time off. After high school he joined the army and was stationed in Japan during the American occupation. After serving, he attended Kenyon College on the GI Bill, from where he graduated cum laude and Phi Beta Kappa in 1952. Wright went on to earn his MA and PhD at the University of Washington, where he studied with Theodore Roethke and Stanley Kunitz. While Wright was a graduate student, W. H. Auden selected Wright's manuscript *The Green Wall* (1957) for publication in the Yale Younger Poets Series. Wright also contributed to many literary journals during this time, such as the *Sewanee Review*, the *New Yorker*, and *New Orleans Poetry Review*. He went on to teach at the University of Minnesota, Macalester College, and New York City's Hunter College. The subjects of Wright's earlier books, *The Green Wall* and *Saint Judas* (1959), focus on profound, isolating human issues such as lost love and marginalization from society, which Wright had witnessed firsthand during his childhood. Whereas his earlier work is mostly conventional in form, Wright's later works are more open and looser in structure, as seen in *The Branch Will Not Break* (1963) and *Shall We Gather at the River* (1968). In 1971 Wright was elected a fellow of the Academy of American Poets, and his *Collected Poems* (1972) received the Pulitzer Prize for Poetry the following year. He wrote actively during this period, publishing the collections *Two Citizens* (1973), *I See the Wind* (1974), *Old Booksellers and Other Poems* (1976), *Moments of the Italian Summer* (1976), and *To a Blossoming Pear Tree* (1978). He died in New York City in 1980. Three posthumous collections of his work have been published: *This Journey* (1982), *The Temple in Nîmes* (1982), and *Above the River: The Complete Poems* (1992).

LADY MARY WROTH (1587–1651 or 1653)   Wroth's mother was a wealthy heiress from Wales and Sir Walter Raleigh's first cousin; her father was appointed the first Earl of Leicester by King James I. In 1604, it was arranged that Mary would marry Sir Robert Wroth, who turned out to be an alcoholic, a philanderer, and a compulsive gambler. Although Lady Wroth became a fixture in Queen Anne's court and was a close friend, and perhaps lover, of playwright, poet, and actor Ben Jonson, her husband's death in 1614 saddled her with considerable debt. Perhaps in an attempt to earn money to satisfy her creditors, she published *The Countesse of Montgomeries Urania* (1621). Credited as the first substantial work of fiction written by an Englishwoman, it included sonnets interspersed throughout the romantic prose. The work, however, was highly controversial as royal society believed that it bore a striking resemblance to real life and revealed the court's secrets; King James ordered that it be withdrawn. Among her other works, all unpublished during her lifetime, are *The Second Part of the Countesse of Montgomeries Urania*, a few poems, and an unfinished play titled *Love's Victory*. Scholars believe that her financial circumstances and the scandal surrounding *Urania* led to Wroth's departure from royal societal circles; thus, very little about her later life, including the exact date of her death, is known.

SIR THOMAS WYATT (1503–1542)   Though people generally think of William Shakespeare when they hear the word *sonnet*, Sir Thomas Wyatt is the poet generally credited as the "father of the English sonnet." Wyatt's father, Henry Wyatt, was one of Henry VII's privy councillors and remained a friend to the court when Henry VIII assumed the throne in 1509. Wyatt was educated at St. John's College at the University of Cambridge and followed his father to court in 1515 as an ambassador for Henry VIII. In 1522 he married Elizabeth Brooke, sister of George Brooke—a baron—and later traveled to Rome as part of the delegation that petitioned the pope to annul Henry VIII's marriage to his first wife, Catherine of Aragon. Wyatt was knighted in 1535 but came to disgrace the following year when he was imprisoned in the Tower of London after quarreling with the Duke of Suffolk (and possibly for committing adultery with Anne Boleyn, Henry VIII's wife at the time). Excepting a handful of poems included in the miscellany *The Court of Venus*, none of Wyatt's poems were printed during his lifetime; fifteen years after Wyatt's death his poetry finally appeared alongside that of Henry Howard, Earl of Surrey, in printer Richard Tottel's *Songs and Sonnets written by the Right Honorable Lord Henry Howard late Earl of Surrey and other*. Wyatt's poetry often reflects classical and Italian models, especially the Petrarchan sonnet, and he was also adept at other new forms in English. His poetry helped to establish the poetic convention of a cruel mistress who abuses her lover—a form that flourished in the English canon thereafter.

WILLIAM BUTLER YEATS (1865–1939)   Yeats was born in Ireland and educated in both Ireland and London. Much of his poetry and many of his plays reflect his fascination with the history of Ireland—particularly the myths and legends of its ancient, pagan past—as well as his interest in the occult. As Yeats matured, he turned increasingly to contemporary subjects, expressing his nationalism in poems about the Irish struggle for independence from England. In 1891 he became one of the founders of an Irish literary society in London, the Rhymers' Club, and of another in Dublin the following year. Already a recognized poet, Yeats helped to establish the Irish National Theater in 1899; its first production was his play *The Countess Cathleen*, written in 1892. His contribution to Irish cultural and political nationalism led to his appointment as a senator when the Irish Free State was formed in 1922. Yeats's preeminence as a poet was recognized in 1923, when he received the Nobel Prize in Literature. Among his works are *The Wanderings of Oisin and Other Poems* (1889), *The Wind among the Reeds* (1899), *The Green Helmet and Other Poems* (1910), *Responsibilities: Poems and a Play* (1914), *The Tower* (1928), and *Last Poems and Two Plays* (1939).

DEAN YOUNG (b. 1955) Young was born in Columbia, Pennsylvania, and he received his BA in English and his MFA in creative writing from Indiana University. He has taught at various schools and writing programs, including the University of Iowa's Writers' Workshop and the MFA program at Warren Wilson College, before becoming the William Livingston Chair of Poetry at the University of Texas at Austin in 2008. He has been the recipient of fellowships from the Guggenheim Foundation, the National Endowment for the Arts, and Stanford University. He is the author of eight books of poetry, most recently *Skid* (2002), *Elegy on Toy Piano* (2005), *Embryoyo* (2007), and *Primitive Mentor* (2008). About his poems, Young has said, "I think they're very much about misunderstanding. . . . I wrote my first book to be understood, to be accepted. . . . And I realized that the poems in the first book weren't by me—they were instilled in my head. And that not being understood, not being accepted, was my subject." His recent volumes include *The Art of Recklessness: Poetry as Assertive Force and Contradiction* (2010), *Fall Higher* (2011), and *Bender: New and Selected Poems* (2012).

KEVIN YOUNG (b. 1970) Young was born in Lincoln, Nebraska, and earned degrees from Harvard University and Brown University. He was a Stegner Fellow at Stanford University in the interim. He taught at the University of Georgia and Indiana University, before becoming professor of English and creative writing at Emory University. He has edited two collections in the Everyman's Library, *Blues Poems* (2003) and *Jazz Poems* (2006), and has published several volumes of his own poetry, including *Most Way Home* (1998), *To Repel Ghosts: Five Sides in B Minor* (2002), *Jelly Roll: A Blues* (2003), *Black Maria: Poems Produced and Directed* (2005), *For the Confederate Dead* (2007), and *Dear Darkness* (2008). His work has also appeared in a number of periodicals, including the *New Yorker*, the *Paris Review*, *Ploughshares*, and *Poetry*. His most recent works include the poetry collections *Ardency: A Chronicle of the Amistad Rebels* (2011), which won the Before Columbus Foundation American Book Award, and *Book of Hours* (2014), as well as the essay collection *The Gray Album: On the Blackness of Blackness* (2012), a New York Times Notable Book.

TIMOTHY YU (b. 1974) Yu earned his BA from Harvard University and his PhD from Stanford University. He is the author of *Race and the Avant-Garde: Experimental and Asian American Poetry Since 1965* (2009), which "delves into the 1960s social upheaval to trace how language and Asian American writing emerged as parallel poetics of the avant-garde, each with its own distinctive form, style, and political meaning." He has contributed poems and criticism to numerous publications, including *Interlope, Chicago Review*, the *Poetry Project Newsletter, Shampoo*, and *Cordite*. He has also written several chapbooks of poetry, most recently *15 Chinese Silences* (2012). Yu is associate professor of English and Asian American Studies—as well as director of Asian American Studies—at the University of Wisconsin–Madison.

LU XUN (1881–1936) Born into a prosperous Chinese family, Lu Xun was educated in the Confucian classics of poetry, history, and philosophy from a young age. His preference, however, was for the folk tales and traditional stories related to him by Ah Chang, the illiterate servant woman who raised him. Because of his family's declining fortune as he got older, Lu was forced to continue his secondary studies at government-funded military schools that specialized in Western education. In 1902 he moved to Japan and began attending a Western-style medical school, but he abandoned this track in 1906 to become a writer. He returned to China in 1909, taking on some teaching positions and working on traditional Chinese scholarship, which he considered beneath his intellect. After the revolution, which overthrew imperial rule in 1912, Lu began working for the Ministry of Education in Beijing, where he was highly regarded for renovating and expanding the Beijing Library, establishing a Natural History Museum, and establishing the Library of Popular Literature. In 1918 he published "Diary of a Madman," which was praised for being antitraditional; it earned him recognition as one of the leading writers of China's New Culture Movement. In 1920 Lu began teaching fiction and literary theory at colleges including Peking University, Beijing Normal University, and Beijing Women's College. In the 1920s he published two collections of short stories: *A Call to Arms* (1923) and *Wandering* (1926), classics that are often considered to mark the beginning of modern Chinese literature. He also published a volume of prose poetry, *Wild Grass* (1927), and an autobiographical collection of essays about his youth, *Morning Blossoms Plucked at Dusk* (1932). After developing an interest in Marxism, Lu cofounded the League of Left-Wing Writers in 1930. A year later, when the right-wing government passed strict censorship laws, he went into hiding and used a pseudonym to write essays critical of the ruling party. Described by Nobel laureate Kenzaburō Ōe as "The greatest writer Asia produced in the twentieth century," Lu published his final collection of fiction, *Old Tales Retold*, in 1935.

Glossary of Literary Terms

Abstract language Language that describes ideas, concepts, or qualities, rather than particular or specific persons, places, or things. *Beauty, courage, love* are abstract terms, as opposed to such concrete terms as *man, stone, woman.* George Washington, the Rosetta stone, and Helen of Troy are particular concrete terms. Characteristically, literature uses *concrete* language to animate *abstract* ideas and principles. When Robert Frost, in "Provide, Provide," describes the pain of impoverished and lonely old age, he doesn't speak of an old, no longer beautiful female. He writes: "The witch that came (the withered hag) / To wash the steps with pail and rag, / Was once the beauty Abishag."

Alexandrine In poetry, a line containing six iambic feet (iambic hexameter). Alexander Pope, in "An Essay on Criticism," reveals his distaste for the forms in a couplet: "A needless Alexandrine ends the song, / That, like a wounded snake, drags its slow length along." *See* Meter.

Allegory A narrative in verse or prose, in which abstract qualities (*death, pride, greed,* for example) are personified as characters. In Nathaniel Hawthorne's story "Young Goodman Brown" (p. 77), Brown's wife personifies faith and the old man in the forest personifies Satan.

Alliteration The repetition of the same consonant sounds, usually at the beginning of words in close proximity. The *w* sounds in these lines from Robert Frost's "Provide, Provide" alliterate: "The witch that came (the withered hag) / To wash the steps with pail and rag, / Was once the beauty Abishag."

Allusion A reference in a literary work to something outside the work, usually to some famous person, place, thing, event, or other literary work.

Ambiguity A phrase, statement, or situation that may be understood in two or more ways. In literature, ambiguity is used to enrich meaning or achieve irony by forcing readers to consider alternative possibilities. When the duke in Robert Browning's "My Last Duchess" (p. 173) says that he "gave commands; / Then all smiles stopped together. There she stands / As if alive," the reader cannot know exactly what those commands were or whether the last words refer to the commands (as a result of which she is no longer alive) or merely refer to the skill of the painter (the painting is extraordinarily lifelike).

Analogy A comparison that uses a known thing or concept to explain something unfamiliar. *See* Metaphor; Simile.

Anapest A three-syllable metrical foot consisting of two unaccented syllables followed by an accented syllable. *See* Meter.

Antagonist A character in a story, play, or narrative poem who stands in opposition to the hero (*see* Protagonist). The conflict between antagonist and protagonist often generates the action or plot of the story.

Antistrophe *See* Strophe.

Apostrophe A direct address to a person who is absent or to an abstract or inanimate entity. In one of his sonnets (p. 1243), John Donne admonishes: "Death, be not proud!" And in "Lines Composed a Few Miles above Tintern Abbey," Wordsworth speaks to a river in Wales: "How oft, in spirit, have I turned to thee, / O sylvan Wye! thou wanderer through the woods."

Archaism   The literary use of obsolete language. When Keats, in "Ode on a Grecian Urn" (p. 1245), writes: "with brede / Of marble men and maidens overwrought," he uses an archaic word for *braid* and intends an obsolete definition, "worked all over" (that is, "ornamented"), for *overwrought*.

Archetype   Themes, images, and narrative patterns that are universal and thus embody some enduring aspects of human experience. Some of these themes are the death and rebirth of the hero, the underground journey, and the search for the father.

Assonance   The repetition of vowel sounds in a line, stanza, or sentence: *road nowhere*. By using assonance that occurs at the end of words—*my, pie*—or a combination of assonance and consonance (the repetition of final consonant sounds—*fish, wish*), poets create rhyme. Some poets use assonantial and consonantial off rhymes (*see* Near rhyme). W. H. Auden, in a celebrated verse from "Five Songs," writes: "That night when joy began / Our narrowest veins to flush, / We waited for the flash / Of morning's levelled gun." *Flush* and *gun* are assonantial, *flush* and *flash* are consonantial (and, of course, alliterative).

Atmosphere   The general feeling or mood created in the reader by a work. *See* Mood.

Aubade   A love song or lyric to be performed at sunrise.

Ballad   A narrative poem, originally of folk origin, usually focusing on a climactic episode and told without comment. The most common ballad form consists of quatrains of alternating four- and three-stress iambic lines, with the second and fourth lines rhyming. Often, the ballad will employ a *refrain*—that is, the last line of each stanza will be identical or similar. Dudley Randall's "Ballad of Birmingham" (p. 431) is a twentieth-century example of the ballad tradition.

Blank verse   Lines of unrhymed iambic pentameter. Shakespeare's dramatic poetry is written principally in blank verse. *See* Meter.

Caesura   A strong pause within a line of poetry. Note the caesuras indicated by a double vertical line (‖) in these lines from Robert Browning's "My Last Duchess" (p. 173): "That's my last Duchess painted on the wall, / Looking as if she were alive, ‖ I call / That piece a wonder, now: ‖ Frà Pandolf's hands / Worked busily a day, ‖ and there she stands."

Carpe diem   Latin, meaning "seize the day." A work, usually a lyric poem, in which the speaker calls the attention of the auditor (often a young woman) to the shortness of youth and life and then urges the auditor to enjoy life while there is time. Andrew Marvell's "To His Coy Mistress" (p. 977) is among the best of the *carpe diem* tradition in English. The opening stanza of a famous Robert Herrick poem nicely illustrates *carpe diem* principles: "Gather ye rosebuds while ye may, / Old Time is still a-flying / And this same flower that smiles today, / Tomorrow will be dying."

Catharsis   A key concept in the *Poetics* of Aristotle that attempts to explain why representations of suffering and death in drama paradoxically leave the audience feeling relieved rather than depressed. According to Aristotle, the fall of a tragic hero arouses in the viewer feelings of "pity" and "terror"—pity because the hero is an individual of great moral worth and terror because the viewer identifies with and, consequently, feels vulnerable to the hero's tragic fate. Ideally, the circumstances within the drama allow viewers to experience a catharsis that purges those feelings of pity and terror and leaves them emotionally purified.

Central intelligence   *See* Point of view.

Character   A person or figure in a literary work, sometimes classified as either *flat* (quickly describable) or *round* (more developed, complex). *See* Protagonist *and* Antagonist.

Characterization   The means of presenting and developing a character, shown through the author's description, the character's actions or thoughts, or other characters' actions or thoughts.

Chorus   Originally, a group of masked dancers who chanted lyric hymns at religious festivals in ancient Greece. In the plays of Sophocles, the chorus, while circling around the altar to Dionysus, chants the odes that separate the episodes. These odes, in some respects, represented an audience's reaction to, and comment on, the action in the episodes. In Elizabethan drama, and even, on occasion, in modern drama, the chorus appears, usually as a single person who comments on the action.

Comedy   In drama, the representation of situations that are designed to delight and amuse and that end happily. Comedy often deals with ordinary people in their human condition, while tragedy deals with the ideal and heroic and, until recently, embodied only the high born as tragic heroes. *Compare* Tragedy.

Conceit   A figure of speech that establishes an elaborate parallel between unlike things. The *Petrarchan conceit* (named for the fourteenth-century Italian writer of love lyrics) was often imitated by Elizabethan sonneteers until the device became so hackneyed that Shakespeare mocked the tendency in Sonnet 130 (p. 936): "My mistress' eyes are nothing like the sun; / Coral is far more red than her lips' red; / If snow be white, why then her breasts are dun; / If hairs be wires, black wires grow on her head." The *metaphysical conceit* employs strange, even bizarre, comparisons to heighten the wit of the poem. Perhaps the most famous metaphysical conceit is John Donne's elaborate and extended parallel of a drawing compass to the souls of the couple in "A Valediction: Forbidding Mourning" (p. 938).

Concrete language   *See* Abstract language.

Conflict   The struggle of a protagonist, or main character, with forces that threaten to destroy him or her. The struggle creates suspense and is usually resolved at the end of the narrative. The force opposing the main character may be another person—the antagonist—or society (as in Harlan Ellison's "'Repent, Harlequin!' Said the Ticktockman," p. 374), or natural forces (as in Katherine Anne Porter's "The Jilting of Granny Weatherall," p. 1227). A fourth type of conflict reflects the struggle of opposing tendencies within an individual (as in Tolstoy's "The Death of Iván Ilých," p. 1132).

Connotation   The associative and suggestive meanings of a word, in contrast to its literal or *denotative* meaning. One might speak of an *elected official*, a relatively neutral term without connotative implications. Others might call the same person a *politician*, a more negative term; still others might call him or her a *statesman*, a more laudatory term. *Compare* Denotation.

Consonance   Repetition of the final consonant sounds in stressed syllables. In the second poem of W. H. Auden's "Five Songs," lines 1 and 4 illustrate consonance, as do lines 2 and 3. "That night when joy began / Our narrowest veins to flush, / We waited for the flash / Of morning's levelled gun."

Couplet   A pair of rhymed lines—for example, these from Andrew Marvell's "To His Coy Mistress" (p. 977): "Thus, though we cannot make our sun / Stand still, yet we will make him run."

Dactyl   A three-syllable metrical foot consisting of an accented syllable followed by two unaccented syllables. *See* Meter.

Denotation   The literal dictionary definition of a word, without associative and suggestive meanings. *See* Connotation.

Denouement   The final revelations that occur after the main conflict is resolved; literally, the "untying" of the plot following the climax.

Deus ex machina   Latin for "god from a machine." Difficulties were sometimes resolved in ancient Greek and Roman plays by a god, who was lowered to the stage by means of machinery. The term is now used to indicate unconvincing or improbable coincidences that are used to advance or resolve a plot.

Dialect   A variety of a language distinguished by its pronunciation, vocabulary, rhetoric, and grammar. When used in dialogue, dialect reveals a character's membership in certain groups or communities.

Dialogue   The exchange of words between characters in a drama or narrative.

Diction   The choice of words in a work of literature and hence an element of style crucial to the work's effectiveness. The diction of a story told from the point of view of an inner-city child (as in Toni Cade Bambara's "The Lesson," p. 98) will differ markedly from a similar story told from the point of view of a mature and educated adult, like the narrator of James Joyce's "Araby" (p. 125).

Didactic   A term applied to works with the primary and avowed purpose of persuading the reader that some philosophical, religious, or moral doctrine is true.

Dimeter   A line of poetry consisting of two metrical feet. *See* Meter.

Distance   The property that separates an author or a narrator from the actions of the characters he or she creates, thus allowing a disinterested, or aloof, narration of events. Similarly, distance allows the reader or audience to view the characters and events in a narrative dispassionately.

Dramatic irony   *See* Irony.

Dramatic monologue   A type of poem in which the speaker addresses another person (or persons) whose presence is known only from the speaker's words. During the course of the monologue, the speaker (often unintentionally) reveals his or her own character. Such poems are dramatic because the speaker interacts with another character at a specific time and place; they are monologues because the entire poem is uttered by the speaker. Robert Browning's "My Last Duchess" (p. 173), Matthew Arnold's "Dover Beach" (p. 943), and T. S. Eliot's "The Love Song of J. Alfred Prufrock" (p. 651) are dramatic monologues.

Elegy   Usually, a poem that laments the death of a particular person. The term often is used to describe meditative poems on the subject of human mortality. A. E. Housman's "To an Athlete Dying Young" (p. 1258) is an elegy.

End-rhyme   *See* Rhyme.

End-stopped line   A line of verse that embodies a complete logical and grammatical unit. A line of verse that does not constitute a complete syntactic unit is called *run-on*. For example, in the opening lines of Robert Browning's "My Last Duchess" (p. 173): "That's my last Duchess painted on the wall, / Looking as if she were alive. I call / That piece a wonder, now . . . ," the opening line is end-stopped while the second line is run-on, because the direct object of *call* runs on to the third line.

English sonnet   Also called *Shakespearean sonnet. See* Sonnet.

Enjambment   The use of run-on lines. *See* End-stopped line.

Epigraph   In literature, a short quotation or observation related to the theme and placed at the head of the work. T. S. Eliot's "The Love Song of J. Alfred Prufrock" (p. 651) has an epigraph.

Epiphany   In literature, a showing forth, or sudden manifestation. James Joyce used the term to indicate a sudden illumination that enables a character (and, presumably, the reader) to understand his situation. The narrator of Joyce's "Araby" (p. 125) experiences an epiphany toward the end of the story, as does Leo Tolstoy's Iván Ilých (p. 1132).

Epode   *See* Strophe.

Euphony   Language embodying sounds pleasing to the ear.

Exposition   Information supplied to readers and audiences that enables them to understand narrative action. Often, exposition establishes what has occurred before the narrative begins, or informs the audience about relationships among principal characters. The absence of exposition from some modern literature, particularly modern drama, contributes to the unsettling feelings sometimes experienced by the audience.

Farce   A type of comedy, usually satiric, that relies on exaggerated character types, ridiculous situations, and often horseplay.

Feminine rhyme   A two-syllable rhyme in which the second syllable is unstressed, as in the second and fourth lines of these verses from James Fenton's "God, A Poem": "A nasty surprise in a sandwich, / A drawing-pin caught in your sock, / The limpest of shakes from a hand which / You'd thought would be firm as a rock."

Figurative language   A general term covering the many ways in which language is used nonliterally. *See* Hyperbole, Irony, Metaphor, Metonymy, Paradox, Simile, Symbol, Synecdoche, Understatement.

First-person narrator   *See* Point of view.

Foot   *See* Meter.

Free verse   Poetry, usually unrhymed, that does not adhere to the metrical regularity of traditional verse. Although free verse is not metrically regular, it is nonetheless clearly more rhythmic than prose and makes use of other aspects of poetic discourse to achieve its effects.

Heroic couplet   Iambic pentameter lines that rhyme *aa*, *bb*, *cc*, and so on. Usually, heroic couplets are *closed*—that is, the couplet's end coincides with a major syntactic unit so that the line is end-stopped. These lines from Alexander Pope's "Essay on Man" illustrate the form: "And, spite of pride, in erring reason's spite, / One truth is clear; Whatever IS, IS RIGHT."

Hexameter   A line of verse consisting of six metrical feet. *See* Meter.

Hubris   In Greek tragedy, arrogance resulting from excessive pride.

Hyperbole   Figurative language that embodies overstatement or exaggeration. The boast of the speaker in Robert Burns's "A Red, Red Rose" (p. 942) is hyperbolic: "And I will luve thee still, my dear, / Til a' the seas gang dry."

Iamb   A metrical foot consisting of an unstressed syllable followed by a stressed syllable. *See* Meter.

Imagery   Language that embodies an appeal to a physical sense, usually sight, although the words may invoke sound, smell, taste, and touch as well. The term is often applied to all figurative language. *Images* illustrate a concept, thing, or process by appealing to the senses.

Internal rhyme   *See* Rhyme.

Irony   Figurative language in which the intended meaning differs from the literal meaning. *Verbal irony* includes overstatement (hyperbole), understatement, and opposite statement. The following lines from Robert Burns's "A Red, Red Rose" (p. 942) embody overstatement: "As fair art thou, my bonnie lass, / So deep in luve am I; / And I will luve thee still, my dear, / Til a' the seas gang dry." These lines from Andrew Marvell's "To His Coy Mistress" (p. 977) understate: "The grave's a fine and private place, / But none, I think, do there embrace." W. H. Auden's ironic conclusion to "The Unknown Citizen" (p. 430) reveals opposite statement: "Was he free? Was he happy? The question is absurd: / Had anything been wrong, we should certainly have heard." *Dramatic irony* occurs when a reader or an audience knows things a character does not and, consequently, hears things differently. For example, in Shakespeare's *Othello* (p. 984), the audience knows that Iago is Othello's enemy, but Othello doesn't. Hence, the audience's understanding of Iago's speeches to Othello differs markedly from Othello's.

Italian sonnet   Also called *Petrarchan sonnet*. *See* Sonnet.

Lyric   Originally, a song accompanied by lyre music. Now, a relatively short poem expressing the thought or feeling of a single speaker. Almost all the nondramatic poetry in this anthology is lyric poetry.

Metaphor   A figurative expression consisting of two elements in which one element is provided with special attributes by being equated with a second, unlike element. *See* Simile.

Meter   Refers to recurrent patterns of accented and unaccented syllables in verse. A metrical unit is called a *foot*, and there are four basic accented patterns. An *iamb*, or *iambic foot*, consists of an unaccented syllable followed by an accented syllable (bĕfóre, tŏdáy). A *trochee*, or *trochaic foot*, consists of an accented syllable followed by an unaccented syllable (fúnnў, phántŏm). An *anapest*, or *anapestic foot*, consists of two unaccented syllables followed by an accented syllable (in the line "If év ‖ erўthĭng háp ‖ pĕns thăt cán't ‖ bĕ dóne," the second and third metrical feet are anapests). A *dactyl*, or *dactylic foot*, consists of a stressed syllable followed by two unstressed syllables (sýllăblĕ, métrĭcăl). One common variant, consisting of two stressed syllables, is called a *spondee*, or *spondaic foot* (dáybréak, moónshíne).

Lines are classified according to the number of metrical feet they contain (an iambic hexameter line is an *alexandrine*):

one foot	monometer
two feet	dimeter
three feet	trimeter
four feet	tetrameter
five feet	pentameter
six feet	hexameter

Here are some examples of various metrical patterns:

Tŏ eách ‖ hĭs súff ‖ erĭngs: áll ‖ ăre mén,	*iambic tetrameter*
Cŏndemnéd ‖ ă liké ‖ tŏ groán;	*iambic trimeter*
Ónce ŭp ‖ ón ă ‖ mídnĭ ght ‖ dréarў, ‖ whíle Ĭ ‖	
póndĕred ‖ wéak ănd ‖ wéarў	*trochaic octameter*
Thĕ Ăssýr ‖ iăn căme dówn ‖ likĕ ă wólf ‖ ŏn thĕ fóld	*anapestic tetrameter*
Iš thís ‖ thĕ rég ‖ iŏn, thís ‖ thĕ soíl, ‖ thĕ clíme,	*iambic pentameter*
Fóllŏw ĭt ‖ úttĕrlў,	*dactylic dimeter*
Hópe bĕ ‖ yónd hópe:	*dimeter line—trochee and spondee*

Metonymy   A figure of speech in which a word stands for a closely related idea. In the expression "The pen is mightier than the sword," *pen* and *sword* are metonyms for written ideas and physical force.

Monologue   A long, uninterrupted speech by a character.

Mood   The atmosphere or general feeling of a work. *See* Atmosphere.

Muses   The nine daughters of Zeus and Mnemosyne (memory) who preside over various humanities. Although there are some variations, generally they may be assigned as follows: Calliope, epic poetry; Clio, history; Erato, lyric poetry; Euterpe, music; Melpomene, tragedy; Polyhymnia, sacred poetry; Terpsichore, dance; Thalia, comedy; and Urania, astronomy.

Narrator   The speaker of the story, not to be confused with the author. For kinds of narrators, *see* Point of view.

Near rhyme   Also called *off rhyme, slant rhyme,* or *oblique rhyme.* Usually the occurrence of consonance where rhyme is expected, as in *pearl, alcohol,* or *heaven, given. See* Rhyme.

Octave   An eight-line stanza. More often, the opening eight-line section of an Italian sonnet, rhymed *abbaabba,* followed by the sestet that concludes the poem. *See* Sonnet.

Ode   Usually, a long, serious poem on exalted subjects, often in the form of an address. Keats's "Ode on a Grecian Urn" (p. 1245) is representative. In Greek dramatic poetry, odes consisting of three parts—the *strophe,* the *antistrophe,* and the *epode*—were sung by the chorus between the episodes of the play. *See* Strophe.

Off rhyme   *See* Near rhyme.

Omniscient narrator   *See* Point of view.

Onomatopoeia   Language that sounds like what it means. Words like *buzz, bark,* and *hiss* are onomatopoetic. Also, sound patterns that reinforce the meaning may be designated onomatopoetic. Alexander Pope illustrates such onomatopoeia in this passage from "An Essay on Criticism":

> 'Tis not enough no harshness gives offense,
> The sound must seem an echo to the sense:
> Soft is the strain when Zephyr gently blows,
> And the smooth stream in smoother numbers flows;
> But when loud surges lash the sounding shore,
> The hoarse, rough verse should like the torrent roar:
> When Ajax strives some rock's vast weight to throw,
> The line too labors, and the words move slow;
> Not so, when swift Camilla scours the plain,
> Flies o'er the unbending corn, and skims along the main.

Opposite statement   *See* Irony.

Ottava rima   An eight-line, iambic pentameter stanza rhymed *abababcc.* Originating with the Italian poet Boccaccio, the form was made popular in English poetry by Milton, Keats, and Byron, among others.

Oxymoron   Literally, "acutely silly." A figure of speech in which contradictory ideas are combined to create a condensed paradox: *thunderous silence, sweet sorrow, wise fool.*

Paean   In classical Greek drama, a hymn of praise, usually honoring Apollo. Now, any lyric that joyously celebrates its subject.

Paradox   A statement that seems self-contradictory or absurd but is, somehow, valid. The conclusion of Donne's "Death, Be Not Proud" (p. 1243) illustrates: "One short sleep past, we wake eternally / And death shall be no more; Death, thou shalt die." In Holy Sonnet 14, Donne, speaking of his relationship with God, writes: "Take me to You, imprison me, for I, / Except You enthrall me, never shall be free, / Nor ever chaste, except You ravish me."

Parody   An imitation of a work using the original's form or content as a model, meant to criticize or create a humorous effect.

Pastoral   *Pastor* is Latin for "shepherd," and the pastoral is a poetic form invented by ancient Roman writers that deals with the complexities of the human condition as if they exist in a world peopled by idealized rustic shepherds. Pastoral poetry suggests that country life is superior to urban life. In the hands of such English poets as Marlowe and Milton, the pastoral embodies highly conventionalized and artificial language and situations.

Pentameter   A line containing five metrical feet. *See* Meter.

Persona   Literally, "actor's mask." The term is applied to a first-person narrator in fiction or poetry. The persona's views may differ from the author's.

Personification   The attribution of human qualities to nonhuman things, such as animals, aspects of nature, or even ideas and processes. When Donne exclaims in "Death, Be Not Proud" (p. 1243), "Death, thou shalt die," he uses personification.

Petrarchan sonnet   Also called *Italian sonnet*. *See* Sonnet.

Plot   A series of events in a story or drama that bear a significant relationship to each other. E. M. Forster illuminates the definition: "'The King died, and then the Queen died,' is a story. 'The King died, and then the Queen died of grief,' is a plot."

Poetic license   Variation from standard word order to satisfy the demands of rhyme and meter.

Point of view   The person or intelligence a writer of fiction creates to tell the story to the reader. The major techniques are: (1) *first person*, where the story is told by someone (often, though not necessarily, the principal character) who identifies himself or herself as "I," as in James Joyce's "Araby" (p. 125); (2) *third person*, where the story is told by someone (not identified as "I") who is not a participant in the action and who refers to the characters by name or as "he," "she," and "they," as in Harlan Ellison's "'Repent, Harlequin!' Said the Ticktockman" (p. 374); (3) *omniscient*, a variation on the third person, where the narrator knows everything about the characters and events, can move about in time and place as well as from character to character at will, and can, whenever he or she wishes, enter the mind of any character, as in Tolstoy's "The Death of Iván Ilých" (p. 1132); (4) *central intelligence*, another variation on the third person, where narrative elements are limited to what a single character sees, thinks, and hears, as in Toni Cade Bambara's "The Lesson" (p. 98). *See also* Unreliable narrator.

Prose   Ordinary written or spoken expression, resembling everyday language or speech.

Prosody   The study of the elements of versification, such as *rhyme, meter, stanzaic patterns*, and so on.

Protagonist   Originally, the first actor in a Greek drama. In Greek, *agon* means "contest." Hence, the protagonist is the hero, the main character in a narrative, in conflict either with his or her situation or with another character. *See* Antagonist.

Quatrain   A four-line stanza.

Refrain   The repetition within a poem of a group of words, often at the end of ballad stanzas.

Rhyme   The repetition of the final stressed vowel sound and any sounds following (*cat, rat; debate, relate; pelican, belly can*) produces perfect rhyme. When the last stressed syllable rhymes, the rhyme is called masculine (*cat, rat*). Two-syllable rhymes with unstressed last syllables are called feminine (*ending, bending*). When rhyming words appear at the end of lines, the poem is *end-rhymed*. When rhyming words appear within one line, the line contains *internal rhyme*. When the correspondence in sounds is imperfect (*heaven, given; began, gun*), *off rhyme, slant rhyme*, or *near rhyme* is produced.

Rhythm   The quality created by the relationship between stressed and unstressed syllables. A regular pattern of alternation between stressed and unstressed syllables produces *meter*. Irregular alternation of stressed and unstressed syllables produces *free verse*. Compare the rhythm of the following verses from Robert Frost's "Stopping by

Woods on a Snowy Evening" (p. 1272) and Walt Whitman's "Out of the Cradle Endlessly Rocking":

> Whose woods these are I think I know.
> His house is in the village though;
> He will not see me stopping here
> To watch his woods fill up with snow.

> Out of the cradle endlessly rocking,
> Out of the mocking-bird's throat, the musical shuttle,
> Out of the Ninth-month midnight,
> Over the sterile sands and the fields beyond, where the child leaving his bed
>   wander'd alone, bareheaded, barefoot,
> Down from the shower'd halo.

Run-on line   *See* End-stopped line.

Satire   Writing in a comic mode that holds a subject up to scorn and ridicule, often with the purpose of correcting human vice and folly. Harlan Ellison's "'Repent, Harlequin!' Said the Ticktockman" (p. 374) satirizes a society obsessed with time and order.

Scansion   The analysis of patterns of stressed and unstressed syllables to establish the metrical or rhythmical pattern of a poem.

Sestet   The six-line resolution of a Petrarchan sonnet. *See* Sonnet.

Setting   The place, time, and social context in which a work occurs. Often the setting contributes significantly to the story; for example, the tawdry gloom at the fair in James Joyce's "Araby" (p. 125) destroys the narrator's expectations.

Shakespearean sonnet   Also called *English sonnet*. *See* Sonnet.

Simile   Similar to metaphor, the simile is a comparison of unlike things introduced by the words *like* or *as*. For example, Robert Burns, in "A Red, Red Rose" (p. 942), exclaims, "O My Luve's like a red, red rose," and Shakespeare mocks extravagant similes when he admits in Sonnet 130, "My mistress' eyes are nothing like the sun" (p. 936).

Slant rhyme   *See* Rhyme.

Soliloquy   A dramatic convention in which an actor, alone on the stage, speaks his or her thoughts aloud. Iago's speech that closes act I of Shakespeare's *Othello* (p. 984) is a soliloquy, as is Othello's speech in act III, scene 3, lines 258–79.

Sonnet   A lyric poem of fourteen lines, usually of iambic pentameter. The two major types are the Petrarchan (or Italian) and Shakespearean (or English). The Petrarchan sonnet is divided into an octave (the first eight lines, rhymed *abbaabba*) and sestet (the final six lines, usually rhymed *cdecde* or *cdcdcd*). The Shakespearean sonnet consists of three quatrains and a concluding couplet, rhymed *abab cdcd efef gg*. In general, the sonnet establishes some issue in the octave or three quatrains and then resolves it in the sestet or final couplet. Robert Frost's "Design" (p. 1265) is a Petrarchan sonnet; several Shakespearean sonnets appear in the text.

Spondee   A metrical foot consisting of two stressed syllables, usually a variation within a metrical line. *See* Meter.

Stanza   The grouping of a fixed number of verse lines in a recurring metrical and rhyme pattern. Keats's "Ode on a Grecian Urn" (p. 1245), for example, employs ten-line stanzas rhymed *ababcdecde*.

Stream-of-consciousness technique   The narrative technique that attempts to reproduce the full and uninterrupted flow of a character's mental process, in which ideas, memories, and sense impressions may intermingle without logical transitions. Writers using this technique sometimes abandon conventional rules of syntax and punctuation.

Strophe   In Greek tragedy, the unit of verse the chorus chanted as it moved to the left in a dance rhythm. The chorus sang the *antistrophe* as it moved to the right and the *epode* while standing still.

Style   The way an author expresses his or her matter. Style embodies, and depends upon, all the choices an author makes—the diction, syntax, figurative language, and sound patterns of the piece.

Subplot   A second plot, usually involving minor characters. The subplot is subordinate to the principal plot but is often resolved by events that figure in the main plot. For example, Iago's manipulation of Roderigo in Shakespeare's *Othello* (p. 984) is a subplot that enters the main plot and figures prominently in the play's climax.

Symbol   An object, an action, or a person that represents more than itself. The urn in Keats's "Ode on a Grecian Urn" (p. 1245) symbolizes the cold immortality of art. The symbolism arises from the *context*. *Public symbols*, in contrast to these *contextual symbols*, are objects, actions, or persons that history, myth, or legend has invested with meaning—the cross, Helen of Troy, a national flag.

Synecdoche   A figure of speech in which a part is used to signify the whole. In "Elegy Written in a Country Churchyard," Thomas Gray writes of "Some heart once pregnant with celestial fire; / Hands that the rod of empire might have swayed." That heart, and those hands, of course, refer to whole persons who are figuratively represented by significant parts.

Synesthesia   An image that uses a second sensory impression to modify the primary sense impression. When one speaks of a "cool green," for example, the primary *visual* evocation of green is combined with the *tactile* sensation of coolness. Keats, in "Ode to a Nightingale," asks for a drink of wine "Tasting of Flora and the country green, / Dance, and Provençal song, and sunburnt mirth!" Here, the *taste* of wine is synesthetically extended to the sight of flowers and meadows, the movement of dance, the sound of song, and the heat of the sun.

Tetrameter   A verse line containing four metrical feet. *See* Meter.

Theme   The statement or underlying idea of a literary work, advanced through the concrete elements of character, action, and setting. The theme of Harlan Ellison's "'Repent, Harlequin!' Said the Ticktockman" (p. 374), in which an ordinary person defies an oppressive system, might be that to struggle against dehumanizing authority is obligatory.

Third-person narrator   A voice telling a story who refers to characters by name or as "he," "she," or "they." *See* Point of view.

Tone   The attitude embodied in the language a writer chooses. The tone authors take in a work toward readers, the subject matter, or themselves might be sad, joyful, ironic, solemn, playful. Notice, for example, the somber tone of Matthew Arnold's "Dover Beach" (p. 943).

Tragedy   The dramatic representation of serious and important actions that culminate in catastrophe for the protagonist, or chief actor, in the play. Aristotle saw tragedy as the fall of a noble figure from a high position and happiness to defeat and misery as a result of *hamartia*, some misjudgment or frailty of character. *Compare* Comedy.

Trimeter   A verse line consisting of three metrical feet. *See* Meter.

Triplet   A sequence of three verse lines that rhyme.

Trochee   A metrical foot consisting of a stressed syllable followed by an unstressed syllable. *See* Meter.

Understatement   A figure of speech that represents something as less important than it really is—hence, a form of irony. When in Robert Browning's "My Last Duchess" (p. 173) the duke asserts, "This grew; I gave commands; / Then all smiles stopped together," the words ironically understate what was likely an order for his wife's execution.

Unreliable narrator   The speaker or voice of a work who is not able to accurately or objectively report events, as in Charlotte Perkins Gilman's "The Yellow Wallpaper" (p. 548).

Verse   A stanza of a poem. More generally, verse can be used interchangeably with the term *poetry*.

Villanelle   A French verse form of nineteen lines (of any length) divided into six stanzas— five tercets and a final quatrain—employing two rhymes and two refrains. The refrains consist of lines 1 (repeated as lines 6, 12, and 18) and 3 (repeated as lines 9, 15, and 19). Dylan Thomas's "Do Not Go Gentle into That Good Night" (p. 1267) is a villanelle.

Acknowledgments (continued from p. ii)

Chris Abani. "Blue" from *Dog Woman*. Copyright © 2004 by Chris Abani. Reprinted by permission of Red Hen Press.

Chimamanda Adichie. "My American Jon." Copyright © 2007 by Chimamanda Adichie, used by permission of The Wylie Agency LLC.

Dilruba Ahmed. "Snake Oil, Snake Bit" from *Poetry* (November 2013). Copyright © 2013 by Dilruba Ahmed. Reprinted with the permission of the author, www.dilrubaahmed.com.

Edward Albee. *The Sandbox* from *Three Plays* by Edward Albee. Copyright © 1959, 1960, 1988 by Edward Albee. Published in 2013 by Overlook Duckworth, Peter Mayer Publishers, Inc., New York and London. www.overlookpress.com. All rights reserved.

Sherman Alexie. "War Dances" from *War Dances*. Copyright © 2009 by Sherman Alexie. Used by permission of Grove/Atlantic, Inc. Any third party use of this material, outside of this publication, is prohibited.

Julia Alvarez. "Woman's Work" from *Homecoming*. Copyright © 1984, 1996 by Julia Alvarez. Published by Plume, an imprint of Penguin Group (USA); originally published by Grove Press. By permission of Susan Bergholz Literary Services, New York, NY and Lamy, NM. All rights reserved.

Maggie Anderson. "Long Story" from *A Space Filled with Moving* by Maggie Anderson. Copyright © 1992. Reprinted by permission of the University of Pittsburgh Press.

Anonymous. "Edward" 56 lines from *The First Poems in English*, translated and edited by Michael Alexander (Translations first published 1966, revised and expanded 1991. This edition first published in 2008.) Copyright © Michael Alexander 1966, 1977, 1991, 2008. Reprinted by permission of Penguin Books Ltd.

Hanan Mikha'il 'Ashrawi. "Night Patrol" from *Anthology of Modern Palestinian Literature* 12/e. Copyright © 1992 Columbia University Press, Reprinted with permission of the publisher.

W. H. Auden. "Musée des Beaux Arts" and "The Unknown Citizen" copyright © 1940 and renewed 1968 by W. H. Auden; from *W. H. Auden Collected Poems* by W. H. Auden. Used by permission of Random House, an imprint and division of Penguin Random House LLC. All rights reserved.

Kofi Awoonor. "Africa" from *The Promise of Hope: New and Selected Poems, 1964–2013* by Kofi Awoonor by permission of the University of Nebraska Press. Copyright © 2014 by the Board of Regents of the University of Nebraska.

James Baldwin. "Sonny's Blues" copyright © 1957 by James Baldwin, was originally published in *Partisan Review*. Copyright renewed. Collected in *Going to Meet the Man*, published by Vintage Books. Reprinted by arrangement with the James Baldwin Estate.

Toni Cade Bambara. "The Lesson" copyright © 1972 by Toni Cade Bambara from *Gorilla, My Love* by Toni Cade Bambara. Used by permission of Random House, an imprint and division of Penguin Random House LLC. All rights reserved.

Robin Bernstein. "Inventing a Fishbowl: White Supremacy and the Critical Reception of Lorraine Hansberry's *A Raisin in the Sun*." *Modern Drama* 42 (1999) 16–27. Copyright © 1999. Reprinted by permission of the University of Toronto Press (www.utpjournals.com).

Elizabeth Bishop. "The Fish" and "One Art" from *The Complete Poems 1927–1979* by Elizabeth Bishop. Copyright © 1979, 1983 by Alice Helen Methfessel. Reprinted by permission of Farrar, Straus and Giroux, LLC.

Eula Biss. "Time and Distance Overcome" from *The Iowa Review*, Vol. 38. No. 1 (Spring, 2008). Reprinted by permission of The Iowa Review.

Richard Blanco. "América" from *City of a Hundred Fires*, by Richard Blanco, copyright © 1998. Reprinted by permission of the University of Pittsburgh Press.

Adrian Blevins. "Case Against April" from *The Brass Girl Brouhaha*. Copyright © 2003 by Adrian Blevins. Reprinted with the permission of The Permissions Company, Inc., on behalf of Copper Canyon Press. www.coppercanyonpress.org.

Gwendolyn Brooks. "We Real Cool" reprinted by consent of Brooks Permissions.

1429

Alan Feldman. "My Century" from *A Sail to Great Island*. Copyright © 2004 by the Board of Regents of the University of Wisconsin System. Reprinted by permission of The University of Wisconsin Press.

Lawrence Ferlinghetti. "Constantly Risking Absurdity" and "In Goya's Greatest Scenes" from *A Coney Island of the Mind*. Copyright © 1958 by Lawrence Ferlilnghetti. Reprinted by permission of New Directions Publishing Corp.

Annie Finch. "Coy Mistress" from *Eve*, Story Line Press. Copyright © 1997 by Annie Finch. Reprinted by permission of Rob Weisbach Creative Management.

Donald Finkel. "The Great Wave: Hokusai" from *Selected Shorter Poems*. Copyright © 1987 by Donald Finkel. Reprinted by permission.

Carolyn Forché. All text [prose poem] from "The Colonel" from *The Country Between Us* by Carolyn Forché. Copyright © 1981 by Carolyn Forché. Originally appeared in *Women's International Resource Exchange*. Reprinted by permission of HarperCollins Publishers.

Daisy Fried. "Econo Motel, Ocean City" from *Women's Poetry: Poems and Advice* by Daisy Fried. Copyright © 2013 by Daisy Fried. Reprinted by permission of the University of Pittsburgh Press.

Robert Frost. "A Semi-Revolution," "Nothing Gold Can Stay" and "Stopping By Woods on a Snowy Evening" from *The Poetry of Robert Frost*, edited by Edward Connery Lathem. Copyright © 1923, 1969 by Henry Holt and Company. Copyright © 1942, 1951 by Robert Frost. Copyright © 1970 by Lesley Frost Ballantine. Reprinted by permission of Henry Holt and Company, LLC. All rights reserved. "Design," "After Apple-Picking," "The Road Not Taken," "Fire and Ice," "Birches," and "Out, Out—" from *The Poetry of Robert Frost*, edited by Edward Connery Lathem. Copyright © 1923, 1930, 1939, 1969 by Henry Holt and Company. Copyright © 1936, 1944, 1951, 1958 by Robert Frost. Copyright © 1964, 1967 by Lesley Frost Ballantine. Reprinted by permission of Henry Holt and Company, LLC. All rights reserved.

Rivka Galchen. "Wild Berry Blue" from *American Innovations* by Rivka Galchen. Copyright © 2014 by Rivka Galchen. Reprinted by permission of Farrar, Straus and Giroux, LLC, and HarperCollins Publishers Ltd. All rights reserved.

Tess Gallagher. "I Stop Writing the Poem" from *Midnight Lantern: New and Selected Poems*. Copyright © 1976 by Tess Gallagher. Reprinted with the permission of The Permissions Company, Inc. on behalf of Graywolf Press, Minneapolis, Minnesota, www.graywolfpress.org.

Deborah Garrison. "Sestina for the Working Mother" from *The Second Child: Poems* by Deborah Garrison. Copyright © 2006 by Deborah Garrison. Used by permission of Random House, an imprint and division of Penguin Random Hosue LLC. All rights reserved.

Shirley Geok-lin Lim. "Learning to Love America" from *What the Fortune Teller Didn't Say*. Copyright © 1998 by Shirley Geok-lin Lim. Reprinted with the permission of The Permissions Company, Inc., on behalf of West End Press, Albuquerque, New Mexico, http://www.westendpress.org.

Dagoberto Gilb. "I Knew She Was Beautiful" first published in *The New Yorker*. Reprinted by permission of the author.

Allen Ginsberg. "A Supermarket In California" from *Collected Poems 1947–1980* by Allen Ginsberg. Copyright © 1955 by Allen Ginsberg. Reprinted by permission of HarperCollins Publishers.

Nikki Giovanni. "Revolutionary Dreams" from *The Collected Poems of Nikki Giovanni: 1968–1998*. Copyright compilation © 2003 by Nikki Giovanni. Chronology and notes copyright © by Virginia C. Fowler. Reprinted by permission of HarperCollins Publishers.

Malcolm Gladwell. "Small Change" from *The New Yorker*, October 4, 2010. Reprinted by permission of the author.

Louise Glück. "The School Children" from *The First Four Books of Poems* by Louise Glück. Copyright © 1968, 1971, 1972, 1973, 1974, 1975, 1976, 1977, 1978, 1979, 1980, 1985, 1995 by Louise Glück. Reprinted by permission of HarperCollins Publishers. "A Myth of Innocence" from *Poems 1962–2012* by Louise Glück. Copyright © 2012 by Louise Glück. Reprinted by permission of Farrar, Straus & Giroux, LLC.

Allegra Goodman. "Apple Cake" from *The New Yorker*, July 7, 2014. Copyright © 2014. Reprinted by permission of Irene Skolnick Literary Agency.

William Greenway. "Pit Pony" from *Where We've Been* by William Greenway. Reprinted by permission of the author.

Donald Hall. "Affirmation" from *The Painted Red: Poems* by Donald Hall. Copyright © 2002 by Donald Hall. Reprinted by permission of Houghton Mifflin Harcourt Publishing Company. All rights reserved.

Mark Halliday. "Chicken Salad" from *The Gettysburg Review* and *Keep This Forever* (Tupelo Press, 2008). Reprinted by permission of the author.

Lorraine Hansberry. Entire Play from *A Raisin in the Sun* by Lorraine Hansberry, copyright © 1958 by Robert Nemiroff, as an unpublished work. Copyright © 1959, 1966, 1984 by Robert Nemiroff. Copyright renewed 1986, 1987 by Robert Nemiroff. Used by permission of Random House, an imprint and division of Penguin Random House LLC. All rights reserved.

Robert Hayden. "Those Winter Sundays" from *Collected Poems of Robert Hayden* by Robert Hayden, edited by Frederick Glaysher. Copyright © 1966 by Robert Hayden. Used by permission of Liveright Publishing Corporation.

Terrance Hayes. "Root" from *Wind in a Box* by Terrance Hayes. Copyright © 2006 by Terrance Hayes. Used by permission of Penguin Books, an imprint of Penguin Publishing Group, a division of Penguin Random House LLC.

Seamus Heaney. "Mid-Term Break" and "Valediction" from *Opened Ground: Selected Poems 1966–1996* by Seamus Heaney. Copyright © 1998 by Seamus Heaney. Reprinted by permission of Farrar, Straus and Giroux LLC. and Faber and Faber Ltd.

Anthony Hecht. "After the Rain" from *Collected Earlier Poems* by Anthony Hecht. Copyright © 1990 by Anthony E. Hecht. Used by permission of Alfred A. Knopf, an imprint of the Knopf Doubleday Publishing Group, a division of Penguin Random House LLC. All rights reserved.

Ernest Hemingway. "Hills Like White Elephants" reprinted with the permission of Scribner, a division of Simon & Schuster, Inc. from *The Short Stories of Ernest Hemingway* by Ernest Hemingway. Copyright © 1927 by Charles Scribner's Sons. Copyright renewed © 1955 by Ernest Hemingway. All rights reserved.

Juan Filipe Herrera. "187 Reasons Mexicanos Can't Cross the Border (remix)" from *187 Reasons Mexicanos Can't Cross the Border: Undocuments 1971–2007* by Juan Filipe Herrera. Copyright © 2007. Reprinted by permission of City Lights Books.

Tony Hoagland. "I Have News for You" from *Unincorporated Persons in the Late Honda Dynasty*. Copyright © 2010 by Tony Hoagland. Reprinted with the permission of The Permissions Company, Inc., on behalf of Graywolf Press, Minneapolis, Minnesota, www.graywolfpress.org.

Andrea Hollander. "Betrayal" © 2009 by Andrea Hollander. Reprinted by permission of the author.

A. D. Hope. "His Coy Mistress to Mr. Marvell" by A. D. Hope. Reprinted by permission of Curtis Brown Australia.

Marie Howe. "What the Living Do" from *What the Living Do* by Marie Howe. Copyright © 1997 by Marie Howe. Used by permission of W. W. Norton & Company, Inc.

Langston Hughes. "Mother to Son," "I, Too" and "Harlem (2)" from *The Collected Poems of Langston Hughes* by Langston Hughes, edited by Arnold Rampersad with David Roessel, Associate Editor. Copyright © 1994 by the Estate of Langston Hughes. Used by permission of Alfred A. Knopf, an imprint of the Knopf Doubleday Publishing Group, a division of Penguin Random House LLC. All rights reserved. "Salvation" from *The Big Sea* by Langston Hughes. Copyright © 1940 by Langston Hughes. Copyright renewed 1968 by Arna Bontemps and George Houston Bass. Reprinted by permission of Hill and Wang, a division of Farrar, Straus and Giroux, LLC.

David Henry Hwang. *Trying to Find Chinatown* by David Henry Hwang from *Trying to Find Chinatown: The Selected Plays of David Henry Hwang*. Copyright © 2000 by David Henry Hwang. Published by Theatre Communications Group. Used by permission of Theatre Communications Group.

Shirley Jackson. "The Lottery" from *The Lottery* by Shirley Jackson. Copyright © 1948, 1949 by Shirley Jackson. Coyright renewed 1976, 1977 by Laurence Hyman, Barry Hyman, Mrs. Sarah Webster, and Mrs. Joanne Schnurer. Reprinted by permission of Farrar, Straus and Giroux, LLC.

Ha Jin. "The Bridegroom" from *The Bridegroom: Stories* by Ha Jin. Copyright © 2000 by Ha Jin. Used by permission of Pantheon Books, an imprint of the Knopf Doubleday Publishing Group, a division of Penguin Random House LLC. All rights reserved.

James Weldon Johnson. "A Poet to His Baby Son" from *James Weldon Johnson: Complete Poems* by James Weldon Johnson, edited by Sondra Kathryn Wilson. Copyright 1935 by James Weldon Johnson, copyright renewed © 1963 by Grace Nail Johnson. Used by permission of Penguin Books, an imprint of Penguin Publishing Group, a division of Penguin Random House LLC.

Lacy M. Johnson. "White Trash Primer" first appeared in *Memoir Journal*; adapted for inclusion in *Trespasses: A Memoir*. Copyright © 2012 University of Iowa Press. Reprinted by permission.

Ruth Margalit. "The Unmothered" from *The New Yorker*, May 9, 2014. © Condé Nast. Reprinted by permission.

Bill McKibben. "A Call to Arms: An Invitation to Demand Action on Climate Change" by Bill McKibben, *Rolling Stone*, Issue 1210, June 5, 2014. Copyright © Rolling Stone LLC 2014. All rights reserved. Used by permission.

Peter Meinke. "Advice to My Son" from *Liquid Paper: New and Selected Poems* by Peter Meinke, © 1991. Reprinted by permission of the University of Pittsburgh Press.

W. S. Merwin. "Thanks" from *The Rain In the Trees* by W. S. Merwin. Copyright © 1988 by W. S. Merwin. Used by permission of Alfred A. Knopf, an imprint of the Knopf Doubleday Publishing Group, a division of Penguin Random House LLC. All rights reserved.

Robert Mezey. "My Mother" from *Collected Poems 1952–1999*. Copyright © 2000 by Robert Mezey. Reprinted with the permission of The Permissions Company, Inc, on behalf of the University of Arkansas Press, www.aupress.com.

Lydia Millet. "Love in Infant Monkeys" from *Love in Infant Monkeys*. Copyright © 2009 by Lydia Millet. Reprinted by permission of Counterpoint.

Czesław Miłosz. "Voices of Poor People: A Song on the End of the World" from *The Collected Poems 1931–1987* by Czeslaw Milosz. Copyright © 1988 by Czeslaw Milosz Royalties, Inc. Reprinted by permission of HarperCollins Publishers.

Lisel Mueller. "Happy and Unhappy Families I" from *Alive Together* by Lisel Mueller. Copyright © 1996 by Lisel Mueller. Reprinted with permission of Louisiana State University Press.

Bharati Mukherjee. "Two Ways to Belong in America" by Bharati Mukherjee. Copyright © 1996 by Bharati Mukherjee. Originally published in *The New York Times*. Reprinted by permission of the author.

Taslima Nasrin. "Things Cheaply Had" from *The New Yorker*, October 9, 1995. Translated from the Bengali by Carolyne Wright, with Mohammad Nurul Huda and the author. Copyright © 1995 by Carolyne Wright. Reprinted with permission of Carolyne Wright.

Maggie Nelson. "Thanksgiving" from *Something Bright, Then Holes* by Maggie Nelson. Copyright © 2007 by Maggie Nelson. Reprinted by permission of Counterpoint.

Howard Nemerov. "Money" from *The Collected Poems of Howard Nemerov*. Copyright © 1977 by Howard Nemerov. Reprinted by permission of The University of Chicago Press.

Pablo Neruda. "The Dead Woman" by Pablo Neruda from *The Captain's Verses*. Copyright © 1972 by Pablo Neruda and Donald D. Walsh. Reprinted by permission of New Directions Publishing Corp.

John Frederick Nims. "Love Poem" from *Selected Poems* by John Frederick Nims. Copyright © 1982 by John Frederick Nims. Reprinted by permission of the University of Chicago Press.

Jean Nordhaus. "A Dandelion for My Mother" from *Innocence* (Ohio State University Press, 2006). Reprinted by permission of The Ohio State University Press.

Lynn Nottage. *Poof!* by Lynn Nottage. Copyright © 1993, 2004 by Lynn Nottage. Published by Theatre Communications Group. Used by permission of Theatre Communications Group.

Joyce Carol Oates. "Where Are You Going, Where Have You Been?" by Joyce Carol Oates. Copyright © 1970 Ontario Review, Inc. Reprinted by permission of John Hawkins & Associates, Inc.

Tim O'Brien. "The Things They Carried" from *The Things They Carried* by Tim O'Brien. Reprinted by permission of Houghton Mifflin Harcourt Publishing Company. All rights reserved.

Flannery O'Connor. "A Good Man Is Hard to Find" from *A Good Man Is Hard To Find and Other Stories* by Flannery O'Connor. Copyright © 1953 by Flannery O'Connor and renewed 1981 by Regina O'Connor. Reprinted by permission of Houghton Mifflin Harcourt Publishing Company. All rights reserved. Excerpt from *Mystery and Manners* by Flannery O'Connor, edited by Sally and Robert Fitzgerald. Copyright © 1969 by the Estate of Mary Flannery O'Connor. Reprinted by permission of Farrar, Straus and Giroux, LLC.

Frank O'Hara. "My Heart" from *The Collected Poems of Frank O'Hara* by Frank O'Hara. Copyright © 1971 by Maureen Granville-Smith, Administratrix of the Estate of Frank O'Hara, copyright renewed 1999 by Maureen O'Hara Granville-Smith and Donald Allen. Used by permission of Alfred A. Knopf, an imprint of the Knopf Doubleday Publishing Group, a division of Penguin Random House LLC. All rights reserved.

Sharon Olds. "Sex Without Love" from *The Dead & The Living* by Sharon Olds. Copyright © 1987 by Sharon Olds. "My Father's Diary" from *Blood, Tin, Straw: Poems* by Sharon Olds. Copyright © 1999 by

Sharon Olds. Used by permission of Alfred A. Knopf, an imprint of the Knopf Doubleday Publishing Group, a division of Penguin Random House LLC. All rights reserved.

Mary Oliver. "When Death Comes" from *New and Selected Poems* by Mary Oliver. Published by Beacon Press, Boston. Copyright © 1992 by Mary Oliver. Reprinted by permission of The Charlotte Sheedy Literary Agency Inc.

Daniel Orozco. "Orientation." Reprinted by permission of The Seattle Review.

George Orwell. "Shooting an Elephant" from *A Collection of Essays* by George Orwell. Copyright © 1950 by Sonia Brownell Orwell and renewed 1978 by Sonia Pitt-Rivers. Reprinted by permission of Houghton Mifflin Harcourt Publishing Company. All rights reserved.

Alicia Suskin Ostriker. "Daffodils" from *No Heaven* by Alicia Suskin Ostriker, copyright © 2005. "The Dogs at Live Oak Beach, Santa Cruz" from *The Little Space: Poems Selected and New, 1968–1998* by Alicia Suskin Ostriker, copyright © 1998. Both are reprinted by permission of the University of Pittsburgh Press.

Dorothy Parker. "One Perfect Rose" from *The Portable Dorothy Parker* by Dorothy Parker, edited by Marion Meade. Copyright © 1926, renewed © 1954 by Dorothy Parker. Used by permission of Viking Books, an imprint of Penguin Publishing Group, a division of Penguin Random House LLC.

Suzan-Lori Parks. *Father Comes Home from the Wars* by Suzan-Lori Parks from the book *365 Days/365 Plays*. Copyright © 2006 by Suzan-Lori Parks. Published by Theatre Communications Group. Used by permission of Theatre Communications Group.

Omar Pérez. "Contributions to a Rudimentary Concept of Nation" from *Something of the Sacred*. Copyright © 2007 by Omar Pérez, translated by Roberto Tejada. Reprinted by permission of the author and translator from *Something of the Sacred* (Factory School, 2007).

Carl Phillips. "Blue" from *In the Blood*. Copyright © University Press of New England, Lebanon, NH. Reprinted with permission.

Marge Piercy. "Barbie Doll" and "The Market Economy" from *Circles on the Water* by Marge Piercy. Copyright © 1982 by Middlemarsh, Inc. Used by permission of Alfred A. Knopf, an imprint of the Knopf Doubleday Publishing Group, a division of Penguin Random House LLC. All rights reserved.

Sylvia Plath. "Daddy" from *Ariel* by Sylvia Plath. Copyright © 1963 by Ted Hughes. Reprinted by permission of HarperCollins Publishers and Faber and Faber Ltd.

Katherine Anne Porter. "The Jilting of Granny Weatherall" from *Flowering Judas and Other Stories* by Katherine Anne Porter. Copyright © 1930 and renewed 1958 by Katherine Anne Porter. Reprinted by permission of Houghton Mifflin Harcourt Publishing Company. All rights reserved.

Kevin Powers. "Letter Composed During a Lull in the Fighting" by Kevin Powers. Copyright © 2013 by Kevin Powers. Published by Little, Brown, 2013. First appeared in *Poetry*, February, 2009. Reproduced by permission of the author c/o Rogers, Coleridge & White, 20 Powis Mews, London W11 1JN.

Wyatt Prunty. "Learning the Bicycle" from *The American Scholar*, Volume 58, No. 1, Winter 1989. Copyright © 1988 by the author. Reprinted by permission of The American Scholar.

Dudley Randall. "Ballad of Birmingham" reprinted by permission of the Dudley Randall Literary Estate. From *Roses and Revolutions: The Selected Writings of Dudley Randall*, Melba Joyce Boyd, Ed. (Detroit: Wayne State University Press, 2009).

Barbara Ras. "You Can't Have It All" from *Bite Every Sorrow*. Reprinted by permission of Louisiana State University Press.

Spencer Reece. "The Manhattan Project" (*Poetry Magazine*). Reprinted by permission of the author.

Adrienne Rich. "Living in Sin" from *The Fact of a Doorframe: Selected Poems 1950–2001* by Adrienne Rich. Copyright © 2002, 1955 by Adrienne Rich. Used by permission of W. W. Norton & Company, Inc.

Ranier Maria Rilke. "Archaic Torso of Apollo" translation copyright © 1982 by Stephen Mitchell; from *Selected Poetry of Ranier Maria Rilke* by Ranier Maria Rilke, translated by Stephen Mitchell. Used by permission of Random House, an imprint and division of Penguin Random House LLC. All rights reserved.

Theodore Roethke. "I Knew a Woman" from *Collected Poems* by Theodore Roethke. Copyright © 1954 by Theodore Roethke. "My Papa's Waltz" from *Collected Poems* by Theodore Roethke. Copyright © 1942 by Hearst Magazines, Inc. Both poems are used by permission of Doubleday, an imprint of the Knopf Doubleday Publishing Group, a division of Penguin Random House LLC. All rights reserved.

Salman Rushdie. "Imagine There's No Heaven" from *Step Across This Line: Collected Nonfiction 1992–2002* by Salman Rushdie. Copyright © 2002 by Salmlan Rushdie. Used by permission of Random House, an imprint and division of Penguin Random House LLC. All rights reserved.

INDEX OF AUTHORS AND TITLES

A & P, 92
Abani, Chris: Blue, 679
'Abbasi, Riza: *Two Lovers*, 858
Adjectives of Order, 683
Adichie, Chimamanda Ngozi: My
    American Jon, 915
Advice to My Son, 200
Affirmation, 1268
After Apple-Picking, 1261
After great pain, a formal feeling comes, 1247
After Making Love We Hear Footsteps, 951
Afternoon Happiness, 949
Ahmed, Dilruba: Snake Oil, Snake Bite,
    1282
Albee, Edward: *The Sandbox*, 1296
Alexie, Sherman: War Dances, 594
All Shall Be Restored, 660
Alvarez, Julia: Woman's Work, 697
America, 705
América, 707
American History, 287
Anderson, Maggie: Long Story, 666
Anonymous: Edward, 1239
Antigonê, 450
Apparently with no surprise, 1248
Apple Cake, 1213
Araby, 125
Archaic Torso of Apollo, 1289
Arnold, Matthew: Dover Beach, 943
'Ashrawi, Hanan Mikha'il: Night Patrol,
    446
Auden, W. H.: Musée des Beaux Arts,
    1249; The Unknown Citizen, 430
Awoonor, Kofi: America, 705

Baldwin, James: Sonny's Blues, 561
Ballad of Birmingham, 431
Bambara, Toni Cade: The Lesson, 98
Barbie Doll, 659
Bartleby, the Scrivener, 319
Battle Royal, 355
Because I could not stop for Death, 1257

Behind Grandma's House, 203
Behn, Aphra: Love in Fantastique
    Triumph satt, 972
Be Near Me, 974
Betrayal, 975
Birches, 178
Bishop, Elizabeth: The Fish, 1283; One
    Art, 946
Biss, Eula: Time and Distance Overcome,
    844
Bitch, 948
Blake, William: The Chimney Sweeper
    (Songs of Experience), 169; The
    Chimney Sweeper (Songs of
    Innocence), 168; The Garden of
    Love, 171; The Lamb, 170; London,
    171; A Poison Tree, 941; The
    Shepherd, 170; The Tyger, 172
Blanco, Richard: América, 707
Blevins, Adrian: Case against April, 960
Blue, 679
Blue, 692
Book of the Dead, The, 614
Bradstreet, Anne: To My Dear and Loving
    Husband, 941
Bridegroom, The, 630
Brooks, Gwendolyn: We Real Cool, 432
Brosh, Allie: This Is Why I'll Never Be an
    Adult, 296
Browning, Robert: My Last Duchess, 173
Brueghel, Pieter, the Elder: *Landscape
    with the Fall of Icarus*, 1250
Bryant, Hallman B.: Reading the Map in
    "A Good Man Is Hard to
    Find," 157
Bullet in the Brain, 1234
Burns, Robert: A Red, Red Rose, 942
But Men Loved Darkness rather than
    Light, 417

Call to Arms, A: An Invitation to Demand
    Action on Climate Change, 506

Cambridge ladies who live in furnished souls, the, 655

Carver, Raymond: What We Talk About When We Talk About Love, 876

Case against April, 960

Cask of Amontillado, The, 1126

Castillo, Sandra M.: Christmas, 1970, 195

Catullus: 85, 933; 70, 972

Chicken Salad, 1278

Chierici, Gaetano: *The Veteran*, 74

Chimney Sweeper, The (Songs of Experience), 169

Chimney Sweeper, The (Songs of Innocence), 168

Chin, Marilyn: How I Got That Name, 672

Chinese Silence No. 22, 694

Chopin, Kate: The Storm, 861; The Story of an Hour, 1174

Christman, Jill: The Sloth, 1311

Christmas Comes to Moccasin Flat, 210

Christmas, 1970, 195

Chung, Sonya: Getting It Right, 1109

Cisneros, Sandra: My Wicked Wicked Ways, 194

Clark, Michael: Flannery O'Connor's "A Good Man Is Hard to Find": The Moment of Grace, 163

Clifton, Lucille: There Is a Girl Inside, 956

Clover, Joshua: The Nevada Glassworks, 675

Cofer, Judith Ortiz: American History, 287; Latin Women Pray, 670

Collins, Billy: Monday, 691; The Sandhill Cranes of Nebraska, 1291; Sonnet, 958

Colonel, The, 436

"Come darkest night, becoming sorrow best," 964

Commencement Speech, Kenyon College, 309

Constantly Risking Absurdity, 185

Contributions to a Rudimentary Concept of Nation, 678

Coy Mistress, 982

Crashaw, Richard: But Men Loved Darkness rather than Light, 417

Cruz, Victor Hernández: Problems with Hurricanes, 1277

Cullen, Countee: Incident, 182

cummings, e. e.: the Cambridge ladies who live in furnished souls, 655; in Just-, 180

Daddy, 953

Daffodils, 1272

Dandelion for My Mother, A, 189

Danticat, Edwidge: The Book of the Dead, 614

Davie, Donald: The Nonconformist, 432

Dead Woman, The, 1265

Dear John Wayne, 671

Death and Life, 1122

Death, Be Not Proud, 1243

Death of Iván Ilých, The, 1132

Dennis, Carl: Thanksgiving Letter from Harry, 205

Design, 1265

DeVries, Peter: To His Importunate Mistress (Andrew Marvell Updated), 981

Diary of a Madman, 537

Díaz, Junot: Drown, 906

Dickinson, E. L.: Why We Are Infidels, 498

Dickinson, Emily: After great pain, a formal feeling comes, 1247; Apparently with no surprise, 1248; Because I could not stop for Death, 1257; I felt a Funeral, in my Brain, 175; I heard a Fly buzz—when I died, 1248; I'm Nobody! Who are you?, 648; Much Madness is divinest Sense, 420; She rose to His Requirement, 421; There is no Frigate like a Book, 2

Djanikian, Gregory: Sailing to America, 669

Doctorow, E. L.: Why We Are Infidels, 498

Dogs at Live Oak Beach, Santa Cruz, The, 189

Dog's Death, 1286

Doll's House, A, 213

Donne, John: Death, Be Not Proud, 1243; The Flea, 937; Holy Sonnets: "If poisonous minerals, and if that tree," 416; Meditation XVII, from Devotions upon Emergent Occasions, 1303; A Valediction: Forbidding Mourning, 938

Do Not Go Gentle into That Good Night, 1267

Doshi, Tishani: The Immigrant's Song, 683; Lament—I, 685

Dover Beach, 943

Dove, Rita: My Mother Enters the Work Force, 698

Dowell, Bob: The Moment of Grace in the Fiction of Flannery O'Connor, 155

Doyle, Brian: Pop Art, 294

Dreams, 439

Drown, 906

Dulce et Decorum Est, 445

Dum Dum Boys, 113

Dunbar, Paul Laurence: We Wear the Mask, 650

Easter 1916, 422

Eating Alone, 970

Econo Motel, Ocean City, 962

Edward, 1239

Egan, Jennifer: Safari, 393

85, 933

Eliot, T. S.: The Love Song of J. Alfred Prufrock, 651

Ellison°, Harlan: "Repent, Harlequin!" Said the Ticktockman, 374

Ellison, Ralph: Battle Royal, 355

End of FIRPO in the World, The, 411

Erdrich, Louise: Dear John Wayne, 671

Everyday Use, 586

Facing It, 1276

Faiz, Faiz Ahmed: Be Near Me, 974

Father Comes Home from the Wars, 270

Faulkner, William: A Rose for Emily, 623

Fear No More the Heat o' the Sun, 1242

Feet in Smoke, 1312

Feldman, Alan: My Century, 192

Ferlinghetti, Lawrence: Constantly Risking Absurdity, 185; In Goya's Greatest Scenes, 1251

Fern Hill, 183

Finch, Annie: Coy Mistress, 982

Finkel, Donald: The Great Wave: Hokusai, 1255

Fire and Ice, 944

Fish, The, 1283

Flannery O'Connor's "A Good Man Is Hard to Find": The Moment of Grace, 163

The Flea, 937

Flounder, 437

Forché, Carolyn: The Colonel, 436

Fried, Daisy: Econo Motel, Ocean City, 962

Frost, Robert: After Apple-Picking, 1261; Birches, 178; Design, 1265; Fire and Ice, 944; Nothing Gold Can Stay, 1263; 'Out, Out—,' 1262; The Road Not Taken, 178; A Semi-Revolution, 439; Stopping by Woods on a Snowy Evening, 1264

Galchen, Rivka: Wild Berry Blue, 130

Gallagher, Tess: I Stop Writing the Poem, 696

Garden of Love, The, 171

Garrison, Deborah: Sestina for the Working Mother, 699

Getting It Right, 1109

Gilb, Dagoberto: I Knew She Was Beautiful, 1111

Gilman, Charlotte Perkins: The Yellow Wallpaper, 548

Ginsberg, Allen: A Supermarket in California, 442

Giovanni, Nikki: Dreams, 439

Girl, 105

Gladwell, Malcolm: Small Change: Why the Revolution Will Not Be Tweeted, 513

Glück, Louise: The Myth of Innocence, 190; The School Children, 190

God's Grandeur, 1257

Golconde, 316

Goodman, Allegra: Apple Cake, 1213

Good Man Is Hard to Find, A, 141

Good People, 927

Goya, Francisco de: The Third of May, 1808, Madrid, 1252

Great Day, The, 438

Great Wave, The: Hokusai, 1255

Great Wave Off Kanagawa, The, 1256

Greenway, William: Pit Pony, 1287

Ha Jin: The Bridegroom, 630

Half a Day, 88

Hall, Donald: Affirmation, 1268

Halliday, Mark: Chicken Salad, 1278

Hanging Fire, 187
Hansberry, Lorraine: *A Raisin in the Sun*, 710
Happy and Unhappy Families I, 947
Hard Rock Returns to Prison from the Hospital for the Criminal Insane, 658
Hardy, Thomas: The Man He Killed, 32, 445; Men Who March Away, 175
Harlem, 429
Hawthorne, Nathaniel: Young Goodman Brown, 77
Hayden, Robert: Those Winter Sundays, 969
Hayes, Terrance: Root, 681
Heaney, Seamus: Mid-term Break, 1273; Valediction, 957
Hemingway, Ernest: Hills Like White Elephants, 923
Herrera, Juan Felipe: 187 Reasons Mexicanos Can't Cross the Border (remix), 661
Herrick, Robert: To the Virgins, to Make Much of Time, 940
Hills Like White Elephants, 923
His Coy Mistress to Mr. Marvell, 978
Hoagland, Tony: I Have News for You, 1294
Hokusai, Katsushika: *The Great Wave Off Kanagawa*, 1256
Hollander, Andrea: Betrayal, 975
Holy Sonnets: "If poisonous minerals, and if that tree," 416
Hope, A. D.: His Coy Mistress to Mr. Marvell, 978
Hopkins, Gerard Manley: God's Grandeur, 1257; Spring and Fall, 176
Housman, A. E.: When I Was One-and-Twenty, 177; To an Athlete Dying Young, 1258
Howe, Marie: What the Living Do, 1279
How I Got That Name, 672
Hughes, Langston: Harlem, 429; I, Too, 441; Mother to Son, 199; Salvation, 284
Hunger Artist, A, 347
Hurston, Zora Neale: Sweat, 866

I Am the People, the Mob, 425
Ibsen, Henrik: *A Doll's House*, 213
I felt a Funeral, in my Brain, 175

If We Must Die, 429
I Have News for You, 1294
I heard a Fly buzz—when I died, 1248
I Knew a Woman, 944
I Knew She Was Beautiful, 1111
I know I am but summer to your heart (Sonnet XXVII), 973
"Imagine There's No Heaven": A Letter to the Sixth Billionth World Citizen, 501
Immigrant's Song, The, 683
I'm Nobody! Who are you?, 648
Incident, 182
In Goya's Greatest Scenes, 1251
in Just-, 180
I Stop Writing the Poem, 696
I, Too, 441

Jackson, Shirley: The Lottery, 367
Jilting of Granny Weatherall, The, 1227
Johnson, Georgia Douglas: Old Black Men, 650
Johnson, James Weldon: A Poet to His Baby Son, 648
Johnson, Lacy M.: White Trash Primer, 852
Jones, Sabrina: Little House in the Big City, 833
Jonson, Ben: Song, To Celia, 940
Joy, Camden: Dum Dum Boys, 113
Joyce, James: Araby, 125

Kafka, Franz: A Hunger Artist, 347
Keats, John: Ode on a Grecian Urn, 1245
Kenyon, Jane: Let Evening Come, 1275
Kincaid, Jamaica: Girl, 105; On Seeing England for the First Time, 489
Kingston, Maxine Hong: No Name Woman, 1097
Kinnell, Galway: After Making Love We Hear Footsteps, 951
Kizer, Carolyn: Afternoon Happiness, 949; Bitch, 948
Klimt, Gustav: *Death and Life*, 1122
Klotz, Marvin: Requiem, 1270
Knight, Etheridge: Hard Rock Returns to Prison from the Hospital for the Criminal Insane, 658
Komunyakaa, Yusef: Facing It, 1276

Lamb, The, 170

Lament—I, 685

Landscape with the Fall of Icarus, 1250

Larkin, Philip: A Study of Reading Habits, 186; This Be the Verse, 187

Latin Women Pray, 670

Lau, Evelyn: Solipsism, 197

Lawrence, Jacob: *This Is Harlem,* 534

Lazarus, Emma: The New Colossus, 702

Learning to Love America, 443

Learning the Bicycle, 959

Lee, Li-Young: Eating Alone, 970

Lesson, The, 98

Let Evening Come, 1275

Lethem, Jonathan: 13, 1977, 21, 1319

Letter Composed During a Lull in the Fighting, 448

Levine, Philip: What Work Is, 433

Life, Love, Happiness: A Found Essay from the Twitterverse, 1119

Lim, Shirley Geok-Lin: Learning to Love America, 443

Lipsyte, Sam: The Naturals, 1196

Little House in the Big City, 833

Living in Sin, 952

London, 171

Long Story, 666

Lorde, Audre: Hanging Fire, 187

Lottery, The, 367

Love in Fantastique Triumph satt, 972

Love in Infant Monkeys, 900

Love Poem, 946

Love Song of J. Alfred Prufrock, The, 651

Lying in a Hammock at William Duffy's Farm in Pine Island, Minnesota, 1290

Magritte, René: *Golconde,* 316

Mahfouz, Naguib: Half a Day, 88

Manhattan Project, The, 196

Man He Killed, The, 32, 445

Man to Send Rain Clouds, The, 1209

Man Who Built This House, The, 1280

Margalit, Ruth: The Unmothered, 1325

Market Economy, The, 435

Market Women's Cries, 646

Marvell, Andrew: To His Coy Mistress, 977

McKay, Claude: If We Must Die, 429

McKibben, Bill: A Call to Arms: An Invitation to Demand Action on Climate Change, 506

Meditation XVII, from Devotions upon Emergent Occasions (selection), 1303

Meinke, Peter: Advice to My Son, 200

Melville, Herman: Bartleby, the Scrivener, 319

Men Who March Away, 175

Merwin, W. S.: Thanks, 204

Mezey, Robert: My Mother, 201

Mid-term Break, 1273

Millay, Edna St. Vincent: I know I am but summer to your heart (Sonnet XXVII), 973

Millet, Lydia: Love in Infant Monkeys, 900

Miłosz, Czesław: A Song on the End of the World, 1266

Modest Proposal, A, 481

Moment of Grace in the Fiction of Flannery O'Connor, The, 155

Monday, 691

Money, 656

Mother to Son, 199

Moths, The, 1191

Much Madness is divinest Sense, 420

Mueller, Lisel: Happy and Unhappy Families I, 947

Mukherjee, Bharati: Two Ways to Belong in America, 849

Musée des Beaux Arts, 1249

My American Jon, 915

My Century, 192

My Father's Diary, 965

My Father's Noose, 1107

My Heart, 690

My Last Duchess, 173

My Mother, 201

My Mother Enters the Work Force, 698

My Papa's Waltz, 968

Mystery and Manners (selection), 153

Myth of Innocence, The, 190

My Wicked Wicked Ways, 194

Nasrin, Taslima: Things Cheaply Had, 677

Naturals, The, 1196

Negative, 680

Nelson, Maggie: Thanksgiving, 211

Nemerov, Howard: Money, 656

Neruda, Pablo: The Dead Woman, 1265
Nevada Glassworks, The, 675
New Colossus, The, 702
Night Patrol, 446
Nims, John Frederick: Love Poem, 946
No Name Woman, 1097
Nonconformist, The, 432
Nordhaus, Jean: A Dandelion for My
    Mother, 189
Nothing Gold Can Stay, 1263
Nottage, Lynn: Poof!, 1087
Not Waving but Drowning, 180

Oates, Joyce Carol: Where Are You Going,
    Where Have You Been?, 886
O'Brien, Tim: The Things They Carried,
    1177
O'Connor, Flannery: A Good Man Is
    Hard to Find, 141; Mystery and
    Manners (selection), 153
Ode on a Grecian Urn, 1245
O'Hara, Frank: My Heart, 690
Old Black Men, 650
Olds, Sharon: My Father's Diary, 965; Sex
    without Love, 958
Oliver, Mary: When Death Comes, 1270
On Being Brought from Africa to America,
    702
Once More to the Lake, 1305
One Art, 946
1 Corinthians 13, 1095
187 Reasons Mexicanos Can't Cross the
    Border (remix), 661
One Perfect Rose, 944
One Song, America, Before I Go, 440
On Seeing England for the First Time, 489
Orientation, 107
Ostriker, Alicia: Daffodils, 1272; The Dogs
    at Live Oak Beach, Santa Cruz, 189
Orozco, Daniel: Orientation, 107
Orwell, George: Shooting an Elephant, 827
Othello, 984
'Out, Out—', 1262
Owen, Wilfred: Dulce et Decorum Est, 445
Ozymandias, 1245

Parker, Dorothy: One Perfect Rose, 944
Parks, Suzan-Lori: Father Comes Home
    from the Wars, 270

Paul: 1 Corinthians 13, 1095
Pérez, Omar: Contributions to a
    Rudimentary Concept of Nation,
    678
Peter Quince at the Clavier, 426
Phillips, Carl: Blue, 692
Piercy, Marge: Barbie Doll, 659; The
    Market Economy, 435
Pit Pony, 1287
Plath, Sylvia: Daddy, 953
Poe, Edgar Allan: The Cask of Amontil-
    lado, 1126
Poet to His Baby Son, A, 648
Poison Tree, A, 941
Political Power of Social Media, The, 522
Poof!, 1087
Pop Art, 294
Porter, Katherine Anne: The Jilting of
    Granny Weatherall, 1227
Powers, Kevin C.: Letter Composed
    During a Lull in the Fighting, 448
Problems with Hurricanes, 1277
Prunty, Wyatt: Learning the Bicycle,
    959

Raisin in the Sun, A, 710
Randall, Dudley: Ballad of Birmingham,
    431
Ras, Barbara: You Can't Have It All, 1292
Reading the Map in "A Good Man Is Hard
    to Find," 157
Red, Red Rose, A, 942
Reece, Spencer: The Manhattan Project,
    196
"Repent, Harlequin!" Said the
    Ticktockman, 374
Requiem, 1270
Revolutions Per Minute, 510
Rich, Adrienne: Living in Sin, 952
Richard Cory, 1261
Rilke, Rainer Maria: Archaic Torso of
    Apollo, 1289
Road Not Taken, The, 178
Robinson, Edwin Arlington: Richard
    Cory, 1261
Roethke, Theodore: I Knew a Woman,
    944; My Papa's Waltz, 968
Root, 681
Rose for Emily, A, 623

Rushdie, Salman: "Imagine There's No Heaven": A Letter to the Sixth Billionth World Citizen, 501
Ryan, Kay: All Shall Be Restored, 660

Safari, 393
Sailing to America, 669
Sailing to Byzantium, 1259
Salvation, 284
Sandbox, The, 1296
Sandburg, Carl: I Am the People, the Mob, 425
Sandhill Cranes of Nebraska, The, 1291
Sappho: With His Venom, 933
Satirical Elegy on the Death of a Late Famous General, A, 1243
Saunders, George: The End of FIRPO in the World, 411
School Children, The, 190
Second Coming, The, 424
Secret Life of Walter Mitty, The, 407
Sedaris, David: What I Learned and What I Said at Princeton, 304
Semi-Revolution, A, 439
Senghor, Léopold Sédar: To New York, 703
Sestina for the Working Mother, 699 70, 972
Sexton, Anne: The Starry Night, 1253
Sex without Love, 958
Shakespeare, William: *Othello,* 984; Fear No More the Heat o' the Sun, 1242; Sonnet 18, "Shall I compare thee to a summer's day?" 934; Sonnet 116, "Let me not to the marriage of true minds," 936; Sonnet 130, "My mistress' eyes are nothing like the sun," 936; Sonnet 73, "That time of year thou mayst in me behold," 1241; Sonnet 64, "When I have seen by Time's fell hand defac'd," 935; Sonnet 29, "When, in disgrace with fortune and men's eyes," 31, 934
Shelley, Percy Bysshe: Ozymandias, 1245
Shepherd, The, 170
She rose to His Requirement, 421
Shirky, Clay: The Political Power of Social Media, 522
Shooting an Elephant, 827

Silko, Leslie Marmon: The Man to Send Rain Clouds, 1209
Sloth, The, 1311
Small Change: Why the Revolution Will Not Be Tweeted, 513
Smith, Stevie: Not Waving but Drowning, 180; To Carry the Child, 181
Snake Oil, Snake Bite, 1282
Solipsism, 197
Solnit, Rebecca: Revolutions Per Minute, 510
Song of Myself (selection), 686
Song on the End of the World, A, 1266
Song, To Celia, 940
Sonnet, 958
Sonnet 18, "Shall I compare thee to a summer's day?" 934
Sonnet 116, "Let me not to the marriage of true minds," 936
Sonnet 130, "My mistress' eyes are nothing like the sun," 936
Sonnet 73, "That time of year thou mayst in me behold," 1241
Sonnet 64, "When I have seen by Time's fell hand defac'd," 935
Sonnet 29, "When, in disgrace with fortune and men's eyes," 31, 934
Sonny's Blues, 561
Sophocles: *Antigonê,* 450
Soto, Gary: Behind Grandma's House, 203
Spring and Fall, 176
Stafford, William: Traveling through the Dark, 1285
Starry Night, The, 1253
Starry Night, The, 1254
Stella's Birth-Day, 167
Stevens, Wallace: Peter Quince at the Clavier, 426
Stillmann, Pablo Piñero: Life, Love, Happiness: A Found Essay from the Twitterverse, 1119
Stopping by Woods on a Snowy Evening, 1264
Storm, The, 861
Story of an Hour, The, 1174
Study of Reading Habits, A, 186
Sullivan, John Jeremiah: Feet in Smoke, 1312
Supermarket in California, A, 442

Sweat, 866

Swift, Jonathan: Market Women's Cries, 646; A Modest Proposal, 481; A Satirical Elegy on the Death of a Late Famous General, 1243; Stella's Birth-Day, 167

Talusan, Grace: My Father's Noose, 1107
Tan, Amy: Two Kinds, 384
Taylor, Sheila Ortiz: The Way Back, 207
Teague, Alexandra: Adjectives of Order, 683
Tennyson, Alfred, Lord: Ulysses, 418
Thanks, 204
Thanksgiving, 211
Thanksgiving Letter from Harry, 205
There Is a Girl Inside, 956
There is no Frigate like a Book, 2
They Flee From Me, 963
Things Cheaply Had, 677
Things They Carried, The, 1177
Third of May, 1808, Madrid, The, 1252
13, 1977, 21, 1319
This Be the Verse, 187
This Is Harlem, 534
This Is Why I'll Never Be an Adult, 296
Thomas, Dylan: Do Not Go Gentle into That Good Night, 1267; Fern Hill, 183
Those Winter Sundays, 969
Thurber, James: The Secret Life of Walter Mitty, 407
Time and Distance Overcome, 844
To an Athlete Dying Young, 1258
To Carry the Child, 181
To His Coy Mistress, 977
To His Importunate Mistress (Andrew Marvell Updated), 981
Tolstoy, Leo: The Death of Iván Ilých, 1132
To My Dear and Loving Husband, 941
To New York, 703
To the Virgins, to Make Much of Time, 940
Traveling through the Dark, 1285
Trethewey, Natasha: Flounder, 437
Turpin, Mark: The Man Who Built This House, 1280
Two Kinds, 384
Two Lovers, 858
Two Ways to Belong in America, 849
Tyger, The, 172

Ulysses, 418
Unknown Citizen, The, 430
Unmothered, The, 1325
Updike, John: A & P, 92; Dog's Death, 1286

van Gogh, Vincent: *The Starry Night,* 1254
Valediction, 957
Valediction, A: Forbidding Mourning, 938
Veteran, The, 74
Viramontes, Helena María: The Moths, 1191

Walker, Alice: Everyday Use, 586
Wallace, David Foster: Commencement Speech, Kenyon College, 309; Good People, 927
War Dances, 594
Way Back, The, 207
Welch, James: Christmas Comes to Moccasin Flat, 210
We Real Cool, 432
We Wear the Mask, 650
What If Shakespeare Had Had a Sister?, 819
What I Learned and What I Said at Princeton, 304
What the Living Do, 1279
What We Talk About When We Talk About Love, 876
What Work Is, 433
Wheatley, Phillis: On Being Brought from Africa to America, 702
When Death Comes, 1270
When I Heard the Learn'd Astronomer, 10
When I Was One-and-Twenty, 177
Where Are You Going, Where Have You Been?, 886
White, E. B.: Once More to the Lake, 1305
White Trash Primer, 852
Whitman, Walt: One Song, America, Before I Go, 440; Song of Myself (selection), 686; When I Heard the Learn'd Astronomer, 10
Why We Are Infidels, 498
Wild Berry Blue, 130
Winged Purposes, 966
With His Venom, 933
Wolff, Tobias: Bullet in the Brain, 1234